Supply chain for Wavefarer Board Shorts by Patagonia, a Los Angeles-based clothing designer and distributor.

Design (colour & pattern)
Patagonia, Ventura, California &
Yagi (fabric wholesaler), Japan

Design (style)
Patagonia, Ventura, California

Nylon plant

Toray Industries,
Japan

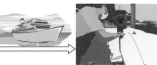

Cutting and sewing
Castle Peak Co., Bangkok

Weaving plant

Dyeing and printing plant

Distribution & warehousing
Patagonia, Reno, Nevada

Legend: Information - - ➤ Trucking ——➤ Ocean Freight ⟹

fourth canadian edition

OPERATIONS MANAGEMENT

William J. Stevenson
Rochester Institute of Technology

Mehran Hojati
University of Saskatchewan

McGraw-Hill
Ryerson
Connect. Learn. Succeed.

Operations Management
Fourth Canadian Edition

Copyright © 2011, 2007, 2004, 2001 by McGraw-Hill Ryerson Limited, a Subsidiary of The McGraw-Hill Companies. Copyright © 2005, 2002, 1999 by The McGraw-Hill Companies, Inc. All rights reserved. Previous copyright editions 1996, 1992, 1986, 1982 by Richard D. Irwin, a Times-Mirror Higher Education Group, Inc. company. No part of this publication may be reproduced or transmitted in any form or by any means, or stored in a database or retrieval system, without the prior written permission of McGraw-Hill Ryerson Limited, or in the case of photocopying or other reprographic copying, a license from The Canadian Copyright Licensing Agency (Access Copyright). For an Access Copyright licence, visit www.accesscopyright.ca or call toll-free to 1-800-893-5777.

Statistics Canada information is used with the permission of Statistics Canada. Users are forbidden to copy the data and redisseminate them, in an original or modified form, for commercial purposes, without permission from Statistics Canada. Information on the availability of the wide range of data from Statistics Canada can be obtained from Statistics Canada's Regional Offices, its World Wide Web site at www.statcan. gc.ca, and its toll-free access number: 1-800-263-1136.

The Internet addresses listed in the text were accurate at the time of publication. The inclusion of a Web site does not indicate an endorsement by the authors or McGraw-Hill Ryerson, nor does McGraw-Hill Ryerson guarantee the accuracy of information presented at these sites.

ISBN-13: 978-0-07-096957-5
ISBN-10: 0-07-096957-4

3 4 5 6 7 8 9 QDB 1 9 8 7 6 5 4 3 2

Printed and bound in the United States of America.

Care has been taken to trace ownership of copyright material contained in this text; however, the publisher will welcome any information that enables them to rectify any reference or credit for subsequent editions.

Vice-President and Editor-in-Chief: Joanna Cotton
Sponsoring Editor: Kimberley Veevers
Marketing Manager: Jeremy Guimond
Managing Editor, Development: Kelly Dickson
Developmental Editors: Sarah Fulton and Christopher Cullen
Photo/Permission Editor: My Editor Inc.
Senior Editorial Associate: Christine Lomas
Supervising Editor: Kara Stahl
Copy Editor: Karen Rolfe
Production Coordinator: Michelle Saddler
Cover and Interior Design: Kyle Gell
Cover Image Credits: (airport) Charles Thatcher/RM; (hotel) Tom Merton/RF; (kitchen) Greg Pease/RM; (factory) Monty Rakusen/RF; (hospital) Brand X Pictures/RF; (gears) Christian Lagerek/RF
Page Layout: S R Nova Pvt Ltd., Bangalore, India
Printer: Quad/Graphics

Library and Archives Canada Cataloguing in Publication

Stevenson, William J.
    Operations management / William J. Stevenson, Mehran Hojati. –4th Canadian ed.
    Includes index.

First ed. had title: Production/operations management.
ISBN 978-0-07-096957-5

1. Production management–Textbooks. I. Hojati, Mehran, 1958- II. Title.

TS155.S785 2010   658.5   C2010-903453-8

About the Authors

William Stevenson
Rochester Institute of Technology

This book is dedicated to you.

Dr. William Stevenson is an associate professor of Decision Sciences in the College of Business at Rochester Institute of Technology. He teaches graduate and undergraduate courses in operations management, management science, quality concepts, and quality applications.

He is the author of textbooks in management science and statistics, as well as operations management. His articles have appeared in *Management Science*, *Decision Sciences, Quality Progress*, and other journals.

Dr. Stevenson received a bachelor's degree in industrial engineering, an M.B.A. and a Ph.D. in production/operations management from Syracuse University.

Mehran Hojati
University of Saskatchewan

I dedicate this book to my parents, Hossein Hojati and Zahra Hedayati.

Dr. Hojati is an associate professor of operations management in the Edwards School of Business at the University of Saskatchewan. He teaches operations management and purchasing and supply management. He has taught and prepared teaching materials for the Purchasing Management Association of Canada. His articles have appeared in *International Journal of Production Economics, Production & Inventory Management Journal*, and others. His research interests are in the applications of operations research techniques in operations.

Dr. Hojati received a bachelor's degree in economics and a master's degree in operational research from London School of Economics, and a Ph.D. in management science from the University of British Columbia. He is certified in Production and Inventory Management (CPIM), awarded by APICS (the Association for Operations Management).

Brief Contents

Chapter Supplements Available on *Connect*

Contents

PART FOUR Quality

CHAPTER 9 Management of Quality 285

CHAPTER 10 Statistical Quality Control 321

CHAPTER 13 Aggregate Operations Planning 468

CHAPTER 14 Material Requirements Planning and Enterprise Resource Planning 504

Chapter Supplements Available
on *Connect*

Preface

The field of operations management is dynamic and an integral part of many of the good things that are happening in organizations. The material in this book is intended as an introduction to operations management and shows its interesting, realistic, and practical applications to service and manufacturing operations.

The subject matter represents a blend of concepts from industrial engineering, cost accounting, marketing, general management, management science, quantitative methods, and statistics. The topics covered include both strategic issues and operational decisions. Activities such as forecasting, designing goods and services, choosing a location for an office or factory, allocating resources, scheduling activities, and assuring and improving quality are core issues in organizations. Some of you are or will be employed directly in these areas, while others will have jobs that are indirectly related to operations. So, whether this is your field of study or not, knowledge of operations management will certainly benefit you and the organization you work for.

The advantages of using a Canadian version of an operations management textbook are numerous, including:

- Use of Canadian data
- Canadian location decisions are described
- Examples of Canadian organizations, more familiar and interesting to students, are given
- Issues important for Canadian instructors and reviewers are addressed

WHAT'S NEW IN THE FOURTH CANADIAN EDITION?

The fourth Canadian edition of *Operations Management* has been developed for the Canadian market with several key features:

New and Updated Canadian and International Content. A new selection of relevant Canadian and international readings (OM in Action boxes), mini-cases, examples, and problems fill the text with real-world applications. There are over **60** new readings (OM in Action boxes), examples, and mini-cases replacing old material; all the other readings and mini-cases have been updated.

Profiles of diverse organizations such as MHR Warehouse Operations, Dell Computers, and Holland College provide students with a realistic understanding of manufacturing and service organizations both inside and outside Canada.

Tightened Exposition. The fourth Canadian edition of *Operations Management* has been further revised to bring you a tighter, shortened text while maintaining the wide topical coverage and student-friendly style.

Updated Coverage and Organization. The fourth Canadian edition features an increased number of end-of-chapter questions and problems, topics requested by the Canadian reviewers, and other material deemed necessary by the Canadian author. A fourth type of Taking Stock question (on ethics) and a new type of question (Experiential Learning Exercises) are added at the end of each chapter. Some other important additions and changes are as follows:

Chapter	Title	Important Changes/Additions
2	Competitiveness, Strategic Planning, and Productivity	Expands the Strategy section to Strategic Planning.
3	Demand Forecasting	Changes have been made to Formula 3-7 for Trend-adjusted Exponential Smoothing (to match the common method used).
4	Product Design	Includes a new section on Design for Environment.
5	Strategic Capacity Planning	A bottleneck example has been added.
8	Location Planning and Analysis	Includes a new section on Voronoi polygons to determine trade areas for retail/restaurant sectors.
9	Management of Quality	Detailed requirements for the Canada Awards for Excellence have been added.
11	Supply Chain Management	Includes examples of real supply chains (e.g., Patagonia, NYK Logistics)
12	Inventory Management	Revisions have been made to the Amount of Shortage and Annual Service Level sections. Includes a new subsection on Determining the Order Interval. The Coordinated Periodic Review model has been added.
14	Material Requirements Planning and Enterprise Resource Planning	The "ERP vs. Accounting Software" and "The ABCs of ERP" readings have been moved into the text of chapter.
15	Just-in-Time and Lean Production	A new section on Implementing JIT/Lean, including Value Stream Mapping, has been added.
16	Job and Staff Scheduling	Coverage of long- and medium-term scheduling has been deleted in order to focus on short-term scheduling. A new subsection on "Dealing with Infinite Loading" has been added to relate this chapter to the results of MRP.
17	Project Management	The section on Using Microsoft Project has been updated from the 2003 to the 2010 version.
18	Waiting-Line Analysis	Includes both single-server and multi-server models for "finite number in system."

HIGHLIGHTS OF THE FOURTH CANADIAN EDITION

Balanced Content. The text strives to achieve a careful balance in the presentation of operations management. Care has been taken to balance definitions and concepts with quantitative, hands-on problems; to balance theoretical material with real-life applications; and to balance classical topics in operations management with new developments that particularly interest students.

Problem-Solving Approach. To further students' hands-on experience of OM, the text contains examples with solutions throughout. At the end of most chapters is a group of solved problems to illustrate concepts and techniques. Some of the end-of-chapter problems have answers at the end of the book.

Renowned Style. Always favoured among instructors, the writing style in *Operations Management* is clear, concise, and student-friendly, while maintaining the technical rigour necessary for the subject matter. From step-by-step problem solving, to theoretical exposition, to in-depth mini-cases and readings, the book is designed to promote student understanding of the role of operations management in successful businesses—which, in turn, promotes student success in class.

MAJOR STUDY AND LEARNING FEATURES

A number of key features in this textbook have been specifically designed to help introductory students learn, understand, and apply operations concepts and problem-solving techniques. All of these have been carefully developed over four Canadian editions and ten U.S. editions and have proven successful.

Learning Objectives. Every chapter and supplement lists the learning objectives as a short guide to studying the chapter. These objectives are incorporated within each chapter and at the end of each chapter in the questions and problems.

Figures and Photos. The fourth Canadian edition includes extensive photographs and graphic illustrations to support student study and provide interest and motivation.

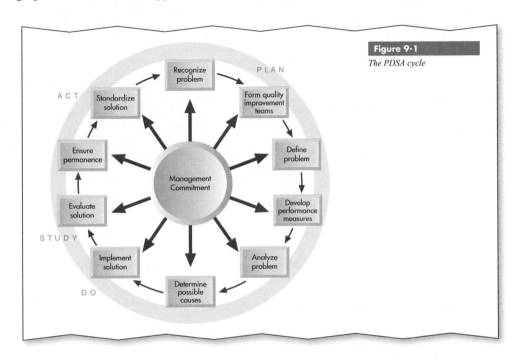

Figure 9-1

The PDSA cycle

In Canada, High Liner Foods uses eight deep-sea trawlers to fish around Nova Scotia and Newfoundland. Its two primary processing plants are nearby in Lunenburg, NS, and Burin, NF.

OM in Action. Throughout the textbook are readings about applications of OM. These OM in Action boxes highlight important real-world applications, provide examples of operations issues, and offer further elaboration of the textbook material. They also provide a basis for classroom discussion and generate interest in the subject matter.

OM in *ACTION*   http://www.marks.com

Mark's Work Wearhouse

Mark's Work Wearhouse is a large chain of work wear in Canada. The demand for most of Mark's products, such as winter clothing and boots or summer shorts, is affected by the season. Mark's uses a software called Inforem to forecast demand for its products and to make inventory decisions. Here, we describe the forecasting module of Inforem, whereas the Mini-Case at the end of Chapter 12 provides information on inventory decisions in Mark's.

Inforem facilitates adoption of a seasonal-relatives profile for each product by providing typical profiles for each product family. The forecasting method deseasonalizes the past demand, fits adaptive exponential smoothing (a variation of exponential smoothing where the smoothing constant α is automatically adjusted after each period to best fit the data) to the deseasonalized data, forecasts using the fitted model, then reseasonalizes the forecasts.

Recently, Mark's has started using weather intelligence information from Planalytics to fine-tune its seasonal merchandising, assortment, and allocation planning for some of its products. Mark's buyers have found this information useful. For example, recently a men's buyer had to decide the discount price for shorts for a Father's Day flyer to be printed in May. Usually, all shorts would have been offered at a 50 percent discount. However, the prediction from Planalytics was for a colder-than-usual spring and warmer-than-usual summer. Based on this, the buyer took a chance and discounted only some types of the shorts 25 percent. The weather prediction came true, resulting in fewer sales of shorts in spring; however, all the remaining shorts were sold in the summer at full price. This action resulted in $50,000 more profits to Mark's. Also, because the forecast called for warmer summer in Western Canada, 8,000 additional shorts were diverted to the Western Canada stores, and subsequently were all sold.

In another example, winter was predicted to be less severe. This resulted in Mark's buying more removable-liner jackets and fewer fixed-liner jackets. Planalytics also provides how much more or less a product will sell during a season; for example 20 percent more demand for cotton fleece.

Sources: Inforem User's Manual; J.K. Speer, "Rain or Shine, Mark's Work Wearhouse Has the Right Stuff: Thanks to Weather-based Business Intelligence from Planalytics, the Scramble Factor at Mark's Work Wearhouse Has Been Drastically Reduced," *Apparel* 48(2) Oct 2006, 20–22.

Mini-Cases. Many chapters include short cases, selected to provide a broader, more integrated thinking opportunity for students.

MINI-CASE

WhiteWater West Industries

Whitewater West Industries was founded by Geoff Chutter in early 1980s. An accountant working in Vancouver, Geoff got interested in waterslides in 1980 while visiting his uncle in Kelowna who had done consulting on a waterslide in a local park. Geoff quit his job, bought 18 acres of land in Penticton, 60 km south of Kelowna, and built his own water park. More interested in creative aspects of design, he sold his water park in 1983 and bought half-ownership of a Kelowna fibreglass factory. Slides are made by manually spraying melted fibreglass and resin on moulds.

Whitewater West entered the wave pool business in 1987 through a technology agreement with a Scottish company. Due to this and various other design and manufacturing innovations, Whitewater West kept growing. Most of its sales was international and was trucked to Vancouver and shipped from there. Whitewater moved its headquarters to Richmond, B.C., and expanded its design and engineering staff.

In 1995, the Kelowna plant was getting too small for Whitewater West's sales volume. Geoff needed a larger factory. He had to decide its location: In or near Kelowna or near its headquarters in Richmond? List the advantages and disadvantages of each alternative location and recommend one.

Sources: http://www.whitewaterwest.com; http://www.formashape.com; C. Clark, "He Turns Water into Fun," *CA Magazine,* January 1993, 126(1), pp. 6–7; R. McQueen, "Canada's 50 Best Managed Companies: Whitewater West Industries Ltd," *Financial Post,* December 13, 1997, p. 48.

Examples with Solutions. Throughout the textbook, wherever a quantitative technique is introduced, an example is included to illustrate the application of that technique. These are designed to be easy to follow.

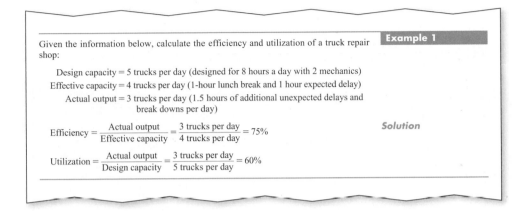

Given the information below, calculate the efficiency and utilization of a truck repair shop:

Example 1

Design capacity = 5 trucks per day (designed for 8 hours a day with 2 mechanics)
Effective capacity = 4 trucks per day (1-hour lunch break and 1 hour expected delay)
Actual output = 3 trucks per day (1.5 hours of additional unexpected delays and break downs per day)

Solution

$$\text{Efficiency} = \frac{\text{Actual output}}{\text{Effective capacity}} = \frac{3 \text{ trucks per day}}{4 \text{ trucks per day}} = 75\%$$

$$\text{Utilization} = \frac{\text{Actual output}}{\text{Design capacity}} = \frac{3 \text{ trucks per day}}{5 \text{ trucks per day}} = 60\%$$

Service Icons. Where service topics are addressed in the textbook, a service "S" icon appears in the corresponding margin to flag the attention of both students and instructors.

Web Links. Web addresses of relevant Web sites are highlighted in the margin with a Web icon.

Global Icons. Where a concept or example has worldwide effect, it is flagged with a globe icon.

END-OF-CHAPTER RESOURCES

For student study and review, the following items are provided at the end of each chapter.

Summaries. An overview of the material covered.

Key Terms. Key terms are highlighted in the text, repeated in the margin with brief definitions for emphasis, and listed at the end of each chapter with page references to aid in reviewing.

Solved Problems. At the end of most chapters, solved problems illustrate problem solving and the core concepts of the chapter. These have been carefully prepared to enhance student understanding, as well as to provide additional examples of problem solving.

Problem 3

Type I error (alpha risk). After several investigations of points outside control limits revealed nothing, a manager began to wonder about the probability of the Type I error for the control limits used, which were based on $z = 1.90$.

a. Determine the alpha risk for this value of z.

b. What z would provide an alpha risk of about 2 percent?

Solution

a. Using Appendix B, Table A, we find that the area under the curve between $z = 0$ and $z = +1.90$ is .4713. Therefore, the area (probability) of values within 1.90 to +1.90 is 2(.4713) = .9426, and the area beyond these values is $1 - .9426 = .0574$. Hence, the alpha risk is 5.74 percent.

b. Because half of the risk lies in each tail, the area under the curve between $z = 0$ and the value of z you are looking for is .49. The closest value is .4901 for $z = 2.33$. Thus, control limits based on $z = 2.33$ provide an alpha risk of about 2 percent.

Excel Spreadsheet Solutions. Where applicable, the solved problems include screen shots of a spreadsheet solution. These are taken from the Excel templates, which can be found on *Connect*.

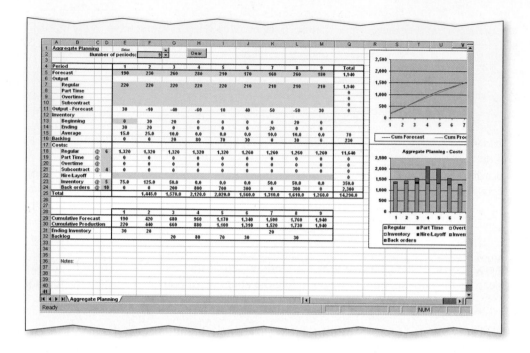

Discussion and Review Questions. These are intended to serve as a student self-review or as class discussion starters.

Taking Stock, Critical Thinking, Experiential Learning, and Internet Exercises. These activities encourage analytical thinking and help broaden conceptual understanding.

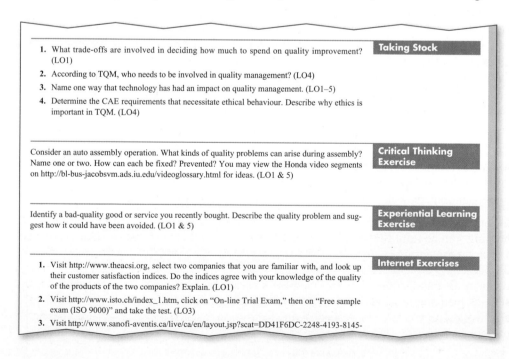

Taking Stock

1. What trade-offs are involved in deciding how much to spend on quality improvement? (LO1)
2. According to TQM, who needs to be involved in quality management? (LO4)
3. Name one way that technology has had an impact on quality management. (LO1–5)
4. Determine the CAE requirements that necessitate ethical behaviour. Describe why ethics is important in TQM. (LO4)

Critical Thinking Exercise

Consider an auto assembly operation. What kinds of quality problems can arise during assembly? Name one or two. How can each be fixed? Prevented? You may view the Honda video segments on http://bl-bus-jacobsvm.ads.iu.edu/videoglossary.html for ideas. (LO1 & 5)

Experiential Learning Exercise

Identify a bad-quality good or service you recently bought. Describe the quality problem and suggest how it could have been avoided. (LO1 & 5)

Internet Exercises

1. Visit http://www.theacsi.org, select two companies that you are familiar with, and look up their customer satisfaction indices. Do the indices agree with your knowledge of the quality of the products of the two companies? Explain. (LO1)
2. Visit http://www.isto.ch/index_1.htm, click on "On-line Trial Exam," then on "Free sample exam (ISO 9000)" and take the test. (LO3)
3. Visit http://www.sanofi-aventis.ca/live/ca/en/layout.jsp?scat=DD41F6DC-2248-4193-8145-

Problems. Most chapters have numerous Problems, ranging from simple practice problems that apply techniques to more difficult conceptual problems that provide a challenge and require students to integrate concepts.

Operations Tours. These readings give students a descriptive look at operations in action at manufacturing or service organizations. These real-life illustrations show direct application to reinforce the importance of the concepts described in the textbook.

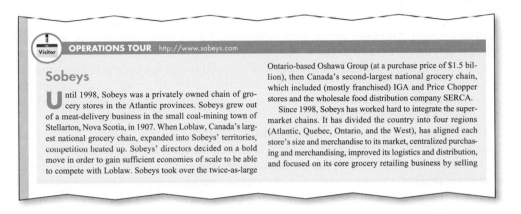

OPERATIONS TOUR   http://www.sobeys.com

Sobeys

Until 1998, Sobeys was a privately owned chain of grocery stores in the Atlantic provinces. Sobeys grew out of a meat-delivery business in the small coal-mining town of Stellarton, Nova Scotia, in 1907. When Loblaw, Canada's largest national grocery chain, expanded into Sobeys' territories, competition heated up. Sobeys' directors decided on a bold move in order to gain sufficient economies of scale to be able to compete with Loblaw. Sobeys took over the twice-as-large Ontario-based Oshawa Group (at a purchase price of $1.5 billion), then Canada's second-largest national grocery chain, which included (mostly franchised) IGA and Price Chopper stores and the wholesale food distribution company SERCA.

Since 1998, Sobeys has worked hard to integrate the supermarket chains. It has divided the country into four regions (Atlantic, Quebec, Ontario, and the West), has aligned each store's size and merchandise to its market, centralized purchasing and merchandising, improved its logistics and distribution, and focused on its core grocery retailing business by selling

SUPERIOR SERVICE

Service takes on a whole new meaning with McGraw-Hill Ryerson and *Operations Management*. More than just bringing you the textbook, we have consistently raised the bar in terms of innovation and educational research—both in operations management and in education in general. These investments in learning and the education community have helped us to understand the needs of students and educators across the country, and allowed us to foster the growth of truly innovative, integrated learning.

Integrated Learning. Your Integrated Learning Sales Specialist is a McGraw-Hill Ryerson representative who has the experience, product knowledge, training, and support to help you assess and integrate any of our products, technology, and services into your course for optimum teaching and learning performance. Whether it's helping your students improve their grades, or putting your entire course online, your *i*Learning Sales Specialist is there to help you do it. Contact your *i*Learning Sales Specialist today to learn how to maximize all of McGraw-Hill Ryerson's resources!

i-Learning
ADVANTAGE
McGraw-Hill Ryerson

iLearning Services. McGraw-Hill Ryerson offers a unique *i*Services package designed for Canadian faculty. Our mission is to equip providers of higher education with superior tools and resources required for excellence in teaching. For additional information, visit www.mcgrawhill.ca/highereducation/iservices.

McGraw-Hill Ryerson
iLearning
Services Program

Teaching & Learning Conference Series. The educational environment has changed tremendously in recent years, and McGraw-Hill Ryerson continues to be committed to helping you acquire the skills you need to succeed in this new milieu. Our innovative Teaching & Learning Conference Series brings faculty together from across Canada with 3M Teaching Excellence award winners to share teaching and learning best practices in a collaborative and stimulating environment. Pre-conference workshops on general topics, such as teaching large classes and technology integration, will also be offered. We will also work with you at your own institution to customize workshops that best suit the needs of your faculty.

**Teaching & Learning
Conference Series**

COMPREHENSIVE TEACHING AND LEARNING PACKAGE

We have developed a number of supplements for both teaching and learning to accompany this text:

Mc Graw Hill connect™

Connect is a web-based assignment and assessment platform that gives students the means to better connect with their coursework, with their instructors, and with the important concepts that they will need to know for success now and in the future. *Connect* embraces diverse study behaviours and preferences with breakthrough features that help students master course content and achieve better results. The powerful course management tool in *Connect* also offers a wide range of exclusive features that help instructors spend less time managing and more time teaching.

With *Connect*, you can deliver assignments, quizzes, and tests online. A robust set of questions and problems are presented and tied to the textbook's learning objectives. Track individual student performance—by question, assignment, or in relation to the class overall—with detailed grade reports. Integrate grade reports easily with Learning Management Systems (LMS) such as WebCT and Blackboard. And much more.

Stevenson *Connect*, written by Trent Tucker, helps you teach for today's needs:

Unlimited Practice, Instant Feedback. Provide instant feedback to unlimited textbook practice problems, acknowledging correct answers and pointing to areas that need more work.

Automatic Grading. Focus on teaching instead of administrating with electronic access to the class roster and gradebook, which easily sync with your school's course management system.

Direct Textbook and Testbank Questions. Assign students online homework, and test and quiz questions with multiple problem types, algorithmic variation, and randomized question order.

Integrated eBooks. Connect directly integrates the McGraw-Hill textbooks you already use into the engaging, easy-to-use interface.

Dedicated Canadian Support and Training. The *Connect* development team and customer service groups are located in our Canadian offices and work closely together to provide expert technical support and training for both instructors and students.

Mc Graw Hill connect™ for Students

Connect provides students with a powerful tool for improving academic performance and truly mastering course material, plus 24/7 online access to an interactive and searchable eBook. *Connect* allows students to practise important skills at their own pace and on their own schedule. Importantly, students' assessment results and instructors' feedback are all saved online—so students can continually review their progress and plot their course to success.

Instructor Resources

Instructor's Manual. Prepared by the author, the instructor's manual includes a brief description of the McGraw-Hill OM video series, "teaching notes" for each chapter and supplement, complete solutions to all text problems, mini-cases, and cases.

Computerized Test Bank. Prepared by Paul Callaghan, Acadia University, the computerized test bank includes over 2,000 questions and problems for exams. The computerized test bank is available through EZ Test Online—a flexible and easy-to-use electronic testing program—that allows instructors to create tests from book-specific items. EZ Test accommodates a wide range of question types and allows instructors to add their own questions. Test items are also available in Word format (Rich text format). For secure online testing, exams created in EZ Test can be exported to WebCT and Blackboard. EZ Test Online is supported at www.mhhe.com/eztest where users can download a Quick Start Guide, access FAQs, or log a ticket for help with specific issues.

Microsoft® PowerPoint® Lecture Slides. Prepared by Laurel Donaldson, Douglas College, the PowerPoint slides draw on the highlights of each chapter and provide an opportunity for the instructor to emphasize the most relevant visuals in class discussions.

Additional Content. Data files and Excel templates are also available on *Connect*.

Video Library. The MH OM Video Series includes professionally developed videos showing students real applications of key manufacturing and service topics. Each video contains plant tours to help students see how companies are using operations management concepts and techniques to be productive and competitive.

The OM Center. The OM Center, edited and maintained by Byron Finch, provides additional operations management resources for both students and instructors. Consider this as your site for pedagogical support or reference and for students seeking current OM information. Among its features, the site covers OM resources by topic, contains links to the "top 50" company tours, offers Internet published articles and business news, and lists OM publications and organizations. The site also contains articles from BusinessWeek and other journals available exclusively to users of the site, daily news feeds on topics such as supply chain management, and links to many other McGraw-Hill operations management resources.

Course Management

McGraw-Hill Ryerson offers a range of flexible integration solutions for **WebCT** and **Blackboard** platforms. Please contact your local McGraw-Hill Ryerson *i*Learning Sales specialist for details.

Create Online

McGraw-Hill's Create Online places the most abundant resource at your fingertips—literally. With a few mouse clicks, you can create customized learning tools simply and affordably. McGraw-Hill Ryerson has included many of its market-leading textbooks within Create Online for e-book and print customization as well as many licensed readings and cases. For more information, go to www.mcgrawhillcreate.com.

CourseSmart

CourseSmart brings together thousands of textbooks across hundreds of courses in an eTextbook format providing unique benefits to students and faculty. By purchasing an eTextbook, students can save up to 50 percent off the cost of a print textbook, reduce their impact on the environment, and gain access to powerful Web tools for learning, including full text search, notes and highlighting, and email tools for sharing notes among classmates. For faculty, CourseSmart provides instant access to review and compare textbooks and course materials in their discipline area without the time, cost, and environmental impact of mailing print examination copies. For further details, contact your *i*Learning Sales Specialist or visit www.coursesmart.com.

Acknowledgements

We gratefully acknowledge the input of reviewers and contributors who so vitally helped to shape the fourth Canadian edition of *Operations Management*, including:

Mohammed Fazle Baki,
Windsor University

Paul Callaghan,
Acadia University

Richard K. Cho,
University of New
   Brunswick

Romulus Cismaru,
University of Regina

Avninder Gill,
Thompson Rivers
   University

Rajan Gupta, Memorial
University of
   Newfoundland

Neil Holt,
University of Western
   Ontario

Kalinga Jagoda,
Mount Royal College

Dennis Kira,
Concordia University

Wieslaw Kubiak,
Memorial University

Abdur Rahim,
University of New
   Brunswick

David Slichter,
Conestoga College

Rick Sparkman,
Acadia University

Reena Yoogalingam,
Brock University

We also appreciate the work of reviewers and contributors for the third Canadian edition:

Kirk Bailey,
Ryerson University

Walid Belassi,
Athabasca University

George Dracalopoulos,
Vanier College

Brent McKenzie,
University of Western
   Ontario

Ron McLachlin,
University of Manitoba

Saibal Ray,
McGill University

Mahesh C. Sharma,
Concordia University

Rob Shepherd,
Niagara College

Manish Verma,
Memorial University

And the reviewers and contributors for the second Canadian edition:

Mitali De,
Wilfrid Laurier University

Conrad D'Souza,
Centennial College

Stephen Dudra,
British Columbia Institute
   of Technology

Albert Ersser,
Mohawk College

Wieslaw Kubiak,
Memorial University of
   Newfoundland

Shanling Li,
McGill University

Jim Mason,
University of Regina

Dave Meston,
Ryerson University

Ragu Nayak,
Centennial College

Saibal Ray,
McGill University

Austin Redlack,
Memorial University

Jane Rotering,
George Brown College

Mahesh Sharma,
Concordia University

Bill Wedley,
Simon Fraser University

Sajjad Zahir,
University of Lethbridge

We would like to thank the McGraw-Hill Ryerson staff, including Sponsoring Editor Kimberley Veevers; Managing Editor of Development Kelly Dickson; Developmental Editors Sarah Fulton and Christopher Cullen; Supervising Editor Kara Stahl, and copy editor Karen Rolfe for their excellent work.

Mehran Hojati
William J. Stevenson

CHAPTER 1

Introduction to Operations Management

hapter 1 introduces you to the field of operations management. It describes the nature and scope of operations management, and how operations management relates to other parts of the organization. Among the other important topics it covers are a comparison of production of goods versus performance of services, a brief history of operations management, and a list of major trends that affect operations. After you have read this chapter, you will have a good understanding of what the operations function of an organization encompasses.

Chapter 2 discusses operations management in a broader context, and presents the issues of competition, strategic planning, and productivity. After you have read Chapter 2, you will understand the importance of the operations function relative to the goals of an organization, and how performance of production function can be measured.

LEARNING OBJECTIVES

After completing this chapter, you should be able to:

LO1 Define the term *operations management* and identify operations management jobs.

LO2 Identify the three major functional areas of organizations and describe how they interrelate.

LO3 Describe the scope of operations management and provide an overview of this book, including differentiating between design and operations decisions.

LO4 Compare goods versus services.

LO5 Discuss the operations manager's job.

LO6 Describe the key aspects of operations management decision making.

LO7 Briefly describe the historical evolution of operations management.

LO8 Identify some of the major trends that affect operations management.

Up until the late 1990s, Sobeys was a regional chain of supermarkets in Atlantic Canada. Then Loblaw started opening up stores in Sobeys' backyard. Sobeys' top management decided that the only way the company could compete was by expanding nationally. The company is now the second-largest grocery chain in Canada, competing effectively with Loblaw, mainly due to improvements in operations and use of technology.

When Walmart, renowned for its supply chain/operations efficiency and effectiveness, expanded into Canada in the mid-1990s, it caught Zellers by surprise. Zellers had been operating with almost no competition, carrying old merchandise, and offering little customer service; nevertheless, it made money. Then its profits started to shrink and losses piled up. Its parent company, Hudson's Bay Company, had to change the strategic and operations direction of Zellers. Despite some improvements in its operations, Zellers was not able to fully recover. Now, Zellers and its parent, HBC, are part of a private U.S. company.

This book is about operations management. The subject matter is fascinating and timely: productivity, quality, e-commerce, global competition, supply chain management, and customer service are very much in the news. All are part of operations management. This first chapter presents an introduction and overview of operations management. Among the issues it addresses are the following: What is operations management? Why is it important? What are major functions in an organization? What is the scope of operations management? How can we differentiate between production of goods and performance of services? What do operations managers do? What decision-making approaches do they take? The chapter also provides a brief description of the historical evolution of operations management and a discussion of the major trends that affect operations management.

LO 1 INTRODUCTION

operations management
The management of processes or systems that create goods and/or provide services.

process   A series of linked actions, changes, or functions bringing about a result.

Operations management is the management of processes and the systems that create goods and/or provide services. A system is a set of interrelated parts that must work together. A **process** is a series of linked actions, changes, or functions bringing about a result. There are three types of processes: core, support, and managerial. Core or operational processes directly create goods and/or services. Support processes support core processes, and managerial processes govern the system.

We use an airline to illustrate the system and processes involved. The system includes staff, airplanes, airport facilities, and maintenance facilities, sometimes spread out over a wide territory. Most of the activities performed by management and administrative employees fall into the realm of operations management:

Forecasting things such as seat demand for flights, the growth in air travel, and weather and landing conditions.

Capacity planning such as deciding the number of planes and where to use them.

Scheduling of planes for flights and for routine maintenance; scheduling of pilots and flight attendants; and scheduling of ground crews, counter staff, and baggage handlers.

Managing inventories of items such as food and beverages and spare parts.

Assuring quality, essential in flying and maintenance operations, where the emphasis is on safety. Also important in dealing with customers at ticket counters, check-in, telephone and electronic reservations, and in-flight service, where the emphasis is on efficiency and courtesy.

Employee motivation and training in all phases of operations.

Location of facilities according to top managers' decisions on which cities to provide service for, where to locate maintenance facilities, and where to locate major and minor hubs.

Buying materials such as fuel, food, and spare parts. Buying aircraft and maintaining it.

For an airline, core processes include reservations, boarding and flying the planes, handling the luggage, and performing maintenance. Support processes include forecasting, scheduling, managing inventories, assuring quality, and buying material. Managerial processes include capacity planning, locating facilities, and employee motivation.

Now consider a bicycle factory. This might be primarily an *assembly* operation: buying components such as frames, tires, wheels, gears, and other items from suppliers, and then assembling bicycles. The factory might also do some of the *fabrication* work itself (forming frames, making the gears and chains) and buy mainly raw materials and a few parts and materials such as paint, nuts and bolts, and tires. Among the key operations management activities in either case are scheduling production, deciding which components to make and which to buy, ordering parts and materials, deciding on the style of bicycle to produce and how many, purchasing new equipment to replace old or worn-out equipment, maintaining equipment, motivating workers, and ensuring that quality standards are met.

Obviously, an airline and a bicycle factory are completely different types of operations. One is primarily a service operation, the other a producer of goods. Nonetheless, these two operations have much in common. Both involve scheduling of activities, motivating employees, ordering and managing supplies, selecting and maintaining equipment, and satisfying quality standards. And in both businesses, the success of the business depends on planning.

Many companies use operations management strategies, tactics, and actions in order to improve their efficiency and effectiveness. **Efficiency** refers to operating at minimum cost and time, whereas **effectiveness** refers to achieving the intended goals (quality and responsiveness). This text contains many practical and real-life examples of operations management in the form of tours, cases, photos, readings in the form of OM in Actions, and video clips (see *Connect*). For example, there is a description of how Stone Consolidated, the paper manufacturer (now part of Abitibi Bowater), chose a location for a landfill (Chapter 8), how Toronto East General Hospital implemented total quality management (Chapter 9), how Sears Canada uses supply chain tools to improve their operation (Chapter 11), how various companies such as Eli Lilly Canada use warehouse management systems to operate efficiently (Chapter 12), and how companies such as Celestica use just-in-time systems to work efficiently (Chapter 15).

efficiency Operating at minimum cost and time.

effectiveness Achieving quality and responsiveness.

OM in ACTION

Operations Management Job Ads

Buyer—Supply Management

Responsibilities:

You will be responsible for the complete procurement process for assigned oilfield or corporate purchases, up to delivery to the end user. And be responsible for providing your clients with superior service, and the timely acquisition of materials and services, in an honest and ethical manner. This includes the extensive use of SAP and ProCon systems. As part of your daily activities, you will gather supplier and market knowledge, to aid in the creation of supply strategies that allow us to lower the Total Cost of Ownership for purchases. Over time you will progress through positions designed to give you learning opportunities and experience on the equipment and services used by the Oil & Gas industry. As well as opportunities to learn the general operating practices used by our main clients: Corporate, Operations, Drilling and Facilities. This will allow you to increasingly add commercial and technical value in the various phases of Western Canadian oilfield operations. You will ensure that top quality material is obtained, while maintaining the highest levels of ethics and integrity as you initiate and close out various purchasing agreements and orders. You will develop an above average understanding of all the technical standards and relevant equipment specifications for these commodities. You will be required to initiate, maintain and provide SAP related statistics and continuously analyze these purchasing activities for process improvement opportunities.

Qualifications & Requirements:

- Please indicate your GPA and rating scale (e.g., GPA of 3.5 out of 4) when applying for this position. Also, include a cover letter as the first page of your resume in one Word document.

- Students graduating in 2010 and recent graduates with a Bachelor's degree (Business, Economics, Engineering) and desire [sic] a career in supply chain management. Ideally you are also working towards your CPP designation, or are willing to undertake Purchasing Management Association of Canada (PMAC) studies upon completion of your university studies.

- Additional Requirements/Preferences:
  - A motivated self-starter;
  - Some exposure to the oil and gas industry would be an asset but not necessary;
  - Microsoft software skills (Excel, Word, and PowerPoint);
  - Exposure to SAP, or other integrated computer systems, would be an asset.
  - Eligible to work in Canada.

Supervisor, Manufacturing

Essential Duties and Responsibilities:

- Leads and manages all operational functions involved in the production and distribution of complex scientific instruments (Laboratory Automation) in support of business unit and division strategic and annual operating plans

- Meets customer satisfaction objectives in the areas of order communications, on-time delivery, and installation as well as ongoing quality and reliability standards

- Drives continuous improvement and productivity

- Leads the Operation to high levels of Operational Excellence, productivity, and inventory turnover through contemporary Lean Manufacturing and Supply Chain Management concepts

- Drives improvement in material costs through value engineering, supply base consolidation, and Low-Cost Region sourcing

- Ensures the Operations Organization is a key participant and stakeholder in the New Product Development process, with the goal of development and on-time launch of high quality products that meet cost, feature, and quality objectives

- Manages up to 12 direct reports

Minimum Education and Experience Requirements:

- Bachelor's degree in engineering or business preferred

- Minimum of two to five years of progressive manufacturing operations experience with a solid track record of advancement and a variety of functional experiences

Knowledge, Skills, and Abilities necessary to perform essential functions:

- Demonstrate 4-I values: Integrity, Intensity, Innovation and Involvement

- Excellent knowledge of manufacturing fabrication and production assembly and test processes

- Excellent knowledge of quality theory, continuous improvement, and Lean Manufacturing methodologies and tools; prior six sigma experience is desired

- Working knowledge of lean replenishment approaches with both external and internal supply chain partners

- Prior experience is desired working in an organization with complex products containing both hardware and software where a structured New Product Development PhaseGate review process is in use with high levels of process compliance and effectiveness

- Excellent written and oral communications skills

- Be willing to travel as required (estimate 10%, including international)

- Strong relationship building and influencing skills in a matrix environment are a must

- Prior formal training and implementation experience in lean manufacturing concepts (5S, pull systems/kanban, DFT, value stream mapping, kaizen)

- Prior ERP experience is a must, with SAP experience highly desired

- Demonstrated Role Model Leader Characteristics:
  - Embody the 4-I values
  - Delight customers
  - Communicate openly and honestly
  - Focus on growth
  - Champion employee development

Sources: http://sesd.usask.ca/students/posting/list/target/business_-_operations_mgmt/1/view/21329 accessed Nov. 7, 2009; Thermo Fisher Scientific, "About Us," https://careers.thermofisher.com/viewjob.html?optlink-view=view-115786&ERFormID=newjoblist&ERFormCode=any accessed Nov. 7, 2009.

Why Study Operations Management?

There are a number of very good reasons. First, because a large percentage of a company's expenses occur in the operations area, such as purchasing materials and workforce salaries, more efficient operations—even a small reduction in operations costs—can result in large increases in profits. Second, a large number of management jobs are in operations management—areas such as purchasing, quality assurance, production planning and control, scheduling, logistics, inventory management, and many more (see the "Operations Management Job Ads" OM in Action). Third, activities in all of the other areas of business organizations, such as finance, accounting, human resources, management information systems (MIS), and marketing are all interrelated with operations management activities. So it is essential for people who work in these areas to have a basic understanding of operations management.

Careers in Operations Management

If you are thinking of a career in operations management, you can benefit by joining one or more of the following associations.

Purchasing Management Association of Canada (PMAC)

Supply Chain & Logistics Association Canada (SCL)

Canadian Supply Chain Sector Council (CSCSC)

American Production and Inventory Control Society (APICS) (now called the Association for Operations Management)

American Society for Quality (ASQ)

Canadian Operational Research Society (CORS)

Production and Operations Management Society (POMS)

Project Management Institute (PMI)

Decision Sciences Institute

Global Association of Productivity and Efficiency Professionals (previously Institute of Industrial Engineers)

APICS, PMAC, and ASQ all offer certification programs that can enhance your qualifications. Information about job opportunities can be obtained from all of these associations.

http://www.pmac.ca

http://www.sclcanada.org

http://www.supplychaincanada.org

http://www.apics.org

http://www.asq.org

http://www.cors.ca

http://www.poms.org

http://www.pmi.org

http://www.decisionsciences.org

http://www.iienet.org

LO 2 FUNCTIONS WITHIN ORGANIZATIONS

Organizations are formed to pursue goals that are achieved more efficiently and effectively by the concerted efforts of a group of people rather than by individuals working alone. Organizations are devoted to producing goods and/or providing services. They may be for-profit (i.e., business) or non-profit organizations (e.g., hospitals). Their goals, products, and services may be similar or quite different. Nonetheless, their functions and the way they operate are similar.

A typical organization has three basic functions: operations, finance, and marketing (see Figure 1-1). These three functions, and other supporting functions, perform different but related activities necessary for the operation of the organization. The functions must interact to achieve the goals and objectives of the organization, and each makes an important contribution. For instance, unless operations and marketing work together, marketing may promote goods or services that operations cannot profitably deliver, or operations may turn out goods or services for which there is no demand. Similarly, unless finance and operations work closely, funds for materials, expansion, and new equipment may not be available when needed.

Let's take a closer look at these functions.

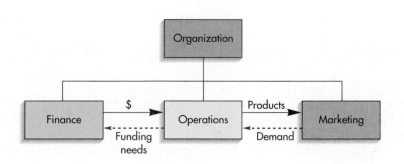

Figure 1-1

The three basic functions of organizations and flows between them

Operations

The operations function performs all the activities *directly* related to producing goods or providing services. Hence, it exists both in fabrication and assembly operations, which are *goods-oriented*, and in areas such as health care, transportation, restaurant, and retailing, which are primarily *service-oriented* (see Table 1-1).

Table 1-1	Type of Operations	Examples
Examples of types of operations	Goods producing	Farming, mining, construction, manufacturing
	Services	Warehousing, trucking, airlines
		Retailing, wholesaling, banking
		Films, radio, and television
		Telephone

The operations function is the core of most organizations; it is responsible for the creation of an organization's goods or services. Inputs are used to obtain finished goods or services using one or more *transformation/conversion processes* (e.g., storing, transporting, and cutting). To ensure that the desired outputs are obtained, measurements are taken at various points (*feedback*) and then compared with previously established standards to determine whether corrective action is needed (*control*). Figure 1-2 shows the conversion process. Table 1-2 provides two examples of inputs, transformation processes, and outputs.

Figure 1-2

The operations function involves the conversion of inputs into outputs.

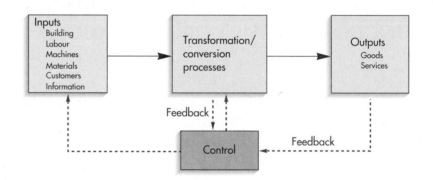

Table 1-2	Food Processor	Inputs	Processes	Output
Illustrations of the transformation process		Raw vegetables	Cleaning	Canned vegetables
		Metal sheets	Making cans	
		Water	Cutting	
		Energy	Cooking	
		Labour	Packing	
		Building	Labelling	
		Equipment		
	Hospital	**Inputs**	**Processes**	**Output**
		Sick patients, doctors, nurses	Examination	Healthy patients
		Building	Surgery	
		Medical supplies	Monitoring	
		Equipment	Medication	
		Laboratories	Therapy	

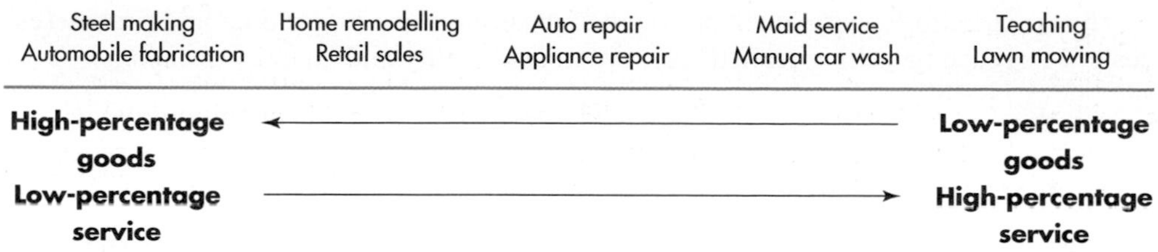

Steel making Automobile fabrication	Home remodelling Retail sales	Auto repair Appliance repair	Maid service Manual car wash	Teaching Lawn mowing

Figure 1-3

The goods–service continuum

High-percentage   ← ————————————————   Low-percentage
    goods   goods

Low-percentage ———————————————— →   High-percentage
    service   service

It is important to note that goods and services often occur jointly. For example, having the oil changed in your car is a service, but the new oil is a good. Similarly, house painting is a service, but the paint is a good. The goods–service package is a continuum. It can range from primarily goods, with little service, to primarily service, with few goods (see Figure 1-3).

The essence of the operations function is to *add value* during the transformation process: **Value added** is the term used to describe the difference between the cost of inputs and the value or price of outputs. In non-profit organizations, the value of outputs (e.g., highway construction, police, and fire protection) is their value to society; the greater the value added, the greater the efficiency of these operations. In for-profit organizations, the value of outputs is measured by the prices that customers are willing to pay for those goods or services. Companies use the money generated by value added for research and development, investment in new facilities and equipment, to pay workers, and to pay out to owners as *profits*. Consequently, the greater the value added, the greater the amount of funds available for these purposes.

value added The difference between the cost of inputs and the value or price of outputs.

One way that businesses attempt to become more productive (i.e., make more output with the same or fewer inputs) is to examine critically whether the operations performed by their workers add value. Businesses consider those that do not add value wasteful. Eliminating or improving such operations decreases the cost of inputs or processing, thereby increasing the value added. For instance, a company may discover that it is producing an item much earlier than the scheduled delivery date to a customer, thus requiring the storage of the item in a warehouse until delivery. In effect, additional costs are incurred by storing the item without adding to the value of the item. Reducing storage time would reduce the transformation cost and, hence, increase the value added. A similar comment applies for receiving raw material/parts too early. Obviously, working with suppliers and customers can lead to productivity for all sides. This is called supply chain management. More information on this will be provided later in the chapter and in Chapter 11.

Finance

The finance function performs activities related to securing resources at favourable prices and allocating those resources throughout the organization. Finance and operations management personnel cooperate by exchanging information and expertise in activities such as:

1. *Provision of funds.* The necessary funding of operations and the amount and timing of funding can be important and even critical when funds are tight. Careful planning can help avoid cash flow problems. Most for-profit companies obtain the majority of their funds through the revenues generated by sales of their goods and services.

2. *Economic analysis of investment proposals.* Evaluation of alternative investments in plant and equipment requires inputs from both operations and finance people.

Marketing

Marketing is responsible for assessing customer wants and needs, and for communicating those needs and feedback to operations people and to product design people (usually engineers in manufacturing companies). That is, operations needs information about demand so that it can plan accordingly (e.g., purchase materials or schedule work), while product design people need information that relates to improving current products and services, and designing new ones. Marketing, design, and production must work closely together to successfully implement design changes and to develop and produce new products. One important piece of information marketing needs from operations is the manufacturing or service **lead time** in order to give customers realistic estimates of how long it will take to fill their orders.

lead time The time between ordering a good or service and receiving it.

Figure 1-4

Operations interfaces with a number of supporting functions.

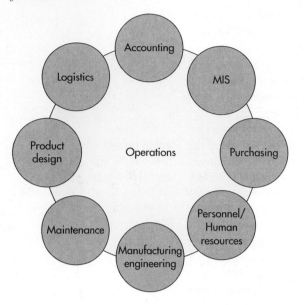

Thus, marketing, operations, and finance must interface on product and process(es) design, forecasting, setting realistic schedules, and quality and quantity decisions.

Other Functions

There are a host of other supporting functions that interface with operations (see Figure 1-4).

Accounting supplies information to management on costs of labour, materials, and overhead, and may provide reports on items such as scrap, downtime, and inventories. Accounting includes accounts payables and accounts receivables. Accountants gather the information needed for financial statements as well.

Management information systems (*MIS*) is concerned with providing management with the information it needs to effectively manage. This occurs mainly through designing systems (hardware and software) to capture relevant information and preparing reports.

Purchasing has responsibility for procurement of materials, supplies, equipment, and services. Close contact with operations is necessary to ensure correct quantities and timing of purchases. The purchasing department is often called on to evaluate vendors for quality, delivery-time reliability, service, price, and flexibility. Purchasing may also be involved in arranging incoming transportation, receiving, and inspection of the purchased goods.

The *personnel* or *human resources* department is concerned with recruitment and training of personnel, labour relations, contract negotiations, wage and salary administration, and ensuring the health and safety of employees.

Manufacturing engineering is responsible for design or purchase of the machines and equipment needed in the production processes. Also called process engineers, they are mainly trained as mechanical engineers, but other fields such as electrical and chemical may also be needed.

Maintenance is responsible for general upkeep and repair of equipment, buildings and grounds, heating and air-conditioning; removing toxic wastes; parking; and perhaps security.

Product design in manufacturing companies usually is done by engineers, but in other companies it could be done by people such as architects, scientists, chemists, and chefs. Designers create goods and services from information given to them on markets by marketing people and provide product specifications to operations to make the products.

Logistics involves the transportation of raw material to the plant; storage; and transportation of goods to warehouses, retail outlets, or final customers.

Many of these interfaces are elaborated on in later chapters.

LO3 THE SCOPE OF OPERATIONS MANAGEMENT

We have already noted that operations management is responsible for the creation of goods and services. This encompasses acquisition of resources and the conversion of raw material into outputs using one or more transformation processes. This involves designing, planning, executing, and controlling the elements that make up the processes.

A primary function of operations management is to guide the system by decision making. Certain decisions affect the *design* of the system, and others are *operational* (planning, scheduling, execution, control). Design decisions are usually strategic and long term (1–5 years ahead), whereas planning decisions are tactical and medium term (1–12 months ahead), and scheduling, execution and control decisions are short term (1–12 weeks ahead).

System design involves decisions that relate to product and service design, system capacity, the geographic location of facilities, arrangement of departments and placement of equipment within physical structures, and acquisition of equipment. *Operational activities* involve management of personnel, inventory planning and control, production planning, scheduling, project management, and quality assurance. In many instances, operations management is more involved in day-to-day operating decisions than with decisions relating to system design. However, operations management has a vital stake in system design because *system design essentially determines many of the parameters of operations*. For example, costs, space, capacities, and quality are directly affected by design decisions. Even though operations management is not solely responsible for making all design decisions, it can provide a wide range of information that will have a bearing on the decisions. Table 1-3 provides additional details on the design and operations decisions, and indicates where the topics are discussed in this text.

One factor that influences these decisions is whether the output is a good or a service.

Decision Area	Basic Questions	Chapter
Forecasting	What will the demand be?	3
Design		
Product and service Design	What do customers want? How can products and services be designed?	4
Capacity (long term)	How much capacity will be needed? How can the organization best meet capacity requirements?	5
Process design	What processes should the organization use?	6
Layout	What is the best arrangement for departments, machines, and equipment, in terms of work flow?	6
Design of work systems	What is the best way to motivate employees? How can productivity be improved? How to measure work? How to improve work methods?	7
Location	What is a satisfactory location for a facility (factory, store, etc.)?	8
Operational (planning, scheduling, execution, and control)		
Quality	How is quality defined? How are quality goods and services achieved and improved?	9
Quality control	Are processes performing adequately? What standards should be used? Are standards being met?	10
Supply chain management	Which supplier to choose? How to transport goods?	11
Inventory management	How much to order? When to reorder? Which items should get the most attention?	12
Aggregate planning	How much capacity will be needed over the medium term? How can capacity needs best be met?	13
Material requirements Planning	What material, parts, and subassemblies will be needed, and when?	14
Just-in-time manufacturing	How to manage production so that it is fast and lean?	15
Scheduling	How can jobs best be scheduled? When to schedule staff?	16
Project management	Which activities are the most critical to the success of a project? What resources will be needed, and when will they be needed?	17
Waiting lines	What service capacity is appropriate?	18

Table 1-3

Design and operations decisions

LO4 DIFFERENTIATING PRODUCTION OF GOODS VERSUS PERFORMANCE OF SERVICES

Production of goods results in a *tangible output*, such as an automobile, a building, wheat, lumber, fish, and gasoline—anything that we can see or touch. Production of goods can be categorized as follows:

- Manufacturing
- Construction
- Agriculture
- Forestry
- Fisheries
- Mining, and oil and gas.

Among these, manufacturing is the largest sector. Manufacturing includes:

- Food and beverage
- Textile and clothing
- Wood products and furniture
- Paper and printing
- Petroleum, chemicals, and plastics
- Primary metals and nonmetals
- Fabricated metals and non-metals
- Machinery
- Computer and electronic products
- Electrical equipment and appliances
- Transportation equipment.

Service, on the other hand, generally implies an *act*. A physician's examination, auto repair, lawn care, and projecting a film in a theatre are examples of services. The majority of services fall into these categories:

- Government services (federal, provincial, municipal)
- Wholesale/retail (clothing, food, appliances, stationery, toys, etc.)
- Finance and insurance (banking, stock brokerage, insurance, etc.)
- Real estate, rental, and leasing
- Health care (doctors, dentists, hospitals, etc.)
- Professional and technical services (lawyers, accountants, architects, auto mechanics)
- Personal services (laundry, dry cleaning, hair/beauty, lawn care, etc.)
- Business support services (data processing, e-business, advertising, employment agencies, etc.)
- Education (schools, colleges, universities, etc.)
- Hotels and restaurants
- Information, culture, and recreation
- Transportation and warehousing
- Utilities.

Production of goods and performance of services are often similar in terms of *what* is done but different in terms of *how* it is done. For example, both involve design and operation decisions, e.g., both must decide what size facility is needed. Both must make decisions on location, scheduling and control of operations, and allocation of scarce resources.

Production of goods and performance of services differ in:

1. Customer contact, use of inventories, and demand variability
2. Uniformity of input
3. Labour content of jobs
4. Uniformity of output
5. Measurement of productivity
6. Quality assurance.

Let us consider each of these differences.

1. Often, by its nature, service involves a much higher degree of customer contact than goods production. The performance of a service often occurs at the point of consumption. For example, repairing a leaky roof must take place where the roof is, and surgery requires the presence of the patient. On the other hand, goods production allows a separation between production and consumption, so that goods production may occur away from the consumer. This permits a fair degree of latitude in selecting work methods, assigning jobs, scheduling work, and exercising control over operations. In addition, goods producers can build up inventories of finished goods (e.g., cars, refrigerators), enabling them to absorb some of the shocks caused by variable demand. Service operations, however, cannot build up inventories and are much more sensitive to demand variability—banks and supermarkets alternate between lines of customers waiting for service and idle tellers or cashiers waiting for customers.

2. Service operations are subject to greater variability of inputs than typical goods-producing operations. Each patient, each lawn, and each auto repair presents a specific problem that often must be diagnosed before it can be remedied. Goods producers often have the ability to carefully control the amount of variability of inputs.

3. Services often require a higher labour content whereas goods production typically can be more capital intensive (i.e., mechanized).

4. Because high mechanization generates products with low variability, goods production tends to be smooth and efficient; service activities sometimes appear to be slow and awkward, and output is more variable. Automated services are an exception to this.

5. Measurement of productivity (i.e., ratio of outputs to inputs) is more straightforward in goods production due to the high degree of uniformity of most produced items. In service operations, variations in demand intensity and in requirements from job to job make productivity measurement considerably more difficult. For example, compare the productivity of two doctors. One may have a large number of routine cases while the other does not, so their productivity appears to differ, unless a very careful analysis is made.

6. Quality assurance is more challenging in services when performance and consumption occur at the same time. In goods production, errors can be corrected before the customer receives the output.

Although it is convenient to think in terms of systems devoted exclusively to producing goods or performing services, most real systems are a blend of both. For instance, maintenance and repair of equipment are services performed by virtually every goods producer. Similarly, most service organizations typically sell goods that complement their services. Thus, a lawn care business usually sells goods such as weed killers, fertilizers, and grass seeds. Hospitals dispense drugs along with health services. Restaurants sell food. Movie theatres sell popcorn, candy, and beverages.

The service sector and the goods-producing sector are both important to the economy. However, the service sector has been growing faster and now accounts for more than 75 percent of jobs in Canada. See Figure 1-5.

Figure 1-5

*Percentage of total labour
force by industry*

Source: Adapted from Statistics
Canada CANSIM database,
http://cansim2.statcan.ca, Table
282–0094, various series, June 30,
2010; and census data.

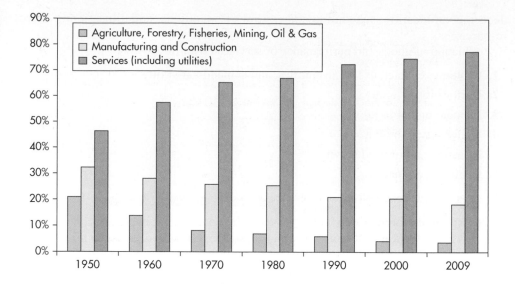

LO 5 THE OPERATIONS MANAGER'S JOB

The operations manager is the key figure in the system: he or she has the ultimate responsibility for the creation of goods or performance of services.

The kinds of jobs that operations managers oversee vary tremendously from organization to organization largely because of the different products or services involved. Thus, managing a banking operation obviously requires a different kind of expertise than managing a steelmaking operation. However, in a very important respect, the jobs are the same: They are both essentially *managerial*. In every case, the operations manager must coordinate the use of resources through the management activities of planning, organizing, directing, and controlling.

Examples of the responsibilities of operations managers according to these classifications are given in Table 1-4. Note that operations managers require both technical and behavioural competence.

In a survey of production/operations managers of approximately 250 Australian companies (two-thirds manufacturing), the following characteristics were discovered: approximately half joined the company after trade school and were promoted through the ranks; thus, they were deficient in business management, accounting/finance, and computer skills. Approximately half had total responsibility over planning, quality, and maintenance, whereas the other half provided major inputs into these decisions. Approximately

Table 1-4

*Responsibilities of operations
managers*

Planning	Organizing
Capacity	Degree of centralization
Location	Departments
Mix of products and services	Subcontracting
Production processes	Suppliers
Layout	Staffing
Controlling	**Directing**
Inventory control	Scheduling
Quality control	Issuance of work orders
Production pace	Job assignments
Motivation	Purchasing
Cost control	Logistics

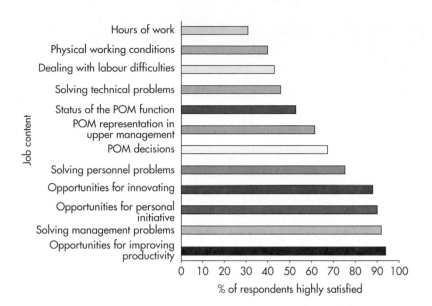

Figure 1-6

Level of job satisfaction

half would like more control over planning, information systems, personnel, and quality decisions. Most production/operations managers were given targets for cost reduction and productivity improvement. A list of job content and satisfaction of respondents for each is given in Figure 1-6. Most enjoy these challenges, whereas more than half are not happy with the heavy hours of work, working conditions, dealing with labour difficulty, and solving technical problems. Further questions revealed that most are happy with their compensation, work variety, work importance, and autonomy, whereas most are unhappy with their benefits and feedback from top management.

(LO 6) OPERATIONS MANAGERS AND DECISION MAKING

The chief role of an operations manager is that of a decision maker. In this capacity, the operations manager exerts considerable influence over the degree to which the goals and objectives of the organization are realized.

Throughout this book, you will encounter the broad range of decisions that operations managers must make, and you will be introduced to the tools necessary to handle those decisions. This section describes general approaches to decision making, including the use of models, quantitative approaches, analysis of trade-offs, the systems approach, establishing priorities, and ethics.

Models

A **model** is an abstraction of reality, a simplified representation of something. For example, a child's toy car is a physical model of a real automobile. Mathematical models represent important characteristics of the object by mathematical symbols and their relationship by mathematical equations and inequalities. Examples of mathematical models include formulas and sets of equations. Schematic models are graphs, charts, and drawings. Common statistical models include Normal distribution and regression equations.

Real life involves an overwhelming amount of detail, much of which is irrelevant for any particular problem. Models ignore the unimportant details so that attention can be concentrated on the most important aspects of a situation, thus increasing the opportunity to understand a problem and its solution.

Because mathematical, schematic, and statistical models play a significant role in operations management decision making, they are heavily integrated into the material of this text. For each model, try to learn (1) its purpose, (2) how it is used to generate results, (3) how these results are interpreted and used, and (4) what assumptions and limitations apply.

model An abstraction of reality; a simplified representation of something.

Quantitative Approaches

Quantitative approaches to problem solving often embody an attempt to obtain optimum solutions to the mathematical models of managerial problems. This is sometimes done by solving a set of equations. A popular example is *linear programming*, which is widely used for optimum allocation of scarce resources. *Queuing techniques* are useful for analyzing situations in which waiting lines form. *Inventory techniques* are widely used to control inventories. *Project scheduling techniques* such as PERT (program evaluation and review technique) are useful for planning, coordinating, and controlling large-scale projects. *Forecasting techniques* are widely used in forecasting demand. *Statistical techniques* are currently used in many areas of decision making, including quality control.

Many of these quantitative techniques require computers, and are somewhat time consuming. In contrast, a heuristic approach is a quick way to find a good solution. For example, in designing the work of an assembly-line worker, a good heuristic is to choose the longest possible (eligible and will-fit) activity first. For many decisions, a heuristic may be the only practical solution.

Analysis of Trade-offs

One type of heuristic approach is *trade-off* analysis. For example, (a) in deciding on the amount of inventory to stock, the manager may take into account the trade-off between the increased level of customer service that the additional inventory would yield and the increased costs required to stock that inventory; (b) in selecting a piece of equipment, a manager may evaluate the merits of extra features relative to the cost of those extra features; (c) in the scheduling of overtime to increase output, the manager may weigh the value of the increased output against the higher costs of overtime (e.g., higher labour costs, lower productivity, lower quality, and greater risk of accidents).

Throughout this book you will be presented with solution methods that reflect these kinds of trade-offs. Managers sometimes deal with these decisions by listing the advantages and disadvantages—the pros and cons—of a course of action to better understand the consequences of the decisions they must make. In some instances, managers add weights to the items on their list that reflect the relative importance of various factors. This can help them "net out" the potential impacts of the trade-offs on their decision. An example of this is the factor-rating approach described in Chapter 8 on location planning and analysis.

The Systems Approach

system   A set of interrelated parts that must work together.

A **system** can be defined as a set of interrelated parts that must work together. The systems approach emphasizes interrelationships among these parts. Hence, from a systems viewpoint, the output and objectives of the organization as a whole take precedence over those of any one part.

The systems approach is essential whenever something is being designed, redesigned, implemented, improved, or otherwise changed. It is important to take into account the impact on all parts of the system. For example, to investigate if the upcoming model of an automobile will have antilock brakes, a designer must take into account how customers will view the change, instructions for using the brakes, chances for misuse, the cost of producing the new brakes, installation procedures, recycling worn-out brakes, and repair procedures. In addition, workers will need training to make and/or assemble the brakes, production scheduling may change, inventory procedures may have to change, quality standards will have to be established, advertising must be informed of the new features, and parts suppliers must be selected.

Establishing Priorities

Pareto phenomenon   A few factors account for a high percentage of results achieved.

In virtually every situation, managers discover that certain elements are more important than others. Recognizing this fact of life enables the managers to direct their efforts to where they will do the most good and to avoid wasting time and energy on insignificant elements. This is referred to as the **Pareto phenomenon**, which means some things (a few) will be very important for achieving an objective or solving a problem, and other things (many) will not.

This is also known as 80-20 rule, meaning that approximately 20 percent of factors will impact approximately 80 percent of the results achieved. The implication is that a manager should examine each situation, searching for the few factors that will have the greatest impact, and give them the highest priority. This is one of the most important and pervasive concepts in operations management. In fact, this concept can be applied at all levels of management and to every aspect of decision making, both professional and personal.

Ethics

Operations managers, like all managers, have the responsibility to make ethical decisions. Ethical issues arise in many aspects of operations management, including:

- Worker safety: providing adequate training, maintaining equipment in good working condition, maintaining a safe working environment
- Product safety: providing products that minimize the risk of injury to users or damage to property or the environment
- The environment: not doing things that will harm the environment
- Closing facilities: taking into account the impact on a community, and honouring commitments that have been made.

In making decisions, managers must consider how their decisions will affect shareholders, employees, customers, the community at large, and the environment. Finding solutions that will be in the best interests of all of these stakeholders is not always easy, but it is a goal that all managers should strive to achieve.

(LO7) THE HISTORICAL EVOLUTION OF OPERATIONS MANAGEMENT

Systems for production have existed since ancient times. The Great Wall of China, the Egyptian pyramids, the ships of the Spanish empire, and the roads and aqueducts of the Romans provide examples of the human ability to organize for production. Even so, most of these examples could be classified as "public works" projects.

In the earliest days, goods were produced using **craft production**: highly skilled workers using simple, flexible tools produced goods according to customer specifications. Goods were produced in small shops by craftsmen and their apprentices. Under that system, it was common for one person to be responsible for making a product, such as a horse-drawn wagon or a piece of furniture, from start to finish. Only simple tools were available; the machines that we use today had not been invented.

craft production System in which highly skilled workers use simple, flexible tools to produce small quantities of customized goods.

Craft production had major shortcomings. Because products were made by skilled craftsmen who custom-fitted parts, production was slow and costly. And when parts failed, the replacements also had to be custom made, which was also slow and costly. Another shortcoming was that production costs did not decrease as volume increased; there were no *economies of scale*, which would have provided a major incentive for expansion. Instead, many small shops emerged, each with its own set of standards.

Prior to the 1700s, business activities in Canada were limited to fishing and fur trade. Under a practice called *mercantilism*, raw materials were exported to Europe for further processing and manufacturing. Companies such as the Hudson's Bay Company imported British-made goods to trade with local populations. All manufactured products came from Europe. The production of goods for sale, at least in the modern sense, and the modern factory system had their roots in the Industrial Revolution.

The Industrial Revolution

The Industrial Revolution began in the 1770s in England and spread to the rest of Europe and to North America during the nineteenth century. A number of innovations changed the face of production forever by substituting machine power for human or animal power.

Perhaps the most significant of these was the steam engine, made practical by James Watt around 1769, because it provided a source of power to operate machines in factories. The spinning jenny (1770) and power loom (1785) revolutionized the textile industry. Supplies of coal and iron ore provided material for generating power and making machinery. The new machines, made of iron, were much stronger and more durable than the simple wooden machines they replaced. Two concepts assisted in large-scale production: division of labour and interchangeable parts.

division of labour Breaking up a production process into small tasks so that each worker performs a small portion of the overall job.

Division of labour, which Adam Smith wrote about in *The Wealth of Nations* (1776), means that an operation is divided up into a series of many small tasks and individual workers are assigned to one of those tasks. Unlike craft production, where each worker was responsible for doing many tasks and thus required skill, with division of labour the tasks were so narrow that virtually no skill was required.

interchangeable parts Parts of a product made to such precision that they do not have to be custom fitted.

The **interchangeable parts** concept is sometimes attributed to Eli Whitney, an American inventor who applied the concept to assembling muskets in the late 1700s. The basis for interchangeable parts is to standardize parts so that any part in a batch of parts would fit. This meant that parts did not have to be custom fitted, as they were in craft production. The standardized parts could also be used for replacement parts. The result was a tremendous decrease in assembly time and cost.

Soon after their invention in Britain, the iron-making and steam engine technologies were imported into North America. In Canada, a few small mills began operating in the first half of the 1800s. By the second half of the 1800s, canals and railways were built, and timber was being exported.

The discovery of electricity by Edison in the late 1800s allowed replacement of electricity for steam as a power source, improving the efficiency and working environment of factories.

Despite the major changes that were taking place, management theory and practice had not progressed much from early days. What was needed was an enlightened and more systematic approach to management.

Scientific Management

The scientific management era brought widespread changes to the management of factories. The movement was spearheaded by American efficiency engineer and inventor Frederick Taylor, who is often referred to as the father of scientific management. Taylor believed in a "science of management" based on observation, measurement, analysis and improvement of work methods, and economic incentives. He studied work methods in great detail to identify the best method for doing each job. Taylor also believed that management should be responsible for planning, carefully selecting and training workers, finding the best way to perform each job, achieving cooperation between management and workers, and separating management activities from work activities.

Taylor's methods emphasized maximizing output. They were not always popular with workers, who sometimes thought the methods were used to unfairly increase output without a corresponding increase in compensation. Certainly some companies did abuse workers in their quest for efficiency. Eventually, the public outcry reached the halls of the U.S. Congress, and hearings were held on the matter. Taylor himself was called to testify in 1911, the same year in which his classic book *The Principles of Scientific Management* was published. The publicity from those hearings actually helped scientific management principles to achieve wide acceptance in industry.

A number of other pioneers also contributed heavily to this movement, including the following:

Frank Gilbreth was an industrial engineer who is often referred to as the father of time and motion study. He developed the principles of motion economy that could be applied to incredibly small portions of a task.

Lillian Gilbreth, a psychologist and the wife of Frank Gilbreth, worked with her husband, focusing on the human factor in work. (The Gilbreths were the subject of a classic 1950s film, *Cheaper by the Dozen*.) Many of her studies in the 1920s dealt with worker fatigue.

Henry Gantt recognized the value of nonmonetary rewards to motivate workers, and developed a widely used tool for scheduling, called a Gantt chart.

During the early part of the twentieth century, automobiles were just coming into vogue in North America. Ford's Model T was such a success that the company had trouble keeping up with orders for the cars. In an effort to improve the efficiency of operations, Henry Ford adopted the scientific management principles espoused by Frederick Taylor. He also introduced the *moving assembly line*, a type of assembly line in which the product is pulled along the line while the workers assemble its parts.

Ford introduced **mass production** to the automotive industry, a system of production in which large volumes of standardized goods are produced by low-skilled or semiskilled workers using highly specialized, and often costly, equipment. Ford was able to do this by taking advantage of a number of important concepts. Perhaps the key concept that launched mass production was interchangeable parts. Ford accomplished this by standardizing the gauges used to measure parts during production and by using newly developed processes to produce uniform parts. A second concept used by Ford was the division of labour in a moving assembly line. Together, these concepts enabled Ford to tremendously increase the production rate at his factories using readily available inexpensive labour.

mass production System in which lower-skilled workers use specialized machinery to produce high volumes of standardized goods.

The Industrial Revolution and scientific management allowed some industrialization in Canada at the beginning of the twentieth century. These changes allowed for more effective exploitation of Canada's resources, such as minerals and agriculture. The National Policy import tariffs encouraged foreign entrepreneurs and companies, mainly Americans, to set up factories and sales offices in Canada; the transfer of technology helped both countries. For example, Massey Ferguson established and grew as one of the world leaders in agricultural harvesting machinery, and McLaughlin Motor Co. was established in partnership with Buick and later became General Motors of Canada. The United States replaced Britain as the largest trading partner and investor in Canada in 1926.

The Human Relations Movement

Both Taylor and Ford expected workers to perform like robots. This paved the way for the human relations movement. Whereas the scientific management movement heavily emphasized the technical aspects of work design, the human relations movement emphasized the importance of the human element in job design. In the following decades, there was much emphasis on motivation. During the 1930s, Elton Mayo conducted studies at the Hawthorne division of Western Electric. His studies revealed that in addition to the physical and technical aspects of work, giving special attention to workers is critical for improving productivity. During the 1940s, Abraham Maslow developed motivational theories, which Frederick Hertzberg refined in the 1950s. Douglas McGregor added to this in the 1960s. In the 1970s, William Ouchi combined the Japanese approach, with such features as lifetime employment, employee problem solving, and consensus building, and the traditional Western approach that features short-term employment, specialists, and individual decision making and responsibility.

Decision Models and Computers

The factory movement was accompanied by the development of several quantitative techniques. F.W. Harris developed one of the first models in 1913: a mathematical model for inventory management. In the 1930s, three coworkers at Bell Telephone Labs—Dodge, Romig, and Shewart—developed statistical procedures for sampling and quality control.

At first, these quantitative models were not widely used in industry. However, the onset of the Second World War changed that. The war generated tremendous pressures on manufacturing output, and specialists from many disciplines combined efforts to achieve advancements in the military and in manufacturing. This area became known as operations research. After the war, efforts to develop and refine quantitative tools for decision making continued, facilitated by the advent of the mainframe computer in 1951. This resulted in decision models for forecasting, production planning (using the linear program of Dantzig), project management, and other areas of operations management.

During the 1960s and 1970s, quantitative techniques were highly regarded (these modelling and solutions for business are called *management science*); in the 1980s, they lost some favour. However, the widespread use of personal computers (invented in the late 1970s by Apple Computers) and user-friendly software in the workplace is causing resurgence in the popularity of these techniques. In 1975, Orlicky proposed Material Requirements Planning (MRP), mainly for assembly operations.

The advent of the computer resulted in its use in machine automation starting in the 1960s. In the middle to late 1980s, network computing began to increase, with applications such as electronic data interchange (EDI) and the ability to instantaneously receive point-of-sale data. This has led to more cooperation with the suppliers in the form of partnering, and formation of supply chains. In the mid-1990s, the Internet began to play a major role in business operations, and more and more companies are using enterprise resources planning (ERP) software to coordinate their sales, materials management, production planning/manufacturing, and accounting/finance activities.

The Influence of Japanese Manufacturers

A number of Japanese manufacturers developed or refined management practices that increased the productivity of their operations and the quality of their products. This made them very competitive, sparking interest in their approaches by companies outside Japan. One of their approaches, **total quality management**, emphasized quality and continual improvement, worker teams and empowerment, and achieving customer satisfaction. A related approach is using lean production system and just-in-time manufacturing.

Lean production systems use much fewer resources than mass production systems—less space, less inventory, and fewer workers—to produce a comparable amount of output. They use a highly skilled workforce and flexible equipment. In effect, they incorporate advantages of both mass production (high volume, low unit cost) and craft production (high variety and flexibility). And quality is higher than in mass production. Lean production is a broad approach to just-in-time manufacturing.

The skilled workers in lean production systems are more involved in maintaining and improving the system than their mass production counterparts. They are taught to stop production if they discover a defect, and to work with other employees to find and correct the cause of the defect so that it won't recur. This results in an increasing level of quality over time, and eliminates the need to inspect and rework at the end of the line.

Because lean production systems operate with lower amounts of inventory, additional emphasis is placed on anticipating when problems might occur *before* they arise, and avoiding those problems through careful planning. Even so, problems still occur at times, and quick resolution is important. Workers participate in both the planning and correction stages. Technical experts are still used, but more as consultants rather than substitutes for workers. The focus is on designing a system so that workers will be able to achieve high levels of quality and quantity.

Compared to workers in traditional systems, much more is expected of workers in lean production systems. They must be able to function in teams, playing active roles in operating and improving the system. Individual creativity is much less important than team success. Responsibilities also are much greater, which can lead to pressure and anxiety not present in traditional systems. Moreover, a flatter organizational structure means career paths are not as steep in lean production organizations. Workers tend to become generalists rather than specialists, another contrast to more traditional organizations.

Unions often oppose conversion from a traditional system to a lean system because they view the added responsibility and multiple tasks as an expansion of job requirements without comparable increases in pay. In addition, workers sometimes complain that the company is the primary beneficiary of employee-generated improvements.

Table 1-5 provides a comparison of craft production, mass production, and lean production. Keep in mind that all three of these modes of production are in existence today.

total quality management
Involving every employee in a continual effort to improve quality and satisfy the customers.

lean production System that uses minimal amounts of resources to produce a high volume of high-quality goods with some variety.

Table 1-6 provides a chronological summary of some of the key developments in the evolution of operations management.

Table 1-5

A comparison of craft, mass, and lean production

	Craft Production	**Mass Production**	**Lean Production**
Description	High variety, customized output, with one or a few skilled workers responsible for an entire unit of output.	High volume of standardized output, emphasis on volume. Capitalizes on division of labour, specialized equipment, and interchangeable parts.	Moderate to high volume of output, with more variety than mass production. Fewer mass production buffers such as extra workers, inventory, or time. Emphasis on quality. Employee involvement and teamwork are important.
Examples of Goods and Services	Home remodelling and landscaping, tailoring, portrait painting, diagnosis and treatment of injuries, surgery.	Sugar, steel, movie theatres, airlines, hotels, mail sorting, paper.	Automobiles and their components, electronics, logistics services, industrial equipment, batteries, furniture.
Advantages	Wide range of choice, output tailored to customer needs.	Low cost per unit, requires mostly low-skilled workers.	Flexibility, variety, high quality of goods.
Disadvantages	Slow, requires skilled workers, few economies of scale, high cost, and low standardization.	Rigid system, difficult to accommodate changes in output volume, product design, or process design. Volume may be emphasized at the expense of quality.	No safety nets to offset any system breakdowns, fewer opportunities for employee advancement, more worker stress, requires higher-skilled workers than mass production.

Table 1-6

Historical summary of operations management

Approximate Date	Contribution/Concept	Originator
1769	Steam engine	James Watt
1776	Division of labour	Adam Smith
1790	Interchangeable parts	Eli Whitney
1911	Principles of scientific management	Frederick W. Taylor
1911	Time and motion study	Frank Gilbreth
1912	Chart for scheduling activities	Henry Gantt
1913	Moving assembly line	Henry Ford
1915	Mathematical model for inventory management	F.W. Harris
1930	Hawthorne studies on worker motivation	Elton Mayo
1935	Statistical procedures for sampling and quality control	H.F. Dodge, H.G. Romig, W. Shewhart
1940	Operations research applications in warfare	Operations research groups
1947	Linear programming	George Dantzig
1951	Commercial digital computers	Sperry Univac
1960s	Computer-aided automation	Numerous
1970s	Personal computers	Apple
1975	Material requirements planning	Joseph Orlicky
1980s	Total quality management and lean production/just-in-time	Quality gurus; Toyota, and Taiichi Ohno
1990s–	Internet and e-business, technology, globalization, supply chains, and outsourcing	Numerous

LO8 MAJOR TRENDS

Organizations must constantly monitor current trends and take them into account in their strategies and operations management. The following are some long-term trends affecting operations management. Recently, however, there has been a slowdown in the world economy affecting these trends. No one knows how long the slowdown will last.

e-commerce Use of the Internet and other electronic networks to buy and sell goods and services.

1. *The Internet and e-commerce.* The *Internet* offers great potential for organizations and in many cases, and it has altered the way companies compete in the marketplace.

   Electronic commerce, or **e-commerce**, involves the use of Internet and other electronic networks to buy and sell goods and services. E-commerce is changing the way organizations interact with their customers and their suppliers. E-commerce is receiving increased attention from managers in developing strategies, planning, and decision making.

2. *Technology.* Technological advances have led to a vast array of new products and processes. Undoubtedly the computer has had—and will continue to have—the greatest impact on organizations. It has revolutionized the way companies operate. Applications include product design, processing technology, information processing, and communication. Obviously there have been—and will continue to be—many benefits from technological advances. However, technological advance also places a burden on management. For example, management must keep abreast of changes and quickly assess both their benefits and risks. Predicting advances can be tricky at best, and new technologies often carry a high price tag and usually a high cost to operate or repair. And in the case of computer operating systems, as new systems are introduced, support for older versions is discontinued, making periodic upgrades necessary. Conflicting technologies can exist that make technological choices even more difficult. Technological innovations in both *products* and *processes* will continue to change the way organizations operate, and hence, require continuing attention.

3. *Globalization.* Global competition, global markets, global supply chains, and global operations are having a growing impact on the strategies and operations of organizations, large and small, around the world. The General Agreement on Tariffs and Trade (GATT) of 1994 and later agreements of the World Trade Organization reduced the tariffs and subsidies in many countries, expanding world trade. China has become the factory of the world (see e.g., http://www.americanchronicle.com/articles/view/105125). This has led to long international supply chains and the importance of managing them.

   In addition, the Free Trade Agreement and NAFTA have increased trade with the United States to as much as 80 percent of total foreign trade of Canada. The implication is the need for improved efficiency and increased quality. However, occasionally there is protectionism, such as U.S. tariffs on Canadian softwood lumber.

supply chain A sequence of activities and organizations involved in producing and delivering a good or service.

4. *Supply chains.* A **supply chain** is the sequence of organizations—their facilities and activities—that are involved in producing and delivering a good or service. The sequence begins with basic suppliers of raw materials and extends all the way to final consumers. Facilities might include warehouses, factories, processing centres, offices, distribution centres, and retail outlets. Activities include forecasting, purchasing, inventory management, information management, quality assurance, scheduling, production, distribution, delivery, and customer service.

   Figure 1-7 provides an illustration of a supply chain: a chain that begins with wheat growing on a farm and ends with a customer buying a loaf of bread in a grocery store. Notice that the value of the product increases as it moves through the supply chain. Obviously, if members of a supply chain work together, they can all benefit. This is called supply chain management (see Chapter 11).

Figure 1-7

A supply chain for bread

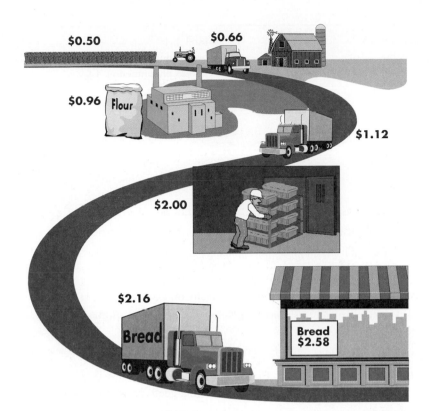

A growing aspect of supply chains is *outsourcing*—that is, buying a part of goods/ services or a segment of production/service process rather than producing or performing it within the organization. As more and more manufacturing has been shifted overseas, especially to China, supply chains have become longer, adding to cost and lead time of products. Also, increasing global competition has boosted the amount of outsourcing. These factors have resulted in the increased importance of coordination and collaboration of members of each supply chain.

These trends are having a major influence on organizations (including accounting, finance, international business, marketing, and MIS), as well as on operations management. Their impact on operations management is discussed throughout this text.

Summary

Operations management is responsible for planning and coordinating the use of the organization's resources to convert inputs into outputs. The operations function is one of three primary functions of organizations; the other two are marketing and finance.

The operations function is present in both service- and goods-producing organizations. Operations decisions involve design decisions and operations decisions. Design decisions relate to capacity planning, product design, processes design, layout of facilities, and selecting locations for facilities. Operation decisions relate to quality assurance, production planning, scheduling and control, inventory management, and project management. Service performance differs from goods production in customer contact and labour content, lack of inventories, variation in inputs and outputs, and difficulties in productivity measurement and quality assurance. Operations managers plan, organize, control, and direct. They use models, trade-off analysis, systems approach, priorities, and ethics in decision making.

The chapter provides a brief discussion of the historical evolution of operations management, including craft, mass, and lean production systems, and recent trends in the field. Among these trends are e-commerce, technology, globalization, and supply chains.

Key Terms

craft production, 15
division of labour, 16
e-commerce, 20
effectiveness, 3
efficiency, 3
interchangeable parts, 16
lead time, 7
lean production, 18
mass production, 17

model, 13
operations management, 2
Pareto phenomenon, 14
process, 2
supply chain, 20
system, 14
total quality management, 18
value added, 7

Discussion and Review Questions

Note: An asterisk indicates that a question or problem may be more challenging.

1. Briefly describe the term *operations management*. (LO1)

2. Name the title of three jobs in operations management. (LO1)

3. Why is operations management important to any organization? (LO1)

4. Identify the three major functional areas of organizations and briefly describe how they inter-relate. (LO2)

5. Describe the operations function and the nature of the operations manager's job. (LO2 & 5)

6. Explain the difference between design and operational decisions. (LO3)

7. List five important differences between producing goods and performing services. (LO4)

*8. Give an example of a pure service (i.e., one where no goods are exchanged). What do you think is being transformed? (LO2 & 4)

9. Give three types of activities an operations manager is likely involved in. (LO5)

10. Briefly discuss each of these terms related to the historical evolution of operations management: (LO7)

    a. Industrial Revolution
    b. Scientific management
    c. Interchangeable parts
    d. Division of labour

*11. Why are services important? Why is manufacturing important? (LO4)

*12. What are models and why are they important? (LO6)

*13. Name three people who have contributed to the development of operations management. (LO7)

*14. List the trade-offs you would consider for each of these decisions: (LO6)

    a. Driving your own car versus using public transportation.
    b. Buying a computer now versus waiting for an improved model.
    c. Buying a new car versus buying a used car.
    d. Speaking up in class versus waiting to get called on by the instructor.

15. Describe each of these systems: craft production, mass production, and lean production. (LO7)

16. Why might some people prefer not to work in a lean production system? (LO7)

*17. How have technological changes affected you? Are there any downsides to technological change? Explain. (LO8)

18. Identify some of the current trends in operations management and relate them to recent news or to your personal experience. (LO8)

*19. Why do people do things that are unethical? (LO6)

20. Explain the term *value added*. (LO2)

*21. What is a supply chain and why is it important to manage it? (LO8)

This item appears at the end of each chapter. It is intended to focus your attention on four key issues for organizations in general, and operations management, in particular. Those issues are trade-off analysis, collaboration among various functional areas of the organization, the impact of technology, and ethical issues. You will see four questions relating to these issues.

1. What are trade-offs? Why is careful consideration of trade-offs important in decision making? (LO6)

2. Why is it important for the various functional areas of an organization to collaborate? (LO2)

3. In what general ways does technology have an impact on operations management decision making? (LO8)

4. Why is employing child labour (10- to16-year-olds) in developing countries unethical? (LO6)

This item also will appear in every chapter. It allows you to critically apply information you learned in the chapter to practical situations.

1. Many organizations offer a combination of goods and services to their customers. As you learned in this chapter, there are some key differences between production of goods and delivery of services. What are the implications of these differences relative to managing operations? (LO4)

2. Some people who work in knowledge or arts sectors argue that the operation of their organization cannot be defined as a process, i.e., a set of predetermined activities. Discuss. (LO1)

These exercises also appear at the end of each chapter. They are designed to help you see the relevance of operations management firsthand. (LO3)

Visit a fast-food restaurant and answer these questions:

1. In what ways is quality, or lack of quality, visible?

2. What items must be stocked in addition to the food?

3. How important do you think employee scheduling is? Explain.

4. How might capacity decisions affect the success or failure of the restaurant?

This item will appear at the end of each chapter. It allows you to use the Internet to gain additional knowledge about chapter material. Here are the first exercises.

1. Visit the Web page of one of the associations listed on page 5 and briefly list the targeted members and the services that they provide to their members. (LO1)

2. Visit http://www.dofasco.ca/bins/content_page.asp?cid=339-342-352&lang=1 and watch the video of steel making by Dofasco. Answer the following questions. (a) What are the inputs, processes, and outputs of ArcelorMittal Dofasco? (b) Where in the process is quality determined? (c) What inventories are kept? (LO2 & 3)

Lynn

Lynn had worked for the same major Canadian company for almost 15 years. Although the company had gone through some tough times, things were starting to turn around. Customer orders were up, and quality and productivity had improved dramatically from what they had been only a few years earlier due to a companywide quality improvement program. So it came as a real shock to Lynn and about 400 of her co-workers when they were suddenly terminated following the new CEO's decision to downsize the company.

After recovering from the initial shock, Lynn tried to find employment elsewhere. Despite her efforts, after eight months of searching she was no closer to finding a job than the day she started. Her funds were being depleted and she was getting more discouraged. There was one bright spot, though: She was able to bring in a little money by mowing lawns for her neighbours. She got involved quite by chance when she heard one neighbour remark that now that his children were on their own, nobody was around to cut the grass. Almost jokingly, Lynn asked him how much he'd be willing to pay. Soon Lynn was mowing the lawns of five neighbours. Other neighbours wanted her to work on their lawns, but she didn't feel that she could spare any more time from her job search.

However, as the rejection letters began to pile up, Lynn knew she had to make an important decision in her life. On a rainy Tuesday morning, she decided to go into business for herself—taking care of neighbourhood lawns. She was relieved to give up the stress of job hunting, and she was excited about the prospect of being her own boss. But she was also fearful of being completely on her own. Nevertheless, Lynn was determined to make a go of it.

At first, business was a little slow, but once people realized Lynn was available, many asked her to take care of their lawns. Some people were simply glad to turn the work over to

her; others switched from professional lawn care services. By the end of her first year in business, Lynn knew she could earn a living this way. She also performed other services such as fertilizing lawns, weeding gardens, and trimming shrubbery. Business became so good that Lynn hired two part-time workers to assist her and, even then, she believed she could expand further if she wanted to. During winter months (January and February), Lynn takes her vacation in Florida.

Questions

1. Lynn is the operations manager of her business. Among her responsibilities are forecasting, inventory management, scheduling, quality assurance, and maintenance.
   a. What kinds of things would likely require forecasts?
   b. What inventory items does Lynn probably have? Name one inventory decision she has to make periodically.
   c. What scheduling must she do? What things might occur to disrupt schedules and cause Lynn to reschedule?
   d. How important is quality assurance to Lynn's business? Explain.
   e. What kinds of maintenance must be performed?

2. What are some of the trade-offs that Lynn probably considered relative to:
   a. Working for a company instead of for herself?
   b. Expanding the business?
   c. Launching a Web site?

3. Lynn decided to offer the students who worked for her a bonus of $25 for ideas on how to improve the business, and they provided several good ideas. One idea that she initially rejected now appears to hold great promise. The student who proposed the idea has left, and is currently working for a competitor. Should Lynn send that student a cheque for the idea?

4. Lynn is thinking of making her operations sustainable and environment friendly. Name one or two ideas she might consider.

Sobeys

Until 1998, Sobeys was a privately owned chain of grocery stores in the Atlantic provinces. Sobeys grew out of a meat-delivery business in the small coal-mining town of Stellarton, Nova Scotia, in 1907. When Loblaw, Canada's largest national grocery chain, expanded into Sobeys' territories, competition heated up. Sobeys' directors decided on a bold move in order to gain sufficient economies of scale to be able to compete with Loblaw. Sobeys took over the twice-as-large

Ontario-based Oshawa Group (at a purchase price of $1.5 billion), then Canada's second-largest national grocery chain, which included (mostly franchised) IGA and Price Chopper stores and the wholesale food distribution company SERCA.

Since 1998, Sobeys has worked hard to integrate the supermarket chains. It has divided the country into four regions (Atlantic, Quebec, Ontario, and the West), has aligned each store's size and merchandise to its market, centralized purchasing and merchandising, improved its logistics and distribution, and focused on its core grocery retailing business by selling

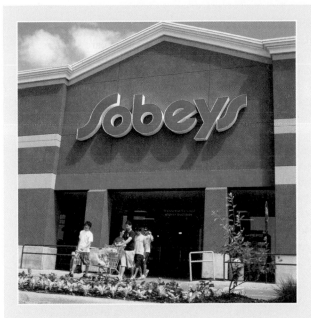

SERCA to Sysco, the giant food distribution company. Sobeys now manages more than 1,300 owned or franchised grocery stores, has annual revenue of more than $15 billion, and employs over 75,000 people. Sobeys' strategy is to emphasize ready-to-serve quality food and fresh produce along with exceptional customer service in attractive stores.

Sobeys operates grocery stores of varying sizes in every region of Canada with a range of services suitable for the market. It runs more than 320 full-service supermarkets under the names Sobeys and IGA Extra. These stores are over 60,000 square feet in size and feature farm-fresh produce, a full-line bakery, meat and poultry, deli, extensive home-style meal selections, a pharmacy, and a variety of innovative in-store retail services such as photo finishing, florist, Western Union money wiring, dry-cleaning, and banking (TD Canada Trust). They usually have between 10 and 14 checkout lanes. A Sobeys store of this size typically employs 200 to 250 people.

Some smaller "Fresh-service" Sobeys and IGA stores (approximately 180) are designed primarily for mid-sized communities with store sizes in the range of 15,000 to 40,000 square feet. The emphasis in these stores is on fresh produce, meat, dairy, and bakery goods, and highly personalized service. Stores of this size often have 8 to 10 checkout lanes and employ 50 to 120 people. Price Chopper stores (about 120) are also approximately the same size but are for value-conscious consumers.

In smaller one-store communities, Sobeys runs approximately 310 stores under the banners IGA, Foodland, and Food Town, which offer consumers convenient, full-service grocery stores on a smaller scale.

Sobeys also runs approximately 285 Needs, Les Marchés Tradition, and Marché Boni choix convenience stores, and approximately 110 other stores such as Lawton's Drugstores; Sobeys Fuel; and Sobeys Spirits, Wines, and Cold Beer.

Products

The produce department of a Sobeys store is set up in a farmers' market style, with most of its produce unpacked and available for customer evaluation and selection. Its produce is sourced mainly nationally, but sometimes locally. As part of its wide produce selection, Sobeys also sells organically grown vegetables. Two features of the store's deli are the hot case foods, such as Grade A whole chickens, and the service case, which holds a wide variety of fresh salads and sliced meats. In addition, it carries a wide variety of international cheeses.

One characteristic of its East Coast origin is Sobeys' fresh seafood market. It stocks a number of fresh fish and seafood delicacies such as whole, portioned, and fillet fish; shellfish; store-made chowder ingredients; and live lobster cooked at a customer's request. Sobeys offers a wide assortment of premium-cut meats available from the service case and boxed meats that it sells under its private label. As well, a meat cutter is on duty to provide personalized service for special-order needs. Years ago Sobeys raised the standard of quality beef by introducing the "Aged for Flavour" program. It has gone a step further with its "Canadian Select Beef." Sobeys now provides only the highest-quality Certified AAA and AA grades of beef.

Sobeys' private-label products, Compliments, number more than 3,000, bringing in 20 percent of sales. The Meals Made Easy program offers time-pressed shoppers a variety of ready-to-serve, home-style meals. At the Courtyard Café, shoppers can take the time to sample an appetizing range of premium-quality foods including fresh-baked pizza, rotisserie chicken, hot and cold pasta entrées, a wide selection of fruit and vegetables, gourmet coffees, and a variety of desserts.

Technology and Operations

At Sobeys, using new technology and improving operations is part of its approach to doing business. In the 1990s, both Sobeys and IGA started using Electronic Data Interchange (EDI) to communicate with their major suppliers, the food manufacturers. This helped with information accuracy and speed. The acquisition of IGA stores provided Sobeys the opportunity to streamline all its operations. Sobeys renovated the Milton warehouse (west of Toronto) and built a large state-of-the-art warehouse in Whitby (east of Toronto), closed five old warehouses in Ontario, installed a warehouse management system (Exceed, by EXE) in its warehouses, used automated ordering systems, established productivity standards in the warehouses, reduced costs of transportation and distribution to its more than 20 regional distribution centres by using a truck-route optimization software by Manugistics, started using multi-temperature trucks to save on the number of trips, and outsourced operations of the Milton and Whitby distribution centres to Axis (a member of Tibbett and Britten group) and Ryder Logistics, respectively. Deliveries vary from one to two times a week for the smaller stores to daily for the largest stores.

In 2000, Sobeys tried to install SAP's Enterprise software to integrate all its stores, warehouses, and headquarters. However, the system crashed in late November 2000 for five days, resulting in lost sales of more than $20 million. As a result, Sobeys' new CEO, Bill McEwan, decided to discontinue the use of SAP. However, in 2005, Sobeys implemented SAP again, first in its Atlantic Canada stores, and later in 2007 in its Ontario stores.

In 2005, Sobeys initiated "Smart Retailing," a productivity improvement program that aimed to reduce wastes by improving inventory management. Smart Retailing includes:

a. Produce wheel (multi-level produce display on wheels)

b. Level block facing and case cutting (cut one side of the case of cans, place the case on the shelf, and frequently align the cans in the front row)

c. Just-in-time production system (for perishable items in deli and prepared food)

d. Backroom grocery stock levels (using visual guides for piles of cans and bottles in the back of the store)

e. Kanbans (a visual method of replenishment for bakery and salad products)

f. Communication boards (for transmitting messages, instructions, schedules, and monitoring improvement data)

Smart Retailing has been implemented in most stores. Sobeys is continuing its Smart Retailing by adding Peer-to-Peer management (sharing best practices across stores), Fresh Food Management (forecasting the hourly demand for freshly prepared meals in each store), and Workforce Management software (forecasting the level of service needed and scheduling adequate staff in each store).

Sobeys has continued to expand its portfolio of stores westward by building new stores and acquiring smaller chains. For example, Sobeys bought Thrifty Foods chain of B.C. and replaced its Manitoba distribution centre with a larger one (380,000 square feet) in Headingly, just west of Winnipeg. In 2007, the Sobey family bought the 28 percent of the outstanding shares of Sobeys for over $1 billion, thus making Sobeys a private company again (under the name Empire Company Ltd.). In 2008, Sobeys continued its expansion into Quebec by buying the 25-store chain Achille de la Chevrotiere. In 2009, Sobeys continued its technology and operations improvement by opening a new automated distribution centre in Vaughn, just north of Toronto.

Questions

1. What are the inputs, processes, outputs, and feedback/control for a grocery store such as Sobeys or IGA?

2. What are the operations decisions for running a grocery store such as Sobeys or IGA?

Sources: Sobeys Annual Reports, 1999–2006; Empire Co. Ltd. Annual Reports, 2007–2009; M. Love, "Sobey's to Build New Distribution Centre in Manitoba," *Canadian Grocer* 121(7), September 2007, p. 12; "Sobeys Reports Efficiencies from EDI," *Canadian Grocer* 109(7), July 95, p. 5; P. D'Souza and S. Silcoff, "On Special This Week: Supermarkets," *Canadian Business* 71(21), December 24, 1998–January 8, 1999, pp. 32–40; R. Robertson "Delivering Food Value," *Materials Management and Distribution* 45(4), May 2000, p. 18; M. Evans, "Grocery Gateway Inks Supply Deal with Sobeys: 'It Allows Us to Be Aggressive,'" *Financial Post* (*National Post*), October 23, 2002, p. FP4; J. Tutunjian, "The Passion of Bill McEwan," *Canadian Grocer* 118(4), May 2004, pp. 22–23, P. Brent, "Empire Building," *CA Magazine* 140(6), August 2007, pp. 20–26.

CHAPTER 2
Competitiveness, Strategic Planning, and Productivity

LEARNING OBJECTIVES

After completing this chapter, you should be able to:

LO1 List and briefly discuss the primary ways that organizations compete.

LO2 Describe a company's strategic planning, mission/vision/values, strategies, and operations strategy, and list the steps involved in formulating an operations strategy.

LO3 Define and measure the term *productivity,* describe factors affecting productivity, and explain why measuring the productivity of services is difficult.

When Richard Currie was appointed as the president of Loblaw in 1976, Loblaw was only a regional chain of grocery stores in Ontario, making little profit and having cash-flow problems. Now, Loblaw is Canada's largest national grocery store chain. How did the company accomplish this?

WestJet was founded in 1996, but is now challenging Air Canada as the leading airline in Canada. WestJet's operating costs are almost half Air Canada's. How did WestJet achieve this when so many other airlines couldn't?

These are the types of questions answered in this chapter. We will see that organizational and operations strategies contribute to competitiveness of organizations.

competitiveness Ability and performance of an organization in the marketplace compared to other organizations that offer similar goods or services.

strategy The long-term plans that determine the direction an organization takes to become (or remain) competitive.

strategic planning The managerial process that determines a strategy for the organization.

key purchasing criteria The major elements influencing a purchase: price, quality, variety, and timeliness.

This chapter discusses competitiveness, strategic planning, and productivity: three related topics that are vitally important to organizations. **Competitiveness** relates to the ability and performance of an organization in the marketplace compared to other organizations that offer similar goods or services; **strategy** is the long-term plans that determine the direction an organization takes to become (or remain) competitive; **strategic planning** is the managerial process that determines a strategy for the organization; and productivity is a measure of how efficiently the resources are being used.

Slumping productivity gains in recent years and the impressive successes of foreign competition in the marketplace have caused many North American companies to rethink their strategies and to place increased emphasis on operations.

LO1 COMPETITIVENESS

Companies must be competitive to sell their goods and services in the marketplace. Competitiveness is the reason a company prospers, barely gets by, or fails. Competitiveness depends on the capabilities and performance of the company in its marketplace. Capabilities can be developed over time by focusing on a limited range of goods or services, and/or on a technology. Using teamwork and rewards, an organization can develop its capabilities (also called core competencies). Companies should use past experience and expertise in design, operations/manufacturing, or marketing, and leverage them to introduce new goods and services.[1]

An organization's performance in the marketplace depends on the expectation of its customers for purchase of goods or services, mainly price, quality, variety, and timeliness. These are **key purchasing criteria**. A customer can be a consumer (i.e., the final customer) or another company.

Price is the amount a customer must pay for the good or service. If all other factors are equal, customers will choose the good or service that has the lowest price.

Quality refers to characteristics of a good or service determined by its design, material, workmanship, performance, and consistency. Most customers desire high-quality goods and services, but are willing to settle for goods or services that serve their intended purpose (specification).

Variety refers to the choices of models and options available to customers. The more variety, the wider the range of potential customers.

Timeliness refers to the availability of goods or services when they are needed by the customer. This means being on time (as in just-in-time purchasing) or becoming available quickly.

Other purchasing factors include customer service and convenient location.

At Hertz, there is no paperwork and no waiting line once the customer is enrolled in the company's "Gold" services. Car keys to a pre-selected vehicle are provided, along with a copy of the rental agreement, as soon as the driver's licence is shown. Hertz emphasizes timeliness and customer service attributes.

---

[1]R.H. Hayes, et al., *Strategic Operations—Competing through Capabilities*, New York: The Free Press, 1996.

Most customers tend to trade off price against the other purchasing criteria and choose the "best buy" or best "value":

$$\text{value} = \frac{\text{quality, timeliness, etc.}}{\text{price}}$$

In complex purchases, customers may use two categories of purchasing criteria: order qualifiers and order winners.[2] **Order qualifiers** are those purchasing criteria that customers perceive as minimum standards of acceptability for purchase. However, these may not be sufficient to get a customer to purchase from the organization. **Order winners** are those purchasing criteria that cause the organization to be perceived as better than the competition.

Purchasing criteria such as price, on-time delivery, delivery speed, and quality can be order qualifiers or order winners. Over time, a characteristic that once was an order winner may become an order qualifier, and vice versa.

Obviously, it is important to determine the set of order qualifiers and order winners, and the relative importance of each for each market so that appropriate attention can be given to them. Marketing must make that determination and communicate it to operations. Quality consistency and on-time delivery are order qualifiers for most customers.

Organizations compete by emphasizing one or more of the key purchasing criteria in their goods or services. From an organization's point of view, these are called **competitive priorities**:

Cost is the unit production of a good or performance of a service to the organization. Organizations that compete based on cost (i.e., price from a customer's perspective) emphasize lowering their operating costs.

Quality from an organization's perspective means determining customers' quality requirements, translating these into specifications for goods or services, and consistently producing goods or performing services to these specifications.

Flexibility refers to being able to produce a variety of goods or services in the same facility. This also includes customization, which is modifying goods or services to meet the requirements of individual customers. It may also refer to being able to easily increase or decrease the production quantity of goods or services (quantity flexibility). Flexibility is usually achieved by having general-purpose equipment, excess capacity, and multiskilled workers, resulting in easy changeover between production of goods or services.

Delivery refers to being able to consistently meet promised due dates by producing goods or performing services on time or quickly. Delivery is usually achieved by using communication networks, planning and control systems, reliable equipment and workers, and just-in-time production.

If an organization is far from being competitive, it may be able to improve many or all of its competitive priorities simultaneously. However, as the organization becomes more competitive, it tends to reach a point where improving one priority can be achieved only by reducing the emphasis on another priority, i.e., a trade-off is required. The result of this is a focus on only one priority at a time. It has been observed that most companies first emphasize quality, and only after their quality has reached a competitive level, then focus on delivery reliability, next on low-cost operations, and finally on flexibility.

Table 2-1 lists the competitive priorities and examples of companies that emphasize them.

Understanding competitive issues can help managers develop successful strategies.

---

[2]T. Hill, *Manufacturing Strategy: Text and Cases*, 3rd ed. New York: McGraw-Hill, 2000.

Toyota, Japan's largest automobile manufacturer, makes and markets the upscale, award-winning Lexus line. Quality is paramount, and workers have the authority to stop the production line if quality problems are encountered.

order qualifiers Purchasing criteria that customers perceive as minimum standards of acceptability to be considered for purchase.

order winners Purchasing criteria that cause the organization to be perceived as better than the competition.

competitive priorities The importance given to operations characteristics: cost, quality, flexibility, and delivery.

Costco's competitive priorities are cost, quality, and a certain kind of flexibility. It provides a number of carefully selected products in big packages at low prices (due to its large purchase quantities) in a warehouse setting. The products are high quality, and can be returned indefinitely. There are frequent changes in products, which provides customers with weekly variety.

Table 2-1

Examples of competitive priorities used by companies

Competitive Priority	Emphasis	Examples of Organization
Cost	Low cost	The Great Canadian Superstore (Loblaw), WestJet Walmart
Quality	High performance	Sony, Samsung Lexus, Cadillac
	Consistent quality	Coca-Cola, Pepsi Cola Xerox, Toyota Pizza Hut
Flexibility	Variety	Dell Computers Hospital emergency room
	Quantity flexibility	Potash Corp, Air Canada
Delivery	Rapid delivery	McDonald's Purolator Domino's Pizza
	On-time delivery	WestJet Just-in-time suppliers, e.g., Magna International

www.costco.ca

STRATEGIC PLANNING

Strategic planning is the process of determining a strategy, long-term plans that will set a new direction for an organization, and implementing it through allocation of resources and action plans. Some companies perform strategic planning only when they face a crisis, e.g., when they face a significant drop in their sales. More progressive organizations perform strategic planning on a regular basis, usually annually.

Briefly, strategic planning starts with top management soliciting the performance of current strategy from department managers, and commissioning a market research study of the industry and where it is headed in the next one to five years. Then, the management team may form/adjust the organization's mission and vision, based on the organization's values, determine a set of goals, and brainstorm and evaluate alternative ways (strategies) to achieve them. Finally, the chosen strategy is implemented by determining a set of action plans at the operating department level.

The analysis usually concerns the competitiveness of the organization. A well-known decision aid is the SWOT (Strengths, Weaknesses, Opportunities, and Threats) analysis. The organization will try to identify these and to use/build up its strengths to take advantage of market opportunities, and to avoid/neutralize its weaknesses to defend against the threats.

A more detailed strategic planning process for a business has been proposed.[3] It involves answering the following questions:

1. Getting started
   a. What is the scope of business?
   b. Is the current strategy working?
   c. What are the issues/problems?
2. Analyze the industry and source of competitive advantage (i.e., earning above-average profit)
   a. How intense is the competitive rivalry?
   b. How large is the bargaining power of suppliers?

---

[3]S. Early, "Issues and Alternatives: Key to FMC's Strategic Planning System," *Planning Review* 18(3), May/June 1990, pp. 26–33.

    c. How hard is it for new entrants to enter the industry?

    d. How easily can substitute goods or services be developed?

    e. How large is the bargaining power of customers?

    f. How would trends and changes (demand, technology, regulation, etc) affect the industry?

    g. How can generic strategies of niche market, low cost, and product differentiation be used in this industry?

    h. How can we gain and sustain competitive advantage?

3. Analyze customers

    a. What are the market segments?

    b. What are customers' key purchasing criteria?

4. Analyze competitors (established rivals)

    a. What are the strategies and positions (i.e., relative competitive comparison of products) of winners and losers?

    b. Why do competitors behave as they do? Can we influence them?

    c. How has their strategy been changing through time?

5. Assess our relative position

    a. What are our products' strengths and weaknesses as customers see them? Profitability?

6. Assess the state of our business

    a. What are the major issues (in order of importance)?

    b. What should our goals be?

    c. Should we grow, maintain, or sell off part of our business?

7. Develop and evaluate alternative strategies

    a. Can strategies be found for each major issue?

    b. What investments should we make? What actions should we take?

    c. For each alternative, do financial returns justify it?

8. Choose and refine the recommended strategy

    a. What strategy should we choose?

    b. What actions and policies are required? Do they fit together? Are they reinforcing?

    c. What resources are required? Timetables? Expected results?

9. Identify major actions and implement them

    a. How can we coordinate the actions and monitor overall progress?

Mission, Vision, and Values

Some organizations determine and use a mission, vision, and values statement during their strategic planning process. This may help build consensus within the organization as well. An organization's **mission** is where the organization is going now, its products, and its markets. Missions vary from organization to organization, depending on the nature of their business. **Vision** is where the organization desires to be in the future. **Values** are the shared beliefs of the organizations' stakeholders (mainly shareholders/owners, customers, employees, suppliers, and community) which should drive everything else such as culture, mission/vision, and strategy.

It is important that an organization have a clear and simple mission/vision/values statement. Table 2-2 provides some sample mission/vision/values statements.

mission Where the organization is going now.

vision Where the organization desires to be in the future.

values Shared beliefs of the organization's stakeholders.

Table 2-2

Selected company mission/ vision/values statements

http://www.loblaw.ca

http://www.westjet.ca

http://www.mcdonalds.com

Loblaw	**Our mission:** To be Canada's best food, health and home retailer by exceeding customer expectations through innovative products at great prices. **Driven by our responsibility to:** • Respect the environment • Source with integrity • Make a positive difference in our community • Reflect our nation's diversity • Be a great place to work Source: http://www.loblaw.ca
WestJet	**Our mission:** To enrich the lives of everyone in WestJet's world by providing safe, friendly and affordable air travel. **Our vision:** By 2016, WestJet will be one of the five most successful international airlines in the world, providing our guests with a friendly and caring experience that will change air travel forever. **Our values:** Commitment to safety Positive and passionate in everything we do Appreciative of our People and Guests Fun, friendly and caring Align the interests of WestJetters with the interests of the company Honest, open and keep our commitments Source: http://www.westjet.ca
McDonald's Restaurants	McDonald's vision is to be the world's best quick service restaurant experience. Being the best means providing outstanding quality, service, cleanliness and value, so that we make every customer in every restaurant smile. To achieve our vision, we are focused on three worldwide strategies: • Be the best employer for our people in each community around the world. • Deliver operational excellence to our customers in each of our restaurants. • Achieve enduring profitable growth by expanding the brand and leveraging the strength of the McDonald's system through innovation and technology. (Used with permission from McDonald's Corporation.) Source: http://www.mcdonalds.com

Goals and Objectives. Mission/vision provides a general direction for an organization and should lead to organizational *goals*, which provide substance to the overall mission/vision. For example, one goal of an organization may be to capture more market share for a product; another goal may be to achieve profitability. An objective is a specific goal containing numerical values. For example, an objective of a company may be a 25% reduction in operating costs.

Strategies, Tactics, and Action Plans. A strategy is the long-term plans that will determine the direction an organization will take to become (or remain) competitive. A strategy is determined during the strategic planning process. An organization usually has an overall organizational *strategy*. In the past, organizational strategies were dominated by long-term financial and marketing plans, but recently long-term operating plans have dominated. Long-term functional plans are sometimes called *functional strategies*, e.g., financial

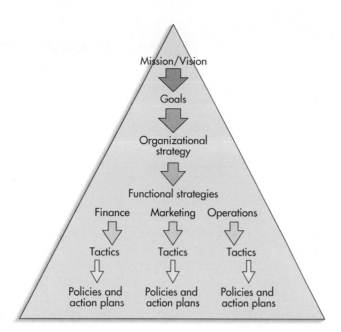

Figure 2-1

Strategic planning is hierarchical in organizations.

strategy or marketing strategy or operations strategy. The functional strategies, if different from organizational strategy, should obviously be congruent with it.

Tactics are medium-term plans sometimes used as components of a strategy. They are more specific in nature than a strategy, and they may provide guidance and direction for determining policies and carrying out **action plans**. An action plan is usually a medium- or short-term project to accomplish a specific objective, assigned to an individual, with a deadline and the resources needed.

It should be apparent that the overall relationship that exists from the mission/vision down to actual policies and action plans is *hierarchical* in nature. This is illustrated in Figure 2-1.

A simple example may help to put this hierarchy into perspective.

tactics Medium-term plans used as components of a strategy.

action plan A medium- or short-term project to accomplish a specific objective, assigned to an individual, with a deadline and the resources needed.

Example 1

Ashley is a high school student in Saskatoon. She would like to live comfortably. A possible scenario for achieving her mission/vision might look something like this:

- Mission/vision: Live a good life.
- Goal: Successful career, good income.
- Strategy: Obtain a college/university education.
- Tactics: Select a college/university and a major; decide how to finance her education.
- Action plans: Register, buy books, take courses, study.

The following example shows the use of an action plan.

Example 2

Wilson Sporting Goods' management decided in the late 1980s to become the leader in the special-order golf-ball business (golf balls that have customized and personalized logos). This mission/vision was to be accomplished over a five-year period by improving quality and delivery. Specific improvement objectives were decided for each competitive priority, and these objectives were cascaded down the organization to appropriate departmental teams, where action plans were established for each needed activity. The objectives and an example of an action plan are shown in Figure 2-2.[4]

---

[4]Based on J.H. Sheridan, "America's Best Plants: Wilson Sporting Goods," *Industry Week* 241(20), October 19, 1992, pp. 59–62.

*An example of objectives and
an action plan*

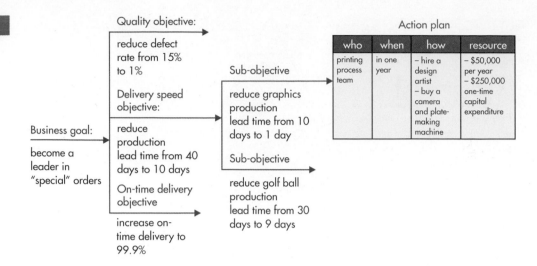

The following example summarizes the whole strategic planning process for a chain
of restaurants.

Example 3

Ruby Tuesday is a chain of full-service but affordable restaurants, mainly in the southeastern United States.[5] Ruby Tuesday performs strategic planning annually. A team of
approximately 24 restaurant and corporate managers conduct the process. To gather
information, the team commissions a market research company to collect market and
competitor data. These include customer surveys, focus groups, and secondary data.
Market data include population growth, changes in population age due to baby boomers,
median income, labour force availability, household food expenditure, ethnic population
growth, lifestyle trends, and customers' price-value awareness. Also, restaurant managers
and assistant managers are asked what Ruby Tuesday's goals and objectives should be,
if there are any problems with the menu, prices, marketing, operations, human resources,
finance, or planning and control. Also, they are asked to identify three most important
strategic issues.

Then the strategic planning team spends approximately two days to synthesize the
data, discuss issues, rank them, come to a consensus, and determine organizational goals.
For example, during one strategic planning process, they determined the following three
goals: (a) exceed customer expectations (b) develop best service teams, and (c) reward
the shareholders. Then, each goal is subdivided into sub-goals or objectives. For example,
to achieve goal (a), a sub-goal was "produce good, high-quality, and consistent food."
Then, for each sub-goal or objective, some policies and action plans are determined. For
example, for "produce good, high-quality, and consistent food," the policies and action
plans included (i) food must be tasteful, wholesome, and visually appealing—change it
if it is not; (ii) hire and train chefs to develop new meals; and (iii) maintain restaurant
equipment.

Then, the newly developed policies are communicated and action plans are assigned.
Some of the policies and action plans relate to corporate staff, some to restaurant managers,
and some to restaurant employees. Employees receive a summary of what is important,
what not to do, the management philosophy, and a code of conduct. Although restaurant
managers monitor the progress, Ruby Tuesday's corporate office performs semiannual

---

[5]R.H. Woods, "Strategic Planning: A Look at Ruby Tuesday," *Cornell Hotel and Restaurant
Administration Quarterly*, June 1994, 35(3), pp. 41–49.

audits and gets customer and employee feedback. The complete strategic plan is listed in the table below:

Goals	Sub-goals and Objectives	Policies or Action Plans
Exceed customer expectations and therefore increase the number of customers	Produce good, high-quality, and consistent food	− Food must be tasteful, wholesome, and visually appealing. Change it if it is not − Hire and train chefs to develop new meals − Maintain restaurant equipment
	Provide good caring service, wow the customers, and do anything to keep customers coming back	− Respond to every customer request with "my pleasure" − Smile, look sharp − Know customers by name − Managers' priority is the customers
	Provide great value to customers; average cost of a meal should not exceed $10	− Atmosphere adds value; "clean as you go" − If the cost of a meal is too high, change it through menu management (e.g., smaller portions) and continuous product development
Develop best service teams	Improve communication	− Communicate plans clearly − Encourage suggestions
	Build loyal and motivated teams	− Hire the best people and train leaders 40 hours per year − Treat everyone with respect and compassion − Encourage stock ownership
	Support community-based teams	− Leaders should participate in the community − Don't move leaders to other restaurants
Reward the shareholders	Achieve same-store sales growth of 2% annually	− Develop additional sales of coffee, alcohol, etc
	Reduce operating costs	− Eliminate paperwork − Find faster and less costly ways of doing things
	Invest in projects with return of at least 20%	− Use smaller food distribution vehicles

Operations Strategy

In large organizations, especially multi-plant manufacturers, the operations function plays a proactive role in strategic planning. Basically, the operations function performs its own strategic planning to answer organizational goals. The determined strategy is called operations strategy. **Operations strategy** deals with guiding the operations function of the organization, but should answer organizational goals.

In other words, operations strategy comprises a set of well-coordinated policies, objectives, and action plans, directly affecting the operations function, which is aimed at securing a long-term sustainable advantage over the competition.[6] In order to formulate an operations

operations strategy   The approach that is used to guide the operations function.

---

[6]C.H. Fine and A.C. Hax, "Manufacturing Strategy: A Methodology and an Illustration," *Interfaces* 15(6), November/December 1985, pp. 28–46.

strategy, the operations function has to cooperate with all the other functions of the business and these functions should collectively monitor the external markets. For example, marketing should be aware of competitors' new product development and customers' expectations in the product markets, and engineering/R&D should be aware of new processing technologies in the technology markets.

The creation of operations strategy occurs both at the company level and at the functional level. At the company level, the role of operations should be identified. Usually, operations' objectives/performance measures are determined in terms of competitive priorities such as cost (e.g., unit cost, labour productivity, inventory turnover), quality (e.g., percentage of products defective, cost of quality), delivery (e.g., percentage of on-time deliveries, lead time), and flexibility (e.g., response to product/quantity changes). As mentioned earlier, trade-offs must be made among these priorities because operations cannot excel in all of them simultaneously. For example, a flexible operation cannot produce the products at minimum cost.

Usually, the operations policies, objectives, and action plans are classified into nine strategic decision categories.

Nine Strategic Decision Categories.

Facility. A major decision for multifacility organizations is how to specialize or focus each facility: by market, product group, or production process type. This usually depends on the economics of production and distribution.

Capacity. This decision is related to facility decision. Long-term capacity decisions relate to size of plants and major equipment. The main issue is whether and how to change the capacity in anticipation of future demand.

Vertical Integration. This is the ownership of a major part or the whole of the supply chain. Cost, coordination, and control are the important factors.

Vendor Relations. The two extremes are using competitive arm's-length or cooperative close relationships (e.g., strategic alliance). This decision also determines how the quality of purchased goods will be assured: either work with a supplier to assure/control its production processes or inspect the incoming parts.

Product Mix and New Products. The challenge of operations management increases as the variety of products and the rate of new product introduction increase. These require flexible production systems.

Process Types and Technology. There are four generic process types: job shop, batch, assembly line, and continuous flow. The product-process matrix (described in Chapter 6) can be used to relate product characteristics to process characteristics (and technologies). The matrix also shows the important trade-offs required in process choice. The process type determines the appropriate technologies and degree of process automation.

Human Resources. With cooperation of the personnel department, workers/staff are appraised, selected, developed, motivated, promoted, and rewarded to work as a team to achieve the company's goals. Various types of compensation and incentive decisions can be used.

Quality. Product quality is determined during the design and production. Conformance to specification during production requires quality assurance, control, and improvement. The tools that can be used include cost of quality, statistical quality control, and continuous improvement/six-sigma. A major decision is whether to assign the responsibility of quality control to the workers.

Operations Infrastructure and Systems. These decisions include choosing a computerized planning and control system (including forecasting, material requirements planning, and scheduling), whether to use just-in-time production, operations policies, and the type of production/delivery system used (make-to-stock or make-to-order). These nine strategic decision categories are described in detail in the following chapters.

Formulation of an Operations Strategy.

1. Link the organization goals to the operations strategy: determine operations requirements of the organization goals.

2. Categorize the customers into types: for example, major customers (with whom closer relationship is desirable) and others (with whom transactional relationship is adequate). For each category, determine which of the four competitive priorities (cost, quality, delivery, and flexibility) should be emphasized.

3. Group product lines into types: for example, classify the product lines into low volume and high volume.

4. Conduct an operations audit to determine the strengths/weaknesses of the current operations strategy in each of the nine strategic decision categories. Also, for each customer category, assess the relative standing of products (relative to desired competitive priorities) against those of most relevant competitors.

5. Assess the degree of focus at each plant: note that a focused plant is more efficient. We can use the product-process matrix (described in Chapter 6) to detect the degree of congruence between a product line and its "natural" process. For example, a low volume–high variety product line should be produced using a job shop process.

6. Develop an operations strategy and re-allocate product lines to plants if necessary. For each of the nine strategic decision categories, state the objectives, policies, and action plans. Deploy these policies and action plans.

The following brief example illustrates the formulation of an operations strategy. A more detailed example is given in the Rohm and Haas case at the end of this chapter.

Example 4

Inland Steel was an integrated steel producer and metal distributor in Indiana Harbour, Indiana (close to Chicago), founded in 1893.[7] In the mid-1980s, Inland Steel had 700–800 customers and 9 million tons per year of steel-making capacity (in addition to coke, limestone, and iron ore mills). But then Japanese steel producers started selling steel in North America at a significantly lower price. This and the reduction in usage of steel in cars led to large losses in Inland Steel. This caused top management, with the assistance of corporate development office, to search for a new operations strategy. They studied the market and customers, competitors, suppliers, and competing products. The competitive analysis of Japanese mills identified a target cost for Inland Steel: the landed cost of Japanese steel in the United States, which was 25 percent lower than Inland Steel's cost. This became the objective. Next, the company segmented the market, and identified where the competitive advantage was. Management also determined the company's management efficiencies and core competencies. Next, they evaluated alternatives. The operations strategy they chose was (a) negotiate a strategic alliance with Nippon Steel (this involved mutual investments in each other's facilities and assistance in research and development, and took five agreements over eight years to finalize); (b) focus on approximately 12 major customers; (c) focus on specialized value-added products such as cold rolled and coated galvanized steel used in car bodies; and (d) reduce the steelmaking capacity by 3 million tons per year, sell the coke and limestone mills, but spend $1.5 billion in new capital investments (two joint venture plants with Nippon Steel in Indiana, to further process sheet metals). In 1994, Inland Steel invested in 18 joint venture service centres in Mexico. Unfortunately, all these moves could not   in 1998. Ispat is now part of ArcelorMittal, the largest steel producer in the world.

---

[7]C. Gebelein, "Strategic Planning: the Engine of Change," *Planning Review* 21(5), September–October 1993, pp. 17–19, and "Ispat Buys Inland Steel, Becomes No. 4 World Producer," *Purchasing*, April 9, 1998, 124(5), p. 28 B13.

Generic Operations Strategies. Generic operations strategies are theme-based operations improvement programs and plans such as just-in-time production and total quality management/continuous improvement. These are generic because they have been frequently used irrespective of the market conditions and competitive situation. If every company in an industry pursues the same generic strategy, every company becomes more efficient and/or more effective without gaining competitive advantage. Therefore, these are, strictly speaking, not strategies, though they are commonly considered so.

The popular generic operations strategies have been changing over time. To illustrate, the generic operations strategies some Japanese manufacturing companies have used since the Second World War are:

- *Low labour cost strategy*. Immediately after the war, exploited the (then) inexpensive labour pool.
- *Scale-based strategy*. During the 1960s, used capital-intensive methods to achieve higher labour productivity and lower unit costs.
- *Focused factories strategy*. During the 1970s, used smaller factories that focused on narrow product lines to take advantage of specialization and achieve higher quality.
- *Flexible factories strategy*. During the 1980s, reduced the time needed to add new product and process designs. Used flexible equipment that allowed volume and design changes, as well as product variety. Continued to stress quality.
- *Continuous improvement strategy*. In the 1990s, introduced new product features and continuous improvement of both products and processes.[8] (See Chapter 9 for more on continuous improvement tools.)

We will briefly describe two generic operations strategies that have been popular recently.

time-based competition
Strategy that focuses on reduction of time needed to accomplish tasks.

Time-based competition focuses on reducing the time required to accomplish various activities (e.g., develop new products or services and market them, respond to a change in customer demand). By doing so, organizations seek to improve service to the customer and gain a competitive advantage over rivals that take more time to accomplish the same tasks. Also costs are generally less, productivity is higher, and quality tends to be higher. Just-in-time production is a special case.

An example of a Canadian company using a time-based strategy is Standard Aero, based in Winnipeg. By redesigning its processes into u-shaped cells, and controlling the activities using a visual system, Standard Aero performs repairs/overhauls of small airplane engines in only two weeks, much faster than its competitors. More on just-in-time and lean production appears in Chapter 15.

outsourcing Buying a part of a good/service or a segment of production/service process from another company, a supplier.

Outsourcing has been increasingly used by many companies to reduce costs, gain flexibility, and take advantage of suppliers' expertise. Outsourcing involves buying a part of a good/service or a segment of production/service process from another company, a supplier. Dell Computers provides a good example of some of the potential benefits of outsourcing and using the supply chain as part of an operations strategy. As well, Dell has become the second largest computer producer by using the Internet to reach and do business with its customers (called mass customization). See the "Dell Computers" OM in Action. There will be more on outsourcing in the purchasing section of Chapter 11.

Minimizing operating costs through becoming more efficient is a common strategy for most organizations. A topic related to efficiency is productivity.

---

[8]G. Stalk Jr. and T. Hout, "Competing Against Time," *Research and Technology Management* 33(2), March–April 1990, pp. 19–24.

OM in ACTION http://www.dell.ca

Dell Computers

In 1984, Michael Dell, then a college student, started selling personal computers from his dorm room. He didn't have the resources to make computer components, so he let others do that, choosing instead to concentrate on selling the computers. And, unlike the major computer producers, he didn't sell to dealers. Instead, he sold directly to consumers, eliminating intermediaries, which permitted lower cost and faster delivery. Although direct selling of PCs is fairly commonplace now, in those days it was a major departure from the norm.

He had little inventory, little capital cost, no R&D, and relatively few employees. This allowed Dell to grow. Because he was in direct contact with his customers, he gained tremendous insight into their expectations and needs, which he communicated to his suppliers.

Having little inventory gave Dell several advantages over his competitors. Aside from the lower costs of carrying inventory, when new faster computer chips became available, there was little inventory to work off, so he was able to offer the newer models much sooner than competitors with larger inventories. Also, when the prices of various components dropped, as they frequently did, he was able to take advantage of the lower prices, which kept his average costs lower than competitors'.

Dell uses the Internet to sell its computers directly to customers. Dell allows customers to choose their many options. This is an example of mass customization. Dell makes the computer to order and uses couriers to send it to the customer. In the 1990s Dell experimented with selling through computer resellers such as Best Buy, but the amount of these sales were so small (< 1% of revenue) that Dell abandoned them. However, recently Dell restarted selling a limited number of products through Best Buy/Future Shop and Staples.

Today the company is worth billions, and so is Michael Dell.

Source: J. Magretta, "The Power of Virtual Integration: An Interview with Dell Computer's Michael Dell," *Harvard Business Review*, March/April 1998, pp. 73–84; B. Francis, "Dell Abandons Its PC Retail Channel," *InfoWorld*, Jul 18, 1994, 28(29), p. 10; J. Jedras, "Dell Expands Its Canadian Retail Play to Staples Business Depot," *Computer Dealer News*, March 21, 2008, 24(2), p. 10.

LO3 PRODUCTIVITY

One of the primary responsibilities of a manager is to achieve *productive use* of an organization's resources. The term *productivity* is used to describe this. **Productivity** measures output (goods and services) per unit input (machine, labour, materials, energy) used to produce them. It is usually expressed as the ratio of output to input:

$$\text{Productivity} = \frac{\text{Output}}{\text{Input}} \qquad (2\text{-}1)$$

productivity A measure of productive use of resources, usually expressed as the ratio of output to input.

A productivity ratio can be computed for a worker, a department, an organization, or an entire country.

A related measure is the rate of *productivity growth*. Productivity growth is the increase in productivity from previous period to the current period relative to the productivity in the previous period. Thus,

$$\text{Productivity growth} = \frac{\text{Current period productivity} - \text{Previous period productivity}}{\text{Previous period productivity}} \qquad (2\text{-}2)$$

For example, if productivity increased from 80 to 84, the growth rate would be

$$\frac{84 - 80}{80} = .05 \text{ or } 5\%$$

Productivity growth is a key factor in a country's standard of living. Productivity increases add value to the economy while keeping inflation in check.

Table 2-3				
Some examples of different types of productivity measures				

Partial measures	$\dfrac{\text{Output}}{\text{Labour}}$	$\dfrac{\text{Output}}{\text{Machine}}$	$\dfrac{\text{Output}}{\text{Material}}$	$\dfrac{\text{Output}}{\text{Energy}}$
Multifactor measures		$\dfrac{\text{Output}}{\text{Labour} + \text{Machine}}$		$\dfrac{\text{Output}}{\text{Labour} + \text{Material} + \text{Energy}}$
Total measure		$\dfrac{\text{Goods or services produced}}{\text{All inputs used to produce them}}$		

Measuring Productivity

Productivity measures can be based on a single input (partial productivity), on more than one input (multifactor productivity), or on all inputs (total productivity). Table 2-3 lists some examples of different types of productivity measures. The choice of productivity measure depends primarily on the purpose of the measurement. If the purpose is to track improvements in labour productivity, then labour becomes the obvious input.

Partial measures are often of greatest use in operations management. Table 2-4 provides some examples of partial productivity measures.

The unit of output used in productivity measure depends on the type of job performed. The following are examples of labour productivity:

$$\frac{\text{Square metres of carpet installed}}{\text{Labour hours}} = \text{Square metres of carpet installed per labour hour}$$

$$\frac{\text{Number of offices cleaned}}{\text{Number of shifts}} = \text{Number of offices cleaned per shift}$$

$$\frac{\text{Board feet of lumber cut}}{\text{Number of weeks}} = \text{Board feet of lumber cut per week (Board foot} = \text{volume of lumber that covers 1 foot} \times 1 \text{ foot} \times 1 \text{ inch)}$$

Similar examples can be listed for *machine productivity* (e.g., the number of pieces turned out by a machine per hour).

Table 2-4	
Some examples of partial productivity measures	

Labour Productivity	Units of output per labour hour Units of output per shift Value-added per labour hour Dollar value of output per labour hour
Machine Productivity	Units of output per machine hour Dollar value of output per machine hour
Material Productivity	Units of output per unit material input, e.g., miles per gallon. Note: litres per 100 km is the inverse of the productivity measure we have defined, but it is still used to measure productivity. Dollar value of output per unit material input
Energy Productivity	Units of output per kilowatt-hour Dollar value of output per kilowatt-hour

Example 5	

Determine the productivity for these cases:

a. Four workers installed 720 square metres of carpet in eight hours.

b. A machine produced 68 usable (i.e., good quality) pieces of a part in two hours.

a. Productivity $= \dfrac{\text{Square metres of carpet installed}}{\text{Labour hours worked}}$

$= \dfrac{720 \text{ square metres}}{4 \text{ workers} \times 8 \text{ hours}}$

$= \dfrac{720 \text{ square metres}}{32 \text{ worker hours}}$

$= 22.5$ square metres/worker hour

b. Productivity $= \dfrac{\text{Usable pieces}}{\text{Production time}}$

$= \dfrac{68 \text{ pieces}}{2 \text{ hours}}$

$= 34$ pieces/hour

Calculations of inputs in a multifactor productivity measure use a common unit of measurement, such as dollars. For example:

$$\dfrac{\text{Quantity of production}}{\text{Labour cost (\$)} + \text{Materials cost (\$)} + \text{Machine overhead (\$)}} \qquad (2\text{-}3)$$

Example 6

Determine the multifactor productivity for the combined inputs of labour, materials, and machine time using the following data:

Output: 7,040 units

Input costs:

Labour (line and support staff, including benefits): $1,000

Materials: $520

Machine overhead: $2,000

$$\dfrac{\text{Multifactor}}{\text{productivity}} = \dfrac{\text{Output}}{\text{Labour} + \text{Materials} + \text{Machine overhead}} = \dfrac{7{,}040 \text{ units}}{\$1{,}000 + \$520 + \$2{,}000}$$

$= 2$ units/dollar

Solution

Please note that some organizations use a different way to measure productivity, e.g., input over output, which gives the input cost per unit of output. As an example, see the "Monsanto" OM in Action.

Even though labour cost as a proportion of total cost has been decreasing in manufacturers, labour productivity is still the main measure used to gauge the performance of individuals, processes, and plants. In addition, its use in services has been increasing as services are employing more workers.

We should not confuse productivity with *efficiency*. Efficiency is a narrower concept that pertains to getting the most out of a *fixed* set of resources; productivity is a broader concept that pertains to better use of overall resources. For example, an efficiency perspective on mowing a lawn if given a hand mower would focus on the best way to use the hand mower; a productivity perspective would include the possibility of using a power mower.

Labour productivity and average operation time for tasks are related concepts. For example, if it takes an average of five minutes to produce one unit, this implies a productivity of (60 minutes per hour)/(5 minutes per unit) = 12 units per hour.

Productivity measures are useful on a number of levels. For an individual, process, department, or organization, productivity measures can be used to track performance *over*

Monsanto

Monsanto, a large producer of seeds and weed control for agriculture, uses productivity indices to measure the efficiency of certain segments of its production process. In particular, it measures the productivity of raw materials, labour, capital (both fixed assets and inventory), energy, and maintenance, and the overall productivity. However, the ratios it uses differ from our definition (i.e., output over input). Raw material productivity is measured by yield (i.e., output) over expected yield. Labour productivity is measured by labour cost (both direct and indirect) over output, i.e., labour cost per kg produced. Energy productivity and maintenance productivity are calculated similarly. Capital productivity is a weighted average of fixed-assets productivity and inventory productivity. Fixed-assets productivity is calculated as output over replacement cost of fixed assets. Inventory productivity is calculated as output over average inventory value. Finally, overall productivity is calculated as weighted average of raw materials, labour, energy, maintenance, and capital productivities.

Source: R.C. Cole Jr. and H.L. Hales, "How Monsanto Justified Automation," *Management Accounting*, 73(7) Jan 1992, pp. 39–43.

time. This allows managers to judge performance and to decide where improvements are needed. For example, if a manager finds that productivity has slipped in a certain area, the manager can examine the factors used to compute productivity to determine what has changed and then devise a means of improving productivity in subsequent periods. Labour productivity is sometimes used in labour wage negotiations where wage raises are tied to productivity growth.

Total productivity and profit of a company are directly related: Total productivity is revenue/total cost, whereas profit is revenue – total cost.

Productivity measures can also be used to judge the performance of an entire industry or a country as a whole. These productivity measures are *aggregate* measures.

In essence, productivity measurements serve as scorecards of the efficient use of resources. Business leaders are concerned with productivity as it relates to *competitiveness*: if two companies both have the same level of output, but one requires less input because of higher productivity, that one will be able to charge a lower price and consequently increase its share of the market, or it might elect to charge the same price, thereby reaping a greater profit.

Productivity Measurement of Services

Service productivity measurement is more problematic than manufacturing. In some services where there is also a large goods component, a measure of output is not hard to find. For example, in the transport (hauling) sector ton-miles is used, in the power sector KWH is used, and in the communication sector number of phone calls is used. In other situations, it is more difficult to measure output because it is partly intangible (e.g., state of health of a patient), involves intellectual activities (e.g., learning operations management), or the output has a high degree of variability (e.g., getting legal advice). Because the outcome is usually an improved state of customer, and customers start off in different states, the inputs can also be variable. Think about medical diagnosis, surgery, consulting, legal services, education, hotels and restaurants, and recreation.

As an illustration, consider the "Examples of Health Care Productivity Measurement" OM in Action, which considers productivity measurement for treating/managing four common diseases.

Sometimes measures of output used in services could result in misleading conclusions about productivity growth. For example, a hospital's aggregate output is usually measured by the number of patient-days of care provided. Suppose that the hospital becomes more productive, resulting in faster patient discharge. This reduces number of patient-days, which will reduce the productivity measure of the hospital!

OM in *ACTION*

Examples of Health Care Productivity Measurement

Diabetes, the imbalance of blood sugar, has no cure. The patient has to monitor his diet and blood sugar, and possibly use insulin to restore it to normal range. Hospital visits are usually confined to out-patient care, but if not in check, diabetes results in serious complications that require inpatient care in hospitals. The output of health care system can be measured as quality-adjusted life years, i.e., the expected life years minus complication rates × their impact. The complication rate depends on clearly identifying serious cases and assisting them intensively. The input cost is measured as cost of staff (doctors, nurses, etc.) at hospitals for both outpatient and inpatient needs (which depend on staffing level and length of stay), plus cost of insulin. Cost of diagnosis (blood test) is not significant; neither is the cost of continuous monitoring of blood sugar (usually self-paid).

Gallstones develop in the gallbladder, and result in abdominal pain. If the case is serious enough, the only treatment is surgery, by removing the gallbladder. Then, patient is cured for life. Because seriousness of this disease is subjective, the choice of surgery is also rather subjective. There are two types of surgery: traditional surgery of opening the stomach and laparoscopic surgery (which results in only three small incisions). Using laparoscopic surgery will result in a considerably shorter hospital stay, which reduces the input cost (cost of the surgery and hospital stay) significantly. The output, quality-adjusted life years, depends on the timing of the decision to go for surgery.

Breast cancer is the most common type of cancer among women. The only treatment is removing the malignant lump, and likely the whole breast, before it spreads. This requires identifying it first. The screening is done by physical exams and mammography. If the initial test indicates possible cancer, a biopsy is performed. Biopsy and surgery can be performed together in one step, or sequentially in two steps. The two-step procedure is less costly because (a) biopsy can be done on outpatient basis, and (b) some biopsies indicate no cancer, thus making step two redundant. Cost of screening and diagnosis can be significantly reduced if only 50-year-old or older women are targeted. Output can be measured in percentage of diagnosed patients who survive at least five years. This depends on how early cancer is detected.

Lung cancer is fatal in approximately 25 percent of the cases. The diagnosis may use expensive CT scanners. If it is treatable, surgery and chemotherapy are used. Chemotherapy is usually done on an outpatient basis. Output can be measured by a five-year survival rate. Input costs include cost of diagnosis, surgery, hospital stay, and chemotherapy.

Source: M.N. Bailey et al., "Healthcare Productivity," *Brookings Papers on Economic Activity*, 1997, pp. 143–202.

Factors that Affect Productivity

Numerous factors affect productivity. Generally, they are methods and management, equipment and technology, and labour. Consider a student who plans to type a lengthy term paper. The student is an average typist and can turn out about three pages per hour. How could the student increase her productivity (i.e., turn out more pages per hour)? One way would be to enrol in a short course to improve typing skills (labour). Another way might be to replace her old computer with a more expensive computer and word-processing package (equipment and technology). Still other productivity improvements might be achieved through improving organization and preparation for the actual typing (methods and management). The incentive of receiving a good grade and the pride of doing a good job might also be important. The point is that all these factors are potential sources of productivity, not only for typing papers but also for any kind of work, and it is generally up to the manager to see that they are fully exploited.

A commonly held misconception is that workers are the main determinant of productivity. According to that theory, the route to productivity gains involves getting employees to work harder. However, the fact is that many productivity gains in the past have come from *equipment and technological* improvements. Familiar examples include automation and computers, text processing, spreadsheets, CAD software, bar codes and scanners, and Internet and e-mail.

Management and methods result in better design, planning, and operating decisions, standardizing and improving processes, improving quality, reducing waste (as in just-in-time production), providing better layout, and using technology, equipment, and labour more effectively and efficiently.

Summary

Competition is the driving force in many organizations. Companies compete by emphasizing one or more competitive priorities, such as cost, quality, flexibility, and delivery. From a customer's perspective, these competitive priorities are price, quality, variety, and timeliness. These are called key purchasing criteria. To develop an effective strategy for the organization, it is essential to determine the key purchasing criteria of customers, and to identify which are order qualifiers, and which are order winners.

Strategies are plans for directing the organization to achieve its mission/vision/goals. Mission/vision is what the company wants to achieve, its products and services, and its markets (now and in the future, respectively). Organizations generally have overall strategies that pertain to the entire organization and functional strategies that pertain to each of the functional areas. Functional strategies are narrower in scope and should be linked to overall strategy. An operations strategy is a coordinated set of policies, objectives, and action plans directly affecting the operations function. These can be classified into nine strategic decision categories: facility, capacity, vertical integration, vender relations, process types and technology, product mix and new products, human resources, quality, and operations infrastructure and systems. Time-based competition and outsourcing are among the most widely used generic operations strategies.

Productivity is a measure of efficient use of resources. Organizations want higher productivity because it yields higher profits and helps them become more competitive. Productivity is measured as output/input. The most common productivity measure is labour productivity, e.g., number of units produced per hour. Productivity of services is hard to measure because outputs are usually intangible and variable, and inputs are variable, too. Factors affecting productivity include methods and management, equipment and technology, and labour.

Key Terms

action plan, 33	outsourcing, 38
competitive priorities, 29	productivity, 39
competitiveness, 28	strategic planning, 28
key purchasing criteria, 28	strategy, 28
mission, 31	tactics, 33
operations strategy, 35	time-based competition, 38
order qualifiers, 29	values, 31
order winners, 29	vision, 31

Solved Problems

Problem 1

A company that processes fruits and vegetables is able to produce 400 cases of canned peaches in one-half hour with four workers. What is labour productivity?

Solution

$$\text{Labour productivity} = \frac{\text{Quantity produced}}{\text{Labour hours}} = \frac{400 \text{ cases}}{4 \text{ workers} \times 1/2 \text{ hours}}$$

$$= 200 \text{ cases per worker hour}$$

Problem 2

A wrapping paper company produced 2,000 rolls of paper in one day. Labour cost was $160, material cost was $50, and overhead was $320. Determine the multifactor productivity.

Solution

$$\text{Multifactor productivity} = \frac{\text{Quantity produced}}{\text{Labour cost} + \text{Material cost} + \text{Overhead}}$$

$$= \frac{2,000 \text{ rolls}}{\$160 + \$50 + \$320}$$

$$= 3.77 \text{ rolls per dollar input}$$

A variation of the multifactor productivity incorporates the price in the numerator by multiplying the units by the price.

Problem 3

A pottery manufacturer that sells to flower stores and department stores had the following output and costs during the last three weeks. Average labour cost is $10 per hour during regular time (first 40 hours of a week) and $15 per hour during overtime (any hours in excess of 40 hours a week), and pottery clay cost was $2 per kg. Calculate the multifactor productivity for each week and comment on the results.

Week	1	2	3
Units produced	1,000	1,500	1,500
No. of workers	2	2	3
Hours per week per worker	40	60	40
Material (kg)	150	250	300

Multifactor productivity = units produced/(labour cost + material cost)

Solution

Week	1	2	3
Units produced	1,000	1,500	1,500
Labour cost	2(40)($10) = $800	$800 + 2(20)($15) = $1,400	3(40)($10) = $1,200
Material cost	150($2) = $300	250($2) = $500	300($2) = $600
Total cost	$1,100	= $1,900	= $1,800
Multifactor productivity	1,000/$1,100	= 1,500/$1,900	= 1,500/$1,800
(pots per $ input)	= 0.91	= 0.79	= 0.83

Multifactor productivity decreased as overtime was used in Week 2 but increased as another worker was added in Week 3 and no overtime was used. However, material cost increased in Week 3 due to mistakes of the new worker.

1. How do you use the four key purchasing criteria personally when buying goods and services? Give an example. (LO1)
2. List the four ways that organizations compete, and give an example for each. (LO1)
3. Explain the difference between order qualifiers and order winners. (LO1)
*4. Explain how a company can gain competitive advantage. (LO1)
5. What is strategic planning and why is it important? (LO2)
6. Briefly list the steps used in strategic planning. (LO2)
7. Describe what an operations strategy is. (LO2)
8. List the nine strategic decision categories. (LO2)
9. Describe how an operations strategy is formulated. (LO2)
10. Give an example of a policy and an action plan. (LO2)
11. Explain the term *time-based competition* and give two examples of companies using it. (LO2)
*12. Boeing's strategy appears to focus on its 777 mid-size plane and its ability to fly into smaller, non-hub airports. Rival European Airbus's strategy appears to focus on large planes. What assumption about future demand for air travel is each company making? (LO2)
13. What is productivity and why is it important? (LO3)
14. List some factors that can affect productivity and an example of each improving productivity. (LO3)
15. A typical Japanese automobile manufacturing plant in North America produces more cars with fewer workers than a typical Big 3 North American plant; see, for example, http://www.oliverwyman.com/content_images/OW_EN_Automotive_Press_2008_HarbourReport08.pdf. What are some possible explanations for this? (LO3)
16. A century ago, most people worked in agriculture, but now less than 4 percent of workers work in agriculture in Canada. Yet due to mechanization and automation, the agricultural output is much more now than a century ago. The majority of people now work in other industries making other

products and rendering services. Also, the standard of living is much higher now than a century ago. Discuss the statement "if productivity increases, fewer workers will be needed." (LO3)

17. Explain the difference between productivity and efficiency. (LO3)

18. Give two reasons that productivity measurement in health care is difficult. (LO3)

Taking Stock

1. Who needs to be involved in formulating organizational strategy? (LO2)

2. Name some of the competitive trade-offs that might arise in a fast-food restaurant. (LO1)

3. How does technology improve each of these?
   a. Competitiveness (LO1)
   b. Productivity (LO3)

4. How can ethics be included in strategic planning? (LO2)

Critical Thinking Exercise

A company has two manufacturing plants, one in Canada and another in China. Both produce the same product. However, their labour productivity figures are quite different. The analyst thinks that this is because the Canadian plant uses more automated equipment for production while the Chinese plant uses a higher percentage of labour. Explain how that factor can cause labour productivity measures to be misleading. Is there another way to compare the two plants that would be more meaningful? (LO3)

Experiential Learning Exercises

1. Select one store that you shop at regularly. What advantage does this store have over its competitors that causes you to shop there? Try to use a purchasing criterion or competitive priority given in the chapter. (LO1)

2. Name one of your personal goals. Determine a plan to reach it (this is the strategy). (LO2)

3. Pick an organization and determine one of its goals and the associated strategy. Hint: Its goal may be discerned from its mission/vision statement. Its strategy may be discerned from its strategic actions. (LO2)

Internet Exercises

1. Find the mission/vision statement of a company (e.g., Wilson Sporting Goods). Does the mission/vision contain the company's products and target market segment? Long-term goals? Explain. (LO2)

2. Visit http://www.timbuk2.com/wordpress_cms/customer-service/about/. What is Timbuk2's competitive priority? (LO1)

Problems

1. Suppose that a company produced 300 standard bookcases last week using seven workers and it produced 240 standard bookcases this week using five workers. In which period was labour productivity higher? Explain. (LO3)

2. The manager of a crew that installs carpets has tracked the crew's output over the past several weeks, obtaining these figures: (LO3)

Week	Crew Size	Square Metres Installed
1	4	960
2	3	702
3	4	968
4	2	500
5	3	696
6	2	500

Calculate the labour productivity for each of the weeks. On the basis of your calculations, what can you conclude about crew size and productivity?

3. Calculate the multifactor productivity measure for each of the weeks shown below. What do the productivity figures suggest? Assume 40-hour weeks and an hourly wage rate of $12. Overhead is 1.5 times weekly labour cost. Material cost is $6 per kilogram. Selling price is $140 per unit. (LO3)

Week	Output (units)	Workers	Material (kg)
1	300	6	45
2	338	7	46
3	322	7	46
4	354	8	48

4. A company that makes shopping carts for supermarkets and other stores recently purchased some new equipment that reduces the labour content of the jobs needed to produce the shopping carts. Prior to buying the new equipment, the company used four workers, who produced an average of 80 carts per hour. Labour cost was $10 per hour and machine cost was $40 per hour. With the new equipment, it was possible to transfer one of the workers to another department. Machine cost increased by $10 per hour while output increased by four carts per hour. (LO3)

   a. Calculate labour productivity before and after the new equipment. Use carts per worker per hour as the measure of labour productivity.
   b. Calculate the multifactor productivity before and after the new equipment. Use carts per dollar cost (labour plus machine) as the measure.
   c. Comment on the changes in productivity according to the two measures. Which one do you believe is more pertinent for this situation?

5. An operation has a 10 percent scrap rate. As a result, only 82 good pieces per hour are produced. What is the potential increase in labour productivity that could be achieved by eliminating the scrap? (LO3)

6. A manager checked production records and found that a worker produced 160 units while working 40 hours. In the previous week, the same worker produced 138 units while working 36 hours. Calculate the labour productivity growth. Explain. (LO3)

*7. Teradyne Connection Systems makes "backplanes" (large printed circuit-board assemblies) for communication and storages devices. Recently, the company converted its production process from batch into assembly line. It also used computers to assist the workers at workstations. As a result, productivity has shot up. The site manager, Mark Galvin, says: "Operators made 300 backplanes in seven days using three shifts by a batch process (i.e., 7 days, 24 hours a day). Later, they assembled 500 backplanes in five days using just two shifts with the new assembly-line approach (i.e., 5 days, 16 hours a day)." Assuming that the same number of workers worked during each shift, and before and after the conversion, what is the percentage growth in labour productivity? (LO3)

8. A land title search office had a staff of three, each working eight hours per day (for a total payroll cost of $480/day) and overhead costs of $300 per day. This office processed an average of seven titles each day. The office recently purchased a computerized title-search system that will allow the processing of an average of 12 titles per day. Although the staff, work hours, and pay will be the same, the overhead costs will be $600 per day. (LO3)

   a. Calculate the labour productivity in the old and the new systems. How much (in percentage) has the labour productivity grown?
   b. Calculate the multifactor productivity in the old and the new systems. How much (in percentage) has the multifactor productivity grown?
   c. Which productivity measure is more appropriate for the land title search office?

9. When Henry Ford introduced moving assembly lines in his Ford Motor Company plants in 1913, the productivity soared.[9] An example of this is the coil line. A coil is an electrical component that makes high voltage for ignition. Before, a skilled worker took approximately 20 minutes to make a coil from start to finish. After an assembly line was set up and the job was divided into 29 different operations performed by 29 workers, it took only approximately 13 minutes to assemble one coil. (Note: Because workers work simultaneously, approximately every 0.5 minute a coil is produced.) (LO3)

   a. Calculate the labour productivity before and after the conversion into an assembly line.
   b. Calculate the percentage increase in labour productivity due to the assembly line.

10. **(i)** One person using a hammer will take five days to nail new shingles on the roof of a 300 m² house.

    (ii) Two persons using a hammer but working together (one holds a shingle, the other swings the hammer) will take two days to do the same job.

    (iii) One person using a nail gun will take one day to do the same job. (LO3)

      a. Define a labour productivity measure and determine its value for each of the above cases.
      b. Calculate the percentage increase in productivity due to method improvement, i.e., from (i) to (ii).
      c. Calculate the percentage increase in productivity due to using technology, i.e., from (i) to (iii).

11. Southwest Tube of Oklahoma[10] is a small fabricator of specialty tubes used in boilers and other equipment. Southwest buys the tubes in long segments and cuts, bends, cold draws, and welds the pieces to make what is needed for the products. A few years ago Southwest Tube was facing tough competition. The prices were falling while the costs were rising. To improve productivity, consultants were brought in. They pointed out problems with labour turnover, absenteeism, weak supervision, staffing mismatch, lack of performance goals, and a dislike for the weekly rotating schedule as causes of the problem. One of the solutions tried, in addition to other improvements, was changing the work schedule to four 12-hour days followed by three days off. The productivity seemed to improve gradually. To ascertain this, the following data for two physically demanding work centres were collected starting the year before the change in work schedule. (LO3)

    Question: Has workers' productivity in the two work centres increased? Explain.

	Cold Draw Dept			Weld Mill Dept	
	Labour	Output		Labour	Output
Year	(1,000 hr)	(1,000 ft)	Year	(1,000 hr)	(1,000 ft)
0	228	18,269	0	132	22,434
1	234	19,576	1	157	34,777
2	183	17,633	2	102	26,715
3	150	18,870	3	77	25,227

*12. The following data (all in billion $) are the sales and profit of Hudson's Bay Company (parent of The Bay and Zellers).[11] (LO3)

---

[9]J.C. Wood and M.C. Wood, eds., *Henry Ford: Critical Evaluations in Business and Management*, London: Routledge, 2003.

[10]J.M. Shirley and T.M. Box, "Productivity Gains at Southwest Tube," *Production and Inventory Management Journal*, Fourth Quarter 1987, 28(4), pp. 57–60. Also see http://www.webcoindustries.com. Reprinted with permission of the APICS, The Association for Operations Management.

[11]Hudson's Bay Company, 2003–5 Annual Reports, http://media.corporate-ir.net/media_files/irol/92/92910/pdfs/04FINANCIALS_ENG.pdf, accessed April 15, 2010.

	2005	**2004**	**2003**
Total Sales & Revenue	7.1	7.3	7.3
EBIT	0.13	0.17	0.18

EBIT = earnings before interest and tax
Hint: Inputs = Total cost = Total Sales & Revenue − EBIT

The following data (all in billion $) are the sales, cost of sales (=cost of goods sold), and operating and overhead expenses of Walmart[12]:

	2005	**2004**	**2003**
Net Sales	285	256	230
Cost of Sales (COS)	220	199	178
Operating, selling, general & admin costs (OSGA)	51	45	40

Hint: Inputs = Total cost = COS + OSGA

Calculate an appropriate measure of productivity for each company and compare. Which company was more productive? Explain.

*13. The following data (all in billion $) are the sales and costs (excluding selling and general and administrative costs) of McDonalds for company-operated restaurants (i.e., excluding franchise restaurants).[13] (LO3)

   a. Calculate the labour productivity (in $ sales over $ payroll & benefits costs) and its growth over time. Interpret your results.

   b. Calculate the multifactor productivity (in $ sales over $ all operating costs given) and its growth over time. Interpret your results.

	2007	**2008**	**2009**
Sales	16.6	16.6	15.5
Operating costs Food & paper	5.5	5.9	5.2
Payroll & benefits	4.3	4.3	4.0
Occupancy (lease, etc)	3.9	3.8	3.5

*14. The following data are the production of potash (KCl), in 1,000 tonne units, and number of active mine-site employees for two mine/mill facilities of The PotashCorp (of Saskatchewan).[14] (LO3)

Calculate the labour productivity (in 1,000 tonnes per employee per year) and its changes over time for each facility, and interpret your results (over time and across the two facilities).

	Lanigan		**Rocanville**	
Year	**Production**	**Employees**	**Production**	**Employees**
2004	2,025	364	1,833	328
2005	2,023	378	2,573	340
2006	1,471	402	1,897	343
2007	1,907	441	2,647	354

[12]http://walmartstores.com/Media/Investors/2005AnnualReport.pdf, accessed April 15, 2010.
[13]McDonald's Annual Report, http://www.aboutmcdonalds.com/etc/medialib/aboutMcDonalds/investor_relations0.Par.17264.File.dat/2009%20AR%20Report%20-%20Print.pdf, accessed April 15, 2010.
[14]PotashCorp, http://www.potashcorp.com/annual_reports/2007/our_story; http://www.potashcorp.com/annual_reports/2006/our_company; http://www.potashcorp.com/annual_reports/2005/business/introduction; http://www.potashcorp.com/annual_reports/2004, accessed April 15, 2010.

15. Frank Gilbreth is the "father" of motion study. One of the first operations he studied was bricklaying. He noticed that there was unnecessary stooping, walking, and reaching. Also some bricks were damaged, which required the bricklayer to inspect each brick and find the better side before laying it. Stooping per brick laid was once for the mortar, and another for the brick. Gilbreth designed a non-stooping scaffolding platform that was raised by a lifting jack as work progressed up the wall so that the mortar and bricks were always at easy reach of the bricklayer. Motions per brick were reduced from 18 to 5, and average time went down from approximately 29 seconds per brick laid to approximately 10 seconds per brick laid. Calculate the labour productivity before and after the improvement, and the percentage of increase. (LO3)

 CASE

Zellers

Zellers is Canada's largest mass merchandise discount store chain. It has approximately 300 stores throughout Canada with annual sales of approximately $4.6 billion. Up until a few years ago, Zellers was owned by the Hudson's Bay Company (HBC), which also owned The Bay, a major department store with approximately 100 stores. Prior to the late 1990s, Zellers targeted budget-minded customers with the slogan, "Lowest Price is the Law."

Zellers was doing well up until 1993 when its earnings (before interest and tax) started to steadily decline from $256 million to $73 million in 1998, mainly due to stiff competition from Walmart. Walmart entered Canada in 1994 by purchasing more than 100 Woolco stores. Walmart's efficient operations involve an integrated computerized inventory record-keeping system, which is accessed by suppliers regularly, and an efficient supply and distribution network. In addition, Walmart has the broadest selection of merchandise, purchased in large volumes at discounted prices.

In addition to competition from Walmart, Zellers had numerous operations problems, including having too many outdated products but being frequently out of stock on popular products, slow checkout lines due to missing product bar codes or having the wrong price in the computer, and lack of customer assistants on the store floor (making the stores essentially self-service).

The dive in profits forced management to take some drastic actions starting in 1998:

- HBC purchased the more than 100 Kmart Canada stores. Based on location, size, performance, lease arrangements, and local market considerations, HBC closed approximately 40 of these stores and converted the remainder into Zellers.

- A major program to clean up inventories was undertaken. Substantial quantities of aged merchandise were cleared out of the system through heavy promotion and high markdowns.

- Zellers' mission was changed to becoming "Mom's store" (with children under 12 years old) and providing "fair value," not the lowest price.

- Exclusive contracts were signed to sell famous brands such as Cherokee, Mossimo, and Hillary Duff, and private brands such as Truly and ToGo were added.

- Larger floor space, over 9,290 m^2, were used for the new stores (as opposed to approximately 4,645 m^2 previously). Zellers expanded and renovated approximately half its stores.

- The layout and decoration of stores were redesigned to give a more open feel by removing tables and other obstructions from the aisles and widening them, and instituting new and clearer colour-coded signage. Checkout was centralized.

- HBC combined the purchasing functions of The Bay and Zellers and created the position of VP merchandising.

- Zellers installed an integrated computer system (IBM), merchandising software (Retek), an inventory-control software (Inforem), and a financial enterprise resources planning software (Oracle) at a cost of approximately $50 million.

- Zellers moved away from promotions (discounts) to everyday low pricing (like Walmart) on 95 percent of its merchandise.

- Zellers moved away from its policy of self-service to one of having several customer service assistants available in the aisles.

Even though in the early 2000s, profit (before interest and tax) crept back up to approximately $150 million per year, it again declined to approximately $70 million per year by 2003. In 2005, Zellers and its parent, HBC, were sold to a private U.S. investor, and in 2008 resold again to a U.S. investment company, the owner of Lord & Tayor, a 47-store upscale U.S. retail chain.

Questions

1. What competitive priority is important for a discount store such as Zellers?

2. Three generic strategies are low cost, niche market, and product differentiation. Which one of these was Zellers using before 1998? After 1998?

3. Do you think Zellers' actions after 1998 fit its new mission? Explain.

Sources: HBC Annual Reports, 1998–2003; M. Duff, "Zellers Reorganizes Stores, Adopts EDLP Strategy," *DSN Retailing Today*, February 25, 2002, pp. 3, 27; M. Duff, "Zellers Debuts Marketing Driven, 'Airy' Prototype," *Discount Store News*, September 6, 1999, pp. 3, 17; D. Gill, "Zellers Fashions Its New Format," *Home Textiles Today*, August 9, 1999, pp. 1, 8 ff; V.L. Facenda, "At Zellers, Mom's the Word," *Discount Merchandiser*, August 99, pp. 87–91.

MINI-CASE

Lynn Revisited

(Refer to Chapter 1, p. 24 for the Lynn case.)

Questions

1. What advantage, if any, does Lynn have over a professional lawn care service?

2. Lynn would like to increase her profits, but she doesn't believe that it would be wise to raise her prices considering the current state of the local economy. Instead, she has given some thought to increasing productivity.

    a. Explain how increased productivity could be an alternative to increased prices.

    b. What are some ways that Lynn could increase productivity?

3. Lynn is thinking about the purchase of new equipment. One piece of equipment would be power sidewalk edgers.

She believes edgers will lead to an increase in productivity. Another piece of equipment would be a chain saw, which would be used for tree pruning. What trade-offs should she consider in her analysis?

4. Lynn has been fairly successful in her neighbourhood and now wants to expand to other neighbourhoods, including some that are five kilometres away. What would be the advantages and disadvantages of doing this?

5. Lynn does not have a mission/vision statement or goals. Which one of the following positions is correct? Explain.

    a. Lynn doesn't need a formal mission/vision statement and goals. Many small businesses don't have them.

    b. She definitely needs a mission/vision statement and goals. They would be extremely beneficial.

    c. These may be of some benefit to Lynn's business, and she should consider developing them.

CASE   http://www.loblaw.ca

Competing the Loblaw Way

Loblaw is Canada's largest national grocery store chain. Its mission is to provide consumers with the best in one-stop shopping for everyday household needs. Besides food, some stores sell housewares, electronics, clothing, pharmacy, photo finishing, and gasoline. Loblaw also offers financial services, including a MasterCard. Loblaw is one of the largest companies in Canada, with over 139,000 full-time and part-time employees.

When Richard J. Currie was appointed the president of Loblaw in 1976, Loblaw was only a regional chain (mainly in Ontario), with low profits and cash flow problems. Most store buildings were leased on a long-term basis and the company had no strategic direction.

Currie closed some unprofitable stores and concentrated on maximizing sales per square foot of the other stores. Loblaw did not open new stores. Although it appeared weak to its competitors, this strategy allowed Loblaw to survive.

Currie believed that Loblaw should own its stores, rather than lease them. The leases were long-term and inflexible. This frequently resulted in the company having to pay for the building well after the store was closed. Also, changing a leased building to accommodate new departments was problematic. So, Loblaw gradually reduced its leases and increased its real estate ownership. Loblaw now owns more than 70% of the buildings it uses.

Currie also believed that controlling the buying activities and labour costs was most important. Given that cost of goods is

approximately 90 percent of the selling price in the grocery business, there is not much margin for labour and overhead costs. Also, he believed that union workers were much more costly than non-union workers. Given that most stores were already unionized, the way around the low margin was to expand the high-volume large stores.

Another problem in the food retailing business was that competitors competed using periodic sales (promotions), following a "high-low" pricing strategy. Currie believed that selling anything below cost was absurd, but he could not convince his competitors. He believed that customers just needed "quality products, reliably available, and priced competitively."

His solution was to introduce the No-Name private label brand in 1978. This way, Loblaw could provide reasonable quality products at reduced prices every day. This was very successful. Later Loblaw continued its private brand (or "control label" products as it calls them) with President's Choice in 1984, and others later, including the Joe Fresh Style line of clothing in 2006.

Currie also believed in the advantage of an online in-store computerized information system. The use of bar codes and scanners allowed efficient data gathering that was used to identify profitability of items. This allowed Loblaw to control costs back up its supply chain.

Throughout the years, Loblaw has grown immensely through buying smaller regional chains and opening new stores. It now owns over 600 and franchises over 400 grocery stores in Canada under different banners, including large superstores such as The Real Canadian Superstore in the West, Dominion in Newfoundland, and Atlantic Superstore; medium-size food-focused stores (called "Great Foods") such as Loblaw's and Zehrs (mainly in Ontario), and Provigo (in Quebec); discount food stores such as Extra Foods (in the West), No Frills (franchised), and Maxi and Maxi & Co in Quebec; and wholesale stores such as Real Canadian Wholesale Club, Cash & Carry, and Presto.

The different store banners sell basically the same products, approximately 24 percent being Loblaw's private brands. However, the general merchandise is sold only through large superstores. Until recently, pricing was not coordinated across different banners and regions. Relations with unions are fairly good. Loblaw has obtained wage cuts from its employees several times.

Until the early 2000s, Loblaw's supply and distribution network was fairly efficient. It has 33 warehouses throughout Canada, including a new 58,560 m^2 distribution centre in Cambridge, Ontario. The information system was working fine but was not centralized. In fact, the purchasing, merchandising, and marketing functions were store banner– and regionally based. Loblaw's revenues were growing at 10 percent annually, and its profit margin was 2.5 percent per year, high for a grocery chain. Loblaw's low prices did not allow Walmart to expand its grocery retailing in Canada. Then, in 2002 Richard Currie retired. Expansion continued, but unfortunately, new management has taken some bold moves that have caused problems for the organization. Management decided the following:

- All Loblaw stores would become larger superstores, selling general merchandise as well as food. Already, more than 13 Ontario stores have been converted to this format.

- To increase efficiencies, all administrative activities would be centralized into one huge office (for 2,000 employees) in Brampton, Ontario. This resulted in relocation problems for

hundreds of the general merchandise buyers in Calgary. Many quit rather than relocate. Later, Loblaw fired 800–1000 of the employees due to redundancy.

- To increase efficiencies in the supply network, Loblaw closed approximately eight smaller warehouse/distribution centres in Ontario, and rerouted inventories to other larger warehouses. However, this transition was not managed well, resulting in many out-of-stock situations in the stores.

- Information technology (for store ordering, purchasing, and inventory tracking) would be centralize and use forecasting. However, the implementation has been unsuccessful.

- Control label products would be expanded, with the objective that they constitute 30 percent of sales.

- Fresh image, health and beauty products, organics, friendly staff, standard store procedures, daily store employee communication meeting, weekly competitor price checking, and management training are important now.

The drastic reorganization resulted in reduced revenue growth during the mid 2000s and even a loss in 2006. Top management has recently changed again, and it appears that Loblaw is doing well again.

Questions

1. What competitive priority does Loblaw emphasize?

2. List and evaluate Loblaw's operations strategy. Use the nine strategic decision categories.

Sources: Loblaw Annual Reports 1998–2009. http://www.loblaw.ca /en/inv_ar.html; Richard J. Curry, "Loblaw's: Putting the Super in Supermarket," *Business Quarterly*, Summer 1994, pp. 24–30; P. Foster, "Three's a Crowd at Loblaw," *National Post*, Apr 23, 2008, p. FP 15.

 CASE http://www.westjet.ca

WestJet's Strategy

WestJet is a fast-growing Canadian discount airline headquartered in Calgary. It started in 1996 with three used airplanes targeting short trips in Western Canada (between Calgary, Edmonton, Kelowna, Winnipeg, and Vancouver). Clive Beddoe, one of the founders of WestJet, got the idea for WestJet after having to pay exorbitant fares to Air Canada for his frequent flights between Calgary (his hometown) and Edmonton and Vancouver, where he owned plastic manufacturing plants. According to Beddoe, "the key to expanding the market and luring masses of people who don't travel and those who drive is to charge

them bargain-basement fares." He called this market the "visiting friends and relatives" market. In order to be able to offer low prices, WestJet needed to run low-cost operations. WestJet studied successful discount airlines in the United States such as Southwest Airlines, and copied most of their operating principles.

How could WestJet have planned for an operating cost per available seat mile approximately half that of Air Canada? The main principles of WestJet's plan were:

- Short-distance flights

- Single class of passengers (no first or business class)

- Purchase only one type of aircraft: Boeing 737

- Fly to smaller cities
- Recruit young enthusiastic employees whose salary is slightly lower than average, but who receive profit-sharing bonuses
- Emphasize "fun and friendly culture" and empower the employees (i.e., bottom-up management)
- Use equity financing and tight financial controls
- Use paperless tickets
- No connecting flights and no baggage transfers
- No frequent flyer program.

To further motivate its employees, WestJet later introduced an employee share purchase program.

WestJet has gradually and carefully added to its flights. In 2000 WestJet expanded eastward to Hamilton, Ontario, then to Windsor, Halifax, Montreal, Gander, St. John's, and in 2002 to Toronto. Now, WestJet has flights to 47 Canadian, U.S., Mexican, and Caribbean cities. The sun destinations flights are seasonal, offered in winter, when travel inside Canada dips. However, this expansion in flights has resulted in WestJet's flying some medium-distance flights (e.g., to Hawaii), flying to big cities, and performing baggage transfers.

In concert with increased flights, WestJet has been gradually adding to its fleet of planes, simultaneously replacing the old 737-200 (with 125 seats) with new next-generation 737s in three sizes: 737-600 (119 seats), 737-700 (136 seats), and 737-800 (166 seats). Now it has 74 next-generation 737 planes, which are 30 percent more fuel efficient. The average age of WestJet planes is only 3–4 years now. New planes can be operated close to 12 hours a day vs. 10 hours for the old planes. Clearly, their maintenance cost is lower than the old planes. The new planes have leather seats and individual live seat-back satellite TV for each passenger. WestJet owns most of its planes.

WestJet is not afraid to spend money on useful technology. An example is the installation of blended winglets on the end of the wings of new planes, which will increase lift and reduce drag, thus increasing fuel economy by approximately 5 percent. The approximately $600,000 investment per plane pays back in about four years. Another example is the use of dual boarding bridges in certain airports such as Calgary and Vancouver. This allows boarding and un-boarding from both front and back doors simultaneously, halving the time.

WestJet now employs approximately 6,700 employees (still non-unionized, but over 80 percent own WestJet shares) and has about 35 percent of the air travel market in Canada. WestJet has one of the best on-time (within 15 minutes of the scheduled time) arrival performances and is one of the most profitable airlines in North America, despite the sharp increase in jet fuel cost in recent years. Its load factor (percentage of seats occupied) has been increasing from 70 percent in the late 1990s to 80–85 percent, and its revenue is over $2 billion.

Questions

1. What market segment does WestJet compete in? Name an order qualifier and order winner for this market.

2. What competitive priority does WestJet have?

3. What were the advantages of each of the initial principles used by WestJet in 1996 to reduce its operating costs?

4. How has WestJet kept its low operating costs and increased the utilization of its planes, while growing more than 10% per year?

Sources: WestJet's 1999–2007 Annual Reports, http://c3dsp. westjet.com/guest/media/investorMedia.jsp?id=Investor#financial; http://www.WestJet.ca, accessed April 15, 2010.

Rohm and Haas's Operations Strategy

Rohm and Haas (R&H), based in Philadelphia, is a major producer of specialty chemicals such as polymer emulsions used in water-based paint. In the-mid 1990s, R&H was being squeezed between suppliers (petrochemical companies) and major customers such as Walmart and Home Depot. Furthermore, competitors were taking market share. R&H's selling price had remained the same for five years whereas costs were going up. In addition, the production and order fulfillment was chaotic and stressful. The 11 U.S. plants each made all of the approximately 800 products. All customers, approximately 4,000, received the same service such as customized certificate of analysis or packaging/labelling. There was no fixed lead time; the due date was negotiated between the customer service rep (CSR) and the schedulers. The production schedule kept changing, with less than a day's notice.

To fix these problems, R&H spent $100 million on Enterprise Resource Planning software, but after three years of implementation, there was no real change to its business processes. Then, a management team was formed consisting of sales, marketing, manufacturing, operations, and logistics managers, and some internal consultants. The team analyzed R&H's customer base, dividing them into four categories: (1) partners or potential partners, (2) strategically important, (3) important, and (4) others.

It was decided that the approximately 3,200 customers in Tier 4 would be supplied by three exclusive distributors and not by R&H directly. This would save CSRs/schedulers' time and save production/transportation costs as larger batches to the distributors would be cheaper per unit.

Sales and marketing people interviewed Tier 1 customers to find out what service they valued most and what R&H's competitors were offering. The services were categorized, their cost estimated, and a matrix was formed that related each tier with the service categories it would receive. For example, Tier 1 customers would receive special services such as customized packaging/labelling, Tier 2 would receive standard services, and Tier 3 would receive limited services.

Also, the team studied the demand characteristic of the approximately 800 products. The results showed that most high-volume products were ordered regularly, whereas most low-volume products were ordered irregularly. The team mathematically modelled one of the facilities and performed a simulation study to find out the effect of dedicating chemical reactors to either high-volume or low-volume products, given various lead times. The results showed that the capacity would increase by 20 percent and on-time delivery would improve.

The team recommended specializing some of the plants/reactors to make the high-volume products and the others to make the low-volume products. Also, the high-volume products, which can be forecasted accurately, are to be made to stock, with a lead time of two days. On the other hand, it was decided not to carry any stocks of the low-volume variable-demand products. These are made to order with a lead time of seven days, and a minimum-order quantity equal to the production batch size. Tier 1 customers have accepted the increase in lead time for low-volume products because it is certain.

As a result of these changes, R&H has saved millions of dollars, increased its production capacity, and improved its on-time delivery rates.

Questions

1. What was an important organizational goal for Rohm and Haas in the mid-1990s?

2. What competitive priorities of Rohm and Haas were important for its Tier 1 customers?

3. Compare the above steps with the steps of operations strategy formulation given in the chapter. What are the similarities and differences?

4. What policies and actions were used by Rohm and Haas in any of the nine strategic decision categories?

Source: A.J. D'Alessandro and A. Baveja, "Divide and Conquer: Rohm and Haas' Response to a Changing Specialty Chemicals Market," *Interfaces* 30(6), November/December 2000, pp. 1–16.

Demand Forecasting | PART TWO

CHAPTER 3
Demand Forecasting

LEARNING OBJECTIVES

After completing this chapter, you should be able to:

LO1 Identify uses of demand forecasts, distinguish between forecasting time frames, describe common features of forecasts, list the elements of a good forecast and steps of forecasting process, and contrast different forecasting approaches.

LO2 Describe at least three judgmental forecasting methods.

LO3 Describe the components of a time series model, and explain averaging techniques and solve typical problems.

LO4 Describe trend forecasting and solve typical problems.

LO5 Describe seasonality forecasting and solve typical problems.

LO6 Describe associative models (regression) and solve typical problems.

LO7 Describe three measures of forecast accuracy and two ways of controlling forecasts, and solve typical problems.

LO8 Identify the major factors to consider when choosing a forecasting technique.

This part is devoted solely to demand forecasting. It is presented early in the book because demand forecasts are the basis for a wide range of decisions that are described in the following chapters. In fact, demand forecasts are basic inputs for many kinds of decisions in business organizations. Consequently, it is important for *all* managers to be able to understand and use demand forecasts. Although product demand forecasts are typically developed by the sales/marketing function, the operations function, through production planning, will receive and use the demand forecasts. Also, the operations function develops demand/usage forecasts for supplies and spare parts.

Chapter 3 provides important insights on demand forecasting as well as information on how to develop and monitor demand forecasts.

efore 1998, Ocean Spray, the cranberry cooperative, had problems meeting retailer orders because it was not able to plan production effectively. Sales and operations functions in effect had two different forecasts of each product. Then Ocean Spray changed its forecasting process. This improved the accuracy of forecasts from 55 percent to 75 percent, resulting in much improved customer service. How did Ocean Spray do this?

Spare parts are required for machines and equipment. They break down randomly. When they do, the spare part should be available soon to reduce the shut-down period. How do companies such as Caterpillar's Spare Parts Distribution or the maintenance warehouse of a chemical company such as Sterling Pulp Chemicals (now part of ERCO Worldwide) forecast the need for their spare parts?

These are the types of questions answered in this chapter.

🔵LO1 INTRODUCTION

demand forecast The estimate of expected demand during a specified future period.

Planning is an integral part of an operations manager's job. If uncertainties cloud the planning process, operations managers will find it difficult to plan effectively. Demand forecasts help operations managers by reducing some of the uncertainty, thereby enabling them to develop more meaningful plans. A **demand forecast** is the estimate of expected demand during a specified future period.

People make and use demand forecasts in their everyday life. They forecast e.g., "How much food and drink will I need?" when visiting a grocery store or "How much cash or gas will I need?" when visiting a bank or gas station. To make these forecasts, they take into account two kinds of information. One is current factors or conditions. The other is past experience in a similar situation. Sometimes they will rely more on one than the other, depending on which approach seems more relevant at the time. Demand forecasting for business purposes involves similar approaches. However, more formal methods are used to make demand forecasts and to assess forecast accuracy. Demand forecasting basically involves modelling the past pattern of demand for an item and projecting it into the future while taking new developments into account.

There are three types of uses for demand forecasts in operations. One is to help managers design the system, the other is to help them plan the medium-term use of the system, and the third is to schedule the short-term use of the system. Designing the system involves long-term plans about which goods and services to offer; capacities, facilities, and equipment to have; where to locate, and so on. Planning the medium-term use of the system involves tasks such as planning overall inventory and workforce levels, and planning production at the aggregate product family level. See the "Duracell Forecasting" OM in Action on page 61 for an example of the use of long- and medium-term forecasting, and the "Colgate-Palmolive Co." OM in Action on page 89 for an example of medium-term forecasting. Scheduling the short-term use of the system involves scheduling of production, purchasing of parts and raw materials, and staff scheduling (see Figure 3-1.)

Business forecasting pertains to more than predicting demand. Financial and economic forecasts are used to predict variables such as profits, revenues, costs, stock prices, and GDP. This chapter will focus on the forecasting of demand (sales of goods/services or usage of spare parts/supplies). Keep in mind, however, that the concepts and techniques presented in this chapter apply equally well to the other types of business forecasting.

In spite of its use of computers and sophisticated mathematical models, forecasting is not an exact science. Instead, successful forecasting often requires a skilful blending of art and science. Experience, judgment, technical expertise, information, and communication all play a role in developing useful forecasts. Along with these, a certain amount of luck and a dash of humility can be helpful, because the worst forecasters occasionally produce a very good forecast, and even the best forecasters sometimes miss completely.

Generally speaking, the responsibility for preparing demand forecasts for finished goods or services lies with the marketing or sales departments rather than operations. Nonetheless, because demand forecasts are major inputs for many operations decisions, operations managers must be knowledgeable about the kinds of forecasting techniques available, the assumptions that underlie their use, and their limitations. Also the operations

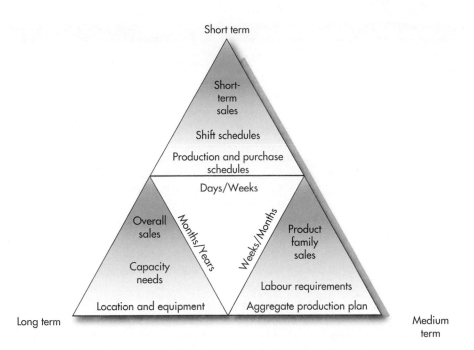

Figure 3-1

The uses of demand forecasts in operations in terms of time frame

function provides feedback about the feasibility of producing the demand forecasts. See the "Forecasting in Ocean Spray Cranberries" OM in Action on page 58. In addition, inventory managers (see Chapter 12) make forecast of usage of supplies and spare parts.

Recently, supply chain partners have started to collaborate on the forecasting process. The customer company makes the forecast in consultation with the supplier, allowing for both sides to provide inputs such as the expectation of customer for increased quantities during a promotion, the capacity limitations of the supplier, etc. This is called Collaborative Planning, Forecasting, and Replenishment (CPFR) (more on this in Chapter 11 on Supply Chain Management).

Features Common to All Forecasts

A wide variety of forecasting techniques are in use. In many respects, they are quite different from one another, as you shall soon discover. Nonetheless, certain features are common to all techniques and forecasts, and it is important to recognize them.

1. Forecasting techniques generally assume that the same underlying causal system that existed in the past will continue to exist in the future.

Comment. A manager cannot simply delegate forecasting to models or computers and then forget about it, because unplanned or special occurrences can wreak havoc with forecasts. For instance, weather-related events, sales promotions, and changes in features or prices of the company's own and competing goods or services can have a major impact on demand. Consequently, a manager must be alert to such occurrences and be ready to override forecasts.

2. Forecasts are rarely perfect; actual results usually differ from predicted values. No one can predict *precisely* how related factors will impinge upon the variable in question; this, and the presence of randomness, preclude a perfect forecast. Allowances should be made for inaccuracies.

3. Forecasts for groups of items tend to be more accurate than forecasts for individual items, because forecasting errors among items in a group usually have a cancelling effect. For example, the forecast for total sales of a new T-shirt will be more accurate than the forecast for each size and colour.

4. Forecast accuracy decreases the farther the forecasted time period is into the future. Generally speaking, short-term forecasts must contend with fewer uncertainties than longer-term forecasts, so they tend to be more accurate. The **forecasting horizon** is the range of time periods we are forecasting for.

forecasting horizon   The range of time periods we are forecasting for.

Forecasting in Ocean Spray Cranberries

Ocean Spray is an agricultural cooperative owned by approximately 800 cranberry growers and 100 grapefruit growers in the United States and Canada (British Columbia and Quebec). It produces juices in bottles and cans in different flavour mixes and container sizes. When all the combination of products, sizes, and types of containers are taken into account, the number of different products ranges in the hundreds. For example, a case of eight 1.89 litre Cran-Apple juice drink bottles is a product. The company also keeps track of groups of similar products, called categories, and groups of same-size products, e.g., a group of all 1.89 litre cranberry drink bottles. Also, the products and groups in each of company's four North American manufacturing plants and for the major customers, the retail chains, are tracked separately.

Forecasting is performed by the demand planning group, which is located in the Logistics and Planning department. It consists of a manager and five demand planners, each responsible for a combination of approximately 300 different products and category/size/manufacturing plant/major customer groupings. Forecasts are primarily used for production planning, purchasing, and shipment of the products. The planning process is called sales and operations planning, discussed in more detail later under the heading "Aggregate Operations Planning" in Chapter 13.

Every month during the first week, the demand planners use a software by Manugistics, which uses the past three years' history of shipments and time series models to forecast shipments for the next six months. These forecasts are shared with local sales managers to check and adjust, based on local knowledge of customer intentions, inventory, and promotions. During the second week, the adjusted forecasts are further examined and adjusted by regional and divisional marketing managers in a group meeting, called the Forecast Alignment meeting. During the third week, the aligned forecasts are passed to the production/supply planning for review in the Supply Alignment meeting. Finally, during the last week of the month, upper management from sales, marketing, operations, and finance meet with demand planners (in a Sales and Operations Planning meeting) to review and implement the results of the alignment meetings.

Before setting up the above formal process and using Manugistics in 1998, Ocean Spray did not have one unique forecast for each product and groupings. The accuracy of forecasts was low—mean absolute percentage error (MAPE) was approximately 45 percent at the product level. Now, MAPE is approximately 25 percent.

A challenge for the demand planners is the seasonality of sales of cranberries. Approximately 90 percent of sales occur during the fall, primarily before Thanksgiving and Christmas. Ocean Spray constantly introduces new products such as a new mix of another fruit with cranberry. If a similar product had been introduced before, this product's sales history will be used as a guide for the new product's demand. Otherwise, the services of the consumer research department will be needed.

Sources: http://www.oceanspray.com; P. Gelly, "Managing Bottom Up and Top Down Approaches: Ocean Spray's Experience," *Journal of Business Forecasting Methods & Systems* 18(4), Winter 1999/2000, pp. 3–5; J. Malehorn, "Forecasting at Ocean Spray Cranberries," *Journal of Business Forecasting Methods & Systems* 20(2), Summer 2001, pp. 6–8; http://www.manugistics.com/documents/collateral/Ocean_Spray_ManuCS.pdf; H. Landi, "Straight from the Bog to the Bottle," *Beverage World* 124(1757) Dec 15, 2005, 38–42.

An important consequence of the last point is that flexible business organizations—those that can respond quickly to changes in demand—require a shorter forecasting horizon and, hence, benefit from more accurate short-term forecasts than competitors that are less flexible and who must therefore use longer forecasting horizons. Flexibility can be achieved by shortening the lead time required to produce goods/services, and purchase raw materials/parts/supplies, and related approaches such as postponement (i.e., waiting until customer order is received to add differentiating features to standard components or products).

Elements of a Good Forecast

A forecast should fulfill certain requirements:

1. The forecasting horizon must be long enough so that its results can be used.
2. The degree of accuracy of the forecast should be stated.
3. The forecasting method/software chosen should be *reliable*; it should work consistently.
4. The forecast should be expressed in *meaningful units*. Financial planners need to know demand in *dollars*, whereas demand and production planners need to know demand in *units*.

5. All functions of an organization should be using the same forecast.

6. The forecasting technique should be *simple to understand and use*.

Steps in the Forecasting Process

There are six basic steps in the forecasting process (only steps 4 to 6 are used on a continuing basis):

1. *Determine the purpose of the forecast*, the level of detail required, the amount of resources (personnel, computer time, dollars) that can be justified, and the level of accuracy necessary.

2. *Establish a forecasting horizon.*

3. *Select a forecasting technique.*

4. *Gather and analyze relevant historical data.* Ensure that the data is of past demand rather than sales or shipments, which will be different if there were stock-outs. Identify any assumptions that are made.

5. *Prepare the forecast.*

6. *Monitor the forecast.* If it is not performing in a satisfactory manner, re-examine the parameters of the technique or use a different technique.

Approaches to Forecasting

There are two general approaches to forecasting: judgmental and quantitative. Judgmental methods consist mainly of subjective inputs, which may defy precise numerical description (but may still depend on historical data). Quantitative methods involve either the use of a time series model to extend the historical pattern of data into the future or the development of associative models that attempt to utilize *causal (explanatory) variables* to make a forecast.

Judgmental techniques permit inclusion of *soft* information (e.g., human factors, personal opinions, hunches) in the forecasting process. Those factors are often omitted or downplayed when quantitative techniques are used because they are difficult to quantify. Quantitative techniques consist mainly of analyzing objective, or *hard*, data. They usually avoid personal biases that sometimes contaminate judgmental methods. In practice, either or both approaches might be used to develop a forecast.

Judgmental methods rely on non-quantitative analysis of historical data and/or analysis of subjective inputs obtained from various sources, such as consumers (surveys), similar products (historical analogies), the sales staff, managers and executives, and panels of experts. Quite frequently, these sources provide insights that are not otherwise available, e.g., for new product development, promotions, etc. Long-term forecasting typically uses judgmental methods because quantitative techniques may be inaccurate in this case.

Some forecasting techniques simply attempt to project past data into the future. These techniques use historical, or time series, data with the assumption that the future will be like the past. **Time series models** identify specific patterns in the data and project or extrapolate those patterns into the future, without trying to identify causes of the patterns.

Associative models use equations that consist of one or more *explanatory* variables that can be used to predict future demand for the variable of interest. For example, demand for a particular paint might be explained by variables such as the price, the amount spent on advertising it, and the season, as well as specific characteristics of the paint (e.g., quality).

judgmental methods
Use non-quantitative analysis of historical data and/or analysis of subjective inputs from consumers, sales staff, managers, executives, similar products, and experts to help develop a forecast.

time series models   Extend the pattern of data into the future.

associative models   Use explanatory variables to predict future demand for the variable of interest.

Overview of Demand Forecasting by Forecasting Horizon

Forecasting *long-term* demand typically involves annual data for, e.g., the next five years. It requires knowledge of the specific market and judgment of experts/managers. For new products, either consumer surveys and test markets are undertaken, or demand for an analogous product is used. A common approach is to forecast the demand for the whole market, estimate the market share for the new product, and multiply the two to get the demand forecast. If historical data are available, the trend is estimated and projected into future, e.g., using regression.

Forecasting *medium-term* demand typically involves monthly demand for, e.g., the next 12 months. A mix of judgmental and quantitative methods is used. *Seasonal* effects are taken into account.

Forecasting *short-term* demand typically involves daily or weekly demand for, e.g., the next 12 weeks. Usually there are thousands of products/parts to forecast. Therefore, a simple quantitative method, e.g., an averaging technique, is used. Sales promotions are forecasted separately.

(LO2) JUDGMENTAL METHODS

In some situations, forecasters may rely solely on judgment and opinion to make forecasts. The introduction of new products, the redesign of existing products, or sales promotions are situations where judgmental forecasting is needed, as well as when analyzing future actions of customers and competitors. In such instances, forecasts may be based on collective executive opinions, opinions of the sales staff, consumer surveys, historical analogies, or opinions of experts. See the "McCormick" OM in Action for a case where the forecaster uses his own judgment to determine the base forecast.

Executive Opinions

A small group of upper-level managers (e.g., VPs of marketing, operations, and finance) may meet and collectively develop a forecast. This approach is often used as a part of long-term strategic planning and new-product development. It has the advantage of bringing together the considerable knowledge and talents of various managers.

Sales Force Opinions

The sales staff or the customer service staff is often a good source of information because of their direct contact with customers. They are often aware of any plans that the customers may be considering for the future, including the current level of customer inventory.

Consumer Surveys

Because it is the potential consumers who ultimately determine sales, it seems natural to solicit input from them. This could be in the form of questionnaires conducted by mail or phone to a large sample of potential consumers. It also could be through group meetings with a small number of potential consumers (focus groups).

 OM in ACTION   http://www.mccormick.com

McCormick

McCormick is the largest spice manufacturer in North America. The sales (in units) of approximately 3,500 spices are forecasted by the production forecaster (located in the marketing/sales department) every month for the next two years. The functions that use these forecasts are purchasing, material management, and production. The production forecaster uses strictly judgmental forecasting. First, he looks at the past three years of sales history and from that he develops the base forecasts. Then, he considers any sales/marketing information on price increases, promotions, fads, and trends, and modifies the base forecasts. These forecasts are reviewed (for some products monthly and for others quarterly) by marketing/sales and production staff during regular monthly meetings.

To forecast sales during promotion of a spice, sales during past promotions of the same product are used. To forecast sales of new products, past sales of a similar product are used.

The production forecaster finds the forecasting of new items and low-volume items most challenging because their sales are dependent on only a few customers. Items being promoted and those subject to price change are also hard to forecast. The forecast errors range from approximately 20 percent for high-volume items to as high as 45 percent for low-volume and new items.

Sources: C.L. Jain, "Forecasting at McCormick & Company," *Journal of Business Forecasting Methods & Systems* 10(4), Winter 1991–92, pp. 3–5.

Duracell Forecasting

Duracell, a Procter and Gamble company, is the largest manufacturer of alkaline batteries in the world. Although it has a limited number of common (e.g., AA, C) and specialty (e.g., for cameras, watches) batteries, the various regular pack sizes (e.g., 2, 4, etc.) and special promotion packs result in hundreds of different stock-keeping units (SKUs). Each SKU is considered distinct for the purpose of inventory control. Forecasting is performed by the market and sales forecasting group located in the finance department. There are a manager and six forecasters. The forecasting group performs two types of forecasting: strategic and tactical.

Strategic forecasting involves both projecting competitors' sales and Duracell's sales, by pack size and trade channel, for the next three years. Size of market and its growth, share of Duracell and its growth, and retail inventory changes are forecasted and used to arrive at Duracell's shipment forecasts. Marketing approves the growth plan and view of marketplace. Duracell finds the Point of Sale (POS) data and Nielsen's market information valuable. Also used are economic data and industry data on battery-powered devices. Scenarios based on competitor and Duracell's actions are developed and their effect on forecasts is examined using techniques such as regression. The strategic plan becomes the basis for the tactical plan.

In tactical planning, monthly forecasts (called latest estimates) are made at the SKU level for the next 12 months. Performance in the market during the previous month is reviewed, issues and assumptions are analyzed, and forecasts are updated. Information from salespeople regarding future promotions, in-store display changes, and competitors' actions are used in this process. The aggregate forecasts are approved by VPs of marketing, sales, and finance by the fourth day of each month. By the sixth day, manufacturing also approves the plan. Later, SKU level forecasts are discussed with middle-level managers responsible for the required actions.

Source: R. Gordon, "A Role for the Forecasting Function," *Journal of Business Forecasting Methods & Systems* 16(4), Winter 1997/98, pp. 3–7; http://www.Duracell.com.

Historical Analogies

Sometimes the demand for a similar product in the past, after some adjustment, can be used to forecast a new product's demand. For example, the demand for cranberry-apple drink can be used to forecast the demand for cranberry-grape drink.

Expert Opinions

The forecaster may solicit opinions from a number of experts. One way of doing this is called the **Delphi method**. It involves circulating a series of questionnaires among experts. Responses are kept anonymous, which tends to encourage honest responses and reduces the risk that one person's opinion will prevail. Each new questionnaire is developed using the information extracted from the previous one, thus enlarging the scope of information on which participants can base their judgments. The goal is to achieve a consensus forecast.

Delphi method   Experts complete a series of questionnaires, each developed from the previous one, to achieve a consensus forecast.

One application of the Delphi method is for *technological* forecasting, i.e., assessing changes in technology and their impact on an organization. Often the goal is to predict *when* a certain event will occur. For instance, the goal of a Delphi forecast might be to predict when video telephones might be installed in at least 50 percent of residential homes or when a vaccine for a disease might be developed. For the most part, these are long-term, single-time forecasts, which usually have very little hard information to go by.

 ## TIME SERIES MODELS: INTRODUCTION AND AVERAGING

Introduction

A **time series** is a time-ordered sequence of observations taken at regular intervals over a period of time (e.g., hourly, daily, weekly, monthly, quarterly, annually). Forecasting

time series   A time-ordered sequence of observations taken at regular intervals of time.

techniques based on time series data are made on the assumption that future values of the series can be estimated from their own past values. Although no attempt is made to identify variables that influence the series, these methods are widely used, often with quite satisfactory results.

Analysis of time series data requires the analyst to identify the underlying behaviour of the series. This can often be accomplished by merely *plotting* the data and visually examining the plot. One or more patterns might appear: level (i.e., average), trend, seasonal variation, and cycle. In addition, there can be random and irregular (one-time) variations. These behaviours can be described as follows:

level (average) A horizontal pattern of time series.

trend A persistent upward or downward movement in data.

seasonality Regular wavelike variations related to the calendar, weather, or recurring events.

cycle Wavelike variation lasting more than one year.

irregular variation Caused by unusual one-time explainable circumstances, not reflective of typical behaviour.

random variation Residual variations after all other behaviours are accounted for (also called noise).

1. **Level (average)**, or constant, refers to a horizontal pattern of time series.
2. **Trend** refers to a persistent upward or downward movement in the data. Population growth, increasing incomes, and cultural changes often account for such movements.
3. **Seasonality** refers to regular repeating wavelike variations generally related to factors such as the calendar, weather, or recurring events. For example, sales of ice cream are higher in the summer. Restaurants, supermarkets, and theatres experience weekly and even daily "seasonal" variations.
4. **Cycles** are wavelike variations lasting more than one year. These are often related to a variety of economic, political, and even agricultural conditions, such as supply of cattle.
5. **Irregular variations** are due to unusual one-time explainable circumstances, not reflective of typical behaviour, such as severe weather conditions, strikes, or sales promotions. They do not reflect typical behaviour, and whenever possible should be identified and removed from the data.
6. **Random variations** are residual variations that remain after all other behaviours have been accounted for (also called noise). This randomness arises from the combined influence of many—perhaps a great many—relatively unimportant factors, and it cannot be reliably predicted. Time series techniques smooth random variations in the data.

Some of these behaviours are illustrated in Figure 3-2. The small "bumps" in the plots represent random variations.

The following sections have descriptions of the various approaches to the analysis of time series data.

Naïve Methods

naïve forecast For a stable series, the naïve forecast for the period equals the previous period's actual value.

A simple, but widely used approach to forecasting is the naïve method. The naïve method can be used with a stable series (level or average with random variations), with seasonal variations, or with trend. With a stable series, the last data point becomes the **naïve forecast** for the next period. Thus, if the demand for a product last week was 20 cases, the forecast for this week is 20 cases. With seasonal variations, the naïve forecast for this "season" is equal to the value of the series last "season." For example, the forecast for demand for turkeys this Christmas is equal to demand for turkeys last Christmas. For data with trend, the naïve forecast is equal to the last value of the series plus or minus the difference between the last two values of the series. For example, suppose the last two values were 50 and 53:

Period	Actual	Change from Previous Value	Naïve Forecast
$t-1$	50		
t	53	+3	
$t+1$			$53+3=56$

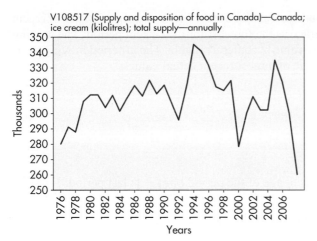

Source: Statistics Canada CANSIM 2 database, Series v108517; accessed January 26, 2010.

Figure 3-2

Level, trend, and seasonal variations (from top to bottom)

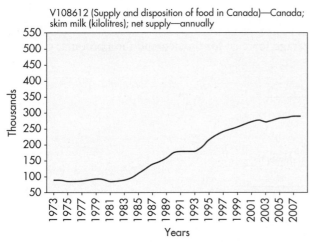

Source: Statistics Canada CANSIM 2 database, Series v108612; accessed January 26, 2010.

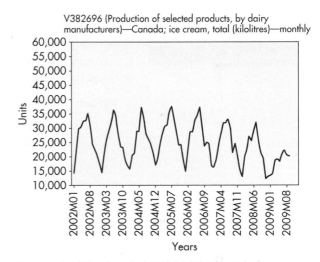

Source: Statistics Canada CANSIM 2 database, Series v382696; accessed January 26, 2010.

Although at first glance the naïve method may appear *too* simplistic, it is nonetheless a legitimate forecasting tool used by some businesses such as restaurants and retail stores. Consider the advantages: It has virtually no cost, it is quick and easy to prepare, and it is easily understandable. The main objection to this method is its inability to provide highly accurate forecasts.

The accuracy of a naïve forecast can serve as a standard of comparison against which to judge the cost and accuracy of other techniques.

One weakness of the naïve method is that the forecast just *traces* the actual data, with a lag of one period; it does not smooth the random variations out at all. But by expanding the number of historical data a forecast is based on, this difficulty can be overcome.

Averaging Methods

Averaging methods generate forecasts that reflect recent level (i.e., an average) of a time series. They can handle stable series (i.e., a level series with random variations around it), where there is no trend or seasonality. Three techniques for averaging are described in this section:

1. Moving average

2. Weighted moving average

3. Exponential smoothing

moving average Technique that averages a number of recent actual values as forecast for current period. It is updated as new values become available.

Moving Average. The **moving average** technique technique averages a *number* of recent actual data values and uses the average as the forecast for the current period. The moving average forecast is updated as a new value becomes available. The *n*-period moving average forecast for period *t* is the average of *n* most recent actual values.

$$F_t = MA_n = \frac{\sum_{i=t-1}^{t-n} A_i}{n} \tag{3-1}$$

where

i = An index that corresponds to age of the period ($i = t - 1$: last period; $i = t - 2$: two periods back, ...)

n = Number of periods (data points) in the moving average

A_i = Actual value in period i

MA_n = n period moving average

F_t = Forecast for this period (i.e., period t)

Example 1

Calculate a three-period moving average forecast for the demand for a product, given its demand for the last five periods.

Period	Demand
1	42
2	40
3	43
4	40 } the 3 most recent demands
5	41

Solution

$$F_6 = \frac{43 + 40 + 41}{3} = 41.33$$

If actual demand in period 6 turns out to be 39, the moving average forecast for period 7 would be

$$F_7 = \frac{40 + 41 + 39}{3} = 40.00$$

Note that in a moving average, as each new actual value becomes available, the forecast is updated by adding the newest value and dropping the oldest and then calculating the average. Consequently, the forecast "moves" by reflecting only the most recent values.

Figure 3-3 illustrates a three-period moving average forecast plotted against the actual demand during 31 periods. Note how the moving average forecast *lags* behind the actual values and how smooth the forecasted values are compared with the actual values.

The moving average forecast can incorporate as many data points as desired. In selecting the number of periods to include, the decision maker must take into account that the number of data points in the moving average determines its sensitivity to each new data point: the fewer the data points in a moving average, the more sensitive (responsive) to most recent data the moving average tends to be. (See Figure 3-4.) If responsiveness is important, a moving average with relatively few data points should be used. This will permit quick adjustment to a change in the data, but it will also cause the forecast to be somewhat

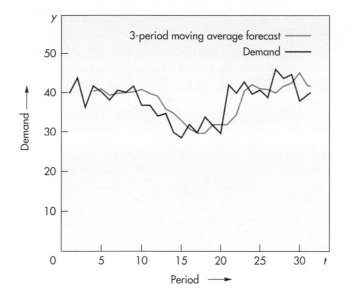

Figure 3-3

A moving average forecast tends to smooth the data but lags behind the data.

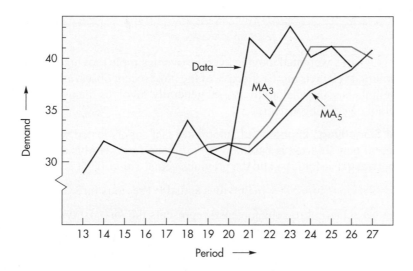

Figure 3-4

The fewer time periods in a moving average, the greater the responsiveness of the forecast to the most recent data.

responsive even to random variations. Conversely, moving averages based on more data points will be smoother but less responsive to "real" changes. Hence, the decision maker must weigh the cost of responding more slowly to changes in the data against the cost of responding to what might simply be random variations. A review of forecast errors (later in the chapter) can help in this decision.

The advantages of a moving average forecast are that it is easy to calculate and easy to understand. A possible disadvantage is that all values in the moving average forecast are weighted equally. For instance, in a five-period moving average forecast, each value has a weight of 1/5. Hence, the oldest value has the *same weight* as the most recent value.

Weighted Moving Average. A **weighted moving average** is similar to a moving average, except that it assigns larger weight to the most recent values in a time series in calculating a forecast. For instance, the most recent value might be assigned a weight of .40, the next most recent value a weight of .30, the next after that a weight of .20, and the next after that a weight of .10. Note that the weights sum to 1.00 (because averaging methods assume that there is no trend), and that the heaviest weights are assigned to the most recent values.

weighted moving average
A variation of moving average where more recent values in the time series are given larger weight in calculating a forecast.

Example 2

Given the following demand data,

a. Calculate a weighted moving average forecast for period 6 using a weight of .40 for the most recent period, .30 for the next most recent, .20 for the next, and .10 for the next.

b. If the actual demand for period 6 is 39, forecast the demand for period 7 using the same weights as in part a.

Period	Demand
1	42
2	40
3	43
4	40
5	41

Solution

a. $F_6 = .40(41) + .30(40) + .20(43) + .10(40) = 41.0$

b. $F_7 = .40(39) + .30(41) + .20(40) + .10(43) = 40.2$

Note that if four weights are used, only the *four most recent* demand values should be used to prepare the forecast.

The advantage of a weighted moving average over a simple moving average is that the weighted moving average is more reflective of the most recent observations. However, the choice of weights is somewhat arbitrary and generally involves the use of trial and error to find a suitable weighting scheme.

exponential smoothing

Weighted averaging method based on previous forecast plus a percentage of the difference between that forecast and the previous actual value.

Exponential Smoothing. Exponential smoothing is a sophisticated weighted averaging method where a new forecast is based on the previous forecast plus a percentage of the difference between that forecast and the previous actual value. That is:

Forecast = Previous forecast + α(Previous actual − Previous forecast)

where (Previous actual − Previous forecast) represents the *forecast error* and α is a proportion less than one. More concisely,

$$F_t = F_{t-1} + \alpha(A_{t-1} - F_{t-1}) \tag{3-2a}$$

where

F_t = Forecast for period t

F_{t-1} = Forecast for period $t-1$

α = Smoothing constant, $0 < \alpha < 1$

A_{t-1} = Actual demand in period $t-1$

For example, suppose that the previous forecast was 42 units, previous actual demand was 40 units, and $\alpha = .10$. The new forecast would be computed as follows:

$$F_t = 42 + .10(40 - 42) = 41.8$$

Then, if the actual demand turns out to be 43, the next forecast would be:

$$F_t = 41.8 + .10(43 - 41.8) = 41.92$$

An alternate form of formula 3-2a reveals the weighting of the previous forecast and the previous actual demand:

$$F_t = (1 - \alpha) F_{t-1} + \alpha A_{t-1} \tag{3-2b}$$

For example, if $\alpha = .10$, this would be

$$F_t = .90 F_{t-1} + .10 A_{t-1}$$

The quickness of adjustment by forecast error is determined by the smoothing constant, α. The closer its value is to zero, the slower the forecast will adjust by forecast error (i.e., the greater the smoothing). Conversely, the closer the value of α is to 1.0, the greater the responsiveness and the less the smoothing. This is illustrated in Example 3.

Example 3

The following table illustrates two series of exponential smoothing forecasts for a data set, and the resulting (Actual − Forecast) = Error, for each period. One forecast uses $\alpha = .10$ and the other uses $\alpha = .40$. The following figure plots the actual data and both sets of forecasts. It can be observed that the .10 forecast plot is smoother and less responsive than the .4 forecast plot.

Period (t)	Actual Demand	$\alpha = .10$ Forecast	$\alpha = .10$ Error	$\alpha = .40$ Forecast	$\alpha = .40$ Error
1	42	—	—	—	—
2	40	42	−2	42	−2
3	43	41.8	1.2	41.2	1.8
4	40	41.92	−1.92	41.92	−1.92
5	41	41.73	−0.73	41.15	−0.15
6	39	41.66	−2.66	41.09	−2.09
7	46	41.39	4.61	40.25	5.75
8	44	41.85	2.15	42.55	1.45
9	45	42.07	2.93	43.13	1.87
10	38	42.36	−4.36	43.88	−5.88
11	40	41.92	−1.92	41.53	−1.53
12		41.73		40.92	

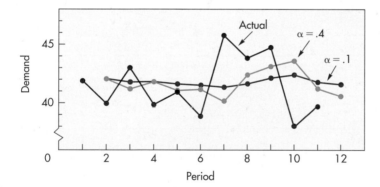

Selecting a smoothing constant is basically a matter of judgment or trial and error (or one can use the forecast errors to guide the decision). The goal is to select a smoothing constant that balances the benefits of smoothing random variations with the benefits of responding to real changes if and when they occur. Commonly used values of α range from .05 to .50. Low values of α are used when the underlying average tends to be stable; higher values are used when the underlying average is susceptible to change.

Some computer packages include a feature that permits automatic modification of the smoothing constant so that the forecast errors do not become unacceptably large. This method is called **adaptive** (or variable response) **exponential smoothing**.

Exponential smoothing is one of the most widely used techniques in forecasting, partly because of its ease of computation and partly because of the ease with which the weighting scheme can be altered—simply by changing the value of α.

Note. A number of different approaches can be used to obtain a starting forecast for period 2, such as the average of the first several periods, a subjective estimate, or the first actual value (i.e., the naïve approach). For simplicity, the naïve approach is used in this book. In practice, using an average of, say, the first three values as a forecast for period 4 would provide a better starting forecast because it would be more stable.

adaptive exponential smoothing   A version of exponential smoothing where the smoothing constant is automatically modified in order to prevent large forecast errors from occurring.

(LO4) TECHNIQUES FOR TREND

Analysis of trend involves developing an equation that will suitably describe the trend (assuming that trend is present in the data). The trend component may be linear or it may be nonlinear. Some commonly encountered nonlinear trend types are illustrated in Figure 3-5. A simple plot of the data can often reveal the existence and nature of a trend. We will first focus on *linear* trend because this is fairly common. Linear trend is usually fitted using regression. Microsoft Excel facilitates this, in addition to many types of nonlinear trend.

linear trend equation

$\hat{y}_t = a + bt$, used to develop forecasts when linear trend is present.

Linear Trend Equation. This equation has the form

$$\hat{y}_t = a + bt \tag{3-3}$$

where

t = Index of time periods, starting from $t = 1$ for the first period

$\hat{y}_t$ = Value of trend line at period t

a = Value of trend line at $t = 0$ (intercept)

b = Slope of the trend line

Forecast for period t: $F_t = a + bt$

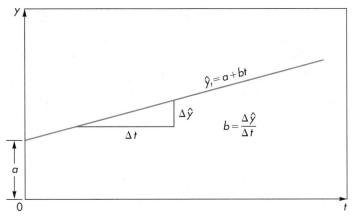

The line intersects the y axis where $\hat{y}_t = a$. The slope of the line $= b$.

Figure 3-5

Graphs of some nonlinear trends

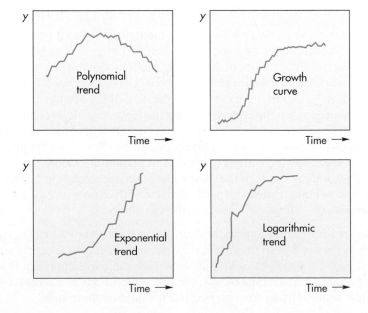

For example, consider the trend equation $\hat{y}_t = 45 + 5t$. The intercept (i.e., value of $\hat{y}_t$ when $t = 0$) is 45, and the slope is 5, which means that, on the average, the value of forecast will increase by five units for each time period. If $t = 10$, the forecast, F_t, is $45 + 5(10) = 95$ units. The equation can be plotted by finding two points on the line. One can be found by substituting some value of t into the equation (e.g., $t = 10$). The other point is $(0, a)$ (i.e., $\hat{y}_t$ at $t = 0$). Plotting those two points and drawing a straight line through them yields the graph of the linear trend line.

The coefficients of the line, a and b, can be computed from data using these two equations:

$$b = \frac{n\sum ty - \sum t \sum y}{n\sum t^2 - \left(\sum t\right)^2} \tag{3-4}$$

$$a = \frac{\sum y - b \sum t}{n} \quad \text{or} \quad \bar{y} - b\bar{t} \tag{3-5}$$

where

n = Total number of periods

y = Value of the demand time series

Note that these equations are identical to those used for computing a linear regression line, except that t replaces x in the equations.

Example 4

Cell phone sales of a company over the last 10 weeks are shown below. The data appear to have a linear trend. Determine the equation of the linear trend and predict the sales of cell phones for weeks 11 and 12. Plot the data and trend line.

Week	Unit Sales
1	700
2	724
3	720
4	728
5	740
6	742
7	758
8	750
9	770
10	775

Solution

Week (t)	y	ty	t²
1	700	700	1
2	724	1,448	4
3	720	2,160	9
4	728	2,912	16
5	740	3,700	25
6	742	4,452	36
7	758	5,306	49
8	750	6,000	64
9	770	6,930	81
10	775	7,750	100
55	7,407	41,358	385

Using formulas 3-4 and 3-5, we can calculate the coefficients of the trend line:

$$b = \frac{10(41{,}358) - 55(7{,}407)}{10(385) - 55(55)} = \frac{6{,}195}{825} = 7.51$$

$$a = \frac{7{,}407 - 7.51(55)}{10} = 699.40$$

Thus, the trend line is $\hat{y}_t = 699.40 + 7.51t$.

Substituting values of t into this equation, the forecasts for the next two weeks (i.e., $t = 11$ and $t = 12$) are:

$$F_{11} = 699.40 + 7.51(11) = 782.01$$

$$F_{12} = 699.40 + 7.51(12) = 789.52$$

The original data (in black), the trend line (in blue), and the two projections (forecasts) are shown on the following graph. It is evident that the data exhibit a linear trend.

We can use the Excel template on *Connect* to solve this problem. Alternatively, we can set up our own Excel template. In fact, Excel has a feature that makes fitting a trend line very easy. If you are using Excel 2003, click "Insert" pull-down menu and then click "Chart." Next, follow the instructions to chart the time series as a line plot, then click on a white space on the chart ("Chart" pull-down menu will appear). In the "Chart" pull-down menu, choose "Add Trendline ...," which can fit six types of trends to the data. The default is the "Linear trend." Then click the "Options" tab, and tick the "Display equation on chart."

In Excel 2007, click on the "Insert" tab and follow the instructions to draw a line chart, then click on a white space on the chart ("Layout" tab will appear). Next, click on the "Layout" tab and then "Trendline," and finally in "More Trendline Options" tick "Display Equation on chart."

Note that the equation computed by Excel, which is displayed on the graph, has a more accurate value for the intercept.

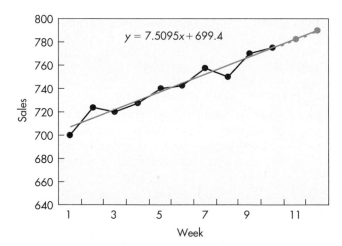

Nonlinear Trend

Although linear trend is appropriate for some series, it is inadequate for others such as demand for a new product that has a faster growth or for an old product that has a slower growth. Example 5 illustrates an exponential trend.

Example 5

PHH Fantus Corp. (now part of Deloitte) was involved in facility location and capacity planning consulting work.[1] One project involved a manufacturer of audio products with a production facility in the United Kingdom that needed more production capacity. From this plant, the company was supplying all of Europe. The question was where to locate a second plant and what capacity to build it for. The historical sales for all major European countries were available. From these, Fantus forecasted 1991–95 sales. The largest sales market was in Germany, and it appeared to have exponential trend (see the graph in the margin). We wish to find out the equation for this trend and extend it one year further.

Year (x)	Projected Sales in Germany (in million units)
1991	11.3
1992	13.4
1993	16.1
1994	19.2
1995	22.9

Solution

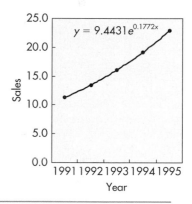

After entering the data in Excel and drawing the time series line plot using "Chart," we use the "Trendline" function to fit the best exponential trend to the data. The equation will also be displayed if you select the "Display equation on chart" option. The exponential trend equation is approximately, $\hat{y}_t = 9.4431 e^{0.1772x}$, where $e = 2.7182818$. Note that this exponential trend assumes a constant *percentage* increase in sales from one year to the next. This constant growth rate can be determined as follows: take the coefficient of year index x from regression, raise e to the power of the coefficient, subtract 1, and multiply by 100. For this example, $e^{0.1772} = 1.194$, so the constant percentage yearly increase in sales is 19.4 percent. This can be confirmed by subtracting any year's sales from the following year's sales and dividing by the same year's sales. For example (forecast sales 1995 − forecast sales 1994)/forecast sales 1994 = (22.9 − 19.2)/19.2 = 0.193, or 19.3 percent (the difference to 19.4 percent is rounding error). The forecast for 1996 is $F_{96} = 9.4431 e^{0.1772(6)} = 27.3$ million units.

Trend-Adjusted Exponential Smoothing

A variation of simple exponential smoothing can be used when a time series exhibits trend. It is called **trend-adjusted exponential smoothing** or *double exponential smoothing*. If a series exhibits trend, and exponential smoothing is used on it, the forecasts will all lag behind the trend: if the data are increasing, each forecast will be too low; if the data are decreasing, each forecast will be too high.

The trend-adjusted forecast (TAF) for period $t + 1$ is composed of two forecasts:

$$TAF_{t+1} = S_t + T_t \qquad (3\text{-}6)$$

where

S_t = Smoothed series at the end of period t

T_t = Smoothed trend at the end of period t

trend-adjusted exponential smoothing Variation of exponential smoothing used when a time series exhibits trend.

[1]M.P. Butler, "Facility and Capacity Planning Using Sales Forecasting by Today's Industrial Engineer," *Industrial Engineering* 22(6), June 1990, pp. 52–55.

which are in turn estimated by:

$$S_t = \text{TAF}_t + \alpha(A_t - \text{TAF}_t) \qquad (3\text{-}7)$$

$$T_t = T_{t-1} + \beta(S_t - S_{t-1} - T_{t-1})$$

where α and β are smoothing constants, and A_t = actual value in period t. In order to use this method, one must select values of α and β (usually through trial and error) and make an estimate of starting smoothed series and smoothed trend. We will use the first few data points to estimate the smoothed series and smoothed trend.

Example 6

Using the cell phone data from Example 4 (where it was concluded that the data exhibited a linear trend), use trend-adjusted exponential smoothing to prepare forecasts for periods 5 through 11, with $\alpha = .4$ and $\beta = .3$. Use the first four weeks to estimate starting smoothed series and smoothed trend.

Solution

Table 3-1 displays the data again in the Actual column. We will use the average of the first four weeks as the starting smoothed series:

$$S_4 = (700 + 724 + 720 + 728)/4 = 718.$$

The starting smoothed trend can be based on the net change of $728 - 700 = 28$ for the *three* changes from week 1 to week 4, for an average of $T_4 = 28/3 = 9.33$.

The trend-adjusted forecast for week 5 is:

$$\text{TAF}_5 = S_4 + T_4 = 718 + 9.33 = 727.33$$

After observing the actual sales in week 5 (740 units), we can calculate the smoothed series and smoothed trend at the end of week 5:

$$S_5 = \text{TAF}_5 + \alpha(A_5 - \text{TAF}_5)$$
$$= 727.33 + .4(740 - 727.33)$$
$$= 732.40$$
$$T_5 = T_4 + \beta(S_5 - S_4 - T_4)$$
$$= 9.33 + .3(732.40 - 718 - 9.33)$$
$$= 10.85.$$

Table 3-1

Trend-adjusted forecast calculations for Example 6

t (Week)	A_t (Actual)	$\text{TAF}_t + \alpha(A_t - \text{TAF}_t) = S_t$	$T_{t-1} + \beta(S_t - S_{t-1} - T_{t-1}) = T_t$	$\text{TAF}_{t+1} = S_t + T_t$
1	700			
2	724	Starting values:		
3	720	$S_4 = (700+724+720+728)/4 = 718$, $T_4 = (728-700)/3 = 9.33$		
4	728	$\text{TAF}_5 = 718 + 9.33 = 727.33$		
5	740	$727.33 + .4(740 - 727.33) = 732.40$	$9.33 + .3(732.40 - 718 - 9.33) = 10.85$	743.25
6	742	$743.25 + .4(742 - 743.25) = 742.75$	$10.85 + .3(742.75 - 732.40 - 10.85) = 10.70$	753.45
7	758	$753.45 + .4(758 - 753.45) = 755.27$	$10.70 + .3(755.27 - 742.75 - 10.70) = 11.25$	766.52
8	750	$766.52 + .4(750 - 766.52) = 759.91$	$11.25 + .3(759.91 - 755.27 - 11.25) = 9.27$	769.18
9	770	$769.18 + .4(770 - 769.18) = 769.51$	$9.27 + .3(769.51 - 759.91 - 9.27) = 9.37$	778.88
10	775	$778.88 + .4(775 - 778.88) = 777.33$	$9.37 + .3(777.33 - 769.51 - 9.37) = 8.90$	786.23

Therefore, the trend-adjusted forecast for week 6 is:

$$\text{TAF}_6 = S_5 + T_5 = 732.40 + 10.85 = 743.25.$$

After observing the actual sales in week 6 (742 units), we can calculate the smoothed series at the end of week 6:

$$S_6 = \text{TAF}_6 + \alpha(A_6 - \text{TAF}_6)$$
$$= 743.25 + .4(742 - 743.25)$$
$$= 742.75$$

and the smoothed trend at the end of week 6 is:

$$T_6 = T_5 + \beta(S_6 - S_5 - T_5)$$
$$= 10.85 + .3(742.75 - 732.40 - 10.85)$$
$$= 10.70.$$

Therefore, the trend-adjusted forecast for week 7 is:

$$\text{TAF}_7 = S_6 + T_6 = 742.75 + 10.70 = 753.45.$$

This process is continued until the trend-adjusted forecast for week 11, TAF11 = 786.23, is determined (see Table 3-1).

Although calculations for trend-adjusted exponential smoothing are somewhat more involved than for a linear trend line, trend-adjusted exponential smoothing has the ability to adjust to *changes* in trend. A manager must decide if this benefit justifies the extra calculations.

The following figure shows the graph of the actual demand and the trend-adjusted exponential smoothing forecasts.

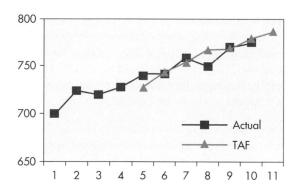

Demand for products such as Sea-Doos watercraft and boats, Can-Am roadsters, all-terrain and side-by-side vehicles, Ski-Doo and Lynx snowmobiles, as well as Evinrude outboard engines are subject to seasonal fluctuations. BRP offsets these fluctuations by alternating its manufacturing capacity to deliver a diverse product portfolio.

LO5 TECHNIQUES FOR SEASONALITY

Seasonal variations in time series data or seasonality are regularly repeating wavelike movements in series values that can be tied to recurring events, weather or calendar. Familiar examples of data with seasonality are retail trade, ice cream sales, and residential natural gas sales. Most seasonal variations repeat annually. However, the term *seasonal variation* is also applied to shorter lengths of repeating patterns. For example, rush-hour traffic occurs twice a day—incoming in the morning and outgoing in the late afternoon. Theatres and restaurants often experience weekly repeating demand patterns, with higher demand on Fridays or weekend. Banks may experience daily repeating "seasonal" variations (heavier traffic during the noon hour and just before closing), weekly repeating variations (heavier toward the end of the week), and monthly repeating variations (heavier around the beginning of the month because of payroll cheques being cashed or deposited). Most products and services have seasonality.

seasonal variations
Regularly repeating wavelike movements in series values that can be tied to recurring events, weather, or calendar.

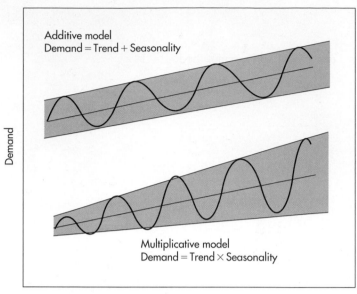

Additive model
Demand = Trend + Seasonality

Multiplicative model
Demand = Trend × Seasonality

Demand

Time

Seasonality: the additive and multiplicative models compared using a linear trend

seasonal relative Proportion of average or trend for a season in the multiplicative model.

Seasonality in a time series is expressed in terms of the amount that actual value during a season deviates from the *average* value of a series during the length of a repeating pattern, e.g., a year. If trend is present, seasonality is measured relative to the trend value.

There are two different models of seasonality: additive and multiplicative. In the *additive* model, seasonality is expressed as a *quantity* (e.g., 20 units), which is added or subtracted from the series average (or trend). In the *multiplicative* model, seasonality is expressed as a *proportion* of the average (or trend) amount (e.g., 1.10), which is then multiplied by the average (or trend) of the series. Figure 3-6 illustrates the two models for a linear trend line. In practice, most organizations use the multiplicative model, so we shall focus exclusively on the multiplicative model.

The seasonal proportions in the multiplicative model are referred to as **seasonal relatives** or *seasonal indexes*. Suppose that the seasonal relative for the quantity of toys sold in November at a store is 1.20. This indicates that toy sales for that month are 20 percent above the monthly average (i.e., annual sales/12). A seasonal relative of .90 for July indicates that July sales are 90 percent of the monthly average. Figure 3-7 displays a variety of seasonal variations.

Knowledge of seasonal variations is an important factor in retail planning and scheduling. Moreover, seasonality can be an important factor in capacity planning for systems that must be designed to handle peak loads (e.g., public transportation, electric power plants, highways, and bridges).

Knowledge of the extent of seasonality in a time series can enable one to *remove* seasonality from the data (i.e., to seasonally adjust or deseasonalize the data) in order to discern other patterns. Thus, one frequently reads or hears about, for example, the "seasonally adjusted unemployment rate."

The next section briefly describes how seasonal relatives are used, and the following section describes how seasonal relatives are computed.

Using Seasonal Relatives. Seasonal relatives are used first to *deseasonalize* the data, and later to *incorporate seasonality* in the forecast of deseasonalized data (i.e., to reseasonalize the data).

To deseasonalize the data is to remove the seasonal component from the data in order to get a clearer picture of the non-seasonal components. Deseasonalizing data is accomplished by *dividing* each data point by its seasonal relative (e.g., divide November demand by the November relative, divide December demand by the December relative, and so on).

Reseasonalizing the forecasts of the deseasonalized demand is accomplished by multiplying each forecast by its seasonal relative.

The complete steps of forecasting seasonal demand, called *time series decomposition*, are as follows:

1. Compute the seasonal relatives.
2. Deseasonalize the demand data.
3. Fit a model to the deseasonalized demand data, e.g., moving average or trend.
4. Forecast using this model (to obtain the deseasonalized forecasts).
5. Reseasonalize the deseasonalized forecasts.

Example 7 illustrates steps 3 and 5 of this approach.

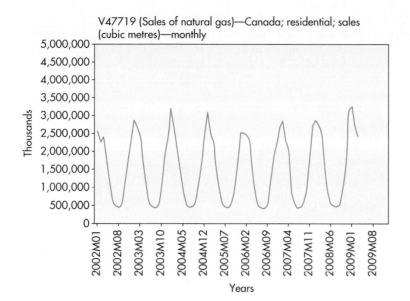

V47719 (Sales of natural gas)—Canada; residential; sales (cubic metres)—monthly

Figure 3-7

Examples of seasonal variation

Source: Statistics Canada CANSIM 2 database, Series v47719; accessed January 26, 2010.

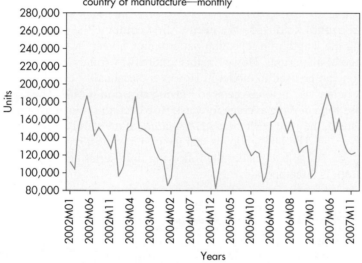

V2452 (New motor vehicle sales, Canada, provinces and territories)—Canada; total, new motor vehicles; units; total, country of manufacture—monthly

Source: Statistics Canada CANSIM 2 database, Series v2452; accessed January 26, 2010.

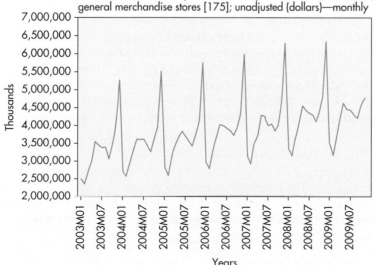

V32955919 (Retail trade, sales by trade group based on the North American industry classification system (NAICS))—Canada; general merchandise stores [175]; unadjusted (dollars)—monthly

Source: Statistics Canada CANSIM 2 database, Series v32955919; accessed January 26, 2010.

Example 7

A furniture manufacturer wants to predict quarterly demand for a certain loveseat for quarters 15 and 16, which happen to be the second and third quarters of a particular year. The series has both trend and seasonality. Quarter relatives are $Q_1 = 1.20$, $Q_2 = 1.10$, $Q_3 = .75$, and $Q_4 = .95$. The trend portion of deseasonalized demand data is projected using the equation $\hat{y}_t = 124 + 7.5t.$, where t is the index of quarter and $\hat{y}_t$ is the estimate of the trend component of demand in quarter t. Use this information to predict demand for quarters 15 and 16.

Solution

The trend values at $t = 15$ and $t = 16$ are:

$$\hat{y}_{15} = 124 + 7.5(15) = 236.5$$
$$\hat{y}_{16} = 124 + 7.5(16) = 244.0$$

Multiplying the trend value by the appropriate quarter relative yields a forecast that includes both trend and seasonality. Given that $t = 15$ is a second quarter and $t = 16$ is a third quarter, the forecasts are:

$$F_{15}: \ 236.5(1.10) = 260.15$$
$$F_{16}: \ 244.0(0.75) = 183.00$$

Computing Seasonal Relatives. We need to first compute the average (or trend) of all periods during the length of a repeating pattern, e.g., a year. A simple method is to just use the average of all periods. However, this ignores any trends. If there is a linear trend, then regression can be used to model it. However, seasonality could influence the slope of the line. A better way is to use **centred moving average (CMA)**. The computations are similar to those for a moving average forecast. However, the values are not projected as in a forecast; instead, they are *positioned in the middle* of the set of periods used to compute the moving average. The implication is that the CMA is most representative of that point in the series. For example, consider the following time series data where the length of a repeating pattern is three periods:

centred moving average (CMA) A moving average positioned at the centre of the data that were used to compute it.

Period	Demand	Three-Period Centred Average	
1	40		
2	46	42.67	Average = $\dfrac{40 + 46 + 42}{3}$ = 42.67
3	42		

The three-period average is 42.67. As a centred average, it is positioned at period 2; the average is most representative of the series at that point.

The ratio of demand at period 2 to this centred average at period 2 is an estimate of the seasonal relative at that point. Because the ratio is $46/42.67 = 1.08$, the series is 8 percent above average at that point. However, to achieve a reliable estimate of seasonality for any season, it is necessary to compute seasonal ratios for a number of seasons and then average these ratios. For example, average the ratios of two or three Fridays for the Friday relative, average two or three Saturdays for the Saturday relative, and so on.

Example 8

The manager of a parking lot has calculated the daily relatives for the number of cars per day in the parking lot. The length of a repeating pattern is a week. The calculations are displayed below (about three weeks are shown for illustration). A seven-period centred moving average is used because there are seven days (seasons) per week.

Day	No. of Cars	Centred MA₇	No. of Cars/CMA₇
Tues	67 ⎫		
Wed	75 ⎪		
Thur	82 ⎪		
Fri	98 ⎬	71.86	$98/71.86 = 1.36$ (Friday)
Sat	90 ⎪	70.86	$90/70.86 = 1.27$
Sun	36 ⎪	70.57	$36/70.57 = .51$
Mon	55 ⎭	71.00	$55/71.00 = .77$
Tues	60	71.14	$60/71.14 = .84$ (Tuesday)
Wed	73	70.57	$73/70.57 = 1.03$
Thur	85	71.14	$85/71.14 = 1.19$
Fri	99	70.71	$99/70.71 = 1.40$ (Friday)
Sat	86	71.29	$86/71.29 = 1.21$
Sun	40	71.71	$40/71.71 = .56$
Mon	52	72.00	$52/72.00 = .72$
Tues	64	71.57	$64/71.57 = .89$ (Tuesday)
Wed	76	71.86	$76/71.86 = 1.06$
Thur	87	72.43	$87/72.43 = 1.20$
Fri	96	72.14	$96/72.14 = 1.33$ (Friday)
Sat	88		
Sun	44		
Mon	50		

The estimated Friday relative is $(1.36 + 1.40 + 1.33)/3 = 1.36$. Relatives for other days can be calculated in a similar manner. For example, the estimated Tuesday relative is $(.84 + .89)/2 = .87$. The sum of average ratios of the seven days of the week should be 7 (because an average day has a seasonal relative of 1 and there are 7 average days in a week). If it is not, the average ratios should be adjusted by rescaling them.

The number of periods needed in a centred moving average is equal to the number of "seasons" involved. For example, with quarterly data, a four-period centred moving average is needed. When the number of periods is even, one additional step is needed because the middle of an even set of periods falls between two middle periods. The additional step requires taking a centred two-period moving average of the even-numbered centred moving average, which results in averages that "line up" with data points and, hence, permit determination of seasonal ratios. The following example illustrates this case, as well as the other steps of the time series decomposition.

Example 9

Below are quarterly data for production of ice cream in Canada from quarter 1 of 2006 to quarter 3 of 2009.[2]

a. Calculate the quarterly relatives using the centred moving average method.

b. Deseasonalize the data, fit an appropriate model, project it four quarters ahead, and reseasonalize to obtain forecasts for ice cream demand for the 4th quarter of 2009 and Q1 to Q3 of 2010.

---

[2]Adapted from CANSIM 2, Series v382696. Note that timing of production of a perishable product such as ice cream is close to its sales.

Solution

a.

Quarter		Production (million litres)	CMA₄	CMA₂	Production/CMA₂
2006	1	66			
	2	96			
	3	91	79.75	78.875	91/78.876 = 1.154
	4	66	78	77.375	66/77.375 = 0.853
			76.75		
2007	1	59		75.875	0.778
			75		
	2	91		74.250	1.226
			73.5		
	3	84		73.000	1.151
			72.5		
	4	60		71.375	0.841
			70.25		
2008	1	55		69.500	0.791
			68.75		
	2	82		66.875	1.226
			65		
	3	78		63.875	1.221
			62.75		
	4	45		59.750	0.753
			56.75		
2009	1	46		54.875	0.838
			53		
	2	58			
	3	63			

Year	QUARTER 1	2	3	4	Total
2006			1.154	0.853	
2007	0.778	1.226	1.151	0.841	
2008	0.791	1.226	1.221	0.753	
2009	0.838				
Average	0.802	1.226	1.175	0.816	4.019
Adjusted	.802(4/4.019) = 0.798	1.226(4/4.019) = 1.220	1.170	0.812	4.000

b.

Quarter		Production (million litres)	Seasonal Relatives	Deseasonalized Production
2006	1	66	0.798	66/.798 = 82.707
	2	96	1.220	96/1.220 = 78.689
	3	91	1.170	77.778
	4	66	0.812	81.281
2007	1	59	0.798	73.935
	2	91	1.220	74.590
	3	84	1.170	71.795
	4	60	0.812	73.892
2008	1	55	0.798	68.922
	2	82	1.220	67.213
	3	78	1.170	66.667
	4	45	0.812	55.419
2009	1	46	0.798	57.644
	2	58	1.220	47.541
	3	63	1.170	53.846

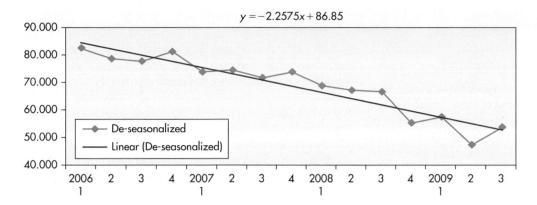

$$y = -2.2575x + 86.85$$

The deseasonalized data has a (decreasing) linear trend. Therefore, a linear trend is fitted to the deseasonalized data using regression, and its equation is displayed at the top of the chart above.

Using the regression equation, the trend forecasts for periods 16 to 19 (Q4 of 2009 and Q1 to Q3 of 2010) are:

$$Y_{16} = -2.2575(16) + 86.85 = 50.730$$
$$Y_{17} = -2.2575(17) + 86.85 = 48.473$$
$$Y_{18} = -2.2575(18) + 86.85 = 46.215$$
$$Y_{19} = -2.2575(19) + 86.85 = 43.958$$

The reseasonalized forecasts for the fourth quarter of 2009 and Q1 to Q3 of 2010 are:

$$F_{16} = 50.730(0.812) = 41.193$$
$$F_{17} = 48.473(0.798) = 38.681$$
$$F_{18} = 46.215(1.220) = 56.382$$
$$F_{19} = 43.958(1.170) = 51.431$$

Techniques for Cycles

Cycles are wavelike movements, similar to seasonal variations, but of longer duration—say, two to six years long. When cycles occur in time series data, their irregularity makes it difficult or impossible to project them from past data because turning points are difficult to identify. A short moving average or a naïve approach may be of some value, although both will produce forecasts that lag cyclical movements by one or several periods.

The most commonly used approach is associative models: Search for another variable that relates to, and *leads*, the variable of interest. For example, the number of housing starts (i.e., permits to build houses) in a given month often is an indicator of demand a few months later for products and services directly tied to construction of new homes (e.g., sales of new major appliances). Thus, if an organization is able to establish a high correlation with such a *leading variable*, it can develop an equation that describes the relationship, enabling forecasts to be made. It is important that a persistent relationship exist between the two variables. Moreover, the higher the correlation, the better the chances that the forecast will be accurate.

LO6 ASSOCIATIVE MODELS

Associative models rely on identification of related variables that can be used to predict values of the variable of interest. For example, sales of beef is related to the price of beef and the prices of substitutes such as chicken, pork, and lamb; sales during promotions

Mark's Work Wearhouse

Mark's Work Wearhouse is a large chain of work wear in Canada. The demand for most of Mark's products, such as winter clothing and boots or summer shorts, is affected by the season. Mark's uses a software called Inforem to forecast demand for its products and to make inventory decisions. Here, we describe the forecasting module of Inforem, whereas the Mini-Case at the end of Chapter 12 provides information on inventory decisions in Mark's.

Inforem facilitates adoption of a seasonal-relatives profile for each product by providing typical profiles for each product family. The forecasting method deseasonalizes the past demand, fits adaptive exponential smoothing (a variation of exponential smoothing where the smoothing constant α is automatically adjusted after each period to best fit the data) to the deseasonalized data, forecasts using the fitted model, then reseasonalizes the forecasts.

Recently, Mark's has started using weather intelligence information from Planalytics to fine-tune its seasonal merchandising, assortment, and allocation planning for some of its products. Mark's buyers have found this information useful. For example,

recently a men's buyer had to decide the discount price for shorts for a Father's Day flyer to be printed in May. Usually, all shorts would have been offered at a 50 percent discount. However, the prediction from Planalytics was for a colder-than-usual spring and warmer-than-usual summer. Based on this, the buyer took a chance and discounted only some types of the shorts 25 percent. The weather prediction came true, resulting in fewer sales of shorts in spring; however, all the remaining shorts were sold in the summer at full price. This action resulted in $50,000 more profits to Mark's. Also, because the forecast called for warmer summer in Western Canada, 8,000 additional shorts were diverted to the Western Canada stores, and subsequently were all sold.

In another example, winter was predicted to be less severe. This resulted in Mark's buying more removable-liner jackets and fewer fixed-liner jackets. Planalytics also provides how much more or less a product will sell during a season; for example 20 percent more demand for cotton fleece.

Sources: Inforem User's Manual; J.K. Speer, "Rain or Shine, Mark's Work Wearhouse Has the Right Stuff: Thanks to Weather-based Business Intelligence from Planalytics, the Scramble Factor at Mark's Work Wearhouse Has Been Drastically Reduced," *Apparel* 48(2) Oct 2006, 20–22.

depend on the discount and size of the ad; and crop yields are related to soil conditions and the amounts and timing of rain and fertilizer applications.

The essence of associative models is the development of an equation that summarizes the effects of **predictor variables** on the variable of interest. The primary method of analysis is **regression**.

predictor variables
Variables that can be used to predict values of the variable of interest.

regression   Technique for fitting a line to a set of points.

least squares line
Minimizes the sum of the squared deviations around the line.

Simple Linear Regression

The simplest and most widely used form of regression involves a linear relationship between two variables. A plot of the values might appear like that in Figure 3-8. The objective in linear regression is to obtain an equation of a straight line that minimizes the sum of squared vertical deviations of data points (x, y) from the line. This **least squares line** has the equation

$$\hat{y} = a + bx \tag{3-8}$$

where

$\hat{y}$ = Predicted (dependent) variable

Figure 3-8

A straight line is fitted to a set of points, each a pair (x, y).

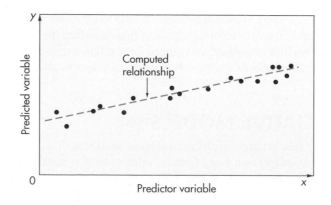

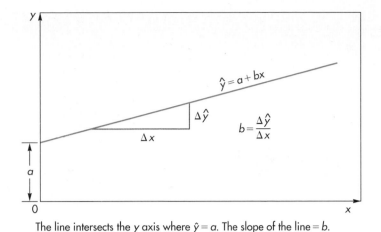

Figure 3-9

Equation of a straight line

The line intersects the y axis where $\hat{y} = a$. The slope of the line $= b$.

$x =$ Predictor (independent) variable

$b =$ Slope of the line

$a =$ Value of $\hat{y}$ when $x = 0$ (i.e., the height of the line at the y intercept)

(Note: It is conventional to represent values of the predicted variable on the y axis and values of the predictor variable on the x axis.) Figure 3-9 illustrates the linear regression equation.

The coefficients a and b of the line are computed using these two equations:

$$b = \frac{n\left(\sum xy\right) - \left(\sum x\right)\left(\sum y\right)}{n\left(\sum x^2\right) - \left(\sum x\right)^2} \tag{3-9}$$

$$a = \frac{\sum y - b\sum x}{n} \quad \text{or} \quad \bar{y} - b\bar{x} \tag{3-10}$$

where

$n =$ Number of paired observations

$(x, y) =$ the symbols showing a pair of observations

Example 10

Healthy Hamburgers has a chain of 12 stores. Revenue and profit for the stores are given below. Obtain a regression line for the data, and predict profit for a store with revenue of $10 million.

Revenue, x	Profit, y
(in millions of dollars)	
7	.15
2	.10
6	.13
4	.15
14	.25
15	.27
16	.24
12	.20
14	.27
20	.44
15	.34
7	.17

Figure 3-10

A linear model seems reasonable for Example 10.

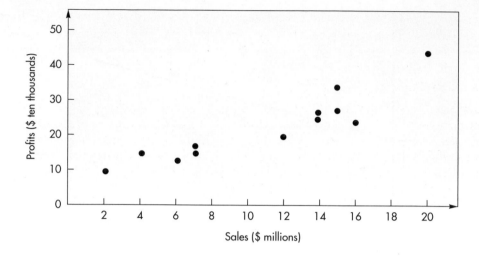

Solution

First, plot the data and decide if a linear model is reasonable (i.e., do the points seem to scatter around a straight line? Figure 3-10 suggests they do). Next, compute the quantities Σx, Σy, Σxy, and Σx^2 and substitute into the (3-9) and (3-10) equations to find:

$$b = \frac{n\left(\sum xy\right) - \left(\sum x\right)\left(\sum y\right)}{n\left(\sum x^2\right) - \left(\sum x\right)^2} = \frac{12(35.29) - 132(2.71)}{12(1,796) - 132(132)} = .01593$$

$$a = \frac{\sum y - b\left(\sum x\right)}{n} = \frac{2.71 - 0.01593(132)}{12} = .0506$$

Thus, the regression equation is: $\hat{y} = .0506 + .01593x$. For revenue of $x = 10$ (i.e., $10 million), estimated profit is: $\hat{y} = .0506 + .01593(10) = .2099$, or \$209,900. (It may appear strange that substituting $x = 0$ into the equation produces a predicted profit of \$50,600 because it seems to suggest that profit will occur with no sales. However, the value of $x = 0$ is *outside the range of observed values*. The regression line should be used only for the range of values from which it was developed; the relationship may be non-linear outside that range. The purpose of the a value is simply to establish the height of the line where it crosses the y axis.)

The Excel template of this problem on *Connect* is shown in Table 3-2. The symbol r represents correlation between x and y, and will be described next. The regression coefficients b and a can also be directly obtained in Excel using "=slope(RangeY,RangeX)" and

Table 3-2

Excel template for Example 10

Simple Linear Regression				
<Back			Clear	
Slope =	0.0159	r =	0.9166657	
Intercept =	0.0506008	r² =	0.840276	
x	y	Forecast	Error	
7	0.15	0.1621124	−0.0121124	
2	0.1	0.0824612	0.0175388	
6	0.13	0.1461822	−0.0161822	
4	0.15	0.1143217	0.0356783	
14	0.25	0.273624	−0.023624	
15	0.27	0.2895543	−0.0195543	
16	0.24	0.3054845	−0.0654845	
12	0.2	0.2417636	−0.0417636	
14	0.27	0.273624	−0.003624	
20	0.44	0.3692054	0.0707946	
15	0.34	0.2895543	0.0504457	
7	0.17	0.1621124	0.0078876	

x =	10	
Δx =	1	Forecast: 0.2099031

"=intercept(RangeY,RangeX)" functions, respectively, where RangeY is the range of Excel cells containing the y values and RangeX is the range of Excel cells containing the x values.

Correlation Coefficient

Correlation coefficient measures the strength of relationship between two variables. Correlation coefficient can range from -1.00 to $+1.00$. A correlation coefficient of $+1.00$ indicates that changes in one variable are always matched by changes in the other variable in the same direction; a correlation coefficient of -1.00 indicates that increases in one variable are matched by decreases in the other variable; and a correlation coefficient close to zero indicates little *linear* relationship between two variables. If a causal model is to be used to forecast the demand for an item (y), it is important that the relationship between x and y variables is strong. The correlation coefficient between two variables can be computed using the equation:

correlation coefficient A measure of the strength of relationship between two variables.

$$r = \frac{n\left(\sum xy\right) - \left(\sum x\right)\left(\sum y\right)}{\sqrt{n\left(\sum x^2\right) - \left(\sum x\right)^2} \cdot \sqrt{n\left(\sum y^2\right) - \left(\sum y\right)^2}} \qquad (3\text{-}11)$$

The square of the correlation coefficient, r^2, provides a measure of the proportion of variability in the values of y that is "explained" by the independent variable. The possible values of r^2 range from 0 to 1.00. The closer r^2 is to 1.00, the greater the proportion of explained variation. A high value of r^2, say .80 or more, would indicate that the independent variable is a good predictor of values of the dependent variable. A low value, say .25 or less, would indicate a poor predictor, and a value between .25 and .80 would indicate a moderate predictor.

The correlation coefficient can be obtained in Excel using "=CORREL(RangeY,RangeX)" function, where RangeY is the range of Excel cells containing the y values and RangeX is the range of Excel cells containing the x values. Similarly, r^2 can be obtained in Excel using "=RSQ(RangeY,RangeX)" function.

Example 11

Monthly sales of LCD television sets in a store and the unemployment rate in the region are shown below for 11 months. Determine if unemployment levels can be used to predict demand for LCD TVs and, if so, derive the correlation coefficient and the predictive equation.

Month	1	2	3	4	5	6	7	8	9	10	11
Units sold (y)	20	41	17	35	25	31	38	50	15	19	14
Unemployment % (x)	7.2	4.0	7.3	5.5	6.8	6.0	5.4	3.6	8.4	7.0	9.0

1. Plot the data to see if a linear model seems reasonable. In this case, a linear model seems somewhat appropriate.

Solution

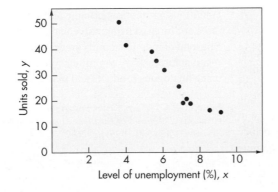

2. Compute the correlation coefficient:

$$r = \frac{11(1,750.8) - 70.2(305)}{\sqrt{11(476.3) - (70.2)^2} \cdot \sqrt{11(9,907) - (305)^2}} = -.966$$

This is a high negative correlation, indicating a strong downward-sloping linear relationship.

3. Compute the regression line:

$$b = \frac{11(1,750.8) - 70.2(305)}{11(476.4) - 70.2(70.2)} = -6.91$$

$$a = \frac{305 - (-6,9145)(70.2)}{11} = 71.85$$

$$y = 71.85 - 6.91x$$

Note that the equation pertains only to unemployment levels in the range 3.6 to 9.0 percent, because sample observations cover only that range.

Multiple Regression

Simple linear regression may prove inadequate to handle certain problems because more than one predictor variable is needed. Models that involve more than one predictor require the use of multiple regression. While this is beyond the scope of this text, you should be aware that it is often used. The computations lend themselves more to computers than to hand calculation. It is necessary to weigh the additional cost and effort against potential improvements in accuracy of predictions. For examples of the use of multiple regression, see the "Mary Kay Cosmetics" and "Michigan AAA" OM in Actions.

(LO7) ACCURACY AND CONTROL OF FORECASTING PROCESS

Accuracy and control of forecasting process are vital aspects of forecasting. Forecasting accuracy is the degree of correctness of the forecasts generated by the forecasting process. The large number of factors usually influencing the demand for a product or spare part, and random variations, makes it almost impossible to correctly predict future values of demand on a regular basis. Consequently, it is important to include the extent to which the forecast might deviate from the actual value. This will allow the forecast user to better prepare for probable values of demand, provided that this deviation is not too large (i.e., the forecasting process is accurate enough).

OM in ACTION   http://www.marykay.com

Mary Kay Cosmetics

The financial planning and analysis office of Mary Kay Cosmetics performs monthly sales forecasts, both in dollars and in individual units. The individual unit data are sent to the distribution function, which modifies them as new information is received. The revenues in dollars are forecast using a set of regression equations, in which the explanatory variables include the size of sales force, each salesperson's order size, economic conditions, promotion, pricing, and seasonality. The individual units are forecast using naïve and moving average techniques. The total of individual units times their prices is reconciled with revenue forecasts. A committee forecasts the new-product sales using analogous products and market research.

Source: R.C. Wiser, "Sales Forecasting System at Mary Kay Cosmetics," *Journal of Business Forecasting Methods & Systems*, 14(3) Fall 1995, pp. 26–27.

Michigan AAA

The number of incoming calls to the emergency road service call centre of Michigan AAA varies by month of the year (higher during winter months) and day of the week. But even for a specific day of the week the number of calls varies significantly from one week to the next. For example, during winter months (December to March) on Mondays, the number of calls during each half hour has 25th, 50th, 75th, and 90th percentiles as shown below. During mornings, the number of calls during a given half-hour period can vary from almost 0 to over 400 calls. This depends mainly on weather conditions such as average temperature and snowfall. Therefore, Michigan AAA uses multiple regression to determine this relationship and uses forecasts of weather condition in the next few days to plan the number of staff and other resources needed to assist its members.

Interestingly, the percentage of calls of a day throughout the day is fairly stable, though it has a strong "seasonality," and is highest around 10 am and lowest during the night. Also, the large week-to-week variability for a given day of the week does not exist in seasons other than winter.

Source: R. Klungle and J. Maluchnik, "Call Center Forecasting at AAA Michigan," *Journal of Business Forecasting*, Winter 1997/1998 16(4), 8–13.

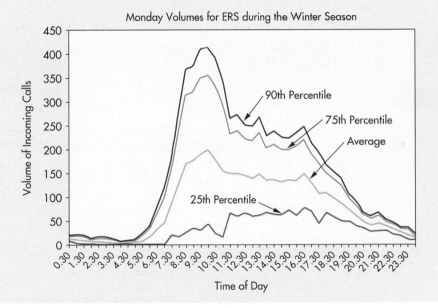

Accurate forecasts are necessary for the success of daily activities of every organization. Forecasts are the basis for an organization's schedules, and unless the forecasts are accurate enough, schedules will be generated that may provide for too few or too many resources, too little or too much output, the wrong output, or the wrong timing of output, all of which can lead to additional costs, dissatisfied customers, and headaches for managers.

A related concept is control of forecasting process. Assuming that a forecasting process was initially accurate enough, it is important to monitor forecast errors through time to ensure that the errors remain within reasonable bounds (i.e., forecasting process remains accurate enough). If they are not, it will be necessary to take corrective action. Both accuracy and control of forecasting process requires measurement of forecast errors. **Forecast error** is the difference between the value that actually occurs and the value that was forecasted for a given time period. Hence, Forecast error = Actual value − Forecast value:

forecast error Difference between the actual value and the forecast value for a given period.

$$e_t = A_t - F_t \tag{3-12}$$

Positive errors result when the forecast is too low relative to the actual value, whereas negative errors result when the forecast is too high relative to the actual value. For example, if actual demand for a month is 100 units and forecast demand was 90 units, the forecast was too low; the forecast error is $100 - 90 = +10$.

Accuracy of Forecasting Process

mean absolute deviation (MAD) The average of absolute value of forecast errors.

mean squared error (MSE) The average of square of forecast errors.

mean absolute percent error (MAPE) The average absolute percent forecast error.

Accuracy (or better, inaccuracy) of the forecasting process is measured using three alternative forecast-error summaries: **mean absolute deviation (MAD)**, **mean squared error (MSE)**, and **mean absolute percent error (MAPE)**. MAD is the average absolute forecast error, MSE is the average of squared forecast errors, and MAPE is the average absolute percent forecast error. The formulas used to compute MAD, MSE, and MAPE are[3]:

$$MAD = \frac{\sum |Actual - Forecast|}{n} \tag{3-13}$$

$$MSE = \frac{\sum (Actual - Forecast)^2}{n} \tag{3-14}$$

$$MAPE = \frac{\sum \left[\frac{|Actual - Forecast|}{Actual} \right] \times 100}{n} \tag{3-15}$$

where n is the number of periods. MAD and MSE are similar to the standard deviation and variance of the forecast error, respectively. Example 12 illustrates the calculation of MAD, MSE, and MAPE.

Example 12

Calculate MAD, MSE, and MAPE for the following data.

Period	Actual	Forecast	Forecast Error	$(A - F)$ $\|Error\|$	Forecast Error^2	$\frac{\|Error\|}{Actual} \times 100$
1	217	215	2	2	4	.92%
2	213	216	−3	3	9	1.41
3	216	215	1	1	1	.46
4	210	214	−4	4	16	1.90
5	213	211	2	2	4	.94
6	219	214	5	5	25	2.28
7	216	217	−1	1	1	.46
8	212	216	−4	4	16	1.89
			−2	22	76	10.26%

Solution

Using the numbers shown in the above table,

$$MAD = \frac{\sum |e|}{n} = \frac{22}{8} = 2.75$$

$$MSE = \frac{\sum e^2}{n} = \frac{76}{8} = 9.5$$

$$MAPE = \frac{\sum \left[\frac{|e|}{Actual} \times 100 \right]}{n} = \frac{10.26\%}{8} = 1.28\%$$

From a computational standpoint, the difference between these three measures is that MAD weighs all errors equally, MSE weighs errors according to their *squared* values, and MAPE weighs errors relative to their actual values.

Because MAD and MSE depend on the scale of data, it is not meaningful to compare the MAD or MSE of two different time series variables. However, we can compare the accuracy of two different forecasting techniques for the same time series variable: A lower value for MAD or MSE implies a more accurate forecasting technique. For an example, see Solved Problem 7.

---

[3]The absolute value, represented by the two vertical lines in formula 3-13, ignores minus signs; all data are treated as positive values. For example, −2 becomes +2.

MAPE can be used to measure forecasting accuracy irrespective of the specific time series data used. For example, the accuracy of the forecasting process resulting in the forecasts given in Example 12 is $100 - \text{MAPE} = 100 - 1.28 = 98.72\%$, a very accurate forecasting process. In practice, accuracy above 70 percent is considered satisfactory. A related concept to forecasting accuracy is the sum of forecast errors, sometimes called **bias**. A persistently positive bias implies that forecasts frequently underestimate the actual values, and a persistently negative bias implies that forecasts frequently overestimate the actual values. Bias occurs because either demand pattern has changed or the way forecasts are determined is flawed. For example, if forecasts are based on salespersons' opinions, the way their budget is determined tends to influence their forecasts: for new products they tend to underestimate the demand and for declining products they tend to overestimate the demand.[4]

bias The sum of forecast errors.

The above statements about MAD, MSE, and MAPE assume negligible bias. If bias is substantial, it will reduce the accuracy of the forecasting process. For Example 12, bias $= -2$, which is very small relative to the scale of demand (over 210). It is important to reduce the bias in order to improve the accuracy of the forecasting process.

Controlling the Forecasting Process

It is necessary to monitor forecast errors to ensure that the forecasting process is performing adequately and remains accurate enough. If not, corrective action should be taken.

Monitoring forecast errors is usually accomplished by either control chart or tracking signal.

Control Chart. A **control chart for forecast errors** is a time series plot of forecast errors where they are compared to two predetermined values, or *control limits*, as illustrated in Figure 3-11. Forecast errors that fall outside either control limits signal that corrective action is needed.

control chart for forecast errors A time series plot of forecast errors that has limits for individual forecast errors.

Also, corrective action is needed if there is strong evidence against the following two assumptions:

1. Forecast errors are randomly distributed around a mean of zero (i.e., there is no bias).

2. The distribution of forecast errors is normal. See Figure 3-12.

The control limits are usually chosen as a multiple of the standard deviation of forecast errors. The square root of MSE is used in practice as an estimate of the standard deviation of forecast errors.[5] That is,

$$s = \sqrt{\text{MSE}} \tag{3-16}$$

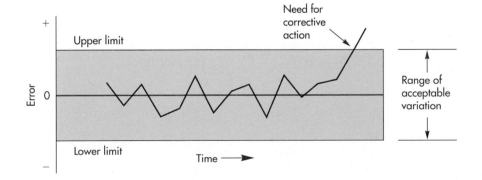

Figure 3-11

Monitoring forecast errors

---

[4]H. Petersen, "Integrating the Forecasting Process with the Supply Chain: Bayer Healthcare's Journey," *Journal of Business Forecasting Methods & Systems* 22(4), Winter 2003/2004, pp. 11–16.

[5]The actual value could be computed as $s = \sqrt{\dfrac{\Sigma(e - \bar{e})^2}{n-1}}$ (where e = forecast error and $\bar{e}$ = sample average of forecast errors).

Figure 3-12

Conceptual representation of a control chart

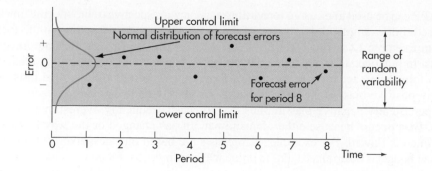

Recall from your statistics course that for a normal distribution, approximately 95 percent of the values (forecast errors in this case) fall within limits of $0 \pm 2s$ (i.e., 0 ± 2 standard deviations), and approximately 99.7 percent of the values fall within $\pm 3s$ of zero. Hence, if the forecasting process is "in control," 99.7 percent or 95 percent of the forecast errors should fall within the control limits, depending on whether $3s$ or $2s$ control limits are used.

Example 13

Monthly sales of leather jackets at a store for the past 24 months, and forecasts and forecast errors for those months, are shown below. Determine if the forecasting technique is satisfactory using a control chart with $2s$ limits. Use data from the first eight months to develop the control chart, then evaluate the remaining data with the control chart.

Month	A (Sales)	F (Forecast)	A − F (Error)
1	47	43	4
2	51	44	7
3	54	50	4
4	55	51	4
5	49	54	−5
6	46	48	−2
7	38	46	−8
8	32	44	−12
9	25	35	−10
10	24	26	−2
11	30	25	5
12	35	32	3
13	44	34	10
14	57	50	7
15	60	51	9
16	55	54	1
17	51	55	−4
18	48	51	−3
19	42	50	−8
20	30	43	−13
21	28	38	−10
22	25	27	−2
23	35	27	8
24	38	32	6
			−11

1. Make sure that the average forecast error is approximately zero: *Solution*

$$\text{Average error} = \frac{\sum \text{errors}}{n} = \frac{-11}{24} - = -0.46 \sim 0 \text{ relative to magnitude of sales.}$$

2. Compute the standard deviation of forecast errors using the first 8 months:

$$s = \sqrt{\text{MSE}} = \sqrt{\frac{\sum e^2}{n}}$$

$$= \sqrt{\frac{\sum 4^2 + 7^2 + 4^2 + 4^2 + (-5)^2 + (-2)^2 + (-8)^2 + (-12)^2}{8}} = 6.46$$

3. Determine $2s$ control limits:

$$0 \pm 2s = 0 \pm 2(6.46) = -12.92 \text{ to } +12.92$$

4. **i.** Check that all forecast errors are within the control limits. Month 20's forecast error (-13) is just below the lower control limit (-12.92).

ii. Check for non-random patterns. Note the runs of positive and negative errors in the following plot. This suggests non-randomness (and that a better forecasting technique is possible). (We present more on control charts in Chapter 10.)

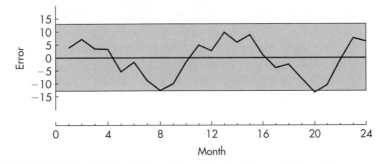

Tracking Signal. An alternative measure to control the forecasting performance is **tracking signal**:

$$\text{TS} = \frac{\sum e}{\text{MAD}}.$$

tracking signal   A measure used to control the forecasting process: sum of forecast errors divided by mean absolute forecast error.

OM in *ACTION*   http://www.colgate.com

Colgate-Palmolive Co.

The sales forecasting office in Colgate-Palmolive's finance department performs monthly sales forecasts of shipments for the next year, using the past two years' data. There are five regional sales forecasters in the United States, who report to four national forecast managers, each responsible for one product line. Every month, Colgate-Palmolive uses a sophisticated software package called STSC (now Manugistics) to forecast individual item sales. The sales forecasters then aggregate the individual products into families, and evaluate each family's reasonableness in consultation with marketing/sales functions using information on promotion, price, economic trends, Nielsen data, and competition, making adjustments if necessary. The adjusted family sales forecasts are then disaggregated into individual-item forecasts. Separate monthly production planning meetings are held with the production people. Because forecasting promotion sales is more difficult, these are monitored daily. For brand items that have loyal customers and are not promoted, the forecast accuracy is better than 95 percent. For forecasting sales of a new product, first a panel of potential consumers is used to estimate the market size, then the market share for the product is estimated and finally the annual sales are estimated by multiplying the two. These are further tested using selected test markets.

Source: C.L. Jain, "Forecasting at Colgate-Palmolive Company," *Journal of Business Forecasting Methods & Systems* 11(1), Spring 1992, pp. 16–20.

When TS values exceed 4 in absolute value,[6] the analyst should study the model and make changes. For example, reset the initial values to eliminate the bias (the top of TS ratio), change parameters such as smoothing constant α to make the forecasting technique more responsive, use a different forecasting technique, etc.

(LO 8) CHOOSING A FORECASTING TECHNIQUE

Many different kinds of forecasting techniques are available, and no single technique works best in every situation. When selecting a technique for a given situation, the manager or analyst must take a number of factors into consideration.

The two most important factors are *cost* and *accuracy*. Cost is affected by the preparation time and complexity. Questions to ask are: How much money is budgeted for generating the forecast? What are the possible costs of errors, and what are the benefits that might accrue from an accurate forecast? Generally speaking, the higher the accuracy, the higher the cost, so it is important to weigh cost–accuracy trade-offs carefully. The best forecast is not necessarily the most accurate or the least costly; rather, it is some combination of accuracy and cost deemed best by the management.

Other factors to consider in selecting a forecasting technique include the availability of historical data, the forecasting horizon, and pattern of data.

Some techniques are more suited to long-term forecasts while others work best for the shorter term. For example, moving average and exponential smoothing are essentially short-term techniques, since they produce forecasts for the *next* period. Regression trend models can be used to project over much longer time periods. If there is a strong and stable cause-and-effect relationship, then causal regression models could be used. Also, if the objective of forecasting is to understand what drives sales, then regression should be used. Several of the judgmental techniques are well suited for long-term forecasting because they do not require historical data. The Delphi method and executive opinion methods are often used for long-term planning. New products and services lack historical data, so forecasts for them must be based on subjective estimates. Table 3-3 provides a guide for

Table 3-3

A guide to selecting an appropriate forecasting method

Forecasting Method	Amount of Historical Data	Data Pattern	Forecasting Horizon	Preparation time	Complexity
Simple exponential smoothing	5 to 10 observations	Data should be stationary	Short	Short	Little sophistication
Trend-adjusted exponential smoothing	10 to 15 observations	Trend	Short to medium	Short	Moderate sophistication
Regression trend models	10 to 20	Trend	Short, medium, long	Short	Moderate sophistication
Seasonal	Enough to see 2 peaks and troughs	Seasonal patterns	Medium	Short to moderate	Moderate sophistication
Causal regression models	10 observations per independent variable	Can handle complex patterns	Medium or long	Long	Considerable sophistication

Source: J. Holton Wilson and D. Allison-Koerber, "Combining Subjective and Objective Forecasts Improves Results," *Journal of Business Forecasting Methods & Systems*, 11(3) Fall 1992, p. 4.

---

[6]G.W. Plossl and O.W. Wight. *Production and Inventory Control*. Upper Saddle River, NJ: Prentice Hall, 1967.

Factor	Short Term	Medium Term	Long Term
1. Frequency	Daily, weekly	Monthly, quarterly	Annual
2. Level of aggregation	Item	Product family	Total output
3. Type of model	Smoothing Trend Regression	Trend and Seasonal Regression	Managerial Judgment, Trend Regression
4. Degree of management involvement	Low	Moderate	High
5. Cost per forecast	Low	Moderate	High

Table 3-4

Forecast perspectives, by forecasting horizon

Source: C.L. Jain, "Benchmarking Forecasting Models," *Journal of Business Forecasting Methods & Systems*, Fall 2002, pp. 18–20, 30.

selecting an appropriate forecasting method. Table 3-4 provides additional perspectives on forecasts in terms of the forecasting horizon.

In some instances, a manager might use more than one forecasting technique to obtain independent forecasts. If the different techniques produced approximately the same predictions, that would give increased confidence in the results; disagreement among the forecasts would indicate that additional analysis may be needed. The chosen forecasting technique should be tested before use to ascertain the level of accuracy.

The Institute of Business Forecasting and Planning (http://www.IBF.org) surveyed over 5,000 companies about their forecasting practices. Time series techniques are popular (61 percent use them), especially moving average (15 percent), exponential smoothing (15 percent), and linear trend (21 percent). Also used are regression (16 percent) and surveys (7 percent).[7]

Using Forecast Information

A manager can take a *reactive* or a *proactive* approach to a forecast. A reactive approach views forecasts as probable descriptions of future demand, and a manager reacts to meet that demand (e.g., adjusts production rates, inventories, the workforce). Conversely, a proactive approach seeks to actively influence demand (e.g., by means of advertising, pricing, or goods/service changes).

Generally speaking, a proactive approach requires either a causal model (e.g., regression) or a subjective assessment of the influence on demand. It is possible that a manager might use two forecasts: one to predict what will happen under the status quo and a second one based on a "what-if" approach.

Computers in Forecasting

Computers play an important role in preparing forecasts based on quantitative data. Their use allows managers to develop and revise forecasts quickly and without the burden of manual calculations. There is a wide range of software packages available for forecasting.[8]

---

[7]C.L. Jain, "Benchmarking Forecasting Models," *Journal of Business Forecasting Methods & Systems* 21(3), Fall 2002, pp. 18–20, 30.

[8]For a survey, see F. Elikai et al., "A Review of 52 Forecasting Software Packages," *The Journal of Business Forecasting Methods & Systems*, Summer 2002, 21(2), pp. 19–27.

TimeTrends

Alt-C Systems Inc. is a Montreal-based software company whose forecasting software, TimeTrends, is being used by some large companies. The software is simple, flexible, and easy to use. It performs all the techniques we have described in this chapter and more. It can access SQL, Microsoft Access, and other databases. It allows grouping of items for forecasting aggregate product families. For a given time series data, it can automatically determine the most accurate technique and its parameter(s). In addition to forecasting, TimeTrends assists in replenishment (inventory control) decisions. An optional module assists in forecasting sales promotions.

Another optional module, e-forecasting, allows use of the software over the Internet. This feature was the reason Compaq Direct bought TimeTrends. Compaq Direct was Compaq Computer's direct fulfillment subsidiary that sold customized computer solutions (configurations) to large accounts. The forecasting software was used by sales people (client service personnel) located in three call centres (in Indiana, California, and Nebraska) to forecast their customers' future demand. In the headquarters these forecasts were gathered and then sent to Compaq's assembly facility in California for production planning.

Molson (Coors) Canada also purchased TimeTrends. It is used by three regional forecasters who forecast each product's demand in each market. Then the manager of demand planning accumulates the forecasts and sends them to be used in the planning of production and sales. They forecast 80 weeks into the future, and update the forecasts every week. TimeTrends automatically identifies the start and stop forecast dates for products that are offered only part of the year. It allows override of forecasts and automatically updates all the groups of products affected.

Parmalat Canada, the largest producer and distributor of dairy products in Canada (formed from Ault Foods and Beatrice), also uses TimeTrends to forecast demand. The forecast coordinator in the trade marketing office in Etobicoke, Ontario, especially likes the ability of TimeTrends to import the seasonal relatives from Excel. The forecasts are transmitted to the production plant in Belleville, Ontario, for use in sales and operations planning, and then purchase planning. TimeTrends is installed on a desktop computer that is connected to the sales database on the AS/400 server. The computer regularly updates the data from the server. The use of TimeTrends has resulted in 10 percent more of the products (from 40 to 50 percent) having forecasts that are accurate within plus or minus 30 percent of actual demand (i.e., have MAPE = 30%).

Sources: "Forecasting in the Field: Compaq Leverages the Web with Canadian Solution," *Manufacturing Automation* 16(5), September 2001, pp. 12–15; Molson case study, http://www.Alt-C.com; and Parmalat case study, http://www.Alt-C.com.

A Canadian software company is Alt-C Systems of Montreal. Its TimeTrends forecasting software and some of its uses in industry are illustrated in the "TimeTrends" OM in Action.

Summary

Forecasts are vital inputs for the design and operation of the productive systems because they help managers anticipate the future. Forecasting horizons are classified into long, medium, and short term.

Forecasting techniques can be classified as judgmental or quantitative. Judgmental methods rely on judgment, experience, and expertise of executives, sales staff, experts, or consumers to formulate forecasts; quantitative techniques use precise numerical calculations to develop forecasts. Some of the techniques are simple and others are complex. Some work better than others, but no technique works in every case. All techniques assume that the same underlying system that existed in the past will continue to exist in the future.

The judgmental methods include executive opinions, sales force estimates, consumer surveys, historical analogies, and expert opinions. Two major quantitative approaches are described: time series and associative (causal) techniques. The time series techniques rely strictly on the examination of historical data; predictions are made by projecting past pattern of a variable into the future. Important time series techniques include averaging techniques (moving average and exponential smoothing), linear trend, and time series decomposition for seasonal data. Associative techniques such as regression attempt to explicitly identify influencing factors and to incorporate that information into equations that can be used for predictive purposes.

All forecasts tend to be inaccurate; therefore, it is important to provide a measure of accuracy. Measures of forecast accuracy include Mean Absolute Deviation (MAD), Mean Squared Error (MSE), and Mean Absolute Percent Error (MAPE). Control of forecasts involves deciding whether a forecast is performing adequately, using, for example, a control chart.

When selecting a forecasting technique, a manager must choose a technique that will serve the intended purpose at an acceptable level of cost and accuracy.

Table 3-5 lists the formulas used in the forecasting techniques and in the methods of measuring their accuracy.

Technique	Formula	Definitions
Naïve forecast for stable data	$F_t = A_{t-1}$	F = Forecast A = Actual data t = Index of time period
Moving average forecast	$F = \dfrac{\sum\limits_{i=1}^{n} A_i}{n}$	n = Number of periods
Exponential smoothing forecast	$F_t = F_{t-1} + \alpha(A_{t-1} - F_{t-1})$	α = Smoothing constant
Linear trend forecast	$\hat{y} = a + bt$ where $b = \dfrac{n\sum ty - \sum t \sum y}{n \sum t^2 - \left(\sum t\right)^2}$ $a = \dfrac{\sum y - b \sum t}{n}$ or $\bar{y} - bt$	a = Intercept b = Slope y = Demand value $\hat{y}$ = Trend line value t = Index of time period
Trend-adjusted exponential smoothing forecast	$\text{TAF}_{t+1} = S_t + T_t$ where $S_t = \text{TAF}_t + \alpha(A_t - \text{TAF}_t)$ $T_t = T_{t-1} + \beta(S_t - S_{t-1} - T_{t-1})$	TAF_{t+1} = Trend-adjusted forecast for next period $(t+1)$ S_t = Smoothed series at the end of current period (t) T_t = Smoothed trend at the end of current period (t) β = Smoothing constant for trend
Linear regression forecast	$\hat{y} = a + bx$ where $b = \dfrac{n\left(\sum xy\right) - \left(\sum x\right)\left(\sum y\right)}{n\left(\sum x^2\right) - \left(\sum x\right)^2}$ $a = \dfrac{\sum y - b \sum x}{n}$ or $\bar{y} - b\bar{x}$	x = Predictor (independent) variable
MAD	$\text{MAD} = \dfrac{\sum\limits^{n} \lvert e \rvert}{n}$	MAD = Mean absolute deviation e = Forecast error = $A - F$
MSE	$\text{MSE} = \dfrac{\sum\limits^{n} e^2}{n}$	MSE = Mean squared error
MAPE	$\text{MAPE} = \dfrac{\sum\left[\dfrac{\lvert e \rvert}{\text{Actual}} \times 100\right]}{n}$	MAPE = Mean absolute percent error
Control limits	$\text{UCL} = 0 + z\sqrt{\text{MSE}}$ $\text{LCL} = 0 - z\sqrt{\text{MSE}}$	$\sqrt{\text{MSE}}$ = standard deviation z = Number of standard deviations; 2 and 3 are typical values
Tracking signal	$\text{TS} = \dfrac{\sum e}{\text{MAD}}$	

Table 3-5

Summary of formulas

Key Terms

adaptive exponential smoothing, 67
associative models, 59
bias, 87
centred moving average (CMA), 76
control chart for forecast errors, 87
correlation coefficient, 83
cycle, 62
Delphi method, 61
demand forecast, 56
exponential smoothing, 66
forecast error, 85
forecasting horizon, 57
irregular variation, 62
judgmental methods, 59
least squares line, 80
level (average), 62
linear trend equation, 68

mean absolute deviation (MAD), 86
mean absolute percent error (MAPE), 86
mean squared error (MSE), 86
moving average, 64
naïve forecast, 62
predictor variables, 80
random variation, 62
regression, 80
seasonal relative, 74
seasonal variations, 73
seasonality, 62
time series, 61
time series models, 59
tracking signal, 89
trend, 62
trend-adjusted exponential smoothing, 71
weighted moving average, 65

Solved Problems

Problem 1

Forecasts based on averages. Given the following data:

Period	Number of Complaints
1	60
2	65
3	55
4	58
5	64

Prepare a forecast using each of these approaches:

a. The appropriate naïve approach.

b. A three-period moving average.

c. A weighted average using weights of .50 (most recent), .30, and .20.

d. Exponential smoothing with a smoothing constant of .40.

Solution

a. This time series is stable. Therefore, the most recent value of the series can be used as the next forecast: 64.

b. $MA_3 = \dfrac{55 + 58 + 64}{3} = 59$

c. $F_6 = .50(64) + .30(58) + .20(55) = 60.4$

d.

Period	Number of Complaints	Forecast	Calculations
1	60		[The actual value of series in
2	65	60	Period 1 is used as the forecast for period 2]
3	55	62	$60 + .40(65 - 60) = 62$
4	58	59.2	$62 + .40(55 - 62) = 59.2$
5	64	58.72	$59.2 + .40(58 - 59.2) = 58.72$
6		60.83	$58.72 + .40(64 - 58.72) = 60.83$

You can also obtain the exponential smoothing forecasts using the Excel template on *Connect*:

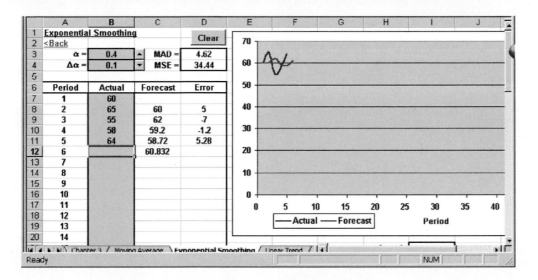

Using *seasonal relatives*. An orchard ships boxed fruit regionally. Using the following infor-   **Problem 2**
mation, forecast shipments for the first four months of next year.

Month	Seasonal Relative	Month	Seasonal Relative
Jan.	1.2	Jul.	.8
Feb.	1.3	Aug.	.6
Mar.	1.3	Sep.	.7
Apr.	1.1	Oct.	1.0
May	.8	Nov.	1.1
Jun.	.7	Dec.	1.4

The monthly trend forecast equation is estimated to be:

$$y_t = 402 + 3t$$

where

$t = 0$ corresponds to January of two years ago

y_t = trend value (no. of boxes of fruits to ship) in month t

a. Determine trend amounts for the first four months of next year: January, $t = 24$; February,   *Solution*
$t = 25$; etc. Thus,

$Y_{\text{Jan}} = 402 + 3(24) = 474$

$Y_{\text{Feb}} = 402 + 3(25) = 477$

$Y_{\text{Mar}} = 402 + 3(26) = 480$

$Y_{\text{Apr}} = 402 + 3(27) = 483$

b. Multiply each monthly trend by the corresponding seasonal relative for that month.

Month	Seasonal Relative	Forecast
Jan.	1.2	474(1.2) = 568.8
Feb.	1.3	477(1.3) = 620.1
Mar.	1.3	480(1.3) = 624.0
Apr.	1.1	483(1.1) = 531.3

Problem 3

Linear trend line. Plot the following data on a graph, and verify visually that a linear trend line is appropriate. Develop a linear trend equation. Then use the equation to predict the next two values of the series.

Solution

Period	Demand
1	44
2	52
3	50
4	54
5	55
6	55
7	60
8	56
9	62

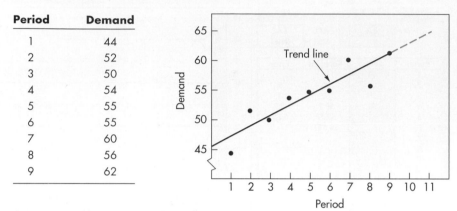

A time series plot of the data indicates that a linear trend line is appropriate:

Period, t	Demand, y	ty	t^2
1	44	44	1
2	52	104	4
3	50	150	9
4	54	216	16
5	55	275	25
6	55	330	36
7	60	420	49
8	56	448	64
9	62	558	81
45	488	2,545	285

$$b = \frac{n\sum ty - \sum t \sum y}{n\sum t^2 - \left(\sum t\right)^2} = \frac{9(2,545) - 45(488)}{9(285) - 45(45)} = 1.75$$

$$a = \frac{\sum y - b\sum t}{n} = \frac{488 - 1.75(45)}{9} = 45.47$$

Thus, the trend equation is $y_t = 45.47 + 1.75t$. The next two forecasts are:

$$y_{10} = 45.47 + 1.75(10) = 62.97$$
$$y_{11} = 45.47 + 1.75(11) = 64.72$$

You can also use the Excel template on *Connect* to obtain the regression coefficients and plot. Simply replace the existing data in the template with your data.

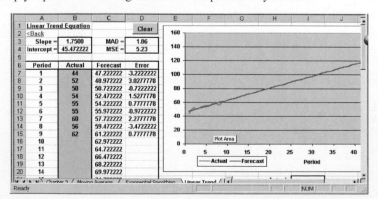

Calculating seasonal relatives. Obtain estimates of quarterly relatives for these data:

Year:			1				2				3			4
Quarter:	1	2	3	4	1	2	3	4	1	2	3	4	1
Demand:	14	18	35	46	28	36	60	71	45	54	84	88	58

Year	Quarter	Demand	CMA$_4$	CMA$_2$	Demand/CMA$_2$		*Solution*
1	1	14				
	2	18				
			28.25			
	3	35		30.00	1.17	
			31.75			
	4	46		34.00	1.35	
			36.25			
2	1	28		39.38	.71	
			42.50			
	2	36		45.63	.79	
			48.75			
	3	60		50.88	1.18	
			53.00			
	4	71		55.25	1.29	
			57.50			
3	1	45		60.50	.74	
			63.50			
	2	54		65.63	.82	
			67.75			
	3	84		69.38	1.21	
			71.00			
	4	88				
4	1	58				

		Quarter		
	1	**2**	**3**	**4**
			1.17	1.35
	.71	.79	1.18	1.29
	.74	.82	1.21	
	.145	.161	3.56	2.64
Average for the quarter:	.725	.805	1.187	1.320

The sum of these relatives is 4.037. Multiplying each by 4.00/4.037 will scale the relatives, making their total equal 4.00. The resulting relatives are quarter 1, 0.718; quarter 2, .798; quarter 3, 1.176; quarter 4, 1.308.

Casual regression analysis. A large retailer has developed a graph that displays the effect of advertising expenditures on sales volume. Using the graph, determine an equation of the form $\hat{y} = a + bx$ that describes this relationship.

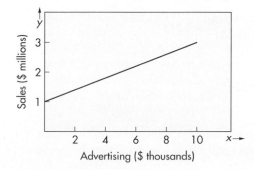

Solution

The linear equation has the form $\hat{y} = a + bx$, where a is the value of $\hat{y}$ when $x = 0$ (i.e., where the line intersects the y axis) and b is the slope of the line (the amount by which $\hat{y}$ changes for a one-unit change in x).

Accordingly, $a = 1$ and considering the points $(x = 0, y = 1)$ and $(x = 10, y = 3)$, $b = (3 - 1)/(10 - 0) = .2$, so $\hat{y} = a + bx$ becomes $\hat{y} = 1 + .2x$. [*Note:* $(3 - 1)$ is the change in y, and $(10 - 0)$ is the change in x.]

Problem 6

Causal regression analysis. The owner of a small hardware store has noted a weekly sales pattern for door locks that seems to move in parallel with the number of break-ins reported each week in the newspaper. The data are:

Sales:	46	18	20	22	27	34	14	37	30
Break-ins:	9	3	3	5	4	7	2	6	4

a. Plot the data to determine which type of equation, linear or nonlinear, is appropriate.

b. Obtain a linear regression equation for the data.

c. Estimate sales if the number of break-ins in a week is five.

Solution

a.

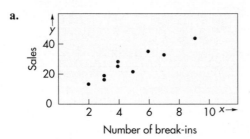

The graph supports a linear relationship.

b. The computations for a straight line regression equation are:

x	y	xy	x²
9	46	414	81
3	18	54	9
3	20	60	9
5	22	110	25
4	27	108	16
7	34	238	49
2	14	28	4
6	37	222	36
4	30	120	16
43	248	1,354	245

$$b = \frac{n\left(\sum xy\right) - \left(\sum x\right)\left(\sum y\right)}{n\left(\sum x^2\right) - \left(\sum x\right)^2} = \frac{9(1,354) - 43(248)}{9(245) - 43(43)} = 4.275$$

$$a = \frac{\sum y - b\left(\sum x\right)}{n} = \frac{248 - 4.275(43)}{9} = 7.129$$

Hence, the equation is: $\hat{y} = 7.129 + 4.275x$.

You can also obtain the regression coefficients using the appropriate Excel template on *Connect*. Simply replace the existing data for x and y with your data. Note: be careful to enter the values for the variable you want to predict as y values. In this problem, the objective is to predict sales, so the sales values are entered in the y column.

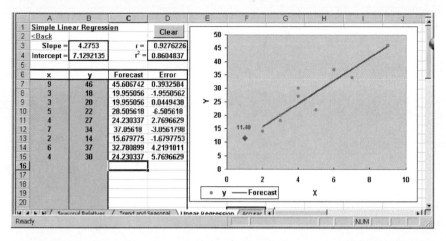

c. For $x = 5$, $\hat{y} = 7.129 + 4.275(5) = 28.50$ units.

Accuracy and control of forecasting process. The manager of a large manufacturer of industrial pumps must choose between two alternative forecasting techniques to forecast the demand for its top-selling pump. Both techniques have been used to prepare forecasts for a six-month period. Using MAD as a criterion, which technique produces more accurate forecasts?

Problem 7

Month	Demand	Forecast Technique 1	Forecast Technique 2
1	492	488	495
2	470	484	482
3	485	480	478
4	493	490	488
5	498	497	492
6	492	493	493

Check that each forecast has an average error (= sum of errors/6) of approximately zero (see computations that follow.)

Solution

Month	Demand	Technique 1	e	$|e|$	Technique 2	e	$|e|$
1	492	488	4	4	495	−3	3
2	470	484	−14	14	482	−12	12
3	485	480	5	5	478	7	7
4	493	490	3	3	488	5	5
5	498	497	1	1	492	6	6
6	492	493	−1	1	493	−1	1
			−2	28		+2	34

$$\mathrm{MAD}_1 = \frac{\sum |e|}{n} = \frac{28}{6} = 4.67$$

$$\mathrm{MAD}_2 = \frac{\sum |e|}{n} = \frac{34}{6} = 5.67$$

Technique 1 produces more accurate forecasts because its MAD is smaller.

Problem 8

Control chart. Given the following demand data for a product, prepare a naïve forecast for periods 2 through 10. Then determine each forecast error, and use those values to obtain $2s$ control limits. If demand in the next two periods turns out to be 125 and 130 units, can you conclude that the forecasting process is not in control?

Period:	1	2	3	4	5	6	7	8	9	10
Demand:	118	117	120	119	126	122	117	123	121	124

Solution

For a naïve forecast, each period's demand becomes the forecast for the next period. Hence, the forecasts and forecast errors are:

Period	Demand	Forecast	Error	Error²
1	118	—	—	—
2	117	118	−1	1
3	120	117	3	9
4	119	120	−1	1
5	126	119	7	49
6	122	126	−4	16
7	117	122	−5	25
8	123	117	6	36
9	121	123	−2	4
10	124	121	3	9
			+6	150

The average forecast error ($+6/9$) is fairly small relative to size of demand (over 110).

$$s = \sqrt{\frac{\sum \text{error}^2}{n}} = \sqrt{\frac{150}{9}} = 4.08 \, (n = \text{Number of errors})$$

The control limits are $\pm 2(4.08) = \pm 8.16$.

The forecast for period 11 is 124. Demand turned out to be 125, for a forecast error of $125 - 124 = +1$. This is within the limits of ± 8.16. The next demand turned out to be 130 and the naïve forecast is 125 (based on the period 11 demand of 125), the forecast error is $+5$. Again, this is within the limits, so you cannot conclude that the forecasting technique is not in control. With more values—at least five or six—you could plot the forecast errors as a time series plot in a control chart to see whether you could detect any patterns suggesting the presence of non-randomness or non-normality.

Discussion and Review Questions

1. What are the differences between quantitative and judgmental approaches to forecasting? What are the advantages and disadvantages of each approach? (LO1)

2. Name and explain, if not obvious, one feature common to all forecasts. (LO1)

3. Name one element of a good forecast and, if not obvious, explain why it is important. (LO1)

4. What are the three forecasting horizons? For each forecasting horizon, name one operations management decision that needs the forecast. (LO1)

5. Briefly describe the steps of forecasting process. (LO1)

*6. How can *shipments* to a customer differ from *demand* by the customer? (LO1)

7. Explain how flexibility in production systems relates to the forecasting horizon and accuracy. (LO1)

8. Pick one judgmental method and describe it. (LO2)

9. What is a time series? (LO3)

10. Generally, how do time series models forecast? (LO3)

11. How does the naïve method forecast a seasonal time series such as sales dollars during every hour of a particular day in a fast-food restaurant? (LO3)

12. Describe the moving average and exponential smoothing techniques, and explain why they are not suitable for seasonal or trend forecasting. (LO3)

13. What advantages does exponential smoothing have over moving average? (LO3)

14. How does the number of periods in a moving average affect the responsiveness of the forecast? (LO3)

15. How does the size of smoothing constant in exponential smoothing affect the responsiveness of the forecast? (LO3)

16. How is regression used in forecasting linear trend? (LO4)

*17. Explain the equation for an exponential trend. (LO4)

*18. Explain the three formulas used in trend-adjusted exponential smoothing. (LO4)

19. What is a seasonal relative? Give a numerical example and interpret it. (LO5)

20. Describe the centred moving average method and explain how it eliminates seasonality from a time series. (LO5)

21. Describe how seasonal relatives are determined using the centred moving average method. (LO5)

22. List the steps of time series decomposition for a seasonal time series with trend. (LO5)

23. Describe how the causal (associative) regression model is used for forecasting. (LO6)

24. What is the correlation coefficient and how it is used in associative regression model? What does it mean if correlation coefficient is negative? (LO6)

25. What is forecasting accuracy and how is it measured? (LO7)

26. Define and contrast MAD, MSE, and MAPE. (LO7)

27. Define control chart for forecast errors. What is the purpose of establishing control limits for forecast errors? (LO7)

*28. What factors would you consider in deciding whether to use a wide or narrow range of acceptable variation in a control chart? (LO7)

29. What is the tracking signal? Contrast it with the control chart. (LO7)

*30. Explain how control chart and tracking signal can be used to monitor bias. (LO7)

31. Contrast the reactive and proactive approaches to forecasting. Give an example of an organization or situation in which each type is used. (LO8)

*32. Choose a forecasting technique appropriate for predicting: (LO8)

    a. Demand for Mother's Day greeting cards.
    b. Popularity of a new television series.
    c. Demand for vacations on the moon.
    d. The impact of price increase on sales of Mary Kay cosmetics.
    e. Demand for toothpastes in a particular supermarket.

Taking Stock

1. Explain the trade-off between cost and accuracy in a forecasting system. (LO8)

2. Who needs to be involved in preparing forecasts? (LO1)

3. How has technology had an impact on forecasting? (LO8)

*4. Forecasts are sometimes manipulated by managers to accomplish goals such as higher budget, capacity increases, etc. Also, sales persons may underestimate the demand in order to beat it to receive a bonus, or they may overestimate it to keep their job. How can a company combat these unethical behaviours?[9] (LO2)

[9]A. Michail, "How to Identify and Correct Politically-motivated Forecasts," *Journal of Business Forecasting Methods & Systems* 23(4), Winter 2004/2005, pp. 3–9.

Critical Thinking Exercise

It has been said that forecasting using a time series averaging method is like driving a car by looking in the rear-view mirror. What are the conditions that would have to exist for driving a car that are analogous to the assumptions made when using time series averaging methods? (LO3)

Experiential Learning Exercises

*1. Obtain next-day temperature forecasts (daily highs) in your town/city for three days (you can visit http://www.theweathernetwork.com, choose your city, and use the Short Term Forecast in the afternoon of the same day and next day, in the middle of the Web page). Compare the accuracy of the next-day forecasts with naïve forecasts. Interpret your result. (LO7)

*2. Gather data on 1-, 2-, and 3-day temperature forecasts (daily highs) and actual highs in your town/city for 4 days and compare the accuracy of each 1-, 2-, and 3-day temperature forecasts (you can visit http://www.theweathernetwork.com, choose your city, and use the Long Term Forecast highs in the bottom of the Web page). Interpret your results. (LO7)

*3. Pick your favourite stock on the Toronto Stock Exchange and choose a forecasting method to forecast its next-day closing price. Repeat this for each of the next three days. (Hint: Go to http://www.tmx.com, click on Symbol Lookup at top left, find out the symbol for your company, then enter it under Get Quote... on the top left, and click Go. You can also get past prices (to choose and fine-tune your forecasting method) by clicking the Price History tab.) Are you satisfied with the results? Explain why you feel the forecasting method you chose worked or didn't work. (LO8)

Internet Exercise

Go to the Institute of Business Forecasting and Planning Web site (http://www.IBF.org) and look into jobs in forecasting (click on "Forecasting Jobs" on the top and "Search Job Listings" on the right). Select a job in Canada and briefly summarize it. You will have to fill in some information about yourself (i.e., register with IBF) to access the job description. (LO1)

Problems

1. A commercial bakery has recorded sales (in dozens) for three products during the last 15 workdays: (LO3)

Workday	Blueberry Muffins	Cinnamon Buns	Cupcakes
1	30	18	45
2	34	17	26
3	32	19	27
4	34	19	23
5	35	22	22
6	30	23	48
7	34	23	29
8	36	25	20
9	29	24	14
10	31	26	18
11	35	27	47
12	31	28	26
13	37	29	27
14	34	31	24
15	33	33	22

a. Plot the three time series variables to determine their pattern.
b. Forecast workday 16 sales for each of the products using an appropriate naïve method.
c. If you could use a more sophisticated method than naïve, what technique would you use for each variable?

2. A can opener manufacturer has had monthly sales for a seven-month period as follows: (LO3 & 4)

Month	Sales (000 units)
Feb.	19
Mar.	18
Apr.	15
May	20
Jun.	18
Jul.	22
Aug.	20

a. Plot the data.

b. Forecast September's sales volume using each of the following:

  i A linear trend equation. (Use of Excel's Trendline, with display Equation on chart option, is recommended).

  ii A four-month moving average.

  iii Exponential smoothing with a smoothing constant .10, assuming a March forecast of 19(000).

  iv The naïve approach.

  v A weighted average using .50 for August, .30 for July, and .20 for June.

c. Which method seems *least* appropriate? Why?

d. What does use of the term *sales* rather than *demand* presume?

3. A dry cleaner uses exponential smoothing to forecast equipment usage as a percentage of capacity (i.e., utilization) at its main plant. August usage was forecast to be 88 percent of capacity, whereas actual usage turned out to be 89.6 percent of capacity. A smoothing constant of .2 is used. (LO3)

a. Prepare a forecast for September.

b. Assuming actual September usage of 92 percent, prepare a forecast for October's usage.

4. An electrical contractor's records during the last five weeks indicate the following number of job requests: (LO3)

Week:	1	2	3	4	5
Requests:	20	22	18	21	22

Predict the number of requests for week 6 using each of these methods:

a. Naïve.

b. Four-week moving average.

c. Exponential smoothing with $\alpha = .30$.

5. Freight car loadings during an 18-week period at a port are: (LO4)

Week	Number	Week	Number	Week	Number
1	220	7	350	13	460
2	245	8	360	14	475
3	280	9	400	15	500
4	275	10	380	16	510
5	300	11	420	17	525
6	310	12	450	18	541

a. Compute a linear trend line for freight car loadings. (Use of Excel's Trendline, with display Equation on chart option, is recommended).

b. Use the trend equation to predict loadings for weeks 19 and 20.

c. The manager intends to install new equipment when the volume reaches 700 loadings per week. Assuming the current trend continues, the loading volume will reach that level in approximately what week?

6. Suppose it is the beginning of 2008 and you are trying to assist the forecaster in Case New Holland, an international agricultural and construction equipment manufacturer, forecast total agricultural equipment industry sales in Canada for the year. You have accessed Statistics Canada's CAN-SIM 2 database and found the agricultural equipment manufacturing industry's GDP (in 2002 constant prices) in series v41881336. The data between 2000 and 2007 are as follows: (LO3)

Year	Agricultural Equipment Manufacturing Industry's GDP (in billion 2002$)
2000	9.8
2001	10.3
2002	11.4
2003	9.8
2004	10.4
2005	10.3
2006	9.4
2007	10.4

   a. Plot the time series data.
   b. Identify its patterns and suggest a forecasting technique.

7. a. Develop a linear trend equation for the following data on demand for white bread loaves at a bakery (use of Excel's Trendline, with display Equation on chart option, is recommended), and use it to forecast demand on day 16. (LO4)

Day	Loafs	Day	Loafs	Day	Loafs
1	200	6	232	11	281
2	214	7	248	12	275
3	211	8	250	13	280
4	228	9	253	14	288
5	235	10	267	15	310

   b. The variations around the linear trend line seem to have above- and below-the-line runs. Therefore, use trend-adjusted exponential smoothing with $\alpha = .3$ and $\beta = .2$ to model the bread demand. Use the first four days to estimate the initial smoothed series (use the average of the first four days) and smoothed trend (use the increase from day 1 to day 4 divided by 3). Start forecasting day 5. What is the forecast for day 16?

*8. The agronomist in charge of canola seed production for a major seed-producing and marketing company is wondering if the forecast for production of seed #1234 for 2008, made by the head office, is a little too low. The sales of seed #1234, in thousand tonnes, for the past eight years are shown below. The company regularly improves its seeds, and has recently introduced a new seed. Given the life-cycle decline in the sales of #1234, the head office's 2008 forecast sales for #1234 is 10 percent lower than 2007 sales. Fit an appropriate model to the data and forecast sales of #1234 in 2008. Do you agree with the head office's forecast? Explain. (LO3 & 4)

Year	#1234 sales
2000	0.1
2001	2.1
2002	2.8
2003	3.1
2004	3.9
2005	3.7
2006	3.5
2007	3.4
2008	

9. After plotting the following demand data, a manager has concluded that a trend-adjusted exponential smoothing model is appropriate to predict future demand. Use period 1 to 4 to estimate the initial smoothed series (use the average of the first four periods) and smoothed trend (use the increase from day 1 to day 4 divided by 3). Use $\alpha = .5$ and $\beta = .4$ to develop forecasts for periods 5 through 10. (LO4))

Period, t	A, Actual
1	210
2	224
3	229
4	240
5	255
6	265
7	272
8	285
9	294
10	

10. A manager of a store that sells and installs hot tubs wants to prepare a forecast for the number of hot tubs demanded during January, February, and March of next year. Her forecasts are a combination of trend and seasonality. She uses the following equation to estimate the trend component of monthly demand: $y_t = 70 + 6t$, where $t = 0$ in June of last year. Seasonal relatives are 1.10 for January, 1.02 for February, and .95 for March. What demands should she forecast? (LO5)

11. A gift shop in a tourist centre is open only on weekends (Friday, Saturday, and Sunday). The owner–manager hopes to improve scheduling of part-time employees by determining seasonal relatives for each of these days. Data on recent activity at the store (sales transactions per day) are shown in the following table: (LO5)

	Week					
	1	2	3	4	5	6
Friday	149	154	152	150	159	163
Saturday	250	255	260	268	273	276
Sunday	166	162	171	173	176	183

a. Develop seasonal relatives for each day using the centred moving average method.
b. Deseasonalize the data, fit an appropriate model to the deseasonalized data, project three days ahead, and reseasonalize the projections to forecast the sales transactions for each day, Friday to Sunday, of next week.

12. The manager of a fashionable restaurant open Wednesday through Saturday says that the restaurant does about 35 percent of its business on Friday night, 30 percent on Saturday night, and 20 percent on Thursday night. What are the seasonal relatives for each day? (LO5)

13. Coal shipments from a mine for the past 17 weeks are: (LO3 & 4)

Week	Tonnes Shipped	Week	Tonnes Shipped
1	405	10	440
2	410	11	446
3	420	12	451
4	415	13	455
5	412	14	464
6	420	15	466
7	424	16	474
8	433	17	476
9	438		

a. Plot the data as time series, determine the pattern, and explain why an averaging technique would not be appropriate in this case.

b. Use an appropriate technique to develop a forecast for week 18.

14. **a.** Calculate daily seasonal relatives for the number of customers served at a restaurant, given the following data. (Hint: Use a seven-day centred moving average.) (LO5)

b. Deseasonalize the data, fit an appropriate model to the deseasonalized data, project it 7 days ahead, and reseasonalize the projections to forecast daily demand next week.

Day	Number Served	Day	Number Served
1	80	15	84
2	75	16	77
3	78	17	83
4	95	18	96
5	130	19	135
6	136	20	140
7	40	21	37
8	82	22	87
9	77	23	82
10	80	24	98
11	94	25	103
12	125	26	144
13	135	27	144
14	42	28	48

*15. Echlin Inc. is an after-market supplier of automotive spare parts.[10] A part is usually made specifically for a particular model of a car. In order to forecast the demand for a part, Echlin tries to use the following process: (a) determine the total number of new vehicles using this part sold each year, (b) determine the replacement probability by age for the first replacement, second replacement, and so on of the part for current and future years, (c) calculate the total number of replacement units for each year, (d) break this down into original equipment manufacturer market and aftermarket manufacturer market, (e) calculate Echlin's annual share using its market share, and, finally (f) break down the annual forecast into quarterly and monthly sales forecasts using seasonal relatives.

Consider a specific part. Echlin makes brake callipers for a particular model of a car, first introduced in 1986. Suppose it is now the end of 1992, and using steps *a* to *e* above Echlin has forecasted its own sales of this calliper for 1993. (LO5)

Year	Echlin's Sales of Callipers
1990	10,444
1991	10,319
1992	8,477
1993	6,334 (forecast)

Echlin also has quarterly sales of these callipers for the past three years.

Quarter	1990	1991	1992
Q_1	2370	2641	2281
Q_2	2058	2198	1814
Q_3	2778	2518	2127
Q_4	3238	2962	2255
Total	10,444	10,319	8,477

[10]See J.A.G. Krupp, "Forecasting for the Automotive Aftermarket," *Journal of Business Forecasting Methods & Systems* 12(4), Winter 1993–94, pp. 8–12.

a. Use the 1990–92 quarterly data above to determine the quarterly seasonal relatives.

b. Use your answer to part *a* and 1993 forecast sales (6,334 units) to forecast quarterly sales for 1993.

c. Deseasonalize the data, fit an appropriate model to the deseasonalized data, project it four quarters ahead, and reseasonalize the projections to forecast quarterly demand in 1993. Contrast your results with part (b).

16. A pharmacist has been monitoring sales of a certain over-the-counter (i.e., no prescription is needed) pain reliever. Daily sales during the last 15 days were: (LO4)

Day:	1	2	3	4	5	6	7	8	9
Number sold:	36	38	42	44	48	49	50	49	52
Day:	10	11	12	13	14	15			
Number sold:	48	52	55	54	56	57			

a. If you learn that on some days the store ran out of this pain reliever, would that knowledge cause you any concern regarding the use of sales data for forecasting demand? Explain.

b. Assume that there was no stock-outs. Plot the data. Is the linear trend model appropriate for this item? Explain.

c. Using trend-adjusted exponential smoothing with initial smoothed series and trend determined from days 1 to 8 and $\alpha = \beta = .3$, develop forecasts for days 9 through 16.

17. New-car sales of a dealer during the past year are shown in the following table, along with monthly seasonal relatives. (LO5)

Month	Units Sold	Seasonal Relative	Month	Units Sold	Seasonal Relative
Jan.	640	0.80	Jul.	765	0.90
Feb.	648	0.80	Aug.	805	1.15
Mar.	630	0.70	Sept.	840	1.20
Apr.	761	0.94	Oct.	828	1.20
May	735	0.89	Nov.	840	1.21
Jun.	850	1.00	Dec.	800	1.21

a. Plot the data. Does there seem to be a trend?

b. Deseasonalize the new car sales.

c. Plot the deseasonalized data on the same graph as the original data. Comment on the two plots.

18. The following data shows a small tool and die shop's quarterly sales (in $000s) for the current year. What sales would you predict for the first quarter of next year? Quarterly seasonal relatives are $Q_1 = 1.10$, $Q_2 = .99$, $Q_3 = .90$, and $Q_4 = 1.01$. (*Hint*: First deseasonalize the data, then observe the trend and project it ahead one quarter, and finally reseasonalize.) (LO5)

Quarter	1	2	3	4
Sales	88	99	108	141

19. A farming cooperative's manager wants to forecast quarterly grain shipments for each quarter of next year (Year 6), based on the data shown below (quantities are in metric tonnes): (LO5)

	Quarter			
Year	**1**	**2**	**3**	**4**
1	200	250	210	340
2	210	252	212	360
3	215	260	220	358
4	225	272	233	372
5	232	284	240	381

a. Determine quarterly seasonal relatives using the centred moving average method.

b. Deseasonalize the data, fit an appropriate model to the deseasonalized data, extend it four quarters, and finally reseasonalize the projections.

*20. Federated Cooperatives Limited (FCL) is the largest wholesaler of grocery, hardware, and agricultural supplies in Western Canada, and operates warehouses in Saskatoon, Edmonton, Calgary, and Winnipeg. In the Calgary warehouse, a particular golf club is carried in stock. The demand for this golf club during each month of the period 2003–05 is listed below (note that FCL uses weekly time buckets, but for simplicity we have combined these into monthly data): (LO5)

Month	2003	2004	2005
Jan	0	2	3
Feb	52	8	20
Mar	29	44	12
Apr	49	74	31
May	47	75	61
Jun	58	87	28
Jul	0	145	107
Aug	64	11	57
Sep	3	24	21
Oct	17	9	10
Nov	10	5	0
Dec	1	6	1

   a. Determine the monthly relatives using the 12-period centred moving average method.

   b. Deseasonalize the data, fit an appropriate model to the deseasonalized data, project it 12 months ahead, and reseasonalize the projections to forecast monthly sales for 2006. (These forecasts will be used to plan purchases of the golf club from the manufacturer.)

21. The following data are quarterly sales of natural gas in Saskatchewan by SaskEnergy (in peta joules ≈ 1 billion cubic feet) from Q1 of 2005 to Q3 of 2009.[11] (LO5)

Year	Q1	Q2	Q3	Q4
2005	49	24	18	37
2006	42	20	20	43
2007	48	24	20	40
2008	51	25	19	43
2009	51	24	15	

   a. Compute the seasonal relative for each quarter using the centred moving average method.

   b. Deseasonalize the data, fit an appropriate model to the deseasonalized data, extend the model four quarters, and reseasonalize these in order to forecast the sales of natural gas by SaskEnergy from Q4 2009 to Q3 2010.

*22. For planning production in the medium term, vehicle manufacturers need to forecast the demand for new motor vehicle sales. The following data are the number (in thousands) of Honda Ridgeline trucks manufactured by Honda during each quarter, starting from first quarter of 2005 (when Ridgeline was introduced) until the 3rd quarter of 2008.[12] Assume that all Ridgelines produced in a quarter were sold in the same quarter. (LO5)

Year	Q1	Q2	Q3	Q4
2005	11.5	19.2	17.4	12.7
2006	11.9	15.1	17.4	12.1
2007	10.6	19.1	13.9	11.5
2008	10.2	6.2	5.6	

---

[11]http://www.saskenergy.com/about_saskenergy
[12]CANSIM series V429850230.

a. Compute the seasonal relative for each quarter using the centred moving average method.

b. Deseasonalize the data, fit an appropriate model to the deseasonalized data, extend the model four quarters, and reseasonalize these in order to forecast the sales of Ridgeline trucks in the 4th quarter of 2008, and 1st, 2nd, and 3rd quarters of 2009.

*23. Mountain Aquaculture and Producers Association (MA&PA) is a small trout producers' cooperative in West Virginia.[13] Its main product is boned, head-removed trout sold to local stores. One of the problems MA&PA is facing is that the demand for its products is seasonal (see the sales in pounds of boned, head-removed trout from Q1 1997 to Q3 2000 below). The manager would like to plan production better. (LO5)

Year	Q1	Q2	Q3	Q4
1997	664	1,338	1,170	259
1998	422	1,098	1,939	1,069
1999	803	1,430	1,206	843
2000	698	1,076	1,149	

a. Compute the seasonal relative for each quarter using the centred moving average method.

b. Deseasonalize the data, fit an appropriate model to the deseasonalized data, extend the model four quarters, and reseasonalize these in order to forecast the sales of boned, head-removed trout from the 4th quarter of 2000 to 3rd quarter of 2001.

24. The manager of a seafood restaurant wants to establish a price on shrimp dinners. Experimenting with prices produced the following data: (LO6)

Average Number Sold per Day, y	Price, x	Average Number Sold per Day, y	Price, x
200	$6.00	155	$8.25
190	6.50	156	8.50
188	6.75	148	8.75
180	7.00	140	9.00
170	7.25	133	9.25
162	7.50		
160	8.00		

a. Plot the data as a scatter plot, determine the regression equation, and plot the regression line on the same graph as data. (You may use Excel's "=slope(RangeY,RangeX)" and "=intercept(RangeY, RangeX)" to obtain the regression coefficients b and a, respectively, where RangeY is the range of Excel cells containing the y values and RangeX is the range of Excel cells containing the x values. Alternatively, use Trendline in the Layout menu.)

b. Determine the correlation coefficient and interpret it. (You may use Excel's "=CORREL (RangeY,RangeX)" to determine r).

25. The following data were collected during a study of consumer buying patterns. (LO6)

Observation	X	Y	Observation	X	Y
1	15	74	8	18	78
2	25	80	9	14	70
3	40	84	10	15	72
4	32	81	11	22	85
5	51	96	12	24	88
6	47	95			
7	30	83			

a. Plot the data as a scatter plot.

b. Obtain a linear regression line for the data. (You may use Excel's "=slope(RangeY,RangeX)" and "=intercept(RangeY,RangeX, where RangeY is the range of Excel cells containing the y values and RangeX is the range of Excel cells containing the x values)" to obtain the regression coefficients b and a, respectively. Alternatively, use Trendline in the Layout menu.)

---

[13] R.M. Fincham. A Break-even Analysis of Trout Processing in West Virginia: A Case Study Approach, M.S. thesis, West Virginia University, 2001.

c. What percentage of the variation is explained by the regression line? (You may use Excel's "=RSQ(RangeY,RangeX)" to obtain r^2).

d. Use the equation determined in part *b* to predict the value of *y* for *x* = 41.

26. A lawn and garden centre intends to use sales of lawn fertilizer to predict lawn mower sales. The store manager wishes to determine the relationship between fertilizer and mower sales. The pertinent data are: (LO6)

Period	Fertilizer Sales (tonnes)	Number of Mowers Sold	Period	Fertilizer Sales (tonnes)	Number of Mowers Sold
1	1.6	10	8	1.3	7
2	1.3	8	9	1.7	10
3	1.8	11	10	1.2	6
4	2.0	12	11	1.9	11
5	2.2	12	12	1.4	8
6	1.6	9	13	1.7	10
7	1.5	8			

a. Determine the correlation between the two variables. Does it appear that a relationship between these variables will yield good predictions? Explain. (You may use Excel's "=CORREL (RangeY,RangeX)" to determine *r*, where RangeY is the range of Excel cells containing the *y* values and RangeX is the range of Excel cells containing the *x* values. You also need R^2, RSQ(RangeY,RangeX).

b. Obtain a linear regression line for the data. (You may use Excel's "=slope(RangeY,RangeX)" and "=intercept(RangeY,RangeX)" to obtain the regression coefficients *b* and *a*, respectively. Alternatively, use Trendline in the Layout menu.)

c. Predict lawn mower sales, given fertilizer sales of 2 tonnes.

27. Columbia Gas Company of Ohio distributes natural gas to residential, business, and industrial customers in Ohio.[14] In order to secure enough gas supply, Columbia Gas forecasts daily demand for the next five days using regression. It has identified the average daily temperature as the most important explanatory variable for daily demand for natural gas. The regression is estimated using daily data from the past two years. For brevity, we consider only a subset of this period as follows. (LO6)

a. Plot the average temperature and demand data for the past 10 days. Does there appear to be a linear relationship?

b. Estimate the regression coefficients. (You may use Excel's "=slope(RangeY,RangeX)" and "=intercept(RangeY,RangeX)" to obtain the regression coefficients *b* and *a*, respectively, where RangeY is the range of Excel cells containing the *y* values and RangeX is the range of Excel cells containing the *x* values.).

c. If the average temperature tomorrow is expected to be 54 degrees Fahrenheit, what is the forecast for demand for natural gas tomorrow?

Day	Avg. Temp (F)	Demand (thousand dekatherm)
−10	33	1005
−9	46	501
−8	41	612
−7	47	499
−6	37	692
−5	36	709
−4	32	951
−3	34	1053
−2	38	746
−1	43	458

[14]Based on A.H. Catron, "Daily Demand Forecasting at Columbia Gas," *Journal of Business Forecasting* 19(2) Summer 2000, 10–15

28. An analyst must decide between two different forecasting techniques for weekly sales of inline skates: a linear trend equation and the naïve approach. The linear trend equation is $y_t = 124 + 2t$, and it was developed using data from periods 1 through 10. Based on data for periods 11 through 19 as shown below, which of these two methods has greater accuracy? (You can use any one of the three measures of forecast errors). (LO7)

t	Units Sold	t	Units Sold
11	147	16	152
12	148	17	155
13	151	18	157
14	145	19	160
15	155		

29. Two different forecasting techniques were used to forecast demand for cases of bottled water in a store. Actual demand and the two sets of forecasts for seven periods are as follows: (LO7)

Period	Demand	Forecast Demand F1	Forecast Demand F2
1	68	66	66
2	75	68	68
3	70	72	70
4	74	71	72
5	69	72	74
6	72	70	76
7	80	71	78

  a. Calculate the MAD for each set of forecasts. Which technique appears to be more accurate?
  b. Calculate the MSE for each set of forecasts. Which technique appears to be more accurate?
  c. Calculate the MAPE for each set of forecasts. Which technique appears to be more accurate?
  d. Do all three measures of forecast errors provide the same conclusion (i.e., are they consistent) in this case? Do you expect consistent results for every case? Explain.
  e. In practice, *either* MAD, MSE, or MAPE would be employed to compute a measure of forecast errors. What factors might lead a manager to favour one?

30. Two independent set of forecasts based on judgment and experience have been prepared each month for the past 10 months. The forecasts and actual demand are as follows: (LO7)

Month	Demand	Forecast 1	Forecast 2
1	770	771	769
2	789	785	787
3	794	790	792
4	780	784	798
5	768	770	774
6	772	768	770
7	760	761	759
8	775	771	775
9	786	784	788
10	790	788	788

  a. Calculate the MSE, MAD, and MAPE for each forecast. Does one forecast seem superior? Explain.

b. Do all three measures of forecast errors provide the same conclusion (i.e., are they consistent) in this case? Do you expect consistent results in every case? Explain.

c. Calculate 2s control limits for each forecast and determine if each forecasting process is in control. Explain.

31. The classified department of a monthly magazine has used a combination of quantitative and judgmental methods to forecast sales of advertising space. The forecast errors over an 18-month period are as follows: (LO7)

Month	Forecast Error	Month	Forecast Error
1	−8	11	1
2	−2	12	6
3	4	13	8
4	7	14	4
5	9	15	1
6	5	16	−2
7	0	17	−4
8	−3	18	−8
9	−9		
10	−4		

a. Using the first half of the data (Months 1 to 9), construct a control chart with 2s limits.

b. Plot the last nine forecast errors on the control chart. Is the forecasting process in control? Are the forecast errors random? Explain.

32. A textbook publishing company has compiled data on total annual sales of its business textbooks for the preceding eight years: (LO4 & 7)

Year:	1	2	3	4	5	6	7	8
Sales (000):	40.2	44.5	48.0	52.3	55.8	57.1	62.4	69.0

a. Plot the data and fit an appropriate model to it. Forecast the preceding eight years, and determine the forecast errors. Finally, construct a 2s control chart.

b. Using the model, forecast textbook sales for each of the next five years.

c. Suppose actual sales for the next five years turn out as follows:

Year:	9	10	11	12	13
Sales (000):	73.7	77.2	82.1	87.8	90.6

Calculate the forecast errors for years 9 to 13. Is the forecasting process in control? Explain.

33. A manager has just received an evaluation from an analyst on two potential forecasting methods. The analyst is indifferent between the two methods, saying that they should be equally accurate and in control. The demand and the forecasts using the two methods for nine periods follow: (LO7)

Period:	1	2	3	4	5	6	7	8	9
Demand:	37	39	37	39	45	49	47	49	51
Method 1:	36	38	40	42	46	46	46	48	52
Method 2:	36	37	38	38	41	52	47	48	52

a. Calculate the MSE for each method and compare the two methods.

b. Construct a 2s control chart for each method and interpret them. Do you agree with the analyst? Explain.

*34. Consider the usage of item #14-46-506: 4 ft. Supersaver fluorescent lamps in Sterling Pulp Chemicals (now part of ERCO Worldwide) in the first 10 months of 2008.

Month	2008
Jan	10
Feb	10
Mar	66
Apr	32
May	34
June	18
July	24
Aug	9
Sep	14
Oct	48

Fit a model to the data using each of the following techniques and forecast the November usage in each case. Also, plot the two moving average forecasts and the actual, the two exponential smoothing forecasts and the actual, and the linear trend and the actual (three graphs altogether). (LO3 & 4)

a. Three-month moving average.
b. Five-month moving average.
c. Exponential smoothing with smoothing constant = 0.1.
d. Exponential smoothing with smoothing constant = 0.3.
e. Linear trend (regression).
f. Just by observing the plots, which of the above techniques would you use to forecast the usage of fluorescent lamps and why? (Hint: the plot overall closest to actual demand will be most accurate).
g. Alternatively, compute the MAD for each forecasting technique and determine the most accurate technique.

*35. Consider the total production (and sales) of ice cream in Canada (in millions of litres) for the period 1995 until 2007 (from left to right)[15]:

341, 331, 317, 315, 321, 278, 298, 311, 302, 302, 335, 320, 309

Fit a model to ice cream production data using each of the following techniques and forecast the 2008 production in each case. Also, plot the two moving average forecasts and the actual, the two exponential smoothing forecasts and the actual, and the linear trend and the actual (three graphs altogether). (LO3 & 4)

a. Two-year moving average.
b. Four-year moving average.
c. Exponential smoothing with smoothing constant = 0.2.
d. Exponential smoothing with smoothing constant = 0.4.
e. Linear trend (regression).
f. Just by observing the plots, which of the above techniques would you use to forecast the ice cream production and why? (Hint: The plot overall closest to actual demand will be most accurate).
g. Alternatively, compute the MAD for each forecasting technique and determine the most accurate technique.

*36. The number of Toyota Corollas produced in the Cambridge, Ontario, plant during each month of January 2008 to December 2009 period was as follows[16]:

---

[15]CANSIM 2 database series v108517.
[16]CANSIM 2 series V42190663.

Month	No. Produced	Month	No. Produced
2008–01	4,959	2009–01	6,733
2008–02	8,463	2009–02	1,006
2008–03	11,706	2009–03	9,328
2008–04	9,907	2009–04	9,072
2008–05	9,354	2009–05	8,738
2008–06	11,297	2009–06	12,259
2008–07	8,905	2009–07	9,519
2008–08	12,249	2009–08	12,113
2008–09	19,160	2009–09	14,044
2008–10	14,264	2009–10	16,650
2008–11	13,687	2009–11	16,912
2008–12	8,657	2009–12	13,851

Assume that the cars are sold in the same month they are produced. Identify an appropriate forecasting technique, briefly state the reason(s) you chose it, and forecast Corolla demand in January 2010. (LO3, 4, 5, 7, 8)

MINI-CASE   http://www.acadianbakers.com

Acadian Bakers

Week	Sales
1	461
2	450
3	463
4	458
5	476
6	492
7	482
8	491
9	488
10	488

Acadian Bakers is a small sweets bakery in Houston, Texas. One of its products is a croissant. Acadian bakes the croissants from frozen croissants that it buys. For the sake of quality, the company don't want to store its frozen goods for more than one week. For orders of more than 576 cases, the delivery is free (saving $15 per order). A case contains 144 frozen croissants. Acadian has collected its total weekly sales for croissants (in cases) for the last 10 weeks. Management feels that the sales of croissants are increasing. Determine if and when Acadian can take advantage of the quantity discount.

CHAPTER 4
Product Design

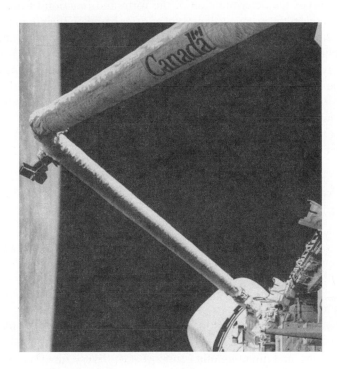

LEARNING OBJECTIVES

After completing this chapter, you should be able to:

LO1 Describe the product design process.

LO2 Name some sources of ideas for new or revised designs.

LO3 Discuss key issues in product design.

LO4 Discuss special considerations for service design.

LO5 Describe and perform quality function deployment (QFD).

Satisfying customers begins with product (good and service) design. Moreover, decisions made in this area impact operations and organizations' overall success.

Similarly, production process design and capacity planning impact the ability of the production system to perform and satisfy customers, in addition to affecting cost of production. Process design and layout are closely related. Layout decisions involve the arrangement of the workplace, which affects the flow of work through the system. Facility layout is an important part of most services.

Work design focuses on the human element in production systems. Increasingly, managers are realizing that workers are a valuable asset and can contribute greatly to the organization's success.

The location decision influences operating costs, transportation costs, labour availability, and access to markets.

Design decisions have strategic significance for organizations. Many of these decisions are made jointly with the CEO and top managers of other functional areas of the organization.

Computer manufacturers such as Dell and car manufacturers such as Ford need to introduce new models or redesign existing models every year because of intense competition and continuous technological innovation. How do some companies manage to introduce successful new products quickly when others can't? This is the type of question we will be answering in this chapter.

The essence of any organization is the goods and services it offers. There is an obvious link between the *design* of those goods and services and the *success* of the organization. In addition, the quality of the product is mainly, perhaps as much as 80 percent, determined during the design. Further, product design is usually expensive and time consuming, and many new product ideas die before being marketed. Hence, organizations have a vital stake in achieving good product design.

product design Determining the form and function of the product.

Product design involves the determination of the form and function of the product. Business organizations select the products they want to offer based on their expected profit contribution. In most cases, products are redesigned to invigorate their demand and to take advantage of new technology.

In this chapter you will find many insights into good and service design. Among the topics covered are the steps involved in product design or redesign; sources of ideas for design or redesign; some design issues, service design; and quality function deployment, a method for translating the "voice of customers" into design attributes.

Product design—or redesign—should be closely tied to an organization's strategy. It is a major factor in customer satisfaction and competitive advantage.

(LO1) PRODUCT DESIGN PROCESS

Successful organizations use four elements to rapidly create new goods and services and bring them to consumers (see Figure 4-1).

The product approval committee consists of top management and oversees and directs the design/development activities. It is responsible for authorizing new products, reviewing their progress at phase (or stage) review points, allocating resources across different projects, and ensuring consistency between company strategy and design/development projects.

Core teams are cross-functional teams empowered to plan and lead the design/development projects from idea to commercialization. This involves resolving issues and conflicts, making trade-off decisions, and directing other support staff. Every function involved in the design/development should be represented in the core team, but the team should not be large (maximum of eight members) in order to be effective. It is important to clearly define every core member's role and responsibility, and those of the functional managers,

Figure 4-1

Four basic elements required to bring new products from idea to consumers

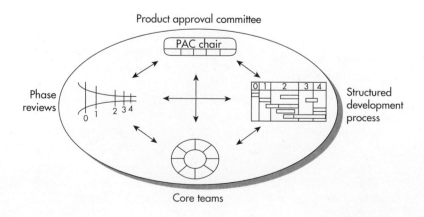

to ensure that the core team is empowered. The limits of authority of the core team should be defined. Many core teams also include a legal and regulatory member.

Phase reviews (or stage-gates) are milestones during a new product design/development project when the progress of the core team is reviewed by the product approval committee. The decision will be to approve, cancel, or redirect the project. Reviews help top management acquire better understanding of the project, guide the project, and force closure of issues arising during each phase of the project. Phase reviews result in recognizing the problems and making necessary changes earlier, reducing the cost of changes and time to market. Cost of changes tends to multiply with each phase—changing a sketch is a lot easier than changing a prototype, and changing a prototype is a lot easier than changing the first production unit. This is called the "escalator effect."[1]

The structured development process is the use of project management techniques. It involves breaking each phase (stage) into steps and each step into activities, determining their precedence relationships, scheduling, and execution and control. The steps are most critical and are planned and managed by the core team. An activity relates to one functional area and is planned and managed by the core team member from that function. Activities may be broken down into day-to-day tasks. It is important that the amount of structure is just right: too much structure results in bureaucracy and too little structure results in ineffective design/development process.

The usual phases (stages) for product design, and a brief description for each, are:

1. Idea generation and preliminary assessment (or scoping): ideas can come from customers' feedback, research and development staff, suppliers, and competitors. Preliminary assessment involves market, technical, and financial evaluation.

2. Building a business case: Determine what customers want ("voice of the customer"), determine the nature of product and assess its technical feasibility, establish product goals and objectives (performance, price, quality, quantity, launch date, etc.), plan the nature of the production process (determine the inputs, process objectives, and production process in general), and perform a complete financial analysis.

3. Development of product and process: Translate the "voice of the customer" into technical (physical) product specifications, such as product size, features, and so on. As part of this, several concepts (sketch of product) are developed. Each concept represents a slightly different product form and/or function, and its components. Choose one concept and complete the design. Build product prototypes, test, and revise the design if necessary. Design the production/service delivery process: develop a few process concepts (sketches), evaluate them and choose one concept and complete the design, build a prototype of the process and evaluate it, and revise the process if necessary. Determine the machines and equipment, plant layout, and work centre designs.

4. Testing and validation: perform external testing, finalize the product and process specifications, and buy the machines and equipment and start trial runs.

5. Launch.

A core team usually consists of a product manager, product designers (usually stylists, also called industrial designers, and engineers), and manufacturing/operations representatives. The team is expanded during each phase of design with marketing representatives (at the start and at the end), accountants (to establish cost goals), process engineers (for process design, tooling/equipment), quality control, and purchasing and supplier representatives (component design and manufacturing).

This team-based approach of simultaneously designing the product and process is called *concurrent engineering*. In contrast, in the past, because of time pressure and the "silo" mentality, each functional area performed its part of design in isolation and "threw" the work "over the wall" to the next department in design. The order was (1) marketing,

(2) product design/engineering, (3) manufacturing, and (4) purchasing. This frequently resulted in late launches and costly design revisions. Concurrent engineering is further discussed later in the chapter. The new product design/development process is illustrated in Figures 4-2A (the stage-gate model) and 4-2B (process used by Dell Computers).

In the stage-gate model, *Scoping* involves preliminary market, financial, and technical assessment; *Building Business Case* involves determining customer requirements, competitive analysis, detailed financial and technical analysis, product definition, and operations assessment; *Development* involves further developing the product concept, making and testing prototypes, and operations process development; and *Testing and Validation* involves further in-house testing and customer trials, acquisition of production equipment, and operations trials.

Figure 4-2A

The stage-gate model of the new product design and development process

Source: Stage-Gate® © Product Development Institute Inc. http://www.prod-dev.com/stage-gate.php.

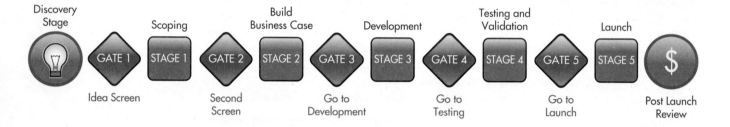

Figure 4-2B

Dell's new product design/development process chart

Source: S. Thomke et al., *Product Development at Dell Computer Corporation*, Case no. 9-699-010. Boston: Harvard Business School, 2000. Copyright © 2000 by the President and Fellows of Harvard College. Reprinted by permission.

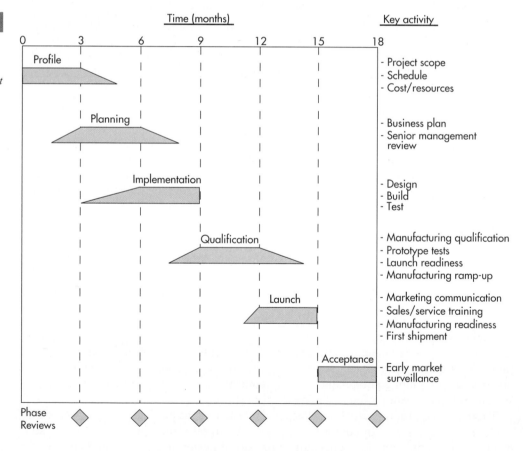

(LO2) SOURCES OF IDEAS FOR NEW OR REDESIGNED PRODUCTS

Ideas for new or improved goods and services can come from a wide range of sources, both from within the organization and from outside it: front-line employees, the suppliers and purchasing function, customers and sales/marketing functions, competitors (through reverse engineering), and the research and development (R&D) function.

Front-line employees—those who make the goods or deliver services to customers—have seen the problems in manufacturing/assembly operations or service delivery system caused by faulty design of the parts and products. Their feedback could improve the redesigned product. Suppliers of materials and parts/components and their contact within the organization, the purchasing agents, can be a rich source of ideas about the design/redesign of purchased items. Customers and their contact within the organization, the customer service and marketing/sales employees, are aware of problems with products. Similarly, product failures and warranty claims indicate where improvements are needed. Marketing employees are often sources of ideas based on their studies of markets, buying patterns, and familiarity with demographics. Also, marketing can help craft a vision of what customers are likely to want in the future. Customers may submit suggestions for improvements of existing products or need for new products, or they may be queried through the use of surveys or focus groups.

One of the strongest motivators for new and improved products is competitors' products. Some companies purchase a competitor's product and dismantle it to discover what it is composed of and how the components work, searching for ways to improve their own product. This is called **reverse engineering**. The following are some examples of reverse engineering. Xerox, despite inventing the copy machine, came under competitive pressure from cheaper Japanese copiers such as Toshiba in 1980s. Xerox tore down the competitor's copiers and learned their secrets. When IBM created its personal computer in 1980s, the only component that was not publicly available was the ROM-Bios chip. It did not take its competitors, such as Compaq, too long to produce a similar chip and make IBM clones. Ford Motor Company used reverse engineering in developing its highly successful Taurus model: it examined competitors' automobiles, searching for best-in-class components (e.g., best hood release, best dashboard display, best door handle). Sometimes reverse engineering can enable a company to "leapfrog" the competition by developing an even better product.

The **research and development (R&D)** function within an organization consists of lab scientists and engineers who are involved in creative work on a systematic basis in order to increase knowledge directed toward product or process innovation.

The costs of R&D can be high. Large companies in the automotive (such as Magna International), computer (such as IBM Canada), communications (such as BCE), aerospace (such as Pratt & Whitney Canada), and pharmaceutical/biotech (such as Apotex) spend a lot of money on R&D. For a list of Canada's top 100 R&D spenders, see http://www.researchinfosource.com/2008-top100.pdf. For a list of top 100 R&D spenders worldwide, see http://www.spectrum.ieee.org/images/dec07/images/12.RDchart.pdf. Hewlett-Packard is considered one of the most innovative companies in the world. In a study of innovative projects in HP, it was discovered that having skilled and helpful people who work well together, and management support, as well as using a systematic product design process (to provide discipline and focus) are the required ingredients for a high degree of innovation.[2]

R&D also contributes to a company by developing the prototypes, testing the prototypes in engineering labs, and improving product's reliability.

The following OM in Action box illustrates some market-related sources of ideas for product design.

reverse engineering
Dismantling a competitor's product to discover what it is composed of and how the components work, searching for own-product improvements.

This 3.78 litre space-efficient square plastic twist and pour paint container with a hollow handle on one side, a snap-in pour spout, and a twist-off lid, is a significant innovation in paint packaging. Dutch Boy is a brand of Sherwin-Williams group.

research and development (R&D) Lab scientists and engineers involved in creative work on a systematic basis to increase knowledge directed toward product and process innovation.

[2]R. Rivas and D.H. Gobeli, "Accelerating Innovation at Hewlett-Packard," *Research Technology Management* 48(1), January/February 2005, pp. 32–39.

OM in ACTION

Searching for New Product Ideas

What is the best way to find new product ideas? Consider the following approaches that have shown success in the past:

1. Listening to the Market Complaints

Many companies have made their products successful by listening to consumer complaints about products already on the market. Complaints about the inadequacies of two-ply tissues inspired Kimberly-Clark to create three-ply Cold Care Tissues, and Gillette found it could satisfy customers with complaints about white residue from its deodorants by creating the Clear Stick.

An equivalent complaint about lipstick smearing on coffee cups and shirt collars resulted in Lancome's transfer-resistant Rouge Idole lipsticks.

2. Gaps in the Market

3M used focus groups to create its Pop-up Tape Dispenser—it noticed consumers were one hand short of being able to hold wrapping paper, scissors, and tape when wrapping gifts. The new patented creation fit like a wristwatch, precutting tape strips and otherwise giving gift-wrappers a hand up. Black & Decker introduced its cordless DeWalt power tools for professionals who needed powerful equipment (such as drills) and could get this only from corded tools. The Black & Decker Snakelite twistable flashlight allows for hands-free use during repairs in tight-fitting spaces such as bathrooms or furnaces.

John Deere Co.'s "Gator" is an inexpensive, six-wheel, off-road all-terrain utility vehicle suitable for transporting everything from personnel and equipment to farming debris to wounded soldiers from the battlefield. The Gator simply doesn't have any direct competitors.

3. Exploring Niche Markets

For drivers who have been dropped by their insurance carriers because they are considered risky, Kingsway Financial Services Company of Mississauga, Ontario, provides an unparalleled service: offering car insurance to drivers like these, Kingsway has seen its annual revenue rocket from less than $20 million to more than $92 billion in a mere 10 years.

Coleman, traditionally a manufacturer of camping gear, found a lucrative niche in the market when it produced smoke detectors with large "broom button" alarm testers. Using a broom handle to shut off nuisance alarms triggered by burnt toast appealed especially to the elderly and gave Coleman a 40 percent market share as a result.

4. Using New Technology

Many new products have found that they could attract the attention of the market by exploiting a new science or art, whether it is a once-a-month pill to rid cats and dogs of fleas (Novartis), or frosted windows that clear up with the flip of a switch (3M). Research in Motion (RIM) founders managed to use their capability with pagers to invent Blackberry, a portable e-mail communicator, in the late 1990s at the peak of the high-tech boom.

5. Creating New Market Space

Westjet started by targeting a new market, the "friends and relatives" visitors who normally drive to visit. Sony Walkman created the new market of personal portable stereo market for joggers and commuters. Starbucks emphasizes the emotional value of drinking coffee by providing a chic "caffeine-induced oasis." Body Shop did the reverse by selling natural ingredients and healthy living instead of glamour and beauty.

Question

Can you name some more examples of the above sources of product ideas?

Sources: Adapted from Allan J. Magrath, "Mining for New Product Successes," *Business Quarterly* 62(2), Winter 1997, pp. 64–68; "The Edison Best New Product Awards," *Marketing News* 31(6), March 17, 1997, pp. E4–E12; W.C. Kim & R. Mauborgne, "Creating New Marketplace," *Harvard Business Review* 77(1), January/February 1999, pp. 83–93.

KEY ISSUES IN PRODUCT DESIGN

Designers must take into account issues such as product life cycle, standardization, mass customization product reliability, robust design, legal and ethical issues, design for environment, concurrent design of product and production process, computer-aided design, design for easy manufacturing and assembly, and component commonality. These topics are discussed in this section. We begin with life cycles.

Life Cycle

life cycle   Incubation, growth, maturity, saturation, and decline.

The decision to design a new substitute product or to redesign an existing product, and its timing, depends on the nature and length of the product's life cycle. Most products go through a **life cycle**: incubation, growth, maturity, saturation, and decline.

Incubation. When an item is introduced, it may be treated as a curiosity. Demand is generally low because potential buyers are not yet familiar with the item. Many potential buyers recognize that all of the bugs have probably not been worked out and that the price may drop after the introductory period. Production methods are generally designed for low volumes.

Growth. With the passage of time, design improvements usually create a more reliable and less costly product. Demand then grows for these reasons and because of increasing awareness of the product. Higher production volume will involve automated production methods and contribute to lower costs.

Maturity. There are few, if any, design changes, and demand levels off.

Saturation. Saturation leads to a decline in demand.

Decline. In decline, companies attempt to prolong the useful life of a product by improving its reliability, reducing costs of producing it (and, hence, the price), redesigning it, or introducing a new substitute product. These stages are illustrated in Figure 4-3.

Consider the portable computer data storage products in various stages of the life cycle: Memory keys are in the growth stage, DVDs are in the saturation stage, and CDs are in the decline stage.

Some products do not exhibit life cycles: wooden pencils; paper clips; nails, knives, forks, and spoons; drinking glasses; and similar items. However, most new products do.

Services, too, experience life cycles. For example, in banking, using tellers is in saturation stage, using ABMs is in its maturity, and Internet banking is in its growth stage.

Wide variations exist in the amount of time a particular product takes to pass through a given phase of its life cycle: some pass through various stages in a relatively short period; others take considerably longer. Often it is a matter of the basic *need* for the item and the *rate of technological change*. Some toys, novelty items, personal computers, and style items have a life cycle of less than one year, whereas other items, such as clothes washers and dryers, may last for decades before yielding to technological change.

OXO Good Grips Corn Stripper is an example of a product filling a need in the market.

Standardization

Standardization refers to the extent to which there is absence of variety in a part or product, that is, having limited types, sizes, and colours. Standardized products are made in large quantities of identical items; paper, gasoline, and 2 percent milk are examples. Standardized service implies that every customer or item processed receives essentially the same service. An automatic car wash is a good example; each car, regardless of how clean or dirty it is, receives the same service.

Large-volume production and purchase of only a few types of standardized parts would reduce costs due to economies of scale. For example, auto manufacturers have standardized

standardization Extent to which there is absence of variety in a part or product.

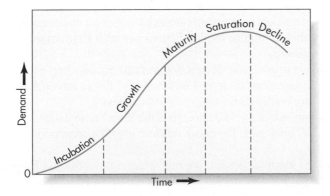

Figure 4-3

Most products exhibits a life cycle over time.

key components of their automobiles across similar product lines; components such as brakes, electrical systems, and other "under-the-skin" parts would be the same. By reducing variety, they save time and money while increasing quality and reliability in their products.

Another benefit of standardization is reduced time and cost to train employees. Similarly, inventory, purchasing, and accounting activities become much more routine. WestJet's using only Boeing 737 airplanes is an example, where costs of training the pilots and maintenance workers, and inventory of spare parts, are reduced.

Lack of standardization can at times lead to serious difficulties and competitive struggles, particularly when systems are incompatible. For example, lack of standardization in computer software and operating systems (Apple versus IBM) has presented users with hard choices because of the difficulty in switching from one system to the other.

Standardization also has disadvantages. A major one relates to the reduction in variety. This can limit the range of customers to whom a product appeals. Another disadvantage is that a manufacturer may lock in obsolescence and resist modification of a part.

Design for Mass Customization

Companies like standardization because it enables them to produce high volumes of relatively low-cost products, albeit products with little variety. Customers, on the other hand, typically prefer more variety, although they like the low cost. The question for producers is how to resolve these issues without (1) losing the benefits of standardization and (2) incurring the problems that are often linked to variety. The answer, at least for some companies, is **mass customization**, a strategy of producing standardized goods or services but incorporating some degree of customization in the final product. Several tactics make this possible. One is *delayed differentiation*, and another is *modular design*.

Delayed differentiation is a *postponement* tactic: the process of producing but not quite completing a product until customer preferences or specifications are known. In case of goods, almost-finished units might be held in inventory until customer orders are received, at which time customized features are incorporated according to customer requests. For example, furniture makers can produce dining room sets but not apply stain, allowing customers a choice of stains. Once the choice is made, the stain can be applied in a relatively short time. Another example is HP printers, made in Singapore, for the European market. By postponing country-specific customization, e.g., labels, packaging, and manuals, and doing this in its distribution centre in Stuttgart, HP saved 25 percent in total costs of manufacturing, shipping, and inventory costs. Finally, manufacturers of men's clothing produce dress pants that have legs that are unfinished, allowing the customers to choose the exact length.

Modular design is grouping of parts into modules that are easily interchanged or replaced. The product is composed of a number of modules or components instead of a collection of individual parts. One familiar example of modular design is computers with modular components that can be replaced if they become defective. By arranging modules in different configurations, different computer capabilities can be obtained. This is the major reason that Dell Computers can assemble and have custom-ordered computers delivered to its Internet customers in a matter of days. For mass customization, modular design enables producers to quickly assemble modules to achieve a customized configuration for an individual customer, avoiding the long customer wait that would occur if individual parts had to be assembled.

Another advantage of modular design is that failures are often easier to diagnose and remedy because modules can be tested individually. Other advantages include simpler purchasing, inventory control, and assembly operations.

The main disadvantage of modular design is the inability to disassemble some modules in order to replace a faulty part; the entire module must be scrapped—usually at a higher cost.

For an example of modular design, see the "Magna Powertrain's Engine Module" OM in Action.

mass customization
Producing basically standardized goods or services but incorporating some degree of customization.

delayed differentiation
Producing, but not quite completing, a product until customer preferences are known.

modular design Parts are grouped into modules that are easily replaced or interchanged. The product is composed of a number of modules or components instead of a collection of individual parts.

OM in ACTION   http://www.magna.com

Magna Powertrain's Engine Module

Automakers are increasingly looking to reduce the number of parts under the hood by moving to larger and more sophisticated engine modules. Magna Powertrain's front-engine cover module is one of the most advanced and value-added engine modules. The module incorporates a wide range of components, including the front engine cover, water pump, oil pump, idler, tensioner, pulleys, and fasteners. Magna Power-train provides vehicle manufacturers with one-stop shopping in terms of concept design, development, prototyping, testing, and manufacturing, as well as complete program management. The module provides significant reductions in assembly time, which in turn results in cost savings.

Source: *Magna 2001 Annual Report*, pp. 12–13.

A relatively new way of mass customization uses computer technology. For example, Amazon.com uses a software program that analyzes a customer's browsing history and suggests other books that people with similar interests have bought.

Reliability

Reliability is a measure of the ability of a product, a part, or an entire system to perform its intended function under normal conditions.

The term **failure** is used to describe a situation in which an item does not perform as intended. This includes not only instances in which the item does not function at all, but also instances in which the item's performance is substandard or it functions in a way not intended. For example, a smoke alarm might fail to respond to the presence of smoke (not operate at all), it might sound an alarm that is too faint to provide an adequate warning (substandard performance), or it might sound an alarm even though no smoke is present (unintended response).

New products are tested to find their breaking points. If this is low, the reliability of the product must be improved. For example, laptop and notebook computers need to be tough enough to absorb unintentional drops, and trucks, cars, and motorcycles need to endure bumps in the roads for many years. For more on reliability, see the chapter supplement on *Connect*.

reliability The ability of a product, part, or system to perform its intended function under normal conditions.

failure Situation in which a product, part, or system does not perform as intended.

Robust Design

Some products will function as designed only within a narrow range of conditions, while others will perform over a much broader range of conditions. The latter have **robust design**. Consider a pair of fine leather boots—obviously not made for trekking through mud or snow. Now consider a pair of heavy rubber boots—just the thing for mud or snow—as well as other conditions. The rubber boots have a design that is more *robust* than the fine leather boots.

The more robust a product, the less likely it is to fail due to a change in the environment in which it is used or in which it is performed. Hence, the more designers can build robustness into the product, the better it should hold up, resulting in a higher level of customer satisfaction.

robust design Design that can function over a broad range of conditions.

Taguchi's Approach. Japanese engineer Genichi Taguchi's approach is based on robust design. His premise is that it is often easier to design a product that is insensitive to environmental factors, either in manufacturing or in use, than to control the environmental factors.

The central feature of Taguchi's approach—and the feature used most often by North American companies—is *parameter design*. This involves determining the specification settings for the product that will result in robust design in terms of manufacturing variations, product deterioration, and conditions during use.

The Taguchi approach modifies the conventional statistical methods of experimental design. Consider this example. Suppose a company intends to use 11 chemicals in a new product. There are two suppliers for these chemicals, and the chemical concentrations vary slightly between the two suppliers. Classical design of experiments would require $2^{11} = 2,048$ test runs to determine which combination of chemicals would be optimum. Taguchi's approach would involve testing only 12 combinations.[3]

Legal and Ethical Issues

Designers must be careful to take into account a wide array of legal and ethical considerations. Organizations have been faced with many government (federal, provincial, municipal) acts and regulations, administered by government agencies and boards designed to regulate their activities. Among the more familiar ones are the Food and Drug acts (Health Canada), the *Canadian Environmental Protection Act* (Environment Canada), the *Motor Vehicle Safety Act* (Transport Canada), and the *Hazardous Products Act* (Industry Canada). Bans or regulations on materials such as saccharin, CFC, phosphate, and asbestos have sent designers scurrying back to their drawing boards to find alternative designs acceptable to both government regulators and customers. Similarly, automobile pollution standards and safety features, such as seat belts, air bags, safety glass, and energy-absorbing bumpers and frames, have had a substantial impact on automotive design. Much attention also has been directed toward toy design to remove sharp edges, small pieces that can cause choking, and toxic materials. In construction, government (municipal) regulations require access to public buildings for persons with disabilities, and standards for insulation, electrical wiring, plumbing, and fire protection.

Designers should not infringe on patents, trademarks, and copyright of competitors. If the product is not significantly different from a patented/copyrighted product in functional and operational characteristics or appearance (if this results in undeserved benefit), the company can be sued.[4]

Product liability can be a strong incentive for design improvements. **Product liability** means that a manufacturer is liable for any injuries or damages caused by a faulty product because of poor workmanship or design.

Ethical issues often arise in the design of products. Designers are often under pressure to speed up the design process and to cut costs. These pressures often require them to make trade-off decisions, many of which involve ethical considerations. One example is: should a software company release a product as scheduled when it struggles with bugs in the software, or wait until most of the bugs have been removed?

Design for Environment

Design for Environment (DFE) is an umbrella term describing techniques used to incorporate environmental concerns, including the three Rs of reduce, reuse, and recycle, into product design. The most common DFE practices include:

- Design for energy efficiency of product and energy used in manufacturing
- Design for hazardous material minimization, including emissions and wastes in manufacturing
- Design for biodegradable disposal, including packaging
- Design for re-use, including packaging

product liability

A manufacturer is liable for any injuries or damages caused by a faulty product.

http://www.gc.ca

---

[3]See for example, http://controls.engin.umich.edu/wiki/index.php?title=Design_of_experiments_via_taguchi_methods:_orthogonal_arrays&printable=yes (accessed April 19, 2010).
[4]See, for example, W.M. Fitzpatrick and S.A. DiLullo, "Attack of the Clones: Reverse Engineering, R&D, and the Law," *Competition Forum*, 2006, 4(2), pp. 501–514.

Some Applications of Design for Environment

Through its "Considered Index," Nike has started to measure its products' impact on the environment, including use of solvents as cleaners and primers, wastes in cutting materials, and impact of materials manufacture and end-of-life. It uses some products that contain recycled materials. For example, recycled polyester contains recycled plastic drink bottles, clothing scraps, uniforms, etc. Nike also uses organic cotton in all its apparels. It also has stopped using PVC in its products.

Patagonia is a high-end environmentally conscious outdoor/sports garments, shoes, and luggage company in Los Angeles. Patagonia designs its products and has them made by various manufacturers throughout the world but is intimately involved in the supply chain starting with sourcing of raw materials. Patagonia's products use organic cotton, recycled polyester, and little glue.

Xerox is a leader in design for the environment. Its printer cartridges are designed for refurbish. Customers are given a prepaid package to facilitate the return of empty cartridges. In addition, Xerox has a take-back program for old copiers. The copiers are designed for easy disassembly. If a copier can be remanufactured, faulty components are replaced. Good components are put through a test called "Signature Analysis" to ensure that they perform as well as new components. If a copier cannot be refurbished, it will be used as a source for components/parts. Parts are coded to facilitate recycling. Parts are cleaned using CO_2 blasts instead of solvents. Only a small percentage of a copier will be wasted. Xerox has invented small "cartridge free" solid-ink sticks to replace cartridges. Finally, Xerox factories are energy efficient, and produce minimal waste and emissions by recycling, using as fuel, and burning byproducts and wastes.

Sources: http://www.nikebiz.com/responsibility/considered_design/index.html; http://www.patagonia.com/web/us/footprint/index.jsp; .xerox.com/about-xerox/environment/enca.html.

- Design for disassembly and remanufacture
- Design for recycling, including packaging

We will expand on some of these. **Remanufacturing** refers to refurbishing used products by replacing worn-out or defective components, and reselling the products. This can be done by the original manufacturer, or another company. Among products that have remanufactured components are automobiles, printers, copiers, cameras, computers, and telephones.

Designing products so that they can be taken apart more easily is **design for disassembly**, which includes using fewer parts and less material; using snap-fits and fewer screws, nuts, and bolts; and using no glue. It also means accessible screws and bolts, and requiring only common hand tools to disassemble.

Recycling means recovering materials for future use. This applies not only to manufactured parts but also to materials used during production, such as lubricants and solvents. Reclaimed metal or plastic parts may be melted down and used to make different products. Recycling requires using materials that can be recycled, e.g., thermoset plastics vs. thermoplastics, not adding fillers in plastics, and identifying the material on the part.

remanufacturing
Refurbishing used products by replacing worn-out or defective components.

design for disassembly
Design so that used products can be easily taken apart.

recycling Recovering materials for future use.

Concurrent Engineering

To achieve a smoother transition from product design to production, and to decrease product development time, many companies are using *simultaneous development*, or concurrent engineering. In its narrowest sense, **concurrent engineering** means bringing design and manufacturing engineers together early in the design phase to simultaneously develop the product and the processes for creating the product. More recently, this concept has been enlarged to participative design/engineering, which includes manufacturing, marketing, and purchasing personnel in a cross-functional team. In addition, the views of suppliers are frequently sought.

Traditionally, designers developed a new product without any input from manufacturing, and then turned over the design to manufacturing, which would then have to develop a process for making the new product. This "throw-over-the-wall" approach created tremendous challenges for manufacturing, generating numerous conflicts and greatly increasing the time needed to successfully produce a new product. It also contributed to an "us vs. them" mentality.

concurrent engineering
Bringing engineering design, manufacturing engineers, and staff from marketing, manufacturing, and purchasing together early in the design phase.

For these and similar reasons, the simultaneous development approach has great appeal. Among the key advantages of this approach are the following:

1. Manufacturing engineers and personnel are able to identify production capabilities. Very often, there is some latitude in design in terms of selecting suitable materials and processes. Knowledge of production capabilities can help in this selection. In addition, cost and quality considerations can be greatly influenced.

2. There are early opportunities for design or procurement of critical machines or components, some of which might have long lead times. This can result in a major shortening of the product development process, which could be a key competitive advantage.

Computer-Aided Design (CAD)

computer-aided design (CAD)   Product design using computer graphics.

Computer-aided design (CAD) uses computer graphics for product design. The designer can modify an existing design or create a new one on a display unit by means of a light pen, keyboard, joystick, or mouse. Once the design is entered into the computer, the designer can manoeuvre it on the screen as if it was a three-dimensional object: it can be rotated to provide the designer with different perspectives, it can be split apart to give the designer a view of the inside, and a portion of it can be enlarged for closer examination.

A major benefit of CAD is the increased productivity of designers. No longer is it necessary to laboriously prepare manual drawings of products or parts and revise them repeatedly to correct errors or incorporate revisions. A rough estimate is that CAD increases the productivity of designers from 3 to 10 times. A second major benefit of CAD is the creation of a database for manufacturing that can supply needed information on product geometry and dimensions, and tolerances.

Some CAD systems allow the designer to perform engineering and cost analysis on proposed designs. For instance, the computer can determine the weight and volume of a part and do stress analysis as well. When there are a number of alternative designs, the computer can quickly go through the possibilities and identify the best one, given the designer's criteria. For a tour of capabilities of the SolidWorks 3D CAD software, see http://www.solidworks.com/pages/onlinetour2/.

Computer-aided design (CAD) is used to design components and products to exact measurement and detail. This sprinkler was designed to exact specifications.

Design for Manufacturing and Assembly

Designers need to clearly understand the capabilities of the production function (e.g., equipment, skills, types of materials, and technologies). This will help in choosing designs that match capabilities. When opportunities and capabilities do not match, management must consider the potential for expanding or changing capabilities to take advantage of those opportunities.

Manufacturability is a key concern for manufactured goods: ease of fabrication and/or assembly is important for cost, productivity, and quality.

design for manufacturing (DFM)   Takes into account the organization's manufacturing capabilities when designing a product.

design for assembly (DFA)   Focuses on reducing the number of parts in a product and on assembly methods and sequence.

The term **design for manufacturing (DFM)** is used to indicate the designing of products that are compatible with manufacturing capabilities. A related concept is **design for assembly (DFA)**. Design for assembly focuses on reducing the number of parts in an assembly, as well as on the assembly methods and sequence that will be employed. See Figure 4-4 for some examples.

Component Commonality

Companies can realize significant benefits when a component can be used in multiple products. For example, car manufacturers use the same chassis (platform) and internal components, such as engines and transmissions, on several models. In addition to the savings in design time, companies reap benefits through standard training for assembly and installation, increased opportunities for savings by buying in bulk from suppliers,

Figure 4-4

*Examples of design for
manufacturing and assembly*

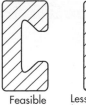

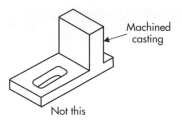

Feasible   Less expensive and
therefore preferable

Avoid undercuts and re-entrant
angles in the cross-section of special
cold-finished-steel stock if possible,
since these are more costly to produce.

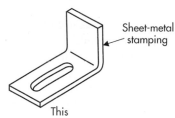

Machined
casting

Not this

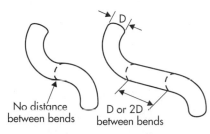

No distance
between bends   D or 2D
between bends

Not this   This

Allow a straight length between bends in tubes,
because of metal fatigue as a result of bending.

Sheet-metal
stamping

This

Stampings are often less costly
than machined castings.

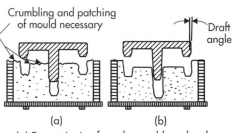

Crumbling and patching
of mould necessary

Draft
angle

(a)   (b)

(a) Poor stripping from the mould results when no
allowance is made for draft.
(b) Ample draft permits easy and safe stripping for
castings made in sand moulds.

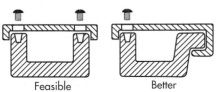

Feasible   Better

Minimize the number of fasteners by
incorporating lips or other hooking elements
in the basic parts. (Design for assembly.)

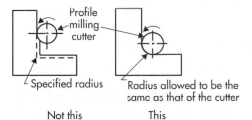

Profile
milling
cutter

Specified radius   Radius allowed to be the
same as that of the cutter

Not this   This

Product design should permit the use of the radii
provided by the cutting tools in milling machines.

and commonality of parts for repair, which reduces the inventory dealers and auto parts
stores must carry, and training needed by technicians. Computer software often comprises
a number of modules that are commonly used for similar applications, thereby saving
the time and cost to write the code for major portions of the software. Tool manufacturers use
a design that allows tool users to attach different power tools to a common power source.

Hewlett-Packard's Design-for-Supply-Chain program includes a simple quantitative
decision-making tool for designers to make commonality trade-off decisions.[5] The trade-off
is between annual holding cost saved by using commonality versus extra cost of manufacturing to provide commonality. An example of a unique part is a power adapter that works

[5]J. Amaral and B. Cargille, "How "Rough-cut" Analysis Smoothes HP's Supply Chain," *Supply Chain
Management Review* 9(6), September 2005, pp. 38–45.

RIM

Research in Motion (RIM) of Waterloo, Ontario, is one of the most successful high-tech Canadian companies, even though it has only one product, the BlackBerry wireless handheld device. The continuous improvement of the technology of pagers for more than 15 years paid off in 1999 when RIM decided to convert its two-way pager to work with e-mail programs.

The market accepted BlackBerry as the best device of its kind, resulting in ever-increasing sales. One distinguishing feature of BlackBerry is that as it receives or sends e-mails, it automatically updates the e-mail program on the desktop using data communication lines. This eliminates the duplication of using the e-mail program. Similarly, the BlackBerry automatically updates the personal calendar on the desktop.

The competition in this market segment is fierce, with most products converging to handle e-mail, voice, and video. BlackBerry was also modified in 2002 to work like a phone, and more recently to have a colour display and touch screen.

Given the stiff competition, RIM is "protecting" itself by licensing its excellent wireless e-mail software to its competitors. This strategic move (i.e., if you can't beat them, join them) seems to be paying off. RIM handles the subscription of its customers to a wireless telecommunication service.

RIM had revenues of more than $11 billion and more than 1,000 R&D employees in 2009.

http://www.cadillac.com

with 110V electricity (for North America), and another that works with 220V electricity (for Europe). If commonality is used, the universal power adapter will work with either 110 or 220V electricity. To make the decision whether a universal power adapter will be cheaper in terms of both manufacturing and after-sale service, an analysis similar to the following is used: Based on number of products sold that need this adapter (e.g., 10,000), number of service locations throughout the world (e.g., 400), and annual failure rate of the adapter (e.g., 1%), it follows that average annual demand for this power adapter in a service location will be $10,000(.01)/400 = .25$ unit. Given replenishment lead time of 4 days (from the supplier or other locations), average demand during lead time is only $.25(4)/365 = .003$ unit. Therefore, to provide, for example, a four-hour service response, keeping one unit of this adapter in stock at each service location is more than sufficient. Now, if one universal adapter is kept in stock instead of two unique adapters, there will be a saving of one unit at each service location. If each adapter costs $100 and annual holding cost rate is 20% of unit cost, the savings in the annual holding cost will be $(400)(1)(\$100)(.20) = \$8,000$. If the extra cost of manufacturing a universal adapter (relative to a unique adapter) is $.50 per unit, annual additional cost will be $\$.50 \times 10,000 = \$5,000$. Because $\$5,000 < \$8,000$, using the universal adapter is cheaper than using two unique adapters.

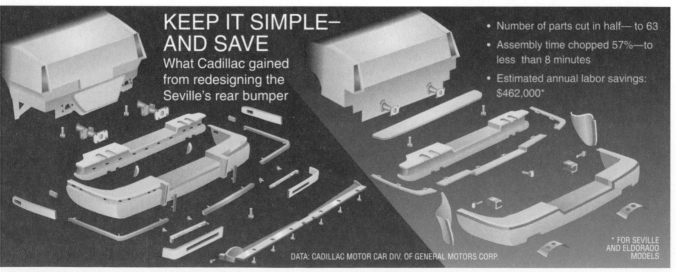

By redesigning the Seville's rear bumper for easy assembly, Cadillac cut the number of parts in half. The new design also led to higher quality as there were fewer parts and steps that might be defective.

LO4 DIFFERENCES IN DESIGNING SERVICES

Most of this chapter so far also applies to service design. However, there are some key differences between goods and services that warrant special consideration for service design:

1. Goods are generally tangible; services are intangible. Consequently, service design often includes secondary factors such as peace of mind, ambiance, and convenience. Another consequence of this is that it is hard to sketch a service. A new service must rely on faith and trust of customers; thus, the importance of image.

2. In many instances, services are created and delivered at the same time. For example, if a bus company makes changes to the bus schedule, or the bus routes, or the types of buses used, those changes will not be hidden to the riders. Obviously, this service redesign could not be done realistically without considering the *process* for delivering the service. In such instances, there is less latitude in finding and correcting errors *before* the customer has a chance to discover them. Consequently, training, process design, and customer relations are particularly important; hence, the increased role of operations. Quality is measured by measuring customer satisfaction.

3. Most services involve some degree of customization (variety). Because of this, there will be variability in length of service. When there is little or no contact, service can be much more standardized, whereas high contact provides the opportunity to tailor the service to the precise needs of individual customers. For example, see Figure 4-5, which shows different types of clothes retailing.

4. Services have lower barriers to entry and exit. Even in capital-intensive services such as air travel, introducing a new service, e.g., a new type of ticket with new restrictions on its use, is relatively easy because it uses the current resources of the airline. The disadvantage of this is that the company cannot easily measure the cost of introducing the service because of the shared resources. Too many similar services will no doubt increase the complexity and cost of operations. This places pressure on service design to be innovative but selective. Because of its relative ease of introduction, many new services are copies of competitors' services.

5. Location is often important to service design, with convenience as a major factor. Hence, design of services and choice of location are often closely linked.

To illustrate service design process further, let's look at service design process in the financial sector.

The Service Design Process in the Financial Sector

The financial services sector is one of the largest service sectors in Canada and introduces most new services. In a survey of 82 North American financial institutions (banks,

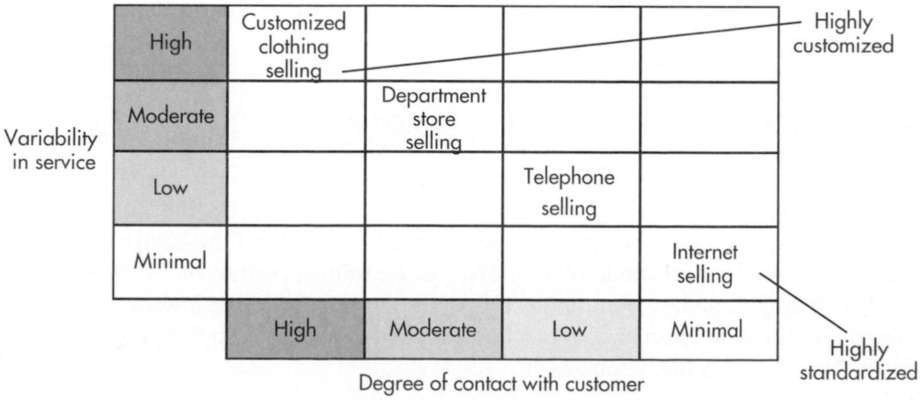

Figure 4-5

The relationship between service variability and customer contact in retail clothes selling

Figure 4-6

Frequency of new service design activities typically conducted by financial institutions

Source: Figure 4-6 reprinted from *Industrial Marketing Management* 25, 1996, S.J. Edgett, "The New Product Development Process from Commercial Financial Services," pp. 507–515. Copyright 1996, with permission from Elsevier.

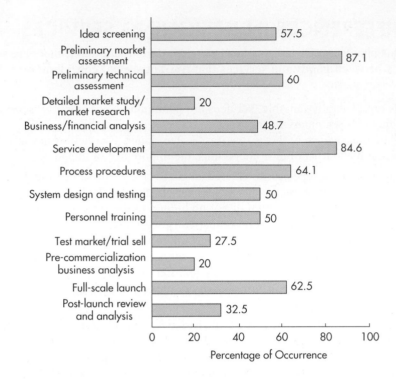

insurance, trust, leasing, reinsurance, and mutual fund companies), it was discovered that some financial institutions do not perform some of the activities given in the product design process (see Figure 4-6). In particular, few do "detailed market study/market research" and "pre-commercialization business analysis." The reason for this is that most new services offered by a company are copies of successful services offered by a competitor or the company itself.

In comparing high and low performers, it was found that the difference is "better idea screening," "preliminary market assessment," "market research," "service development," and "post-launch review."

Service Design Guidelines

A number of simple but highly effective rules are often used to guide the design of services:

1. Have a single, unifying theme, such as convenience or speed. This will help personnel work together rather than at cross-purposes.

2. Ensure that the service delivery system has the capability to handle any expected variability in service requirements.

3. Include design features and checks to ensure that service will be reliable and will provide consistently high quality.

4. Design the service delivery system to be user-friendly. This is especially true for self-service systems.

LO5 QUALITY FUNCTION DEPLOYMENT

quality function deployment (QFD) A structured approach that integrates the "voice of the customer" into product design.

Quality function deployment (QFD) is a structured approach for integrating the "voice of the customer" into product design. Customer requirements often take the form of a general statement such as "It should be easy to adjust the cutting height of the lawn mower." Once the customer requirements are known, they must be translated into measurable technical terms. For example, a statement about changing the height of the lawn mower may be translated into the characteristics of mechanism used to accomplish that, e.g., tightness of the spring that controls the mechanism.

The structure of QFD is based on a set of matrices. The main matrix relates customer requirements (what) to their corresponding technical requirements (how). Technical requirements are measurable physical and functional characteristics of the product. This concept is illustrated in Figure 4-7. Additional features are usually added to the basic matrix to broaden the scope of analysis. Typical additional features include competitive evaluation of customer requirements, a correlation matrix for technical requirements (this can reveal conflicting technical requirements), and target values (product specs) for technical requirements. The matrix is often referred to as the *house of quality* because of its house-like appearance.

An example of a house of quality is shown in Figure 4-8. The data relate to a commercial printer (customer) and the company that produces the paper rolls. To start, a key part is the list of customer requirements on the left side of the matrix. Next, note the technical requirements, listed vertically near the top. The key relationships are shown in the centre of the figure. The circle with a dot inside it indicates the strongest relationship; that is, it denotes the most important technical requirement(s) for satisfying the customer requirement (see the lower right-hand side for relationship weights). Now look at the "customer requirements importance" weights that are shown next to each customer requirement (3 is most important).

Next, consider the correlation matrix at the top of the "house." Of special interest is the strong negative correlation between "paper thickness" and "roll roundness." Designers will have to find some way to overcome that or make a trade-off decision.

On the right side of the figure is the competitive evaluation of customer requirements, comparing the paper roll manufacturing company's performance on the customer requirements with each of its two key competitors (A and B). For example, the company (X) is worst on the first customer requirement and best on the third customer requirement. A line connects the X performances. Ideally, design will cause all of the Xs to be in the highest positions.

Across the bottom of Figure 4-8 are technical requirements importance weights, target values, and competitive evaluations of technical requirements, which can be interpreted in a manner similar to that of the competitive evaluation of customer requirements. The target values typically contain technical specifications that are the result of the design process.

A technical value (or specification) may have a norm (midpoint) and a tolerance ($\pm$). A tolerance is established to (a) make the fabrication and/or assembly of the product easier and (b) enable the product to perform its function with minimum adjustment. Usually, these two objectives are in conflict. Too-tight a tolerance can ensure functional requirements, but is not cost-effective. Too-loose a tolerance can reduce fabrication and assembly costs, but requires frequent rework to maintain product's performance. Technical requirements importance weights are the sums of values assigned to the relationships multiplied by customer requirements importance. For example, the 3 in the first column is the product of the importance to the customer, 3, and the weak (Δ) relationship, 1. These help designers focus on important technical requirements. In this example, the first technical requirement has the lowest importance while the next four technical requirements all have high importance.

The house of quality approach involves a sequence of "houses," beginning with house of quality (Figures 4-7 and 7-8), which determines the product design characteristics and target values (House 1), which in turn lead to specific component design characteristics and target values (House 2), which in turn leads to production process design characteristics and target values for each component (House 3), and finally, a quality plan for each production process (House 4). This sequence is illustrated in Figure 4-9. The construction of House 2 to House 4 is basically similar to construction of House 1, but the details are beyond the scope of this textbook.

"A QFD Snapshot" OM in Action contains another example of House of Quality.

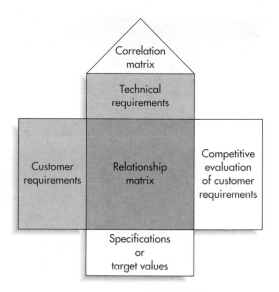

Figure 4-7

The house of quality

Figure 4-8

An example of the house of quality for paper rolls used by a commercial printer

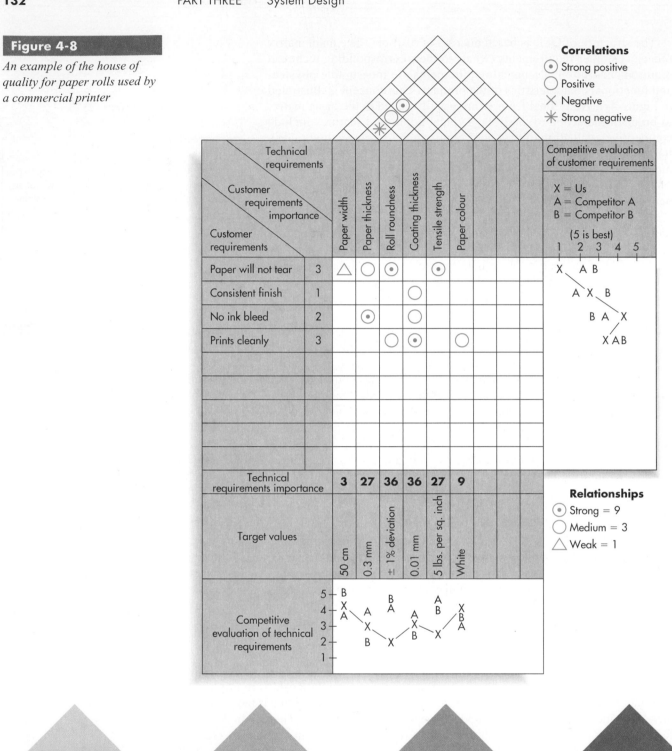

Figure 4-9

The house of quality sequence

A QFD Snapshot

*H*ow a pencilmaker sharpened up its product by listening to "the voice of the customer" through quality function deployment.

Devised by Japan's Professor Yoji Akao, QFD has been winning adherents since it was transplanted to North America in the late 1980s. In this example of how it works, Writesharp Inc. is imaginary, but the technique in the accompanying diagram is real.

First, Writesharp's customers were surveyed to determine what they value in a pencil and how they rate the leading brands. Each wish list item was correlated with a pencil's physical and functional characteristics. Reverse engineering—tearing down a competitors' product to see what makes it tick—produced the competitive evaluation of technical requirements.

An analysis of the matrix quickly revealed that the improvement with the biggest potential was "point lasts" (see competitive evaluation of customer requirements). This is largely correlated with "Time between sharpenings" and "Lead dust." It was determined that these characteristics could be improved by using a better-quality lead. An interdepartmental team was assigned the task of evaluating new lead formulations that would last longer and generate less dust. The lead-formulation team organized its work with a similar matrix, segmented to show the physical and functional contributions of the ingredients in pencil lead. This revealed that the binder, or glue, used in forming the lead was the key variable. Tests found a polymer that dramatically reduced dusting by retaining more moisture and also wore down more slowly. While this binder was more expensive, better production controls promised to reduce waste enough to trim total per-pencil manufacturing costs by 1¢.

Technical requirements
- ⊙ Strong correlation
- △ Possible correlation
- ○ Some correlation

Competitive evaluation of customer requirements
Scale: 1 to 5 (5 = best)

Customer requirements		Pencil length (inches)	Time between sharpenings (written lines)	Lead dust (particles per line)	Hexagonality	Customer requirements importance rating (5 = highest)	Writesharp (now)	Competitor X	Competitor Y	Writesharp (target)
	Easy to hold	○			○	3	4	3	3	4
	Does not smear		○	⊙		4	5	4	5	5
	Point lasts	△	⊙	○		5	4	5	3	5
	Does not roll	△			⊙	2	3	3	3	4

Competitive evaluation of technical requirements		Pencil length	Time between sharpenings	Lead dust	Hexagonality
	Writesharp (now)	5	56	10	70%
	Competitor X	5	84	12	80%
	Competitor Y	4	41	10	60%
	Writesharp (target)	5.5	100	6	80%

	Writesharp (now)	Competitor X	Competitor Y	Writesharp (target)
Market price	15¢	18¢	14¢	16¢
Market share	16%	12%	32%	20%
Profit per unit	2¢	3¢	2¢	4¢

Source: Reprinted from October 25, 1991, issue of *BusinessWeek* by special permission, copyright © 1991 by The McGraw-Hill Companies, Inc.

Summary

Product design is a key factor in satisfying the customers. To be successful, organizations must be continually aware of what customers want, what the competition is doing, what government regulations are, and what new technologies are available.

The design process involves market/competitor analysis, goal setting (product, performance, cost, quality), quality function deployment, concept design, product specification, and building and testing prototypes. The idea for a new or a redesigned product can come from customers, employees, suppliers, competitors, and the research and development department. The stage of life cycle of a product influences the nature of its redesign. Using standard parts and common modules saves operating costs, but it is possible to provide some mass customization by allowing customers options on modules and postponement. The reliability of well-designed products has to be extensively tested and improved. It may be cheaper to design robust products that perform consistently in varied production and use conditions. It is faster and less costly for the product team to perform both product and process designs concurrently. CAD has helped reduce the design time significantly. It is cheaper overall to design products that have fewer parts and are easier to manufacture and assemble. Services need to deal with customer presence and involvement, and the inherent variability in service requirements. QFD is a multifunctional process for product design that starts with the "voice of the customer" and ends with its translation into product characteristics.

Key Terms

computer-aided design (CAD), 126
concurrent engineering, 125
delayed differentiation, 122
design for assembly (DFA), 126
design for disassembly, 125
design for manufacturing (DFM), 126
failure, 123
life cycle, 120
mass customization, 122
modular design, 122

product design, 116
product liability, 124
quality function deployment (QFD), 130
recycling, 125
reliability, 123
remanufacturing, 125
research and development (R&D), 119
reverse engineering, 119
robust design, 123
standardization, 121

Discussion and Review Questions

1. What are some of the factors that cause organizations to redesign their products? (LO1)

2. What are the stages (phases) of the product design process? (LO1)

3. What is CAD? Describe some of the ways a product designer can use it. (LO3)

4. What is standardization? Give an example. Name some of the main advantages and disadvantages of standardization. (LO3)

5. What is modular design? Give an example. What are its main advantages and disadvantages? (LO3)

6. Explain the terms *design for manufacturing* and *design for assembly*, give an example of each, and briefly explain why they are important. (LO3)

7. What is concurrent engineering and what are some of the competitive advantages of concurrent engineering? (LO3)

8. What is the *stage-gate or phase-review* model? What are the stages? (LO1)

9. What is meant by the term *life cycle*? Give an example. Why would this be a consideration in product design? (LO3)

10. Name some ways the R&D department of a company contributes to produce design. (LO2)

11. What is *mass customization*? What is *delayed differentiation*? Give an example. (LO3)

12. Name two factors that make service design different from goods design. (LO4)

13. Explain the term *robust design*. Give an example. (LO3)

14. Explain what *quality function deployment* is, briefly how it is done, and what its objective is. (LO5)

15. What is reverse engineering? Give an example. Do you feel it is unethical? (LO2)
16. Name a service organization and describe the basic service(s) they provide. (LO4)

Taking Stock

1. Describe some of the trade-offs that are encountered in product design. (LO5)
2. Who needs to be involved in the design of products? Explain. (LO1)
3. How has technology had an impact on product design? (LO2 & 3)
4. Is designing products that are not refurbishable or recyclable, such as computers and electronics that end up in city garbage dumps, unethical? Discuss. (LO3)

Critical Thinking Exercise

Think of a new or revised good or service that you would like to see on the market. Discuss the implications of designing and producing that product relative to legal, profitability, competitiveness, design, and production issues. (LO3)

Experiential Learning Exercise

Visit http://www.baddesigns.com/examples.html and read about some bad designs. Describe one example from your own experience. (LO1 & 5)

Internet Exercises

1. Go to http://bits.me.berkeley.edu/develop and write a brief summary of important design elements in the design of Boeing 777. (LO3)
2. Watch the Design Overview video at http://www.wescast.com/en/engineering_design. Summarize the technologies used in Wescast's engineering design process. (LO1)
3. Watch the video at http://solutions.3m.com/wps/portal/3M/en_WW/History/3M/Company/century-innovation. List two innovative products that 3M has invented. (LO1)

Problems

1. Prepare a table similar to Figure 4-5 on page 129 and place each of these banking transactions in the appropriate cell of the table: (LO4)
   a. Make a cash withdrawal from an automated banking machine (ABM).
   b. Make a savings deposit using a teller.
   c. Open an account.
   d. Apply for a mortgage loan.

2. Prepare a table similar to Figure 4-5 on page 129. Then place each of these transactions in the appropriate cell of the table: (LO4)
   a. Buy stamps from a postal clerk.
   b. Mail a package that involves checking different rates.
   c. Send money using Western Union.

3. Refer to Figure 4-8 on page 132. What two technical requirements have the highest impact on the customer requirement "Paper will not tear"? Explain why. (LO5)

4. Prepare a house of quality for chocolate chip cookies made in a bakery. List what you believe are the three most important customer requirements and the three most relevant technical requirements. Next, indicate by a checkmark which customer requirements and which technical requirements are related. Finally, determine the target values. No need to fill in the other parts of the house. (LO5)

5. Determine a house of quality for a ballpoint pen. In the house of quality, fill in three customer requirements. Determine one technical requirement for each customer requirement and fill it in. Relate the pair by a checkmark, and determine a reasonable target value for each technical requirement and fill it in. (LO5)

*6. In 2002 Wilson Sporting Goods wanted to enter the market for youth baseball batting helmets with a durable, strong, stylish youth batting helmet with improved ventilation and a quick and simple adjustment feature for a one-size-fits-all youth batting helmet. Wilson commissioned the product design firm Designconcepts to design and develop the helmet. Designconcepts's sketch for the adjustment mechanism of helmet is shown below.[6] The finished helmet is now marketed as Cat Osterman's Signature Series.

   For each of the five customer requirements given above, find a measurable technical requirement and enter both in a house of quality. Relate them by placing a checkmark at their intersection. Also fill in the target value (specification) for each technical requirement. (LO5)

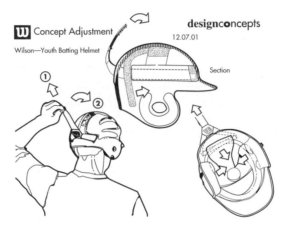

*7. In 2004 Calor (T-Fal), a member of Groupe SEB of France, world's largest kitchen products and small appliances manufacturer, commissioned the product design firm of SeymourPowel to redesign its midline steam iron (http://www.seymourpowell.com/casestudies/view/25). The market for irons was in a slump and Calor wanted to reinvigorate the market. Like its predecessor, Avantis, Aquaspeed was desired to be attractive, easy to handle and ergonomic, and light, but had two additional requirements: (a) a larger hole and less-messy process for filling water in the reservoir, and (b) more stability to reduce chance of toppling off the ironing board. Avantis, like other irons, had a small water hole in the front part of the handle. The result of the redesign, Aquaspeed, is shown below (front and back views)[7]:

---

[6]D. Franchino, "Delivering Success Through Design: Reinventing the Batting Helmet," *Design Management Review* 18(1), Winter 2007, pp. 22–27.
[7]D. Powell, "Innovation in Practice: The Calor Aquaspeed Iron," *Design Management Review* 16(1), Winter 2005, pp. 26–32.

In a house of quality, fill in five customer requirements. Determine one technical requirement for each customer requirement and fill it in. Relate the pair by a checkmark, and determine a reasonable target value for each technical requirement and fill it in (LO5).

*8. In the mid-2000s, DeWalt, a Black and Decker brand, saw the need by carpenters and do-it-yourselfers for a cordless battery-operated nailer.[8] At that time, the only automatic nailers in the market were pneumatic ones that were cumbersome because of the need for a compressor and a hose. DeWalt consulted and observed carpenters at work and determined the following customer requirements: speed, run time (length of time until the battery needs recharging), power (nail penetration), ease of loading nails, ergonomics (size, weight, and balance), being able to see the nail going in, and being able to work in tight spots. One of the eight related nailers in the designed family is shown on the right. In a house of quality, fill in five customer requirements. Determine one technical requirement for each customer requirement and fill it in. Relate the pair by a checkmark, and determine a reasonable target value for each technical requirement and fill it in. (LO5)

*9. Puritan-Bennett is a manufacturer of medical test equipment.[9] In the early 1990s, its PB900A spirometer (equipment to measure lung capacity, see the left photo below) was rapidly losing market share to a competitor's product, which was simpler and half its price. Puritan-Bennett decided to use Quality Function Deployment to redesign PB900A. It surveyed its customers (pulmonologists, allergists, and nurses) to identify customer needs. A total of 26 customer needs were identified. Puritan-Bennett's product design team translated these into 56 design attributes (technical requirements). Here, we will consider a small subset of the customer needs. The following customer needs were most important (importance is in brackets): product is affordable (150), provides accurate readings (100), eliminates technician (administrator) variability (140), is easy to operate (130), and is sanitary (108). Prepare a house of quality with five customer requirements. Determine one technical requirement for each customer requirement and fill it in. Relate the pair by a checkmark. Determine a reasonable target value for each technical characteristic and fill it in. (The redesigned spirometer, PB100, shown in the right photo below, was 1/10th the size and 1/15th the weight of PB900A, shown at left.) (LO5)

*10. Ford and other automakers regularly use house of quality to translate voice of customers (customer requirements) into design characteristics (technical requirements) in areas such as rust prevention (body durability) and car door design.[10] Some of the most important customer requirements for a car door are: easy to close, stays open on a hill, easy to open, does not leak in rain, and doesn't allow road noise in. In a house of quality, fill in these five customer requirements. Determine one technical requirement for each customer requirement and fill it in. Relate the pair by a checkmark, and determine a reasonable target value for each technical requirement and fill it in. (LO5)

---

[8]J. Watson, "Building the Perfect Product: The Story of DeWalt Cordless Nailer," *Design Management Review* 17(1), Winter 2006, pp. 21–27.

[9]J.R. Hauser, "How Puritan-Bennett Used the House of Quality," *Sloan Management Review* 34(3) Spring 1993, pp. 61–70.

[10]J.R. Hauser and D. Clausing, "The House of Quality," *Harvard Business Review*, May–June 1988, pp. 63–73.

MINI-CASE   http://www.paradoxdesign.net

The Redesign of a Snowboarding Helmet

Paradox Design was a medium-sized design company in Barrie, Ontario. One of its recent designs was a snowboarding helmet for Burton Snowboards of Vermont, United States. This new helmet, named Synth, was to be a remodelled version of an older model, Skycap (see photo), which was introduced four years ago and was in need of new styling.

Skycap

Paradox brainstormed to identify the aesthetics and emotional influences on the culture of snowboarders. From this, concept sketches were made:

Concept sketches

A concept was chosen and refined through feedback from marketing and snowboarder groups.

Detailed concept

Once the detailed design was finalized, a foam model was handmade to help visualize the shape and curves of the helmet.

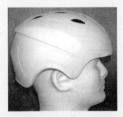

Foam model

Then, the interior of the helmet was designed to ensure comfort and ventilation.

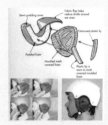

Interior design

Then the ear pad concept was sketched and refined to provide warmth, protection, and simple installation and removal from the helmet.

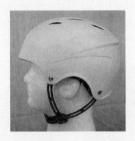

Ear pad design

From the completed design, a CAD model was created. A rapid prototype was created from the CAD model using stereo-lithography. This was shown to Burton for feedback.

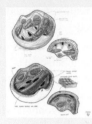

Rapid prototype

The prototype was accepted by Burton, and Synth went into production. It is selling well.

Production model

Question

Compare the product design steps taken by Paradox Design with the steps of the stage-gate model. Is there any difference? If so, briefly explain.

Source: http://www.paradoxdesign.net, accessed January 2005. Paradox Design merged with Spark Innovations of King City, Ontario, in 2005, http://www.sparkinnovations.com. Photos and figures courtesy of Steve Copeland and Roger Ball.

Open Wide and Say "Ultra"

In fourth place behind McDonald's, A&W, and Burger King, Harvey's, the Canadian quick-service hamburger chain with more than 340 restaurants, needed a new idea in the mid-1990s. Harvey's is part of Cara Operations Ltd., the airline food-services company that also owns the Swiss Chalet chain of restaurants, approximately 100 Air Terminal Restaurants, and Summit Food Servitces Distributors. Harvey's had had new ideas before (open grill and fresh vegetables, for one), but these had become old hat by 1995. Gabe Tsampalieros, Cara's new president, who was a major franchisee with 60 Harvey's and Swiss Chalet restaurants, started working on the idea in October 1995, and by the following month the mission was clear: "Create Canada's best-selling hamburger." Tsampalicros and Harvey's vice-president planned the launch of the new burger for May 1996.

Harvey's began polling burger lovers across Canada in January 1996, first by telephone and later in focus groups of 8 to 12 people. While the tradition of burgers had so far led to flattened-out, Frisbee-like burgers that hung over the edges of the buns (giving customers the impression that they were getting more for their money), feedback from the market produced another idea: go thicker, juicier, chewier, and tastier. To bring this simple idea to life, Harvey's brought in chef Michael Bonacini, whose upscale Toronto restaurants had been a big hit.

Bonacini's challenge was not only to produce a tasty burger, but also to produce a burger that could handily survive the fast-food process (mechanically produced, frozen for weeks, and shipped around the country). Bonacini produced 12 "taste profiles"—from the bland to the bizarre—and introduced them to the Harvey's cxccutivcs at a suburban Harvey's training centre. This would be the first in a long series of tasting exercises. (Bonacini thinks he ate 275 bite-sized burgers in a four-month period.)

Each of Harvey's executives tasted a portion of the 12 unlabelled patties and ranked it for "mouth feel," taste, linger, fill factor, and bite. Exotic offerings (Cajun, Oriental, falafel, and so forth) were rejected, leaving three simply seasoned burgers on the short list.

McCormick Canada Inc., Harvey's spice supplier, was employed to determine the final proportions of seasonings and secret ingredients to replicate the taste of Bonacini's samples in a way that could survive the fast-food process. "They [the meat packagers] would give us a 500-pound batch—that's 2,000 burgers—and we would taste them a couple of days after they had been mixed. Then we would also taste them at one-, two-, three-, and four-week intervals to see how the flavours would change," said Bonacini. McCormick's Food Technologists varied the seasonings by slight amounts with different results, and each change was followed by testing. For two months, all of Harvey's head-office workers gathered before breakfast to test the newest batches; it became clear that the May launch date was unrealistic, so they bumped back the launch to mid-September.

Though missing deadlines is rarely advisable, in this case it was fortuitous. On May 9, exactly one week before the original launch date, McDonald's introduced the Arch Deluxe with the most aggrcssivc marketing campaign yet seen from McDonald's.

As the burger making neared completion, Harvey's turned its attention to choosing a name for the new burger. The company considered several (the Ultimate, the Canadian, the Big Burger, the One and Only), but settled wisely on the Ultra, a bilingual name. The company chose a foil packaging for better heat retention (and because the traditional box would appear larger than the burger itself), and reinitiated the advertising campaign, promoting a $1.88 price. Testing the burger in Calgary, Sudbury, and Quebec, Harvey's found customer reaction to be very positive ("It's more like a home-made burger," "It has a steak-like bite"), but went through five more adjustments to the amounts and mixing time of the ingredients.

On September 16, 1996, Ultra was launched and resulted in record sales, transaction counts, and restaurant visits. With over a million sold in the first two weeks, the Ultra resulted in more than 85 percent of Harvey's sales.

Since then, Harvey's has introduced other types of hamburgers such as bacon and cheese, veggie burger, and Big Harv Angus, as well as a chicken sandwich.

Big Harv, introduced in 2003, was an attempt to buck the trend of low-fat, low-calorie burgers offered by the other fast-food restaurants. It had double the calories and fat of the Original burger. Big Harv targeted male customers with craving for thick home-made barbequed burgers.

Cara has expanded its full-service restaurant offerings by purchasing the Kelsey's chain and the Second Cup chain. In 2004, Cara bought back its outstanding shares and became a private company. In 2006, Cara sold Second Cup to Gabe Tsampalieros's new company, Dinecorp Hospitality.

Questions

1. Identify the steps of the product design process used by Harvey's. (Specifically, consider market analysis, concept development, prototype development, and (external) testing and validation).

2. Did Harvey's use any other concepts discussed in the chapter?

3. Prepare a house of quality for Ultra's design. Fill in four customer requirements. For each customer requirement, determine a technical requirement and relate the pair using a checkmark. For each technical requirement, determine a reasonable target value.

Sources: Adapted from P. Roy, "Open Wide and Say 'Ultra' (Harvey's Had a Brilliant Idea About Burgers)," *Canadian Business* 69(12), December 1996, pp. 26–30; "Stay Hungry: Gabe Tsampalieros Knows the Food Business from the Kitchen Floor Up (Will That Be Enough for Cara?)," *Canadian Business* 69(11), September 1996, pp. 104–110; Cara Operations Annual Reports, 1999–2003, http://www.cara.com.

To access "Reliability," the supplement to Chapter 4, please visit *Connect*.

CHAPTER 5
Strategic Capacity Planning

grocerygateway.com

LEARNING OBJECTIVES

After completing this chapter, you should be able to:

LO1 Define capacity, explain the importance of long-term capacity, know how to measure capacity and understand two related performance measures, and describe factors influencing effective capacity.

LO2 Describe the strategic capacity planning process in organizations, know long-term demand patterns and calculate capacity requirements, and discuss major considerations for developing capacity alternatives.

LO3 Describe the break-even analysis approach for evaluating capacity alternatives, and use it to solve problems.

When the Internet became ubiquitous in the 1990s, entrepreneurs scrambled to take advantage of it by starting some form of e-business. Two examples are Grocery Gateway in Toronto and Homegrocer.com in Seattle, specializing in home delivery of supermarket groceries. In search of growth, and thinking growth must eventually lead to profitability, and given the availability of seemingly unlimited investor funds, they kept on expanding, without ever making a profit. Eventually their deficient business model caught up with them. Why is it that some companies make the right capacity decisions and some don't? This is the topic of this chapter.

(LO1) INTRODUCTION

Capacity refers to an upper limit on the workload that an operating unit can handle. The operating unit might be a plant, department, machine, store, or worker.

Capacity is usually measured in terms of the production rate; e.g., the maximum number of motorcycles that can be assembled in a particular plant per day, or the maximum number of customers that can be served in a particular restaurant per day. If output is hard to measure, a major input can be used, e.g., number of seats in a particular restaurant.

Capacity decisions have different time frames: long term, medium term, or short term. Long term usually refers to one to five years into the future. We need to make long-term capacity decisions such as determining the plant size and major machines and equipment. Medium-term usually refers to next 12 months, and medium-term capacity decisions include determining the nature and level of workforce, which in turn determines the aggregate operations plan. Short term relates to the next few days and weeks, up to 12 weeks ahead, and short-term capacity decisions include determining nature and level of staffing and work shifts, which in turn determines the production schedule of products or capacity of service.

Strategic capacity planning is the systematic determination of facility and major equipment requirements to meet long-term demand for goods and services.

In this chapter, we study mainly long-term capacity planning, while deferring medium-term capacity decisions to Chapter 13 (Aggregate Operations Planning) and short-term capacity decisions to Chapter 16 (Job and Staff Scheduling) and Chapter 18 (Waiting Lines Analysis).

capacity The upper limit on the workload that an operating unit can handle. Capacity is also measured as maximum production rate. Alternatively, a major input is used, e.g., size.

strategic capacity planning Systematic determination of facility and major equipment requirements to meet long-term demand for goods and services.

The Importance of Long-Term Capacity

For a number of reasons, long-term capacity decisions are among the most fundamental of all the system design decisions that managers must make. These include:

1. Capacity has a real impact on the ability of the organization to meet future demands for products; capacity essentially limits the rate of output possible. Having capacity to satisfy demand can allow a company to take advantage of opportunities.

2. Capacity affects operating costs and ease of management. Ideally, capacity and demand requirements will be matched, which will tend to minimize operating costs. A production level too close to or exceeding capacity is costlier, requiring using overtime, expediting deliveries, lost sales, etc.

3. Capacity is usually a major determinant of initial capital cost. Typically, the greater the capacity of a productive unit, the greater its capital cost.

4. Capacity involves long-term commitment of resources and, once they are committed, it may be difficult to modify them without incurring major costs.

5. Capacity can affect competitiveness. If a company has excess capacity, or can quickly add capacity, that fact may serve as a barrier to entry of other companies. An example of this is the Potash Corp of Saskatchewan, which, after expanding in the 1970s and

1980s, has been left with some idle potash-processing facilities. For example, the Lanigan mill's old site, after expansion, has been kept idle, and can be brought into operation if needed (at some expense). This excess capacity is a deterrent against new competition.

Measuring Capacity and Two Related Performance Measures

In selecting a measure of capacity, it is better to choose one that does not require updating. For example, dollar amounts are often a poor measure of capacity (e.g., a restaurant may have capacity of $1 million of sales a year) because price changes over time necessitate updating of that measure.

Where only one product is involved, the capacity of the productive unit may be expressed in terms of that item. However, when multiple products are involved, as is often the case, using a simple measure of capacity based on units of output can be misleading. An appliance manufacturer may produce both refrigerators and freezers. If the output rates for these two products are different, it would not make sense to simply state capacity in units without reference to either refrigerators or freezers. The problem is compounded if the company has other products. One possible solution is to state capacities in terms of each product. Thus, the company may be able to produce 100 refrigerators per day *or* 160 freezers per day. Sometimes this approach is helpful, sometimes not. For instance, if an organization has many different products, it may not be practical to list all of the relevant capacities. A better way is to choose a major product, and represent each other product in equivalent units of the major product (more in Chapter 13). Alternatively, one can use the *availability of a major input.* Thus, a hospital has a certain number of beds, a job shop has a number of labour hours available, and a bus has a certain number of seats.

No single measure of capacity will be appropriate in every situation. Rather, the measure of capacity must be tailored to the situation. Table 5-1 provides some examples of commonly used measures of capacity.

There are two types of capacity:

design capacity The maximum output that can possibly be attained under ideal conditions.

effective capacity The maximum possible output that can be sustained given operating hours, product mix, scheduling difficulties and expected delays, and machine maintenance.

1. **Design capacity**: the maximum output that can possibly be attained under ideal conditions.
2. **Effective capacity**: the maximum possible output that can be sustained given operating hours, product mix, scheduling difficulties and expected delays, and machine maintenance.

Effective capacity is less than design capacity owing to realities of working less than 24 hours per day, changing product mix, or periodic maintenance of equipment, lunch and coffee breaks, problems in scheduling and balancing operations, and similar circumstances. Actual output cannot exceed effective capacity and is often less because of machine breakdowns, absenteeism, shortages of materials, and quality problems, as well as other factors that are outside the control of the operations managers.

Table 5-1	Business	Inputs	Outputs
Some examples of commonly used measures of capacity	Auto manufacturing		Number of cars per shift
	Steel mill		Tonnes of steel per day
	Oil refinery	Barrels of crude oil used per day	Barrels of gasoline per day
	Farming	Number of acres	Bushels of grain per acre per year, litres of milk per day
	Restaurant	Number of tables, number of seats	Number of meals per day
	Theatre	Number of seats	Number of tickets sold per day
	Retail sales	Square metres of floor space, sales per square foot	Revenue generated per day

These different measures of capacity are useful in defining two measures of operating unit performance: efficiency and utilization. **Efficiency** is the ratio of actual output to effective capacity. **Utilization** is the ratio of actual output to design capacity, or, equivalently, used time over available time.

efficiency   The ratio of actual output to effective capacity.

$$\text{Efficiency} = \frac{\text{Actual output}}{\text{Effective capacity}} \qquad\qquad (5\text{-}1)$$

$$\text{Utilization} = \frac{\text{Actual output}}{\text{Design capacity}} \quad \text{or} \quad = \frac{\text{Used time}}{\text{Available time}} \qquad\qquad (5\text{-}2)$$

utilization   The ratio of actual output to design capacity, or equivalently used time over available time.

Example 1

Given the information below, calculate the efficiency and utilization of a truck repair shop:

Design capacity = 5 trucks per day (designed for 8 hours a day with 2 mechanics)

Effective capacity = 4 trucks per day (1-hour lunch break and 1 hour expected delay)

Actual output = 3 trucks per day (1.5 hours of additional unexpected delays and break downs per day)

Solution

$$\text{Efficiency} = \frac{\text{Actual output}}{\text{Effective capacity}} = \frac{3 \text{ trucks per day}}{4 \text{ trucks per day}} = 75\%$$

$$\text{Utilization} = \frac{\text{Actual output}}{\text{Design capacity}} = \frac{3 \text{ trucks per day}}{5 \text{ trucks per day}} = 60\%$$

Both efficiency and utilization are normally less than 100 percent. For an example of a case where utilization is greater than 100 percent, see the "Utilization in Canadian Hospitals" OM in Action. For capacity measure and utilization used by airlines, see the "Airline Capacity" OM in Action.

OM in ACTION

Utilization in Canadian Hospitals

Up until early 1990s, the Canadian health care system was the envy of the world. Then came a recession and federal government deficits, which were passed to provinces in the form of drastic cuts in social services transfer payments. In turn, provinces cut hospital budgets. The number of hospital beds in Canada dropped by over 32 percent from 176,000 in 1989 to fewer than 120,000 in 2002. The bed reductions were followed by hospital closures and amalgamations. As a result, there is little slack in the system, especially during the peak flu season.

Most hospitals in Canada are examples of operations where utilization does exceed 100 percent some days. The Royal Columbian Hospital in Vancouver is an example. In peak season, the emergency room fills because there are no beds in the hospital to move patients to. The average stay in the emergency room increases up to three days from the customary two hours. Utilization exceeds 100 percent of capacity because emergency stretchers are used as beds. Another example is Campbell River Hospital on Vancouver Island where during some days in

October 2008, 83 patients crowded the 59-bed hospital, forcing cancellation of two cancer surgeries. The same story holds for most other hospitals such as the Foothills Hospital in Calgary, Pasqua and Regina General Hospitals, York Central and Sunnybrook Health Sciences Centre of Toronto, Ottawa Hospital, and the Queen Elizabeth II Health Sciences Centre of Halifax.

As a result, nurses, physicians, and other health care providers are stressed, and some people requiring emergency care are dying. Examples include a heart attack victim in Weyburn, Saskatchewan; an asthmatic teenager in Toronto; and a construction worker who fell six stories in Mississauga. In all these cases, the ambulance was turned away by the hospitals because the emergency rooms were completely full.

Sources: http://www.cbc.ca/health/story/2007/01/26/hospitals-emerg.html; Hospital Trends in Canada, Canadian Institute for Health Information 2005, http://secure.cihi.ca/cihiweb/dispPage.jsp?cw_page=AR_1215_E; http://www.cbc.ca/health/story/2008/10/29/bc-hospital-surgeries-cancelled-campbell-river.html?ref=rss; http://www.canada.com/topics/news/national/story.html?id=496f0573-e309-403a-8c3d-0768ccb7a372.

OM in ACTION

Airline Capacity

Capacity in the airline industry is measured by Available Seat Miles (the sum over all planes of the number of their seats multiplied by the number of miles each normally flies per year). The capacity utilization is measured by Passenger Load Factor, which is the average percentage of seats occupied. Air Canada, with approximately 340 planes and 1,370 flights per day, had approximately 62.8 billion Available Seat Miles and Passenger Load Factor of 80.6 percent in 2007. A related measure is Revenue Passenger Miles, which is Passenger Load Factor multiplied by Available Seat Miles. In 2007, Air Canada's Revenue Passenger Miles was = 62.8 × 0.806 = 50.6 billion.

Source: Air Canada's Annual Report, 2007, http://www.aircanada.com/en/about/investor/documents/2007_ar.pdf.

Because effective capacity acts as a lid on actual output, the key to improving capacity utilization is to increase effective capacity by identifying what is constraining it.

Factors Influencing Effective Capacity

Many aspects of system design have an impact on effective capacity. The same is true for many planning and operating decisions.

Facilities and Machines. The design of facilities, including floor space and layout, directly influence effective capacity. Layout of the work area often determines how smoothly work can be performed, and environmental factors such as heating, cooling, lighting, and ventilation also play a significant role. Further, machine and equipment speed and their state directly influence capacity, which means their maintenance is important.

Product. Products can have a tremendous influence on effective capacity. For example, when items are similar, the ability of the system to produce those items is much greater than when successive items differ. Thus, a restaurant that offers a limited menu can usually prepare and serve meals at a faster rate than a restaurant with an extensive menu. The more uniform the output, the more opportunities there are for standardization of machines, methods, and materials, which leads to greater effective capacity.

Workers. The tasks that make up a job, the variety of activities involved, and the training, skill, and experience required to perform a job all have an impact on the potential and actual output. In addition, employee motivation has a very basic relationship to effective capacity, as do absenteeism and labour turnover.

Planning and Operational Factors. Hours of operation influence effective capacity. A company using only one eight-hour shift per day in effect forgoes the use of its equipment 67 percent of the time. Scheduling problems may occur when there are differences in equipment capabilities or differences in job requirements. The effective capacity may be constrained by a bottleneck operation, inventory decisions, late deliveries, acceptability of purchased materials and parts, and quality control procedures.

External Factors. Product standards, especially minimum quality and performance standards, can restrict management's options for increasing effective capacity. Also, pollution standards on products and equipment often reduce effective capacity, as does paperwork required by government regulatory agencies. A similar effect occurs when a union contract limits the number of hours and type of work an employee may do.

LO2 STRATEGIC CAPACITY PLANNING PROCESS IN ORGANIZATIONS

Capacity decisions in organizations are usually part of the annual strategic planning process. They directly influence capital budgeting. The steps taken are as follows:

1. Forecast demand for products one to five years, or more, ahead.
2. Calculate capacity requirements to meet the forecasts.

OM in ACTION

Banks Open New Branches in Alberta

Despite the recent signs of recession, banks are going ahead with renovation of their older branches in well-established markets while opening new branches in other growth markets in Alberta. The growth strategy is long term, and plans are set for the next three to four years. The decision on expansion depends on housing and commercial development, and statistics on population, industrial, and real estate growth. For example,

TD Canada Trust opened six new branches in 2007, eight in 2008, and nine in 2009, mostly in Calgary and Edmonton. RBC opened seven new branches in 2009, all in Calgary and Edmonton. Scotiabank opened five new branches in 2009, all in Calgary. Bank of Montreal opened four new branches in 2007, four in 2008, and five in 2009. CIBC opened one new branch in Calgary in 2009. Both this and an existing branch will also be open on Sunday afternoons.

Sources: G. Teel, "Banks Buck the Trend with Expansion Plans; New Alberta Branches in Works," *Calgary Herald*, December 6, 2008, p. E.1.

3. Measure capacity now, and decide if and how to bridge the gap in capacity in the future.

   a. Generate technically feasible alternatives varying in nature (plant, equipment, subcontract, lease), size, location, price changes, etc.

   b. Evaluate each alternative economically.

      i. Initial investment? Annual revenues? Annual operating expenses? Life of investment?

      ii. Method of evaluation: Break-even analysis, payback period, or net present value.

   c. Consider non-economic aspects too, e.g., ease of use, reliability, etc.

   d. Choose the best alternative and implement it.

For an example showing the long-term nature of capacity decisions, see the "Banks Open New Branches in Alberta" OM in Action.

In the rest of this chapter, we will briefly describe Steps 1 and 2, provide some considerations for performing Step 3a, and describe use of breakeven analysis for Step 3b.

Forecasting Long-term Demand

Figure 5-1 illustrates some basic long-term demand patterns. In addition to basic patterns there are more complex patterns, such as a combination of cycles and trends, and s-shaped product life cycle curves.

When trends are identified, the fundamental issues are (1) how long the trend might persist (because few things last forever) and (2) the shape and slope of the trend. If cycles are identified, interest focuses on (1) the approximate length of the cycles, and (2) the amplitude of the cycles (i.e., deviation from average).

Most popular long-term forecasting techniques are judgmental and regression. For details, please refer back to Chapter 3.

For an example of a case where technology changed a trend unexpectedly, see the "Capacity in the Aluminum Industry" OM in Action.

The link between marketing and operations is crucial. Through customer contacts and demographic analyses, marketing can supply vital information to operations.

Figure 5-1

Common long-term demand patterns

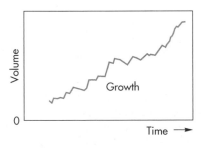

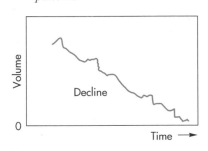

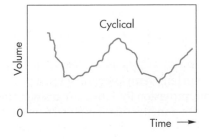

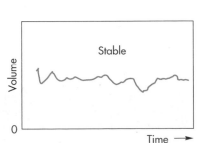

OM in ACTION

Capacity in the Aluminum Industry

Making capacity decisions is hard. Consider the aluminum industry. In the 1970s and 1980s, aluminum can sales were growing at over 10 percent per year. This occurred when aluminum cans grabbed market share from glass bottles as containers used to hold soft drinks. Companies such as Alcan and Alcoa saw no end to the market growth for aluminum cans. Therefore, they invested heavily in mills to make rolled sheets of aluminum from which pop cans are made. But in the early 1990s, market growth stopped because PET (Polyethylene Terephthalate) plastic bottles grabbed market share from aluminum cans. In 2000s, the strong, seemingly

never-ending, demand for aluminum by China (with 9 percent annual growth rate) and its inadequate future electricity supply to process aluminum, resulted in takeover frenzy within major Western aluminum companies looking for available production capacity. For example, Alcan warded off Alcoa's takeover bid only to accept the $38 billion takeover bid of Rio Tinto, a large British/Australian mining company, in late 2007. It remains to be seen if this was a good move.

Source: M. Brooks, President, Alcan Rolled Products, "Insights on the Global Aluminum Industry," December 5, 2003, http://www.alcan.com/web/publishing.nsf/ Content/Insights+on+the+Global+A luminum+Industry, accessed 2005; S. Silcoff, "Chinese Aluminum Demand Triggered Alcan Takeover," *CanWest News*, October 26, 2007, p. 1.

Calculating Capacity Requirements

We will illustrate the case of calculating capacity requirements for the number of machines needed to make some products. One must have reasonably accurate demand forecasts for each product and know the standard processing (run) time per unit for each product on the suggested machine, the number of workdays per year, and the number of hours per day that will be used.

Example 2

A department works one eight-hour shift, 250 days a year, and has the following figures for annual product demands and expected processing time per unit of a type of machine that is currently being considered. How many machines are needed?

Product	Annual Demand	Standard Processing Time per Unit (Hr)	Processing Time Needed (Hr)
#1	400	5.0	2,000
#2	300	8.0	2,400
#3	700	2.0	1,400
			5,800

Solution

Working one eight-hour shift, 250 days a year provides an annual capacity of $8 \times 250 = 2,000$ hours per year for each machine. We can see that three of these machines would be needed to handle the required volume:

$$\frac{5,800}{2,000 \text{ hours/machine}} = 2.90 \text{ machines (round up to 3)}$$

The size of the facility can be determined by summing the area required for machines, inventory, handling material, and the offices required.

Major Considerations for Developing Capacity Alternatives

1. Design Flexibility into System. The long-term nature of capacity decisions and the risks inherent in long-term forecasts suggest potential benefits from designing flexible systems. For example, provision for future expansion in the original design of a structure frequently can be obtained at a small price compared to what it would cost to remodel an existing structure that did not have such a provision. Hence, if future expansion of a restaurant seems likely, water lines, power hookups, and waste disposal lines can be put in place initially so that if expansion becomes a reality, modification to the existing structure can be minimized. Similarly, a new golf course may start as a nine-hole operation, but if provision is made for future expansion by obtaining options on adjacent land, it may progress to a larger (18-hole) course.

2. Differentiate between New and Mature Products. Mature products tend to be more predictable in terms of capacity requirements, and they may have predictable life spans. This means less risk of choosing an incorrect capacity and length of life for the investment. New products tend to carry higher risk because of the uncertainty often associated with predicting the quantity and duration of demand. These uncertainties are due to unknown and changing reaction of customers, evolving technologies, and uncertain competitor reaction. Flexibility and starting small is more important in this case.

3. Take a "Big Picture" Approach to Capacity Changes. When developing capacity alternatives, it is important to consider how parts of the system interrelate. For example, when making a decision to increase the number of rooms in a motel, one should also take into account probable increased demands for parking, entertainment and food, and housekeeping. This is sometimes called *capacity balance*. Capacity *imbalance* results in *bottlenecks*, which restrict the capacity of the whole system. To increase the capacity of the system, the capacity of the bottleneck operation should be increased.

Example 3

The first product created by toy company Spin Master, now the third largest toy manufacturer in North America, was Earth Buddy, a grass head.[1] Spin Master was hoping to sell 5,000 Earth Buddies for Mother's Day and had one week to produce them. The Earth Buddy assembly line consisted of the following operations: A: fill grass seeds and sawdust in a nylon stocking (average time 45 seconds), B: form ears and nose using elastic bands (average time 40 seconds), C: stick on the eyeglass and eyes (average time 25 seconds; eyeglass was formed off line), and D: paint the mouth (average time 10 seconds). Finally, Earth Buddies are left to dry overnight and then packed. If the capacity is desired to be at least 125 Earth Buddies per hour ($= 5,000/40$),

a. How many workers does Spin Master need in each of the operations A to D?

b. Determine the bottleneck operation for your answer to part a, and the line capacity.

Solution

a. $\rightarrow$ Fill 45 Sec $\rightarrow$ Form 40 Sec $\rightarrow$ Eyes 25 Sec $\rightarrow$ Paint 10 Sec $\rightarrow$ dry
125 units/hr $= 2.083$ units/min.

Desired time per unit $= 1/2.083 = .48$ min./unit $= 28.8$ sec/unit

Let $n =$ number of workers in an operation

Fill: $(45/n) \leq 28.8 \rightarrow n \geq 1.56$ round up 2 workers

Form: $(40/n) \leq 28.8 \rightarrow n \geq 1.39$ round up to 2 workers

Eyes: $(25/n) \leq 28.8 \rightarrow n \geq .87$ round up to 1 worker

Paint: $(10/n) \leq 28.8 \rightarrow n \geq .35$ round up 1 worker

Earth Buddy

b. Operation times, given number of workers from part a:

$\rightarrow$ Fill $45/2 = 22.5$ Sec $\rightarrow$ Form $40/2 = 20$ Sec $\rightarrow$ Eyes $25/1 = 25$ Sec $\rightarrow$ paint $10/1 = 10$ Sec

Longest operation time ($=$ lowest capacity) determines the bottleneck: Eyes

Capacity of assembly line $=$ capacity of Eyes $= 60/25 = 2.4$ units/minute $= 144$ units/hour

---

[1]"Company, About Us, Video Biography," http://www.spinmaster.com.

4. Prepare to Deal with Capacity "Chunks." Capacity increases are often acquired in fairly large chunks rather than smooth increments, making it difficult to achieve a match between desired capacity and actual capacity. For instance, the desired capacity of a certain Air Canada Jazz route may be 55 seat, but aircrafts available (Canadair CRJ 100/200 and 705) have 50 and 75 seats, respectively. One CRJ 100/200 would cause capacity to be five seats short of what is needed, but one CRJ 705 would result in an excess capacity of 20 seats. Most airlines would choose the larger aircraft in this case, because cost of shortage (lost profit) is usually larger than cost of excess capacity. This decision becomes more difficult when demand has a trend or cycle. In case of, for example, increasing demand, the timing of aircraft purchase/lease also has to be decided: Should one install capacity ahead of demand (proactive strategy) or after demand has occurred (reactive strategy)? Again, the answer basically depends on expected cost of shortage vs. expected cost of excess capacity.

5. Attempt to Smooth Out Capacity Requirements. Unevenness in capacity requirements can create certain problems. For instance, during periods of inclement weather, public transportation ridership tends to increase substantially relative to periods of pleasant weather. If capacity is set slightly above normal demand, the system tends to alternate between underutilization and overutilization. Again, the answer basically depends on expected cost of shortage vs. expected cost of excess capacity. If the service is critical, spare capacity should be available or be arranged for peak periods. Another solution in some cases such as electricity generation is demand management, i.e., persuading some customers to shift their demand from peak periods to off-peak periods by differential pricing.

Seasonal variations are generally easier to cope with than random variations (e.g., due to weather) because they are *predictable*. One possible solution to uneven demand is to identify products or services that have complementary demand patterns. For instance, demand for Ski-Doos and Sea-Doos complement each other. (More solutions to this problem will be discussed in Chapter 13.)

6. Use Capacity Cushion. When demand is variable, capacity is usually chosen above the average (forecast) demand. The excess of capacity over the average demand is called **capacity cushion** or safety capacity. The size of capacity cushion again depends on the tradeoff between cost of capacity shortage and cost of capacity excess. See Figure 5-2, where a normal (bell-shaped) demand distribution is assumed. For vital services such as electricity, the chosen capacity should be larger than normal *peak* demand, i.e., there should be a large (positive) capacity cushion. For an application of this and some other capacity considerations, see the "Capacity Planning for Electricity Generation" OM in Action later in the chapter.

7. Identify the Optimal Operating Level. Production units typically have an ideal or optimal level of operation in terms of average unit cost of output. At the **optimal operating level**, average cost per unit is the lowest for that production unit; larger or smaller rates of output will result in a higher unit cost, i.e., the average cost curve is "u" shaped.

The explanation for the shape of the cost curve is that at low levels of output, the investment costs of facilities and equipment must be absorbed (paid for) by very few units. Hence, the cost per unit is high. As output is increased, there are more units to absorb the "fixed" cost of facilities and equipment, so unit cost decreases. However, beyond a certain point, unit cost will start to rise. Reasons for this include worker fatigue; equipment breakdowns; the loss of flexibility which leaves less of a margin for error; and, generally, greater difficulty in coordinating operations.

Both optimal operating level and the amount of the minimum average unit cost tend to be a function of capacity of the operating unit. As the capacity of a plant increases, the optimal operating

capacity cushion The excess of capacity over the average demand.

optimal operating level The level of production that has the lowest average unit cost.

Figure 5-2

Capacity cushion

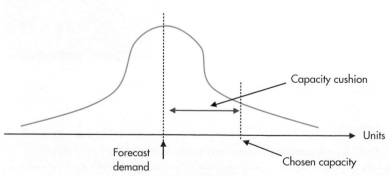

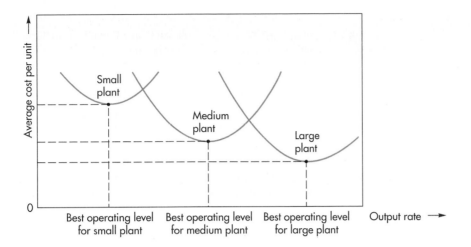

Figure 5-3

Average cost per unit and optimal operating level are functions of size of a production unit (graph shows economies of scale).

level increases and the minimum average cost per unit decreases. Thus, larger plants tend to have higher optimal operating level and lower average cost per unit than smaller plants. Figure 5-3 illustrates this point, called **economies of scale**.

In choosing the capacity of an operating unit, management must take these relationships into account along with the availability of financial and other resources and forecasts of demand.

economies of scale   The economic conditions that favour larger plants and equipment by causing average unit cost to decrease as production increases.

OM in *ACTION*

Capacity Planning for Electricity Generation

Electricity generation is like a service operation because electricity cannot be stored in large amounts. The closest to inventoried electricity is having a water reservoir upstream from a dam equipped with electricity-generating turbines. Because voltage must be close (within ± 3 volts) to 110v (or machines and equipment will not work), automatic fuses/relays will disconnect power (causing a blackout) if supply is not equal to demand. Therefore, to avoid blackouts, supply must equal demand at all times. This requires not only precise monitoring of demand and coordination of supply, but also having enough capacity available at all times.

However, electricity demand has seasonality and is sometimes volatile. Demand is at its highest during hot summer days (when air conditioners are used) and cold winter days (when room and car block heaters are used). Peak usage usually occurs between 4 and 8 p.m. when people return home, plug in their car, start cooking, possibly use the washing machine, and watch TV. In addition, the peak demand can be abnormal/extreme, e.g., the hottest day this summer could be the hottest in 30 years.

The electricity supply can also be variable due to unexpected problems in generation and transmission (e.g., a hurricane can topple trees on transmission lines, ripping them). In addition, the generating plants require downtime for repair and maintenance.

Therefore, to avoid much of the blackouts, the available capacity must not be much smaller than the extreme peak demand. The target for reserve capacity (or capacity cushion) is usually chosen so that the length of blackout is at most two hours per year. However, there are ways to avoid the blackout altogether, e.g., (1) use demand response programs that, through differential pricing, encourage large electricity consumers to shift their demand to off-peak times and (2) buy electricity from a neighbouring provinces/states.

Most provinces have one power company (e.g., Sask-Power, a Crown corporation) or there is a central government-appointed authority to regulate and coordinate power generation and distribution (e.g., Ontario Power Authority/Independent Electricity System Operator IESO/Hydro One). The reason is that generating plants and transmission/distribution lines require significant investment, service to remote communities has to be subsidized, and reliable service is expected by all consumers (imagine no electricity, and hence no heating, in −40 degree temperature).

In the early and middle part of the last century, provinces invested heavily in power generation and transmission/distribution capacities. For example, many hydro dams, coal-powered power plants, and nuclear power plants were built. Unfortunately, during the latter part of last century there was little new investment, letting capacity drop (due to closing of aging plants) while peak demand kept increasing due to population growth. For example, Ontario had 30 gigawatts of capacity and peak demand of 22 gigawatts in 1997, but in 2001 capacity was down to 27 gigawatts and peak demand was up to 25 gigawatts.

The ensuing blackouts and environmental concerns (due to CO_2 gas emissions from coal-fired plants) have forced some provinces to start planning their electricity-generating capacity and to replace coal-fired plants with natural gas–fired plants, wind turbines, and refurbished nuclear plants. For example, in 2005 IESO produced the chart opposite, which forecasts the Required Resources (demand + reserved capacity) for the following 10 years (the 3 lines) and suggested capacity options (coloured areas) to replace all the coal-fired plants. The High line is based on extreme peak demand and the Median line on the average peak demand during the past 30 years. The goal was to shut down all the coal-fired plants between 2007 and 2009, and refurbish Pickering Unit 1 nuclear plant, receive Requests for Proposals for several gas-fired plants and windmills (in two phases), and refurbish Bruce Nuclear Plant Units 1 and 2. As it can be seen, this

would have resulted in High requirements not being met by 2008 and in Median requirements not being met by 2011. Therefore, the government of Ontario has postponed the closing of some of the coal-fired plants (especially Nanticoke) to 2014. In the meantime, Ontario Power Generation is experimenting with burning biomass as fuel in some coke-burning plants such as Nanticoke.

The replacement and refurbishment plans are underway and on time so far. As part of capacity planning it was discovered that downtown Toronto's electricity needs in the next five years could not be met due to transmission lines bottlenecks. Three gas-powered generating plants (a total of 550 megawatts in Portlands Energy Centre) are being built to answer this problem. Also, Western Greater Toronto Area is receiving 1 gigawatt more of capacity through upgrades in transmission equipment and lines.

Source: http://www.ieso.ca; http://www.ieso.ca/imoweb/pubs/media/10yearOutlook-highlights-2005jul.pdf.

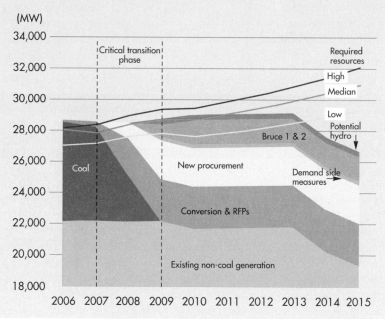

Ontario's replacement scenario for coal-fired plants

Source: http://www.ieso.ca/imoweb/pubs/media/10yearOutlook-highlights-2005jul.pdf.

EVALUATING ALTERNATIVES

An organization needs to evaluate alternatives for future capacity from a number of different perspectives. Most obvious are economic considerations: Will an alternative be economically feasible? How much will it cost? What will operating and maintenance costs be? What will the revenue be? What will its useful life be? Other considerations include, Will it be compatible with present personnel and operations? What is the personal preference of managers?

Less obvious, but nonetheless important, is possible negative public opinion. Any option that could disrupt lives and property (noise, traffic, pollution) is bound to generate hostile reactions. Construction of new facilities may necessitate moving personnel to a new location. Embracing a new technology may mean retraining some people and terminating some jobs. Relocation can cause unfavourable reactions, particularly if a town is about to lose a major employer.

A number of techniques are useful for evaluating capacity alternatives from an economic standpoint. Some of the more common are break-even analysis, payback period, and net present value. Break-even analysis is described in this chapter.

Break-even Analysis

Break-even analysis focuses on relationship between costs, revenue, and volume (i.e., quantity) of output. The purpose of break-even analysis is to determine the quantity at which the investment starts to make a profit. Another name for break-even analysis is cost-volume-profit analysis.

Use of break-even analysis requires identification of all costs related to the production of a given product. These costs are then classified as fixed or variable costs. *Fixed costs* tend to remain constant regardless of quantity of output. Examples include rental costs, property taxes, equipment costs, heating and cooling expenses, and certain administrative costs. *Variable costs* vary directly with quantity of output. The major components of variable costs are generally materials and labour costs. We will assume that variable cost per unit remains the same regardless of quantity of output.

Table 5-2 summarizes the symbols used in the break-even analysis formulas.

FC = Fixed cost

VC = Total variable cost

v = Variable cost per unit

TC = Total cost

TR = Total revenue

R = Revenue per unit (i.e., price)

Q = Quantity or volume of output

Q_{BEP} = Break-even quantity

P = Profit

Table 5-2

Break-even analysis symbols

The total cost associated with a given quantity of output is equal to the sum of the fixed cost and the variable cost per unit times quantity:

$$TC = FC + VC \qquad (5\text{-}3)$$

$$VC = Q \times v \qquad (5\text{-}4)$$

Figure 5-4a shows the relationship between quantity of output and fixed cost, total variable cost, and total (fixed plus variable) cost.

Revenue per unit, like variable cost per unit, is assumed to be the same regardless of quantity of output. Assuming that all output can be sold, total revenue will have a linear

Figure 5-4

Break-even relationships

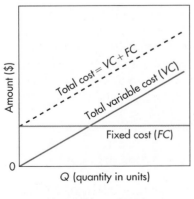

a Fixed, variable, and total costs

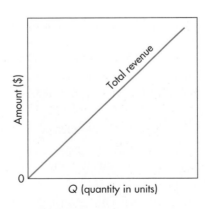

b Total revenue increases
linearly with output

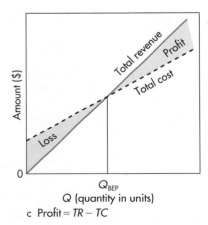

c Profit = $TR - TC$

relationship to output, as illustrated in Figure 5-4b. The total revenue associated with a given quantity of output, Q, is:

$$TR = R \times Q \qquad (5\text{-}5)$$

Figure 5-4c describes the relationship between profit, which is the difference between total revenue and total cost, and quantity of output. The quantity at which total cost and total revenue are equal is referred to as the **break-even point (BEP)**. When quantity is less than the break-even point, there is a loss; when quantity is greater than the break-even point, there is a profit. The greater the deviation from this point, the greater the profit or loss. Total profit can be calculated using the formula:

$$P = TR - TC = R \times Q - (FC + v \times Q)$$

Factorizing Q, we have

$$P = Q(R - v) - FC \qquad (5\text{-}6)$$

Solving for Q, the required quantity needed to generate a specified profit is:

$$Q = \frac{P + FC}{R - v} \qquad (5\text{-}7)$$

A special case of this is the quantity of output needed for total revenue to equal total cost, i.e., when profit $P = 0$. This is the break-even point:

$$Q_{BEP} = \frac{FC}{R - v} \qquad (5\text{-}8)$$

If demand is expected to be greater than the break-even point, then we conclude that it is a good capacity investment decision (i.e., will make a profit). Otherwise, it is not (i.e., will make a loss).

break-even point (BEP)
The quantity of output at which total cost and total revenue are equal.

Example 4

The management of a large bakery is contemplating adding a new line of pies which will require leasing new equipment for a monthly payment of $6,000. Variable costs would be $2.00 per pie, and pies would retail for $7.00 each.

a. How many pies must be sold per month in order to break even?

b. What would the profit (loss) be if 1,000 pies are made and sold in a month?

c. How many pies must be sold to realize a profit of $4,000 per month?

d. If demand is expected to be 1,500 pies per month, is this a good investment?

Solution

$FC = \$6,000$ per month, $v = \$2$ per pie, $R = \$7$ per pie

a. $Q_{BEP} = \dfrac{FC}{R - v} = \dfrac{\$6,000}{\$7 - \$2} = 1,200$ pies/month

b. For $Q = 1,000$, $P = Q(R - v) - FC = 1,000\,(\$7 - \$2) - \$6,000 = -\$1,000$ (i.e., loss of $1,000)

c. $P = \$4,000$; solve for Q using formula 5-7:

$$Q = \frac{\$4,000 + \$6,000}{\$7 - \$2} = 2,000 \text{ pies per month}$$

d. Because $1,500 > 1,200$, this is a good investment.

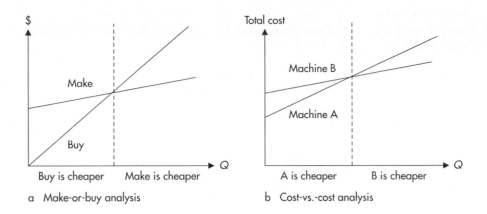

Figure 5-5

Two types of analysis

a   Make-or-buy analysis   b   Cost-vs.-cost analysis

Break-even analysis can also be used for (1) make-or-buy decisions, and (2) deciding between two or more capacity alternatives (cost-vs.-cost analysis).

The make-or-buy decision involves deciding whether to buy a machine (fixed cost) and make the product in-house (variable cost) or to buy the product (variable cost with no fixed cost). See Figure 5-5a. Let v_m = per unit variable cost of make and v_b = per unit variable cost of buy (i.e., purchase price). Then, the break-even point will be:

$$Q = FC/(v_b - v_m) \qquad\qquad (5\text{-}9)$$

The cost-vs.-cost decision involves two (or more) "make" options: machine A vs. machine B. Each machine will have a fixed cost and a variable cost. See Figure 5-5b. Let FC_A and v_A be fixed cost and unit variable cost of machine A, and FC_B and v_B be fixed cost and unit variable cost of machine B. Then, break-even point will be:

$$Q = (FC_A - FC_B)/(v_B - v_A) \qquad\qquad (5\text{-}10)$$

Break-even Problem with Step Fixed Cost

Capacity alternatives may involve *step costs*, which are costs that increase stepwise as potential volume increases. For example, a company may have the option of purchasing one, two, or three machines, with each additional machine increasing the fixed cost, although perhaps not equally. (See Figure 5-6a.) In this case *multiple break-even quantities* may occur, possibly one for each range. This is illustrated in Figure 5-6b, where there is a break-even point in the second and another in the third range. In order to decide how many machines to purchase, a manager must compare forecast demand to the break-even points and choose the most appropriate number of machines, as Example 5 shows.

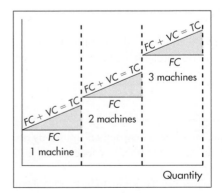

a   Step fixed costs and variable costs

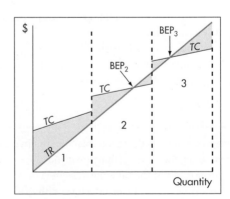

b   Multiple break-even points

Figure 5-6

Break-even problem with step fixed cost

Example 5

A manager has the option of purchasing one, two, or three machines. Fixed costs and potential quantities are as follows:

Number of Machines	Total Annual Fixed Cost	Corresponding Range of Output
1	$ 9,600	0 to 300
2	$15,000	301 to 600
3	$20,000	601 to 900

Variable cost is $10 per unit, and revenue is $40 per unit.

a. Determine the break-even point (if any) for each range.

b. For any value of annual demand between 0 and 900 units, determine how many machines the manager should purchase.

a. Calculate the break-even point for each range using the formula $Q_{BEP} = FC/(R - v)$. For one machine

$$Q_{BEP} = \frac{\$9,600}{\$40/\text{unit} - \$10/\text{unit}} = 320 \text{ units [not in the range, so there is no } BEP]$$

For two machines $Q_{BEP} = \dfrac{\$15,000}{\$40/\text{unit} - \$10/\text{unit}} = 500$ units

For three machines $Q_{BEP} = \dfrac{\$20,000}{\$40/\text{unit} - \$10/\text{unit}} = 666.67$ units

b. For demand $\leq 499 \rightarrow$ use 0 machine (because the first feasible break-even point is 500 units)

For $500 \leq$ demand $\leq 600 \rightarrow$ use 2 machines

For $601 \leq$ demand $\leq 666 \rightarrow$ Do not use 3 machines (because the second feasible break-even point is 666.67). However, the manager should use 2 machines (note: some demand will not be satisfied).

For $667 \leq$ demand $\leq 900 \rightarrow$ use 3 machines

As with any quantitative tool, it is important to verify that the assumptions on which the break-even analysis is based are reasonably satisfied for a particular situation. Note that revenue per unit or variable cost per unit is not always constant. Also, break-even analysis requires that fixed and variable costs are separated, and this is sometimes exceedingly difficult to accomplish.

If a proposal looks attractive using break-even analysis, the next step would be to determine the annual cash flows and calculate the net present value, which is covered in any introductory finance course.

Summary

Design capacity is the theoretical maximum output, but effective capacity is limited by operating hours, maintenance, etc. Efficiency is the ratio of actual output to effective capacity, and utilization is that proportion of the time the system is operating.

A variety of factors can interfere with effective capacity. These include facility design and layout, human factors, product factors, equipment maintenance, scheduling problems, and quality considerations.

Capacity planning is the process of determining alternatives to meet long-term forecast of demand.

Development of capacity alternatives is enhanced by considering the life cycle of the product, designing systems with flexible capacity, taking a systems approach to planning, recognizing that capacity increments are often acquired in chunks, practising demand management, using capacity cushion, and choosing the right capacity and optimal operating level.

In evaluating capacity alternatives, a manager must consider both quantitative and qualitative aspects. Quantitative analysis usually reflects economic factors, and qualitative considerations include intangibles such as operational fit and personal preferences of managers. Break-even analysis determines that quantity beyond which profit will be attained.

break-even point (BEP), 152
capacity, 141
capacity cushion, 148
design capacity, 142
economies of scale, 149

effective capacity, 142
efficiency, 143
optimal operating level, 148
strategic capacity planning, 141
utilization, 143

A manager must decide whether to make or buy (i.e., outsource) a certain item used in the production of its vending machines. Cost and demand estimates are as follows:

	Make	**Buy**
Annual fixed cost	$150,000	None
Variable cost/unit	$60	$80
Annual demand (units)	12,000	12,000

a. Given these numbers, should the company buy or make this item?

b. There is a possibility that demand could change in the future. At what quantity would the manager be indifferent between making and buying?

a. Determine the annual cost of each alternative:

Total cost = Fixed cost + Quantity × Variable cost

Make: $150,000 + 12,000 ($60) = $870,000

Buy: 0 + 12,000 ($80) − $960,000

Because the annual cost of making the item is less than the annual cost of buying it, the manager should choose to make the item.

b. To determine the quantity at which the two choices would be equivalent, set the two total costs equal to each other, and solve for quantity: $TC_{make} = TC_{buy}$. Thus, $150,000 + Q($60) = 0 + Q($80)$. Solving for Q, we get $Q = 7,500$ units. Alternatively, one can use formula (5-9): BEP = $FC/(v_b - v_m) = $150,000/($80 - $60) = 7,500$ units. Therefore, at 7,500 units a year, the manager would be indifferent between making and buying. For lower demand, the choice would be to buy, and for higher demand, the choice would be to make.

A toy company wants to make electric turtles. The line will have a monthly fixed cost of $42,000 and variable costs of $3 per turtle. Turtles would sell for $7 each. Prepare a table that shows total revenue, total variable cost, fixed cost, total cost, and profit for monthly demands of 10,000, 12,000, and 15,000 units. In what range do you expect the break-even point to lie? Calculate the break-even point.

Solution

$$\text{Revenue} = \$7 \text{ per unit}$$
$$\text{Variable cost} = \$3 \text{ per unit}$$
$$\text{Fixed cost} = \$42{,}000 \text{ per month}$$
$$\text{Profit} = Q(R - v) - FC$$
$$\text{Total cost} = FC + v \times Q$$

Demand	Total Revenue	Total VC	Fixed Cost	Total Cost	Profit
10,000	$70,000	$30,000	$42,000	$72,000	$(2,000)
12,000	84,000	36,000	42,000	78,000	6,000
15,000	105,000	45,000	42,000	87,000	18,000

The break-even point would lie between 10,000 and 12,000 units per month. $Q_{BEP} = \dfrac{FC}{R - v} = \dfrac{\$42{,}000}{\$7 - \$3} = 10{,}500$ units per month

Problem 3

Refer to Problem 2. Develop an equation that can be used to calculate monthly profit for any quantity. Use that equation to determine profit when quantity equals 22,000 units per month.

Solution

$$\text{Profit} = Q(R - v) - FC = Q(\$7 - \$3) - \$42{,}000 = \$4Q - \$42{,}000$$

For $Q = 22{,}000$, profit is $\$4(22{,}000) - \$42{,}000 = \$46{,}000$

Problem 4

A manager must decide which type of machine to buy, Type A or Type B, and how many of each. Type A machine costs $15,000 each, and Type B costs $11,000 each. The machines are operated 8 hours a day, 250 days a year. The variable cost of using either machine is negligible.

Either machine can be used to perform two types of chemical analysis, C1 and C2, but the processing times will be different. Annual quantities (i.e., number of analyses) and processing times are shown in the following table. The goal is to minimize total purchase cost but meet annual requirements within the available hours.

Analysis Type	Annual Quantity	Processing Time per Analysis (hr) A	Processing Time per Analysis (hr) B
C1	1,200	1	2
C2	900	3	2

Solution

Total processing time (annual quantity × processing time per analysis) needed by type of equipment:

Analysis Type	A	B
C1	1,200	2,400
C2	2,700	1,800
Total	3,900	4,200 hrs

Total processing time available per machine is 8 hours/day × 250 days/year = 2,000 hours per year. Hence, one machine can handle 2,000 hours of analysis, two machines can handle 4,000 hours, etc.

Given the total processing requirements, two Type A machines would be needed for a total cost of 2 × $15,000 = $30,000, or three Type B machines for a total cost of 3 × $11,000 = $33,000. Thus, two machines of Type A would have lower cost than three Type B machines.

1. Explain the various definitions of capacity. Give an example of each. (LO1)
2. How do long-term, medium-term, and short-term capacity decisions differ? (LO1)
3. Why is the long-term capacity decision important? Give three reasons. (LO1)
4. Contrast design capacity and effective capacity. (LO1)
5. Propose measures of capacity for a hospital and for an airline. In what way are the measures similar and different? (LO1)
6. Contrast efficiency and utilization. (LO1)
7. What is capacity planning and how is it done? (LO1 & 2)
8. How can long-term capacity requirements be determined? (LO2)
9. Give one example of building flexibility into system capacity. (LO2)
10. What is a bottleneck operation? Name two places/operations in an airport that are usually bottlenecks. (LO2)
11. What is meant by the term capacity "chunks"? What are the reactive and proactive strategies for timing capacity increases? Should essential services such as utilities use the reactive or proactive strategy? Explain. (LO2)
12. What are economies of scale? Give an example. Is there a limit to them? Explain. (LO2)
13. How do electrical utilities meet abnormal peak demand? Name three ways. (LO2)
14. What influences effective capacity? (LO1)
15. What is the optimal operating level for a machine and why is it usually less than its design capacity? (LO2)
16. What is capacity cushion? Give an example. (LO2)
17. Discuss how capacity planning for essential services such as utilities differs from capacity planning for other services. (LO2)
*18. When Air Canada emerged from bankruptcy protection in 2004, its top management decided to replace some of its older planes with new ones. In particular, several relatively small Embraer and Bombardier planes (with fewer than 90 seats) and several large Boeing 777 and 787 (with more than 200 seats) were ordered. These are much more fuel efficient than the planes they replace. However, Air Canada operations are still not as low cost as WestJet's. An Available Seat Mile costs Air Canada 16–17¢ whereas it costs WestJet 11–12¢. Recall that WestJet is non-unionized, runs only one type of plane (Boeing 737 which seats 100–150 passengers), and is financially stronger (see the WestJet case at the end of Chapter 2). Discuss the pros and cons of Air Canada's decision. (LO1 & 2)
19. What is break-even analysis and how is it used? (LO3)

1. What are two major trade-offs in capacity planning? (LO2)
2. Who needs to be involved in capacity planning? (LO1)
3. In what ways has mechanization/automation/technology had an impact on capacity planning? (LO2)
4. When Air Canada went into bankruptcy in 2003/2004, a new holding company, ACE, was formed with the goal of breaking up various components of Air Canada such as the Aeroplan customer loyalty plan, the maintenance department, and the regional subsidiary airline Jazz. ACE managed to achieve its goals against the opposition of Air Canada employees, especially its pilots. What was left of Air Canada was practically worthless. Is what has happened to Air Canada unethical? Explain. (LO2)

A computer repair shop has a design capacity of eight repairs per day. Its effective capacity, however, is four repairs per day, and its actual output is three repairs per day. The manager would like to increase the number of repairs per day. Which of the following factors would you recommend that the manager investigate: quality problems, absenteeism, or scheduling and balancing? Explain your reasoning. (LO1)

Experiential Learning Exercises

1. Estimate the hourly capacity of the following two service systems by obtaining their processing times. (LO2)

   a. An automatic car wash.

   b. A cashier in a supermarket, a teller in a bank, or a similar service operation.

   Obtain the processing times for approximately six customers.

2. How confident are you of your estimate for part 1a and how confident are you of your estimate for part 1b? Explain.

Internet Exercise

1. Go to the Web site of Airbus A380, the biggest passenger plane ever built (525 passengers or more on 2 floors, with a range of 15,000 km, and a wingspan of 80 metres), http://www.airbus.com/en/aircraftfamilies/a380. (LO2)

   a. Identify some airlines interested in A380, and try to explain their choice.

   b. Identify the capacity problems this plane causes for airports (e.g., see http://science.howstuffworks.com/transport/flight/modern/a3806.htm).

Problems

1. a. Calculate the utilization and efficiency in each of these situations: (LO1)

   i   A bank processes an average of seven loans per day. It has a design capacity of 10 loans per day and an effective capacity of eight loans per day.

   ii A furnace repair team services an average of four furnaces a day. The design capacity is six furnaces a day and the effective capacity is five furnaces a day.

   b. Would you say that systems with higher efficiency will have higher utilization than other systems? Explain.

2. In a job shop, effective capacity is only 50 percent of design capacity, and actual output is 80 percent of effective capacity. What design capacity would be needed to achieve an actual output of eight jobs per week? (LO1)

3. A producer of pottery is considering the addition of a new factory to absorb the backlog of demand that now exists. The primary location being considered will have fixed cost of $10,000 per month and variable cost of $1 per unit produced. Each item is sold to retailers at a price that averages $2. (LO3)

   a. What quantity per month is required in order to break even?

   b. What profit would be realized on a monthly quantity of 20,000 units?

   c. What quantity is needed to obtain a profit of $16,000 per month?

   d. What quantity is needed to provide revenue of $23,000 per month?

   e. Plot the total cost and total revenue lines against quantity per month.

4. A small company intends to increase the capacity of its bottleneck operation by adding a new machine. Two alternatives, A and B, have been identified, and the associated costs and revenues have been estimated. Annual fixed costs would be $40,000 for A and $30,000 for B; variable costs per unit would be $10 for A and $12 for B; and revenue per unit would be $15 for A and $16 for B. (LO3)

   a. Determine each alternative's break-even point.

   b. At what quantity would the two alternatives yield the same profit?

   c. If expected annual demand is 12,000 units, which alternative would yield the higher profit?

5. The selling price for a type of felt-tip pen is $1 per pen. Fixed cost of the operation is $25,000 per month and variable cost is 50 cents per pen. (LO3)

   a. Find the break-even quantity.

   b. How many pens must be sold to obtain a monthly profit of $15,000?

6. Natalie is considering the purchase a cell phone service plan. There are two service plans to choose from. Plan A has a monthly charge of $20 plus $0.45 a minute for daytime calls and

unlimited evening/night/weekend calls. Plan B has a flat rate of $50 with 200 daytime minutes of calls allowed per month and a cost of $0.40 per daytime minute beyond that, and unlimited evening/night/weekend calls. (LO3)

   a. Determine the total charge under each plan for this case: 120 minutes of daytime calls a month.
   b. Prepare a graph that shows total monthly cost for each plan vs. daytime call minutes.
   c. Over what range of daytime call minutes will each plan be optimal?

7. A company plans to begin production of a new small appliance. The manager must decide whether to purchase the motors for the appliance from a vendor at $7 each or to produce them in-house. Either of two processes could be used for in-house production; one would have an annual fixed cost of $160,000 and a variable cost of $5 per unit, and the other would have an annual fixed cost of $190,000 and a variable cost of $4 per unit. Determine the range of annual quantity for which each of the alternatives would be best. (LO3)

8. A manager is trying to decide whether to purchase a certain part or to have it produced internally. Internal production could use either of two processes. One would entail a variable cost of $16 per unit and an annual fixed cost of $200,000; the other would entail a variable cost of $14 per unit and an annual fixed cost of $240,000. Three vendors are willing to provide the part. Vendor A has a price of $20 per unit for any annual quantity up to 30,000 units. Vendor B has a price of $22 per unit if demand is 1,000 units or less, but $18 per unit (for all units) if demand is greater. Vendor C offers a price of $21 per unit for the first 1,000 units, and $19 per unit for additional units. (LO3)

   a. If the manager anticipates an annual demand of 10,000 units, which alternative would be best from a cost standpoint? For 60,000 units, which alternative would be best?
   b. Determine the range for which each alternative is best. Are there any alternatives that are never best? If so, which ones?

9. A company manufactures a product using two identical machines. Each machine has a design capacity of 250 units per day and an effective capacity of 230 units per day. At present, actual output averages 200 units per machine, but the manager estimates that productivity improvements soon will increase output to 225 units per day. Annual demand for the product is currently 50,000 units, but it is expected that within two years annual demand will triple. How many machines should the company plan to have to satisfy the forecasted demand? Assume 240 workdays per year. (LO2)

10. A manager must decide which type of machine to buy, A, B, or C. Machine fixed costs are: (LO2)

Machine	Cost/Year
A	$40,000
B	$30,000
C	$80,000

The company makes four products. Product forecasts and unit processing times on each machine are as follows:

Product	Annual Demand	Processing Time Per Unit (Minutes)		
		A	B	C
1	16,000	3	4	2
2	12,000	4	4	3
3	6,000	5	6	4
4	30,000	2	2	1

a. How many machines of each type would be needed in order to meet annual demand for all the products? Based on annual fixed costs, which type of machine and how many will cost least to satisfy the demand? Machines operate 10 hours a day, 250 days a year.

b. Consider this additional information: The machines differ in terms of hourly operating costs: The A machines have an hourly operating cost of $10 each, B machines have an hourly operating cost of $11 each, and C machines have an hourly operating cost of $12 each. Which alternative machine should be selected, and how many would be necessary to minimize total cost while satisfying processing requirements?

11. A manager must decide how many machines of a certain type to purchase. Each machine can process 100 customers per day. One machine will result in a fixed cost of $2,000 per day, while two machines will result in a fixed cost of $3,800 per day. Variable costs will be $20 per customer, and revenue will be $45 per customer. (LO3)

a. Determine the break-even points for one machine and two machines.

b. If estimated demand is 90 to 120 customers per day, how many machines should be purchased?

12. The manager of a car wash must decide whether to have one or two wash lines. One line will have a fixed cost of $4,000 a month, and two lines will have a fixed cost of $7,000 a month. Each line would be able to process 15 cars an hour. Variable costs will be $1 per car, and revenue will be $3 per car. The manager projects average demand of between 14 and 18 cars an hour. Would you recommend one or two lines? The car wash will be open 300 hours a month. (LO3)

13. The total demand for polypropylene, a type of plastic, in North America is approximately 11 billion pounds. H. Patrick Jack, VP of Fina Oil & Chemical Co., predicts (based on the previous 10 years) that total demand will grow anywhere between 5 and 8 percent annually. The total capacity is currently 12.3 billion pounds. In addition, a total of 4.5 billion pounds of new capacity is under construction by eight companies in eight locations and will be ready for production within the next four years. Would total capacity be enough to meet expected demand four years from now?[2] (LO2)

14. A parts manufacturer plans to replace its existing facility with a new one. The management is considering two possible capacities for the new facility: 200,000 or 250,000 units per year. The 200,000-unit plant would have an annual fixed cost of $4.0 million and a per unit production cost of $20. The 250,000-unit plant would have an annual fixed cost of $6 million and a per unit cost of $15. The parts will be sold for an average price of $60 per unit. (LO3)

a. Calculate the break-even point for each capacity alternative.

b. Suppose that the company projects its sales to be 220,000 units per year. Which alternative would you recommend? Hint: Calculate the annual profit in each case.

15. The fixed cost of running a gift store (wages, rent, etc.) in a particular mall is $250,000 per year.[3] The gross margin (i.e., sales – cost of goods sold or alternatively revenue – variable cost) is 45 percent of sales. Assuming store is open 364 days a year, (LO3)

a. What are the minimum daily sales to break even?

b. If the owner's profit target is 10 percent of sales, what are the minimum daily sales to breakeven?

c. If the owner's profit target is $100,000 per year, what are the minimum daily sales to break even?

*16. One of the first Internet-based groceries home delivery businesses was Homegrocer.com. In 1998, Mike Donald, president of Concord Sales, one of the largest food brokers in B.C., and two partners thought of starting such a business in Vancouver. However, they had to move it to Seattle in order to get financing from U.S. financiers. Mike thought that because Microsoft and Boeing are located in Seattle, the proportion of households with Internet would be high.

---

[2]D. Richards, "Polypropylene Capacity Soars But All of It May Be Needed," *Chemical Market Reporter* 251(12), March 24, 1997, pp. 7, 9.

[3]G. Cunningham, "Breakeven Analysis Key to Profits: The Next Century Promises More Stress and Retail Unpredictability," *Gifts & Tablewares* 25(1), January 2000, p. 58.

After raising approximately $4 million, and using it to lease a large warehouse, purchase 10 trucks, set up the web page and software, and advertise, Homegrocer.com had fewer than 1,000 regular customers. Mike estimated that an average regular customer purchased 3 times a month and bought approximately $75 each time (below $75, Homegrocer.com charged a delivery fee of $10). The gross margin (i.e., sales – cost of goods sold or alternatively revenue – variable cost) was around 20 percent, and total monthly labour and overhead costs were approximately $300,000. (LO3)

a. How many regular customers did Homegrocer.com need in 1998 to break even?

Despite the slow initial business, Homegrocer.com persevered and even expanded into Portland, Oregon. In the frenzy of dot.com era in 1999, private investors, including Amazon.com, invested approximately $100 million in Homegrocer.com. Homegrocer.com used the money to further expand, trying to compete with Webvan, a California-based competitor. In the beginning of 2000, Homegrocer.com raised over $250 million by issuing shares to the public, and kept on expanding to more cities in the United States. However, its share prices started to decline due to increasing losses. In mid-2000, Webvan bought Homegrocer.com for over $1 billion. Webvan itself went bankrupt in 2001.

b. Why would a startup company want to expand so fast? Why did most Internet grocery businesses fail?[4]

*17. A few years ago, the Toronto plant of a multinational soup producer was in competition with its U.S. sister plant to supply the Northeastern U.S. market. However, its cost of production was not competitive. One source of cost disadvantage was the tin cans. The Toronto plant bought its tin cans for approximately $6.00 per case of 48 cans, whereas the U.S. plant made its own cans at the cost of $5.00 (in Canadian dollars) per case. The manager estimated that installing an automatic can line cost $2.0 million for building expansion and $12 million for equipment. The can line would have a variable production cost of $5.50 per case. (LO3)

a. Assuming a useful life of 10 years, no salvage value, and straight-line depreciation, calculate the annual fixed cost of the canning line.
b. Calculate the annual breakeven quantity between buying and making the cans in-house.
c. Draw a graph of the annual cost of buying and annual cost of making (try to make it to scale), and determine which option is better if the annual requirement of the Toronto plant was 5 million cases of cans.

18. Suppose your friend is thinking of opening a new restaurant, and she hopes that she will have around 20 groups of (on average) 4 customers on a typical busy evening. Each meal will take around 1.5 hours and it is expected that on average a table will be used twice in an evening. Each table and its surroundings will require 4 square metres of space. (LO2)

a. Calculate the required seating area.
b. If each meal will take an average of 12 minutes to cook on a heating element, and each stove will have 4 elements, how many stoves would the restaurant require? Assume that all 10 "tables" could come at the same time and that the kitchen should be able to cook the meal for them during their first hour of visit.

*19. Corner Tavern is a small-town bar that sells only bottled beer. The average price of a bottle of beer at the tavern is $3.00 and the average cost of a bottle of beer to the tavern is $1.00. The tavern is open every night. One bartender and two to three waitresses are on duty each night. The fixed costs (salaries, rent, tax, utilities, etc.) total $260,000 per year. (LO3)

a. The owner wishes to know how many bottles of beer the tavern must sell during the year to start making profit.
b. What is the revenue at the breakeven quantity found in the part a?
c. Draw the annual revenue and total annual cost vs. the number of bottles of beer sold per year. Make sure that the y-axis is to scale. Identify the important points on the graph.

---

[4]J. Schreiner, "Net Grocer Debuts with Little Fanfare Big Backers: …" *National Post*, March 11, 2000, p. C03; J. Greenwood, "Canadians Break Bread with Amazon Online Grocery Store," *National Post*, May 19, 1999, p. C01.

d. Using the graph in part c, answer the following question: If Corner Tavern sells 140,000 bottles of beer a year, would it make a profit? Explain.

e. The owner thinks $50,000 is a reasonable annual profit. How many bottles of beer should the tavern sell to make $50,000 profit?

f. An available option is to open the tavern earlier on the weekends. The attraction would be a discount of $0.50 off the regular price. The extra salaries of waitresses and bartender for the whole year are estimated to be $30,000. How many extra bottles of beer must the tavern sell in order to break even in this option?

*20. A small brewery reuses its own empty bottles, but it does not have a bottle-cleaning machine. The empty bottles are collected from liquor stores and bars, and brought back to the brewery. Once enough empty bottles accumulate, they are trucked to a cleaning facility and clean bottles are brought back. The cleaning facility charges 10 cents to wash a bottle, and cost of trucking is 2 cents per bottle. Management is thinking of buying an automated bottle-cleaning machine. The machine costs $1 million and has a useful life of 10 years. The machine will be used only when enough empty bottles accumulate. The operating cost of the machine is expected to be $108 per hour, washing 60 bottles per minute. (LO3)

a. How many bottles per year would have equal total annual cost of doing the cleaning in-house vs. outsourcing the cleaning? Use straight-line depreciation.

b. What is the total annual cost at the quantity found in part a?

c. Draw the two total annual costs vs. the quantity of bottles per year. Make sure that the y-axis is to scale. If the brewery is expected to have 1 million bottles per year to wash, which decision is less costly?

21. The following diagram shows a four-step process that begins with Operation 1 and ends with Operation 4. The rates shown in each box represent the effective capacity of that operation (LO2).

a. Determine the capacity of this process.

b. Which of the following three actions would yield the greatest increase in process capacity? (i) increase the capacity of Operation 1 by 15 percent; (ii) increase the capacity of Operation 2 by 10 percent; or (iii) increase the capacity of Operation 3 by 10 percent.

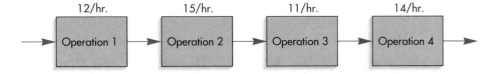

12/hr.   15/hr.   11/hr.   14/hr.

Operation 1 → Operation 2 → Operation 3 → Operation 4

MINI-CASE   http://www.grocerygateway.com

Grocery Gateway

In introducing a new product, the fear of competitors catching up and not knowing exactly what the customers want may result in making the wrong capacity decisions.

Such was the case for Grocery Gateway (GG), the grocery e-tailer in Toronto. In the height of the Internet craze of the late 1990s, GG managed to attract $30 million to start its business. Whereas a small grocery delivery business could just use a few trucks and shop at the local grocery stores, a larger outfit, having given guarantees of availability and quality to its thousands of customers, needs a warehouse with inventories. In 2000, GG managed to find investors to inject another $33 million into its

business, thus enabling it to build a larger (75,000 ft²) warehouse with more inventory. Groceries were purchased from Longo Brothers wholesale and retail chain. GG would deliver a customer's order in a three-hour window specified by the customer at the cost of $6 per delivery.

By the end of 2001, GG hadn't made any profit even though the number of its customers was increasing 30 percent per year and its revenue was $28 million in 2001. Was it because its market was too small or because its costs were too high? Thinking that it was the former reason, GG decided to expand its market to 10 urban centres as far away as Kitchener-Waterloo, moved into an even larger warehouse (280,000 ft²), and purchased the Direct Home Delivery company (GG then had 140 delivery trucks).

The revenue in 2002 almost doubled ($51 million) but with the much higher overhead GG now needed $85 million revenue to break even. Was this because the purchased groceries were too expensive or because customers wanted to also buy other goods such as hardware and liquor? Thinking it was a little of both, GG changed its supplier from Longo Brothers to Sobeys (which had cheaper groceries but that were not necessarily as fresh), and started to offer products from Home Depot and some liquor. This move attracted another $12 million from investors.

However, the customers were not happy with the prices—some claimed that GG's prices were more than those of the brick-and-mortar grocery stores, and others claimed that the quality of the produce was lower than before. Business was not growing and losses were piling up. Finally in August 2004, GG was sold to Longo Brothers for $7 million. Longo Brothers closed GG's warehouse and distributes the orders from its 17 retail stores and one distribution centre.

Questions

1. What mistakes did GG make?

2. Is the concept of grocery e-tailing, as attempted by GG, a sound one? Explain. Hint: You may contrast grocery e-tailing with what Amazon.com does and how it operates.

Source: M. Snider, "Too Good to Be True," *Profit* 23(5), November 2004, pp. 18–19.

MINI-CASE   http://www.shouldice.com

Shouldice Hospital

Shouldice Hospital, in Thornhill just north of Toronto, is a specialized private medical facility. It performs only hernia surgeries. Hernia is the rupture of a stomach muscle, usually in the groin, which results in organs such as intestines bulging out, causing discomfort. Shouldice Hospital was founded in 1945 by Dr. Earle Shouldice after he came back from World War II. Shouldice Hospital is famous internationally for its innovative surgery technique, its effective post-operation recovery methods, and its resort-like friendly and happy atmosphere. Only a local anesthetic is used during the surgery. Then patients are encouraged to move around as much as possible without hurting themselves. For example, food is served only in the common cafeteria, and patients need to use stairs to get to it.

The specialization on hernia results in increased expertise of the surgeons, reducing the operation time but at the same time increasing the quality of surgery. Only 1 percent of the patients need a second surgery later on, whereas more than 10 percent of patients using other hospitals need a second surgery. Another reason for the efficiency of Shouldice is that it utilizes its beds and operating rooms fully. The patient usually spends three days and three nights in the hospital. For example, a patient arrives Sunday afternoon, gets operated on Monday morning, recuperates on Tuesday and leaves on Wednesday after lunch.

Each day, Sunday to Thursday, 29–30 patients check in. Thus, there are 29–30 surgeries every workday. Each surgery, on average, takes just under one hour. Surgeries take place between 7:30 a.m. and 1:30 p.m. There are currently 12 full-time surgeons. A surgeon operates on two to three patients per day, and spends the rest of the time examining new patients (who can just walk in).

Questions

1. How many beds does Shouldice Hospital need?

2. How many operating rooms does Shouldice Hospital need?

3. What is the annual capacity of Shouldice Hospital (in terms of number of hernia operations)?

To access "Decision Analysis," the supplement to Chapter 5, please visit *Connect*.

CHAPTER 6
Process Design and Facility Layout

LEARNING OBJECTIVES

After completing this chapter, you should be able to:

LO1 Describe the basic production process types.

LO2 Discuss automated production technologies.

LO3 Describe steps of production process design and learn to draw process flow diagrams.

LO4 Describe the basic plant/facility layout types.

LO5 Solve simple assembly-line balancing problems.

LO6 Develop simple process (functional) layouts.

acing competition from other fast-food restaurants such as Burger King and Wendy's and to improve its efficiency, in the late 1990s, after doing R&D for six years at the cost of $20 million, McDonald's re-engineered its burger assembly process from make-to-stock to assemble-to-order. In the past, McDonald's would pre-make complete burgers and keep them on heated holding trays until they were either sold or discarded. In the new "made-for-you" system, the meat patties are pre-cooked and kept in special steamers, the universal holding cabinets. When a customer orders a burger, the bun is toasted and the burger is assembled. McDonald's implemented this system in most of its North American restaurants at a cost of $50,000 each. The result was a reduction of 0.25–0.5 percent in the cost of wasted burgers. However, it was discovered that "made-for-you" was too slow for large restaurants during peak times, resulting in lost sales. Recently, McDonald's has modified the system to accommodate large restaurants. How do companies make good process decisions? This is the topic of this chapter.

LO1 INTRODUCTION AND PROCESS TYPES

Product design, strategic capacity planning, process and layout design, and choices about location are among the most important decisions managers must make, because those decisions have long-term consequences for the organization.

Processes convert inputs into outputs; they are at the core of operations management. But the impact of processes goes beyond operations management: they affect the entire organization and its ability to achieve its mission. So process choices have strategic significance.

Process design and facility layout (i.e., the arrangement of the workplace) are closely tied, and for that reason these two topics are presented in a single chapter.

Process design determines the form and function of how production of goods or services is to occur. It has major implications for layout of facilities, equipment, and design of work systems. Process design occurs as a matter of course when new products are being designed or existing products are redesigned. However, process design and redesign also occurs due to technological changes in equipment and methods improvement.

The very first step in process design is to consider whether to **make or buy** some or all of a product or a segment of the production process. If a decision is made to buy a part/product or a segment of the production process, this eliminates the need to produce the part/product or perform that segment of production process.

Make-or-buy decisions are often strategic, based on existing or desired core capabilities. Other factors include available capacity, quality, whether demand is steady or temporary, the secrecy of technology, and cost.

The first part of the chapter covers basic process types, automation, and process design, whereas the second part is devoted to types of layout, assembly-line balancing, and designing process (functional) layouts.

Every production process is different, even in the same industry. However, there are certain similarities between processes based on quantity (volume) and variety of the products that are produced by the process, and the flexibility of the process. This enables us to classify processes into four basic types: job shop, batch, repetitive (assembly line), and continuous. Projects are discussed in Chapter 17.

Job Shop. A **job shop** process is used when a low quantity of high-variety customized goods or services will be needed. The process is *intermittent*; work shifts from one small job to the next, each with somewhat different requirements. High flexibility of equipment and skilled workers are important characteristics of a job shop. A manufacturing example of a job shop is a tool and die shop that is able to produce one-of-a-kind tools and dies (a die is a metal "mould" used to form a part under a press, e.g., to make a coin). A service example is the emergency ward of a hospital, which is able to process a variety of injuries and diseases.

process design Determining the form and function of how goods or services are produced.

make or buy Decide whether to make a part or product in-house or to buy it or a segment of production process from another company.

job shop A process type used when a low quantity of high-variety customized goods or services is needed.

The managerial challenge in a job shop is to schedule the jobs so that the due dates are met and the resources are utilized as much as possible.

Example 1

Hi-Bek Precision Spring Company is a small job shop located in the centre of Hamilton, Ontario. Owned and operated by R.J. Hick, Hi-Bek fills a specialty niche in manufacturing, making custom springs for a variety of distributors and manufacturers, from the springs in Jolly Jumper® baby exercisers, to Delta Faucet products, to Frost fences. Each spring requires a unique design.

Many of Hi-Bek's customers specify the design of the spring they need, sending a blueprint or a sample of the spring with their request, which includes (1) number of pieces desired (varying anywhere from 50 to 500,000); (2) type of material required, gauge of wire, any finishing required, etc.; and (3) the date by which the order is required.

All of these factors are taken into consideration by Hick, who personally quotes on all orders. Naturally, it is easier for Hick to quote on jobs that Hi-Bek has done before. The quoted price is based on cost of raw material, amount of material required, and the amount of time required to run the job. Other factors that influence the quote include delivery dates (rush orders command higher margins) and the total number of units.

After a quote has been accepted by a customer, the job order is sent to the shop floor. The shop operates from 7:30 a.m. to 5:00 p.m., Monday to Friday, employing between six and nine workers depending on the demand. Hick handles prioritization of orders and scheduling of machines and personnel along with the shop foreman. Production on a given job begins with the setup of the appropriate machine. Coiling machines can be custom configured for specific jobs, allowing for alterations to the gauge (thickness) and type of wire, the circumference and length of the spring, the number of coils in the spring, and the length of the spring ends. As well, the machine can be set to wind springs at varying speeds, depending on the level of quality required. Depending on the complexity of the product, a job being run in the machine may or may not require the full-time attention of an operator, and the time required for quality checking by the operator and foreman will vary accordingly. The setup of the job will cost the customer between $140 and $300, depending on complexity, and the skilled labour required to set up the job will cost $35 to $40 per hour. As well, customers are charged a "burden rate"—essentially a cost per hour for use of the machine during setup—of about $12 per hour. Finally, customers are charged for the operator's time to process the job, anywhere from $18 to $40 per hour.

Some jobs are quite simple, and springs are transported directly from the coiling machine to the oven on large metal racks where the steel is heated to temper it, giving the spring its tension (or its bounce, in the case of compression springs). Different springs require different temperatures (from 120°C for phosphor bronze—a low grade of wire—to 315°C for stainless steel), and a different length of time in the oven. The oven must also be scheduled for use for each individual job.

In the simplest jobs, after cooling, the springs can be packaged and arranged for shipping. In most cases, however, there are additional steps both before and after firing in the furnace.

Before firing, some springs require precision adjustments for their custom usage. The coiled springs are transported from the coiling machine to the precision-adjustment area of the shop in metal pails or large plastic drums, depending on the size of the job. An extension spring (the kind you stretch) or a torsion spring (the kind you twist) may require particularly crafted ends to suit its use. Each of these adjustments is done by hand, using a grinder or a press set for the specific job. Like the coiling machine, each press requires a certain amount of setup time and time for a shop worker to actually make the adjustments, all of which is factored into the price of the order. In the case of a press, a customer will be billed the same $140 to $300 per hour for setup though the customer is typically charged less for the labour required in the actual adjustment ($18 to 20 per hour) and the burden rate for the press (about $2 per hour).

Following the furnace, springs may undergo grinding or finishing, for either practical or aesthetic reasons. In some cases, springs are electroplated with zinc. This is a complex process involving electricity and acid or alkaline solutions, and for this reason is outsourced. Depending on the needs of the job, it may be outsourced to a company as near as Cambridge, Ontario (60 km away), or as far as Buffalo, NY (more than 100 km away). In other cases, springs are coated with oil or painted with "Black Japan" (a coating of linseed oil and Gilsonite varnish) for durability, depending on their eventual use. Unlike electroplating, these processes can be done in-house at a competitive rate.

Finally, the product is packaged and readied to be shipped. This, too, can take a good deal of time (10,000 springs can take a half day or more to pack).

The illustration below shows the layout diagram of the shop and the production process for three types of springs. The colours and icons correspond to the departments of the shop.

Job A is the type of compression spring used inside a ballpoint pen. Here, after setting up the coiling machine, the springs are wound, then heat-treated in the furnace and shipped to the customer.

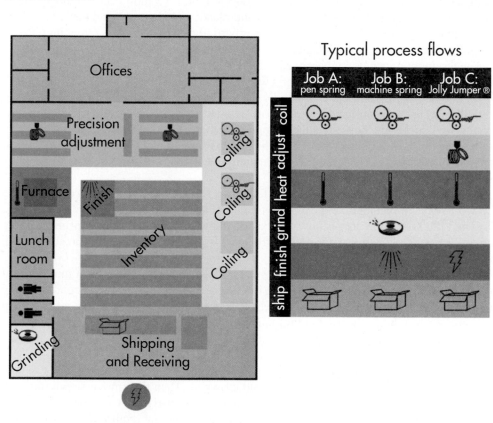

Job B is a typical machine spring, which undergoes the same basic steps as the ballpoint pen spring, but has its ends ground and is coated with oil in the finishing stage to add durability to the spring before shipping.

Job C is Jolly Jumper® springs. In this case, the coiling machine requires a special setup, because the Jolly Jumper® springs require tapered ends. After this, each spring must be precision adjusted to give it a specially looped end. It is heat treated, but before shipping is sent to an outside company to be electroplated. The springs then return to Hi-Bek and are shipped to the customer.

batch process A type of process used when a moderate volume and variety of goods or services is desired.

Batch. Batch process is used when a moderate volume/quantity and variety of goods or services is desired. The equipment need not be as flexible as in a job shop, but process is still intermittent. The skill level of workers doesn't need to be as high as in a job shop because there is less variety in the jobs. Examples of batch process include small bakeries, which make bread, cakes, or cookies in batches; movie theatres, which show movies to groups (batches) of people; and airlines, which carry planeloads (batches) of people from airport to airport. Other examples of products that lend themselves to batch production are beer, paint, ice cream, clothes, magazines, and books. For another example, see Stickley Furniture at the end of Chapter 14.

The managerial challenge in a batch process is scheduling batches in order to meet planned production and demand while utilizing the resources at a high level. Capacity issues and technology management are more important than in job shops.

Example 2

Great Western Brewing Company (GWB) was formed in 1989 when Molson Breweries of Canada decided to close its Saskatoon brewery. Its employees bought the plant and reopened it as a private company. GWB produces light, premium, Pilsner, and six other specialty beers, and packages them in glass and plastic bottles, cans, and kegs.

The main ingredient in beer is malt, which is partially sprouted barley. Other ingredients are grains such as corn or wheat, and hops, which produces its bitter taste.

The production process for beer can be divided into four stages: brewing, fermentation, finishing, and packaging. Brewing starts with mixing ground malt and water in the mash mixer and boiling it. Then, the mash (solid) and the wort (malt sugar liquid) are separated (by filtering) in the lauter tun. Next, the wort is boiled again in the brew kettle for approximately 1.5 hours while hops are added. Hops and other solids are separated from wort (by settlement) in the hot liquor tank. Then, the brew is aerated and cooled in the cold liquor tank. So far, the process has taken approximately five hours. The batch size in the brewing part of the process is about 20,000 litres.

Fermentation starts in one of the many fermenters where yeast is added. Yeast converts the wort sugar into alcohol and carbon dioxide (CO_2). Fermentation is complete in nine days and the fermented beer is now cooled and pumped into one of many primary aging tanks. The yeast, which settled in the fermenter, is recovered and reused in subsequent batches.

The brew kettle

Finishing involves cold aging (about 0 degree Celsius) of the beer for a minimum of one week in a primary aging tank and then filtering and recooling it into a secondary aging tank where it rests a further week. The beer is then ready to be filtered and cooled again and pumped to a bright beer (packing) tank where it is now ready to be packaged. CO_2 that has been collected during fermentation is injected into the beer each time it is moved, to ensure a specific level of CO_2 in the final product.

The bottles used are empty bottles collected from liquor stores. They are washed, electronically inspected, filled with beer, and crowned. Then they move slowly through a pasteurizer, and are labelled, packed, and palletized (approx. 100 cases per pallet). The canning process is similar but uses only new cans, which do not require washing or labelling. GWB's packaging capacity is 360 bottles and 480 cans per minute. Overall capacity of GWB is 45 million litres of beer per year.

Different types of beer differ in terms of taste, colour, and alcohol content. These are influenced by the ingredients, temperature, and length of each step of the process, yeast, hops, separation, and filtration. The chemistry of brewing is very complex and is still not fully understood. The equipment is specialized, with all beer following the same processing route. The remotely activated pumps and gauges are controlled by a central control room. Changeover from one type of beer to another requires washing the tanks, which takes approximately half an hour. The process flow diagram and plant floor plan (layout) are displayed below.

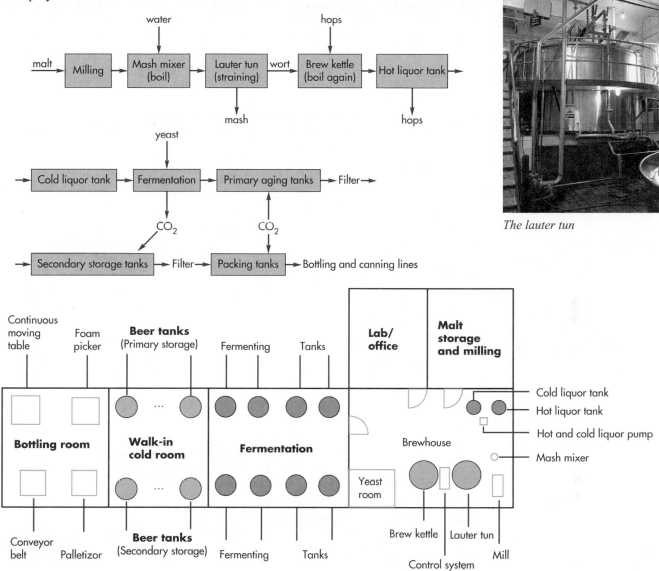

The lauter tun

Repetitive. When higher quantities of more standardized goods or services are needed, **repetitive process** is used. The standardized output means only slight flexibility of equipment is needed. Skill of workers is generally low. Examples of this type of process include **production lines** and **assembly lines**. In fact, this type of process is sometimes referred to as *assembly line.* A production line is a sequence of machines/workstations that perform operations on a part/product. An assembly line is a production line where parts are added to a product sequentially.

The line can be either machine-paced (same speed) or worker-paced (variable speed). Familiar products made by this type of process include automobiles, television sets, and computers. An example of repetitive service is an automatic carwash. Other examples of repetitive service include cafeteria lines and ticket collectors at sports events and concerts.

The managerial challenges in a production/assembly line are capacity balance, technology management, quality, and materials management.

repetitive process   A type of process used when higher quantities of more standardized goods or services are needed.

production line   A sequence of machines/workstations that perform operations on a part/ product.

assembly line   A production line where parts are added to a product sequentially.

Example 3

Paccar Trucks builds some of its high-end Kenworth and Peterbilt medium and heavy-duty trucks at its 360,000 ft^2 assembly plant in Sainte-Therese, Quebec. A truck has two major subassemblies: chassis and cab. The chassis is made up of the bottom frame, the engine and power train, wheels, etc. The Quebec plant receives its engines from Paccar's U.S. engine plants and Paccar buys the other major components from its suppliers. The cab and hood are purchased already fabricated. The Quebec plant paints them and stores them in a buffer area on the second floor (shown by blue lines in the layout diagram below). This is to let the paint dry and because it is more efficient to use a batch process for painting (i.e., a large number of the same colour cabs and hoods are painted one after another). Sixty hoods and 30 cabs can be stored in the buffer area. Typically, a cab and hood are painted two to five days before they are used.

Four out of every five trucks are white. However, the different interior, motor, chassis length, and brand result in approximately 40 different products. In addition, several options are available. Paccar constantly introduces new models offering better technologies such as no-idle solution (to provide heating or cooling to the sleeper cabin while the truck engine is turned off) and hybrid engines. The equipment is specialized but flexible. Most material handling is by overhead conveyors. Workers appreciate this in the frame shop where heavy (1–2.5 tonnes) and long (6–13 metres) beams are assembled. The overhead conveyors also save floor space.

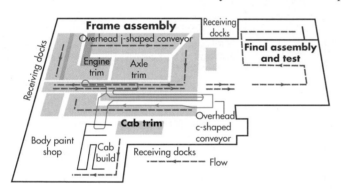

The parts and components are received just-in-time and delivered straight to the point of use. There are 31 receiving docks near the points of use. The two subassembly lines (chassis and cab) join in the middle of the left side of the plant (see the plant layout and the process flow diagram below) and the truck is hauled to the final assembly and test area on the right. Capacity of the plant is 40 trucks per eight-hour shift, which means that, at capacity, every 12 minutes a truck moves up one workstation. The Quebec plant periodically changes its employment level to match its production with North American demand for its trucks. In recent years, 60 to 70 trucks have been assembled per day during two shifts.

Process flow diagram for Paccar's Sainte-Therese, Quebec, Plant

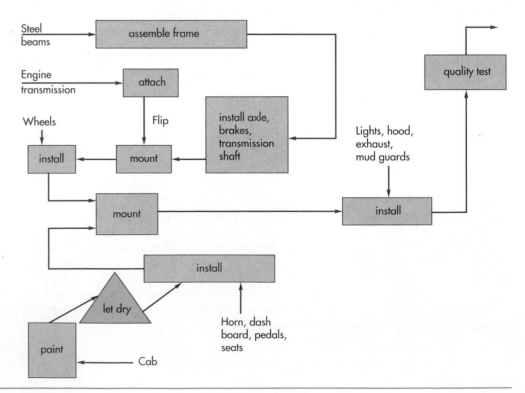

Continuous. When a very high volume of highly standardized output is desired, a **continuous process** is used. There is almost no variety in output and, hence, no need for equipment flexibility. As in assembly lines, workers are generally low skilled. Product is usually also continuous, i.e., it cannot be counted. Examples of products made using continuous process include steel, paper, sugar, flour, and salt. Continuous services include utilities and the Internet.

The managerial challenges in a continuous process are the same as in an assembly line, but because of faster speed of production, greater care is required for automated control of the flow, and start and stop of production are more challenging.

continuous process Used when a high volume of highly standardized output is required.

The Redpath Sugar Refinery is located on the Toronto waterfront. The refinery runs 24 hours a day, 7 days a week.

Raw Materials. Sugar Cane is grown on large plantations in the tropics and processed in huge mills, close to the field, by crushing the cane stalks and extracting the juice (sap). Boiling the juice crystallizes it into "raw sugar," which is purchased by Redpath Sugar and shipped to Toronto in huge cargo ships.

Cargos of raw sugar arrive at the refinery in volumes of up to 25,000 tonnes (this being the limit of ships passing through the St. Lawrence Seaway) and are unloaded by dockside cranes and then transferred by conveyor belt to the refinery's raw sugar shed. This building has a capacity of 65,000 tonnes and has a floor the size of two football fields, which is necessary because the seaway closes in the winter and all stocks of raw sugar must be brought in and stored before then to ensure continuous production year-round.

The Refining Process. Although the raw sugar is of a relatively high quality, it still contains a residue of original cane-trash, ash, waxes, as well as any additional solids or other impurities that might have contaminated the cargo during transportation. Refining is designed to remove all of these unwanted elements and to leave only pure sucrose at the end.

The "mingler"

The process commences with the transfer of the raw sugar into the refinery building, where it is weighed and fed into a mixing trough called a "mingler." Blended together with a solution of molasses and warm water, the resultant slurry ("magma") is spun at high speed in one of a set of oversized washing machines ("affination centrifugals"). The spun-off syrup is recycled, while the crystal ("washed raw sugar") is melted and dissolved in hot water to produce a syrup ("raw liquor"), which is then passed through a sequence of filters to remove the impurities.

Starting with a simple mechanical sieve ("strainer") that removes the larger visible solids, the liquor passes through a "carbonation" and "sweetland" system, whereby chalk (calcium carbonate) encapsulates the remaining solids, making them larger so that they can be removed by fine cloth filters in the sweetland presses. The final filtration, to remove the undesirable yellow colouration in the liquor, is done by the use of absorption in large tanks filled with commercial resin and carbon-based filtration agents, similar to those used in municipal water purification systems. The end result of this series of filtrations is a clear, colourless syrup ("fine liquor") consisting of nothing but sucrose and water.

Vacuum vessels used for re-crystallization

The fine liquor is now recrystallized by boiling it for an hour under vacuum. The resultant "white massecuite" (a combination of recrystallized sucrose, uncrystallized sucrose syrup, and water) is spun in the "white sugar centrifugals" to separate the liquid from the crystals. While the syrups are recycled to create additional crystals, the crystals of pure white sucrose are dried in large rotary driers ("granulators") to reduce their moisture content to less than .03 percent.

The granular sugar is either packaged in a range of weights or sold in larger "bulk" loads and shipped out in road or rail tanker loads (of up to 100 tonnes) for further use in a variety of industrial and commercial applications.

The Redpath Sugar Refinery in Toronto, Ontario

Flow Process Diagram

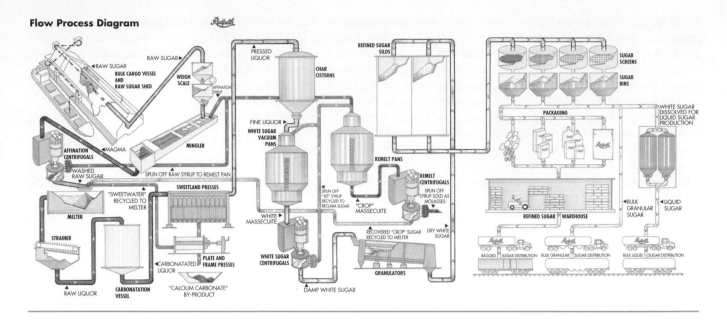

Table 6-1 provides an overview of major characteristics of the four types of production process.

The ideal is to have production process capabilities, such as equipment flexibility, match product requirements, such as product variety and quantity (volume). This relationship is displayed as the shaded main diagonal of the product-process matrix of Figure 6-1.

Failure to match product requirements and production process characteristics can result in inefficiencies and higher costs than are necessary, perhaps creating a competitive disadvantage. For example, using a batch process when there is only one product is usually inefficient because the process does not use enough automation. On the

Table 6-1

Major characteristics of the four types of production process

	Job Shop	Batch	Repetitive/ Assembly	Continuous
Product Variety	Customized	Semi-standardized	Standardized	Highly standardized
Volume	Low	Low-moderate	High	Very high
Equipment flexibility	Very high	Moderate	Low	Very low

Figure 6-1

The product–process matrix

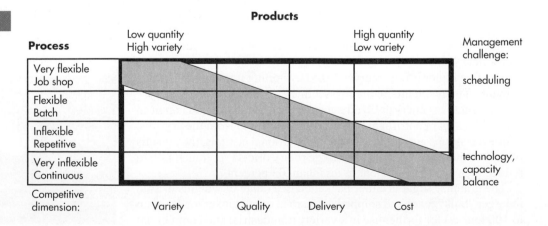

other hand, when there are many products produced on a continuous or assembly process, the frequent product switches will result in long change-over times, which are nonproductive.

Another consideration is that products often go through a *life cycle* that begins with low quantity, which increases as the product becomes better known. When that happens, a manager must know when to shift from one type of production process (c.g., job shop) to the next (e.g., batch).

The processes discussed above do not always exist in their "pure" forms. It is not unusual to find hybrid processes—processes that have elements of other process types embedded in them. For instance, if quantity/volume increases for some items, a process that began as, say, job shop or batch may evolve into batch or repetitive. This may result in having some part of process running as a job shop or batch process and others as repetitive process.

Another point is that processes that produce high quantity of products specialize in these products. This concept is called "focused factory." Recently, however, some companies have managed to handle high quantity and high variety on the same process, e.g., the "made-for you" system of McDonald's or Dell Computer's mass customization.

Within each production process, many individual operations are performed. The choice of operations used in a process depends on nature, shape, size, quantity, variety, and other competitive attributes of the products to be produced by the process. Examples of types of materials include metal, plastic, glass, wood, food ingredients, and yarn. Examples of shape include round, square, and with cavity. Examples of operations include forming (e.g., casting, forging), reshaping (e.g., drilling, cutting, bending, cold-drawing), and assembly (e.g., welding, bolting, gluing). A list of some common metal-working and non-metal-working operations is given in Table 6-2.

Table 6-2

Basic operations

Some Metalworking Operations				
Assembly	**Casting and Moulding**	**Cutting**	**Forming**	**Finishing**
Braze	Cast:	Broach	Draw	Blast
Cement	die, sand,	Drill	Extrude	Buff
Fasten	investment	Grind	Punch	Clean
Press-fit	Mould:	Hone	Roll	Debur
Shrink-fit	injection,	Mill	Trim	Heat treat
Solder	powered metal,	Shape	Swage	Paint
Weld	and permanent	Turn	Spin	Polish

Some Non-metalworking Operations				
Chemicals	**Food**	**Mining**	**Textiles**	**Lumber**
Crack	Can	Dry	Braid	Debark
Cook	Cook	Crush	Knit	Cure
Cure	Crush	Excavate	Polish	Joint
Distill	Freeze	Extract	Shrink	Kiln
Evaporate	Pasteurize	Load	Spin	Plane
Grind	Press	Screen	Wash	Saw
Screen	Sterilize	Smelt	Weave	Turn

Source: PKG Operations Management W/OM Software CD-Rom, 9th edition by Gaither/Fraizer. © 2002. Reprinted with permission of South-Western, a division of Thomson Learning, www.thomsonrights.com. Fax 800-730-2215.

LO2 AUTOMATION

automation Using machinery/equipment with sensing and control devices that enable it to operate automatically.

http://www.essarsteelalgoma.com/facilities/dspc/

A key question in process design is whether to automate. **Automation** is using machinery/equipment with sensing and control devices that enable it to operate automatically. If a company decides to automate, the next question is by how much. Automation can range from factories that are completely automated to a single automated operation.

Automation offers a number of advantages over human labour. It has low variability, whereas it is difficult for a human to perform a task in exactly the same way, rapidly, and on a repetitive basis. In a production setting, variability is detrimental to quality and to meeting schedules. Moreover, automated machines do not get bored or distracted or get injured, nor do they go out on strike, ask for higher wages, or file labour grievances.

Automation is frequently touted as a strategy necessary for competitiveness. For example, in steel-making, a "mini" mill, controlled by an integrated computer system, produces an uninterrupted hot band of steel using scrap metal and electrical charge. Mini mills have a substantial productivity advantage over foundries, which use iron ore in blast furnaces. An example of a mini-mill is the Direct Strip Production Complex of Algoma Steel (now part of Essar Steel, an Indian private company). Another example of using automation for competitiveness is the gigantic automated paper-making machines that automatically sense the thickness of paper and adjust to run at speeds of more than 60 km per hour.

However, automation also has certain disadvantages and limitations compared to human labour. To begin with, it can be costly. Technology is expensive; usually it requires high volumes of output to offset high initial costs. In addition, automation is much less flexible than human labour. Once a process has been automated, it is hard to change it. Moreover, workers sometimes fear automation because they may lose their jobs. That can have an adverse effect on morale and productivity.

An automated guided vehicle used in a John Deere factory

Decision makers must carefully examine the issue of whether to automate or the degree to automate, so that they clearly understand all the ramifications. Also, much thought and careful planning are necessary to successfully integrate automation into a production system. Otherwise, it can lead to major problems. GM invested heavily in automation in the 1980s only to find its costs increasing while flexibility and productivity took a nosedive. Its market had shrunk while it was increasing its capacity! Moreover, automation has important implications not only for cost and flexibility, but also for the fit with overall strategic priorities.

Generally speaking, there are three kinds of automation: fixed, programmable, and flexible.

Fixed automation is the most rigid of the three types. The concept was perfected by the Ford Motor Company in the early 1900s, and it has been the cornerstone of mass production in the auto industry. It uses high-cost, specialized equipment for a fixed sequence of operations. Low unit cost and high volume are its primary advantages; minimal variety and the high cost of making major changes in either product or process are its primary limitations.

Programmable automation involves the use of high-cost, general-purpose equipment controlled by a computer program that provides both the sequence of operations and specific details about each operation. Changing the process is as easy (or difficult) as changing the computer program. This type of automation has the capability of economically producing a fairly wide variety of low-volume products in small batches. Numerically controlled (N/C) machines and some robots are examples of programmable automation.

numerically controlled (N/C) machines Machines that perform operations by following mathematical processing instructions.

Numerically controlled (N/C) machines are programmed to follow a sequence of processing instructions based on mathematical relationships that tell the machine the details of the operations to be performed. The instructions are stored on a device such as a computer disk, magnetic tape, or microprocessor. Although N/C machines have been used for many decades, they are an important part of the new approaches to manufacturing. Individual machines may have their own computer; this is referred to as *computerized numerical control* (*CNC*). Or one computer may control a number of N/C machines, which is referred to as *direct numerical control* (*DNC*). The computer can directly use the dimensions of the item from the CAD software to accelerate machine programming.

N/C machines are best used in cases where parts are processed frequently and in small batches, where part geometry is complex, close tolerances are required, mistakes are costly, and there is the possibility of frequent changes in the design. The main limitations of N/C machines are the higher skill levels needed to program the machines and their high cost.

A **robot** consists of three parts: a mechanical arm, a power supply, and a controller. Unlike movie versions of robots, which vaguely resemble human beings, industrial robots are much less glamorous and much less mobile; most robots are stationary except for their movable arms.

robot A machine consisting of a mechanical arm, a power supply, and a controller.

Robots can handle a wide variety of tasks, including welding, assembly (mainly surface-mounting for circuit boards), loading and unloading of machines, painting, and testing. They relieve humans from heavy, dirty, and unsafe work and often eliminate drudgery.

Some uses of robots are fairly simple, others are much more complex. At the lowest level are robots that follow a fixed set of instructions. Next are programmable robots, which can repeat a set of movements after being led through the sequence. These robots "play back" a mechanical sequence much as a camcorder plays back a visual sequence. At the next level up are robots that follow instructions from a computer. At the top are robots that can recognize objects and make certain simple decisions.

Robots can be powered pneumatically (by air), hydraulically (by fluids), or electrically.

Flexible automation evolved from programmable automation. It uses equipment that is more customized than that of programmable automation. A key difference between the two is that flexible automation requires significantly less changeover time. This permits almost continuous operation of equipment *and* product variety without the need to produce in batches.

In practice, flexible automation is used in several different formats.

A *machining centre* is a machine capable of performing a variety of operations on parts. The machine is numerically controlled.

A **flexible manufacturing system (FMS)** is a group of machining centres, controlled by a computer, with automatic material handling and robots or other automated equipment. They can produce a variety of *similar* products. An FMS may have from three or four machines to more than a dozen. They are designed to handle intermittent processing requirements with some of the benefits of automation and some of the flexibility of individual, or stand-alone, machines (e.g., N/C machines). An FMS offers reduced labour costs and more consistent quality compared with more traditional manufacturing methods, lower capital investment and higher flexibility than "hard" automation, and relatively quick changeover time. An FMS appeals to managers who hope to achieve both the flexibility of job shop and the productivity of repetitive process.

Although the above are important benefits, an FMS also has certain limitations. One is that this type of system can handle a relatively narrow range of part variety, so it must be used for a family of similar parts requiring similar machining. Also, an FMS requires longer planning and development times than more conventional processing equipment because

Aliment Putter's Sainte-Sophie, Quebec, plant uses this Motoman Palletizing robot to arrange its cases of pickle jars into pallets (which can then be moved efficiently by forklifts). Before installing the robot, the palletizing step was a bottleneck in the process. Also, the heavy cases were difficult to handle manually.[1]

flexible manufacturing system (FMS) A group of machining centres controlled by a computer, with automatic material handling and robots or other automated equipment.

[1]http://www.motoman.com/motomedia/articles/Plant%209-06.pdf

Figure 6-2

Applicability of automated systems based on product quantity and variety

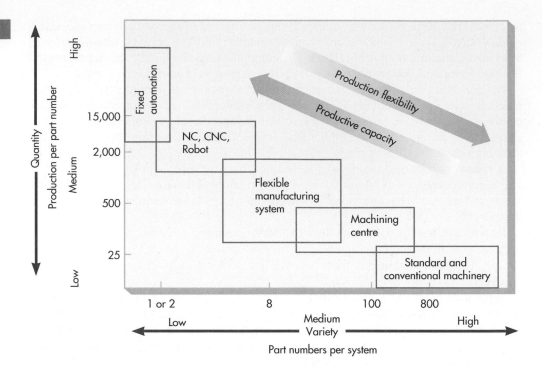

of its increased complexity and cost. Furthermore, companies sometimes prefer a gradual approach to automation, but FMS represents a sizable chunk of technology.

The suitability of these systems to a production environment primarily depends on the variety and quantity of products. See Figure 6-2.

computer-integrated manufacturing (CIM)

A system for linking a broad range of manufacturing and other activities through an integrating computer system.

Computer-integrated manufacturing (CIM) is a system that uses an integrating computer system to link a broad range of manufacturing and other activities, including engineering design and production planning and control. More encompassing CIM systems can link order taking, scheduling, purchasing, inventory control, shop control, and distribution to manufacturing. In effect, a CIM system integrates information from other areas of an organization with manufacturing. The overall goal of using CIM is to link various parts of an organization to achieve rapid response to customer orders and/or product changes, to allow rapid production, and to reduce *indirect* labour costs.

LO3 PROCESS DESIGN

Process Design determines the form and function of how production of goods or services is to occur. It involves identifying the activities and their sequence, resources, and controls directly needed in the production of goods or rendering of services.

There are other activities needed in operating an organization (besides the creation of goods and services) that should also be designed as processes, such as order taking and sales, planning, purchasing, and staffing. These are referred to as "business" processes. Our focus here is the production (or operations) process design.

We assume that this is a new production process for a new product. More often, production processes are only redesigned and this is done by either automating one part of the process or replacing a machine with a newer one. In this case, only some of the following steps need to be performed.

Methodology for Production Process Design

Production process design is part of the product design methodology of Chapter 4, and, as such, was briefly mentioned there. Here, we will expand it.

Given the product quantity, variety, cost, quality, delivery speed (lead time), and product specifications (nature, shape, size, components, and how they fit together),

1. **Define the production process** (called Operations Assessment in Stage 2 of Stage-gate model for product design)
   - Determine how completed the input materials should be. These are make-or-buy decisions.
   - Set production process objectives:
     - Capacity (or production speed), flexibility
     - Type of process (job shop, batch, assembly, continuous)
     - Cost (fixed, variable), process quality capability
     - Technology/extent of automation, production start date
   - Determine the nature of process in general.

2. **Production process development** (in Stage 3 of Stage-gate model)

   2.1 Conceptualize the design

   This answers the question: How do you get from inputs (materials) to output? That is, what is the sequence of major operations (activities) needed?
   - Develop a few alternative process concepts (sketches). Two approaches can be used:
     - Incremental: do one step at a time from start to end.
     - Hierarchical (top down): break the whole job into two operations, then divide each into sub-operations, etc., until the desired level of detail is reached.
   - Usually a *process flow diagram* is used to show the operations and the movement of materials through the operations.
   - Evaluate each alternative process concept.

   2.2 Make an embodiment of the design
   - Choose one process concept and complete the design.
   - Build a prototype process (can use computer modelling) and test it.
     - Determine the resources (machines, equipment, and labour) needed, in general.
     - Estimate the costs, quality, etc., and compare with the objectives.
   - Refine the process and re-evaluate it.

   2.3 Create a detailed design
   - Finalize the process specifications
     - Determine the specific machines, equipment (their capacities and make), and labour.
     - Design the plant layout.
     - Design the work centres.

3. **Buy the machines and equipment, recruit workers, and start trial runs** (in Stage 4 of Stage-gate model)

Drawing a **process flow diagram** starts with identifying the boundaries of the process (inputs and outputs) and the level of detail required. The incremental approach involves following the flow of materials (or customers, in services) through the transformation process, and identifying the activities and resources (machines, labour, and their capabilities) required and their sequence. Experience with a similar process is useful. For technical products, expertise of process/manufacturing engineers is required.

process flow diagram
Shows the operations and movement of material through the operations.

As an example, the process flow diagram for making a cheeseburger in McDonald's is as follows:

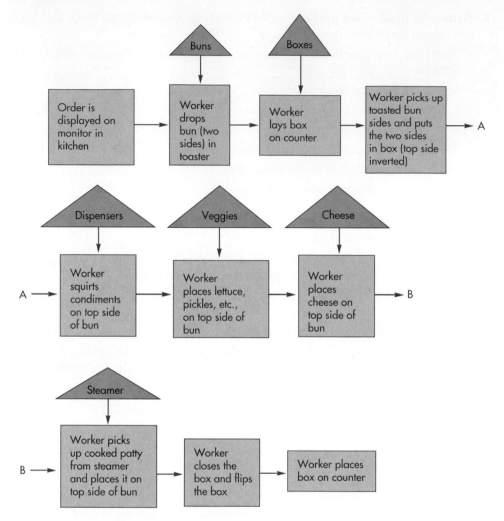

Note that storage is shown by a triangle and an operation is shown by a rectangle. Also note that flows (arrows) are usually from left to right. If there is a need to show the information flows, they could be shown as dashed arrows.

The following two examples illustrate the basics of process design.

Example 5

A company wants to diversify into mass-production of bread. It requires a process flow diagram.

Solution

We start with the recipe for making a loaf of bread:

1. Mix flour, salt, yeast, and water to obtain dough.
2. Knead the dough.
3. Shape the dough into a ball, put in a pan and leave to rise.
4. Bake in oven.
5. Let bread cool and remove from pan.

Because of the large quantity of ingredients (and the economy of quantity buying), a raw material storage room will be used. Because mixing large quantities of ingredients by hand is difficult, a mixing machine is required. The same reason applies to kneading. As it happens, a machine exists that does both mixing and kneading. To automate the shaping, the easiest method is to dump the big lump of dough into a hopper that cuts and drops small pieces of dough in the bread pans, which are then transported on a conveyor belt for a while to let bread rise and then into an open-ended oven (like an automated carwash). Next, the pans are transported on a conveyor belt for a while to cool down. Finally, bread loaves are taken out of the pans, sliced, and bagged.

The following process flow diagram is a good first step:

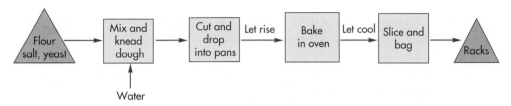

Example 6

Suppose you wish to design a production process to make simple oak tables. The input material is oak planks approximately 2 inches thick by 6 inches wide by 6 feet long. The tables will have square tops with dimensions of 1 inch thick by 3 feet each side. Each of the four legs for the table should be round with a radius of 1 inch and length of 3 feet. All parts are sanded and varnished before assembly. The legs are attached to the top using brackets. The low production quantity implies batch production. Design a production process to manufacture the tables by drawing a process flow diagram. Identify the machines used for each operation. *Hint:* Saw a plank in half thickness and glue the resulting boards side-by-side to form part of table top. To make the legs, saw the planks into 2-inch wide segments and then use a lathe to make them round.

Solution

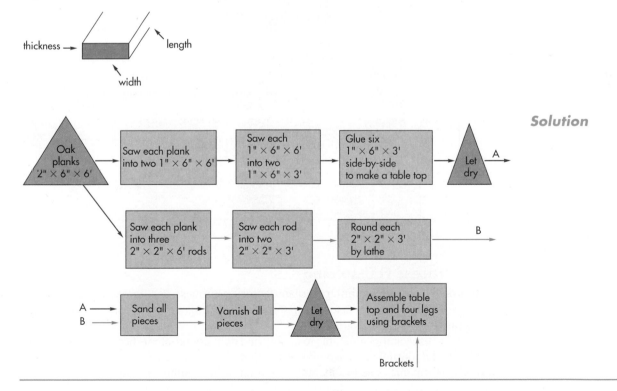

The Integrated Definition (IDEF) method is a hierarchical top-down approach to process design. Starting from the name/function of the process (e.g., "sell insurance"), the process design team decomposes it into its linked components step by step until the level of detail desired is reached. IDEF is a conceptual approach requiring brainstorming rather than recollection of past actual processes. At each stage, the team discusses and either approves the decomposition or backtracks.[2]

Secura Insurance Co. of Switzerland hired Coopers & Lybrand to redesign its processes, one of which was the car insurance sales process. A workshop of the managers was held over three days to teach them the IDEF method. The "sell insurance" process was used as an example. Here is how the stages of decomposition of "sell insurance" progressed.[3]

Day 1:

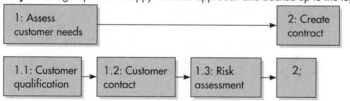

Day 2: The group was unhappy with this approach and backed up to the top:

Day 3: The process was broken into many "short" processes, each starting and ending with customer

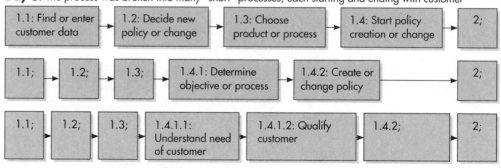

Service Process Fail-safeing

Service process design is similar to manufacturing process design except that instead of material, the flow of the customer or something belonging to the customer should be followed (as illustrated in Example 7).

Services are especially vulnerable to quality and delivery problems because the customer is usually present during service delivery and there is little time to fix any problems then. That is why companies need to identify potential failure points and incorporate features

---

[2]For more information, see http://www.idef.com.
[3]Example 7 is from J. Fulscher and S.G. Powell, "Anatomy of a Process Mapping Workshop," *Business Process Management Journal* 5(3), 1999, pp. 208ff.

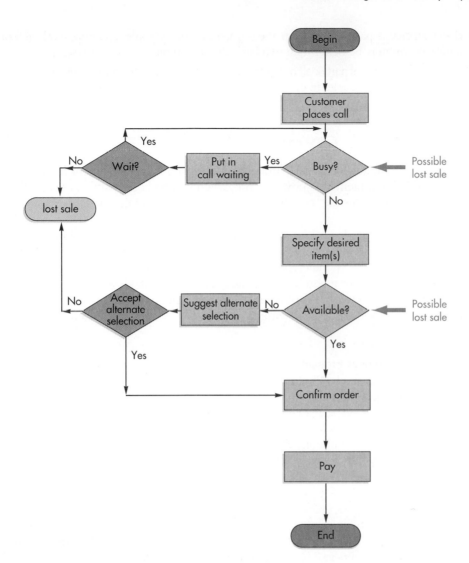

Figure 6-3

Fail-safeing phone order-taking process

that minimize the chance of failure. Figure 6-3 illustrates the fail-safeing of a telephone order-taking process. Ovals show events of interest and diamonds show decision points. The steps of the process are in the sequence from the perspective of a customer. The possible failure points are (1) if all the customer service representatives are busy and (2) if the specific item desired by the customer is not available. A good order-taking process will have backup plans in case of either failure. The usual ones are (1) to use a call-waiting system and (2) to suggest substitute products. These plus well-trained servers result in a robust system that provides consistent performance.

Customer Perception in Service Process Design

Another difference with manufacturing is that a service is usually varied and intangible. This raises the customer perception issue. Some suggestions to improve customer perception in services are:

- Do not raise customer expectations too high in the beginning. This is because customers compare their expectation and the actual service they receive in order to judge the quality of service.
- End the service positively because customers remember the end more.
- If the service is pleasurable, divide it into segments. For example, two short rides in an amusement park may be better than one long ride.

- If the service is painful, combine the segments. For example, cleaning teeth in a one-hour session may be better than two half-hour sessions.
- Let customers control part or all of the process. For example, self-services such as ATMs are preferred by most people. In this case, it is important to make the process user-friendly.
- Communicate the evidence of quality to customers.

LO4 TYPES OF LAYOUT

Layout refers to the location of departments, work centres, or equipment in the facility/plant. A good layout facilitates flow of work, whereas a bad one results in congestion.

This section describes the main types of layout designs and the models used to obtain good layout designs.

The need for layout planning arises both in designing new facilities and in redesigning existing facilities. The most common reasons for redesign of layouts include inefficient operations (e.g., excessive material handling/delay), changes in the design of products, changes in the quantity or mix of outputs, and changes in methods or equipment.

There are generally two types of layout—product (line) layout (for assembly and continuous processes) and process (functional) layout (for job shop and batch processes).

Product (Line) Layout

product layout Arranges production resources linearly according to the progressive steps by which a product is made.

Product layout arranges production resources linearly according to the progressive steps by which a product is made. Product layout is used to achieve a smooth and rapid flow of large quantities of goods or customers through a system. This is made possible by highly standardized goods or services that allow highly standardized, continual production. The work is divided into a series of standardized tasks, permitting specialization of both labour and equipment. Because only one or few very similar items are involved, it is feasible to arrange an entire layout to correspond to the production requirements of the product. For instance, if a portion of a manufacturing operation required the sequence of cutting, sanding, and painting, the appropriate pieces of equipment would be arranged in that sequence. And because each item follows the same sequence of operations, it is often possible to utilize fixed-path material-handling equipment such as conveyors to transport items between operations. The resulting arrangement forms a line like the one in Figure 6-4. In manufacturing environments, a line refers to a production line or an assembly line, depending on the type of activity involved. In services, the term *line* may or may not be used. It is common to refer to a cafeteria line as such but not a car wash, although from a conceptual standpoint the two are nearly identical. Figure 6-5 illustrates the layout of a typical cafeteria line. Examples of this type of layout are less plentiful in services because service requirements usually exhibit too much variability to make standardization feasible. Without high standardization, many of the benefits of a repetitive process are lost. When lines are used, certain compromises must

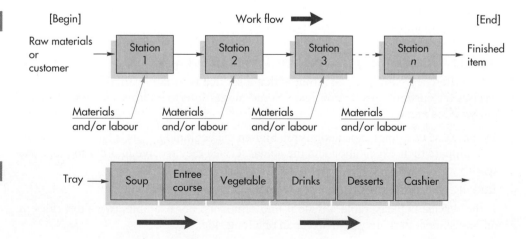

Figure 6-4

A product (line) layout

Figure 6-5

A cafeteria line

be made. For instance, an automatic car wash provides equal treatment to all cars—the same amount of soap, water, and scrubbing—even though cars may differ considerably in cleaning needs. As a result, very dirty cars may not come out completely clean, and relatively clean cars go through the same system with considerable waste of soap, water, and energy.

Product layouts achieve a high degree of labour and equipment utilization, which tends to offset their high equipment cost. Because items move quickly from operation to operation, the amount of work-in-process is often minimal. Consequently, operations are so closely tied to each other that the entire system is highly vulnerable to being shut down because of mechanical failure or absenteeism. *Preventive maintenance*—periodic inspection and replacement of worn parts or those with high failure rates—reduces the probability of breakdowns during the operations. Of course, no amount of preventive maintenance can completely eliminate failures, so management must take measures to provide quick repair. These include maintaining an inventory of spare parts and having repair personnel available to quickly restore equipment to normal operation.

A Cadillac assembly line

Advantages of product layouts include low-cost production and simplified accounting, purchasing, and inventory control.

Disadvantages of product layouts include higher equipment cost; dull, repetitive jobs; repetitive stress injuries; and inflexibility in response to changes in the quantity of output or in product mix.

Process (Functional) Layout

Process layout arranges production resources together according to similarity of function. It processes items that have a variety of production requirements. The variety of jobs requires frequent adjustments to equipment. This causes a discontinuous work flow, which is referred to as *intermittent processing*. A manufacturing example of a process layout is a *machine shop*, which has separate departments for milling, grinding, drilling, and so on. Items that require those operations are frequently moved in lots or batches to the departments in a sequence that varies from job to job. Consequently, variable-path material-handling equipment (forklift trucks, skids on wheels, tote boxes, etc.) is needed.

process layout Arranges production resources together according to similarity of function.

The use of *general-purpose equipment* provides the flexibility necessary to handle a wide range of production requirements. Workers who operate the equipment are usually skilled. Figure 6-6 illustrates the departmental arrangement typical of a process layout.

Process layouts are quite common in services. Examples include the emergency department of a hospital, a grocery store and an auto repair shop. For instance, an emergency department may have areas consisting of emergency rooms, X-ray rooms, surgery rooms, etc.

Because equipment in a process layout is arranged by type rather than by production sequence, the system is much less vulnerable to shutdown caused by mechanical failure or absenteeism. In manufacturing systems, especially, idle equipment is usually available to replace machines that are temporarily out of service. Moreover, because items are often processed in lots, there is considerably less interdependence between successive operations than with a product layout. Maintenance costs tend to be lower because the equipment is less specialized than that of product layouts, and the grouping of machinery permits repair personnel to become skilled in handling that type of equipment. Machine similarity reduces the necessary investment in spare parts. On the negative side, routing and scheduling must be done on a continual basis to accommodate the variety of production requirements typically imposed on these systems. Material handling is inefficient, and unit handling costs are generally much higher than in product layouts. In-process inventories can be substantial due to batch processing. Furthermore, it is not uncommon for such systems to have equipment utilization rates under 50 percent because of routing and scheduling complexities related to the variety of production requirements being handled.

Figure 6-6

Process (functional) layout

| Dept. A | Dept. C | Dept. E |
| Dept. B | Dept. D | Dept. F |

Standard Aero provides a variety of maintenance, repair, and overhaul services to the aviation industry, including repair of gas turbine engines. It has locations in Winnipeg, the United States, Europe, and Asia. In the 1990s, among other things, Standard Aero reorganized its repair facilities into cellular layout. Instead of a job shop layout where similar machines are bunched up together, Standard Aero segmented the repair process and also grouped similar parts into cells. Each cell is operated by a self-managed team whose performance is measured and displayed in front of the cell. Standard Aero has become so proficient at conversion into cellular layout that it started a division that sells this service to other engine repair facilities. In 2007, Standard Aero was purchased by Dubai Aerospace Enterprises.

cellular layout Layout in which different machines are arranged in a cell that can process items that have similar processing requirements.

group technology Grouping items with similar design or manufacturing characteristics into part families.

Cellular Layout

A **cellular layout** is a type of layout in which different machines are arranged in a *cell* that can process items with similar processing requirements, called *part families*. A cell is, in effect, a miniature version of a product layout. A cell may have no conveyorized movement of parts between machines, or may have a flow line connected by a conveyor (automatic transfer). Figure 6-7 compares a typical functional (process) layout and a cellular layout. Observe that in the cellular layout, machines are arranged to handle all of the operations necessary for a group (family) of similar parts. Thus, all parts in the same family follow the same route, although minor variations (e.g., skipping an operation) are possible. In contrast, the functional (process) layout involves multiple paths for these parts.

A cell is usually U-shaped (see Figure 6-8). A U-shaped line permits increased communication among workers on the line, thus facilitating teamwork. Flexibility in work assignments is increased because workers can handle not only adjacent stations but also stations on opposite sides of the line.

There are numerous benefits of cells. These include faster processing time, increased capacity, less material handling, less work-in-process inventory, and reduced setup times.

Grouping of similar items is known as **group technology** and involves identifying items with similarities in either design or manufacturing characteristics, and grouping them into part

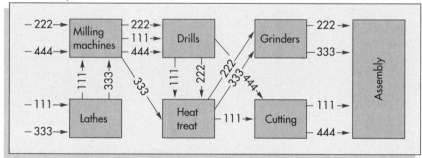

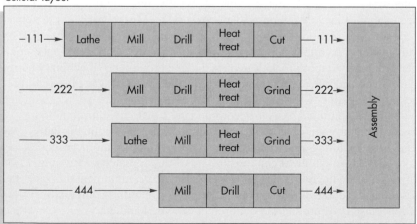

Figure 6-7

Comparison of functional (process) and cellular layouts

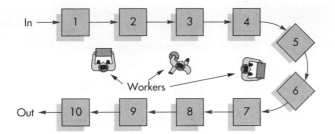

Figure 6-8

A U-shaped cell

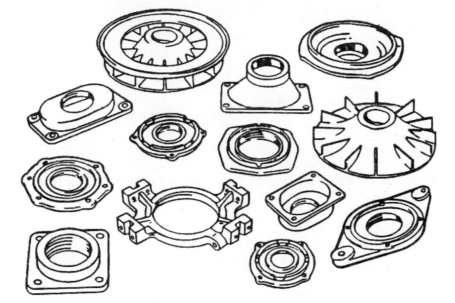

Figure 6-9

A group of parts with similar characteristics

families. Design characteristics include size, shape, material, features (holes, slots, notches, grooves), and function; manufacturing characteristics involve the type/sequence of operations and tolerance (precision) required. Figure 6-9 illustrates a group of parts with similar characteristics.

Once similar items have been identified, items can be classified according to their families, and a system can be developed that facilitates retrieval of these codes from the database for purposes of design and manufacturing. For instance, a designer can use the system to determine if there is an existing part similar or identical to the one that needs to be designed. It may happen that an existing part, with some modification, is satisfactory. This greatly enhances the productivity of design. Similarly, planning the manufacturing of a new part can include matching it with one of the part families in existence, thereby alleviating much of the burden of specific processing details.

The conversion to group technology is often a major undertaking; it is a time-consuming job that involves the analysis of a considerable amount of data. Three primary methods for accomplishing this are visual inspection, examination of design and production data, and production flow sequence and routing analysis. For an example of a cellular layout, see the photo and caption of Standard Aero.

Warehouse Layout

The design of a warehouse is based on a different set of factors than the design of factories. Items requiring cold storage are stored together in freezers and coolers. Frequency and size of orders is an important consideration; items that are ordered frequently and in large amounts should be placed near the entrance to the warehouse (or receiving/shipping area), and those ordered infrequently or in small amounts should be placed toward the rear of the warehouse. Any correlation between items is also significant (e.g., item A is usually ordered with item B), suggesting that placing those two items close together would reduce

Federated Co-op's Warehouse

This 278,000 square foot warehouse/distribution centre in Saskatoon is a hub of activity 24 hours a day. Federated Co-operatives Ltd. is a wholesale grocery and hardware distributor in Western Canada. Most activities occur in the staging area on the north side of the warehouse. Shipments from manufacturers and producers arrive on pallets and are stored either on the dry grocery racks on the right, on the floor in the promotion area in the centre (closest to the staging area), or on racks in the produce, cooler, or freezer areas on the top left. Orders from customers, approximately 270 retail Co-op stores, get picked by order pickers on pallet jacks and are collected in the staging area for trucking. Repack, in the bottom centre, is a secure area for expensive items such as batteries and open

cases of items, where order pickers pick items on foot and place them in baskets.

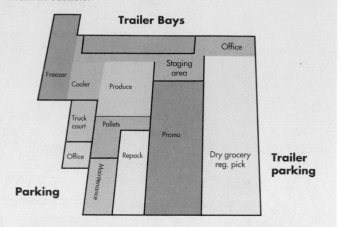

the cost and time of *picking* (retrieving) those items. As an example, see the "Federated Co-op's Warehouse" OM in Action.

Retail Layout

The objectives that guide design of manufacturing layouts often pertain to cost minimization and product flow. However, with retail layouts such as department stores, supermarkets, and specialty stores, designers take into account the presence of customers and the opportunity to influence sales. Customer flow is an important factor to consider.

Office Layout

Office layouts underwent a transformation as the flow of paperwork was replaced with electronic communication. That means that there is less need to place office workers in a layout that optimizes the physical transfer of information or paperwork. A new trend is to create an image of openness; office walls are giving way to low-rise partitions.

LAYOUT DESIGN STEPS

The following steps are used in manufacturing layout design. Other layout designs follow similar steps.

- Determine the location of receiving and shipping.
- For "product layout," fit the process flow diagram onto a sketch of the factory floor, starting from receiving and ending in shipping. Determine the approximate location of each part of the process.
- For "process layout," determine the expected work flow between each pair of departments, and place the two departments with the highest workflows closest to each other.
- Continue until all departments are located.
- Keep special requirements of machines in mind (e.g., a heavy press needs a strong foundation, the paint department needs a clean environment).
- Allow space for machines, in-feeds, out-feeds, workers, and carts/forklifts.
- Keep rearranging the plan using feedback from workers until you find what works best.
- On the factory floor, paint an outline of machines, in-feed and out-feed spaces.

- Walk through the normal sequence of activities.
- Run the electricity and other lines, and move the machines in.

LO5 ASSEMBLY-LINE BALANCING

Assembly lines range from fairly short, with just a few operations, to long lines that have a large number of operations. Automobile assembly lines are examples of long lines. At the assembly line for Ford Mustang, a Mustang travels about 14 kilometres from start to finish! Figure 6-10 illustrates the assembly chart for a typical automobile.

Many of the benefits of a product (line) layout relate to the ability to divide the required work into a series of tasks (e.g., "assemble parts C and D") that can be performed quickly and routinely by low-skilled workers or specialized equipment. The durations of these tasks typically range from a few seconds to a few minutes. Most time requirements are so brief that it would be impractical to assign only one task to each worker. For one thing, most workers would quickly become bored by the limited job scope. For another, the number

http://www.ford.com

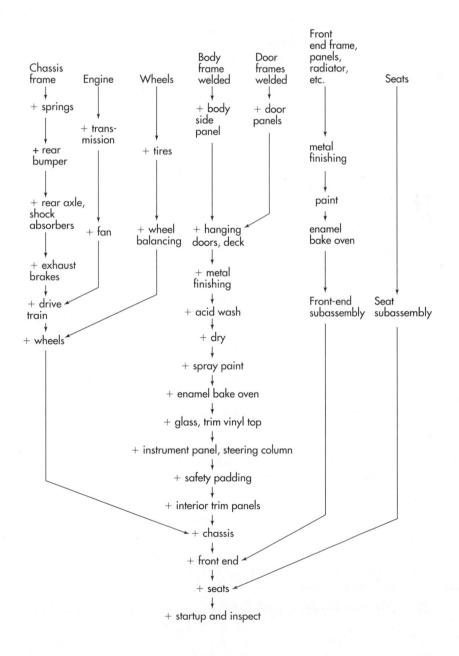

Figure 6-10

Assembly chart for a typical automobile

of workers required to complete even a simple product or service would be enormous. Instead, tasks are usually grouped into manageable bundles and assigned to workstations staffed by one or two operators.

Assigning tasks to workstations in such a way that the workstations have approximately equal time requirements is referred to as **line balancing**. This minimizes the idle time along the line and results in high utilization of labour and equipment. Idle time occurs if task times are not equal among workstations; some stations are capable of producing at higher rates than others. These "fast" stations will experience periodic waits for the output from slower stations or to avoid build-ups of work in downstream stations. Unbalanced lines are undesirable in terms of inefficient utilization of labour and equipment and because they may create morale problems at the slower stations for workers who must work continuously.

The major obstacle to attaining a perfectly balanced line is the difficulty of forming task bundles that have the same duration. One cause of this is that it may not be feasible to combine certain activities into the same bundle, either because of differences in equipment requirements or because the activities are not compatible (e.g., risk of contamination of paint from grinding). Another cause of difficulty is that differences among task lengths cannot always be overcome by grouping the tasks. A third cause of an inability to perfectly balance a line is that the technological sequence may prohibit otherwise desirable task combinations. Consider a series of three operations that have durations of two minutes, four minutes, and two minutes, as shown in the following diagram. Ideally, the first and third operations could be combined at one workstation and have a total time equal to that of the second operation. However, it may not be possible to combine the first and third operations. In the case of an automatic car wash, scrubbing and drying operations could not realistically be combined at the same workstation due to the need to rinse cars between the two operations.

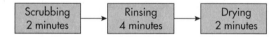

Usually, each workstation has one worker who handles all of the tasks at that station, although an option is to have several workers at a single workstation. For purposes of illustration, however, all of the examples and problems in this chapter have workstations with one worker.

A manager could decide to use anywhere from one to five workstations to handle five tasks. With one workstation, all tasks would be done at that station; with five stations, one task would be assigned to each station. If two, three, or four workstations are used, some or all of the stations will have multiple tasks assigned to them. How does a manager decide how many stations to use?

The primary determinant is the line's **cycle time** (also called **takt time**). The cycle time is the *maximum* time allowed at each workstation to perform its assigned tasks before the unit moves on. The cycle time also establishes the output rate of a line. For instance, if the cycle time is two minutes, units will come off the end of the line at the rate of one every two minutes.

As a general rule, the cycle time is determined by the desired output rate. We can calculate the cycle time using this formula:

$$CT = \frac{OT}{D} \tag{6-1}$$

where

CT = Cycle time

OT = Operating time per day

D = Desired output per day (i.e., demand)

line balancing Assigning tasks to workstations in such a way that the work stations have approximately equal time requirements.

cycle time The maximum time allowed at each workstation to complete its set of tasks on a unit.

For example, suppose that the desired output rate is 480 units per day, and the line will operate for eight hours per day (480 minutes). Using Formula 6-1, the necessary cycle time is

$$\frac{480 \text{ minutes per day}}{480 \text{ units per day}} = 1.0 \text{ minute per unit}$$

The number of workstations that will be needed is a function of the cycle time, the sum of task times, and our ability to combine tasks into workstations. We can determine the *theoretical minimum* number of workstations necessary, given a cycle time, as follows:

$$N_{min} = \frac{\Sigma t}{CT} \qquad\qquad (6\text{-}2)$$

where

N_{min} = Theoretical minimum number of workstations

Σt = Sum of task times

Given cycle time of 1 minute per unit, if sum of task times is 2.5 minutes, the minimum number of workstations required to achieve this goal is:

$$N_{min} = \frac{2.5 \text{ minutes per unit}}{1 \text{ minute per unit per workstation}} = 2.5 \text{ workstations}$$

Because 2.5 workstations is not feasible, it is necessary to *round up* (because 2.5 is the minimum) to three workstations. Thus, the actual number of workstations used will equal or exceed three, depending on how successfully the tasks can be grouped into work bundles.

A very useful tool in line balancing is a **precedence network**. Figure 6-11 illustrates a simple precedence network. It visually portrays the tasks that are to be performed along with the *precedence* requirements; that is, the *order* in which tasks must be performed. The network is read from left to right, so the initial task(s) are on the left and the final task is on the right. In terms of precedence relationship, we can see from the diagram, for example, that the only requirement to begin task *b* is that task *a* must be finished. However, in order to begin task *d*, tasks *b* and *c* must *both* be finished.

Now let's see how a line is balanced. This involves assigning tasks to workstations. Generally, no techniques are available that guarantee an optimal set of assignments. Instead, managers employ rule of thumb or *heuristic (intuitive) rules*, which provide good sets of assignments. A number of line-balancing heuristics are in use, two of which are described here for purposes of illustration:

1. Assign the task with the longest time.

2. Assign the task with the most followers.

The following tasks are all tasks that you would encounter by following all paths (in the direction of arrows) from the task in question through the precedence network.

The general procedure used in line balancing is described in Table 6-3.

precedence network
A diagram that shows the tasks and their precedence requirements.

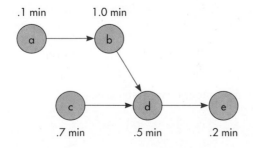

Figure 6-11

A simple precedence network

Table 6-3

Line balancing procedure

1. Identify the cycle time and determine the minimum number of workstations.

2. Make assignments to workstations in order, beginning with workstation 1. Tasks are assigned to workstations moving from left to right through the precedence network. Start each workstation with time left = cycle time.

3. Before each assignment, use the following criteria to determine which tasks are eligible and will fit:

    a. All its preceding tasks in the network have been assigned.

    b. The task time does not exceed the time left at the workstation.

    If no eligible tasks will fit, set idle time = time left and move on to the next workstation.

4. Assign tasks (and break ties) using one of these heuristic rules:

    a. Assign the task with the longest time.

    b. Assign the task with the most followers.

5. After each task assignment, update the time left at the workstation by subtracting the time of assigned task from time left.

6. Continue until all tasks have been assigned to workstations. Calculate total idle time.

Example 8

Assign the tasks shown in Figure 6-11 to workstations using a cycle time of 1.0 minute. Use the heuristic rule "Assign the task with the most followers."

Solution

Workstation	Time Left	Eligible	Will Fit	Task (time)	Idle Time
1	1.0	a, c	a, c*	a (.1)	
	.9	b, c	c	c (.7)	
	.2	b	—		.2
2	1.0	b	b	b (1.0)	
	.0	d	—		.0
3	1.0	d	d	d (.5)	
	.5	e	e	e (.2)	
	.3	—	—		.3
					.5

*Task a was assigned because it has more followers (three, vs. two for task c).

Comment: The initial "Time Left" for each workstation is equal to the cycle time. For a task to be eligible, tasks preceding it on the precedence network must have been assigned, and for it to fit, the task's time must not exceed the workstation's time left.

Two widely used measures of effectiveness of the set of assignments are:

percentage idle time 100 times sum of idle times per unit divided by actual number of workstations times cycle time.

1. The **percentage idle time** of the line. This is sometimes referred to as the *balance delay*. It can be calculated as follows:

$$\text{Percentage idle time} = \frac{\text{Sum of idle times per unit}}{N_{\text{actual}} \times \text{cycle time}} \times 100 \tag{6-3}$$

where N_{actual} = Actual number of workstations.

For the preceding example, the value is:

$$\text{Percentage idle time} = \frac{.5}{3 \times 1.0} \times 100 = 16.7\%$$

2. The *efficiency* of the line. This is calculated as follows:

Efficiency = 100 − percentage idle time   (6-4)

In the preceding example, efficiency = 100% − 16.7% = 83.3%

Example 9

Suppose we were to design an assembly line for assembling the oak accessory table shown in the following photos. Assume the top and legs come as subassemblies and that both leg assemblies need to be screwed to the top before leg braces (cross-bars) can be assembled. The steps of assembly and their estimated times are:

Task	Time (seconds)
a. Place top subassembly upside down on the work surface.	4
b. Place a leg subassembly over the top subassembly as shown in the left-hand photo, insert a screw in the predrilled hole, align, and drive the screw in.	20
c. Insert another screw in the other predrilled hole and drive the screw in.	13
d. Place another leg subassembly over the other side of the top subassembly, insert a screw in the predrilled hole, align, and drive the screw in.	20
e. Insert another screw in the other predrilled hole and drive the screw in.	13
f. Place a leg brace between two leg subassemblies as shown in the right-hand photo, insert a screw in the predrilled hole, align, and drive the screw in.	20
g. Insert another screw in the other side's predrilled hole and drive the screw in.	13
h. Place another leg brace between two leg subassemblies on the other side, insert a screw in the predrilled hole, align, and drive the screw in.	20
i. Insert another screw in the other side's predrilled hole and drive the screw in.	13
j. Tighten all screws.	32

1. Draw the precedence network.
2. Assuming that we need to assemble one table per minute, assign the tasks to workstations using the "assign the task with the most followers" heuristic rule, breaking a tie with the "assign the task with the longest time" heuristic rule. If there is a further tie, break it randomly (i.e., you can choose any one of the tasks tied).

Solution

1. Note: to be able to start f or h (installing a leg brace/cross bar), both leg assemblies should be already installed (c and e). That is why there are two arrows into f and h from c and e.

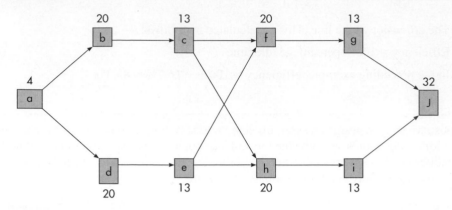

2.

WS	Time Left	Eligible	Will Fit	Assign (time)	Idle Time
1	60s	a	a	a(4)	
	56	b, d	b, d*	b(20)	
	36	c, d	c, d**	d(20)	
	16	c, e	c, e***	c(13)	
	3	E	—	—	3
2	60s	E	e	e(13)	
	47	f, h	f, h****	f(20)	
	27	g, h	g, h*****	h(20)	
	7	g, i	—	—	7
3	60s	g, i	g, i******	g(13)	
	47	i	i	i(13)	
	34	i	i	j(32)	
	2	—	—	—	2
					12s

*b is assigned randomly—both b and d have 6 followers and their time is tied at 20s also.

**d is assigned because it has 6 followers, more than 5 followers of c.

***c is assigned randomly—both c and e have 5 followers and their time is tied at 13s also.

****f is assigned randomly—both f and h have 2 followers and their time is tied at 20s also.

*****h is assigned because it has 2 followers, more than 1 follower of g.

******g is assigned randomly—both g and i have 1 follower and their time is tied at 13s also.

Variable Task Times

Although it is convenient to treat assembly operations as if their time will be the same in each repetition, it is more realistic to assume that task times will be variable. The reasons for the variations are numerous, including worker fatigue, boredom, material shortages, defects, mechanical problems, and product differences.

The following example shows the effect of variation in task times. If three workstations each take 3 minutes to perform their tasks, then the capacity of the line will be 20 units per hour, with percentage idle time = 0 percent (see case (a) in the following figure). However, if each workstation's time is variable: 2 minutes with probability of .5 and 4 minutes with probability of .5, assuming that there is no room for inventory between the workstations, it can be shown, using simulation, that the capacity of the line drops to 16.17 units per hour, with percentage idle time = 19.1 percent (see case (b) in the figure below). Note that the average workstation time is still 3 minutes; however, workstations 1 and 2 can be left idle if their successor workstation is taking 4 minutes and workstations 2 and 3 can be left idle if their predecessor workstation is taking 4 minutes.

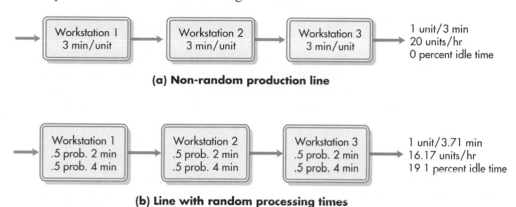

(a) Non-random production line

(b) Line with random processing times

Solutions to the variable task times include:

- Reducing the variability, e.g., by designing the work better, by using high-quality material, and by doing preventive maintenance; and
- Using buffer inventory between workstations.
- Leaving some idle time in workstations that have variable time.

Treatment of Bottlenecks

One approach to dealing with long (bottleneck) tasks/operations is to use *parallel workstations*. Parallel workstations increase the work flow and provide flexibility.

Consider the following example.[4] A job has four tasks; task times are 1 minute, 1 minute, 2 minutes, and 1 minute. Assume each task is assigned to a different workstation and there are no buffer inventories between the workstations. The cycle time for the line will be 2 minutes per unit and the output rate will be 30 units per hour:

$$\frac{60 \text{ minutes per hour}}{2 \text{ minutes per unit}} = 30 \text{ units per hour}$$

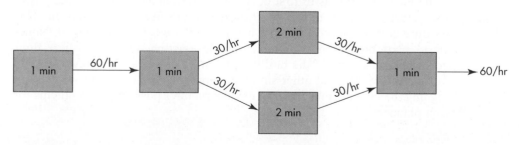

Using parallel workstations for the third task would result in a cycle time of 1 minute per unit because the output rate at the parallel workstations would total 60 units per hour, and this allows an output rate for the line of 60 units per hour:

[4]Adapted from M.P. Groover. *Automation, Production Systems, and Computer Aided Manufacturing*, 2nd ed. Englewood Cliffs, NJ: Prentice Hall, 1987, Chapter 6.

Toyota Mixes and Matches

Toyota decided to produce minivans in the United States in the late 1990s. Wanting to get into production quickly, Toyota took an ambitious step at its Georgetown, Kentucky, manufacturing plant, deciding to produce Sienna minivans at the same time—and at the same workstations—that produce Camry automobiles.

"Although Camry and Sienna are built from the same basic chassis, and share more than 50 percent of their parts, there are key differences. Sienna is five inches longer, three inches wider and a foot taller than Camry. Each Sienna takes up more space on the assembly line and requires more and bigger parts.

"Another automaker might shut down a plant for months to make the changes. But Toyota needed to move quickly. Delay could jeopardize sales of Sienna.

"Out of 300 workstations on the assembly line, Sienna needs different parts at 26. But only seven new production steps are needed. … To save time, Toyota decided not to add workstations. Instead, it selected two teams of workers, one for each shift, that are responsible for attaching Sienna-only parts. Meanwhile, engineers, working with Toyota workers, designed equipment to make those duties easy to perform."

As soon as a Sienna approaches one of the seven spots on the assembly line, a member of the Sienna team is there to take over. Some team members climb inside, where they scoot around on wheeled carts. Others attach roof racks by standing on platforms that put the van's top waist high, eliminating the need to reach, etc.

Toyota may have shortened the time needed to start production by three years by using this innovative approach to the assembly line.

Source: Based on "Camry Assembly Line Delivers New Minivan," *USA Today*, p. B3. Copyright 1997, *USA Today*. Adapted with permission.

Another approach is to *cross-train* workers so that they are able to perform in more than one workstation. Then, when bottlenecks occur, the workers with temporarily increased idle time can assist other workers who are temporarily overburdened, thereby maintaining an even flow of work along the line. This is sometimes referred to as *dynamic line balancing*, and it is used most often in just-in-time systems.

Sometimes a line needs to handle more than one product. This is referred to as a *mixed model line*. This can cause bottlenecks. The "Toyota Mixes and Matches" OM in Action describes one solution to bottlenecks in mixed model lines.

LO6 DESIGNING PROCESS (FUNCTIONAL) LAYOUTS

The main issue in design of process layouts concerns the relative positioning of the departments involved. As illustrated in Figure 6-12, departments must be assigned to locations. The challenge is to develop a reasonably good layout. Some departments may benefit from adjacent locations, whereas others should be separated. For example, a lab with delicate equipment should not be located near a department that has equipment with strong vibrations. Conversely, two departments that share some of the same equipment would benefit from being close together.

The ideal situation is to first develop a layout and then design the physical structure around it, thus permitting maximum flexibility in design. This procedure is commonly followed when new facilities are constructed. Nonetheless, many layouts must be developed in existing structures where floor space, the dimensions of the building, location of entrances, elevators, and re-inforced flooring, and other similar factors must be carefully weighed in designing the layout. Note that multilevel structures pose special problems for layout planners.

Figure 6-12

Departments must be assigned to locations.

Locations

A	B	C
D	E	F

Departments to be assigned
1
2
3
4
5
6

Customers or materials in a process layout may require different operations and different sequences of operations, which causes them to follow different paths through the facility. Because transportation costs or time can be significant, one of the major objectives in process layout design is to minimize total transportation cost, distance, or time.

Minimizing Total Transportation Cost or Distance

In this case, the design of process layouts requires the following information:

1. A list of departments or work centres, their approximate dimensions, and the dimensions of the building that will house the departments.

2. Current and projection of future work flows between the various departments.

3. The distance between centres of locations and the cost per unit of distance to move loads between locations.

4. A list of any special considerations (e.g., operations that must be close to each other or operations that must be separated).

It can be helpful to summarize the necessary data in *from-to charts* like those in Tables 6-4 and 6-5. Table 6-4 indicates the distance between centres of each pair of locations, and Table 6-5 indicates current or projected work flow between each pair of departments. For instance, the distance chart reveals that a trip from the centre of location A to the centre of location B will involve a distance of 20 metres. Oddly enough, the length of a trip between centres of locations A and B may differ depending on the *direction* of the trip, due to one-way routes, elevators, or other factors. To simplify the discussion, we assume a constant distance between centres of any two locations regardless of direction. However, it is not realistic to assume that interdepartmental work flows are equal—there is no reason to suspect that department 1 will send as much work to department 2 as department 2 sends to 1. For example, several departments may send goods to the packaging department, but packaging may send goods only to the shipping department.

Transportation costs can also be summarized in from-to charts, but we shall avoid that complexity, assuming instead that costs are a direct, linear function of distance.

In practice, there are a large number of possible assignments. For example, there are more than 87 billion different ways that 14 departments can be assigned to 14 locations. This makes finding an optimal solution difficult. Often planners must rely on heuristic rules to obtain a good, but not necessarily optimal, solution. A reasonable rule is to locate departments with relatively high interdepartmental work flow as close together as possible.

Table 6-4

Distance between centres of locations (metres)

From	To	Location A	Location B	Location C
A		—	20	40
B		20	—	30
C		40	30	—

Heuristic

1. Assign the pair of departments with the greatest interdepartmental work flow to locations whose centres are closest to each other, keeping the future assignments in mind.

2. Then pick the pair with second highest work flow and assign them to two available locations whose centres are the next two closest, keeping their relationship with those already assigned and future assignments in mind.

3. Continue until all departments have been assigned.

Table 6-5

From-to departmental work flow (loads per day)

From	To	Department 1	Department 2	Department 3
1		—	10	80
2		20	—	30
3		90	70	—

Example 10

Assign the three departments shown in Table 6-5 to locations A, B, and C, which are separated by the distances shown in Table 6-4, in such a way that total transportation cost is minimized. Assume that the cost per metre to move any load is $1. Note that distances between centres of departments are independent of direction of flow (i.e., the distance from-to chart is symmetrical).

Solution

Sum the work flow between every pair of departments in each direction and sort the pairs of departments by the total work flow:

Department Pair	Work Flow	
3–1	90	170
1–3	80	
3–2	70	100
2–3	30	
2–1	20	30
1–2	10	

You can see that departments 1 and 3 have the highest interdepartmental work flow. Also note that centres of locations A and B are the closest. Thus, it seems reasonable to consider assigning 1 and 3 to locations A and B, although it is not yet obvious which department should be assigned to which location. Further inspection of the work flow list reveals that 2 and 3 have higher interdepartmental work flow than 1 and 2, so 2 and 3 should be located more closely than 1 and 2. Hence, it would seem reasonable to place 3 between 1 and 2. The resulting assignments might appear as illustrated in Figure 6-13.

Because the cost per metre to move any load is $1, you can compute the total daily transportation cost for this assignment by multiplying each department's number of loads by the trip distance between their centres, and summing those quantities:

Department	Number of Loads to:	Location	Distance between Centres:	Loads × Distance
1	2: 10	A	C: 40	10 × 40 = 400
	3: 80		B: 20	80 × 20 = 1,600
2	1: 20	C	A: 40	20 × 40 = 800
	3: 30		B: 30	30 × 30 = 900
3	1: 90	B	A: 20	90 × 20 = 1,800
	2: 70		C: 30	70 × 30 = 2,100
				7,600

At $1 per load metre, the cost for this plan is $7,600 per day.

Figure 6-13

Interdepartmental work flows for Example 10

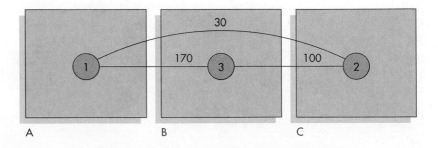

Closeness Ratings

The preceding approach suffers from the limitation of focusing on only one objective (i.e., the total transportation cost), but many situations involve multiple criteria. Richard Muther developed a more general approach to the problem, which allows for subjective input from managers to indicate the relative importance of closeness or remoteness of each department pair.[5] That information is then summarized in a grid like that shown in Figure 6-14. The letters represent the importance of closeness for each department pair, with A being the most important, E being important, and X representing an undesirable pairing. Thus, in the grid below it is "absolutely necessary" to locate 1 and 2 close to each other because there is an A at the intersection of those departments on the grid. On the other hand, 1 and 4 should not be close together because their intersection has an X. In practice, the letters on the grid are often accompanied by numbers that indicate the reason for each closeness rating: they are omitted here to simplify the illustration. Muther suggests the following reasons for need for and undesirability of closeness:

1. Use same equipment or facilities.
2. Share the same personnel.
3. Sequence of work flow.
4. Ease of communication.
5. Unsafe or unpleasant conditions.
6. Similar work performed.

Muther suggests that closeness ratings in the grid be first used to draw a relationship graph, using the A and X ratings, but keeping E ratings in mind. Then this graph is fitted onto the floor plan. Example 11 illustrates this heuristic.

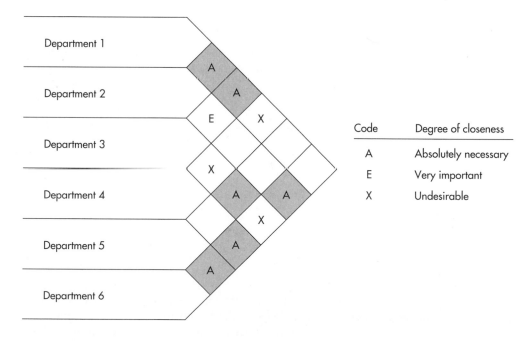

Figure 6-14

A simplified Muther grid

Code	Degree of closeness
A	Absolutely necessary
E	Very important
X	Undesirable

[5]Richard Muther and John Wheeler, "Simplified Systematic Layout Planning," *Factory* 120, nos. 8, 9, and 10 (August, September, October, 1962) pp. 68–77, 111–19, 101–13.

Example 11

Assign the six departments in Figure 6-14 to a 2 × 3 set of locations.

Solution

Prepare a list of A and X ratings by referring to the grid in Figure 6-14:

A	X
1–2	1–4
1–3	3–4
2–6	3–6
3–5	
4–6	
5–6	

Next, form a cluster of A links, beginning with the department that appears most frequently in the A list (in this case, department 6):

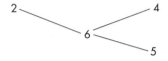

Take the remaining As in order of number of appearance in the list, and add them to the above main cluster, rearranging the cluster as necessary. Form separate clusters for departments that do not link with the main cluster. In this case, all departments link with the main cluster.

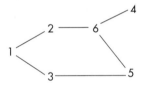

Next, graphically portray the Xs as "separation" cluster(s):

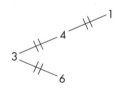

Finally, fit the As cluster into a 2 × 3 arrangement, keeping X separations in mind:

1	2	6
3	5	4

Note that alternative solutions are possible. For this solution, the E rating has also been satisfied, even though no attempt was made to explicitly consider it. Naturally, not every problem will yield the same results, so it may be necessary to do some additional adjusting to see if improvements can be made, keeping in mind that the A and X assignments deserve the greatest consideration.

Note that departments may be considered close not only when they touch side to side, but also when they touch corner to corner. However, side-by-side departments are closer.

Computer Software

The size and complexity of layout problems has led to the development of a number of computer software. An example of these is the Plant Design & Optimization modules of Siemens PLM software. This family (FactoryCAD, FactoryFlow, Plant Simulation, and FactoryMockup) provides icons for graphical display, calculates total material flow distances, uses several heuristics to determine a good layout, performs simulation of material flow, and provides 3-D walk-through displays. For more detail, visit the website in the right margin.

http://www.plm.automation. siemens.com/en_us/products/ tecnomatix/plant_design/index. shtml?&ku=true&a=0

Summary

Production process design involves determining the form and function of the production process, i.e., the activities, their sequence, resources, and controls used to make the product.

Process types include job shop, batch, repetitive, and continuous flow. Job shop is used for many low-quantity customized products, batch process is used for few medium-quantity standard products that are produced in batches, and repetitive and continuous processes are used for one or two high-quantity standard products.

The product-process matrix relates the product quantity and variety to the process type and its flexibility.

Automation is used to reduce the production costs and improve quality. Examples include numerically controlled machines.

Process design involves finding a conceptual sequence of operations to produce the good or service, testing it, and finalizing it by determining the machines and plant layout. A process flow diagram is used to display the sequence of operations.

Facility layout design is used to determine the location of the machines and departments on the facility floor. Product layouts are geared to high-volume outputs of standardized items. Workers and equipment are arranged according to the technological sequence required by the product involved. Emphasis in design is on work flow through the system, and specialized processing and handling equipment is used. Process layouts group similar activities into departments or work centres. These systems can handle a wide range of processing requirements. However, the variety of processing requirements necessitates continual routing and scheduling. The rate of output is generally much lower than that of product layouts. Cellular layouts use a cell that processes a group of similar products or parts using different machines arranged in a "U" shape.

The main effort in product layout design is assembly-line balancing, which focuses on dividing the work required to produce a product into tasks and bundling them so that they are as nearly equal as possible in terms of time. The goal is to achieve a high degree of utilization of labour and equipment.

In process layout design, efforts often focus on the relative positioning of departments to minimize total transportation cost or to meet other requirements concerning the closeness of certain department pairs.

Key Terms

assembly line, 169
automation, 174
batch process, 168
cellular layout, 184
computer-integrated manufacturing
  (CIM), 176
continuous process, 171
cycle time, 188
flexible manufacturing system (FMS), 175
group technology, 184
job shop, 165
line balancing, 188

make or buy, 165
numerically controlled (N/C) machines, 174
percentage idle time, 190
precedence network, 189
process design, 165
process flow diagram, 177
process layout, 183
product layout, 182
production line, 169
repetitive process, 169
robot, 175

Problem 1

The tasks shown in the following precedence network are to be assigned to workstations with the intent of minimizing percentage idle time. Management desires an output rate of 275 units per day. Assume 440 minutes are available per day.

a. Determine the appropriate cycle time.

b. What is the minimum number of workstations possible?

c. Assign tasks using the "assign the task with the longest time" heuristic rule.

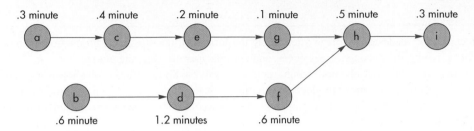

Solution

a. $CT = \dfrac{\text{Operating time}}{\text{Desired output}} = \dfrac{440 \text{ minutes per day}}{275 \text{ units per day}} = 1.6$ minutes per unit per workstation

b. $N_{\min} = \dfrac{\sum t}{\text{Cycle time}} = \dfrac{4.2 \text{ minutes per unit}}{1.6 \text{ minutes per unit per workstation}} = 2.625$, round up to 3 workstations

Workstation	Time Left*	Eligible	Will Fit	Assign Task (time)	Idle Time
1	1.6	a, b	a, b	b(.6)	
	1.0	a, d	a	a(.3)	
	.7	c, d	c	c(.4)	
	.3	e, d	e	e(.2)	
	.1	g, d	g	g(.1)	
	.0	d	—	—	.0
2	1.6	d	d	d(1.2)	
	.4	f	—	—	.4
3	1.6	f	f	f(.6)	
	1.0	h	h	h(.5)	
	.5	i	i	i(.3)	
	.2	—	—	—	.2
					.6

*The initial time for each workstation is the cycle time calculated in part *a*.

The resulting assignments are shown below.

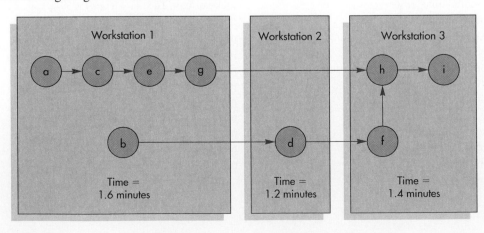

Assign nine automobile service departments to bays in a 3 × 3 floor grid so that the closeness   **Problem 2**
ratings in the following Muther grid are satisfied. Only A and X ratings are shown. The location
of department 4 must be in the middle right-hand side of the floor grid.

Department 1								
Department 2	A	A						
Department 3		A	X	A	A			
Department 4			A	A				
Department 5		A	E	X	A			
Department 6			X	X				
Department 7	X	X						
Department 8								
Department 9								

Department 1 has most A ratings, making it the centre position in the cluster. After connecting   *Solution*
all the other departments with A rating to Department 1 and adding the other A ratings, we get
the following cluster:

Next, we can identify the clusters of departmental pairings that should be avoided:

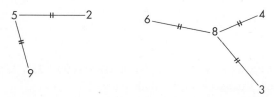

The departments in each X cluster should be spaced around the perimeter of the grid. Placing the
A cluster on the floor plan with dept 1 in the centre room and arbitrarily starting with dept 6 in top
right room, we get:

2	3	6
9	1	4
7	5	

Now, using the X clusters, it follows that we should move dept 5 and 7 one room to the right and
place dept 8 in the bottom left room, so that dept 5 is not close to dept 9 and dept 8 is not close
to dept 4. The following final floor plan results:

2	3	6
9	1	4
8	7	5

Problem 3

Five departments, 1 to 5, are to be assigned to locations B–F in the grid below. For technical reasons, department 6 must be assigned to location A. Transportation cost is $2 per metre. The objective is to minimize total transportation cost. Information on from-to departmental work flows and distances between centres of locations is shown in the following tables. Use the heuristic given in the section "Minimizing Total Transportation Cost or Distance." Calculate total transportation cost.

From \ To	**Distance between Centres of Locations (metres)**					
	A	**B**	**C**	**D**	**E**	**F**
A	—	50	100	50	80	130
B		—	50	90	40	70
C			—	140	60	50
D				—	50	120
E					—	50
F						—

From \ To	**From-To Departmental Workflows (number of trips per day)**					
	1	**2**	**3**	**4**	**5**	**6**
1	—	90	25	23	11	18
2	35	—	8	5	10	16
3	37	2	—	1	0	7
4	41	12	1	—	4	0
5	14	16	0	9	—	3
6	32	38	13	2	2	—

A Dept. 6	B	C
D	E	F

Solution

First, determine the total interdepartmental work flows (e.g., for 1–2 the flow is $90 + 35 = 125$) because the distances are symmetric. Then, arrange them from high to low.

Pair of Dept.	Workflow
1–2	125
1–4	64
1–3	62
2–6	54
1–6	50
2–5	26
1–5	25
3–6	20
2–4	17
4–5	13
2–3	10
5–6	5
3–4	2
4–6	2
3–5	0

From this, we can see that departments 1 and 2 have the greatest interdepartmental work flow, so they should be closest, perhaps at B and E (which have the smallest between-centres distance). However, since work flow between 2 and 6 is larger than between 1 and 6, place department 1 in location E and department 2 in location B. Next, work flow between 1 and 4 is highest. The work flow between 4 and 6 is low, suggesting that they need not be close. Therefore, place department 4 in F. Next, work flow between 1 and 3 is highest. Hence, place department 3 in location D. Finally, department 5 has to be placed at location C.

A Dept. 6	B Dept. 2	C Dept. 5
D Dept. 3	E Dept. 1	F Dept. 4

Total cost:

Pair of Dept.	b Distance		c Workflow	(b × c × $2) Cost
1–2	(B–E)	40	125	$10,000
1–3	(D–E)	50	62	6,200
1–4	(F–E)	50	64	6,400
1–5	(E–C)	60	25	3,000
1–6	(A–E)	80	50	8,000
2–3	(B–D)	90	10	1,800
2–4	(B–F)	70	17	2,380
2–5	(B–C)	50	26	2,600
2–6	(A–B)	50	54	5,400
3–4	(F–D)	120	2	480
3–5	(D–C)	140	0	0
3–6	(A–D)	50	20	2,000
4–5	(C–F)	50	13	1,300
4–6	(A–F)	130	2	520
5–6	(A–C)	100	5	1,000
				$51,080

1. Explain the importance of process design. (LO1)
2. Briefly describe the four basic process types and give a manufacturing example for each. (LO1)
3. Give a service example for each of the four basic process types. (LO1)
4. Briefly discuss the advantages and disadvantages of automation. (LO2)
5. Briefly describe computer-aided approaches to production. (LO2)
6. What is a numerically controlled machine? (LO2)
7. What is the product-process matrix? What is its purpose? (LO1)
8. Describe the approach for process design. (LO3)
9. What is a process flow diagram? (LO3)
10. What are the differences between product and service process design? (LO3)
11. Describe the general approach for layout design. (LO4)
12. Relate process and product layout to process types. (LO4)
13. What are the main advantages of a product layout? The main disadvantages? (LO4)
14. What are the main advantages of a process layout? The main disadvantages? (LO4)
15. Why are routing and scheduling continual problems in process layouts? (LO4)
16. Compare machine/equipment maintenance strategies in product and process layouts. (LO4)
17. Briefly outline the impact that job processing sequence has on each of the layout types. (LO4)

18. The City Transportation Planning Committee must decide whether to begin a long-term project to build a subway system or to upgrade the present bus service. Suppose you are an expert in fixed-path and variable-path material-handling equipment, and the committee seeks your counsel on this matter. What are the advantages and limitations of the subway and bus systems? (LO4)

19. Why are product layouts atypical in service environments? (LO4)

20. According to a study, it costs more than three times the original purchase price in parts and labour to replace a totally wrecked automobile. Explain the reasons for this large discrepancy in terms of the processes used to assemble the original car and those required to reconstruct the wrecked car. (LO1&4)

21. How can a layout help or hinder productivity? (LO4)

22. What is a cellular layout? What are its main benefits and limitations? (LO4)

23. What is group technology? (LO4)

24. What is the goal of line balancing? What happens if a line is unbalanced? (LO5)

25. Explain the consequences of task time variability on line balancing. (LO5)

26. What is the main objective of process layout? (LO6)

Taking Stock

1. Name a major trade-off in (a) process design, (b) layout design. (LO3&5)

2. Who needs to be involved in process design? Layout design? (LO3&4)

3. In what ways does technology have an impact on process design? Layout design? (LO2&6)

4. Use of efficient production processes in raising animals for meat has resulted in factory farms where animals (pigs, hens, etc.) are kept in confinement at high stocking density. For example, female pigs are impregnated and kept in gestation crates (2 feet by 7 feet) for the whole 4 months of pregnancy. This process is repeated after the delivery. Many people consider this practice unethical. In fact, it has been banned in Europe. Smithfield Foods, the largest U.S. pork producer, under pressure from McDonald's, has decided to stop the use of gestation crates in its 187 pig nurseries.[6] Where in the process design methodology should this kind of ethical issue be considered? (LO3)

Critical Thinking Exercises

1. There are several factors that must exist in order to make automation feasible. Name one or two of the most important factors and briefly explain their importance. (LO2)

2. Layout decisions affect a wide range of facilities, from factories, grocery stores, offices, department stores, and warehouses, to malls, parking lots and garages, and kitchens. Layout is also important in the design of some products such as the interiors of automobiles and the arrangement of components inside computers and other electronic devices. Select three different items from this list, or other similar items, and explain for each what the one or two key considerations for layout design are. (LO4)

Experiential Learning Exercises

1. Visit a supermarket and identify an area of the store that has the characteristics of each of these processing types: job shop, batch, repetitive, and continuous. (LO1)

2. Compare the layout of a supermarket to the layout of a convenience store. Explain the differences you observe. (LO4)

3. Design an assembly line for preparing a turkey sub (lettuce, tomato, mayo, and turkey). Use about six workstations. Begin with cutting the bun open, and end with cutting the sub in half. Estimate the time needed in seconds for each workstation. (LO3)

4. Draw the layout of two gas stations you know and compare the two. Which is better? (LO4)

---

[6]M. Kaufman, "Largest Pork Processor to Phase out Crates," *Washington Post*, Jan 26, 2007, p. A06.

1. Visit the Web page of one of the following companies and draw its process flow diagram: (LO3)

   - Kalesnikoff Lumber   http://www.kalesnikoff.com/tour.html
   - Prestige Homes   http://www.prestigehomes.ca/homebuying/factory_tour/#photo_tour
   - Guildcrest Homes   http://www.guildcrest.com/factory_tour/1.php
   - Tata Steel   http://www.tatasteel.com/products-and-processes/processes/steel-making-process.asp
   - Dofasco   http://www.dofasco.ca/HOW_Steel_Is_Made/html
   - Derscher Paper Box   http://www.drescherpuzzle.com/puzzles_process.php
   - Andrews Products   http://www.andrewsproducts.com/technical/plant_tour.htm
   - LA Aluminum   http://www.laaluminum.com/la_aluminum_tour.html
   - Clark Metal   http://www.clark-metal.com/tour/

2. Visit http://manufacturing.stanford.edu, click on "How Everyday Things Are Made," choose a product from the left column (e.g., airplane, motorcycle, cars, jelly beans, bottles, wool, denim), click on it, watch the video, and draw the process flow diagram. (LO3)

3. Visit http://www.patagonia.com/web/us/footprint/index.jsp, click on "Choose a product," then click on a product icon, identify and draw the supply chain, watch the manufacturing video, and draw the process flow diagram. (LO3)

1. An assembly line with 17 tasks is to be balanced. The longest task is 2.4 minutes, and the total time for all tasks is 18 minutes. The line will operate for 450 minutes per day. (LO5)

   a. What is the minimum number of workstations needed if the output rate is to be 180 units per day?
   b. What cycle time will provide an output rate of 125 units per day?
   c. What output will result if the cycle time is (i) 9 minutes? (ii) 15 minutes?

2. A manager wants to assign tasks to workstations to achieve an hourly output rate of 33 units. Assume that the shop works 60 minutes per hour (i.e., no breaks). (LO5)

   a. Assign the tasks shown in the following precedence network (times are on the nodes and are in minutes) to workstations using the following heuristic rules: (i) "Assign the task with the most followers." (ii) Tiebreaker: "Assign the task with the longest time."
   b. What is the efficiency?

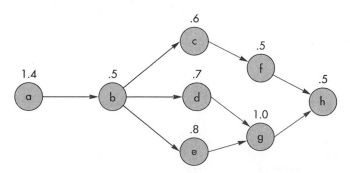

3. A manager wants to assign tasks to workstations in order to achieve an hourly output rate of four units. The department uses a working time of 56 minutes per hour. (LO5)

   a. Assign the tasks shown in the following precedence network (times are on the nodes and are in minutes) to workstations using the following heuristic rules: (i) "Assign the task with the most followers." (ii) Tiebreaker: "Assign the task with the longest time." If a tie still exists, choose randomly.

b. What is the efficiency?

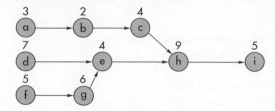

4. A large manufacturer of pencil sharpeners is planning to add a new sharpener, and you have been asked to balance the assembly line, given the following task times and precedence relationships. Assume that cycle time is 1.3 minutes per unit. (LO5)

Task	Duration (minutes)	Immediate Follower
a	.2	b
b	.4	d
c	.3	d
d	1.3	g
e	.1	f
f	.8	g
g	.3	h
h	1.2	—

a. Do each of the following:
   i. Draw the precedence network.
   ii. Assign the tasks to workstations using the heuristic rule "Assign the task with the most followers." Break ties using the heuristic rule "Assign the task with the longest time."
   iii. Determine the percentage idle time.
   iv. Calculate the rate of output that could be expected for this line assuming a 420-minute working day.

b. Answer these questions:
   i. What is the shortest cycle time that will permit use of only two workstations? Identify the tasks you would assign to each workstation.
   ii. Determine the percentage idle time that would result if two workstations were used.
   iii. What is the daily output under this arrangement?

5. As part of a major plant renovation project, the industrial engineering department has been asked to balance a revised assembly operation to achieve an output rate of 240 units per eight-hour day. Task times and precedence relationships are as follows: (LO5)

Task	Duration (minutes)	Precedes Task
a	.2	b
b	.4	d
c	.2	d
d	.4	g
e	1.2	f
f	1.2	g
g	1.0	—

Do each of the following:

a. Draw the precedence network.
b. Determine the required cycle time.
c. Determine the minimum number of workstations needed.
d. Assign the tasks to workstations using the heuristic rule "Assign the task with the most followers." Use the heuristic rule "Assign the task with the longest time" as a tiebreaker. If a tie still exists, choose randomly.
e. Calculate the percentage idle time for the assignments in part *d*.

6. Twelve tasks, with times and precedence requirements as shown in the following table, are to be assigned to workstations using a cycle time of 1.5 minutes. Heuristic rule "Assign the task with the most followers" will be tried. The tiebreaker will be the heuristic rule "Assign the task with the longest time." (LO5)

Task	Duration (minutes)	Follows Task	Task	Duration (minutes)	Follows Task
a	.1	—	g	.4	f
b	.2	a	h	.1	g
c	.9	b	i	.2	h
d	.6	c	j	.7	i
e	.1	—	k	.3	j
f	.2	d, e	l	.2	k

   a. Draw the precedence network.
   b. Assign tasks to workstations.
   c. Calculate the percentage idle time.

7. For the following tasks: (LO5)

   a. Develop the precedence network.
   b. Determine the cycle time (in seconds) for a desired output rate of 500 units in a seven-hour day.
   c. Determine the minimum number of workstations for output rate of 500 units per day.
   d. Balance the line using the "Assign the task with the most followers" heuristic rule. Break ties with "Assign the task with the longest time" heuristic rule. Use a cycle time of 50 seconds.
   e. Calculate the percentage idle time for the line.

Task	Task Time (seconds)	Immediate Predecessors
A	45	—
B	11	A
C	9	B
D	50	—
E	26	D
F	11	E
G	12	C
H	10	C
I	9	F, G, H
J	10	I
	193	

8. A shop works a 400-minute day. The manager of the shop wants an output rate of 200 units per day for the assembly line that has the tasks shown in the following table. Do the following: (LO5)

   a. Construct the precedence network and calculate the cycle time.
   b. Assign tasks according to "Assign the task with the most followers" rule. In the case of a tie, use "Assign the task with the longest time" heuristic rule.
   c. Calculate the balance delay.

Task	Immediately Precedes Task(s)	Task Time	Task	Immediately Precedes Task(s)	Task Time
a	b, c, d	.5	g	h	.4
b	e	1.4	h	k	.3
c	e	1.2	i	j	.5
d	f	.7	j	k	.8
e	g, i	.5	k	m	.9
f	i	1.0	m	—	.3

9. Arrange six departments into a 2×3 floor grid so that these conditions are satisfied: 1 is close to 2; 5 is close to 2, 4, and 6; and 3 is not close to 1 or 2. (LO6)

10. Using the information given in the preceding problem, develop a Muther grid using the letters A and X. Leave any pair of combinations not mentioned blank. (LO6)

11. Using the information in the following Muther grid, determine the department locations on the following floor plan. Note that departments 1 and 7 must be in the locations shown. (LO6)

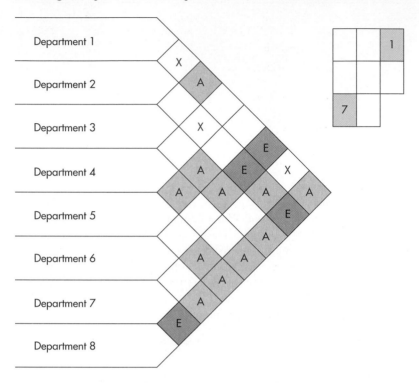

12. Arrange the eight departments shown in the following Muther grid into a 2×4 floor plan. Note: Department 2 must be in the location shown. (LO6)

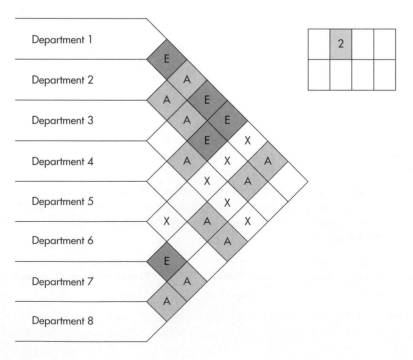

13. Arrange nine departments into a 3×3 floor grid so that they satisfy the conditions shown in the following Muther grid. Place department 5 in the lower left corner of the 3×3 floor grid. (LO6)

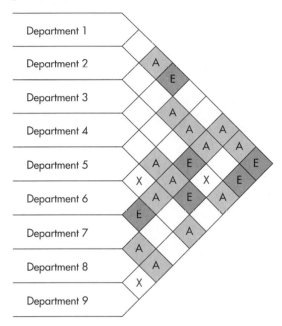

14. Determine the placement of departments in the following floor plan that will minimize total transportation cost using the data in the following tables. Assume that reverse distances are the same. Use a cost of $1 per trip metre. Use the heuristic in the section "Minimizing Total Transportation Cost or Distance." (LO6)

Location A	Location B	Location C
	Location D	

Distance between Centres of Locations (metres)

From \ To	A	B	C	D
A	—	40	80	70
B		—	40	50
C			—	60
D				—

Number of Trips per Day From-To Departments

From \ To	1	2	3	4
1	—	10	20	30
2		—	40	40
3			—	25
4	50	50	30	—

15. Eight work centres must be arranged in an L-shaped building. The locations of work centres 1 and 3 have already been assigned as shown in the following diagram. Assuming

that transportation costs are $1 per load per metre, develop a suitable layout that minimizes total transportation cost using the information given below. (Assume the reverse distances are the same.) Use the heuristic in the section "Minimizing Total Transportation Cost or Distance." (LO6)

A 1	B	
C	D	E 3
F	G	H

Distance (metres)

From	To	A	B	C	D	E	F	G	H
A		—	40	40	60	120	80	100	110
B			—	60	40	60	140	120	130
C				—	45	85	40	70	90
D					—	40	50	40	45
E						—	90	50	40
F							—	40	60
G								—	40
H									—

Loads per Day

From	To	1	2	3	4	5	6	7	8
1		—	10	5	90	365	135	125	0
2		0	—	140	10	0	35	0	120
3		0	220	—	110	10	0	0	200
4		0	110	240	—	10	0	0	170
5		5	40	100	180	—	10	40	10
6		0	80	40	70	0	—	10	20
7		0	45	20	50	0	40	—	20
8		0	0	0	20	0	0	0	—

16. Develop a process layout that will minimize the total distance travelled by patients at a medical clinic, using the following information. Assume a distance of 35 feet between the reception area and each other location A to F. Assume that the reverse distances are the same. Use the floor plan shown on the next page. Use the heuristic in the section "Minimizing Total Transportation Cost or Distance." (LO6)

Distance between Centres of Locations (feet)

From	To	A	B	C	D	E	F
A		—	20	60	80	120	160
B			—	40	60	80	120
C				—	40	60	80
D					—	40	60
E						—	40
F							—

	Trips From–To Departments (per day)						
From \ To	1	2	3	4	5	6	Reception
Reception	10	10	200	20	0	100	—
1	—	0	0	80	20	40	10
2	0	—	0	0	0	20	40
3	40	0	—	10	190	10	10
4	30	50	0	—	10	70	0
5	60	40	60	30	—	20	10
6	10	100	0	20	0	—	30

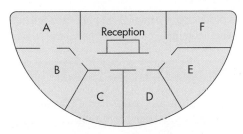

17. Ten labs should be assigned to the circular floor plan shown below. Recalling a similar layout's congestion in the halls, the new lab manager has requested an assignment that will minimize traffic between offices, but movement in the halls is restricted to a counterclockwise route. Develop a suitable layout using the following information. Assign Lab 1 to Location A, Lab 2 to Location I, and Lab 8 to Location E. (LO6)

	Number of Trips per Day From–To Labs									
From \ To	1	2	3	4	5	6	7	8	9	10
1	—	40	1	20	20	4	0	2	6	5
2	0	—	2	15	25	10	2	12	13	6
3	50	35	—	10	13	4	0	4	7	1
4	6	1	8	—	0	14	10	20	22	11
5	3	2	7	35	—	22	5	9	19	10
6	5	5	10	0	2	—	15	0	1	20
7	20	16	50	4	9	2	—	1	3	0
8	10	6	14	2	4	44	13	—	1	25
9	5	5	18	1	2	40	30	42	—	32
10	30	30	35	20	15	5	40	10	15	—

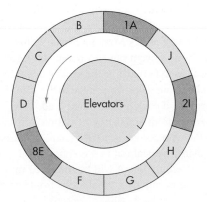

18. For the process of conducting a bank transaction using a teller in your bank:

   a. Draw a process flow diagram. Start when customer arrives at the bank. Fail-safe this process.

   b. Use IDEF method to design this process. (LO3)

19. Draw a process flow diagram for customer service/eating in a full-service restaurant. Start when a customer arrives at the restaurant. (LO3)

20. Draw a process flow diagram for preparing a personal income tax return. (LO3)

21. Draw a process flow diagram for mass producing potato chips. Start with trucks bringing potatoes to the plant. (LO3)

22. Draw a process flow diagram for batch production of bagels, as done by e.g., Great Canadian Bagel Company. (LO3)

23. **a.** A pencil is made from a graphite rod and wooden body (plus a metal band and eraser at one end). Given the graphite rod, come up with two different ways (concepts) of manufacturing a pencil (ignore the metal band and eraser). (LO3)

    b. Draw a process flow diagram for mass producing a pencil. You may use the photos and descriptions from http://www.generalpencil.com/gpc_ourpencils_how.html.

24. Draw a process flow diagram for making a yarn (thread) from fleece (sheep wool). Use approximately 4 major steps. You may use http://www.blackberry-ridge.com/prosdscr.htm as a source.

25. **a.** Chocolate is toasted, ground (and heated), refined, and moulded seeds of cocoa beans. Draw a process flow diagram (approximately five operations) for making chocolate from cocoa beans at home. State what equipment (if any) you plan to use for each operation. (LO3)

    b. View the video at http://www.hersheys.com/discover/tour_video.asp, and draw the process flow diagram for mass producing milk chocolate with almond (approximately eight operations).

26. Paper is made from wood pulp. Wood pulp is made from wood chips by either cooking it with chemicals (called Kraft pulp) or grinding the wood chips into its fibres (called Thermomechanical pulp). Pulp is cleaned and possibly bleached before papermaking. If one were to make paper at home, the following process could be used: (LO3)

    "The pulp is poured into a large tub and the fibres are suspended in the water. A framed screen is dipped into the water and is lifted to the surface, catching the fibres onto the screen. The screen can either be left in the sun to dry, or be transferred to boards, pressed, smoothed and then dried."[7]

    Design a continuous process for mass producing paper. Assume pulp has already been made. Draw the process flow diagram.

27. Audio Innovations of Stillwater, Oklahoma, makes car speaker cabinets and enclosures. Before 2001, it made 12,000 cabinets per month using 130 workers and a labour-intensive process. Then, it was purchased by Rockford Corp of Arizona, which strove to increase its capacity and productivity. (LO3)

    Before the change the process was as follows: 5/8 inch–thick Medium Density Fiberboard (MDF) was cut into individual sides of the cabinet using a beam saw (a circular saw on a table guided by beams). Then, for each piece a router was used to machine the slanted edges. Next, to cover the four sides a strip of carpet was cut, and the four sides were glued to the strip. Then, the strip ends were glued together. Finally, the front and back pieces were glued.

    The process change involved both the nature of operations and their automation. A machine (called a laminator) was bought to glue carpet to the whole sheet of MDF. Then, the carpeted board is cut into a piece the size of the four sides using the beam saw. A computerized grooving line was purchased to make three V-grooves where the piece will be folded to form the sides of the box. After this, a worker glued the strip ends together. Finally, the front and back pieces were glued.

    As a result of the change, the company can make 20,000 cabinets per month using the same number of workers.

[7]http://www.hqpapermaker.com/paper-history

1. Draw the process flow diagram before the change.
2. Draw the process flow diagram after the change.
3. Determine the productivity before and after the change.[8]

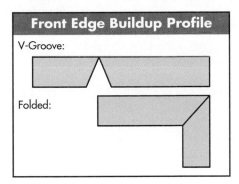

28. Draw a process flow diagram for packing six 227-gram cartons of baby cereal into cardboard cases. Assume that filled cartons arrive from the manufacturing process on a conveyor, collapsed cases are on a close-by cart, and packed cases are put on a conveyor to palletizing area.[9] (LO3)

29. The tasks performed in a cafeteria to serve a customer and the average service times are as follows: (LO5)

Tasks	Service Time per Customer (seconds)
Serve vegetables	25
Serve entrée	30
Serve soup	20
Serve dessert	15
Serve drink	10
Collect money	60

The only precedence relationship is that "collect money" has to be last. The current layout performs these tasks in the sequence given; each task is performed by one worker except that only one worker serves both dessert and drink.

a.   i. Draw the precedence network.
   ii. What is the maximum number of customers who can be served per hour (capacity) using the current layout?
  iii. Assuming that capacity in part *ii* equals desired output, what are the cycle time and minimum number of workstations (workers) needed?
  iv. Suppose that capacity has to be increased. Where can the sixth worker be employed, assuming that equipment is not a constraint?
   v. How can we keep the same number of workers (five) but change the process in order to increase the capacity?

b. Using cycle time = 35 seconds and "Assign the task with the longest time" heuristic rule, balance the assembly line, and calculate the percentage idle time.

30. Suppose you need to assemble 72 Quickline Guest tables in one hour (see the photos on the next page). The assembly activities and their standard times are listed below. Using common sense,

[8]L. Ohm, "Automation Boosts Production 65 Percent," *FDM—The Magazine of Woodworking Production Management*, Aug 2003, 75(12), pp. 48–54.
[9]An automated case packer can be seen at http://www.trinamics.com/616sl.html and its use in H. J. Heinz is described in J. Mans, "Servos Increase Case-packing Efficiency," *Packaging Digest*, 43(7), July 2006, pp. 26–29.

draw a precedence network and calculate the cycle time. Then, perform assembly-line balancing using "Assign the task with the longest time" heuristic rule, breaking ties using "Assign the task with the most followers" heuristic rule. Any further ties can be broken randomly. (LO5)

Activity		Standard Time (seconds)
A.	Lay the top face down on a clean surface.	10
B_1.	Attach a mounting bracket to a corner of the top using three screws.	35
C_1.	Add a compression ring on the bracket.	5
D_1.	Slide one end of a leg over the compression ring and turn it so that the hole is aligned with the Allen screw.	10
E_1.	Tighten the screw with Allen wrench.	15
B_2.	Attach another mounting bracket to another corner of top using three screws.	35
C_2.	Add another compression ring.	5
D_2.	Slide one end of another leg over the compression ring and turn it.	10
E_2.	Tighten with Allen wrench.	15
B_3.	Attach another mounting bracket to another corner of top using three screws.	35
C_3	Add another compression ring.	5
D_3.	Slide end of another leg over the compression ring and turn it.	10
E_3.	Tighten with Allen wrench.	15
B_4.	Attach another mounting bracket to another corner of top using three screws.	35
C_4.	Add another compression ring.	5
D_4.	Slide end of another leg over the compression ring and turn it.	10
E_4.	Tighten with Allen wrench.	15
F.	Turn the table over on its legs.	30

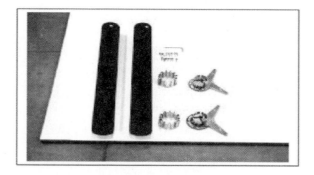

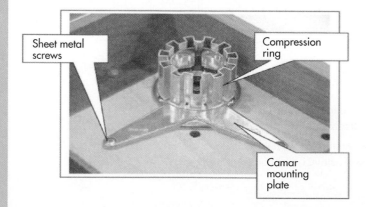

Sheet metal screws

Compression ring

Camar mounting plate

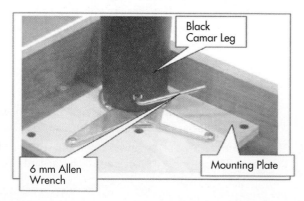

Black Camar Leg

6 mm Allen Wrench

Mounting Plate

31. Consider the Scoot & Go Rider shown on the next page and made by the Processed Plastic Company (PPC). Suppose that PPC has received a rush order from Walmart for 8,800 units to be shipped in five days. (LO5)

a. Assuming 16 hour workdays, calculate the cycle time.

b. Start with the body on the table, and assume all parts are within reach. Also assume that the steering wheel subassembly has already been made. Using common sense, draw a precedence network for the following activities, which are required to assemble a Scoot & Go Rider.

Activity	Standard time (seconds)
a. Insert the steering wheel subassembly in the body.	7
b. Hammer the front (short) axle into a pal nut (using the pal nut tool).	10
c. Slide a wheel in the component resulting from b.	5
d. Pass component resulting from c through the steering shaft hole.	5
e. Slide a wheel into component resulting from d.	4
f. Hammer the component resulting from e into a pal nut (using the pal nut tool).	12
g. Hammer the rear (long) axle into a pal nut (using the pal nut tool).	10
h. Slide a wheel in the component resulting from g.	6
i. Pass component resulting from h through the body's rear axle holes.	7
j. Slide a wheel into component resulting from i.	4
k. Hammer the component resulting from j into a pal nut (using the pal nut tool).	13
l. Place walker bar on the body and attach using one screw.	15
m. Insert another screw into walker bar to attach it to the body.	11
n. Insert another screw into walker bar to attach it to the body.	11
o. Insert another screw into walker bar to attach it to the body.	11
p. Perform final quality check and box it.	30

c. If the cycle time is 33 seconds, what is the minimum number of workstations needed?

d. Perform assembly-line balancing using 33 seconds cycle time, the standard times, and the precedence network from part b. Use "Assign the task with the longest time" heuristic rule, breaking ties using "Assign the task with the most followers" heuristic rule. Any further ties can be broken arbitrarily.

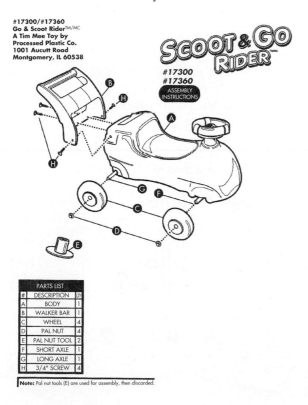

#17300/#17360
Go & Scoot Rider™/MC
A Tim Mee Toy by
Processed Plastic Co.
1001 Aucutt Road
Montgomery, IL 60538

SCOOT & GO RIDER™

#17300
#17360
ASSEMBLY INSTRUCTIONS

PARTS LIST		
#	DESCRIPTION	QTY
A	BODY	1
B	WALKER BAR	1
C	WHEEL	4
D	PAL NUT	4
E	PAL NUT TOOL	2
F	SHORT AXLE	1
G	LONG AXLE	1
H	3/4" SCREW	4

Note: Pal nut tools (E) are used for assembly, then discarded.

32. Consider the Playskool Storage Studio below. We wish to design an assembly line to assemble several units. The assembly tasks and their standard times (in seconds) are listed below. (LO5)

Tasks		Standard Time (seconds)
a.	Place the Toy Chest (A), with the Lid/Art Board (F) already attached, on the conveyor.	8
b_1.	Slide one Side Support (B) in the holes on one side of top of Toy Chest.	9
b_2.	Slide the other Side Support (B) in the holes on the other side of top of Toy Chest.	9
c_1.	Attach one Bin Support (C) to Side Supports in the front using 2 pins (D).	20
c_2.	Attach another Bin Support (C) to Side Supports in the front using 2 pins.	20
d.	Insert 4 pins in the Brace (G).	15
e_1.	Place one Bin Support (C) in the back on Side Supports.	8
e_2.	Place another Bin Support (C) in the back on Side Supports.	8
f.	Attach the Brace (with pins) to the Bin and Side Supports in the back.	40
g_1.	Place a Storage Bin (E) on the Bin Supports.	7
g_2.	Place another Storage Bin on the Bin Supports.	7
g_3.	Place another Storage Bin on the Bin Supports.	7
g_4.	Place another Storage Bin on the Bin Supports.	7
g_5.	Place another Storage Bin on the Bin Supports.	7
g_6.	Place another Storage Bin on the Bin Supports	7

The parts are to be assembled according to the following precedence network:

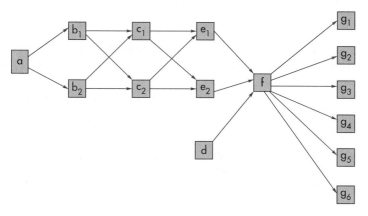

a. Calculate the cycle time if 75 units per hour are to be assembled.
b. What is the minimum number of workstations?
c. Using your answer to part a, perform assembly-line balancing using "Assign the task with the longest time" heuristic rule, breaking any ties using "Assign the task with the most followers" rule. If there is still a tie, break it randomly.

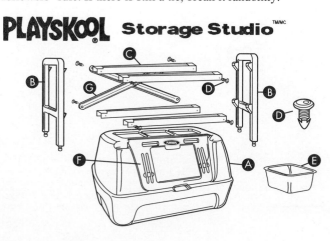

33. To assemble the plastic chair (shown below) using an assembly line, the following activities with estimated standard times are required. (LO5)

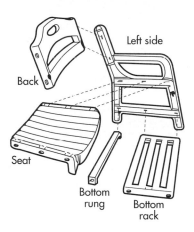
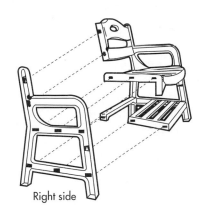

Activity		Standard Time (seconds)
A	Place left side inside up on the work area	5 seconds
B	Tap back in	8
C	Tap seat in	13
D	Tap bottom rung in	7
E	Tap bottom rack in	9
F	Align all slots and tap right side in	15

a. Draw a precedence network for this assembly.

b. If the desired output rate of the assembly line is 120 chairs per hour, what is the minimum number of workstations required?

c. Using a cycle time of 30 seconds per chair, and "Assign the task with the longest time" heuristic rule, design the assembly line (i.e., balance the line).

MINI-CASE

School Chairs

School chairs are usually made of plastic and metal, costing anywhere from $30 to $100 each. You wish to evaluate the idea of manufacturing wooden chairs for sale to schools, churches, etc. You have found the following design for a chair.

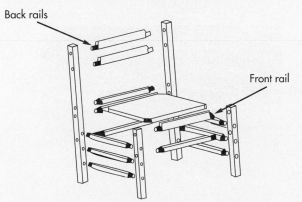

Most wooden chairs are made of hardwoods such as oak, maple, cherry, or cedar. Suppose that cedar is cheaper where you live. The dimensions of the parts of the chair are as follows:

Item	Number	Dimension (inches) (thickness, width, length)
Back post	2	$2 \times 2 \times 36$
Front post	2	$2 \times 2 \times 18$
Crossbar	10	$1 \times 1 \times 14$
Rails	3	$2 \times 1 \times 14$
Seat	1	$1 \times 16 \times 16$

The most economical size of cedar lumber is $2'' \times 4'' \times 8'$ (i.e., 2 inches thick by 4 inches wide by 8 feet long). Therefore, you intend to buy only this size.

Questions

1. Calculate the number of this lumber you will need per chair.

2. Determine the operations needed to make the chair and draw a process flow diagram. Note that the crossbars and rails have a tenon (a small round tip) on each end that will go in the mortise (the hole) of the posts. These have to be made. Also, the seat's corners have to be cut to allow for the posts.

Source: Based on H. Quesada and R. Gazo, "Development of a Manufacturing System for Construction of School Furniture," *Forest Products Journal* 53(9), September 2003, pp. 47–54.

MINI-CASE

The Double-D Cell

Sometimes converting an assembly line into two or more cells will actually reduce the staffing requirements. Such was the case in the hardware (mechanical parts) subassembly of recliners in the Franklin Corp. plant in Houston, Mississippi.

The Initial Subassembly Frames (ISF) were assembled by four workers. Then, the ISFs were stored in the ISF queue until they were needed by the circular line, at which time a material handler mounted ISFs on wheeled tables, which were secured to the outer ring of the line with rollers (see the photo below on the left). Five workers worked inside the ring. The cycle time in the ring was approximately 30 seconds, but there was a total of 35 seconds of idle time per subassembly assembled in the ring. There were four types of subassemblies but they were similar.

In order to improve the efficiency of the circular line, the Double-D layout was proposed (see the photo below on the right).

Questions

1. What are the advantages of the Double-D cells over the circular line?

2. Suppose that the task times of the five workstations in the ring were 30, 25, 20, 20, and 20 seconds, respectively. Explain how four workers, two in each D, can produce the same output as the five workers in the ring.

Source: http://fwrc.msstate.edu/pubs/doubled.pdf

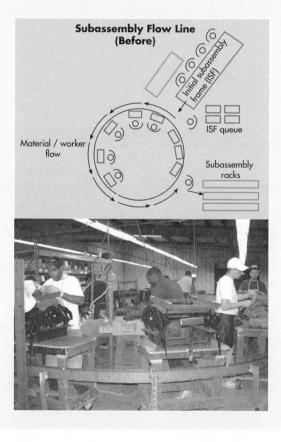

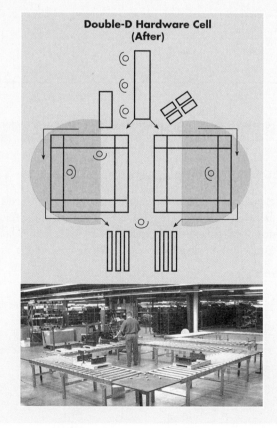

Rockland Cook/Chill Facility Layout Design

In the early 1990s, the New York State Office of Mental Health decided to centralize food production (i.e., kitchen) for its 29 mental hospitals. A small consulting firm was contracted to design the facility. It was determined that the production process should be decomposed into the following departments and desired area for each:

Department	Desired Area (ft²)
Receiving area	800
Vegetable fridges	600
Dry storeroom and dairy fridges	2,300
Poultry and meat freezers	1,500
Vegetable prep	600
Poultry and meat thaw fridges	400
Raw meat prep	800
Ingredient control (can openers, scales)	900
Salad/pasta/dessert prep	1,500
Cook-chill area	3,800
Cooked meat prep	700
Office	1,800
Ware-wash (utensils, carts, etc)	1,500
Finished products coolers and fridges	2,800
Test Kitchen	1900
Shipping area	600

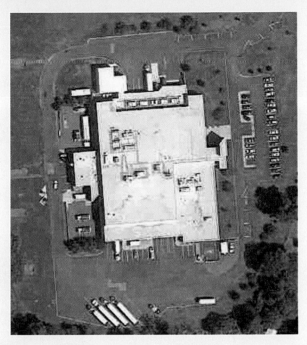

Google Earth aerial view of the Rockland facility

Source: Based on D. Arey, "Steam Power Produces for N.Y. Psych Centres," *Foodservice Equipment & Supplies Specialist*, Aug 25, 1996, p. 51–54.

Questions

1. Using common sense, determine a Muther grid for the departments.

2. Determine the location of the departments on a 200 ft long by 150 ft wide floor plan. Locate the receiving area on the top and shipping area in the bottom. Allow for two north-south and two to three east-west corridors.

To access "Linear Programming," the supplement to Chapter 6, please visit *Connect.*

CHAPTER 7
Design of Work Systems

LEARNING OBJECTIVES

After completing this chapter, you should be able to:

LO1 Briefly describe efficiency and behavioural approaches to job design.

LO2 Explain the purpose of methods analysis and describe how methods analysis is performed.

LO3 Discuss the impact of working conditions on job design.

LO4 Describe time study methods and perform calculations.

LO5 Describe various compensation methods.

ork content and method, working conditions, and health and motivation of workers directly affect the productivity of an organization. Successful companies such as Bombardier and Decoma (Magna Exterior Systems) realize this. How do these companies design work system for their employees? Questions such as this are answered in this chapter.

LO1 INTRODUCTION AND JOB DESIGN

This chapter covers work system design, the last step in process design. Work system design involves *job design* (content and method), determination of working conditions, *work measurement* (i.e., establishment of standard times), and *compensation*.

Work design is one of the oldest activities in operations management, and was the main focus of scientific management (later called industrial engineering) of Frederick Taylor at the beginning of last century. Work system design is important because it directly affects an organization's productivity.

Job design involves specifying the content (what) and method (how) of a job. The objective of job design is to increase long-term productivity.

job design Specifying the content and method of a job.

The factors that affect job design and the implications of various alternatives are often so complex that a person without a good background in job design is likely to overlook important aspects of it. Workers and managers alike should be consulted in order to take advantage of their knowledge and to keep them informed.

Current practice in job design contains elements of two basic schools of thought. One is the *efficiency* school, which emphasizes a systematic, logical approach to labour cost reduction; the other is called the *behavioural* school and emphasizes satisfaction of wants and needs of workers as a motivator for increased productivity.

The efficiency approach is a refinement of Frederick Taylor's scientific management. The behavioural approach emerged during the 1950s and includes job enlargement, enrichment, rotation, and teams. It is noteworthy that specialization is a primary issue of disagreement between the efficiency and behavioural approaches.

Efficiency Approach

Efficiency approach includes specialization, methods analysis, and time standards. We will discuss specialization here and cover methods analysis and time standards later in the chapter.

Specialization focuses jobs to a narrow scope. Examples range from assembly-line jobs to medical specialties. For instance, an assembly-line worker could be installing windshields the whole shift (i.e., hundreds of them, same task repeated every minute). College/university professors often specialize in teaching certain courses, some auto mechanics specialize in transmission repair, and some bakers specialize in wedding cakes. The main rationale for specialization is the ability to concentrate one's efforts and thereby become proficient at that type of work.

specialization Focusing the job to a narrow scope.

Unfortunately, some of these jobs, e.g., assembly-line jobs, can be monotonous and boring. The advantages and disadvantages of assembly-line specialization for company and worker are summarized in Table 7-1.

Advantages	
For company:	For worker:
1. Simplifies training	1. Low education and skill requirements
2. High productivity	2. Minimum responsibilities
3. Low wage costs	3. Little mental effort needed
Disadvantages	
For company:	For worker:
1. Difficult to motivate quality	1. Monotonous/boring work
2. Worker dissatisfaction, possibly resulting in absenteeism, high turnover, disruptive tactics	2. Limited opportunities for advancement
	3. Little control over work
	4. Little opportunity for self-fulfillment

Table 7-1

Advantages and disadvantages of assembly-line specialization

The seriousness of the problems with assembly-line specialization caused job designers to seek the behavioural approach.

Behavioural Approach

In an effort to make jobs more interesting and meaningful, job designers frequently consider job enlargement, job rotation, job enrichment, and teams.

job enlargement Giving a worker a larger portion of the total task.

Job enlargement means giving a worker a larger portion of the total task of making the good or providing the service. This constitutes *horizontal loading*—the additional work is on the same level of skill and responsibility as the original job. The goal is to make the job more interesting by increasing the variety of skills required and by letting the worker make a more recognizable contribution to the overall output. For example, a production worker's job might be expanded so that he is responsible for a *sequence* of activities instead of only one activity.

job rotation Workers periodically exchange jobs.

Job rotation means having workers periodically exchange jobs. A company can use this approach to avoid having one or a few employees stuck in monotonous/repetitive jobs. Job rotation allows workers to broaden their learning experience and enables them to fill in for others in the event of sickness or absenteeism. Also, repetitive motion injuries may be avoided by periodically doing a different type of physical work. An example of job rotation is an assembly-line worker who rotates with his team mates every hour.

job enrichment Increasing responsibility for planning and coordination.

Job enrichment involves an increase in the level of responsibility for planning and coordination. It is sometimes referred to as *vertical loading*. An example of this is an operator who is also responsible for the maintenance, set up, and quality control of the machine/process she uses.

self-directed teams Groups who perform the same function and are empowered to make certain decisions and changes in their work.

A **self-directed team**, sometimes referred to as *an autonomous team*, is a group of employees who perform the same function, e.g., the milling operation in a plant. They are empowered to make decisions involving their work as a group. The underlying concept is that the workers, who are close to their work and have the best knowledge of it, are better suited than management to make the most effective decisions involving their work. Moreover, they tend to work harder to ensure that the desired results are achieved. For these teams to function properly, team members must be trained in new skills, including communication and leadership. Self-directed teams have a number of benefits. One is that fewer managers are necessary.

Other benefits include higher quality, productivity, and worker satisfaction. However, middle managers often feel threatened as teams assume more of their traditional functions. See the "Ralston Foods" OM in Action for an example and more details.

OM in ACTION

Ralston Foods

Ralston Foods's plant in Sparks, Nevada, makes store-brand breakfast cereals, e.g., for IGA. The plant follows a team-based work management approach. The operating work groups are maintenance, milling, extrusion, flaking, packing, warehousing, and logistics. The support work groups are human resources, accounting, engineering services, and tech services. Each group consists of 8–50 members. Groups larger than 10 are further divided into teams. All groups are either autonomous or semi-autonomous, and have a self-appointed group leader. Each group decides its own interviewing, hiring, work assignments, schedules, job rotation, performance appraisals, discipline, termination, cost control, quality, safety, continuous improvement, food

safety, service results, capital projects, communications, counselling, customer relations, security, and temperature management. The management also works as a group, acting both as enforcer and facilitator, and is involved in activities such as communication of business trends, production scheduling and prioritization, cost/budget management, benefits and wage adjustments, mass meetings, and support for programs for continuous improvement, safety, counselling/discipline, substance abuse, and employee assistance. The Sparks plant's participatory management has resulted in it achieving its goals on productivity, cost reduction, and quality, while keeping its employees happy.

Source: D.R. Kibbe and J. Casner-Lotto, "Ralston Foods—from Greenfield to Maturity in a Team-based Plant," *Journal of Organizational Excellence*, Summer 2002, 21(3), pp. 57–67.

METHODS ANALYSIS

Methods analysis breaks down the job into a sequence of tasks and elements and tries to make it more efficient.

If methods analysis is done for an existing job, the procedure is to have the analyst observe the job as it is currently being performed and then devise improvements. For a new job, the analyst must rely on the method being used for similar jobs.

The basic procedure in methods analysis is:

1. Identify the job to be studied and gather all pertinent facts about its operations, machines, equipment, materials, and so on.

2. Discuss the job with the operator and supervisor.

3. Analyze and document the present method of performing the job.

4. Question the present method and propose a new method.

Analyzing and questioning the method and proposing a new method requires careful thought about the what, why, when, where, and who of the job. Often, simply going through these questions will clarify the review process by encouraging the analyst to take a devil's advocate attitude toward both present and proposed methods. Frequently, technology assists in the method improvement; see the "Sobeys Reorganizes" OM in Action for an example.

Analyzing and improving methods is facilitated by the use of various charts, such as *process charts* and *worker–machine charts*.

Process charts are used to review and examine the overall sequence of an operation by focusing on the movements of the operator or the flow of material. These charts are helpful in identifying the non-productive steps of the process (e.g., delays, temporary storages, distances travelled). Figure 7-1 illustrates a process chart for "Requisition of petty cash" in a company. The petty cash is used for minor expenses such as buying a hand tool or stationery.

Experienced analysts usually develop a checklist of questions they ask themselves to generate ideas for improvements. Some representative questions are:

1. Why is there a delay, storage, or inspection at this point?

2. How can travel distances be shortened or avoided?

3. Can an operation be eliminated?

4. Can the sequence of operations be changed?

5. Can similar activities be grouped?

6. Would the use of additional or improved equipment be helpful?

methods analysis   Breaks down the job into a sequence of tasks and elements and improves it.

process chart   Chart used to examine the overall sequence of an operation by focusing on movements of the operator or flow of material.

OM in *ACTION*

Sobeys Reorganizes

When Sobeys bought the Oshawa Group in 1998, the food distribution centre in North Montreal, which supplies IGA and small independent chains, was already in the middle of work reorganization to streamline the supply chain and increase its operating efficiency. Five joint union–management improvement committees were formed: Technology Change and Working Methods; Perishable Sector; Non-perishable Sector; Transportation; and Occupational Health and Safety. One of the projects was the job assignment activity done at the beginning of each night shift. The assignment was done based on seniority; because the volume and type of work varied every night, it took approximately 30 minutes. The new approach uses a job assignment software that takes only five minutes to run.

Another new work procedure concerns the job of order pickers. Before, they were given a customer order list showing the names of items and the number of cases to pick from each location in the warehouse. A minimum of 145 pickups per hour in the grocery section and 130 in the frozen section was required. The order pickers, using their pallet jacks, raced through the aisles of warehouse, following their own chosen routes; this resulted in accidents and errors. Sobeys installed a computer order-picking system that directs each order picker to his next pickup position and specifies the standard time for doing so.

Source: M. Brossard, "Reorganizing the Sobeys Distribution Centre in Montreal," *Workplace Gazette* 4(2), 2001, pp. 34–43.

Figure 7-1

Example of a process chart

Source: Elias M. Awad, *Systems Analysis and Design*, 4th ed. (Burr Ridge, IL: Richard D. Irwin, 1985), p113. © 1985 by Richard D. Irwin, Inc. Reprinted by permission of the McGraw-Hill Companies Inc.

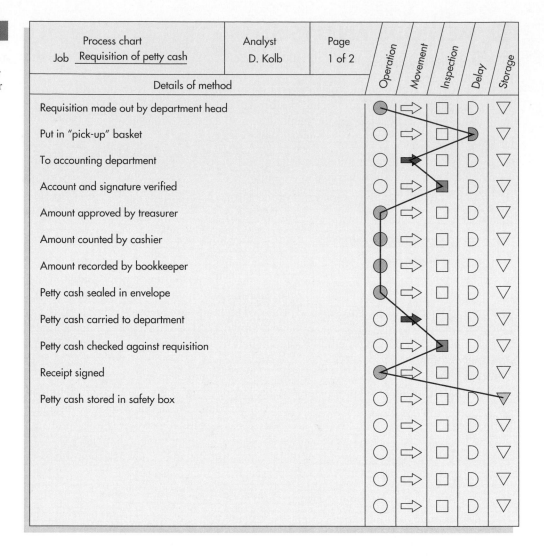

For the example of "Requisition of petty cash," after considering the amount of work involved and the high frequency of requisitions, a solution may be to issue a corporate credit card (with a certain limit) to the department heads.

worker–machine chart
Used to determine portions of a work cycle during which an operator and equipment are busy or idle.

A **worker–machine chart** is helpful in visualizing the portions of a work cycle during which an operator and machine are busy or idle. The analyst can easily see when the operator and machine are working independently and when their work overlaps or is interdependent. One use of this type of chart is to determine how many machines the operator can manage.

Figure 7-2 presents an example of a worker–machine chart for weighing and pricing bulk food. As evident, the machine can be used by more than one operator (if needed) because it is idle most of the time.

Motion Study

motion study   Systematic study of the human motions used to perform an operation or task.

Motion study is the systematic study of the human motions used to perform an operation or a task. The purpose is to eliminate unnecessary motions and to identify the best sequence of motions for maximum efficiency. Hence, motion study can be an important tool for methods analysis and productivity improvement. Present practice evolved from the work of Frank Gilbreth, who originated the concept in the bricklaying trade in the early twentieth century. Through the use of motion study, Gilbreth increased the number of bricks laid per hour by a factor of 3. Usually, motion study is performed in conjunction with time study (described later in "Work Measurement").

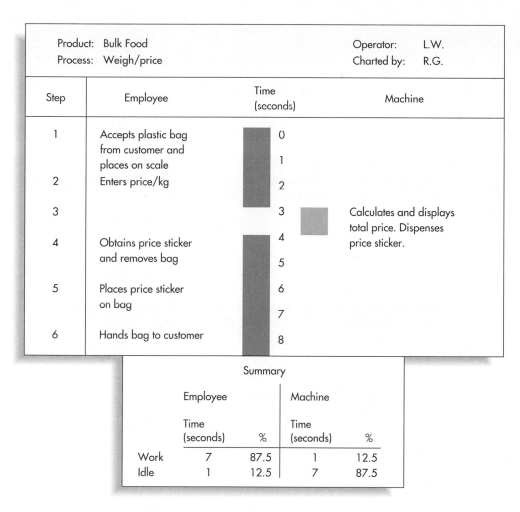

Figure 7-2

Example of a worker-machine chart

There are a number of different techniques or tools that motion study analysts can use to develop efficient procedures. The most used techniques or tools are:

1. Motion economy principles
2. Analysis of elementary motions
3. Micro-motion (slow-motion video) study
4. Simultaneous hands motion chart.

Gilbreth's work laid the foundation for the development of **motion economy principles**, which are guidelines for designing motion-efficient work procedures. The guidelines are divided into three categories: use of arms and body, arrangement of the workplace, and design of tools and equipment. Table 7-2 lists some examples of the principles.

A list of some common basic elementary motions (*elements* for short) includes reach, grasp, move, and disengage. Breaking the task into elements enables motion analysis and also easy timing of the elements. Describing a job using elements often takes a substantial amount of work. However, for short, repetitive jobs, element analysis may be justified.

Frank Gilbreth and his wife, Lillian, an industrial psychologist, were also responsible for introducing motion pictures for studying motions, called **micro-motion study**. This approach is applied not only in industry but also in some other areas such as sports. Use of camera and slow-motion replay enables analysts to study motions that would otherwise be too rapid to see. In addition, the resulting films provide a permanent record that can be referred to not only for training workers and analysts but also for settling disputes involving standard times.

motion economy principles Guidelines for designing motion-efficient work procedures.

micro-motion study Use of motion pictures and slow motion to study motions that otherwise would be too rapid to analyze.

A. The use of arms and body.

   1. Both hands should begin and end their activity simultaneously and should not be idle at the same instant, except during frequent but short rest periods.

   2. The motions made by the hands should be minimal and symmetrical.

   3. Momentum should assist workers wherever possible and should be minimized if it must be overcome by muscular effort.

   4. Continuous natural curved motions are preferable to straight-line motions involving sudden and sharp changes in direction.

   5. Strength requirements should be much less than the maximum available. Avoid lifting heavy objects. Use slow movements for maximum muscle strength.

   6. Eliminate bend and rise, awkward positions, and make the tasks easier to reduce fatigue.

   7. Eliminate eye travel and avoid losing eye focus.

B. The arrangement of the workplace.

   1. Fixed locations for all tools and material should be provided to permit the best sequence and to eliminate or reduce search and selection.

   2. Gravity bins and drop delivery should reduce reach and move times; wherever possible, ejectors should remove finished parts automatically.

   3. All materials and tools should be located within easy reach.

   4. Provide a chair or stool if possible.

C. The design of tools and equipment.

   1. Where possible, power tools should replace hand tools.

   2. All levers, handles, wheels, and other control devices should be readily accessible to the operator and designed to give the best possible mechanical advantage and to utilize the strongest available muscle group.

   3. Parts should be held in position by fixtures.

Source: Adapted from Benjamin W. Niebel, *Motion and Time Economy* (Burr Ridge, IL: Richard D. Irwin, Inc., 1993), pp. 206–207. Reprinted with permission of the McGraw-Hill Companies Inc.

simo chart A chart that shows the elementary motions performed by each hand, side-by-side, over time.

Motion study analysts may use a simultaneous hands motion chart or **simo chart** (see Figure 7-3a) to study the elementary motions performed by each hand, side-by-side, through time. Here, the methods analyst studies a trim/blanking job on a hand-operated press with an accompanying die. He breaks the job down into a right- and left-hand process chart (aligned through time). A review of the process charts shows that delays are occurring because the motions of the right and left hand are not balanced: the left hand is waiting while the right hand raises the handle of the press, again while the right hand removes the part from the die, and again when the right hand regains control of the press handle. If the operator did not have to remove the finished piece from the die, he would be freed from the action of re-grasping the press handle. The improved method is shown in Figure 7-3b. A fixture was developed to lift the part clear from the die while the press is being raised and eject it through the back of the press by an air blast. Simo charts are invaluable in studying operations such as data entry, sewing, surgical and dental procedures, and certain fabrication and assembly operations.

LO3 WORKING CONDITIONS

Working conditions are an important aspect of work system design. In many instances, government standards and regulations apply. Physical factors such as temperature and humidity, ventilation, illumination, noise and vibration, work breaks, safety, ergonomics, workers' well-being, and a healthy workplace can have significant impacts on worker performance in terms of productivity and quality of output.

a. *Right- and left-hand analysis of a blanking operation*

The Airfelt Mfg. Corp.
Right and Left Hand Analysis

Operation ___Blank supporting strip on hand arbor press___

Part No. ___P-1107-7___   Dwg. No. ___PB-1107___   Date ___1-12-___

Drawn By ___W. Eitele___   Dept. ___13___   Plant ___Bellefonte___   Sheet ___1___ of ___1___

Sketch

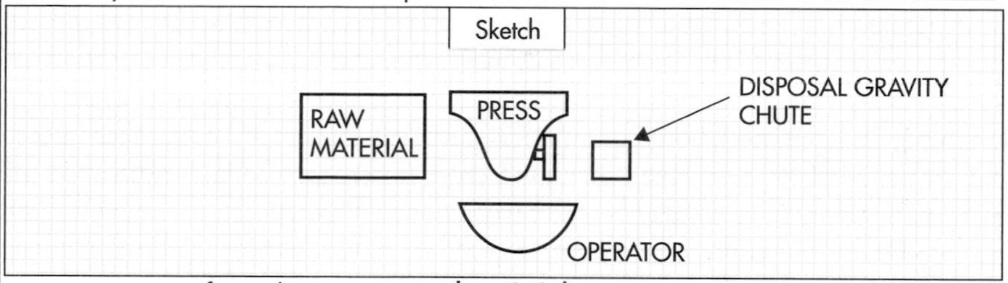

RAW MATERIAL   PRESS   DISPOSAL GRAVITY CHUTE

OPERATOR

Left Hand	Symbols		Right Hand	
1. Pick up part from hopper			Pull press handle down	1.
Reach for part	Re	H	Hold handle	
Grasp part	G	H	Hold handle	
Move part adjacent to die	M	M	Move press handle down	
2. Wait for right hand			Raise press handle up	2.
Unavoidable delay	UD	M	Move press handle up	
Unavoidable delay	UD	RI	Release press handle	
3. Wait for right hand			Get part from die	3.
Unavoidable delay	UD	Re	Reach for part in die	
Unavoidable delay	UD	G	Grasp part	
4. Place part in die			Drop part in chute	4.
Move part to die	M	M	Move part to chute	
Position part in die	P	RI	Release part	
Release part	RI	UD	Wait for left hand	
5. Wait for right hand			Get press handle	5.
Unavoidable delay	UD	Re	Reach for handle	
Unavoidable delay	UD	G	Grasp handle	

b. *Right- and left-hand analysis of a blanking operation in which unavoidable delays have been omitted*

The Airfelt Mfg. Corp.
Right and Left Hand Analysis

Operation ___Blank supporting strip on hand arbor press___

Part No. ___P-1107-7___   Dwg. No. ___PB-1107___   Date ___1-12-___

Drawn By ___W. Eitele___   Dept. ___13___   Plant ___Bellefonte___   Sheet ___1___ of ___1___

Sketch

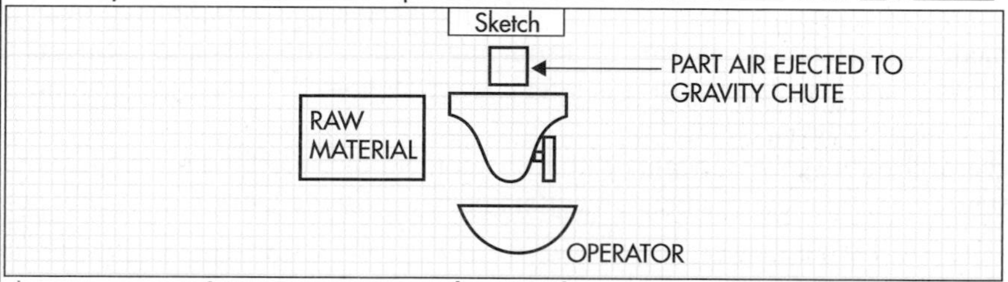

PART AIR EJECTED TO GRAVITY CHUTE

RAW MATERIAL

OPERATOR

Left Hand	Symbols		Right Hand	
1. Get part from hopper			Pull press handle down	1.
Reach for part	RE	H	Hold handle	
Grasp part	G			
Move part to die	M	M	Move press handle down	
2. Place part in die				2.
Move part to die	M		Raise press handle up	
Position part	P	M	Move handle up	
Release part	RI	H	Hold handle	

Figure 7-3

A simultaneous hands motion chart

Source: B.W. Niebel, *Motion and Time Study*, 5th ed. (Homewood, IL: Richard D. Irwin, 1972). Reprinted by permission.

http://www.hrsdc.gc.ca/eng/
labour/health_safety/index.shtml

Brief History of Government Regulation of Workplace. Working conditions have sometimes been detrimental to the health of workers, and work injuries and fatalities sometimes occur, although the numbers have been declining. Historically, the mechanization and creation of factories in the nineteenth century was the start of increasing health and safety problems. The government passed worker protection acts that required guards on the machines, fire safety, boiler and elevator inspection, sanitation, ventilation, and adequate heating and lighting. The Canadian Labour Code of 1966 included safety as well as other work standards such as minimum wage. In 1978, the Labour Code was amended to give three rights to workers: (a) to refuse dangerous work, (b) to participate in improving safety and health problems (through joint management/labour committees), and (c) to know about hazards in the workplace. Also created in 1978 was the Canadian Centre for Occupational Health and Safety. In 1988, the right to know about hazards in the workplace was shaped into the requirement for a Workplace Hazardous Materials Information System (WHMIS), which mandates proper labelling of hazardous material and making available the material safety data sheets.

Temperature and Humidity. Many operations need to be performed in high temperatures, such as in an iron foundry, and some others need to be performed in low temperatures, such as in a slaughterhouse. Although human beings can function under a fairly wide range of temperatures, work performance tends to be adversely affected if temperatures are outside a very narrow *comfort band.* That comfort band depends on how strenuous the work is; the more strenuous the work, the smaller the comfort range.

For most work activities, the comfort band is about 10°C to 21°C at a relative humidity of between 30 to 80 percent. Productivity drops sharply below 0°C and above 30°C and at relative humidity close to 100 percent. Solutions range from selection of suitable clothing to space heating or cooling devices.

Ventilation. Some factories (such as lumber mills and grinding operations) create much dust; some others (such as pulp and paper mills) generate gases and foul odours. These are unhealthy and unpleasant. Large fans and air-conditioning equipment are commonly used to exchange and recondition the air.

Illumination. The amount of illumination required depends largely on the type of work being performed; the more detailed the work, the higher the level of illumination needed for adequate performance. Other important considerations are the amount of glare and contrast.

Sometimes natural daylight can be used as a source of illumination. It is not only free, but also provides some psychological benefits. Workers in windowless rooms may feel cut off from the outside world and experience various psychological problems. On the down side, the inability to control natural light (e.g., cloudy days) can result in dramatic changes in light intensity.

Noise and Vibrations. Noise is caused by the movement and vibrations of machines or equipment. Noise can be annoying or distracting, leading to errors and accidents. It can also damage or impair hearing if it is loud enough. Figure 7-4 illustrates loudness level of some typical sounds.

Successful sound control begins with measurement of the offending sounds. In a new operation, selection and placement of equipment can eliminate or reduce many potential

---

Figure 7-4

Decibel values of typical sounds (db)

Source: From Benjamin W. Niebel, *Motion and Time Study,* 8th ed. Copyright © 1988 Richard D. Irwin, Inc. Used by permission of McGraw-Hill Companies, Inc., p. 248.

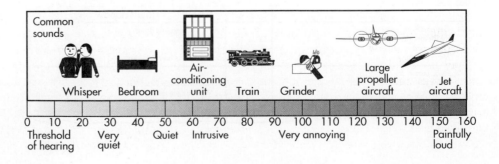

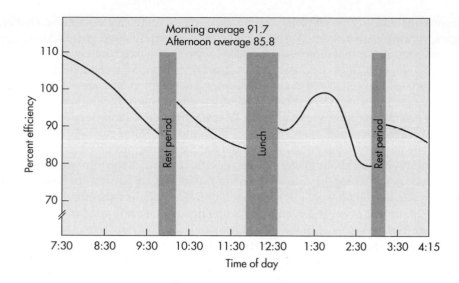

Figure 7-5

A typical relationship between worker efficiency and time of day

Source: Benjamin W. Niebel, *Motion and Time Study,* 8th ed. (Burr Ridge, IL: Richard D. Irwin, 1988), p. 270 © 1988 by Richard D. Irwin, Inc. Reprinted by permission of the McGraw-Hill Companies Inc.

problems. In the case of existing equipment, it may be possible to redesign or substitute equipment. In some instances, the source of noise can be isolated from other work areas. If that isn't feasible, acoustical walls and ceilings that deflect sound waves may prove useful. Sometimes the only solution is to provide earplugs or earmuffs for those in the immediate vicinity.

Vibrations can be a factor in work system design even without a noise component. Vibrations can come from tools, machines, vehicles, air-conditioning systems, pumps, and other sources. Corrective measures include padding, stabilizers, shock absorbers, cushioning, and rubber mountings.

Work Breaks. The frequency, length, and timing of work breaks (i.e., rests) can have a significant impact on both productivity and quality of output. One indication of the relationship between worker efficiency and work breaks is illustrated in Figure 7-5. It reveals that efficiency generally declines as the day wears on, but it also shows how breaks for lunch and rest can cause an upward shift in efficiency.

An important variable in the rate of decline of efficiency and potential effects of work breaks is the amount of physical and/or mental requirements of the job. Steelworkers, for instance, may need rest breaks of 15 minutes per hour due to the strenuous nature of their jobs. In fact one of Taylor's experiments showed that for men carrying 92-pound pig-irons up a ramp, maximum output was quadrupled when the workers rested 58 percent of the time. For 40-pound pig-irons, optimal rest was 48 percent of the time. Physical effort is not the only condition that indicates the need for work breaks. People working at computer monitors also need periodic breaks, and students need study breaks.

Safety. Worker safety is one of the most basic issues in work system design. This area needs constant attention from management, employees, and job designers. Workers cannot be effectively motivated if they feel they are in physical danger.

From an employer standpoint, accidents are undesirable because they are expensive (insurance and compensation); they usually involve damage to equipment and/or products; they require hiring, training, and makeup work; and they generally interrupt work.

The two basic causes of accidents are worker carelessness and unsafe conditions. Carelessness includes unsafe acts. Examples include failure to use protective equipment, overriding safety controls (e.g., taping control buttons down), disregarding safety procedures, improper use of tools and equipment, and failure to use reasonable caution in danger zones. Unsafe conditions include unprotected pulleys, chains, material-handling equipment, machinery, and so on. Also, poorly lit walkways, stairs, and loading docks constitute hazards. Toxic wastes, gases and vapours, and radiation hazards must be contained. In many instances, these cannot be detected without special equipment, so they would not be obvious to workers or emergency personnel. Protection against hazards involves use

____

_____

_____

_____

of proper lighting, clearly marked danger zones, use of protective equipment (hardhats, goggles, earmuffs, gloves, heavy shoes, and clothing), safety devices (machine guards, dual-control switches that require an operator to use both hands), emergency equipment (emergency showers, fire extinguishers, fire escapes), and thorough instruction and training in safety procedures and use of regular and emergency equipment. Housekeeping (clean floors, open aisles, waste removal) is another important safety factor. Workers must be trained in proper procedures and attitudes. Management must enforce safety procedures and use of safety equipment.

The enactment of Occupational Health and Safety regulations emphasizes the importance of safety considerations in work system design. It provides specific safety regulations with inspectors to see that they are adhered to. Inspections are carried out both at random and to investigate complaints of unsafe conditions. The officials are empowered to issue warnings, to impose fines, and even to order shutdown for unsafe conditions.

A more effective way to deal with management of safety issues is to incorporate it into the company's management planning and control activities, just as product quality is managed. A safety management system based on the guidelines of BSI OHSAS 18000 can be used. This is similar to ISO 9000 (for quality systems) and ISO 14000 (for environment systems).

The OHSAS 18000 requires that health and safety activities be planned.[1] This process requires that, after an annual risk assessment, realistic objectives and targets be set and that the roles, responsibilities, and timelines necessary to achieve the targets be clearly communicated to—and understood by—all those involved in achieving them. Operational controls (procedures) and emergency plans must be developed and documented for those risks found to be intolerable. Employees must be trained.

Performance and compliance with system requirements must be measured in order to ensure that they are controlled. Any incident, accident, or other nonconformance within the system needs to be investigated at a level appropriate to its impact on the system. The resulting corrective and preventive action developed from this process ensures that the standards of practice are complied with and are adequate. Finally, senior management must periodically review the system (e.g., internal or external audits every six months) to ensure that it is meeting the objectives stated in its policy and that it is effectively implemented. Improvements in the overall system are identified and implemented through the planning process.

In March 2001, Compaq's Fremont, California, plant was one of the first plants in North America to implement OHSAS 18000. After obtaining its ISO 9002 and ISO 14000 registrations, it was easy for Compaq to use the same management systems to manage health and safety. In fact, the same person led the environment, health, and safety systems. As a result, Compaq reduced its accident rate by 30 percent (twice its goal of 15 percent) in less than a year.[2]

ergonomics Fitting the job to the worker's capability and size.

http://www.bsi-global.com

Ergonomics. **Ergonomics** involves fitting the job to the worker's capability and size. It relates to the design of equipment, work methods, and work space to remove awkward reaching and bending, forceful gripping of tools, heavy lifting, and endless repetition of motions. Among other things, ergonomics seeks to prevent common workplace injuries such as back injuries and repetitive motion injuries by taking into account the fact that people vary in their physical dimensions and capabilities, and that some activities, when continually repeated, result in strains in muscles and joints (called *musculoskeletal injuries*, *repetitive motion injuries*, or *cumulative trauma disorders*). Most ergonomic problems are unintentional mistakes that develop because no one had the knowledge or the time to design the work system properly. Companies have compelling interests in reducing worker injuries: injuries result in lower productivity, lost workdays, and increases in workers' compensation premiums.

[1] J.J. Janssen, "OHSAS 18001: Another @#$%& Standard?" *OH&S Canada* 18(1), January/February 2002, p. 58.
[2] "Compaq Facility Reaps Benefits From OHSAS 18001," *OH&S Canada* 71(2), February 2002, p. 14.

Nexgen Ergonomics

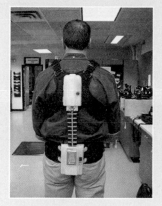

Nexgen Ergonomics is a well-known Canadian company, located in Montreal, involved in producing or reselling (under distribution agreement) software and products used in ergonomics. The products include a virtual mannequin that can be dimensioned according to average or extreme sizes of a male or female body, to be used in testing CAD drawings of products that directly interact with a human body. Also, Nexgen sells lumbar motion measurement products (see photos on the right), video analysis software, 2D to 3D conversion, and many types of medical and safety equipment.

Mother Hubbard's Kitchens

In the sanding operation of Mother Hubbard's Kitchens in Dartmouth, Nova Scotia, the worker held the sander with his operating hand and a piece of cabinet on a table with the other hand (see the two sketches below), and the work required reaching and exerting force from the shoulder. There was a chance of repetitive motion injuries and shoulder pain.

Ergonomic solution: a tilted work space with a piece-holding jig:

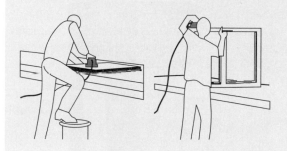

Source: http://www.ccohs.ca/oshanswers/occup_workplace/cab_manu.html.

Some common examples of ergonomic problems in the office are as follows. A common problem in using the computer mouse is that it is usually placed beside the keyboard. This results in the need for constant reaching and stretching of the arm, which can result in long-term joint problems. A solution is using a rotating platform for the mouse so that it can be moved closer to the body. The arm should be at a right angle close to the body and the wrist should not be bent. Another common problem is bad sitting posture. An ergonomic chair that can be adjusted for the user's body dimensions should be used. After adjustment, the height of its back should fit in the "small" of the back of the user and the height of the seat should be just below the knees of the user (while standing). There should be approximately a 5-cm gap between the back of the knee and the chair (while sitting; see the illustration to the right). The display monitor should be just below the horizontal eyesight so that there is no need for slouching. It should be approximately 60 to 80 cm from the eyes. Because monitors emit light, one should look away from the screen every few minutes for a few seconds (preferably at distant objects). If a document is being read, it, and not the monitor, should be lit using a lamp. Also, because monitors act like mirrors, their angle should be adjusted to avoid glare. For more information on ergonomics, see the Canadian Centre for Occupational Health and Safety Web site at http://www.ccohs.ca.

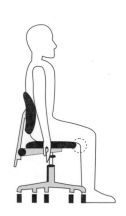

Two industrial application of ergonomics are described in the "Mother Hubbard's Kitchens" and "Honda Motorcycles" OM in Actions (on the last page and below, respectively), and some ergonomics products are mentioned in the "Nexgen Ergonomics" OM in Action on the last page.

Workers' Well-being and a Healthy Workplace

Many companies are realizing that productivity of employees depends on their general health and well-being. The National Quality Institute, in cooperation with Health Canada, developed the Healthy Workplace award in 1998 to recognize companies that have a holistic system for a healthy workplace, including physical, mental, safety, personal, and social aspects. The criteria include four "drivers" of a healthy workplace: leadership role (having a policy and being involved in a healthy workplace); planning process (needs assessment, setting goals, designing programs); fostering worker involvement (respecting workers, training to use the programs); and process management (collecting and using feedback). The outcomes—the results of a healthy workplace system such as reduction in absenteeism, turnover, and accident rates—should be measured and compared with goals. The programs can affect the physical environment (safety, cleanliness, protective equipment, ergonomics, lighting, air quality, noise, wheelchair accessibility, etc.), health practices (assistance to give up smoking and alcohol abuse, promoting healthy nutrition in the cafeteria, a fitness facility, etc.), and social environment (developing self-respect and a sense of belonging and control over work, protection against harassment and workplace violence, coping with stress, fairness in job assignment and evaluation, reasonable pace of work, flexible hours, benefits plan, etc.). For an application of Healthy Workplace, see the "Magna Exterior's Healthy Workplace" OM in Action, For an overview of the NQI's Healthy Workplace Checkup, see http://www.nqi.ca/services/HW_Checkup.aspx.

http://www.nqi.ca

Correct positioning of equipment and tools can help reduce fatigue and increase employee productivity. Here, an ergonomist from Humantech Inc., in Ann Arbor, Michigan, collects a workstation's measurements to ensure proper height and accessibility for employees.

OM in ACTION

Honda Motorcycles

One of the operations studied by the ergonomics team of the Honda motorcycle plant in, Marysville, Ohio, in the early 2000s was the finishing/grinding operation for fenders in the welding department. The fender, weighing approximately 6 kg, had to be lifted and repositioned on a stationery stand several times, and the operator had to assume awkward positions and reach up to .7 metre to do the work. These added approximately 30 minutes of work per fender. The team installed an adjustable positioner, which reduced the awkward positions and limited the reach to .4 metre, hence reducing the time to 15 minutes per fender.

Source: D. Abbott, "Show Us the Money," *The Safety & Health Practitioner*, May 2003, 21(5), pp. 32–34.

Magna Exterior's Healthy Workplace

Magna Exteriors designs and manufactures automotive exterior components. It has several facilities in Canada and other countries.

In Canada, each plant has a health program designed according to employee needs. Employees periodically receive a health and wellness newsletter. Health education and awareness are also developed through short, monthly seminars offered on a variety of topics (fitness, nutrition, back care, repetitive strain, shift work, etc.). The seminars are accompanied by corresponding screening clinics. For example, the Healthy Heart (cardiovascular) seminar is followed by a blood pressure clinic. Healthy workplace policies and programs such as discounts on local gyms, smoking cessation programs, and stretch break programs further support employees as they move toward better health. There are intramural sports (hockey, baseball, and soccer). Magna is committed to an operating philosophy based on fairness and a concern for its people, put in the form of an Employee Charter. It includes the following principles: job security, a safe and healthful workplace, fair treatment, competitive wages and benefits, employee equity and profit participation, communication and information, a hotline, and an employee relations advisory board. Magna offers a vast array of career training opportunities to employees at all levels. Employee input is encouraged through anonymous suggestions, monthly meetings with the plant and human resources managers, and an employee satisfaction survey.

Source: G. McKeown, "Case Study: Decoma International Inc.: Commitment to a Healthy Workplace, http://www.nqi.ca/articles/article_details.aspx?ID=55, July 28, 2001.

LO4 WORK MEASUREMENT

Work measurement or time study is concerned with determining the *length of time* it should take to complete the job. Job times are vital inputs for personnel planning, estimating labour costs, assembly-line balancing, and designing incentive systems. For an application, see the "Rebalancing at Ford's St. Thomas Plant" OM in Action.

A **standard time** is the amount of time it should take a qualified worker to complete a specified task, working at a sustainable rate, and using given methods, tools and equipment, raw materials, and workplace arrangement. Whenever a standard time is developed for a job, it is essential to provide a complete description of the parameters of the job because the actual time to do the job is sensitive to all of these factors; changes in any one of the factors can materially affect time requirements. For instance, changes in product design or changes brought about by a methods analysis should trigger a new time study to update the standard time. As a practical matter, though, minor changes do not justify the expense of restudying the job. Consequently, the standard time for many jobs may be slightly inaccurate. Periodic time studies may be used to update the standard times.

Organizations develop standard times in a number of ways. The most commonly used methods are:

1. Stopwatch time study
2. Predetermined element times
3. Work sampling.

Stopwatch Time Study

Stopwatch time study is used to develop a standard time for a job based on observations of one worker taken over a number of cycles. It is then applied to the work of all others in the organization who perform the same job. The basic steps in a stopwatch time study are:

1. Define the job to be studied, and inform the worker who will be studied.
2. Determine the number of cycles to observe.
3. Time the job, and rate the worker's performance.
4. Calculate the standard time, allowing for rest periods.

The analyst who studies the job should be thoroughly familiar with it because it is not unusual for workers to attempt to include extra motions during the study in the hope of gaining a standard that allows more time per piece. Furthermore, the analyst will need to

work measurement
Determining how long it should take to do a job.

standard time   The amount of time it should take a qualified worker to complete a specified task, working at a sustainable rate, and using given methods, tools and equipment, raw materials, and workplace arrangement.

stopwatch time study
Development of a standard time based on observations of one worker taken over a number of cycles.

Rebalancing at Ford's St. Thomas Plant

One of the uses of standard time is in auto assembly plants, specifically in assembly-line balancing. Because of work method and technology changes, the line needs to be rebalanced periodically. This work redistribution needs to be negotiated with the unions. At Ford's assembly plant in St. Thomas,

Ontario, according to the collective agreement the management can rebalance the line during a four-month period every year (called the balance-out period). Ironically, many workers refuse their new work assignment using the right to refuse "unsafe" work.

Source: R. Sinclair, "Health and Safety Work Refusals: A Case Study of Ford of Canada's St. Thomas Assembly Plant," *Workplace Gazette* 1(4), 1998, pp. 54–58.

check that the job is being performed efficiently (i.e., a methods analysis should first be performed on the job) before setting the standard time.

In most instances, an analyst will break all but very short jobs down into tasks and obtain times for each task. There are several reasons for this: One is that some tasks are not performed in every cycle and the breakdown enables the analyst to get a better perspective on them. Another is that the worker's proficiency may not be the same for all tasks of the job. A third reason is to build a file of task times that can be used to set times for other jobs.

Workers sometimes feel uneasy about being studied and fear changes that might result. The analyst should make an attempt to discuss these things with the worker prior to studying an operation to reduce such fears and to enlist the cooperation of the worker.

The number of cycles that must be timed is a function of three things: (1) the variability of observed times, (2) the desired accuracy (maximum acceptable error proportion), and (3) the desired level of confidence for the estimated job time. Very often the desired accuracy is expressed as a percentage of the mean of the observed times. For example, the goal of a stopwatch time study may be to achieve an estimate that is within 10 percent of the actual mean. The sample size needed to achieve that goal can be determined using:

$$n = \left(\frac{zs}{a\bar{x}} \right)^2 \tag{7-1}$$

where

z = Number of normal standard deviations needed for desired confidence

s = Sample standard deviation

a = Maximum acceptable error proportion (= percentage/100)

$\bar{x}$ = Sample mean

n = number of observations (= sample size)

Typical values of z used are:[3]

Desired Confidence (%)	z Value
90	1.65
95	1.96
95.5	2.00
98	2.33
99	2.58

Of course, the value of z for any desired confidence can be obtained from the Normal table in Appendix B, Table A, working backward (first divide the desired confidence

---

[3]Theoretically, a t rather than a z value should be used because the population standard deviation is unknown. However, the use of z is simpler and provides reasonable results when the number of observations is 30 or more, as it generally is. In practice, z is used almost exclusively.

by 200). For example, if a 97% confidence is required, then $97/200 = .485$, which relates to $z = 2.17$ in the table.

To make a preliminary estimate of sample size, it is typical to take a small number of observations (i.e., 10 to 20) and calculate values of $\bar{x}$ and s to use in the formula for n. Toward the end of the study, the analyst may want to recalculate n using revised estimates of $\bar{x}$ and s based on the increased data available.

An alternate formula used when the desired accuracy is stated as an *amount* (e.g., within one minute of the true mean) instead of a proportion is:

$$n = \left(\frac{zs}{e}\right)^2 \qquad (7\text{-}2)$$

where

$e = $ Accuracy amount or maximum acceptable error amount

Example 1

An industrial engineer wants to estimate the time required to perform a certain job. A preliminary study yielded a mean of 6.4 minutes and a standard deviation of 2.1 minutes for the job. The desired confidence is 95 percent. How many observations will she need (including those already taken) if the maximum acceptable error is:

a. ± 10 percent of the sample mean?

b. .5 minute?

Solution

a. $s = 2.1$ minutes $z = 1.96$

$\bar{x} = 6.4$ minutes $a = .10$

$$n = \left(\frac{zs}{a\bar{x}}\right)^2 = \left(\frac{1.96(2.1)}{.10(6.4)}\right)^2 = 41.36 \text{ (round up to 42)}$$

b. $e = .5$ $n = \left(\frac{zs}{e}\right)^2 = \left(\frac{1.96(2.1)}{.5}\right)^2 = 67.77 \text{ (round up to 68)}$

Development of a standard time actually involves calculation of three times: *observed time (OT), normal time (NT)*, and *standard time (ST)*.

Observed Time. The observed time is simply the average of the recorded times. Thus,

$$OT = \frac{\sum x_i}{n} \qquad (7\text{-}3)$$

where

$OT = $ Observed time

$\sum x_i = $ Sum of recorded times

$n = $ Number of observations

Note: If a task does not occur during each cycle, its average time should be determined separately.

Normal Time. The normal time is the observed time adjusted for the worker's performance. It is calculated by multiplying the observed time by a *performance rating*. That is,

$$NT = OT \times PR \qquad (7\text{-}4)$$

where

$NT = $ Normal time

$PR = $ Performance rating

This assumes that a single performance rating has been determined for the entire job. If ratings are made on a task-by-task basis, the normal time is obtained by multiplying each task's average time by its performance rating and then summing those values:

$$NT = \sum (\bar{x}_j \times PR_j) \qquad (7\text{-}5)$$

where

$\bar{x}_j$ = Average time for task j

PR_j = Performance rating for task j

The reason for including this adjustment factor is that the worker being observed may be working at a rate different from a "normal" rate, either to deliberately slow the pace or because his or her natural abilities differ from the norm. For this reason, the analyst assigns a performance rating to adjust the observed times to an "average" pace. A normal performance rating is 1.00. A performance rating of .9 indicates a pace that is 90 percent of normal, whereas a rating of 1.05 indicates a pace that is slightly faster than normal. For long jobs, each task may be rated; for short jobs, a single rating may be made for an entire cycle.

When assessing performance, the analyst must compare the observed performance to her concept of normal. Obviously, there is room for debate about what constitutes normal performance, and performance ratings are sometimes the source of considerable conflict between labour union and management. Although no one has been able to suggest a way around these subjective evaluations, sufficient training and periodic *recalibration* of analysts using training films can provide a high degree of consistency in the ratings of different analysts.

Standard Time. Normal time is the length of time a worker should take to perform a job if there are no delays or rest breaks. It does not take into account such factors as personal needs (getting a drink of water or going to the washroom), unavoidable delays (machine adjustments and repairs, talking to a supervisor, waiting for materials), or rest breaks to recover from fatigue. The standard time for a job is the normal time multiplied by an *allowance* for these factors.

$$ST = NT \times AF \qquad (7\text{-}6)$$

where

ST = Standard time

AF = Allowance factor

Allowance can be based on either job time or time worked (e.g., a workday). If allowance is based on the *job time*, the allowance factor must be calculated using the formula

$$AF_{\text{job}} = 1 + A \qquad A = \text{Allowance proportion based on job time} \qquad (7\text{-}7)$$

This is used when different jobs have different allowances. If allowances are based on a proportion of the time worked (i.e., the *workday*), the appropriate formula is

$$AF_{\text{day}} = \frac{1}{1 - A} \qquad A = \text{Allowance proportion based on workday} \qquad (7\text{-}8)$$

This is used when jobs are the same or similar and have the same allowance factor.

Time Study Observation Sheet. Usually a standard form is used to record the observations in a stopwatch time study. In the following example, the job is attaching 2 feet by 3 feet chart sheets together. The job has been decomposed into four tasks (the left column). Under each task in parentheses is the event that signifies the end of the task. For example, grasping the stapler signifies the end of task 1 and the start of task 2. Focusing on these events makes measuring the times easier. Also note that to the right of each task are two rows. The top row is the individual time of the task in each of the 10 cycles, whereas the bottom row is the cumulative times. For example, for task 2 in cycle 1, the cumulative time is .23 minutes. The individual time for this task is therefore .23 − .07 = .16 minutes, where .07 was the (cumulative) time at the end of task 1 in cycle 1. The cumulative time steadily advances as more cycles are timed. However, the minute digit of the cumulative time has been omitted in order to save recording time. For example, the cumulative time for task 4 in cycle 2 is actually 1.09, but only .09 is shown. It is clearly easier, faster, and more accurate to record the cumulative times first, and then calculate the individual times after the completion of the study.

Time Study Observation Sheet																
Identification of operation		Assemble 24" × 36" Chart Blanks								Date 10/9						
Began Timing: 9:26 Ended Timing: 9:32		Operator 109				Approval				Observer						
Task description and Breakpoint		Cycles											Summary			
		1 .00	2	3	4	5	6	7	8	9	10	ΣT	T	PR	NT	
1	Fold over end (grasp stapler)	.07	.07	.05	.07	.09	.06	.05	.08	.08	.06	.68	.07	.90	.06	
		.07	.61	.14	.67	.24	.78	.33	.88	.47	.09					
2	Staple five times (drop stapler)	.16	.14	.14	.15	.16	.16	.14	.17	.14	.15	1.51	.15	1.05	.16	
		.23	.75	.28	.82	.40	.94	.47	.05	.61	.24					
3	Bend and insert wire (drop pliers)	.22	.25	.22	.25	.23	.23	.21	.26	.25	.24	2.36	.24	1.00	.24	
		.45	.00	.50	.07	.63	.17	.68	.31	.86	.48					
4	Dispose of finished chart (touch next sheet)	.09	.09	.10	.08	.09	.11	.12	.08	.17	.08	1.01	.10	.90	.09	
		.54	.09	.60	.15	.72	.28	.80	.39	.03	.56			.55 normal minute for cycle			
5																
6																
10																
Normal cycle time .55 + Allowance (.55 × .143) or .08 = Std. time .63 min/pc.																

Example 2

Calculate the allowance factor for these two cases:

a. The allowance is 20 percent of *job* time.

b. The allowance is 20 percent of *work* time.

$A = .20$

Solution

a. $AF_{job} = 1 + A = 1.20$, or 120%

b. $AF_{day} = \dfrac{1}{1 - A} = \dfrac{1}{1 - .20} = 1.25$, or 125%

Table 7-3 illustrates some typical allowances. In practice, the allowance may be based on the judgment of the analyst, work sampling (described later in the chapter), or negotiations between labour unions and management.

Example 3

A time study of an assembly job yielded the following observations for a job for which the analyst gave a performance rating of 1.13. Using an allowance of 20 percent of job time, determine the standard time for this job.

i Observation	Time, x (minutes)	i Observation	Time, x (minutes)
1	1.12	6	1.18
2	1.15	7	1.14
3	1.16	8	1.14
4	1.12	9	1.19
5	1.15	Total	10.35

Solution

$$n = 9 \qquad PR = 1.13 \qquad A = .20$$

a. $OT = \dfrac{\sum x_i}{n} = \dfrac{10.35}{9} = 1.15$ minutes.

b. $NT = OT \times PR = 1.15(1.13) = 1.30$ minutes.

c. $ST = NT \times (1 + A) = 1.30(1.20) = 1.56$ minutes.

Note: If an abnormally short time has been recorded, it typically would be assumed to be an observation error and thus discarded. If one of the observations in Example 3 had been .10, it would have been discarded. However, if an abnormally *long* time has been recorded, the analyst would want to investigate that observation to determine whether some irregularly occurring aspect of the task (e.g., retrieving a dropped tool or part) exists, which should legitimately be factored into the job time.

Despite the obvious benefits that can be derived from stopwatch time study, some limitations also must be mentioned. One limitation is the fact that only those jobs that can be observed can be studied. This eliminates most managerial and creative jobs, because these involve mental as well as physical aspects. Also, the cost of the study rules out its use for irregular operations and infrequently occurring jobs. Finally, it disrupts the normal work routine, and workers resent it.

Table 7-3

Allowance percentages for different working conditions recommended by the International Labour Organization, a UN agency

	Percent		Percent
A. Constant allowances for work breaks:		**4.** Bad light:	
1. Personal	5	**a.** Well below	2
2. Basic fatigue	4	**b.** Very inadequate	5
B. Variable allowances:		**5.** Atmospheric conditions (heat and humidity, cold)—variable	0–10
1. Standing	2		
2. Abnormal position		**6.** Close attention required:	
a. Awkward (bending)	2	**a.** Fine or exacting	2
b. Very awkward (lying, stretching)	7	**b.** Very fine or very exacting	5
3. Use of force or muscular energy (lifting, pulling, or pushing):		**7.** Noise level:	
Weight lifted (in pounds):		**a.** Intermittent–loud	2
5	0	**b.** Intermittent–very loud	5
10	1	**c.** High-pitched–loud	5
15	2	**8.** Mental strain:	
20	3	**a.** Fairly complex process	1
25	4	**b.** Complex or wide span of attention	4
30	5	**c.** Very complex	8
35	7	**9.** Monotony:	
40	9	**a.** Medium	1
45	11	**b.** High	4
50	13	**10.** Tediousness:	
60	17	**a.** Tedious	2
70	22	**b.** Very Tedious	5

Source: Benjamin W. Niebel, *Motion and Time Study*, 8th ed. (Burr Ridge, IL: Richard D. Irwin, 1988), p. 416. © 1988 by Richard D. Irwin, Inc. Reprinted with permission of the McGraw-Hill Companies Inc.

Bombardier

Bombardier Aerospace's de Havilland plant in Toronto tried the AutoMOST software package from H.B. Maynard and Co. in order to become more efficient in its sheet metal, machining, and assembly operations. AutoMOST uses the MOST (Maynard Operation Sequence Technique) work measurement method, a newer and simpler version of MTM. A Maynard consultant and five de Havilland methods engineers used some frame and ribs subassembly work centres as test areas for using AutoMOST. After getting the cooperation of the workers' union (Canadian Auto Workers union), they introduced the project and its goals to the work centres' operators. Then, they identified the work elements performed in each work centre and improved the work methods to make them more efficient. They included activities such as locating inputs, verifying inputs, and deburring drilled holes as standard practices. The elements and their difficulty index were entered in AutoMOST, which generated standard times for various operations. The project took about four months. Both the employees and the company were satisfied

with the results. Later on, de Havilland methods engineers, having learned how to use AutoMOST, continued expanding the use of work measurement to other work centres.

Source: http://www.hbmaynard.com/ClientArticles/dehavilland.asp

Predetermined Element Times

Predetermined element times are published data based on extensive research on element times.

A commonly used set of tables is *methods-time measurement* (MTM), which was developed in the late 1940s by the Methods Engineering Council. To use this approach, the analyst must divide the job into its basic elements (e.g., reach, grasp, move, turn, disengage), measure the distances involved, rate the difficulty of the element (e.g., into three types of move: against stop; to approximate location; and to exact location), and then refer to the appropriate table of data to obtain the time for that element. The time for the job is obtained by adding the times for all of the basic elements. Times of the basic elements are measured in Time Measurement Unit (TMU); one TMU equals .036 second. One minute of work may cover a few basic elements; a typical job may involve several tens or more of these basic elements. The analyst needs a considerable amount of skill to adequately analyze the operation and develop realistic time estimates. Table 7-4 presents a portion of the MTM tables for "move" to give you an idea of the kind of information they provide.

For example, suppose that an element is to move a tape measure 12 inches to the end of a plank of lumber. This is a Case B move: move object to approximate location. It is not an Exact move (Case C) because there are many possible locations at the end of the plank. Note that the next element, not included here, will be position, which is exact. The table says that this move should take 13.4 TMUs or approximately .5 second.

The weight allowances on the right of the table are for moving heavier objects. In this case, the formula for calculating the predetermined time is:

Predetermined time = static constant + dynamic factor × time from the left of table.

For example, a hammer weighing 3 pounds is to be moved 12 inches. Because 2.5 < 3 < 7.5, the second category on the right of the table applies. Hence,

Predetermined time = 2.2 + 1.06 × 13.4 = 16.4 TMUs or .6 seconds.

predetermined element times Published data based on extensive research on element times.

Table 7-4

The MTM table for "move"

Distance Moved (inches)	Time (TMU)				Weight Allowance			Case and Description
	A	B	C	Hand in Motion B	Weight (pounds) up to:	Dynamic Factor	Static Constant TMU	
¾ or less	2.0	2.0	2.0	1.7				
1	2.5	2.9	3.4	2.3	2.5	1.00	0	
2	3.6	4.6	5.2	2.9				A. Move object to other hand or against stop.
3	4.9	5.7	6.7	3.6	7.5	1.06	2.2	
4	6.1	6.9	8.0	4.3				
5	7.3	8.0	9.2	5.0	12.5	1.11	3.9	
6	8.1	8.9	10.3	5.7				
7	8.9	9.7	11.1	6.5	17.5	1.17	5.6	
8	9.7	10.6	11.8	7.2				
9	10.5	11.5	12.7	7.9	22.5	1.22	7.4	B. Move object to approximate or indefinite location.
10	11.3	12.2	13.5	8.6				
12	12.9	13.4	15.2	10.0	27.5	1.28	9.1	
14	14.4	14.6	16.9	11.4				
16	16.0	15.8	18.7	12.8	32.5	1.33	10.8	
18	17.6	17.0	20.4	14.2				
20	19.2	18.2	22.1	15.6	37.5	1.39	12.5	
22	20.8	19.4	23.8	17.0				
24	22.4	20.6	25.5	18.4	42.5	1.44	14.3	C. Move object to exact location.
26	24.0	21.8	27.3	19.8				
28	25.5	23.1	29.0	21.2	47.5	1.50	16.0	
30	27.1	24.3	30.7	22.7				

Source: MTM Association for Standards and Research. Copyrighted by the MTM Association for Standards and Research. No reprint permission without written consent from MTM Association, 1111 E. Touhy Ave., Des Plaines, IL 60018.

A high level of skill is required to generate a predetermined element time. Analysts take training or certification courses to develop the necessary skills to do this kind of work.

There are many MTM tables. There is a table for reach, move, turn, apply pressure, grasp, position, release, disengage, eye travel and eye focus, and body, leg, and foot motions. Each table has various values depending on the distance, difficulty (e.g., reach to fixed location or to variable location, etc.), whether the hand was in motion before or not, weight carried, degree turned, and size of object. Obviously, using the MTM tables is very time consuming and requires many years of experience.

We will instead use the Simplified MTM Table (see Table 7-5), which contains approximate values for most elements.

Example 4

Suppose a carpenter needs a two-foot-long piece of a 2″ × 4″ × 8″ plank of lumber that is located on his work table in front of him. First he needs to mark the two-foot location from one end of the lumber. His retractable measurement tape is in one of his pockets, and his pencil is in the other pocket. After marking the lumber, both tape and pencil should be returned to the respective pockets. Decompose this marking activity into elements and

Table 7-5

The simplified methods-time-measurement (MTM) Table

METHODS-TIME MEASUREMENT APPLICATION DATA

SIMPLIFIED DATA

(All times on this Simplified Data Table include 15% allowance)

HAND AND ARM MOTIONS	BODY, LEG, AND EYE MOTIONS

REACH or MOVE   TMU
  1"...................................... 2
  2"...................................... 4
  3" to 12" 4 + length of motion
  over 12" 3 + length of motion
  (For TYPE 2 REACHES AND MOVES
  use length of motion only)
	TMU
	Simple foot motion 10
	Foot motion with pressure 20
	Leg motion............................ 10

POSITION
  Fit   Symmetrical   Other
  Loose   10   15
  Close   20   25
  Exact   50   55
	Side step case 1 20
	Side step case 2 40

	Turn body case 1 .... 20 Turn body case 2 45
	Eye time 10

TURN—APPLY PRESSURE
  TURN............................. 6
  APPLY PRESSURE........... 20
	Bend, stoop or kneel on
	  one knee......................... 35
	Arise................................... 35

GRASP
  Simple 2
  Regrasp or Transfer 6
  Complex 10
	Kneel on both knees 80
	Arise................................... 90

	Sit .... 40 Stand 50
	Walk per pace..................... 17

DISENGAGE
  Loose 5
  Close 10
  Exact 30
	1 TMU = .00001 hour
	         = .0006 minute
	         = .036 second

Source: Harold Maynard, *Industrial Engineering Handbook*, 2nd ed. (New York: McGraw-Hill, 1963). Reprinted with permission of the McGraw-Hill Companies.

determine a standard time for marking the wood using Table 7-5. We assume a right-handed person (i.e., mark with the right hand).

Solution

Element	Standard Time (TMU)
Reach for the measuring tape in pocket using the left hand (assume 12 inches)	$4 + 12 = 16$
Grasp (simple)	2
Move it to the end of the lumber (assume 12 inches)	$4 + 12 = 16$
Reach and grasp the end of the tape with the right hand (assume 12 inches)	$(4 + 12) + 2 = 18$
Position the end of the tape on the end of lumber (assume loose, symmetrical)	10
Move the measuring tape left across the lumber and locate (eye time) the two-foot mark	$(3 + 24) + 10 = 37$
Disengage the right hand, reach, and grasp pencil in the other pocket (assume 12 inches; assume complex grasp)	$5 + (4 + 12) + 10 = 31$
Move it close to the location of two-foot mark on the tape (assume 12 inches)	$4 + 12 = 16$
Position the pencil exactly and mark the location of two-foot mark (move 1 inch)	$50 + 2 = 52$
Put the pencil back into the pocket, disengage, and return hand	$(4 + 12) + 5 + (4 + 12) = 37$
Move the tape up 1 inch and wait until it retracts into its case (assume 1 second = 28 TMU retracting time)	$2 + 28 = 30$
Put the tape back into the pocket, disengage, and return hand	$(4 + 12) + 5 + (4 + 12) = \underline{37}$
	302 TMUs
	or 10.9 seconds

Work Sampling

work sampling Technique for estimating the proportion of time that a worker spends on each activity or is idle.

Work sampling is a technique for estimating the proportion of time that a worker spends on each activity or is idle.

Unlike time study, work sampling does not require timing an activity, nor does it even involve continuous observation of the activity. Instead, an observer makes brief observations of a worker at random intervals and simply notes the nature of the activity. For example, a secretary may be typing, filing, talking on the telephone, and so on; and a carpenter may be carrying supplies, taking measurements, cutting wood, and so on. The resulting data are *counts* of the number of times each activity or idle time was observed.

Although work sampling is occasionally used to set standard times, its primary use is for analysis of non-repetitive jobs. In a non-repetitive job, such as secretarial work or maintenance, it may be important to establish the percentage of time an employee is doing a particular activity. Work sampling can also be an important tool in developing the job description.

Work sampling estimates include some degree of error. Hence, it is important to treat work sampling estimates as *approximations* of the actual proportion of time devoted to a given activity. The goal of work sampling is to obtain an estimate that provides a specified confidence of not differing from the true value by more than a specified error proportion. For example, we may desire an estimate of idle time that will provide a 95-percent confidence of being within 4 percent of the actual percentage. Hence, work sampling is designed to produce a value, $\hat{p}$, which estimates the true proportion, p, within some acceptable error proportion, a: $\hat{p} \pm a$. The variability associated with sample estimates of p tends to be approximately normal for large sample sizes.

The amount of acceptable error proportion is a function of the sample size, the desired level of confidence, and sample proportion. For large samples, the acceptable error proportion a can be calculated using the formula

$$a = z\sqrt{\frac{\hat{p}(1-\hat{p})}{n}} \tag{7-9}$$

where

z = Number of standard deviations needed to achieve the desired confidence

$\hat{p}$ = Sample proportion (the number of occurrences divided by the sample size)

n = Sample size

a = maximum acceptable error proportion

In most instances, management will specify the desired confidence level and amount of acceptable error proportion, and the analyst will be required to determine a sample size sufficient to obtain these results. The appropriate value for n can be determined by solving formula 7-9 for n, which yields

$$n = \left(\frac{z}{a}\right)^2 \hat{p}(1-\hat{p}) \tag{7-10}$$

Example 5

The manager of a small supermarket chain wants to estimate the proportion of the time the stock clerks spend making price changes on previously marked merchandise. The manager wants a 98-percent confidence that the resulting estimate will be within 5 percent of the true value. What sample size should she use?

Solution

$a = .05$ $z = 2.33$ (for 98% confidence) $\hat{p}$ is unknown

When no sample estimate of p is available, a preliminary estimate of sample size can be obtained using $\hat{p} = .50$. After 20 or so observations, a new estimate of $\hat{p}$ can be obtained from those observations and a revised value of n calculated using the new $\hat{p}$. It would be prudent to recalculate the value of n at two or three points during the study to obtain a better indication of the necessary sample size. Thus, the initial estimate of n is:

$$n = \left(\frac{2.33}{.05}\right)^2 (.50)(1-.50) = 542.89, \quad \text{or } 543 \text{ observations}$$

Suppose that, in the first 20 observations, stock clerks were found to be changing prices twice, making $\hat{p} = 2/20 = .10$. The revised estimate of n at that point would be:

$$n = \left(\frac{2.33}{.05}\right)^2 (.10)(1 - .10) = 195.44, \quad \text{or } 196$$

Suppose a second check is made after a total of 100 observations, and $\hat{p} = .11$ at this point (including the initial 20 observations). Recalculating n yields:

$$n = \left(\frac{2.33}{.05}\right)^2 (.11)(.89) = 212.60, \quad \text{or } 213$$

The overall procedure consists of the following steps:

1. Clearly identify the worker(s) to be studied.
2. Notify the worker(s) of the purpose of the study to avoid arousing suspicion.
3. Calculate an initial estimate of sample size using a preliminary estimate of p, if available (e.g., from analyst experience or past data). Otherwise, use $\hat{p} = .50$.
4. Develop a random observation schedule.
5. Begin taking observations. Recalculate the required sample size several times during the study.
6. Determine the estimated proportion of time spent on the specified activity.

Observations must be spread out over a period of time so that a true indication of variability is obtained. For two applications of work sampling, see the following "Work Sampling" and "Scotiabank" OM in Action boxes.

OM in ACTION

Work Sampling

Work sampling can be performed in the construction industry in order to identify opportunities for productivity improvement. This is in the interest of both the owner of the building and the construction company. A work sampling study was performed on a construction job in Tippecanoe, Indiana, in June 2002.

The trades involved were pipe fitters, electricians, sheet-metal workers, insulators, carpenters, and painters, working under the general contractor Shambaugh and Son. It was decided to classify the activities into three categories:

- Primary or productive (direct) work such as demolition, fabrication, installation, and inspection
- Supportive work such as material handling, clean-up, receiving instructions, communications, reading blueprints/making calculations/marking (called layout work), and doing safety work
- Recoverable (wasted) work such as late start/early finish, personal needs, waiting, and not being there (called missing in action).

Each day, a random start time was determined using the computer. A pre-planned tour was followed through the job site, recording the activity of each worker observed. Each tour took 25–30 minutes. The tours were repeated a few times each day, collecting 200–300 observations. Using two observers, approximately 5,000 observations were collected in 10 days.

The counts were summarized and are presented below. As can be observed, material handling (18 percent) and waiting (17 percent) are the largest supportive and recoverable components. To reduce these activities, a temporary building for material storage was set up on site and supervisors were trained in using scheduling techniques.

Breakdown of overall productivity for work sampling study

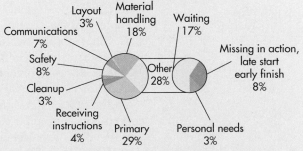

Source: J.L. Jenkins and D.L. Orth, "Productivity through Work Sampling," *AACE International Transactions* 2003, pp. CSC.05.1–7. Reprinted with the permission of AACE International, 209 Prairie Ave., Suite 100, Morgantown, WV 25601 USA. Phone 800-858-COST/304-296-8444. Fax: 304-291-5728. Internet: http://www.aacei.org. E-mail: info@aacei.org. Copyright © by AACE International; all rights reserved.

Scotiabank

TimeCorder® Time Tracking System is a calculator-like device that keeps track of activity times of an employee. It is self-administered: when the employee starts a new activity, he/she pushes the associated code in the TimeCorder® Time Tracking System. After two or more weeks, the device is returned to Pace Productivity Inc. in Toronto and an anonymous report is issued to the employer. Scotiabank used the TimeCorder® Time Tracking System to find out what percentage of the time of its personal banking officers was actually spent on selling. This was discovered to be only 29 percent. The rest of the time was spent on administrative duties, such as documenting calls and reviewing reports, and servicing, planning, and sales management. After centralizing some administrative work and performing some training, the TimeCorder® Time Tracking System was

used again. This time it showed that selling percentage was 37 percent of the employees' time.

Source: http://www.paceproductivity.com/results.htm: case study.

(LO 5) COMPENSATION

It is important for organizations to develop suitable compensation plans for their employees. If wages are too low, organizations may find it difficult to attract and hold competent workers. If wages are too high, the increased costs may result in lower profits, or may force the organization to increase its prices, which might adversely affect demand for the organization's products.

Organizations use two basic approaches for compensating employees: time-based pay and output-based pay. **Time-based pay**, also known as hourly pay, compensates the employee for the time he has worked. Salary also represent a form of time-based pay. **Output-based (piece rate) pay** compensates employees according to the amount of output they produce, thereby tying pay directly to performance.

Time-based pay is more widely used than output-based pay, particularly for office, administrative, and managerial employees, but also for blue-collar workers. One reason for this is that calculation of compensation is straightforward. Employees often prefer time-based pay because the pay is steady and they know how much compensation they will receive for each pay period. In addition, employees may resent the pressures of the output-based pay.

Another reason for using time-based pay is that many jobs do not lend themselves to the use of piece rate. In some cases, it may be difficult or impossible to measure output. For example, jobs that require creative or mental work cannot be easily measured on an output basis. Other jobs may include irregular activities or have so many different forms of output that measuring output and determining pay are fairly complex. Finally, *quality* considerations may be as important as *quantity* considerations. In health care, for example, emphasis is placed on both the quality of patient care and the number of patients processed.

On the other hand, situations exist where piece rate is desirable. Piece rate rewards workers for their output, causing some workers to produce more than they might under time-based pay. On the negative side, piece rate involves a considerable amount of paperwork. Calculation of wage is more difficult than under time-based pay, because output has to be measured and standards set.

In order to obtain maximum benefit from piece rate pay, it should be:

1. Accurate
2. Easy to apply

time-based pay
Compensation based on length of time an employee has worked.

output-based (piece rate) pay Compensation based on amount of output an employee produces.

3. Consistent

4. Easy to understand

5. Fair.

In the past, piece rate pay was fairly popular. Now minimum-wage legislation makes it somewhat impractical. Even so, many of the compensation plans currently in use represent variations of the piece rate pay. They typically incorporate a base rate that serves as a floor: workers are guaranteed that amount as a minimum, regardless of output. The base rate is tied to an output standard; a worker who produces less than the standard will be paid at the base rate. However, if the worker produces more than the standard output, she will receive a *bonus*.

The basic compensation may be topped off by group bonus and/or skill/knowledge bonus.

Group Bonus Plans. A variety of group bonus/incentive plans, which stress sharing of productivity gains with employees, are in use. Some focus exclusively on output (called group incentive), while others reward employees for output and for reductions in costs (called gain sharing), or increases in profit (called profit sharing).

A survey of major collective agreements has shown that although (individual) piece rate pay is still popular, use of profit sharing is increasing.[4]

Skill/Knowledge Bonus Plans. Organizations are increasingly setting up bonus plans to reward workers who undergo training to increase their skill/knowledge. This is referred to as a **skill/knowledge bonus plan**. A skill/knowledge bonus plan has three dimensions: *horizontal skills* reflect the variety of tasks the worker is capable of performing; *vertical skills* reflect managerial tasks the worker is capable of; and *depth skills* reflect quality and productivity results.

skill/knowledge bonus plan Rewarding workers who undergo training to increase their skills/knowledge.

An example of a skill/knowledge bonus plan is that used in the Molson Breweries (Montreal) plant, where a multi-skill premium of $4 per day is paid to client service truck drivers and a $0.50 per hour premium is paid to multi-skilled brewing operations employees. The team leaders in warehouse, shipping, and garage operations receive a team leader premium of $15 per week.[5]

Summary

The design of work systems involves job design, methods analysis, working conditions, work measurement, and compensation.

Job design is concerned with the content of jobs and work methods. In the past, job design tended to focus on efficiency, but now there seems to be an increasing awareness and consideration of the behavioural approach. This includes job enlargement, rotation, enrichment, and teamwork.

Analysts often use methods analysis and motion study techniques to make the job more efficient. Charts such as process chart, worker–machine chart, and simo chart are used to document how work is done. Working conditions such as temperature, illumination, and work breaks affect productivity and health and safety of workers. Ergonomics, i.e., fitting the job to workers' capabilities, is also important.

Work measurement is concerned with specifying the length of time needed to complete a job (i.e., its standard time). Commonly used approaches include stopwatch time study and predetermined element times. A related technique is work sampling, which is used to estimate the proportion of time a worker spends on a certain aspect of the job. Table 7-6 provides a summary of the formulas used in time study and work sampling.

---

[4]B. Fawcett, "Wage Incentive Plans—1988–1998," *Workplace Gazette* 1(3), 1998, pp. 41–44.
[5]S. Payette, "What's New in Workplace Innovations?" *Workplace Gazette* 3(1), 2000, pp. 110–119.

Table 7-6	**Time Study**		**Work Sampling**	
Summary of formulas	A. Sample size		A. Maximum acceptable error proportion	
	$n = \left(\dfrac{zs}{a\overline{x}}\right)^2$	(7-1)	$a = z\sqrt{\dfrac{\hat{p}(1-\hat{p})}{n}}$	(7-9)
	$n = \left(\dfrac{zs}{e}\right)^2$	(7-2)		
	B. Observed time		B. Sample size	
	$OT = \dfrac{\sum x_i}{n}$	(7-3)	$n = \left(\dfrac{z}{a}\right)^2 \hat{p}(1-\hat{p})$	(7-10)
	C. Normal time		**Symbols:**	
	$NT = OT \times PR$	(7-4)	a = Maximum acceptable error proportion	
	$NT = \sum(\overline{x}_i \times PR_i)$	(7-5)	A = Allowance proportion	
	D. Standard time		e = Maximum acceptable error amount	
	$ST = NT \times AF$	(7-6)	n = Number of observations needed	
	E. Allowance factor		NT = Normal time	
	$AF_{job} = 1 + A$	(7-7)	OT = Observed time	
	$AF_{day} = \dfrac{1}{1-A}$	(7-8)	PR = Performance rating	
			$\hat{p}$ = Sample proportion	
			s = Standard deviation of observed times	
			ST = Standard time	
			x_i = Time for ith observation (i = 1, 2, 3,..., n)	
			z = No. of standard deviations needed to achieve desired confidence	

Time-based (hourly, salaried) pay is most common. Output-based (piece rate) pay is used in some industries. Group bonus plans, such as profit sharing, and skill/knowledge bonus plans are becoming more common.

Key Terms

Solved Problems

Problem 1

A time study analyst timed an assembly operation for 30 cycles, and then computed the average time per cycle, which was 18.75 minutes. The analyst assigned a performance rating of 0.96 to the operator, and decided that an appropriate allowance was 15 percent. Assume that the allowance factor is based on the *workday*. Determine the observed time (OT), the normal time (NT), and the standard time (ST).

Solution

OT = Average time = 18.75 minutes

$NT = OT \times$ Performance rating = 18.75 minutes $\times$ .96 = 18 minutes

$AF = \dfrac{1}{1-A} = \dfrac{1}{1-.15} = 1.176$

$ST = NT \times AF = 18 \times 1.176 = 21.17$ minutes

Problem 2

A time study analyst wants to estimate the number of observations that will be needed to achieve a specified maximum error, with a confidence of 95.5 percent. A preliminary study yielded a mean of 5.2 minutes and a standard deviation of 1.1 minutes for the job. Determine the number of observations needed for these two cases:

a. A maximum acceptable error of $\pm 6\%$ of the sample mean.

b. A maximum acceptable error of .40 minute.

Solution

a. $\bar{x} = 5.2$ minutes $z = 2.00$ for   95.5%
     $s = 1.1$ minutes $a = .06$

$$n = \left(\frac{zs}{a\bar{x}}\right)^2 = \left(\frac{2.00(1.1)}{.06(5.2)}\right)^2 = 49.72 \text{ (round up to 50 observations)}$$

b. $e = .40$

$$n = \left(\frac{zs}{e}\right)^2 = \left(\frac{2.00(1.1)}{.40}\right)^2 = 30.25 \text{ (round up to 31 observations)}$$

Problem 3

Work sampling. An analyst has been asked to prepare an estimate of the proportion of time that a lathe operator spends adjusting the machine, with a 90-percent confidence level. Based on previous experience, the analyst believes the proportion will be approximately 30 percent.

a. If the analyst uses a sample size of 400 observations, what is the maximum possible error percentage that will be associated with the estimate?

b. What sample size would the analyst need in order to have maximum error of no more than ± 5 percent?

Solution

a. $\hat{p} = .30$ $z = 1.65$ (for 90-percent confidence)

$$a = z\sqrt{\frac{\hat{p}(1-\hat{p})}{n}} = 1.65\sqrt{\frac{.3(.7)}{400}} = .038 \quad \text{or} \quad 3.8\%$$

b. $n = \left(\frac{z}{a}\right)^2 \hat{p}(1-\hat{p}) = \left(\frac{1.65}{.05}\right)(.3)(.7) = 228.69, \quad \text{or} \quad 229$

Problem 4

A supervisor timed a hotel maid performing the four main tasks necessary to clean a room. These times (in minutes) for five rooms and the performance rating of the maid for each task are given below. Assuming a 10% allowance factor based on job time, calculate the standard time for cleaning a room.

Task	Performance Rating	Room 1	Room 2	Room 3	Room 4	Room 5
Replenishing the mini-bar	100	2	2.5	1.5	1	2
Making the bed	90	2.5	3	4	3	2.5
Vacuuming the floor	110	3	4	2.5	3	2.5
Cleaning the bathroom	80	4	4.5	3.5	4	6

Solution

Task	Performance Rating PR	Observations X_i (min. per cycle) 1	2	3	4	5	$OT = (X_1 + \dots + X_5)/5$	$NT = OT(PR)$	$ST = NT(AF)$
1	100%	2.0	2.5	1.5	1.0	2.0	1.80	1.8	1.98
2	90%	2.5	3.0	4.0	3.0	2.5	3.00	2.7	2.97
3	110%	3.0	4.0	2.5	3.0	2.5	3.00	3.3	3.63
4	80%	4.0	4.5	3.5	4.0	6.0	4.40	3.52	3.87
								Job Standard Time:	12.45

Discussion and Review Questions

1. What is job design and why is it important? (LO1)

2. What are some of the main advantages and disadvantages of specialization from a company's perspective? From a worker's perspective? (LO1)

3. Contrast the meanings of the terms *job enlargement* and *job enrichment*. (LO1)

4. What is the purpose of behavioural approach to job design? (LO1)

5. What are self-directed work teams? What are some potential benefits of using these teams? (LO1)

6. Some Japanese companies have a policy of rotating their managers among different managerial jobs. In contrast, North American managers are more likely to specialize in a certain area (e.g., finance or operations). Discuss the advantages and disadvantages of each of these approaches. Which one do you prefer? Why? (LO1)

7. Name some reasons methods analysis is needed. How is methods analysis linked to productivity improvements? (LO2)

8. How are tools such as a process chart and a worker–machine chart useful? (LO2)

9. What are the motion economy principles? (LO2)

10. What is a standard time? What does it assume? (LO4)

11. What are the main uses of standard times? (LO4)

12. Could problems with determining performance rating be avoided by studying a group of workers and averaging their times? Explain briefly. (LO4)

13. If an average worker could be identified, what advantage would there be in using that person for a stopwatch time study? What are some reasons an average worker might not be studied? (LO4)

14. What are the main limitations of stopwatch time study? (LO4)

15. Comment on the following. "At any given instant, the standard times for many jobs will not be strictly correct." (LO4)

    a. Why is this so?
    b. Does this mean that those time standards are useless? Explain.

16. Why do workers sometimes resent time studies? (LO4)

17. What is work sampling? How does it differ from time study? (LO4)

18. What are the key advantages and disadvantages of: (LO5)

    a. Time-based pay? (i) for management and (ii) workers?
    b. Piece rate (output-based) pay? (i) for management and (ii) workers?

19. Explain the skill/knowledge bonus plan. (LO5)

20. The temperature in the meat department of a grocery store is usually kept about 10–11 degrees Celsius. The activities include cutting and packaging the meat. Explain how the workers could cope with this low temperature. (LO3)

21. Why should a company care about the health and safety of its workers? Is it possible to operate profitably without this concern? Give an example of a company that cares about its workers and another that doesn't. (LO3)

22. What is ergonomics? Give an example. (LO3)

23. What is a healthy workplace? Give an example. (LO3)

Taking Stock

1. What are the trade-offs in each of the following situations?

    a. Using self-directed teams exclusively instead of a more conventional approach with occasional use of teams. (LO1)
    b. Deciding how often to update standard times due to minor changes in work methods. (LO4)

2. Who uses the results of work measurement in an organization? (LO4)

3. In what ways does technology have an impact on job design? (LO1, 3, 4)

4. In Canada, the health and safety of workers are protected by the *Occupational Health and Safety Act* of each province, which is enforced by the ministry (or department) of Labour of the province. For example, http://www.labour.gov.on.ca/english/news/courtbulletins.php describes recent court cases brought under *OHSA* in Ontario. As it can be seen from reading some of the cases, the employer is responsible for any accidents; for example, a mechanic's hand being pulled between rollers of a conveyor while greasing it from underneath, an explosion inside a tank due to methane gas when a welder started work in it, or a load of steel bars falling on a delivery driver helping a forklift driver to unload it. In addition, lack of procedures, training, and warning signs also make the employer responsible for any injuries to the worker. An employee not wearing a hard hat, or low light that can cause a fall, is grounds to fine the company. Moreover, a supervisor can personally be fined if he did not inform an employee of the right procedure or training. Do you think that the *Occupational Health and Safety Act* has overreached and is now being unfair to companies and supervisors? Discuss. (LO3)

Critical Thinking Exercise

Can a work system be of strategic importance to a company? Explain and give examples. (LO1 & 5)

Experiential Learning Exercises

1. Select one of the following operations and prepare a worker–machine chart that describes the activities and their times: (LO2)

   a. Visit an ATM and make a withdrawal or other transaction.
   b. Visit a gas station and put fuel into your vehicle.

2. Develop a standard time for preparing a ham and cheese sandwich: (LO4)

   a. List the steps (tasks) required to prepare the sandwich.
   b. Observe the job for several repetitions and make improvements if necessary.
   c. Time each task for several repetitions.
   d. Assign a performance rating to the overall job.
   e. Develop the standard time.

Internet Exercises

1. Go to the Association of Canadian Ergonomists Web site (http://www.ace-ergocanada.ca) and identify the types of activities ergonomists undertake. (LO3)

2. Go to http://www.ergoweb.com/resources/casestudies to find an interesting ergonomics case study and summarize it. (LO3)

3. Visit http://www.osha.gov/SLTC/ergonomics/outreach.html#etools, choose an industry-specific etool, and identify an ergonomic lesson for work design in that industry. (LO3)

Problems

1. An analyst has timed a metal-cutting operation for 50 cycles. The average time per cycle was 10.40 minutes, and the standard deviation was 1.20 minutes for a worker with a performance rating of 125 percent. Assume an allowance of 16 percent of job time. Calculate the standard time for this operation. (LO4)

2. A job was timed for 60 cycles. It took an average of 1.2 minutes per cycle. The performance rating was 95 percent, and workday allowance is 10 percent. Determine each of the following: (LO4)

   a. Observed time.
   b. Normal time.
   c. Standard time.

3. A time study was conducted on a job that contains four tasks. The observations and performance ratings for six cycles are shown in the following table. (LO4)

Task	Performance Rating	Observations (minutes per cycle)					
		1	2	3	4	5	6
1	90%	.44	.50	.43	.45	.48	.46
2	85	1.50	1.54	1.47	1.51	1.49	1.52
3	110	.84	.89	.77	.83	.85	.80
4	100	1.10	1.14	1.08	1.20	1.16	1.26

a. Calculate the average time for each task.
b. Calculate the normal time for each task.
c. Assuming an allowance factor of 15 percent of workday, calculate the standard time for this job.

4. Given these observations (in minutes) for four tasks of a job, determine the observed time (OT) for each task. Note: The second task occurs only in every other cycle. (LO4)

	Cycle					
	1	2	3	4	5	6
Task 1	4.1	4.0	4.2	4.1	4.1	4.1
Task 2	—	1.5	—	1.6	—	1.4
Task 3	3.2	3.2	3.3	3.2	3.3	3.3
Task 4	2.7	2.8	2.7	2.8	2.8	2.8

5. Given these observations (in minutes) for five tasks of a job, determine the observed time (OT) for each task. Note: Some of the tasks occur only periodically. Also, using a performance rating of 90 percent for each task and allowance of 15 percent of job time, calculate the standard time for the job. (LO4)

	Cycle					
	1	2	3	4	5	6
Task 1	2.1	2.0	2.2	2.1	2.1	—
Task 2	—	1.1	—	1.0	—	1.2
Task 3	3.4	3.5	3.3	3.5	3.4	3.3
Task 4	4.0	—	—	4.2	—	—
Task 5	1.4	1.4	1.5	1.5	1.5	1.4

6. Using Table 7-3, develop an allowance percentage for a job that requires the worker to lift a weight of 10 pounds while (1) standing, (2) in light that is well below recommended standards, and (3) with intermittent loud noises occurring. The monotony for this job is high. Include a personal allowance of 5 percent and a basic fatigue allowance of 4 percent. (LO4)

7. A worker–machine operation was found to involve 3.3 minutes of machine time per cycle. In the course of 40 cycles of a stopwatch time study, the worker's time loading and unloading the machine averaged 1.9 minutes per cycle, and the worker was given a rating of 120 percent. Assuming an allowance factor of 12 percent of job time, determine the standard time for this job (including the machine time). (LO4)

8. A recently negotiated union contract allows workers in a shipping department a total of 24 minutes for rest, 10 minutes for personal time, and 14 minutes for delays for each four-hour shifts worked. A time study analyst observed a job in the shipping department that is performed continuously and found an average time of 6.0 minutes per cycle for a worker she rated at 95 percent. What standard time is applicable for that operation? (LO4)

9. The data in the following table represent time study observations for a woodworking operation. (LO4)

a. Based on the observations, determine the standard time for the operation, assuming an allowance of 20 percent of job times.

b. How many observations would be needed to estimate the mean time for task 1 within 1 percent of its true value with a 95.5-percent confidence?

c. How many observations would be needed to estimate the mean time for task 1 within .01 minute of its true value with a 95.5-percent confidence?

		Observations (minutes per cycle)					
Task	Performance Rating	1	2	3	4	5	6
1	110%	1.20	1.17	1.16	1.22	1.24	1.15
2	115	.83	.87	.78	.82	.85	1.32*
3	105	.58	.53	.52	.59	.60	.54

*Unusual delay, disregard time.

10. How many observations should a stopwatch time study analyst plan for in an operation that has a standard deviation of 1.5 minutes per piece if the goal is to estimate the mean time per piece to within .4 minute with a confidence of 95.5 percent? (LO4)

11. How many work cycles should be timed to estimate the average cycle time to within 2 percent of the sample mean with a confidence of 99 percent if a pilot study yielded these times (in minutes): 5.2, 5.5, 5.8, 5.3, 5.5, and 5.1? (LO4)

12. In an initial survey designed to estimate the percentage of time air-express cargo loaders are idle, an analyst found that loaders were idle in 6 of the 50 observations. (LO4)

    a. What is the estimated percentage of idle time?

    b. Based on the initial results, approximately how many observations would you require to estimate the actual percentage idle time to within 4 percent with a confidence of 95 percent?

13. A job in an insurance office involves telephone conversations with policyholders. The office manager estimates that about half of the employee's time is spent on the telephone. How many observations are needed in a work sampling study to estimate that time percentage to within 4 percent and have a confidence of 95 percent? (LO4)

14. The killing and disassembly of a hog in a slaughter plant is very labour-intensive, because the tasks cannot easily be automated. This is because each hog is slightly different and the carcasses cannot in general be held in place in a consistent way in order to automate the work. To achieve the target production (which is high in order to make a profit), tasks need to be very specialized. For example, one task is called "snatching guts." Suppose you are helping the industrial engineer to determine the standard time for this task. The videotape of five cycles revealed the following task times (in seconds): 14, 13, 13, 12, and 14. Assume performance rating of .90 and allowance of 15 percent of job time. Calculate the standard time for this task.[6] (LO4)

15. The following two activities are commonly used to train stopwatch time study observers to get a feel for an average performance rating, i.e., performance rating of 1.0. (LO4)

    a. Walk at 3 miles per hour (= 80 metres per minute = 1.34 metres per second).

    b. Deal a deck of 52 cards into 4 equal piles one foot apart (make a square) in .5 minute.

    Choose one of these and time yourself trying to achieve these times. If you are too slow, repeat the exercise faster until you reach these speeds. Do you believe that these times are sustainable? Explain.

16. We wish to time installing new shingles on our house. To start, we will try to time driving one nail into a shingle. Assume that the shingle is already in place. You have squatted on your roof facing the shingle. The hammer is on the roof next to the shingle. Nails are in your

---

[6]Based on J.S. Moore and A. Garg, "Participatory Ergonomics in a Red Meat Packing Plant, Part II: Case Studies," *Americam Industrial Hygiene Association Journal* 58(7), July 1997, pp. 498–508.

pocket. Use the Simplified MTM technique (Table 7-5) to determine the time of driving one nail into the shingle. (LO4)

17. Using the simplified MTM times given in Table 7-5 and watching the JIT at McDonald's video (Volume 08, OM McGraw-Hill Video Library; http://bl-bus-jacobsvm.ads.iu.edu/videoglossary.html), estimate the time it should take a McDonald's employee to:

   a. Pick up a bun from the rack and drop its two sides into the toaster (the 9:20th–9:22nd minutes of the video). (LO4)

   b. Squirt the second condiment on the bun, side step, and place small pieces of the first vegetable on the bun. Start from just after the first condiment dispenser is put back in its place and end just after the first vegetable pieces are placed on the bun (the 9:42nd–9:49th minutes of the video).

   You can slow down the speed of video play by choosing "Full screen" in view menu, then right-clicking and setting play speed to Slow.

18. In the bottle-recycling department of Labatt's Brewery in St. Johns, Newfoundland, the "throw on" task involved lifting cases of empty bottles from a pallet and putting them on a conveyor.[7] A case weighed approximately 6 kg. "Throw on" sometimes involved reaching up above shoulder-height or bending and lifting elements (see the two sketches below). Each "throw on" took between two and five seconds, and the pallet was unloaded in about three minutes. Even though the workers rotated out of this task every half hour, there was still chance of repetitive motion injuries and lower back pain. Propose an ergonomic solution for this problem. (LO3)

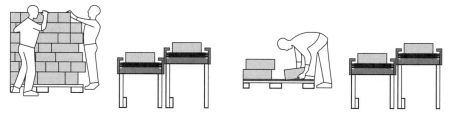

19. In the assembly operation of Mother Hubbard's Kitchens in Dartmouth, Nova Scotia, the worker held the tool with his operating hand and the piece of cabinet with the other hand (see the three sketches below), and the work required reaching and bending, exerting force from shoulder, and awkward positions for arms and body.[8] There was chance of repetitive motion injuries and shoulder and lower back pain. Propose an ergonomic solution for this problem. (LO3)

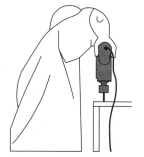

[7]Canadian Centre for Occupational Health and Safety. "Bottle Recycling Department of a Brewery." http://www.ccohs.ca/oshanswers/occup_workplace/brewery.html (accessed May 7, 2010).
[8]Canadian Centre for Occupational Health and Safety. "Cabinet Manufacturing." http://www.ccohs.ca/oshanswers/occup_workplace/cab_manu.html (accessed May 7, 2010).

20. In the Buttered Sole line of Burin's Secondary Processing plant of Fishery Products International, Newfoundland, the "spreading" operation involved spreading the sole on the conveyor belt.[9] The job involved standing in a stooped position and reaching. Propose an ergonomic solution for this problem. (LO3)

To access "Learning Curves," the supplement to Chapter 7, please visit *Connect*.

---

[9]Canadian Centre for Occupational Health and Safety. "Fish Processing." http://www.ccohs.ca/oshanswers/occup_workplace/fish_pro.html (accessed May 7, 2010).

CHAPTER 8
Location Planning and Analysis

LEARNING OBJECTIVES

After completing this chapter, you should be able to:

LO1 Explain the nature and importance of location decisions, and outline the decision process for making these kinds of decisions.

LO2 Describe some of the major factors that affect location decisions, and explain why a foreign company would locate in Canada.

LO3 Use the techniques presented to evaluate location alternatives.

When Cara Operations Limited purchased five more chains of restaurants (in addition to Harvey's and Swiss Chalet) in the early 2000s, it needed to become more efficient in determining the trade area and demographics for each restaurant and the site selection process in general. Fleetguard, a division of Cummins Engine Company, makes filters, exhaust tubes, and mufflers. In the early 2000s, Fleetguard was looking for a site to make a new product. How do companies like these make location decisions? This chapter answers this question.

LO1 INTRODUCTION

New companies obviously need a plant or store/office in which to make or provide their new goods or services. Existing organizations may also need to make location decisions. Companies such as banks, fast-food chains, supermarkets, and retail stores view location as part of their marketing strategy and look for locations that will help them expand their markets. Basically, the location decisions in those cases reflect the *addition* of new locations to an existing system. A similar situation occurs when an organization experiences a growth in demand for its products that cannot be satisfied by expansion at an existing location.

Some companies face location decisions because of depletion of their basic input. For example, fishing and logging operations are often forced to relocate due to the exhaustion of fish and forests at a given location. Mining and petroleum operations face the same sort of situation.

For other companies, a shift in market causes them to consider relocation, or the cost of doing business at a particular location reaches a point where other locations begin to look more attractive. Another reason may be centralizing dispersed locations to gain economies of scale.

There are several reasons that location decisions are an important part of production or service systems design. First, they entail a long-term commitment that makes mistakes difficult to overcome. Second, location decisions impact investment requirements, operating costs, and revenues. Third, a poor choice of location might result in a shortage of qualified labour, inadequate supplies of raw materials, or some similar condition that is detrimental to operations.

Because, by its nature, a location decision is usually based on many factors, no single location may be significantly better than the others. There may be numerous acceptable locations from which to choose, as shown by the wide variety of locations in which successful organizations can be found.

Location factors can depend on where a business is in the *supply chain*. For instance, at the retail end of a chain, site selection tends to focus more on accessibility, consumer demographics (population, age distribution, average income), and traffic patterns. Businesses at the beginning of a supply chain, supplying raw materials, are often located near the source of the raw materials. Businesses in the middle of a chain may locate near suppliers or near their customers, depending on a variety of circumstances. For example, businesses involved in storing and distributing goods often choose a central location to minimize distribution costs. However, Web-based and phone-based businesses are much less dependent on location decisions; they can exist just about anywhere.

Location Decision Process

The way an organization approaches location decisions often depends on its size and the nature and scope of its operations. New or small organizations tend to adopt a rather informal approach. New/small companies typically locate in a certain area simply because the owner/manager lives there. Large established companies, particularly those that already operate in more than one location, tend to take a more formal approach. Moreover, they

Fleetguard

Fleetguard makes various types of filters, exhaust tubes, and mufflers. A subsidiary of Cummins Engine Company, Fleetguard employs 6,000 people in 23 plants in nine countries. In August 2002, Fleetguard was looking for a site, approximately 250,000 square feet for about 400 workers, to make exhaust products for recreational vehicles. Specifically, the objective was to be close to (within one-day truck delivery distance of) its customers (recreational vehicle manufacturers), which were mostly located in the southeast United States. Fleetguard preferred a vacant building that required minimal structural changes.

A real estate advisor identified eight vacant buildings in various communities in the southeastern United States. Then, WDG Consulting was hired to assist in site/building selection. Four green-field sites were also identified and evaluated for comparison. WDG collected preliminary information for each of 12 alternative sites/buildings to ensure that adequate qualified available workers live in the vicinity of each site,

that each had only a small threat of unionization, that a retrofit or building permit application process would be short (less than six months), and that electricity supply would be stable. The information came from WDG files and local economic development agencies.

WDG chose three sites/buildings that satisfied the above requirements. In order to investigate further, interviews were conducted with managers of other plants, personnel agencies, real estate agents, and economic development officers in each area in order to determine the business climate and collect more accurate information. Government officials were asked to provide an incentive package. Each site/building was inspected in order to identify any site-related problems such as land pollution. The three alternatives were compared in terms of wage rates, labour turnover rate, land/building cost, transportation cost, tax rate, electricity rate, and incentive dollars. Waynesboro, Georgia, came out on top, and was recommended to Fleetguard in August 2003.

Source: http://www.wdgconsulting.com/WDGC_Project_case_studies_FleetgardNelson.htm

---

usually consider a wider range of geographic locations. The discussion here pertains mainly to a formal approach to location decisions.

Whether a company chooses to use a location/site selection consultant or assign the project to someone in-house, the basic steps to a successful location decision will be similar:

1. Identify important search parameters and factors, such as location of markets or raw materials.

2. Gather information on appropriate sites (e.g., through telephone and Internet inquiries, reading literature, etc.).

3. Eliminate some to obtain a short list of three or four sites.

4. Visit the short-listed sites, meeting with local authorities and real estate agents.

5. Evaluate the alternatives and make a selection.

Typically, the process will take six months to a year. For an application, see the "Fleetguard" OM in Action.

LO 2 FACTORS THAT AFFECT LOCATION DECISIONS

Many factors influence location decisions. However, often one or two factors dominate the decision. For example, in manufacturing, the potentially dominating factors may include availability of abundant energy and proximity to raw materials (e.g., aluminum production needs large amounts of electricity). Cost of transportation to market can be a major factor (e.g., most soft drinks are produced in local bottling plants). In service organizations, possible dominating factors are market-related. For example, car rental agencies locate in airports and downtowns where their customers are.

This section contains a description of regional/country factors, community and site factors, and advantages of Canadian locations for foreign companies.

Regional/Country Factors

The primary regional factors involve raw materials, markets, and labour considerations.

Location of Raw Materials. Companies locate near or at the source of their raw materials for three primary reasons: necessity, perishability, and transportation costs. Mining operations, farming, forestry, and fishing fall under *necessity*. Obviously, such operations must locate close to the raw materials. Companies involved in canning or freezing of fresh fruit and vegetables, processing of dairy and meat products, and so on must consider *perishability* when considering location. *Transportation costs* are important in industries where processing eliminates much of the bulk in a raw material, making it much less expensive to transport after processing. Examples include potash, lumber, and pulp and paper production. Being close to raw materials is the reason many forest-products companies such as Catalyst Paper and Canfor have plants in British Columbia. Many petrochemical plants are located in Alberta, many farms are located in the prairies, and many fish-processing plants are located in the Atlantic provinces. For two more examples, see the "Two Examples of Closeness to Raw Material and Utilities" OM in Action.

Location of Markets. Retailers and service providers are usually found near the centre of the markets they serve. Examples include fast-food restaurants, gas stations, and supermarkets. Quite often their products and those of their competitors are so similar that they rely on convenience to attract customers. Hence, these businesses seek locations with high population densities or traffic. This is also true for banks, drugstores, and convenience stores.

 OM in ACTION   http://www.mccain.com   http://www.recgroup.com

Two Examples of Proximity to Raw Material and Utilities

McCain Foods

The keys to success in growing potatoes are the quality of the soil and growing conditions. Because of their bulk and perishability, it is best to process potatoes where they are grown. The $20-billion world French fry market is growing at the rate to support three new factories per year.

McCain Foods represents approximately one-third of that market, so to keep its share of the global marketplace, the company has to build an average of one facility every year. By the late 1990s, McCain Foods had potato-processing plants in PEI, New Brunswick, Manitoba, and outside Canada. In 1997, the Manitoba plant in Portage la Prairie was expanded, doubling its capacity. However, McCain soon realized that more capacity was needed to supply the northwestern United States and Asian markets.

McCain had been involved in southern Alberta for many years and purchased some of the potatoes for its Manitoba plant there. Alberta potatoes are firmer than their competitors from the northwestern United States and have lower water content, adding at least 1 percent to profitability.

McCain built a $94-million French fry plant near Coaldale, 30 km east of Lethbridge, Alberta, in 2000. The company had owned land in the area for 25 years. According to Arnold Park, president of McCain Foods, "There are excellent farmers in southern Alberta, and that particular area gives McCain good freight lanes to the ports of Vancouver and the markets of Asia Pacific."

REC Silicon

REC is a Norwegian manufacturer of solar panels, silicon, and wafers for semiconductors and solar panels. In 2006, REC was searching for a location for a new silicon plant. It started off with 100 potential sites in 16 countries, but reduced it first to 40 and then to 5, with which it negotiated. REC chose Becancour Industrial Park just outside Montreal. It plans to build a US$1.2 billion polysilicon plant there, starting in 2012. The main factor in the location decision was the inexpensive electric power supplied by Hydro Quebec—upto 95 megawatts for 20 years.

Sources: "McCain Announces Location of $93 M French Fry Plant," *Daily Commercial News* 72(6), January 11, 1999, p. A5; http://www.siteselection.com/issues/2008/nov/North-American.

In Canada, High Liner Foods uses eight deep-sea trawlers to fish around Nova Scotia and Newfoundland. Its two primary processing plants are nearby in Lunenburg, NS, and Burin, NF.

Competitive pressure on retail operations can be extremely high. In some cases, the market served by a particular location may be too small to justify two competitors (e.g., one burger franchise per block), so the search for potential locations tends to concentrate on locations without competitors. The opposite also might be true; it could be desirable to locate near competitors. Examples include car dealers and clothing stores.

Some companies must locate close to their markets because of the perishability of their products. Examples include bakeries, flower shops, and fresh seafood stores. For others, distribution (transportation) cost is the main factor in closeness to market (for example, sand and gravel retailers and bottling plants). Another example is regional warehouses used by supermarkets and other retail operations to supply multiple outlets. Still other companies require close customer contact. Typical examples are custom tailor shops, home remodellers, home repair services, rug cleaners, lawn and garden services, and component suppliers to just-in-time manufacturers.

Location of many government services should be near the centre of the markets they are designed to serve. For instance, police patrols often concentrate on high-crime areas, and emergency health care facilities are usually found in central locations.

Labour Factors. Primary labour considerations are availability of workers, the wage rates and productivity, and whether unions are a potential problem. Large plants usually locate in or near population centres. Some companies target regions with high unemployment in order to tap the large pool of unemployed workers.

Labour costs are very important for labour-intensive companies and they can differ significantly across regions.[1] Labour rates are related to the cost of living, which also varies across regions. Internationally, Canadian average hourly compensation is close to the United States, lower than many European countries, but higher than Mexico and Asian countries (see http://www.bls.gov/news.release/ichcc.t02.htm). See "Dell's Short-lived Call Centres in Canada" OM in Action as an example of influence of the labour in location decisions.

Other Factors. Electric power sometimes plays a role in location decisions. For instance, many aluminum smelting plants are located in Quebec because they use a large amount of electricity, which is inexpensive in Quebec. The same is true for British Columbia.

---

[1]See CANSIM's "Labour Force Survey Estimates" Table #2820074 for wage rates in each province.

OM in *ACTION*

Dell's Short-lived Call Centres in Canada

Before 2004, Dell Computers used to outsource its North American customer service to India. However, some customers were not happy with the excessive waits; being passed to other representatives, sometimes in other countries; and not having their problems resolved. In the 2004, Dell opened a call centre in Edmonton, and later one in Ottawa, employing approximately 500 people in each location. Dell was so impressed with the performance of its educated and bilingual labour force in Ottawa that it acquired the neighbouring building (about 150,000 ft^2) and added another 1,200 people in 2007. However, the recent recession has forced Dell to cut its workforce by 10 percent worldwide. Unfortunately, Dell decided to close both its Edmonton and Ottawa call centres. The strong Canadian dollar seems to have been a factor.

Sources: J. Lyne, "Growing by Degrees: 1200 More Call Centre Jobs Coming to Ottawa," *Site Selection*, November 20, 2006; http://www.itworldcanada.com/news/cutbacks-at-dell-canada-span-edmonton-to-ottawa/01899; http://www.cbc.ca/canada/story/2008/04/23/dellkanata.html.

OM in *ACTION*

Some Examples of Subsidies

An example of a company obtaining a large subsidy is GM of Canada when it invested $2.5 billion to renovate its Oshawa assembly complex in 2005. GM received $235 million from the federal and Ontario governments. Subsidies have been a fact of life in the auto industry, with southern U.S. states being the prime example of securing auto investment by this means. More recently, with the downturn in economy and sharp drop in auto sales, GM has laid off several thousand employees, despite receiving a huge bailout of several billion dollars.

Another example of government subsidy is a US$40 million grant by the Government of Ontario to Linamar, Canada's second largest auto-parts manufacturer, to build a R&D/training centre and five to six parts/components manufacturing plants in Guelph, costing a total of approximately $1 billion. Linamar, which started in the garage of its founder, Frank Hasenfratz, in Guelph, has 50 parts/components manufacturing plants in 8 countries employing over 10,000 workers, most of which are located in Guelph itself. For this last expansion decision, Linamar was looking to Michigan; however, the Ontario Government subsidy enticed Linamar to invest more in Guelph.

In 2005, Bombardier decided to assemble its new C series mid-size (110–130 seat) planes in Mirabel, a Montreal suburb, close to its main plant and headquarters. However, the rising Canadian dollar forced it to reconsider the location decision. In particular, Bombardier considered Kansas City, the location of its subsidiary, Lear Jets. The decision criteria included accessibility to an international airport, financial considerations and tax benefits, and access to a trained labour pool. After two years of studies and receiving US$350 million from the federal government and $117 million from the Québec government, Bombardier decided that Mirabel is the best location for the C series after all. Construction of the $500 million, 1.3 million ft^2 plant is planned for 2011. The wings of the C series, however, will be made by Short Brothers, the subsidiary of Bombardier in Belfast, Northern Ireland.

Sources: http://www.siteselection.com/ssinsider/bbdeal/bd050307.htm; http://www.siteselection.com/ssinsider/bbdeal/bd060615.htm; http://www.siteselection.com/features/2008/sep/Quebec.

Also, both business and personal taxes in some provinces can reduce or enhance a province's attractiveness to companies seeking new locations. Provinces such as Alberta and Quebec have used lower taxes to attract companies. Federal and provincial governments give tax incentives to encourage more research and development, manufacturing, and investment. For examples, see the "Some Examples of Subsidies" OM in Action.

Land and building costs are also usually significant and can differ across regions. The presence of unions usually results in higher wages and less flexible work rules. Therefore, many companies prefer to locate in regions where unions are not strong.

Bravado Designs

Bravado Designs is a Toronto-based maternity bra manufacturer that sells its products worldwide. When in the mid-2000s the Canadian dollar was soaring against the U.S. dollar, Bravado saw its cost of manufacturing (when converted into U.S. dollars) soar and its profits disappear. At the suggestion of one of its staff, Bravado looked and found a Mexican manufacturer of lingerie in Toluca, one hour from Mexico City. The plant was making lingerie for Victoria's Secret, but had excess capacity. Bravado outsourced some of its products to this contractor. As a result, manufacturing cost dropped by 30 percent immediately. Bravado staff visits the contractor plant once every two weeks and are happy with its quality. The advantage of Mexico over China is that the Mexican plant is able to produce in small quantities (as small as 4,000 bras per month), is closer to Toronto for visiting, and its products can be sold in North America tariff-free.

Source: J. White Bardwell, "Say Hola! to Mexico," *PROFIT*, November 2007, 26(5), pp. 69–70.

Foreign Locations. Some Canadian companies are attracted to foreign locations to exploit their natural resources. Others view foreign locations as a way to expand their markets. Many developing countries offer an abundant supply of cheap labour. For example, many North American companies have plants in China.

A company contemplating a foreign location must carefully weigh the potential benefits against the potential problems. A major factor is the stability of a country's government and its attitude toward foreign companies. Some of the problems of a foreign location can be caused by language and cultural differences. One factor that has negatively impacted the bottom line of some Canadian companies operating plants in foreign countries is the level of corruption (i.e., abuse of entrusted power for private gain). Transparency International, a non-profit international organization based in Germany, annually publishes a Corruption Perception Index for over 180 countries.[2] Canada is one of the least corrupt countries.

Further, it is much harder to coordinate the activities of foreign locations with domestic locations. The "Bravado Designs" OM in Action provides an example of a foreign location decision. The "Is It Best to Export or Manufacture Overseas?" OM in Action explores the choice of foreign locations further.

Community/Site-related Considerations

Usually workers live close to their place of work. Blue-collar workers tend not to relocate to find a job. Therefore, companies should make sure that there are sufficient numbers of potential applicants living near a site. If there are other large employers in the vicinity, then the pool of available workers will be smaller. Large employers usually locate in or around a big city for this reason. Companies employing office workers, engineers, lab researchers, and specialized trades need the services of a college, university, or technical institution in the community. White-collar employees may relocate, but they usually require a high quality of life.

From a company standpoint, a number of factors determine the desirability of a community as a place for its workers and managers to live. They include facilities for education, shopping, recreation, transportation, entertainment, and medical services.

Many communities actively try to attract new businesses because they are viewed as potential sources of future tax revenues and new job opportunities. Communities offer tax abatements, low-cost loans, and grants for worker training. However, communities do not, as a rule, want companies that will create pollution problems or otherwise lessen the quality of life in the community. Examples of this include community resistance to airport expansion, changes in zoning, construction of nuclear facilities, "factory farms," and highway construction.

---

[2]http://www.transparency.org/news_room/in_focus/2008/cpi2008/cpi_2008_table.

OM in ACTION

Is It Best to Export or Manufacture Overseas?

While exporting is often the least risky method of selling overseas, it frequently involves significant transportation cost and tariffs that may make it uneconomical when compared with foreign manufacturing.

With exporting, a company must evaluate the various modes of transportation that would be involved in getting the goods there, and how this relates to the cycle time of putting the product in the marketplace. Some products are time-sensitive; others are less so.

Sometimes companies run into government contracts where the only way to distribute a product in that country is to have it made locally. In China, for instance, companies have to build something there in order to enter that market.

On the other hand, foreign manufacturing, while potentially a more competitive way of entering an overseas market, has its own problems. Political instability, fluctuating market conditions, and the huge capital costs to set up an overseas manufacturing operation are daunting challenges. For example, companies wanting to sell in Russia face political instability as their biggest single operating risk.

The maturity of a company's product affects this decision. A product that is expected to require design changes, for example, may not fit well with foreign manufacturing plans. Tactically, companies want to be moving products offshore that are relatively stable.

The best way for many companies to enter a foreign market is to first export there, but with an eye toward building there in the future. Exporting gives them a feel for the product and its market potential.

Such a strategy worked well for IPSCO. In the early 1980s, the Regina, Saskatchewan–based steel producer exported its steel pipes and flats to the United States from Canada—despite significant transportation costs. Once the company realized that there was significant U.S. demand for its products, it decided to set up shop there.

"Fundamentally it is very expensive to transport steel pipe from Canada to the United States," explained Mario Dalla-Vicenza, IPSCO senior vice-president. "Unlike flat steel, which you're able to transport up to the maximum load-bearing capability of a railcar, steel pipe—because it is hollow—fills the volume of a railcar before it fills the maximum load bearing capability. So, there's a fundamental freight cost disadvantage." To overcome this drawback and make the company more competitive with U.S. pipe producers, IPSCO acquired pipe mills in Camanche, Iowa, and Geneva, Nebraska.

Later, IPSCO built three more pipe mills in Arkansas, Texas, and Minnesota, and two mini-mills in Alabama and Iowa. In 2007, IPSCO itself was bought by Swedish Steel company Svenskt Stal AB (SSAB). In 2008, SSAB sold IPSCO to Russian steel companies EVRAZ and TMK.

Questions

1. What advantages does exporting have over foreign manufacturing?

2. What advantages does foreign manufacturing have over exporting?

Source: Adapted from R. Banham, "Not-So-Clear Choices," *International Business*, November/December 1997, pp. 23–25.

OM in ACTION

Toyota in Woodstock

In the mid-2000s, Toyota was looking for a location to build its RAV4 in North America. After considering several locations, Toyota decided on Woodstock, 40 km from Cambridge, the location of Toyota's existing Canadian plant. Toyota was looking for a green-field location close to one of its existing plants in order to share some of the management and workers, and reduce duplication of facilities. The reasons for choosing Woodstock are as follows: the Cambridge plant was at half the capacity of Toyota's Kentucky plant (therefore, it has room to grow); the federal and Ontario governments provided $100 million in grants; the local government assisted in purchasing the 1,000 acre land from 20 farmers; the site is just off Highway 401 and is connected to both CN and CP rail lines; and there is sufficient labour force in the Woodstock area. The $650 million plant opened in 2008.

Source: http://www.siteselection.com/issues/2005/sept/p524/pg02.htm.

For heavy industries, it is important to be close to a railway line, just at the outskirt of a city or town, usually on a green-field site (i.e., on a vacant out-of-town lot). Light industries usually need to be close to highways. Offices may want to be close to airports. Call and data centres need to be close to major telephone and data transmission lines.

Minacs

Minacs is a customer relationship management and IT services outsourcing company (recently bought by the Aditya Birla company of India). In 2007, Minacs opened a contact centre (a call centre that deals with e-mails, as well as phone calls) in Mississauga, employing 300 employees. Mississauga was chosen because of the great pool of immigrants who live in the greater Toronto area. One of Minacs' automotive customers requires Minacs to be able to communicate with its customers in 19 different languages.

Source: http://www.siteselection.com/features/2007/nov/ontario.

Liquor Store Location

In a study of survival of Alberta liquor stores since privatization in 1993, it was discovered that location, among other factors such as population of trade area and age of the store, is an important determinant of a liquor store's survival. Those liquor stores located near a grocery store had an almost 100 percent chance of survival. The next best location was in shopping centres. Locating in a downtown area or near pubs did not help with survival.

Source: A. Eckert and D.S. West, "Firm Survival and Chain Growth in a Privatized Retail Liquor Store Industry," *Review of Industrial Organization*, February 2008, 32(1), pp. 1–18.

Land and building prices may differ significantly across cities/communities. See http://www.colliers.com/Default.aspx (Canada Locations, click city of your choice, then Market Reports) for commercial real estate prices in major cities in Canada.

The primary considerations related to sites are land and access. Usually a company first estimates the size of land and building required. In many cases, both vacant buildings and undeveloped sites are considered. Other site-related factors include room for future expansion, utility and sewer capacities, and sufficient parking space for employees and customers. In addition, for many companies, access roads for trucks or rail spurs are important.

Industrial parks may be worthy alternatives for companies involved in light manufacturing or assembly, warehouse operations, and customer-service facilities. Typically, the land is already developed—power, water, and sewer hookups have been attended to, and zoning restrictions do not require special attention.

For an example of community/site-related factors, see the "Toyota in Woodstock" OM in Action.

Service and Retail Locations

Services and retailers are typically governed by somewhat different considerations than manufacturers in making location decisions. For one thing, proximity to raw materials is not a factor. Customer access is sometimes a prime consideration, as it is with banks and supermarkets, but not a consideration in others, such as call centres, catalogue sales, and online services. Manufacturers tend to be cost focused, and concerned with labour, energy, and material costs and availability, as well as distribution costs. Services and retailers tend to be profit or revenue focused, concerned with demographics such as age, income, and education; population/drawing area; competition; traffic volume/patterns; and customer access/parking.

Retail and service organizations typically place traffic volume and convenience high on the list of important factors. Generally, retail businesses prefer locations that are near other retailers (although not necessarily competitors) because of the higher traffic volumes and convenience to customers. Thus, restaurants and specialty stores often locate in and around malls, benefiting from the high traffic.

Medical services are often located near hospitals for patients' convenience. Doctors' offices may be located near hospitals, or grouped in other, centralized areas with other doctors' offices.

Good transportation and/or parking facilities can be vital to retail establishments. Downtown areas have a competitive disadvantage in attracting shoppers compared to malls because malls offer ample free parking and proximity to residential areas.

Competitors' locations can be important. In some cases, services and retailers will want to locate near competitors to benefit from the concentration of potential customers. Mall stores and auto dealers are good examples. In other cases, it is important *not* to be near a competitor (e.g., another franchise operation of the same fast-food chain).

Among the questions that should be considered to make a location decision for a multi-facility service or retail company are the following:

1. How can sales, market share, and profit be optimized for the entire set of locations? Solutions might include some combination of upgrading facilities, expanding some sites, adding new outlets, and closing or changing the locations of some outlets.

2. What are the potential sales to be realized from each potential solution?

3. Where should outlets be located to maximize market share, sales, and profits without negatively impacting other outlets? This can be a key cause of friction between the operator of a franchise store and the franchising company.

4. What probable effects would there be on market share, sales, and profits if a competitor located nearby?

For an example of retail location, see the "Liquor Store Location" OM in Action.

WHY SHOULD FOREIGN COMPANIES LOCATE IN CANADA?

Foreign companies locate plants in Canada to shorten delivery time and reduce delivery costs to markets in Canada and the United States, as well as to exploit Canadian natural resources and use Canadian skilled labour. We have already seen some examples of these companies in previous OM in Actions (REC Silicon, Dell computers, and Toyota). Also see the "Minacs" OM in Action. Notable Canadian natural resources are energy (oil, gas, electricity), forestry (lumber, newsprint, pulp), and minerals (nickel, copper, zinc, aluminum, gold, diamond, potash, uranium). See http://www.nrcan-rncan.gc.ca/stat/docs/important-eng.pdf.

Canadian workers are educated, basic health care is free, and the country is politically stable. Canada is generally safe and secure. Energy costs are low and governments provide R&D tax incentives. Canada has good phone and Internet infrastructure. According to the latest study by KPMG,[3] Canada is the cheapest of nine major industrialized countries in which to operate a plant. According to country competitiveness rankings (based on a survey of executives' opinions in each country) by World Economic Forum (a non-profit organization), Canada ranks tenth in the world.[4]

---

[3]http://www.competitivealternatives.com/highlights/international.aspx.
[4]http://www.weforum.org/pdf/gcr/2008/rankings.pdf.

Microsoft Canada

In 2007 Microsoft decided to open a software development centre in Vancouver, employing 200–300 people initially. Other foreign Microsoft software development centres are in the U.K., India, China, Ireland, Denmark, and Israel. The main reason for locating the new centre outside the United States was that Microsoft was not able to convince the U.S. legislature to grant enough H1B visas for Microsoft to bring foreign programmers to work in the United States. Canada was chosen because it has a liberal immigration legislation for high-tech workers, and Vancouver was chosen because it is very close to Microsoft's headquarters near Seattle.

Source: Microsoft Cites US Immigration Restrictions as Primary Reason Behind Decision to Open Vancouver Software Development Centre," *Research Money*, July 23, 2007, 21(12), p. 4.

Many companies, mainly from the United States, have set up plants in Canada over the last century, thus helping to industrialize Canada. One industry greatly benefiting Canada is the auto industry. The Big Three U.S. automakers, Toyota, and Honda have several assembly and component plants in Canada, mainly in Southern Ontario.

Every province has something to offer. For example, Quebec has been promoting the development of its high-tech industries (which include e-commerce, multimedia, and biotech firms) for decades. It gives a 40 percent income tax credit for employee salaries of high-tech firms, and also a 40 percent tax credit on specialized machinery. This entices innovative companies to locate in Quebec and to take more risk in developing high-tech products.

The "Microsoft Canada" OM in Action provides another example of foreign companies setting up facilities in Canada.

(LO3) EVALUATING LOCATION ALTERNATIVES

A number of techniques are helpful in evaluating location alternatives. They include locational break-even analysis, transportation method, factor rating, centre of gravity method, and Voronoi polygons to determine trade areas.

Locational Break-even Analysis

locational break-even analysis Identifies the least (fixed and variable) cost location choice based on quantity to be produced.

Locational break-even analysis identifies the least (fixed and variable) cost location choice based on quantity to be produced. This is similar to the cost-vs-cost analysis done in Chapter 5, and illustrated in Figure 5-5B. The analysis can be done numerically or graphically. The graphical approach will be demonstrated here because it enhances understanding of the concept and indicates the ranges over which one of the alternatives is superior to the others.

The procedure for locational break-even analysis involves these steps:

1. Determine the fixed and variable costs associated with each location alternative.
2. Plot the total-cost lines for all location alternatives on the same graph.
3. Determine which location will have the lowest total cost for the expected level of output.

This method assumes that fixed and variable costs are constant for the range of probable output, and only one product is involved.

The total cost for each location is represented mathematically as:

$$\text{Total cost} = FC + v \times Q \tag{8-1}$$

where

FC = Fixed cost

v = Variable cost per unit

Q = Quantity of output

Example 1

Fixed and variable costs for four potential plant locations are shown below:

Location	Fixed Cost per Year	Variable Cost per Unit
A	$250,000	$11
B	100,000	30
C	150,000	20
D	200,000	35

a. Plot the total-cost lines for these locations on a single graph.

b. Identify the range of output for which each alternative is superior (i.e., has the lowest total cost).

c. If the expected output at the selected location is 8,000 units per year, which location would provide the lowest total cost?

Solution

a. To plot the total-cost lines, select an output that is approximately equal to the expected output level (e.g., 10,000 units per year). Calculate the total cost for each location at that level:

	Fixed Cost	+	Variable Cost	=	Total Cost
A . . .	$250,000	+	$11(10,000)	=	$360,000
B . . .	100,000	+	30(10,000)	=	400,000
C . . .	150,000	+	20(10,000)	=	350,000
D . . .	200,000	+	35(10,000)	=	550,000

Plot each location's fixed cost (at output = 0) as a point and the total cost at 10,000 units as another point; and connect the two points with a straight line. (See the graph.)

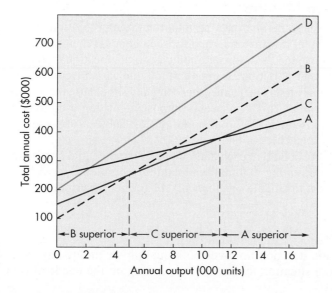

b. The *approximate* ranges for which the various alternatives will yield the lowest total cost are shown on the graph. Note that location D is never superior. The *exact* ranges can be determined by finding the output level at which lines B and C and lines C and A cross. To do this, set their total cost equations equal and solve for Q, the break-even output level. Thus, for B and C:

$$\begin{array}{cc} \text{(B)} & \text{(C)} \end{array}$$
$$\$100{,}000 + \$30Q = \$150{,}000 + \$20Q$$

Solving, you find $Q = 5{,}000$ units per year.
   For C and A:

$$\begin{array}{cc} \text{(C)} & \text{(A)} \end{array}$$
$$\$150{,}000 + \$20Q = \$250{,}000 + \$11Q$$

Solving, $Q = 11{,}111$ units per year.

c. From the graph you can see that for 8,000 units per year, location C provides the lowest total cost.

Similar analysis can be performed using profit instead of total cost. Note that if the selling price and demand is the same across the sites, then the answer will be the same as when using total cost.

For a profit analysis, calculate the total profit for each location:

$$\text{Total profit} = Q(R - v) - FC \tag{8-2}$$

where

   R = Revenue per unit

Solved Problem 2 at the end of the chapter illustrates profit analysis.

Where the expected level of output is close to the middle of the range over which one alternative is superior, the choice is readily apparent. If the expected level of output is very close to the edge of a range, it means that the two alternatives will yield comparable annual costs, so management would be indifferent in choosing between the two *in terms of total cost*. However, it is important to recognize that, in most situations, other factors besides production cost must also be considered (such as transportation cost and availability of labour).

Transportation Method

Transportation costs sometimes play an important role in location decisions. These stem from the movement of raw materials and finished goods. When there is only one facility, the company can include the transportation cost in the locational break-even analysis by incorporating the transportation cost per unit into the variable cost per unit.

When there is more than one facility, the company should use the *transportation method* of linear programming. This is a special-purpose algorithm used to determine the shipments in order to minimize total transportation cost subject to meeting the demands and not exceeding the capacities of facilities.

Various models can be run, each adding one of the potential sites to the set of existing facilities. The site resulting in minimum total transportation cost will be chosen. See the chapter supplement (available on *Connect*) for further description of the transportation method.

Factor Rating

A typical location decision involves both qualitative and quantitative factors, which tend to vary from situation to situation depending on the needs of each organization.

Factor rating involves scoring the factors (both quantitative and qualitative) and determining the weighted score for each location, and choosing the location with highest weighted score.

The following procedure is used in factor rating:

1. Determine which factors are relevant (e.g., location of market, labour supply, parking facilities, revenue potential).
2. Assign a weight to each factor that indicates its relative importance compared with all other factors. Typically, weights sum to 1.00.
3. Decide on a common scale for all factor scores (e.g., 0 to 100).
4. Score all factors for each location.
5. Multiply the factor weight by the score for each factor, and sum the results for each location.
6. Choose the location that has the highest composite score.

This procedure is illustrated by the next example.

factor rating Involves scoring the factors (both quantitative and qualitative) and determining the weighted score for each location, and choosing the location with highest weighted score.

Example 2

A retailer intends to open another store in the same city. The table below contains information on two potential sites. Which is the better alternative?

Solution

Factor	Weight	Scores (Out of 100)		Weighted Scores	
		Alt. 1	Alt. 2	Alternative 1	Alternative 2
Lease cost[1]	.10	100	60	.10(100) = 10.0	.10(60) = 6.0
Renovation cost[1]	.05	80	80	.05(80) = 4.0	.05(80) = 4.0
Traffic volume[2]	.40	70	90	.40(70) = 28.0	.40(90) = 36.0
Operating cost[1]	.10	86	92	.10(86) = 8.6	.10(92) = 9.2
Distance from existing store[2]	.20	40	70	.20(40) = 8.0	.20(70) = 14.0
Size[1]	.15	80	90	.15(80) = 12.0	.15(90) = 13.5
	1.00			70.6	82.7

[1]Lower gets a higher score.
[2]Higher gets a higher score.

Alternative 2 is better because it has higher composite score.

In some cases, managers may prefer to establish minimum *thresholds* for composite scores. If an alternative fails to meet that minimum, they can reject it without further consideration. If none of the alternatives meets the minimum, this means that additional alternatives must be identified.

Centre of Gravity Method

Centre of gravity method determines the location of a distribution centre/warehouse that will minimize total distribution cost. It treats distribution cost as a linear function of the distance and the quantity shipped.

The method uses a map that shows the locations of destinations (demand points). The map must be accurate and drawn to scale. A coordinate system is overlaid on the map to determine relative locations. The location of the (0,0) point of the coordinate system, and its scale, are unimportant. Once the coordinate system is in place, you can determine the coordinates of each destination. (See Figure 8-1a and b.)

centre of gravity method Method for locating a distribution centre/warehouse that minimizes total distribution cost.

Figure 8-1

Centre of gravity method

a. Map showing destinations

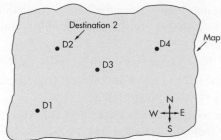

b. Add a coordinate system

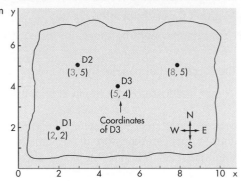

c. Centre of gravity

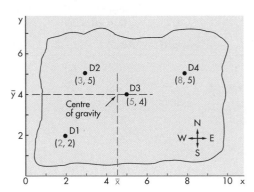

If distance is rectilinear (i.e., travel is east-west and north-south only), then we can decompose the problem into x-axis and y-axis problems and solve them independently. We assume that distance is rectilinear.

If the quantities to be transported to every destination are *equal*, you can obtain the coordinates of the centre of gravity (i.e., the location of the distribution centre/warehouse) by finding the average of the x coordinates and the average of the y coordinates (see Figure 8-1c).

These averages can be easily determined using the following formulas:

$$\bar{x} = \frac{\sum x_i}{n}$$

$$\bar{y} = \frac{\sum y_i}{n}$$

(8-3)

where

$x_i = x$ coordinate of destination i

$y_i = y$ coordinate of destination i

$n =$ number of destinations

When the number of units to be transported is not the same for all destinations, which is usually the case, a *weighted average* must be used to determine the centre of gravity, with the weights being the *quantities* to be transported.

The appropriate formulas in this case are:

$$\bar{x} = \frac{\sum x_i Q_i}{\sum Q_i}$$

$$\bar{y} = \frac{\sum y_i Q_i}{\sum Q_i}$$

(8-4)

where

Q_i = Quantity to be transported to destination i

Example 3

Determine the coordinates of the centre of gravity for the problem that is depicted in Figure 8-1a. Assume that the shipments from the centre of gravity to each of the four destinations will be equal quantities.

Solution

The coordinates of the destinations can be obtained from Figure 8-1b:

Destination	x,	y
D1	2,	2
D2	3,	5
D3	5,	4
D4	8,	5
	18,	16

$$\bar{x} = \frac{\sum x_i}{n} = \frac{18}{4} \qquad \bar{y} = \frac{\sum y_i}{n} = \frac{16}{4}$$

$$= 4.5 \qquad\qquad = 4$$

Hence, the centre of gravity is at (4.5, 4), which places it just west of destination D3 (see Figure 8-1c).

Example 4

Suppose that the shipments for the problem depicted in Figure 8-1a are not all equal, but instead are the following:

Destination	x, y	Weekly Quantity
D1	2, 2	800
D2	3, 5	900
D3	5, 4	200
D4	8, 5	100
		2,000

Determine the centre of gravity in this case.

Solution

Because the quantities to be shipped differ among destinations, you must use the weighted average formulas.

$$\bar{x} = \frac{\sum x_i Q_i}{\sum Q_i} = \frac{2(800) + 3(900) + 5(200) + 8(100)}{2,000} = \frac{6,100}{2,000} = 3.05 \,[\text{round to 3}]$$

$$\bar{y} = \frac{\sum y_i Q_i}{\sum Q_i} = \frac{2(800) + 5(900) + 4(200) + 5(100)}{2,000} = \frac{7,400}{2,000} = 3.7$$

Hence, the coordinates of the centre of gravity are approximately (3, 3.7). This would place it south of destination D2. (See Figure 8-2.)

Figure 8-2

Centre of gravity

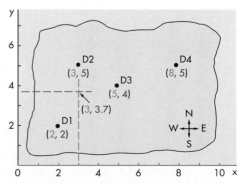

Voronoi Polygons to Determine Trade Areas

The trade or service area for a retail store, restaurant, bank branch, etc, of a multi-facility company is usually determined by a Voronoi or Thiessen polygon. The city or town is divided into non-overlapping polygons so that each polygon contains one facility (as its centre) and any point within a polygon is closest (in terms of Euclidian distance) to the centre of the polygon (than any other polygon centres). Euclidian distance between two points (x_1, y_1) and (x_2, y_2) is $\sqrt{(x_1 - x_2)^2 + (y_1 - y_2)^2}$.

There are many ways Voronoi polygons can be determined. An efficient method, Lawson's algorithm, first determines which facilities' polygons share borders by connecting those facilities by specific triangles (called Delaunay triangles) and then constructing the polygons from the triangles.

Lawson's Algorithm to Determine Delaunay Triangles. Given the set of facilities or points V:

Lawson Algorithm

- form a *super triangle*, enclosing all points p in V
- as long as not all points p of V have been considered do:
  1. insert point p into triangulation
  2. triangulate new p (i.e., draw edges to p from the enclosing triangle, creating new triangles)
  3. for all the new triangles t created recursively:
     - check the circumcircle of t, if it contains a neighbouring point, then *flip*
- remove *super triangle*

Source: http://www.henrikzimmer.com/VoronoiDelaunay.pdf.

A circumcircle is the unique circle that goes through the three vertices of a triangle. "Flip" involves deleting the longest side of the triangle and creating a new line between the vertex facing it and a vertex of the previous triangle.

An iteration of Lawson algorithm, including the "flip" operation, is illustrated below. Suppose that graph (A) below is the current solution of Lawson algorithm (another example, Example 6 below, starts from the beginning). Point (facility) q is added in graph (B). All vertices of the triangle where q is located are connected to q in graph (C). The new triangles created by q are circumcircled one at a time (i.e., a circle is passed through the three vertices of the triangle). If the circle contains other point(s) (facility(ies)), then q is connected to that (those) facility(ies) directly and the edges that it (they) cross is (are) removed. In graph (C), if the triangle (a, q, c) is circumcircled, the circle will contain point (facility) b. Therefore, b is connected directly to q and edge (a, c) is removed (see graph D). The circle which circumcircles triangle (a, q, d) does not contain any other vertex. However, the circle circumcircling triangle (d, q, c) will contain both vertices e and f. Therefore, both are connected directly to q and the edges they cross, (d, c) and (e, c) are removed (see graph E).

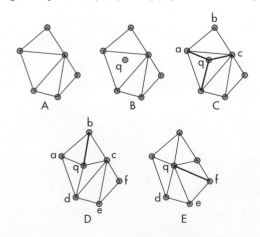

At the end of the Lawson algorithm, the Delaunay triangles can be used to construct Voronoi polygons by drawing a perpendicular line segment in the midpoint of each edge to where these lines intersect. For example, if the triangles in graph (E) above are the final solution to the Lawson algorithm, the associated Voronoi polygons are as follows:

Example 5

Locations of four Burger King Restaurants in Saskatoon are shown in the following map (with red circles). Determine the trade area for each restaurant using the Voronoi polygons.

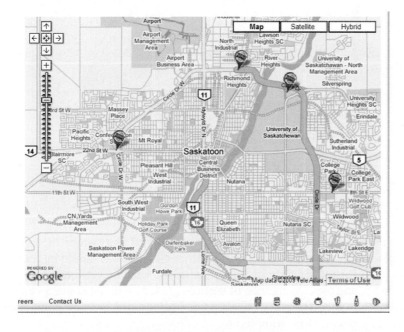

First determine a super triangle that includes all four points.

Solution

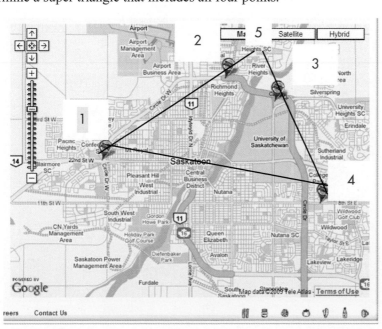

To accelerate the solution, we used points 1 and 4 as two vertices of the super triangle, and used the lines connecting points 1 and 2 and points 3 and 4 as the sides of the super triangle. These intersect at vertex 5 (see the figure above). The super triangle has vertices (1, 4, 5). Because points 1 and 4 are already a vertex of the super triangle, they have already been considered in the Lawson's algorithm. Now, points 2 and 3 have to be added to the super triangle by Lawson's algorithm. Adding point 2 results in just adding a line from point 4 to point 2 (because 2 is already connected to vertices 1 and 5 by the edge (1, 5).) See the figure below.

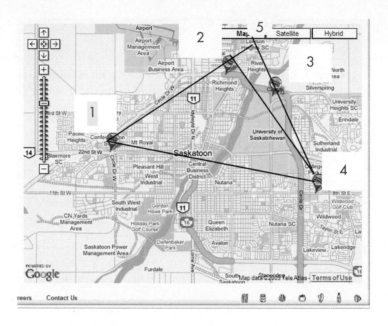

Because none of the circumcircles containing point 2 and two of the super triangle vertices will contain the other vertex of super triangle, no lines should be removed (i.e., there is no need for a flip). Specifically, the circumcircle of vertices (2, 1, 4) will not contain vertex 5, and the circumcircle of vertices (2, 4, 5) will not contain vertex 1. Now, add point 3 to the super triangle. Connect point 3 to vertex 2 because point 3 falls in the triangle (2, 4, 5). See the following figure.

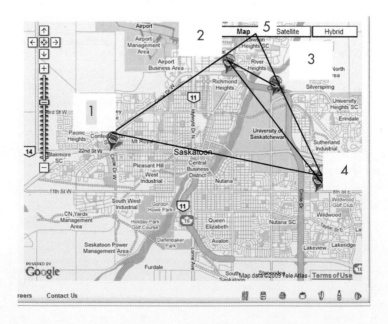

The circle circumcircling the triangle (2, 3, 5) will not contain points 1 or 4, so there is no need for flip. However, the circle circumcircling (2, 3, 4) will contain vertex 1. Therefore, line (2, 4) should be removed and line (1, 3) should be added. This is the end of Lawson's algorithm. See the diagram below.

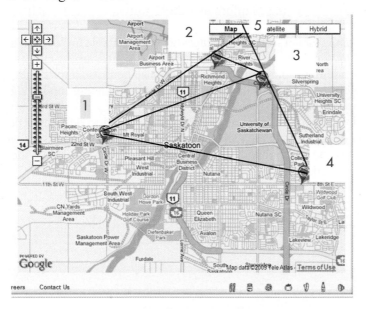

Now, omit point 5 and line segments (3, 5) and (2, 5). Then, construct the Voronoi polygons by drawing perpendicular thick lines to each edge of the triangles at their midpoints. The thick lines surrounding each restaurant in the following figure mark the boundaries of the trade area of the restaurant.

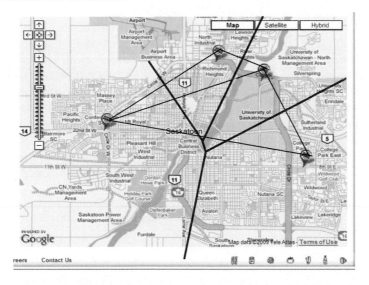

You can check the accuracy of the above Voronoi polygons by inputting the locations of restaurants in the solution software given at http://www.cs.cornell.edu/Info/People/chew/Delaunay.html.

Location Analysis Software

Two types of software are used in location analysis: geographic information system and modelling/optimization. **Geographic information system (GIS)** is a computer-based tool for collecting, storing, retrieving, and displaying location-dependent demographic data

geographic information system (GIS) A computer-based tool for collecting, storing, retrieving, and displaying location-dependent demographic data on maps.

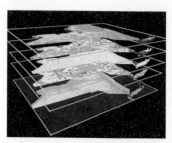

A Geographic Information System (GIS) is a tool that can be used for location planning. This graphic of New York State combines information from different databases to answer demographic questions about the state. This information also can be broken down into smaller units, such as counties.

on maps. The data might involve age, incomes, type of employment, type of housing, or other similar data deemed useful for decision at hand. The intuitive graphical maps facilitate communication of facts and hence decision making. Companies providing GIS software and services are MapInfo (now part of Pitney Bowes) and ESRI. For some applications involving MapInfo and ESRI software, see the "GIS Case Studies" OM in Action.

Modelling/optimization software packages are also available for location analysis. Many packages employ linear programming or a variation called mixed integer programming algorithms. In addition, some software packages use heuristic approaches to obtain reasonable solutions to location problems. A company producing modelling/optimization location software is MicroAnalytics.

MicroAnalytics OptiSite uses the transportation model to determine the optimal use and allocation of suppliers, warehouses, and customer demand points, as well as optimal location of plants and warehouses. Other software from Micro-Analytics includes Bustops and TruckStops used for optimal routing (http://www.bestroutes.com).

 OM in ACTION

GIS Case Studies

Cara

When Cara Operations purchased five more restaurant chains in the beginning of the 2000s (in addition to Harvey's and Swiss Chalet), the Director of Market Planning in the Real Estate Department needed assistance to keep up. Cara purchased MapInfo's site selection software AnySite. The software provides not only electronic maps of trade areas but also demographic information such as the number of people and their spending habits for eating out. Cara also uses a plug-in software called Site Matcher that assists in matching a new trade area with a similar one that already has an existing restaurant in it. MapInfo has reduced the analysis time per site from half a day down to one hour.

Source: http://resource.mapinfo.com/static/files/document/1086796426697/Cara.5.7.pdf.

Scotiabank Mexico

Scotiabank is Canada's most international bank. In the mid-1990s, Scotiabank was expanding quickly in Mexico, but was rather unfamilar with the demographics and locations there. It employed the services of MapInfo and WinSITE software. WinSITE provides demographic, geographic, customer, and small business information, and uses behavioural (retail gravity) models to identify potential markets, market shares, and sites for new branch networks and ATMs. This information is used by local branch managers, together with in-person visits, to determine profitable sites. The results have been very good so far. Scotiabank has over 600 branches and 1,400 ATMs in Mexico.

Sources: http://www.mapinfo.com/americas/us/case_studies/financial/collateral/Scotiabank_CaseStudy.pdf; http://www.scotiabank.com.mx/QuienesSomos/quien/Quienes/Historia/Pages/Quienes_somos.aspx.

The Co-operators

The Co-operators, based in Guelph, consists of 33 insurance co-operatives in Canada. It uses over 430 independent insurance agents to acquire clients. To each agent, The Co-operators has made available MapInfo's TargetPro (for target marketing) and PSYTE Advantage (market segmentation system). These tools help the agents to understand their service market better and to target the right insurance service to each consumer. For example, clients with auto insurance but not home insurance are targeted for home insurance. Also, using the software, The Co-operators is able to identify the closest agent to a potential client.

Source: http://www.mapinfo.com/americas/us/case_studies/insurance/collateral/Co-Operators_CaseStudy.pdf.

Levi Strauss

In 2004, Levi Strauss decided to maximize its distribution by also selling its jeans in specialty stores such as workwear and western apparel outfitters. In order to not impact the sales of its existing retailers, Levi Strauss purchased BusinessMAP and Business Analyst Online services from ESRI. For each existing retailer, the software detremines a 1-, 3-, and 5-mile ring (or square if driving distance is used) around the retailer (similar to Voronoi polygons). Any new potential retailer is also geocoded, and if it is too close to an existing retailer, it will not be approved.

Source: http://www.esri.com/library/casestudies/levistrauss.pdf.

Summary

Location decisions confront both new and existing organizations. Growth, market shifts, depletion of raw materials, and the introduction of new products are among the reasons organizations are concerned with location decisions. The importance of these decisions is underscored by the long-term commitment necessary and by their impact on costs.

A common approach to location analysis is to first identify a country or region that seems to satisfy overall needs and then identify a number of community/site alternatives for more in-depth analysis.

In practice, the major influences on location decisions are location of raw materials, labour supply, market considerations, and community/site-related factors. Most retailers decide on a site far from locations of their other stores and the competitors' stores, taking potential sales into account. Foreign locations may be attractive in terms of labour cost, abundance of raw material, or as potential market for a company's products. Canada is one of the best locations for a foreign plant/facility, because it is close to the U.S. market, has an educated labour force, and has abundant natural resources.

A variety of methods are used to evaluate location alternatives. Those described in the chapter include locational break-even analysis, factor rating, centre of gravity method, and Voronoi polygons for determining trade areas.

Key Terms

centre of gravity method, 267   geographic information system (GIS), 273
factor rating, 267   locational break-even analysis, 264

Solved Problems

Problem 1

Locational Break-even Cost-vs.-cost Analysis. A manufacturer that sells its products in Saskatchewan is looking for a production location there. There are three potential locations: Saskatoon, Regina, and Yorkton. Saskatoon would involve a fixed cost of $4,000 per month and a variable cost of $4 per unit; Regina would involve a fixed cost of $3,500 per month and a variable cost of $5 per unit; and Yorkton would involve a fixed cost of $5,000 per month and a variable cost of $6 per unit. Use of the Saskatoon location would decrease the manufacturer's distribution costs by $19,000 per month, Regina by $22,000 per month, and Yorkton by $18,000 per month. Which location would result in the lowest total cost to distribute 800 units per month in Saskatchewan?

Solution

Given: Quantity = 800 units per month

	FC per Month	Variable Cost per Unit, v	Decrease in Distribution Cost per Month
Saskatoon	$4,000	$4	$19,000
Regina	3,500	5	22,000
Yorkton	5,000	6	18,000

Monthly total cost $= FC + VC -$ Decrease in distribution cost

Saskatoon: $4,000 + $4 per unit $\times$ 800 units $-$ $19,000 $= -$11,800
Regina: 3,500 $+$ 5 per unit $\times$ 800 units $-$ 22,000 $=$ $- 14,500$
Yorkton: 5,000 $+$ 6 per unit $\times$ 800 units $-$ 18,000 $=$ $- 8,200$

Hence, Regina would have the lowest total cost.

Problem 2

Locational Break-even Profit-vs.-profit analysis. A manufacturer is about to lose its lease, so it must move to another location. Two locations are currently under consideration. Fixed costs would be $8,000 per month at location A and $9,400 per month at location B. Variable costs are expected to be $5 per unit at location A and $4 per unit at location B. Monthly demand has been steady at 8,800 units for the last several years and is not expected to deviate from that amount in the foreseeable future. The product sells for $6 per unit. Determine which location would yield higher profit under these conditions.

Solution

$$\text{Profit} = Q(R - v) - FC$$

Location	Q	R	v	Q(R − v)	FC	Monthly Profit
A	8,800	$6	$5	$8,800	$8,000	$ 800
B	8,800	$6	$4	$17,600	$9,400	$8,200

Hence, location B is expected to yield higher monthly profit.

Problem 3

Factor rating. Determine which location, A or B, has a higher composite score given the following information:

Factor	Weight	Score A	B
Labour cost	.50	20	40
Material cost	.30	10	30
Supplier base	.20	50	10
	1.00		

Solution

Multiplying the weights with the location scores and adding, we can see that location B has higher composite score:

Factor	Weight	Score A	B	Weighted Scores A	B
Labour cost[1]	.50	20	40	.50(20) = 10	.50(40) = 20
Material cost[1]	.30	10	30	.30(10) = 3	.30(30) = 9
Supplier base[2]	.20	50	10	.20(50) = 10	.20(10) = 2
	1.00			23	31

[1]lower gets a higher score
[2]higher gets a higher score

Problem 4

Centre of gravity. Determine the centre of gravity location for these destinations:

Destination	(x,y) Coordinate	Weekly Quantity
D1	3,5	20
D2	6,8	10
D3	2,7	15
D4	4,5	15
		60

Solution

Because the weekly quantities are not all equal, we must use the formulas in formula 8-4.

$$\bar{x} = \frac{\Sigma xQ}{\Sigma Q} = \frac{3(20) + 6(10) + 2(15) + 4(15)}{60} = \frac{210}{60} = 3.5$$

$$\bar{y} = \frac{\Sigma yQ}{\Sigma Q} = \frac{5(20) + 8(10) + 7(15) + 5(15)}{60} = \frac{360}{60} = 6.0$$

Hence, the centre of gravity has the coordinates $x = 3.5$ and $y = 6.0$

Discussion and Review Questions

1. In what ways can the location decision have an impact on the production system? (LO1)
2. Respond to this statement: "The importance of the location decision is often vastly overrated; the fact that virtually every type of business is located in every region of the country means that there should be no problem in finding a suitable location." (LO1)
3. Outline the general approach for developing location alternatives. (LO1)
4. What regional/country factors influence location decisions? (LO2)

5. What community/site-related factors influence location decisions? (LO2)

6. How are manufacturing and service location decisions similar? Different? (LO2)

7. What are the potential benefits of locating in foreign countries? Potential drawbacks? (LO2)

8. What is the factor rating method, and how does it work? (LO3)

9. What are the basic assumptions in locational break-even analysis? (LO3)

10. What is the centre-of-gravity method, and when should it be used? (LO3)

11. What are Voronoi polygons and when should they be used? (LO3)

12. The problem of finding a hub for an airline or for a package delivery service such as FedEx (for which Memphis is the hub) can be modelled and solved by the centre-of-gravity method. Explain how. (LO3)

13. Crude oil in Canada that was first explored near Sarnia, Ontario, is long gone by now. Still, Sarnia is known as the Chemical Capital of Canada, having 16 chemical and 3 major oil refineries. Explain what advantage Sarnia has relative to locations in Alberta that are closer to oil and petrochemical feedstock production. (LO2)

14. Determine the main factors that might be used for locating each of the following facilities:

   a. hospital
   b. chemical factory
   c. fire station
   d. high-end hotel
   e. motel (LO2)

Taking Stock

1. What trade-offs are involved in deciding to have a single large centrally located facility instead of several smaller dispersed facilities? (LO2)

2. Who needs to be involved in facility location decisions? (LO1)

3. Name two ways that technology has had an impact on location decisions. (LO3)

4. Governments compete with each other to attract businesses to create jobs in their jurisdictions. Some examples of these subsidies are given in the "Some Examples of Subsidies" OM in Action. There is no doubt that some of these have helped keep jobs in Canada. However, some people argue that subsidies are not in the long-term interest of taxpayers. For example, between 1982 and 2005, Pratt & Whitney Canada, the largest recipient of government subsidies, received over $1.5 billion in low-interest loans and Bombardier received over $0.75 billion. However, they have repaid only a small percentage of the loans and at the same time are laying off thousands of employees.[5] Also, there have been abuses. For example, Morgan Stanley received tax credits from the Government of Quebec for opening a 300-employee software development centre in Montreal although 200 of them were working for a contractor, Compuware, in Montreal, and simply transferred from Compuware to Morgan Stanley. Another example is Videotron, which created a subsidiary and transferred 100 of its employees to it (without physically moving them) to take advantage of Quebec tax credits.[6] Are government subsidies appropriate? Discuss. (LO2)

Critical Thinking Exercise

The owner of a franchised fast-food restaurant has exclusive rights to operate in a city. The owner currently has a single outlet, which has proved to be very popular and there are often waiting lines of customers. The owner is therefore considering opening one or more other restaurants in the area. What are the key factors that the owner should investigate before making a final decision? (LO2 & 3)

Experiential Learning Exercise

Identify a nearby location that has seen several businesses fail. Visit the location and try to determine what were the reasons for failures. Alternatively, visit a new business in your area and determine why it located there. (LO2 & 3)

[5]http://www.taxpayer.com/federal/federal-misery-corporate-welfare.
[6]D. MacPherson, "Quebec Gives Money to Company for Existing Jobs," *The Gazette*, May 8, 2008, p. A21.

1. Visit http://www.pbinsight.com/products/location-intelligence/applications/mapping-analytical/ mapinfo-professional. View the MapInfo Professional multimedia tour (link is on the right hand side) and briefly summarize what MapInfo software does. (LO3)

2. Visit http://www.SiteSelection.com, type "Canada" in the search box on the top right, and press Enter. In the Search Engine, choose "Site Selection" in the Category box. Find an article about a location decision involving Canada. Identify the company and the major factors it used to find a suitable site. (LO2)

1. A newly formed company must decide on a plant location. There are two alternatives under consideration: locate near the major raw materials or locate near the major customers. Locating near the raw materials will result in lower fixed and variable costs than locating near the market, but the owners believe that there would be a loss in sales volume because customers tend to favour local suppliers. Revenue per unit will be $180 in either case. Using the following information, determine which location would produce greater profit. (LO3)

	Near Raw Materials	Near Customers
Annual fixed costs ($ millions)	$1.2	$1.4
Variable cost per unit	$36	$47
Expected annual demand (units)	8,000	12,000

2. The owner of a sandwich shop hopes to add one new outlet. She has studied three locations. Each would have the same labour and materials costs (food, serving containers, napkins, etc.) of $1.76 per sandwich. Sandwiches sell for $2.65 each in all locations. Rent and equipment costs would be $5,000 per month for location A, $5,500 per month for location B, and $5,800 per month for location C. (LO3)

   a. Determine the quantity necessary at each location to realize a monthly profit of $10,000.
   b. If expected sales at locations A, B, and C are 21,000, 22,000, and 23,000 sandwiches per month, respectively, which location would yield the greatest profit?

3. A manufacturer of industrial machines wants to move to a larger plant, and has identified two alternatives. Location A has annual fixed cost of $800,000 and variable cost of $14,000 per unit; location B has annual fixed cost of $920,000 and variable cost of $12,000 per unit. (LO3)

   a. At what quantity of output would the two locations have the same total cost?
   b. For what range of output would location A be superior? For what range would B be superior (i.e., have lower total annual cost)?

4. A company that produces pleasure boats has decided to expand one of its lines. The current facility is insufficient to handle the increased workload, so the company is considering three alternatives, A (new location), B (subcontract), or C (expand the existing facility).
   Alternative A would involve substantial fixed cost but relatively low variable cost: fixed cost would be $250,000 per year and variable cost would be $500 per boat. Subcontracting would involve a cost per boat of $2,500, and expansion would require an annual fixed cost of $50,000 and a variable cost of $1,000 per boat. (LO3)

   a. Find the range of output for each alternative that would yield the lowest total cost.
   b. Which alternative would yield the lowest total cost for an expected annual quantity of 150 boats?
   c. What other factors might be considered in choosing between expansion and subcontracting?

5. Rework Problem 4b using this additional information: Expansion would result in an increase of $70,000 per year, subcontracting would result in an increase of $25,000 per year, and adding a new location would result in an increase of $40,000 per year in transportation costs. (LO3)

6. A company that has recently experienced growth is seeking to lease a small plant in Winnipeg, Montreal, or Toronto. Prepare an economic analysis of the three locations given

the following information: annual cost for building, equipment, and administration would be $40,000 for Winnipeg, $60,000 for Montreal, and $100,000 for Toronto. Labour and materials are expected to be $8 per unit in Toronto, $4 per unit in Winnipeg, and $5 per unit in Montreal. The Montreal location would increase total transportation cost by $50,000 per year, the Winnipeg location by $60,000 per year, and the Toronto location by $25,000 per year. Expected annual quantity is 10,000 units. (LO3)

7. A retired auto mechanic hopes to open a rustproofing shop. Customers would be local dealers. Two locations are being considered, one in the centre of the city and one in the outskirts. The central city location would involve fixed monthly cost of $7,000 and labour, materials, and transportation costs of $30 per car. The outskirt location would have fixed monthly costs of $4,700 and labour, materials, and transportation costs of $40 per car. Price at either location will be $90 per car. (LO3)

   a. Which location will yield the greatest profit if monthly demand is (i) 200 cars? (ii) 250 cars?

   b. At what quantity of cars will the two sites yield the same monthly profit?

8. For each of the four types of organizations shown below, rate the importance of each factor given in the left column in terms of making location decisions using L = low importance, M = moderate importance, and H = high importance. (LO2)

Factor	Local Bank	Steel Mill	Grocery Warehouse	Public School
Convenience for customers	_____	_____	_____	_____
Attractiveness of building	_____	_____	_____	_____
Proximity to raw materials	_____	_____	_____	_____
Large amounts of power	_____	_____	_____	_____
Labour cost and availability	_____	_____	_____	_____
Transportation cost	_____	_____	_____	_____
Construction cost	_____	_____	_____	_____

9. Using the following factor ratings (100 points is the maximum), determine which location for a clothing store, A, B, or C, should be chosen. (LO3)

		Location		
Factor	Weight	A	B	C
Convenience of access ..	.15	80	70	60
Parking facility	.20	72	76	92
Frontage	.18	88	90	90
Shopper traffic	.27	94	86	80
Operating cost	.10	98	90	82
Neighbourhood	.10	96	85	75
	1.00			

10. A manager has received an analysis of several cities being considered for a new office complex. The data (10 points is the maximum) are: (LO3)

	Location		
Factor	A	B	C
Business services.	9	5	5
Community services. . .	7	6	7
Construction cost	5	6	5
Cost of living	4	7	8
Personal taxes	5	5	4
Commuting ease.	6	7	8

a. If the manager weighs the factors equally, how would the locations compare?

b. If business services and construction cost are given weights that are double the weights of the other factors, how would the locations compare?

11. A toy manufacturer distributes its toys from five distribution centres (DCs) throughout the country. A new plant is to be built for a new line of toys. The monthly quantities to be shipped to each DC are approximately the same. A coordinate system has been established and the coordinates of each DC have been determined as shown below. Determine the optimal coordinates of the plant. (LO3)

Location	(x,y)
A	3,7
B	8,2
C	4,6
D	4,1
E	6,4

12. A clothing manufacturer produces women's clothes at four locations. A coordinate system has been determined for these four locations as shown below. The location of a central warehouse for rolls of cloth must now be determined. Weekly quantities to be shipped to each location are shown below. Determine the coordinates of the location that will minimize total transportation cost. (LO3)

Location	(x,y)	Weekly Quantity
A	5,8	15
B	6,9	20
C	3,9	25
D	9,4	30

13. A company that handles hazardous waste wants to open up a central disposal centre. The objective is to minimize the total shipping cost to the disposal centre from five receiving stations it operates. Given the locations of the receiving stations and the volumes to be shipped daily below, determine the location of the disposal centre. (LO3)

Location of Receiving Station, (x, y)	Volume, Tonnes per Day
10, 4	26
4, 1	9
4, 7	25
2, 6	30
8, 7	40

14. Determine the centre of gravity of the destinations shown on the following map. Monthly shipments will be the quantities listed below. (LO3)

Destination	Quantity
D1	900
D2	300
D3	700
D4	600
D5	800

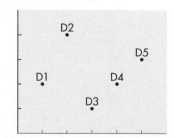

MINI-CASE http://acadianbakers.com

Acadian Bakers

A cadian Bakers is a small but well-known bakery, making and selling cakes and croissants in Houston. Its major customers, their locations on a coordinate system, and their weekly purchases are listed below.

Acadian's coordinates are (27, 36). Is Acadian centrally located to serve its customers?

Customer	Coordinates		Weekly Purchases ($)
	X	Y	
B. Catering	22	31	80
B. Bar & Grill	38	38	70
H's	38	36	90
H Club	38	37	120
H.C. Club	30	33	90
J's Hideaway	−10	12	60
M's	38	36	140
M. Club	−10	44	140
N.M.	47	33	300
K.S. Catering	33	33	50

MINI-CASE http://www.bowater.com

Stone Consolidated

I n 1990, Stone Consolidated (now part of AbitibiBowater) decided to develop new landfills for six of its seven mills in eastern Canada. Three of its mills in the St. Maurice Valley area of Quebec were closely situated: the Laurentide mill in Grand-Mere produced uncoated ground-wood papers; the Belgo mill in Shawinigan (10 km south) produced newsprint and de-inked pulp; and the Wayagamack mill in Trois-Rivières (40 km further south) produced Kraft specialty paper. Given their proximity, Stone Consolidated began a search for a landfill site that could hold the combined waste generated by these three mills.

Stone Consolidated forecasted its total waste output over the next 25 years. It was calculated that the required landfill would need to take up a 58-hectare area.

Stone Consolidated began its search in a 45 × 60 km area containing the three mills, identifying all parcels of land that were at least 58 hectares and satisfied the Quebec Ministry of Environment's landfill guidelines; 175 potential sites were found. This number was reduced by consulting zoning restrictions affecting each of the potential sites, excluding sites within or close to residential and commercial areas as well as those in agricultural areas, which would have required zoning modification and a public hearing at the Quebec Commission for the Protection of Agricultural Territories. Still further sites were excluded for political reasons, being in municipalities that had negative histories with landfills. Of the original 175 potential sites, 67 were still viable after this initial exclusion phase.

To further exclude sites, Stone Consolidated consulted available geological and geotechnical reports and aerial photographs. Sites predominantly of water-bearing sand and those with shallow bedrock were thus excluded because of risks of groundwater contamination and the costs of implementing measures in line with environmental protection. After this second exclusion phase, six potential sites remained.

Each of these six sites was subjected to tests to confirm viable subsoil conditions. No unexpected conditions were uncovered, so a decision table containing nine criteria was prepared to help select the optimum site: topography, road access, visual impact, weighted average distance to mills, geology and soil condition, groundwater, surface water, actual or potential land use, and population density. Each criterion was assigned a weight varying between 3 and 8. For each evaluation criterion, a specific site was rated as follows:

- Favourable = 4
- Acceptable = 2
- Marginally acceptable = 1

The numerical ranking system is explained in Table 1. The scores of each of the six potential sites are shown in Table 2.

Table 1

Numerical ranking system

Criteria	Weighting	Favourable Factor (4)	Acceptable (2)	Marginally Acceptable (1)
Topography	5	Natural relief and slopes favourable to development	Acceptable relief and slopes—not seriously complicated for development	Abrupt relief—difficult or complicated development
Road access	6	Provincial highways bordered by few or no houses	Road network through areas with few houses	Road network through high-density population areas
Visual impact	3	Site not readily noticeable by passersby	Site could be readily noticeable to passersby; visual screening measures may be required	Site readily noticeable to passersby; screening measures necessary
Weighted avg. distance to mills	3	Average distance less than 15 km	Average distance less than 20 km	Average distance more than 20 km
Geology and soils	7	Low permeable soils	Moderately permeable soils	Permeable soils
Groundwater	8	Favourable depth to groundwater	Probably acceptable depth to groundwater	Potentially unacceptable depth to groundwater
Surface water	6	Drainage network a fair distance from the site	Drainage network at minimal distance from the site	Drainage network to be altered
Actual or potential land use	8	Forestry or industrial zoning—few or no houses	Adjacent to agricultural zoning	Site close to residential area
Population density	6	Minimal residential development	Scattered residential development	Moderate to dense residential development

Table 2

Site evaluation matrix

Criteria	Weight	St-Georges-de-Champlain	Ste-Geneviere	St-Barnabe	St-Mathieu	St-Gerard	Grandes-Piles
Topography	5	4	4	4	1	2	1
Road access	6	4	2	1	1	1	4
Visual impact	3	4	2	2	4	1	4
Weighted avg. distance to mills	3	4	1	2	2	4	2
Geology and soils	7	4	2	1	1	2	2
Groundwater	8	4	2	2	2	2	4
Surface water	6	1	2	2	4	2	2
Actual or potential land use	8	4	4	1	4	1	2
Population density	6	4	2	1	2	1	2

Question

Calculate the total weighted score for each site. Which one is the best?

Sources: Based on F. Villeneuve, D. Dallaire, and V.G. Fournier, "Site Location and Open Communications Are the Keys to a Successful Landfill Permitting: How One Company Handled Its Expansion Needs," *Pulp & Paper Canada* 99(2), February 1998, pp. 29–31ff.

MINI-CASE

WhiteWater West Industries

hitewater West Industries was founded by Geoff Chutter in early 1980s. An accountant working in Vancouver, Geoff got interested in waterslides in 1980 while visiting his uncle in Kelowna who had done consulting on a waterslide in a local park. Geoff quit his job, bought 18 acres of land in Penticton, 60 km south of Kelowna, and built his own water park. More interested in creative aspects of design, he sold his water park in 1983 and bought half-ownership of a Kelowna fibreglass factory. Slides are made by manually spraying melted fibreglass and resin on moulds.

Whitewater West entered the wave pool business in 1987 through a technology agreement with a Scottish company. Due to this and various other design and manufacturing innovations, Whitewater West kept growing. Most of its sales was international and was trucked to Vancouver and shipped from there. Whitewater moved its headquarters to Richmond, B.C., and expanded its design and engineering staff.

In 1995, the Kelowna plant was getting too small for Whitewater West's sales volume. Geoff needed a larger factory. He had to decide its location: In or near Kelowna or near its headquarters in Richmond? List the advantages and disadvantages of each alternative location and recommend one.

Sources: http://www.whitewaterwest.com; http://www.formashape. com; C. Clark, "He Turns Water into Fun," *CA Magazine*, January 1993, 126(1), pp. 6–7; R. McQueen, "Canada's 50 Best Managed Companies: Whitewater West Industries Ltd," *Financial Post*, December 13, 1997, p. 48.

MINI-CASE   http://www.palliser.com/companyinfo.php

Palliser Furniture

alliser Furniture is the largest furniture manufacturer in Canada, but it grew out of the basement of its founder, A.A. DeFehr, who made simple wood products in Winnipeg in the 1940s. It grew steadily until 1963 when it moved to a 40 acre site in McLeod Industrial Park in northeast Winnipeg, the location of most of its current plants. Palliser's revenue was approximately $50 million and it employed approximately 800 workers in 1963.

The growth was steady but the furniture market in Canada was limited. In 1968, Palliser bought a bankrupt furniture upholsterer in Airdrie, north of Calgary, and started selling in the United States. However, it did not have much success there. In 1981, Palliser opened a furniture factory in Fargo, North Dakota, near Winnipeg, to make selling in the United States easier. In 1985, seeing the surge of cheap imports from Asia, Palliser got into wholesale trade by creating the World Trade division which bought furniture from the Far East and sold it to North American furniture retailers.

Later, Palliser opened a particle board plant on its site in Winnipeg, becoming more vertically integrated in order to control quality and costs. In 1991, Palliser bought a bankrupt North Carolina furniture plant. Later, seeing the attractive prices for leather sofas and chairs, it started making more leather furniture. It also started a line of furniture for children's bedroom, called Logic. Palliser had grown to 1,800 employees and $200 million revenue. After NAFTA, in1994, Palliser took advantage of free trade with the United States by doubling its sales and employees. It also built a plant in Mexico to reduce its costs and to get closer to the southern U.S. market for leather furniture. Mexico was chosen over a plant in China because Palliser chose to follow the customization and fast (2–4 weeks) delivery strategies, knowing that the transport time from China would be 6–8 weeks for its competitors, even though labour cost would be cheaper there. Also, because of NAFTA, there would be no duties for goods produced in Mexico.

In 2001, Palliser introduced a line of trendy furniture for youth, called EQ3, and got into retailing furniture. Later, the rising Canadian dollar and cheap imports from China put pressure on solid wood furniture business, forcing Palliser to differentiate itself by making veneer products on machine-driven processes in Canada, but buying labour-intensive traditional wood products from the Far East. To reduce costs, Palliser built more factories in Mexico, and shifted more of the production of leather furniture from Winnipeg to Mexico. Currently it has 4 factories in Mexico employing approximately 1,400 employees and 4 factories in Canada employing approximately 2,800 employees.

Question

How has Palliser competed internationally? How have its location strategies helped it?

Sources: J. Rusen, "From Humble Beginnings . . .," *Manitoba Business*, September 1988, 10(7), Sec. 1, p. 6; J.E. Watson, "Entrepreneur of the Year," *Manitoba Business*, May 1, 2000, 22(4), p. 7; M.J. Knell, "Palliser to Shift some Leather Mfg. to Mexico," *Furniture Today*, April 4, 2005 (http://www.furnituretoday.com/ article/28738-Palliser_to_shift_some_leather_mfg_to_Mexico.php); M.J. Knell, "Palliser Restructures into Five Operating Companies," *Furniture Today*, August 10, 2006 (http://www.furnituretoday.com/ article/36914-Palliser_restructures_into_five_operating_companies. php?q=Palliser).

Burger King

Burger King (BK) has a director of development for each country or region it operates in. Most BK restaurants are free-standing buildings with drive-through, parking area, and inside seats. However, there are some store-front restaurants in downtowns, corner restaurants in shopping strips, and co-brand restaurants e.g., with a Shell gas station. BK locates restaurants in key sites in a town or city. Key sites include major intersections and large shopping malls.

The site selection process is as follows:

- The market is reviewed and all acceptable sites are identified. A map is divided into grids, separated by major arteries, bridges, etc. A grid is further subdivided by major streets (having a traffic count of over 25,000 cars per day). On the map, shopping malls and the location of any existing BK restaurants and competitor fast-food restaurants are marked. Traffic flow estimates are obtained. A site is acceptable if its "trade area" (the source of 80 percent or more of its customers) is a residential area with a population of 30,000 or more, or is

on a major street with traffic flow of at least 25,000 cars per day, or is close to a mall. An acceptable site for a full-size restaurant is between 20,000 and 40,000 ft^2.

- Annual sales are affected by trade area population and traffic, location of competitors and any existing BK locations, visibility, accessibility, whether the site is a corner lot, etc. Cost of site development includes land, building, and equipment. This involves getting a permit, determining the building plan, and issuing tenders to construction contractors.

Question

Get a map of your city/town, and identify the location of all the Burger King restaurants on the map.

1. Determine the trade area for each restaurant based on the Voronoi method.

2. Based on your local knowledge, determine which of the criteria given in the BK site selection process are satisfied for each BK location.

Source: http://www.bk.com/companyinfo/realestate.aspx.

Trade Area of McDonald's Restaurants in Saskatoon

The locations of 10 McDonald's restaurants in Saskatoon are shown by red circles in the following map.

Question

Determine the trade area for each restaurant by determining Voronoi polygons.

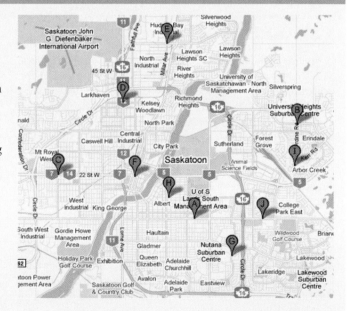

To access "The Transportation Model," the supplement to Chapter 8, please visit *Connect*.

CHAPTER 9
Management of Quality

The topics in this part relate to quality. There are two chapters: Chapter 9, Management of Quality, introduces quality concept, quality awards and certificates such as ISO 9001, HACCP, and Canada Awards for Excellence, and quality tools. Chapter 10 explains statistical quality control.

LEARNING OBJECTIVES

After completing this chapter, you should be able to:

LO1 Define the term *quality,* describe evolution of quality management, discuss dimensions and determinants of quality, describe various costs associated with quality, and discuss philosophies of quality gurus.

LO2 Describe ISO 9001 and apply it.

LO3 Describe HACCP and apply it.

LO4 Describe Canada Awards for Excellence and TQM, and apply them.

LO5 Give an overview of problem solving and process improvement, and describe and use various quality tools.

oronto East General Hospital (TEGH), like other hospitals in Canada, is under pressure to improve its service and reduce the waiting times. Delta Hotels has become a leading high-end Canadian hotel chain. How do organizations such as TEGH and Delta Hotels succeed? Focusing on quality management is a major reason. This is the topic of this chapter.

LO1 INTRODUCTION

quality The ability of a good or service to consistently meet or exceed customer expectations.

Broadly defined, **quality** refers to the ability of a good or service to consistently meet or exceed customer expectations. Prior to the increased level of Japanese competition in the North American marketplace in the 1980s, quality was not uppermost in the minds of the management. They tended to focus on quantity, cost, and productivity rather than on quality. It wasn't that quality was *un*important, it just wasn't *very* important.

Partly because of this thinking, foreign companies, many of them Japanese, captured a significant share of the North American market. In the automotive sector, leading Japanese manufacturers Toyota and Honda became major players in the North American market.

Many North American companies changed their views about quality after that. Stung by the success of foreign competitors, they embraced quality in a big way. They hired consultants, sent their people (including top executives) to seminars, and initiated a vast array of quality improvement programs. These companies clearly recognized the importance of quality and the fact that quality isn't something that is tacked on as a special feature, but is an *integral part* of a good or service. In the 1990s, North American automakers began to close the quality gap.

Evolution of Quality Management

Prior to the Industrial Revolution, skilled craftsmen performed all stages of production. Pride of workmanship and reputation often provided the motivation to see that a job was done right. Lengthy guild apprenticeships caused this attitude to carry over to new workers. Moreover, one person or a small group of people were responsible for an entire product.

Division of labour accompanied the Industrial Revolution; each worker was then responsible for only a small portion of each product. Pride of workmanship became less meaningful because workers could no longer readily identify with the final product. However, producing to specifications (e.g., product dimensions) became more important because of requirement for inter changeable parts. The responsibility for **quality control** (monitoring, testing, and correcting quality problems after they occur) shifted to the foremen and full-time quality inspectors. In many instances, 100-percent inspection was performed at the end of the production line.

quality control
Monitoring, testing, and correcting quality problems after they occur.

During the 1950s, the quality movement started to evolve into **quality assurance** (providing confidence that product's quality will be good), which aims to prevent defects before they occur rather than finding them after they occur. Operators were given more responsibility for quality during the production process.

quality assurance
Providing confidence that a product's quality will be good by preventing defects before they occur.

Various quality gurus such as Deming, Juran, Feigenbaum, and Crosby contributed to the evolution of quality assurance.

In the 1970s, NASA and the Pillsbury company created a quality management system to assure and control food safety. Later, International Organization of Standards created ISO 9000 set of standards for a quality management system.

The evolution of quality took a dramatic shift from quality control and assurance to a strategic management approach to quality in the 1980s, called total quality management (TQM). This approach places greater emphasis on customer satisfaction, and it involves all levels of management as well as workers (all functions of the organization) in a continuing effort to increase quality (called **continuous improvement**, never-ending improvements to key processes as part of TQM)

Recently, some companies are pursuing a problem solving/process improvement approach called Six Sigma, which uses sophisticated statistical tools.

continuous improvement
Never-ending improvements to key processes as part of total quality management.

Dimensions of Quality

The term *quality* is used in a variety of ways. Sometimes it refers to the characteristics of material or grade of a product, such as "Canada Choice" or "grade A" eggs. At other times, it refers to workmanship, or performance, or reliability, or special features such as "waterproof" or "subtle aroma." We first describe product quality and then service quality.

The implication in these various connotations of quality is that customers value certain aspects of a good or service, and therefore associate those aspects with the quality that they perceive a good or service has.

Quality of Goods. The aspects or **dimensions of quality of goods** include:[1]

Performance—main characteristics or function of the product
Aesthetics—appearance, feel, smell, taste
Special features—extra characteristics or secondary functions
Safety—reduction or elimination of risk of injury or harm
Reliability—consistency of performance over time (not failing for certain length of time)
Durability—long life
Perceived quality—subjective evaluation of quality (e.g., reputation, image)
Service after sale—warranties, maintenance, and handling of complaint
Latent quality—assumed quality (not expressed by customers but important)

dimensions of quality of goods Performance, aesthetics, special features, safety, reliability, durability, perceived quality, service after sale, and latent.

These dimensions are illustrated by the examples of quality dimensions for a car in Table 9-1. In a broader sense, the term *fitness for use* is used to define quality. This means quality is whatever customer expects in the product, including such things as on-time delivery.

Dimension	Example
1. Performance	Everything works, ride, handling, leg room
2. Aesthetics	Interior design, soft touch, fit and finish, grade of materials used
3. Special features	
Convenience	Placement of gauges and controls
High tech	GPS, DVD player
4. Safety	Antilock brakes, airbags
5. Reliability	No breakdowns in the first 5 years
6. Durability	Long life, resistance to rust and corrosion
7. Perceived quality	Top-rated car, e.g., Cadillac
8. Service after sale	Warranty, handling of complaints, maintenance
9. Latent	Roadworthiness (satisfies government regulations)

Table 9-1

Examples of quality dimensions for a car

[1]Adapted from David Garvin, "What Does Quality Really Mean?" *Sloan Management Review* 26(1), 1984, pp. 25–43.

Service Quality. The dimensions of quality of goods above don't adequately describe service quality. Instead, service quality is often described using the following dimensions:[2]

Tangibles—the physical appearance of facility, equipment, personnel, and communication materials.

Convenience—the availability and accessibility of the service.

Reliability—the ability to perform a service dependably, consistently, and accurately for a certain length of time.

Responsiveness—the willingness of service provider to help customers in unusual situations and to deal with problems.

Time—the speed with which service is delivered.

Assurance—the knowledge exhibited by personnel and their ability to convey trust and confidence.

Courtesy—the way customers are treated by employees.

Table 9-2 illustrates the dimensions of service quality for car repair.

Table 9-2	Dimension	Examples
Examples of service quality dimensions for car repair	**1.** Tangibles	Clean facilities and neat personnel
	2. Convenience	Convenient location of repair shop and open evenings and weekends
	3. Reliability	Problem fixed right every time
	4. Responsiveness	Willing and able to answer questions
	5. Time	Reasonable wait time
	6. Assurance	Staff knowledgeable about the repair
	7. Courtesy	Friendly and courteous treatment of customers by staff

We have already seen the dimensions of product quality in the quality function deployment (described in Chapter 4). They are the types of customer requirements in the house of quality.

Customers evaluate a good or service's quality relative to their expectation. If the quality, as perceived by a customer, is higher than expected, he will be delighted; if it is the same, the customer is satisfied, but if it is less, he will be dissatisfied.

Determinants of Quality

A product's quality is determined during:

1. Product design
2. Process design
3. Production

Product design phase is the starting point for the level of quality eventually achieved. Product design involves decisions about the characteristics and specifications of a product such as size, shape, and material. Note that quality is what the customers require. Quality function deployment (house of quality in Chapter 4) should be used to translate the customer requirements into technical attributes of the product and their target values (specifications). For example, in creating a new burger, the customer requirement of "juicy" can be translated into "moisture content of a burger" with target value of "1 milliliter."

During process design, technical (product) characteristics should be translated into process characteristics and specifications. For example, "moisture content = 1 ml" can be

---

[2]Adapted from Valerie A. Zeithhaml, A. Parasuraman, and Leonard L. Berry, *Delivering Quality Service and Balancing Customer Expectations* (New York: The Free Press, 1990), and J. R. Evans and W. M. Lindsey, *The Management and Control of Quality*, 3rd ed. (St. Paul, MN: West Publishing, 1996).

OM in ACTION

Diversicare

Achieving customer and employee satisfaction in the retirement and nursing home industry is not an easy task. Diversicare, based in Mississauga, Ontario operates 7 long-term-care and 20 retirement homes across Canada. Some of these are owned by Diversicare and the others are managed by Diversicare, some with staff from another company. As a result, there were huge discrepancies in services offered across its facilities and a lot of staff turnover. In 1993, a committee of Diversicare employees met to identify how to improve the quality of operations. The result was the "Continuous Quality Improvement" (CQI) initiative, designed to encourage employees to achieve excellence in quality of care.

CQI required four crucial elements:

1. *Key indicators*: Continual measuring and monitoring of specific health care issues to ensure the effectiveness of programs and services.

2. *Human resources*: Training of management and staff, and development of management systems to achieve optimal use of human resources.

3. *Commitment*: Active encouragement of individual initiatives to implement improvements in the quality of care.

4. *Empowerment*: Empowering caregivers to review existing mechanisms and to make recommendations to improve the quality of life for residents.

CQI involved focus on the customers, but also on the processes. In order to accomplish this, a common mission and vision was created. The company focused its quality initiative on improving customer satisfaction and employee recruitment, development, and reward. For example, Diversicare looked at recruitment, selection, and retention processes. Each home identified the best workers and set up a "talent team." The talent teams took a central role in recruitment and selection, and mentored the new staff. Management took a cheerleader role, encouraging staff to participate in the CQI program.

CQI had 16 key indicators that measured a host of employee and resident concerns such as safety (e.g., falls, bedsores, work injuries). The company also added eight quality of life indicators, including a "key wish" for residents. Diversicare constantly looks for ways to improve these indicators. Initiatives from all levels within the organization are celebrated and shared through an annual CQI conference, which promotes the exchange of best practices within the organization. Diversicare, Ontario Region, won a 2001 Canada Award for Excellence Quality Trophy, and a 2006 Order of Excellence (reaffirming its maintenance of quality excellence).

Sources: 2001 Recipient Profiles: http://www.nqi.ca/articles/article_details.aspx?ID=47; http://www.diversicare.ca/corporate.shtml.

---

translated into "use a grill capable of maintaining 350 ± 10 degrees Fahrenheit" (which will be used for 8 minutes (4 minutes per side) to grill a meat patty). The ± 10 is the tolerance allowed.

During production, **conformance to design specifications** refers to the degree to which the produced goods or services conform to (i.e., *achieve*) the specifications of the designers. This is affected by factors such as documentation of processes and procedures, the skills and training of operators, the stability and monitoring of processes, taking corrective actions (e.g., through problem solving) when necessary, communication and meeting of staff, record keeping and verification (audits), and having good quality suppliers.

conformance to design specifications during production   The degree to which produced goods or services conform to the specifications of the designers.

Costs of Quality

To show the importance of dealing with quality issues and to manage quality, one must estimate the various costs associated with quality. Those costs can be classified into four categories:

Internal failure costs   *Appraisal* (detection) costs

External failure costs   *Prevention* costs

Failure costs are incurred by defective parts or products. **Internal failures** are those discovered during production; **external failures** are those discovered after delivery to the customer.

failure costs   Costs caused by defective parts or products.

internal failures   Failures discovered during production.

external failures   Failures discovered after delivery to the customer.

Internal failures occur for a variety of reasons, including defective material from vendors, incorrect machine settings, faulty equipment, incorrect methods, incorrect processing, and faulty or improper material handling procedures. The costs of internal failures include lost production time, scrap and rework, possible equipment damage, and possible employee injury.

External failures are defective products that go undetected by the producer. Resulting costs include warranty work, handling of complaints, replacements, liability/litigation, payments to customers or discounts used to offset the inferior quality, loss of customer goodwill, and opportunity costs related to lost sales.

appraisal (detection) costs
Costs of inspection and testing.

Appraisal (detection) costs relate to inspection, testing, and other activities intended to uncover defective products. They include the cost of inspectors, testing, test equipment, and labs.

prevention costs   Costs of preventing defects from occurring.

Prevention costs relate to attempts to prevent defects from occurring. They include costs such as quality planning and administration, working with vendors, standard operating procedures, and training.

Internal and external failure costs represent costs related to poor quality, whereas (some) appraisal and prevention costs represent investments for achieving good quality. Also, it is generally believed that spending $1 on prevention may save as much as $10 on detection and as much as $100 on fixing failures.

Quality Gurus

A core of quality experts has shaped modern quality practices. Among the most famous are Deming, Juran, Feigenbaum, and Crosby. Together, they have had a tremendous impact on the management of quality, and the way companies operate.

W. Edwards Deming. A statistics professor at New York University in the 1940s, Deming went to Japan after the Second World War to assist the Japanese in improving their quality and productivity. His contributions were so much appreciated that an annual quality prize, the Deming Prize, was established in his name in 1951.

Although the Japanese revered Deming, he was largely unknown to business leaders in North America. In fact, he worked with the Japanese for almost 30 years before North American companies turned their attention to Deming, embraced his philosophy, and requested his assistance in setting up quality improvement programs.

Deming compiled a list of 14 points he believed were the prescription needed to achieve quality in an organization (see Table 9-3). His message is basically that the cause of inefficiency and poor quality is the *system,* not the employees. Deming felt that it was *management's responsibility* to correct the system to achieve the desired results. Deming stressed the need to reduce variation in output, which can be accomplished by distinguishing between *special causes* of variation (i.e., correctable) and *common causes* of variation (i.e., random). This is the foundation of statistical process control (SPC), covered in the next chapter. Deming also promoted the plan-do-study-act (PDSA) cycle of problem solving (covered later in this chapter).

Deming believed that workers want to create and learn, but that management unintentionally often does things such as establishing rating systems that rob workers of their internal motivation. He believed that management's greatest challenge in achieving quality was in motivating workers to contribute their collective efforts to achieve a common goal.[3]

Joseph M. Juran. Juran, like Deming, taught Japanese manufacturers how to improve the quality of their goods, and he, too, can be regarded as a major force in Japan's success in quality. He made his first trip to Japan a few years after the publication, in 1951, of his *Quality Control Handbook.*

[3]For a three-part video about Deming, see http://www.youtube.com/watch?v=GHvnIm9UEoQ, http://www.youtube.com/watch?v=mKFGj8sK5R8, and http://www.youtube.com/watch?v=6WeTaLRb-Bs.

Table 9-3

Deming's 14 points

1. Create constancy of purpose toward improvement of goods and services with a plan to become competitive and to stay in business. Decide to whom top management is responsible.

2. Adopt the new philosophy. We are in a new economic age. We can no longer live with commonly accepted levels of delays, mistakes, defective materials, and defective workmanship.

3. Cease dependence on mass inspection. Require instead statistical evidence that quality is built in. (*Prevent* defects rather than *detect* defects.)

4. End the practice of awarding business on the basis of price tag. Instead, depend on meaningful measures of quality along with price. Eliminate suppliers that cannot qualify with statistical evidence of quality.

5. Find problems. It is management's job to work continually on the system (design, incoming materials, composition of material, maintenance, improvement of machines, training, supervision, retraining).

6. Institute modern methods of training on the job.

7. The responsibility of foremen must be changed from sheer numbers to quality ... [which] will automatically improve productivity. Management must prepare to take immediate action on reports from foremen concerning quality barriers such as inherent defects, machines not maintained, poor tools, and fuzzy operational definitions.

8. Drive out fear so that everyone may work effectively for the company.

9. Break down barriers between departments. People in research, design, sales, and production must work as a team to foresee problems of production that may be encountered with various materials and specifications.

10. Eliminate numerical goals, posters, and slogans for the work force, asking for new levels of productivity without providing methods.

11. Eliminate work standards that prescribe numerical quotas.

12. Remove barriers that stand between the hourly worker and his right to pride of workmanship.

13. Institute a vigorous program of education and retraining.

14. Create a structure in top management that will push every day on the above 13 points.

Source: W. Edwards Deming, *Quality, Productivity, and Competitive Position* (Cambridge, MA: MIT, Center for Advanced Engineering Study, 1982), pp. 16–17.

Juran viewed quality as fitness-for-use. He also believed that roughly 80 percent of quality defects are controllable; thus, management has the responsibility to correct this deficiency. He described quality management in terms of a *trilogy* consisting of quality planning, quality control, and quality improvement. According to Juran, quality planning is necessary to establish processes *capable* of meeting quality standards; quality control is necessary in order to know when corrective action is needed; and quality improvement will help to find better ways of doing things. A key element of Juran's philosophy is the commitment of management to continuous improvement.

Juran is credited as one of the first to measure the cost of quality, and he demonstrated the potential for increased profits that would result if costs of poor quality could be reduced.

Juran proposed 10 steps for continuous improvement, shown in Table 9-4.

Armand Feigenbaum. Feigenbaum was General Electric's top expert on quality. He recognized that quality was not only a collection of tools and techniques, but also a "total field." He saw that when improvements were made in a process, other areas of the company also achieved improvements. Feigenbaum's understanding of systems theory led him to create an environment in which people could learn from each other's successes, and his leadership and open work environment led to cross-functional teamwork. Also, he introduced the concept of **quality at the source**, meaning that every worker is responsible for his own work. For example, a worker can stop the assembly line if there is a defect.

http://www.juran.com

quality at the source Every employee is responsible for inspecting his own work.

Table 9-4

Juran's 10 steps for continuous improvement

1. Build awareness for the need and opportunity for quality improvement.
2. Set goals for improvement.
3. Organize people to reach the goals.
4. Provide training throughout the organization.
5. Carry out projects to solve problems.
6. Report progress.
7. Give recognition.
8. Communicate results.
9. Keep score.
10. Maintain momentum by making annual improvement part of the regular systems and processes of the company.

Source: Joseph M. Juran, ed. "The Quality Trilogy," *Quality Progress*, Aug. 1986, 19(8), pp. 19–24. Reprinted with Permission from Quality Progress © 1986 ASQ American Society for Quality. No further distribution allowed without permission.

In 1961 his book *Total Quality Control* was published. In it, Feigenbaum laid out 40 quality principles. Table 9-5 lists some of his key principles.

Table 9-5

Key principles of Feigenbaum's philosophy of total quality control

1. Total quality control is a system for integrating quality development, maintenance, and improvement efforts in an organization that will enable engineering, marketing, production, and service to function at optimal economic levels while achieving customer satisfaction.
2. The "control" aspect of quality control should involve setting quality standards, appraising performance relative to these standards, taking corrective action when the standards are not met, and planning for improvement in the standards.
3. Factors that affect quality can be divided into two major categories: technological and human. The human factor is the more important one.
4. Costs of quality can be divided into four categories: prevention costs, appraisal costs, internal failure costs, and external failure costs.
5. It is important to control quality at the source.

Source: Adapted from Peter Capezio and Debra Morehouse, *Taking the Mystery Out of TQM,* 2nd ed. (Franklin Lakes, NJ: Career Press, © 1995) pp. 100–101.

Philip B. Crosby. Crosby worked at Martin Marietta Company in the 1960s. While he was there, he developed the concept of *zero defects* and popularized the phrase "Do it right the first time." He stressed prevention and argued against the idea that "there will always be some level of defectives."

zero defects The philosophy that any level of defects is too high.

In accordance with the concept of **zero defects**, Crosby believed that any level of defects is too high, and that management must install programs that help the organization move toward zero defects. Among some of his key points are the following:[4]

1. Top management must demonstrate its commitment to quality and its willingness to give support to achieve good quality.
2. Management must be persistent in efforts to achieve good quality.

_____

[4]Philip Crosby, *Quality without Tears: The Art of Hassle-Free Management* (New York: McGraw-Hill, 1984).

3. Management must spell out clearly what it wants in terms of quality and what workers must do to achieve that.

4. Make it (or do it) right the first time.

Unlike the other gurus, Crosby maintained that achieving quality can be relatively easy. Crosby's quality-is-free concept is based on the following: costs of poor quality are much greater than traditionally recognized and these costs are so great that rather than viewing quality efforts as costs, organizations should view them as a way to reduce costs, because the improvements generated by quality efforts will more than pay for themselves.

Table 9-6 provides a summary of the important contributions of the gurus to modern quality management.

 OM in ACTION   www.deltahotels.com/en/about

Delta Hotels

With 38 hotels and 7,000 employees located in every major Canadian city, Delta is one of the top hotel chains in Canada. Delta Hotels is a subsidiary of Fairmont Hotels & Resorts.

Since 1995, the company has developed formalized procedures for hotels' daily operations. These are based on the NQI's Criteria for Canada Awards for Excellence.

Delta Hotels trains internal assessors to conduct individual hotel assessments and develop a quality improvement plan. Every two years, a hotel will undergo an initial three-day assessment and a subsequent five-day assessment to ensure that ongoing quality measures are incorporated into the hotel's culture and all aspects of operations. External assessors are also invited, ensuring that assessments meet the professional standards of NQI. According to the senior vice president (people and quality), "Our goal is to ensure a seamless approach to quality, so that it is part of our culture." Assessments, their frequency, and their outcome are listed in the table below.

From their first days, employees are told that they are key to the hotel's success and that their opinions matter. Trust between management and employees has developed to the extent that an employee can walk in her manager's office and say, "I think this really needs to be changed" or "This is what I need in order to get my job done." Employees receive an additional week's pay if they participate in a certain number of training hours per year.

Delta internally delivers over 40 programs on topics ranging from conflict resolution to valuing leadership.

There are also annual reviews of each employee's performance.

There is an employee assistance program (to deal with personal problems). The return-to-work program offers a modified workload, flexible hours, and personal days off.

Delta has also created management development reviews, including 360° feedback, that examine specific managerial competencies such as flexibility, ability to handle stress, ability to work with a team, and interpersonal sensitivity. The results, including employee satisfaction, are tied to managers' bonuses.

Employee satisfaction and professional development have risen dramatically. Employee accomplishments are recognized during regular "town hall" meetings.

Problem-solving teams regularly monitor processes for improvement opportunities. One result of these improvements is Delta's "one-minute check-in guarantee" for Delta Privilege members. Delta's power-to-please program empowers employees to have control over a customer's experience.

As a result of all these initiatives and improvements, Delta has realized improved results in guest satisfaction and won a Canada Award for Excellence Quality Trophy in 2000, Healthy Workplace Gold Trophy in 2004, and Order of Excellence in Quality (renewing the Quality Trophy) in 2007.

Sources: "Canada Awards for Excellence," *Canadian Business*, December 11, 2000, pp. 93–96; http://www.deltahotels.com.

Assessment	Frequency	Outcome
Quality business assessment (QBA)	Once in 24 months	Quality improvement plan (QIP)
Employee opinion survey (EOS)	Once in 12 months	People action plan (PAP)
Minimum standard checklist	Once in 24 months	People resources plan
Benefits/pension/compensation reports	Once a month at each hotel and corporate office	Security/wellness plan

Table 9-6	Contributor	Key Contributions
A summary of key contributions to quality management	Deming	14 points; special versus common causes of variation, SPC, PDSA cycle
	Juran	Quality is fitness-for-use; quality trilogy
	Feigenbaum	Quality is a total field; quality at the source
	Crosby	Quality is free; zero defects

LO2 ISO 9001

The purpose of the International Organization for Standardization (ISO) is to promote worldwide standards that will improve operating efficiency and productivity, and reduce costs. The ISO is composed of the national standards bodies of over 100 countries. The Canadian representative body is the Standards Council of Canada. The work of the ISO is conducted by some 180 technical committees. ISO 9001 is the work of Technical Committee 176 (Quality Management and Quality Assurance Committee).

ISO 9001 is the international standard for a quality management system. This standard is critical for companies doing business internationally, particularly in Europe. A company wanting to be certified must document its processes and procedures, and undergo an external on-site assessment by accredited auditors. The process often takes 12 to 18 months. With certification comes registration in an ISO directory that companies seeking suppliers can refer to. They are generally given preference over unregistered companies. Approximately one million companies are registered worldwide; almost half of them are located in Europe, but China has the most numbers (see http://www.iso.org/iso/survey2007.pdf).

The ISO 9001 review process involves considerable self-appraisal, resulting in problem identification and improvement. Registered companies face an ongoing series of audits, and they must be re-registered every three years. A graphical representation of major ISO 9001 activities and their interaction is shown below. A summary of elements of ISO 9001 standard (updated in the year 2000) is listed in Table 9-7.

ISO 9001   The international standard for a quality management system, critical to international business.

www.iso.org

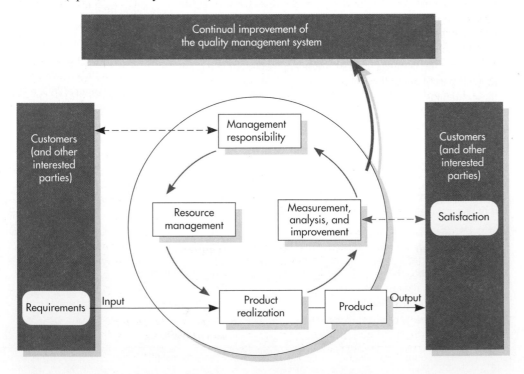

There are usually three types of documents created for ISO 9001: a quality manual, a procedures manual, and detailed work instructions and other supporting documents. The procedures manual includes all critical processes of the organization, and for each process

ISO 9001:2000 Summary

1. Quality Management System (QMS)

1.1 General Requirements

Create and document a quality policy, objectives, quality manual, quality planning, processes, procedures, and records. Also identify parts and processes outsourced and control their quality. Justify any exclusions. Describe the interaction between different processes.

1.2 Documentation Requirements

Quality Manual

Procedures Manual

Work Instructions, etc.

Control the issue and use of documents and records.

2. Management Responsibility

2.1 Management Commitment

Communicate the commitment to QMS to all employees, provide resources, establish a quality policy and deploy it as departments' objectives, and conduct management reviews of the QMS.

2.2 Customer Focus

Understand and meet customer requirements; enhance satisfaction.

2.3 Quality Policy

2.4 Planning

Establish objectives for functions and products

Plan the QMS

2.5 Responsibilities, Authority, and Communication

- Foster open communication and culture of employee involvement in the organization.
- Define and communicate the responsibilities and authority of all personnel. Ensure that customers' requirements are understood.
- Appoint a management representative who ensures that the QMS is established and functions, reports its performance to top management, and promotes quality awareness.

2.6 Management Review

- Review QMS, audit results, customer feedback, and performance.
- Implement preventive and corrective actions, follow up.
- Implement QMS and product improvements, provide needed resources.

3. Resource Management

3.1 Provision of Resources

Determine and provide the QMS and the customer satisfaction the resources needed.

3.2 Human Resources

Provide competent people, education, and training.

3.3 Infrastructure

Provide infrastructure (building, equipment, etc.).

3.4 Work Environment

Work environment must be appropriate to meet product requirements.

4. Product Realization

4.1 Planning of Product Realization

Plan and develop processes needed for producing the product, including quality requirements and inspection/testing requirements. This may include drawing process flow diagram, determining routing/process sheet, etc.

4.2 Customer-related Processes

Ensure that product requirements are defined and reviewed before acceptance of order (including unstated and regulatory requirements) and that the organization has the ability to meet the requirements. Establish effective communication with the customers regarding product information, inquiries, changes, feedback, and complaints.

4.3 Design and Development

Plan the product design and development process. Define the review and validation stages of product design and development. Review inputs, such as functional requirements, to ensure that all the requirements are complete, unambiguous, and not in conflict with each other. Ensure that the design and development process meets the requirements and provides clear information for the purchase of required material. Also, control the design and development changes.

4.4 Purchasing

Use a systematic supplier evaluation and selection procedure. Ensure to provide complete and accurate purchasing information. Ensure that purchased products conform to the specified purchase requirements.

4.5 Production and Service Provision

- Produce under controlled conditions. Ensure product drawing, specifications, and work instructions are provided to the workers.
- Process the product on capable equipment. Make available suitable monitoring and measuring devices.
- Validate the process.
- Identify product testing status and track products.
- Protect customer-owned property.
- Prevent damages during handling, storage, packaging, and delivery.

4.6 Control of Monitoring and Measurement Devices

Provide appropriate measurement and test equipment and calibrate them periodically.

5. Measurement, Analysis, and Improvement

5.1 General

Determine the methods for measurement and analysis, including statistical techniques.

5.2 Monitoring and Measurement

Monitor and measure customer satisfaction, the processes, and the products. When results are unsatisfactory, undertake corrective action. Keep records. Conduct periodic and systematic internal audits of the QMS.

5.3 Control of Nonconforming Products

Segregate defective products. Repair, use as-is (with concession to the customer), or scrap the product. Keep records of the nonconformance and the action taken.

5.4 Analysis of Data

Collect and analyze appropriate data on customer satisfaction, conformity to product requirements, product trends, processes, and supplier performance.

5.5 Improvement

Continuously improve the QMS. Investigate the causes of exiting or potential nonconformity and take corrective and preventive actions.

Sources: http://www.conestogac.on.ca/~dmcintos/introduction.htm; www.ulc.ca/downloads/ulc_management_RP2-2000.pdf; D.L. Goetsch and S.B. Davis, *Understanding and Implementing ISO 9000:2000*, 2nd ed. (New Jersey: Pearson Prentice-Hall, 2002).

Table 9-7

Elements of the ISO 9001 quality management system (updated in the year 2000)

Holland College, PEI

Holland College is a large community college with campuses in seven towns in PEI. Holland College offers both competency-based (career-oriented) diploma/certificate programs and continuing education. It considers its products to be the programs it offers. Its primary customers are the students while its secondary customers are the future employers of the students. Holland College is one of the few colleges/universities in Canada that are ISO 9001 certified.

The quality management system (QMS) set up by Holland College includes quality policies (e.g., involve industry/business leaders in development and evaluation of the programs) and quality objectives (e.g., more than 80 percent of students should recommend their program to someone they know). QMS also includes a quality manual that delineates how Holland College provides and manages its resources, and designs, delivers, controls, and improves its programs. This is done by setting up several processes for its major activities. The processes and other information/instructions are described in a set of procedures. A procedure has the following sections: purpose, scope, related procedures, documents/definitions/responsibilities, and sections that describe guidelines and instructions, possibly including a process flow diagram.

Adequate funding is provided for resources such as staff and faculty, and buildings and equipment (e.g., computers and audiovisuals). There is a procedure for recruiting qualified staff/faculty based on education, training, skills, and experience. There are several procedures for appraisal and training

of employees to improve their services to the students and to maintain the relevance and appeal of the programs. Computers are periodically replaced with new ones.

To design and deliver its programs and services, and to deal with its customers (the students), Holland College has several processes: Marketing and recruitment, admissions and registration, student exit and graduation, career counselling/accommodation/disability services, design and development of programs and curriculum, delivery of programs and courses, purchasing of equipment, and library/bookstore/computer services/student-finance services. These processes are provided under controlled conditions. Some of the procedures used to control some of the above processes include using course outlines, taking attendance, assessing students, using transcripts, dealing with student misconduct, and equipment maintenance and repair.

The programs are measured, analyzed, and improved by getting feedback from students and employers. Instructors and managers continuously review the performance of their programs and take corrective action. The executive committee annually reviews the programs' performance against the objectives and prescribes action plans to improve them.

For a list of links to Holland College QMS, visit https://sam. hollandcollege.com/AngelUploads/Content/Quality_Management_System/_assoc/3BD141D6699D44C593DF73C5A236438 F/QMS-Welcome.pdf.

Sources: www.hollandc.pe.ca/quality; https://sam.hollandcollege. com/AngelUploads/Content/Quality_Management_System/_assoc/ 9F99DA3D6BED484E8C5DBA903BBDB366/HC_Quality_ Manual.pdf.

---

a description (in general terms) of how it is to be done (using a process flow diagram) and what to do if there is a problem.

For two videos on ISO 9001, see http://www.iso.org/iso/pressrelease.htm?refid=Ref1174 and http://www.youtube.com/watch?v=G8WI2MgyS7w. For an application of ISO 9001, see the "Holland College, PEI" OM in Action above.

LO3 HAZARD ANALYSIS CRITICAL CONTROL POINT (HACCP)

HACCP A quality management system designed for food processors.

HACCP is a quality management system, similar to ISO 9001, designed for food processors, especially meat, poultry, and fish processors. It originated with the Pillsbury company when it had to design and manufacture food for the NASA space missions in 1970s. HACCP is mandatory for fish processors in Canada and is becoming mandatory for meat and poultry processors. Meat exporters to other countries, such as the United States and Japan, need to have HACCP certification too. HACCP is enforced by the Canadian Food Inspection Agency (CFIA). Other food-related industries such as dairies, fruit and vegetable processors, and egg producers are also encouraged to implement HACCP.

HACCP deals with food safety, in particular, biological, chemical, and physical hazards.[5] HACCP is implemented by a multidisciplinary team, including a food biologist

---

[5]http://www.inspection.gc.ca/english/fssa/polstrat/haccp/haccpe.shtml; http://www.omafra.gov.on.ca/english/food/foodsafety/processors/haccp.htm.

and sanitation expert in addition to representatives from production, engineering, quality assurance, etc. As in ISO 9001, top management's commitment is essential.

First, the HACCP team inspects various construction and/or sanitary aspects of the plant, equipment, and personnel. For example, the land should have good drainage and water source, and no garbage or odours. The building should have easy-to-clean walls, floors, and ceilings; sloped floors to drains; screened windows; close-fitting doors; self-closing washroom doors; good ventilation; and be pest proof.

If there is any shortcoming, corrective action is undertaken. Also, the team ensures that there is a regular system of work instructions, inspection, and prevention in place for the building, equipment, and personnel. Guidelines and standard operating procedures (SOP) are provided by the CFIA and other government agencies. Further, there should be a procedure for product recall, i.e., a product coding system and records.

The following product and process background information is required:

1. Describe the product, source of raw material, product characteristics, ingredients, packaging, how the product is used, shelf life, where the product will be sold, labelling instructions, and distribution control.

2. Draw the process flow diagram and number the steps of the process. Also, draw the plant layout diagram, identifying each operation by its number and showing the material flows by arrows.

3. Identify all the Regulatory Action Points (RAP), i.e., points in the process where safety control is mandated by the government. These usually include the receiving point(s) of raw material(s) and the shipping point of the products, but may also include other critical points such as where thawing of fish and the labelling of fish cans take place. SOPs are provided for most of these activities, specifying parameters such as time and temperature. If there is no SOP for a RAP, the company needs to define one. The RAP plan specifies the control measures (such as SOPs), the inspection (detection) procedures (what, how, frequency, and who), and corrective actions.

There are three main HACCP steps:

1. Perform Hazard Analysis:
   - For each ingredient/processing step, identify potential hazard(s). To do this, one can use the reference database of CFIA; books on microbiology, food processing, and plant sanitation; Health Canada reports on illnesses, recalls, and complaints; and scientific papers. Hazards are classified into biological, chemical, and physical.
   - Determine if the potential hazard is significant and provide your justification.
   - Provide preventive measures for significant hazards in process design (e.g., include pasteurization operation).

2. Determine the Critical Control Points (CCPs):
   - For every ingredient/processing step with one or more significant hazard(s), if there will not be a subsequent step that would eliminate the hazard, then this step is a CCP. The receiving point of raw material, the closing point of the cans, and the sterilization point are typical CCPs.

3. Establish the HACCP Plan:
   - For each CCP/significant hazard, determine a control/preventive measure, the critical limits, the monitoring procedure (what, how, frequency, and who), the corrective action and records, and the verification procedures.

Example 1

The product description is chunk-style tuna, canned in small cans, sealed at the bottom and top, packaged in brine (salt water) or oil, ready-to-eat, with a five-year shelf life, and sold in retail stores.

A simplified process flow diagram for this product is shown on the next page. The company buys the cans, with the bottom already sealed to the wall, but separate can tops. For simplicity, we assume that the tuna is canned fresh (If the tuna is frozen, it has to be thawed first). The process briefly is as follows: after receiving, the fish's head and tail are cut off, and racks of fish are precooked in order to make skinning and deboning easier. Then, the automated canning line cuts the fish into chunks, fits a chunk in a can, adds ingredients, and vacuum-seals the top. Next, baskets of fish cans are sterilized and cooked further in pressurized steam rooms, washed, dried, and individually weighed and labelled.

Government regulations require that the tuna not be tainted or decomposed (i.e., should be safe and wholesome), and the can should be accurately labelled with a product code (including the date canned). In addition to sanitation and hygiene at the plant, equipment, and operator levels, HACCP requirements can be satisfied by the following critical control points and quality control/assurance plans:

Critical Control Point	Quality Assurance Plan	Quality Control Plan
Receiving	Vessel records of cooling	Visual inspection and tests for toxins (60 fish per lot)
Precooking	Standard operating procedures (SOP), cooking time and temperature	
Cans and Tops	Manufacturing record of material and SOP	Visual inspection
Close cans		Visual (every half hour) and teardown tests (every four hours) for seams
Pasteurize	SOP, temperature, time, pressure	
Wash with chlorine		Test residual chlorine in water
Label		Inspect continuously for accuracy

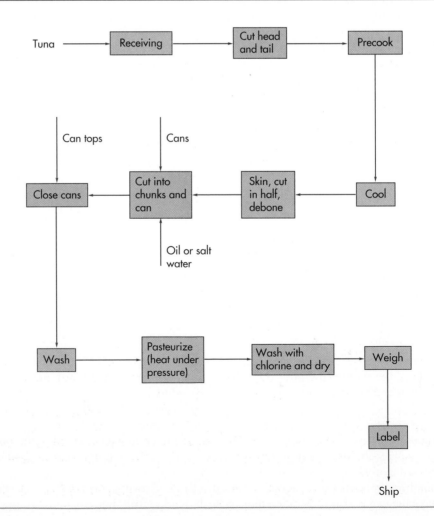

LO4 CANADA AWARDS FOR EXCELLENCE (CAE) AND TOTAL QUALITY MANAGEMENT (TQM)

Canada Awards for Excellence recognize outstanding quality achievement by Canadian organizations, administered annually by the National Quality Institute (NQI), an independent not-for-profit organization (NQI also presents *CAE Healthy Workplace®* awards). NQI investigated the workings of successful organizations and developed a set of criteria for business excellence. The criteria also provide a comprehensive, practical, and well-tested framework for continuous improvement. The six main categories of the criteria are displayed below. Note that quality is embedded in strategic management of the organization, i.e, all functions of the organization are engaged in quality management.

In recent years, to make the implementation of the quality management system easier for organizations, NQI has divided the implementation into four stages or levels (called Progressive Excellence Program; see the following figure): Level 1: Foundation, Level 2: Transformation, Level 3: Role Model, and Level 4: World Class.

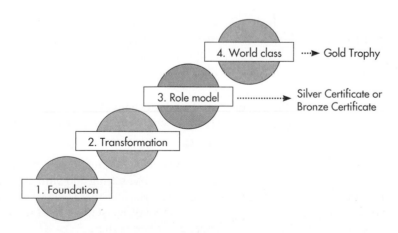

For each level, NQI provides the requirements to certify in that level (minor differences are made between private and public organizations, education, and hospitals).

Level 1 CAE certification requires developing a mission statement, defining customers, planning training in management principles and practices, and performing an assessment of the above activities.

Level 2 CAE certification involves strategic planning; identifying customer needs; human resource planning; identifying, documenting, and improving key processes; and supplier/partner planning. These activities start after an initial gap analysis and internal/ external assessment using questionnaires, used to determine an improvement plan, and end with review of improvement results.

At Level 3 CAE certification, the organization demonstrates shared commitment; performs periodic planning, sets priorities, and communicates performance; measures customer satisfaction and receives feedback; involves employees in health and safety, provides training and measures its effectiveness, and measures employee satisfaction; analyzes, improves, and documents processes, involves customers and suppliers and benchmarks process management; and shares information with suppliers and involves them in new product design. Also, all activities are continuously improved. These activities start after an initial gap analysis and internal/external assessment using questionnaires, used to determine an improvement plan, and end with review of improvement results.

Level 4 CAE requirements build on the other levels, and the organization demonstrates that it has achieved good to excellent overall results and at least three years of positive trends from the improvement efforts.[6]

Since 1989, the awards have honoured more than 50 Canadian organizations for outstanding quality achievement. For three examples, see the "Toronto East General Hospital" on the next page, and "Diversicare" and "Delta Hotels" OM in Actions earlier in the chapter.

Total Quality Management

total quality management (TQM) An approach to quality management that involves everyone in an organization in quality management and continual effort to improve quality and customer satisfaction.

Total quality management (TQM) is an approach to quality management that involves everyone in an organization in quality management and continual effort to improve quality and customer satisfaction. There are three key features in TQM. One is a never-ending push to improve quality, which is referred to as *continuous improvement*; the second is the *involvement of everyone* in the organization in quality management; and the third is the goal of ever-increasing *customer satisfaction*.

We can describe the TQM approach as follows:

1. Find out what customers want. This might involve the use of surveys, focus groups, interviews, or some other technique that integrates the customer's voice in the decision-making process.

2. Design a product that will meet (or exceed) what customers want.

Poka-yoke or **fail-safing** Incorporating process design elements that prevent mistakes.

3. Design processes that facilitate doing the job right the first time (called "quality at the source"). Determine where mistakes are likely to occur and try to prevent them (called **Poka-yoke** or **fail-safing**, i.e., incorporating process design elements that prevent mistakes). Involve and empower the workers in quality management. When mistakes do occur, find out why, and implement corrective actions so that they are less likely to occur again.

4. Keep track of results (TQM is data driven), and use them to guide improvement in the system. Never stop trying to improve (called "continuous improvement").

5. Extend these concepts to suppliers/partners.

Many companies have successfully implemented TQM. Management must be totally committed and involved by becoming educated in quality, setting and enforcing improvement goals, providing resources, and reviewing progress. If it isn't, TQM will become just another fad that quickly dies and fades away. The above five steps should remind you of the criteria for Canada Awards for Excellence, described earlier.

It would be incorrect to think of TQM as merely a collection of techniques. Rather, TQM reflects a whole new attitude toward quality. It is about the *culture* of an organization. To truly reap the benefits of TQM, the culture of an organization must change.

Table 9-8 illustrates the differences between cultures of a TQM organization and a more traditional organization.

---

[6]See http://www.for.gov.bc.ca/hfp/frep/qmgmt/index.htm for an example of applications and assessments for Levels 1 to 3 of CAE requirements by the Forest and Range Evaluation Program (FREP) of BC.

Toronto East General Hospital

Toronto East General Hospital (TEGH), with 470 beds, is one of the full-service teaching hospitals serving Toronto, and one of two hospitals in Canada that have passed Level 4 certification of NQI. TEGH received a gold trophy for quality and healthy workplace in 2008. TEGH defines its vision, mission, values, success factors, and priorities and performance measures (indicators) during its strategic planning process, which is performed every three years (led by the board of directors/top management). The latest plans are given below:

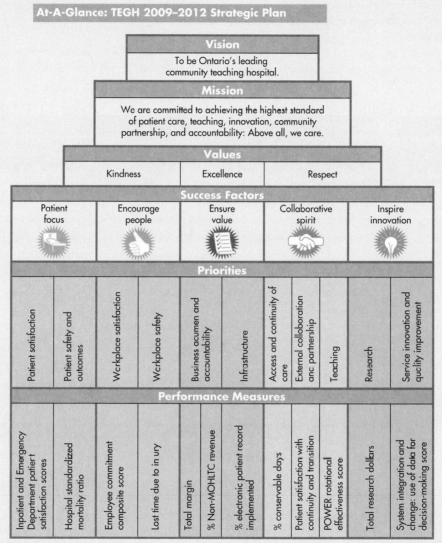

Note: *MOHLTC = Ministry of Health and Long Term Care; Conservable days = number of days a patient stays in the hospital above the average days for community hospitals; Power rotational effectiveness score = overall score for TEGH given by University of Toronto medical residents working in TEGH.*

These are determined after collecting data on patient needs, Toronto health district priorities (to coordinate services with other Toronto hospitals), and Ontario health priorities. Both strategic plans and annual reviews are shown on the TEGH Web site for patients and employees to see. The above performance measures and others deemed of interest to patients and employees (e.g., wait times) are measured annually and posted on the TEGH Web site. The performance measures are compared with other Toronto and Ontario hospitals as benchmarks. For those measures that require improvement, action plans are determined by top management, and each action plan is assigned to a corporate support manager. Also, there are funds for departments/programs to apply for projects.

TEGH has commissioned a demographic study of its catchment area and is familiar with its patients. It performs surveys of its patients' satisfaction with quality of care they received, performs post-discharge phone calls, collects testimonials from its satisfied patients, and has a community advisory council.

TEGH has no difficulty recruiting physicians (it has approximately 400) and nursing staff (it has approximately 2,500). Also, TEGH has approximately 500 volunteers. TEGH has introduced a violence prevention program and has enhanced its wellness facilities and programs. It offers a foundation of leadership program for both its physicians and nurses (so far more than 350 have taken the course). It offers a 2.5 year onsite program for its nurses to get a bachelor's degree from Ryerson University. TEGH has also increased its online training programs. Employee and physician satisfaction scores are annually determined by sampling staff.

TEGH has designed and documented many processes and procedures, e.g., patient flow (to reduce patient stay), continuity of care (to reduce the time until patient is transferred to the right place for care), patient preparation for various tests or surgeries, research study funding, "Good catch" program for staff to identify errors or safety risks before they occur, and standards for service delivery, appearance, etc.

TEGH has partnered with North York General Hospital and Sunnybrook Health Science Centre to perform thoracic (spine) surgery on their patients, and with University of Toronto Medical School to train residents and supervise student projects, etc.

Sources: http://www.tegh.on.ca/bins/doc.aspx?id=7828; http://www.tegh.on.ca/bins/doc.asp?rdc_id=5234.

Table 9-8

Comparing the cultures of TQM and traditional organizations

Aspect	Traditional	TQM
Overall mission	Maximize return on investment	Meet or exceed customer expectations
Objectives	Emphasis on short term	Balance of long term and short term
Management	Not always open; sometimes inconsistent objectives	Open; encourages employee input; consistent objectives
Role of manager	Issue orders; enforce	Coach, remove barriers, build trust
Customer requirements	Not highest priority; may be unclear	Highest priority; important to identify and understand
Problems	Assign blame; punish	Identify and resolve
Problem solving	Not systematic; individuals	Systematic; teams
Improvement	Erratic	Continuous
Supplier relations	Adversarial	Partners
Jobs	Narrow, specialized; much individual effort	Broad, more general; much team effort
Focus	Product-oriented	Process-oriented

LO5 PROBLEM SOLVING AND CONTINUOUS IMPROVEMENT

Problem solving is one of the basic activities in quality improvement. In order to be successful, problem-solving efforts should follow a standard approach. Table 9-9 describes the basic steps and quality tools (explained later) used in the problem-solving process. This methodology, when used in continuous quality improvement, is called the plan-do-study-act cycle.

Plan-Do-Study-Act Cycle

plan-do-study-act (PDSA) cycle (or Deming cycle) The problem-solving and quality improvement methodology used in the continuous improvement.

The **plan-do-study-act (PDSA) cycle**, also referred to as the **Deming cycle**, is the problem-solving and quality improvement methodology used in continuous improvement. The cycle is illustrated in Figure 9-1. Representing the cycle with a circle underscores the continuing nature of its use in the continuous improvement.

There are four basic steps in the PDSA cycle:

Plan. Begin by studying the current problem (or opportunity for quality improvement). Document the problem. Then collect data. Next, analyze the data and develop a plan for improvement. Specify measures for evaluating the plan.

Table 9-9

Step 1 Define the problem.

Give problem definition careful consideration. Quality tools include benchmarking.

Step 2 Collect data.

The solution must be based on facts. Quality tools include check sheet, scatter diagram, histogram, run chart, and control chart.

Step 3 Analyze the problem.

Find the root cause. Quality tools include Pareto chart, cause-and-effect diagram, design of experiments, and analysis of variance.

Step 4 Generate potential solutions.

Tools include brainstorming, interviewing, and surveying.

Step 5 Choose a solution and implement it.

Keep everyone informed.

Step 6 Monitor the solution to see if it accomplishes the goal.

If not, modify the solution, or return to Step 1. Quality tools include control chart and run chart.

Table 9-9

Basic steps in problem solving and quality tools used

Figure 9-1

The PDSA cycle

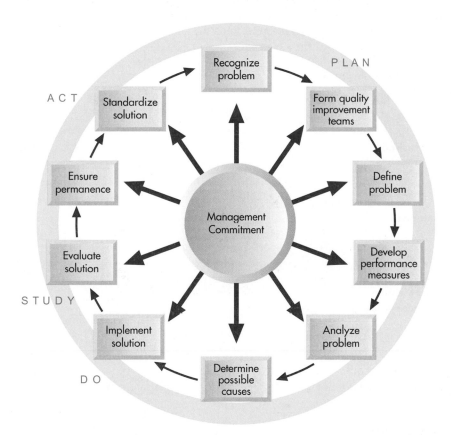

Do. Implement the plan, on a small scale if possible. Document any changes made during this phase. Collect data systematically for evaluation.

Study. Evaluate the data collected during the *do* phase. Check how closely the results match the original goals of the *plan* phase.

Act. If the results are acceptable, *standardize* the new solution and communicate it to all people associated with the problem. Implement training for the new solution. If the results are unacceptable, revise the plan and repeat the cycle or cease the project.

SIX SIGMA

Six Sigma is a more sophisticated statistical approach to problem solving and quality improvement than used in the PDSA cycle of the continuous improvement. The problem-solving and quality improvement methodology in Six Sigma has five steps: define, measure, analyze, improve, and control (DMAIC). In Six Sigma the best employees are trained to become full-time change agents, called black belts, who act like internal consultants with considerable power and resources at their disposal. Consequently, Six Sigma projects are more coordinated than the improvement projects of TQM/Continuous Improvement. Each project chosen should significantly increase the value for customers, shareholders, or employees. In a narrower sense, Six Sigma refers to having very capable and precise processes that make only three or four defects per million parts produced. Companies such as Motorola, GE, Allied Signal, Boeing, and American Express have implemented Six Sigma projects successfully.[7] There will be more on Six Sigma in the next chapter.

BASIC QUALITY TOOLS

An organization can use a number of quality tools for problem solving and quality improvement. The tools aid in data collection and interpretation, and provide the basis for decision making.

The first seven tools are often referred to as the *seven basic quality tools*. Figure 9-2 provides a quick overview of the seven tools.

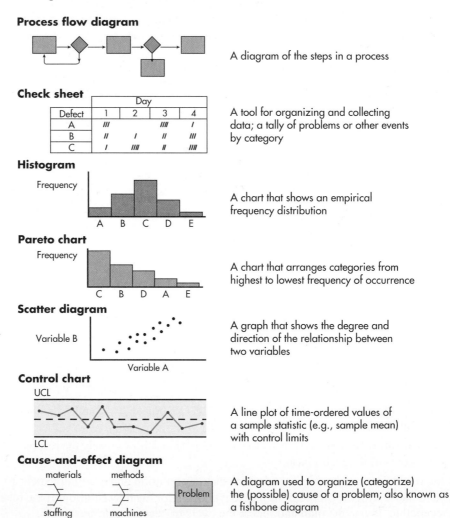

Process flow diagram

A diagram of the steps in a process

Check sheet

A tool for organizing and collecting data; a tally of problems or other events by category

Histogram

A chart that shows an empirical frequency distribution

Pareto chart

A chart that arranges categories from highest to lowest frequency of occurrence

Scatter diagram

A graph that shows the degree and direction of the relationship between two variables

Control chart

A line plot of time-ordered values of a sample statistic (e.g., sample mean) with control limits

Cause-and-effect diagram

A diagram used to organize (categorize) the (possible) cause of a problem; also known as a fishbone diagram

---

[7]T. Pyzdek, *The Six Sigma Handbook*, 2nd ed. (New York: McGraw-Hill, 2003).

Process Flow Diagram. A **process flow diagram** is a diagram of the steps in a process. As a problem-solving or quality improvement tool, a process flow diagram can help investigators identify possible points in a process where problems or opportunities for improvement occur. Process flow diagrams were described in Chapter 6.

Check Sheets. A **check sheet** is a sheet of paper that provides a format for recording and organizing data in a way that facilitates collection and analysis. Check sheets are designed on the basis of what the users are attempting to learn by collecting data. Many different formats can be used for a check sheet and there are many different types of check sheets. One frequently used form of check sheet deals with types of defects and when they occur, another with location of defects. These are illustrated in Figures 9-3 and 9-4.

Figure 9-3 shows tallies that denote the types of defects in a product's labels and the time of day each occurred. Problems with missing labels tend to occur early in the day and smeared print tends to occur late in the day, whereas off-centre labels are found throughout the day. Identifying types of defects and when they occur can help in pinpointing causes of the defects.

Figure 9-4 makes it easy to see where defects on a product are occurring. In this case, defects seem to be occurring on the tips of the thumb and first finger, in the finger valleys (especially between the thumb and first finger), and in the centre of the gloves. Again, this may help determine why the defects occur and lead to a solution.

Histograms. A **histogram** is a chart of the frequency distribution of observed values. Among other things, one can see if the distribution is symmetrical, what the range of values is, and if there are any unusual values. Figure 9-5 illustrates a histogram for repair times of a machine. Note the two peaks. A possible cause might be that there are two types of breakdowns, those requiring minor repairs and others requiring major repairs.

Pareto Analysis. **Pareto analysis** is a technique for focusing attention on the most important problem (or opportunity for improvement). The Pareto concept is that relatively few

process flow diagram
A diagram of the steps in a process.

check sheet   A sheet of paper that provides a format for recording and organizing data in a way that facilitates collection and analysis.

histogram   A chart of the frequency distribution of observed values.

Pareto analysis   Technique for focusing attention on the most important problem (or opportunity for improvement).

Day	Time	Type of Defect					
		Missing label	Off-centre	Smeared print	Loose or folded	Other	
M	8–9	IIII	II				6
	9–10		III				3
	10–11	I	III	I			5
	11–12		I		I	I (Torn)	3
	1–2		I				1
	2–3		II	III	I		6
	3–4		II	HHI			8
Total		5	14	10	2	1	32

Figure 9-3

An example of a check sheet identifying the type and time of defect occurring in a product's labels.

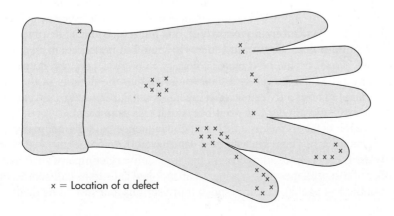

x = Location of a defect

Figure 9-4

A check sheet that identifies the location of defects on a rubber glove.

Figure 9-5

A histogram of a machine's repair times

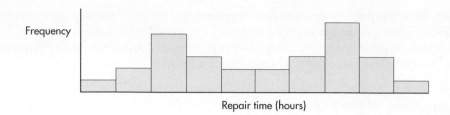

Figure 9-6

A Pareto chart based on data in Figure 9-3

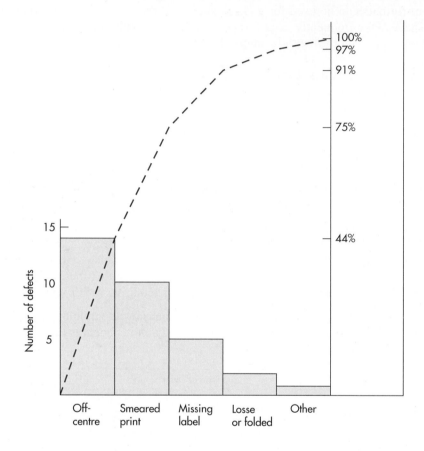

factors account for a large percentage of the total problems (e.g., complaints, defects), thus making these few factors important. More specifically, the Pareto concept states that approximately 80 percent of the problems are from 20 percent of the types of problems. For instance, 80 percent of machine breakdowns are from 20 percent of the types of breakdowns, and 80 percent of the product defects are from 20 percent of the types of defects. The idea is to focus on resolving the most important problems, leaving the less important.

Often, it is useful to prepare a chart that shows the number of occurrences by category (type), arranged in order of frequency. Figure 9-6 illustrates such a chart corresponding to the check sheet shown in Figure 9-3. The dominance of off-centre labels becomes apparent. Presumably, the manager and employees would first focus on trying to resolve this problem. Once they accomplish that, they could address the remaining defects in a similar fashion; "smeared print" would be the next major category to be resolved, and so on. Additional check sheets would be used to collect data to verify that the defects in these categories have been eliminated or greatly reduced. Hence, in later Pareto diagrams, categories such as "off-centre" may still appear but would be much less prominent.

Sometimes each defect type has a different consequence, and the company may assign different weights to each. Then, the weighted value (weight × frequency) will be used in the Pareto analysis. For example, an overnight package delivery company such as FedEx has lower number of lost packages than number of abandoned calls to its call centres due to busy operators, but the lost package error is much more serious and should be dealt with first.

Scatter Diagrams. A **scatter diagram** is a plot of pairs of observations of two variables and can show the correlation between the two variables. A correlation may point to a cause of a problem. Figure 9-7 shows an example of a scatter diagram. In this particular diagram, there is a *positive* (upward-sloping) relationship between the humidity and the number of errors per hour. High values of humidity result in high numbers of errors. On the other hand, a *negative* (downward-sloping) relationship would mean that when values of one variable are high, values of the other variable are low.

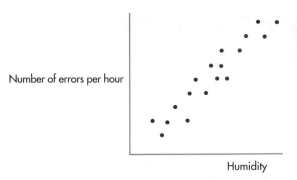

Number of errors per hour

Humidity

Figure 9-7

A scatter diagram

The higher the correlation between the two variables, the less scatter in the points; the points will tend to line up. Conversely, if there were little or no relationship between two variables, the points would be completely scattered. In Figure 9-7, the correlation between humidity and errors seems high, because the points appear to scatter closely along an imaginary line.

Control Charts. A **control chart** is a line plot of time-ordered values of a sample statistic with control limits. It can be used to monitor a process to see if the process output is stable. It can help detect the presence of *assignable* or *correctable* causes of variation. Figure 9-8 illustrates a control chart. Note that the variations for this control chart seem random, with no assignable causes. Control charts can also indicate when a problem occurred and thus give insight into what caused the problem. Control charts are described in detail in Chapter 10.

UCL

LCL

Time

Figure 9-8

A control chart

Cause-and-Effect Diagrams. A **cause-and-effect diagram** or **fishbone** or **Ishikawa diagram** is a diagram used to organize (categorize) the (possible) causes of a problem (the effect). Usually 4Ms—machine (and equipment), method, manpower, and materials—are used as categories. Often this tool is used in the brainstorming sessions to organize the ideas generated.

An example of a cause-and-effect diagram is shown in Figure 9-9. Each of the factors listed in the diagram is a potential source of ticket defects. Note that related factors are bunched up; for example, maintenance frequency and tension adjustment of the printer. Some factors are more likely causes than others. If the cause is still not obvious at this point, additional investigation into the *root cause* may be necessary, involving a more in-depth data collection and analysis. For an application of the cause-and-effect diagram, see the "Kentucky Fried Chicken" OM in Action.

In addition to the seven basic quality tools above, another useful tool is the run chart.

scatter diagram A plot of pairs of observations of two variables and can show the correlation between the two variables.

control chart A line plot of time-ordered values of a sample statistic with control limits.

cause-and-effect diagram A diagram used to organize (categorize) the (possible) causes of a problem (the effect); also called a *fishbone diagram.*

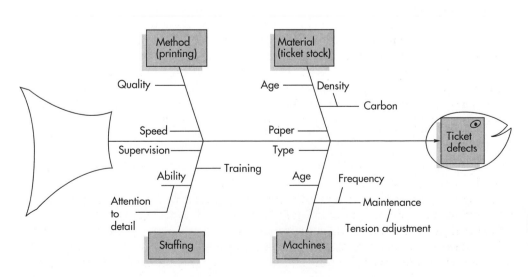

Figure 9-9

Cause-and-effect diagram for ticket defects

Figure 9-10

A run chart

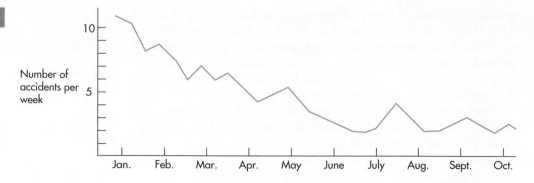

Number of accidents per week

run chart A time plot that can be used to track the values of a variable over time.

Run Charts. A **run chart** is a time plot that can be used to track the values of a variable over time. This can aid in identifying trends or other patterns that may be occurring. Figure 9-10 provides an example of a run chart showing a decreasing trend in accident frequency over time.

The "Improvement of Free-throw Shooting" and "Honda" OM in Actions are two applications of problem-solving using some of the quality tools above.

OM in ACTION

Kentucky Fried Chicken (KFC)

In the 1990s, KFC implemented an improvement program in its four Oklahoma City restaurants to reduce the drive-through service times, which were considered excessive. KFC bought and installed electronic timers to measure wait times. The window "hang time" was about two minutes on average. The regional manager set goals to reduce this time by 10 percent at a time. When the window hang time exceeded the goal, a buzzer would go off and the employee had to write down the reason for the delay in a "blocker log." This information was collected and organized in a cause-and-effect diagram (DTW = Drive through window):

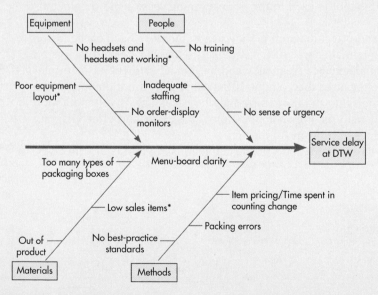

The more frequent causes were identified and solutions were sought for them by the improvement team. For example, sufficient working headsets and spare batteries were provided, layout was changed to reduce the distance employees walked, and rarely ordered items were discontinued and variety of desserts was reduced. This process of continued improvement was continued for about a year (several more solutions were implemented such as pricing items so that they cost whole dollars after tax) until the average hang time was reduced to one minute.

Source: U.M. Apte and C.C. Reynolds, "Quality Management at Kentucky Fried Chicken," *Interfaces* 25(3), May/June 1995, pp. 6–21.

OM in *ACTION*

Improvement of Free-throw Shooting

I used the PDSA cycle to improve my son's basketball free-throw shooting.

Plan

I had observed, over a three-year period from 1991 to 1993, that in basketball games, my son Andrew's free-throw shooting percentage averaged between 45 percent and 50 percent.

Identify and define the process. Andrew's process for shooting free throws was simple: Go to the free-throw line, bounce the ball four times, aim, and shoot.

Plot the points. To confirm my observations on the results of the current process, we went to the YMCA and Andrew shot five sets of 10 free throws for a total of 50 shots. His average was 42 percent. Results were recorded on a run chart (see Figure 1). I concluded the process was stable.

Identify the causes. A cause-and-effect diagram was used to graphically illustrate the relationship between the effect—a low free-throw shooting percentage—and the principal causes (see Figure 2).

In analyzing my son's process, I noticed that he did not stand at the same place on the free-throw line every time. I believed his inconsistent shooting position affected the direction of the shot. If the shot goes left or right, there is a smaller probability that the ball will have a lucky bounce and go in. I also noticed that he didn't seem to have a consistent focal point.

Develop and select alternatives. The alternative selected for Andrew, a right-handed shooter, was for him to line up his right foot on the middle of the free-throw line, bounce the ball four times, focus on the middle of the front part of the rim, and visualize the perfect shot before he released the ball.

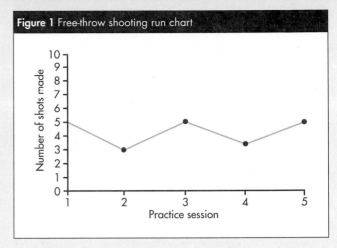
Figure 1 Free-throw shooting run chart

Do and Study

The course of action at this point was for Andrew to shoot five more sets of 10 free throws to test the effectiveness of the changes.

This and the results of another 20 practice sessions are compared with before-improvement results in Figure 3. The new process was first implemented in games toward the end of the 1994 season, and in the last three games, Andrew hit nine of his 13 free throws for a free-throw shooting average of 69 percent.

Act

As we monitored Andrew's process from March 17, 1994 to Jan. 18, 1996, we plotted the total number of practice shots made out of 50 (see Figure 4). It shows that the process is stable. Similar free-throw shooting percentage occurred during actual games.

Source: Based on T. Clark and A. Clark, "Continuous Improvement on the Free-Throw Line," *Quality Progress* 30(10), October 1997, pp. 78–80.

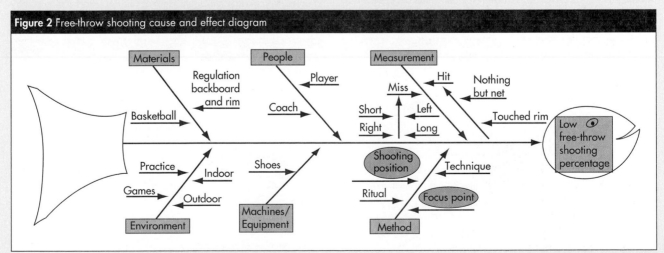
Figure 2 Free-throw shooting cause and effect diagram

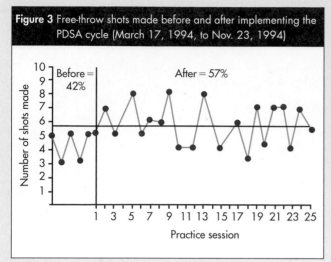

Figure 3 Free-throw shots made before and after implementing the PDSA cycle (March 17, 1994, to Nov. 23, 1994)

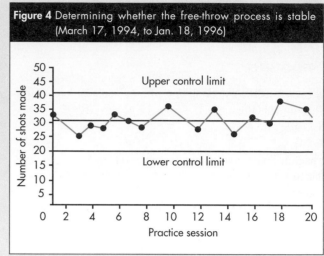

Figure 4 Determining whether the free-throw process is stable (March 17, 1994, to Jan. 18, 1996)

OM in ACTION

Honda

At the Honda plant in Marysville, Ohio, an improvement project was undertaken to solve the excessive use of primer by Line 1. The problem was discovered by comparing Line 1 with Line 2. On both lines, primer was coated on the body of a car by first charging the body with electricity and then lowering it in a primer bath. To identify why there was a difference in primer thickness, data was collected on the two lines and compared.

Note from the histograms in Figure 1 below that the average thickness of primer in Line 1 is greater than Line 2. Also, the variability of primer thickness is higher in Line 1 than Line 2. Because every car's primer thickness should be higher than the minimum specification (shown by the dashed vertical line on the left), the higher variability forces the average primer

thickness for Line 1 to be greater than Line 2. To identify the cause for this, the team looked into factors such as time-in-bath, cleanliness of bath, and primer density. Measurements showed no significant difference between the two lines for these factors. Finally, the temperature of the primer solution was measured over four shifts.

As can be observed from the run charts and histograms in Figure 2, Line 1 has higher temperature variability. Thus, temperature must be the cause of the primer thickness variability. A new temperature control device was purchased and installed on Line 1, lowering the variability in temperature, and therefore in average primer thickness.

Source: G.P. Maul and J.S. Gillard, "Solving Chronic Problems with Simple Tools," *Quality Progress*, July 1994, pp. 51–55. Figures reprinted with permission from Quality Progress, American Society for Quality.

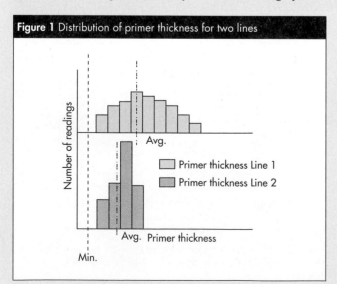

Figure 1 Distribution of primer thickness for two lines

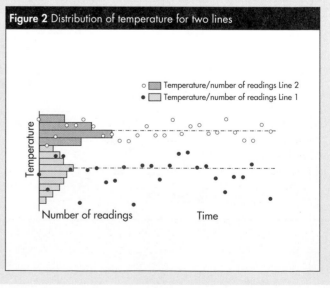

Figure 2 Distribution of temperature for two lines

Methods for Generating Ideas and Reaching Consensus

Some additional tools that are useful for generating ideas in problem solving/quality improvement are brainstorming, quality circles, interviewing, benchmarking, and the 5W2H approach.

Brainstorming. **Brainstorming** is a technique for generating a free flow of ideas on finding causes, solutions, and implementing solutions in a group of people. In successful brainstorming, criticism is absent, no single member is allowed to dominate sessions, and all ideas are welcomed.

brainstorming Technique for generating a free flow of ideas on finding causes, solutions, and implementing solutions in a group of people.

Quality Circle. A **quality circle** is a group of workers, usually in the same department, who meet to discuss ways of improving the products and processes. Quality circles are not only a valuable source of worker input, but also they can motivate workers by demonstrating management interest in worker ideas. Quality circles are usually less structured and more informal than teams involved in continuous improvement, but in some organizations quality circles have evolved into continuous improvement teams. Perhaps a major distinction between quality circles and teams is the amount of authority given to the teams. Typically, quality circles have had very little authority to implement any but minor changes; continuous improvement teams are sometimes given a great deal of authority. Consequently, continuous improvement teams have the added motivation generated by empowerment.

quality circle A group of workers who meet to discuss ways of improving the products or processes.

Interviewing. Another technique that an improvement team can use to collect information about a problem (or opportunity for improvement) is interviewing. Internal problems may require interviewing employees; external problems may require interviewing customers and suppliers.

Benchmarking. **Benchmarking** is the process of measuring an organization's performance against the best in the same or another industry. Its purpose is to establish a standard against which performance is judged, and to possibly learn how to improve. Once a benchmark has been identified, the goal is to meet or exceed that standard through improvements.

benchmarking Process of measuring an organization's performance against the best in the same or another industry.

Selecting an industry leader provides insight into what competitors are doing; however, competitors may be reluctant to share this information. Selecting organizations that are world leaders in other industries is another alternative. For example, Xerox uses many benchmarks: for employee involvement, Procter & Gamble; for quality process, Florida Power & Light and Toyota; for high-volume production, Kodak and Canon; for bill

OM in ACTION

Benchmarking the Student Residence Application Process at Carleton University

The office of Quality Initiatives at Carleton University uses benchmarking to improve various university processes. One such project was the students residence application process. Three-quarters of rooms were reserved for new students who indicated such a need in their entrance application form. When they received conditional acceptance in February, they also received a form for residence. However, they had until June to apply. Other students could also apply but were put on a waiting list. All applicants were assigned to residences in July in a batch operation. However, reassignment of rooms continued until the end of August. This resulted in a 3–4 percent vacancy rate at the beginning of September. Benchmarking involved studying the process used by other Canadian universities. The information was collected from their Web pages and by making phone calls (interviewing). Eventually, the process used at McGill University was chosen. This involved bringing the deadline for application for residence by new students from June to March. Students were assigned a room then. Other students were assigned as they applied after that. Also, an online application form was created to make the process easier. The new process resulted in a vacancy rate of less than 1 percent at the beginning of September.

Sources: M.J. Armstrong, "Benchmarking Goes to School," *Quality Progress*, May 2007, 40(5), pp. 54–58; http://www.carleton.ca/qualityinitiatives.

collection, American Express; for research and development, AT&T and Hewlett-Packard; for order filling and distribution, L.L. Bean and Hershey Foods; and for daily scheduling, Cummins Engine. For an example of benchmarking, see the "Benchmarking Student Residence Application Process at Carleton University" OM in Action.

The 5W2H Approach. Asking questions about the problem (or opportunity for improvement) can lead to important insights about the cause of the problem, as well as potential ways to improve it. One method is called the **5W2H** (5 "w" words and 2 "h" words) **approach**, which asks questions about a problem that begin with: what, why, where, when, who, how, and how much.

Sometimes posing the questions in a negative way may help. For example, in addition to asking, "Where is the defect on the object?" also ask, "Where else could the defect have been on the object, but isn't?" In addition to asking, "When did the defect occur?" also ask, "When else could the defect have occurred, but didn't?"

5W2H approach A method of asking questions about a problem that begin with: what, why, where, when, who, how, and how much.

Reaching Consensus. The team approach works best when it reaches decisions based on consensus. This may be achieved using one or more of the following methods:

1. *List reduction* is applied to a list of possible solutions. Its purpose is to clarify items and, in the *process*, reduce the list of items by posing questions about affordability, feasibility, and likelihood of solving the problem (or improving the quality).

2. A *balance sheet* approach lists the pros and cons of each item and focuses discussion on important issues.

3. *Paired comparisons* is a process by which each item on a list is compared with every other item, two at a time. For each pair, team members select the preferred item. This approach forces a choice between items. It works best when the list of items is small: say, five or fewer.

Summary

Quality has evolved from artisan's workmanship to quality control inspectors, to quality assurance and prevention of defects, and finally to incorporation of quality in the company strategy as total quality management.

Quality is defined according to various dimensions such as performance, esthetics, reliability, and durability. Quality is determined during product design, process design, and production. Costs of quality include external and internal failure, detection, and prevention costs. Modern quality management is directed at preventing mistakes (i.e., quality assurance) rather than finding them after they occur (i.e., quality control).

The chapter includes a description of the key contributors (gurus) to quality management: Deming, Juran, Feigenbaum, and Crosby. ISO 9001 is a standard for quality management system, which is made up of elements such as a quality manual and procedures; management responsibility; resource management; product realization, and measurement; analysis, and improvement.

Hazard Analysis Critical Control Point (HACCP) is also a quality management system (QMS), but its focus is on food safety. It involves finding control points for hazards and setting up quality assurance and control plans at each control point.

The Canada Awards for Excellence (CAE) are given annually to organizations that have shown great achievement in quality management. Its criteria involve areas of leadership, planning, customer focus, people focus, process management, and supplier/partner focus. The Progressive Excellence Program has divided the implementation of the QMS efforts into four levels to make it easier to achieve. CAE requirements lead to total quality management.

Total quality management (TQM) is a never-ending pursuit of higher quality that involves everyone in an organization. The driving force is customer satisfaction; a key activity is continuous improvement. Training of managers and workers in quality concepts, tools, and procedures is an important aspect of the approach. Improvement teams are an integral part of TQM/continuous improvement. A major activity is problem-solving. The methodology used is the plan-do-study-act (PDSA) or the Deming cycle. The seven basic quality tools used in problem-solving and quality improvement include checksheet, histogram, cause-and-effect diagram, and control and run charts.

Key Terms

Solved Problems

A city's police department handed out the following traffic tickets on a summer weekend. Make a check sheet and a Pareto diagram for the types of infraction. If the police department wants to reduce the number of traffic infractions, what type of traffic infraction should the department focus on?

Problem 1

Ticket Number	Infraction	Ticket Number	Infraction
1	Excessive speed	11	Expired licence
2	Expired licence	12	DUI
3	Improper turn	13	Improper turn
4	Excessive speed	14	DUI
5	DUI	15	Excessive speed
6	DUI	16	DUI
7	Excessive speed	17	DUI
8	DUI	18	DUI
9	Improper turn	19	Excessive speed
10	DUI	20	DUI

Check sheet (list the types of infractions, tally, summarize frequencies):

Solution

Infraction	Tally	Frequency
Excessive speed	ЖЖ	5
Expired licence	//	2
Improper turn	///	3
Driving under influence (DUI)	ЖЖ ЖЖ	10

Pareto diagram (array infractions from highest frequency to lowest):

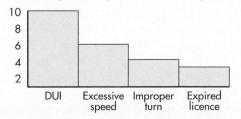

The police department should focus on reducing driving under influence (DUI). It is 50 percent of all traffic infractions.

Problem 2

A friend of yours has told you that no matter how much she studies, she does badly in exams. Help her set up a cause-and-effect diagram for her problem.

Solution

The "effect" is "does not do well in exams." The possible causes can be categorized as in 4M's: machine, method, manpower, and material. Some of the causes under each category are:

Machine: Does not know how to use computer/Internet/library effectively to study

Method: Does not know how to study effectively; does not spend enough time studying

Manpower: Does not have the right background (e.g., lacks math skills); has problem memorizing things

Material: Does not know what is important to study (types of questions in the exam); does not have the textbook and study guide

---

Discussion and Review Questions

1. List and briefly explain the dimensions of goods and service quality. (LO1)

2. Explain the terms *conformance to design specifications during production.* (LO1)

3. Contrast quality assurance, control, and improvement. (LO1)

4. Use the dimensions of quality to describe typical characteristics of these goods and services: (LO1)

   a. A television set
   b. A restaurant meal (a good)
   c. A restaurant meal (a service)
   d. Painting a house

5. Describe the cost of quality, and its categories. Give an example for each category for a fast-food restaurant. (LO1)

6. Describe the evolution of quality management. (LO1)

7. Select one of the quality gurus and briefly describe his contributions to quality management. (LO1)

8. What is ISO 9001, and why is it important for global businesses to have ISO 9001 certification? (LO2)

9. Briefly summarize the elements of ISO 9001. (LO2)

10. Describe HACCP. (LO3)

11. Briefly describe the criteria for the Canada Awards for Excellence. (LO4)

12. What are the key elements of TQM? (LO4)

13. Briefly describe each of the seven basic quality tools. (LO5)

14. Briefly explain each of these tools: (LO5)

    a. Brainstorming
    b. Benchmarking
    c. Run chart

15. Explain each of these methods: (LO5)

    a. The plan-do-study-act (PDSA) cycle
    b. The 5W2H approach

16. List the steps of problem solving. (LO5)

17. Is there a specific set and sequence of basic quality tools used in problem solving/continuous improvement? Compare the "Improvement of Free-throw Shooting," and "Honda" OM in Actions in this regard. (LO5)

18. Contrast ISO 9001, HACCP, and CAE. (LO2, 3, & 4)

1. What trade-offs are involved in deciding how much to spend on quality improvement? (LO1)

2. According to TQM, who needs to be involved in quality management? (LO4)

3. Name one way that technology has had an impact on quality management. (LO1–5)

4. Determine the CAE requirements that necessitate ethical behaviour. Describe why ethics is important in TQM. (LO4)

Consider an auto assembly operation. What kinds of quality problems can arise during assembly? Name one or two. How can each be fixed? Prevented? You may view the Honda video segments on http://bl-bus-jacobsvm.ads.iu.edu/videoglossary.html for ideas. (LO1 & 5)

Identify a bad-quality good or service you recently bought. Describe the quality problem and suggest how it could have been avoided. (LO1 & 5)

1. Visit http://www.theacsi.org, select two companies that you are familiar with, and look up their customer satisfaction indices. Do the indices agree with your knowledge of the quality of the products of the two companies? Explain. (LO1)

2. Visit http://www.isto.ch/index_1.htm, click on "On-line Trial Exam," then on "Free sample exam (ISO 9000)" and take the test. (LO3)

3. Visit http://www.sanofi-aventis.ca/live/ca/en/layout.jsp?scat=DD41F6DC-2248-4193-8145-DDE77042A743, and click on "Begin the tour." After viewing the manufacturing operations of Sanofi-Aventis, prepare an HACCP analysis for a blister pack or bottle of the drug shown. (LO3)

4. Visit http://www.trilliumhealthcentre.org/newsroom/news_releases/September9_2008.html and http://www.trilliumhealthcentre.org/quality_safe_care/index.html, and identify how Trillium Health Centre's quality management system matches the CAE requirements. (LO3)

5. Visit http://www.kamloops.ca/pdfs/news/2008/08-08-nqi-backgrounder.pdf , and identify how City of Kamloop's quality management system matches the CAE requirements. (LO3)

1. Make a check sheet and then a Pareto chart for the following car service repair shop data. (LO5)

Ticket No.	Work	Ticket No.	Work	Ticket No.	Work
1	Tires	11	Brakes	21	Lube & oil
2	Lube & oil	12	Lube & oil	22	Brakes
3	Tires	13	Battery	23	Transmission
4	Battery	14	Lube & oil	24	Brakes
5	Lube & oil	15	Lube & oil	25	Lube & oil
6	Lube & oil	16	Tires	26	Battery
7	Lube & oil	17	Lube & oil	27	Lube & oil
8	Brakes	18	Brakes	28	Battery
9	Lube & oil	19	Tires	29	Brakes
10	Tires	20	Brakes	30	Tires

2. An air-conditioning repair department manager has compiled data on the primary reason for 41 service calls during the previous week, as shown on the next page. Using the data, make

a check sheet for the problem types for each customer type, and then construct a Pareto chart for each type of customer. (LO5)

Job Number	Problem/ Customer Type	Job Number	Problem/ Customer Type	Job Number	Problem/ Customer Type
301	F/R	315	F/C	329	O/C
302	O/R	316	O/C	330	N/R
303	N/C	317	W/C	331	N/R
304	N/R	318	N/R	332	W/R
305	W/C	319	O/C	333	O/R
306	N/R	320	F/R	334	O/C
307	F/R	321	F/R	335	N/R
308	N/C	322	O/R	336	W/R
309	W/R	323	F/R	337	O/C
310	N/R	324	N/C	338	O/R
311	N/R	325	F/R	339	F/R
312	F/C	326	O/R	340	N/R
313	N/R	327	W/C	341	O/C
314	W/C	328	O/C		

Key: Problem type:
    N = Noisy
    F = Equipment failure
    W = Runs warm
    O = Odour
Customer type:
C = Commercial customer
R = Residential customer

3. Prepare a run chart for the number of defective computer monitors produced in a plant shown below. Workers are given a 15-minute break at 10:15 A.M. and 3:15 P.M., and a lunch break at noon. What can you conclude? (LO5)

Interval Start Time	Number of Defects	Interval Start Time	Number of Defects	Interval Start Time	Number of Defects
8:00	1	10:45	0	2:15	0
8:15	0	11:00	0	2:30	2
8:30	0	11:15	0	2:45	2
8:45	1	11:30	1	3:00	3
9:00	0	11:45	3	3:30	0
9:15	1	1:00	1	3:45	1
9:30	1	1:15	0	4:00	0
9:45	2	1:30	0	4:15	0
10:00	3	1:45	1	4:30	1
10:30	1	2:00	1	4:45	3

4. Prepare a run chart for the following 911 call data. Use five-minute intervals (i.e., count the calls received in each five-minute interval. Use intervals of 0–4, 5–9, etc.). Note: Two or more calls may occur in the same minute; there were three operators on duty this night. What can you conclude from the run chart? (LO5)

Call	Time	Call	Time	Call	Time
1	1:03	15	1:43	29	2:03
2	1:06	16	1:44	30	2:04
3	1:09	17	1:47	31	2:06
4	1:11	18	1:48	32	2:07
5	1:12	19	1:50	33	2:08
6	1:17	20	1:52	34	2:08
7	1:21	21	1:53	35	2:11
8	1:27	22	1:56	36	2:12
9	1:28	23	1:56	37	2:12
10	1:29	24	2:00	38	2:13
11	1:31	25	2:00	39	2:14
12	1:36	26	2:01	40	2:14
13	1:39	27	2:02	41	2:16
14	1:42	28	2:03	42	2:19

5. Suppose that a table lamp fails to light when turned on. Prepare a cause-and-effect diagram to analyze possible causes. Use categories such as lamp, cord, etc. (LO5)

6. Prepare a cause-and-effect diagram to analyze why a machine has produced a defective part. (LO5)

7. Prepare a scatter diagram for each of the following pairs of variables and then express in words the apparent relationship between the two variables. Put the first variable on the horizontal axis and the second variable on the vertical axis. (LO5)

a.

Age	24	30	22	25	33	27	36	58	37	47	54	28	42	55
Days absent	6	5	7	6	4	5	4	1	3	2	2	5	3	1

b.

Temperature (°C)	18	17	22	19	28	14	24	30	25	18	26
Error rate		1	2	0	0	3	3	1	5	2	1	3

8. The local police department has responded to a vehicle accident along a stretch of highway. Prepare a cause-and-effect diagram for this accident. Use categories such as vehicle, driver, weather, etc. (LO5)

9. Suppose you are going to have a prescription filled at a local pharmacy. Referring to the dimensions of service quality, for each dimension, give an example of how you would judge the quality of the service. (LO1)

10. Prepare a HACCP analysis for burgers made in a fast-food restaurant such as McDonald's. (LO3)

11. Consider the processing of the Northern (cold water) shrimp. They are caught off the East and West coast, be-headed at sea and frozen or iced, and then further processed on shore. Consider a processing which results in cooked, peeled, and frozen small shrimps. Government regulations require that product not be tainted (rancid; bad taste and odour) or unsafe, or decomposed (rotten), and the bag/box should be accurately weighed and labelled with a product code (including place and date of processing). A process flow diagram for processing shrimp is given on the layout diagram below. Identify hazards/defects, and determine a Critical Control Point and a quality assurance/control plan for each hazard/defect.[7] (LO3)

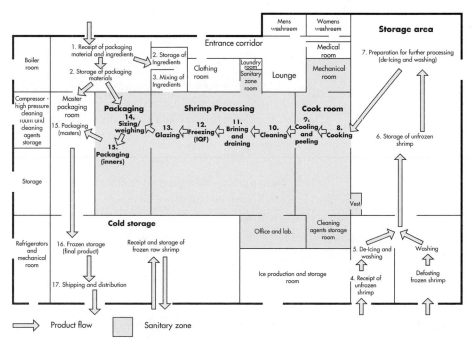

[7]http://www.inspection.gc.ca/english/anima/fispoi/qmp/files/cookshrp.doc, accessed 2006; removed 2007; similar plans are in http://seafood.ucdavis.edu/haccp/Plans.htm.

MINI-CASE

North Shore University Hospital

North Shore University Hospital in New York has initiated some improvement projects in order to accommodate the increasing number of patients. One project involved reducing the turnaround time of patient-discharge-to-bed-ready process, displayed below.

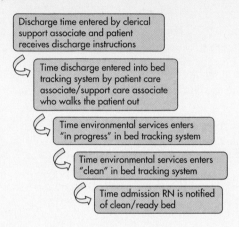

The process seemed to take many hours with significant variations. To study this process, the times between pairs of consecutive steps of the process for 195 patient discharges were computed and plotted (see distributions below). For example, Discharge-bed tracking system (step 1 to step 2) took from 200 to 850 minutes.

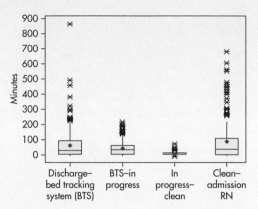

Identify which part(s) of the process could be targeted for time reduction and suggest some solutions.

Source: A. Pellicone and M. Martocci, "Faster Turnaround Time," *Quality Progress*, March 2006, 39(3), pp. 31–36.

MINI-CASE

Walkerton Tragedy

In May 2000, seven residents of Walkerton, a small town in southern Ontario, died of E. coli poisoning transmitted through the town's water. The water had been drawn from a well that was usually a safe source of water supply. Although well water treatment was rather simple—just added chlorine to disinfect it—the town water works' manager, Stan Koebel, believed that the water was so safe that chlorine did not have to be used.

This conclusion may have been true under normal circumstances; however, during April 2000 the farm adjacent to the well fertilized its fields with cattle manure. Unfortunately, during the second week of May, the area received unusually high levels of rain, which washed E. coli from the manure into the well. The usual level of chlorine was inadequate to kill the high level of the bacteria. Compounding this, Koebel did not follow the Ontario Ministry of the Environment's guideline

for checking the level of residual chlorine in treated water (in fact a minimum of .5 mg per litre should remain to continue disinfecting the water through the distribution pipes).

During the third week of May, people started to get sick. Water was finally tested and E. coli was found in the samples. Koebel kept quiet for a few days, hoping the nightmare would end. Unfortunately, the situation got worse: almost half the town's population got sick and eventually seven people died.

Questions

1. State the quality characteristics of drinking water.

2. Draw a process flow diagram for water treatment of a town like Walkerton that uses well water.

3. Apply the HACCP analysis to develop a quality management system for water treatment of such a town.

Source: © Queen's Printer for Ontario, 2007.

MINI-CASE

Chick-n-Gravy Dinner Line

The operations manager of a company that produces frozen dinners had received numerous complaints from supermarkets about the company's Chick-n-Gravy dinners. The manager

asked her assistant, Ann, to investigate the matter and to report her recommendations.

Ann's first task was to determine what problems were generating the complaints. The majority of complaints centred on five defects: underfilled packages, a missing item, spilled/mixed items, unacceptable taste, and improperly sealed packages.

Next, she took 800 samples of dinners from the two production lines and examined each sample, making note of any defects that she found. A summary of those results is shown in the table below.

What should Ann recommend to her boss?

			Defect Observed				
Date	Time	Line	Under filled	Missing Item	Spilled/Mixed	Unacceptable Taste	Improperly Sealed
5/12	0900	1		√√	√	√√√	
5/12	1330	2			√√		√√
5/13	1000	2				√	√√√
5/13	1345	1	√√		√√		
5/13	1530	2		√√	√√√		√
5/14	0830	1		√√√		√√√	
5/14	1100	2	√√		√	√√	
5/14	1400	1			√		√
5/15	1030	1		√√√		√√√√√	
5/15	1145	2			√	√√	
5/15	1500	1	√		√		
5/16	0845	2				√√	√√
5/16	1030	1		√√√	√	√√√	
5/16	1400	1					
5/16	1545	2	√	√√√√√	√	√	√√

MINI-CASE

Tip Top Markets

Tip Top Markets is a regional chain of supermarkets. On July 28, Karen Martin, manager of one of the stores, was disturbed by the large number of recent complaints from customers at her store, particularly on Tuesdays, so she obtained complaint records from the store's customer service desk for the last three Tuesdays. These are shown below.

Analyze the data and make a recommendation to Karen.

July 13

wrong price on spaghetti	overcharged
water on floor	out of brown rice
store looked messy	out of mushrooms
store too warm	overcharged
checkout lines too long	checkout wait too long
cashier not friendly	shopping cart broken
out of feta cheese	couldn't find Aspirin
overcharged	out of brown lunch bags
out of Saran Wrap	out of straws
out of Haagen-Dazs Bars	

July 20

out of low-salt pickles	out of large eggs
checkout lines too slow	out of cran-apple juice
found keys in parking lot	out of pretzels
lost keys	out of apricot jam
wrong price on sale item	telephone out of order
overcharged on corn	out of cocktail sauce
wrong price on baby food	water on floor
out of 500-mL Tide	out of frozen onion rings
out of green tea	out of frozen squash
checkout lines too long	out of powdered sugar
out of romaine lettuce	out of nonfat peanut butter

July 27

out of dill pickles	wanted to know who won the lottery
reported accident in parking lot	store too warm
wrong price on cran-apple juice	oatmeal spilled in bulk section
out of carrot juice	telephone out of order
out of licorice sticks	out of Lava soap
out of chocolate milk	water on floor
out of Lava Bars	out of glazed doughnuts
windows dirty	out of baby carrots
out of iceberg lettuce	spaghetti sauce on floor
dislike store decorations	out of Skippy crunchy peanut butter
out of St. John's wort	out of butter
out of vanilla soy milk	

Staples' Extended-Service Warranty Process

Ron bought a Toshiba laptop with a two-year extended warranty from Staples Store number 52 in Saskatoon on November 8, 2007. The laptop developed a problem in January 2009: a broken wire in the AC power supply. In the beginning of February 2009, Ron went to Store 52 with his power supply and showed the staff the problem. They said that he should call the Toronto service center to get a claim number. Ron called the Toronto service centre and explained the problem. After about 10 minutes he received a repair number. He found out that he has to also turn in the laptop even though the problem was only with the power supply. On February 11, 2009, Ron took his laptop and power supply, in the original box, to Store 52. It took the employee about 20–25 minutes to issue a Repair Depot Technician Service Request (he had difficulty completing the form on the computer). Ron waited until March 23, when he went to Store 52 around 1 pm. He told the employee that it had been more than six weeks since he turned in his laptop and power supply, and he was wondering what had happened. First, the employee brushed off Ron's question by saying that repairs may take two to six weeks. Ron pointed out that it had been more than six weeks and the repair was a simple replacement of a common power supply. Reluctantly, the employee tried to pull up the service request on the computer. He had trouble locating it. After five minutes, he found the service request, which appeared to be cancelled. The employee couldn't explain what happened and said that Ron should return and talk to Dylan after 4 pm. Unfortunately, Ron didn't have time to do that. The next day, he went to Store 52 around 7 pm, and asked for Dylan. The manager, Jen, said that Dylan wasn't working then. Ron asked Jen if she could help. She couldn't find the service request on her computer, so she checked in her office in the back. After 10 minutes, she returned and said that the laptop had been shipped last Friday from Winnipeg and should arrive soon. On April 3, Ron received a phone call from Store 52 saying that the laptop had arrived. Ron went there the next day. An employee gave him his laptop and power supply. Ron pointed out that he had also turned in the box (which contained some installation CDs, manuals, etc.). She read the Service Request form and said that she didn't think that was correct. Ron left the store with his laptop and power supply. On April 9, Ron received a phone call from Store 52 saying that his laptop box was there to be picked up.

Questions

1. State the quality problems incurred during the Extended Service Warranty Process described above.

2. For each quality problem, determine a quality assurance plan that could have prevented it in the first place.

CHAPTER 10
Statistical Quality Control

LEARNING OBJECTIVES

After completing this chapter, you should be able to:

LO1 List and briefly explain the elements of the statistical process control planning process.

LO2 Explain how control charts are designed and the concepts that underlie their use, and solve problems that involve control chart design and use.

LO3 Assess process capability, and solve problems involving process capability.

LO4 Describe Six Sigma quality and design of experiments.

elphi is a parts supplier to General Motors and, like all other companies in the auto industry, is in a very competitive business. Buffalo General Hospital, like other hospitals, tries to meet the increasing demand for its services safely and efficiently but with limited resources. Harley Davidson is the only U.S. motorcycle company left. How do organizations such as these survive and grow? While some other factors are also relevant, quality control is certainly an important contributor.

LO1 INTRODUCTION

The best companies emphasize *designing quality into the process (e.g., by undertaking continuous improvement and Six Sigma quality projects), thereby greatly reducing the need for inspection/tests.* The least progressive companies rely heavily on receiving and shipping inspection/tests. Many occupy a middle ground that involves some receiving and shipping inspection/tests and some process control (i.e., inspection during the process). The most progressive have achieved an inherent level of quality that they can avoid any inspection/test and process control. That is the ultimate goal.

statistical quality control
Use of statistical techniques and sampling in monitoring and testing of quality of goods and services.

Statistical quality control uses statistical techniques and sampling in monitoring and testing of quality of goods and services.

The part of statistical quality control that relies primarily on inspection/tests of previously produced items is referred to as *acceptance sampling.* This is described in the chapter supplement, which can be accessed at *Connect.* The part of statistical quality control that occurs during production are referred to as statistical process control, and we examine these in this chapter (see Figures 10-1 for phases of statistical quality control in a company and 10-2 for location of use of acceptance sampling and statistical process control within production).

Statistical quality control is important because it provides an economical way to evaluate the quality of products and meet the expectations of the customers.

inspection   Appraisal of a good or service against a standard.

Inspection is an appraisal activity that compares the quality of a good or service to a standard. To determine whether a process is functioning as intended or to verify that a batch or lot of raw materials or final products does not contain more than a specified percentage of defective goods, it is necessary to physically examine at least some of the items in question.

Statistical Process Control Planning Process

Effective statistical process control requires the following planning steps:

1. Define the quality characteristics important to customers, and how each is measured.
2. For each characteristic,
   a. Determine a quality control point
   b. Plan how inspection is to be done, how much to inspect, and whether centralized or on-site
   c. Plan the corrective action

Define the Quality Characteristics. The first step is to define, in sufficient detail, what is to be controlled. It is not enough, for example, to simply refer to a painted surface. The

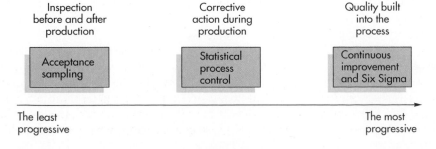

Figure 10-1

Phases of statistical quality control/improvement in a company

Inspection before and after production	Corrective action during production	Quality built into the process
Acceptance sampling	Statistical process control	Continuous improvement and Six Sigma

The least progressive ———————————————————————→ The most progressive

Figure 10-2

Location of use of an acceptance sampling and statistical process control within production

paint can have a number of important characteristics such as its colour, gloss, thickness, and resistance to fading or chipping. Different characteristics may require different approaches for control purposes. Only those characteristics that can be measured are candidates for control. Thus, it is important to consider how measurement will be accomplished. There must be a standard that can be used to evaluate the measurement. This relates to the level of quality being sought.

Determine a Quality Control Point. Many operations have numerous possible inspection points. Because each inspection adds to the cost of a product, it is important to restrict inspection efforts to the points where they can do the most good. In manufacturing, some of the typical inspection points are:

1. *At the beginning of the process.* There is little sense in paying for goods that do not meet quality standards and in spending time and effort on material that is bad to begin with.

2. *At the end of the process.* Customer satisfaction and company's image are at stake here, and repairing or replacing products in the field is usually much more costly than doing it at the factory.

3. *At the operation where a characteristic of interest to customers is first determined.* In particular, before a costly, irreversible, or covering (e.g., painting) operation.

The HACCP system described in the previous chapter also provides some guidelines for determining the quality control points.

In the service sector, inspection points include where personnel and customer interface (e.g., service counter) and the parts of the facility that customer sees. Table 10-1 illustrates some examples of inspection points and quality characteristics inspected in some businesses.

How Inspection Is to Be Done. This is usually technical and needs engineering knowledge. For example, to test clarity of beer, a white light is shined through it and its dispersion is measured.

How Much to Inspect. The amount of inspection can range from no inspection whatsoever to inspection of each item. Low-cost, high-volume items such as paper clips, nails, and pencils often require little inspection because (1) the cost associated with passing defective items is quite low and (2) the processes that produce these items are usually highly reliable, so that defects are rare. Conversely, items that have large costs associated with passing defective products require inspection. Thus, critical components of a vehicle are closely scrutinized.

The majority of quality control applications lie somewhere between the two extremes. Most require some inspection, but it is neither possible nor economically feasible to examine every product. The cost of inspection and resulting interruptions of a process (if inspection is not automated) typically outweigh the benefits of 100 percent inspection. However, the cost of letting undetected defects slip through is sufficiently high that inspection cannot be completely ignored. The amount of inspection needed is governed by the cost of inspection and the expected cost of passing defective items.

As illustrated in Figure 10-3, if inspection activities increase, inspection cost increases, but the cost of passing defective decreases. The goal is to minimize the sum of these two costs.

As a rule of thumb, operations with a high proportion of human involvement necessitate more inspection than mechanical operations, which tend to be more reliable. The frequency of inspection depends largely on the rate at which a process may go out of control. A stable process will require only infrequent checks, whereas an unstable one

OM in *ACTION*

Delphi

The Delphi plant in Brookhaven, Mississippi, makes fuse and relay boxes for GM trucks and SUVs. The plastic fuse tray is produced by injection-moulding presses. The rectangular holes on the tray and holes for terminals must have tolerance of 0.3 mm in order to hold fuses and metal terminals in place, and they must be located correctly on the tray. To check the accuracy of the trays, each moulding press's output is tested every two hours in a lab by sampling one tray. The tray is put in a vision inspection machine and secured into a fixture. The machine magnifies the image 12 times, digitizes it, and compares it with a good tray. The positions of fuse and terminal holes are checked. The vision system is Smartscope Flash by Optical Gaging Products, Inc. It uses the Measure-X software to perform the analysis, and reports the results to the QC-Calc SPC software, which produces control charts, etc. The fixture was carved out from acrylic material

using laser to maximize its accuracy (5–7 percent tolerance), thus reducing measurement errors.

A plastic tray for fuse box of GM trucks and SUVs.

Sources: L. Adams, "Making Complex Parts That Fit Together," *Quality* 41(1), January 2002, pp. 24–26; http://www.ogpnet.com.

Figure 10-3

The amount of inspection is optimal when the sum of the costs of inspection and passing defectives is minimized.

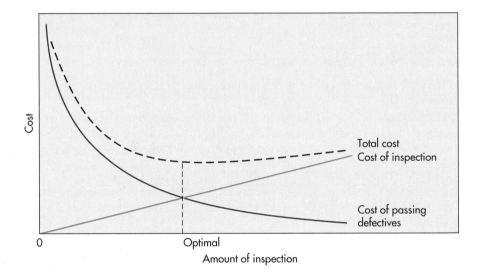

or one that has recently given trouble will require more frequent checks. Likewise, many small lots will require more samples than a few large lots because it is important to obtain sample data from each lot.

Centralized versus On-site Inspection. Some situations require that inspections be performed *on site*. For example, inspecting the hull of a ship for cracks requires inspectors to visit the ship. If the test is simple enough (e.g., measuring dimensions), it can be done by a handheld caliper or micrometer. Alternatively, automated inspection, e.g., using a vision system or laser gauge, can be installed on the machine (which can perform 100 percent inspection). At other times, specialized tests need to be performed and can best be performed in a lab (e.g., medical tests, analyzing food and water samples, testing metals for hardness or paper for tensile strength and tear resistance, running viscosity tests on lubricants, and measuring dimensions that require large expensive coordinate measuring machines).

The central issue in the decision concerning on-site or lab inspections is whether the advantages of specialized lab tests are worth the time and interruption needed to obtain the results. Specialized equipment, skilled quality control inspectors, and a more favourable test environment (less noise, vibrations, and dust) offer strong arguments for using a lab. More companies are now relying on self-inspections by operators on-site.

Type of Business	Inspection Points	Quality Characteristics	Table 10-1
Fast food	Service counter	Appearance, friendliness of server, waiting time	*Examples of inspection points and quality characteristics in some businesses*
	Eating area	Cleanliness	
	Kitchen	Cleanliness, quality of food, temperature and time of food storage, temperature and time of cooking, health regulations, and hygiene	
Supermarket	Cashiers	Accuracy, courtesy, waiting time	
	Aisles and stockrooms	Clutter	
	Shelf stock	Availability, rotation of perishables, appearance	
Brewery	Hot/cold liquor tanks	Bitterness	
	Filtering	Clarity	
	Fermentation tank	Alcohol content	

See the "Delphi" OM in Action for an example of centralized inspection and the "Harley-Davidson" OM in Action later in the chapter for an example of on-site inspection.

Plan the Corrective Action.   When a process is judged out of control for an important characteristic, the process should be stopped and corrective action must be taken. This involves uncovering the cause (e.g., worn-out tool bits, or failure to follow specified procedures) and correcting it. Also, any potentially off-specification (i.e., defective) parts or products should be tested, and if defective, should be either reworked or scrapped. To ensure that corrective action is effective, the output of a process must be monitored for a sufficient period of time to verify that the problem has been eliminated.

(LO2) STATISTICAL PROCESS CONTROL

Statistical process control (SPC) is concerned with statistical evaluation of the product in the production process. To do SPC, the operator takes periodic samples from the process and compares them with predetermined limits. If the sample results fall outside the limits, the operator stops the process and takes corrective action. If the sample results fall within the limits, the operator allows the process to continue.

statistical process control (SPC)   Statistical evaluation of the product in the production process.

Types of Variations and Sampling Distributions

All processes that produce a good or service exhibit a certain amount of "natural" variation in their output. The variations are created by the combined influences of countless minor factors, each one so unimportant that even if it could be identified and eliminated, the decrease in process variability would be negligible. In effect, this variability is inherent in the process. It is often referred to as a *chance* or **random variation**. In Deming's terms, this is referred to as *common variability* of the process. The amount of random variation differs from process to process. For instance, older machines generally exhibit a higher degree of random variation than newer machines, partly because of worn parts and partly because new machines may incorporate design improvements that lessen the variability in their output.

random variation   Natural variation in the output of a process, created by countless minor factors.

A second kind of variability in process output is non-random and is called **assignable variation**. In Deming's terms, this is referred to as *special variation*. Unlike random variation, the main sources of assignable variation can usually be identified (assigned to a specific cause) and eliminated. Excessive tool wear, equipment that needs adjustment, defective materials, and human errors (e.g., failure to follow correct procedures) are typical sources of assignable variation.

assignable variation   Non-random variability in process output; a variation whose cause can be identified.

The main task in SPC is to distinguish assignable from random variation. Taking a sample of two or more observations and calculating a sample statistic such as sample mean makes the task easier. This is because random variations are reduced in sample statistics.

The variability of a sample statistic is described by its *sampling distribution*, which is the theoretical distribution of the values of the statistic for all possible samples of a given size from the process. Consider the process for filling bottles with soft drink. If the amount of soft

Figure 10-4

The sampling distribution of the sample mean, for a given sample size, has less variability than the process.

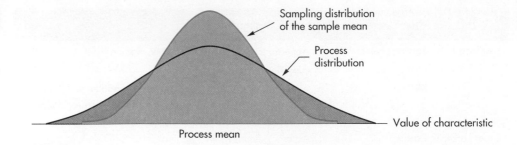

drink in a large number of bottles is measured accurately, we would discover slight differences among the bottles. If these amounts were arranged on a graph, the frequency distribution would reflect the *process variability*. The values would be clustered close to the process average (e.g., 2 litres), but some of the values would vary somewhat from the mean.

If we take *samples* of three bottles at a time and compute, for example, the *mean* amount of soft drink in each sample, we would discover that these values also vary, just as the *individual* values varied. However, the distribution of the sample mean is more concentrated around process mean (2 litres) than the distribution of process (i.e., individual bottles; see Figure 10-4).

The sampling distribution of the sample mean exhibits less variability (i.e., it is less spread out) than the process distribution. This reflects the *averaging* that occurs in computing the sample means: high and low values in samples tend to offset each other, resulting in less variability among sample means than among individual values. Note that both distributions have the same mean. Finally, note that most process distributions and sampling distributions are approximately *Normal*. Furthermore, the *central limit theorem* implies that sampling distributions will be approximately Normal, even if the population (i.e., the process) is not.

The sampling distribution of the sample mean can be used to judge whether a process has shifted (i.e., there is an assignable cause). If the process has not shifted then the sample mean should fall between ±2 (with 95.5 percent probability) or ±3 (with 99.7 percent probability) standard deviations of the long-standing and known process mean (see Figure 10-5). If it doesn't, then we can conclude that the process most likely has shifted, and hence there is an assignable cause.

Control Charts

control chart A time-ordered plot of a sample statistic with limits.

A **control chart** is a *time-ordered* plot of a sample statistic, with limits. It is used to distinguish between random and assignable variation (or equivalently no shift and a shift in the process). The basis for a control chart is the sampling distributions. We will illustrate this concept by focusing on the sample mean as the sample statistic. As mentioned before, because the sampling distribution of the sample mean will be Normal, 99.7 percent of the sample means will fall within ±3 standard deviations of its mean, which is the same as the process mean. Therefore, we could decide to set the limits at ±3 standard deviations from the long-standing known process mean, and conclude that any sample mean that was farther away from the long-standing known process mean than these limits reflects a shift

Figure 10-5

Percentage of values under the curve within given ranges in a Normal sampling distribution of the sample mean

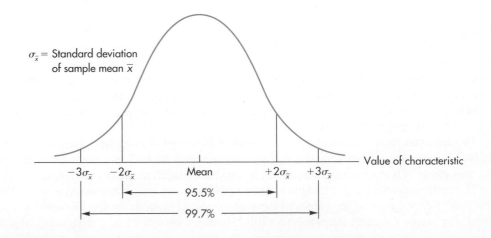

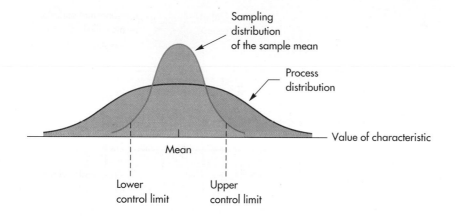

Figure 10-6

Control limits are based on the sampling distribution of the sample mean.

in the process, and hence an assignable variation. In effect, these limits are called **control limits**. Figure 10-6 illustrates how control limits for a sample mean control chart are based on the sampling distribution of the sample mean.

The larger value is the *upper control limit* (UCL), and the smaller value is the *lower control limit* (LCL). A sample statistic that falls between these two limits suggests random variation (i.e., no process shift) while a value outside or on either limit suggests assignable variation (i.e., the deviation from the long-standing known process mean is so large that the process must have shifted).

Note that the control limits are not directly related to specification limits. Control limits are based on the characteristic of the process, whereas the specification limits are based on the desired characteristic of the product. The process is capable if the process values fall within the specification limits. However, control limits are for sample statistics, so they should fall well within the specification limits. This will be further explained in the "Process Capability" section later in the chapter.

It is important to recognize that because any control limits will leave some area in the *tails* of the distribution, there is a small probability that a sample statistic value will fall outside the limits *even though only random variations are present* (i.e., there is no process shift). For example, if ±2 Sigma (standard deviation) limits are used, they would include 95.5 percent of the values. Consequently, the complement of that number (100 percent − 95.5 percent = 4.5 percent) would not be included. That percentage (or *probability*) is sometimes referred to as the probability of a **Type I error**, where the "error" is concluding that a process has shifted (i.e., an assignable variation is present) when it has not (i.e., only random variation is present). This is also referred to as *alpha* risk, where alpha (α) is the sum of the probabilities in the two tails. Figure 10-7 illustrates this concept.

Using wider limits (e.g., ±3 Sigma limits) reduces the probability of a Type I error because it decreases the area in the tails of the distribution. However, wider limits make it more difficult to detect assignable variations (i.e., a shift in the process) *if* they are present. For example, the process might shift (an assignable cause of variation) enough to be detected by Two Sigma limits, but not enough to be readily apparent using Three Sigma limits. That

control limits The dividing lines for the value of sample statistic between concluding no process shift and a process shift, hence random and assignable variations.

Type I error Concluding that a process has shifted (i.e., an assignable variation is present) when it has not (i.e., only random variation is present).

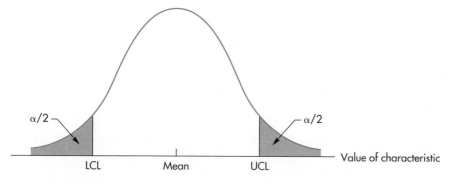

Figure 10-7

The probability of a Type I error

α = Probability of a Type I error

The components of a sample mean control chart

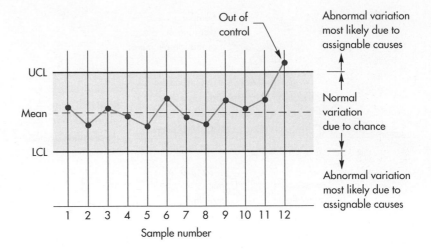

Concluding that a process has not shifted (i.e., only random variation is present) when it has (i.e., an assignable variation is present).

could lead to a second kind of error, known as a **Type II error**, which is concluding that a process has not shifted (i.e., only random variation is present) when it has (i.e., an assignable variation is present). In theory, the costs of making each error should be balanced by their probabilities. However, in practice, Two Sigma limits and Three Sigma limits are commonly used without specifically referring to the probability of a Type II error.

The sample statistic values are usually plotted against time, together with the upper and lower control limits. This produces a record of the process control activity, as well as helps to prevent the process from going out of control. Figure 10-8 illustrates the components of a sample mean control chart. Each sample mean is represented by a single red dot on the chart. Moreover, each sample mean is compared to the control limits to judge if it is within the acceptable (random) range. Figure 10-9 illustrates this concept.

Designing Control Charts. The following steps are usually taken to design control charts:

1. Determine a sample size n (usually between 2 and 20). The choice of n depends on the cost of inspection versus the expected cost of Type II error. The larger n is, the smaller the probability of Type II error.

2. Obtain 20 to 25 samples of size n. Compute the appropriate sample statistic for each sample (e.g., sample mean).

3. Establish preliminary control limits using appropriate formulas (given in following sections), and graph them.

4. Plot the sample statistic values on the control chart, and note whether any points fall outside the control limits.

5. If you find no points outside control limits, assume that there is no assignable cause and therefore the process is stable and in control (other cases showing instability will be illustrated at the end of this section). If not, investigate and correct assignable causes of variation; then repeat the process from step 2 on.

Each sample mean (a red dot) is compared to the control limits

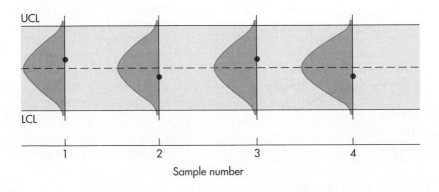

Sample Mean and Range Control Charts

The **sample mean control chart**, sometimes referred to as an $\bar{x}$ chart, is used to monitor the process mean. The centre line used in $\bar{x}$ chart represents the process mean. This is estimated by taking a few samples, computing their mean, and then averaging these means. These samples are used to ensure that the process is stable and in control. It can be shown that the average of means is the mean of all the observations in the samples, and hence is called the grand mean. The control limits can be determined in two ways. The choice depends on what information is available.

sample mean ($\bar{x}$) control chart   The control chart for sample mean, used to monitor the process mean.

The first approach to calculate the control limits is to use the standard deviation of the process, σ.

$$\text{Upper Control Limit (UCL}_{\bar{x}}) = \bar{\bar{x}} + z\sigma_{\bar{x}}$$

$$\text{Lower Control Limit (LCL}_{\bar{x}}) = \bar{\bar{x}} - z\sigma_{\bar{x}}$$

(10-1)

where

$\sigma_{\bar{x}}$ = Standard deviation of the sampling distribution of the sample mean = $\sigma/\sqrt{n}$

σ = Process standard deviation

n = Sample size

z = Standard Normal deviate (usually $z = 3$)

$\bar{\bar{x}}$ = Average of sample means = grand mean

The following example illustrates the use of these formulas.

Example 1

A quality inspector took five samples, each with four observations, of the length of a part (in cm). She computed the mean of each sample (see table below).

a. Use the following data to obtain Three Sigma (i.e., $z = 3$) control limits for sample mean. Is the process in control?

b. If a new sample has values 12.10, 12.19, 12.12, and 12.14, using the sample mean control chart in part a, has the process mean changed (i.e., is there an assignable variation)?

It is known from previous experience that the standard deviation of the process is .02 cm.

		Sample				
		1	**2**	**3**	**4**	**5**
	1	12.11	12.15	12.09	12.12	12.09
	2	12.10	12.12	12.09	12.10	12.14
Observation	**3**	12.11	12.10	12.11	12.08	12.13
	4	12.08	12.11	12.15	12.10	12.12
	$\bar{x}$	12.10	12.12	12.11	12.10	12.12

a. $\bar{\bar{x}} = \dfrac{12.10 + 12.12 + 12.11 + 12.10 + 12.12}{5} = 12.11\,\text{cm}$

Solution

Using formula 10-1, with $z = 3$, $n = 4$ observations per sample, and $\sigma = .02$, we find:

$$\text{UCL}_{\bar{x}}:\ 12.11 + 3\left(\frac{.02}{\sqrt{4}}\right) = 12.14$$

$$\text{LCL}_{\bar{x}}:\ 12.11 - 3\left(\frac{.02}{\sqrt{4}}\right) = 12.08$$

Because all 5 sample means fall between the control limits (12.08 and 12.14), the process is in control.

b. $\bar{x}_6 = \dfrac{12.10 + 12.19 + 12.12 + 12.14}{4} = 12.1375\,\text{cm}$

Because $12.08 < 12.1375 < 12.14$, the process mean has not changed (i.e., there is only random variation).

Note: The fact that some of the *individual* measurements fall outside of the control limits (e.g., the first observation in Sample 2, the last observation in Sample 3, and the second observation in Sample 6) is irrelevant. You can see why by referring back to Figure 10-6: *individual* values are represented by the process distribution, a large portion of which lies outside of the control limits for the sample *mean*.

A second approach to calculate the control limits is to use the sample *range* (i.e., maximum value – minimum value in the sample) as a measure of process variability (instead of σ). The appropriate formulas for sample mean control limits in this case are:

$$UCL_{\bar{x}} = \bar{\bar{x}} + A_2\bar{R}$$
$$LCL_{\bar{x}} = \bar{\bar{x}} - A_2\bar{R}$$

(10-2)

where

A_2 can be obtained from Table 10-2

$\bar{R}$ = Average of sample ranges of a few samples

Table 10-2

Factors for Three Sigma control limits for $\bar{x}$- and R-charts

Number of Observations in Sample, n	Factor for $\bar{x}$ Charts, A_2	Factors for R-Charts Lower Control Limit, D_3	Factors for R-Charts Upper Control Limit, D_4
2	1.88	0	3.27
3	1.02	0	2.57
4	0.73	0	2.28
5	0.58	0	2.11
6	0.48	0	2.00
7	0.42	0.08	1.92
8	0.37	0.14	1.86
9	0.34	0.18	1.82
10	0.31	0.22	1.78
11	0.29	0.26	1.74
12	0.27	0.28	1.72
13	0.25	0.31	1.69
14	0.24	0.33	1.67
15	0.22	0.35	1.65
16	0.21	0.36	1.64
17	0.20	0.38	1.62
18	0.19	0.39	1.61
19	0.19	0.40	1.60
20	0.18	0.41	1.59

Source: Adapted from Eugene Grant and Richard Leavenworth, *Statistical Quality Control,* 4th ed. (New York: McGraw-Hill, 1972), p. 645.

Example 2

Twenty samples of $n = 8$ have been taken of the weight of a part. The average of sample ranges for the 20 samples is .016 kg, and the average of sample means is 3 kg. Determine Three Sigma control limits for sample mean of this process.

Solution

$\bar{\bar{x}} = 3$, $\bar{R} = .016$, $A_2 = .37$ for $n = 8$ (from Table 10-2)

$$\text{UCL}_{\bar{x}} = \bar{\bar{x}} + A_2\bar{R} = 3 + .37(.016) = 3.006 \text{ kg}$$

$$\text{UCL}_{\bar{x}} = \bar{\bar{x}} - A_2\bar{R} = 3 - .37(.016) = 2.994 \text{ kg}$$

Sample Range Control Chart. The **sample range (R) control chart** is used to monitor process dispersion or spread. Although the underlying sampling distribution is not Normal, the concept for design and use of sample range control chart is much the same as that for $\bar{x}$ chart. Control limits for sample range control chart are found using these formulas:

sample range (R) control chart The control chart for sample range, used to monitor process dispersion or spread.

$$\text{UCL}_R = D_4\bar{R}$$
$$\text{LCL}_R = D_3\bar{R}$$

(10-3)

where values of D_3 and D_4 are obtained from Table 10-2.

Example 3

Twenty-five samples of $n = 10$ observations have been taken from a milling process. The average of sample ranges is .01 centimetre. Determine upper and lower control limits for the sample range.

Solution

$\bar{R} = .01 \text{ cm}$, $n = 10$

From Table 10-2, for $n = 10$, $D_4 = 1.78$ and $D_3 = .22$

$\text{UCL}_R = 1.78(.01) = .0178 \text{ cm}$

$\text{LCL}_R = .22(.01) = .0022 \text{ cm}$

In Example 3, a sample range of .0178 centimetre or more would suggest that the process variability has increased. A sample range of .0022 cm or less would imply that the process variability has decreased. In the former case, this means that the process is producing too much variation; we would want to investigate this in order to remove the assignable cause of variation. In the latter case, even though decreased variability is desirable, we would want to determine what is causing it: Perhaps an improved method has been used, in which case we would want to identify it.

If the standard deviation of process σ is not known but the average of sample ranges $\bar{R}$ is known, then σ can be estimated from $\bar{R}$ as follows: Equate the two UCLs in formulas 10-1 and 10-2, substitute 3 for z, and simplify:

$$\bar{\bar{X}} + 3\sigma_{\bar{x}} \approx \bar{\bar{X}} + A_2\bar{R}$$
$$3\sigma_{\bar{x}} \approx A_2\bar{R}$$
$$3\frac{\sigma}{\sqrt{n}} \approx A_2\bar{R}$$

(10-4)

$$\sigma \approx \frac{\sqrt{n}}{3}A_2\bar{R}$$

Why Use Both Sample Mean and Sample Range Control Charts? Sample mean and sample range control charts provide different perspectives on a process. Sample mean control charts are sensitive to shifts in the process mean, whereas sample range control charts are sensitive to changes in process dispersion or spread. Because of this difference in perspective, both charts must be used to monitor a process. The logic of using both

Figure 10-10

Sample mean and sample range control charts used together complement each other

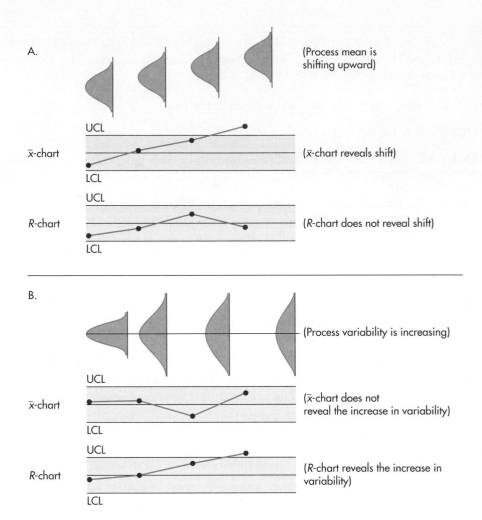

is readily apparent from Figure 10-10. In 10-10A, the sample mean control chart picks up the shift in the process mean, but because the dispersion is not changing, the sample range control chart fails to indicate a problem. Conversely, in 10-10B, a change in process dispersion is not detected by the sample mean control chart, but is detected by the sample range control chart. Thus, use of both control charts provides more information than either chart alone.

Individual Unit and Moving Range Control Charts

individual unit (X) control chart Control chart for individual unit, used to monitor single observations ($n=1$).

When the rate of production is low, testing is expensive, or there is no reason to expect additional information by taking more observations, only one unit (i.e., $n = 1$) is used for inspection. In this case, the sample mean control chart reduces to **individual unit (X) control chart**, and its control limits can be determined by:

$$UCL_x = \bar{X} + z\sigma$$
$$LCL_x = \bar{X} - z\sigma \tag{10-5}$$

moving range (MR) control chart Control chart for moving range, i.e., the difference between consecutive observations, used to monitor the dispersion or spread when $n=1$.

where $\bar{X}$ is the mean of a few individual observations (that estimates the process mean), σ is the process standard deviation, and z is the standard Normal deviate. It is important to note that the above formulas assume a Normal process distribution.

The "sample" range cannot be calculated in the usual way in this case because there is only one observation in each sample. Instead, the differences between consecutive observations, called moving range (MR), are calculated and used in the **moving range (MR) control chart** to control the dispersion or spread. We can still use the formula for the sample range control limits (10-3) but determine D_4 and D_3 from Table 10-2 using $n = 2$. Thus, the control limits for the moving range control chart are:

$$\text{UCL}_{\text{MR}} = 3.27\bar{R}$$

$$\text{LCL}_{\text{MR}} = 0\bar{R} = 0 \tag{10-6}$$

where $\bar{R}$ is the average of the moving ranges (the absolute value of the difference between two consecutive observations). It is important to note that consecutive moving range values are not independent and that this fact has to be considered when analyzing the moving range control chart.

Example 4

The following data are the (Brinell) hardness measures of 10 individual steel screws produced by a screw machine.

a. Determine the Three Sigma control limits for the X-chart and the moving range control chart. Is the process in control?

Sample Number	Hardness
1	36.3
2	28.6
3	32.5
4	38.7
5	35.4
6	27.3
7	37.2
8	36.4
9	38.3
10	30.5

b. If the 11th observation is 38.7, using the control charts in part a, is the process still in control?

Solution

a. We have to compute the average and standard deviation of the individual observations (estimate of process standard deviation). Also, we need to calculate the difference of consecutive observations (absolute value) to obtain the moving ranges, and then average these to get $\bar{R}$. These are displayed below:

Sample Number	Hardness	Moving Range
1	36.3	—
2	28.6	7.7
3	32.5	3.9
4	38.7	6.2
5	35.4	3.3
6	27.3	8.1
7	37.2	9.9
8	36.4	0.8
9	38.3	1.9
10	30.5	7.8
Average =	34.12	5.51
Std dev =	4.11	

The control limits for X-chart are:

$$\text{UCL}_x = \bar{X} + z\sigma = 34.12 + 3(4.11) = 46.45$$

$$\text{LCL}_x = \bar{X} - z\sigma = 34.12 - 3(4.11) = 21.79$$

The control limits for moving range control chart are:

$$UCL_{MR} = 3.27(5.51) = 18.02$$

$$LCL_{MR} = 0$$

All 10 hardness values fall within the X-chart control limits and all nine moving range values fall within the moving range control limits. Therefore, the process is in control.

b. $21.79 < 38.7 < 46.45$, therefore the 11th observation is within its control limits. The new moving range $= 38.7 - 30.5 = 8.2$. Because $0 < 8.2 < 18.02$, the new moving range is also within its control limits. Therefore, the process is still in control.

Note that if formula 10-4 were used to estimate σ from $\bar{R}$ in the above example instead of calculating it directly, we would have obtained:

$$\sigma \approx \frac{\sqrt{n}}{3} A_2 \bar{R} = \frac{\sqrt{2}}{3} (1.88)(5.51) = 4.88$$

The relatively large discrepancy between 4.88 and 4.11 (estimate of σ derived directly from samples) is due to the fact that the data are not distributed Normally, as evident from the histogram below (note that formula 10-4 assumes that process distribution is Normal).

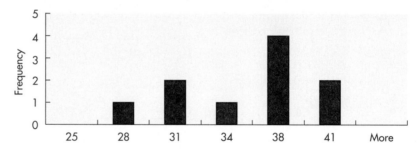

Control Charts for Attributes

Control charts for attributes are used when the process characteristic is *counted* rather than measured, i.e., when an item in a sample is either defective or not. There are two types of attribute control charts, one for the fraction of defective items in a sample (*p*-chart) and one for the number of defects per unit (*c*-chart).

p-chart Control chart for sample proportion of defectives, used to monitor the proportion of defective items generated by a process.

p-Chart. The **p-chart** is the control chart for the sample proportion of defectives, and is used to monitor the proportion of defective items generated by the process. The theoretical basis for a *p*-chart is the Binomial distribution, although for large sample sizes the Normal distribution provides a good approximation to it. Conceptually, a *p*-chart is constructed and used in much the same way as an $\bar{x}$-chart.

The centre line on a *p*-chart is the average proportion of defectives in the population, *p*. The standard deviation of the sampling distribution of the sample proportion, when *p* is known, is

$$\sigma_p = \sqrt{\frac{p(1-p)}{n}}$$

Control limits for *p*-chart are calculated using the formulas

$$UCL_p = p + z\sigma_p$$
$$LCL_p = p - z\sigma_p$$

(10-7)

If *p* is unknown, it can be estimated from a few samples. That estimate, $\bar{p}$, replaces *p* in the preceding formulas, as illustrated in the following example.

Note: Because formula (10-7) is an approximation, sometimes LCL_p will be negative. In this case, zero should be used as the lower control limit.

Example 5

A quality inspector counted the number of defective parts a prototype machine made in samples of 100 taken every hour during a 20 hour period.

a. Using the following data, construct a Three Sigma control chart for the sample proportion of defectives.

b. Is the machine producing a stable proportion of defectives?

Sample	Number of Defectives	Sample	Number of Defectives
1	4	11	8
2	10	12	12
3	12	13	9
4	3	14	10
5	9	15	21
6	11	16	10
7	10	17	8
8	22	18	12
9	13	19	10
10	10	20	16
			220

Solution

a. $\bar{p} = \dfrac{\text{Total number of defectives}}{\text{Total number of observations}} = \dfrac{220}{20(100)} = .11$

$\hat{\sigma}_p = \sqrt{\dfrac{\bar{p}(1-\bar{p})}{n}} = \sqrt{\dfrac{.11(1-.11)}{100}} = .03$

Control limits are:

$\text{UCL}_p = \bar{p} + z(\hat{\sigma}_p) = .11 + 3(.03) = .20$

$\text{LCL}_p = p - z(\dot{\sigma}_p) = .11 - 3(.03) = .02$

b. Plotting the control limits and the sample proportion of defectives, you can see that the process is not in control: sample 8 ($^{22}/_{100} = .22$) and sample 15 ($^{21}/_{100} = .21$) are above the upper control limit. Therefore, the machine operation should be investigated for assignable causes, and after corrective action, new data should be collected and new p-control limits should be calculated.

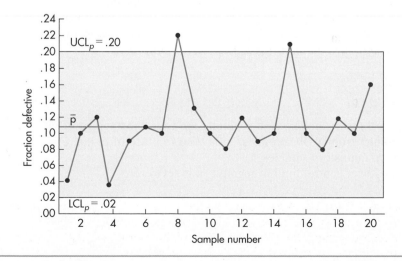

Buffalo General Hospital

n the 1990s, when Buffalo General Hospital was implementing continuous improvement, management introduced

control charts for monitoring safety incidents such as intravenous (IV) and medication incidents (see two examples below where dashed lines show 1, 2, and 3 standard deviations from the centre line):

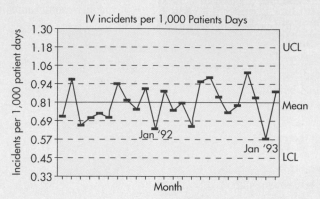

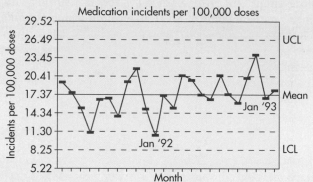

The incidents could be any one of the following:

1. Adverse reaction	9. Incorrect route
2. Delay	10. Incorrect times
3. Extra dose	11. Omission
4. Failure to initiate	12. Therapy, no order
5. Failure to follow policy	13. Transcription error
6. Incorrect dosage	14. Incorrect rate of flow
7. Incorrect drug	15. Wrong solution
8. Incorrect patient	

Question

What type of control chart, *p*- or *c*-, is each of the above control charts?

Source: L. Gothard and N.E. Wixson, "Charting a Course for Continuous Quality Improvement," *Risk Management*, Jan 1994, 41(1), pp. 27–33.

---

c-chart Control chart for sample number of defects per unit product, used to monitor the number of defects per unit product.

c-Chart. When the goal is to control the number of *occurrences* of defects *per unit product*, a **c-chart** (the control chart for the sample number of defects per unit product) is used. A unit might be an automobile, a hotel room, a typed page, or a roll of carpet. In this case, there is no sample size, only occurrences may be counted: the non-occurrences cannot be. The underlying sampling distribution is the Poisson distribution. Use of the Poisson distribution assumes that defects occur over some *continuous* region and that the probability of more than one defect at any particular spot is negligible. The mean number of defects per unit product is c and the standard deviation is $\sqrt{c}$. For practical reasons, the Normal approximation to the Poisson is used. The control limits are:

$$\text{UCL}_c = c + z\sqrt{c}$$
$$\text{LCL}_c = c - z\sqrt{c}$$

(10-8)

If the value of c is unknown, as is generally the case, the average of number of defects per unit product from a few samples, $\bar{c}$, is used in place of c, i.e., $\bar{c}$ = total number of defects ÷ total number of samples.

When the lower control limit is negative, it is set to zero.

Rolls of coiled wire are monitored using a *c*-chart. Eighteen rolls have been examined, and the number of defects per roll has been recorded in the following table.

Example 6

a. Is the process in control? Plot the values on a *c*-chart using three standard deviation control limits.

b. Suppose a new roll has seven defects. Using the *c*-chart of part a, is the process still in control?

Sample	Number of Defectives	Sample	Number of Defectives
1	3	10	1
2	2	11	3
3	4	12	4
4	5	13	2
5	1	14	4
6	2	15	2
7	4	16	1
8	1	17	3
9	2	18	1
			45

a. $\bar{c} = 45/18 = 2.5$

Solution

$$UCL_c = \bar{c} + 3\sqrt{\bar{c}} = 2.5 + 3\sqrt{2.5} = 7.24$$

$$LCL_c = \bar{c} - 3\sqrt{\bar{c}} = 2.5 - 3\sqrt{2.5} = \rightarrow 0$$

As shown in the *c*-chart below, the process is in control.

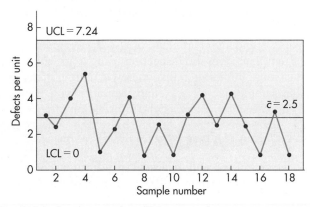

b. Because $0 < 7 < 7.24$, the process is still in control.

For an application of control charts for attributes, see the "Buffalo General Hospital" OM in Action.

Using Control Charts

So far we have used the rule that a process should be investigated when sample statistic falls outside the control limits. There are other cases when a process should be investigated. These relate to non-random patterns in the control chart plots. These are shown in Figure 10-11.

Some examples of non-random patterns in control chart plots.

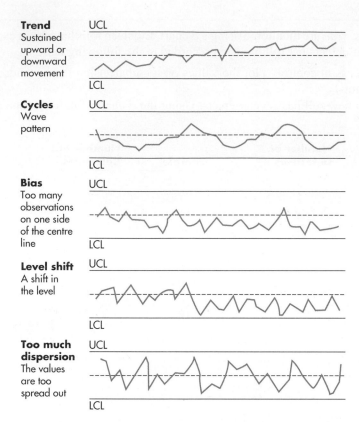

Trend
Sustained upward or downward movement

UCL
- - -
LCL

Cycles
Wave pattern

UCL
- - -
LCL

Bias
Too many observations on one side of the centre line

UCL
- - -
LCL

Level shift
A shift in the level

UCL
- - -
LCL

Too much dispersion
The values are too spread out

UCL
- - -
LCL

Standardization is a key component of McDonald's strategy and all foods are prepared according to a strict reference manual. Farmers even have special guidelines to follow in growing potatoes for French fries. Here, quality control staff check all aspects of French fries, from the taste to their length.

http://www.mcdonalds.com

design specification
A range of acceptable values established by engineering design or customer requirements.

process variability   Actual variability in a process for a product.

process capability   The ability of a process to meet the design specification.

In some instances, a manager can choose between using a $\bar{x}$-chart and a p-chart. If she is monitoring the diameter of a drive shaft, either the diameter could be measured and a $\bar{x}$-chart used for control, or the shafts could be inspected using a *go, no-go gauge*—which simply indicates whether a particular shaft is within specification or not, without giving its exact dimensions—and a p-chart could be used. Measurement is more costly and time-consuming per unit than a yes–no inspection using a go, no-go gauge, but because measurement supplies more information than merely counting items as good or bad, one needs a much smaller sample size for a $\bar{x}$-chart than a p-chart. Hence, a manager must weigh the time and cost of sampling against the information provided.

LO3 PROCESS CAPABILITY

Three terms relate to the process capability: design specification, control limits, and process variability. Each term represents a slightly different aspect of variability, so it is important to differentiate these terms.

Design specification, established by engineering design or customer requirements, is a range of values in which a product must fall in order to be acceptable.

Control limits are statistical limits that reflect the extent to which *sample statistics* such as mean and range can vary due to randomness alone.

Process variability is the actual variability in a process for a product.

Control limits and process variability are directly related: control limits are based on sampling distribution variability, and sampling distribution variability is a function of process variability. On the other hand, there is no direct link between design specification and either control limits or process variability. The output of a process may or may not conform to design specification, even though the process may be statistically in control. That is why it is also necessary to take into account the *capability* of a process. The term **process capability** refers to the ability of a process to meet the design specification. Measuring this capability is called capability analysis.

Capability Analysis

Capability analysis determines whether the process output falls within the design specification. If it is within the design specification for all its output, then the process is said to

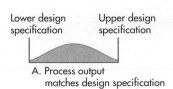
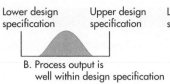
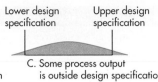

be "capable." If it is not, the process is said to be incapable and the manager must decide how to correct the situation.

Consider the three cases illustrated in Figure 10-12. In case A, process output and design specification are well matched, so that nearly all of the process output can be expected to meet the design specification. In case B, 100 percent of the output is within the design specification limits. In case C, however, the design specification is tighter than what the process is capable of, so a few percentage of the output fail to meet the design specification.

In instances such as case C in Figure 10-12, a manager might consider a range of possible solutions: (1) redesign the process or reduce its variability by, for example, performing experiments to find the best settings for the controllable factors; (2) use an alternative process that can achieve the desired accuracy; (3) retain the current process but attempt to eliminate unacceptable output using 100 percent inspection; and (4) examine the design specification to see whether it could be relaxed without adversely affecting customer satisfaction.

Process variability is typically measured as the interval ±3 standard deviations from the process mean. To determine whether the process is capable, compare this ±3 standard deviations value to acceptable range of variation (i.e., design specification range or width), assuming that the process mean is centred at the midpoint of design specification. For example, suppose that the ideal length of time to perform a service is 10 minutes, and an acceptable range of variation around this time is ±1 minute. If the process has a standard deviation of .5 minute, it would not be capable because ±3 standard deviations would be ±1.5 minutes, which exceeds ±1 minute. An alternative way is to compare six standard deviations of the process with the design specification width (upper design specification − lower design specification). For the above example, 6 sigma of the process is 6(.5) = 3 minutes, and the design specification width is 2(1) = 2 minutes.

Example 7

A manager has the option of using any one of three machines, A, B, or C, for making a part. The machines and their standard deviations of outputs (in millimetres) are listed below. Determine which machines are capable if the design specification for the part's length is between 101.00 mm and 101.60 mm.

Machine	Standard Deviation (mm)
A	.10
B	.08
C	.13

Determine the output variability of each machine (i.e., 6 standard deviations) and compare that value to the specification width of .60 mm (= 101.60 − 101.00).

Machine	Standard Deviation (mm)	Machine Variability = 6σ
A	.10	.60
B	.08	.48
C	.13	.78

We can see that both machine A and machine B are capable of producing output that is within the specification (assuming they can be centred at the midpoint of the design specification 101.30) but that machine C is not, because its variability of .78 exceeds the design specification width of .60. See Figure 10-12 for a visual portrayal of these results.

OM in ACTION   http://www.harley-davidson.com

Harley-Davidson

Harley-Davidson implemented a PC–based networked statistical process control system in two of its power-train plants a few years ago. Harley controls approximately 500 critical dimensions such as bore diameter, hole location, flatness, and surface finish of motorcycle parts. Upgrading from paper control charts, Harley installed more than 60 personal computers in strategic locations throughout both plants and connected the on-site coordinate measuring machines and other gauges into the network. As soon as an operator completes a measurement, an updated control chart is displayed on the monitor. If

the process is out of control but the part's characteristic is still within tolerance, a yellow status flag is shown. If it is outside the specification limits, a red flag is displayed.

Whenever a process goes out of control, or a part is produced outside specification limits, a dialogue box pops up and the operator is prompted to enter an assignable cause. In many cases the cause of the problem is readily apparent to the operator and is immediately fixed. If the operator can't find the cause of the problem, he or she contacts the workgroup quality adviser. If additional assistance is needed, then a manufacturing engineer is brought in.

Source: R. Della, "Harley Rides High on SPC Changes," *Quality* 39(1), January 2000, pp. 40–43.

OM in ACTION

Imperial Bondware

Imperial Bondware of Kenton, Ohio, makes paper cups for hot and cold drinks. It has 62 large automated machines, each making cups starting from rolls of printed paperboard strip. The dimensions (rim diameter, rim thickness, and cup height) are important because the cups have to work flawlessly in automated drink machines (i.e., they must be released from the stack just before a drink is poured). Before automating the data gathering and analysis, Imperial Bondware used to take four hours just to print the quality control charts. After installing automated laser gauges and Zontec's Synergy software, the manager can access the performance of each machine quickly. Of particular interest is the process capability of each machine. Two examples of the charts used by Imperial Bondware to control rim diameters produced by a cup-making machine are shown. The individual unit chart (without showing the control limits but showing the design specification limits) is displayed on the top, and a process distribution with the design specification limits are shown in the bottom. This particular machine makes cups that have diameters 97.7 percent within specification.

Question

Using the information given in the charts, can you verify that $C_p = 0.875$ and $C_{pk} = 0.6656$?

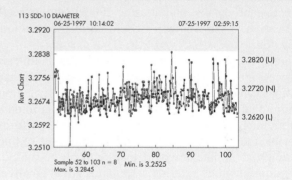

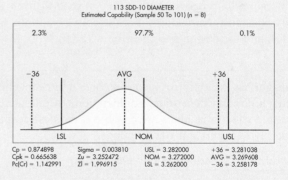

Source: K. Aldred, "Paper Cup Manufacturer Slashes Report Time," *IIE Solutions* 30(8), August 1998, pp. 44–45. Reprinted with permission of the Institute of Industrial Engineers, 3577 Parkway Lane, Suite 200, Norcross, GA, 720-449-0461.

C_p

To express the capability of a machine or process, some companies use the ratio of the design specification width to the process width (= 6 sigma). This can be calculated using the following formula:

$$\text{Process capability ratio, } C_p = \frac{\text{Design specification width}}{\text{Process width}}$$

$$= \frac{\text{Upper design specification} - \text{Lower design specification}}{6\sigma} \tag{10-9}$$

Example 8

Calculate the process capability index for each machine in Example 7.

The design specification width in Example 7 was .60 mm. Hence, to determine the capability index for each machine, divide .60 by the process width (i.e., 6 standard deviations) of each machine. The results are:

Machine	Standard Deviation (mm)	Machine Capability	C_p
A	.10	.60	.60/.60 = 1.00
B	.08	.48	.60/.48 = 1.25
C	.13	.78	.60/.78 = 0.77

Using the capability ratio, you can see that for a process to be capable, it must have a capability ratio of at least 1.00. A ratio of 1.00 implies that 99.74 percent of the output of a process can be expected to be within the design specification limits, hence only 0.26 percent, or 2,600 parts per million, fall outside the design specification. Moreover, the greater the process capability ratio, the greater the probability that the output of a machine or process will fall within design specification.

C_{pk}

If a process is not centred between design specification limits, or if there is no design specification limit on one side, a slightly different measure is used to calculate its capability. This ratio is represented by the symbol C_{pk}. It is calculated by finding the difference between each of the specification limits and the process mean, dividing that difference by three standard deviations of the process, and identifying the smaller ratio. Thus, C_{pk} is equal to the *smaller* of:

$$\frac{\text{Upper design specification} - \text{Process mean}}{3\sigma} \tag{10-10}$$

and

$$\frac{\text{Process mean} - \text{Lower design specification}}{3\sigma}$$

Example 9

A process's output has a mean of 9.20 kg and a standard deviation of .30 kg. The lower design specification is 8.00 kg and the upper design specification is 10.00 kg. Calculate the C_{pk}.

1. Calculate the ratio for the lower design specification:

$$\frac{\text{Process mean} - \text{Lower design specification}}{3\sigma} = \frac{9.20 - 8.00}{3(.30)} = \frac{1.20}{.90} = 1.33$$

2. Calculate the ratio for the upper design specification:

$$\frac{\text{Upper design specification} - \text{Process mean}}{3\sigma} = \frac{10.00 - 9.20}{3(.30)} = \frac{.80}{.90} = .89$$

The smaller of the two ratios is .89, so this is the C_{pk}. Because the C_{pk} is less than 1.00, the process is *not* capable. Note that if C_p had been used, it would have given the false impression that the process was capable:

$$C_p = \frac{\text{Upper design specification} - \text{Lower design specification}}{6\sigma} = \frac{10.00 - 8.00}{6(.30)} = \frac{2.00}{1.80} = 1.11 > 1.00$$

See the "Imperial Bondware" OM in Action for an application of process capability analysis.

The Global Six Sigma Awards

The Global Six Sigma Awards are given annually by World-wide Conventions and Business Forums, a consulting firm, to companies that have carried out excellent business improvement work through Six Sigma projects. Both TD Canada Trust and Bank of Montreal have won the award. TD Canada Trust's first Six Sigma project involved looking into excessive complaints received from customers who used TD Visa's call centres in London (Ontario) and Montreal. The complaints were because of lengthy and complicated identity verification process. Besides asking for name and address, customers were asked other personal questions, and every time they were rerouted they had to go through the authentification process again. The solution identified and implemented by the Six Sigma team was to design a standard and short authentification process and to eliminate unnecessary reauthentifications.

Bank of Montreal got into Six Sigma when top management recruited an experienced Master black belt in May 2005 to improve the efficiency and effectiveness of the back office part of the bank, called product operations. He trained other black belts who help local teams carry out Six Sigma projects. So far, more than 250 projects have been completed successfully.

Sources: http://www.tgssa.com/TGSSA-Supplement-Final.pdf; http://www.tgssa.com/WCBFfull.pdf

SIX SIGMA QUALITY

Six Sigma quality

A more advanced version of problem solving/continuous improvement. It also refers to the goal of achieving process variability so small that the half-width of design specification equals six standard deviations of the process.

Six Sigma quality is a more advanced version of problem solving/continuous improvement that was discussed in the previous chapter. It also refers to the goal of achieving process variability so small that the half-width of design specification equals six standard deviations of the process. That means that the process capability ratio equals 2.00, resulting in an extremely small probability (.00034 percent, or 3.4 units per million) of getting any output outside design specification. This is illustrated in Figure 10-13 on the next page.[1]

The differences of Six Sigma quality and Continuous Improvement are:[2]

	Six Sigma Quality	**Continuous Improvement**
Objective	Product and process perfection	Product and process improvement
Tools	Statistical, e.g., design of experiments and analysis of variance	Simple data analysis, e.g., Pareto chart, cause-and-effect diagram
Methodology	Define, measure, analyze, improve, control (DMAIC)	Plan, do, study, act (PDSA)
Team leader	Black belt	Champion
Training	Long/formal	Short/informal
Culture change	Usually enforced	Sometimes enforced
Project time frame	Months/years	Days/weeks

The Six Sigma improvement methodology DMAIC involves:

Define	Determine the customers and critical-to-quality procedures
Measure	Identify and measure the quality problem, determine the baseline Sigma, and identify possible influencing factors
Analyze	Test the influencing factors and identify the vital few
Improve	Select the solution method, prove its effectiveness, and implement it
Control	Develop a process control plan

---

[1] Actually 3.4 defects per million corresponds to 4.5σ. The other 1.5σ is to allow process mean to be off-centre by up to 1.5σ.

[2] "Baldrige, Six Sigma, & ISO: Understanding Your Options," http://www.baldrige.nist.gov/Issue_Sheet_Options.htm, Summer 2002; J. Bossert et al., "Your Opinion: Are Six Sigma and Lean Manufacturing Really Different?," *ASQ Six Sigma Forum Magazine* 2(1), November 2002, pp. 38–43.

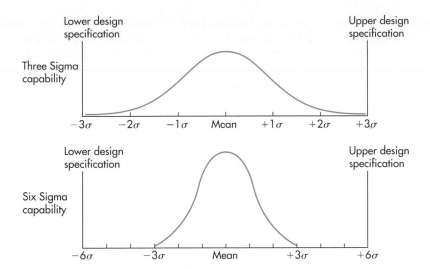

Figure 10-13

Three Sigma versus Six Sigma capability. (Blue curves show the process output; note x-axis scales are different in the two charts.)

For two applications of Six Sigma quality in banks, see the "The Global Six Sigma Award" OM in Action.

Example 10

The North Shore-Long Island Jewish Health System[3] consists of several hospitals and nursing homes around New York City. A central lab performs blood tests for the health system as well as for other private clinics. The Six Sigma consultants are housed in the Center for Learning and Innovation of the health system. Although the health system has a very large and capable Quality Management Department, the Six Sigma group decided to remain separate. The Six Sigma group focuses on chronic issues that cannot be solved easily and uses systematic statistical and change management techniques.

One project the Six Sigma group worked on in 2002/2003 was the labelling of test specimens in the central lab. The tests are done by automated machines, so most errors occur before the test. The critical-to-quality procedures for labelling are (a) receiving the requisition of blood test and specimen, (b) entering patient information into the computer, (c) delivering the specimen to the automated machines, (d) obtaining results, and (e) sending the results to the requisitioner.

The Six Sigma team consisted of some members of the Six Sigma group, lab management, and representatives from Compliance, Quality, and Marketing. The objective was to reduce the errors and missing data. The data accompanying the specimens were patient name, social security number, date of birth, gender, physician's name, name of test, and a code name for the diagnosis.

The percentage of errors and omissions was 5 percent. The major problem was identified to be omission of the code name for diagnosis. The solution was rather simple: a pocket guide to the diagnosis code for the requisioners. This reduced the error and omission rate to 0.7 percent.

To further reduce labelling errors and omissions, the next common error (approximately 50 percent of remaining errors or omissions) was identified as the social security number. A pattern was easily found: most of these errors originated from units that used a special set of codes (called addressograph) which presented the information in a confusing way. Again, an easy solution was discovered: peel off the bar code at the bottom of patient's chart and attach it to the requisition.

The team also performed a benchmarking study of the productivity of the labelling staff (accessioners). A labeller prepared an average of 17 labels per hour, whereas the industry norm was 20. Although some workers were faster than the others, there was no statistically significant difference in their productivity. The team decided to look at the method

---

[3]N.B. Riebling et al., "Toward Error Free Lab Work," *ASQ Six Sigma Forum Magazine* 4(1), 2004, pp. 23–29.

of labelling. A meeting of all staff was called. Their opinion was that there was quite a bit of walking and moving involved and sometimes it was confusing to find the right machines for the particular test needed for a specimen. Solutions suggested were (a) provide a colour-coded book of tests and machines that perform each, (b) put up same colour signs over machines, and (c) employ a runner to move the batch of specimens to the machines. The team decided to try these and also to create a position of lead labeller who would take 20 requisitions/specimen per hour to each labeller and answer any questions they might have.

An experiment was designed to measure the influence of (a) using barcodes, (b) expertise of individual labellers (accessioners), and (c) the new work process (called distribution) on the productivity of labellers. This is done by collecting data under various levels of the factors above. The results are shown in the figure below.

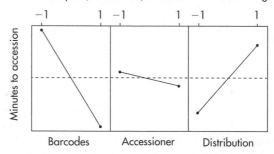

Main effects plot (data means) for minutes to accessioning

As can be seen, the use of barcodes (barcodes = 1) and the new work process (distribution = −1) reduces minutes to accession, i.e., increases productivity. Finally, the individual unit and moving range control charts were constructed to monitor the productivity of each labeller. Productivity has been improving and has exceeded 20 labels per hour per accessioner.

Design of Experiments

design of experiments

Performing experiments by changing levels of factors to measure their influence on output and identifying best levels for each factor.

Design of experiments involves performing experiments by changing levels of factors to measure their influence on output and identifying best levels for each factor. However, if this is done by changing the level of one factor at a time, while keeping the levels of other factors constant, an extremely large number of experiments will be required.

Factorial design suggests a more concise set of experiments by changing the level of more than one factor at a time. For example, suppose we have three factors, each having two levels. Then, if we change one factor's level at a time, in order to determine the best levels for each factor, we will need $2^3 = 8$ different experiments. However, factorial design suggests that, in this case, the following four experiments are adequate (the body of the table shows the level of each factor; this is called fractional factorial design):[4]

	Experiment			
Factor	**(i)**	**(ii)**	**(iii)**	**(iv)**
A	1	1	2	2
B	1	2	1	2
C	1	2	2	1

In general, the number of experiments (runs) one needs to perform, given the number of factors (at 2 levels), are given on the next page, where white (and one black) cells are for full factorial experiments (which can also identify interaction between factors) and other colours show progressively more restrictive analyses (green, yellow, and red, respectively) whose results may be less reliable. For example, a full factorial experiment with 4 factors (at 2 levels) requires 16 experiments (runs).

---

[4]G.S. Peace, *Taguchi Methods* (Reading, Massachusetts: Addison-Wesley, 1993).

Runs	2	3	4	5	6	7	8	9
4	2^2	2^{2-1}_{III}						
8		2^3	2^{4-1}_{IV}	2^{5-2}_{III}	2^{6-3}_{III}	2^{7-4}_{III}		
16			2^4	2^{5-1}_{V}	2^{6-2}_{IV}	2^{7-3}_{IV}	2^{8-4}_{IV}	2^{9-5}_{III}
32				2^5	2^{6-1}_{VI}	2^{7-2}_{IV}	2^{8-3}_{IV}	2^{9-4}_{IV}
64					2^6	2^{7-1}_{VII}	2^{8-2}_{V}	2^{9-3}_{IV}
128						2^7	2^{8-1}_{VIII}	2^{9-2}_{VI}
256							2^8	2^{9-1}_{IX}
512								2^9

Example 11

In the early 1990s, Navistar's Indianapolis engine plant had a problem with the flatness of its cylinder heads (the top part of the engines). The specification width was a lot smaller than process variability, rendering the process incapable. The final machining operation shaved a small amount of metal from the top of cylinder heads. The variation in the flatness resulting from this operation needed to be reduced. Possible factors were thought to be:

a. Feed rate for broach that shaved the metal

b. The thickness of metal removed

c. The pressure of clamp holding the cylinder head down

For each factor, two levels were determined:

a. (1 = 80 feet/minute, 2 = 120 feet/minute)

b. (1 = .020 inch, 2 = .0028 inch)

c. (1 = 600 pounds, 2 = 500 pounds)

Four experiments were used (see the design given on the previous page). Each experiment (i) to (iv) was repeated six times in order to improve the accuracy of the results. For example, in the first experiment, all factors were set to level 1. For each cylinder head produced, the height of 32 points on its flat surface was measured and the difference between the maximum height and the minimum height was calculated. This high-low difference was averaged over the six pieces produced using the same experiment. The results are:

	Experiment			
	(i)	**(ii)**	**(iii)**	**(iv)**
Average high-low difference (in 1/10,000 inch):	33.32	45.93	25.88	27.17

From these results, the influence of each level of each factor can be determined. For example, Factor 1, level 1 was used in experiments (i) and (ii). Therefore, its average high-low difference is (33.32+45.93)/2 = 39.62. The other results were calculated in a similar manner:

Factor	Level 1	Level 2
a	39.62	26.52
b	29.60	36.55
c	30.24	35.90

It can be shown that the levels of all three factors have significant influence on average high-low difference. Therefore, to reduce the variation in cylinder head flatness, this operation should use Level 2 of factor *a* (i.e., 120 feet/minute tool speed), Level 1 of

Factor *b* (i.e., remove .020 inch metal), and Level 1 of Factor *c* (i.e., use 600 pounds of clamp pressure). This will reduce the variation in flatness as much as possible.

Source: Based on R.W. Schmenner, *Production/Operations Management*, 5th ed. (New York: MacMillan, 1993, pp. 118–119).

Summary

This chapter describes statistical process control planning process, statistical process control and control charts, process capability, and Six Sigma quality. Key issues in statistical process control planning include defining the quality characteristic, where to inspect in the process, how much to inspect, whether to inspect on-site or in a laboratory, and the corrective action plan.

Statistical process control focuses on detecting departures from stability in a process. Control charts are commonly used for this. There are two types of variations: random and assignable. Several types of control charts are described in the chapter: sample mean and range, individual unit and moving range, *p*- and *c*-charts. Process capability analysis is used to determine if the output of a process will satisfy design specification. Six Sigma quality is the approach that improves process capability to very high levels (3.4 defects per million). Design of experiments is a major tool in Six Sigma quality. Factorial design provides an efficient method for design of experiments. Figure 10-14 can be used to choose the right control chart. Table 10-3 provides a summary of formulas.

Figure 10-14
Choosing the right control chart

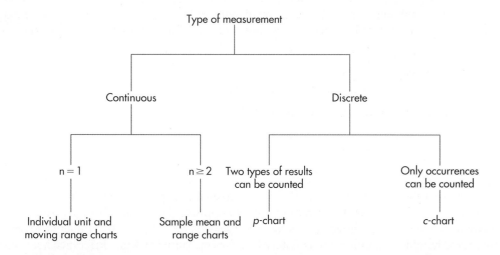

Table 10-3
Summary of formulas

Control Charts		
Name	**Symbol**	**Control Limits**
Sample mean	$\bar{x}$	$\bar{\bar{x}} \pm z \dfrac{\sigma}{\sqrt{n}}$ or $\bar{\bar{x}} \pm A_2\bar{R}$
Sample range	R	$UCL = D_4\bar{R},\ \ LCL = D_3\bar{R}$
Sample proportion of defectives	P	$\bar{p} \pm z\sqrt{\dfrac{\bar{p}(1-\bar{p})}{n}}$
Sample number of defects	C	$\bar{c} \pm z\sqrt{\bar{c}}$
Process Capability		
Name	**Symbol**	**Formula**
Capability index for a centred process	C_p	$\dfrac{\text{Design specification width}}{6\sigma \text{ of process}}$
Capability index for a non-centred process	C_{pk}	Smaller of $\left\{\begin{array}{l}\dfrac{\text{Process mean} - \text{Lower design specification}}{3\sigma} \\[2mm] \dfrac{\text{Upper design specification} - \text{process mean}}{3\sigma}\end{array}\right.$

Key Terms

Solved Problems

Process distribution and sampling distribution. An industrial process makes 3 feet plastic pipes with an average inside diameter of 1 inch and a standard deviation of .05 inch.

Problem 1

a. If you randomly select one piece of pipe, what is the probability that its inside diameter will exceed 1.02 inches, assuming that the process distribution is Normal?

b. If you select a random sample of 25 pieces of pipes, what is the probability that the sample mean will exceed 1.02 inches?

Solution

$\mu = 1.00$, $\sigma = .05$

a. $z = \dfrac{x - \mu}{\sigma} = \dfrac{1.02 - 1.00}{.05} = .4$

Using Appendix B, Table A, $P(z > .4) = .5000 - .1554 = .3446$.

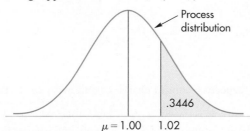

b. $z = \dfrac{\bar{x} - \mu}{\sigma / \sqrt{n}} = \dfrac{1.02 - 1.00}{.05 / \sqrt{25}} = 2.00$

Using Appendix B, Table A, $P(z > 2.00) = .5000 - .4772 = .0228$.

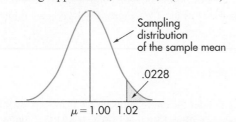

Control charts for sample mean and range. Processing new accounts at a bank is intended to average 10 minutes each. Five samples of four observations each have been taken. Use the sample data below in conjunction with Table 10-2 to construct upper and lower control limits for both sample mean and sample range control charts. Do the results suggest that the process is in control?

Problem 2

	Sample 1	Sample 2	Sample 3	Sample 4	Sample 5
	10.2	10.3	9.7	9.9	9.8
	9.9	9.8	9.9	10.3	10.2
	9.8	9.9	9.9	10.1	10.3
	10.1	10.4	10.1	10.5	9.7
Totals	40.0	40.4	39.6	40.8	40.0

Solution

a. Determine the mean and range of each sample.

$$\bar{x} = \frac{\sum x}{n}, \quad \text{Range} = \text{Largest} - \text{Smallest}$$

Sample	Mean	Range
1	$40.0/4 = 10.0$	$10.2 - 9.8 = .4$
2	$40.4/4 = 10.1$	$10.4 - 9.8 = .6$
3	$39.6/4 = 9.9$	$10.1 - 9.7 = .4$
4	$40.8/4 = 10.2$	$10.5 - 9.9 = .6$
5	$40.0/4 = 10.0$	$10.3 - 9.7 = .6$

b. Calculate the average sample mean and average sample range:

$$\bar{\bar{X}} = \frac{10.0 + 10.1 + 9.9 + 10.2 + 10.0}{5} = \frac{50.2}{5} = 10.04$$

$$\bar{R} = \frac{.4 + .6 + .4 + .6 + .6}{5} = \frac{2.6}{5} = .52$$

Note that one can use Excel to compute these quantities. For average, " = average(cells)" should be used where "cells" is the coordinates of cells where data are located. For example, if data are in cells A2 to A5, then use "= average(A2:A5)." Similarly, for range, "max(A2:A5) – min(A2:A5)" should be used.

c. Obtain factors A_2, D_4, and D_3 from Table 10-2 for $n = 4$: $A_2 = .73$, $D_4 = 2.28$, $D_3 = 0$.

d. Calculate upper and lower limits:

$$\text{UCL}_{\bar{x}} = \bar{\bar{x}} + A_2\bar{R} = 10.04 + .73(.52) = 10.42$$
$$\text{LCL}_{\bar{x}} = \bar{\bar{x}} - A_2\bar{R} = 10.04 - .73(.52) = 9.66$$
$$\text{UCL}_R = D_4\bar{R} = 2.28(.52) = 1.19$$
$$\text{LCL}_R = D_3\bar{R} = 0(.52) = 0$$

e. Plot sample means and ranges on their respective control charts, or otherwise verify that points are within limits.

All sample means (10.0, 10.1, 9.9, 10.2, 10.0) are larger that LCL of $\bar{X}$ (9.66) and smaller than UCL of $\bar{X}$ (10.42). Similarly, all sample ranges (.4, .6, .4, .6, .6) are larger than LCL of R(0) and smaller than UCL of R(1.19). Hence, the process is in control.

Problem 3

Type I error (alpha risk). After several investigations of points outside control limits revealed nothing, a manager began to wonder about the probability of the Type I error for the control limits used, which were based on $z = 1.90$.

a. Determine the alpha risk for this value of z.

b. What z would provide an alpha risk of about 2 percent?

Solution

a. Using Appendix B, Table A, we find that the area under the curve between $z = 0$ and $z = +1.90$ is .4713. Therefore, the area (probability) of values within 1.90 to +1.90 is 2(.4713) = .9426, and the area beyond these values is $1 - .9426 = .0574$. Hence, the alpha risk is 5.74 percent.

b. Because half of the risk lies in each tail, the area under the curve between $z = 0$ and the value of z you are looking for is .49. The closest value is .4901 for $z = 2.33$. Thus, control limits based on $z = 2.33$ provide an alpha risk of about 2 percent.

Problem 4

p-chart and c-chart. Using the appropriate control chart, determine Two Sigma control limits for each case:

a. An inspector found an average of 3.9 scratches in the exterior paint of each of the automobiles being prepared for shipment to dealers.

b. Before shipping lawn mowers to dealers, an inspector attempts to start each mower and notes the ones that do not start on the first try. The lot size is 100 mowers, and an average of 4 did not start on the first try based on a few samples (4 percent).

Solution

The choice between these two types of control charts relates to whether *two* types of results can be counted (*p*-chart) or whether *only occurrences* can be counted (*c*-chart).

a. The inspector can count only the scratches that occurred, not the ones that did not occur. Consequently, a *c*-chart is appropriate. The sample average is 3.9 scratches per car. Two Sigma control limits are found using the formulas

$$UCL = \bar{c} + z\sqrt{\bar{c}}$$
$$LCL = \bar{c} - z\sqrt{\bar{c}}$$

where $\bar{c} = 3.9$ and $z = 2$. Thus,

$$UCL = 3.9 + 2\sqrt{3.9} = 7.85 \text{ scratches}$$
$$LCL = 3.9 - 2\sqrt{3.9} = -.05, \text{ So the lower limit is 0 scratches}$$

b. The inspector can count both the lawn mowers that started and those that did not start. Consequently, a *p*-chart is appropriate. Two Sigma control limits can be calculated using the following:

$$UCL = \bar{p} + z\sqrt{\frac{\bar{p}(1-\bar{p})}{n}}$$
$$LCL = \bar{p} - z\sqrt{\frac{\bar{p}(1-\bar{p})}{n}}$$

where
$\bar{p} = .04$
$n = 100$
$z = 2$

Thus,

$$UCL = .04 + 2\sqrt{\frac{.04(.96)}{100}} = .079$$
$$LCL = .04 - 2\sqrt{\frac{.04(.96)}{100}} = .001$$

Problem 5

Determine if these three processes are capable:

Process	Mean	Standard Deviation	Lower Spec	Upper Spec
1	7.5	.10	7.0	8.0
2	4.6	.12	4.3	4.9
3	6.0	.14	5.5	6.7

Solution

Notice that the means of the first two processes are exactly in the centre of the upper and lower specs. Hence, the C_p index (Formula 10-9) is appropriate. However, the third process is not centred, so C_{pk} (Formula 10-10) is appropriate.

$$\text{For processes 1 and 2: } C_p = \frac{\text{Upper spec} - \text{Lower spec}}{6\sigma}$$

In order to be capable, C_p must be at least 1.0.

$$\text{Process 1: } \quad C_p = \frac{8.0 - 7.0}{6(.10)} = 1.67 \text{ (capable)}$$

$$\text{Process 2: } \quad C_p = \frac{4.9 - 4.3}{6(.12)} = 0.83 \text{ (not capable)}$$

For Process 3, C_{pk} must be at least 1.0. It is the lesser of these two:

$$\frac{\text{Upper spec} - \text{Mean}}{3\sigma} = \frac{6.7 - 6.0}{3(.14)} = 1.67$$

$$\frac{\text{Mean} - \text{Lower spec}}{3\sigma} = \frac{6.0 - 5.5}{3(.14)} = 1.19$$

$$\text{Minimum } \{1.67, 1.19\} = 1.19 > 1.0 \rightarrow \text{capable.}$$

Discussion and Review Questions

1. What is statistical quality control and why is it important? (LO1)

2. List the steps in the statistical process control planning process. (LO1)

3. Answer these questions about inspection: (LO1)

    a. What level of inspection is optimal?
    b. What are the main considerations in choosing between centralized inspection and on-site inspection?
    c. What points are potential candidates for inspection?

4. What are the key concepts that underlie the construction and interpretation of control charts? (LO2)

5. What is the purpose of a control chart? (LO2)

6. Classify each of the following as either a Type I or a Type II error: (LO2)

    a. Putting an innocent person in jail.
    b. Releasing a guilty person from jail.

7. Why is order of observation important in control charts? (LO2)

8. What are the steps for designing a control chart? (LO2)

9. Briefly explain the purpose of each of these control charts: (LO2)

    a. $\bar{x}$
    b. R
    c. Individual unit
    d. Moving range
    e. p
    f. c

10. Why are $\bar{x}$ and R charts used together? (LO2)

11. If all the observations are within control limits, does that guarantee that the process variation contains only randomness? (LO2)

12. Identify a process in a bank and one in a retail store that control charts can be used to monitor. (LO2)

13. Define and contrast control limits and design specification limits. (LO3)

14. A customer has recently tightened the design specification for a part your company supplies. The design specification is now much tighter than the machine being used for the job is capable of. Briefly identify alternatives you might consider to resolve this problem. (LO3)

15. Define and contrast C_p and C_{pk}. (LO3)

16. Can the value of C_{pk} exceed the value of C_p for the same process and specification limits? Explain. (LO3)

17. A process can be capable but out of control. Another process can be in control but incapable. Explain. (LO2 & 3)

18. What is Six Sigma quality and how does it differ from continuous improvement's PDSA? (LO4)

19. What is design of experiments and why is it useful for Six Sigma quality? (LO4)

Taking Stock

1. What trade-offs are involved in each of these decisions?

    a. Deciding whether to use Two Sigma or Three Sigma control limits. (LO2)

    b. Choosing between a large sample size and a smaller sample size. (LO1)

2. Who needs to be involved in statistical process control (SPC)? (LO1)

3. Name two ways that technology has had an impact on SPC. (LO1)

4. What kind of ethical issues arise in SPC when the operators are put in charge of quality control at their own workstations? How can these concerns be addressed? Explain. (LO1)

Critical Thinking Exercise

Analysis of the output of a process has suggested that the variability was non-random on several occasions recently. However, each time the investigation has not revealed any assignable causes. What are some of the possible explanations for not finding any causes? What should the manager do? (LO3)

Experiential Learning Exercise

Obtain approximately 10 small bags of M&M candies (multicoloured), or similar candies. Arrange the unopened bags in a single row, and treat each bag as a sample from an ongoing process, in the order you have placed them. Treat the yellow candies (or another colour that is the fewest in number in each bag) as defects. (LO1, 2, 3)

a. List the four or five steps needed to obtain sample information for each bag, beginning with opening the bag.

b. Determine the upper and lower control limits for the sample proportion of defectives using Three Sigma control limits. Note: the number of candies in each bag may not be exactly the same. You can ignore that.

c. Is the process variation random? Explain how you reached your conclusion.

Internet Exercises

1. Visit http://jobs.isixsigma.com, choose a job announcement related to Six Sigma quality, and describe the job description. (LO4)

2. Visit http://www.qualitymag.com, find the case study from the current issue (under Departments on the lower right side) and summarize it. (LO1)

3. Visit http://www.tgssa.com, register, then look into the case studies. Find one Six Sigma project and summarize it. (LO4)

4. Visit http://www.statease.com/pubs/breaddoe.pdf and summarize the design of experiment to determine the ingredients for bread. (LO4)

Problems

1. Design specification for a motor housing states that it should weigh between 24 and 25 kgs. The process that produces the housing yields a mean of 24.5 kg and a standard deviation of .2 kg. The distribution of output is Normal. (LO2 & 4)

   a. What percentage of housings will not meet the design specification?

   b. Within what values should 95.44 percent of sample means of this process fall if samples of $n = 16$ are taken?

2. An automatic filling machine is used to fill two-litre bottles of cola. The machine's output is known to be approximately Normal with a mean of 2.0 litres and a standard deviation of .01 litre. Output is monitored using means of samples of five observations. (LO2)

   a. Determine the upper and lower control limits that will include roughly 95.5 percent of the sample means.

   b. If the means for 6 samples are: 2.005, 2.001, 1.998, 2.002, 1.995, and 1.999, is the process in control?

3. Process time at a workstation is monitored using sample mean and range control charts. Six samples of $n = 10$ observations have been obtained and the sample means and ranges computed (in minutes): (LO2)

Sample	Mean	Range
1	3.06	.42
2	3.15	.50
3	3.11	.41
4	3.13	.46
5	3.06	.46
6	3.09	.45

   a. Using the factors in Table 10-2, determine the upper and lower limits for sample mean and range control charts.

   b. Is the process in control?

4. Six samples of five observations each have been taken of 80 kg concrete slabs produced by a machine, and the results are displayed below. (LO2)

   a. Using factors from Table 10-2, determine the upper and lower control limits for sample mean and range, and decide if the process is in control.

   b. A new sample results in the following slab weights: 81.0, 81.0, 80.8, 80.6, and 80.5. Use the control limits determined in part a to decide if the process is still in control.

			Sample			
	1	**2**	**3**	**4**	**5**	**6**
	79.2	80.5	79.6	78.9	80.5	79.7
	78.8	78.7	79.4	79.4	79.6	80.6
	80.0	81.0	80.4	79.7	80.4	80.5
	78.4	80.4	80.3	79.4	80.8	80.0
	81.0	80.1	80.8	80.6	78.8	81.1

5. In a refinery, the octane rating of gasoline produced is measured by taking one observation from each batch. Twenty observations follow. (LO2)

   a. Construct Three Sigma control charts for the individual unit and moving range. Is the process in control?[5]

---

[5]Adapted from Amitava Mitra. *Fundamentals of Quality Control and Improvement*, 2nd ed. (Englewood Cliffs, NJ: Prentice Hall, 1998).

b. A new batch has octane rating of 94.0. Using the control charts in part a, is the process still in control?

Observation Number	Octane Rating	Observation Number	Octane Rating
1	89.2	11	85.4
2	86.5	12	91.6
3	88.4	13	87.7
4	91.8	14	85.0
5	90.3	15	91.5
6	87.5	16	90.3
7	92.6	17	85.6
8	87.0	18	90.9
9	89.8	19	82.1
10	92.2	20	85.8

6. Using four samples of 200 credit card statements each, an auditor found the following number of erroneous statements in each sample: (LO2)

	Sample			
	1	2	3	4
Number of errors	4	2	5	9

   a. Determine the proportion of defectives in each sample.

   b. If the true proportion of defectives for this process is unknown, what is your best estimate of it?

   c. What is your estimate of the mean and standard deviation of the sampling distribution of the sample proportion of defectives for samples of 200?

   d. What control limits would give an alpha risk of .03 for this process?

   e. What alpha risk would control limits of .047 and .003 provide?

   f. Using control limits of .047 and .003, is the process in control?

   g. Suppose that the long-term proportion of defectives of the process is known to be 2 percent. What are the values of the mean and standard deviation of the sampling distribution?

   h. Construct a p-control chart for the process, assuming a proportion of defectives of 2 percent, and Two Sigma control limits. Is the process in control?

7. A medical facility does MRIs for sports injuries. Occasionally a test yields inconclusive results and must be repeated. Using the following 13 sample results for the number of retests in $n = 200$ observations each, construct a control chart for the proportion of retests using Two Sigma limits. Is the process in control? (LO2)

	Sample												
	1	2	3	4	5	6	7	8	9	10	11	12	13
Number of retests	1	2	2	0	2	1	2	0	2	7	3	2	1

$= 25$

8. The administrator of a small town received a certain number of complaints during the last two weeks. (LO2)

   a. Construct a control chart with Three Sigma limits for the number of complaints received each day using the following data. Is the process in control?

   b. If 16 complaints are received today (day 15), using the control chart of part a, is there a change in the average number of complaints per day?

Day														
	1	**2**	**3**	**4**	**5**	**6**	**7**	**8**	**9**	**10**	**11**	**12**	**13**	**14**
Number of complaints	4	10	14	8	9	6	5	12	13	7	6	4	2	10

9. a. Construct a control chart with Three Sigma limits for the number of defects per spool of cable based on the following data. Is the process in control? (LO2)

   b. If a new spool has five defects, using the control chart of part a, has the process changed?

Observation														
	1	**2**	**3**	**4**	**5**	**6**	**7**	**8**	**9**	**10**	**11**	**12**	**13**	**14**
Number of defects	2	3	1	0	1	3	2	0	2	1	3	1	2	0

10. After a number of complaints about its directory assistance, a telephone company examined samples of calls to determine the frequency of wrong numbers given to callers. Each sample consisted of 100 calls. The manager stated that the error rate is about 4 percent. Construct a control chart using 95 percent limits and using $\bar{p} = .04$. Is the process in control? Is the manager's assertion about the error rate correct? Explain. (LO2)

Observation																
	1	**2**	**3**	**4**	**5**	**6**	**7**	**8**	**9**	**10**	**11**	**12**	**13**	**14**	**15**	**16**
Number of errors	5	3	5	7	4	6	8	4	5	9	3	4	5	6	6	7

11. Specification for the diameter of a metal shaft is much wider than the machine used to make the shafts is capable of. Consequently, the decision has been made to allow the cutting tool to wear a certain amount before replacement. The tool wears at the rate of .004 centimetre per metal shaft produced. The process has a natural variation, σ, of .01 centimetre and is Normally distributed. Specification for the diameter of the metal shafts is 15.0 to 15.2 centimetres. How many shafts can the process turn out before tool replacement becomes necessary (i.e., before the process makes an out-of-spec shaft)? (See diagram below.) (LO3)

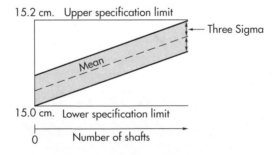

12. Design specification for the concrete slabs in Problem 4 is between 78 and 81 kg.

   a. Based on the data given in Problem 4, is the specification being met? (LO3)

   b. Estimate the process standard deviation from the average range in Problem 4 using formula 10-4. Then, calculate the C_p. Is the process capable? Compare with your answer to part a.

13. The time needed for performing a machining operation is to be investigated. Historically, the process has had a standard deviation equal to .146 minute. The means (in minutes) of 39 samples of $n = 6$ are: (LO2)

Sample	Mean	Sample	Mean	Sample	Mean
1	3.86	14	3.81	27	3.81
2	3.90	15	3.83	28	3.86
3	3.83	16	3.86	29	3.98
4	3.81	17	3.82	30	3.96
5	3.84	18	3.86	31	3.88
6	3.83	19	3.84	32	3.76
7	3.87	20	3.87	33	3.83
8	3.88	21	3.84	34	3.77
9	3.84	22	3.82	35	3.86
10	3.80	23	3.89	36	3.80
11	3.88	24	3.86	37	3.84
12	3.86	25	3.88	38	3.79
13	3.88	26	3.90	39	3.85

Construct an $\bar{x}$-chart for this process with Two Sigma limits. Is the process in control?

14. A company has just negotiated a contract to produce a part for another company. In the process of manufacturing the part, the inside diameter of successive parts becomes smaller and smaller as the cutting tool wears. However, the specification is so wide relative to machine capability that it is possible to set the diameter initially at a large value and let the process run for a while before replacing the cutting tool. (LO3)

   The inside diameter decreases at an average rate of .001 cm per part, and the process has a standard deviation of .01 cm and the variability is approximately Normally distributed. After how many parts must the tool be replaced if the design specification is between 3 cm and 3.5 cm, and the initial setting is 3 standard deviations below the upper design specification?

15. Refer to Solved Problem 2. Suppose that the design specification is between 9.65 and 10.35 minutes. Based on the data given in the Solved Problem 2, does it appear that the design specification is being met? If not, what should one do? (LO3)

16. A technician in a quick oil change shop had the following service times (in minutes) for 20 randomly selected cars: (LO2)

	Sample		
1	**2**	**3**	**4**
4.5	4.6	4.5	4.7
4.2	4.5	4.6	4.6
4.2	4.4	4.4	4.8
4.3	4.7	4.4	4.5
4.3	4.3	4.6	4.9

   a. Determine the mean of each sample.

   b. Estimate the mean and standard deviation of the process.

   c. Estimate the mean and standard deviation of the sampling distribution of the sample mean.

   d. What would Three Sigma control limits for the sample mean be? What alpha risk would they provide?

   e. What alpha risk would control limits of 4.14 and 4.86 for the sample mean provide?

   f. Using the control limits of 4.14 and 4.86, are any sample means beyond these control limits? If so, which one(s)?

   g. Construct the control charts for sample mean and sample range using Table 10-2. Are any sample means and ranges beyond the control limits? If so, which one(s)?

h. Explain why the control limits are different for sample mean in parts *d* and *g*.

i. If the process has a known mean of 4.4 and a known standard deviation of .18, what would Three Sigma control limits be for a sample mean chart? Are any sample means beyond the control limits? If so, which one(s)?

17. A process screens a certain type of potash granules resulting in a mean diameter of .03 cm and a standard deviation of .003 cm. The allowable variation in granule in diameter is from .02 to .04 cm. (LO3)

    a. Calculate the capability ratio C_p for the process.

    b. Is the process capable?

18. Given the following list of machines, the standard deviation for their output, and specification half-width for the job that may be processed on that machine, using C_p determine which machines are capable of performing the given jobs. (LO3)

Machine	Standard Deviation (cm)	Job Half-Width Specification (± cm)
001	.02	.05
002	.04	.07
003	.10	.18
004	.05	.15
005	.01	.04

19. Suppose your manager presents you with the following information about machines that could be used for a job, and wants your recommendation on which one to choose. The design specification width is .48 mm. Calculate the C_p index for each machine, and explain what additional information you will need to make a choice. (LO3)

Machine	Cost per Unit ($)	Standard Deviation (mm)
A	20	.079
B	12	.080
C	11	.084
D	10	.081

20. Each of the processes listed below is non-centred with respect to the design specification. Calculate the C_{pk} index for each, and decide if the process is capable. (LO3)

Process	Process Mean	Process Standard Deviation	Lower Design Specification	Upper Design Specification
H	15.0	.32	14.1	16.0
K	33.0	1.00	30.0	36.5
T	18.5	.50	16.5	20.1

21. As part of an insurance company's training program, participants learn how to conduct a fast but effective analysis of clients' insurability. The goal is to have participants achieve a time less than 45 minutes. There is no minimum time, but the quality of assessment should be acceptable. Test results for three participants were: Armand, a mean of 38 minutes and a standard deviation of 3 minutes; Jerry, a mean of 37 minutes and a standard deviation of 2.5 minutes; and Melissa, a mean of 37.5 minutes and a standard deviation of 2.5 minutes.

    Which of the participants would you judge to be capable? Explain. (LO3)

*22. The following data (in ohms) are the resistance of resistors made on an automated machine. The mean and range of each sample are given in the right two columns, and the mean of sample means and the mean of sample ranges are given below these. (LO2)

    a. Develop sample mean and sample range control charts for resistance of resistors using the first 10 samples. Is the process in control?

    b. Use the control charts developed in part a to decide if the eleventh sample (also given below) indicates an out-of-control situation.

Resistance of Resistors (in Ohms)

Sample	Obs 1	Obs 2	Obs 3	Obs 4	Mean	Range
1	1,010	991	985	986	993.00	25
2	995	996	1,009	994	998.50	15
3	990	1,003	1,015	1,008	1,004.00	25
4	1,015	1,020	1,009	998	1,010.50	22
5	1,013	1,019	1,005	993	1,007.50	26
6	994	1,001	994	1,005	998.50	11
7	989	992	982	1,020	995.75	38
8	1,001	986	996	996	994.75	15
9	1,006	989	1,005	1,007	1,001.75	18
10	992	1,007	1,006	979	996.00	28
					1,000.03	22.30
11	996	1,006	997	989		

*23. Essex Corp. of St. Louis is a small manufacturer of parts for Boeing's Aircraft and Missile Systems. In the late 1990s, Essex was trying to establish a SPC program. Part number 528003-N was typical. The following samples[6] of two were observed for a critical dimension of the part (in inches). The lower specification, nominal, and upper specification values were .4160, .4185, .4210 inches, respectively. (LO2)

a. Is the process capable?

b. Construct sample mean and sample range control charts. Is the process in control?

					Sample					
1	2	3	4	5	6	7	8	9	10	
.4190	.4190	.4180	.4180	.4175	.4180	.4175	.4173	.4183	.4185	
.4190	.4185	.4180	.4179	.4175	.4179	.4175	.4176	.4184	.4185	

*24. When Polaroid reduced the number of quality inspectors and increased operator responsibility for statistical process control in its R2 plant (which made instant film cartridges with 10 films in each) in Waltham, Massachusetts, in 1985, it encountered an unexpected result.[7] Instead of quality improving, it actually got worse. To identify the problem, Bud Rolfs, quality control manager, asked an operator from each shift to sample six observations of the critical characteristics of the product and report these to him. One important characteristic of instant films is the pod weight. A pod is a small capsule at the end of each film that contains chemicals. When the film is pulled out, the pod bursts and releases the chemicals that will develop the film. Too much chemical overdevelops the film and too little underdevelops it. (LO2)

a. Use the following three samples of six observations each (in grams) from the first day of the data collection period to develop a sample mean and sample range control chart for the pod weight. Is the process in control?

b. The first sample from the second day is 2.841, 2.802, 2.802, 2.806, 2.807, and 2.807. Is the process still in control?

Sample	Shift	1	2	3	4	5	6	Average
1	A	2.800	2.799	2.760	2.802	2.805	2.803	2.795
2	B	2.750	2.820	2.850	2.740	2.850	2.790	2.800
3	C	2.768	2.807	2.807	2.804	2.804	2.803	2.799

*25. A small manufacturer of metal ring seals for aircraft engines has been asked by its major customer to implement SPC. One major type of ring requires cutting a one-eighth inch wide slot using a milling machine. The following six samples of five observations each, taken every half hour, are the width of the slots (in inch) made by the milling machine on the rings. (LO2)

---
[6]Data retrieved from S.K. Vermani, "SPC Modified with Percent Tolerance Pre-control Charts," *Quality Progress* 33(10), October 2000, pp. 43–48.
[7]Process Control at Polaroid (A), 1987, HBS case: 9-693-047.

1	2	3	4	5	6
0.1261	0.1259	0.1239	0.1225	0.1259	0.1255
0.1253	0.1263	0.1265	0.1249	0.1243	0.1273
0.1245	0.1247	0.126	0.1265	0.1242	0.1245
0.1249	0.124	0.1257	0.1248	0.1257	0.1268
0.1248	0.1251	0.1243	0.1256	0.1251	0.1263

  a. Set up the sample mean and range control charts for this operation. Is the process in control?

  b. The seventh sample contains the following values: 0.124, 0.1252, 0.1295, 0.1262, and 0.1275. Using the control charts from part a, is the process still in control?

*26. The management of a dried milk manufacturer wanted to evaluate the process capability of its packaging lines. A can line was studied for weight of filled cans. The specification is 974 grams plus or minus 14 grams (including the weight of the can itself). Thirty-five samples of six cans were weighed, and sample mean and range were calculated. The process was in control. The grand mean was 975.7 grams and process standard deviation was 4.7581 grams. (LO3)

  a. Calculate the C_p and C_{pk} ratios. Is the filling line capable?

  b. After changing the wearable parts of the line, including the piston cylinders, 46 samples of 6 cans were weighed. The grand mean was 976.19 grams and process standard deviation was 2.891 grams. Calculate the new values of C_p and C_{pk} ratios. Has the filling line become capable?

*27. Suppose a process capability study was conducted on a punch-press operation. One of the characteristics of interest is the width of the slot having a specification of 0.4040 ± 0.007 inch. Twenty-five samples of five pieces were obtained during a shift, and the sample means and ranges are plotted below. Determine if the process is capable of meeting the specification. (LO3)[8]

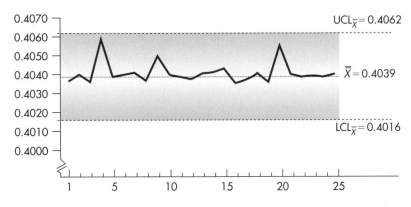

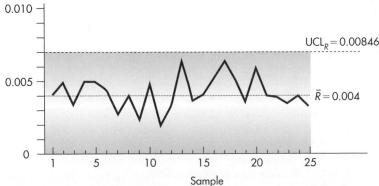

Sample

---

[8]J. Heinricks and M.M.K. Fleming, "Quality Statistical Process Control at Cherry Textron," *Industrial Management*, May/June 1991, 33(3), pp. 7–10.

*28. Royal North Shore Hospital, a 650-bed teaching hospital in Sidney, Australia, uses control charts for quality management.[9] One control chart used shows the number of outpatients waiting more than 30 days for elective surgery (see below). Because the number was increasing (see the plot to the left of X up to 3 months before X), the hospital appointed a waiting list coordinator (3 months before X) who helped reduce the number (see the plot between 3 months before X and Y), and later reduced further by reducing the holidays for elective surgery from six weeks to three weeks during Christmas (see the plot to the right of Y). The control limit lines are 3 standard deviations of the values during each of the 3 subperiods from their centre lines. Determine what type of control chart this is. (LO2)

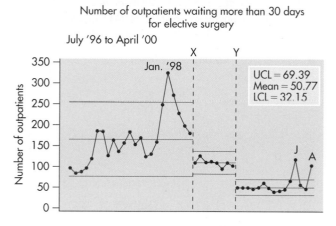

*29. Lexington, Kentucky's Shriners Hospital for children is a small hospital specializing in orthopedics.[10] The chief of staff uses various control charts to monitor the performance of the physicians such as the number of patient days a specific doctor works in a month. For example, see the two charts below for Doctor X. Determine (a) what type of chart the left chart below is and (b) verify the upper control limit for the chart on the right. Note: the upper control limit of the left chart is 3 standard deviation of all the values shown (Jan 02–July 03) from its centre line (the average). (LO2)

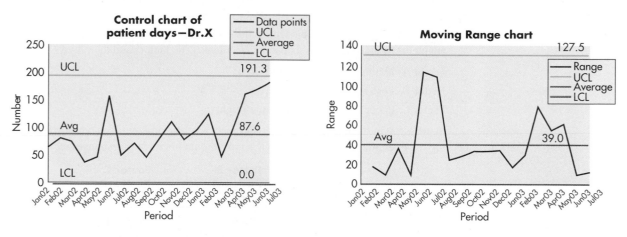

*30. A design of experiments was conducted to study the effect of various factors on the yield and taste of microwave popcorn.[11] The factors and their settings were as follows: (LO4)

---

[9]H.E. Ganley and J. Moxey, "Making Informed Decisions in the Face of Uncertainty," *Quality Progress*, October 2000, 33(10), pp. 76–78.

[10]D.E. Lighter and C.M. Tylkowski, "Case Study: Using Control Charts to Track Physician Productivity," *Physician Executive*, September/October 2004, 30(5), pp. 53–57.

[11]http://www.statease.com/pubs/popcorn.pdf.

Table 1

Factors and Levels

Factor	Low(−1)	High(+1)
Price	Generic	Brand
Time	4 min.	6 min.
Power	Medium	High
Preheat	No	Yes
Elevate	No	Yes

Preheat involves heating water in the microwave for 1 minute prior to popcorn. Elevate means put a plate or something similar under the popcorn bag to raise the bag.

Fractional factorial design was used to obtain two responses: (a) Bullets = weight of non-popped pop corns, in ounces; and (b) taste (a score between 1 and 10, 10 = best).

A	B	C	D	E	Bullets	Taste
−1	−1	−1	−1	1	1.5	7.5
1	−1	−1	−1	−1	1.4	8.0
−1	1	−1	−1	−1	1.9	9.0
1	1	−1	−1	1	0.6	6.5
−1	−1	1	−1	−1	1.8	7.0
1	−1	1	−1	1	0.3	7.5
−1	1	1	−1	1	0.2	2.5
1	1	1	−1	−1	0.9	1.0
−1	−1	−1	1	−1	1.7	7.0
1	−1	−1	1	1	0.8	6.0
−1	1	−1	1	1	0.6	4.5
1	1	−1	1	−1	0.9	4.0
−1	−1	1	1	1	0.6	9.0
1	−1	1	1	−1	1.3	7.5
−1	1	1	1	−1	Missing	—
1	1	1	1	1	Missing	—

The last two experiments were botched and produced no results.

Determine the influence of each level of each factor on each response and prescribe the best levels for each response (Bullets to be minimized and Taste to be maximized).

*31. Stat-Ease Inc, the producer of a Design of Experiments software, performed an experiment a few years ago to identify the factors that were important in increasing the response rate of engineers to Stat-Ease workshop announcements. The factors and their levels were:[12]

Factor A: Number of colors (two vs. four)

Factor B: Postcard size (4″ × 6″ vs. 5.5″ × 8.5″)

Factor C: Paper stock (index vs. heavyweight)

Stat-Ease made eight types of its announcement postcard and sent each type to 1/8 of this mailing list of engineers. The levels of each type and number of fax responses received were:

Version	Factor A Number of Colors	Factor B Postcard Size	Factor C Postcard Thickness	Response
1	2-colour (−)	4″ × 6″ (−)	Index (−)	34
2	4-colour (+)	4″ × 6″ (−)	Index (−)	18
3	2-colour (−)	5.5″ × 8.5″ (+)	Index (−)	44
4	4-colour (+)	5.5″ × 8.5″ (+)	Index (−)	26
5	2-colour (−)	4″ × 6″ (−)	Heavyweight (+)	26
6	4-colour (+)	4″ × 6″ (−)	Heavyweight (+)	17
7	2-colour (−)	5.5″ × 8.5″ (+)	Heavyweight (+)	29
8	4-colour (+)	5.5″ × 8.5″ (+)	Heavyweight (+)	21

---

[12]Source: http://www.statease.com/pubs/marketingvoodoo.pdf.

Determine the influence of each level of each factor on the response and prescribe the best levels for each factor. What do you recommend Stat-Ease should do? (LO4)

*32. A chocolate manufacturer makes a variety of chocolate products including large chocolate bars (340 grams) and boxes of six smaller chocolate bars (170 grams in total). (LO3)

    a. Specification for a large bar is 330 grams to 350 grams. What is the largest standard deviation (in grams) that the machine that fills the bar moulds can have and still be considered capable if its average fill is 340 grams?

    b. The machine that fills the bar moulds for the smaller bars has a standard deviation of .80 grams. The filling machine is set to deliver an average of 28.5 grams per bar. Specification for the 6-bar box is 160 to 180 grams. Is the process capable? Hint: The variance of the box's weight is equal to six times the variance of each smaller bar's weight.

    c. What is the lowest setting (in grams) for the smaller-bar filling machine that will leave the process for the 6-bar box capable?

MINI-CASE

Cereal Manufacturer

The plant manager of a cereal manufacturer is wondering if the company could save some cereal by slightly lowering the cereal content of each box. Studying a major product, a 454 gram (net weight) ready-to-eat cereal, he discovers that four boxes are routinely taken from the filling machine every 10 minutes and weighed. Data for approximately 2.5 hours of inspection are shown below.

Questions

1. Is the process in control?
2. Determine what weight the filler head is likely set to.
3. If the *Weights and Measures Act* dictates that the tolerance for weight of a product of approximately 454 grams is 2 grams, what is the probability that an inspector will find a legally defined underweight box (i.e., weighing less than 452 grams)?
4. Has the filler head been set too conservatively? Discuss.

Samples

1	2	3	4	5	6	7	8	9	10	11	12	13	14	15
455.5	456.0	456.0	452.5	456.0	452.0	457.5	454.5	456.0	453.0	455.0	458.0	457.5	458.0	460.0
460.0	455.5	453.0	455.0	456.0	455.0	455.5	453.0	454.0	455.0	457.5	456.0	456.5	453.0	455.5
456.5	456.0	454.0	453.0	455.0	453.0	457.0	453.0	453.0	456.0	456.5	454.5	453.0	456.5	454.5
456.5	456.0	455.0	455.0	454.5	456.0	452.0	458.0	455.0	456.5	456.5	454.0	455.5	456.0	457.0

MINI-CASE   http://company.ingersollrand.com/aboutus/Pages/default.aspx

Quality Control at Ingersoll-Rand

The Ingersoll-Rand plant in Davidson, North Carolina, assembles air compressors for air tools. A few years ago it installed a SPC software that collects critical information about the quality of its air compressors. This made tracking of the percentage of defectives (for each compressor type, components in each compressor, and parts of each component) much easier. Note that percentage defective is just 100 times proportion defective. It also made it possible to monitor these percentages using *p*-charts (sample percentage defective control charts). Using the previous month's percentage defective *p*, Ingersoll-Rand monitored the percentage of defective compressors that it made on each day; if this number was larger than two standard deviations above *p*, Ingersoll-Rand would try to identify the

cause of the most frequent defect and find a solution for it. For example, the portable line showed an increased percentage of defectives on January 6. First the 69 defects were classified according to defect types (see Figure 1): air leaks (30), motors (15), pumps (3), pressure switch (14), cosmetic (2), miscellaneous (3), and bad check valve (2). Given that each of these defects had a control chart in the software, Ingersoll-Rand found out that air leaks' percentage defective was more than two standard deviations above its previous month's percentage defective (3 percent). Then, the company classified the 30 air leak defects by location of air leak (see Figure 2): tanks weld (5), manifold (12), discharge elbow (1), discharge tube (11), and drain valve (1). Using the control charts for each of these, manifold percentage defective was more than two standard deviations above its previous month's percentage defective

(0.7 percent). Having identified the most frequent defect source (air leak from manifold), Ingersoll-Rand contacted the manifold manufacturer and provided this information. The manufacturer found the root cause and fixed the problem. Use of SPC in Ingersoll-Rand facilities continues.

Questions

1. Verify that the percentage of defective portable compressors produced on January 6 was more than twice its standard deviation above the expected proportion (*Hint:* use $\bar{p} = 8\%$ and $n = 578$).

2. Do the same for air leaks (*Hint:* use $\bar{p} = 3\%$ and $n = 578$).

3. Do the same for manifolds (*Hint:* use $\bar{p} = .7\%$ and $n = 578$).

Sources: P.J. Cooper and N. Demos, "Losses Cut 76 Percent with Control Chart System," *Quality* 30(4), April 1991, pp. 22–24. Reprinted with permission from *Quality Magazine*.

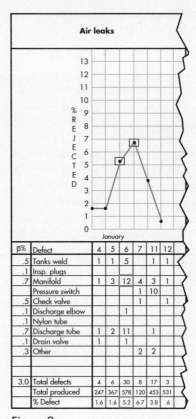

Portable line

p̄%	Defect	4	5	6	7	11	12
3.0	Air leaks	4	6	30	8	17	3
2.6	Motors	4	3	15	6	9	8
.4	Pumps		1	3	1	1	1
.1	Sheaves				1		
.3	Pressure switch	2	3	14			5
.2	Cosmetic			2	1		
1.0	Misc.	2	2	3			
.4	Bad check valve		1	2			2
8.0	Total defects	12	16	69	16	28	19
	Total produced	247	367	578	120	453	531
	% Defect	4.9	4.5	11.9	13.3	6.2	3.6

Figure 1

Portable Line

Air leaks

p̄%	Defect	4	5	6	7	11	12
.5	Tanks weld	1	1	5		1	1
.1	Insp. plugs						
.7	Manifold	1	3	12	4	3	1
	Pressure switch				1	10	
.5	Check valve				1		1
.1	Discharge elbow			1			
.1	Nylon tube						
.7	Discharge tube	1	2	11		1	
.1	Drain valve	1		1			
.3	Other				2	2	
3.0	Total defects	4	6	30	8	17	3
	Total produced	247	367	578	120	453	531
	% Defect	1.6	1.6	5.2	6.7	3.8	.6

Figure 2

Air Leaks

To access "Acceptance Sampling," the supplement to Chapter 10, please visit *Connect*.

CHAPTER 11
Supply Chain Management

Supply chain management refers to collaboration and coordination of the facilities and activities, both within and outside the organization, that make up a value chain, starting from raw material and ending with the consumers, linking across supplier–customer companies.

LEARNING OBJECTIVES

After completing this chapter, you should be able to:

LO1 Explain what a supply chain is, discuss the need to manage a supply chain including outsourcing, and identify strategic and tactical/ operational supply chain activities.

LO2 Describe what logistics is, know how to select a transportation mode, and discuss some fast delivery methods, third-party logistics, reverse logistics, and global supply chains.

LO3 Discuss three technologies used in supply chain management.

LO4 Outline the key steps in creating an effective supply chain, including Collaborative Planning, Forecasting, and Replenishment (CPFR) and performance metrics.

LO5 Explain the purchasing function in organizations.

LO6 Discuss supplier management and partnership.

ygard International, based in Winnipeg, is the largest ladies' wear manufacturer in Canada. Nygard has been very successful and is continuously expanding. When NAFTA was being negotiated, Nygard was one of the few Canadian clothing manufacturers that supported it. Now, while competition from the Far East has threatened most other apparel makers, Nygard is able to compete. How does Nygard do this? It is not just the design of clothing, workmanship, or quality of fabric. It is Nygard's supply chain management.

(LO1) INTRODUCTION

supply chain Sequence of organizations—their facilities and activities—that are involved in producing and delivering a product.

A **supply chain** is the sequence of organizations—their facilities and activities—that are involved in producing and delivering a product. The sequence may begin with suppliers of raw materials and extends all the way to the final customer. Facilities include factories, warehouses/distribution centres, retail outlets, and offices. Activities may include forecasting, product design, facility design, quality assurance, scheduling, purchasing, transportation, inventory management/warehousing, production, distribution/delivery, and customer service. There are two kinds of movement in these systems: the physical movement of material (generally toward the end of the chain, the consumer) and the exchange of information and money (mainly toward the beginning of the chain, the source of material).

The term "chain" in supply chain signifies the importance of close relationship between suppliers and buyers (i.e., inseparable as in a chain). This is a relatively new term, first used approximately two decades ago when quick replenishment systems such as Quick Response were introduced between some retailers and their suppliers (e.g., manufacturers).

Every organization is part of at least one supply chain, and many are part of multiple supply chains. Figure 11-1a illustrates a typical supply chain for a product. Figure 11-1b is the supply chain for Wavefarer Board Shorts by Patagonia, a Los Angeles-based clothing designer and distributor. Note that all manufacturing activities are outsourced to Far East companies (this is called offshoring). In Chapter 1, Figure 1-7, a typical supply chain for a loaf of bread was displayed.

Supply chains are sometimes referred to as value chains, a term that reflects the concept that value is added as goods progress through the chain. Supply or value chains typically comprise separate organizations, rather than just a single organization. However, the objective of a supply chain is that these organizations integrate their activities so that the supply chain acts as one.

supply chain management Collaboration and coordination of all components of the supply chain so that market demand is met as efficiently and effectively as possible.

Supply chain management is collaboration and coordination of the components of the supply chain so that market demand is met as efficiently and effectively as possible.

OM in *ACTION*

Some Examples of Best Supply Chain Practices

In addition to being efficient and fast, a supply chain should be agile (i.e., react quickly to sudden changes in supply or demand), adaptable (i.e., change its structure over time as markets change), and align its members' interests. As an example of agility, Dell Computers continually changes the price of various computers/options so that the components that are abundant are demanded more and those in short supply are demanded less.

As an example of adaptability, Gap Inc. has adapted the supply chains of its three brands (Gap, Old Navy, and Banana Republic) to their competitive attributes (speed and variety, cost, and quality, respectively). Gaps suppliers are in Central America, Old Navy's suppliers are in China, and Banana Republic's suppliers are in Italy. As an example of alignment, R.R. Donnelly, the largest book printer in the world, is sharing the cost savings suggested by its paper and ink suppliers with them.

Source: H.L. Lee, "The Triple-A Supply Chain," *Harvard Business Review*, Oct 2004, pp. 102–112.

a.

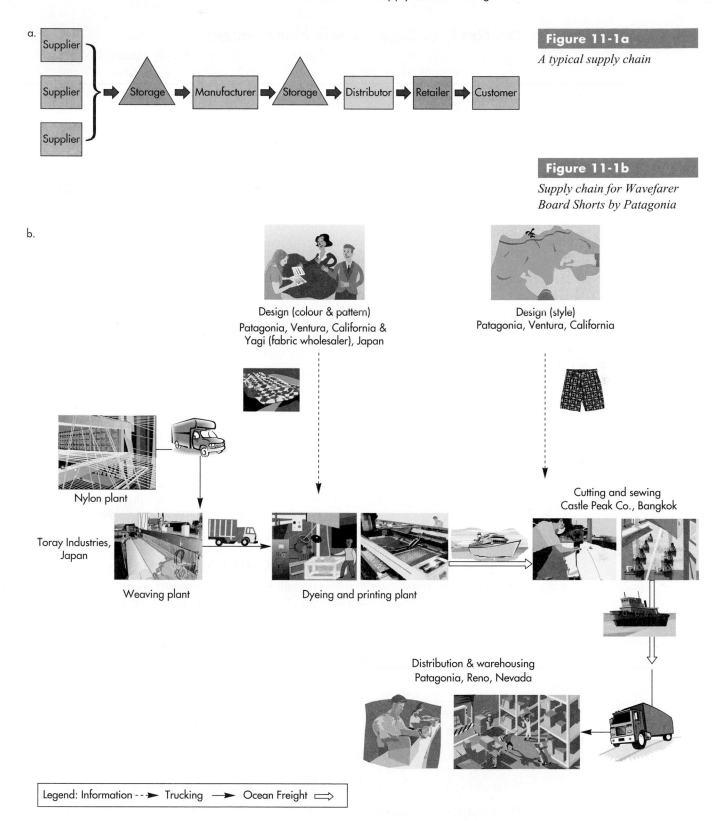

Figure 11-1a
A typical supply chain

Figure 11-1b
Supply chain for Wavefarer Board Shorts by Patagonia

b.

Design (colour & pattern)
Patagonia, Ventura, California &
Yagi (fabric wholesaler), Japan

Design (style)
Patagonia, Ventura, California

Nylon plant

Toray Industries,
Japan

Weaving plant

Dyeing and printing plant

Cutting and sewing
Castle Peak Co., Bangkok

Distribution & warehousing
Patagonia, Reno, Nevada

Legend: Information - - ➤   Trucking ──➤   Ocean Freight ⇨

The same competitive attributes that were given for the products of a company in Chapter 2 are important for supply chains: product cost, timeliness, quality, and service. Therefore, supply chains should be efficient (reduce costs) and effective (meet timeliness and quality requirements). See the "Some Examples of Best Supply Chain Practices" OM in Action for other desirable characteristics of supply chains.

The Need for Supply Chain Management

In the past, most organizations did little to manage their supply chains. Instead, they tended to concentrate on their own operations (silo mentality). However, a number of factors have made it desirable for organizations to actively manage their supply chains. The major factors are:

1. *The need to improve operations.* During the last three decades, many organizations have adopted practices such as Just-In-Time (JIT) and TQM. As a result, they have achieved improved quality while wringing much of the excess costs out of their operations. For many organizations the major gains within their own operations have already been realized. Opportunity now lies largely with procurement, distribution, and logistics—the supply chain.

outsourcing Buying goods or services instead of producing or providing them in-house.

2. *Increasing level of outsourcing.* Organizations are increasing their level of **outsourcing**, buying goods or services instead of producing or providing them in-house (called in-sourcing). As companies are reducing their costs and increasing their product quality, they are focusing on their core activities and subcontracting the others.

   Some companies engage in extensive outsourcing. For example, personal computer manufacturers buy most of their parts from suppliers and merely assemble the computers. Some companies also outsource support services, e.g., data processing, payroll, maintenance, security, legal, and accounting.

   Organizations may outsource for a variety of reasons: a supplier may have lower cost (due to economies of scale), more expertise and knowledge, or patent; demand may be temporary or seasonal; or the company may not have idle capacity. Outsourcing carries some risk: reduction in control and expertise. Strategic considerations may outweigh other factors: companies should in-source those parts or processes that are or should be their core competencies, i.e., long-term organizational capabilities that help the organization to compete.

   In some cases, a company might do both: make a portion of the quantity needed in-house and let a supplier make the rest. The benefits include maintaining expertise and flexibility, and hedging against loss of a supplier or higher prices.

   The following simple example (Example 1) illustrates how one might compare the costs of in-sourcing (make) versus outsourcing (buy) of a part.

   For two applications of outsourcing, see the "Nikon's Supply Chain" OM in Action on the next page and the "Challenger 300" OM in Action later in the chapter.

3. *Increasing globalization.* Increasing globalization has expanded the physical length of supply chains, and the quantity of materials and products being transported.

Example 1

Analyze the following data to determine the total annual cost of in-sourcing (make) and outsourcing (buy) for a part.

	Make (in-source)	Buy (outsource)
Expected annual quantity	20,000 units	20,000 units
Variable cost per unit	$5.00	$6.00
Annual fixed costs	$30,000	

Solution

Total annual cost = Fixed cost + Variable cost per unit × Estimated annual quantity

Make (in-source): $30,000 + $5 × 20,000 = $130,000
Buy (outsource): $0 + $6 × 20,000 = $120,000

In this instance, outsourcing (buy) would save $10,000 a year. This information should be combined with information on other relevant factors to decide which alternative, make or buy, would be better.

OM in ACTION

Nikon's Supply Chain

Nikon manufactures most of its cameras in the Far East. Because of a short product life cycle and high value, Nikon uses air cargo to transport its cameras to North American. Many retail chains require customization of packaging or a kit, e.g., camera, lens, batteries, and a charger. Until recently, after the air cargo arrived from Asia in Los Angeles, the shipment was sent to a contract kitter near LA that took days or weeks to do its job. Then, the shipment was received back, and half was distributed by trucks and the other half put on a plane to New York City. Now, Nikon has a contract with UPS, which transports the shipment from Asia directly to its hub in Louisville, Kentucky, and performs kitting in its facility there. Then it distributes the shipments in North America. UPS also provides customs brokerage service, advance shipping notice, and real-time tracking to Nikon. This integrated supply chain has reduced the total delivery time to 2–3 days.

Source: R. Morton, "Keeping the Supply Chain in Focus," *Logistic Today*, Jul 2007, pp. 12–15.

4. *Increasing e-commerce.* Increasing e-commerce has resulted in more Internet purchasing, which requires more and faster package delivery/logistics services.

5. *The need to manage inventories across the supply chain.* Inventories play a major role in the success or failure of a supply chain, so it is important to coordinate inventory levels throughout a supply chain. Shortages can severely disrupt the timely flow of work and have far-reaching impacts, while excess inventories add unnecessary holding costs. It would not be unusual to find inventory shortages in some parts of a supply chain and excess inventories in the other parts of the same supply chain.

The **bullwhip effect** or demand amplification is the phenomenon in which the demand variability progressively increases for companies upstream in the supply chain. While the demand at a retail store for a particular product is fairly stable, the demand at the wholesaler/distribution centre (DC) is more variable, containing large spikes and wavelike patterns. These variations are even more magnified at the manufacturer. Clearly, the bullwhip effect causes inefficiencies at the manufacturer and DC, such as excess inventory holding cost and overtime, and leads to lower customer service.

> **bullwhip effect** Demand variability is progressively larger moving backward through a supply chain.

Causes of the bullwhip effect range from using large order quantities downstream to slow reactions to changes in demand upstream (due to lack of demand visibility and large lead times). The slow reactions can be part of the demand forecasting/production control system. For example, time series methods have a lag and the effect of one jump in demand endures for many future periods. Also, production decisions are affected by inventory on hand, which, together with lead-time delays, can result in bad decisions. Other causes are manufacturer price discounts that lead to surges in demand, and gaming by retailers when there is a shortage by inflating their orders in anticipation of receiving only a portion of them.

Figure 11-2 shows the orders received by HP for its inkjet printers from a computer reseller (a retail chain) and the actual sales of the reseller. It can be observed that while the final customer demand for HP inkjet printers is fairly stable, the orders placed by the reseller have spikes and dips, which make order forecasting difficult for HP.

Effective supply chain management offers numerous benefits. For example, Campbell Soup doubled its inventory turnover rate and Hewlett-Packard cut deskjet printer supply costs by 75 percent.[1] Also, effective supply chain management helped Walmart become the largest and most profitable retailer in the world, Dell to become the second largest computer company (HP is the largest), and Amazon.com to become the largest e-tailer.

---

[1]Marshall Fisher, "What Is the Right Supply Chain for Your Product?" *Harvard Business Review*, March/April 1997, pp. 105–116.

Figure 11-2

Order amplification relative to sales of a reseller (retail chain) of HP inkjet printers

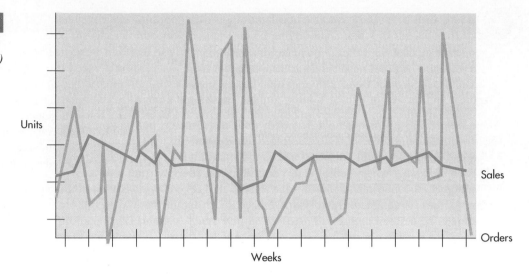

Units

Sales

Orders

Weeks

OM in ACTION   http://www.midas.ca

Midas Canada

Midas Canada's approximately 240 auto service shops, mostly franchises, repair mainly mufflers. The mufflers are mainly produced in Midas factories in the United States and trucked to Canada. Midas Canada has three distribution centres (DC) in Toronto, Montreal, and Vancouver, and two third-party-operated DCs in Edmonton and Moncton. Before 1997, Toronto's DC, located in Agincourt under the same roof as the national headquarters, supplied all the other DCs as well as repair shops in Ontario and Manitoba. In 1997, the installation of better forecasting/inventory control software enabled Midas Canada to have most manufacturers ship directly to the other four DCs. This reduced the total shipment cost by 12 percent and speeded up deliveries to the other four DCs. Direct shipment is an example of "dis-intermediation," one way to reduce costs in supply chains.

Source: G. Guidoni, "Midas Touch: Forecasting Software Installation Pays Off for Auto Service Giant," *Materials Management & Distribution* 42(5), May 1997, pp. 16–19.

Supply Chain Activities

Strategic (Design) Activities. Strategic decisions have long-term impacts on a supply chain. First, goals and competitive characteristics such as quality, cost, variety (flexibility), timeliness (speed), customer service, and fill rate (i.e., percentage of demand filled from stock on hand) should be determined by the members of the supply chain. Then, products may be designed/redesigned with these competitive characteristics in mind. Next, supply chains are designed/redesigned for these products, goals, and competitive characteristics. This involves determining the number, location, capacity, and process types of the facilities. Quality assurance, workforce, and information systems should also be considered. For examples of redesign of supply chains, see the "Midas Canada," "Delco," and "Kodak" OM in Actions.

Determining the extent of vertical integration (i.e., the ownership of a segment of supply chain), which is affected by outsourcing decisions, is also a strategic decision. Recently, instead of ownership, customer–supplier partnerships are becoming more widespread.

Tactical (Planning)/Operational Activities. The important tactical/operational activities in supply chains relate to production planning and control, including forecasting, purchasing, transportation of material, inventory control/warehousing, and scheduling of production and distribution/deliveries, movement of products (replenishment), and customer service. Questions such as "should a product be manufactured at this plant, today or later, or shipped from another location, today or later?" should be answered.

OM in *ACTION*

Delco

Some years ago, Delco Electronics, now part of Delphi, a major supplier of parts and components to General Motors, studied its supply chain in order to reduce its costs. Delco had manufacturing plants in Matamoros, Mexico, Milwaukee, and Kokomo, Indiana. Before the study, all shipments from the manufacturing plants were trucked to Kokomo and then put on dedicated trucks to each GM assembly plant. The team studying the supply chain looked at various alternatives such as direct shipment from a manufacturing plant to one or more assembly plants. In the end, the lowest cost option was to design "milk routes" where a truck carries shipments of a group of assembly plants in a geographic area from each manufacturing plant.

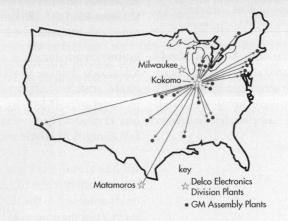

Source: D.E. Blumenfeld, et al., "Reducing Logistics Costs at General Motors," *Interfaces* 17(1), January/February 1987, pp. 26–47.

OM in *ACTION*

Kodak

Kodak makes a variety of products including digital cameras, photo printers, photo kiosks, and radiography equipment for hospitals. Kodak has hundreds of field engineers (FE) dispersed throughout North America who repair Kodak equipment. Some of the inventory of spare parts used in repairs is in the central warehouse in Rochester. The rest are in the trunks of the cars that the FEs use. Until recently, the proportion of inventory split between the central warehouse and the trunks of the FEs was 50–50. A study team was set up to reduce the supply chain costs. The team discovered that 50 percent of the items in the FEs' trunks were expensive items costing more than $700 (mostly refurbishable), but they accounted for only 5 percent of the demand. The process used by the FEs after a repair to have a part refurbished is shown in the diagram below.

Kodak's old way of supplying parts

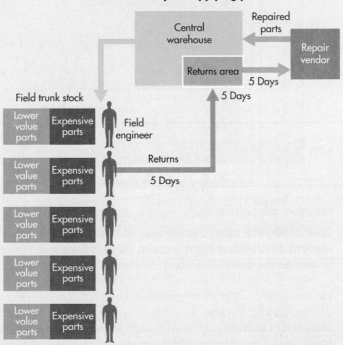

The FE would send the repairable expensive part to the central warehouse, which then would send it to a repair vender for repair. The total time averaged 15 days. The study team decided to pool trunk inventories of the FEs who were located near one another and set up Forward Stock Locations (FSL). The team determined these locations with the help of the Prophet software of Baxter Planning Systems. Kodak contracted with UPS to perform the delivery from the closest FSL to the location of repair or the FE when the need arises (FEs don't carry expensive slow-moving parts in their trunk anymore). The new supply chain reduced the inventory carrying costs by more than 50 percent. The new process is shown in the following diagram.

Source: M. Brienzi and S. Kekre, "How Kodak Transformed its Service Parts Supply Chain," *Supply Chain Management Review* 9(7), Oct 2005, pp. 25–32.

The new way of supplying parts

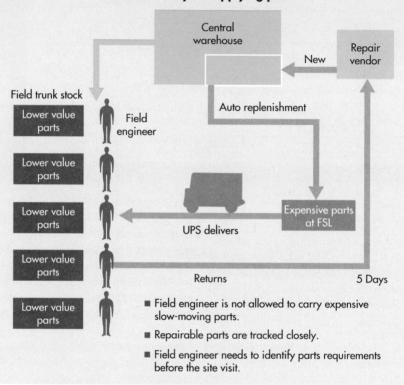

One important tactical/operational decision is where in the supply chain the inventory should be held. Two general rules apply to this decision:

1. Value of inventory increases as materials move down the supply chain toward the consumers (thus it becomes more valuable/responsive to consumer demand).

2. The nature of inventory becomes more specific (thus it loses flexibility of use) as inventory moves down the supply chain.

risk pooling Holding safety stocks in one central location rather than in multiple locations.

These two rules often conflict. Managers must strike a balance to determine the location of inventories in the supply chain.

Another factor for inventory decisions is **risk pooling**: holding safety stocks in one central location rather than in multiple locations. Risk pooling can provide better service (availability) to customers, because the variations in demands in various locations typically cancel each other out for the central location.

delayed differentiation/ postponement Waiting until late in the process to add differentiating features to standard components and products.

Finally to reduce the costs of increasing product variety and small lot sizes, **delayed differentiation** or **postponement** can be used, i.e., waiting until late in the process to add differentiating features to standard components and products. For example, in the paint industry, manufacturers send only white base paint to retail stores where a small quantity of colour paint is mixed into white to get the customer's desired colours when demanded.

(LO2) LOGISTICS

Logistics refers to the movement and warehousing of materials/products and information, both within the production facility and outside. In addition to raw materials and manufacturing parts and components, incoming materials include maintenance, repair, and operating (MRO) supplies such as fuels, spare parts, lubricants, and office supplies. Logistics management is a major part of supply chain management.

Logistics costs can be separated into three categories: internal (within a company) logistics costs, cost of outsourcing to logistics service providers, and inventory carrying or holding cost (cost of money tied up in inventory + storage cost + shrinkage cost + obsolescence cost) outside the company (incoming material transportation and outgoing product distribution). The logistics costs of a company in Canada usually range between 3 and 8 percent of its sales (see Figure 11-3): pharmaceutical and chemical companies tend to have the highest and petroleum and motor vehicle manufacturers tend to have the lowest logistics costs relative to their sales revenue.

logistics   The movement and warehousing of materials/products and information, both within the production facility and outside.

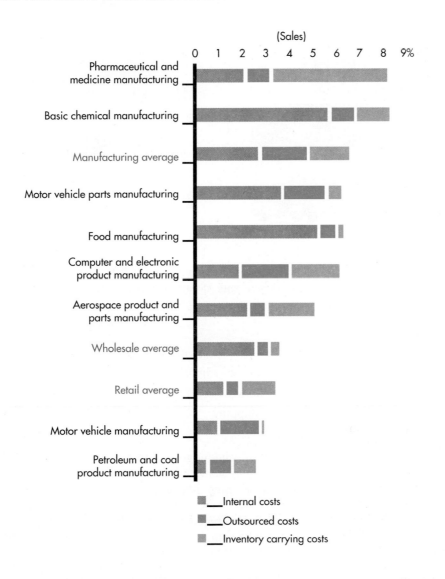

Figure 11-3

2007 key sector total SCM and logistics–costs breakdown

Movement within a Facility

Movement of goods within a manufacturing facility is part of production control. Depending on the nature of goods, the volume, and the production process, different material

Figure 11-4

Movements of goods within a facility

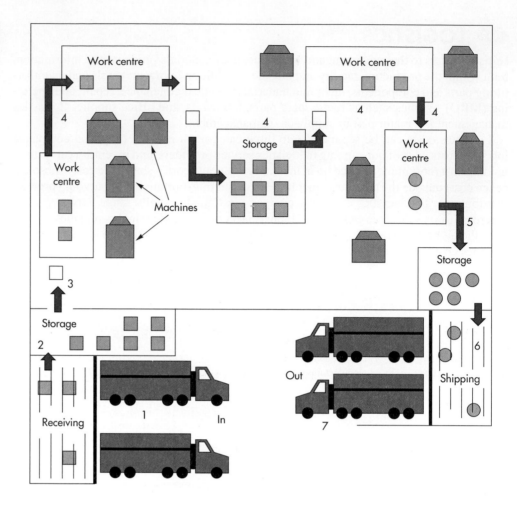

handling equipment is used. Common equipment includes forklifts, carts, baskets, and bins. Figure 11-4 shows the following movements of parts in a batch manufacturing facility:

1. From incoming vehicles to receiving.
2. From receiving to storage.
3. From storage to the point of use (e.g., a work centre).
4. From one work centre to the next or to temporary storage.
5. From the last operation to final storage.
6. From final storage to packaging/shipping.
7. From shipping to outgoing vehicles.

Shipping is the term used for the act of sending goods out for delivery. In an assembly line/Just-In-Time (JIT) system, there are fewer or no storage/inventories. In a continuous process, there are more receiving and shipping inventories. In a job shop, there are more work-in-process inventories.

Movements of materials must be coordinated so that they arrive at the appropriate destinations at appropriate times. Workers and supervisors must take care so that items are not lost, stolen, or damaged during movement.

Incoming and Outgoing Deliveries

traffic management
Overseeing the delivery of incoming and outgoing goods.

Overseeing the delivery of incoming and outgoing goods comes under the heading of **traffic management**. This function handles schedules and decisions on delivery methods and times, taking into account costs of various alternatives, government regulations,

OceanGuaranteed

APL logistics, a major ocean freight mover, and Conway Freight, a major trucking company, together now offer a combined ocean and trucking service from the Far East, primarily China, that does not suffer from delivery time unreliability of the past. OceanGuaranteed delivers shipments within a promised date 99 percent of the time, or they will subtract 20 percent from the invoice. APL delivers the shipment to the port of Los Angeles (or Long Beach) on its ships and Conway uses its trucks to deliver the shipment to any point in North America. The shipment time varies depending on the port of origin and location of destination. For example, from Shanghai or Shenzhen to Sioux Falls, South Dakota, the service is guaranteed to take 18 days. Many medium-value shipments are being diverted from air cargo to ocean/trucking because it is much cheaper and now as reliable.

Source: P. Burnson, "Ocean Shipping Strategies: Risk versus Reward," *Logistics Management*, September 2007, 46(9), pp. 35–36.

---

the needs of the organization relative to quantities and timing, and external factors such as potential delivery delays or disruptions (e.g., highway construction, truckers' strikes).

Modes of transportation, the equipment used for delivery, include ships, trains, trucks, and airplanes. The order of modes given above is from least costly to most costly and from slowest to fastest. The most common delivery method inland is trucking (which is most flexible), followed by railways, which are used for bulk transport of heavy goods. Ocean freight is used for bulk transport of goods on oceans. Some cargo ships are used on the Great Lakes, and pipelines transport crude oil and natural gas. Some logistics companies use a combination of these modes. For example, multimodal parcel delivery companies such as Purolator, FedEx, and UPS use air and trucks.

In terms of delivery reliability, the order from most to least reliable is air cargo, trucking, railway, and ocean freight. Because of low delivery reliability, until recently JIT manufacturers have been hesitant to use ocean freight (see the "OceanGuaranteed" OM in Action above).

> **modes of transportation**
> The equipment used for delivery, including ships, trains, trucks, and airplanes.

Selecting a Transportation Mode

For some businesses, a situation that often arises is the need to make a choice between rapid (but more expensive) delivery such as overnight or second-day air and slower (but less expensive) alternative such as using trucks. In some instances, an overriding factor justifies sending the goods by the quickest means possible, so there is little or no choice involved. However, in other instances urgency is not the primary consideration, so there is a choice. The decision in such cases often focuses on the total transportation and inventory holding costs of each alternative. An important assumption is that the buyer takes ownership at the supplier's location and pays for delivery, which is the case in most business purchases. Initially, we make the assumption that the two alternative modes of transportation are equally reliable; hence they require the same level of safety stock; safety stocks are extra inventory kept when supply lead time and/or demand quantity are variable.

The in-transit holding cost incurred by an alternative is calculated as:

$$\text{In-transit Holding cost} = \frac{H(d)}{365} \tag{11-1}$$

where H = annual holding cost of items being transported
d = duration of transport (in days)

Total delivery cost = transportation (freight) cost + in-transit holding cost

$$= \text{transportation (freight) cost} + \frac{H(d)}{365}$$

Example 2

Determine which delivery alternative, one day or three days, is best when the holding cost of the item is $1,000 per year, the one-day delivery transportation cost is $40, and the three-day delivery transportation cost is:

a. $35   **b.** $30

Solution

$H = \$1,000$ per year
Total cost of 1-day delivery $= \$40 + \$1000(1/365)$
$$= \$42.74$$

Total cost of 3-day delivery

a. $= \$35 + \$1000(3/365)$
$= \$43.22 > \$42.74$
Therefore, 1-day delivery is cheaper.

b. $= \$30 + \$1000(3/365)$
$= \$38.22 < \$42.74$
Therefore, 3-day delivery is cheaper.

When the modes of transportation are different (e.g., air vs. ocean freight), the unequal reliability of these modes requires different levels of safety stocks. Therefore, the cost of holding safety stocks at the destination should also be included in the total cost of a mode.

Example 3

Consider a part that is to be transported from China to Europe. The annual demand for the part is 23,000 units. Price is $210 per unit. Annual holding cost rate is 20% of unit price. There are two transportation options.

Air cargo: Takes 7 days (door to door) and costs $52 per unit.
Ocean freight: Takes 35 days and cost $10 per unit.

Because of variability of transportation time and demand, 2 weeks of demand will be kept at destination as safety stock [(2/52)(23,000) units] if air cargo is used. On the other hand, 8 weeks of demand will be kept at destination as safety stock if ocean freight is used. Assume that order quantity will be the same in either case. Calculate the total annual freight, in-transit holding, and safety stock costs for each mode, and choose the cheaper mode.

Solution

Annual costs:

Air

Freight $= \$52(23,000)$	$=$	$\$1,196,000$
In-transit holding $= 23,000(\$210)(.20)(7/365)$	$=$	$18,526.03$
Safety stock $= (2/52)(23,000)(\$210 + \$52)(.20)$	$=$	$46,353.85$
		$\$1,260,879.88$

Note: Cost of the part at the destination includes air transportation cost: $210 + $52.

Ocean

Freight $= \$10(23,000)$	$=$	$\$230,000$
In-transit holding $= 23,000(\$210)(.20)(35/365)$	$=$	$92,630.14$
Safety stock $= (8/52)(23,000)(\$210 + \$10)(.20)$	$=$	$155,692.31$
		$\$478,322.45$

Note: Cost of the part at the destination includes ocean transportation cost: $210 + $10.

Ocean is much cheaper.[2]

[2] T. Miller, "The International Modal Decision (Part 1)," *Chilton's Distribution*, October 1991, 90(11), pp. 82–92; T. Miller, "Air vs. Ocean: Two Critical Factors (Part 2)," *Chilton's Distribution*, November 1991, 90(12), pp. 46–52.

Warehousing

Besides storage of goods, warehouses are used for consolidating shipments, deconsolidating shipments, and cross docking. Consolidating shipments means collecting the incoming shipments from various geographic areas headed toward another geographic area and combining them into a larger shipment in order to take advantage of economies of scale in transportation. Deconsolidating shipments is the opposite: splitting a large incoming shipment into smaller shipments that are headed to different customers.

In **cross-docking**, goods arriving at a warehouse from a supplier are directly loaded onto outbound trucks, thereby avoiding warehouse storage. Walmart initiated cross-docking to reduce inventory holding costs and delivery lead times.

cross-docking Loading goods arriving at a warehouse from a supplier directly onto outbound trucks, thereby avoiding warehouse storage.

Fast Delivery Methods

Just-In-Time (JIT) replenishment started in the auto industry in the 1980s, and for an automobile manufacturer it means that parts/components are received in small lots and frequently, only a few hours before they will be used. Soon later, JIT replenishment was modified and applied to apparel/textile and wholesale/retail sectors under the name "quick response."

Quick response (QR) involves making sales information available to vendors. The purpose is to create a Just-In-Time replenishment system that is keyed to consumer buying patterns, as opposed to periodic orders by retailers. Another name for quick response is *continuous product replenishment*. QR results in frequent small-lot shipments.

quick response (QR) Just-in-time replenishment system used in retailing where orders are based on actual sales, not periodic orders by retailers.

Quick response has several benefits. Among them are reduced dependency on forecasts and the ability to achieve a closer match between supply and demand. In addition, there are savings on inventory holding costs. For applications, see the "Sears Canada," "Zara," and "Nygard" OM in Actions.

Efficient consumer response (ECR), initiated in 1992, is an expanded version of quick response, used in the grocery industry. In addition to continuous product replenishment, ECR includes further collaboration on replenishment, forecasting, and planning of store assortments, promotions, and product introductions.

efficient consumer response (ECR) An expanded version of quick response, used in the grocery industry, which includes further collaboration.

Vendor-managed inventory (VMI) is a related, though not necessarily fast-delivery, initiative that reduces the inventories in the supply chain. In VMI, the vendor's employee periodically comes on the buyer's premise, counts the inventories of her company on the buyer's shelves, and replenishes them to the previously agreed-upon level. VMI has been used by soft drink companies supplying convenience stores, electrical distributors supplying small maintenance warehouses, etc.

vendor-managed inventory An agreement in which the supplier has access to the customer's inventory and is responsible for maintaining the inventory level required by the customer

JIT Delivery Problems. JIT systems such as quick response often require frequent deliveries of small shipments. This can place a tremendous burden on the delivery system in several respects. One is the increased traffic that results. Instead of one large delivery per week, a company switching to JIT may require many smaller loads every day. Multiply that by the number of items obtained from various suppliers, and you can begin to appreciate the potential traffic nightmare and resulting delays in the receiving area. Also, there is an increase in transportation cost per unit because there is a fixed cost per delivery (e.g., per truck), even if only a partial load is delivered. Smaller trucks are one possibility, but that, too, will generate a fixed cost. There is always a chance of disruption of deliveries due to labour strikes, equipment problems, etc. Because of these factors, it is necessary to carefully weigh the costs and benefits of using frequent, small deliveries, and select a lot size that *balances* all relevant costs.

Distribution Requirements Planning

Distribution requirements planning (DRP) is a system for synchronizing replenishment schedules across the supply chain. It is especially useful in multi-echelon distribution networks (hierarchical levels of factory, regional warehouses, and retail stores). It uses a concept similar to material requirements planning (see Chapter 14) for distribution. Starting with forecast demand at the end of the distribution network (retail stores), DRP works

distribution requirements planning (DRP) DRP is a distribution planning system that starts with the forecast demand at the end of the distribution network (retail stores), and works backward through the network to obtain time-phased replenishment schedules for moving goods from the factory through each level of the distribution network.

backward through the network to obtain time-phased replenishment schedules for moving goods from the factory through each level of the distribution network. Note that DRP is a push system (it produces and ships based on demand forecasts and plans) whereas quick response is a pull system (it produces and ships based on actual demand).

OM in ACTION   http://www.sears.ca

Sears Canada

Sears Canada has two words of advice for retailers that spend a lot of time trying to forecast sales of specific items, seeking to avoid out-of-stocks: Don't bother.

This is what you'd have to infer from the success the Toronto-based division of Chicago-based Sears, Roebuck and Co. has achieved by implementing new procurement processes founded on quick response.

In doing so, the retailer has effectively removed the burdens of forecasting from itself and placed them squarely on the shoulders of its suppliers.

Sears Canada, with 124 department stores, 39 furniture and appliance stores, and 2,150 catalogue pick-up locations, is the highest-volume retailer in Canada. In 1994, with the help of Andersen Consulting, the chain began an initiative to redesign its merchandise procurement processes, seeking to streamline activities from purchase to delivery to payment.

There was ample reason to move quickly. Walmart had entered Canada, acquiring 120 former Woolco stores, and other competitors, including The Home Depot and Costco, were expanding their Canadian presence.

Sears Canada had been proud of its sophisticated but often complex procurement capabilities. Many different methods were employed to accomplish the same basic business functions.

In simplifying, the company went from 37 distinct procurement methods to four standard models; from many distribution methods to total flow-through (the name sometimes used for quick response); and from 31 ways to pay to one.

Other changes included using more negotiations, cross-docking, advance shipping notices (ASNs), and electronic fund transfer.

For example, under the old approach there were large monthly shipments of large appliances from suppliers to Sears's warehouses, from which customer orders were filled. This required a large, expensive inventory, high storage costs, and extensive handling with the commensurately higher possibility of damage.

Now, when a customer in a store decides to buy a Whirlpool dishwasher, for example, the sales associate connects online to Whirlpool via a store terminal to confirm the availability of the item. The associate then places the order (via EDI) and commits to a fast and firm delivery date.

Whirlpool then sends an ASN and ships the next day. The product is cross-docked at a Sears warehouse and put on an outbound route. Nearly 100 big-ticket suppliers, including Whirlpool, GE, Sanyo, and Goldstar, have been converted to the new approach.

Results include $65 million in inventory takeout and an 11 percent improvement in the customer fill rate.

ASNs have become a vital part of the overall supply chain process vision, with the top 700 suppliers—representing 85 percent of all purchases—converted in the first six months.

Gone with this new approach are attempts by Sears Canada to forecast customer demand. Instead, the chain agrees to provide its suppliers with its sales information and its promotional marketing plans. The suppliers then must agree to decrease lead time and be responsive to actual demand by replacing what is sold.

Source: Based on "Sears Canada on Forecasts: Let the Manufacturer Do It," *Chain Store Age* 71(8), August 1995, pp. 44–46.

OM in ACTION

Zara

Zara is a brand name for men, women, and childrens' clothes, owned by Inditex, a Spanish clothing company. Inditex owns over 20 factories in Coruna, Spain, and over 4,000 retail stores around the world. It is one of the largest clothing chains in the world. Inditex is unique in the clothing

industry in emphasizing speed to market as its competitive attribute, even though its clothes are good quality and reasonably priced. Also, Inditex is different in that it owns the manufacturing plants, as opposed to outsourcing the manufacturing. Inditex has divided its business into three units: men's, women's, and children. Each unit has its own designers, buyers, production planners, and sales staff. Within each unit, the staff (except production and distribution staff who are shared) work under the same roof in large halls. There is a weekly communication with store managers regarding what is selling. Inditex produces and sells more than 10,000 different types of clothes every year. The design-to-display takes only two to three weeks because Inditex's factories have excess capacity (from colouring/printing, to cutting and sewing), the giant warehouse (about 5 million sq. ft) has excess capacity, and Inditex uses air cargo to transport its clothes overseas. The emphasis is on small lots and speed, rather than cost minimization. It seems that this strategy is paying off because Inditex is growing at the rate of over 20 percent per year and its net margin is 10 percent, higher than any rivals.

Source: K. Ferdows, et al., "Rapid-fire Fulfillment," *Harvard Business Review*, November 2004, pp. 104–110.

Third-Party Logistics

Some companies are outsourcing their logistics requirements, turning over warehousing and deliveries to companies that specialize in these areas such as Purolator, UPS, FedEx, PBB Global Logistics, and Ryder Trucks. This is called *third-party logistics*. One possible reason for outsourcing logistics is a desire to concentrate on the core business. Employing a company that specializes in logistics provides other benefits such as a well-developed logistics information system, experienced logistics personnel, customs facilities, foreign locations, and the ability to provide lower transportation rates.

Reverse Logistics

Reverse logistics refers to the backward flow of goods returned to the supply chain from their final destination. Goods may be returned because they are defective, because they are unsold, or because customers simply change their minds. Reverse logistics includes returns management. Returns management involves processing returned goods, which generally involves sorting items, examining/testing items, restocking items that are in good condition, repairing defectives, reconditioning products, recycling materials, and disposing of obsolete or hazardous materials. The goal of reverse logistics management is to recapture or create value in returned goods or to properly dispose of goods that cannot be resold.

Two key elements of reverse logistics are gate-keeping and avoidance. **Gate keeping** oversees the acceptance of returned goods with the intent of reducing the cost of returns by screening returns at the point of entry into the system and refusing to accept goods that should not be returned or goods that are returned to the wrong destination. Effective gate-keeping enables organizations to control the rate of returns without negatively impacting customer service. **Avoidance** refers to preventing returns by dealing with their causes. It can involve product design and quality assurance issues. It may also involve careful monitoring of forecasts during promotional programs to avoid overestimating demand.

reverse logistics   Backward flow of goods returned to the supply chain from their final destination.

gate keeping   Screening returned goods at the point of entry into the system to prevent incorrect acceptance of goods.

avoidance   Preventing returns by dealing with their causes.

Global Supply Chains

As international trade barriers fall, more companies are expanding their global operations. This is presenting tremendous opportunities and opening up previously untapped markets for raw materials, goods, and services. It has also increased the number of competitors. Even companies that operate only within a single country are faced with increased foreign competition.

OM in ACTION

NYK Logistics

NYK Logistics is a large global logistics company with strength in ocean freight. NYK has over 100 cargo ships, over 100 car transport ships, and over 400 bulk and oil tanker ships. It also performs various logistics services such as warehousing/distribution, freight forwarding, and supply chain consulting. The following diagrams show supply chains for a typical automobile manufacturer and a typical retail chain, with NYK services performed for each in ovals (W/H = warehouse; CKD = completely knocked down; PDI = pre-distribution inspection; Drayage = loading/unloading and locally transporting the ocean containers).

Sources: http://www.nyklogistics.com/regional/industry_auto_map.shtml?page=auto0; http://www.nyklogistics.com/regional/industry_supplyChain_map.shtml?page=retail0.

Supply Chain for an Automobile Manufacturer

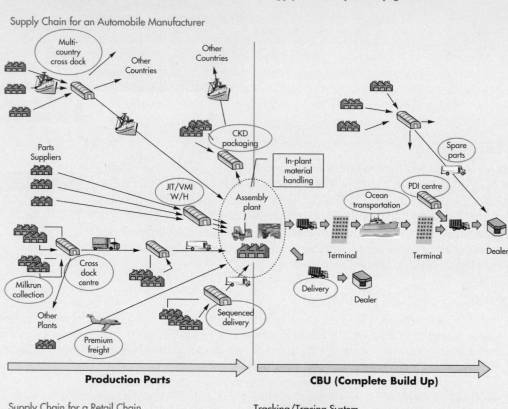

Supply Chain for a Retail Chain

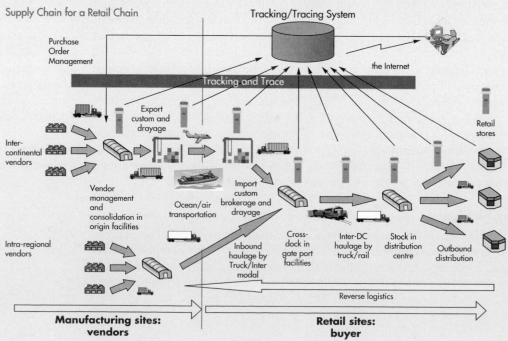

Managing a global supply chain that may have far-flung customers and/or suppliers magnifies some of the challenges of managing a domestic supply chain. Obviously, distances and lead times increase as the supply chain becomes longer. In addition, there is the possibility of having to deal with different languages and cultures, currencies, and possibly additional modes of transportation.

The ability to export to other countries, as opposed to making the product there, has allowed multinational companies to centralize the production of families of their products in one location. This allows economies of scale, but requires localization of the product for different markets, which have different feature preferences. For example, most people buy front-load washing machines in the U.K., whereas in North America, top-loading washing machines are popular. The "NYK Logistics" OM in Action shows two typical global supply chains.

LO3 SOME SUPPLY CHAIN TECHNOLOGIES

Two computer technologies used in supply chain management are electronic data interchange (EDI) and radio frequency identification (RFID). Also, Internet, directly or through e-commerce, is important for supply chain management.

Electronic Data Interchange

Electronic data interchange (EDI) is the direct, computer-to-computer transmission of interorganizational transactions and information, including purchase orders, sales data, advance shipping notices, invoices, engineering drawings, and more. Among the reasons companies are increasingly using EDI (especially the Internet-based version of it; see the "Sterling Commerce" and "QLogitek" OM in Actions) are:

- Reduction in clerical labour (no need for receiving, storing, and manipulating data manually)
- Reduction of Paperwork
- Increased accuracy (avoids re-entry of data, thus reducing errors)
- Increased Speed

In most JIT systems, EDI is used to signal a replenishment to the supplier. There are many applications of EDI in retailing involving electronic communication between retailers and vendors. Walmart has a satellite network for EDI that allows retail store point-of-sale data to be downloaded every night to the Walmart main database, which vendors can also access. This enables the vendors to improve their forecasting, production scheduling, and inventory management; Walmart saves money on carrying inventory; and fill rates go up. For more information, see the "Walmart" OM in Action on the next page.

RFID

Radio frequency identification (RFID) is a technology that uses radio waves to identify objects such as goods in a supply chain. This is done through the use of an RFID tag that

electronic data interchange (EDI) The direct transmission of interorganizational transactions and information, computer-to-computer, including purchase orders, sales data, advance shipping notices, invoices, and engineering data.

radio frequency identification (RFID) A technology that uses radio waves to identify objects such as goods in a supply chain.

OM in ACTION

Sterling Commerce

Sterling Commerce provides electronic commerce capability between a company and its suppliers that do not have an EDI system. For a fee, the supplier can join the community of suppliers of the customer and use a secure environment (using Sterling's Value Added Network) to receive electronic purchase orders of the customer, acknowledge them, as well as send advance shipping notices and invoices. This system bypasses the problems associated with faxing the P.O., and the subsequent communications, which have to be manually entered in the customer's computer system. Instead, the transactions are fully integrated in the customer's computer system. The Web forms used also reduce the inaccuracies of a manual/fax system for the customer company. For more information on Sterling's software, see http://www.sterlingcommerce.com/products/all-products, and for some case studies, see http://www.sterlingcommerce.com/customers/by-product/?id=100.

Source: http://www.sterlingcommerce.com.

OM in ACTION

Walmart

Walmart uses a satellite to transmit store point-of-sale and other data (shelf-space and local sales decisions captured by handheld devices from store staff) to Walmart's computers in Bentonville, Arkansas, several times a day. There are three supply chains: (1) Some suppliers (of mainly soft lines such as apparel, footwear, etc.) have access to the POS data and perform vendor-managed inventory and replenish the stores directly. (2) Other suppliers receive orders from Walmart and ship to the distribution centres, which cross-dock most items to the retail stores. (3) Walmart replenishes fast-moving items in the stores according to their POS data from inventory kept in the distribution centres. See the following diagram.

Source: F.A. Kuglin, *Customer-centered Supply Chain Management*. New York: AMACOM (American Management Association), 1998, p. 175.

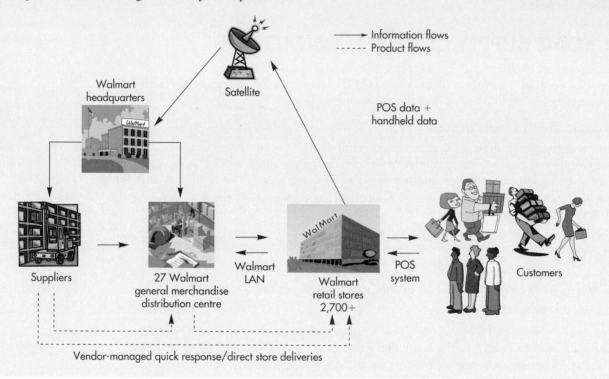

is attached to an object. The tag has an integrated circuit chip and an antenna that emits information to network-connected RFID readers using radio waves. The illustration on the left shows a RFID tag. It looks like a label, although the centre of the middle layer contains a microchip surrounded by a thin metal object which acts as antenna.

There are two kinds of RFID tags: (1) Active tags have a battery and emit radio waves by themselves; hence they have a longer range (perhaps up to 50 metres or so) but are more expensive, (2) Passive tags do not have a battery but work by responding to electromagnetic waves emitted by the RFID reader; hence have a shorter range (perhaps up to 5 metres or so).

RFID tags can be attached to pallets, cases, or individual items. They provide unique identification, enabling businesses to identify, track, monitor, or locate practically any object in the supply chain that is within the range of a tag reader. These tags are similar to bar codes, but have the advantage of conveying much more information and they do not require the line-of-sight reading that bar codes require. And unlike bar

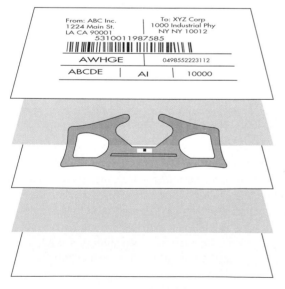

codes, which must be scanned individually and usually manually, multiple RFID tags can be read simultaneously and automatically. Furthermore, an RFID tag provides more precise information than a bar code: tags contain detailed information on each object, whereas bar codes convey only an object's classification, such as its stock keeping unit (SKU).

RFID eliminates the need for manual counting and bar-code scanning of goods at receiving docks, in warehouses, and on retail shelves. This eliminates errors and greatly speeds up the process.

The costs involved in setting up an RFID system include the cost of the tags themselves as well as the cost of programming and fixing individual tags to the objects, the cost of readers, and the cost of hardware and software to transmit and analyze the data generated. Other than the cost (currently a passive RFID tag costs approximately 10 cents), the downside of RFIDs is that the radio waves are affected by the nature of some objects (e.g., liquid and metal objects interfere with the proper working of the RFID tags).

For two applications of RFID, see the "NYK Yard (Long Beach)" and "American Apparel" OM in Actions. For further information on RFID, see http://rfid.averydennison.com/faq.php.

OM in ACTION

NYK Yard (Long Beach)

NYK is a logistics management company. In its 70 acre yard in Long Beach, California, it deconsolidates ocean freight containers from 11 ocean freight lines and transloads (i.e., transfers) them into the trailer trucks of 12 to 15 domestic carriers heading to 22 Target distribution centres in the United States. Before 2003, NYK used a manual system to keep track of the containers. The drivers did not always drop off their containers/trailers in the specified parking slot (many times because the designated slot was already occupied). Yard personnel used a clipboard and walkie-talkie to roam the yard and record the correct location of the containers/trailers. In 2003, NYK asked WhereNet (now part of Zebra Enterprise Solutions) to install

35 wireless antennas throughout the yard (covering 1,200 parking slots and 250 distribution docks) and bought 1,000 active (battery-operated) RFID WhereTags. These tags are attached at the gate to each container and trailer that comes in the yard using a clamp and are removed when the container or trailer is about to exit the yard. The RFID tags, real-time locating system, and yard management system, all from WhereNet, have increased the accuracy of container/trailer parking slot locations to 100 percent and the daily throughput of the yard by 40 percent. The wireless antennas are also used by the yard (hostler) tractors that move the containers/trailers back and forth between the parking slots and the distribution centre.

Sources: http://zes.zebra.com/customers/cs-nyk.jsp; http://zes.zebra.com/customers/cs-nyk-v.jsp

OM in ACTION

American Apparel

American Apparel (AA) is an LA–based vertically integrated manufacturer (i.e., performs weaving of fabric, dyeing, cutting, and sewing itself) and retailer of T-shirts and other clothes for youth. AA's policy is to display one unit of each colour and size of each style of its clothes in each of its 200 + stores. However, because many of them look similar and many of them are misplaced by customers in the store and change rooms, each store uses approximately six employees the whole day to perform physical inventory and replace the misplaced items, or if sold, to replenish them from the back room. To solve this problem, AA has tested placing a passive

(without battery) RFID tag on each of its merchandise at one store in NY City. Thousands of passive RFID tags were purchased from Avery Dennison, a major label and RFID tag manufacturer. Each item received from the distribution centre in LA was tagged with a RFID tag that was programmed with the identity of the item. Also, a few RFID readers were purchased from Motorola (MC9090-G). The RFID readers are used to zoom in toward any particular clothes (they beep as they get closer) or identify any item in their vicinity. The use of RFID has reduced the need for physical inventory to only two employees and the length of this activity to two hours per day.

Source: C. Robbins Gentry, "RFID Speeds Replenishment," *Chain Store Age* 84(6), Jun 2008, pp. 54–56.

E-Commerce

e-commerce The use of computers and Internet to conduct buying and selling.

E-commerce refers to the use of computers and Internet to conduct buying and selling. E-commerce involves business to business (B2B) and business to consumer (B2C) commerce. Delivery companies have seen the demand for their services increase dramatically due to e-commerce. Thus, e-commerce has promoted the use of supply chains and supply chains have enabled e-commerce. Table 11-1 lists some of the numerous advantages of e-commerce.

Table 11-1
Advantages of e-commerce

Companies have a global presence and customers have global choices and easy access to information.

Companies can improve competitiveness and quality of service by allowing access to their services any time.

Companies can analyze the interest in various products based on the number of hits and requests for information.

Companies can collect detailed information about clients' choices, which enables mass customization and personalized products. An example is the purchase of Dell Computers over the Web, where the buyer specifies the final configuration.

Supply chain response times are shortened. The biggest impact is on products that can be delivered directly on the Web, such as software distribution.

disintermediation Reducing one or more steps in a supply chain by cutting out one or more intermediaries.

The roles of the intermediary and sometimes the traditional retailer or service provider are reduced or eliminated entirely in a process called **disintermediation**. This process reduces costs and adds alternative purchasing options.

Substantial cost savings and substantial price reductions related to the reduction of transaction costs can be realized. Companies that provide purchasing and support through the Web can save significant personnel costs.

E-commerce allows the creation of virtual companies that distribute only through the Web, thus reducing costs. Amazon.com and other net vendors can afford to sell for a lower price because they do not need to maintain retail stores and, in some cases, warehouse space.

The playing field is leveled for small companies which lack significant resources to invest in infrastructure and marketing.

There are two essential features of e-commerce businesses: the Web site, and order fulfillment. Companies may invest considerable time and effort in front-end design (the Web site), but the back end (order fulfillment) is at least as important. It involves order processing, inventory management, warehousing, packaging, billing, and delivery.

In the early days of Internet selling, many organizations thought that they could avoid bearing the costs of holding inventories by acting solely as intermediaries, having their suppliers ship directly to their customers. Although this approach worked for some companies, it failed for others, usually because suppliers ran out of certain items. This led some companies to rethink the strategy. Industry giants such as Amazon.com built huge warehouses so they could maintain greater control over their inventories. Still others are outsourcing fulfillment, turning over that portion of their business to third-party fulfillment operators that perform third-party logistics functions as well as take customer orders and fill the order from their warehouse. Besides logistics, UPS and FedEx also perform order fulfillment.

To facilitate e-commerce, including finding a buyer or a seller, some e-marketplaces or exchanges have been created. Table 11-2 describes some mainly B2B e-exchanges. For an example of a software that can be used to set up private exchanges, see the "Ariba" OM in Action later in this chapter.

Type	Description	Web site	**Table 11-2**
Buyer-initiated exchanges			
CareNet Services Inc.	Has over 450 hospitals using EDI for ordering and receiving invoices from more than 95 health care vendors.	http://www.carenet.ca	
Quadrem	Set up by 14 large mining companies to facilitate their purchasing transactions.	http://www.quadrem.com	
Avendra	Set up by Marriott and Hyatt; buys for about 4,500 hotels from 900 suppliers.	http://www.avendra.com	
Seller-initiated exchanges			
Global Healthcare Exchange	Set up by a few large pharmaceutical and medical/surgical equipment suppliers.	http://www.ghx.com	
1SYNC	Set up by few large manufacturers of consumer packaged goods.	http://www.gs1us.org/1sync	
Bank-sponsored exchange			
Online Mart	TD Bank's small-business storefront; it provides a safe marketplace for a variety of products.	http://www.onlinemart.ca	

LO4 CREATING AN EFFECTIVE SUPPLY CHAIN

Creating an effective supply chain requires linking distribution channels, production, and suppliers to customers. It should enable all participants in the chain to achieve significant gains, hence giving them an incentive to cooperate.

Requirements for a Successful Supply Chain

Successful supply chain management requires forming close relationships, trust, willingness to cooperate, agreement on common goals, alignment of incentives; effective communication and coordination of activities; supply chain visibility and information sharing; event management capability; and performance metrics.

Forming Close Relationships, Trust, Willingness to Cooperate, Agreement on Common Goals, Alignment of Incentives. It is important for the members of a supply chain to form close relationships (even partnerships). This requires trust, willingness to cooperate, sharing similar goals, and confidence that they will take actions that are mutually beneficial. See the "Aligning Incentives" OM in Action for an example of how economic incentives of supply chain members can be aligned.

Effective Communication and Coordination of Activities. Effective supply chains require close and regular communication among members at all levels in order to coordinate activities for effective operations. This requires integrated technology and standardized ways and means of communicating among members. One approach to achieve this is the collaborative planning, forecasting, and replenishment (CPFR), explained in a sub-section below.

Supply Chain Visibility and Information Sharing. Supply chain visibility means that a member can connect to any part of its supply chain to access data in real time on forecasts and sales data, inventory levels, shipment status, impending shortages, and other problems that could impact the timely flow of products through the chain. Thus, instead of each organization in a supply chain making plans based on a combination of actual orders plus forecasts of demand of its immediate customer, by sharing data on end-customer sales on a real-time basis, each organization in the supply chain can develop plans that contribute to synchronization across the supply chain.

supply chain visibility
A member can connect to any part of its supply chain to access data in real time.

OM in ACTION

Aligning Incentives

For the members of a supply chain to have the economic incentive to work together for the good of all members of the supply chain, the risks, costs, and rewards of doing business should be divided fairly.

To illustrate, suppose a newspaper vendor buys newspapers from a printer for 80 cents each and sells them for $1 each. Also, suppose that it costs the printer 45 cents to print a newspaper, demand for the vendor's newspapers is uniform between 100 and 200 units per day, and that any unsold papers have no value at the end of the day. In the next chapter on inventory management, we will model this problem as the single-period model and provide a formula for its optimal solution. In this case, the optimal solution for the vendor is to buy 120 newspapers. It can be shown that this would result in an expected daily profit of $21.92 for the vendor and $42 for the printer (a total of $63.92 profit). Note that in this case the vendor is bearing all the risk of demand variability.

Now, if both agree that the printer sells each paper to the vendor at cost (45 cents each) and shares in the revenue (e.g., 35% printer, 65% vendor), it can be shown that the optimal solution will be 131 copies, with expected daily profit of $23.01 for the vendor and $44.13 for the printer (a total of $67.14 profit). In this case, vendor and printer will be sharing the risk of demand variability.

Better still, if the printer agrees to buy back any unsold papers for 60 cents each, it can be shown that the optimal solution will be 150 copies, with expected daily profit of $24.95 for the vendor and $49.34 for the printer (a total of $74.29 profit). In this case also, vendor and printer will be sharing the risk of demand variability.

Source: V.G. Narayanan and A. Raman, "Aligning Incentives in Supply Chains," *Harvard Business Review*, November 2004, pp. 94–102.

---

event management The ability to detect and respond to unplanned events.

Event Management Capability. **Event management** is the ability to detect and respond to unplanned events such as delayed shipment or a warehouse running low on a certain item.

Performance Metrics. Performance metrics are necessary to confirm that the supply chain is functioning as expected, or that there are problems that must be addressed. A variety of measures can be used. These are presented in a following section.

Steps in Creating an Effective Supply Chain

Creation of an effective supply chain entails several key steps:

strategic partnering Two or more organizations agree to collaborate so that each may realize a strategic benefit.

1. Develop strategic objectives and tactics. These will guide the process.
2. Integrate and coordinate activities in the internal portion of the chain. This requires (a) overcoming barriers caused by functional thinking that lead to attempts to optimize a sub-set of a system rather than the system as a whole, and (b) sharing data and coordinating activities.
3. Coordinate activities with suppliers and with customers. This involves addressing supply and demand issues.
4. Coordinate planning and execution across the supply chain. This requires a system for sharing data across the supply chain, allowing access to data to those who engage in operations to which it will be useful.
5. Consider the possibility of forming *strategic partnerships*. **Strategic partnering** occurs when two or more organizations agree to collaborate so that each may realize a strategic benefit. There are different degrees of partnership. A basic version occurs when a supplier agrees to hold inventory for a customer, thereby reducing the customer's cost of holding the inventory in exchange for the customer agreeing to a long-term commitment, thereby relieving the supplier of the costs of continually finding new customers, negotiating prices and services, and so on. It is important that the number of partners in a supply chain be small and the number of chains a company belongs to be limited so that working relationships and trust can be established.

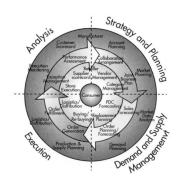

CPFR A process for communicating and agreeing on forecasts between the manufacturer and the customer (distributor).

Collaborative Planning, Forecasting, and Replenishment (CPFR)

CPFR is the latest effort to increase the effectiveness and efficiency of supply chains. It moves quick response one step further by establishing a process for communicating and agreeing on forecasts and plans between the manufacturer and the customer (the distributor/retail chain). The two parties exchange data and written comments electronically—for example, they communicate the reasons for their forecast or reasons for disagreeing with the other's forecast. Some companies such as Walmart, HP, Procter & Gamble, Kimberly-Clark, and Nabisco have been involved in pilot tests of CPFR.

Below is a summary of the implementation guideline prepared by the Voluntary Inter-Industry Commerce Standards Association (VICS; http://www.vics.org/committees/cpfr):

- Planning
  - Decide which product category to collaborate on, the objectives, resources, information sharing, forecast horizon, promotions, minimum order size, lead time, and review period.
- Forecasting
  - Buyer collects POS data, forecasts sales, and shares them with supplier (including promotion plans).
  - Supplier compares the forecasts with capacity. Will there be any significant shortfall?
  - Supplier tries to resolve the difference; may contact buyer
  - Buyer/supplier jointly create order forecasts (taking inventory into account).
- Replenishment
  - Buyer generates order for next week.
  - Supplier issues acknowledgement; executes delivery.
- For an application of CPFR, see the "Whirlpool's CPFR" OM in Action.

Performance Metrics

The following performance metrics are commonly used to measure performance of a supply chain (note their similarity with the competitive attributes of Chapter 2):

1. Quality
2. Cost (unit cost, inventory turnover, logistics costs)
3. Variety/flexibility (production and product changes)
4. Delivery (lead time, on-time delivery)
5. Customer service (fill rate, response time)

Inventory turnover refers to the rate at which inventory (material) goes through the system. Faster is better: The quicker materials pass through the supply chain, the lower inventory costs will be, and the quicker products and services will be delivered to the customer. **Fill rate** is the percentage of demand filled from stock on hand.

A similar set of performance metrics has been determined by the Supply Chain Council, a not-for-profit association of companies and consultants interested in supply chain management. The metrics are part of the Supply Chain Operations Reference (SCOR) model and are shown in Table 11-3. The SCOR model reflects an effort to standardize measurement of supply chain performance. Cash-to-cash cycle time is the number of days of working capital tied up in the supply chain. It is calculated by adding the number of days of inventory to number of days of receivables outstanding and subtracting the number of days of payables outstanding.

inventory turnover The rate at which inventory (material) goes through the supply chain.

fill rate Percentage of demand filled from stock on hand.

LO5 PURCHASING

The purchasing function is responsible for obtaining the raw materials, manufacturing parts, supplies, machines and equipment, and services needed to produce a good or provide a service. Purchasing is a major part of supply chain management. You can get some idea of the importance of purchasing when you consider that most of the cost of

Perspective	Metrics
Reliability	On-time delivery
	Lead time
	Fill rate (fraction of demand met from stock)
	Perfect order fulfillment
Flexibility	Response time
	Upside production flexibility
Expenses	Supply chain management cost
	Warranty cost as a percentage of revenue
	Value added per employee
Assets/utilization	Total inventory days of supply
	Cash-to-cash cycle time
	Net asset turns

Table 11-3

Supply Chain Operations Reference (SCOR) model metrics

OM in ACTION

Whirlpool's CPFR

In 2002 Whirlpool's Logistics Department was reorganized into the Supply Chain Department so that it could improve its customer service performance. As part of that, Whirlpool tested CPFR with two of its major customers (retail chains). Even though there was informal collaboration before, the lack of a shared-files database and a predetermined collaboration schedule (specific hourly and daily plan in a weekly cycle) meant that the process of forecast reconciliation was not effective. After getting internal and external buy-in, the project manager formed two separate CPFR teams, one for each customer, and prepared a training manual on CPFR.

The teams included Whirlpool's demand managers dealing with each customer, some production planners, deployment planners (responsible for inventory levels in Whirlpool's regional distribution centres), and marketing forecast managers (who generated top-down forecasts based on industry trends and market shares). The customers each also formed a team including inventory managers/planners, buyers, and information system staff. One team chose i2 Technologies' Supply Chain Collaborator (now called Collaborative Supply Execution), while the other used another software used by the customer with another supplier.

The CPFR process actually affected Whirlpool's internal forecasting and planning process. Instead of monthly sales and operations planning, Whirlpool executives review the weekly forecast generated jointly with the customer. Sales and Marketing are alerted with short-supply and excess-supply stock keeping units (SKUs) in order to shape the demand.

After only a few months, the forecast inaccuracy has significantly decreased (Mean Absolute Percentage Error for SKUs at store-level have decreased from an average of 69 percent to 44 percent) and the week-to-week changes in order quantities and units shipped are closer together and to the week-to-week changes in store sales (see the figure below). Also, CPFR has given better understanding of Whirlpool-customer problems. The improvement process continues.

Whirlpool; Week-to-week changes in order quantities, units shipped, and store sales

The order and corresponding shipment variability has come closer to actual store sales variability (which is considerably lower) since CPFR went live.

Source: N. Sagar, "CPFR at Whirlpool Corporation: Two Heads and an Exception Engine," *Journal of Business Forecasting Methods & Systems* 22(4), Winter 2003/2004, pp. 3–10.

QLogitek

QLogitek is a supply chain collaboration software company in Toronto, which also provides hosting (private trading exchange [PTE]) service. QLogitek's set of software uses SaaS (Software-as-a-Service) model, based on Microsoft's .NET technology, which allows a company to communicate with its suppliers over the Internet, instead of using EDI on a dedicated value-added network (VAN).

HMV uses QLogitek's SaaS supply chain software and PTE, which allows HMV's approximately 100 stores to send purchase orders to and receive invoices from its small suppliers (the larger suppliers and all the stores are connected using a VAN and EDI). Use of QLogitek's SaaS and PTE has reduced the purchasing/accounts payable staffing needs of HMV by 75 percent.

A company that uses QLogitek's SaaS Inbound Management System is Hudson's Bay Company (HBC), where it is used to receive advance shipping notices and invoices from small suppliers. Before QLogitek's SaaS, HBC had 57 receiving schedulers in its seven distribution centres making appointments for approximately 3,000 weekly deliveries with 2,000 suppliers and 100 common carriers using phone/fax/e-mail. QLogitek's SaaS has made three-quarters of the schedulers redundant.

Sources: G. Hilson, "Harmonious Supply Chain," *Computing Canada* 28, January 18, 2002, p. 19; http://www.qlogitek.com/Libraries/Case_Studies/HMV-EDI-Case_study-CanadaComputing.sflb.ashx; http://www.qlogitek.com/Libraries/Case_Studies/HBC-IMS-CaseStudy-MMD-Article.sflb.ashx.

---

many finished goods comes from purchased parts and materials. Furthermore, all goods sold by retailers and wholesalers have to be purchased first. Nonetheless, the importance of purchasing is more than just the cost of goods purchased; other important factors include the *quality* of goods and services, and *timing* of deliveries of goods or services, both of which can have a significant impact on operations. Also, purchasing plays the central role in forming partnerships.

The basic goal of purchasing is to develop and implement purchasing plans for goods and services that support the business plan. Among the duties of a buyer are identifying sources of supply, negotiating contracts, maintaining a database of suppliers, obtaining goods and services that meet operations' requirements in a timely and cost-efficient manner, managing suppliers, establishing partnerships, and acting as liaison between suppliers and various internal departments.

Purchasing is taking on increased importance as organizations place greater emphasis on supply chain management, quality improvement, Just-In-Time, and outsourcing.

Purchasing's Interfaces

Purchasing interfaces with a number of other functional areas within an organization, as well as with outside suppliers. Purchasing is the connecting link between the organization and its suppliers. In this capacity, it exchanges information with suppliers and with functional areas.

The *operations* department constitutes the main source of requests for purchased materials (manufacturing parts and operating supplies), and close cooperation between operations and the purchasing department is vital if quality, quantity, and delivery goals are to be met. Cancellations, changes in specifications, or changes in quantity or delivery times must be communicated to the other side, the requisitioner or supplier, immediately. Another user of purchasing services is the *maintenance* department, which requires spare parts and repair supplies. New machines and equipment are also needed.

The purchasing department may require the assistance of the *legal* department in interpreting regulations, writing up contracts, and providing advice in case of a dispute (see Figure 11-5).

Accounting is responsible for handling payments to suppliers. In many organizations, *data processing* is handled by the accounting department, which keeps inventory records and checks invoices.

Design engineering usually prepares material/part specifications, which must be communicated to suppliers. On the other hand, because of its contacts with suppliers, purchasing is often in a position to pass information about product and material improvements on

OM in ACTION

Nygard

Nygard International is the largest ladies' wear manufacturer in Canada (revenues of $300 million). Its main manufacturing facilities are in Winnipeg, California, and Mexico. Founder Peter J. Nygard is considered a visionary in the apparel industry. In the early 1990s, he computerized the design and production activities in his Winnipeg facilities using CAD, computerized cutting, and planning/control systems with a computer at every workcentre, and computerized receiving and shipping using bar codes. All the programming, equivalent to a full-blown Enterprise Resource Planning software, was done in-house. By 2000, the entire operation was paperless.

In the mid-1990s, Nygard turned his attention to the supply chain. He asked his major customers, such as Hudson's Bay Company, to let an EDI software be installed on their system so that when an item was sold at a store, this information was immediately relayed to a Nygard factory and routed to the right workcentre to start production. Nygard guarantees 24-hour response time, from the time of receiving an order to shipment. This is revolutionary in the apparel industry, where the usual lead time is at least two weeks. Nygard's system also has EDI connection to its major suppliers of fabric, zipper, buttons, etc. Nygard has spent approximately $50 million on its information technology during the last two decades.

Source: http://www3.nygard.com/corporate/company_profile.html.

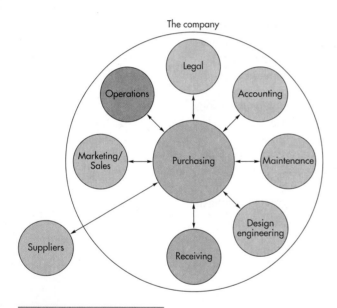

Figure 11-5

Purchasing's interfaces

to design personnel. Also, design and purchasing people may work closely to determine whether changes in specifications, design, or materials can reduce the cost of purchased items (see the section below on value analysis).

Receiving staff check incoming shipments, and material handling staff move the goods to their destination (the requisitioner). Accounting must be notified when shipments are received so that payments can be made.

Marketing/sales staff sometimes need some products for resale. In this case, purchasing and marketing should have a close relationship in order to satisfy the customer. In retail/wholesale, this relationship is vital. In fact, in many retail/wholesale companies, the functions of marketing and purchasing are combined into one job, that of the merchandise buyer. Merchandise buyers should have a good sense of marketing in order to buy items that will be purchased by companies' customers.

Suppliers or vendors work closely with purchasing to learn what materials/parts are needed by the organization and when. Purchasing must rate vendors on cost, quality, reliability, and so on (see the later section on choosing suppliers). Good supplier relations can be important for rush orders and changes. Figure 11-5 summarizes purchasing's interfaces.

Purchasing Cycle

purchasing cycle A series of steps that begins with a request for purchase and ends with paying the supplier.

The **purchasing cycle** is a series of steps that begins with a request from within the organization to purchase material, equipment, supplies, or other items, and ends with paying the supplier. The main steps in the purchasing cycle are:

1. *Purchasing receives the requisition.* The requisition includes (a) a description of the item desired, (b) the quantity and quality necessary, and (c) desired delivery dates. Having a catalogue of approved products will accelerate the purchasing cycle. See the "SciQuest" OM in Action later in the chapter, which explains how the company sets up e-catalogues for organizations.

2. *Purchasing selects a supplier.* The buyer must identify suppliers that have the capability of supplying the desired goods. If no suppliers are currently in the files, new ones

must be sought. Trade directories may be referenced. Usually potential suppliers are asked to quote a price (more on this in the following section on determining price). If the order involves a large expenditure, particularly for a one-time purchase of equipment, for example, vendors will usually be asked to submit a proposal saying how they will meet the need, and operating and design personnel will be asked to assist in the purchase.

3. *Purchasing places the order with the supplier.* Large-volume, continuously used manufacturing-parts purchases are negotiated using long-term contracts. If the item is critical to the product, partnership with suppliers may be investigated. Large-volume, continuously used supplies may be purchased by blanket purchase orders (or standing orders), which often involve annual negotiation of prices for a total annual purchase dollar amount, with deliveries subject to operating units' direct request throughout the year. Many companies have an established EDI connection (or its Internet equivalent) with some of their suppliers, reducing the cost and time of purchasing. Electronic purchasing is commonly referred to as e-procurement. Small purchases should be handled directly between the operating unit and the supplier. Using corporate credit cards simplifies paying the suppliers because there is only one bill per requisitioner per month.

4. *Monitoring orders* (and expediting). Routine follow-up on orders, especially large orders or those with lengthy lead times, allows the buyer to prevent delays.

5. *Receiving orders.* Receiving staff must check the incoming shipment against the purchase order, and material handling moves it to its destination (the requisitioner). Receiving must notify purchasing and accounting departments by preparing a receiving report. If the quality of the incoming shipment is in doubt, quality control staff must inspect the shipment. If there are a large number of items in the shipment, sampling should be used. If the goods are not satisfactory, they should be returned to the supplier for credit or replacement.

6. *Paying the supplier.* Upon receipt of shipment, accounts payable must pay the invoice. If a discount is given for early payment, this should be taken advantage of.

Value Analysis

Value analysis refers to the examination of the *function* of a product in an effort to reduce its cost. Typical questions that would be asked include, Could a cheaper part or material be used? Is a function necessary? Can the function of two or more parts be performed by a single part for a lower cost? Can the product be simplified? Could specifications be relaxed? Could standard parts be substituted for nonstandard parts? Table 11-4 provides the value analysis process.

value analysis Examination of the function of a product in an effort to reduce its cost.

1. Select a product that has a high annual dollar value.
2. Identify the basic function of the item (in a verb–noun form, e.g., a bolt "joins things.")
3. Obtain answers to these kinds of questions:
   a. Can the function be performed in another way?
   b. Could another material or part be used instead?
   c. Can specifications be less stringent to save cost or time?
   d. Can two or more parts of the item be combined?
   e. Can a different process be used on the item to save cost or time?
   f. Do suppliers have suggestions for improvement?
   g. Can packaging be improved or made less costly?
4. Evaluate the answers obtained, and make a recommendation.

Table 11-4

The value analysis process

Naturally, the buyer cannot perform value analysis each time items are ordered. However, it should conduct value analysis periodically on large annual dollar-value items because of the potential savings.

Although the buyer does not ordinarily have the authority to implement changes on the basis of a value analysis, it can make suggestions to operating units and designers, which may lead to reduction of the cost of those goods. Purchasing can offer a different perspective to the analysis, because of its association with suppliers. If a fair amount of technical knowledge is required to review a product or service, a team can be formed with representatives from design engineering, operations, and cost accounting to work with purchasing to conduct the value analysis.

Determining Prices

Organizations typically determine prices in one of three ways: published price lists, competitive bidding, and negotiation.

In many instances, organizations buy goods and services that have fixed or *predetermined prices*. This is generally the case for standard items that are bought infrequently and/or in small quantities.

For large orders of standard goods and services, getting quotes or *competitive bidding* are common. The buyer calls (in the informal version) or sends written requests (in the formal version) for bids to potential suppliers, asking vendors to quote a price for a specified quantity and quality of items or for a specified service to be performed. Large government purchases of goods or services are usually made through formal competitive bidding. Usually, the lowest quote or bid wins the contract. Large orders usually receive price breaks (called quantity discounts). Recently, some companies have started using *reverse auctions* to purchase supplies: A set of potential suppliers are prequalified, then an auction start time and day is specified, and a software is used by bidders through Internet to bid. This is called a reverse auction because in this case the bidders bid to sell something as opposed to a regular auction where bidders bid to buy something. During the reverse auction, the suppliers reduce their bids over time, unlike in a regular auction, where buyers raise their bids.

Negotiated purchasing is used for special purchases—when specifications are vague, when one or a few customized goods or services are involved (e.g., building a new all-purpose military jet), or when only few potential sources exist. Several *myths* concerning negotiated purchasing should be recognized:

1. Negotiation is a win–lose confrontation.
2. The main goal is to obtain the lowest possible price.
3. Each negotiation is an isolated transaction.

No one likes to be taken advantage of. Furthermore, contractors and suppliers need a reasonable profit to survive. Therefore, a take-it-or-leave-it approach or one that capitalizes on the weaknesses of the other party will serve no useful purpose and may have detrimental effects that surface later. The most reasonable approach is one of give and take, with each side giving and receiving some concessions.

Centralized versus Decentralized Purchasing

centralized purchasing
Purchasing is handled by the purchasing department.

decentralized purchasing
Individual departments or separate locations handle their own purchasing requirements.

Centralized purchasing means that purchasing is handled by the purchasing department. **Decentralized purchasing** means that individual departments or separate locations handle their own purchasing requirements.

The purchasing department may be able to obtain lower prices than decentralized units if the higher volume created by combining orders enables the company to take advantage of quantity discounts offered on large orders. It may also be able to obtain better service and closer attention from suppliers. In addition, centralized purchasing often enables companies to assign certain categories of items to specialists, who tend to be more efficient because they are able to concentrate their efforts on relatively few items instead of spreading themselves across many items. See the "Chinook Health Region" OM in Action later in the chapter.

OM in ACTION

Ariba

Ariba is a major purchasing and business-to-business commerce software company producing software that costs between $1 and $4 million and is created primarily for large enterprises. Ariba's software is compatible with the Internet and different computer systems. Ariba can create a private supplier network or an exchange for a buying company to be used to house suppliers' catalogues, conduct auctions, and send and receive purchasing documents. In addition to automating basic purchasing activities (e.g., creating a requisition and purchase order, transmitting it to a supplier, and receiving and paying invoices), Ariba's software modules assist in purchasing-data collection and spend analysis, and sourcing activities including conducting online auctions. Ariba also has the Ariba Network, consisting of over 120,000 suppliers in 115 countries, an exchange used primarily for small- to medium-size buyers to find and do business with suppliers.

Sources: J. Kerstetter, "How Ariba Got Airborne: Timely Acquisitions Have Made the Upstart a Leader in B2B E-commerce," *BusinessWeek* 36, Sept 18, 2000, p. 126; http://www.ariba.com.

OM in ACTION

SciQuest

SciQuest, headquartered in Cary, North Carolina, provides purchasing software for education, government, health care, and life sciences sectors. The software can be integrated with an Enterprise Resource Planning software or with an even larger purchasing software such as Ariba. SciQuest Catalog Management makes customized supplier e-catalogues available to the requisitioner and the Spend Director directs the requisitioner to products of preferred suppliers by bringing them up first in the search for a product. Then products can be put in a shopping cart as in consumer Internet buying such as from Amazon.com. SciQuest's Requisition Manager enables online approval for the purchase from managers, and the Order Manager streamlines order processing. For more details of SciQuest modules, see http://www.sciquest.com/solutions/index.php, and for some cases see http://www.sciquest.com/resources.php?c=2.

Source: http://www.sciquest.com.

OM in ACTION

Challenger 300

The Challenger 300 business jet is the result of a partnership between Bombardier, Mitsubishi, and Taichung, the three main structural manufacturers. Each company makes a piece of the plane, which is then assembled in just four days in Bombardier's Dorval facility in Quebec. Mitsubishi makes the wings and Taichung makes the tail. The mid-fuselage is made at the Belfast site of Bombardier and the front is made at the Montreal site. The engines are made by Honeywell, the avionics by Rockwell Collins, and there are another 30 suppliers of the interior equipment. The Challenger 300 is a mid-size business jet that seats 8 to 9 people. Normally, small planes are made by one facility. However, Bombardier wanted to integrate the operations of its different facilities—most were bought in the late 1980s. The Montreal site was Canadair, the Belfast site was Short Brothers, and the Kansas City site was Learjet. Parts of the plane were outsourced to Japanese and Taiwanese companies because they agreed to incur the development cost.

Sources: http://www.bombardier.com/en/3_0/3-2/pdf/challenger_300_factsheet.pdf; P. Siekman, "The Snap-Together Business Jet," *Fortune* 145(2), January 21, 2002, pp. 104Aff.

OM in *ACTION*

Chinook Health Region

When Chinook Health Region around Lethbridge, Alberta, centralized the purchasing and warehousing functions of its 10 facilities in one location in the late 1990s, inventory was reduced by half and the number of purchasing staff was reduced, which reduced the materials management's budget by 20 percent. The centralization permitted the smaller rural hospitals to take advantage of quantity-discount buying, up to five to six times cheaper! Among the items centralized were medical supplies, laundry services, and sterilization of surgical equipment.

Source: L. Young, "Finding the Right Supply Chain Medicine," *Data Capture Communications & Commerce*, April 1999, pp. DC9–DC10.

OM in *ACTION*

Mountain Equipment Co-op

Mountain Equipment Co-op (MEC) was established in 1971 by a small group of outdoor enthusiasts in Vancouver who wanted to have quality outdoor equipment available for sale in Canada. MEC now has stores in 10 Canadian cities and two million members. MEC designs and manufactures approximately 60 percent of the items it sells. Other items are purchased from manufacturers. MEC has a strong ethical sourcing policy which requires suppliers to have respect for the environment and the health/safety/dignity of their workers. It requires that a supplier not employ children under 15 or forced labour such as prisoners. The supplier should not abuse its workers, prevent unions, and force its workers to work more than 48 hours regular-time and 12 hours overtime per week. Workers should have at least one in seven days off and should be paid fairly. There should be no discrimination or harassment. New potential suppliers and current suppliers (annually) get audited by an MEC team or external auditors. This entails a one-day visit and a 200-question survey.

Sources: http://www.mec.ca, About MEC, Sustainability, Ethical Sourcing, Factory Conditions; R. Shaw, "Peak Performance [Mountain Equipment Co-op]," *Alternatives Journal* 31(1), January/February 2005, p. 19.

Decentralized purchasing has the advantage of awareness of differing "local" needs and being better able to respond to those needs. Decentralized purchasing usually can offer quicker response than centralized purchasing. Where locations are widely scattered, decentralized purchasing may be able to save on transportation costs by buying locally, which has the added attraction of creating goodwill in the community.

Some organizations manage to take advantage of both centralization and decentralization by permitting individual units to buy certain items while other items are bought centrally. For example, small orders and rush orders may be handled locally or by departments, while centralized purchasing is used for high-volume, high-value items/commodities for which quantity discounts are applicable or for corporate services such as payroll, personnel, information systems, legal, etc.

Spend Analysis

Many businesses fail to collect accurate and useful purchasing data. This is because (1) different stock codes may be used to describe the same supplier or item in different plants, (2) there may not be an easy way to relate and aggregate similar items using their stock codes and description (no product classes or types are defined), (3) relationship between suppliers may have been missed (Note: expenditure with all subsidiaries of a company should be aggregated when negotiating quantity discounts). These problems can be rectified by undertaking spend analysis.

spend analysis Collecting, cleansing, classifying, and analyzing expenditure data with the purpose of reducing procurement costs, improving efficiency, and monitoring compliance with purchasing policies.

Spend analysis involves collecting, cleansing (i.e, amending or removing data that is incorrect, incomplete, improperly formatted, or duplicated), classifying, and analyzing (e.g., using charts) expenditure data with the purpose of reducing procurement costs, improving efficiency, and monitoring compliance with purchasing policies. Spend analysis can provide answers to questions such as: What was bought? From which suppliers? What is the total expenditure on a part? How much is the total expenditure with a supplier?

Before any changes are implemented as a result of spend analysis, its potential savings should be estimated. Only if savings exceed costs of change should a change in the purchasing process be made. For example, if a frequently used part is purchased from different suppliers by different plants (in different regions), then consolidating the purchase of this part with one national/global supplier should lead to significant cost savings. The same is true for similar parts (because most suppliers give discounts for total annual expenditure with them).

It is important that deficiencies of data collection and/or purchasing practice be fixed (e.g., using a spend analysis software) so that the need for spend analysis in future is diminished. For example, maverick buying (users buying from non-preferred suppliers; a preferred supplier is a pre-qualified or certified supplier) should be minimized. Companies have realized up to 5 percent reduction in their total expenditure by performing spend analysis.[3]

Ethics in Purchasing

Ethical behaviour is particularly important in purchasing where the temptations for unethical behaviour can be enormous. Buyers often hold great power, and salespeople are often eager to make a sale. Unless both parties act in an ethical manner, the potential for abuse is very real. Furthermore, with increased globalization, the challenges are particularly great because a behaviour regarded as customary in one country might be regarded as unethical in another country.

The Purchasing Management Association of Canada has established a set of norms of ethical behaviour and code of conduct. (See Table 11-5.) As you read through the list, you'll gain insight into the scope of ethical issues in purchasing. A company known for its ethical purchasing is Mountain Equipment Co-op (see the "Mountain Equipment Co-op" OM in Action).

Table 11-5

Norms of ethical behaviour and code of conduct in purchasing

1. To consider first the interests of one's organization in all transactions and to carry out and believe in its established policies.

2. To be receptive to competent counsel from one's colleagues and to be guided by such counsel without impairing the responsibility of one's office.

3. To buy without prejudice, seeking to obtain the maximum value for each dollar of expenditure.

4. To strive for increased knowledge of the materials and processes of manufacture, and to establish practical procedures for the performance of one's responsibilities.

5. To participate in professional development programs so that one's purchasing knowledge and performance are enhanced.

6. To subscribe to and work for honesty in buying and selling, and to denounce all forms of improper business practice.

7. To accord a prompt and courteous reception to all who call on a legitimate business mission.

8. To abide by and to encourage others to practice the Professional Code of Ethics of the Purchasing Management Association of Canada and its affiliated institutes and corporation.

9. To counsel and assist fellow purchasers in the performance of their duties.

10. To cooperate with all organizations and individuals engaged in activities that enhance the development and standing of purchasing and materials management.

LO6 SUPPLIER MANAGEMENT AND PARTNERSHIP

Reliable and trustworthy suppliers are a vital link in an effective supply chain. Timely deliveries of high-quality goods or services contribute to effective operations. A buyer functions as an "external operations manager," working with suppliers to coordinate the supplier's operations and the buyer's needs.

---

[3]http://www.supplychainbrain.com/content/headline-news/single-article/article/spend-analysis-how-to-squeeze-every-dime-out-of-procurement/.

In this section, various aspects of supplier management are described, including choosing suppliers, supplier certification, supplier relationship, and supplier partnership.

Choosing Suppliers

In many respects, choosing a supplier involves taking into account many of the same factors associated with making a major purchase (e.g., a car or stereo system). A person considers price, quality, availability of product or timely delivery, the supplier's reputation, past experience with the supplier, and service after sale. The main difference is that a company, because of large purchase quantities and production requirements, often orders the materials or parts it wants instead of buying them off-the-shelf. Also, the items are usually delivered to the buyer's location later, and the invoice can be paid a few weeks later. The factors a company takes into account when it selects a supplier and typical questions to ask are outlined in Table 11-6.

Table 11-6 *Factors and typical questions to ask when selecting a supplier*	**Factor**	**Typical Questions**
	Quality	Is the supplier technically capable of achieving the desired quality? What procedures does the supplier have for quality control and quality assurance?
	Flexibility	How flexible is the supplier in handling changes in delivery schedules, quantity, and product or service?
	Location	Is the supplier nearby?
	Price	Are prices reasonable given the entire package the supplier will provide? Is the supplier willing to cooperate to reduce costs?
	Reputation	If used previously, how was the supplier's performance? What is the reputation of the supplier? Is the supplier financially stable?
	Lead time	What lead time can the supplier provide? What policies does the supplier have for keeping items in stock? Is the supplier reliable?
	Other customers	Is the supplier heavily dependent on other customers, causing a risk of giving priority to their needs over ours?
	Service after sale	How much after-sale support does the supplier provide?

Because different factors are important for different situations, purchasing must decide, with the help of the requisitioner, the importance of each factor (i.e., how much weight to give to each factor), and then rate potential suppliers according to how well they can be expected to perform against this list. This process is called **supplier analysis**.

supplier analysis
Evaluating a supplier in terms of factors such as price, quality, delivery, and service.

Supplier Certification

Supplier certification is a detailed examination of the policies, capabilities, and performance of a supplier. The certification process verifies that a supplier meets or exceeds the requirements of a buyer. This is particularly important when buyers are seeking to establish a long-term relationship with suppliers. One advantage of using certified suppliers is that the buyer can eliminate much or all of the inspection and testing of delivered goods from these preferred suppliers.

Rather than develop their own certification program, some companies rely on standard industry certifications such as ISO 9001, perhaps the most widely used international certification.

Supplier Relationship

Purchasing has the ultimate responsibility for establishing and maintaining a good supplier relationship. The type of relationship desired is often related to the length of a contract between the buyer and the seller. In short-term contracts, suppliers are kept at arm's length and the relationship is minimal. Medium-term contracts often involve ongoing relationships. Long-term contracts may evolve into partnerships, with buyers and sellers cooperating on various strategic issues that tend to benefit both parties.

North American companies have become increasingly aware of the importance of building good relationships with their suppliers. In the past, too many companies regarded their suppliers as adversaries and dealt with them on that basis. One lesson learned from the Japanese is that numerous benefits derive from a good supplier relationship, including supplier flexibility in terms of accepting changes in delivery schedule, quality, and quantity. Moreover, suppliers can often help identify improvements in the design of an item purchased from them or suggest better substitutes (i.e., perform value analysis). In fact, they can be involved in the design of new products (called *early supplier involvement*). Thus, simply choosing and switching suppliers on the basis of price is a very shortsighted approach to handling an ongoing need.

Many Japanese companies rely on only one or two suppliers to handle their needs for a group of items. In contrast, many North American companies tend to deal with numerous suppliers. Perhaps they want to remain flexible, and possibly there are advantages in playing off one against the others. However, the advantages of single-sourcing include lower number of orders, deliveries, and invoices, and being able to work with the supplier to reduce lead time, for example. In recent years, North American companies are moving in the direction of reducing the number of their suppliers.

Supplier Partnership

More and more business organizations are seeking to establish partnerships with their suppliers. This implies fewer suppliers, longer-term relationships, sharing of information

---

OM in ACTION

Grand & Toy

Grand & Toy Company provides office supplies, paper, furniture, and computer supplies to Canadian organizations. It carries approximately 6,000 stock-keeping units in its eight regional distribution centres. It also has 75 retail locations and 21 sales offices. Its 230,000 square foot Toronto distribution centre has automated carousels and sorting capability using bar codes, controlled by a warehouse management system (WMS) software. Grand & Toy provides EDI service to its customers using its own wide area network, IBM AS/400 computer, and an ERP software. It also allows its customers to order over the Internet (using its OrderPoint system), where they can use Grand & Toy's electronic catalogue. For example, Nova Corp. of Calgary, the natural gas producer, buys its stationery from Grand & Toy over the Internet. Grand & Toy also keeps records of customer purchase quantities and allows them to access this data, in effect providing inventory record keeping for its customers. Grand & Toy provides next-day delivery in major cities, and has in-stock rate of 98 percent.

Grand & Toy also helps organizations develop EDI connection with their other suppliers. For example, the University of Calgary is now connected to 25 of its largest suppliers using Grand & Toy's EDI network, which also provides a Web-based catalogue for the university buyers who now buy 50 to 60 percent of their purchases using it. In 1996, Grand & Toy was purchased by Boise Cascade, the large U.S. office supplies distributor and paper/lumber producer. This development provides Grand & Toy with paper and preferred pricing on its other purchases.

Sources: "Gearing up for Full Value: Grand & Toy's Value-added Supply Chain Solution," *Modern Purchasing*, 41(8), July/August 1999, pp. S1–S28; "Grand & Toy: Your Partner in the Supply Chain," *Modern Purchasing* 41(2), January/February 1999, pp. S1–S34; "Grand & Toy: A Boise Cascade Office Products Company," *Modern Purchasing* 38(8), July/August 1996, pp. S1–S18; and T. Venetis, "Office Supplies Online: Internet Ordering Cuts Time, Paperwork," *PurchasingB2B*, September 2000, p. 43ff; http://www.grandandtoy.com/sites/Corp/Services/AboutUs_Main.aspx?name=AboutUs_History.

St. Mary's Hospital

The purchasing function can provide cost savings and improved services for an organization. When St. Mary's Hospital Centre of McGill University wanted to save costs, it signed a five-year contract to buy all its intravenous (IV) products requirements from Baxter Corp. Even before the contract, Baxter was the major supplier of IVs to the hospital for many years. In addition, Baxter provided a nurse who communicated with the hospital nurses in order to find suitable substitutes for the non-Baxter-supplied IVs. The standardization process took approximately four months.

Sources: http://www.smhc.qc.ca/english1/About/about-en.htm; M.S. Kamel, "Montreal Hospital Gets Shot in the Arm," *Summit* 3(4), December 2000, pp. 42–43.

(forecasts, sales data, replenishments, problem alerts), and cooperation in planning. Assistance from suppliers could:[4]

1. Reduce the cost of making a purchase.
2. Reduce the transportation cost.
3. Reduce the production cost.
4. Improve the product quality.
5. Improve the product design.
6. Reduce the time to market.
7. Reduce the inventory costs.

Supplier partnerships are required for JIT relationships such as quick response and CPFR.

Professor D.M. Lambert and others in the Global Supply Chain Forum (GSCF) at Ohio State University have developed a partnership model that has been used dozens of times.[5] The partnership model is as follows. After the number of suppliers is reduced, those that provide key materials/services and with whom a company does a lot of business are approached for partnership discussion. Top executives and managers from functional areas from each company are invited to a retreat, facilitated by a third-party consultant.

During 1.5 days, each company's managers first determine the key reasons they should get into partnership (e.g., cost reduction, customer service enhancement, etc.), and provide a metric and target for each reason, and then share these with the other company's managers. There should be frank discussions to clarify the issues. These key expectations are called partnership drivers.

Next, if both sides agree that partnership will likely meet their expectations, they proceed to identify the facilitators. These include compatibility of cultures and management philosophy, and other factors that influence the ease of coordination of activities required for partnership.

Then, if coordination appears to be reasonably easy, based on the level of expectation of benefits of partnership (i.e., attainment of partnership drivers), the intended partnership can be classified as Type I (low benefits), Type II (moderate benefits), or Type III (high benefits).

---

[4]Based on Jim Morgan, "Nine Ways Suppliers Can Improve Competitiveness," *Purchasing*, November 24, 1994, pp. 7–9.

[5]D.M. Lambert and A.M. Knemeyer, "We're in This Together," *Harvard Business Review*, December 2004, pp. 114–122.

Finally, based on the type of intended partnership, both sides have to identify the extent of cooperation in planning, control, communication, and risk/reward sharing, and implement activities to achieve this. For example, joint planning can range from ad hoc (sharing plans for a project) to regularly scheduled (joint planning for key processes); performance-measures determination can range from separate (but shared) to joint (i.e., joint performance); communication can range from ad hoc (one way) to linked electronic communication system (two ways); short-term loss tolerance can range from low to high; and desire to help the other party gain financially can range from limited to high.

For examples of partnership, see "Grand & Toy" (probably a Type I partnership) OM in Action two pages before and "St. Mary's Hospital" (probably a Type II partnership) OM in Action.

Summary

A supply chain consists of the sequence of organizations—their facilities and activities—that are involved in producing and delivering a good or service, from the initial suppliers to the final customer. Supply chain management (SCM) is collaboration and coordination of all components of the supply chain so that market demand is met as efficiently and effectively as possible.

Supply chain management offers the benefits of lower operating costs, reduced inventories (e.g., by avoiding the bullwhip effect), better product availability, and customer satisfaction. The need for SCM has increased due to increased outsourcing (buying as opposed to making), globalization, and e-commerce.

Activities in supply chain management can be classified as strategic (e.g., network design), and tactical/operational (e.g., production planning and control, replenishment).

Logistics involves the movement and warehousing of goods, material, and information in a supply chain. This includes incoming materials, movement within a facility, and outgoing goods. A major decision in supply chain management is to determine the shipping mode: basically, the faster mode results in higher freight cost, but the slower mode, though cheaper in terms of freight cost, results in higher in-transit holding cost.

Retailers/wholesalers and manufacturers have initiated quick (Just-In-Time) replenishment systems with their suppliers under the names of *quick response* and *efficient consumer response*.

Electronic data interchange is being increasingly used for purchasing, order confirmation and payment, and arranging shipments. Radio frequency identification (RFID) is just starting to replace bar codes as a tool for fast identification of items in supply chains. The explosion of e-commerce (i.e., the use of computers and the Internet to conduct buying and selling) has introduced tremendous opportunities, and it underscores the importance of effective supply chain management.

The key to an effective supply chain is to link companies, develop trust, have common goals, share information, and measure performance. Collaborative planning, forecasting, and replenishment (CPFR) is a new initiative that links planning, forecasting, and replenishment activities of the company and its major suppliers.

The purchasing function in organizations is becoming increasingly important. Among purchasing responsibilities are obtaining the materials, manufacturing parts, supplies, equipment and machines, and services needed to produce a good or provide a service. Price, quality, and timely delivery are important factors for a purchase and for choosing a supplier. Purchasing selects suppliers, negotiates contracts, helps establish partnerships, and acts as liaison between suppliers and various internal departments. It also is involved in value analysis, spend analysis, and supplier certification.

In many business organizations there is a move to reduce the number of suppliers and to establish and maintain longer-term relationships with suppliers. Supplier partnership is the closest form of relationship where both buyer and seller benefit by assisting each other. The Global Supply Chain Forum partnership model provides a process for deciding if partnership between a buyer and a supplier is desirable and, if so, to what extent.

Key Terms

avoidance, 377	modes of transportation, 373
bullwhip effect, 367	outsourcing, 366
centralized purchasing, 390	purchasing cycle, 388
CPFR, 384	quick response (QR), 375
cross-docking, 375	radio frequency identification (RFID), 379
decentralized purchasing, 390	reverse logistics, 377
delayed differentiation/postponement, 370	risk pooling, 370
disintermediation, 382	spend analysis, 392
distribution requirements planning (DRP), 375	strategic partnering, 384
e-commerce, 382	supplier analysis, 394
efficient consumer response (ECR), 375	supply chain, 364
electronic data interchange (EDI), 379	supply chain management, 364
event management, 384	supply chain visibility, 383
fill rate, 385	traffic management, 372
gate keeping, 377	value analysis, 389
inventory turnover, 385	vendor-managed inventory, 375
logistics, 371	

Solved Problems

Problem 1

a. Determine which shipping alternative is best if the annual holding cost of an item is 25 percent of its unit price, and a single unit with a price of $6,000 is to be delivered, either by the two-day delivery at a cost of $400 or by the five-day delivery at a cost of $350.

b. At what unit price would the two-day delivery be less costly?

Solution

a. $H = .25(\$6,000) = \$1,500$ per year

Total two-day delivery cost $= \$400 + \$1,500(2/365)$
$$= \$408.22$$

Total five-day delivery cost $= \$350 + \$1,500(5/365)$
$$= \$370.55 < \$408.22$$

Hence, use the five-day delivery.

b. Let $p =$ unit price. Total 2-day delivery cost $= \$400 + .25p(2/365)$

Total 5-day delivery cost $= \$350 + .25p(5/365)$.

Set the two total costs equal: $\$400 + .25p(2/365) = \$350 + .25p(5/365)$

Or $50 = .25p(3/365)$ or $p = 50(365)/3(.25) = \$24,333.34$

Discussion and Review Questions

1. What is a supply chain? (LO1)

2. What is supply chain management? (LO1)

3. What factors have made it desirable to manage supply chains? What are some potential benefits of doing so? (LO1)

4. When should a company outsource the production of a part or performance of a service? Give an example. What are the disadvantages? (LO1)

5. What does supply chain design mean? (LO1)

6. What are the advantages and disadvantages of pushing inventory downstream closer to consumers? (LO1)

7. What is the bullwhip effect, and why does it occur? How can it be overcome? (LO1)

8. Explain how the need to reduce inventory holding costs would be a good reason to (re)design a supply chain, and give an example. (LO1)

9. What is risk pooling? Delayed differentiation? (LO1)

10. What is logistics? (LO2)

11. Explain the quick response, efficient consumer response, and vendor-managed inventory. (LO2)

12. What is the trade-off in selecting a transportation mode? (LO2)

13. What is reverse logistics? (LO2)

14. What is third-party logistics? Give an example. (LO2)

15. What is cross-docking? (LO2)

16. What is e-commerce and what impact has it had on supply chain management? (LO3)

17. What are some of the advantages of e-commerce? (LO3)

18. What is RFID? What are its advantages and disadvantages for a company? (LO3)

19. What is EDI? What are its advantages and disadvantages for a company? (LO3)

20. What are the requirements for effective supply chain management? (LO4)

21. Name two supply chain performance metrics and explain them. (LO4)

22. What is CPFR? What are its advantages and disadvantages? (LO4)

23. Explain the importance of the purchasing function in organizations. (LO5)

24. Describe what a buyer does. Name at least five activities. (LO5)

25. Describe how purchasing interacts with two other functional areas of an organization. (LO5)

26. How is price determined in B2B purchasing? Give an example for each way price is determined. (LO5)

27. Describe value analysis. (LO5)

28. Discuss centralization versus decentralization in purchasing. What are the advantages of each? (LO5)

29. What is spend analysis? Why is it necessary? (LO5)

30. Describe supplier analysis. What are the common factors used in selecting a supplier? (LO6)

31. What is a preferred supplier? What are the advantages and disadvantages of using preferred suppliers? (LO6)

32. Why is good supplier relations important? (LO6)

33. What are the advantages and disadvantages of a partnership to the buyer? To the supplier? (LO6)

34. Describe the Global Supply Chain Forum partnership model. (LO6)

Taking Stock

1. What trade-offs are involved in sharing information with a supplier? With a customer? (LO4)

2. Who needs to be involved in supply chain management? (LO1)

3. Name two different ways that technology has improved the ability to manage supply chains. (LO3)

4. Name one ethical issue in a buyer's job, and explain it. (LO5)

Critical Thinking Exercises

1. Find and describe an example of RFID that you have seen in your daily life or work. (LO3)

2. For the last item you bought (a) determine its supply chain, (b) and describe the criteria you used to select the product/supplier. (LO1 & 5)

3. Visit http://www.patagonia.com/web/us/footprint/index.jsp, click "Choose a Product," then click a garment's icon (other than a board short), study its supply chain and draw it. (LO1)

1. Visit http://www.jda.com/real_results/case-studies.html, choose a client company, and briefly describe how JDA (including Manugistics) software is helping the company. (LO1)

2. Visit http://www.varsitylogistics.com/customers, pick a customer, and describe how it has benefited from the Varsity shipping software. (LO2)

3. Visit http://www.careersinlogistics.ca/case/index.html, click "How do Bananas Get to the Store," follow the tour, and draw the supply chain for Chiquita bananas. (LO1)

4. Visit http://www.supplychaincanada.org/en/JLI-conference2008, watch the two videos by the VP of Logistics of Walmart Canada, and summarize Walmart's supply chain efforts for environment sustainability. (LO2)

5. Visit http://fisher.osu.edu/centers/scm, find and watch the video of Dr. Lambert's overview of his partnership framework, and summarize it. (LO6)

6. Visit http://www.irwebcasting.com/NYKLINE/2008/en/fs_nb.html, watch the video of NYK operations, and summarize the supply chain/logistics services NYK Logistics performs for its customers. (LO2)

7. Visit http://zes.zebra.com/customers/index.jsp, view a customer success video, read the PDF file in http://zes.zebra.com/customers/success-stories.jsp (if it exists), and summarize how RFID has helped the customer. (LO3)

8. Visit http://business.motorola.com/enterprisemobility/video/index.html?vid=1&localeId=33, search for the video on Montreal Transit Authority, view it, and summarize how RFID is being used. (LO3)

9. Visit http://www.purolator.com/global/index.asp and view the video "The Global Supply Chain Process at Work." What service is Purolator offering its customers through its new Richmond, B.C., facility? (LO2)

10. Visit http://www.rfidjournal.com/article/archive/4, choose a case study, and state how RFID is used. (LO3)

11. Visit http://www.sap.com/usa/solutions/business-suite/scm/customers/index.epx, choose a case study (called a customer reference), and summarize it. (LO1)

12. Visit http://www.ups-scs.com/solutions/casestudies.html, pick one case study, and summarize it. (LO2)

13. Visit http://www.ops.fhwa.dot.gov/publications/fhwahop09035/video.htm, view the video "Keeping the Global Supply Chain Moving," and summarize it. (LO2)

1. A manager must choose between two delivery alternatives: two-day freight and five-day freight. Using five-day freight would cost $135 less than using two-day freight for the shipment of 2,000 units. Another consideration is in-transit holding cost, which is $10 per unit per year. Which alternative would you recommend? Explain. (LO2)

2. **a.** Determine which delivery alternative would be most economical for 80 boxes of parts. Each box costs $200 and annual holding cost is 30 percent of cost. Freight costs are: (LO2)

Alternative	Freight Cost (for all 80 boxes)
Overnight	$300
Two-day	260
Six-day	180

b. For what range of unit cost for a box would each delivery alternative be least costly?

3. A manager must make a decision on delivery alternatives. There are two shippers, A and B. Both offer a two-day rate. In addition, A offers a three-day rate and a nine-day rate, and B offers a four-day rate and a seven-day rate. Three hundred boxes are to be delivered and the freight cost

for the whole lot for each option are given below. Annual holding cost is 35 percent of unit cost, and each box has a cost of $140. Which delivery alternative would you recommend? (LO2)

Shipper A		Shipper B	
Options	Freight Cost	Options	Freight Cost
2 days	$500	2 days	$525
3 days	460	4 days	450
9 days	400	7 days	410

4. An appliance manufacturer has a plant near Toronto that receives small electric motors from a manufacturer located in Winnipeg. The demand for motors is 120,000 units per year. The cost of each motor is $120. The motors are purchased in lots of 3,000 units. The ownership of motors transfers to the appliance manufacturer in Winnipeg. The question is which mode of transportation, truck or train, the appliance manufacturer should use to bring the motors from Winnipeg to Toronto. The railroad company charges $2 per motor, and it takes approximately seven days by train. The trucking company charges $4 per motor, but it takes only three days. The appliance manufacturer will keep 1,000 units as safety stock if a truck is used and 3,000 units as safety stock if a train is used for transportation. If the holding cost rate is 25 percent of unit cost per year, which mode of transportation will minimize total transportation and in-transit and safety holding cost? (LO2)

5. Pratt & Whitney, a major aircraft engine manufacturer, wants to re-evaluate the transportation mode it uses to send unfinished parts to its joint-venture facility in Chengdu, China.[6] Annual demand is 2,900 units. At present the company uses air freight. It takes approximately six days from Los Angeles to Chengdu (due to pickup and delivery and customs delays). There are 20 parts in a lot, each weighing 30 kilograms. The air freight cost per part is $90. The pickup and delivery charges at origin and destination add up to $15 per part. The alternative is to use an ocean liner to ship the parts to Shanghai and from there to either use a truck or a train (a 1,000 km distance). The ocean freight for this lot size will cost $30 per part and will take 15 days. The truck from Shanghai to Chengdu will cost $20 per part and will take six days (due to pickup and delivery and customs delays). Transportation by rail will cost $15 per part and will take 14 days (due to pickup and delivery, customs, and transfer delays). In addition, for rail there is a $10 per part charge for pickup and delivery. The company's inventory holding cost rate is 12 percent per year, and the value of each part is $1,000. (LO2)

    Due to variability of lead times, at the destination, safety stocks of 60, 210, and 290 units will be kept if air, ship and truck, and ship and train are used, respectively. Determine the cheapest (total freight, delivery, and in-transit and safety holding cost) mode of transportation for these parts.

6. A brick maker (BM) in Alberta mixes dry ink into its bricks to make them brown.

    BM's demand for dry ink is 60 tons per year. Currently, BM buys the dry ink from an import merchant that buys the ink from a East Coast U.S. manufacturer. The shipments arrive in lot size of 30 tons by rail. The current cost of dry ink is $C612.22 per ton, including rail transportation cost to BM's location. BM currently keeps 6 tons of dry ink as safety stock. BM's buyer has asked the import merchant to quote a price for truck deliveries in smaller lot sizes. The merchant has quoted C$567.78 per ton for a lot size of 20 tons.

    In the meantime, BM's buyer has contacted the manufacturer directly and asked if BM could purchase dry ink directly from the manufacturer. The answer was affirmative and the cost would be US$386.89 per ton (assume US$1 = C$1.05). A common carrier has quoted a price of C$2,600 to haul a full truckload of dry ink (20 tons) from the manufacturer to BM's location in Alberta. The trip will take 7 days.

---

[6]Based on A.Z. Zeng and C. Rossetti, "Developing a Framework for Evaluating the Logistics Costs in Global Sourcing Processes," *International Journal of Physical Distribution & Logistics Management* 33(9/10), 2003, pp. 785–803.

The holding cost rate for BM is 20 pecent of unit cost per year. For truck deliveries, BM will only hold 2 tons of safety stocks. Which alternative has the lowest total annual purchase, transport, in-transit, safety stock, and cycle (batch) holding cost? (LO2)

7. Given the following data, determine the total annual cost of making and of buying from each of vendor A and B. Estimated demand is 15,000 units a year. Which alternative is best? (LO1)

	Make	Vendor A	Vendor B
Variable cost per unit	$ 8	$11	$ 10
Annual fixed cost	$20,000	$ 0	$5,000 (annual charge)

8. Given the following data, determine the total annual cost of making with each of process A and B and of buying. Estimated demand is 10,000 units a year. Which alternative is best? (LO1)

	Make		Buy
	Process A	Process B	
Variable cost per unit	$ 50	$ 52	$51
Annual fixed cost	$40,000	$36,000	
Transportation cost per unit			$ 2

9. For the previous problem, suppose that the operations manager has said that it would be possible to achieve a 10 percent reduction in the fixed cost of Process B and a 10 percent reduction in B's variable cost per unit. Would that be enough to change your answer if the estimated annual cost to achieve those savings was $8,000? Explain. (LO1)

MINI-CASE   http://www.clearwater.ca

Crusty Cargo

In the late 1990s, Clearwater Fine Foods of Bedford, Nova Scotia, the supplier of live lobsters to many of North America's finest restaurants, was seriously considering opening a large live-lobster holding facility (with a capacity of 22,500 lobsters) in Louisville, Kentucky. Clearwater was experiencing some difficulties shipping lobsters from Bedford to the United States, because of delays due to paperwork mix-ups, technology interruptions, and customs backlogs. The idea was to truck live lobsters once or twice a week from Bedford to Louisville on special trucks, hold the lobsters in Louisville waiting for customer orders, and then courier them via UPS. Louisville is the main U.S. air hub for UPS.

Question

What are the advantages and disadvantages of opening up a Louisville warehouse/distribution centre versus shipping via courier from Halifax (within 20 km of Bedford)?

Source: Based on P.C. Pethick, "Crusty Cargo—Clearwater Fine Foods Scores with Fishy Supply Chain," *Materials Management & Distribution*, August 2001, p. 27.

MINI-CASE

HP's CD-RW Device

In the late 1990s, Hewlett-Packard was under competitive pressure in its CD-RW Device markets. The supply chain from the manufacturers of the CD-RW devices in Japan and Malaysia to the customers (computer resellers) in Americas and Europe took approximately 126 days: the shipment of the base units from the Far East took about 30 days; there was a 75-day supply kept in the two regional localization and conversion centres (U.S., Netherlands) in order to hedge against the variability of supply lead time; localization and conversion, i.e., adding a case for external units and putting on labels and packaging in various languages, took only 1 day; 15 days of finished goods inventory was also kept to hedge against demand variability; and ground transportation within North America and Europe took 5 days on average. The total of 126 days cost HP 8 percent per year in holding cost, which amounted to $5.50 per unit (using a unit selling price of $200).

HP's Strategic Planning and Modelling Group was asked to redesign the supply chain. The group evaluated eight different supply networks and found the lowest-cost one. The localization and conversion activities have been centralized in one place (Singapore), and air freight, instead of ships, is used to transport the CD-RW devices to Singapore. Also, air freight is used to transport the finished CD-RW devices to regional distribution centres. The use of air has resulted in elimination of safety stocks at the localization and conversion centre in Singapore. The supply chain cycle time is reduced to approximately eight days.

Other advantages of a single worldwide centre are that forecasting is brought under one roof and the variation in aggregate demand is less (*risk pooling*). Another advantage of the new supply chain is that HP can introduce new products to markets faster. HP also reduced the number of suppliers of CD-RW devices from eight down to one, and got into partnership and collaborative planning, forecasting, and replenishment (CPFR) with the suppler, reducing the manufacturing lead time significantly. HP is using the same supply chain for the new DVD-RW devices.

Question

Draw the supply chain for HP's CD-RW device before and after the redesign. Show the duration of each link on each supply chain.

Source: T. Hammel et al., "The Re-engineering of Hewlett-Packard's CD-RW Supply Chain," *Supply Chain Management* 7(3/4), 2002, pp. 113–118.

CASE http://www.amazon.com

Amazon.com

It is universally accepted that Amazon.com is the company most closely associated with the e-commerce phenomenon. Based in Seattle, Amazon.com started as an online retailer of books in 1995. Since opening for business as "Earth's Biggest Bookstore," Amazon.com has quickly become one of the most widely known, used, and cited commerce sites on the Web. The company has grown at a tremendous rate with revenues rising from about $150 million in 1997 to $19 billion in 2008. Amazon.com's customer base grew from 1.5 million in 1997 to 88 million in 2009. However, the rise in revenue and number of customers was not accompanied by a rise in profits. After several years in which large operational losses were accumulated, it was only in the fourth quarter of 2001 that the company made its first quarterly profit of $5 million and this was achieved during the holiday season.

The company was founded by Jeff Bezos, a computer science and electrical engineering graduate from Princeton. After seeing a statistic about the unprecedented growth rate of 2,300 percent in the number of Internet users, he quit his job as senior vice president of a Wall Street investment bank and decided to pursue the business opportunity of selling books solely on the Web. Bezos moved to Seattle to be close to competent software development talent, and started the company out of his garage in a Seattle suburb, packing orders and then delivering them to the post office in the family car. Jeff Bezos understood immediately the huge growth opportunity of Internet retailing: "The key trade that we make is that we trade real estate for technology. Real estate is the key cost of physical retailers. Real estate gets expensive every year, but technology gets cheaper every year."

Initially, Amazon.com sold only books. Selling books on the Internet makes sense for three reasons: books are easy to ship (have reduced bulkiness), are reasonably low-value items (low risk to ship), and many online features such as sample chapters and editorial and customer reviews make books suitable for online sales. As an online seller, Amazon.com has virtually unlimited online shelf space and can offer a vast selection through an efficient search and retrieval interface. Amazon.com offers a huge selection (millions of books), while the biggest brick-and-mortar bookstore can offer a maximum of 175,000 titles.

Initially Amazon.com was intended to be a "virtual retailer" with no inventory, no warehouses, and no overhead, just a network of computers taking orders and asking others to fill them, but the reality turned out to be quite different. In order to satisfy a huge increase in demand and offer a reliable and fast delivery schedule, Amazon.com could not rely entirely on book wholesalers such as Ingram Books, and decided to build its own regional warehouses. Currently, it has several warehouses/fulfillment centres in the United States (a total of 12 million ft^2) and internationally (a total of 5 million ft^2 in the U.K., Germany, France, Japan, and China).

The following factors gave Amazon.com a competitive advantage over the physical bookstores:

1. Having only a few warehouses, its inventory turnaround was much quicker than that of a brick-and-mortar store.

2. By designing an efficient browsing, reviewing, and ordering system, Amazon.com reduced book return rates from about 30 percent, the industry average, to only 3 percent, with a huge impact on profitability.

3. Retailers bear the cost of displaying the product in a brick-and-mortar bookstore, while Amazon.com passes these cost savings to customers in the form of price reductions.

4. Physical stores have to stock up to 160 days' worth of inventory to provide a reasonable in-store selection for customers; they have to pay the publishers and distributors 45 to 90 days after they buy the books, thus, on average, they carry the cost of the books for up to four months. On the other hand, Amazon.com carries only 15–30 days' worth of inventory, which is paid immediately by credit card. So, Amazon.com can use the money for one to two months interest-free.

From the beginning, Bezos emphasized a customer-centric business strategy: widest selection, convenient searching, and "one-click" ordering; fast delivery (24 hours UPS delivery is a shipping option on items in a Amazon.com warehouse); and very competitive prices. Customers appreciate the value they are getting. The domination of Amazon.com in the online book market became clear in 2001 with the capitulation of a major competitor, Borders. Borders had become a force in book retailing due to its superior computerized inventory management system and had sought in vain to offer a Web site that would effectively compete with Amazon.com. In 2001, Borders eliminated all staff positions at Borders.com and announced that Amazon.com will handle its online bookselling. Borders.com is one example of Amazon Enterprise Solutions, where Amazon.com manages all the Web and back-office programs (and optionally fulfillment) of another company's online business for a fee. Other examples are Target.com (which also uses Amazon.com's fulfillment services), Sears.ca, and Timex.com.

Buoyed by early successes in the book-selling business, Amazon.com decided to diversify its offerings and to expand internationally. In 1998, Amazon.com started selling music, DVDs and videos, toys, electronics, home and garden products, software, and video games. Now, Amazon.com also sells apparel and accessories, jewellery and watches, shoes, musical instruments, gourmet food, health and personal care products, beauty products, computers, cell phones and service, tools, automotive accessories, sports and outdoors supplies, and even pet supplies. It also has its own online music (MP3) store. Recently, Amazon.com designed and manufactured Kindle, an e-book reader, a wireless tablet that can download e-books from the Amazon.com Web site for a fee.

Amazon.com also launched international operations in France, the U.K., Japan, Germany, China, and Canada. Unfortunately, the Canadian branch, Amazon.ca, offers only a limited selection (*Note:* Amazon.com no longer sells to Canadian addresses). The fulfillment is outsourced to Assured Logistics, a Canada Post affiliate, which has a warehouse in Mississauga.

The major argument for the expansion of product offerings was a technological one. The company has already incurred the fixed costs of developing a comprehensive set of integrated software for its Web site and back office, including warehousing, transportation, demand forecasting, inventory planning, and more (*Note:* Web software development is continuing with the objective of perfecting the system). The software has minimized the need for human intervention: when an online customer buys an item, the order management system communicates with inventory and warehouse management systems to find the closest distribution centre for fulfilling the order. The customer knows immediately how long it will take to receive the item.

Expanding into other categories spread the fixed costs of software across a larger number of transactions, leading to greater profits through economies of scale. Says Bezos: "When we open a new category, we use basically the same software. We get to leverage the same customer base, our brand name, and the infrastructure. It's very low cost for us to open a new category because our earlier stores are already covering those costs."

However, many of the new offerings are bulky products that are expensive to stock and ship. Moreover, in the electronics business, leading manufacturers have stringent requirements on how the retailer will display and sell their products. Large manufacturers did not want to jeopardize existing relationships with retailers by selling through Amazon.com (which sold the products at lower prices). At the same time, many manufacturers wanted to set up their own online stores. By moving into new products, Amazon.com exposed itself to new levels of competition. Many established brick-and-mortar players (e.g., Best Buy, JC Penney) had decided to compete in the online arena, too. Nevertheless, many other manufacturers such as HP, Canon, Fisher-Price, Mattel, and Microsoft welcomed Amazon's new marketing channel.

Amazon.com strives to offer its customers compelling value through innovative use of technology, broad selection, high-quality content, high level of customer service, competitive pricing, and personalized service. The following features are intended to enhance the shopping experience: one-click ordering (the Web site remembers all relevant information about the customer and reduces the transactional burden), product description and customer reviews, "Search Inside the Book" (scans of the first few pages of 250,000 books), recommendations, wish list and recently viewed items by each customer. Also, Super Saver Shipping provides free shipping for items costing more than $25 and Amazon Prime provides free shipping for one year for $79.

Besides the Amazon Enterprise Solutions (which runs other company's Web pages), there is the Merchants@Amazon.com program, which sells small merchants' products on Amazon's Web page (there is a link to the merchant's online store). Even individuals can offer their used products to be displayed beside the identical new Amazon product for sale (this is called Amazon

Marketplace, and has over a million members). In addition, Amazon Web Services provides software and system assistance to Web developers for a fee. Finally, the Associate or Syndicated program consists of other online businesses referring customers to Amazon.com for a fee.

Jeff Bezos, founder of Amazon.com.

Questions

1. Should Amazon.com have remained an online bookstore? What are the advantages and disadvantages of diversification?

2. Identify the strategic and tactical/operational activities of supply chain management for Amazon.com and explain how each was used to achieve competitive advantage over a brick-and-mortar store.

Sources: S. Krishnamurthy, "Amazon.com—A Business History," in *E-commerce Management: Text and Cases*, September 27, 2002, pp. 1–45; B. Bacheldor, "From Scratch: Amazon Keeps Supply Chain Close to Home," *InformationWeek*, March 8, 2004, p. 40; H. Green, "How Amazon Aims to Keep you Clicking," *BusinessWeek*, March 2, 2009, 34; http://www.amazon.com/Careers-University-Recruiting/b/ref=gw_m_b_careers?ie=UTF8&node=203348011; http://phx.corporate-ir.net/phoenix.zhtml?c=97664&p=irol-reportsAnnual; A. Deutschman, "Inside the Mind of Jeff Bezos," *Fast Company* 85, August 2004, pp. 52–58; http://en.wikipedia.org/wiki/Amazon.com.

PART SIX

Operations Planning

The chapters in this part relate to the management of inventories, planning, and scheduling—often key factors in the success or failure of operations management to achieve profit and/or cost objectives while satisfying customers. The basic issue is how to best manage resources to effectively match supply and demand.

CHAPTER 12
Inventory Management

LEARNING OBJECTIVES

After completing this chapter, you should be able to:

LO1 Define the term *inventory*, list major reasons for holding inventory, and discuss the objectives of inventory management.

LO2 List the main requirements for effective inventory management, and describe A-B-C classification and perform it.

LO3 Describe the basic EOQ model, the economic production quantity model, the quantity discount model, and the planned shortage model, and solve typical problems.

LO4 Describe how to determine the reorder point and solve typical problems.

LO5 Describe the fixed order interval model and solve typical problems.

LO6 Describe the single period model and solve typical problems.

grocery and hardware distributor such as Federated Co-op holds tens of thousands of parts and products. It competes with grocery chains such as Loblaw, hardware stores such as Home Depot, and general merchandise stores such as Walmart. It is costly to carry excess inventory and poor customer service to not carry enough. How has Federated Co-op remained competitive? One important factor is good inventory management.

Good inventory management is important for the successful operation of most organizations and their supply chains. Operations, marketing, and finance have interests in good inventory management. Poor inventory management hampers operations, diminishes customer satisfaction, and increases operating costs.

This chapter describes inventory management of finished goods, some raw materials, supplies and spare parts, and retail items. The demand for these items is unknown and has to be forecasted. For this reason, these items are called *independent demand* items. Management of manufacturing parts and components will be described in later chapters on material requirements planning and just-in-time. Demand for manufacturing parts and components depends on the production schedule for the finished goods. For this reason, these items are called *dependent demand* items. Topics in this chapter include functions of inventory, the objectives, requirements for effective inventory management, and models for determining *how much* to order and *when* to order. Emphasis is on inventory analysis.

LO 1   INTRODUCTION

An **inventory** or stock is any material or product sitting idle, not being used, usually in a warehouse or storeroom, and kept for use or sale in the future. Companies typically store hundreds or even thousands of items in inventory, ranging from small things such as pencils, paper clips, screws, nuts, and bolts to large items such as equipment. Naturally, many of the items a company carries in inventory relate to the kind of business it engages in. Thus, manufacturing companies carry supplies of raw materials, purchased manufacturing parts and components, partially finished items (i.e., work-in-process [WIP]), and finished goods, as well as spare parts for machines, tools, and other supplies. Retail stores carry items for sale. Hospitals stock drugs, surgical supplies, life-monitoring equipment, sheets and pillow cases, and more. Supermarkets stock foods and other items.

Inventory management is concerned with planning and controlling inventories.

> **inventory** An idle material or product, usually in a warehouse or storeroom.

Importance of Inventories

A typical company probably has about 30 percent of its current assets and perhaps as much as 90 percent of its working capital invested in inventories. One widely used measure of business performance is *return on investment* (ROI), which is profit after taxes divided by total assets. Because inventories may represent a significant portion of total assets, a reduction of inventories can result in a significant increase in ROI.

The major source of revenues for retailers and wholesalers is the sale of merchandise (i.e., inventories). In fact, in terms of dollars, the inventory of goods held for sale is one of the largest assets of a merchandising business.

Service companies do not carry as many inventories, although they do carry inventories of supplies and equipment.

To understand why organizations have inventories at all, you need to be aware of the various functions (purposes) of inventory.

> **inventory management** Planning and controlling the inventories.

Functions (Purposes) of Inventories

Inventories serve a number of functions. Among the most important are the following:

1. To wait while being transported
2. To protect against stock-outs

3. To take advantage of economic lot size and quantity discount
4. To smooth seasonal demand or production
5. To decouple operations
6. To hedge against price increases

Let's take a closer look at each of these.

1. *To wait while being transported.* Raw materials and parts from suppliers, and finished goods from manufacturers heading to markets need to be transported. This is usually done by ship, rail, truck, or planes. Depending on the mode of transportation, the freight could take up to a month to reach its destination. Also, there are sometimes long waits in the distribution centres, terminals, and borders. Items being transported are called *in-transit inventory.*

2. *To protect against stock-outs.* Delayed deliveries and unexpected increases in demand increase the risk of stock-outs or shortages. Delays can occur because of weather conditions, supplier stock-outs, deliveries of wrong materials, quality problems, and so on. The risk of shortage can be reduced by holding *safety stocks,* which are stocks in excess of average demand to compensate for *variabilities* in demand and delivery lead time.

3. *To take advantage of economic lot size and quantity discount.* To minimize purchasing, receiving, material handling, and accounts payable costs, an organization often buys in quantities that exceed their immediate requirements. This necessitates storing some or all of the purchased goods for later use. Similarly, it is usually economical to produce in large rather than small quantities. Again, the excess output must be stored for later use. Thus, inventory storage enables an organization to buy or produce in *economic lot sizes.* This results in consecutive orders occurring after some interval of time, called *order* or *replenishment cycle.* The resulting inventory is hence known as *cycle stock (or lot or batch inventory).* The ability to store extra goods also allows a company to take advantage of price discounts for larger orders.

4. *To smooth seasonal demand or production.* Manufacturers that experience seasonal patterns in demand (e.g., agricultural implements or beer manufacturers) often build up inventories during off-season periods to meet high requirements during peak seasons. Also, when supply is seasonal, such as in grain, fruit, and vegetable production, the producer may keep some of the production for later sales (possibly after freezing/canning). These inventories are aptly named *seasonal inventories.*

5. *To decouple operations.* Historically, manufacturers have used inventories as *buffers* between successive operations to maintain continuity of production that would otherwise be disrupted by events such as breakdowns of equipment and accidents that cause a portion of the operation to shut down temporarily. The work-in-process buffers permit other operations to continue temporarily while the problem is resolved.

6. *To hedge against price increases.* Occasionally a buyer or manager will suspect that a substantial price increase is about to occur and will purchase larger-than-normal amounts to avoid the price increase. This is called *anticipation inventory.*

Importance and Objectives of Inventory Management

Inadequate management of inventories can result in both under- and overstocking of items. Under stocking results in missed deliveries, lost sales, dissatisfied customers, and production stoppage; overstocking unnecessarily ties up funds that might be more productive elsewhere and also ties up storage space. Although overstocking may appear to be the lesser of the two evils, the price tag for excessive overstocking can be staggering. It is not unheard of for managers to discover that their company has a 10-year supply of some item. (No doubt they got a good deal on it!)

Inventory management has two main concerns. One is the *level of customer service (availability)*; that is, to have the right goods, in sufficient quantities, in the right place, at the right time. The other is the inventory costs: the *costs of ordering and holding inventories.*

OM in ACTION

SYSPRO

Agood Enterprise Resource Planning (ERP) software for medium-size organizations is SYSPRO®. The first step in using the software is to define the inventory items. This is done in the Stock Codes under Setup of the Inventory module. Each item will have a file (see the screenshot below). The typical information needed is: Stock code, Warehouse to use, Part category (Bought out or Made-in), Product class (e.g., raw material), and Lead time (Days) or Batching rule (e.g., Lot-for-lot).

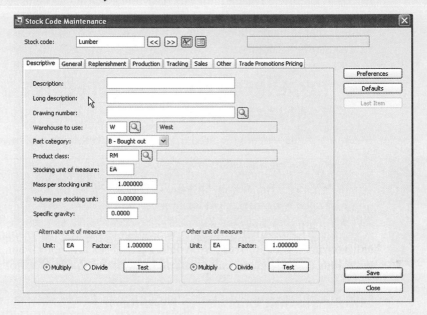

OM in ACTION   http://www.lilly.ca

Eli Lilly Canada

Eli Lilly Canada manufactures pharmaceuticals and medical devices. From its Scarborough, Ontario, distribution centre, Eli Lilly ships products to 200 wholesale and key accounts across Canada. In order to improve lot traceability, inventory record accuracy, and customer service, as well as to eliminate time-consuming paper procedures, in 1997 Eli Lilly installed a radio-frequency (RF) based warehouse management system (WMS), which is integrated with its manufacturing software.

As a product enters the warehouse, an employee uses an RF terminal's scanner to read the lot number and item code, and enters the quantity in the scanner. This information is transmitted instantly to the computer, where it is immediately entered into the inventory database. Upon verification, the WMS generates a bar-code label that provides product tracking as it is stored.

In the picking function, the software first assigns a box number to a specific customer order. Once an operator logs on to the system, the box number label is first printed and attached to a box. The software then directs the picker to retrieve the order in the sequence that minimizes total distance travelled. Once at the picking location, the picker scans the bar-code location ID to confirm the location, and then confirms the product before picking the quantity requested. Once the WMS confirms a correct pick, it directs the picker to the next pick location until the order is filled. The order is then conveyed to a packing station where weight of the order is determined. Upon verification of the weight, the order box number is scanned and assigned to a specific carrier for shipment to the customer.

Source: Based on "A Remedy for Inventory Ailments," *AS/400 Systems Management* 26(2), February 1998, pp. 46–47.

The overall objective of inventory management is to achieve satisfactory levels of customer service (availability) while keeping inventory costs within reasonable bounds. Toward this end, a buyer or inventory analyst must make two fundamental decisions: the *timing* and *size* of orders (i.e., when to order and how much to order). The greater part of this chapter is devoted to models that can be applied to assist in making those decisions.

Managers have a number of measures of performance they can use to judge the effectiveness of their inventory management. The most obvious, of course, is customer satisfaction, which they might measure by the in-stock or *fill rate* (i.e., the percentage of demand filled from stock on hand). Another measure is related to inventory costs: **inventory turnover**, which is the ratio of annual cost of goods to average inventory investment. The inventory turnover ratio indicates how many times a year the inventory is sold or used. Generally, the higher the ratio the better, because that implies more efficient use of inventories. A benefit of this measure is that it can be used to compare companies of different size in the *same* industry. A related measure is *days of inventory* on hand, a number that indicates the expected number of days of sales or usage that can be supplied from existing inventory.

inventory turnover   Ratio annual cost of goods to average inventory investment.

(LO2) REQUIREMENTS FOR EFFECTIVE INVENTORY MANAGEMENT

Inventory managers are required to perform the following activities:

1. Safely storing and using inventories
2. Tracking inventories and using inventory control models
3. Forecasting demands and lead times
4. Estimating inventory costs
5. Performing A-B-C classification

Let's take a closer look at each of these requirements.

Safely Storing and Using Inventories

Most inventory items need to be protected from harsh outdoor environments such as rain and snow. Therefore, inventory is usually stored indoors, in a warehouse or storeroom. Depending on the nature of the item, racks, shelves, or bins may be used to hold them. Heavy items or fast-moving items are stored on the floor. To save moving items long distances, warehouses usually use the vertical space, i.e., they are as high as a three- or four-storey building. Forklifts and high-reach industrial trucks are used to access the top locations.

A warehouse/storeroom should be uncluttered so that items can be stored and retrieved easily. In addition to difficulty in finding a particular item, a cramped warehouse/storeroom will result in excessive damage to stocks. Depending on the flow of items into and out of the warehouse/storeroom, the right level of automation should be used. Most warehouses use forklifts, which move cases of items piled on pallets. Some use conveyors and some use carousels. A **warehouse management system**, or WMS, is a computer software that controls the movement and storage of materials within a warehouse, and processes the associated transactions, including receiving, put-away, replenishment, picking, and shipping. For applications of warehouse management systems, see the "Eli Lilly Canada" OM in Action earlier in the chapter, and the "B.C. Hot House" OM in Action later in the chapter.

warehouse management system   A computer software that controls the movement and storage of materials within a warehouse, and processes the associated transactions.

Some inventoried items are expensive, so access to the building should be controlled, and items that are prone to theft (e.g., small valuable items such as batteries) should be locked up in secure areas. Also, because full pallets are heavy, racks in the warehouse can be high, and equipment such as forklifts and pallet jacks are large and fast moving, safety is an important issue in warehouse management.

A common problem in most warehouses/storerooms is the existence of a considerable amount of obsolete items. These include parts for machines that no longer exist, wrong parts, excess material, used machines, etc. To be efficient, outdated items should be either sent back to the supplier (to be restocked by the supplier) or sold at a discount (salvaged). Obsolete items are a drag on company's assets and take space in the warehouse.

For another application of warehouse management, see the "The McGraw-Hill Ryerson Warehouse in Whitby, Ontario" Operations Tour at the end of this chapter.

Tracking Inventories and Using Inventory Control Models

If inventories are not continually tracked, then they must be periodically counted. **Periodic counting** or review is a physical count of items in inventory made at periodic intervals (e.g., weekly, monthly) in order to decide how much of each item to order. Many small retailers use this approach: a manager periodically checks the shelves and stockroom to determine the quantities on hand. Then, the manager estimates how much of it will be demanded prior to the next delivery and bases the order quantity on this information. This replenishment model is called the *fixed order interval model*. An advantage of this method is that orders from the same supplier can be issued at the same time, which can result in economies in processing and shipping. There are also several disadvantages of periodic review. One is the possibility of stock-out between reviews. To protect against this, extra stock should be carried. Another disadvantage is the time and cost of a physical count.

Perpetual tracking (or *continual* tracking) keeps track of removals from and additions to inventory on a continuous basis, so the system can provide information on the current level of inventory for each item. Usually, a **fixed order quantity/reorder point model** is used with perpetual tracking. When the amount on hand reaches a predetermined minimum (called the reorder point), a fixed quantity is ordered. An obvious advantage of this method is that shortages can be avoided. Another advantage is that the order quantity is fixed; management can determine an optimal order quantity and use it for every order (provided that demand does not vary seasonally or has a trend). A disadvantage of this approach is the added cost of continual record keeping. Bank accounts are kept using this method, i.e., transactions such as customer deposits and withdrawals are instantly recorded and balance is determined continually. All business and manufacturing software programs keep track of inventories continually. For example, see the "SYSPRO" OM in Action earlier in the chapter.

A simple implementation of the fixed order quantity/reorder-point model that does not require inventory counting is the **two bin system**. Items are withdrawn from the first bin until its contents are exhausted. It is then time to reorder. The second bin contains enough stock to satisfy expected demand until the order is filled plus an extra cushion of safety stock that will reduce the chance of stock-outs if the order is late and/or if usage is greater than expected. When the order arrives, top off the second bin and leave the rest in the first bin. Start drawing inventory from the first bin until it is empty again, and repeat. Sometimes an order card is placed at the bottom of the first bin. The advantage of this method is that there is no need to record each withdrawal from inventory or keep track of inventory on hand; the disadvantage is that the reorder card may not be turned in.

Most warehouses and storerooms use laser scanning devices that read bar codes assigned to items, cases, pallets, etc. and the storage location (rack, shelf, bin, etc.). A **bar code** is a number assigned to an item or location, made of a group of vertical bars of different thickness that are readable by a scanner. There are approximately five different types of bar codes. A typical grocery Universal Product Code (UPC) is illustrated to the right. The zero on the left of the bar code identifies this as a grocery item, the first five numbers (14800) indicate the manufacturer, and the last five numbers (23208) indicate the specific item (natural-style applesauce). For more information on bar codes, see http://www.gs1us. org/barcodes_and_ecom. Bar-code scanners represent a major change in the inventory management of warehouses and storerooms because they have increased the speed and accuracy of transactions significantly.

Radio frequency identification (RFID) is a technology that uses radio waves to identify items. This is done through the use of an RFID tag attached to the item. The tag has an integrated circuit chip and an antenna that emits information to a network-connected RFID reader using radio waves. Use of RFID has been increasing, especially for identifying a case of an item and equipment. It is expected that RFID tags will replace

periodic counting   Physical count of items in inventory made at periodic intervals (e.g., weekly, monthly).

perpetual tracking   Keeps track of removals from and additions to inventory continuously, thus providing the current inventory level of each item.

fixed order quantity/reorder point model   An order of a fixed size is placed when the amount on hand drops to or below a minimum quantity called the *reorder point*.

two bin system   Reorder when the first bin is empty; use the second bin until order arrives; Top off the second bin and leave the rest in the first bin; Start drawing inventory from the first bin until it is empty again, and repeat.

bar code   A number assigned to an item or location, made of a group of vertical bars of different thickness that are readable by a scanner.

OM in *ACTION*

Air Canada's RFID

A few years ago, Air Canada realized that out of its 14,000 food trolleys, 2,000 were missing. Each trolley costs about $1,000. The galley trolleys, used to carry food in the airplanes, are handled by caterers, undergo maintenance, may be stored in Air Canada warehouses, and are used in in-flight training centres, altogether more than 50 locations worldwide. The trolleys could be lost in a warehouse, hoarded by a caterer, misidentified and used by another airline, or stolen. Air Canada's manager of equipment design, maintenance, and repair, Barry Wilkins,

first wanted to put a bar code on each trolley. But, because the caterers were too busy to use bar code readers, he looked into RFID tags and readers. Semi-active RFID tags cost about $20 each. Each trolley reports its presence dozens of times a day through RF readers that are installed at the entrance and exit of caterers and other facilities. The system is connected to the Air Canada database, which can be consulted by Air Canada employees and caterers to determine the inventory of trolleys in each location.

Source: J. Stoller, "Sorting out the Details," *CMA Management*, June/July 2004, 78(4), pp. 22–25.

bar codes in the near future. For more information on RFID and two applications, see Chapter 11 on supply chain management. For another application, see the "Air Canada's RFID" OM in Action.

Forecasting Demands and Lead Times

Inventories are used to satisfy future demand requirements, so it is essential to have reliable estimates of the amount and timing of future demand. Also, it is essential to know the **purchase lead time**, the time it will take for orders to be delivered. Similarly, manufacturing lead time is the time it will take for a batch of a product to be manufactured. In addition, managers need to know the extent to which demand and lead time might vary: the greater the potential variability, the greater the need for additional safety stock to reduce the risk of a shortage between deliveries. Thus, there is a crucial link between forecasting and inventory management.

purchase lead time Time interval between ordering and receiving the order.

Point-of-sale (POS) systems electronically record actual sales at the time and location of sale, which, after accumulation into daily or weekly or monthly sales for each stock-keeping unit (SKU), are used in forecasting.

point-of-sale (POS) system Software for electronically recording sales at the time and location of sale.

Given the large number of items kept in inventory of a typical organization, a simple time-series forecasting technique such as exponential smoothing (and its variants) is commonly used to forecast demand of items kept in inventory.

Estimating Inventory Costs

Three basic costs are associated with inventories: holding, ordering, and shortage costs.

Holding or **carrying cost** relates to physically having items in storage. Costs include warehousing costs (rent or building depreciation, labour, material-handling equipment depreciation, heating/cooling, light, etc.) and the opportunity cost associated with having funds, which could be used elsewhere, tied up in inventory. Other holding costs include insurance, obsolescence, spoilage, pilferage, and breakage.

holding (carrying) cost Cost to keep an item in inventory.

The significance of some of the components of holding cost depends on the type of item involved. Items that are easily concealed or are fairly expensive are prone to theft and need to be locked up. Items such as meats and dairy are subject to rapid spoilage and need freezing or cooling.

Holding cost is stated in either of two ways: as a percentage of unit cost or as a dollar amount per unit. Typical annual holding cost rates range from 20 percent to 40 percent of the cost of an item. In other words, to hold a $100 item for one year could cost from $20 to $40.

ordering cost Cost of the actual placement of an order (not including the purchase cost).

Ordering cost is the cost of the actual placement of an order (not including the purchase cost). This includes the time of purchasing/inventory control staff determining how much is needed, periodically evaluating sources of supply, preparing purchase orders; and the fixed-cost portion of transportation, receiving, inspecting, and moving the goods to storage. It also includes the cost of time spent paying the invoice. Ordering cost is generally expressed as a fixed dollar amount per order, regardless of order size.

When a company produces its own inventory instead of ordering it from a supplier, the cost of machine setup is analogous to ordering cost; that is, it is expressed as a fixed charge per production run, regardless of the size of the run. Machine **setup** involves preparing the machine for the job by adjusting it, changing cutting tools, etc.

setup   Preparing the machine for the job by adjusting it, changing cutting tools, etc.

Shortage cost results when demand exceeds the supply of inventory on hand. This cost can include the opportunity cost of not making a sale (i.e., unrealized profit), loss of customer goodwill, late charges, and expediting costs. Furthermore, if the shortage occurs in an item carried for internal use (e.g., to supply an assembly line), the cost of lost production or downtime is considered a shortage cost, which can easily run into hundreds of dollars a minute or more.

shortage cost   Cost of demand exceeding supply of inventory on hand; includes unrealized profit per unit, loss of goodwill, etc.

Performing A-B-C Classification

Items held in inventory are typically not of equal importance in terms of dollars invested, profit potential, sales or usage quantity, or shortage cost. For instance, a producer of electrical equipment might have electrical generators, coils of wire, and miscellaneous nuts and bolts among the items carried in inventory. It would be inefficient to devote equal attention to each of these items. Instead, a more reasonable approach would be to allocate control efforts according to the *relative importance* of various items in inventory.

The **A-B-C classification** groups inventory items into three classes according to some measure of importance, usually annual dollar value (i.e., cost per unit multiplied by annual usage or sales quantity), and then allocates inventory control efforts accordingly. The three classes are: A (very important), B (moderately important), and C (least important). A items generally account for about 15 to 20 percent of the *types* of items (SKUs, not counting multiples of the same part/product) in inventory but about 70 to 80 percent of the annual *dollar value (ADV)*. At the other end of the scale, C items might account for about 50 to 60 percent of the SKUs but only about 5 to 10 percent of the ADV. These percentages vary from company to company, but in most instances a relatively small number of items will account for a large share of ADV, and these items should receive a greater share of inventory control efforts. For instance, A items should receive close attention through better forecasting, more frequent ordering, and better safety stock determination. The C items should receive only loose control (e.g., using a two-bin system, bulk orders), and the B items should have controls that lie between the two extremes.

A-B-C classification   Grouping inventory items into three classes according to some measure of importance, and allocating inventory control efforts accordingly.

OM in *ACTION*   http://www.sourcemedical.com

Source Medical

Source Medical is the largest medical, surgical, and lab products distributor in Canada. It offers over 60,000 items to its customers: hospitals, clinics, doctor's offices, nursing homes, clinical labs, etc. These items satisfy more than 85 percent of the customers' needs. The items include anything from bandages to operating tables. Source Medical has over 300 suppliers, such as 3M Canada, Procter & Gamble, and Kimberly-Clark.

Source Medical has a National Supply Centre (NSC), a 220,000 ft² warehouse/distribution centre, in Mississauga, and 7 regional warehouse/distribution centres (DC), from

Vancouver to St. John's. The regional DCs provide daily delivery service to customers. The NSC carries approximately 30,000 Stock Keeping Units (SKU). The rest are low-demand items (e.g., equipment) that are bought when necessary and are either cross-docked to the DC/customer or directly shipped to the customer. Some of the SKUs are also inventoried in regional DCs (these are called national stocks) and others, used less frequently, are only kept in NSC (called central stocks).

The materials management team forecasts customer demand, monitors and improves supplier delivery performance, and controls the levels of inventory in each facility. Any low or high levels are investigated to identify its cause and the problem is solved with the cooperation of suppliers and/or customers. For example, the cause for a low inventory of a SKU may be an incorrect purchase order or a problem at a supplier. Using this method, Source Medical has reduced its inventories by 15 percent while increasing its fill rate by 8 percent.

Shipments from suppliers to the NSC (30–35 full truckloads and 50–60 less than full truckloads per day) and from NSC to regional warehouses are by contract carriers whereas local deliveries to the customers are by Source Medical's own trucks. The NSC is divided in two parts: approximately 2,000 full case SKUs (A items) are kept on one side, and 28,000 other SKUs (B and C items) are kept on shelves on the other side. Radio frequency communication and bar code scanners are used for receiving, put away, replenishment, and order picking. Source Medical uses Witron warehouse management system and Scancode Logistics freight management system.

Source Medical has JIT or stockless inventory arrangement with its customers. This means that an order is received by EDI from a ward of a hospital, and it is delivered the next day directly to the ward, hence relieving the hospital of the need for a stockroom. Source Medical's Online ordering system provides custom pricing and allows the use of a bar code scanner (the system is called OrderConnect) which makes ordering faster and easier. Also, rush deliveries are possible. The Advanced Customer Logistics team works with customers to improve the efficiency and effectiveness of the supply system, e.g., by performing product standardization. EDI is also used for communication within Source Medical and with its suppliers.

Sources: R. Robertson, "Saving Lives," *Materials Management and Distribution*, July/August 2003, 48(6), pp. 14–20; http://www.sourcemedical.com/en/pages/supply_chain.aspx.

Example 1

Classify the following inventory items as A, B, or C based on annual dollar value (ADV):

Item	Annual Demand	×	Unit Cost	=	Annual Dollar Value (ADV)
1........	3,000		$10		$30,000
2........	9,000		3		27,000
3........	1,000		710		710,000
4........	2,500		250		625,000
5........	1,900		500		950,000
6........	400		200		80,000
7........	500		100		50,000
8........	1,000		4,300		4,300,000
9........	200		210		42,000
10........	5,000		720		3,600,000
11........	2,500		192		480,000
12........	1,000		35		35,000

Solution

Sort the rows by decreasing values of ADV and calculate the percentage of total ADV for each SKU:

Item	Annual Demand	×	Unit Cost	=	Annual Dollar Value (ADV)	% of Total ADV	
8.......	1,000		$4,300		$4,300,000	39.3	A
10......	5,000		720		3,600,000	32.9	
5.......	1,900		500		950,000	8.7	
3.......	1,000		710		710,000	6.5	
4.......	2,500		250		625,000	5.7	B
11......	2,500		192		480,000	4.4	
6.......	400		200		80,000	.7	
7.......	500		100		50,000	.5	
9.......	200		210		42,000	.4	
12......	1,000		35		35,000	.3	C
1.......	3,000		10		30,000	.3	
2.......	9,000		3		27,000	.3	
					$10,929,000	100.0	

Proceed down the list, adding percentage of total ADVs until you get close to 80 percent of total ADV. The first two items have 72.2 percent of total ADV and 2/12 = 17 percent of SKUs, so it seems reasonable to classify them as A items. (Also note the sharp drop in ADV from the second to third rows.) The next four items have moderate ADV (25.3 percent of total ADV and 4/12 = 33 percent of SKUs) and should be classified as B items. (Also note the sharp drop in ADV between the sixth and seventh rows.) The remainder are C items, based on their relatively low ADV (2.5 percent of total ADV and 6/12 = 50 percent of SKUs).

Although annual dollar value may be the primary factor in classifying inventory items, a manager may take other factors into account in making exceptions for certain items (e.g., changing the classification of a C item to A). Factors may include the risk of obsolescence, the consequence of a stock-out, the distance of a supplier, and so on.

Managers use the A–B–C concept in many different settings to improve operations. In fact, A–B–C classification is related to the 80–20 rule and Pareto analysis discussed in Chapter 9. For example, the A–B–C concept is sometimes used to guide **cycle counting**, which is a regular actual count of the items in inventory on a cyclic schedule rather than once a year. The purpose of cycle counting is to (1) reduce discrepancies between inventory records and the actual quantities of inventory on hand, and (2) investigate the causes of inaccuracy and fix them. Accuracy is important because inaccurate records can lead to wrong inventory control decisions, which then lead to disruptions in production, poor customer service, or unnecessarily high inventory carrying cost.

> **cycle counting** Regular actual count of the items in inventory on a cyclic schedule.

The key questions concerning cycle counting for management are:

1. How much accuracy is needed?
2. What kind of counting cycle should be used?
3. Who should do it?

APICS, the American Production and Inventory Control Society (now Association for Operations Management), recommends the following guidelines for inventory record accuracy: ± 0.2 percent for A items, ± 1 percent for B items, and ± 5 percent for C items. Therefore, A items should be counted more frequently than C items. For example, A items should be counted every month, B items quarterly, and C items annually.

http://www.apics.org

Some companies use regular stockroom personnel to do cycle counting during periods of slow activity, while others contract with outside companies to do it on a periodic basis. Use of an outside company provides an independent check on inventory and may reduce the risk of problems created by error-prone employees.

The "Source Medical" OM in Action uses the A–B–C classification in another way.

LO3 FIXED ORDER QUANTITY/REORDER POINT MODEL: DETERMINING THE ECONOMIC ORDER QUANTITY

In the fixed order quantity/reorder point model, the fixed order quantity is ordered when the amount on hand drops to or below the reorder point. The fixed order quantity used is usually the optimal or **economic order quantity (EOQ)**. EOQ is determined by minimizing the total inventory control cost. Four EOQ-related models are described here:

> **economic order quantity (EOQ)** The order size that minimizes total inventory control cost.

1. Basic economic order quantity
2. Economic production quantity
3. EOQ with quantity discounts
4. EOQ with planned shortages

Basic Economic Order Quantity (EOQ)

The basic EOQ model is used to identify the order size for an item that will minimize the sum of the annual costs of holding and ordering inventory. The annual purchase price of units is not included in the total cost in this case because it is assumed that purchase price is unaffected by the order size.

The basic EOQ model is based on a number of assumptions. They are listed in Table 12-1.

Inventory ordering and usage occur in cycles. Figure 12-1 illustrates several inventory (or order) cycles. A cycle begins with receipt of an order of Q units, which are then withdrawn at a constant rate over time. When the quantity on hand is just sufficient to satisfy demand during the lead time, another order for Q units is submitted to the supplier. Because it is assumed that both the demand rate and the lead time do not vary, the order will be received at the precise instant that the inventory on hand falls to zero. Thus, orders are timed to avoid both excess stock and stock-outs.

The optimal order quantity reflects a trade-off between annual holding and annual ordering costs: If the order size is relatively small, the average inventory will be low, resulting in low holding cost. However, a small order size will necessitate frequent orders, which will drive up annual ordering cost. Conversely, ordering large quantities at infrequent intervals can reduce annual ordering cost, but that would result in higher average inventory levels and therefore increased annual holding cost. Figure 12-2 illustrates these two extremes.

Table 12-1	
Assumptions of the basic EOQ model	**1.** Only one product is involved.
	2. Annual demand requirements are known.
	3. Demand is spread evenly throughout the year so that the demand rate is reasonably constant.
	4. Lead time does not vary.
	5. Each order is received in a single delivery.
	6. There are no quantity discounts. This includes the assumption that transportation cost per unit is fixed and does not depend on order size.
	7. Shortage is not allowed.

Figure 12-1

Inventory (or order) cycles: profile of inventory level over time

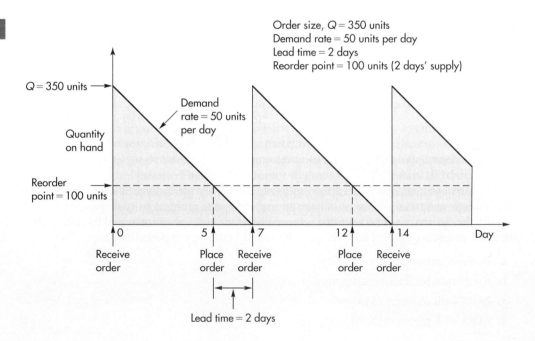

OM in *ACTION*   http://www.bchothouse.com

B.C. Hot House

Vancouver's B.C. Hot House Foods works with 50 local growers of cucumbers, tomatoes, and peppers to grade, package, distribute, and sell their produce. B.C. Hot House moved into a 127,000 ft² facility in the late 1990s. Until then, it was manually tracking the inventory. The new technology, including 15 Intermec hand-held scanners, has improved put-away, processing, and inventory counting.

When produce is received, a tag printer prints a bar-code label for each pallet, storing the SKU, product description, and date in a database. When the labels are scanned later, the hand-held terminals tell employees in which warehouse location to place the pallets. The system directs staff to the three best locations. Before the new system, employees had to search the racks for empty slots.

After grading the produce and putting them in cases, roller encoders apply a bar code to the bottom of each case identifying its content based on the product's originating lane (one of 32), and the date code. These cases are stored temporarily in the warehouse, awaiting shipment.

B.C. Hot House performs daily inventory counting. It used to take two people a full day to count 70,000 to 80,000 cases. Because of the company's growth, 130,000 to 140,000 cases must now be counted, and yet inventory counting now takes one person just three hours daily with a hand-held terminal. The employee scans a bar-coded tag attached to each location, which identifies the location and its product on his or her hand-held terminal's screen display. Then the employee compares the screen information to the quantity of product actually found at the scanned location. If it matches, he or she moves on to the next location. If it doesn't match, he or she updates the screen display for that location. This new inventory counting system has resulted in labour savings of more than $20,000 annually.

Another benefit of the computerized inventory system is that the salespeople can find out what products are available in the warehouse and what date code is on them.

Source: A. Loudin, "A Greener Garden," *Automatic I.D. News* 14(2), February 1998, p. 26ff.

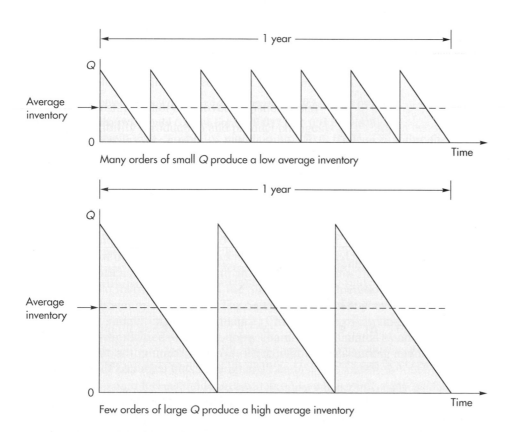

Figure 12-2

Average inventory level and number of orders per year are inversely related: as one increases, the other decreases.

Many orders of small Q produce a low average inventory

Few orders of large Q produce a high average inventory

Thus, the ideal solution is an order size that is neither very large nor very small, but somewhere in between. The exact amount to order will depend on the relative magnitudes of holding and ordering costs.

Figure 12-3

Annual holding, ordering, and total inventory control cost curves

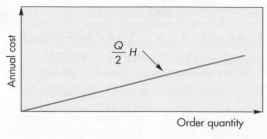

A. Annual holding cost is linearly related to order quantity

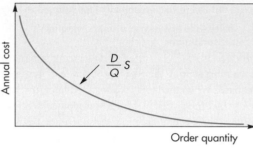

B. Annual ordering cost is inversely and nonlinearly related to order quantity

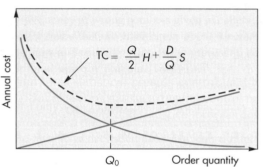

C. The total annual inventory cost curve is U-shaped, and at its minimum annual holding cost equals annual ordering cost

Annual holding cost is calculated by multiplying the average amount of inventory on hand by the cost to hold one unit for one year (even though any given unit would not necessarily be held for a year). The average inventory is simply half of the order quantity: The amount on hand decreases steadily from Q units to 0, for an average of $(Q + 0)/2$, or $Q/2$. Using the symbol H to represent the annual holding cost per unit, the *total annual holding cost* is

$$\text{Annual holding cost} = \frac{Q}{2} H$$

where

Q = Order quantity, units per order

H = Holding (or carrying) cost per unit per year

Annual holding cost is thus a linear function of Q: it increases or decreases in direct proportion to changes in the order quantity Q, as Figure 12-3A illustrates.

On the other hand, annual ordering cost will decrease as order quantity increases, because for a given annual demand, the larger the order quantity the fewer the number of orders needed. For instance, if annual demand is 12,000 units and the order quantity is 1,000 units per order, there will be 12 orders during the year. But if $Q = 2,000$ units, only six orders will be needed; if $Q = 3,000$ units, only four orders will be needed. In general, the number of orders per year will be D/Q, where D = annual demand. Because ordering cost per order is relatively insensitive to order quantity, *annual ordering cost* equals the number of orders per year times the ordering cost per order:

$$\text{Annual ordering cost} = \frac{D}{Q} S$$

where

D = Demand, units per year

S = Ordering cost per order

Because the number of orders per year, D/Q, decreases as Q increases (but not at a constant rate), annual ordering cost is inversely and nonlinearly related to order quantity, as Figure 12-3B illustrates.

The total annual inventory cost of holding and ordering inventory, when Q units are ordered each time is

$$\text{TC} = \begin{matrix}\text{Annual}\\\text{holding}\\\text{cost}\end{matrix} + \begin{matrix}\text{Annual}\\\text{ordering}\\\text{cost}\end{matrix} = \frac{Q}{2}H + \frac{D}{Q}S \qquad (12\text{-}1)$$

Figure 12-3C reveals that the total-cost curve is U-shaped (i.e., convex, with one minimum) and that *it reaches its minimum at the quantity where annual holding and annual ordering costs are equal.* An expression for the optimal order quantity, Q_0, can be obtained using calculus.[1] The result is the formula

$$\text{EOQ} = Q_0 = \sqrt{\frac{2DS}{H}} \qquad (12\text{-}2)$$

The minimum total cost is then found by substituting Q_0 for Q in Formula 12-1. The length of an order cycle (i.e., the time between orders, if Q_0 is used) is

$$\text{Length of order cycle (in years)} = \frac{Q_0}{D} \qquad (12\text{-}3)$$

Example 2

A tire store expects to sell approximately 100 steel-belted radial tires of a certain make, model, and size next year. Annual holding cost is $16 per tire, and ordering cost is $20 per order. The store operates 360 days a year and has ample storage space in the back.

a. What is the EOQ?

b. How many times per year would the store reorder if EOQ units are ordered each time?

c. What is the length of an order cycle if EOQ units are ordered each time?

d. What is the total annual inventory control cost if EOQ units are ordered each time?

Solution

D = 100 tires per year

H = $16 per unit per year

S = $20 per order

a. $Q_0 = \sqrt{\dfrac{2DS}{H}} = \sqrt{\dfrac{2(100)(20)}{16}} = 15.8$,   round to 16

b. Number of orders per year: $D/Q_0 = \dfrac{100 \text{ tires/yr}}{16 \text{ tires each time}} = 6.25$ times per year

---

[1]We can find the minimum point of the total-cost curve by differentiating TC with respect to Q, setting the result equal to zero, and solving for Q. Thus,

$$\frac{d\text{TC}}{dQ} = \frac{dQ}{2}H + d(D/Q)S = H/2 - DS/Q^2$$

$H/2 - DS/Q^2 = 0$, so $Q^2 = \dfrac{2DS}{H}$ and $Q = \sqrt{\dfrac{2DS}{H}}$

Note that the second derivative $\left(\dfrac{2DS}{Q^3}\right)$ is positive, which indicates a minimum has been obtained.

c. Length of order cycle: $Q_0/D = \dfrac{16 \text{ tires}}{100 \text{ tires/yr}} = .16$ year, which is $.16 \times 360$, or 57.6 workdays.

d. TC = Annual holding cost + Annual ordering cost

$= (Q_0/2)H + (D/Q_0)S$

$= (16/2)16 + (100/16)20$

$= \$128 + \$125$

$= \$253$

Note that the annual ordering and annual holding costs are almost equal at the EOQ, as illustrated in Figure 12-3C.

Holding cost is usually stated as a percentage i of the purchase price (or unit cost) of an item rather than as a dollar amount per unit H. However, as long as this percentage is converted into a dollar amount by multiplying it by unit cost R, the EOQ formula is still appropriate.

Example 3

A distributor of security monitors purchases 3,600 black-and-white monitors a year from the manufacturer at the cost of $65 each. Ordering cost is $30 per order, and annual holding cost rate is 20 percent of the unit cost. Calculate the optimal order quantity and the total annual cost of ordering and holding the inventory.

Solution

$D = 3{,}600$ monitors per year

$S = \$30$ per order

$i =$ holding cost rate per year $= 20\%$

$R =$ unit cost $= \$65$

$H = iR = .20(\$65) = \$13$

$Q_0 = \sqrt{\dfrac{2DS}{H}} = \sqrt{\dfrac{2(3{,}600)(30)}{13}} = 128.9, \quad$ round to 129 monitors

TC = Annual holding cost + Annual ordering cost

$= (Q_0/2)H + (D/Q_0)S = (129/2)13 + (3{,}600/129)30 = \$838.50 + \$837.21 = \$1{,}675.71$

Comment. Holding cost per unit per year, ordering cost per order, and annual demand are typically estimated values rather than values that can be precisely determined from, say, accounting records. Holding and ordering costs are sometimes designated rather than computed by managers. Consequently, the EOQ value should be regarded as an approximate quantity rather than an exact quantity. Thus, rounding the calculated value is perfectly acceptable; stating a value to several decimal places would tend to give an unrealistic impression of the precision involved. An obvious question is: How good is this "approximate" EOQ in terms of minimizing total annual inventory control cost? The answer is that the EOQ is fairly robust; the total cost curve is relatively flat near the EOQ, especially to the right of the EOQ. In other words, even if the approximate EOQ differs from the actual EOQ, total cost will not increase much at all. This is particularly true for quantities larger than the real EOQ (see Figure 12-4). Also note that annual demand D is usually estimated by multiplying next month's forecast of demand by 12 or next week's forecast of demand by 52. If there is seasonality in demand, a lot sizing technique, described in Chapter 14, will be more appropriate than EOQ. However, a simple solution commonly used is to determine the length of order cycle for EOQ and set the order quantity equal to the expected demand during that period. For example, for Example 2 above, order the forecast demand for the next 58 days.

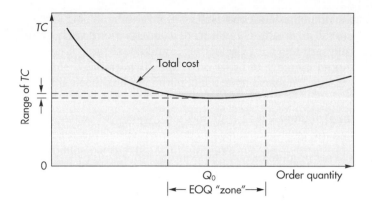

Figure 12-4

The total annual inventory cost curve is relatively flat near the EOQ.

Economic Production Quantity (EPQ)

The equivalent of EOQ in production is the Economic Production Quantity (EPQ). EPQ is used to determine the optimal batch or lot size in a batch process. Batch production is widely used. The reason for this is that, in many instances, the capacity to produce a part on a machine or equipment exceeds the part's usage or demand rate. As long as production continues, inventory will continue to grow. In such instances, it makes sense to periodically produce items in batches or *lots*.

The assumptions of the EPQ model are similar to those of the EOQ model, except that instead of orders being received in a single delivery, units are received incrementally. This is because the production rate is finite. Figure 12-5 illustrates how inventory level is affected by periodically producing a batch of a particular item.

During the production phase of the cycle, inventory builds up at a rate equal to the difference between production and usage rates. For example, if the daily production rate is 20 units and the daily usage rate is 5 units, inventory will build up at the rate of $20 - 5 = 15$ units per day. As long as production continues, the inventory level will grow; when production ceases, the inventory level will begin to decrease. Hence, the inventory level will be maximum, denoted by I_{max}, when production ceases. When the amount of inventory on hand is exhausted, production is resumed and the cycle repeats itself. It can be seen that the average inventory on hand is $.5I_{max}$.

Because the company makes the product itself, there is no ordering cost as such. Nonetheless, with every production run (batch), there is a setup cost—the cost to prepare the equipment for the job, such as cleaning, adjusting, and changing tools and fixtures. Setup costs are analogous to ordering costs because they are independent of the lot (run) quantity. They are treated in exactly the same way, and we use the same symbol, S, to denote setup cost per production run. The larger the run quantity, the fewer the number of runs needed per year and, hence, the lower the annual setup cost. The number of runs or batches per year is D/Q, and the annual setup cost is equal to the number of runs per year times the setup cost per run: $(D/Q) S$.

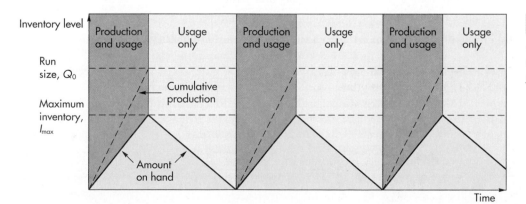

Figure 12-5

Inventory level when a batch of an item is produced periodically

Total annual inventory control cost is:

$$\text{TC} = \text{Annual holding cost} + \text{Annual setup cost} = \left(\frac{I_{max}}{2}\right)H + (D/Q)S \qquad (12\text{-}4)$$

where

I_{max} = Maximum inventory

Q = Production run quantity

S = Setup cost per production run

To calculate I_{max}, let

p = Production rate (e.g., units per day)

d = Usage or demand rate (e.g., units per day)

The production run quantity Q is consumed at the rate of d during the entire cycle length (= the time between the beginnings of two consecutive production runs). Therefore,

$$\text{Cycle length} = \frac{Q}{d} \qquad (12\text{-}5)$$

The production run quantity Q is produced at the rate of p during the production run length (the production phase of the cycle). Therefore,

$$\text{Production run length} = \frac{Q}{P} \qquad (12\text{-}6)$$

Therefore, the maximum inventory level I_{max} is

$$I_{max} = Q - d\left(\frac{Q}{p}\right) = \frac{Q}{p}(p - d) \qquad (12\text{-}7)$$

Substituting (12-7) in (12-4), taking derivatives with respect to Q, setting it equal to zero, and solving for Q, will result in:

$$Q_0 = \sqrt{\frac{2DS}{H}}\sqrt{\frac{p}{p-d}} \qquad (12\text{-}8)$$

Example 4

A toy manufacturer uses 48,000 rubber wheels per year for its popular dump truck series. The company can make its own wheels at a rate of 800 per day. The toy trucks are assembled uniformly over the entire year. Holding cost is $1 per wheel per year. Setup cost for a production run of wheels is $45. The company operates 240 days per year. Determine the:

a. Optimal production run quantity

b. Minimum total annual cost for holding and setup

c. Cycle length for the optimal production run quantity

d. Production run length for the optimal production run quantity

Solution

$D = 48,000$ wheels per year
$S = \$45$ per production run
$H = \$1$ per wheel per year
$p = 800$ wheels per day
$d = 48,000$ wheels per 240 days, or 200 wheels per day

a. $Q_0 = \sqrt{\dfrac{2DS}{H}}\sqrt{\dfrac{p}{p-d}} = \sqrt{\dfrac{2(48,000)45}{1}}\sqrt{\dfrac{800}{800-200}} = 2,400$ wheels

b. $\text{TC}_{min} = \text{Annual holding cost} + \text{Annual setup cost} = \left(\dfrac{I_{max}}{2}\right)H + (D/Q_0)S$

Thus, you must first calculate I_{max}:

$$I_{max} = \frac{Q}{p}(p - d) = \frac{2,400}{800}(800 - 200) = 1,800 \text{ wheels}$$

$$TC_{min} = \frac{1,800}{2} \times \$1 + \frac{48,000}{2,400} \times \$45 = \$900 + \$900 = \$1,800$$

Note again the equality of the annual costs (in this example, setup and holding costs) at the EPQ.

c. Cycle length $= \dfrac{Q}{d} = \dfrac{2,400 \text{ wheels}}{200 \text{ wheels per day}} = 12 \text{ days}$

Thus, a production run of wheels will be made every 12 days.

d. Production run length $= \dfrac{Q}{p} = \dfrac{2,400 \text{ wheels}}{800 \text{ wheels per day}} = 3 \text{ days}$

Thus, each production run will take three days.

EOQ with Quantity Discounts

Quantity discounts are price reductions for large orders, offered to customers to induce them to buy in large quantities. For example, a surgical supply company published the price list shown in Table 12-2 for boxes of extra-wide gauze strips. Note that the price per box decreases as order quantity increases. We consider the all-unit discount case where the price of every unit is the price per unit given for the order quantity. For example, if 60 gauze strips are purchased, the total cost will be 60($1.70) = $102. The alternate method, the "incremental discount" will charge $2.00 for the first 44, $1.70 for each unit above that up to the 69th unit, and $1.40 for each unit above that. For example, for an order of 60 units, 44($2.00) + 16($1.70) = $115.20 will be charged.

quantity discounts Price reductions for large orders.

If quantity discounts are offered, the buyer must weigh the potential benefits of reduced purchase price and fewer orders that will result from buying in large quantities against the increase in holding cost caused by higher average inventory. The buyer's goal is to select the order quantity that will minimize total annual cost, where total annual cost is the sum of annual holding cost, ordering cost, *and* purchase cost:

$$TC = \underset{\text{cost}}{\text{Annual holding}} + \underset{\text{cost}}{\text{Annual ordering}} + \underset{\text{cost}}{\text{Annual purchase}} \tag{12-9}$$

$$\left(\frac{Q}{2}\right)H \quad + \quad \left(\frac{D}{Q}\right)S \quad + \quad RD$$

where

$R = $ Unit price

Recall that in the basic EOQ model, determination of order quantity does not involve the purchase cost. The rationale for not including the purchase cost there is that under the assumption of no quantity discounts, annual purchase cost is not affected by the order quantity. A graph of total annual purchase cost versus order quantity would be a horizontal line. Hence, including purchase cost would merely raise the total cost curve

Order Quantity	Price per Box
1 to 44	$2.00
45 to 69	1.70
70 or more	1.40

Table 12-2

Price list for boxes of extra-wide gauze strips

Figure 12-6

Adding annual purchase cost RD doesn't change the EOQ if there is no quantity discounts

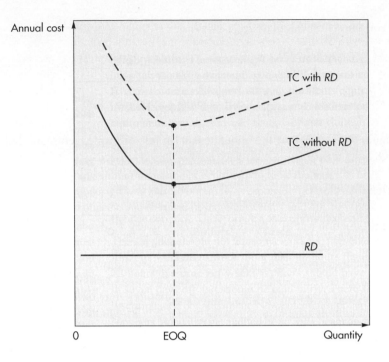

Figure 12-7

The total cost curve with quantity discounts is composed of a portion of the total cost curve for each unit price.

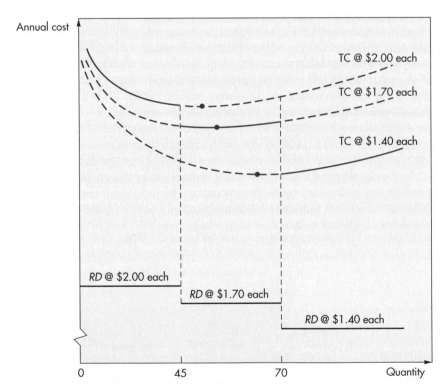

(in Figure 12-3C) by the same amount (*RD*) at every point. That would not change the EOQ (see Figure 12-6).

When quantity discounts are offered, there is a separate U-shaped total cost curve for each unit price. Again, including annual purchase price merely raises each curve by a constant amount. However, because the unit prices are all different, each curve is raised by a different amount: Smaller unit prices will raise the total cost curve less than larger unit prices. Note that no one curve applies to the entire range of quantities; each curve applies to only a *portion* of the range (see Figure 12-7). Hence, the applicable or *feasible* total cost is initially on the curve with the highest unit price and then drops down, curve by curve, at the *break quantities*. Note that from Table 12-2, the break quantities for gauze strips are at 45 and 70 boxes. The result is a total cost curve with *steps* at the break quantities.

Even though each curve has a minimum, those points are not necessarily feasible. For example, the minimum point for the $1.40 curve in Figure 12-7 appears to be around 65 units. However, the price list shown in Table 12-2 indicates that an order size of 65 boxes will receive a unit price of $1.70. The actual total cost curve is denoted by the solid lines; only those price–quantity combinations are feasible. The objective of the quantity discount model is to identify an order quantity that will represent the lowest total cost for the solid lines.

Note that because holding cost is a percentage of price, lower prices will mean lower holding cost which results in larger EOQs. Thus, as price decreases, each curve's minimum point will be to the right of the previous curve's minimum point (see Figure 12-7).

We can determine the best purchase quantity with the following procedure:

1. Beginning with the lowest unit price, calculate the EOQ for each price until you find a feasible EOQ (i.e., until an EOQ falls in the quantity range for its price).

2. If the EOQ for the lowest unit price is feasible, it is the optimal order quantity. If not, compare the total cost at all the break quantities larger than the feasible EOQ with the total cost of the feasible EOQ. The quantity that yields the lowest total cost among these is optimum.

Example 5

A factory uses 4,000 light bulbs a year. Light bulbs are priced as follows: 1 to 499, 90 cents each; 500 to 999, 85 cents each; and 1,000 or more, 80 cents each. It costs approximately $30 to prepare a purchase order and receive and pay the order, and holding cost is 40 percent of purchase price per year. Determine the optimal order quantity and the total annual cost.

Solution

See Figure 12-8 for the graph of total annual cost:

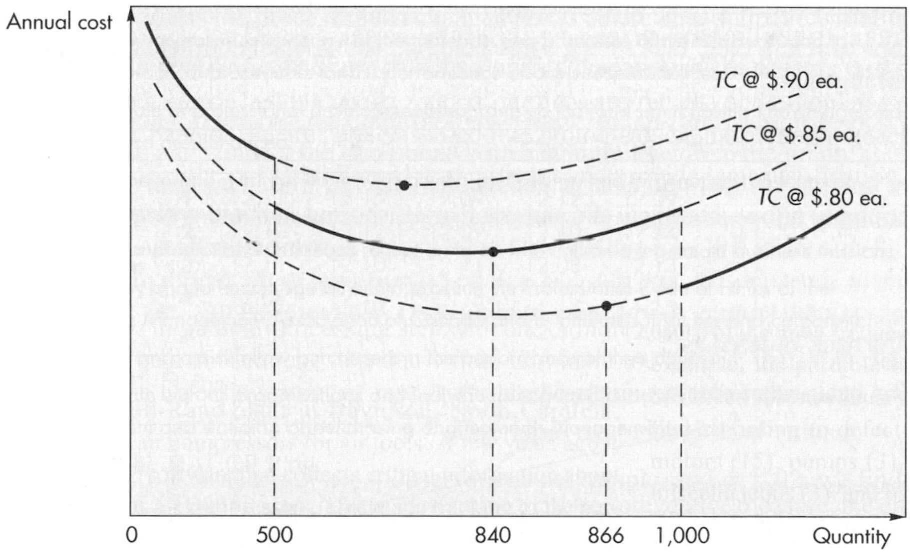

Figure 12-8

Total annual cost for Example 5

$D = 4,000$ light bulbs per year $S = \$30$ $H = .40R$ $R =$ unit price

Range	Unit Price R	H
1 to 499	$.90	$.40(.90) = .36$
500 to 999	$.85	$.40(.85) = .34$
1,000 or more	$.80	$.40(.80) = .32$

Find the EOQ for each price, starting with the lowest price, until you locate a feasible EOQ.

$$EOQ_{.80} = \sqrt{\frac{2DS}{H}} = \sqrt{\frac{2(4,000)30}{.32}} = 866 \text{ light bulbs}$$

Because an order size of 866 light bulbs is less than 1,000 units, 866 is not feasible for the unit price of $.80 per light bulb. Next, try $.85 per unit.

$$EOQ_{.85} = \sqrt{\frac{2(4,000)30}{.34}} = 840 \text{ light bulbs}$$

This EOQ is feasible; it falls in the $.85-per-light-bulb quantity range (500 to 999). Now calculate the total cost for 840 order size, and compare it to the total cost of the break quantity larger than 840, i.e., 1,000 units.

TC = Annual Holding cost + Annual Ordering cost + Annual Purchase cost

$$= \left(\frac{Q}{2}\right)H + \left(\frac{D}{Q}\right)S + RD$$

$$TC_{840} = \frac{840}{2}(.34) + \frac{4,000}{840}(30) + .85(4,000) = \$3,686$$

$$TC_{1,000} = \frac{1,000}{2}(.32) + \frac{4,000}{1,000}(30) + .80(4,000) = \$3,480$$

Because $3,480 < $3,686, the minimum cost order quantity is 1,000 light bulbs.

Comment. Usually the buyer has to pay for transportation cost to his facility. Also, usually larger shipments result in a lower unit transportation cost. It might be possible to represent the structure of transportation cost as price breaks for larger quantities, and hence use the above model to determine the order quantity that minimizes total annual price, transportation, holding, and ordering costs. This will make the model more realistic.

Comment. Even if a large order quantity is purchased, it might be possible to receive portions of it at a time, thus saving some holding cost. A blanket order is an example of this arrangement.

EOQ with Planned Shortages

When holding cost per unit is large and the demand can wait, a company may decide to intentionally allow shortages. We assume that all shorted demand will be back-ordered (i.e., all customers will wait until the next order cycle). However, the back-ordered demand will incur shortage cost, and this cost will be proportional to the length of the time a unit is back-ordered (similar to inventory holding cost). We represent this cost and the number of units back-ordered as:

B = back-order cost per unit per year

Q_b = quantity back-ordered per order cycle

OM in ACTION

Min/Max Model

Another popular inventory model is the min/max model. It is very similar to the fixed order quantity/reorder point model, with the difference that if at the time of order the quantity on hand (i.e., the inventory level) is less than min (i.e., ROP), then the order quantity will be set equal to (max − quantity on hand). Max is approximately equal to the EOQ + ROP. One

facility using min/max model is the Telus warehouse in Calgary, which carries telephones and supplies such as tools for line workers. The system automatically issues purchase orders for most items, but for more expensive items the approval of the buyer is required.

Source: J. Fulcher, "Chain of Events," *Manufacturing Systems* 17(1), January 1999, pp. 85–90.

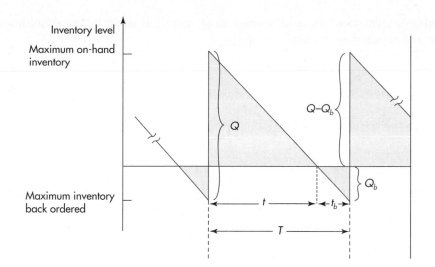

Figure 12-9

Inventory level for the EOQ with planned shortages model

We also make the same assumptions as in the basic EOQ model, except that we allow shortages, which are all back-ordered. The inventory level in this case can be graphed as in Figure 12-9,
    where

T = order interval = length of a order cycle (in days)

   t = time period (during an order interval) when inventory level is non-negative

t_b = time period (during an order interval) when inventory level is negative
(i.e., back-order occurs).

When the next order arrives, the back-ordered demand is satisfied first, i.e., the inventory level just after an order arrival will be $Q - Q_b$. Recall that d = demand rate per day. Because $Q - Q_b$ units are used up at the rate of d units per day, then $Q - Q_b = d \times t$ or

$t = \dfrac{Q - Q_b}{d}$. Similarly, $t_b = \dfrac{Q_b}{d}$ and $T = t + t_b = \dfrac{Q}{d}$. Hence,

$$\frac{t}{T} = \frac{\dfrac{Q - Q_b}{d}}{\dfrac{Q}{d}} = \frac{Q - Q_b}{Q} \text{ and } \frac{t_b}{T} = \frac{\dfrac{Q_b}{d}}{\dfrac{Q}{d}} = \frac{Q_b}{Q}$$

Therefore, average level of inventory during the year is:

$$\frac{Q - Q_b}{2} \times \frac{t}{T} + 0\left(\frac{t_b}{T}\right) = \frac{(Q - Q_b)^2}{2Q},$$

and average level of back orders during the year is:

$$\frac{Q_b}{2} \times \frac{t_b}{T} + 0\left(\frac{t}{T}\right) = \frac{Q_b^2}{2Q}$$

Finally, the total annual inventory control cost

TC = annual ordering cost + annual holding cost + annual back-order cost

$$= \left(\frac{D}{Q}\right)S + \left(\frac{(Q - Q_b)^2}{2Q}\right)H + \left(\frac{Q_b^2}{2Q}\right)B$$

Taking derivative of TC with respect to Q_b, setting it equal to zero, and solving for Q_b, we get

$$Q_b = Q\left(\frac{H}{H + B}\right). \tag{12-10}$$

Taking derivative of TC with respect to Q, setting it equal to zero, multiplying it by $2Q^2$ and rearranging, we get

$$-2DS + Q^2H - Q_b^2(H + B) = 0 \tag{12-11}$$

Substituting (12-10) in (12-11) and solving for Q, we get

$$Q = \sqrt{\frac{2DS}{H}\left(\frac{H + B}{B}\right)} \tag{12-12}$$

Example 6

Annual demand for a particular model of a refrigerator at an appliance store is 50 units. The holding cost per unit per year is $200. The back-order cost per unit per year is estimated to be $500. Ordering cost from the manufacturer is $10 per order. Determine the optimal order quantity and the back-order quantity per order cycle.

Solution

$D = 50$ units per year
$H = \$200$ per unit per year
$B = \$500$ per unit per year
$S = \$10$ per order

$$Q = \sqrt{\frac{2DS}{H}\left(\frac{H + B}{B}\right)} = \sqrt{\frac{2(50)(10)}{200}\left(\frac{200 + 500}{500}\right)} = 2.65, \text{ round to 3 units.}$$

$$Q_b = Q\left(\frac{H}{H + B}\right) = 3\left(\frac{200}{200 + 500}\right) = 0.86, \text{ round to 1.}$$

This model has the following practical implication for this example: Allow the inventory level to drop to zero. Then, when there is a customer demand (for a unit), place an order of 3 fridges from the manufacturer.

LO4 FIXED ORDER QUANTITY/REORDER POINT MODEL: DETERMINING THE REORDER POINT

reorder point (ROP) When the inventory level drops to this amount, the item should be reordered.

The **reorder point (ROP)** is that level of inventory at which an order should be issued. If demand and purchase lead time are both constant, the reorder point is simply

$$\text{ROP} = d \times \text{LT} \tag{12-13}$$

where

$d = $ Demand rate (units per day or week or month)
$\text{LT} = $ Lead time (in days or weeks or months)

Example 7

A patient takes two special tablets per day, which are delivered to his home seven days after an order is called in. At what point should the patient reorder?

Solution

Usage $= 2$ tablets a day
Lead time $= 7$ days
ROP $=$ Usage $\times$ Lead time
$= 2$ tablets per day $\times 7$ days $= 14$ tablets

Thus, the patient should reorder when 14 tablets are left.

Note: Demand and lead time must have the same time units.

When variability is present in demand and/or lead time, it creates the possibility that the actual demand during a lead time will exceed the expected demand during the lead time. Consequently, it becomes necessary to carry additional inventory, called **safety stock**, to reduce the risk of running out of inventory (a stock-out) or to reduce the number of units short. The reorder point then increases by the amount of the safety stock:

$$\text{ROP} = \frac{\text{Expected demand}}{\text{during a lead time}} + \text{Safety stock}$$

safety stock   Stock that is held in excess of expected demand due to variability of demand and/or lead time.

For example, if the expected demand during a lead time is 100 units, and the desired amount of safety stock is 10 units, then the ROP would be 110 units.

Figure 12-10 illustrates how safety stock can reduce shortage or risk of stock-out during a lead time (LT). Note that for the fixed order quantity/ROP model, shortage or stock-out protection is needed only during lead times.

The amount of safety stock that is appropriate for an item depends on:

1. Demand and lead time variability

2. The desired service level

There are two ways to define the service level:

1. Lead time service level

2. Annual service level.

Lead time service level is the probability that demand will not exceed supply (i.e., inventory level) during a lead time. It can be seen that lead time service level is also equal to percentage of the lead time demand filled. **Annual service level** is the percentage of all demand (during the year) filled. Therefore, for the same number of safety stock, lead time service level will be smaller than annual service level (because lead time service level is $1 - (\text{number short/lead time demand})$ whereas annual service level is $1 - (\text{number short/ order cycle demand})$, and lead time demand < order cycle demand).

lead time service level Probability that demand will not exceed supply during a lead time.

annual service level   The percentage of annual demand filled.

The formula commonly used to determine the safety stock, in the presence of demand and/or lead time variability, assumes that demand during a lead time is Normally distributed:

$$\text{Safety stock} = z.\sigma_{d\text{LT}} \tag{12-14}$$

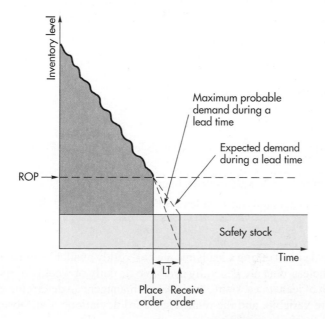

Figure 12-10

Safety stock reduces the risk of a stock-out or the number of units short during a lead time.

Figure 12-11

Distribution of demand during a lead time, lead time service level, and ROP

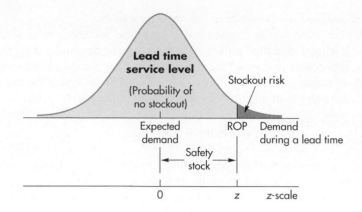

where

z = Safety factor; number of standard deviations above the expected demand

σ_{dLT} = Standard deviation of demand during a lead time

In the above formula, z is related to the service level. However, the exact nature of this relationship depends on the type of service level used: lead time or annual. First, we will describe it for the lead time service level.

ROP Using Lead Time Service Level

Given a desired lead time service level, the value of z can be directly determined from the (standard) Normal probability table, Appendix B, Table B (see Figure 12-11). Note that stock-out risk = 1 − lead time service level. For example, if the desired lead time service level is .95 or 95 percent, stock-out risk will be .05 or 5 percent. Also note that the smaller the stock-out risk the manager is willing to accept, the greater the value of z.

Example 8

The manager of a hardware store has determined, from historical records, that demand for a type and size of bagged cement during its lead time could be described by a Normal distribution that has a mean of 50 bags and a standard deviation of 5 bags. Answer these questions, assuming that the manager is willing to accept a stock-out risk of no more than 3 percent during a lead time:

a. What value of z is appropriate?

b. How many safety stock should be held?

c. What reorder point should be used?

Solution

Expected demand during a lead time = 50 bags
σ_{dLT} = 5 bags
Stock-out risk = 3 percent

a. From Appendix B, Table B, using a service level of $1 - .03 = .97$, we obtain a value of $z = 1.88$.

b. Safety stock = $z\sigma_{dLT}$ = 1.88(5) = 9.40 bags

c. ROP = Expected demand during a lead time + Safety stock = 50 + 9.40 = 59.40 bags

---

When data on demand during a lead time are not readily available, Formula 12-14 cannot be used. Nevertheless, data are generally available on daily or weekly or monthly demand, and on the length of lead times. Using those data, a manager can determine whether demand and lead time are variable, and the related standard deviations. For those situations, one of the following formulas can be used:

If only demand is variable, then $\sigma_{d\text{LT}} = \sqrt{\text{LT}}\sigma_d$, and the reorder point is[2]

$$\text{ROP} = \bar{d}.\text{LT} + z\sqrt{\text{LT}}\sigma_d \tag{12-15}$$

where

$\bar{d} =$ Average daily or weekly or monthly demand

$\sigma_d =$ Standard deviation of daily or weekly or monthly demand

$\text{LT} =$ Lead time in days or weeks or months

If both demand and lead time are variable, then[3]

$$\sigma_{d\text{LT}} = \sqrt{\text{LT}\sigma_d^2 + \bar{d}^2\sigma_{\text{LT}}^2}$$

and the reorder point is

$$\text{ROP} = \bar{d} \cdot \overline{\text{LT}} + z\sqrt{\text{LT}\sigma_d^2 + \bar{d}^2\sigma_{\text{LT}}^2} \tag{12-16}$$

Where $\overline{\text{LT}} = $ *Average* lead time, in days or weeks or months

$\sigma_{\text{LT}} =$ Standard deviation of the lead time, in days or weeks or months

Note: Each of these models assumes that demands and lead time are *independent*.

Example 9

A restaurant uses an average of 50 jars of a special sauce each week. Weekly usage of sauce has a standard deviation of three jars. The manager is willing to accept no more than a 10 percent risk of stock-out during a lead time, which is two weeks. Assume the distribution of usage is Normal.

a. Which of the above formulas is appropriate for this situation? Why?

b. Determine the value of z.

c. Determine the ROP.

Solution

$\bar{d} = 50$ jars per week $\text{LT} = 2$ weeks

$\sigma_d = 3$ jars per week   Acceptable stock-out risk – 10 percent, so lead time service level is .90

a. Because only demand is variable (i.e., has a standard deviation), Formula 12-15 is appropriate.

b. From Appendix B, Table B, using a service level of .90, we obtain $z = 1.28$.

c. $\text{ROP} = \bar{d}.\text{LT} + z\sqrt{\text{LT}}\sigma_d$

---

[2]If daily demand d_i are independent and have the same variance σ_d^2, then it can be shown, using elementary statistics, that $\text{Var}\left(\sum_{i=1}^{\text{LT}} d_i\right) = \left(\sum_{i=1}^{\text{LT}} \text{Var}(d_i)\right) = \text{LT}\,\text{Var}(d_i)$. Taking square root of both sides and substituting chapter notation, we get $\sigma_{d\text{LT}} = \sqrt{\text{LT}}\sigma_d$.

[3]The result follows from the well known variance decomposition formula:

Given two random variables X and Y,

$\text{Var}\,X = E_X X^2 - (E_X X)^2$, by the definition of the variance; $E =$ Expectations

$= E_Y(E_X(X^2|Y)) - E_Y(E_X(X|Y))^2$, conditioning on Y and then taking expectations with respect to Y

$= E_Y(\text{Var}_X(X|Y) + E_X(X|Y)^2) - E_Y(E_X(X|Y))^2$, by the definition of the first term

$= E_Y(\text{Var}_X(X|Y)) + E_Y(E_X(X|Y)^2) - E_Y(E_X(X|Y))^2$, expanding the first term

$= E_Y(\text{Var}_X(X|Y)) + \text{Var}_Y(E_X(X|Y))$, by the definition of the second term

Now let $X = \sum_{i=1}^{\text{LT}} d_i$ and $Y = \text{LT}$. Then the variance decomposition formula becomes:

$$\text{Var} = \left(\sum_{i=1}^{\text{LT}} d_i\right) = E_{\text{LT}}\left(\text{Var}\left(\sum_{i=1}^{\text{LT}} d_i|\text{LT}\right)\right) + \text{Var}_{\text{LT}}\left(E\left(\sum_{i=1}^{\text{LT}} d_i|\text{LT}\right)\right)$$

$= E(\text{LT})\text{Var}(d_i) + E(d_i)^2\text{Var}(\text{LT})$, using elementary statistics

Taking square root of both sides and substituting chapter notation, we get $\sigma_{d\text{LT}} = \sqrt{\text{LT}\sigma_d^2 + \bar{d}^2\sigma_{\text{LT}}^2}$

Figure 12-12

Composition of the demand during a lead time

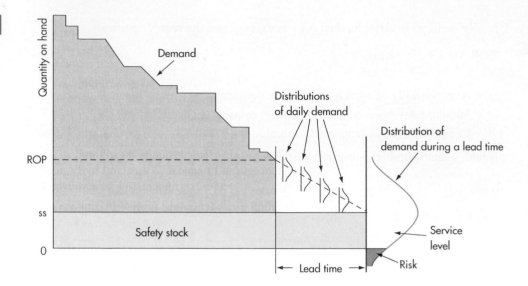

Comment. The logic of formula (12-15) may not be immediately obvious. The first part of the formula is the expected demand, which is the product of daily (or weekly or monthly) demand and the number of days (or weeks or months) of lead time. The second part of the formula is z times the standard deviation of demand during a lead time. Daily (or weekly or monthly) demand is assumed to be Normally distributed and has the same mean and standard deviation (see Figure 12-12). The standard deviation of demand for the entire lead time is found by summing the variances of daily (or weekly or monthly) demands and then finding the square root of that number. Note that, unlike variance, standard deviation is not additive. Hence, if lead time is four days, e.g., the variance of demand during a lead time will equal the sum of the four daily variances, which is $4\sigma_d^2$. The standard deviation of demand during a lead time will be the square root of this, which is equal to $2\sigma_d$. In general, this becomes $\sqrt{LT}\sigma_d$ and, hence, the last part of Formula 12-15.

Example 10

If daily demand is Normally distributed with a mean of 3 units and a standard deviation of 1 unit, and lead time is 2 days, then demand during a lead time will be Normally distributed with a mean of 6 units and a standard deviation of $\sqrt{1^2 + 1^2} = 1.41$ units (see the following charts where the charts on the left and in the middle are the distributions of day 1 and day 2 demands and the right chart is the distribution of the sum of day 1 and day 2 demands):

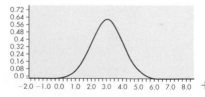 + 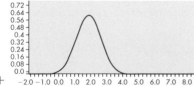 =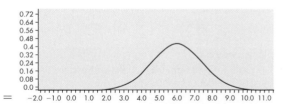

Also note that average demand is usually estimated using the forecast of demand, and standard deviation of demand is usually estimated using standard deviation of forecast error (i.e., square root of MSE or $1.25 \times$ MAD).

Finally, we assumed that a manager has a desired service level from which z, and then safety stocks and ROP, were determined. An alternative method to determine the ROP is based on cost of overstocking and cost of shortage. This analysis will be similar to the single period model later in this chapter.

ROP Using Annual Service Level

Given a desired annual service level (i.e., the percentage of demand filled directly from inventory during the whole year; also known as the *fill rate)*, to find the required ROP, a three-step procedure should be used:

1. Calculate $\qquad E(z) = \dfrac{Q(1 - \text{SL}_{\text{annual}})}{\sigma_{dLT}}$ $\qquad\qquad\qquad$ (12-17)

2. Take the $E(z)$ to Table 12-3 and determine the associated z value.

3. Use the z value in the following general ROP formula or a specific ROP formula (12-15) or (12-16):

$\qquad$ ROP = expected demand during lead time $+ z\sigma_{dLT}$

where $\text{SL}_{\text{annual}}$ = annual service level, and $E(z)$ = Standardized expected number of units short during an order cycle. The derivation of the formula for $E(z)$ in step 1 is rather long and complicated.[4]

Example 11

An inventory item has order quantity $Q = 250$, expected demand during a lead time = 50, and standard deviation of demand during a lead time $\sigma_{dLT} = 16$. Determine the ROP if the desired annual service level is (a) 0.997, and (b) 0.98.

Solution

a. $E(z) = \dfrac{Q(1 - \text{SL}_{\text{annual}})}{\sigma_{dLT}} = \dfrac{250(1 - .997)}{16} = 0.047$

From Table 12-3, $E(z) = .047$ falls between $E(z) = .048$ with $z = 1.28$ and $E(z) = .044$ with $z = 1.32$. Therefore, using interpolation, $z = 1.29$. Finally, ROP $= 50 + 1.29(16) = 7$ 0.64 units.

b. $E(z) = \dfrac{Q(1 - \text{SL}_{\text{annual}})}{\sigma_{dLT}} = \dfrac{250(1 - .98)}{16} = 0.3125$

From Table 12-3, $E(z) = .3125$ falls between $E(z) = .324$ with $z = .16$ and $E(z) = .307$ with $z = .20$. Therefore, using interpolation, $z = .19$. Finally, ROP $= 50 + 0.19(16) = 53.$ 04 units.

---

[4]$\text{SL}_{\text{annual}}$ = expected number of units filled during a cycle (number of cycles per year)/annual demand
$\qquad$ = expected number of units filled during a cycle $(D/Q)/D$
$\qquad$ = expected number of units filled during a cycle/Q
$\qquad$ = $(Q -$ expected number of units short during a cycle)/Q,
$\qquad$ because average demand during an order cycle is Q. Multiplying both side by Q:
Q $(\text{SL}_{\text{annual}}) = Q -$ expected number of units short during a cycle
Rewriting:
Expected number of units short during a cycle $= Q$ $(1 - \text{SL}_{\text{annual}})$
Standardized expected number of units short during a cycle $(\sigma_{dLT}) = Q$ $(1 - \text{SL}_{\text{annual}})$,
This follows from statistics. Let $E(z) =$ Standardized expected number of units short during a cycle.
$E(z)(\sigma_{dLT}) = Q$ $(1 - \text{SL}_{\text{annual}})$

$E(z) = \dfrac{Q(1 - \text{SL}_{\text{annual}})}{\sigma_{dLT}}$

Table 12-3

Normal distribution lead time service levels and standardized expected number short during an order cycle

Z	Lead Time Service Level	E(z)	z	Lead Time Service Level	E(z)	z	Lead Time Service Level	E(z)	z	Lead Time Service Level	E(z)
−2.40	.0082	2.403	−.80	.2119	.920	.80	.7881	.120	2.40	.9918	.003
−2.36	.0091	2.363	−.76	.2236	.889	.84	.7995	.112	2.44	.9927	.002
−2.32	.0102	2.323	−.72	.2358	.858	.88	.8106	.104	2.48	.9934	.002
−2.28	.0113	2.284	−.68	.2483	.828	.92	.8212	.097	2.52	.9941	.002
−2.24	.0125	2.244	−.64	.2611	.798	.96	.8315	.089	2.56	.9948	.002
−2.20	.0139	2.205	−.60	.2743	.769	1.00	.8413	.083	2.60	.9953	.001
−2.16	.0154	2.165	−.56	.2877	.740	1.04	.8508	.077	2.64	.9959	.001
−2.12	.0170	2.126	−.52	.3015	.712	1.08	.8599	.071	2.68	.9963	.001
−2.08	.0188	2.087	−.48	.3156	.684	1.12	.8686	.066	2.72	.9967	.001
−2.04	.0207	2.048	−.44	.3300	.657	1.16	.8770	.061	2.76	.9971	.001
−2.00	.0228	2.008	−.40	.3446	.630	1.20	.8849	.056	2.80	.9974	.0008
−1.96	.0250	1.969	−.36	.3594	.597	1.24	.8925	.052	2.84	.9977	.0007
−1.92	.0274	1.930	−.32	.3745	.576	1.28	.8997	.048	2.88	.9980	.0006
−1.88	.0301	1.892	−.28	.3897	.555	1.32	.9066	.044	2.92	.9982	.0005
−1.84	.0329	1.853	−.24	.4052	.530	1.36	.9131	.040	2.96	.9985	.0004
−1.80	.0359	1.814	−.20	.4207	.507	1.40	.9192	.037	3.00	.9987	.0004
−1.76	.0392	1.776	−.16	.4364	.484	1.44	.9251	.034	3.04	.9988	.0003
−1.72	.0427	1.737	−.12	.4522	.462	1.48	.9306	.031	3.08	.9990	.0003
−1.68	.0465	1.699	−.08	.4681	.440	1.52	.9357	.028	3.12	.9991	.0002
−1.64	.0505	1.661	−.04	.4840	.419	1.56	.9406	.026	3.16	.9992	.0002
−1.60	.0548	1.623	.00	.5000	.399	1.60	.9452	.023	3.20	.9993	.0002
−1.56	.0594	1.586	.04	.5160	.379	1.64	.9495	.021	3.24	.9994	.0001
−1.52	.0643	1.548	.08	.5319	.360	1.68	.9535	.019	3.28	.9995	.0001
−1.48	.0694	1.511	.12	.5478	.342	1.72	.9573	.017	3.32	.9995	.0001
−1.44	.0749	1.474	.16	.5636	.324	1.76	.9608	.016	3.36	.9996	.0001
−1.40	.0808	1.437	.20	.5793	.307	1.80	.9641	.014	3.40	.9997	.0001
−1.36	.0869	1.400	.24	.5948	.290	1.84	.9671	.013			
−1.32	.0934	1.364	.28	.6103	.275	1.88	.9699	.012			
−1.28	.1003	1.328	.32	.6255	.256	1.92	.9726	.010			
−1.24	.1075	1.292	.36	.6406	.237	1.96	.9750	.009			
−1.20	.1151	1.256	.40	.6554	.230	2.00	.9772	.008			
−1.16	.1230	1.221	.44	.6700	.217	2.04	.9793	.008			
−1.12	.1314	1.186	.48	.6844	.204	2.08	.9812	.007			
−1.08	.1401	1.151	.52	.6985	.192	2.12	.9830	.006			
−1.04	.1492	1.117	.56	.7123	.180	2.16	.9846	.005			
−1.00	.1587	1.083	.60	.7257	.169	2.20	.9861	.005			
−.96	.1685	1.049	.64	.7389	.158	2.24	.9875	.004			
−.92	.1788	1.017	.68	.7517	.148	2.28	.9887	.004			
−.88	.1894	.984	.72	.7642	.138	2.32	.9898	.003			
−.84	.2005	.952	.76	.7764	.129	2.36	.9909	.003			

It is important that variations in demands and lead times (with the cooperation of the suppliers) be reduced as much as possible. This will reduce the need for safety stocks. For an application of this, see the "Dell" OM in Action.

Other Related Models

A commonly used variation of the fixed order quantity/reorder point model is the min/max model. The determination of min and max is complicated but min can be approximated by ROP and max by ROP + EOQ. See the OM in Action "Min/Max Model" earlier in the chapter.

Another common model is the base stock model: when the on hand inventory level drops by any x units, order the same x units immediately to bring inventory level back up to the base stock (i.e., max) level.

Another variation of Min/Max model is the Can Order model. In this model, when an item's on-hand inventory level drops to or below Min, all related items (e.g., those bought from the same supplier) are investigated to see if their on-hand inventory level is at or below their can order level. If so, they are ordered too (to bring their inventory level up to Max).

 # FIXED ORDER INTERVAL/ORDER UP TO LEVEL MODEL

fixed order interval/ order up to level model Orders are placed at fixed time intervals to bring the inventory level up to the order up to level.

The **fixed order interval/order up to level model** is used when orders are placed at fixed time intervals (weekly, twice a month, etc.), and inventory level is brought up to the order up to level. This model is widely used by wholesalers and retailers, where usually all items

 OM in ACTION

Dell

Dell buys all the components of its computers and assembles them in its facilities in Austin, Texas. Many of the components come from Asia with lead times of approximately 7 days for air cargo and approximately 30 days for ocean freight. Dell carries little inventories of the components but has set up warehouses, called revolvers, close to its assembly plants. The inventories kept in revolvers are primarily safety stocks and are vendor-owned and managed. To reduce the risk of stockout, Dell may purchase the same component from two to three suppliers. A study of a specific component, supplied by two suppliers, showed that the average inventory level in the revolvers

was equal to 11 days's usage by Dell, and the aggregate annual service level was 98.8 percent. Some of the 11 days' inventory was due to demand fluctuations and the rest was due to supply lead time variability. The study also showed that 20–25 percent of the demand fluctuations was because Dell pulled the components of each supplier in cycles, i.e., for a few days only components of supplier A were used and then for another few days components of supplier B were used, and so on (see the following chart). This increased the variance of demand for each supplier's components. Dell has rectified this situation by pulling the components of each supplier more uniformly.

Source: R. Kapuscinski, et al, "Inventory Decisions in Dell's Supply Chain," *Interfaces*, May/June 2004, 34(3), pp. 191–205.

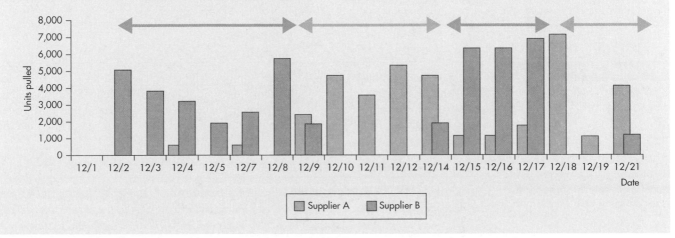

from the same supplier are ordered at the same time. If demand is variable, the order size will tend to vary from interval to interval. This is quite different from the EOQ/ROP model in which the order size remains fixed from cycle to cycle while the length of the cycle varies (shorter if demand is above average, and longer if demand is below average).

Grouping orders for items from the same supplier can produce savings in ordering and shipping costs. Furthermore, some situations do not readily lend themselves to continuous monitoring of inventory levels. Many retail operations (e.g., small drugstores, small grocery stores) fall into this category. The alternative for them is to use fixed interval ordering, which requires only periodic checks of inventory levels.

Two decisions are needed to apply this model for a group of items from the same supplier: (1) the order interval, and (2) the order up to level for each item.

Determining the Order Interval

The order interval can be determined by minimizing total annual holding and ordering costs of all the SKUs received from a particular supplier. The complication is that there are two components to the ordering cost: the cost of issuing a purchase order and the cost of ordering each line item (SKU) in it. In the basic model, we assume that every SKU is ordered at every order time no matter how small its order quantity is. Later, we present the case where not every SKU is ordered at every order time (called the Coordinated Periodic Review model).

Let

OI = order interval (in fraction of a year)

S = fixed ordering cost per purchase order

s = variable ordering cost per SKU included in the purchase order (line item).

For simplicity, we assume s is the same for every SKU

n = number of SKUs purchased from the supplier

R_j = unit cost of SKU_j, $j = 1, ..., n$

i = annual holding cost rate

D_j = annual demand of SKU_j, $j = 1, ..., n$

For each SKU_j from this supplier, we will purchase enough to last until next order, i.e., $Q_j = D_j \cdot OI$

$$\text{Total Annual Inventory Control Cost (TC)} = \sum \left(\frac{D_j \cdot OI}{2} \right) R_j \cdot i + (S + ns)\left(\frac{1}{OI} \right)$$

Taking derivative of TC with respect to OI, setting it equal to 0, and solving for OI, we get the optimal order interval:

$$OI^* = \sqrt{\frac{2(S + ns)}{i \sum D_j R_j}} \qquad\qquad (12\text{-}18)$$

Example 12

Three parts are purchased from the same supplier. The basic cost of placing an order for one of the SKUs is $1.50. The inclusion of each additional SKU costs $.50 more. The annual carrying cost rate is 24 percent of unit cost. The annual demand and unit prices are given below. Assume that the buying company works 250 days a year. Calculate the optimal order interval.

SKU	Demand/year	price/unit
1	12,000	.50
2	8,000	.30
3	700	.10

$S = 1.50 - .50 = \$1.00$

$s = .50$

$i = .24$

$$OI^* = \sqrt{\frac{2(1.00 + 3(.50))}{.24(12,000 \times .50 + 8,000 \times .30 + 700 \times .10)}}$$

$\quad\quad = .0496 \text{ year} = 12.4 \text{ days}$

Solution

Determining the Order up to Level

The order up to level for an item should be enough so that the item lasts until the next order arrives, i.e., after an order interval plus a lead time. This fact is illustrated in the bottom chart in Figure 12-13, which also contracts the fixed order interval model with the fixed order quantity (EOQ/ROP) model. Note that the order quantity (the difference between order up to level and on hand inventory level) for the fixed order interval model will vary from one order time to another (depending on size of demand during the past interval). In the presence of demand and lead time variability, there is a need for safety stocks. The two models also differ in terms of safety stocks. The fixed order interval model must have stock-out protection until the next order arrives, but the fixed order quantity (EOQ/ROP) model needs protection only during lead time. Therefore, the fixed order interval model necessitates a larger amount of safety stock for a given service level.

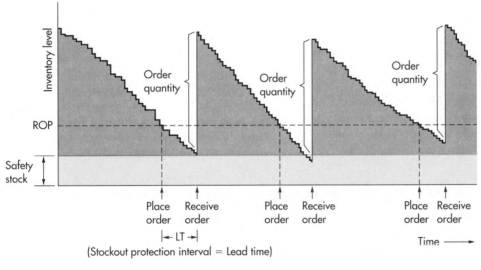

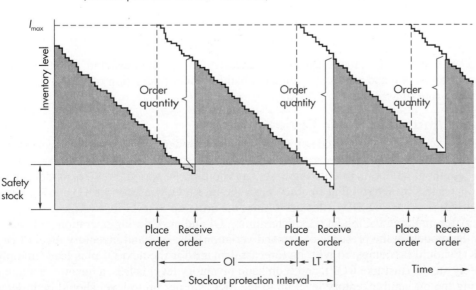

Figure 12-13

Comparison of the fixed quantity (EOQ/ROP) and the fixed order interval models

Therefore, order up to level or I_{max} can be determined by:

I_{max} = Expected demand during an order interval plus a lead time + safety stock   (12-19)

Like the fixed order quantity model, the fixed order interval model can have variations in demand and/or lead time. For the sake of simplicity and because it is the most frequently encountered situation, the discussion here will focus only on *variable demand* and *constant lead time case*. As in the fixed order quantity model, we assume that demand during an order interval and a lead time is Normally distributed.

Therefore, (12-19) becomes

$$I_{max} = \bar{d}(OI + LT) + z\sigma_d\sqrt{OI + LT}$$ (12-20)

where

$\bar{d}$ = *Average* daily or weekly or monthly demand

OI = Order interval (length of time between orders); in days or weeks or months

LT = Lead time in days or weeks or months

z = Safety factor; number of standard deviations above the expected demand

σ_d = Standard deviation of daily or weekly or monthly demand

Note that I_{max} does not have to be recalculated at each order time if demand has no trend or seasonality. Also note that because the period of vulnerability covers the whole order interval, there is only one definition of service level for this model. Order quantity Q can be determined by:

$Q = I_{max}$ − Amount on hand (i.e., inventory level)   (12-21)

| **Example 13** | Given the following information for a SKU, determine its order up to level and amount to order (i.e., order quantity). |

$\bar{d}$ = 30 units per day,   Desired service level = 99 percent

σ_d = 3 units per day,   Amount on hand at reorder time = 71 units

LT = 2 days,   OI = 7 days

Solution

z = 2.33 for 99 percent service level (from Appendix B, Table B)

$$I_{max} = \bar{d}(OI + LT) + z\sigma_d\sqrt{OI + LT}$$

$$= 30(7 + 2) + 2.33(3)\sqrt{7 + 2} = 291 \text{ units}$$

Amount to order = I_{max} − amount on hand = 291 − 71 = 220 units

---

Note that average demand is usually estimated using forecast of demand, and the standard deviation of demand is usually estimated using standard deviation of the forecast error (square root of MSE or 1.25 × MAD).

Coordinated Periodic Review Model

In the fixed order interval model, it might cost less to order some items every two, three, or more order intervals than ordering them at every interval, because their holding cost may be less than the line-item ordering cost. The coordinated periodic review model accommodates this by determining an order interval OI for reviewing every SKU and a multiple m_i of OI for ordering SKU_i (this determines the order up to level for SKU_i).

After planning the model (i.e., determining OI and m_is), during operation and control of the model (in the presence of demand variation), the on-hand inventory level of each SKU should be compared with its forecast demand for the next OI plus lead time plus safety stocks (just like ROP), and if on hand inventory level is less, a quantity enough to bring the on-hand inventory level up to the SKU's order up to level should be ordered.

The order up to level for SKU_i should cover its forecast demand during the next m_i order intervals (OI) plus lead time plus safety stocks only for the next OI + LT.

The determination of optimal values for OI and m_is is complicated. We will use a simple heuristic[5]:

1. Find the SKU with largest annual dollar value D_iR_i. Suppose, it is SKU_k. Let $m_k = 1$.
2. For every other SKU_j, calculate

$$m_j = \sqrt{\frac{s}{D_jR_j}\frac{D_kR_k}{S+s}} \qquad (12\text{-}22)$$

and round it to the nearest integer greater or equal to 1.

3. Calculate OI using:

$$OI^* = \sqrt{\frac{2\left(S + s\sum_{j=1}^{n}\frac{1}{m_j}\right)}{i\sum_{j=1}^{n}m_jD_jR_j}} \qquad (12\text{-}23)$$

The rationale for this heuristic is that both purchase order cost (S) and line item ordering cost (s) are charged to the SKU_k because SKU_k will be ordered at every order interval. Then, m_j for other SKUs are determined using formula (12-22) relative to m_k. Finally, OI is calculated using formula (12-23), which is very similar to formula (12-18) but uses m_jD_j as the order quantity for SKU_j.

Example 14

We use the same data as Example 12 in order to compare the coordinated periodic review model with the fixed order interval model. Recall that $S = \$1.00$, $s = .50$, and $i = .24$.

The annual demand and unit prices are repeated below. Calculate the m_js and OI.

SKU	Demand/year (D_i)	price/unit (R_i)	D_iR_i
1	12,000	.50	$6,000
2	8,000	.30	$2,400
3	700	.10	$70

Solution

The SKU with largest D_iR_i is SKU_1. Therefore, $m_1 = 1$.

$$m_2 = \sqrt{\frac{.5}{2,400}\frac{\$6,000}{1+.5}} = .91 \text{ round to 1. Therefore, } m_2 = 1.$$

$$m_3 = \sqrt{\frac{.5}{70}\frac{\$6,000}{1+.5}} = 5.35 \text{ round to 5. Therefore, } m_3 = 5.$$

$$OI^* = \sqrt{\frac{2(1.00 + .5(1+1+.20))}{.24(1\times 6,000 + 1\times 2,400 + 5\times 70)}}$$

$$= .0447 \text{ year} = 11.2 \text{ days (because the buyer works 250 days a year)}$$

Thus, OI is only slightly smaller, but the plan for SKU_3, because of its small annual dollar usage, is to order it every five order times.

Suppose OI = 11 work days, LT and safety stocks are negligible, demand for SKU_3 during the next 11 work days = 700(11)/250 = 30.8 units. Therefore, the order up to level for SKU_3 should be set to 5(30.8) = 154 units.

---

[5]E.A. Silver, D.F. Pyke, and R. Peterson. *Inventory Management and Production Planning and Scheduling,* 3rd ed. New York: John Wiley and Sons, 1998, pp. 426–429.

LO6 THE SINGLE PERIOD MODEL

The **single period model** (sometimes referred to as the *newsvender problem*) is used for ordering of perishables (e.g., fresh fruits and vegetables, baked goods, seafood, cut flowers) and other items that have a limited useful life (e.g., newspapers, magazines, spare parts for specialized equipment). The *period* for spare parts is the life of the equipment, assuming that the parts cannot be used for other equipment. What sets unsold or unused goods apart is that they are not typically carried over from one period to the next, at least not without penalty. Day-old baked goods, for instance, are often sold at reduced prices, leftover seafood may be discarded, and out-of-date magazines may be offered to used bookstores at bargain rates. There may even be some cost associated with disposal of leftover goods.

Analysis of single period model generally focuses on two costs: shortage and excess. Shortage cost may include a charge for loss of customer goodwill as well as the opportunity cost of lost sale, i.e., unrealized profit per unit. Usually the latter is used:

$$C_{\text{shortage}} = C_s = \text{Revenue per unit} - \text{Cost per unit}$$

We assume $C_s \geq 0$. If a shortage or stock-out relates to an item used in production or to a spare part for a machine, then shortage cost is the cost of lost production.

Excess cost pertains to items left over at the end of the period. In effect, excess cost is the difference between purchase cost and salvage value. That is,

$$C_{\text{excess}} = C_e = \text{Cost per unit} - \text{Salvage value per unit}$$

If there is a cost associated with disposing of excess items, then the salvage value will be negative and will therefore *increase* the excess cost per unit. On the other hand, if salvage value is larger than the original cost, then C_e will be negative. However, in this case, we must have $C_s + C_e > 0$, because salvage value per unit must be less than revenue per unit.

The goal of the single period model is to identify that order quantity, or stocking level, that will minimize the long-run total excess and shortage cost.

There are two general categories of problems that we will consider: those for which demand can be approximated by a continuous distribution (such as Uniform or Normal) and those for which demand can be approximated by a discrete distribution (say, historical frequencies or Poisson). The nature of item can indicate which type of model might be appropriate. For example, demand for liquids and items whose individual units are small but whose demand is large (such as muffins or newspapers), tends to vary over some *continuous scale*, thus lending itself to description by a continuous distribution. Demand for spare parts, expensive flowers, and computers is expressed in terms of the *number of units* demanded and lends itself to description by a discrete distribution.

Continuous Stocking Levels

The concept of identifying an optimal stocking level (i.e., order quantity) is perhaps easiest to visualize when demand is Uniform. Choosing the stocking level is similar to balancing a seesaw, but instead of a person on each end of the seesaw, we have the excess cost per unit (C_e) on one end of the distribution and the shortage cost per unit (C_s) on the other. The optimal stocking level is analogous to the fulcrum of the seesaw; the stocking level equalizes the cost weights, as illustrated in Figure 12-14. If actual demand exceeds the balance point S_o, there is shortage; hence, C_s is on the right end of the distribution. Similarly, if demand is less than S_o, there is excess, so C_e is on the left end of the distribution. When $C_e = C_s$, the optimal stocking level is halfway between the endpoints of the distribution. If one cost is greater than the other, S_o will be closer to the larger cost.

The *service level* is the *probability* that demand will not exceed the stocking level. Calculation of the service level is the key to determining the optimal stocking level, S_o. It can be shown that in order to balance the seesaw on the fulcrum, service level should be chosen so that:

$$\text{Service level SL} = \frac{C_s}{C_s + C_e} \qquad (12\text{-}14)$$

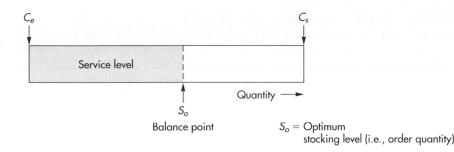

Figure 12-14

The optimal stocking level (i.e., order quantity) balances unit shortage and excess costs.

where

C_s = Shortage cost per unit

C_e = Excess cost per unit

Then, the optimal stocking level, S_o, can be determined from the demand distribution.

Example 15

Muffins are delivered daily to a cafeteria. Demand varies Uniformly between 30 and 50 muffins per day. The cafeteria pays 20 cents per muffin and charges 80 cents for it. Unsold muffins have no salvage value and cannot be carried over into the next day due to spoilage. Find the optimal stocking level and the stock-out risk for that quantity.

Solution

C_e = Cost per unit − Salvage value per unit
    = \$.20 − \$0
    = \$.20 per unit

C_s = Revenue per unit − Cost per unit
    = \$.80 − \$.20
    = \$.60 per unit

$$SL = \frac{C_s}{C_s + C_e} = \frac{\$.60}{\$.60 + \$.20} = .75$$

Thus, the optimal stocking level (i.e., order quantity) must satisfy 75 percent of demand. For the Uniform distribution, this will be at a point equal to the minimum demand plus 75 percent of the difference between maximum and minimum demands:

$S_o = 30 + .75(50 - 30) = 45$ muffins

The stock-out risk is $1.00 - .75 = .25$

A similar approach can be applied when demand is Normally distributed.

Example 16

Suppose the distribution of demand for muffins in the previous example was approximately Normal with a mean of 40 muffins per day and a standard deviation of 5 muffins per day. Find the optimal stocking level for the muffins.

Solution

Recall that $C_s = \$.60$, $C_e = \$.20$,   and $SL = .75$

This indicates that 75 percent of the area under the Normal curve must be to the left of the stocking level. Appendix B, Table B shows that a value of z between .67 and .68, say, .675, will satisfy this. Thus,

$$S_o = 40 + .675(5) = 43.375 \text{ or } 43 \text{ muffins.}$$

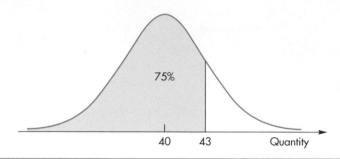

Figure 12-15

The service level for discrete stocking level must equal or just exceed the ratio $C_s/(C_s + C_e)$.

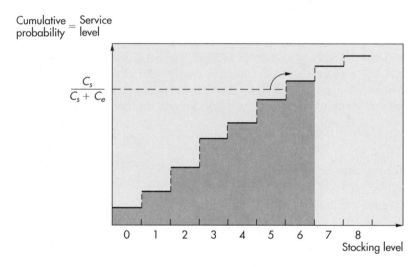

Discrete Stocking Levels

When stocking levels are discrete rather than continuous, the service level calculated using the ratio $C_s/(C_s + C_e)$ usually does not coincide with a feasible stocking level (e.g., the optimal amount may be *between* five and six units). The optimal solution in this case is the *higher level* (e.g., six units). In other words, choose the stocking level so that the desired service level is equalled or just *exceeded*. The service level in this case is compared with the cumulative probability of demand. Figure 12-15 illustrates this concept.

Example 17

Historical records on the use of a spare part for an old press serves as an estimate of usage for the spare part in a similar but new press. Stock-out cost involves downtime expenses and special ordering costs. These average $4,200 per unit short. The spare part costs $1,200 each, and an unused part has $400 salvage value. Determine the optimal stocking level.

Number of Spares Used	Probability	Cumulative Probability
0	.20	.20
1	.40	.60
2	.30	.90
3	.10	1.00
4 or more	.00	
	1.00	

$$C_s = \$4,200 \quad C_e = 1,200 - 400 = \$800 \quad SL = \frac{C_s}{C_s + C_e} = \frac{\$4,200}{\$4,200 + \$800} = .84$$

The Cumulative Probability column indicates the percentage of time that demand was equal to or less than some amount. For example, demand ≤ one spare occurred 60 percent of the time, or demand ≤ two spares occurred 90 percent of the time. Go down the table until cumulative probabilities just exceed service level of 84 percent. This is .90, which relates to two spares.

Example 18

Demand for long-stemmed red roses at a small flower shop can be approximated by a Poisson distribution that has a mean of four dozen roses per day. Profit on the roses is $3 per dozen. Leftover flowers are marked down and sold the next day at a loss of $2 per dozen. What is the optimal stocking level?

Solution

Obtain the cumulative probabilities from the Poisson table (Appendix B, Table C) for a mean of 4.0:

$$C_s = \$3 \quad C_e = \$2 \quad SL = \frac{C_s}{C_s + C_e} = \frac{\$3}{\$3 + \$2} = .60$$

Demand (dozen per day)	Cumulative Probability
0	.018
1	.092
2	.238
3	.434
4	.629
5	.785
⋮	⋮

Compare the service level to the cumulative probabilities. Go down the table until cumulative probability just exceeds SL = .60. This is .629, which relates to 4 dozen.

Summary

Inventory levels must be planned carefully in order to minimize the total cost of holding and ordering them, and provide reasonable levels of customer service (having items available). Inventories serve different functions (or purposes), including meeting seasonal demand, decoupling operations, protection against stock-out, and allowing economic lot size or quantity discounts. Successful inventory management requires keeping them safely, a system to keep track of inventory levels and using inventory control models, accurate information about demand and lead times, realistic estimates of inventory costs, and a priority system for classifying the items in inventory and allocating control efforts (the A-B-C Classification).

Three classes of models are described: fixed order quantity (EOQ)/reorder point (ROP), fixed order interval/order up to level, and the single period models. The first two are appropriate if unused items can be carried over into subsequent periods. The single-period model is appropriate when items cannot be carried over. EOQ models address the question of how much to order. They include the basic EOQ, economic production quantity, quantity discounts, and planned shortages models. The ROP models address the question of when to order (in terms of inventory level on hand) and are particularly helpful in dealing with situations that include variations in either demand or lead time. They involve service level and safety stock considerations. Two types of service level are lead time and annual service levels. When the time between orders is fixed, the fixed order interval model is useful. Coordinated periodic review is a more general model. The formulas presented in this chapter are summarized in Table 12-4.

Table 12-4

Summary of inventory formulas

Model	Formula		Symbols
1. Basic EOQ	$EOQ = Q_0 = \sqrt{\dfrac{2DS}{H}}$	(12-2)	Q_0 = Economic order quantity
	$TC = \dfrac{Q}{2}H + \dfrac{D}{Q}S$	(12-1)	D = Annual demand
			S = Ordering cost per order
	Length of order cycle $= \dfrac{Q_0}{D}$	(12-3)	H = Annual holding cost per unit $= i \cdot R$
			i = Annual holding cost rate
			R = Item unit cost
2. Economic production quantity	$Q_0 = \sqrt{\dfrac{2DS}{H}}\sqrt{\dfrac{P}{p-d}}$	(12-8)	Q_0 = Optimal production run quantity
	$TC = \dfrac{I_{max}}{2}H + \dfrac{D}{Q}S$	(12-4)	P = Production rate
			d = Usage or demand rate
	Cycle length $= \dfrac{Q}{d}$	(12-5)	I_{max} = Maximum inventory level
	Production run length $= \dfrac{Q}{p}$	(12-6)	
	$I_{max} = \dfrac{Q}{P}(p-d)$	(12-7)	
3. Quantity discounts	$TC = \dfrac{Q}{2}H + \dfrac{D}{Q}S + RD$	(12-9)	
4. Planned shortage	$Q_b = Q\left(\dfrac{H}{H+B}\right)$	(12-10)	Q_b = Quantity back-ordered in an order cycle
	$Q = \sqrt{\dfrac{2DS}{H}\left(\dfrac{H+B}{B}\right)}$	(12-12)	B = Annual back-order cost per unit
5. Reorder point under:			d = Demand rate
a. Constant demand and lead time	$ROP = d(LT)$	(12-13)	LT = Lead time
b. Variable demand rate	$ROP = \bar{d}(LT) + z\sqrt{LT}(\sigma_d)$	(12-15)	$\bar{d}$ = Average demand rate
c. Variable lead time and demand	$ROP = \bar{d}(\overline{LT}) + z\sqrt{\overline{LT}(\sigma_d^2) + \bar{d}^2(\sigma_{LT}^2)}$	(12-16)	σ_d = Standard deviation of demand rate
			z = Standard Normal deviate
			$\overline{LT}$ = Average lead time
			σ_{LT} = Standard deviation of lead time
6. Annual service level	$E(z) = \dfrac{Q(1 - SL_{annual})}{\sigma_{dLT}}$	(12-17)	$E(z)$ = Standardized expected number short per order cycle
			σ_{dLT} = Standard deviation of demand during lead time
			SL_{annual} = Annual service level
7. Fixed order interval	$OI^* = \sqrt{\dfrac{2(S + ns)}{i\sum D_i R_i}}$	(12-18)	OI = Order interval
			S = Group ordering cost (i.e., cost of a purchase order)
			s = Individual item ordering cost (i.e., cost of a line item in the purchase order)
			n = Number of SKUs ordered from same supplier
			D_i = Annual demand for SKU_i
			R_i = Unit cost of SKU_i
	$I_{max} = \bar{d}(OI + LT) + z\sigma_d\sqrt{OI + LT}$	(12-20)	
	$Q = I_{max} -$ Amount on hand	(12-21)	
Coordinated periodic review	$m_i = \sqrt{\dfrac{s}{D_i R_i}\dfrac{D_k R_k}{S+s}}$	(12-22)	m_i = Multiple of OI^* used for ordering SKU_i
			k = Index of the SKU with largest annual dollar value $D_i R_i$
	$OI^* = \sqrt{\dfrac{2\left(S + s\sum_{j=1}^{n}\dfrac{1}{m_j}\right)}{i\sum_{j=1}^{n} m_j D_j R_j}}$	(12-23)	
8. Single period	$SL = \dfrac{C_s}{C_s + C_e}$	(12-24)	SL = Service level
			C_s = Shortage cost per unit
			C_e = Excess cost per unit

Solved Problems

Basic EOQ. A small computer manufacturer uses 32,000 computer chips annually. The chips are used at a steady rate during the 240 days a year that the plant operates. Annual holding cost is 60 cents per chip, and ordering cost is $24 per order. Determine:

Problem 1

a. The optimal order quantity.

b. The number of workdays in an order cycle.

Solution

$D = 32{,}000$ chips per year, $S = \$24$

$H = \$.60$ per unit per year

a. $Q_0 = \sqrt{\dfrac{2DS}{H}} = \sqrt{\dfrac{2(32{,}000)\$24}{\$.60}} = 1{,}600$ chips

b. $\dfrac{Q_0}{D} = \dfrac{1{,}600 \text{ chips}}{32{,}000 \text{ chips/yr}} = \dfrac{1}{20}$ year or $1/20 \times 240$ days $= 12$ workdays

Economic production quantity. A company is both a producer and a user of brass couplings. The company operates 220 days a year and uses the couplings at a steady rate of 50 per day. Couplings can be produced at a rate of 200 per day. Annual holding cost is $1 per coupling, and machine setup cost is $35 per production run.

Problem 2

a. Determine the economic production quantity.

b. How many production runs per year will there be?

c. Calculate the maximum inventory level.

d. Determine the length of the pure consumption portion of the cycle.

Solution

$D = 50$ units per day $\times$ 220 days per year $= 11{,}000$ units per year

$S = \$35$ per production run

$H = \$1$ per unit per year

$p = 200$ units per day

$d = 50$ units per day

a. $Q_0 = \sqrt{\dfrac{2DS}{H}}\sqrt{\dfrac{p}{p-d}} = \sqrt{\dfrac{2(11{,}000)35}{1}}\sqrt{\dfrac{200}{200-50}} = 1{,}013$ units.

b. Number of production runs per year: $D/Q_0 = 11{,}000/1{,}013 = 10.86$, or 11.

c. $I_{max} = \dfrac{Q_0}{p}(p-d) = \dfrac{1{,}013}{200}(200-50) = 759.75$ or 760 units.

d. Length of cycle $= \dfrac{Q_0}{d} = \dfrac{1{,}013 \text{ units}}{50 \text{ units per day}} = 20.26$ workdays

Length of production run $= \dfrac{Q_0}{p} = \dfrac{1{,}013 \text{ units}}{200 \text{ units per day}} = 5.06$ workdays

Length of pure consumption portion = Length of cycle − Length of run

$$= 20.26 - 5.06 = 15.20 \text{ workdays}$$

Problem 3

Quantity discounts. A small manufacturer uses roughly 3,400 kg of chemical dye a year. Currently the company purchases 300 kg at a time and pays $3 per kg. The supplier has just announced that orders of 1,000 kg or more will be filled at the price of $2 per kg. The manufacturer incurs a cost of $100 each time it submits an order and uses the annual holding cost of 17 percent of the purchase price.

a. Determine the order quantity that will minimize the total cost.

b. If the supplier offered the discount at 1,500 kg instead of 1,000 kg, what order quantity would minimize total cost?

Solution

$D = 3{,}400$ kg per year, $S = \$100$, $H = .17R$

The quantity ranges are

Range	Unit Price (per kg)
1 to 999	$3
1,000 +	$2

a. Calculate the EOQ for $2 per kg

$$Q_{\$2} = \sqrt{\frac{2DS}{H}} = \sqrt{\frac{2(3{,}400)100}{.17(2)}} = 1{,}414 \text{ kg}$$

Because this quantity falls in the $2 per kg quantity range, it is optimal.

b. If the discount is offered at 1,500 kg, the EOQ for the $2 per kg price is no longer feasible. Consequently, it becomes necessary to calculate the EOQ for $3 per kg and compare the total annual cost for that order quantity with the total annual cost of using the break quantity (i.e., 1,500).

$$Q_{\$3} = \sqrt{\frac{2DS}{H}} = \sqrt{\frac{2(3{,}400)100}{0.17(3)}} = 1{,}155 \text{ kg}$$

$$TC = \left(\frac{Q}{2}\right)H = \left(\frac{D}{Q}\right)S + RD$$

$$TC_{1{,}155} = \left(\frac{1{,}155}{2}\right)(17)(3) + \left(\frac{3{,}400}{1{,}155}\right)100 + 3(3{,}400)$$

$$= \$294.53 + \$294.37 + \$10{,}200 = \$10{,}789$$

$$TC_{1{,}500} = \left(\frac{1500}{2}\right)(17)(2) + \left(\frac{3{,}400}{1{,}500}\right)100 + 2(3{,}400)$$

$$= \$255 + \$226.67 + \$6{,}800 = \$7{,}282$$

Because it would result in a lower total annual cost, 1,500 kg is the optimal order quantity (see the following figure).

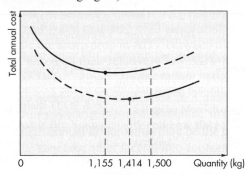

ROP for variable demand and constant lead time. The housekeeping department of a motel uses approximately 400 towels per day. The actual number tends to vary with the number of guests on any given night. Usage can be approximated by a Normal distribution that has a mean of 400 and a standard deviation of 9 towels per day. A linen services company washes the towels with a lead time of three days. If the motel policy is to maintain a stock-out risk of 2 percent for towels, what is the minimum number of towels that must be on hand at reorder time, and how much of that amount can be considered safety stock?

Problem 4

$\bar{d} = 400$ towels per day   LT $= 3$ days

$\sigma_d = 9$ towels per day   Stock-out risk $= 2$ percent, so lead time service level $= 98$ percent

Solution

From Appendix B, Table B, the z value that corresponds to an area under the Normal curve to the left of z of 98 percent is about 2.055.

$$\text{ROP} = \bar{d}\text{LT} + z\sqrt{\text{LT}}\sigma_d = 400(3) + 2.055\sqrt{3}(9)$$

$$= 1,200 + 32.03, \text{ or } 1,232 \text{ towels}$$

Safety stock is 32 towels.

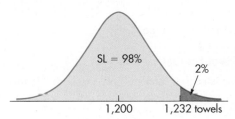

ROP for variable demand and variable lead time. A motel replaces broken glasses at a rate of 25 per day. In the past, this quantity has tended to vary Normally and has a standard deviation of three glasses per day. Glasses are ordered from a distant supplier. Lead time is Normally distributed with an average of 10 days and a standard deviation of 2 days. What ROP should be used to achieve a lead time service level of 95 percent?

Problem 5

$\bar{d} = 25$ glasses per day $\overline{\text{LT}} = 10$ days

$\sigma_d = 3$ glasses per day $\sigma_{\text{LT}} = 2$ days

lead time SL $= 95$ percent, so $z = 1.645$ (Appendix B, Table B)

$$\text{ROP} = \bar{d}\overline{\text{LT}} + z\sqrt{\overline{\text{LT}}\sigma_d^2 + \bar{d}^2\sigma_{\text{LT}}^2}$$

$$= 25(10) + 1.645\sqrt{10(3)^2 + (25)^2(2)^2} = 334 \text{ glasses}$$

Solution

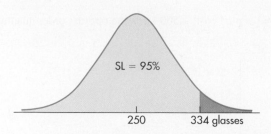

Problem 6

Annual service level. The manager of a store that sells office supplies has decided to set an annual service level of 96 percent for a certain model of telephone answering equipment. The store sells approximately 300 of this model a year. Holding cost is $5 per unit annually, ordering cost is $25, average of demand during a lead time is 20, and standard deviation of demand during a lead time is 7. Calculate the ROP, assuming EOQ is used as the order quantity.

Solution

$SL_{annual} = 96$ percent $D = 300$ units $H = \$5$ $S = \$25$ $\mu_{dLT} = 20$ $\sigma_{dLT} = 7$

First, we need to calculate the EOQ:

$$Q = \sqrt{\frac{2DS}{H}} = \sqrt{\frac{2(300)(25)}{5}} = 54.77 \text{ (round to 55)}$$

$$E(z) = \frac{Q(1 - SL_{annual})}{\sigma_{dLT}} = \frac{55(1 - .96)}{7} = .314$$

Interpolation in Table 12-3 gives $z = .18$.

$ROP = 20 + .18(7) = 21.26$

Problem 7

Fixed order interval model. A lab orders a number of chemicals from the same supplier every 30 days. Lead time is five days. The assistant manager of the lab must determine how much of one of these chemicals to order. A check of stock revealed that eleven 25 mL jars are on hand. Daily usage of the chemical is approximately Normal with a mean of 15.2 mL and a standard deviation of 1.6 mL. The desired service level for this chemical is 95 percent.

a. What should be the amount of safety stock for the chemical?

b. How many jars of the chemical should be ordered at this time?

Solution

$\bar{d} = 15.2$ mL per day, OI $= 30$ days, SL $= 95\%$ or $z = 1.645$

$\sigma_d = 1.6$ mL per day, LT $= 5$ days, Amount on hand $= 11$ jars $\times$ 25 mL per jar $= 275$ mL

a. Safety stock $= z\sigma_d\sqrt{OI + LT} = 1.645(1.6)\sqrt{30 + 5} = 15.57$ mL

b. Amount to order $= I_{max} -$ Amount on hand

$$I_{max} = \bar{d}(OI + LT) + z\sigma_d\sqrt{OI + LT}$$

$$= 15.2(30 + 5) + 15.57 = 547.57 \text{ mL}$$

Amount to order $= 547.57 - 275 = 272.57$ mL
Convert this to number of jars:

$$\frac{272.57 \text{ mL}}{25 \text{ mL per jar}} = 10.90 \text{ or } 11 \text{ jars}$$

Problem 8

Single period model. A cable TV company uses a certain piece of equipment for which it carries two units of a spare part. The part costs $500 and has no salvage value. Part failures can be modelled by a Poisson distribution with a mean of two failures during the useful life of the equipment. Estimate the range of shortage cost per unit for which stocking two units of this spare part is optimal.

C_s is unknown $C_e = \$500$ *Solution*

The Poisson table (Appendix B, Table C) provides these values for a mean of 2.0:

Number of Failures	Cumulative Probability
0..........	135
1..........	406
2..........	677
3..........	857
4..........	947
5..........	983
⋮	⋮

For the optimal discrete stocking level, the service level must be rounded up. Hence, we know that the service level must have been between .407 and .677 in order to make two units the optimal level. By setting the service level first equal to .407 and then to .677, we can establish bounds on the possible range of shortage cost.

$$\frac{C_s}{C_s + \$500} = .407, \text{ so } C_s = .407(\$500 + C_s)$$

Solving, we find $C_s = \$343.17$.
Similarly,

$$\frac{C_s}{C_s + \$500} = .677, \text{ so } C_s = .677(\$500 + C_s)$$

Solving, we find $C_s = \$1,047.99$. Hence, the range of shortage cost per unit is $343.17 to $1,047.99.

---

1. What are the primary reasons for holding inventory? (LO1)

Discussion and Review Questions

2. What are some ways that a company can reduce its needs for inventories? (LO1)

3. Why might it be inappropriate to use inventory turnover ratio to compare the inventory performance of companies in different industries? (LO1)

4. What are the requirements for effective inventory management? (LO2)

5. Define purchase lead time. What factors affect lead time? (LO2)

6. What potential benefits and risks do RFID tags have for inventory management? (LO2)

7. Briefly describe each of the costs associated with inventory. (LO2)

8. Describe briefly the A-B-C classification. (LO2)

9. How would you respond to the criticism that EOQ models tend to provide misleading results because values of D, S, and H are, at best, educated guesses? (LO3)

10. Explain briefly how a higher holding cost can result in more frequent orders. (LO3)

11. Explain how a decrease in machine setup time can lead to a decrease in the average amount of work-in-process inventory a company holds, and why that would be beneficial. (LO3)

12. How is the economic production quantity different from EOQ? (LO3)

13. Why would any company intentionally plan for shortage? Give an example. (LO3)

14. What is safety stock, and what is its purpose? (LO4)

15. Under what circumstances would the amount of safety stock held be (LO4)
    a. Large?
    b. Small?
    c. Zero?

16. What is meant by the term *lead time service level*? Generally speaking, how is lead time service level related to the amount of safety stock held? (LO4)

17. What is annual service level and how is it related to z? (LO4)

18. What is the difference between fixed order interval/order up to level model and fixed order quantity/reorder point model? When would each be preferred? (LO5)

19. What is the difference between fixed order interval/order up to level model and the coordinated periodic review model? When would each be preferred? (LO5)

20. What is the single period model, and under what circumstances is it appropriate? (LO6)

21. Can the optimal stocking level in the single-period model ever be less than median (i.e., 50th percentile) demand? Explain briefly. (LO6)

Taking Stock

1. What trade-offs are involved in each of these aspects of inventory management?
   a. Buying additional amounts to take advantage of quantity discounts.
   b. Conducting actual inventory counts once a quarter instead of once a year. (LO2)

2. Who needs to be involved in inventory decisions? (LO1 & 2)

3. How has technology aided inventory management? (LO2)

4. Employee theft of inventories can be a problem in a wholesaler/distributor warehouse. Name one thing a manager can do to combat this. (LO2)

Critical Thinking Exercise

1. To be competitive, many fast-food chains have begun to expand their menus to include a wider range of foods. Although contributing to competitiveness, this has added to the complexity of operations, including inventory management. Specifically, why has the expansion of menu offerings created problems for inventory management? (LO2)

2. As a supermarket manager, how would you go about evaluating the criticality of an inventory shortage? (LO4)

Experiential Learning Exercises

1. Give three examples of inventory in your personal life. How do you manage them? (LO1)

2. Which inventory model would you use for each of the following? Which has the highest shortage cost? (LO3–6)
   a. Buying gas for your car
   b. Buying groceries
   c. Getting cash from your bank account

3. How can the grocery store you use improve its inventory management? (LO2)

Internet Exercises

1. Visit http://www.inventoryops.com, choose one of the topics below, find and read the relevant information in the Web page, and write a brief summary. (LO2)
   a. Order picking methods
   b. RFID

2. Visit http://www.centor.ulaval.ca/MHMultimediaBank/general.asp, choose a category, click on "videos," pick a video and view it, and describe the equipment shown and its advantages. (LO2)

3. Visit http://www.advanced-planning.eu/advancedplanninge-237.htm, and compare the inventory models illustrated there with our inventory models. (LO4 & 5)

1. The manager of an automobile repair shop hopes to achieve a better allocation of inventory control efforts by adopting A-B-C classification. Given the monthly usages and unit costs in the following table, classify the items in the A, B, and C categories according to monthly dollar value. (LO2)

Item	Monthly Usage	Unit Cost
4021	50	$1,400
9402	300	12
4066	40	700
6500	150	20
9280	10	1,020
4050	80	140
6850	2,000	15
3010	400	20
4400	7,000	25
2307	1,958	14

2. The following table contains the monthly usage and unit costs for a random sample of 15 items from a list of 2,000 inventory items at a health care facility. (LO2)

Item	Unit Cost	Monthly Usage
K34	10	200
K35	25	600
K36	36	150
M10	16	25
M20	20	80
Z45	80	700
F14	20	300
F95	30	800
F99	20	60
D45	10	550
D48	12	90
D52	15	110
D57	40	120
N08	30	40
P05	16	500

   a. Develop an A-B-C classification for these items.
   b. How could the manager use this information?
   c. After reviewing your classification scheme, suppose that the manager decides to place item P05 into the A category. What are some possible explanations for this decision?

3. A large bakery buys flour in 25 kg bags. The bakery uses an average of 4,860 bags a year. Preparing an order and receiving the shipment of flour bags involves a cost of $10 per order. Annual holding cost is $5 per flour bag. (LO3)

   a. Determine the economic order quantity.
   b. What is the average number of bags on hand (i.e., in inventory)?
   c. How many orders per year will there be?
   d. Calculate the total annual cost of ordering and holding flour.
   e. If ordering cost were to increase by 50 percent per order, by what percentage would the EOQ change?

4. A large law firm uses an average of 10 packages of copier paper a day. Each package contains 500 sheets. The firm operates 260 days a year. Storage and handling costs for the paper are $1 per year per package, and it costs approximately $10 to order and receive a shipment of papers. (LO3)

   a. What order quantity would minimize total annual ordering and holding cost?
   b. Calculate the total annual inventory control cost using your order quantity from part a.

c. Except for rounding, are annual ordering and holding costs equal at the EOQ?

d. The office manager is currently using an order quantity of 100 packages. The partners of the firm expect the office to be managed in a cost-efficient manner. Would you recommend that the office manager use the optimal order quantity instead of 100 packages? Justify your answer.

5. A flower shop uses 250 clay pots a month. The pots are purchased for $2 each. Annual holding cost is estimated to be 30 percent of purchase cost, and ordering cost is $20 per order. The manager has been using an order quantity of 250 flower pots. (LO3)

a. Calculate the EOQ.

b. Calculate the EOQ's total annual inventory control cost.

c. What additional annual inventory control cost is the shop incurring by using the current order quantity?

6. A fresh produce distributor uses 800 non-returnable packing crates a month, which it purchases at a cost of $5 each. The manager has assigned an annual holding cost of 25 percent of the purchase price per crate. Ordering cost is $28 per order. Currently the manager orders 800 crates at a time. How much could the firm save annually in ordering and holding costs by using the EOQ? (LO3)

7. Demand for an item is projected to be 100 units per month. The monthly holding cost is $2 per unit, and it costs an estimated $55 to process an order. (LO3)

a. Determine the EOQ.

b. If the vendor is willing to offer the manager a discount of $10 *per order* for ordering in multiples of 50 units (e.g., 50, 100), would you advise the manager to take advantage of the offer? If so, what order quantity would you recommend?

c. Alternatively, if the demand can wait at the cost of $5 per unit per month, what should the order quantity and the amount short per order cycle be?

8. A food processor uses approximately 27,000 non-returnable glass jars a month for its fruit juice product. Because of storage limitations, a lot size of 4,000 jars has been used. Monthly holding cost is one cent per jar, and ordering cost is $20 per order. (LO3)

a. What penalty is the company incurring by using its present order quantity?

b. The manager would like to justify the present order quantity. One possibility is to simplify order processing to reduce the ordering cost. What ordering cost would enable the manager to justify the current order quantity?

9. A sausage factory can produce European wieners at a rate of 500 kg per day. It supplies wieners to local stores and restaurants at a steady rate of 100 kg per day. The cost to prepare the equipment for producing European wieners is $12. Annual holding cost is $4 per kg of wieners. The factory operates 300 days a year. Calculate: (LO3)

a. The optimal production run quantity.

b. The number of production runs per year.

c. The length (in days) of a production run.

10. A chemical plant produces sodium bisulfate in 100 kg bags. Demand for this product is 20 tonnes per day. The capacity for producing this product is 50 tonnes per day. Setup cost is $400, and storage and handling costs are $200 per tonne per year. The company operates 200 days a year. (Note: 1 tonne = 1,000 kg). (LO3)

a. What is the optimal number of bags per production run?

b. What would the average inventory level be for this lot size?

c. Determine the approximate length of a production run, in days.

d. About how many production runs per year would there be?

e. How much could the company save annually in inventory control cost if the setup cost could be reduced to $200 per production run and the optimal production quantity is recalculated and used?

11. A company is about to begin production of a new product. The manager of the department that will produce one of the components for the product wants to know how often his machine will be available for other work. The machine will produce the item at a rate of 200 units a day. Eighty units will be used daily in assembling the final product. The company operates five days a week, 50 weeks a year. The manager estimates that it will take almost a full day

to get the machine ready for a production run, at a cost of $300. Inventory holding cost will be $10 per unit per year. (LO3)

    a. What production run quantity should be used to minimize total annual setup and holding cost?

    b. What is the length of a production run (in days)?

    c. During production, at what rate will inventory build up?

    d. If the manager wants to run another job between runs of this item, and needs a minimum of 10 days per cycle of this job for the other work, will there be enough time?

12. A company manufactures hair dryers. It buys some of the components, but it makes the heating element, which it can produce at the rate of 800 per day. Hair dryers are assembled 250 days a year, at a rate of 300 per day. Because of the disparity between the production and usage rates, the heating elements are periodically produced in batches of 2,000 units. (LO3)

    a. Approximately how many *batches* of heating elements are produced annually?

    b. If production on a batch begins when there is no inventory of heating elements on hand, how much inventory will be on hand (i.e., in inventory) *two days later*?

    c. What will be the average level of inventory of the heating element, assuming each production cycle begins when there are no inventory on hand?

    d. The same equipment that is used to make the heating element could also be used to make a component for another of the company's products. That job would require four days per cycle of the element. Setup time for making a batch of the heating elements is a half day. Is there enough time to do this job between production of batches of heating element? Explain.

13. A small mail-order company uses 18,000 boxes a year. Holding cost rate is 20 percent of unit cost per year, and ordering cost is $32 per order. The following quantity discounts are available. Determine: (LO3)

    a. The optimal order quantity.

    b. The number of orders per year.

Number of Boxes	Price per Box
1,000 to 1,999	$1.25
2,000 to 4,999	1.20
5,000 to 9,999	1.15
10,000 or more	1.10

14. A jewellery manufacturer buys semi-precious stones to make bracelets and rings. The supplier has quoted a price of $8 per stone for order quantities of 600 stones or more, $9 per stone for orders of 400 to 599 stones, and $10 per stone for smaller order quantities. The jewellery manufacturer operates 200 days per year. Usage rate is 25 stones per day, and ordering cost is $48 per order. (LO3 & 4)

    a. If annual holding cost is 30 percent of unit cost, what is the optimal order quantity?

    b. If lead time is six workdays, at what inventory level should the company reorder?

15. A manufacturer of exercise equipment purchases pulleys from a supplier who lists these prices: less than 1,000, $5 each; 1,000 to 3,999, $4.95 each; 4,000 to 5,999, $4.90 each; and 6,000 or more, $4.85 each. Ordering cost is $50 per order, annual holding cost is 20 percent of purchase cost, and annual usage is 4,900 pulleys. Determine the order quantity that will minimize total cost. (LO3)

16. The manager of a large TV store wants to begin stocking a type of remote control device. Expected monthly demand is 800 units. The remote controls can be purchased from either supplier A or supplier B. Their price lists are as follows: (LO3)

Supplier A		Supplier B	
Quantity	**Unit Price**	**Quantity**	**Unit Price**
1–199	$14.00	1–149	$14.10
200–499	13.80	150–349	13.90
500+	13.60	350+	13.70

Ordering cost is $40 per order and annual holding cost is 25 percent of unit price. Which supplier should be used and what order quantity is optimal if the intent is to minimize total annual cost?

17. A manager just received a new price list for boxes from a supplier. It will now cost $1.00 a box for order quantities of 801 or more, $1.10 a box for 200 to 800, and $1.20 a box for smaller quantities. Ordering cost is $40 per order and holding cost rate is 40 percent of unit cost per year. The company uses 3,600 boxes a year. The manager has suggested a "round number" order quantity of 800 boxes. The manager's rationale is that total annual inventory cost is U-shaped and fairly flat at its minimum. Therefore, the difference in total annual cost between 800 and 801 units would be small anyway. How would you reply to the manager's suggestion? What order quantity would you recommend? (LO3)

18. A newspaper publisher uses roughly 800 metres of baling wire each day to secure bundles of newspapers while they are being distributed to carriers. The paper is published Monday through Saturday. Lead time for purchase of wires is six workdays. The stock-out risk for various levels of safety stock is as follows: 1,500 metres, .10; 1,800 metres, .05; 2,100 metres, .02; and 2,400 metres, .01. What is the appropriate reorder point given that the company desires a lead time service level of 95 percent? (LO4)

19. Given the following information: (LO4)
Expected demand during a lead time = 300 units
Standard deviation of demand during a lead time = 30 units
Demand during a lead time is distributed Normally:
   a. Determine the safety stock needed to attain a 1 percent risk of stock-out during a lead time.
   b. Would a stock-out risk of 2 percent require more or less safety stock than a 1 percent risk? Explain.

20. Given the following information: (LO4)
Expected demand during a lead time = 600 kg
Standard deviation of demand during a lead time = 52 kg
Acceptable stock-out risk during a lead time = 4 percent
   a. What amount of safety stock is appropriate?
   b. At what level of inventory should this item be reordered?

21. Demand for the vanilla ice cream at an ice cream store can be approximated by a Normal distribution with a mean of 21 litres per week and a standard deviation of 3.5 litres per week. The ice cream is purchased from an ice cream producer. The store manager desires a lead time service level of 90 percent. Lead time from the producer is two days. The store is open seven days a week. (LO4 & 5)
   a. If the EOQ/ROP model is used for ordering the ice cream from the producer, what ROP would be consistent with the desired lead time service level?
   b. If a fixed order interval model is used instead, what order quantity should be used if the order interval is 7 days and 8 litres are on hand in inventory at the time of order?
   c. Suppose that the manager is using the EOQ/ROP model described in part a. One day after placing an order with the producer, the manager receives a call from the producer that the order will be delayed because of problems at the producer's plant. The producer promises to have the order there in two days. After hanging up, the manager checks the inventory of vanilla ice cream and finds that 2 litres have been sold since the order was placed. Assuming that the producer's promise is valid, what is the probability that the store will run out of vanilla ice cream before the shipment arrives?

22. The injection moulding department of a company uses an average of 30 litres of a special lubricant a day. The lubricant is replenished when the amount on hand is 170 litres. It takes four days for an order to be delivered. The current stock-out risk is 9 percent. What amount of safety stock would be needed if the acceptable risk of stock-out is to be reduced to 3 percent? (LO4)

23. A company uses an average of 85 circuit boards a day in an assembly process. The standard deviation is 5 units per day. The person who orders the boards follows this rule: Order when

the amount on hand drops to 625 boards. Orders are delivered approximately six days after being placed. The delivery time is Normal with a mean of six days and a standard deviation of 1.10 days. What is the probability that the inventory of circuit boards will be exhausted before the order is received? (LO4)

24. One item a computer store sells is supplied by a vendor who handles only that item. Demand for that item recently changed, and the store manager must determine at what inventory level to replenish it. The manager wants a probability of at least 96 percent of not having a stock-out during a lead time. The manager expects demand to average a dozen units a day and to have a standard deviation of two units a day. Lead time is variable, averaging four days with a standard deviation of one day. Assume demand during a lead time is Normal. At what inventory level should the manager reorder to achieve the desired service level probability? (LO4)

25. The manager of a car wash has received a revised price list from the vendor of the liquid soap, and a promise of a shorter lead time for deliveries. Formerly the lead time was four days, but now the vendor promises a reduction of 25 percent in that time (i.e., new lead time is 3 days). Annual usage of soap is 4,500 litres. The car wash is open 360 days a year. Assume that daily usage of soap is Normal, and that it has a standard deviation of two litres per day. The ordering cost is $10 per order and annual holding cost rate is 40 percent of unit cost. The revised price list (cost per litre) is shown below. (LO3 & 4)

Quantity (litres)	Unit Price per litre
1–399	$2.00
400–799	1.80
800+	1.60

   a. What order quantity is optimal?
   b. What ROP is appropriate if the acceptable risk of a stock-out is 1.5 percent?

26. Experience suggests that usage of copy paper at a small copy centre can be approximated by a Normal distribution with a mean of five boxes per day and a standard deviation of one-half box per day. Two days are required to fill an order for paper. Ordering cost is $10 per order, and annual holding cost is $10 per box. (LO3–5)

   a. Determine the economic order quantity, assuming 250 workdays a year.
   b. If the copy centre reorders when the paper on hand is 12 boxes, calculate the risk of a stock-out during a lead time.
   c. If a fixed order interval of seven days, instead of the EOQ/ROP, is used for reordering, what shortage risk does the copy centre incur if it orders 36 boxes when the amount on hand is 12 boxes?

27. A bulk foods store sells unshelled peanuts by the kilogram. Historically, daily demand is Normally distributed with a mean of 8 kg and a standard deviation of 1 kg. The purchase lead time from the supplier also appears to be Normally distributed with a mean of eight days and a standard deviation of one day. What ROP would provide stock-out risk of 10 percent during a lead time? (LO4)

28. A supermarket is open 360 days per year. Daily use of cash register tape averages 10 rolls, Normally distributed, with a standard deviation of two rolls per day. The cost of ordering tapes is $10 per order, and holding cost is 40 cents per roll a year. Lead time is three days. (LO3 & 4)

   a. What is the EOQ?
   b. What ROP will provide a lead time service level of 96 percent?
   c. What ROP will provide an annual service level of 96 percent if $Q = EOQ$?

29. A service station uses 1,200 cases of oil a year. Ordering cost is $20 per order, and annual holding cost is $3 per case. The station owner has specified an *annual* service level of 99 percent.

   a. What is the EOQ? (LO3 & 4)
   b. What level of ROP is appropriate if demand during a lead time is normally distributed with a mean of 80 cases and a standard deviation of 5 cases?

30. A school bus depot operates 250 days a year. Daily demand for diesel fuel at the depot is Normal with an average of 250 litres and a standard deviation of 14 litres. Holding cost for the fuel is $.30 per litre per year, and it costs $10 in administrative time to submit an order for more fuel. It takes one day to receive a delivery of diesel fuel. (LO3 & 4)

   a. Calculate the EOQ.
   b. Determine the amount of ROP that would be needed if the manager wants an annual service level of 99.5 percent.

31. A drugstore uses the fixed order interval model for many of the items it stocks. The manager wants a service level of .98. Determine the order quantity for the following items if the order interval is 14 days and lead time is 2 days: (LO5)

Item	Average Daily Demand	Daily Standard Deviation	Quantity on Hand
K033	60	5	420
K144	50	4	375
L700	8	2	160

32. A manager must set up inventory ordering procedures for two new production items, P34 and P35. P34 can be ordered at any time, but P35 can be ordered only once every four weeks. The company operates 50 weeks a year, and the weekly usage rate for each item is Normally distributed. The manager has gathered the following information about the items: (LO3–5)

	Item P34	Item P35
Average weekly demand	60 units	70 units
Standard deviation	4 units per week	5 units per week
Unit cost	$15	$20
Annual holding cost rate	30%	30%
Ordering cost per order	$70	$30
Lead time	2 weeks	2 weeks
Acceptable stock-out risk	2.5%	2.5%

   a. At what inventory level should the manager reorder P34?
   b. Calculate the economic order quantity for P34.
   c. Calculate the order quantity for P35 if 110 units are on hand at the time the order is placed.

33. Given the following list of items, (LO2 & 3)

   a. Classify the items as A, B, or C.
   b. Determine the economic order quantity for each item.

Item	Estimated Annual Demand	Ordering Cost	Holding Cost (%)	Unit Price
H4-010	20,000	$50	20	$2.50
H5-201	60,200	60	20	4.00
P6-400	9,800	80	30	28.50
P6-401	16,300	50	30	12.00
P7-100	6,250	50	30	9.00
P9-103	4,500	50	40	22.00
TS-300	21,000	40	25	45.00
TS-400	45,000	40	25	40.00
TS-041	800	40	25	20.00
V1-001	26,100	25	35	4.00

34. The distribution of demand for jelly doughnuts on Saturdays at a doughnut shop is shown in the following table. Determine the optimal number of doughnuts, in dozens, to make each Saturday morning if labour, materials, and overhead are estimated to cost $3.20 per dozen, doughnuts are sold for $4.80 per dozen, and leftover doughnuts at the end of each day are sold the next day at half price. What is the *resulting* service level? (LO6)

Demand (dozens)	Relative Frequency
19	.01
20	.05
21	.12
22	.18
23	.13
24	.14
25	.10
26	.11
27	.10
28	.04
29	.02

35. A public utility intends to buy a turbine as part of an expansion plan and must now decide on the number of spare parts to order. One part, X135, can be purchased for $100 each. Holding and disposal costs are estimated to be 145 percent of the purchase price over the life of the turbine. A stock-out would cost roughly $8,000 due to downtime, ordering, and "special purchase" factors. Historical records based on the performance of similar equipment operating under similar conditions suggest that demand for the spare part will tend to approximate a Poisson distribution with a mean of 3.2 units for the useful life of the turbine. (LO6)

    a. What is the optimal number of units of this spare part to order?

    b. Carrying six spare parts would be the best strategy for what range of shortage cost per unit?

36. A fish store buys fresh tuna daily for $4.20 per kg and sells it for $5.70 per kg. At the end of each day, any remaining tuna is sold to a producer of cat food for $2.40 per kg. Daily demand for tuna at the fish store can be approximated by a Normal distribution with a mean of 80 kg and a standard deviation of 10 kg. What is the optimal stocking level? (LO6)

37. A small grocery store sells fresh produce, which it obtains from local farmers. During the strawberry season, demand for fresh strawberries at the store can be reasonably approximated using a Normal distribution with a mean of 40 litres per day and a standard deviation of 6 litres per day. Excess cost is 35 cents per litre. The grocer orders 49 litres per day. (LO6)

    a. What is the implied cost of shortage per litre?

    b. Why might this be a reasonable figure?

38. Demand for a specific type of cake at a local pastry shop can be approximated using a Poisson distribution with a mean of six per day. The manager estimates it costs $9 to prepare each cake. Fresh cakes sell for $12. Day-old cakes sell for $7 each. What stocking level is appropriate? (LO6)

39. A burger restaurant buys top-grade ground beef for $3 per kg. A large sign over the entrance guarantees that the meat is fresh daily. Any leftover meat is sold to the local high school cafeteria for $2 per kg. Eight hamburgers can be prepared from each kilogram of meat. Burgers sell for $2 each. Labour, overhead, meat, buns, and condiments cost $1 per burger. Demand for ground beef is Normally distributed with a mean of 400 kg per day and a standard deviation of 50 kg per day. What daily order quantity is optimal? (LO6)

40. The distribution of daily demand for rug-cleaning machines at a rental store is shown in the following table. Machines are rented by the day only. Profit on a rug cleaner is $10 per day. The store has four rug-cleaning machines. (LO6)

Demand	Frequency
0	.30
1	.20
2	.20
3	.15
4	.10
5	.05
	1.00

a. Assuming that the stocking decision is optimal, what is the implied range of excess cost per machine per day?

b. Your answer from part a has been presented to the manager, who protests that the amount is too low. Does this suggest an increase or a decrease in the number of rug machines he stocks? Explain.

41. A manager wants to purchase a new piece of processing equipment and must decide on the number of a spare part to order with the new equipment. The spares cost $200 each, and any unused spares will have an expected salvage value of $50 each. The probability of usage of parts can be described by the following distribution: (LO6)

Number	0	1	2	3
Probability	.10	.50	.25	.15

If the part fails and a spare is not available, it will take two days to obtain a replacement and install it. The cost for idle equipment is $400 per day. The spare is expected to cost the same in the future ($200 per unit). What quantity of spares should be ordered?

42. A Las Vegas bakery must decide how many wedding cakes to prepare for the upcoming weekend. Cakes cost $33 each to make, and sell for $60 each. Unsold cakes are reduced to half-price on Monday, and typically one-third of those are sold. Any that remain are donated to a nearby senior centre. Analysis of recent demand resulted in the following probability distribution: (LO6)

Demand	0	1	2	3
Probability	.15	.35	.30	.20

How many cakes should be prepared?

*43. The South Texas Center for Pediatric Care in San Antonio wants to reduce its inventory costs. The Centre carries vaccines (e.g., for whooping cough), non-injectable medical supplies (such as examining-table paper, alcohol swabs, tongue depressors), and office supplies (stationery, paper, and forms). Out of the 113 inventory items, seven vaccines account for approximately 70 percent of annual dollar value of $225,000. Approximately 210 whooping cough vaccines are needed per month. An office manager spends a total of approximately one half-hour finding out how much inventory of whooping cough vaccine is on hand and placing an order. She is paid approximately $17 an hour. The cost of capital for the centre is 8 percent per year, and the storage cost (including use of freezers for some items) is estimated to also be approximately 8 percent of item cost per year. A lot of 10 whooping cough vaccines costs an average of $160.[6] (LO3–5)

a. Calculate the EOQ for whooping cough vaccines.

b. Suppose that the purchase lead time is two days and daily demand for whooping cough vaccines is Normally distributed with a mean of seven vaccines and a standard deviation of two vaccines. Calculate the reorder point if lead time service level of 98 percent is desired.

c. Suppose that the office manager wants to make the replenishment of whooping cough vaccines easier for herself by ordering them every two weeks.

   i Using the information in part b, what should the order up to level (I_{max}) be?

   ii Suppose that the Center has 34 whooping cough vaccines on hand. What should the order quantity be, given your answer to part i?

44. The owner of a health food store has decided to intentionally allow shortage of a food supplement. The annual demand is 500 bottles, the ordering cost is $10 per order, and the holding cost is $1 per bottle per year. Cost of back-ordering one bottle is estimated to be $10 per bottle per year.

a. What should the order quantity be? (LO3)

b. How many bottles will be short per order cycle?

*45. Hallmark sells "personal expression" cards and gifts worldwide through either its own stores or other retailers. Most products are single runs. Unsold products are either discounted and sold to discount retailers, or are discarded.

[6]D.M. Burns, M.J. Cote, and S.L. Tucker, "Inventory Analysis of a Pediatric Care Center," *Hospital Materiel Management Quarterly* 22(3), February 2001, pp. 84–90.

A typical problem Hallmark faces is as follows: A Barbie Stationary Gift set, containing 16 notes, envelopes, and foil seals, is to be produced and marketed to celebrate the 50th year of Barbie. The price will be set at $12.99 per unit. The cost of production to Hallmark will be approximately $6 per unit. The product manager, based on previous sales of Barbie stationery products, estimates that demand and its probability for this product will be as follows:

Demand (in 1000s)	90	100	110	120	130
Probability	.1	.2	.4	.2	.1

Any units not sold through regular channels will be sold to discount retailers at $1 less than cost (i.e., $5 per unit). There is no penalty cost for being short. Determine the optimal order quantity for the Barbie Stationery Gift set.[7] (LO6)

*46. Teck (Cominco)[8] is a Canadian metal mining and processing company. The company runs two warehouses in Trail to store thousands of parts and supplies for the machines and equipment used in its mines and operations in western Canada and Alaska. Until a few years ago, the stocks in the warehouses were controlled using an IBM mainframe computer and IBM application software called Inventory Management Program and Control Techniques, IMPACT. IMPACT keeps track of each part, and its usage (withdrawal from the warehouse) over time, and triggers replenishment (addition to the warehouse) from the suppliers. IMPACT determines the reorder point (and the size of the next order) primarily based on the forecast for usage of the part in the future. The forecasting technique used is Exponential Smoothing. For each inventoried part the smoothing constant is found by trial and error. For the order quantity, IMPACT uses the EOQ. The new version of IMPACT, called INFOREM, is used by many companies such as Federated Cooperatives Ltd. and Mark's Work Wearhouse.

For illustration, consider a specific part, which is kept in stock. The following data is the usage of the part during a nine-month period:

Jan	Feb	Mar	Apr	May	Jun	Jul	Aug	Sep
2	5	10	4	12	0	8	16	4

Suppose that now is the end of September and the next reorder point is coming up. Using Exponential Smoothing with $\alpha = 0.2$, the forecast for October will be 6.7 units. The part costs Cominco $15/unit. Holding cost rate is 20 percent of unit cost per year. Ordering cost is $2/order. Purchase lead time for this part is 20 days. Assume 30 days in a month.[8] (LO3 & 4)

a. What should the EOQ be? *Hint*: Use the forecast for October $\times$ 12 to estimate next year's demand.

b. For how many days is the EOQ enough (i.e., what is its time supply)?

c. Calculate the total annual inventory control cost of the EOQ.

d. Suppose now this part is ordered 7 at a time. How much more expensive is this?

e. Suppose there was no variability in demand or lead time. Determine the reorder point.

f. Suppose a 95 percent lead time service level is required. From the forecasting module, the standard deviation of monthly demand = 5.14 units. Determine the reorder point.

*47. Federated Cooperatives Limited (FCL) is the largest wholesaler/distributor of food and hardware in western Canada. FCL uses the Inforem forecasting and inventory software and the fixed order interval model to order products for its four warehouses. As illustration, consider the ordering of Energizer batteries by the Calgary warehouse. The purchase lead time is approximately 15 days. Suppose that there are only two types of Energizer batteries in the warehouse: Item #0378422CA, 6V Lantern battery with annual demand of 5,767 units and price of $3.85 each, and Item #0378539CA, 6V Lantern battery with annual demand of 603 units and price of $7.54 each. (LO5)

a. Suppose that the fixed cost of a purchase order for one SKU is $3.50 and the variable cost of each additional line item (SKU) is $0.50. Also, suppose that holding cost rate is 20 percent of unit cost per year. Determine the optimal order interval.

---

[7]Based on F.H. Barron, "Payoff Matrices Pay off at Hallmark," *Interfaces* 15(4), July/August 1985, pp. 20–25.

[8]K.B. Hustwick and J.W. Merkley, "Cominco's Computerized Inventory Control System," *Canadian Institute of Mining Bulletin*, July 1982.

b. The forecasted demand for Item #0378422CA is 138 units per week for the next few weeks and the standard deviation of demand is estimated to be 37 units per week. Currently there are 555 units on hand in the warehouse. The service level for this SKU is desired to be 98.5 percent. Calculate the I_{max} (order up to level) for this battery, and determine the current quantity to order.

c. If the demand forecast for Item #0378422CA for the next five weeks was in fact 144.2, 144.2, 133.1, 133.1, and 122 units, respectively (i.e., this item has seasonality), how would your answer to part b change? Assume that the standard deviation of demand remains at 37 units per week.

*48. Sterling Pulp Chemicals (ERCO) in Saskatoon produces chemicals for processing pulp, such as caustic soda. In its maintenance warehouse, it keeps all the spare parts for its equipment as well as supplies such as light bulbs. For inventory control, it uses the Min/Max model which is basically the EOQ/ROP model. Every day, the computer system identifies those stocks that have reached their minimum (ROP) level, and the inventory staff orders those items. For illustration, consider the usage of item #14-46-506: four-foot supersaver fluorescent light bulbs in the first ten months of 2008: 10, 10, 66, 32, 34, 18, 24, 9, 14, and 48. The forecast for November using Exponential Smoothing with $\alpha = .3$ is 27.48 units, and the standard deviation of monthly demand for these bulbs is 18.84 units. The lead time from the supplier, EECOL Electric, is 14 days, and the unit cost is $1.40. Holding cost rate for Sterling is estimated to be 20 percent of unit cost per year and ordering cost is $1 per order. Assume 30 days in a month. (LO3–5)

  a. Calculate the EOQ for this item. (*Hint*: D = forecast for November $\times$ 12.)
  b. For how many months is the EOQ enough (i.e., its time supply)?
  c. Calculate the total annual inventory control cost of the EOQ.
  d. Suppose now this part is ordered 55 units at a time. How much more costly is this?
  e. Calculate the reorder point of these bulbs. Use a 95 percent lead time service level.
  f. Suppose that the fixed order interval model is used to order these bulbs. Given an order interval of two months, calculate the order up to level (I_{max}) for these bulbs. Use a 95 percent service level.

*49. The usage of Male Cord End (#4867), purchased from EECOL Electric Ltd, by Sterling Pulp Chemicals (ERCO) during the June to October period of 1998 was 5, 1, 5, 9, and 8. Using Exponential Smoothing with $\alpha = .5$, the forecast usage for November is 7.25 units, and the standard deviation of monthly usage, using the above numbers, is 3.13 units. The price of one unit is $2.48. Suppose Sterling uses 20 percent as its holding cost rate per year, purchase lead time is approximately 14 days, and desired lead time service level is 95 percent. Assume 30 days in a month. (LO3–5)

  a. If this item is ordered individually using the EOQ/ROP model, and ordering cost is $1 per order, calculate the EOQ and ROP for it.
  b. Suppose Sterling orders the Eagle Male Cord Ends jointly with other SKUs supplied by EECOL Electric. For simplicity, assume that there is only one other SKU, item #14-20-390, Eagle Female Cord End. The forecast for usage of Eagle Female Cord End for November is 2.23 units. The price of a female cord end is $5.06. The ordering cost per purchase order for one SKU is $3 and for another line item $.50.

   i Calculate the optimal order interval.
   ii If currently there are 13 units of Male Cord End on hand, how many should be ordered now?

*50. A franchisee of Fuddruckers, a hamburger restaurant chain based in Texas, has contracted to supply food for a day-long music festival in Crystal Beach, North Carolina. Fuddruckers distinguishes itself from other hamburger restaurant chains with on-premise butcher shop and bakery. Fuddruckers' only Canadian restaurant is located in Saskatoon. It is now the Wednesday before the Saturday festival. Approximately 5,000 tickets have been sold so far, and this number should increase because it is predicted that Saturday will be sunny. The manager, based on previous experience, believes that the eventual number of people who will attend the festival, and the associated probabilities, are: (LO6)

Numbers	6,000	7,000	8,000	9,000	10,000
Probability	.1	.2	.4	.2	.1

The manager expects that on average, each person will eat one meal during the seven-hour festival. She has decided to limit the menu to just two meals: one-third-pound burgers and quarter-pound hot dogs. She estimates, based on regular restaurant sales, that 60 percent of people will buy the burger and 40 percent will buy the hotdog. The cost of one burger will be $2.25 and it will sell for $5, whereas the hot dog will cost $1.34 and will sell for $4. Unused food has to be discarded, and there is no penalty for being short. The meat, hot dogs, buns, and vegetables need to be ordered today (three days before the festival so that they will arrive on the day of the festival). Determine the optimal order quantities for burgers and hotdogs.[9] (LO6)

51. A distributor orders four products from a supplier. The fixed cost to place an order for one SKU is $23, and cost of each additional SKU added to the order is $3. The carrying cost rate is 24 percent per year. Lead time is 1 week. Assume a 50-week year. The annual demand and unit cost of the four SKUs are:

SKU	Annual demand	Unit cost
1	450	$8
2	2,000	12.50
3	200	3.52
4	3,000	33.30

The distributor wishes to use the coordinated periodic review model to plan ordering these SKUs. Calculate the multiples m_js and the optimal order interval OI*. (LO5)

*52. Schaan Healthcare Products is a distributor of medical/surgical products in Saskatchewan. Schaan has a warehouse in Saskatoon that carries thousands of items, one of which is item #345-5870, Micro-Touch Surgical Glove, size 7. The demand for this item (in cases) during the September to November 2002 was 25, 57, and 50, respectively. Schaan's inventory manager uses a three-month moving average to forecast next month's demand for the items. The three-month moving average forecast for December's demand for size 7 gloves is 44 cases. Suppose that he uses the EOQ/ROP model to replenish this item. The surgical gloves are purchased from Ansell Limited in cases of 200 units at a cost of $120 per case. Using the three-month moving average forecast for December, ordering cost of $15 per order, inventory holding cost rate of 15 percent per year, and purchase lead time of two days, (LO3–5)

a. Calculate the EOQ for this item (rounded to a whole number).
b. Calculate the total annual holding and ordering cost if order quantity is 30 cases.
c. Using lead time service level of 96 percent and standard deviation of monthly demand of 16.82 cases, calculate the ROP (rounded to a whole number).
d. In fact, Schaan uses the fixed order interval model for replenishing this item. Calculate the order up to level (I_{max}) for this item (rounded to a whole number) if it is ordered every two weeks and the desired service level is 94 percent.

*53. A wholesale bottler and distributor of both imported and domestic alcoholic drinks purchases half its spirits in barrels, which it then blends and bottles (approximately 60 different types of spirit in up to 5 different bottle sizes). The most time-consuming activity is the

---

[9]Based on S.M. Shafer, "Fuddruckers and the Crystal Coast Music Festival," *Case Research Journal* 22(2), 2002.

changeover of the bottling line for a different bottle size. This takes one full day. Therefore, products that have the same bottle size are bottled one batch after another, saving the bottle-size changeover time (however, there is a smaller setup time for spirit, bottle, and label changeover). ROP of the 1-litre (L) bottles is set to one month of demand because they are usually bottled once a month. Each time, approximately 10 different spirits are run one after another. The actual bottling time is negligible (only 2 days for all 10 spirits). Management wants bottling run length (batch size) of each spirit is equal to its EOQ. Note that because production rate is so much faster than the demand rate, we can use the EOQ formula instead of the EPQ formula.

Suppose now is the beginning of June, and there is going to be a changeover to the 1-L bottles tomorrow. The on-hand inventory of the 1-L bottles of vodka is only 144 cases, whereas the demand forecast this SKU in June is 312 cases. Assume that the demand has no trends or seasonality. The setup cost per bottle run for vodka is $73.23. The cost per case of vodka is $29.31. The carrying cost rate is 15 percent of unit cost per year. (LO3 & 4)

a. Calculate the optimal batch size (i.e., EOQ) for vodka

b. After talking to the supervisor, it became clear that he does not use the EOQ to determine the batch size. Instead he produces enough 1-L bottles of a spirit so that this quantity plus any on-hand inventory is expected to last until the next production run for 1-L bottles, which is one month later. However, for items with uncertain demand such as vodka, he produces a quantity that, together with any on-hand inventory, is expected to meet two months of demand. Assuming that the standard deviation of monthly demand for vodka is 98 cases, what service level is the supervisor implicitly using?

*54. A high-end skiwear producer makes parkas for men, women, juniors, and preschoolers. For each "gender," there are tens of styles, and for each style approximately five colours and four sizes. This results in hundreds of parka SKUs for each "gender." This large variety plus the long lead time from design to distributions make the production planning of the skiwear producer very difficult. (LO6)

The design starts in February, concepts are finalized by May, prototypes are made by July, designs are finalized by September, first-half production quantity is determined and fabrics are ordered by November, fabrics are received and production starts by February of next year, retailers place their orders by March, shipments of products arrive from manufacturers in Asia by July, retailers receive their orders by August, sales pick up by December, and unsold goods are discounted by February of the third year.

It is now November and the VP of operations has to decide on the first-half production quantities. The buying committee has met and each of the six members forecasted the first-half demand for the parkas. For each parka, the VP has averaged these forecasts and calculated the standard deviation. To be more conservative, he has doubled the standard deviation.

As an illustration, a specific women's parka has average forecast value of 2,150 units and standard deviation of 807 units (after doubling). Assume a Normal distribution for the demand. Each parka will be sold for $173 to retailers. The unit cost will be approximately $130. If any parkas are left after January two years later, it will be sold at $115 each. Determine the best production quantity for this parka.

*55. A commercial laundromat products manufacturer wants to consolidate the purchase of all the cardboard boxes it needs for the detergents, bleaches, and fabric softeners it sells to laundromats. The total demand for all these boxes is 10,000 units per year (a unit = 1,000 packages). Assume that ordering cost is $50 per order and holding cost rate is 20 percent per year. The following unit prices and the associated order quantity ranges are proposed by the most competitive bidder. If this bidder is chosen, what should the order quantity for the boxes be? (LO3)

Order Quantity Range	Unit Price
1–500 units	$29.50
501–750	26.87
751–1500	24.77
1,501–2,000	23.93

MINI-CASE http://www.bikefriday.com

Bike Friday

Bike Friday is a small manufacturer of high-end folding travel bicycles located in Eugene, Oregon. The bikes can be folded and carried in a Travelcase. In the late 1990s, the controller of Bike Friday was looking into ways to cut costs. At that time, the company purchased the Travelcases in lot sizes of 100, at a unit price of $65 plus $4.50 for shipping expense. A lot would last a little more than one month. The purchase lead time was six to eight weeks. The controller discovered that if the company ordered a full truckload of 500 Travelcases at a time, the unit price would be $50 plus $2.50 for shipping expense. However, Bike Friday would need a bigger storage space (350 square feet) which was not available in-house. Assuming that a nearby storage space could be leased for $400 a month, holding cost rate of 20 percent per unit per year, and order cost

of $50 per order, determine if buying a truckload of Travelcases would have a lower total cost.

Sources: G.A. Horsfall, "How to Leverage a Bad Inventory Situation," *Hospital Materiel Management Quarterly* 20(2), November 1998, pp. 40–46; http://www.bikefriday.com.

MINI-CASE

Alberta Wheat Pool

Alberta Wheat Pool (AWP, now part of Agricore United) sells chemicals and seeds to Alberta farmers and buys their grains. The chemicals are sold at several elevators, which are located near the farms. Before the 1990s, each elevator manager (approximately 300) independently made decisions about the amount of chemicals needed during the coming year. Because the elevator manager was evaluated only based on sales, he ordered the maximum probable amount. Excess chemicals were transported back to a heated regional warehouse. In the early 1990s, AWP changed the performance measure of elevator managers in order to cut the cost of excess transportation and holding cost over the winter. A position was created: Coordinator of Regional Finance and Accounting to assist with coordination across elevators. A tool used was the single-period inventory model, which was to assist elevator managers make

better decisions. To illustrate, consider the ordering of a particular herbicide by a specific elevator. Each unit weighs 50 kg. The selling price is $56.93 per unit, and the purchase cost (including the transportation cost) is $45.54. Any excess herbicide is transported to the Calgary Warehouse at the cost of $1.09 per unit. The holding cost rate is 10 percent of unit cost per year, charged only for half a year (approximate length of winter). It is estimated that 10 percent of shortage will be lost. The rest will incur $2.19 per unit in expediting cost from the Calgary warehouse. The elevator manager estimates that the demand for this herbicide can take values 100, 400, and 1,500 units with probabilities of .1, .5, and .4, respectively. What is the best order quantity?

Source: D.J. Raby et al., "Inventory Management of Chemical Supplies at Alberta Wheat Pool," *Production and Inventory Management Journal* 32(1), First Quarter, 1991, pp. 1–6.

MINI-CASE http://www.marks.com

Mark's Work Wearhouse

From genteel downtown Toronto to the oil fields of Alberta, Mark's Work Wearhouse caters to customers with very different definitions of work wear.

"We're fashion followers, not fashion leaders," comments Colin Laker, VP of systems. We let the customers decide what we should be stocking in our stores. In downtown Toronto, work wear is khaki pants and a golf shirt, but in the oil fields around Edmonton, guys will jump out of pickups covered head-to-foot in oil in search for new clothes.

"We call ourselves a pull organization. We allow the stores to reorder basic commodities. We want them to do that because we want our stores to reflect Canada's regional differences.

We sell a lot more rainwear in Vancouver than we do in Saskatoon."

Sizes also vary regionally. Mark's stores in British Columbia cater to a significant Asian population, and smaller sizes are a steady part of the mix in the stores. In Gallic Quebec, customers tend to be of average stature, while in the prairie and mountain provinces, they "grow' em big."

Tailoring such refined, store-specific merchandising mixes is tough, but Laker says an inventory forecasting and replenishment system, Inforem, is letting the retailer do just that. Mark's installed Inforem/400 in December 1995. The system, which runs on the IBM AS/400 platform, is allowing the chain to maintain its long-standing commitment to locally defined product mixes.

"We allow Inforem to compute the reorders, and then the store managers can review those suggested orders on their screens in the stores," Laker explains.

If the store managers don't alter the suggested order within 24 hours, the system automatically finalizes the order and sends it off to the manufacturer.

"The store managers also have input in setting different service-level parameters for their stores. You can tell the system that a specific store needs to be 99 percent in stock on a particular SKU at all times. Or you can set that parameter at 75 percent."

But the system is not only an inventory replenishment system, it's also a robust forecasting package. "For the past three years, we've been capturing historical data at 16 different levels of hierarchy in each of our stores," Laker says. "We accumulate that information on a store-by-store basis and we use it to do a store-specific forecasting plan twice a year, spring and fall. We call that our merchandising plan."

Mark's is feeding all that historical data into the Inforem/400 system. The chain is building a sort of "mini-data warehouse" on the AS/400. Inforem will allow the company to compare profiles of individual stores and clusters of stores. It is expected to make the forecasting process more consistent across stores.

The retailer also shares forecasting data with suppliers, where prudent. "If a vendor can manage inventory better than we can, we have no qualms about sharing forecasting information with that vendor," Laker says. "We supply them with sales information and model stock information. It's weekly, store-specific information, by style, by size."

"The problem with the concept of vendor-managed inventory in the past was that it didn't take into account the peaks and valleys in the sales patterns of individual stores," he continues. "The kind of forecasting information Inforem will allow us to offer the manufacturers will help them respond to those changes."

Mark's Work Wearhouse was bought by Canadian Tire in 2001.

Source: "Information Is Hard at Work at Mark's Work Wearhouse," *Chain Store Age,* November 1996, pp. 14A–16A.

Questions

1. How is Inforem helping Mark's Work Wearhouse?

2. What kind of service level, lead time or annual, does Mark's use?

 OPERATIONS TOUR

The McGraw-Hill Ryerson Warehouse in Whitby, Ontario

The 85,000 ft² MHR warehouse in Whitby, Ontario, stores approximately 25,000 Stock Keeping Units (SKUs). Approximately 80 percent of inventory is located in the bulk storage area. These are in full boxes on wooden pallets, located on approximately 7,000 racks. The racks have 5 levels, separated by very narrow aisles (see area A on the layout diagram and Photo 1). The remaining 20 percent of inventory is kept in the loose-book pick areas on easily accessible shelves within reach of order-pickers (areas B, Photo 2).

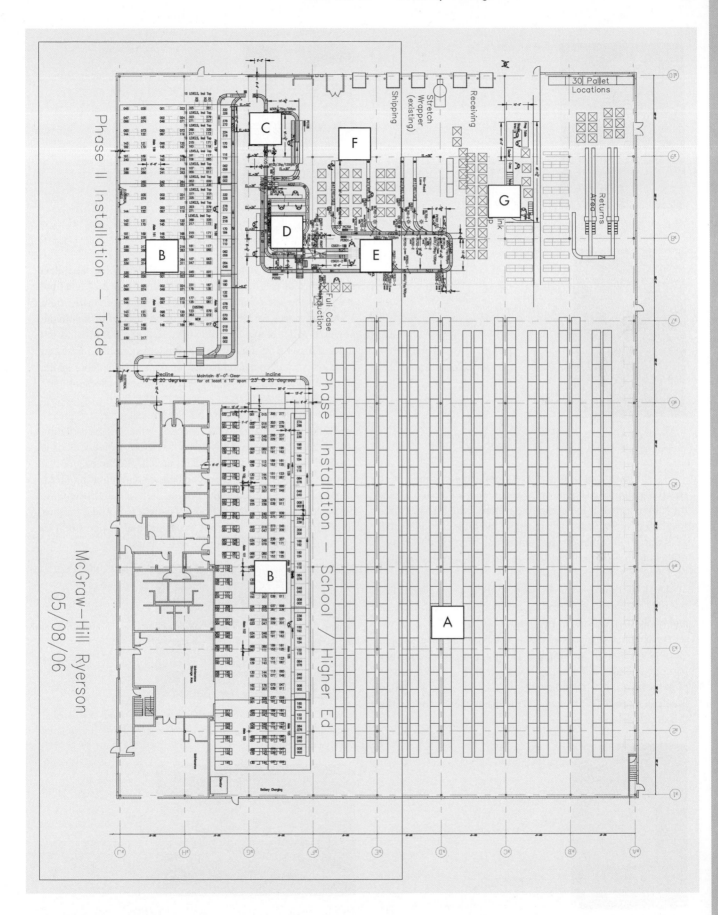

Photo 1: Bulk storage area (with manager Kathleen Ayow)

Photo 2: Loose-book pick area (with powered roller conveyor and shelves on both sides)

As shipments of books arrive from a book printer in the receiving/shipping staging area (area F on the layout diagram), they are entered in the computer system, which issues a rack location in the bulk storage area, and the lot is carried there by a lift truck. Full pallets are placed on first, fourth and fifth levels of racking. Less than full pallets—up to 8 full boxes—are stored in the second- and third-level racks.

The loose-book pick areas are periodically replenished from the bulk storage area when the inventory of a SKU decreases and books are required to fulfill an order.

As a bookstore places an order, a packing list and a shipping label (see Photo 3) are printed. The shipping label contains a barcode and also indicates the type/size of box to be used, the pick locations, ISBN, and quantity. Once the right size of box is selected (one of eight sizes) in the dispatcher's work station, the shipping label is attached.

Photo 3: A packing list (to be inserted inside the box).

Photo 4: A barcode reader reads the shipping label on the box and diverts the box as necessary.

Using an RF device, a picker scans the shipping label barcode, which directs her to the pick location. At the pick location, she picks the book and scans the check digit for verification. Then, she places the book in the box, and places the box on the powered roller conveyor (shown by two parallel lines to the right of areas B in the layout diagram). As the box moves on the conveyor, an optical character reader reads the label on the box and diverts the box to any other relevant loose-book pick aisles (Photo 4).

The conveyor continues to quality control (area C, Photo 5) where the box is scanned and checked by the weigh-in-motion scale for any "no-reads" (missed books). Here, a diverted box is checked for accuracy and the books are checked to ensure that they are in good saleable condition before shipping. If required, the box is then diverted to the pricing area (area D) where the list price is checked and the book is stickered. Then, the box continues to packing where it is packed and sealed (area E, Photo 6) and then to shipping (area F, Photo 7).

Photo 5: This is the quality control area where the boxes are checked for accuracy of item and quantity and to ensure books are in good saleable condition.

Photo 6: An employee fills a box with packing fillers made of recycled paper. Then the box is taped shut automatically.

Photo 7: The shipping area (loose book shelves in the background)

If the order is large, full boxes containing the ordered books are picked up from the bulk storage area by a lift truck (see Photos 8 and 9), and the boxes are moved to the shipping staging area (area F).

Photo 8: A Raymond turret truck is raised to pick up a pallet from a top rack.

Photo 9: The truck driver retrieves a pallet of boxes of books for shipment.

The movement of each lift truck through the aisles is made safer and easier by an electronic guiding system (see Photo 10). The system electronically locks into a wire that runs along the centre of each aisle and keeps the truck centred as it moves (this prevents collision with the racks).

Photo 10: The electronic guiding system (the black box between the front wheels of the truck) and the wire embedded in the floor in front of it.

Area G on the layout diagram is for the returned books (also see Photo 11). Here, boxes are opened, books are checked, and then moved to their shelves in the loose-book pick area.

Photo 11: The returns work centre

The warehouse can fill an order in one day and order picking productivity is approximately 100 SKUs per hour on average.

CHAPTER 13
Aggregate Operations Planning

LEARNING OBJECTIVES

After completing this chapter, you should be able to:

LO1 Explain what sales and operations planning and aggregate operations planning are, and identify the variables and strategies used in aggregate production planning.

LO2 Prepare a good aggregate production plan.

LO3 Prepare a good aggregate service plan.

LO4 Explain what master production scheduling is and how it is performed.

hen DuPont and Merck started a joint venture in early 1990s, the marketing and manufacturing functions of the resulting company had little interaction. Then came the implementation of a software whose main function is to facilitate sales and operations planning. This brought marketing and operations closer. As a result, inventories and lead times have decreased and customer service has improved. What is sales and operations planning and how do companies perform operations planning? That is the subject of this chapter.

(LO1) INTRODUCTION

Organizations make capacity and production decisions on three levels: long term, intermediate term, and short term. Long-term decisions relate to products selection, facility size and location, major equipment decisions, and layout of facilities. These long-term decisions essentially define the capacity constraints within which intermediate planning must function. Intermediate decisions relate to general levels of employment, output, and inventories, which in turn define the boundaries within which short-term capacity and production decisions must be made. Short-term decisions involve scheduling jobs, workers, and equipment. The three levels of capacity and production decisions are depicted in Figure 13-1. Long-term capacity decisions were covered in Chapter 5, and scheduling will be covered in Chapter 16. This chapter covers intermediate capacity and production decisions. These decisions are usually made in the context of an activity called Sales and Operations Planning.

Sales and Operations Planning

Sales and operations planning (S&OP) is the process of integrating sales forecasts with operations plans. It is usually performed once a month and the information is reviewed by the top management at an aggregate (product family) level. The process must reconcile all supply, demand, and new-product plans at both the detail and aggregate level and tie them to the strategic plan. It is for the intermediate term (usually the next 12 months), covering a horizon sufficient to plan for workforce and production changes. Figure 13-2 shows the hierarchy of production planning and the position of S&OP in it. This chapter covers the operations (or aggregate) planning and master scheduling. Material requirements planning will be covered in Chapter 14, and detailed planning and execution systems in Chapter 16.

The process of S&OP begins with recording the sales, production, and inventory levels of the previous month, updating forecasts for the next 12 months or so, seeing if the necessary production changes are feasible, and providing a summary of information to top management for making decisions.

In the top management's meeting, the executives have time only to review a summary of sales, production, and inventory plans of a limited number (e.g., six to eight) families

sales and operations planning Process of integrating sales forecasts with operations plans.

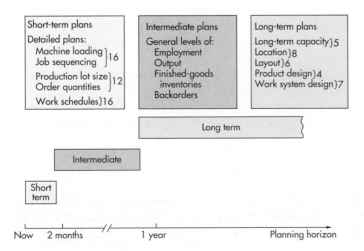

Figure 13-1

Overview of planning levels (chapter numbers are shown)

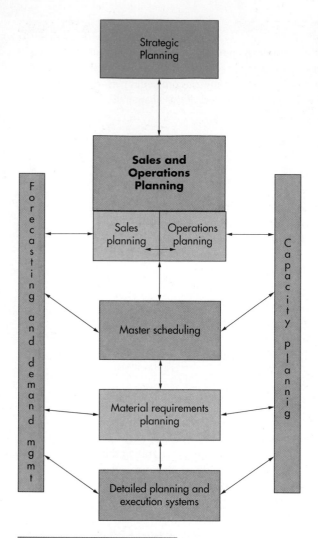

Figure 13-2

Production planning hierarchy

aggregate operations planning   Monthly planning for all the products in the same family (produced in the same facility) for the next 12 months or so.

of products. An example of the summary information for a product family is shown in Figure 13-3. In Location A, the target file rate of 99 percent and finished goods inventory target of 10 days of supply are shown. Note that for make-to-stock products, the company needs to keep safety stocks of finished goods to meet demand variability. The level of finished goods inventory directly affects customer service level through fill rate.

Locations B and E show the old forecast sales for the past three months, and old and new (after update) forecasts for the next six months and the two quarters after that. Locations C and F show the operations plan and the actual production during the past three months, and the old and new (after update) production plan for the next six months and two quarters after that. Locations D and G show the inventory plan and the actual levels during the past three months, and the projected inventory levels resulting from the given forecasts and production plans (and the equivalent days of supply) during the next six months and two quarters after that. Also shown are fill rate performance during the past three months. Finally, in Locations H and J, any major demand and production issues are pointed out.

See the "DuPont Merck" OM in Action for more details of the S&OP process.

Aggregate operations planning is monthly planning for all the products in the same family (produced in the same facility) for the next 12 months or so. It is particularly useful for organizations that experience seasonal fluctuations in demand. The goal of aggregate operations planning is to achieve a production plan that will effectively utilize the organization's resources to satisfy expected demand. Planners must make decisions on output rates, employment levels and changes, inventory levels and changes, and backorders (shortage met from next months' production).

The Concept of Aggregation

In aggregate operations planning, planners focus on a group of similar products, or sometimes an entire product line. For example, planners in a company producing television sets would not concern themselves with 21-inch sets versus 25-inch or 27-inch sets. Instead, planners would lump all models together and deal with them as though they were a single product, a TV; hence, the term *aggregate*. If the products are different, a typical product is chosen and all other products are represented in equivalent units of the chosen product. For example, a brewery may measure the output of its canning line in cases of standard 355-mL beer cans. Any cases of 473-mL beer cans produced are then considered equivalent to 1.33 cases of standard beer cans.

Another example is space allocation in a department store. A manager might decide to allocate 40 percent of the available space in the clothing department to women's wear, 30 percent to juniors, and so on, without regard for what brand names will be offered or how much of juniors will be pants. The aggregate measure or equivalent unit might be racks of clothing.

For labour-intensive services, a common aggregate measure or equivalent unit is full-time equivalent (FTE) of workforce. For example, a half-time worker (working 20 hours a week) is counted as 0.5 FTE.

In each of these examples, an aggregate approach permits managers to make general decisions about intermediate-term capacity and production levels without having to deal with highly specific details.

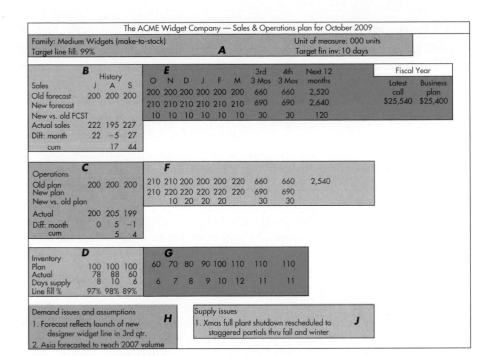

Figure 13-3

An example of the summary information for a product family used in the top management S&OP meeting.

OM in ACTION

DuPont Merck

With three plants in North America and sales offices in eight countries, DuPont Merck Pharmaceutical Company was formed in 1991 as a joint venture between DuPont and Merck.

Business (Strategic) Planning

At DuPont Merck, the strategic planning process involved both marketing and manufacturing. The one-year and five-year objectives of strategic planning were supported by both divisions.

Sales and Operations Planning

This process involved monthly review of plans by senior management; this was where overall levels of manufacturing output and sales were set. The Sales and Operations Planning (S&OP) process reviewed recent past performance and was a forum for confirming or changing future plans, weighing the impact of changes in the market on supply and demand, and deciding how the business will adjust.

The monthly meetings were a touchstone in the cycle of events that made up the S&OP process. The cycle began with extraction and review of sales history from the previous month by demand managers, and forecasting future months. A series of marketing meetings adjusted the aggregate sales forecasts in view of all internal and external factors.

Then, aggregate sales plan data were transmitted to the manufacturing planning groups, which performed reviews and adjusted production plans for the future. Simultaneously, master

schedulers planned the production of each product in concert with demand managers.

Pre-S&OP meetings were held in the middle of each month, where key members of support teams such as customer service, distribution, and quality, as well as marketing and production managers, met to jointly review aggregate past sales and production (with particular attention to the performance metrics such as fill rate, finished goods inventory levels, and lead times) and review sales and operations plans for the coming 39 months. These meetings formed the basis for the S&OP meetings, where company resources were committed by senior management.

Marketing was accountable for implementing the approved sales plans and manufacturing for the approved production plans.

Results

The cooperation between marketing and manufacturing had quantifiable results. The U.S. inventory and manufacturing lead times were reduced by half, while unit sales grew over 15 percent annually. With one product alone, more than $500,000 in business was taken away from a competitor that could not supply the surge in demand—a direct result of the cooperation between divisions.

In 1998 DuPont bought Merck's interest and called the subsidiary DuPont Pharmaceuticals, which was sold to Bristol-Myers Squibb in 2001.

Source: J.R. Dougherty and W. Lerner, "Sales and Marketing's Partnership Role in Class A MRPII," *Hospital Materiel Management Quarterly* 16(1), August 1994, pp. 40–46.

Demand and Capacity Options

Management has a wide range of decision options at its disposal for sales and operations planning. These include demand-influencing actions such as changing prices, promotion, backorders, and producing complementary products during off-season, and capacity-influencing actions such as hiring and laying off permanent workers, using overtime/idle time, hiring and laying off part-time/temporary workers, and stockpiling inventories.

Demand Options. The basic demand options, usually handled by marketing, are:

1. *Pricing.* Pricing differentials are commonly used to shift demand from peak periods to off-peak periods. For example, long-distance phone rates are lower after 6 p.m. and on the weekends.

2. *Promotion.* Price discounts, advertising and other forms of promotion, such as displays and direct marketing, can sometimes be very effective in shifting demand so that it conforms more closely to capacity.

3. *Backorders.* A company can shift demand to future periods by using backorders. That is, orders are taken in one period and deliveries promised for a later period. The success of this approach depends on how willing customers are to wait for delivery. Moreover, the costs associated with backorders include lost sales, annoyed or disappointed customers, and additional paperwork. Backorders can be thought of as negative inventory. Make-to-order companies carry an "inventory" of (back) orders as opposed to finished goods inventory that is carried by make-to-stock companies. A form of backorder is the appointment system, which is an acceptable way to regulate demand in services such as health care.

4. *Complementary products.* Many organizations are faced with the problem of having to provide goods or services for peak demand in situations where demand has seasonality. For instance, demand for bus transportation tends to be more intense during the morning and late-afternoon rush hours but much lighter at other times. Creating new demand for buses at other times (e.g., trips by schools, clubs, and senior citizen groups) would make use of the excess capacity during those idle times. Similarly, many fast-food restaurants are open for breakfast to use their capacities more fully. Manufacturers that experience seasonal demands for certain products (e.g., snow blowers) are sometimes able to develop a demand for a complementary product (e.g., lawn mowers) that makes use of their resources during off-season.

Capacity Options. The basic capacity options are:

1. *Hiring and laying off permanent workers.* Given the operating hours, number of shifts, and size of facility, companies may hire and lay off a limited number of permanent full-time workers (who work approximately 40 hours a week). The nature of operation determines the impact that changes in the workforce level will have on capacity. For instance, if a factory usually has 10 of 14 production lines operating, crews for an additional four lines could be added. Conversely, there may be a lower limit on the number of workers needed to maintain a viable operation (e.g., a skeleton crew).

    Furthermore, a company may be able to add or reduce the number of shifts. For example, instead of working 8 hours a day (i.e., one shift), a company can double its workforce and operate in two shifts (i.e., work 16 hours a day).

    Union contracts may restrict the number of hiring and layoffs a company can do. Moreover, because layoffs can present serious problems for workers, some companies have policies that either prohibit or limit downward adjustments to workforce.

Railway Car Builders

When faced with an increase in business, rail-car builders prefer to use overtime before they would increase the number of workers or start a second shift. The following are comments by top managers of some rail-car manufacturers.

Dick Brown of Trinity Railcar Co. (with facilities in seven U.S. states, five countries in Europe, and Mexico) says that "new people need to be trained to our quality standards and this isn't an overnight accomplishment." What's more, a company doesn't lightly take on new employees with an eye to shedding them when a bulge in business is over. "It takes time to train a workforce, and you like to do it gradually. And the costs of downsizing a workforce are just as formidable as growing one."

Bill Galbraith, senior vice-president, marketing and sales, The Greenbrier Companies (with facilities in Oregon, Mexico,

and Europe), indicates that his company's preferred strategy to deal with capacity constraints is to place the existing workforce on overtime rather than build up additional workforces that the market might not support over the long run. Capacity increases of 12 to 15 percent are possible with this technique.

National Steel Car of Hamilton, Ontario, has the capacity for three shifts, but is operating a single shift. While extra shifts are possible, the company's preference, from the standpoint of human resources, is to develop a competent workforce and maintain employment at a consistent level (we call this level *output strategy*).

Source: A. Kruglinski, "How Tight is 'Capacity' for Car Builders?" *Railway Age* 195(1), January 1994, pp. 16ff.

OM in ACTION

Two Cases from Australia

A Fridge Plant

This plant produces 3 brands of fridges in 15 sizes and 3 colours. Summer months' sales are 20 percent higher than winter months, and there is a peak in November for Christmas sales. Monthly forecast sales for the next 12 months are aggregated at the brand level. There are two assembly lines that work one shift per workday. Holidays are two weeks in Christmas and two weeks in July. The company uses a chase demand strategy because fridges are large and expensive. The union has agreed that 25 percent of workforce can be temporary, on a three-month contract. A new hire needs two to three days of training. Overtime is used only for emergencies.

A Chocolate Plant

This plant produces Easter eggs and Christmas chocolate novelties (300 SKUs). Therefore, the periods before Easter and

Christmas are the busy periods (Easter is busier). There are several chocolate tanks, moulding machines, and foiling/wrapping machines. Change of chocolate type is very time consuming (one to four shifts). The company produces chocolate for Christmas based on forecasts in May and June, and based on firm orders in July and August. Similarly, for Easter, initial production is in September to November based on forecasts, and in December to February based on firm orders. The permanent employment is 120 to 140 workers (on two shifts but not all lines running). However, during the busiest months, October to January, up to 120 to 140 temporary workers on 4- to 50-week contracts are employed. The training period is short. Overtime is used for new product trials and emergencies.

Source: G. Buxey, "Aggregate Planning for Seasonal Demand: Reconciling Theory with Practice," *International Journal of Operations & Production Management*, 2005, 25(11), pp. 1083–1100.

On the other hand, hiring presumes an available supply of workers. This may change from time to time and, at times of low labour supply, has an impact on the ability of an organization to pursue this approach. Another consideration is the skill level of workers. Highly skilled workers are generally more difficult to find than lower-skilled workers, and recruiting them involves greater costs. So the usefulness of this option is limited for highly skilled workers.

Use of hiring and laying off of permanent workers entails certain costs. Hiring costs include screening, recruitment, and training costs to bring new workers "up to speed." And quality may suffer. Some savings may occur if workers who have recently been laid off are rehired. Layoff costs include severance pay, the cost of realigning the remaining workforce, potential bad feelings toward the company on the part of workers who have been laid off, and some loss of morale for workers who are retained (i.e., in spite of company assurances, some workers will believe that in time they too may be laid off).

An increasing number of organizations view workers as assets rather than as variable costs, and would not consider this approach.

2. *Using overtime/idle time.* Overtime and idle time (i.e., nonproductive employment or slack time) can be implemented easily and quickly. Organizations use idle time for training, performing maintenance, problem solving, and process improvement. Overtime (i.e., working longer than 8 hours a day or 5 days a week) permits the employees to increase their earnings (overtime pay is usually 1.5 times the regular-time pay).

On the other hand, overtime often results in lower productivity, poorer quality, more accidents, and increased payroll costs, and idle time results in less efficient use of resources.

3. *Hiring and laying off part-time/temporary workers.* In many instances, the use of part-time/temporary workers is a viable option—much depends on the nature of the work, training and skills needed, and union agreement. Part-time workers, such as high school students, typically work 20 hours a week or less, and do not receive fringe benefits such as dental insurance. Seasonal work requiring low-to-moderate job skills is suitable for temporary workers, who generally cost less than permanent workers in hourly wages and fringe benefits, despite typically being full time, i.e., working 40 hours a week. However, unions may regard such workers unfavourably because they typically do not pay union dues and may lessen the power of unions. Stores, restaurants, resorts, hotels, and other organizations with seasonal demands make use of temporary workers.

Part-time/temporary workers can be added or removed from the workforce with greater ease than permanent workers, giving companies great flexibility in adjusting the size of the workforce.

4. *Stockpiling inventories.* The use of finished-goods inventories allows companies to produce goods in one period and sell or distribute them in a future period. The holding cost includes not only storage costs and the cost of money tied up in inventory, but also the cost of obsolescence, spoilage, and so on. Inventories can be built up during periods when production capacity exceeds demand and drawn down in periods when demand exceeds production capacity. This method is suitable for make-to-stock manufacturing.

For two applications of capacity options, see the "Railway Car Builders" and "Two Cases from Australia" OM in Actions on the previous page.

Inputs to and Outputs from Aggregate Operations Planning

Effective aggregate operations planning requires good *information*. First, the available resources over the planning horizon must be known, and forecasts of demand must be available. Then, planners must take into account company policies, for example regarding changes in employment levels (e.g., some organizations view layoffs of permanent workers as extremely undesirable, so they would use that only as a last resort). Costs of various variables should also be determined.

The outputs of aggregate planning is the level of production (output), which is determined from the level of employment, and in turn determines the amount of inventory or backordering in each period. All these contribute to the total cost of the plan.

Table 13-1 lists the major inputs to and outputs from aggregate operations planning.

Inputs	Outputs
Resources	Total cost of the plan
Workforce/production rates	Projected levels of
Facilities and equipment	Inventory
Demand forecasts	Output
Policy statements	Employment
Overtime	Backordering
Workforce changes, temporary/part-time workers	
Inventory levels/changes	
Backorders	
Costs	
Inventory holding	
Backorder	
Hiring/firing	
Wage rates	
Overtime	

Table 13-1

Aggregate operation planning inputs and outputs

Basic Strategies

As you saw earlier, managers have a wide range of decision options in aggregate operations planning. In this chapter, we will concentrate on the options that directly affect production, such as capacity options and the use of backorders.

Many organizations regard having a fixed number of permanent workers very appealing. Because workforce changes through hiring and firing can have a major impact on the lives and morale of employees and can be disruptive for managers, organizations often prefer to handle uneven demand in other ways. Moreover, changes in permanent workforce size can be very costly, and there is always the risk that there will not be a sufficient pool of workers with the appropriate skills when needed. Therefore, we will not use hiring and layoff of permanent workers to meet demand as a capacity option.

Aggregate planners might adopt a number of strategies. Some of the more prominent ones are:

1. Maintain level output/workforce.
2. Change output to match demand period by period.
3. Use a combination.

The first two strategies are "pure" strategies because each has a single focus; the third strategy is "mixed." Under the **level output/workforce strategy**, a steady rate of output and workforce is maintained while variations in demand are met by using some combination of inventories and backorders. This strategy uses a fixed number of permanent workers that is close to the average full-time worker requirements during the planning horizon (e.g., next 12 months). Level output/workforce strategy assumes that products have a long shelf life. This is true for some products such as durable goods, but not for others such as groceries. Similarly, the use of backorders is usually limited to products that are custom-built.

Matching output to demand is **chase demand strategy**; the planned output for any period is equal to forecast of demand for that period. Chase demand strategy uses a small number of permanent workers equal to the full-time worker requirements during the lowest demand month in the planning horizon, but the main capacity options are part-time/temporary workers and over time/idle time.

level output/workforce strategy Maintaining a steady rate of output and workforce while meeting variations in demand by a combination of inventories and backorders.

chase demand strategy Matching output to demand; the planned output for any period is set at the forecast of demand for that period.

Figure 13-4

Illustration of chase demand and level output/workforce strategies

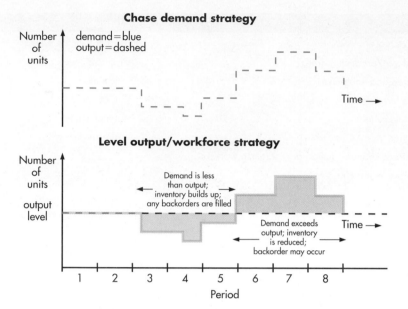

A major advantage of chase demand strategy is that no inventories are carried, which can yield substantial savings for an organization. Service organizations that cannot regulate their demand have to use chase demand strategy. For an application of chase demand strategy, see the "Lands' End" OM in Action.

Figure 13-4 illustrates the two strategies, using a varying demand pattern to highlight the differences in the two approaches.

A mixed strategy uses a combination of the decision variables, e.g., a company can have two levels of output, low in off season and high in busy season, and also use overtime, temporary workers, and inventory buildup and backorders.

Choosing a Strategy. Whatever strategy a company is considering, two important factors are *company policy* and *costs*. Company policy may set constraints on the available options or the extent to which they can be used. For instance, company policy may require that no less than 70 percent of personnel (measured as full-time equivalent) should be permanent. Union agreements often impose restrictions. For example, a union contract may specify maximum numbers of weeks or months temporary workers can be used.

As a rule, aggregate planners seek to match supply and demand within the constraints imposed on them by policies or agreements and at minimum total cost. They usually evaluate alternative aggregate plans in terms of their overall costs. In the next section, two techniques for aggregate production planning are described.

(LO2) TECHNIQUES FOR AGGREGATE PRODUCTION PLANNING

Two different approaches are used for determining the aggregate plan: trial-and-error and optimization. In practice, trail-and-error is used more frequently.

A general procedure for aggregate production planning consists of the following steps:

1. Determine demand forecast for each period in the planning horizon (e.g., next 12 months).

2. Determine capacities and production rates (i.e., the number of units produced by regular time permanent, overtime, part-time/temporary workers).

3. Identify company policies that are pertinent (e.g., maintain a safety stock of 5 percent of demand, maintain a reasonably stable workforce).

4. Determine unit costs for regular time permanent, overtime, and part-time/temporary production; holding inventory; backorder; hiring and layoff (of a temporary worker).

5. If using the trial-and-error approach, develop alternative feasible plans, compute the total cost for each, and select the one with the lowest total cost. If using optimization, the lowest total cost feasible plan will be determined by the computer.

Trial-and-Error

Trial-and-error consists of developing simple tables/worksheets or graphs that enable managers to meet projected demand requirements with production. The chief disadvantage of such techniques is that they do not necessarily result in the optimal (i.e., lowest total cost) aggregate plan.

Very often, graphs can be used to guide the development of alternative aggregate plans. The obvious advantage of a graph is that it provides a visual portrayal of a plan. Some planners prefer cumulative graphs while others prefer to see a period-by-period breakdown of a plan (Figure 13-4 is an example of a period-by-period graph). Figure 13-5A shows a cumulative graph for a plan with level output (the slope of the dashed line represents the production rate) and inventory absorbing demand variations. Figure 13-5B is a cumulative graph used by Blue Bell (Wrangler) jeans (now part of VF Corp.) for a product line (e.g., men's corduroy jeans). Note that the cumulative demand is padded by safety stocks and the cumulative production line is chosen so that it meets the cumulative demand plus safety stock during the planning horizon. In this case, September of next year determines the slope of the cumulative production line, which is linear, indicating a level output strategy.

The three examples below illustrate the development and comparison of simple aggregate plans using worksheets. In the first example, output is held level, with inventory absorbing demand variations. In the second example, a lower rate of regular output is used,

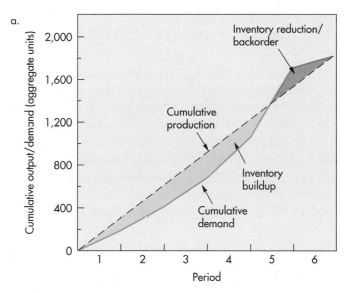

Figure 13-5A

A cumulative graph for level output/workforce strategy

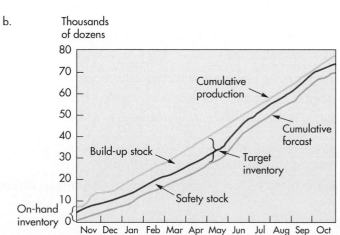

Figure 13-5B

A cumulative graph for level output/workforce strategy used by Blue Bell (Wrangler)

Lands' End

Lands' End is a major phone- and mail-order distributor of clothing and sewn goods located in the small town of Dodgeville, Wisconsin (population 4,000). Sales of Lands' End peak in November and December each year, much like other retailers, due to the holiday shopping season. Lands' End does 40 percent of its business during the fourth quarter. The number of phone calls received jumps from 40,000 a day to more than 100,000 on the busiest days. During the other three quarters, there is also some variation in sales. Lands' End employs customer sales workers (for phone orders), mail-order workers, warehouse workers, customer-service workers, and sewers who perform alterations. Lands' End employs approximately 3,500 permanent and 1,000 part-time workers year-round. How does the company meet its excess demand for labour hours during November and December? First, it employs approximately 2,000 more temporary full-time and part-time workers. The supply of part-time temporary workers comes from high school, college, and university students who can work a six-hour shift after school (three times a week), and the supply of full-time temporary workers comes from some local cheese factories who end their busy season in October. Second, Lands' End encourages its workers to cross-train so that they can work in other jobs when they are needed (called job sharing). Third, employees can work extended schedules during November and December, up to 12 hours a day (the portion above eight hours is performed in a different department and is considered overtime). Approximately one-third of temporary workers return to work for Lands' End again the following year or later. A new hire receives six hours of orientation/training, but a rehire may receive only up to two hours of retraining.

Sources: J.J. Laabs, "Strategic Holiday Staffing at Lands' End," *Personnel Journal* 73(12), December 1994, pp. 28ff; K. Haegele, "Gearing Up for the Holiday Rush," *Target Marketing* 23(6), June 2000, pp. 44–48ff.

supplemented by the use of overtime. The third example is similar, but uses temporary workers instead of overtime. In all three examples, some backorders are allowed during one period but cleared by the end of planning horizon.

These and other examples and problems in this chapter are based on the following assumptions:

1. No allowance is made for holidays and different number of workdays in different months. Also, no allowance is made for safety stocks for each period (but there may be initial and end-of-planning-horizon inventories). These assumptions simplify the computations.

2. We present all production in terms of number of units of the aggregate measure (equivalent unit), not the number of labour hours or workers.

3. The total cost for each of regular time permanent production, overtime production, backorder, inventory, and hire/layoff is a linear function of number of units of the aggregate product; that is, it equals a constant unit cost times the number of units of the aggregate product.

Unit cost of labour should be calculated using the wage rate and number of hours each unit of product will take a worker to make. The hiring cost per unit is the hiring cost per worker divided by the number of units of the product a worker can make during one period, charged to the first period of employment. Layoff cost per unit is determined in the same way, but is charged to the period after the layoff. Cost is charged to the average level of inventory during a period, but to the amount of backorders carried to the next period.

The following relationships are used.

1. To determine the ending inventory and backorder in any period i, first calculate X:

   $$X = \text{Beginning inventory}_i + (\text{Output} - \text{Forecast})_i - \text{Backorder}_{i-1},$$

   where output is the sum of regular permanent, overtime, and part-time/temporary production.

   If $X \geq 0$, then ending inventory$_i$ = X and backorder$_i$ = 0; whereas if $X < 0$, then ending inventory$_i$ = 0 and backorder$_i$ = $-X$.

2. The average inventory for a period is equal to (Beginning inventory + Ending inventory)/2.

3. Beginning inventory$_i$ = ending inventory$_{i-1}$

Example 1

Planners for a company that makes several models of garden tractors are about to prepare an aggregate production plan that will cover the next six months. They have assembled the following information:

Month	1	2	3	4	5	6	Total
Forecast demand	2,000	2,000	3,000	4,000	5,000	2,000	18,000

Permanent workforce = 140

Production per month = 2,800 units or 20 per worker

Initial inventory = 1,000 units

Desired ending inventory at the end of 6th month = 1,000 units

Costs

    Output

        Regular time permanent = $100 per tractor

        Overtime = $150 per tractor

        Temporary = $100 per tractor

        Hire cost = $500 per temporary worker or $25 (=$500/20 units) per unit (charged to the first month of employment)

        Inventory = $10 per tractor per month (charged on the average inventory level)

        Backorder = $150 per tractor per month

They now want to evaluate a plan that calls for level output/workforce (with the current level of permanent workforce, 140), using inventory to absorb the uneven demand but allowing some backorder. They start with 1,000 units inventory on hand in the first month and wish to end with the same amount. Prepare an aggregate production plan and determine its total cost.

The total regular-time output of permanent workers per month is 2,800 units. The filled worksheet for this level output/workforce strategy is shown below. The computations are explained below the worksheet.

Month	1	2	3	4	5	6	Total
Forecast Demand	2,000	2,000	3,000	4,000	5,000	2,000	18,000
Output							
Regular permanent	2,800	2,800	2,800	2,800	2,800	2,800	16,800
Temporary	–	–	–	–	–	–	
Overtime	–	–	–	–	–	–	
Output Forecast	800	800	−200	−1,200	−2,200	800	−1,200
Inventory							
Beginning	1,000	1,800	2,600	2,400	1,200	0	
Ending	1,800	2,600	2,400	1,200	0	0	
Average	1,400	2,200	2,500	1,800	600	0	8,500
Backorder	0	0	0	0	1,000	200	1,200
Costs							
Output							
Regular perm(at $100/unit)	$280,000	280,000	280,000	280,000	280,000	280,000	$1,680,000
Temporary (at $100/unit)	–	–	–	–	–	–	
Overtime (at $150/unit)	–	–	–	–	–	–	
Hire temporary (at $25/unit)	–	–	–	–	–	–	
Inventory (at $10/unit/month)	$14,000	22,000	25,000	18,000	6,000	0	$85,000
Backorder (at $150/unit/month)	$0	0	0	0	150,000	30,000	$180,000
Total	$294,000	302,000	305,000	298,000	436,000	310,000	$1,945,000

Starting with month 1, $(\text{Output} - \text{Forecast})_1 = 2,800 - 2,000 = 800$,

    $X = \text{Beginning inventory}_1 + (\text{Output} - \text{Forecast})_1 - \text{Backorder}_0$

      $= 1,000 + 800 - 0$

      $= 1,800.$

Therefore, ending inventory$_1$ = 1,800 and backorder$_1$ = 0. Also,

$$\text{Average inventory}_1 = (\text{Beginning inventory}_1 + \text{Ending inventory}_1)/2$$
$$= (1{,}000 + 1{,}800)/2$$
$$= 1{,}400.$$

Then, beginning inventory$_2$ = ending inventory$_1$ = 1,800. Continue with the same formulas, but note that in month 5,

$$X = \text{Beginning inventory}_5 + (\text{Output} - \text{Forecast})_5 - \text{Backorder}_4$$
$$= 1{,}200 + (-2{,}200) - 0 = -1{,}000.$$

Therefore, ending inventory$_5$ = 0 and backorder$_5$ = $-(-1{,}000)$ = 1,000. Also, in month 6,

$$X = \text{Beginning inventory}_6 + (\text{Output} - \text{Forecast})_6 - \text{Backorder}_5$$
$$= 0 + 800 - 1{,}000 = -200.$$

Therefore, ending inventory$_6$ = 0 and backorder$_6$ = 200.

The costs were computed as follows. Regular cost in each month equals 2,800 units $\times$ $100 per unit, or $280,000. Inventory cost equals average inventory $\times$ $10 per unit. Backorder cost is $150 per unit times the number of backorders. The total cost for this plan (either sum the row totals of costs or sum the column totals of costs) is $1,945,000.

Example 2	After reviewing the plan developed in the preceding example, planners noticed the large number of backorders in month 5 (1,000 units) and month 6 (200). Furthermore, the desired month 6 ending inventory of 1,000 units is not realized. Therefore, output has to increase by a total of 1,200 units during the planning horizon. The planners decided to investigate the use of overtime to make up for this shortage. It is the policy of the company that the maximum amount of overtime output per month be 400 units. Develop an aggregate production plan in this case and compare it to the previous plan.

Solution

The 1,200 units to be produced during overtime must be scheduled on and before month 5 (when shortage starts to occur). Scheduling it earlier would increase inventory holding costs; scheduling it later would increase the backorder costs. That is why the maximum permitted overtime production is used in months 3 to 5. The completed worksheet is given below.

Month	1	2	3	4	5	6	Total
Forecast	2,000	2,000	3,000	4,000	5,000	2,000	18,000
Output							
Regular	2,800	2,800	2,800	2,800	2,800	2,800	16,800
Temporary	—	—	—	—	—	—	
Overtime	—	—	400	400	400	—	1,200
Output – Forecast	800	800	200	-800	-1,800	800	0
Inventory							
Beginning	1,000	1,800	2,600	2,800	2,000	200	
Ending	1,800	2,600	2,800	2,000	200	1,000	
Average	1,400	2,200	2,700	2,400	1,100	600	10,400
Backorder	0	0	0	0	0	0	0
Costs							
Output							
Regular (at $100/unit)	$280,000	280,000	280,000	280,000	280,000	280,000	$1,680,000
Temporary (at $100/unit)	0	0	0	0	0	0	0
Overtime (at $150/unit)	—	—	60,000	60,000	60,000	—	180,000
Hire temporary (at $25/unit)	—	—	—	—	—	—	
Inventory (at $10/unit/month)	14,000	22,000	27,000	24,000	11,000	6,000	$104,000
Backorder (at $150/unit/month)	$0	0	0	0	0	0	0
Total	$294,000	302,000	367,000	364,000	351,000	286,000	$1,964,000

Note that, even though plan 2 has a larger total cost than plan 1, it produces 1,200 more units and leaves 1,000 units at the end of month 6. Alternatively, the company can use temporary workers to meet the 1,200 units short. The unit cost of temporary-worker production ($100) is lower than unit cost of overtime production ($150), but there is a per unit hire cost of $25. Overall, using temporary workers seems to be less costly than using overtime.

Example 3

A third option is to use temporary workers during months of high demand. For simplicity, we will assume that their productivity is also 20 units per worker per month, and that temporary workers will be working during a second shift, and that up to 60 temporary workers can start at a time, i.e., the temporary production can be 1,200 units in a month. Suppose that it costs an additional $500 to hire and train a temporary worker and nothing to lay off a temporary worker. Therefore, the unit hire cost per unit produced in the first month of employment is $500/20 = $25. Develop an aggregate production plan in this case.

Solution

Dividing the number of units needed (1,200) by the output rate of 20 per temporary worker, you find that 60 temporary worker-months are needed (e.g., 60 temporary workers for 1 month each, or 30 temporary workers for two months each, or 20 temporary workers for three months each, etc.).

Therefore, the planners tried each of the alternatives, i.e., hiring 60 temporary workers in month 5 on a one-month contract, or hiring 30 temporary workers in month 4 on a 2-month contract, or hiring 20 temporary workers in month 3 on a 3-month contract, and so on. The plan with the lowest total cost hires temporary workers in month 4 on a 2-month contract. Later we will describe the trade-off analysis which can assist us in determining the cheapest alternative without actually completing the worksheet for each alternative. The completed worksheet for hiring 30 temporary workers in month 4 on a 2-month contract is given below.

Month	1	2	3	4	5	6	Total
Forecast	2,000	2,000	3,000	4,000	5,000	2,000	18,000
Output							
Regular	2,800	2,800	2,800	2,800	2,800	2,800	16,800
Temporary				600	600		1,200
Overtime	—	—	—	—	—	—	
Output Forecast	800	800	−200	−600	−1,600	800	0
Inventory							
Beginning	1,000	1,800	2,600	2,400	1,800	200	
Ending	1,800	2,600	2,400	1,800	200	1,000	
Average	1,400	2,200	2,500	2,100	1,000	600	9,800
Backorder	0	0	0	0	0	0	0
Costs							
Output							
Regular (at $100/unit)	$280,000	280,000	280,000	280,000	280,000	280,000	$1,680,000
Temporary (at $100/unit)				60,000	60,000		$120,000
Overtime (at $150/unit)	—	—	—	—	—	—	
Hire temporary (at $25/unit)	$0	0	0	15,000	0	0	$15,000
Inventory (at $10/unit/month)	$14,000	22,000	25,000	21,000	10,000	6,000	$98,000
Backorder (at $150/unit/month)	$0	0	0	0	0	0	0
Total	$294,000	302,000	305,000	376,000	350,000	286,000	$1,913,000

Overall, the total cost for this plan is $1,913,000, making it the cheapest of the three alternatives examined (note that the first plan is not feasible). It can be shown (using the trade-off analysis or trial-and-error) that using a combination of temporary workers and overtime (to meet the shortage of 1,200 units) will only increase the cost of the third alternative. Therefore, the third alternative is the optimal aggregate production plan for this company for the next six months.

Procedure for Trial-and-Error. From the three examples above, it is evident that one should follow the steps below to obtain a low- cost aggregate plan:

- Determine the production output by permanent workers (during regular time) for each period.
- Determine total units short and periods short.
- Determine the cheapest way (using the trade-off analysis, described below) to meet the units short, e.g.,
  - Hire temporary and/or part-time workers.
  - Use permanent workers during overtime.
  - Carry inventory from previous periods.
  - Meet demand from following periods (backorder).

Trade-off Analysis. It is possible to use the unit costs of labour, inventory, and backorder in trade-off analyses in order to make good production planning decisions, without having to recalculate the total plan cost. Let's look at some of the decisions we made in the above three examples. In Example 2, overtime should be used in the months when backorders will occur without the use of overtime and, if more overtime production is needed, in the month(s) before them, not after, because backorder cost per unit ($150) is larger than inventory holding cost per unit ($10). Also, because holding inventory costs money, overtime should be used as close to the months with backorder as possible. Therefore, our decision to produce the maximum of 400 units in each of the 3rd, 4th, and 5th month during overtime was correct.

Trade-off analysis would have been able to save us the trouble of even considering the second plan. This is because the cost of a unit made during overtime is $150, whereas the cost of a unit made by a temporary worker (employed say for one month) is less ($100 + hiring cost/number of units produced in a month = $100 + $500/(20) = $125).

Another example is the question of how to use the temporary workers in the third plan. Consider e.g., employing 60 temporary workers for one month in month 5 versus 30 temporary workers for two months starting in month 4. As derived above, the cost of a unit produced by a temporary worker employed for one month is $125. However, the cost of a unit produced by a temporary worker employed for two months is in effect only $100 + $500/(20 \times 2) = $112.50. However, because a unit needs to be carried in inventory for one month (from 4th to 5th month), its total unit cost is $112.50 + $10 = $122.50, which is still < $125. Therefore, using 30 temporary workers for two months starting in month 4 is cheaper than using 60 temporary workers for one month in month 5.

Now consider employing 20 temporary workers for three months starting in month 2. The cost of a unit produced by a temporary worker employed for three months is in effect only $100 + $500/(20 \times 3) = $108.33. However, because a unit needs to be carried in inventory for two months (from 3rd to 5th month), its total unit cost is $108.33 + 2(10) = 128.33, which is > $125. Therefore, using 20 temporary workers for three months starting in month 2 is more expensive than using 30 temporary workers for two months starting in month 3.

The following example further illustrates the trade-off analysis.

Example 4[1]

A food company makes small puddings in a plant. It sells the puddings in cases (a case contains 48 pudding cups). The plant has 15 parallel production lines. The regular operating

---

[1]Based on Bradford Manufacturing case in F.R. Jacobs, R.B. Chase, and N.J. Aquilano, and, *Operations & Supply Management*, 12th ed. (New York: McGraw Hill/Irwin, 2009), pp. 541–542 .

hours is 8 hours a day, 5 days a week, 13 weeks a quarter. Each line is automated but needs 6 workers to operate it and can produce 200 units of output (each unit = 1,000 cases) per quarter. Currently, only 11 production lines are used, for a total quarterly output of 2,200 units. The sales department has forecasted demand for puddings for the next five quarters: 2,000, 2,200, 2,500, 2,700, and 2,200 units. Currently, there are no puddings in the warehouse. The company can change production by changing workforce level but needs to hire or lay off a group of six workers at a time, i.e., by opening or shutting down one production line. Hiring or layoff of one worker costs approximately $1,000 each. Each worker is paid an average of $19.23 per hour. Overtime costs 1.5 times regular-time wages, and is limited to the maximum of 20 percent of regular-time production in any quarter. Holding inventory of a unit for a quarter will cost $50 (charged on the average level of inventory in the quarter). Backorder per unit per quarter is estimated to cost $200.

a. Determine all the relevant unit costs.

b. If the current number of workers is kept for the next five quarters, how many units will the company be short of at the end of Quarter 5?

c. Meet the forecast demand at minimum cost by

   i. Adding another production line

   ii. Adding any number of production lines and/or using overtime

   You may use the trade-off analysis to limit the number of plans considered.

a. Labour cost per unit during regular time

    = Labour cost of one line for one quarter ÷ production of the line in the quarter
    = # of workers for the line × cost per worker per quarter ÷ 200
    = 6 × wage per hour × hours per quarter ÷ 200
    = 6 × $19.23 × hours per day × days per week × weeks per quarter ÷ 200
    = 6 × $19.23 × 8 × 5 × 13 ÷ 200
    = 299.99   round to $300

Solution

Labour cost per unit during overtime

    = proportion of regular time cost × regular time cost
    = 1.5 × $300 = $450

Hiring cost per unit (charged to the first quarter hired)

    = Hiring cost per worker × number of workers per line ÷ production per line per quarter
    = $1,000 × 6 ÷ 200
    = $30

Layoff cost per unit (charged to the quarter after layoff) = same as hiring cost per unit = $30

b. Number short at the end of Quarter 5

    = total demand forecast − 5 × regular production per quarter
    = 11,600 − 5 (2,200)
    = 600 units

c. **i.** The 12th production line should work three quarters because the number short is 600 units (from part b) and the capacity of a line is 200 units per quarter. Note that the quarters with higher-than-average demand are Q3 and Q4. Therefore, the 12th production line should work during Q3 and Q4. Because layoff and rehire costs money and the demand has only one peak, it is evident that the 12th line should work in three consecutive quarters: either Q2 to Q4 or Q3 to Q5. Note that the latter choice will result in backorder from Q5 to Q4. Therefore, choose the former because holding a unit in inventory for two quarters (from Q2 to Q4) costs only 2 × $50 = $100 < $200 = cost of backordering a unit from Q5 back to Q4. The completed worksheet is displayed below. Note that the output of the 12th production line is shown in the "Temporary" row.

Aggregate plan using an additional production line

Quarter	1	2	3	4	5	Total
Forecast	2,000	2,200	2,500	2,700	2,200	11,600
Output						
Permanent	2,200	2,200	2,200	2,200	2,200	11,000
Temporary		200	200	200		600
Overtime						
Output—Forecast	200	200	−100	−300	0	0
Inventory						
Beginning	0	200	400	300	0	
Ending	200	400	300	0	0	
Average	100	300	350	150	0	900
Backorder	0	0	0	0	0	0
Costs						
Permanent @ $300	660,000	660,000	660,000	660,000	660,000	3,300,000
Temporary @ $300	0	60,000	60,000	60,000	0	180,000
Overtime @ $450	0	0	0	0	0	0
Hire temporary/unit @ $30	0	6,000	0	0	0	6,000
Lay off temporary/unit @ $30	0	0	0	0	6,000	6,000
Inventory @ $50	5,000	15,000	17,500	7,500	0	45,000
Backorder @ $200	0	0	0	0	0	0
Total	665,000	741,000	737,500	727,500	666,000	$3,537,000

iv. First we will show that using temporary workers is cheaper than using overtime:

Unit cost of a unit made by a temporary worker hired and laid off after one quarter = $300 + $30 + $30 = $360

< $450 = cost of a unit produced by a permanent worker during overtime.

Now, one way to reduce the total cost of the plan determined in part C_i above is to use two extra production lines during Q4. This will produce 400 units. To produce the remaining 200 units needed, it is clear that we need to start one of these two lines in Q3. As you can see in the worksheet below, the total cost in this case is lower than the plan in C_i. Therefore, the production plan given in the worksheet in c. ii (with 200 units in Q3 and 400 units in Q4 by extra lines) is optimal.

Aggregate plan using two additional production lines

Quarter	1	2	3	4	5	Total
Forecast	2,000	2,200	2,500	2,700	2,200	11,600
Output						
Permanent	2,200	2,200	2,200	2,200	2,200	11,000
Temporary			200	400		600
Overtime						0
Output − Forecast	200	0	−100	−100	0	0
Inventory						
Beginning	0	200	200	100	0	
Ending	200	200	100	0	0	
Average	100	200	150	50	0	500
Backorder	0	0	0	0	0	
Costs						
Permanent @ $300	660,000	660,000	660,000	660,000	660,000	3,300,000
Temporary @ $300	0	0	60,000	120,000	0	180,000
Overtime @ $450	0	0	0	0	0	0
Hire temporary/unit @ $30	0	0	6,000	6,000	0	12,000
Lay off temporary/unit @ $30	0	0	0	0	12,000	12,000
Inventory @ $50	5,000	10,000	7,500	2,500	0	25000
Backorder @ $200	0	0	0	0	0	0
Total	665,000	670,000	733,500	788,500	672,000	$3,529,000

Note that producing 400 units in Q3 and 200 units in Q4 by the extra lines will increase the total cost because 200 more units have to be carried in inventory from Q3 to Q4. Also, producing 600 units in Q3 and nothing in Q4 by the extra lines will increase the total cost because

400 more units have to be carried in inventory from Q3 to Q4, in addition to $30 + $30 extra hiring and laying off costs per unit. Finally, producing nothing in Q3 and 600 units in Q4 by the extra lines will increase the total cost because 100 units have to be backordered from Q4 to Q3, in addition to $30 + $30 extra hiring and laying off costs per unit.

Optimization

Linear Programming Model. A linear programming model is a mathematical representation of the aggregate planning problem. A variable is assigned to each of the number of hires and number of layoffs, amount of overtime, ending inventory, and backorder in each period (e.g., month). All other unknown quantities are represented in terms of these variables. The total cost formula, consisting of the unit costs times the variables, is a linear objective function. Each relationship is represented as a linear equation or inequality constraint. Once the model is entered in a linear programming software, after some iterations, the optimal solution (the lowest cost feasible solution) is found (if it exists). Excel has an add-on program, called Solver, which solves linear programs. See the supplement to Chapter 6 (available on *Connect*) for more information on linear programming.

Transportation Model. When there are no hirings or layoffs, the problem can be formulated as a transportation model, which is even simpler to solve than a linear programming model. See the supplement to Chapter 8 (available on *Connect*) for more information on the transportation model. In order to use this approach, planners must identify capacity (i.e., maximum supply) of regular time, overtime, and part-time/temp, and demand for each period, as well as related costs of production and inventory.

Table 13-2 shows the notation and setup of a transportation table for aggregate production planning. There are n (e.g., 12) set of production rows and n consumption (demand) columns. There is also a row for the beginning inventory (at the top) and a column for unused capacity (in the right). The production quantities, to be determined by the software, will be in each cell. Unit costs are in the little squares in the top right of each cell. Note the systematic way that costs change as you move across a row from left to right. Regular cost, overtime cost, and part-time/temporary costs are at their lowest when the output is consumed (i.e., delivered) in the same month as it is produced. If goods are produced in one month but carried over to later months (i.e., moving across a row to the right), holding costs are incurred at the rate of h per month. Conversely, with backorders, the unit cost increases as you move across a row to the left. For instance, if some goods are produced in month 3 to satisfy backorders from month 2, a unit backorder cost of b is incurred. Unused capacity is generally given a unit cost of 0. Finally, beginning inventory is given a unit cost of 0 if it is used to satisfy demand in month 1. However, if it is held over for use in later months, a holding cost of h per unit is added for each month.

Table 13-2

Transportation model and notation for aggregate production planning

Consumption Month

		Month 1	Month 2	Month 3	. . .	Month n	Unused capacity	Capacity
Month	Beginning inventory	0	h	$2h$	. . .	nh	0	I_0
1	Regular time	r	$r+h$	$r+2h$	. . .	$r+nh$	0	R_1
	Overtime	t	$t+h$	$t+2h$	. . .	$t+nh$	0	O_1
	Part-time/temp	s	$s+h$	$s+2h$	. . .	$s+nh$	0	S_1
2	Regular time	$r+b$	r	$r+h$	. . .	$r+(n-1)h$	0	R_2
	Overtime	$t+b$	t	$t+h$	. . .	$t+(n-1)h$	0	O_2
	Part-time/temp	$s+b$	s	$s+h$	. . .	$s+(n-1)h$	0	S_2
3	Regular time	$r+2b$	$r+b$	r	. . .	$r+(n-2)h$	0	R_3
	Overtime	$t+2b$	$t+b$	t	. . .	$t+(n-2)h$	0	O_3
	Part-time/temp	$s+2b$	$s+b$	s	. . .	$s+(n-2)h$	0	S_3
	.	.	.	.	.	.	.	.
	Demand							Total

Example 5 illustrates the setup and final solution of a transportation model of an aggregate production planning problem.

Example 5

Given the following information, set up the aggregate production planning problem as a transportation table and solve it:

	Month		
	1	**2**	**3**
Demand forecast	550	700	750
Capacity (maximum)			
Regular	500	500	500
Overtime	50	50	50
Part time	120	120	100
Beginning inventory	100		

Costs	
Regular time	$60 per unit
Overtime	$80 per unit
Part time	$90 per unit
Inventory holding cost	$1 per unit per month
Backorder cost	$3 per unit per month

Solution

The transportation table and an optimal solution (using Excel's Solver) are shown in Table 13-3.

Thus, the demand of 550 units in period 1 will be met using 100 units from beginning inventory and 450 units obtained from regular-time output in month 1. The 700 units demanded in month 2 is met by 50 units produced during regular time, 50 units during overtime, and 30 units of part time in month 1 all carried to month 2; and 500 units produced during regular time, 50 units during overtime, and 20 units of part time in month 2. The 750 units demanded in month 3 is met by 100 units of part time in month 2 carried to month 3, and 500 units produced during regular time, 50 units during overtime, and 100 units of part time in month 3. The total cost for this solution is $100(0)+450(60)+50(61)+50(81)+30(91)+500(60)+50(80)+20(90)+100(91)+500(60)+50(80)+100(90)+90(0)=\$124,730$.

Table 13-3

Transportation table and optimal solution for Example 5

	Supply from	Demand for			Unused capacity	Total capacity available (supply)
		Month 1	Month 2	Month 3		
Month	Beginning inventory	[0] 100	[1]	[2]	[0]	100
1	Regular time	[60] 450	[61] 50	[62]	[0]	500
	Overtime	[80]	[81] 50	[82]	[0]	50
	Part-time	[90]	[91] 30	[92]	[0] 90	120
2	Regular time	[63]	[60] 500	[61]	[0]	500
	Overtime	[83]	[80] 50	[81]	[0]	50
	Part-time	[93]	[90] 20	[91] 100	[0]	120
3	Regular time	[66]	[63]	[60] 500	[0]	500
	Overtime	[86]	[83]	[80] 50	[0]	50
	Part-time	[96]	[93]	[90] 100	[0]	100
	Demand	550	700	750	90	2,090

OM in ACTION

Banner Good Samaritan Medical Center

Banner Good Samaritan Medical Center in Phoenix, Arizona, a 662-bed hospital, was in a difficult budgetary situation in the early 1990s. Its nursing budget was based on level work-force (approximately 1,000 FTEs) throughout the year. Because there was little allowance for seasonality, the staff had idle time (approximately 20 percent) during summer months and the hospital employed temporary nurses, hired from external nursing agencies, during winter months. Overtime was also used in winter at 1.5 times regular wage rate plus a premium of $7 per hour. These arrangements cost the hospital a great deal. In addition, the nurses were reluctant to serve as floats, to be traded between units when there was a short-term imbalance in nurse requirements between units. Finally, in 1992—when these extra costs reached $10 million—a consultant was hired to assist the new senior administrator for nursing. Data were gathered on patient days during the year, and a time standard was set for the nursing hours required per patient day. Five levels of work for registered nurses (RNs) were

established. Level 1 RNs, comprising the majority of RNs, work only in one unit (do not float). The number of RNs in Level 1 was based on annual patient days divided by 365. Level 2 RNs, also full time, work in three to four units that share similar skill requirements and are used to meet increases in patient numbers or acuity. Level 2 RNs were paid $.75 per hour more. Level 3 RNs work in many units and are primarily per diem employees. They are used to fill in when regular RNs are sick or if help is needed during winter. Level 4 RNs are part-time, filling in shifts of two hours' duration. Level 5 RNs comprise external agency nurses. Further efforts to reduce the permanent nurses' availability in the summer months were instituted in the form of career enhancement programs and voluntary leaves of absence. The new staffing system was very successful. By 1995, the cost of external agency temporary nurses and overtime declined to $2 million, flexibility increased, patient care improved, and nurses were happier.

Sources: S. Hollabaugh and S. Kendrick, "Staffing: The Five-level Pyramid," *Nursing Management* 29(2), February 1998, pp. 34–36; http://www.bannerhealth.com/Locations/Arizona/Banner+Good+Samaritan+Medical+Center/_Banner+Good+Samaritan+Medical+Center.htm.

Where backorders are not permitted, the cell costs for the backorders can be made prohibitively high so that no backorders will appear in the optimal solution.

LO3 AGGREGATE SERVICES PLANNING

Aggregate planning for production and aggregate planning for services share many similarities, but there are some important differences:

1. *Services occur when they are rendered.* Unlike goods, most services can't be inventoried or backordered. Consequently, it becomes important to be able to match capacity and demand during any month or quarter (i.e., we need to use the chase demand strategy).

2. For labour-intensive services, it may be easier to measure the aggregate plan in terms of time (e.g., hours) or number of workers (FTE) instead of an aggregate measure of output. See the "Banner Good Samaritan Medical Center" OM in Action above and Example 6 below.

Example 6

The director of nursing of a hospital needs to plan the nursing levels for each quarter of next year. She has forecasted the average number of patients per day in each of the hospital wards throughout each quarter of next year. Then she multiplied these numbers by 90 days a quarter × 24 hours a day and divided the result by the number of patients to be assigned to each nurse in each ward (e.g., three patients per nurse in intensive care, etc.) to obtain the aggregate forecast for hours of nursing required in each quarter. Finally, these are converted into number of full-time equivalent (FTE) nurses needed each quarter by dividing them by 480 hours per quarter, and rounding them to the nearest integer. These numbers are displayed as Forecast (FTE) in the following table. There are currently 140 permanent nurses, each working 480 hours a quarter, and being paid an average of $14 an hour. Overtime is allowed up to 50 percent of regular permanent FTEs and is compensated at 1.5 times the regular wage rate. Temporary nurses are available but hospital policy dictates that the maximum number of temporary nurses be at most 20 percent of permanent nurses. Temporary nurses are paid an average of $17 per hour, but no overtime is permitted. The hiring cost is $480 and layoff cost is $240 per temporary nurse. Being a service, no inventory or shortage (backorder) is permitted.

a. Determine all the relevant costs per FTE and fill them in the table.

b. Suppose one temporary nurse is hired and laid off after one quarter. Would this be cheaper than using a permanent nurse during overtime?

c. Determine the minimum total cost (feasible) aggregate service plan, and fill the whole table. Assume that temporary nurses are kept up to 4 quarters.

Solution

Note: The unit of product here is FTE of nursing service.

a. Regular permanent wages = $14/hour × 480 = $6,720 per quarter; temporary nurse wages = $17/hour × 480 = $8,160 per quarter; overtime wages = 1.5 × 6,720 = $10,080 per FTE per quarter. Hiring cost per temporary FTE (charged to the first quarter hired) is $480. Similarly, layoff cost per temporary FTE (charged to the quarter after layoff) is $240.

b. Cost per FTE of temporary nurse kept for a quarter = hire cost per nurse + layoff cost per nurse + wages = $480 + $240 + $8,160 = $8,880 < $10,080 = cost per FTE of overtime. Yes, using temporary nurses is cheaper than using permanent nurses during overtime.

c. Given the result in part b, use up to the maximum hours of temporary nurses in each quarter so that total output equals forecast (recall we cannot have inventory or shortage). Recall that maximum number of temporary workers = 0.20 × 140 = 28 FTE in any quarter. If there is any more need for nurses, we have to use permanent nurses during overtime. In this case, no overtime is necessary. The following aggregate service plan has minimum total cost and is feasible:

Quarter	1	2	3	4	Total
Forecast (FTE)	167	150	158	165	
Output (FTE)					
Reg. perm.	140	140	140	140	
Reg. temporary	27	10	18	25	
Overtime					
Costs per hour					
Reg. perm.@ $6,720	940,800	940,800	940,800	940,800	3,763,200
Reg. temporary @ $8,160	220,320	81,600	146,880	204,000	652,800
Overtime @ $10,080	0	0	0	0	0
Hire temporary @ $480	12,960	0	3,840	3,360	20,160
Layoff temporary @ $240	0	4,080	0	0	4,080
					$4,440,240

yield management The application of variable pricing strategy to allocate capacity based on capacity availability.

Because service capacity is perishable (e.g., an empty seat on an airplane can't be saved for use on another flight), aggregate planners need to take this fact into account when deciding how to match supply and demand. **Yield management** is an approach that seeks to maximize revenue by using a strategy of variable pricing; prices are set relative to capacity availability. Thus, during periods of low demand, price discounts are offered to attract a wider population. Conversely, during peak periods, higher prices are posted to take advantage of limited supply. Users of yield management include airlines, hotels, and resorts.

LO4 DISAGGREGATING THE AGGREGATE PRODUCTION PLAN

For the aggregate production plan to be translated into meaningful terms for production, it is necessary to *disaggregate* it. This involves breaking down the aggregate production plan into specific product's production schedule.

For example, suppose a lawn mower manufacturer's aggregate production plan is to produce 200 lawn mowers in January, 300 in February, and 400 in March. The company produces push mowers, self-propelled mowers, and small riding mowers. Obviously, there are some differences in the materials, parts, and operations that each lawn mower type requires. Hence, the 200, 300, and 400 aggregate lawn mowers must be broken down into specific numbers of mowers of each type and model prior to actually scheduling operations and planning inventory requirements.

The result of disaggregating the aggregate plan is **master production schedule (MPS)**, which shows the anticipated build schedule expressed in the quantity and timing of end items for the next 12 weeks or so. The set of planned productions for all the products is the MPS.

Once a *tentative* MPS has been developed, a planner can do **rough-cut capacity planning**, which converts the MPS into requirements for key resources in order to test the feasibility of a proposed MPS. This means checking capacities of production and warehouse facilities, labour, and vendors to ensure that no gross deficiencies exist that will render the MPS unworkable. It should be noted that, whereas the aggregate plan covers an interval of, say, 12 months (i.e., intermediate term), the MPS covers only a portion of this (i.e., the short term). In other words, only the first three months or so of the aggregate plan is disaggregated. Moreover, the MPS must be updated weekly.

Figure 13-6 illustrates the concept of disaggregating the aggregate plan for the lawn mower manufacturer.

The process of determining the MPS is called *master production scheduling*. Master production scheduling is challenging because each product's anticipated demand should be satisfied while the sum of resource requirements of the MPS should not exceed the capacity determined in the aggregate plan. Like aggregate planning, master scheduling can be done using linear programming. The type of software used for performing master scheduling is known as advanced planning and scheduling (APS) software; see the "Kellogg's" OM in Action. In the following section, we will limit our discussion to the case when capacity is not tight, thus the production schedule for different end-items can be determined independently.

master production schedule (MPS)   The anticipated build schedule expressed in the quantity and timing of specific end items for the next 12 weeks or so.

rough-cut capacity planning   Converting the MPS into requirements for key resources in order to test the feasibility of a proposed master production schedule.

Aggregate plan

*Aggregate units

Month Planned output*	Jan.	Feb.	Mar.
	200	300	400

Master production schedule

Month Planned output*	Jan.	Feb.	Mar.
Push	100	100	100
Self-propelled	75	150	200
Riding	25	50	100
Total	200	300	400

*Actual units—need to further disaggregate into weekly planned output. It is assumed that all products are equivalent.

Figure 13-6

Example of disaggregating the aggregate plan

Master Production Scheduling

Inputs. Master production scheduling has three inputs for each product: the beginning inventory, which is the actual quantity on hand from the preceding week; forecasts for each week of the schedule (next 12 weeks or so); and customer orders, which are quantities already *committed* to customers. Note: we will consider the general case when the product is partly made to stock and partly made to order, thus using both forecast and committed customer orders.

The master production scheduler should work closely with the demand planner to obtain the (committed) customer order and forecast information and to cooperatively determine the MPS.

Consider the following example. A company that makes industrial pumps wants to prepare a master production schedule for June and July. Marketing has forecasted demand of 120 pumps for June and 160 pumps for July for its major product. These will be evenly distributed over the four weeks in each month: 30 per week in June and 40 per week in July, as illustrated in Figure 13-7.

Now, suppose that there are currently 64 pumps in inventory (i.e., beginning inventory is 64 pumps), and that there are customer orders that have been committed (booked) and must be filled (see Figure 13-8).

Outputs. The master production scheduling process uses the inputs on a week-by-week basis for each product to determine the projected inventory (at the end of the week), planned production, and the resulting uncommitted planned inventory, which is referred to as **available-to-promise (ATP) inventory**. Knowledge of the uncommitted (ATP) inventory can enable the sales department to make realistic promises to customers about deliveries of new orders.

available-to-promise (ATP) inventory Uncommitted planned inventory.

Figure 13-7

Weekly forecast demands for the pumps

Weeks

	June				July			
	1	**2**	**3**	**4**	**5**	**6**	**7**	**8**
Forecast	30	30	30	30	40	40	40	40

OM in *ACTION* http://www.kellogs.com

Kellogg's

Kellogg's uses linear programming to perform both aggregate planning and master production scheduling. The Kellogg Planning System (KPS) was written in-house in 1990 to plan production/packaging and distribution of Kellogg's products (hundreds of SKUs including 80 cereals). The operational version of KPS plans the next 30 weeks of production/packaging (90 production and 180 packaging lines in five Kellogg's plants in North America and 15 subcontractor or co-packer plants) and distribution (seven distribution centres, DCs) for master scheduling. The linear program minimizes the production, inventory, and transportation costs subject to safety stocks (equal to two weeks of demand or four weeks of demand if the item is being promoted) and meeting the demand at the DCs.

The solution is used by the plant managers to schedule their production lines and by the logistics managers to schedule their inventories and transportation. The tactical version of KPS plans the next 18 months of production/packaging and distribution for aggregate planning. However, the products are not aggregated in the software (they are in the operational version), but the results are aggregated manually to determine plant budgets, inventory spaces required in distribution centres, etc. KPS also facilitates what-if questions. For example, production of a product over time or in different plants can be combined if its batch sizes are small. Software such as KPS are referred to as Advanced Planning and Scheduling (APS) software.

Sources: G. Brown et al., "The Kellogg Company Optimizes Production, Inventory, and Distribution," *Interfaces* 31(6), November/ December 2001, pp. 1–15; http://www.kelloggs.com.

Weeks

Beginning inventory	June				July			
64	**1**	**2**	**3**	**4**	**5**	**6**	**7**	**8**
Forecast	30	30	30	30	40	40	40	40
Customer orders (committed)	33	20	10	4	2			

Figure 13-8

The table for the pump showing forecast and (committed) customer orders for the next eight weeks, and the beginning inventory

The first step for each product is to calculate the projected on-hand inventory (at the end of the week), one week at a time, until it falls below a specified limit (safety stock). In the above example, the specified limit is assumed to be zero. Hence, we will continue until the projected on-hand inventory (at the end of the week) becomes negative.

The projected on-hand inventory (at the end of the week) is calculated as follows:

$$\text{Projected on-hand inventory} = \text{Inventory from previous week} - \text{Current week's requirements} \tag{13-1}$$

where we use the convention that the current week's requirements is the *larger* of forecast and customer orders (committed).

For the first week, projected on-hand inventory (at the end of the week) equals beginning inventory minus the larger of forecast and customer orders. Because customer orders (33) is larger than the forecast (30), the customer orders amount is used. Thus, for the first week, we obtain:

Projected on-hand inventory (at the end of the week) $= 64 - 33 = 31$

Projected on-hand inventories for the first three weeks (i.e., until the projected on-hand amount becomes negative) are shown in Figure 13-9. When the projected on-hand inventory (at the end of the week) becomes negative, this is a signal that production will be needed to replenish inventory. Suppose that the economic production quantity is 70 pumps, and whenever production is called for, 70 pumps will be planned to be produced. (The determination of economic production quantity was described in Chapter 12.) Hence, the negative projected on-hand inventory at the end of third week will require production of 70 pumps, which will meet the projected shortfall of 29 pumps and leaves 41 (i.e., $70 - 29 = 41$) pumps for future demand.

Weeks

Beginning inventory	June				July			
64	**1**	**2**	**3**	**4**	**5**	**6**	**7**	**8**
Forecast	30	30	30	30	40	40	40	40
Customer orders (committed)	33	20	10	4	2			
Projected on-hand inventory	31	1	−29					

Figure 13-9

Projected on-hand inventory is calculated week by week until it becomes negative (assuming safety stocks = zero).

Customer orders are larger than forecast in week 1; projected on-hand inventory is $64 - 33 = 31$

Forecast is larger than customer orders in week 2; projected on-hand inventory is $31 - 30 = 1$

Forecast is larger than customer orders in week 3; projected on-hand inventory is $1 - 30 = -29$

These calculations continue for the entire scheduling horizon. Every time projected on-hand inventory becomes negative, another production lot of 70 pumps is added to the table. Figure 13-10 illustrates the calculations. The result is the planned production for each week. These can now be added to the table and projected on-hand inventories updated (see Figure 13-11).

It is now possible to determine the amount of inventory that is uncommitted and hence available to promise. Several methods are used in practice. The one we shall employ involves a "look-ahead" procedure: Sum customer orders week by week until (but not including) a week in which there is a planned production. For example, in the first week, this procedure results in summing customer orders of 33 (week 1) and 20 (week 2) and subtracting this from the beginning inventory of 64 pumps plus the planned production (zero in this example). Thus, ATP for week 1 is:

$$64 + 0 - (33 + 20) = 11$$

This inventory is uncommitted and can be delivered in weeks 1 or 2. Note that the ATP quantity is calculated only for the first week and for other weeks in which there is a positive planned production quantity. See Figure 13-12.

Figure 13-10

Determining the planned production and projected on-hand inventory

Week	Inventory from Previous Week	Require-ments*	Net Inventory before Planned Production		(70) Planned Production		Projected Inventory
1	64	33	31				31
2	31	30	1				1
3	1	30	−29	+	70	=	41
4	41	30	11				11
5	11	40	−29	+	70	=	41
6	41	40	1				1
7	1	40	−39	+	70	=	31
8	31	40	−9	+	70	=	61

*Requirements equals the larger of forecast and customer orders in each week.

Figure 13-11

Planned productions are added and projected on-hand inventories are updated.

		Weeks							
		June				July			
	64	1	2	3	4	5	6	7	8
Forecast		30	30	30	30	40	40	40	40
Customer orders (committed)		33	20	10	4	2			
Projected on-hand inventory		31	1	41	11	41	1	31	61
Planned production				70		70		70	70

Weeks

64	June				July			
	1	**2**	**3**	**4**	**5**	**6**	**7**	**8**
Forecast	30	30	30	30	40	40	40	40
Customer orders (committed)	33	20	10	4	2			
Projected on-hand inventory	31	1	41	11	41	1	31	61
Planned production			70		70		70	70
Available-to-promise inventory (uncommitted)	11		56		68		70	70

For weeks other than the first week, the beginning inventory drops out of the calculation, and ATP is the look-ahead customer orders subtracted from the planned production quantity. Thus, for week 3, the customer orders (committed) amounts are $10 + 4 = 14$ and the ATP is $70 - 14 = 56$. For week 5, customer orders (committed) are 2 (future customer orders have not yet been booked), and the ATP is $70 - 2 = 68$. For weeks 7 and 8, there are no customer orders, so for the present all of the planned production amount is available to promise. As additional orders are booked, these would be entered in the table, and the ATP amounts would be updated to reflect those orders. The sales department can use the ATP amounts to provide realistic delivery dates to customers.

Stabilizing the Master Production Schedule

Changes to a master production schedule (i.e., the set of planned productions for all the products) can be disruptive, particularly changes to the near-future portion of the schedule. Typically, the further out in the future a change is, the less it will cause problems.

Master production schedules are often divided into three zones. The dividing lines between zones are sometimes referred to as **time fences**. The emergency zone (see Figure 13-13) is closest to present time and is affected only when something unforeseen and unplanned has happened, such as sudden shifts in demand, or manufacturing problems. Changes in the emergency zone may affect commitment of key resources and therefore require top management level of approval. In addition, such changes should be discouraged unless no other alternatives exist. Next is the trading zone, when changes can be approved at a middle management level and generally involve trading one planned production for another, as opposed to the emergency change that usually sacrifices something in the short term. In the last and farthest forward timeframe, the planning zone, changes are managed without management approval, usually by the demand planner and master scheduler.

time fences   Points in time that separate zones of a master production schedule.

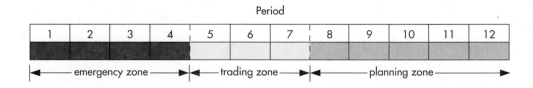

Period

| 1 | 2 | 3 | 4 | 5 | 6 | 7 | 8 | 9 | 10 | 11 | 12 |

|← emergency zone →|← trading zone →|← planning zone →|

Summary

Sales and operations planning is the process of integrating sales forecasts with operations plans. This is usually done monthly when aggregate information is reviewed by top management.

Aggregate operations planning establishes general levels of employment, output, and inventories for the next 12 months or so. In the spectrum of planning, it falls between the broad decisions of long-term strategic planning and short-term planning.

A basic requirement of aggregate planning is the aggregation of a category or family of products into an "equivalent" unit. This permits planners to consider overall levels of employment, output, and inventories without having to become involved with specific details that are better left to short-term planning. The planning variables include using overtime, part-time/temporary workers, carrying inventory, and allowing backorders. Planning strategies range from level output/workforce to chase demand. Planners often use informal (trial-and-error) graphic and worksheet techniques to develop plans, although various mathematical optimization techniques are also used. Aggregate service planning cannot use inventories and backorders and thus relies on chase demand strategy. It also usually uses the amount of workforce (hours or FTE) as the equivalent unit.

After the aggregate plan has been developed, it is disaggregated or broken down into specific product production plans. This leads to a master production schedule, which indicates the planned production quantities and their timing for all the products. Inputs to the master production scheduling are on-hand inventory amounts, forecasts of demand, and committed orders. The outputs are planned productions projected on-hand inventories and uncommitted inventories (available-to-promise).

Key Terms

aggregate operations planning, 470
available-to-promise (ATP) inventory, 490
chase demand strategy, 475
level output/workforce strategy, 475
master production schedule (MPS), 489

rough-cut capacity planning, 489
sales and operations planning, 469
time fences, 493
yield management, 488

Solved Problems

Problem 1

A manager is attempting to put together an aggregate production plan for the coming nine months. She has obtained forecasts of aggregate demand for the planning horizon. The plan must deal with highly seasonal demand; demand is relatively high in months 3 and 4, and again in month 8, as can be seen below:

Month	1	2	3	4	5	6	7	8	9	Total
Forecast	190	230	260	280	210	170	160	260	180	1,940

The company has 20 permanent employees, each of whom can produce 10 units of output per month at a cost of $6 per unit. Inventory holding cost is $5 per unit per month, and backorder cost is $10 per unit per month. The manager is considering a plan that would involve hiring two people to start working in month 1, one on a temporary basis who would work until the end of month 5. The hiring of these two and laying off of one later would cost $500 in addition to production costs. Beginning inventory is 0.

a. What is the rationale for this plan?

b. Determine the total cost of the plan, including production, inventory, and backorder costs.

Solution

a. With the current workforce of 20 people each producing 10 units per month, regular capacity is $20 \times 10 \times 9 = 1,800$ units. That is 140 units less than total demand. Adding one worker would increase regular capacity to $1,800 + 10 \times 9 = 1,890$ units. That would still be 50 units short, or just the amount one temporary worker could produce in five months. Since one of the two seasonal peaks is quite early, it would make sense to start the temporary worker right away to avoid some of the backorder cost.

b. The production plan for this strategy is as follows:

Month	1	2	3	4	5	6	7	8	9	Total
Forecast	190	230	260	280	210	170	160	260	180	1,940
Output										
Regular	220	220	220	220	220	210	210	210	210	1,940
Overtime	—	—	—	—	—	—	—	—	—	—
Subcontract/part time	—	—	—	—	—	—	—	—	—	—
Output – Forecast	30	-10	-40	-60	10	40	50	-50	30	0
Inventory										
Beginning	0	30	20	0	0	0	0	20	0	
Ending	30	20	0	0	0	0	20	0	0	
Average	15	25	10	0	0	0	10	10	0	70
Backorder	0	0	20	80	70	30	0	30	0	230
Costs per unit										
Output										
Regular @ $6	$1,320	1,320	1,320	1,320	1,320	1,260	1,260	1,260	1,260	$11,640
Overtime										
Subcontract/part time										
Inventory @ $5	$75	125	50	0	0	0	50	50	0	$350
Backorder @ $10	0	0	200	800	700	300	0	300	0	$2,300
Total	$1,395	1,445	1,570	2,120	2,020	1,560	1,310	1,610	1,260	$14,290

The total cost for this plan is $14,290 plus the $500 cost for two hirings and later one layoff, giving a total of $14,790. This plan may or may not be good. The manager would need to evaluate other alternative plans before settling on one plan.

You can also use the Excel template on *Connect* to obtain the solution:

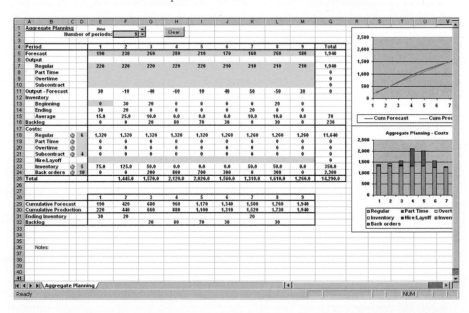

Prepare an MPS table like that shown in Figure 13-12 for the following situation. The forecast for each of the next four weeks is 70 units. The starting inventory is zero. The MPS rule is to

Problem 2

schedule production if the projected inventory on hand will be negative. The production lot size is 100 units. The following table shows customer (committed) orders.

Week	Customer Orders
1	80
2	50
3	30
4	10

Solution

Week	(A) Inventory from Previous Period	(B) Require- ments*	(C = B − A) Net Inventory before Planned Production	Planned Production	(Planned Production + C) Projected Inventory
1	0	80	−80	100	20
2	20	70	−50	100	50
3	50	70	−20	100	80
4	80	70	10	0	10

*Requirements equal the larger of forecast and customer orders in each week.

	Week			
Starting Inv. = 0	**1**	**2**	**3**	**4**
Forecast	70	70	70	70
Customer orders	80	50	30	10
Projected on-hand inventory	20	50	80	10
Planned production	100	100	100	
ATP	20	50	60	

Discussion and Review Questions

1. What is sales and operations planning? How is it done? (LO1)

2. What is aggregate operations planning? What is its purpose? (LO1)

3. Why is there a need for aggregate operations planning? (LO1)

4. What are the most common decision variables for aggregate planning in a manufacturing setting? In a service setting? (LO1)

5. What options are available for changing the medium-term capacity of (a) a school, (b) an airline? (LO1)

6. Under what circumstances would a company use the following strategies? (LO1)

   a. Maintain level output/workforce and let inventories absorb fluctuations in demand.
   b. Vary the size of the workforce to correspond to predicted changes in demand requirements.
   c. Maintain a constant workforce, but vary hours worked (through overtime and idle time) to correspond to predicted demand requirements.

7. What procedure should be used in trial-and-error worksheet approach for aggregate operations planning? (LO2)

8. Give an example of a product with highly seasonal demand and discuss how its manufacturer meets the demand. (LO2)

9. What are the differences between aggregate planning for services and goods? (LO3)

10. What is master production scheduling and how is it done? (LO4)

11. What is ATP, and how is it determined? (LO4)

1. What general trade-offs are involved in master production scheduling for determining the length of emergency zone of the schedule? (LO4)

2. Who needs to interface with the master production schedule and why? (LO4)

3. How has technology had an impact on aggregate planning? (LO1 & 2)

4. Many companies are using temporary workers to meet their peak demand. Is this ethically wrong? Briefly discuss. (LO2 & 3)

Discuss disaggregating an aggregate service plan, and give an example of it in an organization such as a hospital. (LO3 & 4)

Aggregate planning in operations is like budgeting in finance/accounting. Prepare a personal budget for next year following the concept of aggregate planning. Forecast your need for money each quarter and identify the supply of money and its sources. Make sure supply (it could include student loan) meets the demand. (LO2 & 3)

1. Visit http://www.steelwedge.com/solutions/lp_supply_planning.php, and summarize what the Supply Planning module of Steelwedge's S&OP software can do for a company. You may also read and summarize one of the following applications: (LO1)

   a. http://www.steelwedge.com/customers/index.php?z=air_products
   b. http://www.steelwedge.com/newsletter/july05/newsletter_Phull_July05.html

2. Visit http://www.kinaxis.com/operations-performance-solutions/sales-operations-planning. cfm, and summarize what the S&OP module of RapidResponse can do for a company. Also, summarize the application: http://www.kinaxis.com/downloads/customer_spotlight/spotlight-MTD.html. (LO1)

3. Visit http://www.oliverwight-americas.com/cust_profiles, choose a case study, and summarize it. (LO1)

1. Refer to Example 3. Suppose that the new union contract limits the number of temporary workers working in any month to 28 (i.e., 20 percent of number of permanent workers). Recall from Example 2 that up to 400 units can be produced during overtime per month. Using trade-off analysis and trial-and-error, find the minimum cost aggregate production plan in this case. (LO2)

2. A manufacturer of heavy truck engines must develop an aggregate production plan, given the forecasts for engine demand shown below. The company currently has 13 workers and makes 130 engines per month. Regular labour cost is $500 per engine. The beginning inventory is zero. Overtime labour costs $750 per engine. Hiring cost is $2,000 per worker and layoff cost is $1,000 per worker. Inventory holding cost is $50 per engine per month, and backorder cost is $250 per engine per month. Develop the minimum cost aggregate production plan for this company. *Hint*: Start with level output/workforce plan, and use the trade-off analysis to show that changing this plan will only increase the total cost. (LO2)

Month	1	2	3	4	5	6	7	8	Total
Forecast	120	135	140	120	125	125	140	135	1,040

3. A fabric mill has developed the following forecasts (in hundred bolts of cloth). The mill has a normal capacity of 275 units (a unit=hundred bolts) per month, and employs 275 workers. Regular labour cost is $2,000 per unit and overtime labour cost is $3,000 per unit. Up to

50 units per month can be made during overtime. The beginning inventory is zero. Hiring cost is $1,000 per worker and layoff cost is $500 per worker. The inventory holding cost is $1,000 per unit per month, and backorder cost is $5,000 per unit per month. (LO2)

a. Develop a level output/workforce plan.

b. Starting with your answer to part a, use the trade-off analysis to find the minimum cost aggregate production plan.

Month	1	2	3	4	5	6	7	Total
Forecast	250	300	250	300	280	275	270	1,925

4. A small company produces a variety of recreational and leisure vehicles. The marketing manager has developed the following aggregate forecasts: (LO2)

Month	Mar	Apr	May	Jun	Jul	Aug	Sep	Total
Forecast	50	44	55	60	60	40	50	359

Use the following information:

Regular labour cost	$240 per unit
Overtime labour cost	$360 per unit
Regular capacity	40 units per month, using 5 workers
Overtime capacity	8 units per month
Holding cost	$30 per unit per month
Backorder cost	$100 per unit per month
Beginning inventory	0 units
Desired ending inventory	0 units
Hiring cost	$2,000 per worker
Layoff cost	$1,000 per worker

Develop the minimum cost aggregate production plan and compute its total cost.

5. A small company produces whisky. The sales person has developed the following aggregate forecasts for demand (in cases) for the next six months. (LO2)

Month	May	Jun	Jul	Aug	Sep	Oct
Forecast	4,000	4,800	5,600	7,200	6,400	5,000

Use the following information:

Regular labour cost	$20 per case
Regular labour capacity	5,000 cases per month using 50 workers
Overtime labour cost	$30 per case
Part time labour cost	$40 per case
Holding cost	$2 per case per month
Backorder cost	$10 per case per month
Beginning inventory	0

Develop the minimum cost aggregate production plan using a level output/workforce plan, supplemented with each of the following variables, and compute the total cost for each plan. Which plan has the lower total cost?

a. Use overtime (up to 1,000 cases per month).

b. Use a combination of overtime (500 cases per month maximum) and part-time labour (500 cases per month maximum).

6. A company produces a variety of sofas. The manager wants to prepare an aggregate production plan for the next six months using the following information: (LO2)

	MONTH					
	1	**2**	**3**	**4**	**5**	**6**
Forecast Demand	160	150	160	180	170	140

Cost Per Unit	
Regular time	$100
Overtime	$150
Part time	$120
Inventory, per month	$10
Backorder, per month	$50

There are 5 workers, each making 30 sofas a month. The maximum number of sofas produced during overtime is 30 per month. Part-time workers can handle a maximum of 20 units per month. Beginning inventory is zero. Develop a plan that minimizes total cost. No ending inventory or backorders are allowed at the end of month 6.

7. Refer to Solved Problem 1. Start with 20 permanent workers. Prepare a minimum cost aggregate plan that may use some combination of hiring ($200 per worker), laying off ($100 per worker), part-time labour ($8 per unit, maximum of 20 units per month, must use for at least three consecutive months), and overtime ($9 per unit, maximum of 25 per month). The ending inventory in month 9 should be zero with no backorders at the end. Compute the total cost. (LO2)

8. A water bottling company has recently expanded its bottled spring water operations to include several new flavours. The marketing manager is predicting an upturn in demand based on the new offerings and the increased public awareness of the health benefits of drinking more water. She has prepared aggregate forecasts for the next six months, as shown below (quantities are in tank loads): (LO2)

Month	May	Jun	Jul	Aug	Sept	Oct	Total
Forecast	50	60	70	90	80	70	420

The production manager has gathered the following information:

Regular production cost	$1,000 per tank load
Regular production capacity	60 tank loads using 20 employees
Overtime production cost	$1,500 per tank load
Holding cost	$200 per tank load per month
Backorder cost	$5,000 per tank load per month
Beginning inventory	0 tank load

The regular production can be supplemented by up to 30 tank-loads a month from overtime. Determine the aggregate plan that has the lowest total cost.

9. A small company manufactures bicycles in two different sizes. David, the company's owner-manager, has just received the following forecasts for demands for the next six months. (LO2)

	16-inch	**20-inch**
Nov.	1,000 units	500 units
Dec.	900	500
Jan.	600	300
Feb.	700	500
Mar.	1,100	400
Apr.	1,100	600

    a. Under what circumstances is it appropriate to develop just one aggregate production plan rather than two (one for each size bike)?

    b. Suppose the forecasted demands for the two sizes of bikes are summed to obtain one aggregate forecast for each month. Currently David employs 27 full-time, highly skilled employees, each of whom can produce 50 bikes per month. Because skilled labour is in short supply in the area, David would like to keep his 27 workers permanently. There is no inventory of finished bikes on hand at present, but David would like to have 300 on hand at the end of April. A maximum of 200 bikes can be produced during overtime each month. Determine the minimum cost aggregate plan and compute the total cost of your plan using these costs:

Regular	$50 per unit	Inventory	$2.00 per unit per month
Overtime	$75 per unit	Backorder	$10.00 per unit per month

10. A sports goods manufacturer makes baseball and hockey gloves. Suppose now is the end of December and the manager wishes to plan production for the next three quarters. The forecast demand for aggregate units of pairs of gloves is: Q1: 9,400, Q2: 16,200, and Q3: 18,500. There are currently 26 permanent workers. Each worker works 480 hours a quarter and makes 1 pair of gloves per hour. The wage rate is $8 per hour, holding cost per unit per quarter is $1, and the backorder cost per unit per quarter is $10. The manager can hire full-time temporary workers at the cost of $960 per person. Temporary workers also receive $8 per hour and work 480 hours a quarter. There is no layoff cost. Overtime by full-time workers is possible at 1.5 times the regular wage rate up to a maximum of 50 percent of regular time production. Current inventory level is zero and there is no inventory expected at the end of the planning horizon. (LO2)

    a. If 26 permanent workers are kept throughout the planning horizon, how many units will the company be short at the end?

    b. Do tradeoff analysis to show that using temporary workers will be cheaper than using permanent workers during overtime.

    c. Find the aggregate production plan that minimizes total cost.

*11. MR is a manufacturer of industrial fridges, freezes, and air conditioners. In December, the production planner needs to submit a production plan to the plant manager for the next year. The aggregate forecasts for demand for each quarter of next year are Q1: 14,800, Q2: 26,400; Q3: 35,000, and Q4: 19,200 units. The beginning inventory in January is expected to be 0, and the year-end inventory in December of next year can be 0. It costs MR $24 per appliance to hold it in inventory for one quarter. Shortages (demand not met) are undesirable. Assume that any shortage will be backordered (met from future periods), and that backorder cost is $100 per unit per quarter. There are 160 permanent workers who produce 19,200 units per quarter. In busy quarters, they can produce up to 9,600 additional units during overtime. Regular-time labour cost is $60 per unit and overtime labour cost is $83 per unit. MR can hire up to 160 temporary workers to work during a second shift. Assume temporary workers have the same productivity and can produce up to 19,200 units per quarter. A unit produced by temporary workers also costs $60 in labour cost. However, there will be an extra hiring cost of $25 per unit produced by a newly hired temporary worker. There is no layoff cost. (LO2)

    a. If permanent workers are used for the next four quarters during regular time, how many units will MR be short at the end of the year and which quarters will it be short?

    b. Meet units short by hiring temporary workers. Use trade-off analysis to choose the minimum cost plan in this case.

    c. Would using overtime (in addition to some temporary production) be less expensive? Use trade-off analysis to choose the overall minimum cost plan.

*12. MT is a manufacturer of small camping and snowmobile trailers. The demand for camping trailers occurs between January and June of each year (mostly in April and May). MT makes camping trailers during January to June, shuts down in July, and then makes snowmobile trailers from August to November. Suppose now is the end of December. For simplicity, we consider every two months as a period. The aggregate demand forecasts for camping trailers during each of the next three periods (six months) are:

Period 1	Period 2	Period 3
869	1,730	1,374

MT employs 40 permanent workers. The employees are paid an average of $20 per hour (including fringe benefits) and work approximately 320 hours a period (2 months). The 40 permanent workers can make approximately 1,000 camping trailers per period during regular time. They can also work up to 50 percent more as overtime (i.e., up to 12 hours a day vs the regular 8 hours a day) and will be paid 1.5 times the regular wage rate. Alternatively, MT can hire *up to* 40 additional temporary workers to work during a second shift. Hiring cost is $2,000 and layoff cost is $1,000 per temporary worker. Assume temporary workers' wage rate and productivity are the same as permanent workers. Also assume that temporary workers work only during regular time (no overtime) and are kept for whole periods (i.e., for 2 months or 4 months). Inventory holding cost per camping trailer per period is $180, and is charged to average inventory level during each period. Currently there are no camping trailers on hand, and the desired inventory at the end of period 3 is zero (although a small positive number is also acceptable). MT wishes to meet the total forecast demand, but shortage during a period (except last) may be possible, in which case the shortage is backordered at the cost of $600 per camping trailer per period backordered. (LO2)

a. Calculate all the relevant unit costs.

b. Suppose MT uses permanent workers during regular time and overtime. Determine the minimum cost aggregate production plan in this case.

c. Suppose MT hires temporary workers, but decides not to use permanent workers during overtime (just regular time). Determine the minimum cost aggregate production plan in this case. Note: Use multiples of 25 units of production per period (i.e., the production of one temporary worker per period).

d. Would overtime production by permanent workers and regular time production by temporary workers simultaneously result in a lower total cost? Do a trade-off analysis. What is the overall minimum cost aggregate production plan?

13. Refer to Example 5. Suppose that an increase in warehousing and other costs has brought up the inventory holding cost to $2 per unit per month. All other costs and quantities remain the same. Determine a revised optimal solution to this transportation problem. (LO2)

14. Refer to Example 5. Suppose that regular-time capacity will be reduced to 440 units in month 3 to accommodate a companywide safety inspection of equipment. What will the additional cost of the optimal plan be as compared to the one shown in Example 5? Assume all input data are the same as given in Example 5 except for the regular-time capacity in month 3. (LO2)

15. Solve Problem 14 using an inventory holding cost of $2 per unit per month. (LO2)

16. Prepare another master scheduling table for the pumps of Figure 13-12; use the same inputs as the example, but change the master scheduling rule from "schedule production when the projected on-hand inventory would be negative without production" to "schedule production when the projected on-hand inventory would be less than 10 units without production." (LO4)

17. Update the table shown in Figure 13-12 given these updated inputs: It is now the end of week 1; customer orders are 35 for week 2, 16 for week 3, 11 for week 4, 8 for week 5, and 3 for week 6. Inventory on hand is now 33 units. Use the master production scheduling rule of ordering production when projected on-hand inventory would be negative without production. (LO4)

18. Prepare a table like Figure 13-12 using the following information: The forecast for each week of an eight-week schedule is 50 units. The master production scheduling rule is to schedule

production if the projected on-hand inventory would be negative without it. Customer orders (committed) are:

Week	Customer Orders
1	52
2	35
3	20
4	12

Use a production lot size of 75 units and no beginning inventory. (LO4)

19. Verify the available-to-promise (ATP) quantities for each period of the Solved Problem 2. (LO4)

20. Prepare a table like Figure 13-12 for the following situation: The forecast is 80 units for each of the first two weeks and 60 units for each of the next three weeks. The starting inventory is 30 units. The company uses the lot size of 150 units. Also, the desired safety stock is 20 units. Committed orders are:

Week	Customer Orders
1	82
2	80
3	60
4	40
5	20

Hint: If ATP in a week is negative, reduce the previous ATP. (LO4)

21. Minco Inc. is a small company in Midway, Tennessee, which makes fused magnesia and silica.[2] In the beginning of the 1990s, Minco's continuous improvement efforts led it to look for a capacity and production planning software. To prepare for the use of software, a spreadsheet was first used to determine the capacity requirements for the main equipment (the fusion furnaces) and the production schedule for the main products. A major product had the following forecast sales and committed orders (all in thousand pounds):

	January			February			
Week	2	3	4	1	2	3	4
Forecast	56	56	56	66	66	66	66
Committed order	44	0	18				

The initial inventory was 119,000 pounds. The scheduler decided to use a lot size of 100,000 pounds per week and the minimum safety stock at the end of each week was to be 83,000 pounds. (LO4)

a. Prepare a production schedule for this product for the next seven weeks

b. Determine the available-to-promise inventory for the next seven weeks.

*22. Owens Corning makes different size Fiberglas mats in its composite materials facility in Anderson, S. Carolina.[3] For simplicity, consider only two products: light (3/4 ounce per square foot, 76 inches wide), and heavy (1.5 ounces per square foot, 76 inches wide) mats. Both are made on the same production line. The line can make 370,000 pounds of light or 185,000 pounds of heavy mats per week. The forecast weekly demand for the next eight weeks for light mats is 110,000 pounds, and for heavy mats is 120,000 pounds. The economic production quantity (EPQ) for light mats is 370,000 pounds (one week of production), and

[2]W.S. Beversluis and H.H. Jordan, "Using a Spreadsheet for Capacity Planning and Scheduling," *Production and Inventory Management Journal* 36(2), Second Quarter, 1995, pp. 12–16.

[3]M.D. Oliff and E.E. Burch, "Multi-period Production Scheduling at Owens-Corning Fiberglas," *Interfaces*, September/October 1985, pp. 25–34.

for heavy mats is 555,000 pounds (three weeks of production). That is, the line is expected to produce light mats for 1 week, and then produce the heavy mats for 3 weeks, There are 120,000 pounds of inventory of each product currently on hand. Starting with light mats in week 1, determine the planned production for the two products so that neither product's projected on hand becomes negative, but their production lot sizes are close to their EPQ. If one of the products will be short, interrupt the production of the other and start making the short product. (LO4)

MINI-CASE

Lands' End

Lands' End is a mail and phone order company for clothes. Like other retailers, its sales surge close to Christmas. The full-time equivalent (FTE) employee requirements for October to December of last year were as follows: October: 4,000 FTE, November: 6,600 FTE, and December: 7,100 FTE. Lands' End employs 4,000 FTE employees throughout the year (3,500 full time and 1,000 half-time). During November and December, Lands' End can employ up to 1,500 additional FTE part-time and temporary workers (high school students and idle workers from a local cheese factory). Also, Lands' End can use up to 2,000 FTE of overtime work (hours worked beyond an eight-hour shift in a

day). Each FTE permanent employee receives $3,000 a month. Each FTE of overtime work receives $4,500 a month. Each Temporary FTE of part-time and temporary workers receives $3,000 a month, but needs an average of $1,000 of training (charged to the first month of employment).

Questions:

1. Set up this problem as an aggregate planning problem and determine the minimum cost plan. Briefly state the trade-off analysis you used.

2. What factors, other than cost, should be considered in this aggregate planning? Explain.

MINI-CASE

Banner Good Samaritan Medical Center

Banner Good Samaritan Medical Center in Phoenix, Arizona, is a 662-bed hospital. Like other hospitals, the number of its patients increases in the winter. The full-time equivalent (FTE) nurse requirements for Q1 to Q4 of next year are forecasted to be Q1: 1,300 FTE, Q2: 1,000 FTE, Q3: 800 FTE, and Q4: 1,000 FTE. Banner Good Samaritan employs 1,000 FTE permanent nurses throughout the year. During peak season, it can employ up to 500 additional FTE temporary nurses from local temporary personnel agencies. Also, it can use up to 500 FTE of overtime (hours worked beyond an eight-hour shift in a day). Each FTE permanent nurse receives an average of $8,000 a

quarter. Each FTE of overtime work receives $12,000 a quarter. Each Temporary FTE receives $8,000 a quarter, but needs an average of $1,000 for training (charged to the first quarter of employment).

Questions:

1. Set up this problem as an aggregate planning problem and determine the minimum cost aggregate plan. Briefly state the trade-off analysis you used. Calculate the total cost. Note: if demand is less than the number of permanent nurses in a quarter, the nurses will still be paid but the idle time will be used as paid holidays and/or for further training.

2. What factors, other than cost, should be considered in this aggregate planning? Explain.

CHAPTER 14
Material Requirements Planning and Enterprise Resource Planning

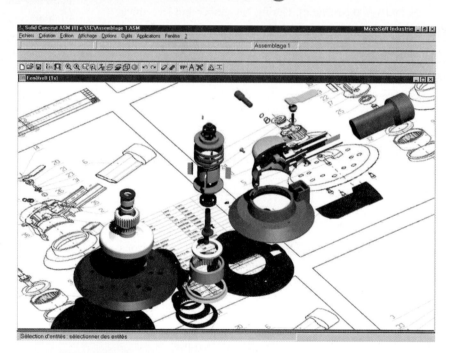

LEARNING OBJECTIVES

After completing this chapter, you should be able to:

LO1 Describe material requirements planning (MRP) and the conditions under which it is most appropriate.

LO2 Describe the inputs to MRP.

LO3 Describe the calculation of MRP, and solve typical problems.

LO4 Describe lot sizing methods, capacity requirements planning, and MRP II.

LO5 Describe enterprise resource planning (ERP).

W escast is a large car exhaust-manifold manufacturer based in Brantford, Ontario. To meet the needs of its just-in-time big car-manufacturer customers, Wescast had to become more efficient and effective in its operations. It needed to be able to track its production and inventories, and to reduce manufacturing lead times and work-in-process inventories. How did Wescast achieve this? The answer to this question and others like this is given in this chapter.

(LO1) INTRODUCTION

This chapter describes MRP (material requirements planning) and ERP (enterprise resource planning). MRP is a planning and scheduling technique primarily used for batch production of the components of assembled items. In this chapter, a component refers to a raw material, part, or sub-assembly. ERP or enterprise software is used to manage and coordinate all the resources, information, and functions of an organization from a shared database. ERP grew out of MRP software, but now also includes business (accounting) modules.

First we will show why plans for components of products require a different treatment than plans for finished goods, supplies, or spare parts.

Dependent Demand

When demand for items is derived from plans to make certain products—as it is with raw materials, parts, and subassemblies used in producing a finished product—those items are said to have **dependent demand**. For example, the parts, materials, and sub-assemblies that go into the production of a particular model of automobile have dependent demand because the amounts needed are a function of the number of cars that is planned to be produced. Conversely, demand for the *finished* cars is *independent*. The customer demand is not known before it occurs and has to be forecasted.

Independent demand of most finished goods and supplies is fairly steady once allowances are made for seasonal variations, but dependent demands tend to be sporadic or "lumpy"; large quantities are used at specific points in time with little or no usage at other times. For example, a company that produces lawn and garden equipment might make a variety of items such as lawn mowers and small tractors, but these are usually made in batches. Suppose that the products are produced as follows—in one month, push mowers; in the next month, mulching mowers; and in the third month, tractors. Some components may be used in most of the items (e.g., nuts and bolts, screws). It makes sense to have a continual inventory of these parts because they are always needed. On the other hand, some parts might be used for only one item. Consequently, demand for those parts occurs only when that item is being produced, which might be once every few months; the rest of the time, demand is zero. Thus, demand is "lumpy." Because of these tendencies, independent-demand items must be carried on a continual basis, but dependent-demand items need only be stocked just prior to the time they will be needed in the production process. Moreover, the predictability of usage of dependent-demand items implies that there is little or no need for safety stock.

Figure 14-1 illustrates key differences between independent and dependent demand, and inventory levels resulting from using inventory control models of Chapter 12 vs. MRP. The inventory control models of Chapter 12 are used for purchasing or production of items with independent demand. In this chapter, we will use MRP for planning the purchasing or production of dependent-demand items.

OVERVIEW OF MRP

Material requirements planning (MRP) is the activity that determines the plans for purchasing and production of dependent-demand components (i.e., raw materials, parts, and sub-assemblies). The production plan for a specified number of each product is converted

dependent demand
Demand for subassemblies, parts, or raw materials that are derived from the plan for production of finished goods.

material requirements planning   The activity that determines the plans for purchasing and production of dependent-demand components.

Figure 14-1

Comparison of independent and dependent demand, and inventory levels resulting from using inventory control models of Chapter 12 vs. MRP

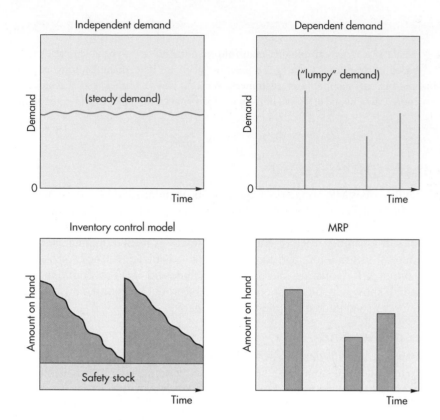

into the requirements for its sub-assemblies, parts, and raw materials, working backward from the due date of the product, using lead times and inventories on hand. This determines when and how much to order of each component. Hence, requirements for end items generate requirements for lower-level components, so that ordering, fabrication, and sub-assembly of components can be scheduled for timely completion of end items while inventory levels for components are kept reasonably low.

Historically, planning purchasing and production of components for assembled products suffered from two difficulties. One was the enormous task of setting up production schedules for products; keeping track of large numbers of raw materials, parts, and subassemblies; and coping with plan changes. The other was a lack of differentiation between independent demand and dependent demand items. All too often, techniques designed for independent-demand items were used to handle dependent-demand items, which resulted in excessive inventories.

OM in ACTION

Prairie Machine & Parts

PM&P is a medium-size industrial machines and component manufacturer for the mining sector in Saskatoon (Potash Corp is a major customer), and repairs equipment such as portable conveyor systems for potash mines. Major operations performed are machining and welding. Before 1998, PM&P used Sage Accounting software and a custom-written module for manufacturing that needed upgrading. Management chose

IndustriOS Enterprise software because it could be easily integrated with the Sage Accounting software. PM&P management is very happy with the IndustriOS software and its assistance. IndustriOS is based in Oakville, Ontario. The benefits include accurate data which is updated in real time, job scheduling and status tracking, and better cost tracking and estimation.

Sources: http://www.industrios.com/successstories/Prairie_Machine_2007_success_story.pdf; http://www.sagepfw.com/products/manufacturingaccounting.aspx; http://www.pmparts.com/index.html.

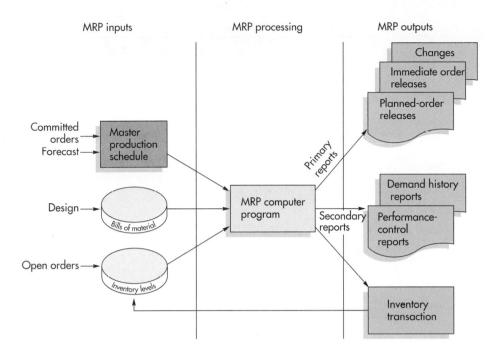

Figure 14-2

Overview of MRP system

In the 1970s, manufacturers began to recognize the importance of the distinction between independent- and dependent-demand items and to approach these two categories in different ways. Much of the burden of record keeping and determining material requirements in many companies has now been transferred to computers. A great deal of the credit for publicizing MRP and educating potential users about MRP goes to Joseph Orlicky,[1] George Plossl, Oliver Wight, and APICS.

The primary inputs to MRP are bills of materials, which tell the composition of products; a master production schedule, which tells how many finished products are desired and when; and inventory levels, lead times, and any open shop or purchase orders (already issued, being executed). Outputs from MRP include immediate and planned order releases and various reports. Figure 14-2 provides overview of MRP system.

For some applications of MRP, see "Hansen Technologies," "Keihin," and "Wescast" OM in Actions later in the chapter.

LO2 MRP INPUTS

An MRP system has three major sources of information: the master production schedule; bills of material; and inventory levels, lead times, and open orders. Let's consider each of these inputs.

Master Production Schedule

A **master production schedule (MPS)**, as described in the previous chapter, is the anticipated build schedule stating which end items are to be produced, when, and in what quantities for the next 12 weeks or so. Figure 14-3 illustrates a portion of an MPS that shows planned output for the end item X for the planning horizon. The schedule indicates that 100 units of X will be needed (e.g., for shipments to customers) at the *start* of week 4 and that another 150 units will be needed at the *start* of week 8.

master production schedule
The anticipated build schedule stating which end items are to be produced, when, and in what quantities for the next 12 weeks or so.

---

[1]Orlicky is the author of *Material Requirements Planning* (New York: McGraw-Hill, 1975).

Figure 14-3

A portion of the master production schedule for the end item X

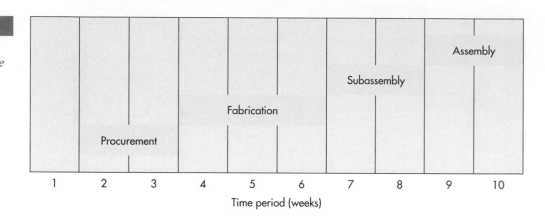

Week number

Item: X	1	2	3	4	5	6	7	8
Quantity				100				150

Figure 14-4

The planning horizon must be longer than the cumulative lead time.

Assembly

Subassembly

Fabrication

Procurement

1   2   3   4   5   6   7   8   9   10

Time period (weeks)

Recall that the quantities in an MPS are determined to satisfy customer orders and forecasts.

The MPS separates the planning horizon into a series of time periods or *time buckets*, which are expressed in weeks or days. However, the time buckets need not be of equal length. In fact, the near-term portion of an MPS may be in days, but later portions may be in weeks or months. Usually, plans for those more distant time periods are more tentative than near-term requirements.

It is important that the planning horizon be longer than the *stacked* or **cumulative lead time** necessary to produce the end items. This amounts to the sum of the lead times that sequential phases of the purchasing and production process require, as illustrated in Figure 14-4, where a total of nine weeks of lead time is needed from ordering components until final assembly is completed.

Some subassemblies are also included in the MPS if they are made to stock (and later used to assemble the final product to order).

cumulative lead time The sum of the lead times that sequential phases of a process require, from ordering of components to completion of final assembly.

Bills of Material

A **bill of material (BOM)** is a listing of all of the subassemblies, parts, and raw material that are needed to produce *one* unit of a finished product. Thus, each finished product has its own bill of material.

A bill of material is related to the assembly diagram and **product structure tree**, which provides a hierarchical diagram of the components needed to assemble a product. Figure 14-5 shows an assembly diagram for a chair, the associated product structure tree, and the indented BOM. The end item (in this case, the chair, the finished product) is shown at the top. For the assembly diagram or product structure tree, just beneath the end item are the back and front subassemblies that must be put together with the two cross bars and a seat to make up the end item; beneath each subassembly are the parts for it. Note that the quantities of each item in the product structure tree refer to the amounts needed to complete one unit of the parent at the next higher level. For example, three back supports are needed for one back assembly. For the indented BOM, the subassemblies are indented one tab to the right, and the components of each subassembly are listed under it and indented one tab further to the right.

bill of material (BOM) A listing of all of the raw material, parts, and subassemblies needed to produce one unit of a product.

product structure tree A hierarchical diagram of the components needed to assemble a product.

Assembly diagram

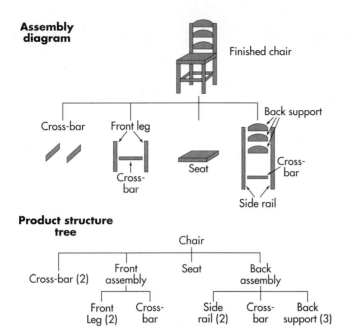

Figure 14-5

Assembly diagram, product structure tree, and indented BOM for a chair

Indented BOM
Chair
    Back Assembly
        Side rail (2)
        Cross-bar
        Back support (3)
    Seat
    Front Assembly
        Front Leg (2)
        Cross-bar
    Cross-bar (2)

OM in ACTION

SYSPRO

SYSPRO is a reasonably priced MRP/ERP software that is easy to use. Suppliers, work centres, all the raw material/parts/subassemblies/products and customers must be defined first. Then, the structure and routing (operations) of each sub-assembly and product that has components are defined. This involves listing each operation to be performed on the item and the "material" used in that operation. Using these structures and routings, customer orders or master production schedule, and inventories, SYSPRO determines the material requirements. Below is the BOM for a table (used in the solution to Problem 23 at the end of chapter).

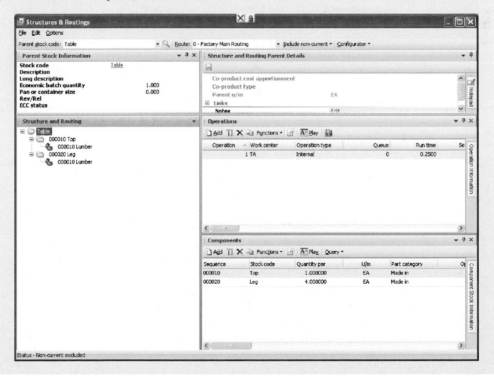

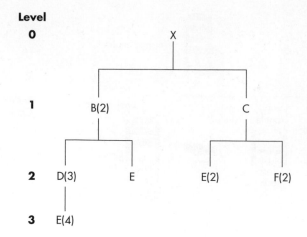

Let's consider the product structure tree shown in Figure 14-6. End item X is composed of two Bs and one C. Moreover, each B consists of three Ds and one E, and each D requires four Es. Similarly, each C is made up of two Es and two Fs. These *requirements* are listed by *level*, beginning with level 0 for the end item, then level 1 for the next level, and so on. The items at each level are *components* of the next level up and, as in a family tree, are *parents* of their respective components. For a software's use of BOM, see the "SYSPRO" OM in Action. Example 1 shows how a BOM can be used in MRP.

Example 1

Use the information presented in Figure 14-6 to do the following:

a. Determine the quantities of B, C, D, E, and F needed to assemble one X.

b. Determine the quantities of these components that will be required to assemble 10 Xs, taking into account the following inventories on hand of various components:

Component	On Hand
B	4
C	10
D	8
E	60
F	5

Solution

a.

```
                                    X: 1
                                     |
        ┌────────────────────────────────────────────────────────────┐
   B: 2×1 = 2   B(2)                                    C: 1×1 = 1   C
                 |                                                    |
        ┌────────────────┐                              ┌────────────────────┐
 D: 3×2 = 6  D(3)  E: 1×2 = 2   E              E: 2×1 = 2  E(2)  F: 2×1 = 2  F(2)
          |
 E: 4×6 = 24   E(4)
```

Thus, one X will require:
B: 2
C: 1

D: 6
E: 28 (Note that E occurs in three places, with requirements of $24 + 2 + 2 = 28$)
F: 2

b.

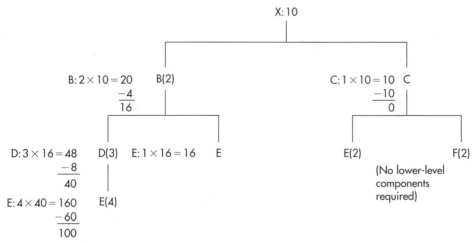

Thus, given the amounts of on-hand inventory, 10 Xs will require:

B: 16
C: 0
D: 40
E: 116 ($= 100 + 16$)
F: 0

Note that the amount on hand for each component is *netted out* (i.e., subtracted from the requirement) before determining the requirements of its children.

Determining net requirements is usually more complicated than Example 1 might suggest. The issue of *timing* is essential (i.e., when must the components be purchased or made) and must be included in the analysis.

OM in *ACTION*

SeaQuest

When there are very similar end products with only minor differences such as different-colour trims, and if the final assembly can be postponed until late in production, then it is possible to simplify the planning process by combining similar end products into an artificial product with a BOM called a planning bill. For example, SeaQuest, now part of AquaLung, a manufacturer of scuba diving equipment and wet suits in California, used the planning bill shown to the right for its Spectrum wet suit.

Each suit required 2 yards (1.8 metres) of fabric. Roughly 75 percent of suits were black and 25 percent were blue. Therefore, in the planning bill 1.5 yards of black and 0.5 yards of blue fabric were specified.

Component	Description	Unit	Qty	Level
1-7001	Fabric, Black	YD	1.5	1
1-7002	Fabric, Blue	YD	.5	1
1-7500	Bind Tape, Black	IN	300	1
1-7600	Bind Tape, Blue	IN	100	1
1-1410	Velcro Hook, Black	IN	33	1
1-1420	Velcro Hook, Blue	IN	11	1
2-3510	Airway Assembly	EA	1	1
2-8-228	Tank Band Assembly	EA	1	1
1-2567	Foam Pad	EA	1	1
1-9001	Box, Spectrum	EA	1	1

Sources: G.H. French, "Linking Design, Marketing, and Shipping for Success: A Case Study in Integration," *Production and Inventory Management Journal*, Third Quarter, 1992, pp. 44–48; http://www.aqualung.com/home.html.

Special Types of BOM. There are three special types of BOM.

A **planning bill**, also called a pseudo bill or a kit, is a combination of several BOMs (see e.g., the "SeaQuest" OM in Action on the previous page). While it does not relate to a real product, its use will result in the calculation of the right number of components to be purchased or produced. Planning bills are used to reduce the number of BOMs necessary for planning when the products have various options.

A **modular bill** is a BOM for a module. Modular bills are used to reduce the number of BOMs when a product consists of various modules, each with a few options. For example, if there are 10 modules each with 2 options, the number of product configurations is $2^{10} = 1,024$, whereas there are only $10(2) = 20$ options. Thus, a company will use the 20 modular bills to plan the purchase or production of the modules and later will assemble the final products to order.

A **phantom bill**, also called a transient bill, is for an item that is usually not kept in inventory. However, it may be sometimes needed, e.g., a spare part or a work-in-process in an assembly line. A phantom item has zero lead time and special stock code so that it will not be regularly ordered. Use of a phantom bill makes planning easier.

Comment. It is important that the bill of material accurately reflect the composition of a product, particularly since errors at one level may become magnified by the multiplication process used to determine quantity requirements of its components. As obvious as this might seem, many companies find themselves with incorrect bills of material. This makes it impossible to effectively determine material requirements; moreover, the task of correcting these records can be complex and time consuming. Accurate records are a prerequisite for effective MRP.

Inventory Levels, Lead Times, and Open Orders

Each item in stock (product, subassembly, part, or raw material) should have a separate description file that contains information about the item and, if purchased, the purchase lead time. Also, the quantity on hand (inventory balance) of each item should be updated continuously as transactions (receipts and issues) occur, and be used to net the requirements as in Example 1b.

Each manufactured or assembled item will have a configuration file that shows the operations necessary and the components used. Each operation will have a standard time for setup and per unit operation time. Using these and the number of items to be produced, the total manufacturing lead time for the batch of the item can be computed. Lead times will be used for timing orders.

Each open shop order and open purchase order (called scheduled receipt in MRP) has a quantity and due date and will be considered projected on-hand inventory on its due date (and used to net the requirements).

(LO3) MRP PROCESSING, UPDATING, AND OUTPUTS

MRP Processing

MRP processing takes the end items' requirements specified by the MPS and "explodes" them into *time-phased* requirements for fabrication or assembly of subassemblies and fabricated parts, and purchase of purchased parts and raw material using the bills of material, offset by the lead times and netted for any inventory on hand or scheduled receipts (on order). You can see the time-phasing of requirements in the *assembly time chart* in Figure 14-7. For example, raw materials D, F, and I must be purchased at the start of week 2, part C at the start of week 4, and part H at the start of week 5 in order for 100 units of the end item to be available for delivery at the start of week 12. The figure also shows the planned fabrication or assembly start times of other items.

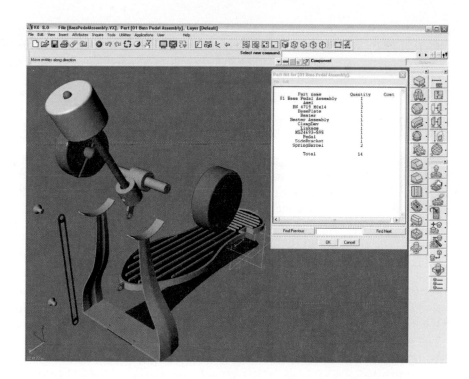

VX Corporation's CAD/CAM software can be used not only for product design, but also to prepare parts lists. This screen shows a parts list for a bass drum pedal along with a three-dimensional view of the product subassemblies.

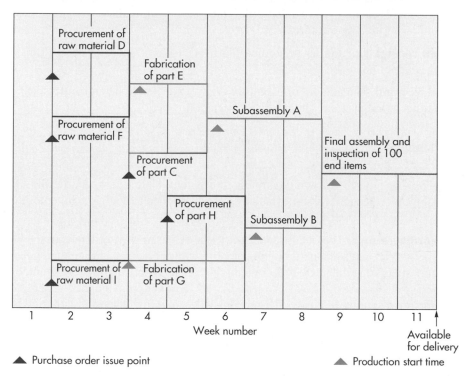

Assembly time chart showing material purchase points and production start times needed to meet scheduled delivery of 100 units of the end item at the start of week 12

Note that the length of horizontal lines represents the lead times. For example, the purchase lead time for raw material D is two weeks, and the manufacturing lead time for 100 units of part E has been calculated to be two weeks. This is based on the speed of the operation(s) involved in fabricating part E.

The quantities that are generated by exploding the bills of material are *gross requirements*; they do not take into account any inventory that is currently on hand or is due to be received (scheduled receipt). The materials that a company must actually acquire to meet the demand generated by the MPS are the *net requirements*.

Lectronic is a small Mississauga-based company with an innovative product: a radio-controlled golf caddy. Lectronic has been using the full version (including the MRP module) of the Business System from Minotaur Software of Brampton for 12 years.

The determination of the net requirements (*netting*) is the core of MRP processing. One accomplishes this by subtracting from gross requirements the sum of inventory on hand and any scheduled receipts, and then adding in safety stock requirements, if applicable:

$$\begin{array}{l} \text{Net} \\ \text{Requirements in} \\ \text{period } t \end{array} = \begin{array}{l} \text{Gross} \\ \text{requirements} \\ \text{in period} \\ t \end{array} - \begin{array}{l} \text{Projected} \\ \text{inventory at} \\ \text{the start of} \\ \text{period } t \end{array} - \begin{array}{l} \text{Scheduled} \\ \text{receipts} \end{array} + \begin{array}{l} \text{Safety} \\ \text{stock} \end{array} \qquad (14\text{-}1)$$

If the formula gives a negative value, then there is no net requirement (i.e., it is 0). For simplicity, we will omit safety stock from the calculations in the examples and most problems. Net requirements are sometimes adjusted to include an allowance for waste; but for simplicity, this too will not be included in the examples or most problems.

The timing and sizes of orders (i.e., material ordered from suppliers or work started within the company) are determined by *planned-order releases*. The timing of the receipts of these quantities is indicated by *planned-order receipts*. Depending on ordering policy, the planned-order releases may have a minimum level, may be multiples of a specified quantity (e.g., 50 units), or may be equal to the quantity needed at that time (called lot-for-lot ordering). Example 2 will illustrate the difference between these ordering policies as well as the general concept of time-phasing material requirements in MRP. As you work through the example, you may find the following list of terms helpful.

Gross requirement. The demand for an item *during* a time period (a week or a day) without regard to the amount on hand. For an end item, this is shown in the MPS; for a component, this is equal to the planned-order release of its immediate "parent" multiplied by the number of item in one parent.

Scheduled receipt. Open order scheduled to arrive from a vendor or shop floor in the *beginning* of a period.

Projected on-hand. The amount of inventory that is expected to be on hand at the *beginning* of a time period: it equals the scheduled receipt this period plus any ending inventory expected from the last period.

Net requirement. The actual amount needed in a time period.

Planned-order receipt. The quantity planned to be received in the *beginning* of a period. Under lot-for-lot ordering, it will equal net requirement. Under lot-size ordering, it may exceed net requirement. We assume that any excess is added to available inventory in the beginning of the *next* time period.

Planned-order release. The quantity planned to be released (i.e., ordered) in the beginning of a period. It equals planned-order receipt offset by lead time. This amount generates gross requirement(s) at the next level down in the BOM. When an order is executed (i.e., the planned-order release of week 1 is released), it is removed from planned-order releases and receipts rows, and is entered in the scheduled receipts row, a lead-time period later.

These quantities are used in a time-phased plan in the following format. The column for period 0 is used to show beginning on-hand inventory.

gross requirement The demand for an item during a time period.

scheduled receipt Open order scheduled to arrive from a vendor or shop floor.

projected on-hand Expected amount of inventory that will be on hand at the beginning of a time period.

net requirement The actual amount needed in a time period.

planned-order receipt Quantity planned to be received in the beginning of a period.

planned-order release Quantity planned to be released (i.e., ordered) in the beginning of a period; that is, planned-order receipt offset by lead time.

Week or day number	0	1	2	3	4	5	6	7	8
Item:									
Gross requirements									
Scheduled receipts									
Projected on-hand									
Net requirements									
Planned-order receipts									
Planned-order releases									

Example 2

A company that produces wood shutters has received two orders for a particular model of wood shutters: 100 units are due for delivery at the start of week 4 and 150 units are due for delivery at the start of week 8. Each shutter consists of two frames and four slatted wood sections. The wood sections are purchased, and the purchase lead time is one week. The frames are also purchased, and the purchase lead time is two weeks. Assembly of the shutters requires one week for lot sizes of 100 to 200 shutters. There is a scheduled receipt of 70 wood sections from the vendor at the beginning of week 1. Currently, there is no on-hand inventory. Determine the size and timing of planned-order releases necessary to meet delivery requirements under each of these conditions:

Lot-for-lot ordering (i.e., order sizes are equal to net requirements).

Lot-size ordering with a minimum lot size of 320 units for frames and multiples of 70 units for wood sections.

a. Develop a production schedule for shutters:

Week number:	1	2	3	4	5	6	7	8
Quantity:				100				150

b. Develop a product structure tree:

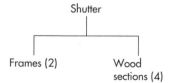

Shutter
Frames (2) Wood sections (4)

c. Using *lot-for-lot ordering*, the processing is shown in Figure 14-8.

At the start of week 4, the production schedule calls for 100 shutters to be ready for delivery and no shutters are projected to be on hand, so the net requirements are 100 shutters. Therefore, planned-order receipt for week 4 equals 100 shutters. Because shutter assembly for 100 units requires one week, this means a planned-order release at the start of week 3. Using the same logic, 150 shutters must be assembled during week 7 in order to be available for delivery at the start of week 8.

The planned-order release of 100 shutters at the start of week 3 means that 200 frames (gross requirement) must be available at that time. Because none are expected to be on hand, this generates net requirement of 200 frames and necessitates planned-order receipt of 200 frames by the start of week 3. With a two-week purchase lead time, this means that the company must order 200 frames at the start of week 1. Similarly, the planned-order release of 150 shutters at the start of week 7 generates gross and net requirements of 300 frames for week 7 as well as planned-order receipt for that time. The two-week purchase lead time means that the company must order frames at the start of week 5.

The planned-order release of 100 shutters at the start of week 3 also generates gross requirement of 400 wood sections at that time. However, because 70 wood sections are expected to be received (scheduled receipt) at the start of week 1 and will be on hand, net requirement is $400 - 70 = 330$ for week 3. This means a planned-order receipt of 330 by the start of week 3. Since purchase lead time is one week, the purchase order must be issued (planned-order release) at the beginning of week 2.

Similarly, the planned-order release of 150 shutters in week 7 generates gross requirement of 600 (150×4) wood sections at that point. Because no on-hand inventory of wood sections is projected for week 7, net requirement is also 600, and planned-order receipt is 600 units at the start of week 7. Again, the one-week purchase lead time means 600 sections should be purchased (planned-order release) at the start of week 6.

Figure 14-8

MRP tables with lot-for-lot ordering for Example 2

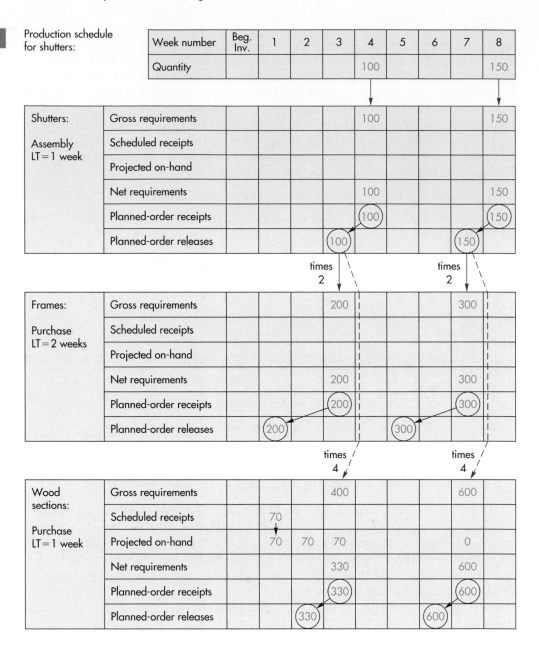

Production schedule for shutters:

Week number	Beg. Inv.	1	2	3	4	5	6	7	8
Quantity					100				150

Shutters:
Assembly
LT = 1 week

	Beg. Inv.	1	2	3	4	5	6	7	8
Gross requirements					100				150
Scheduled receipts									
Projected on-hand									
Net requirements					100				150
Planned-order receipts					(100)				(150)
Planned-order releases				(100)				(150)	

times 2   times 2

Frames:
Purchase
LT = 2 weeks

	Beg. Inv.	1	2	3	4	5	6	7	8
Gross requirements				200				300	
Scheduled receipts									
Projected on-hand									
Net requirements				200				300	
Planned-order receipts				(200)				(300)	
Planned-order releases		(200)				(300)			

times 4   times 4

Wood sections:
Purchase
LT = 1 week

	Beg. Inv.	1	2	3	4	5	6	7	8
Gross requirements				400				600	
Scheduled receipts		70							
Projected on-hand	70	70	70					0	
Net requirements				330				600	
Planned-order receipts				(330)				(600)	
Planned-order releases			(330)				(600)		

d. Under lot-size ordering, the only difference is the possibility that planned receipts will exceed net requirements. The excess is recorded as projected on-hand inventory in the beginning of the following week. For example, in Figure 14-9, the minimum order size for frames is 320 units, but net requirement for week 3 is 200; thus, 320 units are ordered resulting in an excess of $320 - 200 = 120$ units, which become projected on-hand inventory in the start of next week. Similarly, net frame requirement is $300 - 120 = 180$ units in week 7, thus 320 units are ordered, and the excess of $320 - 180 = 140$ units becomes projected on hand inventory in the start of week 8. The same thing happens with wood sections; the excess of planned-order receipts in weeks 3 and 7 is added to projected-on-hand in the start of weeks 4 and 8. Note that the order size for wood sections must be in *multiples* of 70; for week 3 it is 5 times 70 because 350 is the first multiple of 70 larger than 330, and for week 7 it is 9 times 70 because 630 is the first multiple of 70 larger than 580.

Production schedule for shutters:

Week number	Beg. Inv.	1	2	3	4	5	6	7	8
Quantity					100				150

Figure 14-9

MRP tables with lot-size ordering for Example 2

Shutters assembly:

LT = 1 week

Lot size = lot-for-lot

	Beg. Inv.	1	2	3	4	5	6	7	8
Gross requirements					100				150
Scheduled receipts									
Projected on-hand									
Net requirements					100				150
Planned-order receipts					(100)				(150)
Planned-order releases				(100)				(150)	

times 2

Frames purchase:

LT = 2 weeks

Lot size = minimum of 320

	Beg. Inv.	1	2	3	4	5	6	7	8
Gross requirements				200				300	
Scheduled receipts									
Projected on-hand					120	120	120	120	140
Net requirements				200				180	
Planned-order receipts				(320)				(320)	
Planned-order releases		(320)				(320)			

times 4

Wood sections purchase:

LT = 1 week

Lot size = multiples of 70

	Beg. Inv.	1	2	3	4	5	6	7	8
Gross requirements				400				600	
Scheduled receipts		70							
Projected on-hand		70	70	70	20	20	20	20	50
Net requirements				330				580	
Planned-order receipts				(350)				(630)	
Planned-order releases			(350)				(630)		

Example 2 is useful for describing some of the main features of MRP processing, but it understates the enormousness of the task of keeping track of material requirements, especially in situations where the same subassemblies, parts, or raw materials are used in a number of different products. Differences in timing of demands, revisions caused by late deliveries, high scrap rates, and cancelled orders all have an impact on processing.

Consider the two product structure trees shown in Figure 14-10. Note that both products A and C have D as a component. Suppose we want to develop a material requirements plan for D given this additional information: the demand for A is 80 units at the start of week 4 and the demand for C is 50 units at the start of week 5; there is a beginning inventory of 110 units of D on hand, all items have manufacturing or purchase lead times of one week, and we order D using lot-for-lot ordering. The plan is shown in Figure 14-11. Note that the requirements for B and E are not shown because they are not a "parent" of D.

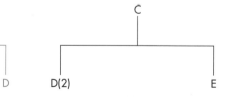

Figure 14-10

Two different products (A and C) having D as a component

Figure 14-11

Material requirements plan for component D

Production schedule

Week number		1	2	3	4	5	6
Quantity (A, C)					80	50	

A Assembly LT=1	Beg. Inv.	1	2	3	4	5	6
Gross requirements					80		
Scheduled receipts							
Projected on-hand							
Net requirements					80		
Planned-order receipts					80		
Planned-order releases				(80)			

times 1

C Assembly LT=1	Beg. Inv.	1	2	3	4	5	6
Gross requirements						50	
Scheduled receipts							
Projected on-hand							
Net requirements						50	
Planned-order receipts						50	
Planned-order releases					(50)		

times 2

D Purchase LT=1	Beg. Inv.	1	2	3	4	5	6
Gross requirements				80	100		
Scheduled receipts							
Projected on-hand	110	110	110	110	30		
Net requirements					70		
Planned-order receipts					70		
Planned-order releases				70			

pegging Identifying the parent items that have generated a given set of requirements for an item.

The term **pegging** denotes working the MRP processing in reverse; that is, identifying the parent items that have generated a given set of requirements for some item such as D. Although this may appear simple enough given the product structure trees and tables shown in this chapter, when multiple products are involved, it is more complex. Pegging enables managers to determine which product(s) will be affected if an order for an item such as D is late.

The importance of the computer becomes evident when you consider that a typical company would have hundreds of end items for which it needs to develop material requirements plans, each with its own set of components. Inventories on hand and on order, planned order releases, and so on must all be updated as changes and rescheduling occur. Without the aid of a computer, the task would be hopeless.

OM in ACTION

Hansen Technologies

Hansen Technologies, Burr Ridge, Illinois, makes components (e.g., valves, pumps, controls) for industrial refrigeration systems. Until a few years ago, Hansen had a custom software that had limited functionality and was expensive to change. A paper work order had to accompany each job through the operations. Then, the company bought Microsoft Dynamics (previously Great Plain) ERP. MS Dynamics has streamlined order processing and manufacturing workflow, which has enabled on-line tracking and has resulted in 15 percent improvement in on-time delivery. The MRP module has resulted in less shortage and in receiving quantity discounts by sharing planned orders with suppliers.

Source: http://www.microsoft.com/dynamics/en/us/products/gp-customer-stories.aspx?casestudyid=48428, accessed August 30, 2009.

Updating the System

A material requirements plan is not a static document. As time passes, some orders will have been completed, other orders will be nearing completion, and new orders will have to be released. In addition, there may have been changes to orders, such as changes in quantity, delays, missed deliveries of parts or raw materials, and so on. Hence, a material requirements plan is a "living" document, one that changes over time. And what we refer to as "Period 1" (i.e., the current period) is continually moving ahead; so what is now Period 2 will soon be Period 1. In a sense, requirements plans such as these have *a rolling horizon*, which means that plans are updated and revised so that they reflect the next set of periods.

The two basic approaches used to update MRP tables are *regenerative* and *net change*. Regenerative MRP is run periodically; Net-change MRP is continuously updated.

Regenerative MRP is essentially a batch-type approach. All inputs to MRP are updated (e.g., inventory on-hand, receipts), the MRP quantities are blanked, and the MRP is processed again.

In **net-change MRP**, the requirements plan is modified to reflect changes as they occur. If some defective purchased parts had to be returned to a vendor, the manager can enter this information into the system as soon as it becomes known. Only the *changes* are "exploded" through the system, level by level; the entire plan would not be regenerated.

Regenerative MRP is best suited for fairly stable situations, whereas net-change MRP is best suited for situations that have frequent changes. The obvious disadvantage of regenerative MRP is the potential amount of lag between the time information becomes available and the time it can be incorporated into the material requirements plan. One way around this is to use a day as the time bucket (instead of a week) and rerun the MRP every night.

Processing costs are typically less using regenerative MRP; changes that occur in a given time period could ultimately cancel each other, thereby avoiding the need to modify and then remodify the plan.

Even a small change in requirements of an item at the top of the product structure tree can have large effects on items down the tree. This is referred to as MRP system *nervousness*. This is especially a problem if it results in changes in purchase or shop orders. MRP system nervousness is similar to the bullwhip effect in supply chains (see Chapter 11). As stated in Chapter 13, one solution to this problem is to freeze the master production schedule for the near future (e.g., next four weeks).

Backflushing is "exploding" an end item's BOM periodically to determine the quantities of the various components that must have been used to make the item (and updating the inventory on-hand quantities for the components). This eliminates the need to collect detailed usage information on the production floor.

MRP Outputs

MRP systems have the ability to provide management with a fairly broad range of outputs, in addition to the MRP tables described previously. These are often classified as *primary reports*, which are the main reports, and *secondary reports*, which are optional outputs.

regenerative MRP Recalculates all the MRP quantities periodically.

net-change MRP Immediately updates only MRP tables affected by a change.

backflushing Exploding an end item's BOM to determine the quantities of the components that must have been used to make the item.

Primary Reports. Immediate order releases, planned-order releases, and changes are part of primary reports:

immediate order releases Authorization for the execution of week 1 planned-order releases.

1. **Immediate order releases** authorize the execution of week 1 planned-order releases.
2. **Planned order releases** indicate the amount and timing of future orders.
3. Changes to open orders: revisions to due dates and quantities, e.g., expedite, de-expedite, move forward, and move backward.

Secondary Reports. Performance-control and demand history reports belong to secondary reports.

performance-control reports Evaluation of system operation, including deviations from plans and cost information.

demand history reports Data useful for forecasting future material requirements.

1. **Performance-control reports** evaluate system operation. They aid managers by measuring deviations from plans, including missed deliveries and stock-outs, and by providing information that can be used to assess cost performance.
2. **Demand history reports** are useful in forecasting future inventory requirements. They include net requirements and other data that can be used to forecast future material requirements.

The wide range of outputs generally permits users to tailor MRP to their particular needs.

(LO4) OTHER CONSIDERATIONS

Safety Stock

Theoretically, inventory systems with dependent demand should not require safety stock below the end-item level. This is one of the main advantages of the MRP approach. Supposedly, safety stock is not needed because the manager can project the requirements once the MPS has been established. Practically, however, there may be exceptions. For example, a bottleneck process or one with varying scrap rates can cause shortages in downstream operations. Furthermore, shortages may occur if orders are late or fabrication or assembly times are longer than expected.

MRP systems deal with these problems in several ways. The manager's first step is to identify activities or operations that are subject to variability and to determine the extent of that variability. When lead times are variable, the concept of safety *time* instead of safety *stock* is often used. This results in scheduling orders for arrival or completion sufficiently ahead of the time they are needed in order to eliminate or substantially reduce the element of chance in waiting for those items. It is important in general to make sure that lead times are accurate. If safety stock is needed because of possible quality problems resulting in scrap, planned order release amounts can be increased by a percentage.

Lot Sizing

lot sizing Choosing a lot size for a purchase or production order.

Determining a lot size to purchase or to produce an order is an important issue in inventory management for both independent- and dependent-demand items. This is called **lot sizing**. For independent-demand items, managers often use economic order quantity or economic production quantity. For dependent-demand systems, however, a wider variety of models is used to determine lot sizes, mainly because no single model has a clear advantage over the others. Some of the most popular models for lot sizing are described in this section.

A primary goal of inventory management for both independent- and dependent-demand items is to minimize the sum of annual ordering cost (or setup cost) and holding cost. With independent demand, the demand is frequently distributed uniformly throughout the year. However, demand tends to be much more lumpy for dependent demand, and the planning horizon is shorter (e.g., three months), so economic lot sizes are usually much more difficult to identify. See Figure 14-12 for an example of lumpy demand for a part.

OM in ACTION

Keihin

Keihin Corp manufactures fuel systems, electronic controls, and heating-ventilation-air-conditioning for Honda. In North America, it has three plants. Before 1995, each plant had stand-alone personal computers running different software, with no coordination among the plants. In view of changing customer schedules and use of JIT ordering by Honda, Keihin adopted Glovia ERP, written by a subsidiary of Fujitsu, as its integrative system that uses Oracle's database. The implementation started in one plant and took only two months. Orders from Honda arrive 10 to 12 times a day by EDI, and go into Customer Releasing module of Glovia from which the production sequence is determined, and then go to the Supplier Releasing module, which allows suppliers to log in and see the daily sequenced requirements of Keihin. The benefits of Glovia include the ability to use 15-minute planning intervals, accuracy, trial-and-error production planning (in the Factory Planning module), constant tracking of inventory, reliability, and ability to display Japanese characters. As a result, inventories have been reduced from four days to half a day. Also, use of the same software in all plants has led to development of expertise by tech staff.

Sources: http://www.glovia.com/html/news/casestudies/keihin. aspx; "Manufacturers Look to ERP for the "Granularity" Needed for Lean, Global Supply Chains," *Manufacturing Business Technology*, January 2007, 25(1), p. 33.

Managers can usually realize economies by grouping consecutive orders. This would be the case if the additional cost incurred by holding the extra units until they were used led to a savings in setup or ordering cost. This determination can be very complex at times for two reasons. First, combining the demands for some of the periods into a single order, particularly for middle-level or end items, has a cascading effect down through the product structure tree; that is, in order to achieve this grouping, you must also group items at lower levels in the tree and incorporate their setup and holding costs into the decision. Second, the uneven period demands and the relatively short planning horizon require continual recalculation and updating of lot sizes.

	Period				
	1	2	3	4	5
Demand	70	50	1	80	4
Cumulative demand	70	120	121	201	205

Figure 14-12

Lumpy demand for a part

The choice of a lot-sizing technique must take into account the nature of demand (degree of uniformity), the relative importance of holding cost versus ordering (or setup) cost, and any other considerations that affect ordering. No single method is suited to all conditions.

Regardless of the lot-sizing method in use, there is always the possibility of adjustments in order sizes due to allowance for shrinkage or scrap, minimum and maximum order quantities established by management or supplier (e.g., do not order more than five months' supply), and operating or shipping constraints (e.g., 200 pieces per run or 12 dozen per shipment). Below are two of the more common lot sizing methods.

Fixed-Interval Ordering. This type of ordering provides coverage for some predetermined number of periods (e.g., two or three weeks). In some instances, the span is simply arbitrary; in other cases, a review of historical demand patterns may lead to a more rational designation of order interval. The rule can be modified when common sense suggests a better way. For example, take a look at the demand shown in Figure 14-12. Using two-period intervals, an order size of 120 units would cover the first two periods. However, the demand in period 3 is so small that it would make sense to combine it with the demand during the first two periods; that is, order 121 units for the first three periods.

Part-Period Method. This method provides a better way to determine the number of periods to order for at the same time. The part-period method, like the EOQ, attempts to balance setup (or ordering) and holding costs. The term *part period* refers to holding a part or parts over a number of periods. For instance, if 10 parts (or units) were held for two periods, this would be $10 \times 2 = 20$ part periods. The economic part period (EPP) can be calculated as the ratio of setup (or ordering) cost to the cost to hold a unit for one period. Thus, the formula for calculating the EPP is:

$$EPP = \frac{\text{Setup (or ordering) cost}}{\text{Unit holding cost per period}}$$

(14-2)

To determine an order size that is consistent with the EPP, various order sizes equal to various cumulative demands are examined, and each one's number of part periods is determined. The one that comes closest to the EPP is selected as the best lot size. Example 3 illustrates this approach.

Example 3

Use the part-period method to determine production run sizes for the following demands (i.e., net requirements) for a manufactured part:

				Period				
	1	**2**	**3**	**4**	**5**	**6**	**7**	**8**
Demand	60	40	20	2	30	—	70	50
Cumulative demand	60	100	120	122	152	152	222	272

Setup cost is $80 per production run for this item, and unit holding cost is $.95 per period.

Solution

1. First calculate the EPP: EPP = $80/$.95 = 84.21, which rounds to 84 part periods. This is the target.

2. Next, try the cumulative lot sizes, beginning with 60, until the part periods approximate the EPP. The calculations of part periods indicate that 122 units should be ordered to be available at period 1 to cover the demand for the first 4 periods (see below). Repeat this process starting at period 5, which results in 100 units to be available at period 5 to cover periods 5 to 7. The next lot will be ordered for period 8, but there is insufficient information now to determine its size.

Period When Order Is Placed	Lot Size	Extra Inventory Carried	× Periods Carried	= Part Periods	Cumulative Part Periods
1	60	0	0	0	0
	100	40	1	40	40
	120	20	2	40	80
	122	2	3	6	86*
5	30	0	0	0	0
	100	70	2	140	140**
8	50	0	0	0	0

*Closer to 84 (than 80)
**Closer to 84 (than 0).

The part-period method worked well for the first lot size because the cumulative number of part periods is close to the EPP, but the effect of lumpy demand is apparent for the second lot size of 100 (140 part periods is not very close to 84 part periods).

Capacity Requirements Planning

capacity requirements planning The process of determining short-term capacity requirements of MRP.

Capacity requirements planning (CRP) is the process of determining short-term capacity requirements of MRP. The inputs to CRP are planned-order releases of MRP for manufactured or assembled items, the current shop load, routing information, and job times. The output of CRP is load reports for each work centre.

A company usually generates an MPS initially, which may or may not be feasible given the capacities of the production system. It is often necessary to run it through MRP and then CRP in order to obtain a clearer picture of actual requirements, which can then be compared to available capacities. If it turns out that the MPS is not feasible, management may either increase the capacity of overloaded work centre(s) (e.g., through overtime) or to revise the MPS. In the latter case, this may entail several revisions, each of which is run through the MRP and CRP system until a feasible plan is obtained. At that point, the master production schedule is *frozen*, at least for the near term, thus establishing a firm schedule from which to plan requirements.

Figure 14-13 presents an overview of the capacity requirements planning process. The process begins with a proposed or tentative master production schedule that must be tested for feasibility and possibly adjusted before it becomes permanent. The proposed schedule is processed using MRP to determine the material requirements. These are then translated into resource (i.e., capacity) requirements for items made in-house involving assembly or fabrication. This is often in the form of a series of **load reports** for each department or work centre, which compares known and expected future capacity requirements with projected capacity availability. Figure 14-14 illustrates the nature of a load report. It shows expected resource requirements (i.e., usage) for jobs currently being worked on and the future planned-order releases. Given this sort of information, the manager can more easily determine whether capacity is sufficient to satisfy these requirements. In the load report illustrated in

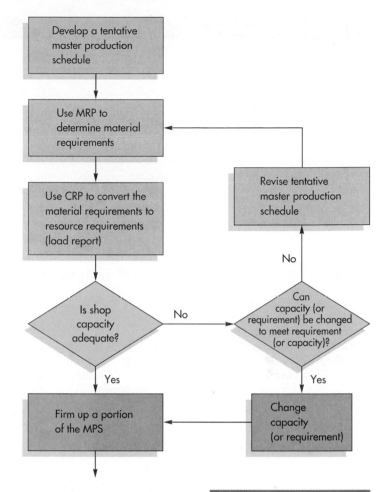

Figure 14-14, planned-order releases in time period 4 will cause an overload. However, it appears possible to accommodate demand by shifting some orders to adjacent periods. In cases where capacity is insufficient, a manager may be able to increase capacity by scheduling overtime or transferring personnel from other areas if this is possible and economical or else revise the master production schedule and repeat the process until an acceptable master production schedule is obtained.

If the master production schedule must be revised, this generally means that the manager must assign priorities to orders if some orders will be finished later than originally planned.

One note of caution is in order concerning the load reports. Often, the load reports are only approximations, and they may not give a true picture because the loading does not take into account scheduling and queuing delays. Consequently, it is possible to experience system backups even though a load report implies sufficient capacity to handle projected loads.

An important aspect of capacity requirements planning is the conversion of quantity requirements into time requirements. This is accomplished by multiplying each period's quantity requirements by standard time per unit plus a setup time per production run. For instance, if 10 units of product A are scheduled in the fabrication department and each unit has a standard time of 2 hours plus a set-up time of 8 hours for the batch, then 10 units of A converts into:

10 units × 2 hours/unit + 8 = 28 hours

By the way, this is the manufacturing lead time for fabricating 10 units of A.

Figure 14-13

The capacity requirements planning (CRP) process

load reports Department or work centre reports that compare known and expected future capacity requirements with projected capacity availability.

OM in ACTION http://www.cat.com

Caterpillar

Caterpillar's Track-type Tractors (CTTT) division makes Bulldozers. In mid-1990s, CTTT went through a long labour strike that destroyed labour–management trust. The new chairman instituted a Common Values program to restore trust, mutual respect, and teamwork. After a few years, there were still too many emergencies and too much time spent searching for parts, and unreliable deliveries of parts to dealers. Also, manufacturing did not trust marketing's forecasts, which frequently overestimated the demand. So in 1999 the division was mandated to certify for Oliver Wight International's Class A certification in Planning and Control. Oliver Wight was one of the originators of MRP, and established a certification program

so that companies could learn to perform effective production planning (called MRP II). To combat communication issues, Oliver Wight consultants served as change agents and independent observers. They instituted formal processes so that people started meeting regularly and working together. The major initiative was Sales & Operations Planning (S&OP, see the previous chapter). Classes were conducted for middle managers and planners/schedulers on S&OP and developing valid schedules. Every operator was trained for two hours on inventory record and BOM accuracy. As a result, CTTT's on-time delivery is now 98 percent, inventory of dealers are down, and use of overtime and expedited freight is down significantly.

Source: As reported at http://www.oliverweight-americas.com/cust_profiles/pdf/caterpillarttt.pdf.

An example of a work centre or department's load report

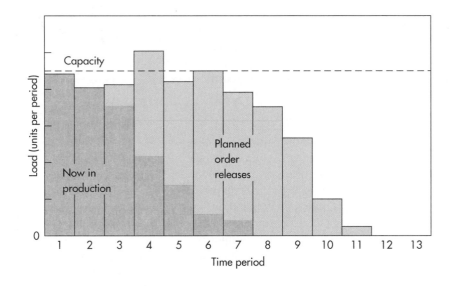

MRP II

manufacturing resource planning (MRP II) Expanded system for production planning and scheduling, involving sales and operations planning, MPS, MRP, CRP, and detailed scheduling.

In the early 1980s, material requirements planning was expanded into a broader system for planning and scheduling the resources of manufacturing companies. This expanded system was dubbed **MRP II** (two), which is also referred to as **manufacturing resource planning**. MRP II is a *closed-loop MRP* which means that it involves the whole production planning process, starting with sales and operations planning; then MPS, MRP, and CRP; and finally detailed scheduling, with feedback going back up (see Figure 14-15).

See the "Caterpillar" OM in Action for an example of the MRP II implementation.

enterprise resource planning (ERP) Or enterprise software, is used to manage and coordinate all the resources, information, and functions of an organization from a shared database.

 ERP

ERP (enterprise resource planning), or enterprise software, is used to manage and coordinate all the resources, information, and functions of an organization from a shared database. ERP involves *standardized* record keeping that will permit *information sharing*.

ERP became popular in the 1990s as MRP II began to fade and when enterprises were revamping their legacy mainframe computer systems in anticipation of possible Year 2000

OM in ACTION

Wescast

Wescast is a large Brantford, Ontario–based car exhaust manifold manufacturer. In the late 1990s, Wescast was looking for a software to integrate its various functions including order taking, production scheduling, and EDI, under pressure from its big automaker customers, which demanded JIT delivery. Wescast bought TRANS4M ERP from Agilisys (now called Infor) and implemented it in phases, module by module. TRANS4M receives orders from automakers, schedules the orders, releases purchase orders to suppliers, and releases shop orders automatically. As a result, inventories have been cut from 10 days down to 3 to 4 days of supply.

Sources: "Supplier Slashed Inventory," *Manufacturing Systems*, October 1999, pp. 25A–28A; http://www.wescast.com; http://www.infor.com/company/news/pressroom/pressreleases/14006.

(Y2K) problems. Tier 1 ERPs at that time, such as SAP, PeopleSoft, J.D. Edwards, BAAN, and Oracle cost millions of dollars to buy and implement, and had a high annual maintenance fee. But top managers felt that they had no choice and jumped on the bandwagon. Because of their complexity, the implementation of most ERPs took many years. The complexity was due to the fact that the software had hundreds of features. For example, Tier 1 ERPs are multi-currency and multi-language.

However, Tier 1 ERPs offered capabilities not offered by accounting software, such as Great Plains and ACCPAC, which primarily kept track of transactions. Tier 1 ERPs included high-volume fast databases that could be connected directly to supplier systems, and modules to perform HR, manufacturing planning and control, material management, customer relationship management (CRM), and e-commerce including Web stores directly connected to the database. They also provided industry-specific solutions and the ability to control work flow such as enforcing the authorization requirement for a high-dollar purchase by a buyer. Since the mid-1990s, many mid-market accounting software programs have moved closer to become complete business systems, even including manufacturing modules. Microsoft has also entered this market by buying Great Plains, Navision, and Solomon accounting software, and even introduced its own Axapta (now these software are called Microsoft Dynamics GP, Nav, Sl, and Ax, respectively).

The difference between Tier 1 ERPs and Tier 2 ERPs has shrunk. At the same time, many companies have realized that the high cost and complexity of Tier 1 ERPs are not worth it. Nowadays, companies are hardly buying Tier 1 ERPs. As a result, ERP companies such as SAP are providing mid-market products such as SAP Business One. Also, there has been heavy consolidation. For example, PeopleSoft bought J.D. Edwards in 2003 and Oracle bought PeopleSoft in 2004, and Baan is now part of Infor. For a

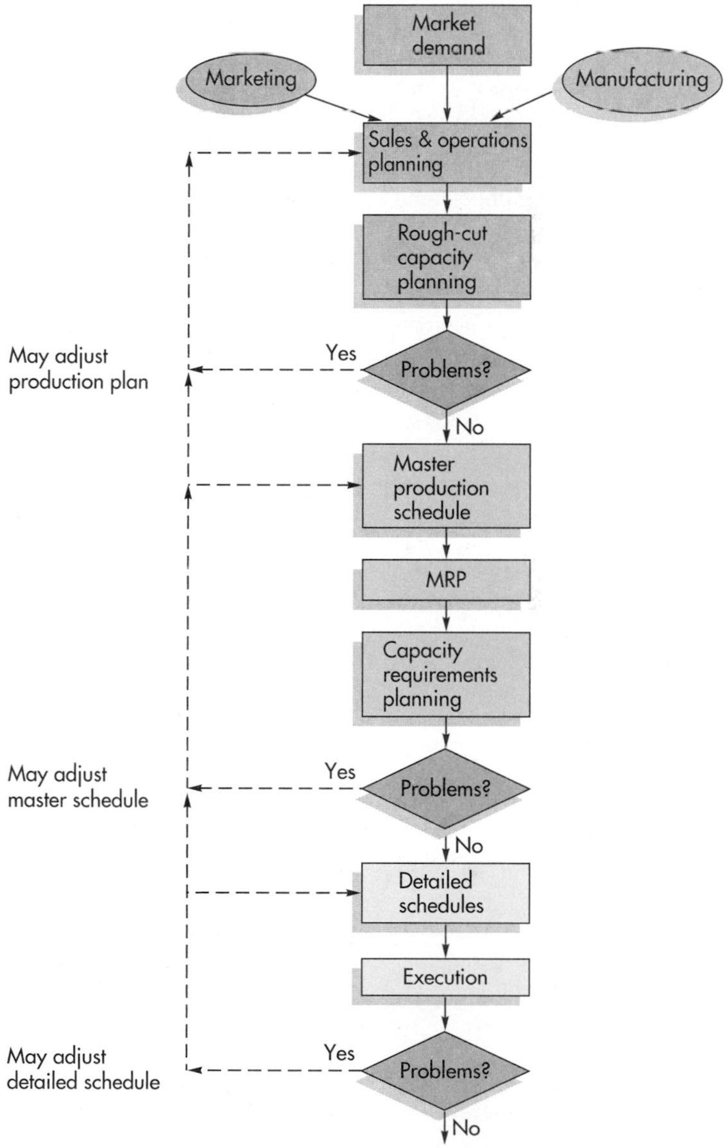

Figure 14-15

An overview of MRP II process

Some SYSPRO Applications

Bonte Foods (http://www.bonte.ca)

Bonte Foods of Dieppe, NB, produces meat for donair/gyro and pizza, bread for pita and pizza, and various sauces for donair and pizza. It employs 150 workers and has a 66,000 ft^2 plant. Being a food processor, Bonte has put in place an HACCP quality management system. However, Bonte did not have a manufacturing or processing software. When Bonte started to use SYSPRO ERP, the greatest benefits were in (1) being able to track production lots for the HACCP system, and (2) being able to keep inventory records and use them in inventory control decision making.

Natural Factors (http://naturalfactors.com/ca/en)

In its plants in Coquitlam, Burnaby, Okanagon, Toronto, and Everett Washington, Natural Factors makes natural personal health tablets and capsules for distribution worldwide. Every day, it packs thousands of bottles for hundreds of sales orders. In 1992, it started using SYSPRO ERP. The advantages are that SYSPRO is intuitive and uses common terminology, it provides lot traceability (back to the raw material) for quality control, and allows central control (from Coquitlam) and decentralized availability. The new WEB service module allows remote inventory status checking, sale order entry, and access to 3PL (Third Party Logistics) tracking within SYSPRO.

Julian Ceramic Tile Inc (http://www.juliantile.com)

Julian Ceramic Tile, a small company, imports ceramic tiles and sells them from its four warehouses in Burnaby, Edmonton, Calgary, and Winnipeg. Since 1994, Julian has used SYSPRO. Although it has only one licence in Burnaby, other locations can access the software to, e.g., order a warehouse transfer and print it on the Burnaby printer. This feature of SYSPRO has saved Julian four days of work per month.

WeighPack Systems (http://www.weighpack.com)

WeighPack Systems, based in Montreal, with show rooms and service facilities in Chicago, Las Vegas, Miami, and Shanghai, manufactures custom weighing and bagging equipment. Weigh-Pack carries a fair amount of inventories of parts and components in its facilities. It started using SYSPRO in 1995, with the server located in Montreal. The benefits of using SYSPRO are that the staff in Montreal can see inventories and financial numbers of all facilities, and perform job costing. WeighPack management likes the accessibility and friendly service of SYSPRO staff.

Sources: "Bonte and SYSPRO: The Right Mix," *Materials Management and Distribution*, March 2005, 50(2), p.51; "Natural Factors Nutritional Products," *CA Magazine*, September 2008, 141(7), p. 22; "Julian Ceramic Tile Inc," *Materials Management and Distribution*, September 2005, 50(7), p. 35; "WeighPack Systems," *CA Magazine*, October 2008, 141(8), p. 21.

list of ERP vendors, see http://www.erp180systems.com. For news on ERPs, see http://www.180systemsblog.com/category/erp/. For some applications of ERP, see the "Some SYSPRO Applications" OM in Action, "Prairie Machine & Parts" OM in Action earlier in the chapter, and other OM in Actions throughout the chapter.

THE ABCs OF ERP[2]

ERP attempts to integrate all departments and functions of a company onto a single computer system that can serve all those different departments' particular needs.

It's a tall order, building a single software program that serves the needs of the people in finance as well as it does the people in human resources and in the warehouse. Each of those departments typically has its own computer system, each optimized for the particular ways that the department does its work. But ERP combines them all into a single, integrated software program that runs off a single database so that the various departments can more easily share information and communicate with each other, and also it reduces redundant data entry.

The integrated approach can have a tremendous payback if companies install the software correctly. Take a customer order, for example. Typically, when a customer places an

---

[2]Most of this section is based on C. Koch, "The ABCs of ERP," http://www.CIO.com/research/erp/edit/erpbasics.html, accessed in 2005.

order, that order begins a mostly paper-based journey from in-basket to in-basket around the company, often being keyed and rekeyed into different departments' computer systems along the way. All that lounging around in in-baskets causes delays and lost orders, and all the keying into different computer systems invites errors. Meanwhile, no one in the company truly knows what the status of the order is at any given point because there is no way for the finance department, for example, to get into the warehouse's computer system to see whether the item has been shipped.

How Can ERP Improve a Company's Business Performance?

ERP automates the tasks involved in performing a business process—such as order fulfillment, which involves taking an order from a customer, making it, shipping it, and billing for it. With ERP, when a customer service representative takes an order from a customer, he or she has all the information necessary to complete the order (the customer's credit rating and order history, the company's MPS and inventory levels, and the shipping/trucking schedule). Everyone else in the company sees the same computer screen and has access to the single database that holds the customer's new order. When one department finishes with the order, it is automatically routed using the ERP system to the next department. To find out where the order is at any time, one needs only to log on to the ERP system and track it down. Customers get their orders faster and with fewer mistakes than before. ERP can apply that same magic to the other major business processes, such as employee benefits or financial reporting.

That, at least, is the dream of ERP. The reality is much harsher. Let's go back to those in-baskets. That process may not have been efficient, but it was simple. Finance did its job, the warehouse did its job, and if anything went wrong outside the department's walls, it was somebody else's problem. Not anymore. With ERP, the customer service representatives are no longer just typists entering someone's name into a computer and hitting the Enter key. The ERP screen makes them business people. It flickers with the customer's credit rating from the finance department and the product inventory levels from the warehouse. Will the customer pay on time? Will we be able to ship the order on time? These are decisions that customer service representatives have never had to make before and that affect the customer and every other department in the company. But it's not just the customer service representatives who have to wake up. People in the warehouse who used to keep inventory in their heads or on scraps of paper now need to put that information online. If they don't, customer service will see low inventory levels on their screens and tell customers that their requested item is not in stock. Accountability, responsibility, and communication have never been tested like this before.

To do ERP right, the ways a company does business will need to change and the ways people do their jobs will need to change too. Real transformational ERP implementation usually runs between one and three years.

Will ERP Fit the Ways a Company Does Business?

It's critical for companies to figure out if their ways of doing business will fit within a standard ERP package before the cheques are signed and the implementation begins. The most common reason that companies walk away from multi-million dollar ERP projects is that they discover that the software does not support one of their important business processes. At that point there are two things they can do: They can change the business process to accommodate the software, which will mean deep changes in long-established ways of doing business and shaking up important people's roles and responsibilities. Or they can modify the software to fit the process, which will slow down the project, introduce dangerous bugs into the system, and make upgrading the software difficult.

What Does ERP Really Cost?

The total cost of ownership of ERP, including hardware, software, professional services, and internal staff costs (for one to two years after installation, which is when the real costs of maintaining, upgrading, and optimizing the system are felt) usually ranges between $50,000 and a few million dollars, depending on the number of licences (seats) and the software (from Tier 1 and Tier 2 vendors).[3]

The Hidden Costs of ERP

ERP practitioners point to the following areas as most likely to result in budget overrun:

1. *Training.* Training expenses are high because workers almost invariably have to learn a new set of processes, not just a new software.

2. *Integration and testing.* A typical manufacturing company may have add-on applications for logistics, production planning, and bar coding. If this laundry list also includes customization of the core ERP package, expect the cost of integrating, testing, and maintaining the system to skyrocket.

3. *Data conversion.* It costs money to move corporate information, such as customer and supplier records, product design data and the like, from old systems to a new ERP system.

4. *Data analysis.* Often, the data from the ERP system must be combined with data from external systems for analysis purposes. Users with heavy analysis needs should include the cost of a data warehouse in the ERP budget—and they should expect to do quite a bit of work to make it run smoothly.

5. *Consultants.* When users fail to plan for disengagement, consulting fees run wild.

How Do You Configure ERP Software?

The packages are built from database tables, thousands of them, that programmers and end users must set to match their business processes; each table has a decision "switch" that leads the software down one decision path or another. By presenting only one way for the company to do each task—say, run the payroll or close the books—a company's individual operating units and far-flung divisions are integrated under one system. But figuring out precisely how to set all the switches in the tables requires a deep understanding of the existing processes being used to operate the business. As the table settings are decided, these business processes are reengineered, ERP's way. Most ERP systems are preconfigured, allowing just hundreds—rather than thousands—of procedural settings to be made by the customer.

Summary

Material requirements planning (MRP) is the activity that determines the ordering of dependent-demand items (i.e., components of assembled products). The planning process begins with a master production schedule. The end items are "exploded" using bills of material, inventory-on-hands are netted, and planned order releases are developed by offsetting for lead times. These show the quantity and timing for purchasing or producing components.

A small number of safety stocks are used in MRP. Various lot-sizing methods are used in MRP, but the main one is lot-for-lot ordering. Capacity requirements planning (CRP) uses the MRP shop order releases and standard operations times to determine the capacity requirements from each work centre.

MRP II is a second-generation MRP that adds a broader scope to planning because it links sales and operations planning, MPS, MRP, CRP, and detailed scheduling. ERP systems build on these linkages even further by integrating all functions of business on a single common database.

---

[3]See http://www.camagazine.com/archives/print-edition/2008/sept/columns/camagazine4469.aspx.

Solved Problems

The following product structure tree shows the components needed to assemble one unit of product W. Determine the quantities of each component needed to assemble 100 units of W.

Problem 1

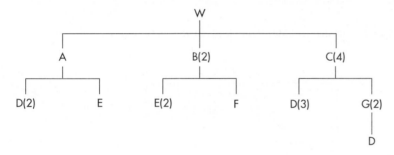

An easy way to calculate and keep track of component requirements is to first do it for 1 end item right on the tree, as shown by the subscripts in the following product structure tree.

Solution

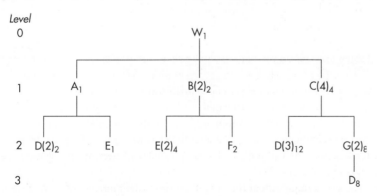

Summary:

Item	(1 W) Quantity	(100 W) Quantity
W	1	100
A	1	100
B	2	200
C	4	400
E	$5 = (1 + 4)$	500
F	2	200
G	8	800
D	$22 = (2 + 12 + 8)$	2,200

Problem 2

The product structure tree for end item E follows. The manager wants to know the material requirements for the purchased part R that will be needed to complete 120 units of E by the start of week 5. Manufacturing lead times for items of this order are one week for level 0 and level 1 items, and purchase lead time is two weeks for level 2 items. There is a scheduled receipt of 60 units of M at the *end* of week 1 and 100 units of R at the *start* of week 1. Lot-for-lot ordering is used, and there are no inventories on-hand.

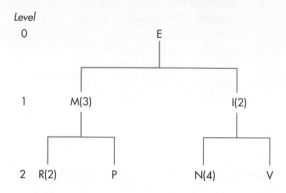

Solution

A partial assembly time chart that includes R and leads to completion of E by the start of week 5 looks like this:

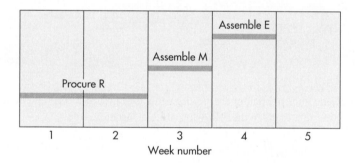

The relevant MRP tables are shown on the next page. The table entries are arrived at as follows:

Production schedule for E: 120 units of E is to be available at the start of week 5.

Table for Item E: Gross requirement equals the quantity specified in the production schedule. Since there is no on-hand inventory, net requirement also equals 120 units. Using lot-for-lot ordering, 120 units must be scheduled to be available at the start of week 5. Because there is a one-week lead time for assembly of 120 units of Es, shop order will need to be released (i.e., work started) at the beginning of week 4.

Table for Item M: The *gross* requirement for M is three times the planned-order release for E ($120 \times 3 = 360$), because each E requires three Ms. These must be available at the start of week 4. The net requirement is 60 units less due to the 60 units of scheduled receipt expected to be on hand at that time. Note that the 60 units expected at the end of week 1 are entered in week 2 because, according to our convention, scheduled receipts occur at the start of the week. Also note that according to our convention, the scheduled receipt goes into projected on-hand immediately. Hence, $360 - 60 = 300$ additional units of M must be available at the start of week 4. With the one-week lead time, there must be a shop order release for 300 Ms at the start of week 3.

Table for Item R: Because each M requires two units of R, 600 Rs will be needed to assemble 300 units of M. However, 100 units of R will be on hand because of the scheduled receipt of 100 units at the start of week 1, so only 500 units of R need to be ordered. Because there is a purchase lead time of two weeks, 500 Rs must be ordered at the start of week 1.

Production schedule for E

Week number	Beg. Inv.	1	2	3	4	5
Quantity						(120)

Item: E LT = 1 week						
Gross requirements						(120)
Scheduled receipts						
Projected on-hand						
Net requirements						120
Planned-order receipts						(120)
Planned-order releases					(120)	

Multiplied by 3
(see product tree)

Item: M LT = 1 week						
Gross requirements					(360)	
Scheduled receipts			(60)			
Projected on-hand			(60)	60	60	
Net requirements					300	
Planned-order receipts					(300)	
Planned-order releases				(300)		

Multiplied by 2
(see product tree)

Item: R LT = 2 weeks						
Gross requirements				(600)		
Scheduled receipts		(100)				
Projected on-hand		(100)	100	100		
Net requirements				500		
Planned-order receipts				(500)		
Planned-order releases		(500)				

Capacity requirements planning. Given the following planned-order releases and the production standard times for a component produced at a work centre, determine the labour hour requirements of the component each week. Are the planned-order releases feasible if capacity is 120 labour hours per week at the work centre?

Problem 3

Planned-order Releases:

Week	1	2	3	4
Quantity	200	300	100	150

Standard Times:

Processing	.5 hour/unit
Machine setup	10 hours (assume one production run per week)

Solution

Convert the quantity requirements into labour requirements by multiplying the quantity requirements by the respective standard times and adding the setup time:

Week	1	2	3	4
Quantity	200	300	100	150
Processing hours	100	150	50	75
Machine setup hours	10	10	10	10
Total labour hours	110	160	60	85

Capacity in week 2 is insufficient because 160 labour hours > 120 labour hours.

Discussion and Review Questions

1. Contrast independent and dependent demand. (LO1)
2. What is MRP, what is its objective, and when is it appropriate? (LO1)
3. How can the use of MRP contribute to profitability? (LO1)
4. What are planning and modular BOMs and why are they used? (LO2)
5. Briefly define or explain each of these terms. (LO2 & 3)
   a. Master production schedule
   b. Bill of material
   c. Manufacturing lead time
   d. Gross requirement
   e. Net requirement
6. What is the difference between the treatment of purchased parts and manufactured parts in MRP? (LO2)
7. Describe MRP processing. (LO3)
8. Contrast planned-order receipts and scheduled receipts. (LO3)
9. Contrast net-change and regenerative MRPs. What is MRP system nervousness? (LO3)
10. How is safety stock included in a material requirements plan? What is safety time? (LO4)
11. What is CRP? What can the planner do if the capacity of a work centre will be exceeded? (LO4)
12. Briefly describe MRP II and indicate how it relates to MRP. (LO4)
13. What is lot sizing and what is its goal? (LO4)
14. If seasonal variations are present, is their incorporation into MRP fairly simple or fairly difficult? Explain briefly. (LO4)
15. How does an ERP system differ from MRP II software? (LO5)
16. What are some unforeseen costs of ERP? (LO5)

Taking Stock

1. What trade-offs are involved in the decision to purchase an ERP software package? (LO5)
2. Who in the organization needs to be involved in MRP? Who needs to be involved in ERP? (LO2, 3 & 5)
3. How important are each of the following considerations in an ERP software? (LO5)
   a. Ease of use
   b. Complete integration
   c. Data reliability
4. Why is trust between labour and management important for effective implementation of MRP, MRP II, or ERP software? (LO4 & 5)

Suppose you work for a furniture manufacturer, one of whose products is the chair depicted in Figure 14-5. Finished goods inventory is held in a central warehouse in anticipation of customer orders. Finished goods are controlled using an EOQ-ROP model. The warehouse manager has suggested using the same model for controlling component inventories. Write him a brief memo outlining your opinion on doing that. (LO1)

Critical Thinking Exercise

Select an assembled item that you can disassemble and has several parts (e.g., a stapler, pencil sharpener, toy car or truck). Develop a product structure tree for the item. (LO2)

Experiential Learning Exercise

Choose one of the following applications of ERP and determine the benefit of using the software: (LO5)

Internet Exercise

a. http://www.coss-systems.com, click Infocenter at the top, then click Case Studies, and finally click on All Stick Label case study.

b. http://www.industrios.com, click Success Stories on the top, then find and click on one of the following:
   i   Frank Zamboni
   ii Cam Tran
   iii Leicatex

c. http://www.minotaursoftware.com/testimonial/testimonial.htm#cs, find and click on one of the following:
   i   Hazekamp Meats
   ii Forsythe Lubrication
   iii Sweet Creations
   iv Ital Pasta

1. a. Given the following product structure tree for product E, determine the quantity of each component required to assemble one unit of E. (LO2)

Problems

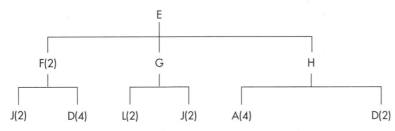

b. Draw the product structure tree for a stapler using its indented BOM below:

Item

Stapler
Top assembly
  Cover
  Spring
  Slide assembly
    Slide
    Spring
Base assembly
  Base
  Strike plate
  Rubber pad (2)

2. The following table shows the components needed to assemble an end item, their manufacturing or purchase lead times for typical lot sizes, and amount on hand. The following product structure tree for the End Item shows the number of each component per parent. (LO2)

Item	End Item	B	C	D	E	F	G	H
LT (wk)	1	2	3	3	1	2	1	2
Amount on hand	0	10	10	25	12	30	5	0

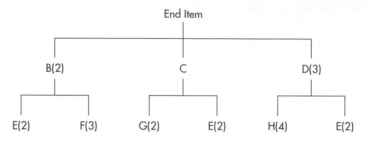

a. If 20 units of the end item are to be assembled, how many additional units of E are needed? (You don't need to develop the MRP tables to determine this.)
b. An order for the end item is scheduled to be shipped at the start of week 11. What is the latest week that production or purchase of the components of the order can be started and the order still be ready to ship on time? (You don't need to develop the MRP tables for this part either.)

3. The following table lists the components needed to assemble an end item, the manufacturing or purchase lead times (in weeks) for typical lot sizes, amount on hand, and the direct components of each item and, in brackets, the number of each component for each parent. (LO2 & 3)

Item	Lead Time	Amount on Hand	Direct Components
End item	1	—	L(2), C(1), K(3)
L	2	10	B(2), J(3)
C	3	15	G(2), B(2)
K	3	20	H(4), B(2)
B	2	30	
J	3	30	
G	3	5	
H	2	—	

a. Draw the product structure tree for the End item.
b. If 40 units of the end item are to be assembled, how many additional units of B are needed? (You don't need to develop the MRP tables.)
c. An order for 40 units of the end item is scheduled to be shipped at the start of week 8. What is the latest week that the components of the order can be started and the order still be ready to ship on time? (You don't need to develop the MRP tables.)

4. Eighty units of product E are needed at the beginning of week 6. Three cases (30 units per case) of J have been ordered and one case is scheduled to arrive in week 3, one in week 4, and one in week 5. *Note*: J must be ordered by the case, and B must be produced in multiples of 120 units. There are 60 units of B and 20 units of J on hand now. Manufacturing lead times are two weeks each for E and B, and purchase lead time is one week for J. (LO3)

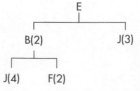

    a. Prepare the material requirements plan for component J.

    b. Suppose that now is week 4 and the quantity of E needed in week 6 has changed from 80 to 70. The planned order releases through week 3 and scheduled receipts have all been executed as in part *a*. How many more (relative to part *a*) Bs and Js will be on hand in week 6?

5. Product P is composed of three subassemblies: K, L, and W. Subassembly K is assembled using 3 Gs and 4 Hs; L is made of 2 Ms and 2 Ns; and W is made of 3 Zs. On-hand inventories are 40 Gs, and 200 Hs. Scheduled receipts are 10 Ks at the start of week 3 and 30 Ks at the start of week 6. (LO2 & 3)

    One hundred Ps must be shipped at the start of week 6, and another 100 at the start of week 7. Manufacturing lead times are two weeks for subassemblies and purchase lead times are one week for the components. Final assembly of P requires one week for 100 units. Include an extra 10-percent scrap allowance in each planned order of G. The minimum order size for H is 200 units. For other items, use lot-for-lot ordering. Develop each of the following:

    a. The product structure tree.

    b. The material requirements plan for P, K, G, and H.

6. A table is assembled using three components, as shown in the following product structure tree. The company that makes the table wants to ship 100 units at the beginning of day 4, 150 units at the beginning of day 5, and 200 units at the beginning of day 7. Receipts of 100 wood sections are scheduled at the beginning of day 2. There are 120 legs on hand. An additional 10 percent of the order size on legs is added for safety stock. There are 60 braces on hand. Lead time (in days) for all items is a function of each order quantity and is shown below. Prepare the material requirements plan using lot-for-lot ordering. (LO3)

Order Quantity	Lead Time (days)
1–200	1
201–550	2
551–999	3

7. Eighty units of product X are needed at the beginning of week 6, and another 30 units are needed at the beginning of week 8. Prepare the material requirements plan for component D, B, and X. D can be ordered only in whole cases (50 units per case). One case of D is automatically received every other week, beginning in week 1 (i.e., week 1, 3, 5, 7). Also, there are 30 units of B and 20 units of D on hand now. Lead times for all items are a function of quantity: one week for up to 100 units, two weeks for 101 to 200 units, three weeks for 201 to 300 units, and four weeks for 301 or more units. (LO3)

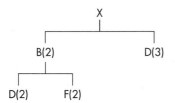

8. A company sells three models of radar detector units. It buys three basic units (E, F, and G) from a Japanese manufacturer and adds one, two, or four lights (component D) to further differentiate the models. D is bought from a domestic producer. (LO3)

Lead times are one week for all items except C, which is two weeks. There are ample supplies of the basic units (E, F, and G) on hand. There are also 10 units of B, 10 units of C, and 25 units of D on hand. Lot sizing rules are lot-for-lot ordering for all items except D, which must be ordered in multiples of 100 units. There is a scheduled receipt of 100 units of D at the start of week 1.

The production schedule calls for 40 units of A to be available at the start of week 4, 60 units of B at the start of week 5, and 30 units of C at the start of week 6. Prepare the material requirements plan for D and its parents.

9. Assume that you are the manager of a shop that assembles power tools. You have just received an order for 50 chain saws, which are to be shipped at the start of week 8. Pertinent information on the chain saw is: (LO2 & 3)

Item	Lead Time (weeks)	On Hand	Direct Components
Chain saw	2	15	A (2), B (1), C (3)
A	1	10	E (3), D (1)
B	2	5	D (2), F (3)
C	2	30	E (2), D (2)
D	1	20	
E	1	10	
F	2	30	

a. Develop the product structure tree for the chain saw and an assembly time chart for this order.

b. Develop the material requirements plan for component E and its parents using lot-for-lot ordering.

c. Suppose that capacity to produce part E is limited to a maximum of 100 units per week. Revise the planned-order releases for weeks 1–4 so that this maximum is not exceeded in any period, keeping in mind the objective of minimizing holding costs. The quantities need not be equal in every period. Note that the gross requirements for E will remain the same. However, quantities in some of the other rows will change. Determine the new values in those rows.

10. Assume that you are the manager of a robot manufacturer. You have just received an order for 40 units of an industrial robot, which is to be delivered at the start of week 7. Using the following information, determine how many units of part G to order and the timing of those orders, given that part G must be ordered in multiples of 80 units and all other components are ordered lot-for-lot. *Hint*: You just need tables for Robot, C, and G. (LO2 & 3)

Item	Lead Time (weeks)	On Hand	Direct Components
Robot	2	10	B, G, C(3)
B	1	5	E, F
C	1	20	G(2), H
E	2	4	—
F	3	8	—
G	2	15	—
H	1	10	—

11. Determine the material requirements plans for parts N and V and subassembly I as described in Solved Problem 2 (see figure there) for each of the following situations: (LO3)

a. Assume that there are currently 100 Ns on hand and scheduled receipts of 40 Is and 10 Vs are expected at the beginning of week 3. Suppose that 120 Es are needed at the start of week 5.

b. Assume on-hand and scheduled receipts are as in part *a*. Now suppose that 100 Es are needed at the start of week 5 and 50 at the start of week 7. Also, use multiples of these order sizes: N, 800; V, 200. Use lot-for-lot ordering for I and E.

c. Using your answer to part *a*, update the MRP for I, N, and V, using the following additional information for each of these cases: (1) one week has elapsed (making it the start of week 2), and (2) three weeks have elapsed (making it the start of week 4). Note: Start your revised plans so that the updated time in each case is designated as week 1. The updated production schedule now has an order for 100 units of E in week 8 of case 1 and in week 6 of case 2 (i.e., week 9 under the former production schedule). Assume all orders are released and received as planned.

12. Information concerning the product structure, lead times, and quantities on hand for an electric golf cart is shown in the following table. Use this information to do each of the following: (LO2 & 3)

    a. Construct the product structure tree.
    b. Construct the assembly time chart.
    c. Develop the material requirements plan that will provide 200 golf carts at the start of week 8, assuming lot-for-lot ordering.

Parts List for Electric Golf Cart	Lead Time (for Typical Order Size)	Quantity on Hand
Electric golf cart	1	0
Top	1	40
Base	1	20
Top		
Supports (4)	1	200
Cover	1	0
Base		
Motor	2	300
Body	3	50
Seats (2)	2	120
Body		
Frame	1	35
Controls	1	0
Wheels (4)	1	240

13. Refer to Problem 12. Assume that unusually mild weather has caused a change in the quantity and timing of orders for golf carts. The revised plan calls for 100 golf carts at the start of week 6, 100 at the start of week 8, and 100 at the start of week 9. (LO3)

    a. Determine the timing and quantities for orders for Top and Base.
    b. Assume that equipment problems have reduced the manufacturer's capacity for assembling Bases to 50 units per week. Revise your material requirements plan for Base to reflect this, but still meet delivery dates.

14. A manufacturing company buys a certain part in varying quantities throughout the year. Ordering cost is $11 per order, and holding cost is $0.14 per piece per month. Given the following demand (net requirements) for the part for the next eight months, determine the order sizes and timing of purchase orders using the part-period method. (LO4)

Month	Demand
1	—
2	80
3	10
4	30
5	—
6	30
7	—
8	30

15. A company periodically produces a part that is a basic component of an assembled product. Each time the part is run, a fixed cost of $125 is incurred. The cost to hold one unit for a

week is estimated to be $1.65. For the demand (net requirements) shown below, determine the quantity and timing of production runs using the part-period method. (LO4)

Week	Demand
1	40
2	20
3	100
4	20
5	—
6	20
7	80

16. A company that manufactures paving material for driveways and parking lots expects the following demand for its product for the next four months. (LO4)

Month number	1	2	3	4
Material (tonnes)	40	80	60	70

The company's machine standard time and available capacity are:

Machine standard time (hours per tonne)	3
Monthly production capacity (hours)	200

a. Determine the capacity requirement for each of the four months.
b. In which months do you foresee a problem? What options would you suggest to resolve any problems?

17. A company produces two very similar products, A and B, that go through a three-step sequence of fabrication, assembly, and packaging. Each step requires one day for a lot to be completely processed and moved to the next department. Processing requirements for the departments (hours per unit) are: (LO4)

	Fabrication		Assembly		Packaging	
Product	Labour	Machine	Labour	Machine	Labour	Machine
A	2	1	1.5	1	1	.5
B	1	1	1	1	1.5	.5

Department capacities are all 700 hours of labour and 500 hours of machine time per day. The following production schedule is for the next three days:

Day	Mon	Tues	Wed
A	200	400	100
B	300	200	200

a. Develop, for each department and day, the capacity requirements for each product and the total load for each day. Ignore changeover time between A and B.
b. Evaluate the projected loads for each day. Is the schedule feasible? What do you suggest for balancing the load?

*18. The systems department has a problem. Its computer died just as it spit out the following information: Planned-order release for item J27 = 640 units in Week 2. The company has been able to reconstruct all the information it lost except the production schedule for the end item 565. The company is fortunate because J27 is used only in 565. Given the following product structure tree and the associated inventory on-hand, lot sizing, and lead-time information, determine what production schedule entry for item 565 was exploded into the material requirements plan that killed the computer. (LO3)

Part Number	On Hand	Lot Sizing	Lead Time
565	0	Lot-for-lot	1 week
X43	60	Multiples of 120	1 week
N78	0	Lot-for-lot	2 weeks
Y36	200	Lot-for-lot	1 week
J27	0	Lot-for-lot	2 weeks

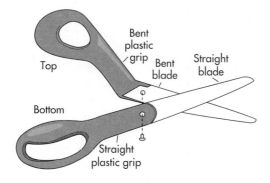

19. Using the drawing of a pair of scissors below, do the following: (LO2 & 3)

    a. Draw the product structure tree for the scissors.

    b. Perform MRP for the scissors and all its components except the screw. Lead times are one day for buying each type of blade, assembling the blades with grips, and for final scissors assembly, but two days for buying each type of plastic grip. Six hundred pairs of scissors are needed on Day 6. *Note:* there are 200 straight blades, 350 bent blades, and 40 top blade assemblies on hand.

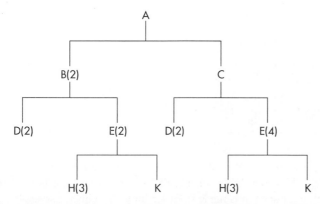

20. Develop the material requirements plan for component H of the end product A that has the following product structure tree. Lead times for A and each component except B are one week. The lead time for B is three weeks. Sixty units of A are needed at the start of week 8. There are currently 15 units of B and 130 units of E on hand, and 50 units of H are in production by a supplier and are scheduled to be received by the start of week 2. (LO3)

*21. Promotional Novelties manufactures a wide range of novelty items for its corporate customers. It has just received an order for 20,000 toy tractor-trailers that will be sold by a gas station chain as part of a holiday promotion. The order is to be shipped at the beginning of week 9. The product structure tree below shows various components of the tractor-trailers and the way it is assembled. (LO3)

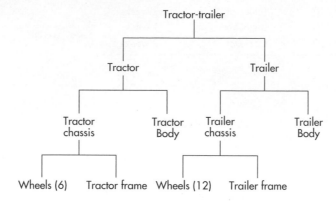

The company can complete final assembly of the tractor-trailers at the rate of 10,000 a week. Assembly time of Tractors and Trailers for this size order, in different departments, is one week each.

The tractors and trailers each have their own chassis departments that can produce chassis at the rate of 100,000 a week. Wheels are purchased from a supplier. Ordered wheels come in sets of 6,400. The lead time for delivery of wheels from the supplier is expected to be three weeks. Perform MRP for the wheels and its parents and answer the following questions:

a. How many wheels will the manager need to order?

b. When should the manager place the order?

c. How many wheels should the manager expect to have left over?

*22. A small furniture maker has just received an order to deliver 250 chairs at the beginning of week 6. The production/purchase planner needs to arrange for the assembly of subassemblies and purchase of parts required for the order. The product structure tree for the chair is displayed below. The chairs, leg assemblies, and back assemblies are to be assembled by one worker each. During an eight-hour day, 25 chairs and 25 legs assemblies can be assembled, whereas 50 back assemblies can be assembled. The company operates five days a week. The seats, spindles, tops, legs, and rails are purchased from another company. Purchase lead time for this size order for each part is one week. The company has some inventory of parts from previous productions: 40 seats, 100 rails, 150 legs, 30 tops, and 80 spindles. (LO3)

a. Calculate assembly lead times for chairs, leg assemblies, and back assemblies required for this order. Assume that chair assembly will start only after the whole batch of its components is available.

b. Develop material requirements plans for this order. Use lot-for-lot ordering. What action should you take now?

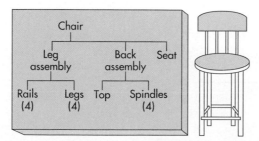

*23. A furniture maker has received an order for 100 units of its kitchen table to be delivered at the beginning of Friday, March 20. The table consists of 1 top and 4 legs, made from purchased lumber (2" by 6" by 6'). Each top is made from 1.5 units of lumber, and each leg is made from 1/6 unit of the lumber. Tops and legs can be made independently in two different workstations, and manufacturing time for 1 top is expected to be 12 minutes and for 1 leg 2 minutes. All 100 tops and 400 legs should be made before any tables are assembled, and final assembly of 1 table is expected to take 4 minutes. The shop works eight hours a day, Monday to Friday. Currently, the company has 20 units of lumber in stock, and purchase lead time for lumber is one work day. (LO2 & 3)

a. Calculate the manufacturing lead time for each operation and draw the product structure tree.

b. Perform material requirements planning for this order. What action should be taken now?

c. How would your answer for lumber change
   i if the safety stock for lumber is 20 units?
   ii if lumber is purchased in batch size of 250 units?
   iii if 250 units are scheduled to be received on March 13?

*24. You wish to plan the assembly and purchase of the components for an order of 4,800 side (accessory) tables (see Example 9 in Chapter 6 on page 191) due at the beginning of week 7. See the product structure tree below. (LO3)

a. Suppose that the assembly of two leg assemblies to a top will take approximately one minute, and the assembly of two leg braces to a WIP will take approximately 1.5 minutes. Assuming that the company works 40 hours a week, calculate the assembly lead times for these two operations for assembling 4,800 tables. Assume that the whole 4,800 units of WIP should be completed before the table assembly starts.

b. Suppose that the tops, leg assemblies, and leg braces are purchased from a vendor, and that purchase lead time is one week each. We have 100 units of top, 200 leg assemblies, and 300 leg braces on hand. A purchase order was released last week for 5,000 tops in anticipation of this order (scheduled receipt = week 1). The leg braces have to be purchased in multiples of 500. Otherwise use lot-for-lot ordering. Develop the MRP tables. What action should you take now?

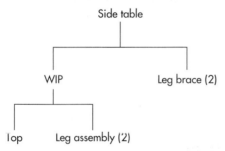

*25. Restaurants need to plan the purchase and production of their food ingredients and components based on the forecast of demand for each meal. Consider the following example for veal picante with linguini in a New Orleans restaurant.[4] (LO2 & 3)

The forecasts for demand for veal picante with linguini during each of the next four days are Thursday, 6; Friday, 10; Saturday, 9; and Sunday, 8. The product structure tree of one veal picante with linguini is as follows: The chef assembles the dish from one serving of cooked linguini and one piece of grilled veal steak. The assistant chef makes the cooked linguini using approximately 100 grams of uncooked linguini (takes approximately 15 minutes). The chef grills the veal steak from a marinated piece of veal (takes approximately 17 minutes). Marinating of a raw veal steak needs to be done the day before (by assistant chef) using some picante sauce, lime juice, oil, salt, and pepper (takes approximately 5 minutes but needs to rest in the fridge overnight). On hand, we have 1 kg of uncooked linguini, six marinated veal steaks and thirteen un-marinated veal steaks. All production lead times are negligible (zero day), except marinating veal steaks which takes one day. All purchase lead times are one day. The restaurant orders uncooked linguini in 10 kg bags and unmarinated veal steaks in 20 piece boxes.

a. Draw the product structure tree for a veal picante with linguini.

b. Develop MRP tables for all items except picante sauce, lime juice, oil, salt, and pepper.

*26. Consider the magazine rack and its pieces shown on the following page. The raw material is 1 inch by 6 inches by 6 feet long planks of oak lumber. The 6 rails and handle are made from

---

[4]Based on John G. Wacker, "Effective Planning and Cost Control for Restaurants: Making Resource Requirements Planning Work," *Production and Inventory Management Journal*, First Quarter, 1985, pp. 55–70.

one plank of lumber, but to make the 2 ends and bottom, first two planks have to be glued together side-by-side. (LO3)

Magazine rack

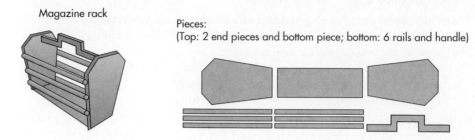

Pieces:
(Top: 2 end pieces and bottom piece; bottom: 6 rails and handle)

The product structure tree below shows that one kit of 6 rails and a handle is made from one plank of lumber, and one kit of 2 ends and a bottom is made from one side-by-side glued piece of lumber which, in turn, is made of 2 planks of lumber. The cutting time of one plank of lumber into one kit of 6 rails and a handle will be 5 minutes. The glue time of 2 planks of lumber will be 5 minutes (assume that the glue will dry overnight). The cutting and router time (for the grooves) of one side-by-side glued piece of lumber into one kit of 2 ends and a bottom will be 10 minutes. Finally, the assembly of one kit of 6 rails and a handle and one kit of 2 ends and a bottom will take 15 minutes. The shop works eight hours a day, five days a week. The purchase lead time for lumber is one work day. The shop has just sold 80 magazine racks to a customer to be delivered on Tuesday, March 31. Assume that each operation is performed by a different operator and each batch should be completed before it is moved to the next operation.

a. Calculate the manufacturing lead time for each operation to make this order.

b. Complete MRP tables for each item. Suppose we currently have 100 planks of lumber in stock. Assume lot-for-lot ordering for all items except lumber, which is purchased in lots of 200 planks.

c. What action should we take now?

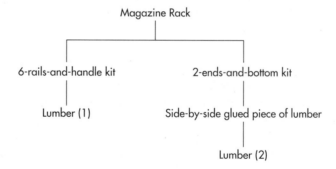

*27. Consider the chair described in Figure 14-5. Suppose that the chair is made by a small furniture manufacturer that has just received an order to deliver 100 chairs on Monday April 20. The production/purchase planner needs to arrange for the purchase of parts and their assembly. The chairs, front assemblies, and back assemblies are to be assembled by one worker each. During an 8-hour day, 100 front assemblies and 50 back assemblies can be assembled. After a batch of 100 front assemblies and 100 back assemblies are produced, the whole chair will be assembled at the rate of 50 per 8-hour day. The company works 5 days a week. The seats, front legs, cross bars, side rails, and back supports are purchased from another company. The purchase lead time for any order is one work day. The company has some inventory of parts from previous purchases: 100 front legs, 160 cross bars, 40 side rails, and 90 back supports. All items are purchased or assembled lot-for-lot, except cross bars, which are purchased in a lot size of 200. In anticipation for this order, an order of 100 seats has already been placed and is expected on Monday April 13. (LO3)

a. Calculate the assembly lead times for the chairs, front assemblies, and back assemblies required for this order.

b. Develop the material requirements plans for this order. What action should you take now?

*28. Consider the School Chairs Mini-case at the end of Chapter 6. Suppose the seat is made in a seat-fabrication work centre, all other parts (posts, cross bars, rails) are made in a post-bar-rail work centre, and the chair is assembled in the chair-assembly work centre. Suppose that a chair takes 15 minutes to assemble and uses 1 seat and one kit of other parts (2 front posts, 2 back posts, 10 cross bars, and 3 rails). A seat takes 5 minutes to make from half a plank (a plank is 2" by 4" by 8'). Assume that glue will be dried overnight. A kit of other parts takes 10 minutes to make from 1 plank. Suppose each work centre is staffed by one worker who works 8 hours a day, 5 days a week (Mon-Fri), and that we promised 90 chairs to a school to be delivered on Friday, December 12. (LO3)

  a. Determine the manufacturing lead times (in day) for assembling 90 chairs, making 90 seats, and making 90 kits of other parts. Round up if a fraction of day is used.

  b. There is no inventory on hand or on order, no safety stocks are needed, lot-for-lot ordering is used, and purchase lead time for lumber is one workday. Use MRP to determine when and how many units of lumber to purchase, seats to make, other parts to make, and chairs to assemble.

  c. What action should be taken now?

  d. If we have 35 planks on hand, how would your answer change?

  e. If we have 35 planks on hand and we order lumber in batch size of 200 planks, how would your answer change?

MINI-CASE

DMD Enterprises

DMD makes specialty bikes. The manager used to order enough bike parts for four months' worth of production, but parts were stacked all over the place, seriously reducing work space and hampering movement of workers. And no one knew exactly where anything was.

The manager heard about MRP, and wants to use it. DMD makes two types of bikes: Arrow and Dart. The manager wants to assemble 15 Arrows and 10 Darts each week from weeks 4 through 8. The product structure trees for the two bikes follow.

```
      Arrow                  Dart
   ┌────┼────┐           ┌────┴───┐
   X    M    W          K(?)      F
   │                  ┌──┴──┐
   F                W(2)    Q
```

He has collected the following information on lead times, inventory on hand, and lot-sizing methods (established by suppliers and/or DMD):

Item	Lead Time (weeks)	On Hand	Lot-Sizing Method
Arrow	2	5	Lot-for-lot
Dart	2	2	Lot-for-lot
X	1	5	Q = 25
W	2*	2	Multiples of 12
F	1	10	Multiples of 30
K	1	3	Lot-for-lot
Q	1	15	Q = 30
M	1	0	Lot-for-lot

*LT = 3 weeks for orders of 36 or more units.

Scheduled receipts are:

Week 1:   20 Arrows, 18 Ws

Week 2:   20 Darts, 15 Fs

Develop the material requirements plans for all the items.

OPERATIONS TOUR   http://www.stickley.com

Stickley Furniture

Introduction

L & J.G. Stickley was founded in 1900 by brothers Leopold and John George Stickley in Manlius, just outside Syracuse, New York. The company is a producer of fine cherry, white oak, and mahogany furniture. In the late 1980s, the company reintroduced its original line of mission oak furniture, which now accounts for over 50 percent of the company's sales.

Over the years, the company experienced both good and bad times, and at one point it employed over 200 people. But by the early 1970s, the business was in disarray: there were only about 25 full-time employees, and the company was on the brink of bankruptcy. The present owners, the Audi family, bought the ailing company in 1974, and under their leadership the company has prospered and grown, and now has over 1,500 employees, with another factory in North Carolina, and a third in Vietnam. Stickley's furniture is sold in North America by some 100 dealers.

Production

The production facility in Manlius is a large, rectangular building with a 9-metre ceiling. Furniture making is labour intensive, although saws, sanders, and other equipment are very much a part of the process. In fact, electricity costs average $40,000 to $50,000 a month. The company has its own tool room where cutting tools are sharpened and replacement tools are produced as needed.

Worker skills range from low-skilled material handlers to highly skilled craftsmen. For example, three master cabinet makers handle customized orders.

The process (see the floor layout diagram below) begins with various sawing operations where planks received from the lumber mills are cut into smaller sizes. The company recently purchased a computer-controlled "optimizer" saw that greatly improves sawing productivity and eliminates some waste. Workers inspect and mark knot locations and other defects they find on each piece of lumber before feeding it into the saw. The computer then determines the optimal set of cuttings, given the location of knots and other defects, and standard lengths needed for subsequent operations. Approximately 29,000 board feet are cut each day. A board foot is equivalent to 1 inch thick by 1 foot wide by 1 foot long. Subsequent sawing operations perform additional cuts for specific jobs.

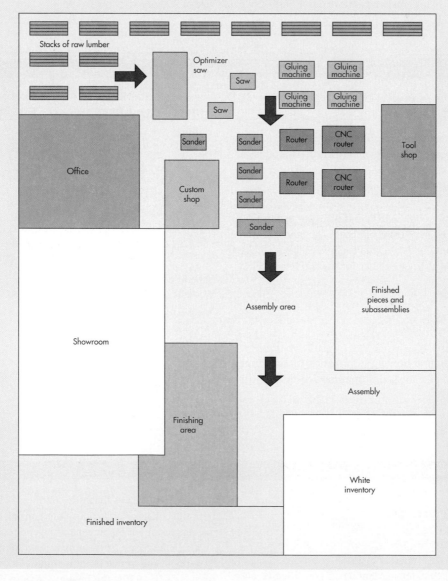

Workers then glue some of the pieces together that will end up as tops of tables, desks, dressers, or similar items. Large presses hold 20 to 30 glued sections at a time. Other pieces that will become table or chair legs, chair backs, or other items go through various shaping operations. Next comes a series of sanding operations which remove excess glue from the glued sections and smooth the surface of both glued and other pieces.

Some of the pieces may require drilling or *mortising*, an operation in which rectangular holes and other shapes are cut into the wood. The company has two CNC (computer numerically controlled) routers that can be programmed to make grooves and other specialty cuts. Some items require carving, which involves highly skilled workers (see the photo above).

Next, workers assemble the various components either into subassemblies or sometimes directly to other components to obtain completed pieces. Each item is stamped with the date of production, and components such as dresser drawers, cabinet doors, and expansion leaves of tables also are stamped to identify their location (e.g., top drawer, left door). Careful records are kept so that if a piece of furniture is ever returned for repairs, complete instructions are available (type of wood, finish, etc.) to enable repair people to closely match the original piece.

The furniture items then usually move to the "white inventory" (unfinished) section, and eventually to the finishing department where workers apply linseed oil or another finish before the items are moved to the finished goods inventory to await shipment to stores or customer locations.

Aggregate Production Planning

The company uses a level output/workforce plan. Demand is seasonal; it is highest in the first and third quarters. During the second and fourth quarters, excess output goes into inventory; during the first and third quarters, excess demand is met using these inventory. The production scheduler uses a (master) schedule that is set for the next 8 to 10 weeks.

Job Scheduling

Job sequence is determined by the amount of remaining inventory (days' supply on hand) and processing time. Lot sizes are determined by factoring in demand, setup costs, and holding costs. Typical lot sizes are 25 to 60 pieces. There are many jobs (lots) being produced concurrently. Each job (lot) is accompanied by a set of bar codes that identify the job and the operation. As each operation is completed, the operator removes a bar-code sticker and delivers it to the scheduling office where it is scanned into the computer, thereby enabling production control to keep track of the progress of a job and to know its location in the shop.

Inventory

In addition to the "white" inventory and a small finished-goods inventory, the company maintains inventories of finished parts (e.g., table and chair legs) and partially assembled items. This inventory serves two important functions. One is to reduce the amount of time needed to respond to customer orders rather than having to go through the entire production process to obtain needed items, and the other is that it helps to smooth production and utilize idle machinery/workers. Because of unequal job times on successive operations, some workstations invariably have slack time while others work at capacity. Slack times are used to build inventories of commonly used pieces and subassemblies. Moreover, because pieces are being made for inventory, there is flexibility in sequencing. This permits jobs that have similar setups to be produced in sequence, thereby reducing setup time and cost.

Quality

Each worker is responsible for checking his work quality, as well as the quality of material received from the preceding operations, and to report any deficiencies. In addition, on several difficult operations, quality control people handle inspections and work with operators to correct any deficiencies. The company is considering a TQM approach (see Chapter 9), but has not yet made a decision on whether to go in that direction. For a virtual tour of Stickley's plant, go to http://www.stickley.com/OurStickleyStory.cfm?SubPgName=FactoryTour.

Questions

1. Which type of production process—job shop, batch, repetitive, or continuous—is the primary mode of operation at Stickley Furniture?

2. Suppose that the company has just received an order for 40 mission oak dining room sets. Briefly list the kinds of information production control will need to plan, schedule, and process this job.

3. Can you suggest any planning tools that might be beneficial to the company? Explain.

CHAPTER 15
Just-in-Time and Lean Production

LEARNING OBJECTIVES

After completing this chapter, you should be able to:

LO1 Explain what is meant by the terms *just-in-time* (JIT) and *lean production*.

LO2 Explain the goals of lean production.

LO3 Describe those aspects of product design that are important for lean production.

LO4 Describe those aspects of process design that are important for lean production.

LO5 Describe those aspects of personnel/organization that are important for lean production.

LO6 Describe those aspects of planning and control that are important for lean production, and solve typical problems for level mixed-model sequencing and determining the number of *kanbans* at a work centre.

LO7 Explain how lean production can be implemented.

elestica is a large electronic manufacturing services provider (i.e., manufactures components for computer and telecom equipment manufacturers) in Canada. Celestica needs to be flexible and fast, but at the same time low cost. How do Celestica and other progressive manufacturers achieve these competitive attributes? Often, they use lean production. This is the subject of this chapter.

(LO 1) INTRODUCTION

The term **just-in-time (JIT)** in a narrow sense, also called *little JIT*, refers to a production system in which both the movement of work-in-process (WIP) during production and deliveries of parts/modules from suppliers are carefully timed so that at each step of the process, the next (usually small, ideally one-unit) batch arrives for processing just as the preceding batch is completed—thus the name, *just-in-time*. The result is a system with few idle items waiting to be processed (i.e., inventory) and a balanced, rapid flow.

In a broader sense, JIT, also called *big JIT*, is a philosophy of "waste" reduction, be it inventory or resources (such as workers, equipment, or floor space), and continuous improvement. In this sense, JIT is identical to **lean production**.

JIT, in the narrow sense, is sometimes contrasted with material requirements planning (MRP; see the previous chapter). MRP relies on a computer-based *component-scheduling* system (using daily or weekly time periods) to trigger and "push" production and deliveries through the process, whereas JIT relies on visual signals to trigger and "pull" production and deliveries (usually hourly) through the process. MRP controls the work centre capacities, whereas JIT controls the inventory (through *kanbans*).

The JIT/lean approach was developed at the Toyota Motor Company by Taiichi Ohno (who eventually became vice-president of manufacturing) and several of his colleagues. The development of JIT/lean in Japan was probably influenced by the fact that Japan is a crowded country with few natural resources. Not surprisingly, the Japanese are very sensitive to waste and inefficiency. They regard rework as waste and excess inventory as evil because it takes up space and ties up resources.

The potential of JIT/lean was first demonstrated in North America by its successful implementation in the Fremont, California, auto plant in the mid-1980s. GM had closed the plant in 1982 because of its low productivity and high absenteeism. A few years later the plant was reopened as a joint venture between Toyota and GM, called NUMMI. About 80 percent of the former plant's workers were rehired, but the Toyota Production System was implemented. By 1985, productivity improved dramatically and absenteeism declined to almost zero.

A few years later, more interest in lean production arouse when *The Machine That Changed the World*, by Womack, Jones, and Roos, was published. Now JIT/lean is being promoted by some government programs, associations, and companies, and being used by most progressive organizations.

Just like the awards for quality, there is a prize for world-class lean systems, called the Shingo Prize. The principles and criteria for a lean system are given in the "Shingo Prize" OM in Action later in the chapter.

A slightly different representation of the JIT/lean principles and tools, which better match the chapters in this textbook, is given in Figure 15-1 on the next page. Displayed are the goals and building blocks of JIT/lean systems. We will describe the goals and each of the building blocks (product design, process design, personnel/organization, and planning and control) in a separate section below. The chapter concludes with a section on implementation of JIT/lean.

just-in-time (JIT) Production system in which processing and movement of parts/modules/work-in-process occur just as they are needed, usually in small batches.

lean production JIT in a broad sense, is a philosophy of waste reduction and continuous improvement.

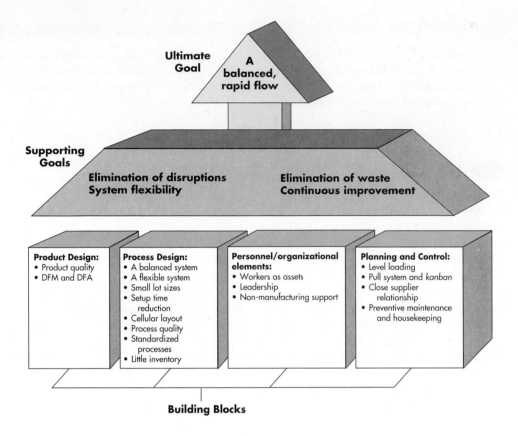

Building Blocks

(LO 2) THE GOALS

The ideal JIT/lean production system produces one piece at a time, defect-free, on-demand, fast, without waste, in a safe production environment. This can be achieved by a balanced rapid flow.

A Balanced Rapid Flow. A *balanced rapid flow* of a family of products is a smooth, even, swift flow of materials, information, or work through the steps of the production process. Here, "balanced" has the same interpretation as in the line balancing of Chapter 6, i.e., the workload should be distributed evenly among the workstations. This goal includes the elimination of unevenness (*mura* in Japanese) and overburden (i.e., using a resource in excess of its optimal operating rate; *muri* in Japanese). A balanced rapid flow can be achieved by the following four supporting goals.

Elimination of Disruptions. Disruptions upset the smooth flow of products through the production system and cause variability. Disruptions are caused by a variety of factors such as poor quality, equipment breakdowns, changes to the schedule/customer demand, and late deliveries of parts/components. All these sources of variability should be eliminated as much as possible.

System Flexibility. A *flexible system* is one that is robust enough to handle a mix of products and changes in the level of output, while still maintaining balance and throughput speed. Reduction of machine setup and lead time will increase system flexibility. Flexibility enables the system to meet changing demand.

Elimination of Waste. Waste (*muda* in Japanese) represents unproductive resources. Eliminating waste can free up resources and enhance production. In the JIT/lean system, wastes include:

a. Overproduction

b. Unnecessary inventory

    c. Waiting

    d. Unnecessary transportation

    e. Overprocessing (i.e., using a complex process instead of a simpler one; work that adds no value)

    f. Inefficient work methods/excess motions

    g. Producing defective products; scrap and rework

    h. Underutilization of employee knowledge/skill

The existence of these wastes is an indication that improvement is possible. For an implementation of JIT/lean system in a service, including examples of waste, see the "RBC" OM in Action.

Continuous Improvement. *Kaizen* (or *continuous improvement*) is continual work to improve the system. In operations, examples include reduce inventories, setup cost and time; improve quality; increase the output rate; and generally cut waste and disruptions. But Kaizen also applies to customer-related processes such as order taking, product development processes such as quality function deployment, supply-related processes such as issuing purchase orders, and support processes such as hiring.
Kaizen is based on the following tenets:

1. Improvement should be done gradually and continuously.

2. Everyone should be involved.

3. It does not require spending great sums of money on technology or consultants.

4. It can be applied anywhere.

5. It involves learning by doing, using scientific thinking.

6. *Kaizen* relies on direct observation and data collection.

One can think of *kaizen* as continuous problem solving (see Chapter 9). Thus, continuous improvement/problem solving becomes a way of life—a "culture" that must be assimilated into the thinking of everyone. It becomes a never-ending quest for improving processes as all members of the organization strive to improve the system. Improvements are made

---

 OM in ACTION   http://www.rbc.com/about-rbc.html

RBC

RBC (Royal Bank of Canada) started using lean and Six Sigma tools to reduce waste and defects, respectively, in 2003 but the projects were led by outside consultants who did not transfer the knowledge of the improvement process to RBC staff. In 2007, RBC started employing some master black belts and black belts who not only lead improvement projects but also train the staff on how to undertake improvement projects themselves. One project was to make the "skimming" fraud investigation more efficient. Skimming is using a counterfeit debit card. The team consisted of a master black belt, 2 fraud agents, and the manager of National Fraud Detection Group in the Enterprise Operations of RBC. The project was in the form of a *kaizen* event (or blitz), which took five days. On day 1, the current skimming fraud investigation process was mapped, and the process was examined for wastes (vs. value to client). On day 2 and 3, possible new processes were mapped and examined.

On day 4, the chosen process was implemented, and on day 5 its improvements were evaluated. Some of the waste reductions were (1) 20 percent reduction in unnecessary data entry, (2) elimination of e-mails to branches, (3) reduction in choices of general ledger accounts required for posting the transaction (from 30 to 2), (4) elimination of duplicate validation of fraudulent transaction, and (5) conversion of manual paper-based process to electronic filing process (saved walking to the shared printer, which caused the agents to batch the cases). The electronic filing process has also cut manual searches, enabled catching missed information (mandatory fields) earlier, and standardized the procedure. The waste reduction has reduced the investigation time from 3 days to 1 day, resulting in happier customers who get their refund faster. It also saved 2,500 hours of work, 14,000 e-mails, 1,000 km of walking, and 315,000 sheets of printed paper per year.

Source: "RBC Embeds Black Belts in a Bid to Get Lean," *Plant,* 2008, pp. 42–46.

at the lowest possible level in the organization (usually front-line workers). Of particular importance are problems that interrupt the smooth flow of work. These must be dealt with quickly, usually by the employee with the help of his supervisor.

For an application of *Kaizen* Blitz (a short-term intensive improvement project by a team), see the "Celestica" OM in Action later in the chapter. The tools (or building blocks) used to achieve the above goals are classified into four classes: product design, process design, personnel and organizational elements, and planning and control. These tools follow.

LO3 PRODUCT DESIGN

Product quality is crucial to JIT/lean systems because poor quality can create major disruptions. Quality must be designed into goods and services. QFD (Quality Function Deployment) should be used to capture the "voice" of customers and deploy it in the product

OM in *ACTION*

Shingo Prize

The Shingo Prize for Operational Excellence was established in 1988 to recognize the achievement of companies worldwide that are implementing JIT/lean systems. It is named after the

Japanese guru on lean manufacturing, Dr. Shigeo Shingo. The criteria currently used to judge a company are principle-based. These are displayed in the following figure. The ten guiding principles (on the left of the figure) are the key concepts or foundations of philosophy of lean/JIT according to the Shingo Prize.

The Shingo Principles of Operational Excellence

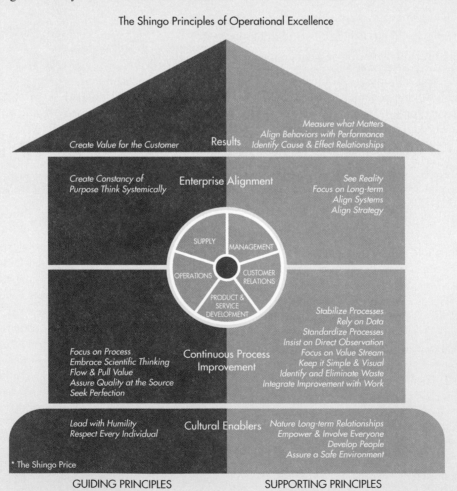

Note that "Flow & Pull value" means shorten lead-time and match supply with demand. The supporting principles (on the right) are the building blocks of the guiding principles. For example, in order to achieve "respect every individual" and 'lead with humility" (which means seek input from everyone), we must have "nurture long-term relationships," "empower and involve everyone," "develop people," and "assure a safe environment." Four categories (or dimensions) of principles are shown, starting from the bottom: Cultural enablers, Continuous process improvement, Enterprise alignment, and Results. Each category has some subcategories, and each is assessed based on how the company has progressed from basic use of tools and techniques, to systems thinking (involving all parts of the company), to incorporating lean approach as part of work principles. Category 2 (i.e., Continuous Process Improvement) is assessed in each of the business process areas: customer relations, product development, operations, supply, and management (other functions of business). Some explanation and the maximum point for each sub-category are given in the table below.

	Max. Points
1. Cultural Enablers	
Leadership	50
People development	
Education, training & coaching	33
Empowerment & involvement	33
Environmental & safety systems	33
2. Continuous Process Improvement	400
Customer relations (having a process for assessing voice of customer, order taking, invoicing, etc)	
Product development (QFD, concurrent engineering, benchmarking, new markets, DFM and DFA, component standardization & modularity, value analysis, innovations, involvement of suppliers/customers, etc.)	
Operations (one-piece flow, demand pull, value stream mapping, total preventive maintenance, SMED, *poka-yoke*, visual systems, cellular layout, *Kaizen*, level loading, 5S, right-sized equipment/facilities, Six Sigma/SPC/design of experiments, tools for quality improvement, etc.)	
Supply (integration with suppliers, a process for making the linkage visible, transport and distribution alliances, respect for suppliers, commitment to supplier development)	

	Max. Points
Management (alignment and integration of other functions in support of production value stream, value stream mapping of other processes, use of JIT/lean/quality improvement tools in other processes)	
3. Enterprise Alignment	200
Enterprise thinking in a global environment (reporting of lean principles/policy, having common management/reporting system, using lean accounting, simple/visual information systems, etc.)	
Policy deployment (scientific thinking, planning process for policy deployment, alignment of objectives, constancy of purpose, etc.)	
4. Results	
Quality (internal quality, quality to the customer, etc.)	50
Delivery (lead time, on-time delivery, etc.)	50
Cost/Productivity (labour productivity, asset productivity, inventory turns, etc.)	50
Customer satisfaction (customer survey, etc.)	50
Morale (employee survey, etc.)	50

Source: http://www.shingoprize.org/files/uploads/Shingo ModelGuidelines.pdf

design. This will create value for the customers. Concurrent engineering should be used to increase functional communications, reduce the need for engineering changes, and speed up the design process.

Products should be designed for easy manufacturing and assembly (DFM and DFA). This speeds up the operations. Value analysis may be used to identify the necessary functions of the product and to cut down product features not valued by the customers. For more information on these and other elements of product design which contribute to a JIT/lean system, see Chapter 4.

(LO 4) PROCESS DESIGN

A Balanced System

takt time The maximum time allowed at each workstation to complete its set of tasks on a unit. Also called cycle time.

In a balanced system, workload is distributed evenly among workstations (see line balancing in Chapter 6). Recall that the maximum time allowed at each workstation to complete its set of tasks on a unit is called cycle time or **takt time**. *Takt* time is changed periodically (e.g., daily) to meet changing demand.

Calculating cycle or takt time was covered briefly in Chapter 6. Here, we illustrate it in more detail. The procedure for obtaining the *takt* time is:

1. Determine the net time available per shift by subtracting any non-productive time from total shift time.
2. If there is more than one shift per day, multiply the net time per shift by the number of shifts to obtain the net available time per day.
3. Calculate *takt* time by dividing the net available time by demand during the day.

Example 1

Given the following information, calculate the *takt* time: Total time per shift is 480 minutes per day, and there are two shifts per day. There are two 20-minute rest breaks and a 30-minute lunch break per shift. Daily demand is 80 units.

Solution

1. Calculate net time available per shift:

Total time	480 minutes
Rest breaks	−40 minutes
Lunch	−30 minutes
	410 minutes per shift

    Calculate the net time available per day:

    410 minutes per shift $\times$ 2 shifts/day = 820 minutes per day

2. Calculate the *takt* time:

    $$Takt \text{ time} = \frac{\text{Net time available per day}}{\text{Daily demand}} = \frac{820 \text{ minutes per day}}{80 \text{ units per day}}$$
    $$= 10.25 \text{ minutes per unit}$$

A Flexible System

Process design can increase *production flexibility* in a variety of ways. Table 15-1 lists some of the techniques used for this purpose.

Table 15-1

Techniques for increasing production flexibility

1. Reduce changeover (set up) time.
2. Cross-train workers so they can help others facing over capacity.
3. Use many small machines rather than few large machines.
4. Use safety stocks.
5. Keep some idle capacity.

Small Lot Sizes

In the JIT/lean system, the ideal lot size is one unit, a quantity that may not always be realistic owing to practical considerations requiring minimum lot sizes (e.g., machines that process multiple items simultaneously, and machines with very long setup times). Nevertheless, the objective is to reduce the lot size as much as possible. Small lot sizes in both the production process and deliveries from suppliers yield a number of benefits that enable JIT/lean systems to operate efficiently. First, with small lots moving through the system, work-in-process (WIP) inventory is considerably less than it is with large lots. This reduces holding cost, space requirement, and clutter in the workplace. Second, inspection and rework costs are less when problems with quality occur, because there are fewer items in a lot to inspect and rework.

Small lots also result in greater system flexibility. Batch systems typically produce a small variety of products. This usually means long production runs of each product, one after the other. Although this spreads the setup cost for a run over many items, it also results in long cycles over the entire range of products. For instance, suppose a company has three product models, A, B, and C. In a batch system, there would be a long run of model A (e.g., covering two or three days or more), then a long run of model B, followed by a long run of model C before the sequence would repeat. In contrast, a JIT/lean system, using small lots, would frequently shift from producing A to producing B and C. This enables JIT/lean systems to respond more quickly to changing customer demands. The contrast between small and large lot sizes is illustrated in Figure 15-2.

It is important to note that the use of small lot sizes is not in conflict with the EOQ approach. The fact is that in JIT/lean, there is an emphasis on reducing the setup time (and hence cost), which reduces the optimal lot size.

Setup Time Reduction

Small lots and changing product mixes require frequent machine setups. An example of a machine changeover or setup is putting a different fixture in a machine to hold a different part or putting in a different die in a press to "stamp" a different part. Another example of a machine changeover/setup is adjusting the heights of fillers and labellers on a beverage bottling line to fill different size bottles. Unless setups are quick and relatively inexpensive, the time and cost to accomplish them can be prohibitive. In JIT/lean systems, workers are often trained to do their own setups. Moreover, some tools and methods are used to reduce setup time.

Multipurpose equipment or attachments can help reduce setup time. For instance, a machine with multiple spindles that can easily be rotated into place for different job requirements can drastically reduce changeover time. Moreover, *group technology* may be used to reduce setup cost and time. This is because parts that are similar in shape, materials, and so on require similar setups.

Another method for setup time reduction is to separate the internal setup activities (i.e., those that cannot be done off line in advance) from the external setup activities (i.e., those

A = units of product A
B = units of product B
C = units of product C

Figure 15-2

Small-lot JIT/lean versus large-lot batch approaches

Small-lot JIT/lean approach

AAA   BBBBBBB   CC   AAA   BBBBBBB   CC   AAA   BBBBBBB   CC   AAA   BBBBBBB   CC

Time ⟶

Large-lot batch approach

AAAAAAAAAAAA   BBBBBBBBBBBBBBBBBBBBBBBBBBB   CCCCCCCCC   AAAAAAAAAA

Time ⟶

Celestica

Celestica is a large electronic manufacturing services company based in Toronto, with 33,000 employees in 20 plants located in 15 countries. Celestica manufactures complex printed circuit assemblies such as PC motherboards and networking cards on contract for computer and communication equipment manufacturers including Dell, IBM, Lucent, and Cisco. Celestica was formed in 1996 and has quickly grown to have over $6.1 billion in annual revenue. Celestica started lean manufacturing initiatives in the Americas plants in 1999. The objective is waste reduction, including defects, overproduction, transportation, waiting, inventory, motion, and any other non-value-adding activity. This is done by *kaizen* teams from each work area, each over a short period of time, e.g., a week. A *kaizen* team includes most operators in an area and the management representatives and facilitators.

An example of a *kaizen* team in Celestica's Toronto plant is the rework group. When the *kaizen* blitz started, the rework area had no organized process flow, with lead time for rework being approximately 14 days. The team rearranged the area into a U-shaped cell, cutting travel distances threefold and number of benches by half (from seven to four). The team wrote standard operating procedures including rules for rejecting a circuit board (previously done by an engineer from outside the group). As a result, the lead time has decreased to two days.

Celestica's Toronto factory

Sources: http://www.advancedmanufacturing.com/Dec04/coverstory.htm, accessed August 30, 2009; http://www.celestica.com/AboutUs/AboutUs.aspx?id=156&ekmensel=17_submenu_0_link_6.

that can be done off line in advance), and to make as many setup activities as possible external; for example, bring the tools and fixtures to the machine before the setup, or preheat the injection mould. Yet, another technique is to streamline the setup. For example, preset the desired settings (one touch setting), use locator pins to prevent misalignment of a die on a press, reduce or eliminate tools, and make movements easier. Finally, train the operators and standardize the set up procedure.

Setup time reduction methods for using presses and dies have been advanced by Shigeo Shingo under the name, "Single Minute Exchange of Die." One approach is to make loading parts and using fixtures faster. For some examples of this, see the "Kubota" OM in Action.

Cellular Layout

Many JIT/lean systems have one or more *cells*. A cell contains the machines and tools needed to process a family of parts that have similar processing requirements (see Chapter 6). In essence, a cell is a highly specialized and efficient production centre.

Conversion to a cell requires

- determining a family of products
- mapping the current process for the family of products
- determining the operations required
- determining the capacity requirements

Kubota

Single Minute Exchange of Die (SMED) is a set of methods and tools for reducing setup time to less than 10 minutes, developed by Shigeo Shingo. When Kubota, a Japanese tractor manufacturer, wanted to implement SMED, it started redesigning the fasteners it used to hold a part to a fixture and/or a fixture (or a die) to a platform (or a press). Displayed below are some of these methods and tools.

Sources: http://www.kubota.com; S. Shingo, *A Revolution in Manufacturing: The SMED System* (Cambridge, Massachusetts: Productivity Press, 1985), p. 196.

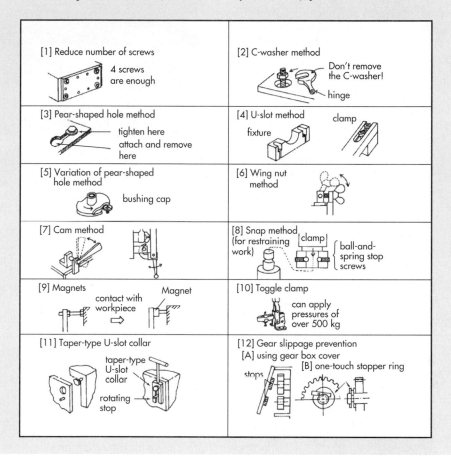

- rearranging the layout and bringing the necessary machines closer together, usually in U-shaped configuration
- determining the capacity of the cell
- upgrading the machines if the capacity is inadequate
- balancing the cell and determining labour requirements
- determining the WIP required between the machines/work stations in the cell

The advantages of cells include faster throughput (i.e., shorter lead times), less material handling, reduced space requirement, and flexibility to increase/decrease the capacity by adding/subtracting workers. The disadvantages of cells are that the machines may not be fully utilized and bringing various machines close together may raise safety/ergonomic issues. For an example of a cell, see Figure 2 of the Mini-Case "Airline Manufacturing" at the end of this chapter.

OM in ACTION http://www.sconatrailers.com

Scona Trailer Manufacturing

Scona Trailer Manufacturing of Edmonton, part of McCoy Corp., manufactures large heavy-duty trailers. In 2003, the demand for trailers was soaring but Scona could not keep up with demand. The new president of McCoy, Jim Rakievich, heard about JIT/lean manufacturing and together with Scona plant manager, Giorgio Overeem, started to study it. Jim brought in a consultant and Giorgio enrolled in a course on JIT/lean manufacturing in Northern Alberta Institute of Technology. In the summer of 2005 they introduced JIT/lean production to Scona, starting with one cell. JIT/lean tools used included value stream mapping, identifying non-value steps and eliminating these wastes, identifying the bottleneck and rearranging the flow to improve the throughput, and tidying up the shop floor (5S). Eventually, the whole plant (25,000 ft^2) was converted into 3–4 cells. The capacity of plant has more than doubled. A trailer can now be produced in only 3 days (down from approximately 25 days before).

Source: K. Laudrum, "McCoy Gets Leaner and Doubles Productivity," *Plant*, March/April 2009, 4(2), p. 8.

Process Quality

Because of low inventories in JIT/lean systems, it is important to prevent defects from occurring; hence, the importance of a capable production process, SPC (Statistical Process Control including control charts) to control and stabilize the production process, Six Sigma to reduce its variability, and *poka-yoke* to mistake-proof it.

poka-yoke Any mechanism that helps an equipment operator avoid mistakes. Its purpose is to eliminate product defects by preventing, correcting, or drawing attention to human errors as they occur.

A **poka-yoke** is any mechanism that helps an equipment operator avoid mistakes. Its purpose is to eliminate product defects by preventing, correcting, or drawing attention to human errors as they occur. Examples of *poka-yoke* include an alarm that sounds if the weight of a package is too low (indicating missing components), an ATM signal if a card is left in the machine, and detectors at department stores that signal if a monitoring tag hasn't been removed from an item, Much of the credit for *poka-yoke* goes to Shigeo Shingo.

autonomation Intelligent automation: if an abnormal situation arises, the machine automatically stops, preventing production of defective products.

A related term is **autonomation** (note the extra syllable *no* in the middle of the word), meaning intelligent automation. It means that if an abnormal situation arises, the machine automatically stops, preventing production of defective products. Another related term is *jidoka*, meaning quality at the source: avoid passing defective products to the following workstation, and stop and fix the problem. Clearly, both *poka-yoke* and autonomation assist in *jidoka*.

jidoka Japanese term for quality at the source: avoid passing defective products to the following workstation, and stop and fix the problem.

Some companies use lights to signal problems; in Japan, this is called **andon**. Each workstation is equipped with a set of three lights. A green light means no problems, an amber light means a worker is falling a little bit behind, and a red light indicates a serious problem. The purpose of the light system is to enable supervisors to immediately see where problems are occurring.

andon A set of lights used at each workstation to signal problems or slowdowns.

Standardized Processes

Processes include customer-related processes such as invoicing, product development processes such as standardization and modularity, supply-related processes such as supplier qualification, and support processes such as capital budgeting. Here we will focus on the production process. The Toyota Production System has rigid rules for work, interaction, work flow, and improvement process.[1]

[1]S. Spear and H.K. Bowen, "Decoding the DNA of the Toyota Production System," *Harvard Business Review*, September/October 1999, pp. 97–106.

The content, sequence, timing, and output of every employee's work are fully specified, even for non-repetitive work such as training or shifting equipment. The worker learns her job primarily by doing it. While in training, the supervisor constantly monitors the worker, compares her performance to the standards, and asks questions to make the worker think and learn her job (e.g., how do you know if you are doing the job right, and what do you do if there is a problem?).

Every connection or link (i.e., people–work interaction) is standardized and specified: it shows the people involved, the form and quantity of product to be supplied, the way the request is made, and the time it should take to meet the request. For example, when a worker cannot do her job, she is supposed to immediately inform her supervisor, and the supervisor should be there promptly to help her (if not, a specified alternative person should be available). *Kanbans* and *andon* are examples of tools used to establish direct link.

Every product or work flows along a simple, specified path (with no loops), not to the next available machine or workstation.

Improvement of all aspects of the work is done by the front-line person, with guidance and teaching of her supervisor, based on scientific method. That is, a hypothesis is formed to predict the outcome of a solution to a problem, and experiments are performed by the worker to see if the hypothesis can be rejected. This will enforce decision making based on data and facts, rather than guesses.

The advantage of these standardizations is that they provide consistency and repeatability, hence the system can be learned and constantly improved. If there was no standard way to, e.g., install a car seat, the variations across workers (and shifts) would confuse the results, making learning and improvement of the operation difficult.

Little Inventory

JIT/lean systems are designed to *minimize* inventory. Recall that in JIT/lean systems inventory is a waste. Inventories are buffers that tend to cover up recurring problems that are never resolved, partly because they aren't obvious and partly because the presence of inventory makes them seem less serious. When a machine breaks down, it won't disrupt the system if there is sufficient inventory of the machine's output to feed into the next workstation. A better solution is to investigate the *causes* of machine breakdowns and focus on eliminating them. Similar situations occur with quality problems, unreliable vendors, and scheduling problems.

A useful analogy is a boat on a pond that has large, hidden rocks (see Figure 15-3). The rocks represent problems that can hinder production (boat's movement). The water in the pond that covers the rocks is the inventory in the system. As the water level is lowered, the largest rocks are the first to appear. At that point, efforts are undertaken to remove these rocks from the water (resolve these problems). Once that has been accomplished, the lower water level (inventory) is adequate.

One way to minimize inventory of raw materials/purchase parts in a JIT/lean system is to have deliveries from suppliers go directly to the production floor, which completely eliminates the need to store incoming parts and materials. At the other end of the process, completed units are shipped out as soon as they are ready, which minimizes storage of finished goods. Coupled with small manufacturing lot sizes resulting in low work-in-process inventory, these features result in systems that operate with very little inventory.

A

B

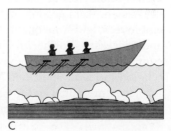
C

Figure 15-3

Large rocks (problems) are hidden by a higher water level (inventory) in A. Lower water level (B) reveals the rocks. Once the large rocks are removed, the lower water level (inventory) is adequate (C).

OM in *ACTION*   http://www.dana.com/wps/wcm/connect/dext/Dana/Home

Dana

When Toyota decided to build a truck assembly plant in Princeton, Indiana, to make Tundra and Sequoia in the late 1990s, it chose Dana Corporation to build its truck frames. Dana built a 129,000-square-foot plant employing about 300 people 73 miles away in Owensboro, Kentucky. To be as lean as possible, Dana makes the frames to the sequence of trucks planned in the Toyota Plant. There are 14 frame models, which are sequenced in batch sizes of one. Therefore, the Dana plant has to be very flexible: it takes a maximum of only three seconds to change over from one model to another in any work centre on the production line. The order information comes via Internet (EDI) from the Toyota plant and is displayed on every work centre. About nine hours later, after operations such as welding, machining, and painting, the frames are trucked to the Toyota plant in batches of 25, about one truck every half hour.

Source: T. Vinas, "In Sync with the Customer," *IndustryWeek* 252(10), October 2002, pp. 46–48.

(LO5) PERSONNEL/ORGANIZATION

Workers as Assets. A fundamental tenet of the JIT/lean is that *workers are assets* and should be respected. Well-trained and motivated workers with high morals are the heart of a JIT/lean system. Education, training, and coaching are essential to develop the workers, as is the promotion of their health and safety. They are given authority (empowered) to make decisions. Workers are expected to participate (be involved) in continuous improvement (*kaizen*). In return, their contribution is recognized and rewarded. Workers are *cross-trained* to perform several steps of a process and operate a variety of machines. This adds to system flexibility because workers are able to help one another when bottlenecks occur or when a co-worker is absent.

Leadership. Top management should take leadership in conversion to JIT/lean because it involves culture change, i.e., the way workers do their job. Goals should be set to progress toward world-class JIT/lean status, their importance should be communicated to the employees to create constancy of purpose, and resources should be allocated so that progress toward JIT/lean is systematic. Employees should be both directed and encouraged to use tools and techniques of JIT/lean and incorporate its principles in their daily work. On the other hand, managers and supervisors are expected to be facilitators, not just order givers. JIT/lean encourages two-way communication between workers and managers. Leaders should lead with humility and seek input from everyone in the organization.

Non-manufacturing Support. Clearly support is needed from sales/marketing for product design, from accounting for product costing, from HR for hiring and training good employees, and from quality assurance and control for improving the quality of products and processes. Further, finance needs to provide the cash for faster but more flexible equipment, purchasing needs to identify qualified JIT/lean suppliers and maintain close relationship with them, and MIS needs to provide the information required to track performance measures and to provide data gathering/communication links. In addition, all these functions should reduce their own department's "wastes."

OM in ACTION   http://www.cglmfg.com

CGL Manufacturing

CGL Manufacturing is a machining, welding, and painting shop in Guelph, Ontario. It started in 1977 as a job shop with five employees. Later, through quality and service, CGL expanded, producing parts for heavy equipment manufacturers such as Raymond lift-trucks. In 2000, CGL had revenue of $10 million and employed approximately 100 workers, but a major customer unexpectedly demanded a 20 percent price cut. The general manager, David Deskur, knew that a major change in CGL had to occur. He attended a JIT/lean manufacturing seminar, was captivated, and acted as the JIT/lean champion. All staff were educated in JIT/lean tools such as value stream mapping, cellular layout, teamwork, and *kaizen*. The plant was reconfigured so that high-volume orders were made in five cells.

During the first year, the distance travelled by forklifts was reduced by 1,000 km, revenues were up by 50 percent, inventories were down by 30 percent, and lead times were down by 20 percent. David believes that the two most important keys to JIT/lean manufacturing are (1) communicate its importance to all staff and (2) tie employee performance measures to their participation in continuous improvement projects. Now, CGL has 170 employees and $35 million in revenue. It has established partnerships with two suppliers: (1) Excel Steel of Cambridge, Ontario, which supplies CGL with sheet metal and (2) a company in China that supplies CGL with castings. CGL has become a role model for JIT/lean manufacturing.

Source: "Get Lean," *Plant*, 2008, pp. 55–64.

 LO 6 **PLANNING AND CONTROL**

Level Loading

JIT/lean places a strong emphasis on achieving stable, level daily mixed-model schedule/ sequence. This will result in *level capacity loading* (*heijunka* in Japanese).

When a company produces different products or models, it is desirable to produce in small lots (to minimize the work-in-process inventories and to maintain flexibility) and to spread out the production of different products or models throughout the day to achieve even smooth production. The ideal case would be to produce one unit of one product or model, then one unit of another, then one unit of another, and so on.

The simplest method for determining a *level mixed-model sequence* is as follows:[2]

a. Determine a "due time" for each unit of each product or model so that the units of the product or model are evenly distributed throughout the day.

b. Sequence the units of all products or models based on their "due times" (from smallest to largest).

The "due times," based on daily demand for each model, are as follows:

Daily Demand	Due Times (start of day = 0, end of day = 1)
1	1/2
2	1/4, 3/4
3	1/6, 3/6, 5/6
4	1/8, 3/8, 5/8, 7/8
5	1/10, 3/10, 5/10, 7/10, 9/10
6	1/12, 3/12, 5/12, 7/12, 9/12, 11/12
7	1/14, 3/14, 5/14, 7/14, 9/14, 11/14, 13/14
8	1/16, 3/16, 5/16, 7/16, 9/16, 11/16, 13/16, 15/16
⋮	

---

[2]R.R. Inman and R.L. Bulfin, "Sequencing JIT Mixed-model Assembly Lines," *Management Science* 37(7), July 1991, pp. 901–904.

In general, if daily demand is n for a product or model, the due times will be:

$$\frac{1}{2n}, \frac{3}{2n}, \frac{5}{2n}, \cdots \frac{2n-1}{2n}.$$

Example 2	Determine a level mixed model sequence if daily demand for product A = 7, B = 16, and C = 5 units.

Solution

The due times for each product are:

A: $1/14 = .071$, $3/14 = .214$, $5/14 = .357$, $7/14 = .5$, $9/14 = .643$, $11/14 = .786$, $13/14 = .929$

B: $1/32 = .031$, $3/32 = .094$, $5/32 = .156$, $7/32 = .219$, $9/32 = .281$, $11/32 = .344$, $13/32 = .406$, $15/32 = .469$, $17/32 = .531$, $19/32 = .594$, $21/32 = .656$, $23/32 = .719$, $25/32 = .781$, $27/32 = .844$, $29/32 = .906$, $31/32 = .969$

C: $1/10 = .1$, $3/10 = .3$, $5/10 = .5$, $7/10 = .7$, $9/10 = .9$

Now, sequence the due times from the smallest to the largest. The smallest due time is .031 for a B, so the first unit to produce is B. The next smallest due time is .071 for an A, so the second unit to produce is A, and so on. The level mixed model sequence is:

B-A-B-C-B-A-B-B-C-B-A-B-B-A-C-B-B-A-B-C-B-B-A-B-C-B-A-B

Pull System and *Kanban*

push system Based on MRP plan, a batch of items is made and pushed to the next work centre as it is completed.

pull system Based directly on customer demand, a work centre pulls items from the preceding work centre as they are needed.

The terms *push* and *pull* are used to describe two different approaches for making and moving items (raw material, parts, subassemblies, products) through a production process. In the traditional production environments that use MRP, a **push system** is used: A batch is started at a work centre according to the production plan derived from MRP. When the batch is finished at the work centre, the output is *pushed* to the next work centre; or, in the case of the final operation, it is pushed on to the finished goods warehouse. Consequently, inventory will pile up at work centres. Conversely, in a **pull system**, control of moving the batch (preferably only one unit) rests with the following operation; each work centre *pulls* the output from the preceding work centre as it is needed; output of the final operation is pulled by customer demand. JIT/lean uses the pull system.

In a pull system, communication moves backward through the system from work centre to work centre. Each work centre communicates its need for more items to the preceding work centre. The batch moves "just in time" to the next operation; the flow is thereby coordinated, and the accumulation of excessive inventories between operations is avoided. Of course, some buffer inventory is usually allowed because operations are not instantaneous. When the buffer inventory decreases to a certain level (i.e., the reorder point), this signals the preceding work centre to produce enough output to replenish the buffer supply. The size of the buffer supply depends on the lead time. If the lead time is short, the buffer can be small. The communication between the two work centres can be done in a variety of ways, including a shout or a wave, but by far the most commonly used method is the use of **kanban** cards. *Kanban* is Japanese for "signal" or "visual card." When a worker needs a batch of an item from the preceding work centre, she uses a *kanban* card. In effect, the *kanban* card is the *authorization* to make the batch. No item can be made without one of these cards.

kanban Card that communicates demand for a batch of an item to the preceding work centre.

The system works this way: A *kanban* card is affixed to each container. When a work centre needs to replenish its supply of a batch of an item, a worker goes to the area where these items are stored and withdraws one container of the item. Each container holds a predetermined quantity. The worker removes the *kanban* card from the container and posts it in a designated spot where it will be clearly visible to the operator of the producing work centre (e.g., a *kanban* board), and the worker moves the container to the using work centre. The posted *kanban* is later picked up by the operator of the producing work centre and another batch of the item is made. Usually because of significant setup time and the desire for high utilization of the producing work centre, a few *kanbans* are first accumulated before production is triggered. Similar withdrawals and replenishments—all controlled by *kanbans*—occur all the way up and down the line from vendors to finished-goods warehouse. Each item will have kanbans between each pair of supplying-using work centres. If supervisors decide the system is too loose because inventories are building up, they may decide to withdraw some *kanbans*. Conversely, if the system seems too tight, they may introduce additional *kanbans*. It is apparent that the number of *kanban* cards in use is an important variable. One can calculate the ideal number of *kanban* cards for each item, between each pair of supplying-using work centres, by this formula:

$$N = \frac{DT(1+X)}{C} \qquad (15\text{-}1)$$

where

N = Total number of *kanbans* (1 *kanban* per container)

D = Average usage rate of using work centre

T = Average lead time for replenishment of one container (includes wait before production, setup, production, and transport times)

X = Policy variable set by the management that represents the safety stocks (as a proportion of average usage during lead time T)

C = Capacity of a standard container

Note that D and T must use the same time unit (e.g., hour, day). The concept underlying the above formula is the same as the concept underlying the reorder point in the EOQ − ROP inventory model (see Chapter 12): ROP = DT(1+X) = average demand during a lead time plus safety stock, where safety stock is a proportion X of the average demand during a lead time.

Example 3

Usage at a work centre is 300 units of a specific part per day, and a standard container holds 25 units. It takes an average of 0.12 day from the time a *kanban* card is posted until the full container is received by the using work centre. Calculate the number of *kanban* cards needed for this part between these two work centres, if $X = 0.20$.

Solution

$N = ?$

D = 300 units per day

T = 0.12 day

C = 25 units per container

X = 0.20

$$N = \frac{300(.12)(1+.20)}{25} = 1.728 \text{ round to 2 containers}$$

Note: Rounding up will cause the system to be looser, and rounding down will cause it to be tighter. Usually, rounding up is used.

Other forms of signal include empty squares on the floor, empty carts or containers, and empty shelves/racks. For an application, see the "Waterville TG" OM in Action on the next page.

OM in ACTION   http://www.wtg.ca

Waterville TG

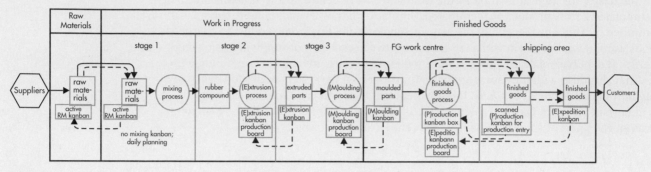

Figure 1

Waterville TG (WTG), of Quebec, designs and manufactures insulation for doors, hoods, and trunks of cars from various types of rubber. Waterville TG is part of Toyoda Gosei Co. Ltd., a division of Toyota Motor Company. WTG has close to 385 different models of insulations designed for almost all types of automobiles. The raw material is synthetic powder rubber. The production process is four stages: mixing, extrusion, moulding, and finishing. WTG uses kanbans for pulling material through most of the production process, as shown in Figure 1 above.

There are raw material (RM) kanbans, WIP extrusion (E) and moulding (M) kanbans, finished goods production (P) kanbans, and shipping or expedition (E) *kanbans*. An example of a RM *kanban* is shown in Figure 2 below:

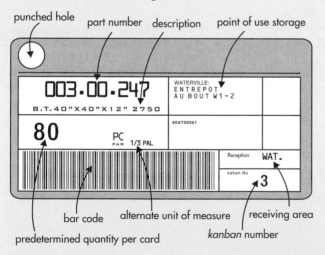

Figure 2

The use of bar codes on a *kanban* is unusual. WTG uses the computer and bar codes to keep track of inventories and changes the number of active *kanbans* as demand varies. The bar codes make this easier. The card itself is printed on plain white paper and inserted in a protective clear plastic pouch that in turn is placed in a self-adhesive pouch. This pouch is then

attached to a container. Soon after a full container is moved to its point of use, the *kanban* is detached and moved back to the originating area. The punched hole in the top left corner is used to hang the card on the *kanban* boards.

Figure 3 shows an example of a WIP E *kanban*. A Ziplock-type seal was added to the pouch for easier maintenance. After trying out several versions of this card, WTG found that *kanban* maintenance was easier when cards included only information that changed little or not at all over time.

At the finished goods level, two cards are used instead of one to allow some excess production (relative to shipment). These kanbans are similar to the WIP *kanbans*.

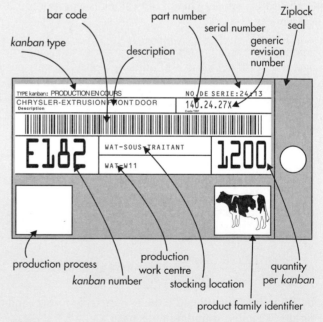

Figure 3

Source: S. Chausse, S. Landry, F. Pasin, and S. Fortier, "Anatomy of a Kanban: A Case Study," *Production and Inventory Management Journal* 41(4), Fourth Quarter 2000, pp. 11–16.

Close Supplier Relationship

JIT/lean companies typically have *close relationships with their suppliers*, who are expected to provide frequent small deliveries of high-quality goods on time. Buyers work with suppliers to help them achieve the desired quality and on-time delivery. The ultimate goal of the buyer is to be able to *certify* a supplier as a reliable producer of high-quality goods, and hence remove the need for inspection of the goods purchased from them.

In effect, the supplier becomes part of an extended JIT/lean system that integrates the facilities of buyer and supplier as part of the value chain. Integration is easier when a supplier is dedicated to only one or few buyers.

Because of the need for frequent small deliveries, many buyers attempt to find local suppliers to shorten the lead time for deliveries and to reduce the lead-time variability. An added advantage of having suppliers nearby is quick response when problems arise. Of course, EDI with the supplier is a must.

Ford is taking a page out of Toyota's JIT/lean book at its Chicago plant that opened in 2004 by having some of its suppliers locate very close to its assembly plant. Ford leased production facilities on its 155 acres land to approximately 10 key suppliers. Suppliers' parts and modules feed directly into Ford's assembly line, carefully coordinated to match the sequence of vehicles Ford is producing, which can range from small cars to SUVs. Not only are suppliers nearby in case problems arise, but also the shortened travel distance and lead times yield tremendous savings in the in-transit inventories of parts and modules.

JIT/lean companies employ a tiered approach for suppliers: They use relatively few first-tier suppliers that work directly with the company and supply major subassemblies. The first-tier suppliers are responsible for dealing with their own suppliers (the second-tier suppliers) that provide parts for the subassemblies, thereby relieving the final buyer from dealing with a large number of suppliers.

The automotive industry provides a good example of this situation. Suppose a certain car model has an electric seat. The seat and its motor together might entail 250 separate parts. A traditional automobile manufacturer might use more than 30 suppliers for the electric seat, but a JIT/lean auto manufacturer will use a single (first-tier) supplier that has the responsibility for the entire seat unit. The auto manufacturer will provide some specification for the overall unit, but leave the details of the motor, springs, and so on, to the supplier. The first-tier supplier, in turn, might subcontract the motor to a second-tier supplier, the track to another second-tier supplier, and the cushions and fabric to another. The second-tier suppliers might subcontract some of their work to third-tier suppliers, and so on. Each tier has to deal with only those just above it and just below it. Suppliers on each level are encouraged to work with each other, and they are motivated to do so because that increases the probability that the resulting item (the seat) will meet or exceed the final buyer's expectations. Figure 15-4 illustrates the difference between the traditional and tiered (JIT/lean) supplier networks.

Figure 15-4

Traditional supplier network compared to supplier tiers used in JIT/lean

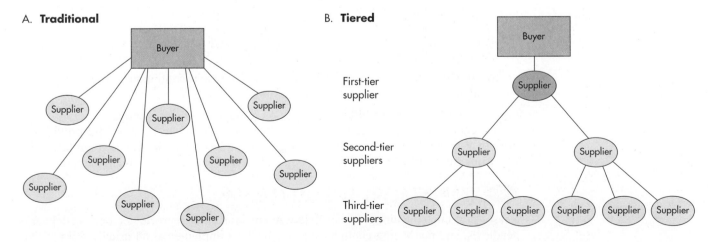

A. **Traditional**

B. **Tiered**

First-tier supplier

Second-tier suppliers

Third-tier suppliers

OM in ACTION

Plains Fabrication & Supply

Plains Fabrication & Supply (PF&S) is a metal shop in Calgary that makes custom industrial heaters, separators, and pressure vessels. It started with 16 people in 1988 and now employs 150 workers and has $20 million revenue. Low profit margin (4 percent) and an old plant brought PF&S to a crossroads in 2005: either it had to become more efficient or had to close down. It decided the former and got help from a provincial government program called Productivity Alberta, which provided JIT/lean manufacturing guidance at a low price. After a four-hour assessment, all employees were put through a four-hour workshop on JIT/lean manufacturing. One area of the shop, the small vessels area, was chosen for lean improvement. The improvements included use of visual and shadow boards, *kanban* cards and shelves, and clean and organized shop floor. After 12 months, the amount of inventory on the shop floor was reduced by 75 percent and lead time was reduced from 44 days to 5 days.

Sources: http://www.albertacanada.com/productivity/lean/plains-fabrication.html, accessed August 30, 2009; C. Lynds, "Making the Most of Time and Space," *Plant*, October 18, 2008, 67(10), p. 20; http://www.productivityalberta.ca/articles/187/plains-speaking.

A very close cooperation with suppliers, called JIT II, has been used by Bose Corporation, the manufacturer of luxury audio equipment, in which a supplier representative is located in Bose's facility and performs the functions of Bose's buyer. This reduces lead times. For another application, see the "Dana" OM in Action earlier in the chapter.

Preventive Maintenance and Housekeeping

preventive maintenance Keeping equipment in good operating condition and replacing parts that have a tendency to fail before they actually do fail.

housekeeping Maintaining the workplace clean and free of unnecessary things.

Because JIT/lean systems have very little work-in-process inventory, equipment breakdowns can be extremely disruptive. To minimize downtime, JIT/lean companies use **preventive maintenance** programs, which emphasize maintaining equipment in good operating condition and replacing parts that have a tendency to fail before they fail.

Even with preventive maintenance, occasional equipment failures will occur. Companies must be prepared for this, so they can quickly return equipment back to working order. This may mean maintaining supplies of critical spare parts and making other provisions for emergency situations, perhaps maintaining a small team of repair people or training workers to do certain repairs themselves.

Housekeeping involves keeping the workplace clean, because it facilitates discovery of problem. For example, clean floors will show oil leak from a machine, which could result in a worker slipping, a safety hazard. Housekeeping also involves keeping the workplace free of anything that is not needed for production, because it takes up space and may cause disruption to the work flow. These and other principles of housekeeping are included in the *5S principles*:

- SORT: remove all objects that do not need to be in the workstation or area.
- SET IN ORDER: tidy up the objects needed and organize them such that they can be seen and therefore found quickly. For example, use a peg or shadow board for hand tools.
- SHINE: clean the workstation completely and eliminate all signs of dust or grime on the floor, machines, and equipment.
- STANDARDIZE: Set standards in cleanliness and organization, and audit the area for compliance.
- SUSTAIN: train workers to perform housekeeping and continuously improve on the standards; make 5S part of the work culture.

http://www.lmsi.ca/5s.htm

For an application, see the "Plains Fabrication & Supply" OM in Action.

JIT/lean systems have been described in the preceding pages. Table 15-2 provides a brief overview of JIT/lean vs. traditional production systems. The next section lists JIT/lean implementation steps and an implementation tool called value stream mapping.

LO7 IMPLEMENTING JIT/LEAN

Reasons for implementing JIT/lean include not making enough profit, not meeting delivery deadlines, and not having enough capacity. JIT/lean implementation usually follows the following steps. Management communicates JIT/lean's importance to the employees and

Factor	Traditional	JIT/lean
Inventory	Much, to offset late deliveries, etc.	Minimal necessary to operate
Deliveries	Few, large	Many, small
Lot sizes	Large	Small
Setups, runs	Few, long runs	Many, short runs
Vendors	Adversaries	Partners
Workers	Replaceable	Assets

Table 15-2

Comparison of JIT/lean and traditional production systems

obtains their cooperation. Usually an outside consultant is brought in as a facilitator. The employees go through a class on JIT/lean tools, techniques, and principles. Implementation is usually piecemeal. A product family is chosen. Usually the products are being produced in batches and excessive material handling is involved. A team of the operators is formed, the product flow is studied and drawn (called the value stream mapping), wastes are identified and eliminated, a cycle (*takt*) time is determined based on demand, and a new streamlined process is designed. This requires re-arranging the equipment into a cellular layout, cross-training the operators, reducing setup times, standardizing the work, balancing the line, applying 5S principles, setting up a demand pull system and arranging *kanban* signals with suppliers, putting in *jidoka* (quality at the source) quality controls, implementing performance-based pay, and continuously improving the line. Then, JIT/lean production is expanded to other products and other business processes such as supplier selection, product design, sales process, and recruiting.

For two implementations of JIT/lean, see the "Scona Trailer Manufacturing" and "CGL Manufacturing" OM in Actions earlier in the chapter.

Value Stream Mapping

A value stream map (VSM) displays the process steps (i.e., the operations), and material and information flows used in the production of a family of products. The information flows control the operations and material flows. A VSM is an extended version of the process flow diagram (see Chapter 6) which also includes the information flows (in the top of the map) and the times of activities (in the bottom of the map). A VSM is best drawn by a multifunctional team of frontline staff. It is important that the map shows what actually happens, and not what should happen. That's why a walk through the process is essential.

A VSM may also show the following for each process step: (a) cycle time, (b) change over (or setup) time, (c) up-time percentage (i.e., utilization), (d) capacity or hours available, and (e) cycle length for production of every part/product (also called Every Part Every or EPE). These are inserted in a data box under each process step.

The team should capture three important attributes of a value stream: (a) flow vs. stagnation (shown by inventories), (b) push vs. pull, and (c) level vs. erratic demand. In addition, the most critical feature of the value stream, usually its throughput time, is also shown on the map (bottom right).

To draw a VSM, the customer is shown by a box on the top right corner of the map, with customer requirements written in a box under it. Similarly, on the top left-hand side of the map the supplier is shown in a box, with the requirements from the supplier written in a box under it. The box for the production control (the function that schedules and controls the production.) is put in the top middle. Electronic information is shown by jagged arrows and paper information by straight arrows. The shipping and receiving are shown under the customer and supplier data boxes, respectively. The production process is drawn in the bottom of the map from left to right. Operations are shown in boxes with their name, etc. Data for each operation is shown below it in a data box. Inventories are shown with a triangle with letter I written in it. Movement of material is shown with a thick arrow. The average processing times and wait times are shown on the time line in the bottom of the map. These two types of times should be distinguished by putting them on different levels. The production lead time (the sum of all times) and the total value-added time (the sum of only processing times) are shown in the bottom right side of the map. See the following example of a VSM for a producer of a simple car part. (Note: C/T = cycle time, C/O = change over time, EPE = every part every).

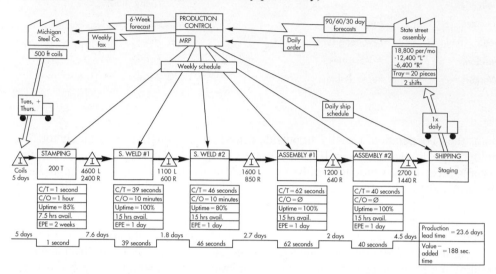

The previous map is the current-state VSM. After drawing it, each step should be challenged for its value. Rework and storage rarely provide value to customers. Increasing the quality capability of a step so that there is no rework and organizing many steps in a continuous flow (by putting capable and available equipment of different technology in a tight sequence as in cellular layout) are good ways to eliminate waste. Another action required is to level the output of the value stream (by e.g., creating some inventory of finished goods before shipment) and, if necessary, divide the value stream into two or more streams (e.g., for standard products and especial products).

The current-state VSM is redrawn to include the desired changes. This is called the future-state VSM. Action plans and programs should be determined and funded to make the necessary changes. Usually, throughput time and costs are reduced and quality is improved. A future-state VSM for producing the above simple car part is shown below. Here, the setup time for the press (in the stamping operation) has been reduced to less than 10 minutes, the welding and assembly operations have been combined in a cell, and the production control is using a pull system instead of the push system. For another application, see the "Canada Post's Calgary Plant" OM in Action.

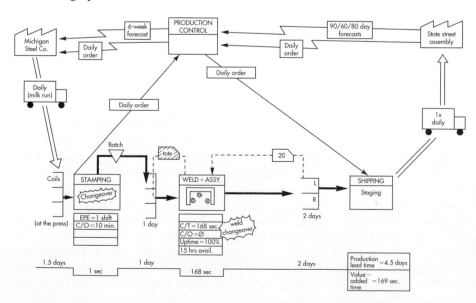

OM in *ACTION*

Canada Post's Calgary Plant

Canada Post has been increasing the efficiency of its operations (letter, parcel, express mail, and publication and advertising mail) since the mid-1990s. Before then, Canada Post used batch processing in many parts of its sorting/distribution plants. Two of the JIT/lean initiatives in its Calgary plant are described below.

a. The Publication and Advertising mail is brought in the plant in 50–60 pound bags placed in large wheeled metal containers. The containers used to be emptied onto a below-floor conveyor at the receiving area that took them to a sorting area where an employee read the tags and rerouted them to be piled up in another container, which was then taken to another part of the 350,000 ft² plant for further sorting. Altogether, a bag was handled four times. This inefficient process was replaced with one that takes the container to an "induction" area where a bag is

picked up every 24 seconds (to match the average number of bags arriving), the tag read, and put on one of the four conveyors (for Calgary, Southern Alberta, Eastern Canada, and needing further processing) depending on the information on the tag. Then the bags are opened and sorted on each conveyor. The whole process now requires 6–7 employees (vs. 10 to 15 employees needed before the change) and the processing lead time has been was reduced from 2 days to 1 day.

b. Value stream mapping was used for most JIT/lean initiatives. An example is the value stream for the current state of express parcel mail processing (shown below; PY = payroll). Again, the parcels are first sorted into East, Edmonton, BC, Others, and Calgary. After this sort, some of the mail is accumulated and moved to another location in the plant for further sorting. This added an average of two hours of waiting. In the Future state, this wait time is eliminated and payroll is reduced by two employees.

Originating Express Parcel Value Stream
CURRENT STATE

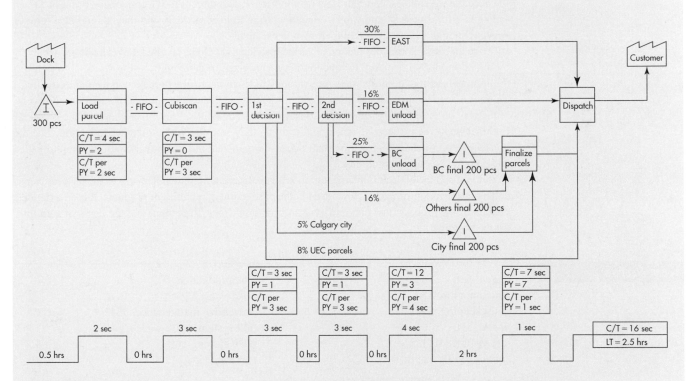

Source: http://www.lean.org/admin/km/documents/d02948c7-1c5c-4b4a-8c0f-989e2ba05e5a-Canada%20Post%20success%20story%202.pdf.

Summary

Just-in-time (JIT), in a narrow sense, is a system of production in which processing and movement of parts/modules/work-in-process occur just as they are needed, usually in small batches. JIT systems require very little inventory because successive operations are closely coordinated. JIT in a broad sense, also called lean production, is a philosophy of eliminating wastes, especially setup, lead times, and inventories, and continuous improvement.

The goals of JIT/lean are a balanced rapid flow, elimination of waste and disruption, a flexible system, and continuous improvement.

The building blocks of a JIT/lean system are various tools and methods used in product design, process design, personnel and organization, and planning and control.

Products should be simple to make and assemble (DFM and DFA). Concurrent engineering and QFD should be used to ensure a fast product design process and that the voice of the customer is reflected in the product's quality.

A JIT/lean system is balanced. One unit is produced every *takt* (or cycle) time to meet the demand. It is flexible (e.g., changeover times are fast) to meet the mix of products and changes in demand.

Small production lot sizes are used in order to reduce the WIP, increase flexibility, and facilitate defect detection. Setup times should be reduced to render small lot sizes economical. Product families are identified and produced in dedicated cells; this reduces material handling and manufacturing lead times. JIT/lean requires the highest quality parts because there is little safety stock. Through *jidoka* or quality at the source, a defective item isn't passed through; workers stop and fix the problem. Standardized work, interaction, and work flow are required in order to learn and improve a JIT/lean system. In addition to WIP, raw material and finished goods inventories should also be minimized.

Workers should be respected and empowered in order to participate in continuous improvement (*kaizen*) and cross-trained in order to help with system flexibility. Top management should assign the necessary resources, communicate its importance, and direct the JIT conversion process. Other functions of business should support manufacturing to become lean, and they should also initiate waste reduction programs within their own departments.

To reduce inventories, production of various products should be levelled. Level loads are achieved by mixed-model sequencing. Production is synchronized to demand by using *kanbans* to pull the minimum amount of parts and materials through the manufacturing process and from the suppliers. There is a need to integrate operations with the suppliers; hence, the number of suppliers should be reduced in order to establish close relationships and partnerships. Preventive maintenance is crucial for JIT/lean systems, because machine downtime may stop the whole plant's production. The 5S housekeeping method is also important because organized and clean workstations operate faster and help in discovering problems.

A tool used in JIT/lean implementation is a value stream map, which displays the process steps, and material and information flows used in the production of a family of products. It is an extended version of the process flow diagram, with information flows (in the top) and the times of activities (in the bottom).

Key Terms

andon, 556	lean production, 547
autonomation, 556	*poka-yoke*, 556
housekeeping, 564	preventive maintenance, 564
jikoda, 556	pull system, 560
just-in-time (JIT), 547	push system, 560
kanban, 560	*takt* time, 552

Solved Problems

Problem 1

Determine the number of *kanbans* needed for a part in a workstation that uses 100 units of the part per hour if the time from posting a *kanban* until receiving a full container (wait, setup, fill, return) is 90 minutes and a standard container holds 84 units. A safety factor of 0.10 is currently being used.

$N = ?$

$D = 100$ units per hour

$T = 90$ minutes (1.5 hours)

$C = 84$ units

$X = .10$

$$N = \frac{D(T)(1 + X)}{C} = \frac{100(1.5)(1 + .10)}{84} = 1.96, \text{round to 2 } kanbans.$$

Determine a level mixed-model sequence for the following set of products and demand. The plant operates five days a week.

Product	Weekly Quantity
A	20
B	40
C	30
D	15

Convert weekly quantities to daily quantities:

Product	Daily Quantity = Weekly Quantity ÷ 5
A	20 ÷ 5 = 4
B	40 ÷ 5 = 8
C	30 ÷ 5 = 6
D	15 ÷ 5 = 3

The due times are:

A: $1/8 = .125, 3/8 = .375, 5/8 = .625, 7/8 = .875$

B: $1/16 = .0625, 3/16 = .1875, 5/16 = .3125, 7/16 = .4375, 9/16 = .5625,$
      $11/16 = .6875, 13/16 = .8125, 15/16 = .9375$

C: $1/12 = .083, 3/12 = .25, 5/12 = .417, 7/12 = .583, 9/12 = .75, 11/12 = .917$

D: $1/6 = .167, 3/6 = .5, 5/6 = .83$

Sort the due times from the smallest to the largest. The smallest due time is .0625 for B, so the first unit in the sequence should be B. The next smallest due time is .083 for C, so the second unit in sequence to produce should be C, and so on:

   B-C-A-D-B-C-B-A-C-B-D-B-C-A-B-C-B-D-A-C-B

Cars are to be assembled on a moving assembly line. Five hundred cars are required per day. Production time per day is eight hours minus a half-hour for lunch break. What is the *takt* time?

$8(60) = 480 - 30 = 450$ minutes per day

Takt time $= 450/500 = 0.9$ minute $= 54$ seconds

1. Distinguish between little JIT and big JIT. (LO1)

2. Explain briefly how a JIT/lean system differs from an MRP-based system. (LO1)

3. What are the main benefits of JIT/lean? Name a company using JIT/lean, and describe how JIT/lean contributes to the company's competitive advantage. (LO1)

4. Contrast the principles of the Shingo prize with the goals of JIT/lean given in Figure 15-1. Why can't a Shingo Prize winner's production process be unbalanced and slow? Explain. (LO1)

5. **a.** What are the goals of JIT/lean system? (LO2)

   b. What are the eight wastes? (LO2)

6. What aspects of product design are important for JIT/lean? (LO3)

7. What are (a) *takt* time, (b) SMED, (c) *jidoka*, and (d) *poka-yoke*? (LO4)

8. What are the benefits of (a) small lot sizes, (b) standardized process, (c) low inventories? (LO4)

9. What is the role of workers in JIT/lean? (LO5)

10. What is a *kanban*? (LO6)

11. Contrast push and pull systems of moving parts/modules/work-in-process through the production system. (LO6)

12. What is level mixed-model sequencing and why is it important? (LO6)

13. Briefly discuss supplier relations in JIT/lean in terms of the following issues: (LO6)

    a. Why are they important?

    b. How do they tend to differ from the more adversarial relations of the past?

14. What is 5S and why is it important? (LO6)

15. What is value stream mapping and why is it important? (LO7)

Taking Stock

1. What trade-offs are involved in shifting from an MRP system to a JIT/lean system? (LO1)

2. Who in the company is affected by a decision to shift from an MRP system to a JIT/lean system? (LO7)

3. To what extent has technology had an impact on JIT/lean systems? (LO4 & 6)

4. A cellular layout contains various machines in close proximity to one another. What kind of health and safety issues can arise in a cell? Give an example. Hint: see e.g., G. D. Brown and D. O'Rourke, "Lean Manufacturing Comes to China: A Case Study of its Impact on Workplace Health and Safety," *International Journal of Occupational and Environmental Health*, 13(3), July/September 2007, pp. 249–257. (LO4)

Critical Thinking Exercises

1. What are the key enablers for successful implementation of JIT/lean? (LO7)

2. Is the service system of WestJet JIT/lean? (See the end of Chapter 2 for a Case on WestJet.) Explain. (LO3–6)

3. In what way is a *kanban* system similar to the EOQ-ROP system of Chapter 12? (LO6)

Experiential Learning Exercise

Visit a McDonald's restaurant and observe its production system. Is it using JIT/lean? Is the production schedule levelled? Is the system flexible (both in terms of equipment and workers)? Is there any visible wastes? Does McDonald's use *kanbans*? Explain. (LO3–6)

Internet Exercises

1. Visit http://www.shingoprize.org/htm/award-info/award-recipients/shingo-prize, choose a recent recipient of the Shingo prize, and briefly summarize its JIT/lean program. (LO1)

2. Read one of the following JIT/lean production cases and summarize it: (LO7)

   a. http://www.leanadvisors.com/index.php/impact2/results_full/lean_aerospace_implementation_at_messier_dowty

b. http://www.leanadvisors.com/index.php/impact2/results_full/lean_implementation_at_
active_burgess_mould_and_design

c. http://www.leanadvisors.com/index.php/impact2/results_full/lean_in_the_haematology_
laboratory

3. View one of the following videos and summarize what value stream mapping is. (LO7)

a. http://www.youtube.com/watch?v=K0fWw9QXk60

b. http://www.youtube.com/watch?v=3mcMwlgUFjU&feature=related

4. Visit http://totalqualitymanagcmcnt.wordprcss.com/2008/10/28/lean-production-system, and
compare the concepts of JIT/lean production system there with that given in the chapter.
(LO1 & 2)

5. Go to http://www2.toyota.co.jp/en/vision/production_system/quiz.html, and take the quiz.
What new concepts did you learn? (LO1–7)

Problems

1. A manager wants to determine the number of *kanbans* to use in a new process for a part. The
process will have a usage rate of 80 pieces of the part per hour. Because the process is new,
the manager has assigned a safety factor of 1.0. Each container holds 45 pieces and a *kanban*
will take an average of 75 minutes to complete a cycle. How many *kanbans* should be used?
As the system improves, will more or fewer *kanbans* be required? Why? (LO6)

2. A JIT/lean system uses *kanban* cards to authorize production and movement of materials.
In one portion of the system, a work centre uses an average of 100 pieces of a part per hour.
The manager has assigned a safety factor of .50. Standard containers are designed to hold
six dozen pieces each. The cycle time for a kanban is 105 minutes. How many *kanbans* are
needed? (LO6)

3. A cell uses 90 kg of a certain material each day. The material is transported in vats that hold
54 kg each. Cycle time for a *kanban* is about two hours. The manager has assigned a safety factor of .50. The plant operates on an eight-hour day. How many *kanbans* are needed? (LO6)

4. Determine a level mixed-model sequence, given the following demand data: (LO6)

Product	Daily Quantity
A	1
B	2
C	3
D	4

5. Determine a level mixed-model sequence, given the following demand data: (LO6)

Product	Daily Quantity
A	2
B	12
C	4
D	5
E	9

6. Determine a level mixed-model sequence, given the following demand data: (LO6)

Product	Daily Quantity
F	9
G	8
H	5
K	6

7. Toyota decided to make its minivan, Sienna, in the same plant as Camry and Avalon. Suppose that during a half-hour period 12 Camrys, 9 Avalons, and 6 Siennas are to be produced. Determine a level mixed-model sequence. (LO6)

*8. The whirlpool factory in Oxford, Mississippi, makes built-in kitchen ovens.[3] In the 1990s, this plant re-engineered its processes to become JIT/lean. One of the parts of a particular oven, Part A, is processed by two 600 ton presses (in series), and then goes through a porcelain system to be coated. Finally, it is stored in the WIP storage location until it is used by the assembly lines. As a container of Part A is to be used, the *kanban* attached to it is taken to the press area and posted on the *Kanban* Post. Demand for Part A is 175 units per workday. A workday is 19 hours. The container size is 30 units. The setup time is 1 hour. Because of the large setup time, 5 *kanbans* are accumulated before production of A begins on the presses (approximately 16 hours of wait time). Production rate for A is 120 units per hour. The safety factor is 120 percent. Determine the number of *kanbans* required for Part A. (LO6)

600 TON PRESSES

1A 2A → PORCELAIN SYSTEM
1B 2B
KANBAN POST

WIP STORAGE LOCATION

ASSEMBLY LINES

→ PART FLOW – ⇢ KANBAN FLOW

9. Calculate the *takt* time for a system where the total time per shift is 480 minutes, there is one shift, and workers are given two 15-minute breaks and 45 minutes for lunch. Daily demand is 300 units. (LO4)

10. What *takt* time would match capacity and demand if demand is 120 units a day, there are two shifts of 480 minutes each, and workers are given three half-hour breaks during each shift, one of which is for lunch or dinner? (LO4)

11. Calculate the *takt* time for a service system that is intended to perform a standardized service. The system will have a total work time of 440 minutes per day, two 10-minute breaks, and an hour for lunch. The service system must process 90 jobs a day. (LO4)

*12. A motor cycle manufacturer produces three models: A, B, and C. This month's master production schedule, divided by 22 work days, has resulted in daily production targets of 54 As, 42 Bs, and 30 Cs. The company works one shift per day, and effective production time is seven hours per day. Determine a level mixed-model sequence. *Hint*: To reduce the size of the problem, divide each production target by their greatest common divisor. (LO6)

MINI-CASE

Airline Manufacturing

Airline Manufacturing is a 275,000-square-foot, 100-employee wood component manufacturer supplying upholsterers (e.g., sofa manufacturers), and is located in Columbus, Mississippi. When Judy Dunaway took the helm of the company following her father in 2000, the company had used a batch production system for 40 years. However, the threat of competition led her to start JIT/lean manufacturing. High-run (quantity) products were identified and grouped together if their required sequences of operations were identical. The machines required for each group were located close together in a dedicated cell (flow line). As a result, the amount of WIP inventory has been cut by more than half, the number of material-handling carts has been reduced from 3,000 to 1,000, and the number of material handlers has been reduced by half. Also, manufacturing lead time is down from four weeks to less than a week.

A high-run product is part #146-3843. Consider the production of a 2,900-unit customer order. Before the layout change, batches of approximately 1,000 units were transported from the warehouse to the CNC Router, and from there batches of approximately 380 units were carried, when ready, from one machine to another by two workers using heavy carts. See the Batch Plant Layout diagram, Figure 1, on the next page. These workers returned the empty carts to the originating machine. After the final operation, Dowel, the finished product was transported in batches of approximately 380 units to the Finished Goods Warehouse using forklifts. The total worker-feet of movement using the forklifts (including the return to their origin) was approximately 5,300.

After the layout change, the only transport is by forklifts bringing in and taking out the product. The total worker-feet of movement using the forklifts has remained at approximately 5,300. However, the amount of machine-to-machine material

---

[3]Based on J.D. Hall et al., "An Optimizer for the Kanban Sizing Problem: A Spreadsheet Application for Whirlpool Corporation," *Production and Inventory Management Journal* 39(1), First Quarter, 1998, pp. 17–22.

handling has been greatly reduced because the machines are located close to each other. See the Cellular Layout, Figure 2, on the right. Due to elimination of delays waiting for material handling, the company can now make the 2,900-unit customer order in one day whereas it used to take six days.

Question

List the benefits of the cellular layout to Airline Manufacturing.

Cellular Layout

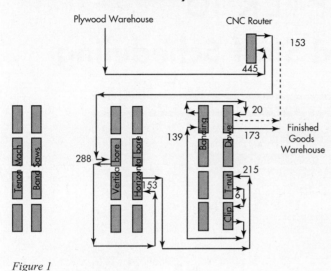

Six of 8 workers (happy faces) add value (was 8 of 25).
Material moves 12 times (was 27)–NO CARTS.
Batch production: 480 parts per day
Flow production: 2,900 parts per day

Figure 2

Sources: W. Duane Motsenbocker et al., "Wood Furniture Components: Implementation of Flow-Line Technology Based on Lean Manufacturing Concepts," *Research Bulletin*, Forest and Wildlife Centre, Mississippi State University; http://www.airlinemfg.com/capabilities.html. Figures courtesy of Mississippi State University.

Batch Plant Layout

Figure 1

Level Operations

L evel Operations is a small company that produces a variety of security devices and safes. The safes come in several different designs. Recently, a number of new customers have placed orders, and the production facility has been enlarged to accommodate the increased demand for the safes. The production manager is currently working on a production plan for the safes. She has obtained the following information from the marketing department on projected average daily demand for each model:

Model	Daily Quantity
A	4
B	3
C	10
D	12
E	5

Question

What might Stephanie determine as the level mixed-model sequence for each day?

To access "Maintenance," the supplement to Chapter 15, please visit *Connect*.

CHAPTER 16
Job and Staff Scheduling

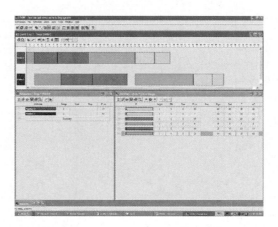

LEARNING OBJECTIVES

After completing this chapter, you should be able to:

LO1 Explain what job and staff scheduling are.

LO2 Explain loading, Gantt charts, and how to deal with infinite loading.

LO3 Discuss and use common priority rules and performance measures for sequencing/scheduling, and perform sequencing/scheduling of

two work centres and setup-dependent cases.

LO4 Explain shop-floor control and input/output control.

LO5 Describe scheduling based on the bottleneck work centre: the theory of constraints.

LO6 Describe some of the approaches used for staff scheduling, including scheduling two consecutive days off and shift scheduling.

When Herman Miller, a major office furniture manufacturer, started the new division Miller SQA (Simple, Quick, Affordable), it tried to change its production system so that it could meet customer orders in two days. How did Miller SQA achieve this? McDonald's is in a competitive market with low margins. How can McDonald's keep its labour costs down? These are the kind of questions answered in this chapter.

INTRODUCTION

Job (or detailed) **scheduling** is establishing the starting and completion hour/date of operations for jobs or orders. It involves assignment of jobs to work centres and to machines within each work centre, sequencing the jobs in front of each machine, and specifying their start, processing, and end times.

A **work centre** is a production area consisting of one or more workers and machines with similar capabilities, which can be considered as one unit for purpose of scheduling.

In the production planning hierarchy, scheduling decisions are the final step before the actual output is produced (see the bottom box in Figure 13-1, called Detailed planning and execution systems; note that detailed planning is the same as detailed scheduling). Many decisions have to be made long before detailed scheduling decisions. They include strategic planning decisions such as the capacity of the system and equipment selected, aggregate planning decisions such as selection and training of workers, and master production scheduling (MPS) and material requirements planning (MRP). Consequently, job scheduling decisions must be made within the constraints established by the above decisions, making them fairly narrow in scope and latitude. Figure 16-1 depicts the location of job scheduling in the production planning system of Black & Decker. It is called *dynamic scheduler* (now Production Scheduler). We will also cover **shop-floor control**, which relates to execution of the schedule and involves maintaining, communicating, and monitoring the status of material, orders, and process, and taking any necessary actions.

Recall that ordinary MRP does not take the load on the component work centres into account during its computation, and thus can result in overload. One has to perform capacity requirement planning to identify the capacity needs of MRP results and accommodate them to make the MRP feasible. However, some advanced planning and scheduling software have the ability to combine and automate these activities. For example, in Figure 16-1, the Capacity-Optimized Planner (now called Factory Planner in i2 Technology) is the capacitated version of MRP (and MPS). For a non-assembly process, there is no need for MRP, and job scheduling is identical to end-product scheduling (i.e., MPS).

MRP schedules the planned order releases backward, starting from the due date for the product. This is an example of **backward scheduling**. However, often scheduling starts from the start time of a job, and works forward into the future. This is called **forward scheduling**.

Staff scheduling involves determining the workdays, and start and end times on each workday, for each employee. This is covered in the last section of this chapter.

Job and staff scheduling are important because they affect customer due dates/service and production/operations costs. For some applications of job scheduling, see the "Beaver Plastics" and "Plastique Micron" OM in Actions later in the chapter.

LOADING

Loading refers to the assignment of jobs to work centres and to various machines within each work centre. In cases where a job can be processed only by a specific line/machine,

job scheduling Establishing the starting and completion hour/date of operations for jobs or orders.

work centre A production area consisting of one or more workers and machines with similar capabilities, that can be considered as one unit for purpose of scheduling.

shop-floor control Execution of the schedule; maintaining, communicating, and monitoring the status of material, orders, and process; and taking any necessary actions.

backward scheduling Scheduling backward from the due date.

forward scheduling Scheduling ahead, starting from the start date of a job.

staff scheduling Determining the workdays, and start and end times on each workday, for each employee.

loading The assignment of jobs to work centres and to various machines within each work centre.

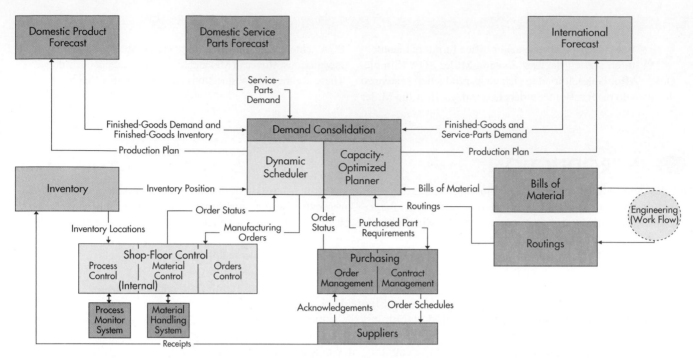

B&D implemented Rhythm from i2 Technologies in the early 1990s. Rhythm (Demand Consolidation, Capacity Optimized Planner, and Dynamic Scheduler) is at the core of Black & Decker's computer integrated manufacturing system. The demand consolidation module (used for forecasting) is now called Demand Manager; Capacity-Optimized Planner (advanced planning and scheduling which performs the function of MRP but keeps production within machine capacities) is now called Factory Planner; and Dynamic Scheduler (the topic of this chapter) is now called Production Scheduler. Rhythm has hundreds of installations around the world. A recent example is the implementation of Factory Planner in all five manufacturing plants of 3M Canada.

Figure 16-1

Black & Decker's production planning system

loading presents little difficulty, except for determining the time of the operation. However, problems arise when two or more jobs are to be processed and there are a number of work centres or machines within a work centre capable of performing the required work. In such cases, the scheduler needs some way of assigning jobs to the work centres or machines within each work centre.

When making an assignment, managers often choose a work centre or machine that will minimize processing and setup costs, minimize idle time among work centres or machines, allow an operator to run two machines simultaneously, or is the least sophisticated work centre or machine that can do the job depending on the situation. For an example, see the "Dell's Austin Plant" OM in Action.

Gantt Chart

Gantt chart A visual aid for loading, scheduling, and control purposes.

A visual aid called **Gantt chart** is used for a variety of purposes related to loading, scheduling, and control. It derives its name from Henry Gantt, who pioneered its use for industrial scheduling in the early 1900s.

There are a number of different types of Gantt chart. Two of the most commonly used are *load/schedule chart* and *schedule/control chart* (described later in the chapter).

load/schedule Gantt chart A Gantt chart that shows the loading and timing of jobs for a resource.

Load/Schedule Gantt Chart. A **load/schedule Gantt chart** depicts the loading and timing of jobs for resources such as machines, work centres, and facilities. This chart is used in services as well. Two examples are illustrated in Figure 16-2, which shows scheduling courses to classrooms and scheduling patients to a hospital's operating rooms. The purpose of a load/schedule Gantt chart is to organize and clarify the actual or intended use of resources over *time*. Time scale is represented horizontally, and resources to be scheduled are listed vertically. The use of the resources is reflected in the body of the chart.

Beaver Plastics

Beaver Plastics, based just outside Edmonton, makes polystyrene construction and packaging products such as egg cartons. The production process starts with polystyrene beads that are cured, and later fed into moulding machines. Large products may be cut using electric-heated wires. Some construction products, such as insulated walls, have reinforcement embedded in them. Beaver Plastics uses Taylor Scheduler to schedule the customer orders on its moulding machines and to also schedule the moulds. The schedule is updated every afternoon with new

orders and order completions. The software is also used to help sales staff promise achievable due dates. Beaver Plastics also uses Taylor Scheduler to enable sharing of some of its expensive moulds among its plants, in Edmonton; Chilliwack, BC; and Mexico. Taylor is also based in Edmonton. Taylor Scheduler has the ability to use optimization (integer linear programming) to perform capacitated master production scheduling and material requirements planning, thus ensuring that machine (and mould) capacities are not exceeded.

Sources: http://www.taylor.com/about/news.php?&flag=3&news=44; http://www.beaverplastics.com/index.html.

Dell's Austin Plant

Dell's Topfer Manufacturing Center (TMC) in Austin, Texas, assembles computers. The operations include kitting (gathering the set of components required for each chassis or case), assembly, testing, and packaging. The kitting is done on several parallel lines. Each kitting line has space for a certain number of chassis types (each chassis type is used for a family of products) called a "lane," and a certain number of bins (each containing a component) that are needed for one or more of the chassis types:

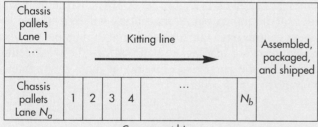

Component bins

The implication of this layout is that any chassis type could be made next, without requiring a setup time. When TMC opened in 2001, the number of kitting lines, and space for lanes and bins, was adequate so that each chassis type was assigned a lane and could be made next, without setup time. In fact high-demand chassis types were assigned one lane each in two kitting lines. The customer orders could be made first-come, first-served. However, since 2001, product variety and types of chassis have doubled. This means that most chassis types do not have a permanent lane and there is a need for setup (replacing the chassis pallet, with a forklift, and the associated bins) when a new chassis type is to be kitted on a kitting line. Because the setup time is long, a batch of a chassis type is made before changing to another. At first, the scheduling staff made decisions on the fly, but this was resulting in too much setup time (and the kitting line was idle while some bins were being changed), thus reducing the productivity of kitting lines. One of the schedulers, with the help of University of Texas faculty,

created some optimization (integer linear programming) and other models to help with the scheduling decisions. The decision making was divided to address three problems: (1) the chassis type to kitting line assignment, (2) the chassis type (within each kitting line) to lane assignment, and sequencing chassis types within each lane, and (3) the scheduling of runs for each chassis type on each kitting line.

Problem 1 assigns chassis types to the kitting lines in order to minimize a combination of the total number of setups required and the maximum bin spaces needed. The constraints include assigning each low-demand chassis type to one kitting line and assigning each high-demand chassis type to two kitting lines. Because demand is fairly stable, this problem is solved only every two weeks.

Problem 2 assigns chassis types to lanes within each kitting line and sequences them in each lane. A linear program balances the demand for chassis types assigned to the lanes so that the demand of the lane with minimum total demand is maximized. The constraints are that the chassis types that ended the last shift first in their lane-sequence are assigned to the same lane as in the previous shift and each lane is assigned at least one chassis type. The sequence within each lane starts with the chassis type that ended the last shift first in its lane, and continues according to the demand of chassis types, largest demand first.

Problem 3 schedules the runs for each chassis type on each kitting line. This is done by calculating the net operating time of each shift (eight hours minus any lunch and maintenance breaks and setup times) and allocating this to each chassis type in the kitting line in proportion to their demand. Thus, every chassis type is produced once a day (a customer service objective). The sequence of chassis types run on the kitting line is flexible as long as the chassis type chosen next is first in its lane and can be kitted while the necessary bins for the chassis type next-in-line are being replaced (to reduce line idle time). Also, the overlap of setup times across kitting lines is reduced so that setup resources are not overloaded.

Source: J.L. Loveland, et al, "Dell Uses a New Production-Scheduling Algorithm to Accommodate Increased Product Variety," *Interfaces*, 37(3), May–June 2007, pp. 209–219.

Figure 16-2

Examples of load/schedule Gantt chart used for scheduling facilities in services

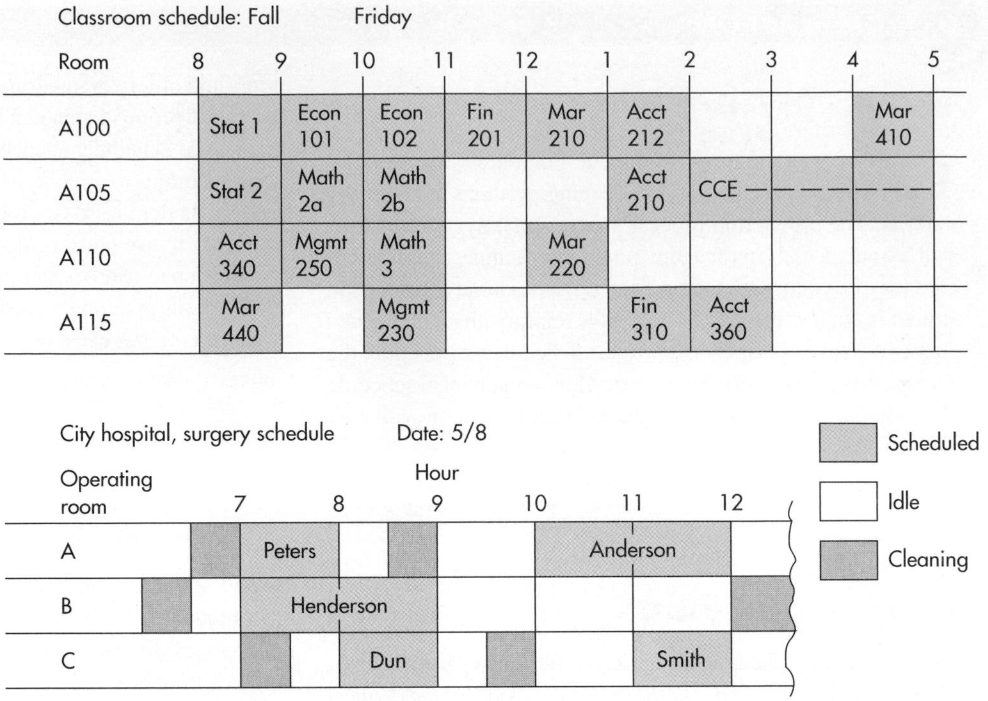

Classroom schedule: Fall   Friday

Room	8	9	10	11	12	1	2	3	4	5
A100	Stat 1	Econ 101	Econ 102	Fin 201	Mar 210	Acct 212				Mar 410
A105	Stat 2	Math 2a	Math 2b			Acct 210	CCE — — — — — —			
A110	Acct 340	Mgmt 250	Math 3		Mar 220					
A115	Mar 440		Mgmt 230				Fin 310	Acct 360		

City hospital, surgery schedule   Date: 5/8

Operating room   Hour

Operating room	7	8	9	10	11	12
A		Peters			Anderson	
B		Henderson				
C		Dun			Smith	

◻ Scheduled

◻ Idle

◻ Cleaning

Managers may use the load/schedule Gantt chart for trial-and-error schedule development. Thus, a tentative surgery schedule might reveal insufficient time allowance for a surgery that may take longer than expected. Use of the chart for classroom scheduling would help avoid assigning two different classes to the same room at the same time. Another example of a load/schedule Gantt chart is given in Figure 16-3. This chart indicates that work centre 3 is completely loaded for the entire week, work centre 4 will be available from Tuesday on, and the other two work centres have idle time scattered throughout the week. This information can help a manager rework loadings to better utilize the work centres. For instance, if all work centres perform the same kind of work, the manager might want to free one work centre for a long job or a rush order.

Figure 16-3

A load/schedule Gantt chart used for scheduling work centres in manufacturing

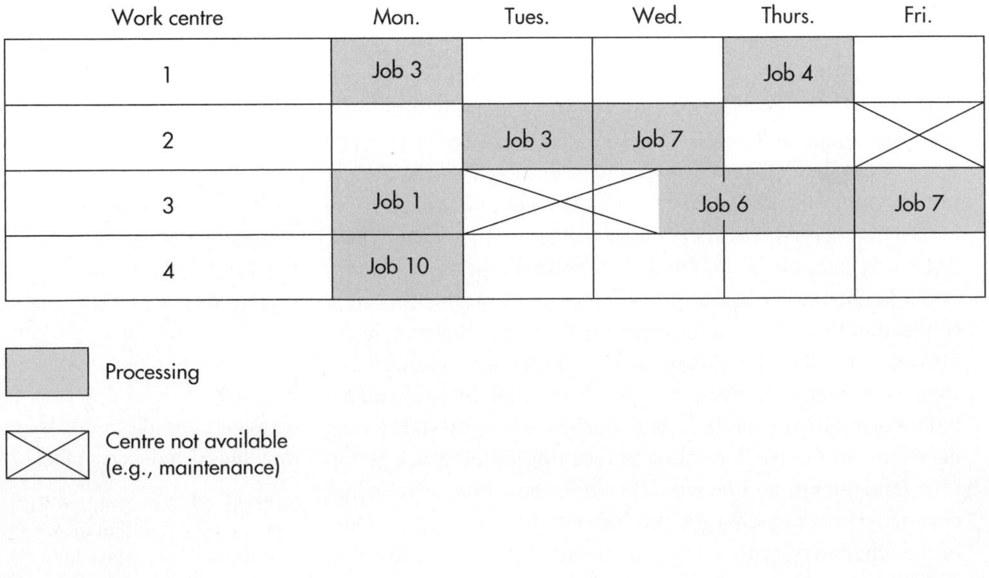

Work centre	Mon.	Tues.	Wed.	Thurs.	Fri.
1	Job 3			Job 4	
2		Job 3	Job 7		✕
3	Job 1	✕	Job 6		Job 7
4	Job 10				

◻ Processing

✕ Centre not available (e.g., maintenance)

Dealing with Infinite Loading

Sometimes it is easier or advantageous to schedule jobs without capacity considerations. An example is MRP scheduling. This is called *infinite loading*. **Infinite loading** assigns jobs to work centres without regard to the available capacity of the work centres.

However, most scheduling is done by finite loading. **Finite loading** assigns jobs to work centres, taking into account the available capacities of work centres and the processing times of jobs, so that the capacities are not exceeded. Schedules based on finite loading may have to be updated often, perhaps daily, due to processing delays at work centres, the addition of new jobs, and completion of current jobs. The following diagram contrasts finite vs. infinite loadings.

infinite loading   Jobs are assigned to work centres without regard to the available capacity of the work centres.

finite loading   Jobs are assigned to work centres taking into account work centres' available capacities and jobs' processing times.

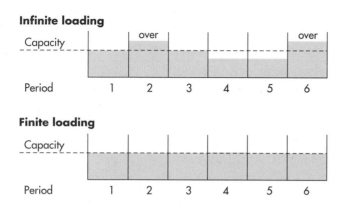

With infinite loading, a manager needs to respond to overloaded work centres. Among the possible responses are shifting work to other periods or other work centres, working overtime, or contracting out a portion of the work. Example 1 illustrates some of these responses.

OM in *ACTION*   http://www.plastiquemicron.com/en

Plastique Micron

Plastique Micron (PM), located in Sainte Claire near Quebec City, is a medium-sized plastic-bottles manufacturer, primarily for the pharmaceutical and cosmetic industry. PM has 29 plastic moulding machines that use the blow moulding method. Each machine melts polyethylene pellets (four types in various colours), forms hollow cylinders of plastic in the right size (called preforms; there are hundreds of sizes), places the preforms in moulds (there are hundreds and they can also be custom made), blows air into the neck of preforms to expand them into the shape of the inside of the moulds, cools the bottles, and finally ejects them. There are several types/models of blow moulding machines, with different capabilities and speeds, some requiring different moulds.

Before 2006, a customer service/planner planned the production, all based on his knowledge of the machines that could produce a particular order and the moulds available. Other required

information for scheduling, such as current load on machines, was also not easily available, despite having a computer system. A production schedule was determined and displayed on a board in the office on a daily basis. The production supervisors had to walk into the office several times a day to find out what they should produce on what machine using what mould. Consequently, customer order promises and follow-up were unsatisfactory and slow.

Then, PM purchased Preactor P300 scheduling software (http://www.preactor.com/Products/Scheduling-Software/Preactor-300-FCS.aspx). The implementation team (the planner, the IT person, and a consultant) started to define the machines and moulds, and their relationship. Because of large varieties and lack of any previous documentation, this process is taking a long time and is ongoing. P300 has brought order and speed to the scheduling of jobs, thus improving customer service.

Source: http://www.preactor.com/Case-Study/Case-Studies/Plastique-Micron.aspx.

Example 1

Suppose that work centres, loads resulting from MRP for Order #1, 100 units of a kitchen table due on Day 5 (see problem 23 of Chapter 14), are:

Order #1	Day 1	Day 2	Day 3	Day 4	Day 5	Day 6	Day 7
Top Fab		▓	▓	▓			
Leg Fab			▓	▓			
Table Assembly					▓		

Also, suppose Order #2, 50 units of a different table due on Day 7, was also promised, with the following additional loads determined by MRP on the same work centres:

Order #2	Day 1	Day 2	Day 3	Day 4	Day 5	Day 6	Day 7
Top Fab				▓			
Leg Fab				▓			
Table Assembly					▓	▓	

Order #2 tables need less time for Top Fab but more time for Table Assembly. Note that Order #2 needs Top Fab for only half a day. Capacity of work centres Top Fab and Leg Fab on Day 4 and Table Assembly on Day 5 are exceeded. What can the scheduler do?

Solution

Many options are possible. Four are tried below. Choose that option which costs least.

1. Move due date for order #2 to Day 8

Order #1	Day 1	Day 2	Day 3	Day 4	Day 5	Day 6	Day 7
Top Fab		▓	▓	▓			
Leg Fab			▓	▓			
Table Assembly					▓		

Order #2	Day 1	Day 2	Day 3	Day 4	Day 5	Day 6	Day 7
Top Fab					▓		
Leg Fab					▓		
Table Assembly						▓	▓

2. Move Leg Fab for order #1 to Day 2–Day 3, if possible, and increase capacity of Top Fab on Day 4 and Table Assembly on Day 5

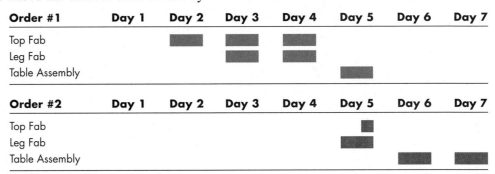

Order #1	Day 1	Day 2	Day 3	Day 4	Day 5	Day 6	Day 7
Top Fab		▓	▓	▓			
Leg Fab		▓	▓				
Table Assembly					▓		

Order #2	Day 1	Day 2	Day 3	Day 4	Day 5	Day 6	Day 7
Top Fab				▓			
Leg Fab				▓			
Table Assembly					▓	▓	

3. Schedule order #2 first (i.e., change the sequence of scheduling)

Order #1	Day 1	Day 2	Day 3	Day 4	Day 5	Day 6	Day 7
Top Fab		▓	▓	▓	▓		
Leg Fab			▓	▓			
Table Assembly					▓	▓	

Order #2	Day 1	Day 2	Day 3	Day 4	Day 5	Day 6	Day 7
Top Fab		▓					
Leg Fab		▓					
Table Assembly				▓	▓		

4. Use solution 3 and Split Top Fab for Order #1 (i.e., move 50 tops to Table Assembly when 50 tops are ready, and start Table Assembly. Move the other 50 tops later when they are ready.)

Order #1	Day 1	Day 2	Day 3	Day 4	Day 5	Day 6	Day 7
Top Fab		▪	▪	▪	▪		
Leg Fab			▪	▪			
Table Assembly					▪		

Order #2	Day 1	Day 2	Day 3	Day 4	Day 5	Day 6	Day 7
Top Fab		▪					
Leg Fab		▪					
Table Assembly			▪	▪			

LO3 SEQUENCING AND SCHEDULING

Although loading decisions determine the machines or work centres that will be used to process specific jobs, they do not necessarily indicate the *order* in which the jobs waiting there are to be processed. **Sequencing** is concerned with determining job processing order.

sequencing Determining the order in which jobs will be processed in a work centre or machine.

If work centres or machines are lightly loaded and if jobs all require the same amount of processing time, sequencing presents no particular difficulties. However, for heavily loaded work centres or machines, especially in situations where relatively lengthy jobs are involved, the order of processing can be very important in terms of costs associated with jobs waiting for processing and in terms of idle time at the work centres/machines. In this section, we will examine some of the ways in which jobs are sequenced.

Priority Rules and Performance Measures

Typically, a number of jobs will be waiting for processing. **Priority rules** or dispatching rules are simple heuristics used to select the order in which jobs will be processed. Some of the most common are listed in Table 16-1. The rules generally rest on the assumption that a job's setup time is *independent* of the processing sequence, and processing time for each job includes its setup time. Due dates may be the result of delivery times promised to customers, MRP planned order releases, or warehouse replenishment. They are subject to revision and must be kept current to give meaning to sequencing choices.

priority rules Simple heuristics used to select the order in which jobs will be processed.

Performance Measures. The effectiveness of any given sequence is judged in terms of one or more *performance measures*. The most frequently used performance measures are:

- *Job flow time*. This is the length of the time a job is in a shop. It includes not only the actual processing time but also any time waiting to be processed, and movement time

Table 16-1

Common priority rules

FCFS (first come, first served): Jobs are processed in the order in which they arrive at a machine/work centre.

SPT (shortest [imminent] processing time): Jobs are processed according to processing time at a machine/work centre, shortest job first.

SRPT (shortest remaining processing time): Jobs are processed according to smallest sum of the processing times at all the remaining required machines/work centres for this job.

EDD (earliest due date): Jobs are processed according to due date, earliest due date first.

MST (minimum slack time): Jobs are processed according to their slack time (i.e., time until due date minus remaining processing time), minimum first.

CR (critical ratio): Jobs are processed according to smallest ratio of time until due date to remaining processing time.

Rush: Emergency or preferred customers first.

between operations. The *average flow time* for a group of jobs is equal to the total flow time for the jobs divided by the number of jobs.

- *Job lateness.* This is the length of time the job completion time/date exceeds the time/date the job was due. We assign zero lateness to jobs that are early. The *average lateness* for a group of jobs is equal to the total jobs lateness divided by the number of jobs.

make-span Time needed to complete a group of jobs from the beginning of the first job to the completion of the last job.

- *Make-span.* **Make-span** is the time needed to complete a *group* of jobs. It is the length of time between the start of the first job in the group and the completion of the last job in the group.

- *Average WIP.* Jobs that are in the shop are considered to be work-in-process inventory. The average work-in-process for a group of jobs can be calculated using the following formula: Average WIP = Total flow time/Make-span

Note that average WIP and average flow time are closely related. If a priority rule results in small average flow time, it will also result in small average WIP and vice versa.

OM in ACTION http://www.hermanmiller.com

Miller SQA

Miller SQA was created by the office-furniture giant Herman Miller Inc. in 1996. The initials SQA stood for "simple, quick, affordable." Miller SQA sold customized products, so the make-to-order production system had to be fast.

When Miller SQA was started, it used its MRP system to plan the fabrication and assembly operations. It offered a premium two-day and a regular two-week delivery service. When a wholesaler or retailer placed an order, the order and its delivery date/time were either electronically (via EDI) or manually entered into Miller SQA's Symix ERP system (now part of Infor). The enhanced MRP module produced a daily schedule based on capacity and materials. Then the supervisors used their experience to sequence the jobs for each work centre. Miller SQA used expediters to accelerate the movement of high-priority late jobs through the operations. But as product demand grew, so did the company's coordination and execution need.

Therefore, Miller SQA reorganized its 27,000-m² manufacturing plant in Holland, Michigan, into 19 workgroups, or "cells." Each cell specialized in a particular product line and oversaw its assembly from start to finish, with little WIP inventory.

Because a customer order typically involved many products that were made in different cells, Miller SQA also needed to ensure that all cells were working on the same order at the same time. The company chose SynQuest's Synchronized Manufacturing to do this. SynQuest combined an MES (manufacturing execution system) with a finite capacity (i.e., loading) scheduler to calculate schedules for all orders through the cells. Orders were frequently downloaded from the MRP system into SynQuest, where it prioritized each order according to its slack time (i.e., due hour—remaining production hours). The order with the least slack time jumped to the top of the dispatch list (i.e., it used the MST rule). The system distributed this dispatch list across the network of 65 PCs located throughout the manufacturing floor.

SynQuest's MES module provided shop-floor operators, planners, schedulers, managers, buyers, and shippers with up-to-the-minute information on job status, projected job completion times, and any problems. SynQuest's scheduler was continually running in the background, adjusting production schedules based on any job status changes. The MES module immediately reflected these changes and shop-floor dispatch lists were adjusted accordingly. If jobs were late, the system warned all users by displaying late jobs in red.

Miller SQA succeeded in reducing its manufacturing lead time to two days and cut its work-in-process inventory to about eight hours' supply.

SynQuest is now part of Viewlocity and Miller SQA is now part of Herman Miller.

Sources: "Software Boosts Manufacturing Process," *FDM, Furniture Design & Manufacturing* 70(4), April 1998, pp. 116–124; "Miller SQA Powers up with Quick Response Manufacturing," *Modern Materials Handling*, 53(2), February 1998, pp. 44–46.

Of the priority rules, the FCFS and rush priority rules are quite simple and need no explanation. The other rules and the performance measures above are illustrated in the following example.

Example 2

Processing times (including setup times) and due dates for six jobs that arrived today and are waiting to be processed at the only machine in a shop are given below. Determine the sequence of jobs, the average flow time, average days late, and average WIP in the shop for each of these priority rules:

a. SPT

b. EDD

c. MST

d. CR

Job	Processing Time (days)	Due Date (end of day)
A	2	7
B	8	16
C	4	4
D	10	17
E	5	15
F	12	18

a. Using the shortest processing time (SPT) rule, the job sequence is A-C-E-B-D-F. So, rearrange the job processing time and due date columns so that jobs appear in the SPT order in the Job column. Also add Completion Time and Days Late columns. See the table below. The completion time column shows the *cumulative* processing times. For example, job C's completion time is 4 days after job A's completion time, i.e., $2 + 4 = 6$. Job A is not late because it is completed at the end of the second day, before its due date, the end of day 7, but Job C is late by 2 days because it is completed at the end of day 6, whereas its due date is the end of day 4. Summing the completion times gives the total flow time (108 days) and completion time of the last job, job F, is the make-span $= 41$ days. The resulting measures of performance are:

   i. *Average flow time*: $108/6 = 18$ days.

  ii. *Average days late*: $40/6 = 6.67$ days.

 iii. *Average WIP*: $108/41 = 2.63$ jobs.

Job Sequence	(i) Processing Time	(ii) Completion Time	(iii) Due Date	(ii)–(iii) Days Late [0 if negative]
A	2	2	7	0
C	4	6	4	2
E	5	11	15	0
B	8	19	16	3
D	10	29	17	12
F	12	41	18	23
		108		40

b. Using the earliest due date (EDD) rule, the job sequence is C-A-E-B-D-F. Repeating the steps in part a results in the table below. The resulting measures of performance are:

   i. *Average flow time*: $110/6 = 18.33$ days.

  ii. *Average days late*: $38/6 = 6.33$ days.

 iii. *Average WIP*: $110/41 = 2.68$ jobs.

Job Sequence	(i) Processing Time	(ii) Completion Time	(iii) Due Date	(ii)–(iii) Days Late [0 if negative]
C	4	4	4	0
A	2	6	7	0
E	5	11	15	0
B	8	19	16	3
D	10	29	17	12
F	12	41	18	23
		110		38

c. Using minimum slack time (due date – processing time) MST rule, the job sequence is C-A-F-D-B-E (see the slack times in the table below; e.g., slack time of Job C = 4 − 4 = 0 and slack time of Job A = 7 − 2 = 5; note the sequence is in increasing size of slack time). Doing the calculations results in the table below. The measures of performance are:

  i. *Average flow time:* 133/6 = 22.17 days

  ii. *Average days late:* 57/6 = 9.5 days

  iii. *Average WIP:* 133/41 = 3.24 jobs

Job Sequence	(i) Slack Time	(ii) Processing Time	(iii) Completion Date	(iv) Due Date	(iii)–(iv) Days Late [0 if negative]
C	0	4	4	4	0
A	5	2	6	7	0
F	6	12	18	18	0
D	7	10	28	17	11
B	8	8	36	16	20
E	10	5	41	15	26
			133		57

d. Using the critical ratio (due date ÷ processing time) CR, the job sequence is C-F-D-B-E-A (see the critical ratios in the table below; e.g., CR for Job C is 4/4 = 1, and CR for Job F is 18/12 = 1.5; note the sequence is in increasing size of CR). Doing the calculations results in the following measures of performance:

  i. *Average flow time*: 160/6 = 26.67 days.

  ii. *Average days late*: 85/6 = 14.17 days.

  iii. *Average WIP*: 160/41 = 3.90.

Job Sequence	(i) Critical Ratio	(ii) Processing Time	(iii) Completion Date	(iv) Due Date	(iii)–(iv) Days Late [0 if negative]
C...............	1.0	4	4	4	0
F...............	1.5	12	16	18	0
D...............	1.7	10	26	17	9
B...............	2.0	8	34	16	18
E...............	3.0	5	39	15	24
A...............	3.5	2	41	7	34
			160		85

The results of these four rules are summarized in Table 16-2.

In this example, the SPT rule is the best according to average flow time and average WIP and a little worse than the EDD rule on average days late. The CR rule is the worst in every case. For a different set of processing time and due date numbers, the performance of priority rules may be a little different.

Rule	Average Flow Time (days)	Average Days Late	Average WIP
SPT	18.00	6.67	2.63
EDD	18.33	6.33	2.68
MST	22.17	9.5	3.24
CR	26.67	14.17	3.90

Table 16-2

Comparison of the four rules for Example 2

Guidelines for Selecting a Priority Rule. The following results apply for every one machine shop: SPT is always superior in terms of minimizing average flow time and, hence, average WIP; if all jobs are late, then the SPT rule will always minimize average days late as well; however, EDD always minimizes the maximum days late.

For multi-machine shops, the following statements about the priority rules can be made. The primary limitation of the FCFS rule is that long jobs may delay the following jobs and machine idle times for downstream work centres will increase. However, for service systems in which customers are directly involved, the FCFS rule is by far the dominant priority rule, mainly because of the inherent fairness, but also because of the difficulty to obtain realistic estimates of processing time for individual jobs. The FCFS rule also has the advantage of simplicity.

Because the SPT rule results in low average flow time, and because it often provides low average days late, it can result in high customer service levels. In addition, since it involves low average WIP in the shop, there tends to be less congestion in the shop. The SPT rule also minimizes downstream idle times. However, due dates are often uppermost in managers' minds, so they may not use SPT or SRPT because it doesn't incorporate due dates. The major disadvantage of the SPT rule is that it tends to make long jobs wait, perhaps for rather long times (especially if new, shorter jobs are continually added to the system). Various modifications may be used in an effort to avoid this. For example, after waiting for a given time period, a long job is automatically moved to the head of the line.

The EDD rule directly addresses due dates and usually results in low maximum days late. Although it has intuitive appeal, its main limitation is that it does not take processing time into account. One possible consequence is that it can result in a long job being processed first, resulting in other jobs waiting a long time, which adds to both in-process inventories and shop congestion.

The MST and CR rules have intuitive appeal. Both use both the due dates and remaining processing times. Although they had the poorest showing in Example 2 for all three measures, they usually do quite well. For an application of scheduling and priority rules, see the "Miller SQA" OM in Action earlier in the chapter.

Sequencing Jobs through Two Work Centres/Machines

Johnson's rule is a technique that schedulers can use to minimize the make-span for a group of jobs to be processed on two successive work centres/machines (sometimes referred to as a two-machine flow shop).[1] It also minimizes the total idle time at the work centres/machines. For the technique to work, several conditions must be satisfied:

Johnson's rule Technique for minimizing make-span for a group of jobs to be processed on two successive work centres/machines.

1. Job time (setup and processing) must be known for each job at each work centre/machine.
2. Job times must be independent of the job sequence.
3. All jobs must follow the same two-step work sequence.
4. All units in a job must be completed at the first work centre/machine before the job is moved to the second work centre/machine.
5. There is adequate space for WIP before the second work centre/machine.

[1]S.M. Johnson, "Optimal Two- and Three-Stage Production with Setup Times Included," *Naval Research Quarterly* 1, March 1954, pp. 61–68.

Determination of the optimum sequence involves these steps:

1. Determine the jobs and their times at each work centre/machine.
2. Select the job with the shortest time. If the shortest time is at the first work centre/machine, schedule that job first; if the time is at the second work centre/machine, schedule the job last. Break ties arbitrarily.
3. Eliminate the job and its time from further consideration.
4. Repeat steps 2 and 3, working toward the centre of the sequence, until all jobs have been scheduled.

Example 3

A group of six jobs is to be processed through a two work-centre flow shop. The first operation involves cleaning and the second involves painting. (1) Determine a sequence that will minimize the make-span for this group of jobs. (2) Determine the make-span. (3) Determine the idle times on work centre 2. Processing times (including setups) are expected to be as follows:

| | **Processing Time (Hours)** | |
Job	Work Centre 1	Work Centre 2
A	5	5
B	4	3
C	8	9
D	2	7
E	6	8
F	12	15

Solution

a. Select the job with the shortest processing time. It is job D, with a time of two hours. Since this time is at the first work centre, schedule job D first. Eliminate job D from further consideration. Job B has the next shortest processing time (3 hours). Since it is at the second work centre, schedule it last and eliminate job B from further consideration. We now have partially identified the following sequence:

1st	2nd	3rd	4th	5th	6th
D					B

The remaining jobs and their times are

Job	1	2
A	5	5
C	8	9
E	6	8
F	12	15

Note that there is a tie for the shortest remaining time (5 hours): job A has the same time at each work centre. It makes no difference whether we place it toward the beginning or the end of the partially filled sequence. Suppose A is placed arbitrarily toward the end. Eliminate job A's time. We now have

1st	2nd	3rd	4th	5th	6th
D				A	B

The shortest remaining time is six hours for job E at work centre 1. Thus, schedule that job toward the beginning of the partially filled sequence (after job D) and eliminate job E's times. Thus, the partially filled sequence is:

1st	2nd	3rd	4th	5th	6th
D	E			A	B

Job C has the shortest time of the remaining two jobs (8 hours). Since it is for the first work centre, place it third in the sequence. Finally, assign the remaining job (F) to the fourth position and the resulting sequence is

1st	2nd	3rd	4th	5th	6th
D	E	C	F	A	B

b. One way to determine the make-span and idle times at work centre 2 is to construct a load/schedule Gantt chart:

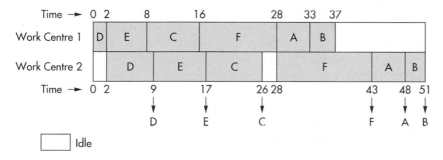

Note that work centre 2 has to wait until the end of the 2nd hour for job D, because job D has to first finish work centre 1 (a job can't be in two places at the same time, unless it can be split). Similarly, work centre 2, after completing job C at the end of the 26th hour, has to wait for job F because work centre 1 will not finish with job F until the end of the 28th hour. Thus, this group of jobs will take 51 hours to complete, i.e., make-span = 51 hours, and the second work centre will wait two hours for its first job and also wait two hours after finishing job C.

When significant idle time at the second work centre occurs, job splitting at the first work centre, just prior to the occurrence of idle time, may alleviate some of the problem and also shorten the throughput time. The use of transfer batches (i.e., splitting jobs) is an important tool in the theory of constraints described later in the chapter. Solved Problem 4 at the end of this chapter illustrates the use of job splitting.

Sequencing Jobs When Setup Times Are Sequence-Dependent

The preceding discussion and examples assumed that machine setup times are independent of processing order, but in many instances that assumption is not true. Consequently, a manager may want to schedule jobs at a work centre or machine while taking those dependencies into account. The goal is usually to minimize total setup time.

Consider the following table, which shows setup times based on job processing order. For example, if job A is followed by job B, the setup time for B will be 6 hours. Furthermore, if job C follows job B, it will have a setup time of 4 hours. If a job is done first, its setup time will be the amount shown in the Initial setup time column to the right of the job. Thus, if job A is done first, its setup time will be 3 hours.

		Initial setup time (hours)	Resulting following job setup time (hours) is		
			A	**B**	**C**
If the	A	3	–	6	2
preceding	B	2	1	–	4
Job is	C	2	5	3	–

The simplest way to determine which sequence will result in the smallest total setup time is to list each possible sequence and determine its total setup time. In general, the number of different alternatives is $n!$ (i.e., n factorial), where n is the number of jobs. Here, n is 3, so $n! = 3 \times 2 \times 1 = 6$. The six alternatives and their total setup times are:

Sequence	Setup Times Total
A-B-C	$3 + 6 + 4 = 13$
A-C-B	$3 + 2 + 3 = 8$
B-A-C	$2 + 1 + 2 = 5$ (smallest)
B-C-A	$2 + 4 + 5 = 11$
C-A-B	$2 + 5 + 6 = 13$
C-B-A	$2 + 3 + 1 = 6$

Hence, to minimize total setup time the scheduler would select sequence B-A-C.

This procedure is relatively simple to do manually when the number of jobs is two or three. However, as the number of jobs increases, the number of sequences increases exponentially. For example, six jobs would have 720 sequences. In such instances, a scheduler should employ a computer to generate the list and identify the best sequence.

(LO4) SHOP-FLOOR CONTROL

Shop-floor control or production activity control involves the execution of the production schedule, and maintenance, communication, and monitoring of the status of material, orders, and process, and taking any necessary actions. Also, providing measurement of efficiency and utilization of the workforce and machines is part of shop-floor control.

Tools for shop-floor control include:

- *Daily dispatch list*: a list of jobs to be run in priority sequence for each work centre.
- *Anticipated delay report*: report issued by manufacturing and purchasing regarding late shop and purchase orders, cause of delay, actions taken, and new due dates.
- *Input/output report*: amount of planned and actual inputs, and planned and actual outputs, for each work centre/machine to monitor workload-capacity relationship. This is explained further below.
- *Schedule/control Gantt chart*: described below.

Manufacturing execution systems usually generate the above list/reports/chart.

Schedule/Control Gantt Chart

schedule/control Gantt chart A Gantt chart that shows the jobs or their components in progress and whether they are on schedule.

A manager often uses a **schedule/control Gantt chart** to monitor the progress of jobs. The vertical axis on this type of Gantt chart shows the jobs or their components in progress, and the horizontal axis shows the time. The chart indicates which jobs or their components are on schedule and which are behind or ahead. A typical schedule/control chart is illustrated in Figure 16-4 for a service. It shows the current status of a landscaping job with planned and actual starting and finishing times for the five components of the job. The chart indicates that approval of the drawings and the ordering of trees and shrubs was on schedule. The site preparation was a bit behind schedule. The trees were received earlier than expected, and planting is ahead of schedule and has already been completed. However, the shrubs have not yet been received. The chart indicates some slack between scheduled receipt of shrubs and shrub planting, so if the shrubs arrive by the end of the week, it appears that the schedule can still be met.

Input/Output Control

input/output (I/O) control Managing work flow and queues at each work centre/machine.

Input/output (I/O) control refers to monitoring and managing the work flow and queue lengths at each work centre/machine. The purpose of I/O control is to manage work flow so that queues and waiting times are kept under control. Without I/O control, demand may exceed processing capacity, causing an overload at the work centre/machine. Conversely,

Component/Week	1	2	3	4	5	6	7
Drawings	[Approval]						
Site		[Preparation]					
Trees		[Order]		[Receive]	[Plant]		
Shrubs		[Order]		[Receive]		[Plant]	
Final Inspection							[Approval]

Scheduled   [   ]

↑
Now

Actual progress

Figure 16-4

Schedule/control Gantt chart for a landscaping job

work may arrive slower than the rate a work centre/machine can handle, leaving the work centre underutilized. Ideally, a balance can be struck between the input and output rates, thereby achieving effective use of work centre/machine capacities without experiencing excessive queues at the work centre/machine.

Figure 16-5 illustrates an input/output report for a work centre. A key portion of the report is the WIP waiting to be processed (in the bottom). The report highlights deviations from planned for both input and output, thereby enabling a manager to determine possible sources of problems.

The deviations in each period are determined by subtracting "Planned" from "Actual." For example, in the first period, subtracting the planned input of 100 hours from the actual input of 120 hours produces a deviation of +20 hours. Similarly, in the first period, the planned and actual outputs are equal, producing a deviation of 0 hours.

The WIP for each period is determined by subtracting the "Actual Output" from the "Actual Input" and adjusting the WIP from the previous period by that amount. For example, in the first period, actual input exceeds actual output by 10 hours. Hence, the current WIP of 40 hours is increased by 10 hours to 50 hours.

The objective is to plan the output based on labour/equipment capacity, then plan the input so that the desired amount of WIP is maintained, and monitor deviations from planned input and output to identify any problems and fix them. The functioning of the input/output control is similar to keeping an unplugged sink at a desired level. In Figure 16-5, it appears that the production controller planned inputs lower than outputs, therefore reducing the WIP to zero, which is not usually desirable in a job shop.

		Period (weeks)					
		1	2	3	4	5	6
Input	Planned	100	100	90	90	90	90
	Actual	120	95	80	88	93	94
	Deviation	+20	−5	−10	−2	+3	+4
	Cum. dev.	+20	+15	+5	+3	+6	+10

Output	Planned	110	110	100	100	100	95
	Actual	110	105	95	101	103	96
	Deviation	0	−5	−5	+1	+3	+1
	Cum. dev.	0	−5	−10	−9	−6	−5

WIP*	40	50	40	25	12	2	0

*Note: Figures represent standard hours of processing time.

Figure 16-5

An input/output report for a work centre.

RELATED ISSUES IN SCHEDULING

Why Scheduling Can Be Difficult

Scheduling can be difficult for a number of reasons. One is that, in reality, an operation must deal with variability in setup times, processing times, interruptions, and changes in the set of jobs. Another major reason is that, except for very small problems, there is no practical method for identifying the optimal schedule, and it would be virtually impossible to sort through the vast number of possible alternatives to obtain the best schedule. Job shops where each job may have a different sequence of operations are especially hard to schedule. See the following example for an illustration.

Example 4

For simplicity, assume that there are exactly one lathe, milling, grinding, and vertical drill machine in the shop. Suppose that the five jobs should be processed in the machine sequence given in the table below (from top down), with standard times given in front of the machine name. For example, for job 1, first one hour of drill is required, then two hours of lathe, etc. To simplify the problem, suppose that the four machines are available starting tomorrow morning and there are no WIP in the shop. Also, suppose that the due hours are all at the end of tomorrow's shift, i.e., the end of hour 8. Hours 9 to 14 correspond to the first six hours of the day after tomorrow. For simplicity, we assume that setup times are included in the operation times and that it is possible to interrupt the processing of a job on a machine (without increasing its setup time), but part of a job cannot be transferred to the next operation. Determine the schedule that meets the due hours.

	Job 1		Job 2		Job 3		Job 4		Job 5	
1.	Drill	1	Lathe	2	Grind	2	Drill	1	Mill	1
2.	Lathe	2	Mill	2	Drill	2	Grind	2	Drill	1
3.	Grind	1	Grind	1	Mill	2	Lathe	1	Lathe	1
4.	Mill	2	Drill	2	Lathe	2			Grind	2
Total (hours)		6		7		8		4		5

Solution

All five jobs have the same due hour, so EDD will not provide a sequence. The shortest remaining processing time (SRPT) rule results in the sequence 4-5-1-2-3. In the following schedule, first job 4 is scheduled all the way on all machines (this is called horizontal loading), then job 5, etc:

4-5-1-2-3   **Hours**

	1	2	3	4	5	6	7	8	9	10	11	12	13	14
Lathe	2	2	5	4	1	1							3	3
Mill	5		2	2				1	1		3	3		
Grind	3	4	4	5	5	2	1	3						
Drill	4	5	1				2	2	3	3				

We observe that the above schedule results in job 3 being six hours late, and job 1 being one hour late. The minimum slack time (MST) rule results in the opposite sequence: 3-2-1-5-4, with the following schedule (using horizontal loading):

3-2-1-5-4   **Hours**

	1	2	3	4	5	6	7	8	9	10	11	12	13	14
Lathe	2	2	1	1	5		3	3			4			
Mill	5		2	2	3	3	1	1						
Grind	3	3			2	1	5	5	4	4				
Drill	1	5	3	3	4	2	2							

Even though the MST rule performs better than the SRPT rule, its schedule still results in job 4 being three hours late.

As you can see, scheduling in a job shop is very difficult. One needs to try various sequences and choose the best. The problem is that there are too many sequences. Note that we made many simplifying assumptions. In general, there are WIP in the shop, the processing time estimates may be inaccurate, a machine could break down, an operator may become ill, set-up times may be sequence-dependent, and jobs could be split and transferred to the next operation in smaller batch sizes.

How to Reduce Scheduling Difficulty

- Set realistic due dates.
- Focus on the bottleneck operation: schedule the bottleneck operation first, and then schedule the non-bottleneck operations around the bottleneck operation. Don't interrupt the bottleneck operation.
- For non-bottleneck operations, consider lot-splitting for large jobs, i.e., transfer a portion of the job to the next operation.
- Use a scheduling software.
- Use shop-floor control, and reschedule every day.

Scheduling Based on the Bottleneck Operation: The Theory of Constraints

Theory of Constraints, developed by Eli Goldratt in the 1980s,[2] focuses on the *bottleneck* operation (i.e., the operation with smallest capacity—in effect, the operation with zero idle time). The output of the system is limited by the output of the bottleneck operation; therefore, it is essential to schedule the non-bottleneck operations in a way that minimizes the idle time of the bottleneck operation. Thus, idle time of non-bottleneck operations is not a factor in overall capacity of the system, as long as the bottleneck operation is used effectively. The result is a technique for scheduling batch production systems that is simpler and less time consuming to use.

Theory of Constraints uses *drum-buffer-rope* conceptualization to manage the system. The "drum" is the master schedule; it sets the pace of the production of the bottleneck operation. The "buffer" refers to inventory just before the bottleneck operation. The "rope" represents the synchronizing of non-bottleneck operations before the bottleneck operation to ensure that these non-bottleneck operations produce the right quantities and at the right times. The goal is to avoid costly and time-consuming multiple setups at the bottleneck operation.

Theory of Constraints also uses varying batch sizes to achieve the greatest output of the bottleneck operation. The term *process batch* denotes the production lot size for a job and the term *transfer batch* denotes a portion of the production lot that could be moved to the bottleneck operation. In effect, a lot could be split into two or more portions. Splitting a large lot at one or more operations preceding a bottleneck operation would reduce the waiting time of the bottleneck operation. The "Oregon Freeze Dry" OM in Action is an application of drum-buffer-rope technique.

[2]Eliyahu M. Goldratt and Jeff Cox, *The Goal: Excellence in Manufacturing* (New York: North River Press), 1984.

Oregon Freeze Dry

Oregon Freeze Dry has three plants on a 35 acre site (with 300 workers) in Albany, Oregon, that freeze-dry vegetables, fruits, and meats by removing their water at low temperature and pressure. After freezing the items, in the low-pressure chambers the ice is evaporated without melting it into water first. Freeze-drying retains the flavour, and the natural structure of the food is regained by adding water at the time of consumption.

Production begins with wet processing of products—a labour-intensive technique involving activities such as cooking or heating. The next step is freezing. This is a capital-intensive operation that uses one of the six very large freezers. The product is then processed through one of 32 dryers (low pressure chambers). The drying operation is also capital intensive and may take from 8 to 50 hours (depending on the product), although 14 to 20 hours is typical. The final step is dry processing—a labour-intensive step including activities such as blending, packaging, and boxing.

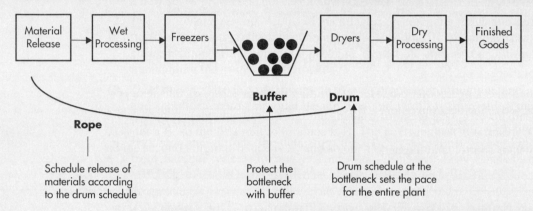

Before 1998, the production was scheduled on a make-to-stock basis according to predetermined batch sizes and sequence. This resulted in large inventories of finished goods and WIP in the freezers, which increased the production lead times and caused the company to be slow in responding to customer orders that could not be satisfied from finished goods. In addition, it resulted in extensive costly overtime and disruptive expediting efforts. Meanwhile, the plants were overstocked with products for which there were no current orders.

Specifically, materials were released for processing according to production schedule, available wet-processing capacity, and available storage space for the accumulated WIP (in the freezers). The wet-processing schedule drove all other operations as in a push system. There were no formal schedules for the freezers, dryers, or dry processing. Typically, about six to eight weeks' worth of demand for each product were processed. The highly variable product times created a "feast or famine" environment in the various operations in which periods of work overload were followed by periods in which there was nothing to do.

In 1998, the company implemented the drum-buffer-rope technique. The capacity analysis clearly indicated that wet processing and dry processing were not constraints. The constraint (i.e., bottleneck) was drying. The dryer schedule was set based on market demand and dryer capacity. All other departments' schedules were subordinated to support the dryer schedule, which fully utilized dryer capacity. Specifically, materials were released to wet processing at the rate dictated by the dryer schedule (offset by lead times). See the above process flow

Bank of dryers at Oregon Freeze Dry

diagram with the drum-buffer-rope illustration. As a result, the wet-processing department could not overproduce and cause excess WIP inventory in the freezers. Furthermore, having a set schedule at the dryers resulted in a predictable product flow to downstream operations at dry processing. The dryer schedule provided greater visibility to future work schedules in wet and dry processing and made the labour requirements in these departments smoother and predictable. Monitoring the buffer inventory in the freezers highlights when the system is having a problem.

Source: M. Umble, E. Umble, and L. Von Deylen, "Integrating Enterprise Resources Planning and Theory of Constraints: A Case Study," *Production and Inventory Management Journal* 42(2), Second Quarter 2001, pp. 43–48.

LO6 STAFF SCHEDULING

Staff scheduling involves determining the work days and the start and end times on each work day for each employee. Staff scheduling in a manufacturing company is usually easy: a typical company works 8 hours a day (e.g., 9 a.m. to 5 p.m.) and 5 days a week (Mon–Fri), a total of 40 hours a week (i.e., full-time employment) for all its employees. If it is very busy, a second shift (e.g., 5 p.m. to 1 a.m., Mon–Fri) will be instituted. Processing companies such as pulp and paper mills operate continuously: 24 hours a day, 7 days a week. They use four full-time shifts, possibly rotating the shifts among employees so that everyone gets to work the unpopular night and weekend shifts.

On the other hand, staff scheduling in services presents certain problems not generally encountered in manufacturing. This is due primarily to (1) the inability to store or inventory services, and (2) the random nature and timing of customer requests for service. For this reason, in this section we will focus on staff scheduling in services such as a restaurant or an airline. Employment can be full time (40 hours a week) or part time (e.g., 20 hours a week). Three staff scheduling problems are considered in this section:

a. Many services operate every day (i.e., seven days a week). However, employees usually work only five consecutive days and then receive two days off. The problem of determining the minimum number of full-time work patterns with five consecutive days of work and two consecutive days off is considered first.

b. Usually a service employee works during a given "shift" (i.e., a period with fixed start and end times). The problem of determining a set of shifts with minimum total duration that meet the hourly staff requirements in a day is considered next.

c. A complex staffing problem arises while scheduling an airline's pilots (and to a lesser degree flight attendants). Besides time, location also plays a role because a pilot has a home base and needs to get back to her home base after a few days. This problem is considered last.

Scheduling Two Consecutive Days Off

First, based on forecast demand for work, the number of staff needed per day is determined. Note that we have assumed that the weekly demand for staff is fairly stable from week to week, but daily demand for staff vary due to "seasonality". For example:

Day	Mon	Tue	Wed	Thu	Fri	Sat	Sun
Staff needed	2	4	3	4	6	5	5

A fairly simple but effective approach for determining the minimum number of workers needed (who work five consecutive days and then take two consecutive days off) is the following[3]:

1. Write "Worker 1" under "Staff needed" and repeat the daily staff needs for Worker 1 (see table below). Choose the first worker's workdays assignment such that the two consecutive days with the lowest maximum daily staff need are designated as his days off. Here Mon–Tue, Tue–Wed, and Wed–Thu all have a maximum of four staff needs. Among these three pairs, choose the one with minimum sum of staff needs: $\min(2 + 4, 4 + 3, 3 + 4) = 6$. Therefore, Mon–Tue should be the two consecutive days off for worker 1. Circle those days. (Note, in case of a further tie, pick the pair whose previous day is not part of the pairs in the tie.)

Day	Mon	Tue	Wed	Thu	Fri	Sat	Sun
Staff needed	2	4	3	4	6	5	5
Worker 1	2	4	3	4	6	5	5

---

[3]R. Tibrewala et al., "Optimal Scheduling of Two Consecutive Idle Periods," *Management Science* 19(1), September, 1972, pp. 71–75.

2. Write "Worker 2" under "Worker 1." Subtract one from each day's staff needs in the row of Worker 1, except for the circled days, and write them in front of worker 2. See the following table. These are the remaining staff needs. Assign worker 2's days off using the lowest maximum daily remaining staff needs of two consecutive days. Wed–Thu has the lowest maximum of any consecutive pair of days of remaining staff needs in front of Worker 2 (3). Circle those days.

Day	Mon	Tue	Wed	Thu	Fri	Sat	Sun
Staff needed	**2**	**4**	**3**	**4**	**6**	**5**	**5**
Worker 1	(2	4)	3	4	6	5	5
Worker 2	2	4	(2	3)	5	4	4

3. Write "Worker 3" under "Worker 2." Subtract one from each day's remaining needs, except for the circled days, and write them in front of worker 3 (see table below). Assign worker 3's days off using the lowest maximum remaining need of two consecutive days. In this case, Mon–Tue, Tue–Wed, Wed–Thu, Sat–Sun, and Sun–Mon all have a maximum remaining need of three employees. The sum of Mon–Tue and Sun–Mon is the smallest (1 + 3 = 4) among these five pairs. The day before Sun (i.e., Sat) is not part of these two tied pairs. Therefore, circle Sun–Mon as the third employee's days off, and repeat the preceding steps for each additional worker until all staffing needs have been met (see below). Note: don't subtract from a value of zero.

Day	Mon	Tue	Wed	Thu	Fri	Sat	Sun
Staff needed	**2**	**4**	**3**	**4**	**6**	**5**	**5**
Worker 1	(2	4)	3	4	6	5	5
Worker 2	2	4	(2	3)	5	4	4
Worker 3	1)	3	2	3	4	3	(3
Worker 4	(1	2)	1	2	3	2	3
Worker 5	1	2	(0	1)	2	1	2
Worker 6	0	1	0	1	(1	0)	1
Worker 7	0	0	0	0	1	(0	0)
Number working:	**4**	**5**	**5**	**5**	**6**	**5**	**5**

To identify the days each worker is working, go across each worker's row to find the values that are not circled. Similarly, to find the workers who are assigned to work during any particular day, go down that day's column to find the values that are not circled. Note: Worker 6 is needed to work only three days, and worker 7 is only needed *one* day. Perhaps two part-time employees can be found to work these days.

Shift Scheduling

Many services have to meet uneven customer demand throughout the day. For example, restaurants have peak lunch and supper demands. To meet the peak demand but save on wages, short shifts, e.g., three to four hours long, staffed by part-time workers, are commonly used. A part-time worker works up to 5 days a week, and usually has limitations on his/her availability times.

Usually, the work schedule is determined for the following week. It involves the following steps:

1. Forecast amount of work to be done during each hour of next week.

2. Convert the work into number of workers required during each hour.

3. Try to cover these with feasible shifts and a minimum number of staff.

4. Assign shifts to staff according to their skill, availability, and agreed-upon total weekly work hours.

For step 2, company standards may exist that specify labour hours required per sales dollar forecasted (This may also be called manning chart).

We will focus on step 3 (called shift scheduling) and illustrate it with an example from McDonald's. We will focus on shifts for the part-time employees and leave out the scheduling of managers who are typically full-time and whose shift determination is straightforward. For example, for a McDonald's restaurant that is open 24 hours a day, a manager's shift could be one of: 6 a.m. → 2 p.m., noon → 8 p.m., 2 p.m. → 10 p.m., or 10 p.m. → 6 a.m., 5 days a week. Note that peak times will be covered by more than one manager.

While we will perform shift scheduling manually, McDonald's Canada uses a sophisticated software called ESP by ThoughtWorks, a Toronto software company. ESP also performs Step 1: forecasting, Step 2: converting the forecasts using manning charts, and Step 4: assignment of employees to the derived shifts using a complex heuristic procedure (called simulated annealing). See the "ESP by ThoughtWorks Inc." OM in Action after the following example.

Example 5

Erindale McDonald's in Saskatoon uses the following manning chart (positional guide) for regular menu (we will focus on the 5 a.m. to 11 p.m. period):

Sales/Hour	Counter	Drive Thru	CSA	Assembly Board	Grill	French Fries
0–$162	1	1			1	
163–223	1	1		1	1	
224–338	1	2		1	1	
339–395	1	2		2	1	
396–492	2	2		2	1	
493–542	2	2		2	1	1
543–621	2	2		3	1	1
622–723	2	3		3	1	1
724–905	2	3	1	4	1	1
906–1,109	3	3	1	4	1	1
>1,110	3	3	1	5	1	1

The hourly forecast sales for May 21, 2004, starting from 5 a.m. until 11 p.m. was:

5–6	6–7	7–8	8–9	9–10	10–11	11–noon	noon–1	1–2	2–3	3–4
$20	$90	$180	$320	$410	$410	$920	$1,260	$630	$420,	$360

4–5	5–6	6–7	7–8	8–9	9–10	10–11
$590	$1,040	$1,040	$810	$390	$340	$240.

a. Determine the number of drive-thru (DT) staff required during each hour.

b. Determine the shifts (three to eight hours long), and number of DT staff on each shift, using the following heuristic.

  1. Start from opening hour:

    i. Determine the length of the shift: begin with a three-hour shift. Increase it by one hour if the number of staff required during this hour is not smaller than the maximum number of staff required so far on the shift. Continue. Stop if the shift is eight hours long.

    ii. Set the number of workers on this shift equal to 1 and reduce the number of staff required for each hour of this shift by 1. Repeat step (i) if the number of staff required (still not met) at the beginning of this shift is not zero.

   2. Move to the next hour with a positive number of staff required (still not met).

   i. Determine the length of the shift as in Step 1 (i).

   ii. Set the number of workers on this shift equal to 1 and reduce the number of staff required (still not met) for each hour of this shift by 1. Repeat Step 2 (i) if the number of staff required (still not met) at the beginning of this shift is not zero. Continue until the number of staff required (still not met) are all zero.

Solution

a. The number of DT staff required during each hour is determined based on the hour's forecast sales and the manning chart (see the following table, the second column from the left). For example, between 8 and 9 a.m., the forecast sales are \$320, which falls within the \$224–\$338 Forecast Sales range. Therefore, 2 DT workers are required then.

b. Shifts S_1, S_2, ... are created to meet or exceed these staff requirements. S_1's length is the maximum 8 hours because the number of DT staff required is not decreasing from 5 a.m. until 1 p.m. Set the number of DT staff on $S_1 = 1$, and calculate number of staff required, still not met, N_1:

N_1 = original requirement − 1, during any hour of S_1
     = original requirement,   during any other hours.

Shift 2 (S_2) starts at 8 a.m. because that is the first hour when N_1 is positive. The length of S_2 is only 6 hours because N_1 starts decreasing after 2 p.m. Set the number of DT staff on $S_2 = 1$ and calculate the number of staff required, still not met, N_2:

$N_2 = N_1 − 1$,   during any hour of S_2
    $= N_1$,   during any other hour.

Shift 3 (S_3) starts at 11 a.m. because that is the first hour when N_2 is positive. The length of S_3 is 8 hours because N_2 does not decrease until 8 p.m. Set the number of DT staff on $S_3 = 1$ and calculate the number of staff required, still not met, N_3:

$N_3 = N_2 − 1$,   during any hour of S_3
    $= N_2$,   during any other hour.

Shift 4 (S_4) starts at 1 p.m. because that is the first hour when N_3 is positive. The length of S_4 is 7 hours because N_3 starts decreasing after 8 p.m. Set the number of DT staff on $S_4 = 1$ and calculate the number of staff required, still not met, N_4:

$N_4 = N_3 − 1$,   during any hour of S_4
    $= N_3$,   during any other hour.

Shift 5 (S_5) starts at 5 p.m. because that is the first hour when N_4 is positive. The length of S_5 is 6 hours because N_4 does not decrease and 11 p.m. is assumed to be the end of the operating time. Set the number of DT staff on $S_5 = 1$ and calculate the number of staff required, still not met, N_5:

$N_5 = N_4 − 1$,   during any hour of S_5
    $= N_4$,   during any other hour.

Shift 6 (S_6) starts at 7 p.m. because that is the first hour when N_5 is positive. The length of S_5 is 4 hours because N_5 does not decrease and 11 p.m. is assumed to be the end of the operating time. Set the number of DT staff on $S_6 = 1$ and calculate the number of staff required, still not met, N_6:

$N_6 = N_5 − 1$,   during any hour of S_6
    $= N_5$,   during any other hour.

Because N_6 is all zeros, all staff requirements have been met. There is no need for another shift.

Time	Forecast Sales	Staff Required	S₁	N₁	S₂	N₂	S₃	N₃	S₄	N₄	S₅	N₅	S₆	N₆
			1		1		1		1		1		1	
5 am	$20	1	0											
6	90	1	0											
7	180	1	0											
8	320	2	1											
9	410	2	1		0									
10	410	2	1		0									
11	920	3	2		1		0							
Noon	1,260	3	2		1		0							
1 pm	630	3	3		2		1		0					
2	420	2	2		2		1		0					
3	360	2	2		2		1		0					
4	590	2	2		2		1		0					
5	1,040	3	3		3		2		1		0			
6	1,040	3	3		3		2		1		0			
7	810	3	3		3		3		2		1		0	
8	390	2	2		2		2		2		1		0	
9	340	2	2		2		2		2		1		0	
10	240	2	2		2		2		2		1		0	
11														

Airline Crew Scheduling

Airlines first schedule the flights for a period (e.g., for the next year) based on market demand, then assign their planes to the flight legs and schedule their maintenance, and finally schedule the crews. Crews are further divided into cabin (flight attendants) and cockpit (pilots and flight engineer). While cabin crew can be scheduled on any flight, cockpit crew is typically licensed for only one type/model of aircraft, so the problem can be decomposed by aircraft type/model for pilots. (Flight engineers are scheduled separately).

OM in ACTION

ESP by ThoughtWorks Inc.

The Employee Scheduling Program (ESP) of ThoughtWorks Software Solutions, of Dundas, Ontario, is used by major fast-food chains such as McDonald's. ESP allows the restaurant manager to enter the information on:

- Each employee, including his skill level and qualifications to work at one or more of the stations (e.g., front counter, assembly board, fries), hours and days available, and maximum hours in a day or in a week she can work.
- Staffing requirements for each station based on expected sales during each hour of next week (called *positioning guide* or *manning chart*).
- Any fixed shifts as deemed necessary by the manager.
- Operating hours, shift lengths and their desirability during various times of the day, and preferences such as desired

average skill level for a station during a particular period, and fairness (giving part-time workers approximately equal number of hours in a week).

- Sales each hour of past weeks.

ESP will use the history of sales from the past few weeks or year to forecast next week's sales on an hourly basis (using e.g., the moving average method). Then, using the positioning guide, it will determine the number of staff (excluding the managers) required in each station. Next, using linear programming, ESP determines feasible shifts to cover the required staff every hour. Finally, ESP will assign the employees to the chosen shifts according to their availability, skill level, maximum hours and days, and fairness.

Source: http://www.thoughtworksinc.com.

The scheduling of pilots (for a given type/model of aircraft) is divided into two steps: (1) determining good crew "pairings," typically one to seven days long, and (2) stringing the pairings together to form a bid line or roster for one month.

In Step 1, a "pairing" or rotation or trip is a sequence of scheduled flights, with short connection times (one to four hours) and overnight layovers, starting from an airline base and ending in the same city. A pairing has to satisfy government, airline, and union rules. For example, the maximum hours of flying per day is eight hours, unless there are long rest periods before and after the flight. A feasible set of pairings covers each flight scheduled during a month. The best set of feasible pairings is the one that minimizes pilot idle times and layover times and costs.

In Step 2, bid lines or rosters are generated, each consisting of a string of the best feasible pairings from Step 1. Bid lines are determined in order to maximize the utilization of crew while satisfying government, airline, and union rules, and presumed preferences of the pilots. An example of a rule for rosters is that in seven days there has to be a continuous rest period of at least 24 hours. Also, there are rules for the maximum and minimum hours of flying per month, minimum number of days off, maximum number of trips, etc. Pilots seem to prefer long blocks of days off, limited time zones crossed, same-city layovers, long rest periods between night followed by day flying, etc.

The rosters are called bid lines because they are presented to pilots for bidding (choosing). If this is done by seniority (most common in North America) and bid lines are constructed according to the pilots' preferences, Step 2 is called a preferential bidding system.

Because of the rules, some of the pairings, called open or unassigned pairings, may not be included in any bid line. These should be limited to 1–5 percent of the pairings. The unassigned pairings, and those dropped by sick pilots, are given to backup or reserve pilots.

Two software companies that provide software for airline crew scheduling are AD OPT (http://www.ad-opt.com) and Navtech Inc. (http://www.navtech.aero/airline_solutions/crew_planning.html).[4]

Summary

Job scheduling involves determining the timing (i.e., start and completion hour/date) of operations for jobs or orders. Staff scheduling involves determining the timing (i.e., start and end times) of work of staff, and the days they work.

A major problem in job scheduling is assigning (loading) jobs to machines/work centres. Load/schedule Gantt chart is frequently employed to help managers visualize workloads. MRP uses infinite loading (i.e., workloads may exceed work centre/machine capacities), and the schedule has to be made feasible by either increasing the work centre/machine capacities or rescheduling.

An important activity in job scheduling is sequencing the jobs. Various priority rules can be used such as shortest processing time (SPT) and earliest due date (EDD). Job scheduling is usually difficult but it can be solved (i.e., the sequence that results in the minimum makespan can be found) for two work-centre/machine problems using Johnson's rule.

Shop-floor control involves execution of the production schedule, and maintenance, communication, and monitoring of the status of material, orders, and process, and taking any necessary actions. Schedule/control Gantt chart is useful for shop-floor control. Input/output control is used to monitor the work flows and WIP (queues) at a work centre/machine. The theory of constraints focuses on the bottleneck operation to perform scheduling.

Staff scheduling is a common problem in services. Determining two consecutive days off for full-time employees and daily shifts for part-time employees are common staff scheduling problems. Another common but complex staff scheduling problem is airline crew scheduling.

[4]S. Yan and J-C Chang, "Airline Cockpit Crew Scheduling," *European Journal of Operational Research*, 136, 2002, pp. 501–511; B. Gopalakrishnan and E.L. Johnson, "Airline Crew Scheduling: State-of-the-Art," *Annals of Operations Research*, 140, 2005, pp. 305–337; A.I.Z. Harrah and J.T. Diamond, "The Problem of Generating Crew Bidlines," *Interfaces*, 27(4), July–August 1997, pp. 49–64; H. Achour, et al., "An Exact Solution Approach for the Preferential Bidding System Problem in the Airline Industry," *Transportation Science*, August 2007, 41(3), pp. 354–365.

Key Terms

Solved Problems

Priority rules. Job times (including setup) and due hours are shown in the following table for five jobs waiting to be processed in a one-machine shop:

Problem 1

Job	Job Time (hours)	Due Hour
a. 12		15
b. 6		24
c. 14		20
d. 3		8
e. 7		6

Determine the processing sequence that would result from each of these priority rules:

a. SPT.

b. EDD.

Solution

	a. SPT		**b. EDD**	
Job	Job Time	Processing Order	Due Hour	Processing Order
A	12	4	15	3
B	6	2	24	5
C	14	5	20	4
D	3	1	8	2
E	7	3	6	1

Priority rules. Using the job times and due hours from the Solved Problem 1 above, determine each of the following performance measures for FCFS sequence (a-b-c-d-e):

Problem 2

a. Make-span.

b. Average flow time.

c. Average hours late.

d. Average WIP.

Solution

Job	Job Time	Completion Time	Hour Due	Hours Late
A	12	12	15	0
B	6	18	24	0
C	14	32	20	12
D	3	35	8	27
E	7	42	6	36
Total		139		75

a. Make-span = 42 hours

b. Average flow time = $\dfrac{\text{Total completion time}}{\text{Number of jobs}} = \dfrac{139}{5} = 27.80$ hours

c. Average hours late = $\dfrac{\text{Total hours late}}{\text{Number of jobs}} = \dfrac{75}{5} = 15$ hours

d. Average WIP = $\dfrac{\text{Total completion time}}{\text{Makespan}} = \dfrac{139}{42} = 3.31$ jobs

Problem 3

Sequencing jobs through two work centres/machines. Use Johnson's rule to obtain the sequence that minimizes the make-span for the jobs shown below through work centre 1 and 2.

Job Times (hours)

Job	Work Centre 1	Work Centre 2
a	2.50	4.20
b	3.80	1.50
c	2.20	3.00
d	5.80	4.00
e	4.50	2.00

Solution

Identify the smallest time: job b (1.50 hours at work centre 2). Because the time is for work centre 2, schedule this job last, and eliminate job b times.

The next smallest time is job e (2.00 hours at work centre 2). Schedule job e next to last, and eliminate job e times.

Identify the smallest remaining job time: job c (2.20 hours at work centre 1). Because the time is for work centre 1, schedule job c first and eliminate job c times. At this point, we have: c, _____, _____, e, b

The smallest time for remaining jobs is 2.50 hours for job a at work centre 1. Schedule this job after job c. The one remaining job (job d) fills the remaining slot. Thus, we have the sequence: c-a-d-e-b

Problem 4

For Solved Problem 3 above, determine what effect splitting jobs c, d, e, and b in work centre 1 would have on the idle time of work centre 2 and on the make-span. Assume that each job can be split into two equal parts.

Solution

The solution from the previous problem is shown in the following load/schedule Gantt chart. The chart below it shows reduced idle time at work centre 2 when splitting is used.

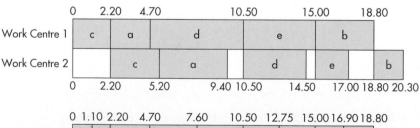

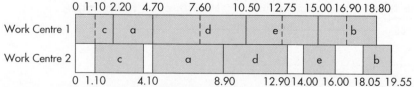

An inspection of these two charts reveals that make-span has decreased from 20.30 hours to 19.55 hours. In addition, the original idle time was 5.6 (= 2.2 + 1.1 + .5 + 1.8) hours. After splitting c, d, e, and b, idle time was reduced to 4.85 (= 1.1 + .6 + 1.1 + 2.05) hours, so some improvement was achieved. Note that processing times at work centre 2 are generally less than at work centre 1 for jobs toward the end of the sequence. As a result, jobs e and b at work centre 2 were scheduled so that they were *centred* around the finishing times of e and b, respectively, at work centre 1, to avoid having to break the jobs due to waiting for the remainder of the split job from work centre 1.

1. What is job scheduling? (LO1)
2. What is a Gantt chart? Name two uses of Gantt chart in scheduling. What are the advantages of using Gantt charts? (LO2 & 4)
3. What is loading? (LO2)
4. MRP assumes infinite loading. Explain. (LO2)
5. Briefly describe each of these priority rules, discuss the advantages and disadvantages of each rule, and suggest a scenario under which each rule may be appropriate: (LO3)

   a. FCFS   b. SPT   c. EDD   d. MST   e. Rush

6. Why are priority rules needed? (LO3)
7. Describe Johnson's rule. (LO3)
8. What is shop-floor control? Name two tools used in shop-floor control. (LO4)
9. What is the input/output control? (LO4)
10. Explain the theory of constraints. (LO5)
11. What is staff scheduling and what are the steps used in staff scheduling? (LO6)
12. What is meant by scheduling two consecutive days off and how is it done? (LO6)
13. What is shift scheduling and how is it done? (LO6)
14. How is airline crew scheduling done? (LO6)

1. What general trade-offs are involved in scheduling decisions? (LO1 & 3)
2. Who needs to be involved in setting job schedules? (LO1)
3. How has technology had an impact on scheduling? (LO1 & 6)
4. Some continuous 24/7 operations rotate the employee shifts on a weekly basis, e.g., day shift → evening shift → night shift → day shift etc, whereas others keep their employee shifts constant. What are the pros and cons of each approach? What ethical issues are involved in this decision? (LO6)

One approach that can be effective in reducing the impact on production bottlenecks is to use smaller transfer lot sizes as in the Theory of Constraints. Explain how small transfer lot sizes can reduce the impact on bottleneck operations. (LO5)

1. Visit a fast-food operation, a supermarket, a hospital, or another service and ask a manager about staff scheduling, covering these questions: (LO6)

   a. Who does it?
   b. How frequently is it done?
   c. Is any software used, and if so, what software?
   d. How easy or difficult is it?
   e. Are demand forecasts used?
   f. Is the manager generally satisfied with the outcome?
   g. Are employees satisfied?

2. How do you schedule your homework assignments of all the courses you are taking now? (LO1–3)
3. How does your city sequence/schedule snow plowing? (LO3)

Internet Exercises

1. Visit http://www.preactor.com/getdoc/bdd42227-1d4b-4660-ab8b-99b0005de92b/North-America.aspx. Choose a case study and summarize it. (LO1)

2. Visit http://www.infor.com/content/casestudies/1376674 (London Health Sciences Centre) or http://www.infor.com/content/casestudies/burlington-coat-factory.pdf and summarize how the Workbrain software helped the organization. (LO6)

3. Visit http://www.taylor.com/industry/case_studies.php, choose a case study, and summarize how Taylor Scheduler has helped the company. (LO1)

Problems

1. The following table contains information concerning four jobs that are waiting for processing at a machine. (LO3)

Job	Job Time (days)	Due Date (days)
A	14	20
B	10	16
C	7	15
D	6	17

a. Sequence the jobs using priority rules (1) SPT, and (2) EDD.
b. For each of the priority rules in part a, determine (1) the average flow time, and (2) the average days late.
c. Is one priority rule superior to the other? Explain.

2. Using the information presented in the following table, identify the processing sequence that would result using (1) MST, (2) SPT, (3) EDD, and (4) CR. For each priority rule, determine (1) average flow time, (2) average hours late, and (3) average WIP. Is one priority rule superior to the others? Explain. (*Hint*: First determine the total job time for each job by calculating the total processing time for the job and then adding in the setup time. All times are in hours.) (LO3)

Job	Processing Time per Unit	Units per Job	Setup Time	Due Hour
a	0.14	45	0.7	4
b	0.25	14	0.5	10
c	0.10	18	0.2	12
d	0.25	40	1.0	20
e	0.10	75	0.5	15

3. The following table shows orders to be processed at a machine as of 8 a.m., Monday. Jobs are listed in the order of arrival. (LO3)

a. Determine the processing sequence using each of these priority rules: (1) CR, (2) MST, (3) SPT, (4) EDD.
b. Determine the performance of each rule using (1) average flow time, (2) average days late.
c. Is one rule superior to the others?

Job	Processing Time (days)	Due Date (days)
A	8	20
B	10	18
C	5	25
D	11	17
E	9	35

4. A production process uses a two-step operation. Tomorrow's work will consist of seven orders as shown below. Determine a job sequence that will minimize the total time required to fill the orders (i.e., the make-span) and determine the make-span. (LO3)

	Time (hours)	
Order	Step 1	Step 2
A.	1.20	1.40
B.	0.90	1.30
C.	2.00	0.80
D.	1.70	1.50
E.	1.60	1.80
F.	2.20	1.75
G	1.30	1.40

5. The times required to complete each of five jobs in a two-machine flow shop are shown in the following table. Each job must follow the same sequence, begin with machine A and end with machine B. (LO3)

   a. Determine a sequence that will minimize the make-span.
   b. Construct a load/schedule Gantt chart for the resulting sequence, and find machine B's idle time.
   c. For the sequence determined in part a, can machine B's idle time be reduced by splitting some jobs in half? If so, which jobs? Draw the new load/schedule Gantt chart.

	Time (hours)	
Job	Machine A	Machine B
a	6	5
b	4	3
c	9	6
d	8	7
e	2	9

6. Given the operation times below in a two-work-centre flow shop:

   a. Develop a job sequence that minimizes total idle time at the two work centres.
   b. Construct a Gantt chart for the activities at the two work centres, and determine work centre 2's idle time. (LO3)

	Job Times (minutes)					
	A	B	C	D	E	F
Work Centre 1	20	16	43	60	35	42
Work Centre 2	27	30	51	12	28	24

7. A two-person shoe repair operation uses a two-step sequence that all jobs follow (first work centre A then work centre B). For the group of jobs listed below, (LO3)

   a. Find the sequence that will minimize the make-span.
   b. Determine the amount of idle time for work centre B.
   c. What jobs are candidates for splitting? Why? If jobs b and c are split in half, how much would the idle time for work centre B be reduced?

	Job Times (minutes)				
	a	b	c	d	e
Work Centre A	27	18	70	26	15
Work Centre B	45	33	30	24	10

8. The following schedules (in hours) were prepared by the production manager of a metal shop. Note that all jobs first go through cutting, then polishing. (LO3)

| | CUTTING | | POLISHING | |
Job	Start	Finish	Start	Finish
A	0	2	2	5
B	2	6	6	9
C	6	11	11	13
D	11	15	15	20
E	15	17	20	23
F	17	20	23	24
G	20	21	24	28

Determine a sequence of jobs that will result in a shorter make-span.

9. A production manager must determine the processing sequence for seven jobs through the grinding and de-burring departments. The same sequence will be followed in each department. The manager's goal is to move the jobs through the two departments as quickly as possible. The site supervisor of the grinding department wants the SPT rule to be used to minimize the work-in-process inventory in his department. (LO3)

PROCESSING TIME (HOURS)

Job	Grinding	Deburring
A	3	6
B	2	4
C	1	5
D	4	3
E	9	4
F	8	7
G	6	2

a. Prepare a schedule using the SPT priority rule for the grinding department (using the grinding times).
b. What is the total flow time in the grinding department for the SPT sequence? What is the make-span for the seven jobs in both the grinding and de-burring departments (using the sequence found in part a)?
c. Determine a sequence that will minimize the make-span in both departments. What total flow time will result for the grinding department?

10. Suppose a body and paint shop has to work on four cars (A, B, C, and D) of a car rental agency. The manager estimated the job times required (in hours) as follows: (LO3)

Cars:	A	B	C	D
Body shop	6	9	7	8
Paint shop	3	5	4	6

The body and paint shop each have dedicated workers. A car has to finish body work before it can be painted. Assume that there are no other cars in the shop.

a. The rental agency is in a hurry to get its cars back. In what order should the shop work on the cars to minimize their make-span?
b. Draw a load/schedule Gantt chart for your sequence in part a, and determine the make-span.

11. A foreman has determined the expected processing times at a machine for a set of jobs and now wants to sequence them. Given the information shown below, do the following: (LO3)

a. Determine the processing sequence using (1) MST, (2) SPT, (3) EDD, and (4) CR. For each sequence, calculate the average days late, the average flow time, and the average WIP.

b. Which rule is best?

Job	Job Time (days)	Due Date (days)
a	4.5	10
b	6.0	17
c	5.2	12
d	1.6	27
e	2.8	18
f	3.3	19

12. Given the information in the following table, determine a processing sequence that would minimize the average flow time. (LO3)

Job	Processing Time (days)	Due Date
A	5	8
B	6	5
C	9	10
D	7	12
E	8	10

13. Given the following information on job times and due hours, determine the processing sequence using priority rules (1) MST, (2) SPT, (3) EDD, and (4) CR. For each rule, find the average flow time and the average hours late. Which rule is best? (LO3)

Job	Job Time (hours)	Due (hours)
A	3.5	7
B	2.0	6
C	4.5	18
D	5.0	22
E	2.5	4
F	6.0	20

14. A shop specializes in heat-treating gears. At 8 a.m., when the shop opened today, five orders were waiting to be processed. Assume that only one unit at a time can be heat-treated. (LO3)

Order	Order Size (units)	Per Unit Time in Heat Treatment (minutes/unit)	Due (minutes from now)
A	16	4	160
B	6	12	200
C	10	3	180
D	8	10	190
E	4	1	220

a. If the earliest due date (EDD) rule is used, what sequence should be used?

b. What will be the average minutes late for the sequence in part *a*?

c. What will be the average WIP in the system for the sequence in part *a*?

d. Would the SPT rule produce better results in terms of average minutes late?

15. A manufacturer has accepted the following jobs for July. Today is Thursday, end of June. The non-working days in July are July 1, 2, 3, 10, 17, 24, 30, and 31. (LO3)

Job	Date Order Received	Production Time Including Setup	Due Date	Due Date in Working Days From Now
A	6/4	6.25 days	11 July	7
B	6/7	2.5 days	8 July	5
C	6/12	8.25 days	25 July	19
D	6/14	3.5 days	19 July	14
E	6/15	9.5 days	29 July	23

Examine the following priority rules, summarizing your findings, and advise on which priority rule to use. FCFS, SPT, EDD, or CR.

16. The following table contains order-dependent setup times for three jobs. Which processing sequence will minimize the total setup time? (LO3)

		Initial Setup Time (hours)	Following Job's Setup Time (hours)		
			A	B	C
	A	2	—	3	5
Preceding Job	B	3	8	—	2
	C	2	4	3	—

17. The following table contains order-dependent setup times for three jobs. Which processing sequence will minimize the total setup time? (LO3)

		Initial Setup Time (hours)	Following Job's Setup Time (hours)		
			A	B	C
	A	2.4	—	1.8	2.2
Preceding Job	B	3.2	0.8	—	1.4
	C	2.0	2.6	1.3	—

18. The following table contains order-dependent setup times for four jobs. For safety reasons, job C cannot follow job A, nor can job A follow job C. Determine the processing sequence that will minimize the total setup time. (*Hint:* There are 12 sequences.) (LO3)

		Initial Setup Time (hours)	Following Job's Setup Time (hours)			
			A	B	C	D
	A	2	—	5	×	4
Preceding Job	B	1	7	—	3	2
	C	3	×	2	—	2
	D	2	4	3	6	—

19. Given the following standard hours of planned and actual inputs and outputs at a work centre, determine the WIP for each period. The beginning WIP is 12 hours of work. (LO4)

		Period				
		1	2	3	4	5
Input	Planned	24	24	24	24	20
	Actual	25	27	20	22	24
Output	Planned	24	24	24	24	23
	Actual	24	22	23	24	24

20. Given the following standard hours of planned and actual inputs and outputs at a work centre, determine the WIP for each time period. The beginning WIP is seven hours of work. (LO4)

	Period	1	2	3	4	5	6
Input	Planned	200	200	180	190	190	200
	Actual	210	200	179	195	193	194

	Period	1	2	3	4	5	6
Output	Planned	200	200	180	190	190	200
	Actual	205	194	177	195	193	200

21. During each four-hour period, a small town police force requires the following number of on-duty police officers: eight from midnight to 4 a.m.; seven from 4 a.m. to 8 a.m.; six from 8 a.m. to noon; six from noon to 4 p.m.; five from 4 p.m. to 8 p.m.; and four from 8 p.m. to midnight. Each police officer works two consecutive four-hour shifts. Determine how to minimize the number of police officers needed to meet the town's daily police requirements. (LO6)

22. Determine the minimum number of workers needed and a schedule for the following staffing requirements, giving workers two consecutive days off per week. (LO6)

Day	Mon	Tue	Wed	Thu	Fri	Sat	Sun
Staff needed	2	3	1	2	4	3	1

23. Determine the minimum number of workers needed and a schedule for the following staffing requirements, giving workers two consecutive days off per week. (LO6)

Day	Mon	Tue	Wed	Thu	Fri	Sat	Sun
Staff needed	3	4	2	3	4	5	3

24. Determine the minimum number of workers needed and a schedule for the following staffing requirements, giving workers two consecutive days off per week. (LO6)

Day	Mon	Tue	Wed	Thu	Fri	Sat	Sun
Staff needed	4	4	5	6	7	8	4

*25. A small grocery store needs the following number of cashiers during each day of a normal week for day (8 a.m. to 4 p.m.) and evening (4 p.m. to midnight) shifts. The store prefers to employ full-time cashiers who work eight hours a day, five days a week, with two consecutive days off. A part-time cashier works four hours a day up to five days a week (with no requirement for consecutive days off). Note that for each unit of cashier requirement below, two part-time cashiers are needed because the periods are eight hours long. Determine the mix of full-time and part-time cashiers and schedule their work in order to minimize total number of cashiers employed but meet the cashier requirements below. (LO6)

Cashiers needed	Mon	Tue	Wed	Thu	Fri	Sat	Sun
8 a.m.–4 p.m.	3	4	3	3	5	8	3

Cashiers needed	Mon	Tue	Wed	Thu	Fri	Sat	Sun
4 p.m.–12 a.m.	2	3	2	2	6	5	3

26. Refer to Example 5. Use the heuristic used in Example 5 to determine shifts for (LO6)
   a. Counter staff
   b. Assembly Board staff

27. Refer to Example 4. Find the optimal solution, i.e., the sequence of jobs that satisfies the due hours (i.e., end of the 8th hour) for all five jobs. (Hint: Switch a pair of jobs in the MST sequence.)

Staff Requirements and Scheduling in Browns Restaurants

Bass PLC, the owner of the Browns Restaurants, a high-end chain in England, was concerned that the restaurants were not achieving their full potential for service speed and efficiency. A consulting team was brought in to look at the operations of one of the restaurants and improve them. The following activities were undertaken:

1. Identify the components of the restaurant production and service-delivery system;

2. Measure the capacity requirements of each component using time study;

3. Measure the historical demand for each component by hour and day of week;

4. Calculate ideal capacity-use levels by factoring steps 2 and 3;

5. Compare current usage with ideal capacity-use levels, determine reasons for the variance, and improve the system.

The project team's first step was to document the details of an ideal experience from the guest's perspective (see Figure 1). Creating the process map allows one to start defining the activities of each staff position (who does what, when, and for whom).

By using a stopwatch, the team conducted a time study for each service and production function. For the kitchen functions, the activities were separated into hands-on assembly and cooking times in order to identify the sequential or parallel nature of activities. Adding the hands-on production time to the elapsed cooking time yields the total production time for each menu item.

The production time was multiplied by historical menu-mix data to determine the workload distribution of cooking effort by cook–function location (e.g., grill, fry). The result was that work was reallocated in a manner that levelled workloads, and bottlenecks plaguing the operation were removed. This line balancing resulted in a reduction of peak-period cooks from 10 to 7.

Browns was staffing its kitchens in a fairly traditional fashion. Day cooks handled the bulk of daily prep work each morning prior to opening. All day cooks arrived at the same time (8 a.m.) and left at the same time (4 p.m.). Because the restaurant was open from noon to midnight, the full complement of evening cooks arrived and departed following a similar eight-hour shift (4 p.m. to midnight). Because the number of customers peaked for lunch around 1:30 p.m. and for dinner around 8:30 p.m., but dipped between 2:30 and 5:30 p.m., the analysis showed that Browns was able to save more than four cooks by shifting the prep work to the middle of the day and staggering the start of the shifts. In effect, no shift before noon was required.

Browns used to assign each server a section comprising six to seven tables. Time studies of service steps revealed that the

Figure 1

Process map—ideal customer experience

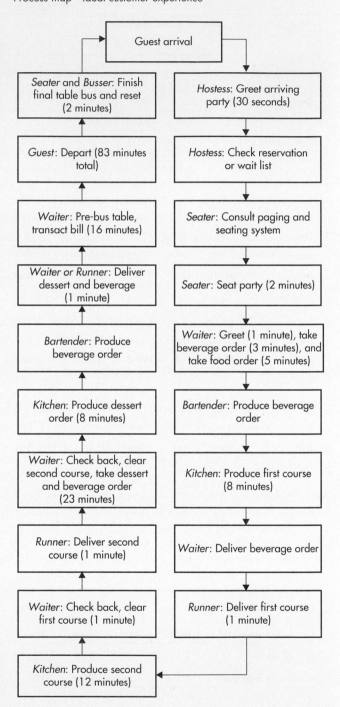

servers could properly handle just five tables each (see Table 1). While management augmented the service coverage with runners, the fact that only two runners supported 15 servers during peak times meant that food often sat in the service window getting cold. Attempting to make up for the labour shortage, the

Table 1

Server time analysis

Process step (per shift)	Time (minutes)	Time (percentage of work time)	Time per table	Number of occurrences	Time per occurrence
Idle	195.6	–	–	91	2.1
Table clearing and bussing	87.3	20%	3.0	78	1.1
Order delivery	77.1	18%	3.3	47	1.6
Beverage delivery	65.3	15%	2.2	42	1.6
Taking order	46.0	11%	1.5	44	1.0
POS operation	45.6	10%	1.6	72	0.6
Silverware setup	36.7	8%	1.2	31	1.2
Transact bill	31.0	7%	1.1	22	1.4
Greet	17.9	4%	0.6	25	0.7
Condiments	13.0	3%	0.4	15	0.9
Print bill	12.3	3%	0.4	21	0.6
Check back	2.8	<1%	0.1	10	0.3
Total	630.6	–	15.4		
Work minutes	435.0	69%			
Idle minutes	195.6	31%			

Total tables attended during study = 29.
Total guests attended during study = 93.
Average guests per table = 3.2.
Target table turns = 4.2 (assuming an 85-minute turn and 75-percent staff-time efficiency).
Suggested section size = 5.

floor managers employed a policy of having the first available server deliver food items as they came up—and frequently the managers themselves had to run food to the guests. With so many service providers delivering orders in such a hurried fashion, guests weren't sure who exactly was the server, were hard pressed to know whom to call for what, and couldn't be sure that their requests would ever be fulfilled if they did ask for something. Moreover, servers rarely had the chance to check back to make sure the customers were satisfied with their entrées. The service studies resulted in a reduction of server sections to five tables to improve service delivery quality, as well as increasing sales potential and tips for servers.

The team also analyzed bar staffing requirements based on historical beverage demand and work effort required for each drink (e.g., bottled beer, premium spirit, wine by the glass and bottle, blended drinks). An example of the time study results is shown in Table 2.

The outcome of the whole study is a graphic overview of the restaurant capacity requirements as a function of guest demand (Figure 2). The graph displays the required capacity of each component as a function of guest demand (in number of tables). For example, during peak hours (50 tables/hour), a total of 15 wait staff, 2 host staff, and 7 cooks are required.

Table 2

Beverage service time analysis (sample)

Product	Process steps	Work time (seconds)
Premium spirit	Take order	7.0
	Stage glass to bar, fill with ice	3.5
	Measure premium spirit to glass	11.1
	Fill glass with post mix	6.0
	Garnish to glass	1.5
	Transact cash	18.2
	Total	47.3

Following the modelling exercise, staff schedules were reworked to better fit the restaurant's business patterns. The revised schedule increased the number of servers by two per shift and reduced the kitchen staff by five cooks per week. Scheduling is assisted by a forecasting system, and a spreadsheet connected to the point-of-sale system facilitates daily transfers of data on guest demand that is used as part of a four-week weighted moving average forecast for demand.

Figure 2

Staff requirements as a function of guest demand (number of tables)

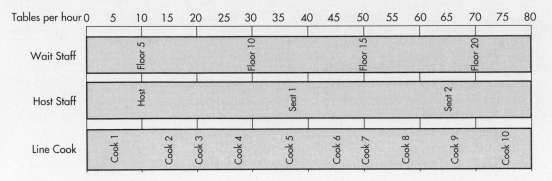

Questions

1. Each guest table takes approximately 15 minutes of a waiter's time. The waiter works with 75 percent staff-time efficiency (i.e., 25 percent allowance factor). Customers spend an average of 85 minutes in the restaurant. How many tables can a waiter be assigned to?

2. The forecast for the number of new tables (guest groups) on a specific day during every half hour from noon to 3 p.m. is 8, 13, 28, 31, 14, and 11. Assuming each table stays 1.5 hours and we assign one waiter to 5 tables, how many waiters would Browns need every half-hour between noon and 3 p.m. period?

3. Suppose that the hourly number of waiters needed on a specific day from noon to midnight is 5, 15, 15, 6, 1, 3, 9, 11, 12, 13, 9, and 6. Determine four-hour shifts to cover these needs with minimum waiter numbers. Hint: Start with noon and use the minimum number of waiters required, still not met, at the start of each shift. However, the last shift should employ the number of waiters required, still not met, during any hour of that shift.

Source: Based on B. Sill and R. Decker, "Applying Capacity-Management Science: The Case of Browns Restaurants," *Cornell Hotel & Restaurant Administration Quarterly* 40(3), June 1999, pp. 22–30.

CHAPTER 17
Project Management

The chapter in this part covers various topics related to successfully managing projects.

LEARNING OBJECTIVES

After completing this chapter, you should be able to:

LO1 Describe what a project is and discuss the nature of a project manager's job.

LO2 Explain what is involved in project planning, how to manage project risks, and what work breakdown structure is.

LO3 Explain what project scheduling is, how schedule/control Gantt charts can be used in project scheduling, and what PERT/CPM and precedence networks are.

LO4 Use PERT/CPM technique with deterministic activity durations to schedule projects, and solve typical problems.

LO5 Schedule activities with probabilistic activity durations, and solve typical problems.

LO6 Describe project "crashing" and solve typical problems.

LO7 Describe what is involved in project execution and control and explain what the earned value is.

LO8 Be able to use Microsoft® Project.

The Information System department of EMCO, the building products manufacturer, had difficulty completing its projects on time. 3M's Medical division could meet only one-third of the launch dates for its new products. Construction management companies such as SNC-Lavalin and Hatch Energy work only on unique construction projects. How do these companies accomplish their projects on time/schedule, within budget, and at expected performance/quality? The answer is effective project management, which is the topic of this chapter.

(LO1) INTRODUCTION

project Unique, large, one-time job requiring special activities to accomplish a specific objective in a limited time frame.

A **project** is a unique, large, one-time job requiring special activities to accomplish a specific objective in a limited time frame. Examples of projects include constructing a store, redesigning a business process, merging two companies, putting on a play, designing new goods or services, and designing an information system. In the above examples, the specific objective is the store, the redesigned business process, the merged company, the play, etc. A related term is *program*. A *program* is a set of projects.

performance goals For a project: keeping the project within schedule, budget, and quality guidelines.

Projects may involve considerable cost. Some have a long time horizon, and some involve a large number of activities that must be carefully planned and coordinated. All projects are expected to achieve the following **performance goals**: to be completed within time/schedule, cost/budget, and quality guidelines. To accomplish this, projects must be authorized, their objectives and scope must be established, a project manager should be appointed, and the project must be planned. Activities/tasks must be identified and time estimates made. Resource requirements must also be estimated and budgets prepared. Once underway, the project's progress must be monitored to ensure that project's performance goals will be achieved.

Projects go through a series of stages or *phases*—a life cycle—which include project initiation (conception, feasibility study/selection), planning and scheduling, execution, control, and closeout. During this life cycle, a variety of skills are needed. The circumstances are analogous to constructing a house. Initially an idea is presented and its feasibility is assessed, then plans must be drawn up by an architect, and approved by the owner and possibly a town's building permits department. Then a succession of activities occurs, each with its own skill requirements, starting with the site preparation, then laying the foundation, erecting the frame, roofing, constructing exterior walls, wiring and plumbing, installing kitchen and bathroom fixtures and appliances, interior finishing and painting and carpeting. Similar sequences occur on large construction projects, in R&D, information technology projects, and in virtually every other instance where projects are being carried out.

In a company, the project initiator/sponsor is usually a senior manager/VP. Project output or deliverable is a good such as a building/software or a service such as merging two databases.

A project is influenced by the company's strategy and policies, and "environment" (e.g., culture, information systems, human resources). The major document used in project initiation is the project *scope* (the work that needs to be accomplished to deliver a good or service, the specified objective).

Deciding which projects to implement is called *project portfolio selection*. This involves factors such as budget, availability of personnel with appropriate knowledge and skill, cost–benefit considerations, financial benefits, e.g., return on investment and net present value, and how the project will contribute to the company's strategy. The following steps for project selection have been suggested[1]:

1. Establish a project council (e.g., the executive committee)
2. Identify some project categories (e.g., long vs. short term, minor vs. major) and criteria (e.g., business value, customer satisfaction, process effectiveness, employee satisfaction)

---

[1]R.L. Englund and R.J. Graham: "From Experience: Linking Projects to Strategy," *Journal of Product Innovation Management*, January 1999, 16(1), pp. 52–64.

SNC-Lavalin

SNC-Lavalin is a large design, engineering, construction, and project management company, based in Montreal, with 35 international offices. Founded in 1911, SNC-Lavalin has performed hundreds of large projects. An example is Phase 2 of the Alouette Aluminum Smelter project in Sept-Iles, Quebec, in 2005. The project increased the facility's capacity to 550,000 tons per annum, the largest aluminum smelter in North America. SNC-Lavalin provided engineering, procurement, and construction management services. A subcontractor was ADF Group (http://www.adfgroup.com) of Terrebonne, near Montreal, that supplied engineering, fabrication, and installation of the steel structures for two new electrolysis halls, each about 1 km long. The project was completed within budget and time.

Source: http://www.snclavalin.com/expertise.php?lang=en&id=25 &sub=1.

3. Collect projects data
4. Assess resources (e.g., labour, dollars) availability
5. Prioritize the projects within categories
6. Select projects to be funded
7. Communicate the results to stakeholders and provide the reasons for selection or non-selection of each project

For an application, see the "Pacific Blue Cross" OM in Action on the next page. For an example of effectiveness of summary reports (scorecards or dashboards) for managing multiple projects, see the "3M Medical Division" OM in Action later in the chapter.

Project planning determines how the project is to be undertaken, and includes breaking down the job into smaller components, called *Work Breakdown Structure* (WBS), determining the resources needed and estimating their costs, scheduling the activities involved or subcontracting the work, planning risk management, and planning material purchases.

Project execution involves purchasing the material, and using the team members and subcontractors to perform the activities/tasks. Project control involves observing the project's progress, issuing performance reports on scope/schedule/cost/quality/risk, and making any necessary changes to the project.

Projects bring various people together, both from the inside and outside of the company. These stakeholders include the project team who perform the activities/tasks, project sponsor/initiator who initiates and gets approval for the project, and customer/users. The project is headed by a project manager, guided by the project sponsor.

Most team members, who have diverse knowledge and skills, will remain associated with the project for less than its full life. Some people go from project to project as their contributions become needed, and others are "on loan," either on a full-time or part-time basis, from their regular jobs.

Certain organizations are involved with projects on a regular basis; examples include consulting firms, architects, lawyers, publishers, and construction companies. For two examples, see the "SNC-Lavalin" OM in Action above and the "Hatch" OM in Action later in the chapter. In these organizations, it is not uncommon for some employees to spend virtually all of their time on projects. These companies have a pure *project organization*.

However, most organizations use a **matrix organization** that temporarily groups together specialists from different departments to work on special projects. Each staff member, for example, a structural engineer or an accountant, works on one or more project(s) part time, but permanently belongs to his department. The project manager and the functional managers share the authority of assigning priorities and directing the work.

matrix organization
An organizational structure that temporarily groups together specialists from different departments to work on special projects.

Finally, some organizations have set up a project management office (PMO) that acts as a department, housing project managers who use team members from functional departments just as in the matrix organization structure. For an example, see the "EMCO" OM in Action.

The Project Manager's Job

project manager The person responsible for planning, scheduling, executing, and controlling a project from inception to completion, meeting the project's requirements and ensuring completion on time, within budget, and to the required quality standards.

The **project manager** is the person responsible for planning, scheduling, executing, and controlling a project from inception to completion, meeting the project's requirements and ensuring completion on time, within budget, and to the required quality standards. She must acquire adequate resources and personnel, and be capable of working through the team members to accomplish the objective of the project. The project manager is responsible for effectively managing each of the following:

1. The *work*, so that all of the necessary activities are accomplished in the desired sequence, and performance goals are met.
2. The *human resources*, so that those working on the project have direction and motivation.
3. *Communications*, so that everybody has the information they need to do their work (usually through regular meetings), and the customer/sponsor is well informed. Logs of actions, issues, and risks should be kept to manage the project, and to have as project history.
4. *Quality*, so that the specific objective is realized.
5. *Time*, so that the project is completed on schedule.
6. *Costs*, so that the project is completed within budget.

To effectively manage a project, a project manager must employ a certain set of skills. The skills include the ability to motivate and direct team members and build a team, make trade-off decisions in project performance goals, expedite the work when necessary, deal with obstacles and team conflicts, put out fires and solve problems, handle failure or fear of failure, and monitor time, budget, and technical details. For projects that involve fairly well defined work, those skills will often suffice. However, for projects that are less well defined, and thus have a higher degree of uncertainty, the project manager must also employ strong leadership skills. These include the ability to adapt to changing circumstances that may involve changes to project performance goals, technical requirements, and project team composition. He must recognize the need for change, decide what changes are necessary in consultation with stakeholders, and work to accomplish them.

OM in *ACTION*

Pacific Blue Cross

Pacific Blue Cross provides extended health and dental insurance to residents of British Columbia. When the new VP of Information Technology (IT) was appointed in 2003, she put in a gate governance process for approving larger projects (lasting over one month), changed the review boards for smaller projects (lasting less than a month), and created a PMO. Each large project is now sponsored by a VP who takes it to the executive committee. If it passes the first gate, cost/benefit analysis is performed on it with the help of the PMO. This result is brought to the executive committee again. If it passes gate 2, it is approved. However, projects costing over half a million dollars need to also go through gate 3, and those costing more than

$1 million need to also go through gate 4. Post-implementation review is gate 5. Smaller projects are prioritized by the department review boards that include department managers. The PMO consists of a manager, three project managers, and two to five contract project managers. All information about processes to follow for a project has been put online. The PMO regularly reports the status of projects to the executives. A "traffic light" report uses green, yellow, and red lights to show the status of each project in terms of time, budget, and performance. The reports are also put online.

Source: Dr. C. Aczel Boivie, "Red Light, Green Light; How One CIO Used Project Management Discipline and the Traffic Light Report to Align Her IT Department with Her Company's Business Goals," *CIO*, June 15, 2006, 19(17), p. 1.

EMCO

EMCO is one of Canada's leading distributors and manufacturers of building plumbing products for residential, commercial, and industrial construction markets.

Before 1998, EMCO's information systems department had trouble estimating internal project durations, progress, and end dates. Red flags often came up too late to have a meaningful impact. Managing multiple projects simultaneously was difficult at best, posing serious resource allocation problems. The result: dissatisfied information systems customers.

In 1998, EMCO created a PMO. Fardin Maknoni, Senior Analyst, Project Management, heads up this department, which handles implementation and support of telecommunications, transaction processing (such as EDI), data processing, systems conversions, and financial system projects for the entire company.

The PMO adopted Deltek's (Welcom) Open Plan. According to Maknoni, "Open Plan was flexible and easy for everyone to use, and it had the features we needed. It allowed us to control and centralize all of our projects." Here are some of the ways EMCO uses Open Plan:

- Before a project begins, managers create six to ten "what-if" scenarios in Open Plan. These allow them to effectively plan ahead, resolve schedule conflicts, and make baseline determinations (such as a project's start date).

- During a project, Open Plan generates weekly progress reports that include time sheets, action items, and project status.

- Time sheet information is uploaded to Open Plan from three sources: an internal data management system, Excel, and manual input.

- Various Gantt, PERT, and spreadsheet reports are created and filtered by criteria meaningful to different tiers of users.

- Progress-analysis reports give critical information to senior management to monitor projects and construct new project proposals.

Source: http://www.deltek.com/pdf/customerstories/cs_emco.pdf#search=%22EMCO%22.

A project manager should accept the political nature of his organization and use it to his advantage. He should be politically sensitive, i.e., realize that people are afraid of change because it might alter their established political relationships.[2]

The job of the project manager can be both difficult and rewarding. He must coordinate and motivate people who sometimes owe their allegiance to other managers in their functional areas. In addition, the people who work on a project possess specialized knowledge and skills that the project manager may lack. Nevertheless, he is expected to guide and evaluate their efforts.

Ethical issues often arise in connection with projects. Examples include the temptation to understate costs or to withhold information in order to get a project approved, pressure to alter or make misleading statements on status reports, falsifying records, compromising workers' safety, and approving substandard work. It is the responsibility of the project manager to maintain and enforce ethical standards.

LO2 PROJECT PLANNING

Project planning involves further elaboration of the project scope (the work to be done) including breaking down the project into smaller components (deliverables, subprojects, work packages, and activities), risk management planning (the identification, analysis, and response plans to what may go wrong), estimating the required resources for the activities (employees, equipment, material), cost estimation (for each activity) and budgeting (calculating total cost per unit time, including subcontracting costs), human resource planning (including assigning team member roles and responsibilities), project scheduling (estimating activity durations, sequencing, and scheduling), quality planning, communications planning, and purchase planning.

It is important to determine the details of work to be done (scope), to formally obtain acceptance of the detailed scope from project customer/sponsor and later, during execution

project planning Analyzing the project into work packages and activities, estimating resources needed and durations, scheduling, etc.

---

[2]For more details, see J.K. Pinto and O.P. Kharbanda, "Lessons for an Accidental Profession," *Business Horizon*, March/April 1995, pp. 41–50.

and control, to control the changes to the project scope. We will describe risk management planning, work breakdown structure (WBS), and project scheduling in more detail in the following sections. In many applications, the design of the good or service, which is the result of project management, is part of the project, performed by architects/engineers, either within the firm or contracted from other firms.

Quality planning involves determining how product quality is to be assured and controlled. It includes deciding the quality policy, objectives, responsibilities, metrics, and tools such as checklists.

Communications planning involves determining the nature of information needed by stakeholders and how to satisfy these needs. It includes plans for information collection/storage, the technology and media used, nature of information distributed (e.g., project performance reports), and methods for accessing and updating the information. For an application, see the "Tim Hortons" OM in Action.

Purchase planning involves determining what to purchase, the statement of work or the specification of the item, supplier evaluation and selection, and the award of contract. The actual delivery and monitoring/controlling of supplier performance are part of the execution and control of the project.

Risk Management Planning

Risks are inherent in projects. They relate to the occurrence of events that can have undesirable consequences, such as delays, increased costs, or an inability to meet technical specifications (quality/performance). In some instances, there is a risk that events will occur that will cause a project to be terminated. Although careful planning can reduce risks, no amount of planning can eliminate chance events due to unforeseen or uncontrollable circumstances.

The probability of occurrence of risk events is highest near the beginning of a project and lowest near the end. However, the cost associated with risk events tends to be lowest near the beginning of a project and highest near the end.

 OM in ACTION

3M Medical Division

3M Medical Division could reach only 34 percent of its milestones (new-product launch-date goals) in 2004. Management was more involved with quickly launched visible products. Even though Microsoft Project was being used by the product teams, there was no standard format for project plans, and managers were not being informed of projects' status in a timely manner. Then in 2006, Microsoft Enterprise Project Management Solution (which includes Microsoft Project, Portfolio, and Web access) and Visio application were used to provide greater visibility of projects status through colour-coded scorecards. This resulted in faster response by managers, doubling the milestone attainment rate.

Source: http://www.microsoft.com/casestudies/Case_Study_Detail.aspx?CaseStudyID=4000000207.

 OM in ACTION   http://www.timhortons.com/ca/en/about/index.html

Tim Hortons

In the early 2000s, Tim Hortons was in the middle of an aggressive expansion plan and needed a faster way to develop new restaurants. Therefore, the engineering services department started using Expesite project management software (http://www.expesite.com/homepage/CaseStudies/TimHortons.pdf), which allowed them to use the Internet to communicate project documents (e.g., blue prints), monitor the schedule, track costs, and receive bids. The system cut the development process for a restaurant from 12 down to 11 months, and saved thousands of dollars a year for couriering blueprints back and forth between architects, engineers, and Tim Hortons' staff. The system has also increased process consistency and accountability (by regular reporting) across regions.

Source: M. Wilson, "Expediting Development," *Chain Store Age*, October 2006, 82(10), p. 92.

Good risk management entails identifying as many potential risks as possible, analyzing and assessing those risks, and planning a response to avoid, transfer, or mitigate the risk. Much of this takes place during planning of a project, although it is not unusual for this process to be repeated during the execution of project as experience grows and new information becomes available.

The first step for risk management planning is to identify the risks. Typically, there are numerous sources of risks, although the more experience an organization has with a particular type of work, the fewer and more identifiable the risks will be. Everyone associated with the project should have responsibility for identifying risks. Brainstorming sessions and questionnaires can be useful in this regard. Another approach to risk identification is to review the documents and analyze the assumptions, looking for inaccuracies, inconsistencies, and incompleteness. The list of risks and other information obtained in the following steps is usually stored in a *risk register*.

Once risks have been identified, each risk must be evaluated to determine its probability of occurrence and its potential consequences if it does occur. Both quantitative and qualitative approaches have merit. All stakeholders can contribute to this effort, and experts might also be called on. Experience with previous projects can be useful. Many tools might be applied, including scenario analysis, simulation, decision trees, and sensitivity analysis. There should be a response to risks with high probability and impact.

Risk response can take a number of forms. Much depends on the nature and scope of a project. First, the root cause of a risk is identified. It will help to categorize risks by either their source (this is called risk breakdown structure) or by the area of work (using the WBS). Risk response includes:

- Redundant (backup) systems; for example, an emergency generator could supply power in the event of an electrical failure

- Using a less complex process or a more stable supplier

- Frequent monitoring of critical project aspects with the goal of catching and eliminating problems in their early stages, before they cause extensive damage

- Transferring risks, say by outsourcing a particular component of a project and requiring performance bonds

- Risk-sharing, for example, as in an oil and gas consortium

- Extending the schedule, creating contingency funds, reducing project scope, clarifying the requirements, obtaining information, and improving communications

Work Breakdown Structure

Because a large project usually involves a large amount of work, it is decomposed into smaller components. **Work breakdown structure (WBS)** is a hierarchical listing of what must be done during the project (see Figure 17-1 for a schematic example); it is for a project what the product structure tree is for a product. The first step in developing a work breakdown structure is to identify the major components of the project. These could be the phases of project, deliverables, or subprojects. The next step is to identify the major subcomponents for each of the major components. This process is repeated until each subcomponent is decomposed into work packages; a work package can be performed by a worker, team, or subcontractor. Then, each work package, possibly with assistance from the worker, team, or subcontractor, is broken down into a list of the activities that will be needed to accomplish it.

A company can use its past experience to determine the WBS. Progressive elaboration can be pursued as the details of work packages become known (this is also called rolling wave planning). Each component in a WBS should be assigned a code for purpose of monitoring its performance.

work breakdown structure (WBS)   A hierarchical listing of what must be done during a project.

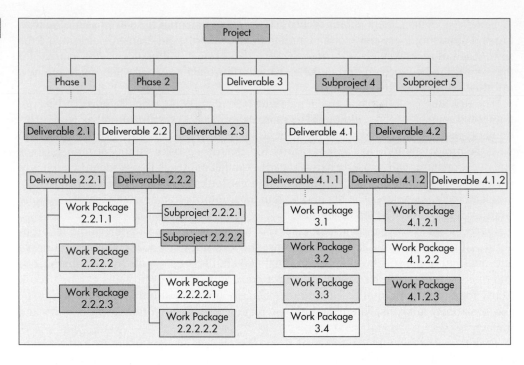

LO3 PROJECT SCHEDULING

project scheduling

Determining the timing of
activities of the project.

Project scheduling involves determining the timing of activities of the project. It starts
with the identification of the activities in the WBS, including their attributes (e.g., physical
location to be performed, person/group/subcontractor responsible) and whether an activity
is a milestone activity (signifying a review/test/approval decision).

Then, any sequential dependencies of every pair of activities should be identified.

Next, the resources (employees or subcontractors, equipment, material) needed for
each activity should be identified. If the needed resources cannot be identified, the activity
should be further decomposed.

Then, the duration of each activity can be estimated using information on the availability
of resources. The risk register could possibly add some contingency time to the duration.
As work is undertaken, more accurate estimates of costs and times become available.
Analogous activities in the past can be used to estimate the activity duration. The 3-point
estimates method, described later under "Probabilistic Activity Durations," can also be
used to estimate the average and standard deviation of an activity's duration.

Finally, the schedule is developed using the activity duration estimates and the sequential
dependencies of activities by the PERT/CPM technique (described later), for both one-point
estimate (deterministic times) and 3-point estimates (probabilistic times). Attempts may be
made to modify the schedule so that a more level use of resources takes place. If the project
will be late, schedule compression methods such as project crashing (accelerating activities) and fast tracking (overlapping predecessor-successor activities) will be performed.
The schedule will be displayed graphically using Gantt or PERT/CPM charts.

We will describe below the schedule/control Gantt chart, PERT/CPM technique using
both deterministic and probabilistic times, and project crashing.

Gantt Chart

The schedule/control Gantt chart, defined in the previous chapter, can be used as a visual
aid for scheduling and control of the activities of a project. It is a popular tool for scheduling and control of *simple* projects. It enables a manager to schedule the activities and
then to monitor their progress over time by comparing their planned progress to their
actual progress. Figure 17-2 illustrates the schedule/control Gantt chart for a bank's plan

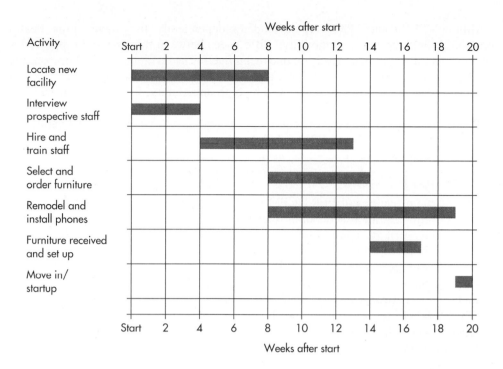

Figure 17-2

A schedule/control Gantt chart for establishing a new bank branch

to establish a new branch. The chart indicates which activities are to occur, their planned duration, and when they are to occur. Then, as the project progresses, the manager is able to see which activities are ahead of schedule and which are behind. This enables the manager to direct attention where it is needed most in order to finish the project on time.

Aside from being a visual tool, an advantage of a schedule/control Gantt chart is its simplicity. However, schedule/control Gantt charts fail to reveal relationships among activities that can be crucial to effective project management. For instance, if one of the early activities in a project suffers a delay, it would be important for the manager to be able to easily determine which later activities are affected. Conversely, some activities may safely be delayed without affecting the overall project completion time. The schedule/control Gantt chart does not directly reveal this. On more complex projects, a *precedence network*, described later, is used for scheduling purposes.

PERT/CPM Technique

PERT (program evaluation and review technique) and **CPM** (critical path method) are two of the most widely used tools for scheduling and control of large-scale projects. By using PERT and CPM, managers are able to obtain:

1. A graphical display of project activities and their sequential relationship
2. An estimate of how long the project will take
3. An indication of which activities are most critical to timely project completion
4. An indication of how long any activity can be delayed without delaying the project

PERT and CPM were developed independently during the late 1950s. PERT evolved through the joint efforts of Lockheed Aircraft, the U.S. Navy Special Projects Office, and the consulting firm of Booz, Allen, Hamilton, in an effort to speed up the Polaris missile project. At the time, the U.S. government was concerned that the Soviet Union might be gaining nuclear superiority, and it gave top priority for the early completion of the project by the U.S. Department of Defense. The project was a huge one, with more than 3,000 contractors and thousands of activities. PERT was quite successful and was generally credited with shaving two years off the length of the project.

CPM was developed by J.E. Kelly of the Remington Rand Corporation and M.R. Walker of DuPont to schedule and control maintenance projects in chemical plants.

PERT   Program evaluation and review technique, used for scheduling and control of large projects.

CPM   Critical path method, used for scheduling and control of large projects.

Although PERT and CPM were developed independently, they have a great deal in common. Moreover, many of the initial differences between them have disappeared as users borrowed certain features from one technique for use with the other. For example, PERT originally stressed probabilistic activity durations because the environment in which it was developed was characterized by high uncertainty. In contrast, the tasks for which CPM was developed were less uncertain, so CPM originally made no provision for variability of duration. To avoid confusion, we will not delve into this difference. For practical purposes, PERT and CPM are the same and we will use the term *PERT/CPM* to refer to either method.

Precedence Network

precedence network
Diagram of project activities and their sequential relationships by use of arrows and nodes.

activity-on-arrow (AOA)
Network in which arrows designate activities.

activity-on-node (AON)
Network in which nodes designate activities.

One of the main features of PERT/CPM is its use of a **precedence network** to depict project activities and their sequential relationships by use of arrows and nodes. There are two slightly different conventions for constructing these networks. Under the original convention, the *arrows* designate activities; under the new convention, the *nodes* designate activities. These are referred to as **activity-on-arrow (AOA)** and **activity-on-node (AON)** network, respectively.

Both types of networks are illustrated in Figure 17-3, using the new bank branch example of Figure 17-2. In the AOA network, the arrows represent both the activities and the sequence in which they must be performed (e.g., Interview precedes Hire and train); in the AON network, the arrows show only the sequence in which activities must be performed, while the nodes represent the activities. Only AON precedence networks will be used in this chapter.

Note that the AON network has a start node, S, which is actually not an activity but is added in order to have a single starting node. Also, an AON network should have only one ending node.

The relationships shown in Figure 17-3 are all of the finish-to-start type (i.e., an activity must finish before its immediate successor can start). Sometimes other types of relationships exist, such as start-to-start (an activity can start only after another has started), finish-to-finish, and start-to-finish. Also, it is possible to require a pre-specified minimum delay (time buffer) in any of these relationships. In addition, some dependencies may be discretionary. Further, there may be external dependencies, e.g., an externally determined start or finish time for an activity. We will consider only finish-to-start relationships, which are most common, in this chapter. Developing and interpreting AON precedence networks requires some familiarity with network conventions; see Figure 17-4.

path   A sequence of activities that leads from the start node to the end node.

Of particular interest are the *paths* or chains in a precedence network diagram. A **path** is a sequence of activities that leads from the start node to the end node. For example, in the AON network of Figure 17-3, S-1-2-6-7 is a path. Note that there are three paths in this

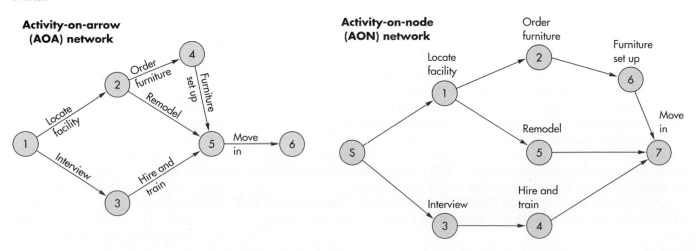

INTERPRETATION	NETWORK RELATIONSHIP

Figure 17-4

AON precedence network conventions

Activities must be completed in sequence: first *a*, then *b*, and then *c*.

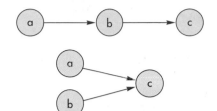

Both *a* and *b* must be completed before *c* can start.

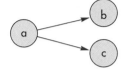

Activity *a* must be completed before *b* or *c* can start.

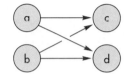

Both *a* and *b* must be completed before *c* or *d* can start.

critical path   The longest path from start to end; determines the expected project duration.

critical activities   Activities on the critical (longest) path.

path slack time   Allowable slippage for a path; the difference between the length of the path and the length of the critical (longest) path.

deterministic durations   Durations that are fairly certain.

probabilistic durations   Durations that allow for variation.

network. One reason for the importance of paths is that they reveal *sequential relationships*. If one activity in a sequence is delayed (i.e., is late) or done incorrectly, all the following activities on that path will be delayed.

Another important aspect of a path is its length (i.e., duration). The length of a path can be determined by summing the expected duration of the activities on it. The path with the largest duration is of particular interest because it governs the project completion time. In other words, expected project duration equals the expected duration of the longest path. Moreover, if there are any delays along the longest path, there will be corresponding delays in the project completion time. Attempts to shorten project completion must focus on the activities on the longest path. Because of its influence on project completion time, the longest path is referred to as the **critical path**, and its activities are referred to as **critical activities**.

Paths that are shorter than the critical path can experience some delays and still not affect the overall project completion time as long as their duration does not exceed the length of the critical path. The allowable slippage for any path is called **path slack time**, and it reflects the difference between the length of the path and the length of the critical path. The critical path, then, has zero path slack time.

LO4 DETERMINISTIC ACTIVITY DURATIONS

The main determinant of the way PERT/CPM networks are analyzed and interpreted is whether activity durations are *probabilistic* or *deterministic*. If durations are fairly certain, we say that the durations are **deterministic**. If durations are subject to variation, we say that the durations are **probabilistic**. Probabilistic durations must include an indication of the extent of probable variation.

This section deals with deterministic activity durations. The next section deals with probabilistic activity durations.

One of the best ways to gain an understanding of the nature of a precedence network and the critical path is to consider a simple example using an intuitive solution method.

The Rogers Centre (formerly known as Sky Dome) in Toronto is one of the few stadiums in the world with a fully retractable roof. It was built in the late 1980s by general contractor Ellis Don Ltd. The project scheduler used Primavera's Project Planner (now part of Oracle) to schedule and control thousands of activities of different trades-people working on this fast-track project. Despite problems with accessibility and a labour strike, the $400-million project was completed on time.

Example 1

Given the information provided below:

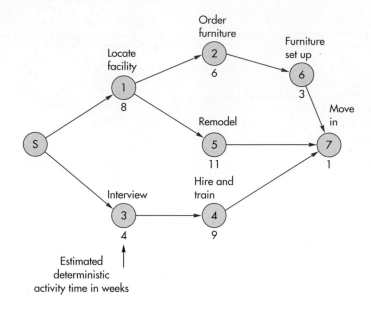

Determine:

a. The length (duration) of each path.

b. The critical path.

c. The expected duration of the project.

d. The slack for each path.

Solution

a. As shown in the following table, the path durations are 18 weeks, 20 weeks, and 14 weeks.

b. The longest path (20 weeks) is S-1-5-7, so it is the critical path.

c. The expected duration of the project is equal to the length of the critical path (i.e., 20 weeks).

d. We find the slack for each path by subtracting its length from the length of the critical path, as shown in the right column of the following table. (*Note*: It is sometimes desirable to know the slack time of the activities. The next section describes a method for obtaining those slack times.)

Path	Duration (weeks)	Path Slack (weeks)
S-1-2-6-7	$8 + 6 + 3 + 1 = 18$	$20 - 18 = 2$
S-1-5-7	$8 + 11 + 1 = 20*$	$20 - 20 = 0$
S-3-4-7	$4 + 9 + 1 = 14$	$20 - 14 = 6$

*Critical path length.

Solution Technique

Many real-life precedence networks are much larger than the simple network illustrated in the preceding example; they often contain hundreds or even thousands of activities and exponentially more paths. Because the necessary calculations can become exceedingly time consuming, large networks are analyzed by a computer program and a solution technique that develops four values for each activity:

- ES, the *earliest* time the activity can *start*.
- EF, the *earliest* time the activity can *finish*.

- LS, the *latest* time the activity can *start* and not delay the project.
- LF, the *latest* time the activity can *finish* and not delay the project.

Once these values have been determined, they can be used to find:

1. Expected project duration
2. Activity slack times
3. The critical path

First, we calculate the earliest start and finish times for each activity, starting from the left at the start node and moving to the right of the precedence network (called a *forward pass*), using the following two simple rules:

1. The earliest finish time for any activity is equal to its earliest start time plus its expected duration, t:

$$EF = ES + t \qquad\qquad (17\text{-}1)$$

2. ES for an activity with one immediate predecessor is equal to the EF of that node. ES for an activity with multiple immediate predecessors is equal to the largest EF of those nodes. Let ES of the start node be zero.

Example 2

Calculate the earliest start time and earliest finish time for each activity in the network shown in Example 1.

Solution

Begin by enlarging each node and placing the activity number and duration inside it as follows:

We determine and place the earliest start time, ES, and the earliest finish time, EF, for the activity inside each node as follows:

ES of the start node is 0. The start node in this example has zero duration. Therefore, $EF_S = ES_S + t = 0 + 0 = 0$. The EF of the start node becomes the ES of the nodes immediately following it. Thus, $ES_1 = 0$ and $ES_3 = 0$:

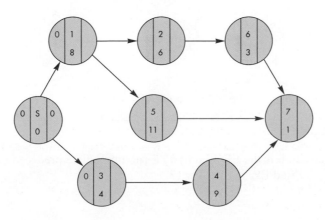

Next, use $EF = ES + t$ for each of the nodes 1 and 3; i.e., $EF_1 = 0 + 8 = 8$ and $EF_3 = 0 + 4 = 4$:

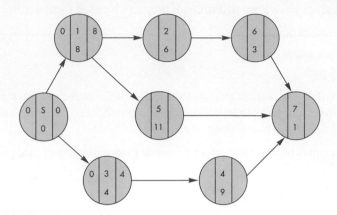

Now, because activity 1 has an EF of 8, both activities 2 and 5 (its immediate successor) will have ES of 8. Similarly, activity 4 will have ES of 4 because EF of node 3, its immediate predecessor, is 4:

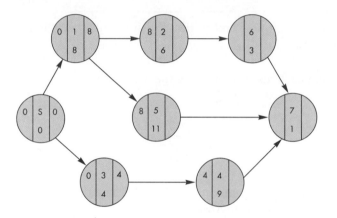

This permits calculation of the EFs for activities 2, 5, and 4: $EF_2 = 8 + 6 = 14$, $EF_5 = 8 + 11 = 19$, and $EF_4 = 4 + 9 = 13$.

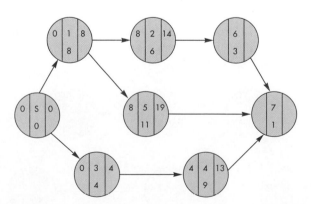

The ES for activity 6 is the EF of activity 2 (its immediate predecessor) which is 14. Using this value, we find $EF_6 = 14 + 3 = 17$.

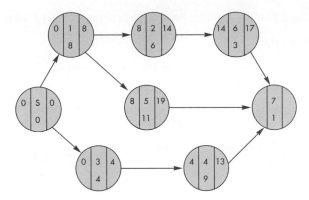

In order to determine the ES for activity 7, we must realize that activity 7 cannot start until *every* activity that immediately precedes it is finished. Therefore, the *largest* of the EFs for the three activities that immediately precede it determines ES_7. Hence, the ES for activity 7 is 19 (i.e., max (17, 19, 13)).

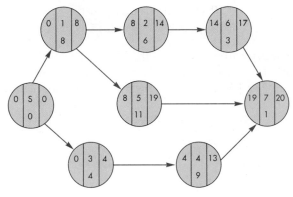

Finally, $EF_7 = 19 + 1 = 20$. Note that the EF for the end node is the expected project duration, 20 weeks.

Now, we calculate the latest start and finish times, starting from the right (i.e., the end node) and moving to the left of the precedence network (called a *backward pass*), using the following two simple rules:

1. The latest start time for any activity is equal to its latest finish time minus its expected duration:

   $$LS = LF - t \qquad\qquad (17\text{-}2)$$

2. For a node with one immediate successor, LF equals the LS of that node. For a node with multiple immediate successors, LF equals the smallest LS of those nodes. Let LF of the end node equal its EF.

Example 3

Calculate the latest finish and latest start times of activities for the precedence network shown at the end of Example 2.

Solution

We will add the LS and LF times to the nodes just below the ES and EF times, respectively, determined in Example 2.

Begin by setting the LF of the last activity (node 7) equal to the EF of that activity. Thus,

$$LF_7 = EF_7 = 20 \text{ weeks}$$

Obtain the LS for activity 7 by subtracting its duration, t, from its LF:

$$LS_7 = LF_7 - t = 20 - 1 = 19:$$

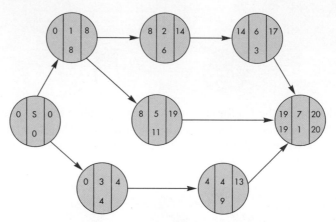

The LS of 19 for activity 7 now becomes the LF for each of the activities that immediately precede it. Thus, $LF_6 = LF_5 = LF_4 = 19$. Now subtract their activity time from their LF to obtain their LS. The LS for activity 4 is $19 - 9 = 10$, for activity 5 is $19 - 11 = 8$, and for activity 6 is $19 - 3 = 16$:

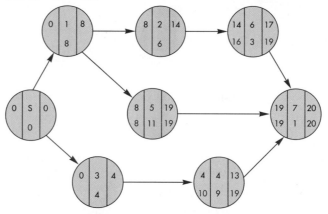

Next, the LS for activity 6, which is 16, becomes the LF for activity 2 (its immediate predecessor), and the LS for activity 4, which is 10, becomes the LF for activity 3 (its immediate predecessor). Using these values, we find the LS for each of these activities by subtracting their activity time from their LF. Therefore, LS for activity 2 is $16 - 6 = 10$, and for activity 3 is $10 - 4 = 6$:

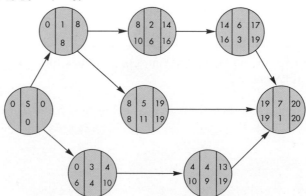

The LF for activity 1 is the *smaller* of the two LSs of the activities that immediately succeed it. Hence, the LF for activity 1 is 8 (i.e., min (8, 10)). The reason you use the smaller time is that activity 1 must finish at a time that permits both the immediately following activities to start no later than their LS.

Once we have determined the LF of activity 1, we find its LS by subtracting its time of 8 from its LF of 8. Hence, LS of activity 1 is 0:

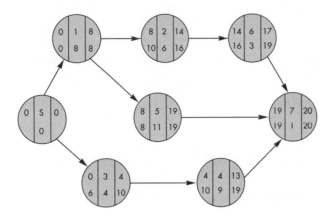

Next, the LF of activity S is the smaller of LS of activities 1 and 3, i.e., $LF_S = \min(0, 6) = 0$. Finally, $LS_S = LF_S - t = 0 - 0 = 0$:

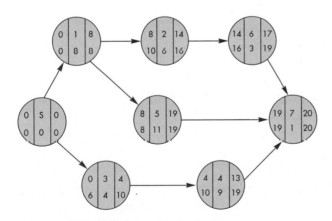

The rules for the above solution technique are reiterated in the following box.

Calculating Activity Slack Times. Activity slack times can be calculated in either of two ways:

$$\text{Slack} = \text{LS} - \text{ES} \quad \text{or} \quad \text{LF} - \text{EF} \tag{17-3}$$

The critical path consists of the activities with zero slack time.

Rules for the PERT/CPM Solution Technique

Forward Pass

Start at the left side of the precedence network (i.e., the start node) and work toward the right side.

For the start activity: ES = 0.

For each activity: ES + Activity duration = EF.

If an activity has a unique immediate predecessor: ES = EF of that activity.

If an activity has multiple immediate predecessors, set its ES equal to the largest EF of its immediate predecessors.

Backward Pass

Start at the right side of the precedence network (i.e., the end node) and work toward the left side.

Use the EF as the LF for the end activity.

For each activity: LS = LF − Activity time.

If an activity has a unique immediate follower: LF = LS of that activity.

If an activity has multiple immediate followers, set the activity's LF equal to the smallest LS of the immediate followers.

Example 4

Calculate activity slack times for the procedence network at the end of Example 3.

Solution

Either the start times or the finish times can be used. Suppose we use the start times. Using ES calculated in Example 2 and LS calculated in Example 3, activity slack times are:

Activity	LS	ES	(LS − ES) Slack
S	0	0	0
1	0	0	0
3	6	0	6
2	10	8	2
5	8	8	0
4	10	4	6
6	16	14	2
7	19	19	0

Example 4 indicates that activities S, 1, 5, and 7 are all critical activities, which agrees with the results of the intuitive approach demonstrated in Example 1.

Knowledge of activity slack times provides managers with information for planning the allocation of scarce resources and for directing control efforts toward those activities that are most susceptible to delaying the project. In this regard, it is important to recognize that activity slack times are based on the assumption that all of the activities on the same path will be started as early as possible and not exceed their expected times. Furthermore, if two activities are both on the same path (e.g., activities 2 and 6 in the preceding example) and have the same slack (e.g., two weeks), this will be the *total* slack available to both. In essence, the activities have *shared slack*. Hence, if the first activity uses all the slack, there will be zero slack left for all the following activities on that same path.

As noted earlier, this solution technique lends itself to computerization. This problem (Examples 2 to 4) will be solved using Microsoft Project at the end of chapter.

Hatch

Hatch is a large Canadian design, consulting engineering, and project management firm specializing in power and energy projects. Hatch (previously Acres) has undertaken hundreds of projects since 1924, both within Canada and internationally. One project was a set of hydroelectric dams over Karun, a major river in southwest Iran, The challenging project started in 1977 and only recently the third dam was completed. The 2000-MW Karun III hydroelectric project includes a 205-metre-high arch dam, a huge underground powerhouse complex, power and water tunnels, and the world's largest concrete-lined plunge pool, all built on a limestone foundation in an area of high seismic activity.

Source: http://www.hatch.ca/energy/hydroelectric/projects/lg_karun.htm.

LO5 PROBABILISTIC ACTIVITY DURATIONS

The preceding discussion assumed that activity durations were known and not subject to variation. While this assumption is appropriate in some situations, there are many others where it is not. Consequently, these situations require a probabilistic approach.

The probabilistic PERT/CPM approach, called the **3-point estimates method**, involves *three* duration estimates for each activity instead of one:

1. **Optimistic duration**: The length of time under the best conditions; represented by t_o.

2. **Pessimistic duration**: The length of time under the worst conditions; represented by t_p.

3. **Most likely duration**: The most probable length of time; represented by t_m.

Managers or others with knowledge about the activity can make these duration estimates.

The **Beta distribution** is a family of continuous positive distributions used to describe the inherent variability of an activity's duration (see Figure 17-5). Although there is no real theoretical justification for using the Beta distribution, it has certain features that make it attractive in practice: The distribution can be symmetrical or skewed to either the right or the left depending on its shape parameters; the mean and variance of the distribution can be readily obtained from the three estimates listed above; and shape parameters can be chosen so that the distribution is uni-modal with a high concentration of probability surrounding the most likely duration estimate.

Of special interest in probabilistic PERT/CPM are the average or expected duration for each activity t_e, and the variance of each activity's duration, σ_{act}^2. The expected duration of an activity, t_e, is an unequally weighted average of the three estimates:

$$t_e = \frac{t_o + 4t_m + t_p}{6} \qquad (17\text{-}4)$$

3-point estimates method PERT/CPM when the activity durations are variable and are determined using three estimates: optimistic, most likely, and pessimistic.

optimistic duration The length of time under the best conditions (t_o)

pessimistic duration The length of time under the worst conditions (t_p).

most likely duration The most probable length of time (t_m).

Beta distribution A family of continuous positive distributions used to describe the inherent variability in activity durations.

Figure 17-5

A Beta distribution is used to describe the variability of an activity's duration.

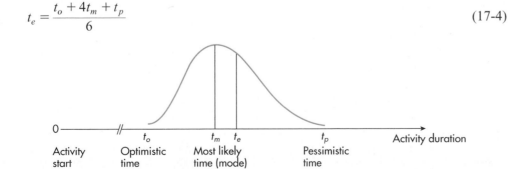

The expected (average) duration of a path is equal to the sum of the expected duration of the activities on it:

Path mean $= \Sigma$(expected duration of activities on the path) $\qquad$ (17-5)

The standard deviation of each activity's duration is estimated as one-sixth of the difference between the pessimistic and optimistic estimates. (Analogously, almost all of the area under a Normal distribution lies within three standard deviations of the mean, which is a range of six standard deviations.) We find the variance by squaring the standard deviation. Thus,

$$\sigma^2_{act} = \left[\frac{(t_p - t_o)}{6} \right]^2 \quad \text{or} \quad \sigma^2_{act} = \frac{(t_p - t_o)^2}{36} \qquad (17\text{-}6)$$

The size of the variance reflects the degree of uncertainty associated with an activity's duration: The larger the variance, the greater the uncertainty.

It is also required to calculate the standard deviation of the duration of a *path*. We can do this by summing the variances of the activity durations on the path and then taking the square root of that number; that is,

$$\sigma_{path} = \sqrt{\Sigma[(\text{variances of activity durations on path}])} \qquad (17\text{-}7)$$

Example 5 illustrates these calculations.

Example 5

The precedence network for a project is shown below, with the three duration estimates for each activity (in weeks) over each node.

a. Calculate the expected duration for each activity and the expected duration for each path.

b. Identify the critical path (based on the expected durations).

c. Calculate the variance of each activity's duration and the standard deviation of each path's duration.

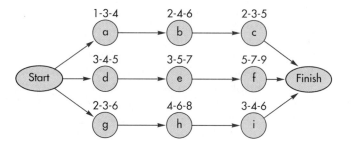

Solution

a. Because the start and finish activities do not take any time in this example, we can ignore them in the following calculations:

| Path | Activity | Durations | | | $t_e = \dfrac{t_0 + 4t_m + t_p}{6}$ | Path Expected Duration |
		t_o	t_m	t_p		
a-b-c	a	1	3	4	2.83 ⎫	
	b	2	4	6	4.00 ⎬	10.00
	c	2	3	5	3.17 ⎭	
d-e-f	d	3	4	5	4.00 ⎫	
	e	3	5	7	5.00 ⎬	16.00
	f	5	7	9	7.00 ⎭	
g-h-i	g	2	3	6	3.33 ⎫	
	h	4	6	8	6.00 ⎬	13.50
	i	3	4	6	4.17 ⎭	

b. The path that has the largest expected duration is the critical path. Because path d-e-f has the largest path expected duration, it is the critical path.

c.

| Path | Activity | Durations | | | $\sigma^2_{act} = \dfrac{(t_p - t_o)^2}{36}$ | σ^2_{path} | σ_{path} |
		t_o	t_m	t_p			
	a	1	3	4	$(4-1)^2/36 = 9/36$	$34/36 = 0.944$	0.97
a-b-c	b	2	4	6	$(6-2)^2/36 = 16/36$		
	c	2	3	5	$(5-2)^2/36 = 9/36$		
	d	3	4	5	$(5-3)^2/36 = 4/36$	$36/36 = 1.00$	1.00
d-e-f	e	3	5	7	$(7-3)^2/36 = 16/36$		
	f	5	7	9	$(9-5)^2/36 = 16/36$		
	g	2	3	6	$(6-2)^2/36 = 16/36$	$41/36 = 1.139$	1.07
g-h-i	h	4	6	8	$(8-4)^2/36 = 16/36$		
	i	3	4	6	$(6-3)^2/36 = 9/36$		

Knowledge of the path's expected duration and standard deviation of duration enables a manager to calculate probabilistic estimates of the project completion time, such as these:

- The probability that the project will be completed by a specified time
- The probability that the project will take longer than its scheduled completion time

These estimates can be derived from the probability that various paths will be completed by the specified time or take longer than the scheduled completion time. Although activity durations are represented by Beta distribution, a path's duration is approximately a Normal distribution. This concept, called the central limit theorem, is illustrated in Figure 17-6.

Determining Path Probabilities

The probability that a given path will be completed in a specified length of time can be determined using the following formula:

$$z = \frac{\text{Specified length of time} - \text{Expected path duration}}{\text{Standard deviation of path duration}} \tag{17-8}$$

The resulting value of z indicates how many standard deviations of the path's duration the specified length of time is beyond the expected path duration. A negative value of z indicates that the specified time is *earlier* than the expected path duration. Once the value of z has been determined, it can be used in Appendix B, Table B, to obtain the probability that the path will be completed by the specified time. Note that the probability is equal to the area under the Normal curve to the left of z, as illustrated in Figure 17-7.

A project is not completed until *all* of its activities, not only those on the critical path, have been completed. It sometimes happens that another path ends up taking more time to complete than the critical path, in which case the project runs longer than expected. Hence, it can be risky to focus exclusively on the critical path. This requires determining the probability that *all* paths will finish by a specified time. To do that, find the probability that each path will finish by the specified time, and then multiply those probabilities.

Figure 17-6

Activity-duration distributions and the path-duration distribution

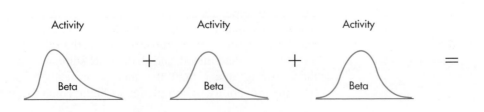

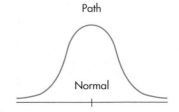

Figure 17-7

The path probability is the area under the Normal curve to the left of z.

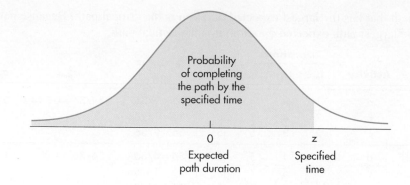

The result is the probability that the *project* will be completed by the specified time. This assumes independence of path durations. The assumption of *independence* of path durations requires two conditions: (a) that the activity durations are independent of each other, and (b) that each activity is on only one path. For activity durations to be independent, the duration for one must not give any information about the duration of the other; if two activities were always early or late together, they would not be considered independent.

Example 6

Using the information from Example 5, answer the following questions:

a. Can the paths be considered independent? Why?

b. What is the probability that the project can be completed within 17 weeks of its start?

c. What is the probability that the project will be completed within 15 weeks of its start?

d. What is the probability that the project will *not* be completed within 15 weeks of its start?

Solution

a. Yes, the paths can be considered independent, since no activity is on more than one path and we have no information suggesting that activity durations are interrelated.

b. To answer questions of this nature, we must take into account the degree to which the path-duration distributions "exceed" the specified completion time. This concept is illustrated in the following figure, which shows the three path-duration distributions, each centred on that path's expected duration, and the specified completion time of 17 weeks.

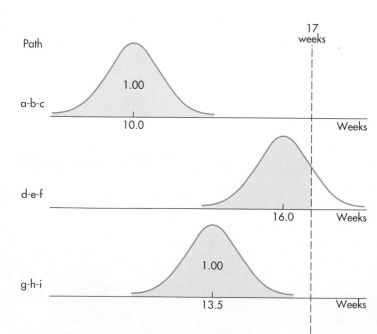

The coloured portion of each distribution corresponds to the probability that the path will be completed within the specified time. Observe that paths a-b-c and g-h-i are well enough to the left of the specified time so that it is highly likely that both will be finished by week 17. In such cases, we essentially need to consider only the distribution of path d-e-f in assessing the probability of completion by week 17. To do so, we must first calculate the value of *z* using formula 17-8 for this path:

$$z = \frac{17 - 16}{1.00} = +1.00$$

Turning to Appendix B, Table B with $z = +1.00$, we find that the area under the curve to the left of z is .8413. To check our intuition, the probabilities for the other two paths are also determined, and all three are summarized in the following table. Note: If the value of z exceeds $+3.50$, treat the probability of completion as being equal to 1.

Path	$z = \dfrac{17 - \text{Expected path duration}}{\text{Standard deviation of path duration}}$	Probability of Completion in 17 Weeks
a-b-c	$\dfrac{17 - 10}{.97} = +7.22$	1.00
d-e-f	$\dfrac{17 - 16}{1.00} = +1.00$	.8413
g-h-i	$\dfrac{17 - 13.5}{1.07} = +3.27$	.9995

Thus, Prob(project finishes by week 17) = Prob(path a-b-c finishes by week 17) ×
Prob(path d-e-f finishes week 17) ×
Prob(path g-h-i finishes by week 17)

$= 1.00 \times .8413 \times .9995 = .8409 \sim 84\%$

c. For a specified time of 15 weeks, the z values are:

Path	$z = \dfrac{15 - \text{Expected path duration}}{\text{Standard deviation of path duration}}$	Probability of Completion in 15 Weeks
a-b-c	$\dfrac{15 - 10}{.97} = +5.15$	1.0000
d-e-f	$\dfrac{15 - 16}{1.00} = -1.00$	.1587
g-h-i	$\dfrac{15 - 13.5}{1.07} = +1.40$	.9192

Paths d-e-f and g-h-i have z values that are less than $+3.50$. From Appendix B, Table B, the area to the *left* of $z = -1.00$ is .1587, and the area to the *left* of $z = +1.40$ is .9192. The path distributions are illustrated in the following figure. The joint probability of all paths finishing within 15 weeks is the product of their probabilities: $(1.00)(.1587)(.9192) = .1459$.

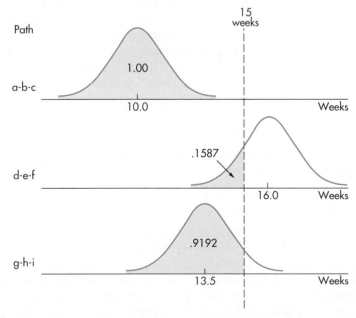

d. The probability of not finishing within 15 weeks is the complement of the probability obtained in part c: $1 - .1459 = .8541$.

Using Simulation. The above discussion assumed that the paths of the project were *independent*, which requires that no activity be on more than one path. If an activity were on more than one path and it happened that the completion time for that activity far exceeded its expected time, all paths that include that activity would be affected and, hence, their durations would not be independent. If only a few activities are on multiple paths, particularly if the paths are *much* shorter than the critical path, the independence assumption may still be reasonable.

Otherwise project schedulers often use *simulation* to find the desired probabilities. This amounts to a form of repeated sampling wherein many passes are made through the precedence network. In each pass, a random value for each activity's duration is selected from the probability distribution of its duration. After each pass, the project duration is determined. After a large number of such passes (e.g., several hundred), there is enough information to prepare a frequency distribution of the project duration. A project scheduler can use this distribution to make a probabilistic assessment of the project duration.

LO6 PROJECT CRASHING

Estimate of an activity's duration is usually made for a given level of resources. In many situations, it is possible to reduce the length of a project, i.e., "crash" the project, by using additional resources. The impetus to shorten projects may reflect efforts to avoid late penalties, to take advantage of monetary incentives for timely or early completion of a project, or to free resources for use on other projects. In new product development, shortening the time may lead to a strategic benefit: beating the competition to the market. In some cases, however, the desire to shorten the length of a project merely reflects an attempt to reduce the indirect costs associated with running the project, such as facilities, equipment, supervision, and personnel costs. Hence, a project manager may be able to shorten a project by increasing *direct* expenses to speed up the project, thereby realizing savings on indirect project costs. *Time–cost trade-off* can be used to identify those activities that will reduce the sum of the indirect and direct project costs.

Only activities on the critical path are potential candidates for crashing (i.e., shortening), because shortening non-critical activities would not have an impact on the project duration. From an economic standpoint, critical activities should be crashed according to crashing cost per period: crash those with the lowest crash cost per period first. Moreover, crashing should continue as long as the cost to crash is less than the benefits derived from crashing. We assume that the indirect costs are a linear function of project duration. Also, we assume (direct) crashing cost per period increases faster the more you crash the project. Figure 17-8 illustrates the basic relationship between indirect, direct, and total project costs due to crashing.

The general procedure for crashing is:

1. Obtain estimates of regular and crash durations and crash cost per period for each activity, and indirect project costs per period.
2. Determine the lengths of all paths.
3. Determine the critical activities.
4. Crash critical activities, starting from the cheapest, as long as crashing cost per period does not exceed the benefits of crashing. Note that two or more paths may become critical as the original critical path becomes shorter, so that subsequent improvements will require simultaneous shortening of two or more paths. In some cases, it will be more economical to shorten an activity that is on two (or more) of the critical paths than two (or more) activities on each critical path.

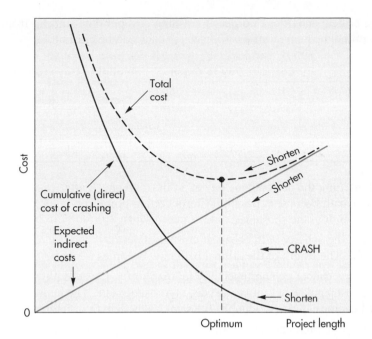

Figure 17-8

Costs related to crashing activities; crashing activities reduces the indirect project costs but increases direct costs; the optimum amount of crashing results in minimizing the sum of these two types of costs.

Example 7

Using the following information and precedence network, develop the optimal project crashing. Indirect project costs are $1,000 per day.

Activity	Normal Duration (days)	Crash Duration (days)	Cost per Day to Crash
a	6	6	—
b	10	8	$500
c	5	4	300
d	4	1	700
e	9	7	600
f	2	1	800

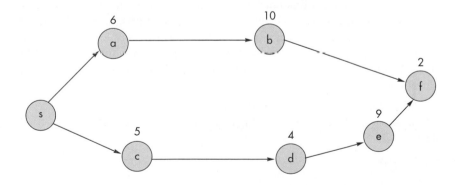

Solution

a. Determine the critical path, its length, and the length of the other path:

Path	Length
s-a-b-f	6 + 10 + 2 = 18
s-c-d-e-f	5 + 4 + 9 + 2 = 20 (critical path)

b. Rank the critical activities in order of crashing cost per day, starting from the lowest, and determine the number of days for which each can be crashed.

Activity	Cost per Day to Crash	Available Days to Crash
c	$300	1
e	600	2
d	700	3
f	800	1

c. Begin shortening the project, one day at a time, and check after each reduction to see if the other path becomes critical. (After a certain point, the other path's length will equal the length of the shortened critical path.) Thus:

  i. Shorten the activity with cheapest crash cost per day, activity c, one day at a cost of $300. The length of the critical path now becomes 19 days.

  ii. Activity c cannot be shortened any more. Shorten the activity with next cheapest crash cost per day, activity e, one day at a cost of $600. The length of path s-c-d-e-f now becomes 18 days, which is the same as the length of path s-a-b-f.

  iii. The paths are now both critical; further improvements will necessitate shortening both paths.

The remaining activities for crashing and their costs are:

Path	Activity	Crash Cost (per day)	Available Days
s-a-b-f	a	—	0
	b	$500	2
	f	800	1
s-c-d-e-f	c	—	0
	e	$600	1
	d	700	3
	f	800	1

At first glance, it would seem that crashing f would not be advantageous, because it has the highest crashing cost per day. However, f is on both paths, so shortening f by one day would shorten *both* paths (and hence, the project) by one day for a cost of $800. The option of shortening the least expensive activity on each path would cost $500 for b for s-a-b-f and $600 for e for s-c-d-e-f, or $1,100 in total. Thus, shorten f by one day. The project duration is now 17 days.

  iv. At this point, no additional crashing is cost-effective. The cost to crash b and e is a total of $1,100, and that would exceed the indirect project costs of $1,000 per day.

The crashing sequence is summarized below:

Path	Length After Crashing *n* Days:			
	n = 0	1	2	3
s-a-b-f	18	18	18	17
s-c-d-e-f	20	19	18	17
Activity crashed		c	e	f
Crash cost		$300	$600	$800

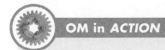

Warner Robins Air Logistics Center

Warner Robins Air Logistics Center (WR-ALC) in Southern Georgia repairs and overhauls U.S. Air Force transport planes such as C-5 Galaxy, C-17 Globemaster, C-130 Hercules, and F-15 fighter jets. Before year 2004, WR-ALC took an average of one year to overhaul a C-5 (resulting in 16-17 WIP) which was deemed to be too slow. Most of the time, a plane was waiting for mechanics, facilities, and/or parts. Then in 2004, WR-ALC implemented lean production, which reduced the throughput time to 240 days. However, this was still too long for the Air Force.

In 2005, WR-ALC implemented the Critical Chain project execution management. Aggressive times for each activity were determined, which added up to only 105 days, with 55 days of project buffer. Similarly, 100 or so non-critical chains each received their own buffers at their end (before feeding into the critical chain). Chains are prioritized daily based on the percentage of buffer time used divided by the percentage of the chain-work completed. The activities on a chain receive the priority of their chain, and those with highest priorities are scheduled for the next five work days. Support services, including parts needed, are prepared/acquired for the schedule.

Also, the WIP is reduced to seven C-5 planes (from 12 in 2004). "Fixer Release Control" points (i.e., the points at which the director could permit the aircraft to move from one phase to the next) have been put in place after each major phase to control the WIP. Also, there is now a "hold" phase of 20 days after strip (i.e., disassembly)/repair phase to ensure that all parts needed have been refurbished before buildup (i.e., reassembly) phase can start. This will reduce the idle time and multitasking of mechanics. Supervisors roam the shop floor solving problems. Bottleneck activities are kaizened.

Source: M.M. Srinvasan, W.D. Best, and S. Chandrasekaran, "Warner Robins Air Logistics Center Streamlines Aircraft Repair and Overhaul," *Interfaces*, 37(1), January/February 2007, pp. 7–21.

LO7 PROJECT EXECUTION AND CONTROL

Project execution involves the actual performance of the activities that were planned in project planning. The project manager directs, coordinates, and manages project activities and team members. The budgeted funds are expended to accomplish the project objective. Resources are obtained, managed, and used.

project execution Involves performance of activities planned.

During execution, quality of the product is assured by applying the planned quality activities.

Team members who are not yet assigned are chosen; their skills are assessed, needed training instituted, and ground rules for team participation are set.

Any purchases or subcontracting plans, whose suppliers are not determined yet, are finalized, and contracts are negotiated. In a construction project, bid packages (e.g., for foundation, frame, roofing, etc.) go out.

The plan for information collection and distribution is executed using clear and timely information in appropriate form (written or oral, formal or informal, using software or manual, etc.). Unexpected requests for information by stakeholders are responded to.

An approach for project execution, especially when multiple projects are underway and require joint resources, is the *critical chain*, proposed by Eli Goldratt in 1997.[3] It is based on two psychological principles: (a) student's syndrome = a student tends to delay the start of an assignment until the last possible time, and (b) Parkinson's law = work expands to fill the time available for its completion. To combat these tendencies, which result in late projects, the critical chain approach does not disclose the due dates of activities to the project workers. Instead, activities are prioritized, scheduled accordingly, and done as soon as possible. Also, estimates of activity duration are examined to ensure that they are not being padded with safety time. Safety or buffer time is added at the end of the critical chain (critical path) and at the end of each feeder chain that feeds into the critical chain. Activity (and chain) priorities are determined daily based on the percentage of buffer time used divided by the percentage of the chain work completed (the activity with a larger ratio gets a higher priority). See the OM in Action "Warner Robins Air Logistics Center."

---

[3]Eliyahu M. Goldratt. *Critical Chain*. Great Barrington, MA: North River Press, 1997, pp. 246.

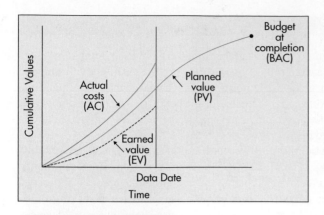

Figure 17-9

Cumulative cost values for a project that is over budget and behind schedule

project control   Comparing a project's progress against plans and taking corrective action if necessary.

Project control involves assessing a project's progress against plans and taking corrective actions, if necessary, in order to bring the project on track. Forecasts of costs and completion time are generated using trend analysis to determine the need for action.

Project control also involves controlling the changes to a project, e.g., to the project's scope. Replanning is usually necessary, but it should be kept to a minimum. Changes to the project's scope should be tightly controlled. If acceptable to the project manager, a change to the scope should be formally verified (i.e., authorized by the customer/sponsor). A common problem is that the customer/sponsor tends to frequently demand changes to the work required. The problem of uncontrolled changes to the project's scope is called *scope creep*.

To control a project's cost and schedule, various measures are used. Work performance information includes the completed and uncompleted deliverables, ongoing and completed activities, percentage of each activity completed, costs authorized/incurred, cost estimates to project completion time, and so on.

A common technique used for cost control is *earned value analysis*. After a project's time and cost are planned (called schedule baseline and cost baseline or budget), the progress of the project is measured, not by the budgeted cost of work scheduled (BCWS; also known as planned value, PV), but by budgeted cost of work performed (BCWP; also known as earned value, EV). The scheduled time overrun is measured by schedule "variance" = PV − EV, and the cost overrun is measured by cost "variance" = actual cost − EV. See Figure 17-9 for an overbudget project that is also behind schedule. Also, forecasts of cost estimate to completion (ETC) and cost estimate at completion (EAC) are made.

Quality control involves using quality tools such as control chart and cause and effect diagram in order to identify quality "variance," find its cause, and implement corrective actions.

The project team is managed by measuring team performance, providing feedback, resolving issues, and recognizing and rewarding good performance.

Software, e-mail, status review meetings, etc., are used to collect and report performance of project in the form of status reports, progress measurements, and forecasts. Communication with project stakeholders is managed by resolving issues promptly.

Risks are tracked, reassessed, and the response plans evaluated. Reserve analysis is performed to determine the adequacy of the contingency fund.

Contracts are managed by measuring the performance of suppliers, comparing them with the contract requirements, and taking corrective actions, if necessary. The relations with suppliers are managed by quickly resolving issues such as contested changes or late payments.

Finally, the project is completed and closed out. It is important to ensure that all contractors/teams have completed their work, and provided warrantees/necessary paper works. Also, it is important to review the project for lessons learned and document these for future reference.

LO8 PROJECT MANAGEMENT SOFTWARE

Many project management software are available such as Microsoft Project and Deltek's (Welcom) EPM suite.

There are many advantages to using project management software. Among them are the following:

- It imposes a methodology and common project management terminology.
- It provides a logical planning structure.
- It enhances communication among team members.
- It flags the occurrence of a problem.
- It automatically formats reports.

- It generates multiple levels of summary reports and detailed reports.
- It enables "what-if" scenarios.
- It generates various charts, including basic schedule/control Gantt chart.

Using Microsoft® Project

Download a free 60-day Trial version of *Microsoft Project* 2010.[4] After registering, downloading, and installing the software, open it:

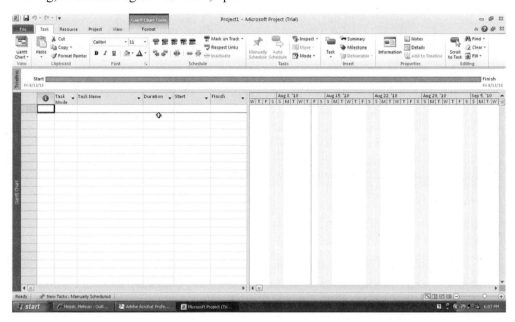

Next, enter the activity (or task) names and their duration. We will enter the data from Example 1. Click the cell under the Task Name and type in "Locate Facility," and press the Enter key. Continue entering the task names until all tasks are entered. Now, click on the cell below Duration and enter 8w (for 8 weeks), and press Enter. As you enter a duration, the Gantt chart on the right assigns a horizontal bar to the activity. Continue entering the durations until all durations are entered:

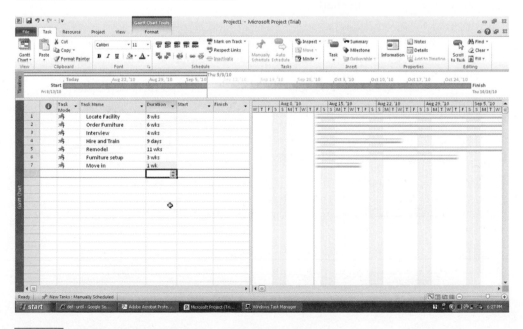

---

[4]http://technet.microsoft.com/en-us/evalcenter/ee404758.aspx.

In order to see the whole Gantt chart, Click on the "View" tab on the top, then click "Entire Project." Note that the bars on the right and the pins under Task Mode are light blue. This indicates that the tasks are currently in Manually Scheduled Mode. This means that Microsoft Project will consider them as fixed tasks, and does not use them in its PERT/CPM solution method. We need to change the Task Modes to Auto Scheduled by clicking on the cell to the left of each task name, then clicking on the blue arrow-down square, and finally clicking on the Auto Scheduled. As you do this, the colour of the pin and the bar on the right will change to dark blue. After all task modes have been changed to Auto Scheduled, the screen looks as follows. Note that in the present form, all the activities start the next day.

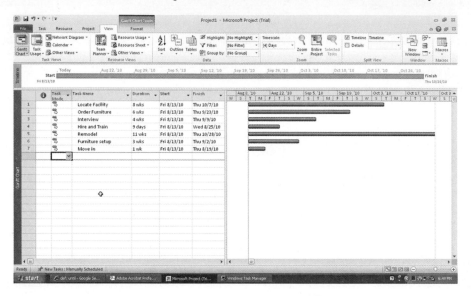

In order to enter the precedence relationships, click on the "Task" tab on the top, then select two activities with finish-start relationship (by keeping the control key pressed), and then clicking on the chain icon above the Schedule in the ribbon on the top. This will move the bar for the successor activity to the right of the bar for the Predecessor activity, and relate them with a short arrow. Continue with all the predecessor-successor pairs until all the precedence relationships have been specified. You can View to the Entire Project again to see the whole Gantt chart:

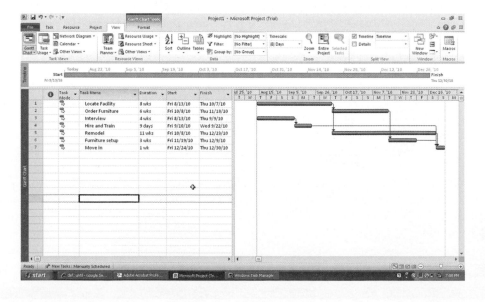

To see the precedence network, (in the "View" tab) click "Network diagram":

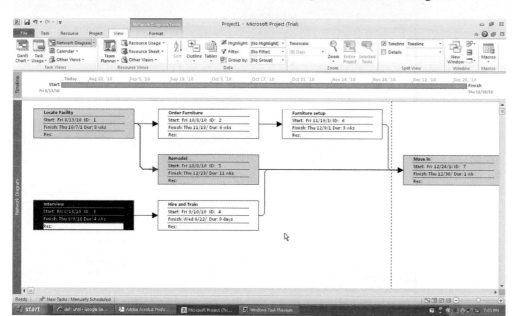

As you can see, the boxes for critical activities are pink.

Microsoft Project also permits us to define resources (i.e., employees and equipment) and to assign these to the activities. This is done by clicking on the "Resources" tab on the top. Also, Microsoft Project allows us to track the progress of activities. This is done by clicking on the "Track" tab on the top, then on "Mark on Track," and finally "Update Tasks." As days pass, team members should enter the percentage of each activity completed. The software will indicate if any activity is behind schedule. For more information on Microsoft Project 2010, including the use of the manually scheduled tasks, see the tutorial in http://office.microsoft.com/en-us/project-help/overview-RZ101831071.aspx?CTT=5& origin=HA010355886&section=1.

Deltek (Welcom)[5]

The Deltek (Welcom) Enterprise Project Management (EPM) software suite is an integrated toolset with modules supporting portfolio analysis, risk management, planning and scheduling, project collaboration, and complete earned value management. This modular, integrated toolset provides timely and selective information to all project participants from chief executives to project managers to team members.

Five products are included in the Deltek EPM suite: WelcomPortfolio™, WelcomRisk™, WelcomHome™, Open Plan®, and Cobra®. Each product can be used as standalone or configured in combination to meet customer requirements. The complete suite supports the full project life cycle from conception through to closure.

Deltek's WelcomPortfolio is a portfolio analysis tool that provides a structured approach to evaluating, selecting, and prioritizing projects so that resources are invested in the projects that best fit current business or organizational strategy. Scoring criteria such as net present value and return on investment are included in a library with the ability to edit or create new ones. Users can also utilize project risk scores generated in Deltek's Welcom-Risk as additional scoring criteria.

---

[5]Courtesy of Deltek staff, 2006.

Typical project financial analysis with user-defined reporting criteria in WelcomPortfolio

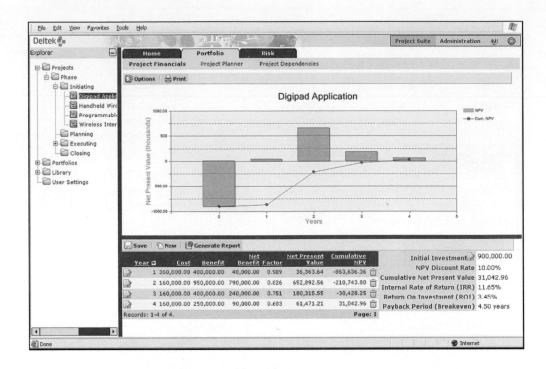

A typical portfolio of potential new projects with respective scores. Note the project risk score from Deltek's WelcomRisk is being used as a ranking criterion.

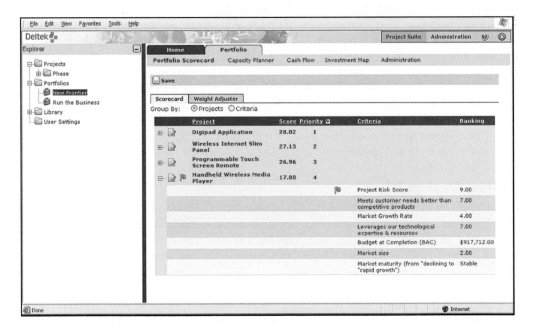

Deltek's WelcomRisk is a risk management solution for the systematic identification, mitigation, and reporting of organizational and project risk on both threats and opportunities. Graphical reports allow executives to assess risk exposure across projects and track mitigation efforts. Project risks are identified, quantified, and tracked to minimize risk exposure. Team members play a collaborative role in identifying and mitigating risks using a formalized process.

WelcomRisk supports a typical five-step process to reduce risk. Risk planning is supported by identifying risk categories (i.e., development, production, technical, political), risk assessment is done by identifying impact types (on cost, quality, schedule, safety), the probability and severity impact of each risk, risk mitigation, and risk monitoring and control.

Risk planning involves determining a risk breakdown structure (also called a Risk Tree) and using it to calculate the risk of a project, working from bottom up using the risk scores. Risk assessment uses each risk, its cause, and potential consequences. The probability and impact severity is estimated and a risk score is generated for each risk event. The risk score is tracked over time and is expected to be reduced as a result of risk mitigation. Risk mitigation involves the steps to reduce the risk score. WelcomRisk has a library of generic response types, and can also recalculate the risk score given the mitigation steps undertaken. Risk Monitoring and Control uses reports such as Risk Tree and "waterfall" diagrams.

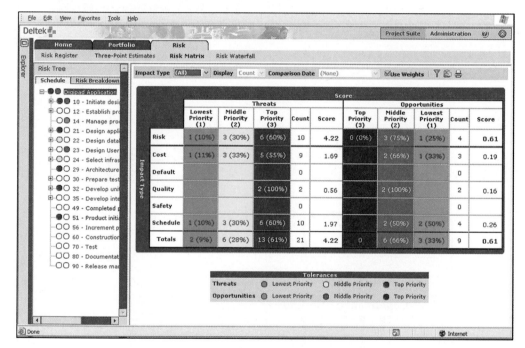

Typical risk tree (on the left) built from a project schedule with a corresponding matrix showing threats and opportunities on a project

Deltek's Open Plan is an enterprise project management software that improves an organization's ability to complete multiple projects on time and on budget. Multiproject analysis, critical path planning, and resource management are supported.

Inter-project constraints are easily modelled in Open Plan. Resource constraints and relationships can be created either at a high level between projects or at a more detailed level between specific activities in different projects. The relative priority of projects can be adjusted to ensure that important projects have access to resources first.

Deltek Open Plan's views can be tailored to create custom reports. For flexible program analysis, projects can be grouped into multi projects, with the ability for a project to belong to more than one multi project.

Open Plan's advanced Gantt chart view automatically shows constraining resources.

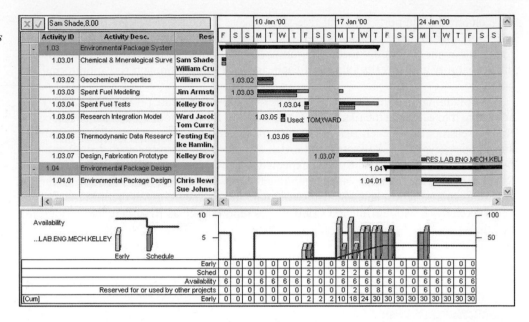

Typical Open Plan logic diagram (i.e., precedence network)

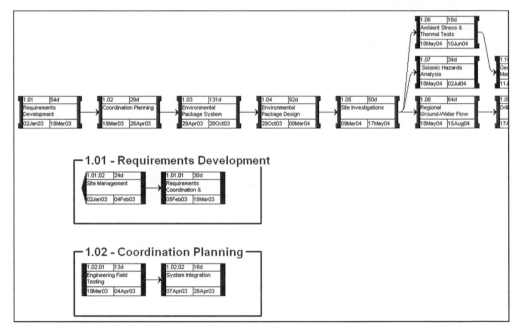

Deltek's Cobra is a robust cost management software for managing project costs, measuring earned value, and analyzing budgets, actuals and forecasts. Earned value is a means of putting a dollar value on project status. This allows managers to formulate a three-way comparison between budget, actual costs, and project status in order to evaluate the true health of project. Simply analyzing budget versus actual costs often gives an incorrect picture of project status. For example, if a contract is 10 percent under budget, this might appear as if the contract is doing very well. Yet, when the project status or earned value is added to the analysis, it shows that only half of the originally planned work has been performed. Thus, the contract is behind schedule and the completed work has cost more than originally planned!

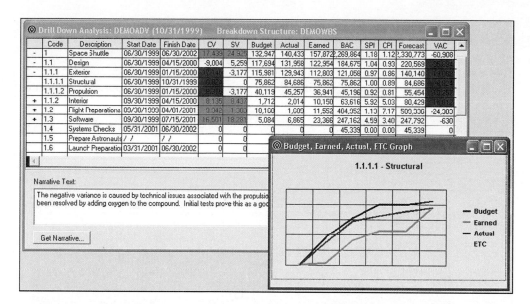

Cobra drill-down report highlights problem areas and an earned value curve

Deltek's WelcomHome is a Web-based project management portal that provides all project participants with easy access to project information. It provides live access to schedules, budgets, action items, and project documents. WelcomHome also allows submission of progress and timesheet information using only a browser.

Graphical dashboards provide executives with high-level summaries at the program level. These views include cost, schedule, and outstanding item metrics in the form of bar charts, line graphs, and pie charts.

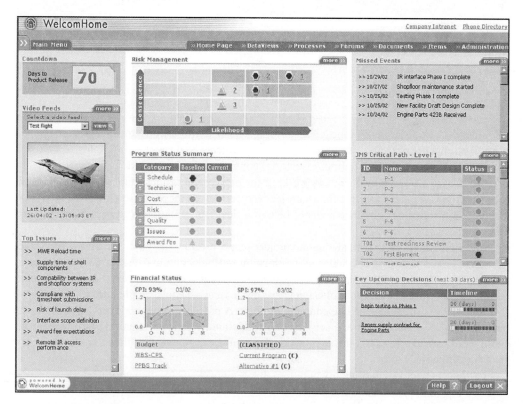

A customized project homepage in Deltek's WelcomHome

Such instruments grouped together within a dashboard provide the user with an easy means of obtaining an overview of a project or program. Dashboards can also serve as an early warning system for potential problems (e.g., red, yellow, green indicators), helping busy executives make timely decisions and take corrective action. Each instrument can be expanded to show additional detailed metric information and can report at a project or program level.

Sample project metrics dashboard in WelcomHome

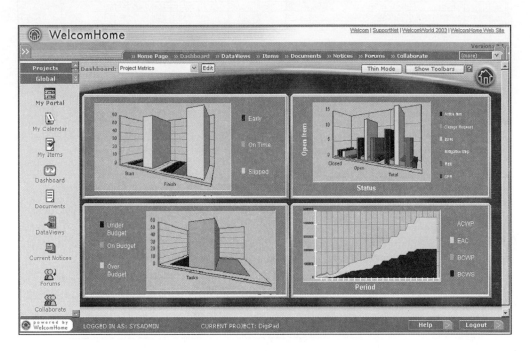

Summary

A project is a unique large one-time job requiring special activities by different people, established to realize a specific objective in a limited time span. Projects go through a life cycle that involves initiation, planning and scheduling, execution, control, and closeout. Most organizations are structured as a matrix, with members working for both projects and a functional department. A project manager is responsible for all project activities from inception to close-out, including meeting the project performance goals of being on time, and within quality specifications and budget.

Project planning involves finalizing the project scope, creating the work breakdown structure, risk management planning, scheduling, cost estimation and budgeting, and quality, communications, and purchase planning. Risk management planning involves risk identification, assessment, and response planning. Schedule/control Gantt charts are used to schedule simple projects.

PERT/CPM is used to schedule complex projects. A precedence network depicts the sequential relationships that exist among activities. The solution reveals the longest (i.e., critical) path and the critical activities, i.e., those activities that must be completed on time to achieve timely project completion.

For projects with variable activity durations, the 3-point estimates method can be used.

In some instances, it may be possible to shorten, or crash, the length of a project by shortening one or more of the critical activities. Typically, such gains are achieved by the use of additional resources, but the shortening will save indirect project costs.

Project execution involves putting the project plans into action, buying materials and assigning team members, or subcontracting the work. Project control means taking measurements of project performance and taking corrective action if necessary. Microsoft Project and Deltek's (Welcom) EPM suite are two widely used types of project management software.

Solved Problems

The following list contains information related to the major activities of a research project. Use the information given to do the following:

a. Draw the precedence network.

Problem 1

b. Find the critical path by identifying all the start-to-end paths and calculating their lengths.

c. What is the expected duration of the project?

Activity	Immediately Precedes	Expected Duration (days)
a	c, b	5
c	d	8
d	i	2
b	i	7
e	f	3
f	m	6
i	m	10
m	End	8
g	h	1
h	k	2
k	End	17

a. In constructing precedence networks, these observations can be useful.

Solution

   i. Use pencil.

   ii. Start and end with a single node.

   iii. Try to avoid having paths cross each other.

   iv. Have arrows go from left to right.

   v. Activities with no predecessors are at the beginning (left side) of the network, immediately after the start node S.

   vi. Activities with multiple predecessors are located at path intersections.

   vii. Go down the activity list in order to avoid overlooking any activities.

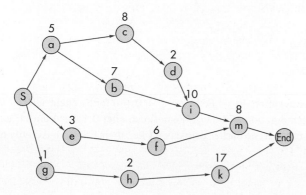

b. and c.

Path	Length (days)
s-a-c-d-i-m-End*	$5+8+2+10+8 = 33$†
s-a-b-i-m-End	$5+7+10+8 = 30$
s-e-f-m-End	$3+6+8 = 17$
s-g-h-k-End	$1+2+17 = 20$

*Critical path.
†Expected project duration.

Problem 2

Using the PERT/CPM solution technique, determine the ES, EF, LF, LS, and slack times for each activity in the following precedence network (durations are in days). Identify the activities that are on the critical path.

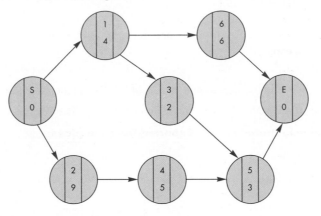

Solution

We will determine and place the ES, EF, LS, and LF times for each activity in its circle as follows:

We determine the earliest start and finish times, working from left to right, as shown in the following network. The explanations follow.

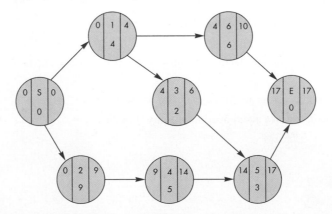

ES for the start node S is 0, by our convention. EF $=$ ES $+ t = 0 + 0 = 0$ for S. Then, activity 1 can start at 0 (i.e., its ES $= 0$). With a duration of 4 days, it can finish after $0 + 4 = 4$ days (i.e., its EF $= 4$). Hence, activity 6 and 3 can start no earlier than day 4 (i.e., their ES $= 4$). Activity 6 has earliest finish of $4 + 6 = 10$ days, and activity 3 has the earliest finish of $4 + 2 = 6$ days. At this point, it is impossible to say what the earliest start is for activity 5; that will depend on which activity, 4 or 3, has the larger EF. Consequently, it is necessary to first calculate ES and EF along the lower path. Using an ES of 0 for activity 2, its EF will be 9, so activity 4 will have an ES of 9 and an EF of $9 + 5 = 14$.

Considering that the two activities immediately preceding node 5 have EF times of 6 and 14, the earliest that activity 5 can start is the *larger* of these, which is 14. Hence, activity 5 has an EF of $14 + 3 = 17$.

Now compare the EFs of the activities immediately preceding the End node. The larger of these, 17, is the ES_{End}, and $EF_{End} = 17 + 0 = 17$. This is also the expected project duration.

The LF and LS times for each activity can now be determined by working backward through the network (from right to left; see the following network). The LF for the End node is 17—the project duration. Then, $LS_{End} = LF_{End} - 0 = 17 - 0 = 17$.

Now, $LF_6 = LF_5 = LS_{End} = 17$. In the case of activity 5, the LS necessary for an LF of 17 is $17 - 3 = 14$. This means that both activities 3 and 4 must finish no later than 14 days. Hence, their LF are 14. Activity 4 has an LS of $14 - 5 = 9$, making the LF of activity 2 equal to 9, and its LS equal to $9 - 9 = 0$.

Activity 3, with an LF of 14, has an LS of $14 - 2 = 12$. Activity 6 has an LF of 17 and therefore an LS of $17 - 6 = 11$. Since activity 1 precedes *both* of these activities, it can finish no later than the *smaller* of 11 and 12, which is 11. Hence, activity 1 has an LS of $11 - 4 = 7$.

Finally, LF of S is the smaller of LS of activities 1 and 2, which is min $(7, 0) = 0$. Hence, LS of S is $0 - 0 = 0$.

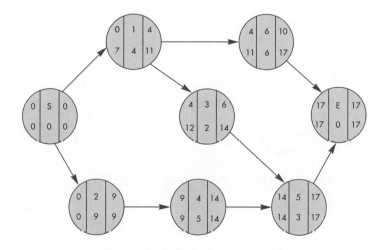

The slack time for an activity is the difference between either LF and EF or LS and ES. Thus,

Activity	LS	ES	Slack	or	LF	EF	Slack
S	0	0	0		0	0	0
1	7	0	7		11	4	7
6	11	4	7		17	10	7
3	12	4	8		14	6	8
2	0	0	0		9	9	0
4	9	9	0		14	14	0
5	14	14	0		17	17	0
E	0	0	0		0	0	0

The activities with zero slack times indicate the critical path. In this case the critical path is S-2-4-5-E.

When working on problems of this nature, keep in mind the following:

a. The ES time for a node with multiple immediate predecessors is the largest EF of the immediate predecessors.

b. The LF for a node with multiple immediate successors is the smallest LS of the immediate successors.

Problem 3

Expected durations (in weeks) and variances for the major activities of an R&D project are depicted on the following precedence network. Determine the probability that the project completion time will be:

a. Less than 50 weeks.

b. More than 50 weeks.

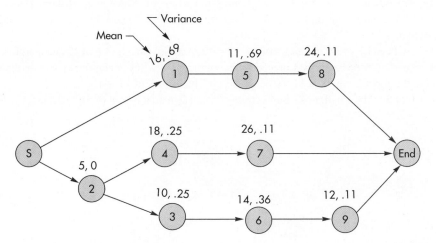

Solution

Because S and End have zero duration, we can ignore them in the following calculations. The mean and standard deviation for each path are:

Path	Expected Time (weeks)	Standard Deviation (weeks)
S-1-5-8-End	$16 + 11 + 24 = 51$	$\sqrt{.69 + .69 + .11} = 1.22$
S-2-4-7-End	$5 + 18 + 26 = 49$	$\sqrt{.00 + .25 + .11} = 0.60$
S-2-3-6-9-End	$5 + 10 + 14 + 12 = 41$	$\sqrt{.00 + .25 + .36 + .11} = 0.85$

a. Calculate the z value for each path for the length specified. Use:

$$z = \frac{50 - t_{path}}{\sigma_{path}}$$

The probability that each path will be completed in 50 weeks or less is shown on the following charts (probabilities are from Appendix B, Table B.) The probability that the project will be completed in 50 weeks or less depends on all three paths being completed in that time. Because z for path S-2-3-6-9-End is greater than $+3.50$, it is treated as having a probability of completion in 50 weeks of 1.00. The probability that *both* other paths will not exceed 50 weeks is the *product* of their individual probabilities of completion within 50 weeks. Thus, $.2061(.9525) = .1963$.

b. The probability that the project will exceed 50 weeks is the complement of this number, which is $1.000 - .1963 = .8037$. (Note that this is not the product of the path probabilities of exceeding 50 weeks.)

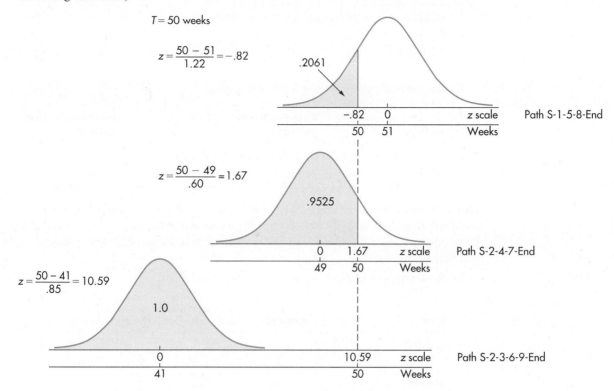

$T = 50$ weeks

$$z = \frac{50 - 51}{1.22} = -.82$$

.2061

−.82   0   z scale   Path S-1-5-8-End
50   51   Weeks

$$z = \frac{50 - 49}{.60} = 1.67$$

.9525

0   1.67   z scale   Path S-2-4-7-End
49   50   Weeks

$$z = \frac{50 - 41}{.85} = 10.59$$

1.0

0   10.59   z scale   Path S-2-3-6-9-End
41   50   Weeks

Indirect cost for a project is $12,000 per week for as long as the project lasts. The project manager has supplied the crash cost and potential information and precedence network shown below. Use the information to: **Problem 4**

a. Determine an optimum crashing plan.

b. Graph the total costs for the plan.

Activity	Crashing Potential (weeks)	Cost per Week to Crash
a	3	$11,000
b	3	3,000 first week, $4,000 after that
c	2	6,000
d	1	1,000
e	3	6,000
f	1	2,000

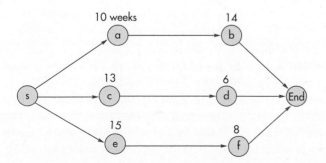

10 weeks   14
a → b

13   6
s → c → d → End

15   8
e → f

Solution

a. i. Calculate path lengths and identify the critical path:

Path	Duration (weeks)
s-a-b-End	24 (critical path)
s-c-d-End	19
s-e-f-End	23

ii. Rank critical activities according to crash costs:

Activity	Cost per Week to Crash	Available Weeks to Crash
b	$3,000 first week, $4,000 after that	3
a	11,000	3

Activity *b* should be shortened one week since it has the lower crashing cost per week. This would reduce indirect costs by $12,000 at a direct cost of $3,000, for a net savings of $9,000. At this point, paths s-a-b-End and s-e-f-End would both have length of 23 weeks, so both would be critical.

iii. Rank activities by crashing cost on the two critical paths:

Path	Activity	Cost per Week to Crash	Available Weeks to Crash
s-a-b-End	b	$4,000	2
. . . .	a	11,000	3
s-e-f-End	f	2,000	1
. . . .	e	6,000	3

Choose one activity (the least costly) on each path to crash: *b* on s-a-b-End and f on s-e-f-End, for a total cost of $4,000 + $2,000 = $6,000 and a net savings of $12,000 − $6,000 = $6,000. Note: There is no activity common to the two critical paths.

iv. Check to see which path(s) might be critical: s-a-b-End and s-e-f-End would be 22 weeks in length, and s-c-d-End would still be 19 weeks.

v. Rank activities on the critical paths:

Path	Activity	Cost per Week to Crash	Available Weeks to Crash
s-a-b-End	b	$4,000	1
. . . .	a	11,000	3
s-e-f-End	e	6,000	3
. . . .	f	(no further crashing possible)	0

Crash b on path s-a-b-End and e on path s-e-f-End one week each for a cost of $4,000 + $6,000 = $10,000, for a net savings of $12,000 − $10,000 = $2,000.

vi. At this point, no further reduction is cost-effective: paths s-a-b-End and s-e-f-End would be 21 weeks in length, and one activity from each path would have to be shortened. This would mean activity a at $11,000 and e at $6,000 for a total of $17,000, which exceeds the $12,000 potential savings in indirect costs. Note that no further crashing for activity (b) is possible.

b. The following table summarizes the results, showing the length of the project after crashing *n* weeks:

Path	n = 0	1	2	3
s-a-b-End	24	23	22	21
s-c-d-End	19	19	19	19
s-e-f-End	23	23	22	21
Project crashed		b	b, f	b, e
Crashing costs ($000)		3	6	10

A summary of costs for the preceding schedule would look like this:

Project Length	Weeks Shortened	Cumulative Crashing Costs ($000)	Cumulative Indirect Costs ($000)	Total Costs ($000)
24	0	0	24(12) = 288	288
23	1	3	23(12) = 276	279
22	2	3 + 6 = 9	22(12) = 264	273
21	3	9 + 10 = 19	21(12) = 252	271
20	4	19 + 17 = 36	20(12) = 240	276

The graph of total cost is as follows.

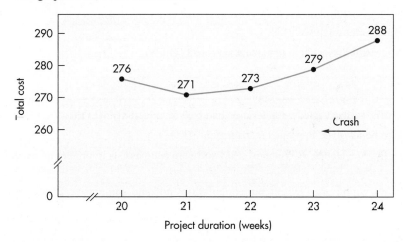

1. What are the phases of a project? (LO1)

2. Explain the difference between matrix and project organization. (LO1)

3. How should a company select its projects? (LO1)

4. What skills would a project manager need? (LO1)

5. What are some aspects of the project manager's job that make it more demanding than the job of a manager working in a more routine organizational framework? (LO1)

6. What does project planning involve? (LO2)

7. List the steps in risk management planning. (LO2)

8. What is a work breakdown structure, and how is it useful for project planning? (LO2)

9. What are some of the reasons an activity might take longer than expected? (LO2)

Discussion and Review Questions

10. Compare a schedule/control Gantt chart and a precedence network. (LO3)

11. Identify the term used for each of the following:

    a. A sequence of activities in a project. (LO3)
    b. The longest sequence of activities in a project. (LO3)
    c. The technique used for probabilistic activity durations. (LO5)
    d. The difference in length of time of any path and the critical path. (LO4)
    e. The statistical distribution used to describe variability of an activity's duration. (LO5)
    f. The statistical distribution used to describe variability of project duration. (LO5)
    g. Shortening an activity by allocating additional resources. (LO6)

12. What are ES, EF, LF, and LS, and how are they calculated? (LO4)

13. What is a critical activity? (LO4)

14. Why might a probabilistic estimate of a project's completion time based solely on the variance of the *critical path* derived using the expected activity durations be misleading? Under what circumstances would it be acceptable? (LO5)

15. Define each of these terms used in the 3-Point Estimates method, and indicate how each is determined. (LO5)

    a. Expected activity duration.
    b. Variance of activity duration.
    c. Standard deviation of a path's duration.

16. Describe the procedure for project crashing. (LO6)

17. Describe project execution. (LO7)

18. What is the critical chain method? (LO7)

19. What does project control involve? (LO7)

20. What is earned value analysis? (LO7)

21. How can Microsoft Project help to manage a project? (LO8)

Taking Stock

1. What trade-offs are associated with duration and cost of an activity? (LO6)

2. Who needs to be involved in project management? (LO1)

3. Explain briefly how Deltek's (Welcom) EPM software suite assists in project management. (LO8)

4. Visit http://www.pmi.org/PDF/ap_pmicodeofethics.pdf and summarize PMI's code of ethics. (LO1)

Critical Thinking Exercise

Project management techniques have been used successfully for a wide variety of projects, including the many NASA space missions, huge construction projects, implementation of major systems such as an ERP, production of movies, development of new goods and services, theatrical productions, and much more. Why not use them for managing the operations function of any business? (LO1)

Experiential Learning Exercise

Select a project you are currently working on, or one that you have recently worked on. (LO1)

    a. List the project objective.
    b. List the main activities.
    c. List the project milestones, such as required progress reports or the completion of major tasks.
    d. How important are (were) behavioural aspects of the project? For example, did the project team agree on project objective, individual work assignments, and so on?
    e. Were there any unforeseen problems? If so, how were they resolved?

1. Visit http://taskcm.com/services/whatiscm and summarize what fast track scheduling is, and visit http://taskcm.com/services/stages and compare the construction project stages with the project stages described in this chapter. (LO1 & 6)

2. Prism Partners is a project management firm. Visit http://www.prismpartners.com/Services.htm and summarize the services it provides to its clients. (LO1)

3. Visit http://www.deltek.com/customers/openplan.asp, choose a customer, and briefly summarize the benefits of using the software for the customer. (LO8)

4. Visit http://www.pmi.org/CareerDevelopment/Pages/AboutCredentialsCAPM.aspx, and briefly summarize the requirements for Certified Associate in Project Management (CAPM). (LO1)

5. Visit one of the following sites, choose a customer, and briefly summarize the benefits of the project (portfolio) management software to the customer: (LO8)

   a. http://www.innotas.com/customers/casestudies.html
   b. http://www.amsrealtime.com/customers/clients.htm

6. Visit http://www.mmm.ca/Careers/Careers_Search.aspx, choose Career Area = Project Management, and summarize the duties of a project manager in the MMM group. (LO1)

7. Visit http://www.bantrel.com/company/services/projectmanagement.aspx and summarize what Bantrel's project management and controls people do. (LO1)

8. Visit http://www.stantec.com/default.htm, click on a Feature Project photo, click on "more information …" and summarize Stantec's project management role. (LO1)

9. Visit http://www.tocc.com/Critical_Chain.htm, and summarize what is written about the Critical Chain approach. (LO7)

10. Organizing an event such as the Vancouver Winter Olympic Games is a monumental project. Planning starts more than seven years ahead, and many different activities/functions are performed, some earlier than the others, such as building the new venues. A brief summary of what the organizing committee is responsible for includes venues (competition stadiums and training halls), arranging for necessary competition equipment, providing lodging for athletes/entourage/officials, scheduling the competitions, organizing medical services, providing transportation, meeting the requirements of media, and organizing cultural events such as the opening and closing shows. Download the business plan of the Vancouver Olympics: http://www.vancouver2010.com/dl/00/08/84/07-05-08-vanoc-business-plan-en-e_14d-dW. pdf, and identify all functions/services (other than construction of new venues) with a budget of more than $10 million that were performed, and list each and its budget. Does the cost of any function/service surprise you? Explain. Hint: See pages 43 to 66 of the 2007 business plan. (LO2)

1. For each of the following precedence networks, determine the critical path and the project duration by determining the length of each path. The numbers above the nodes represent activity durations (in days). (LO4)

   a.
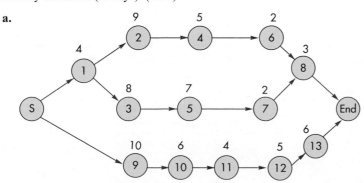

b.

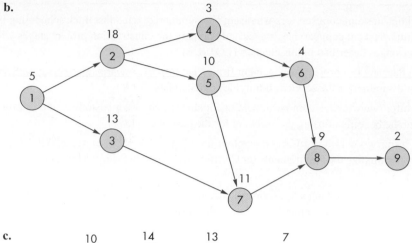

c.

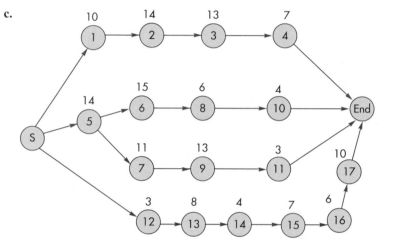

2. Claire received a new word-processing software program for her birthday. She also received a cheque with which she intends to purchase a new computer. Claire's university instructor assigned a paper due next week. Claire decided that she will prepare the paper on the new computer. She made a list of the activities and their estimated durations. Claire's friend has offered to shop for, select, and purchase a computer, and install the software. (LO3 & 4)

   a. Arrange the activities into two logical sequences.
   b. Construct a precedence network.
   c. Determine the critical path by determining the length of each path. What is the expected duration of the project?
   d. What are some possible reasons for the project to take longer than expected?

Estimated Time (hours)	Activity (abbreviation)
.8	Install software (Install)
.4	Outline the paper (Outline)
.2	Submit paper to instructor (Submit)
.6	Choose a topic (Choose)
.5	Use a grammar-checker and make corrections (Check)
3.0	Write the paper using the word-processing software (Write)
2.0	Shop for a new computer (Shop)
1.0	Select and purchase a computer (Select)
2.0	Library research on chosen topic (Library)

3. The following information pertains to a project that is about to commence. Which activities would you be concerned with in terms of timely project completion? Explain. Hint: Determine the length of each path. (LO3 & 4)

Activity	Precedes	Estimated Duration (days)
A	B	15
B	C, D	12
C	E	6
D	End	5
E	End	3
F	G, H	8
G	I	8
H	J	9
I	End	7
I	K	14
K	End	6

4. Construct a precedence network for each of the following two projects. (LO3)

(1) Activity	Precedes Activity	(2) Activity	Precedes Activity
A	D	K	R
B	E, F	L	M
C	G	M	End
D	K	N	P
E	K	P	End
F	H, I	Q	S, T
G	I	R	V
H	End	S	V
I	End	V	End
K	End	T	V, W
J	L, N	W	End

5. For each of the problems listed below, determine the following values for each activity: the earliest start time, earliest finish time, latest finish time, latest start time, and activity slack time. Identify the critical activities, and determine the duration of the project. (LO4)

   a. Problem 1a.
   b. Problem 1b.
   c. Problem 3.

6. Reconsider the precedence network of Problem 1a. Suppose that after 12 days, activities 1, 9, and 2 have been finished; activity 3 is 75 percent finished; and activity 10 is half finished. How many days after the original start time would the project finish? (LO4)

7. Three recent university graduates have formed a partnership and have opened an advertising firm. Their first project consists of activities listed in the following table. (LO5)

   a. Draw the precedence network.
   b. What is the probability that the project can be completed in 24 days or less? In 21 days or less?
   c. Suppose that now is the end of the seventh day and that activities a and b have been completed while activity d is 50 percent completed. Three-point estimates for the remaining duration

of activity d are now 5, 6, and 7 days. Activities c and h are ready to begin. Determine the probability of finishing the project by the end of (a) day 24 and (b) day 21.

Activity	Precedes	Duration in Days		
		Optimistic	Most Likely	Pessimistic
a	c	5	6	7
b	h	8	8	11
c	e	6	8	11
d	f	9	12	15
e	End	5	6	9
f	g	5	6	7
g	End	2	3	7
h	i	4	4	5
i	End	5	7	8

8. The new director of special events at a large university has decided to completely revamp the graduation ceremonies. Toward that end, a precedence network of the major activities has been developed. The network has five paths with expected durations and variances as shown in the following table. Graduation day is 16 full weeks from now. Assuming that the project begins now, what is the probability that the project will be completed before: (LO5)

   a. Graduation day?
   b. The end of week 15?
   c. The end of week 13?

Path	Expected Duration (weeks)	Variance
A	10	1.21
B	8	2.00
C	12	1.00
D	15	2.89
E	14	1.44

9. What is the probability that a project with the following precedence network will take more than 10 weeks to complete if the activity means and standard deviations (both in weeks) are as follows? (LO5)

Activity	Mean	Standard Deviation
a	5	1.3
b	4	1.0
c	8	1.6

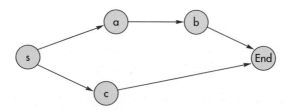

10. The project described in the following table and precedence network has just begun. It is scheduled to be completed in 11 weeks. (LO6)

   a. If you were the manager of this project, would you be concerned? Explain.

b. If there is a penalty of $5,000 a week for each week the project is late, what is the probability of incurring a penalty of at least $5,000?

Activity	Expected Duration (weeks)	Standard Deviation (weeks)
a	4	.70
b	6	.90
c	3	.62
d	9	1.90

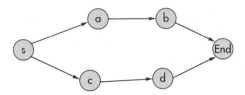

11. The following precedence network displays the 3-Point estimates for each activity of a project. Determine: (LO5)

   a. The expected duration for each path and its variance.
   b. The probability that the project will require more than 49 weeks.
   c. The probability that the project can be completed in 46 weeks or less.

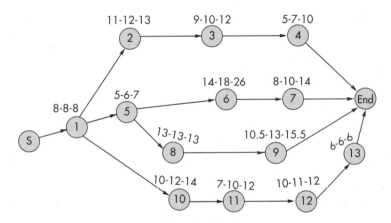

12. A project manager has compiled a list of major activities that will be required to install a computer information system in her company. The list includes 3-point estimates of durations (optimistic, most likely, pessimistic) for activities and the precedence relationships. (LO5)

Activity	Precedes	3-Point Estimates (weeks)
a	d, f	2-4-6
d	e	6-8-10
e	h	7-9-12
h	End	2-3-5
f	g	3-4-8
g	End	5-7-9
b	i	2-2-3
i	j	2-3-6
j	k	3-4-5
k	End	4-5-8
c	m	5-8-12
m	n	1-1-1
n	o	6-7-11
o	End	8-9-13

If the project is finished within 26 weeks of its start, the project manager will receive a bonus of $1,000; and if the project is finished within 27 weeks of its start, the bonus will be $500. Find the probability of each bonus.

13. The project manager of the construction of a domed stadium had hoped to be able to complete the construction prior to the start of the next season. After reviewing the activity duration estimates, it now appears that a certain amount of crashing will be needed to ensure project completion before the season opener. Given the following information, determine the minimum-cost crashing schedule that will shave five weeks off the project length. (LO6)

Activity	Precedes	Normal Duration (weeks)	Crashing Costs	
			First Week	Second Week
A........	B	12	$15,000	$20,000
B........	K	14	10,000	10,000
C........	D, E, F	10	5,000	5,000
D........	G	17	20,000	21,000
E........	H	18	16,000	18,000
F........	I	12	12,000	15,000
G........	M	15	24,000	24,000
H........	N, P	8	—	—
I........	J	7	30,000	—
J........	P	12	25,000	25,000
K........	End	9	10,000	10,000
M........	End	3	—	—
N........	End	11	40,000	—
P........	End	8	20,000	20,000

14. A construction project has indirect costs totalling $40,000 per week. Major activities in the project and their expected durations are shown in the following precedence network: (LO6)

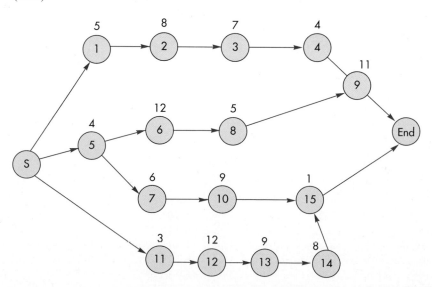

Crashing costs for each activity are:

Activity	Crashing Costs ($000)		
	First Week	Second Week	Third Week
1	$18	$22	$—
2	24	25	25
3	30	30	35
4	15	20	—
9	30	33	36
5	12	24	26
6	—	—	—
8	40	40	40
7	3	10	12
10	2	7	10
15	26	—	—
11	10	15	25
12	8	13	—
13	5	12	—
14	14	15	—

a. Determine the minimum-cost crashing plan that will take off six weeks from the project duration.

b. Plot the total cost curve against project duration. What is the optimum number of weeks to crash the project?

15. A company builds custom equipment. It has landed a contract with a major customer. Relevant data are shown below. The complication is that the delivery has been promised in 32 weeks and the company will have to pay a penalty of $375 for each week the equipment is late. (LO6)

Activity	Precedes	Normal Duration (weeks)	Crashing Costs	
			1st Week	2nd Week
K	L, N	9	$410	$415
L	M	7	125	—
N	J	5	45	45
M	Q	4	300	350
J	Q	6	50	—
Q	P, Y	5	200	225
P	Z	8	—	—
Y	End	7	85	90
Z	End	6	90	—

Develop the minimum cost crashing schedule.

16. The following is the list of activities, their immediate predecessor(s), and their expected duration used by a component supplier to automobile manufacturers to plan for QS 9000 (the auto industry version of ISO 9000) certification (registration).[6] (LO4)

[6]J.K. Bandyopadhyay, "The CPM/PERT Project Scheduling Approach to QS-9000 Registration: A Case Study at a United States Auto Parts Company," *International Journal of Management* 19(3), September 2002, pp. 455–463.

The List of Activities in a QS-9000 Registration Project

Activity	Description	Immediate Predecessor(s)	Estimated Time (weeks)*
A	Appointment of QS-9000 taskforce	None	1
B	Preparation of a feasible plan	A	1
C	Delegation of responsibilities	B	1
D	Searching for a QS-9000 registrar	C	1
E	Preparation of three levels of documentation	C	12
F	QS-9000 awareness training	C	6
G	QS-9000 training of auditors and quality personnel	F	6
H	Preparing the plant for QS-9000 registrar	C	24
I	Conference with lead auditor	D	1
J	Examination of documentation	E, I	3
K	Internal audit of plant sections	G, H, J	12
L	Corrective actions of plant sections	K	12
M	Lead auditor and audit team audit plant	L	1
N	Audit conference and corrective action plan	M	2
O	Implementation of corrective action plans	N	12
P	Lead auditor re-audits corrective actions	O	2
Q	Lead auditor's recommendation	P	1

*These are estimates of time and may vary based upon situation, company, and registrar.

a. Draw the precedence network.
b. Determine the earliest and latest times, and identify the critical activities and the project duration.

17. Use the following activities and their three duration estimates (in days) to do the following: (LO5)

a. Determine the expected duration of the project.
b. Calculate the probability that the project will take at least 18 days.

Path	Activity	t_o	t_m	t_p
	a	4	5	6
a-b-c	b	7	8	10
	c	3	5	9
	d	7	8	11
d-e-f	e	2	3	4
	f	1	4	6

18. Consider the construction of a research building for Eli Lilly & Co., a pharmaceutical company, a few years ago. This 550,000 ft^2, 4-story (in 3 wings), $135 million building was planned to be completed in five years. It required special ventilation for 162 labs, purified water, and special drainage. Consider the following list of major activities/work packages (as seen by Eli Lilly), their expected duration, and their relationship to other activities/work packages for the Eli Lilly building. (LO4)

Activity	Duration (in months)	Immediate Predecessor
A. project approval	3	—
B. decide general requirements	6	A
C. choose A/E firm	2	A
D. preliminary design	3	B, C
E. choose project management firm	2	B
F. decide detailed requirements	6	D, E
G. finalize design	6	F
H. schedule, budget, manual	4	F
I. start bid packages	2	G, H
J. excavate, foundation, steel structure	10	I
K. put up enclosures	7	J
L. HVAC, fire protection, plumbing	6	J
M. Electrical	5	J
N. Interior finishes	12	K, L, M
O. close out project	2	N

a. Draw the precedence network.
b. Determine the ES, EF, LF, and LS times.
c. What is the project duration?
d. What are the critical activities?

*19. A project consists of the following activities, normal durations (days), immediate predecessors, cost per day to crash ($000/day), and available days to crash.[7] (LO6)

Activity	Normal Duration (days)	Immediate Predecessor(s)	Cost per Day to Crash ($000/day)	Available Days to Crash
A	8	—	9	5
B	8	—	2	4
C	6	—	4	3
D	9	A	6	7
E	20	A	3	7
F	11	B, D	1	5
G	9	B, D	7	5
H	12	C, G	8	7

a. Draw the precedence network.
b. Calculate the project duration using normal activity durations.
c. Determine the minimum-cost crashing plan that will take 16 days off the project duration.

---

[7]N. Siemens, "A Simple CPM Time-cost Tradeoff Algorithm," *Management Science*, February 1971, 17(6), pp. B354–363.

Time, Please

"**S**mitty" Smith is a project manager for a large consumer electronics corporation. Although she has been with the company only four years, she has demonstrated an uncanny ability to bring projects in on time, meet technical specifications, and be close to budget.

Her latest assignment is a project that will involve merging two existing technologies. She and her team have almost finished developing the proposal that will be presented to a management committee for approval. All that remains to be done is to determine a duration estimate for the project. Smitty wants an estimated duration that will have a 95 percent probability

of being met. The team has constructed a precedence network for the project. It has three paths. The expected durations and standard deviations for the paths are listed below.

Path	Expected Duration (weeks)	Standard Deviation (weeks)
A	10	4
B	14	2
C	13	2

Question

What project duration (in weeks) should Smitty include in the proposal?

Fantasy Products

Company Background

The Fantasy Products Company (disguised name) is a manufacturer of high-quality small appliances intended for home use. The company's current product line includes irons, a small hand-held vacuum, and a number of kitchen appliances such as toasters, blenders, waffle irons, and coffeemakers. Fantasy Products has a strong R&D department that continually searches for ways to improve existing products as well as developing new ones.

Currently, the R&D department is working on the development of a new kitchen appliance that will chill foods quickly much as a microwave oven heats them quickly, although the technology involved is quite different. Tentatively named The Big Chill, the product will initially carry a price tag of around $125, and the target market consists of upper-income consumers. At this price, it is expected to be a very profitable item. R&D engineers now have a working prototype and are satisfied that, with the cooperation from the production and marketing people, the product can be ready in time for the all-important Christmas buying season. A target date has been set for product introduction that is 24 weeks away.

Current Problem

Fantasy Products' Marketing Vice-President Vera Sloan has recently learned from reliable sources that a competitor is also in the process of developing a similar product, which it intends to bring out at almost the same time. In addition, her source indicated that the competitor plans to sell its product, which will be smaller than The Big Chill, for $99 in the hope of appealing to more customers. Vera, with the help of several of her key people who are to be involved in marketing The Big Chill, has

decided that in order to compete, the selling price for The Big Chill will have to be lowered to within $10 of the competitor's price. At this price level, it will still be profitable, although not nearly as profitable as originally anticipated.

However, Vera is wondering whether it would be possible to expedite the product introduction process in order to beat the competition to the market. If possible, she would like to get a six-week jump on the competition; this would put the product introduction date only 18 weeks away. During this initial period, Fantasy Products could sell The Big Chill for $125, reducing the selling price to $109 when the competitor's product actually enters the market. Since forecasts based on market research show that sales during the first six weeks will be about 400 units per week, there is an opportunity for $25 per unit profit if the early introduction can be accomplished. In addition, there is prestige involved in being first to the market. This should help enhance The Big Chill's image during the anticipated battle for market share.

Data Collection

Since Fantasy Products has been through the product-introduction process a number of times, Vera has developed a list of the tasks that must be accomplished and the order in which they must be completed. Although the duration and costs vary depending on the particular product, the basic process does not. The list of activities involved in product introduction and their precedence relationships are presented in Table 1. Duration and cost estimates for the introduction of The Big Chill are presented in Table 2. Note that some of the activities can be completed on a crash basis, with an associated increase in cost. For example, activity B can be crashed from 8 weeks to 6 weeks at an additional cost of $3,000 (i.e., $12,000 − $9,000). Assume that if B is crashed to 7 weeks, the additional cost will be $1,500 (i.e., $3,000/2).

Table 1
List of activities involved in product introduction and precedence relationships

Activity	Description	Immediate Predecessor(s)
A	Select and order production equipment	—
B	Receive production equipment from supplier	A
C	Install and set up production equipment	B
D	Finalize bill of material	—
E	Order parts	D
F	Receive parts	E
G	First production run	C, F
H	Finalize marketing plan	—
I	Produce magazine ads	H
J	Script for TV ads	H
K	Produce TV ads	J
L	Begin ad campaign	I, K
M	Ship product to consumers	G, L

Table 2
Duration and cost estimates for introduction of The Big Chill

Activity	Normal Duration (weeks)	Normal Cost	Crash Duration (weeks)	Normal & Crash Cost
A	3	$2,000	2	$4,400
B	8	9,000	6	12,000
C	4	2,000	2	7,000
D	2	1,000	1	2,000
E	2	2,000	1	3,000
F	5	0	5	0
G	6	12,000	3	24,000
H	4	3,500	2	8,000
I	4	5,000	3	8,000
J	3	8,000	2	15,000
K	4	50,000	3	70,000
L	6	10,000	6	10,000
M	1	5,000	1	5,000

Fantasy Products needs to decide whether to bring The Big Chill to market 18 weeks from now, as Vera Sloan is recommending. As the project management specialist in the R&D department, you have been asked to answer the following questions:

Questions

1. When would the project be completed using the normal durations?

2. Is it possible to complete the project in 18 weeks? What would the associated additional cost be? Which activities would need to be completed on a crash basis?

3. Is there some time frame shorter than the 18 weeks Vera has recommended that would make more sense in terms of profits?

Source: Adapted from an original case by R.J. Thieraus, M. Cunningham, and M. Blackwell, Xavier University, Cincinnati, Ohio.

PART EIGHT

Waiting-Line Analysis

The chapter in this part covers the analysis of waiting lines. The occurrence of waiting lines in services indicates a temporary imbalance between demand and capacity. Waiting-line analysis can help managers reduce the impact of waiting lines on costs and effectiveness (i.e., customer service).

CHAPTER 18
Waiting-Line Analysis

LEARNING OBJECTIVES

After completing this chapter, you should be able to:

LO1 Explain why waiting lines form, identify the goal of queuing (waiting-line) analysis, explain how waiting line models are used in bank teller staffing, and discuss how to deal with the perception of waiting.

LO2 Describe the system characteristics and measures of performance used in queuing.

LO3 List and distinguish among the queuing models studied in this chapter and understand and use some basic queuing relationships.

LO4 Discuss and use the single-server queuing models presented.

LO5 Discuss and use the multiple-server queueing models presented.

LO6 Discuss and use the finite-source queuing model presented.

ervices such as banks and call centres face variations in customer arrivals and phone calls during the same hour from day to day. How are they able to determine the right level of staffing? This is the type of question answered in this chapter.

(LO1) INTRODUCTION

Those waiting in line would all agree that the solution to the problem is obvious: simply add more servers or do something to speed up service. Although both ideas may be potential solutions, there are certain subtleties that must be dealt with. For one thing, most service systems have the capacity to process customers over the long run. Hence, the problem of customers waiting is a short-term phenomenon. And at certain times the servers are idle, waiting for customers. Thus, by increasing the service capacity, the server idle time would increase even more. Consequently, in designing service systems, the designer must weigh the cost of providing a given level of service capacity against the cost of having customers wait for service. This planning and analysis of service capacity frequently lends itself to **queuing theory**, which is a mathematical approach for the analysis of waiting lines.

The modern queuing theory is based on studies about automatic dialing equipment made in the early part of the last century by Danish telephone engineer A.K. Erlang. Prior to the Second World War, very few attempts were made to apply queuing theory to operations. Since then, queuing theory has been applied to a range of operations problems.

The mathematics of queuing theory can be complex; for that reason, the emphasis here will not be on the mathematics but on the use of formulas and tables for analysis.

Waiting lines are commonly found wherever customers arrive randomly for a service. Some examples of waiting lines we encounter in our daily lives include the line at the supermarket checkout, fast-food restaurant, hospital emergency department, college and university registration, airport check-in counter, movie theatre/concert, post office, call centre, government services, and the bank. In many situations, the "customers" are not people but orders waiting to be filled, trucks waiting to be unloaded, jobs waiting to be processed, equipment awaiting repairs, planes waiting to land or take off, and cars waiting at a traffic light or traffic jam.

One reason that queuing analysis is important is that customers tend to associate waiting with poor service quality, especially if the wait is long. Similarly, for an organization, having employees wait, such as a truck driver waiting to unload, is a waste.

queuing theory
Mathematical approach for the analysis of waiting lines.

Why Is There Waiting?

Many people are surprised to learn that waiting lines tend to form even though a system is under-loaded. For example, a fast-food restaurant may have the capacity to handle an average of 200 orders per hour and yet experience waiting lines even though the number of orders is only 150 per hour. In reality, customers arrive at random rather than at evenly spaced intervals and some orders take longer to fill than others. In other words, both arrival times and service durations exhibit a high degree of variability. As a result, the system at times becomes temporarily overloaded, giving rise to waiting lines; at other times, the system is idle because there are no customers. Thus, although a system may be *underloaded* from a *macro* standpoint, variabilities in arrival times and service durations imply that at times the system is *overloaded* from a *micro* standpoint. It follows that in systems where variability is minimal or non-existent (e.g., because arrivals can be scheduled and service durations are constant), waiting lines do not ordinarily form.

Goal of Waiting-Line Analysis

The goal of queuing analysis is to minimize total costs. There are two types of cost in a queuing situation: "cost" of customers waiting for service and cost of provision of capacity (e.g., determining the number of cashiers at a supermarket or the number of repair people to handle equipment breakdowns). The cost of customers waiting, in addition to loss of

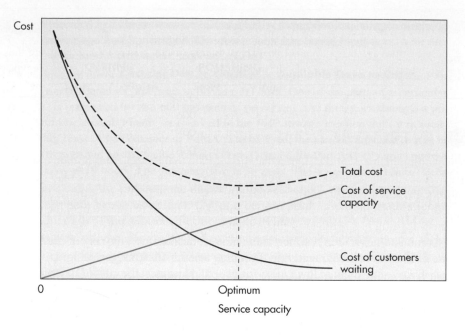

goodwill, includes loss of business due to customers refusing to wait and going elsewhere. Also, if the "customers" are employees, the salaries paid to employees while they wait for service (e.g., mechanics waiting for tools, truck drivers waiting to unload), are part of the cost of customers waiting.

Figure 18-1 shows the two costs and the total cost as a function of service capacity. Note that as capacity increases, its capacity cost increases. For simplicity, the increase is shown as a linear relationship. On the other hand, as capacity increases, the number of customers waiting and the time they wait tend to decrease at a faster rate; also the dissatisfaction of a typical customer is a non-linear function of the waiting time (initially it is insignificant but increases at a faster rate as the wait time increases past a threshold); therefore, waiting cost decreases nonlinearly. Total cost is a U-shaped curve, and the goal of queuing analysis is to identify that level of service capacity that will minimize the total cost. (Unlike the situation in the EOQ model, the minimum point on the total cost curve is *not* necessarily where the two cost lines intersect.)

If pinning down the cost of customers waiting is difficult, another approach is to treat waiting times or line lengths as a policy variable: a manager simply specifies an acceptable level of waiting (e.g., average customer wait time of four minutes before service at a bank) and directs that enough capacity be established to achieve that level of waiting.

Queuing analysis is used in most services. As an example, we will briefly describe its use in bank teller staffing.

Queuing Analysis in Bank Teller Staffing[1]

Most banks have a staffing chart that suggests the minimum number of tellers required based on the forecast of number of customers expected (i.e., arrival rates) during each half-hour. These charts are derived by entering the following data into queuing theory formulas: forecast of average arrival rates, average customer service duration, and a customer service goal (such as an average wait time of approximately four minutes before being served). From branch to branch, the average customer service duration varies because of type of transactions performed (e.g., retail vs. commercial), demographics, and the experience level of tellers. Most of these factors, and the time of day, also affect the customer arrival pattern at each branch during each half-hour. In addition, both service durations and arrival rates change over the years because of technological improvements. For example, Internet/ telephone banking has reduced the need of customers to personally visit their bank.

---

[1]Based on H. Deutsch and V.A. Mabert, "Queuing Theory and Teller Staffing; A Successful Application," *Interfaces* 10(5), October 1980, pp. 63–67.

To check the model assumptions, a sufficiently long data collection period is required; for example, the number of arrivals during each 15-minute period, the queue length at the end of each 15-minute period, and the number of tellers providing service could be recorded. Also, the service durations of at least 1,000 customers needs to be measured. Usually the distributions of number of arrivals and service durations match the assumed shapes (presented later).

The staffing requirements determined for each half-hour during each day of the following week are used to form feasible shifts and staff schedules (as presented in Chapter 16 on Staff Scheduling). For an example of a device that assists in data collection, though not necessarily in banks, see the "Qmatic" OM in Action later in the chapter.

Psychology of Waiting

Even though we focus on quantitative queuing analysis in this chapter, dealing with customers' perception of waiting is also important. Some suggestions in this regard are:

- Determine the acceptable wait time for the operation.
- Try to keep the waiting time experienced by a customer consistent over time.
- Install distractions that entertain and involve customers. For example, provide magazines, TV, mirrors outside elevators, ask the customer to fill out a form, and use the lounge before eating. Make the wait comfortable.
- Inform the customer the cause of an abnormal wait and peak times.
- Keep the line moving continuously.
- Use first come, first served discipline (fairness is important).
- Allow customers to serve themselves.
- Prepare the customers for service before the actual service. For example, encourage customers to print their boarding pass at home the night before their flight.
- Make people conscious of time only if they overestimate the wait time.
- Keep staff who are not serving customers out of sight.
- Try to segment customers by personality; some customers, the "watchers," actually like to spend time in lines, whereas the "impatients" need shorter lines. Some airlines and hotels have club memberships that provide express check-in and check-out for those who want it.
- Never underestimate the power of a friendly and attentive server.[2]

For two examples, see the "Disney World" and "Six Flags" OM in Actions.

LO2 QUEUEING SYSTEM CHARACTERISTICS AND PERFORMANCE MEASURES

There are numerous queuing models from which an analyst can choose. Naturally, much of the success of the analysis will depend on choosing the appropriate model. Model choice is dependent on the characteristics of the waiting line system under investigation. The main characteristics are:

1. Potential number of customers.
2. Number of servers and structure of queuing system.
3. Arrival and service patterns.
4. Queue discipline (i.e., order of service).

Figure 18-2 depicts a simple queuing system.

---

[2]K.L. Katz, B.M. Larson, and R.C. Larson, "Prescription for the Waiting-in-Line Blues: Entertain, Enlighten, and Engage," *Sloan Management Review*, Winter 1991, 32(2), pp. 44–53.

Figure 18-2

A simple queuing system

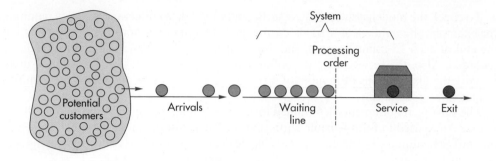

Potential Number of Customers

"infinite"-source The potential number of customers greatly exceeds system capacity.

finite-source The number of potential customers is limited.

The potential number of customers is either limited or is very large. In an **"infinite"-source** situation, the potential number of customers greatly exceeds system capacity. Examples are supermarkets, drugstores, banks, restaurants, theatres, amusement parks, and call centres. Theoretically, a large number of customers can request service at any one time. When the potential number of customers is limited, a **finite-source** situation exists. An example is the maintenance of machines in a company. The potential number of machines that might need repair at any one time is limited. A similar waiting situation occurs when an operator is responsible for loading and unloading a few machines and a nurse is responsible for a few patients.

 OM in ACTION   http://disneyworld.disney.go.com/parks

Disney World

Walt Disney theme parks are leaders in effectively managing waiting lines. Disney analysts are so good that they present seminars to other companies on managing waiting lines. Their success can serve as a benchmark and provide valuable insights for a wide range of services.

Disney's methods are particularly relevant when circumstances make it impossible to quickly add capacity to alleviate waiting times. Here are some of the tactics Disney employs to achieve customer satisfaction:

1. *Provide distractions.* Disney characters may entertain customers, videos provide safety information and build anticipation for the event, vendors move along some lines selling food and drinks, and other vendors sell souvenirs.

2. *Provide alternatives to waiting in line.* Disney offers the "FastPass," which allows customers to reserve a time later in the day for a popular ride when they will be allowed to bypass the regular waiting line. Only one Fastpass is issued to a person at any time.

3. *Keep customers informed.* Signs are clearly posted that give approximate waiting times from that point on, allowing the customers to make a decision on whether or not to join the line or not.

4. *Exceed expectations.* Wait times are usually shorter than the posted times, thereby exceeding customers' expectations.

5. *Other tactics.* Disney maintains a comfortable waiting environment: Waiting lines are often inside, protected from weather. Lines are kept moving, giving the impression of making progress.

Visitors wait to ride the Big Thunder Railroad at Disney World in Florida.

Source: Based in part on "Queuing: Featuring Disney World," McGraw-Hill Irwin OM Video Series.

Number of Servers and Structure of Queuing System

The capacity of a queuing system is a function of the capacity of each server and the number of servers. Each server can handle one customer at a time. (Note: a table of four is considered one "customer"). A queuing system can have either *single* or *multiple servers*. (Note: a group of servers working together as a team such as a surgical team is treated as a "single" server). Other examples of a single-server system are small grocery stores with one cashier, some theatres, and single-bay car washes. Multiple-server systems are commonly found in banks, at airline ticket counters, and at call centres.

Another distinctive characteristic is the number of steps or *phases* in a queuing system. For example, at most fast-food drive-throughs, cars first wait to order at the menu board, and then wait to pay at the pay window, and then wait to pick up the order at the pick-up window. Each stage constitutes a separate phase where queues can form.

Figure 18-3 illustrates some of the most common queuing systems. Because it would not be possible to cover all of these cases in sufficient detail in the limited amount of space available here, our discussion will focus on *single-phase* systems.

If the customers are homogeneous (i.e., similar), then a single line feeding into multiple servers is usually preferred to multiple independent lines each feeding to its own server. The reasons for this are as follows: First, the average wait time will be less because if there is an idle server, the customer waiting at the top of the line will be directed to the idle server right away. This does not happen in multiple independent lines, especially if the other lines cannot be observed. Even if a customer can see and jump to a shorter queue, this process will consume some time and does not guarantee getting to the server first. Second, the customers will be served first-come, first-served, which is more equitable and preferred by most customers. The disadvantages of a joint line are that it might appear too long, it may take a large space, servers may not work as fast as if they were responsible for their own line, and customers cannot choose their favourite server.

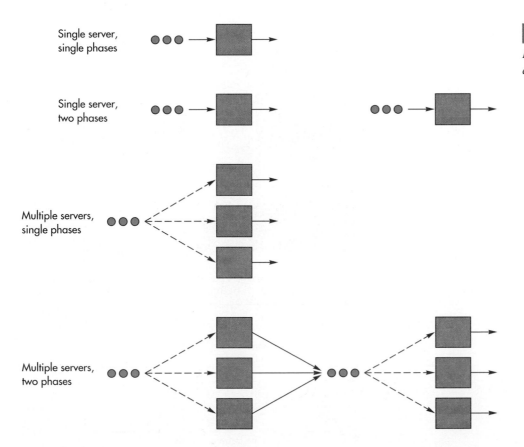

Single server, single phases

Single server, two phases

Multiple servers, single phases

Multiple servers, two phases

Figure 18-3

Four common variations of queuing systems

However, if the customers are heterogeneous (i.e., different), then separate lines could be advantageous. For example, a line for 10 items or less in a grocery store moves faster, resulting in shorter wait times for customers who do not buy a lot. This reduces the total variability of service durations, resulting in reduced average wait time for all customers. In some cases, the company can charge a higher price for providing a faster line; for example, the one-hour photo developing service is more expensive than the five-day economy service in The Real Canadian Superstore.

Arrival and Service Patterns

Poisson distribution A one-parameter discrete probability distribution of a number of events occurring in an interval of time, provided that these events occur with a known average rate and independently of the time since the last event.

Exponential distribution The continuous probability distribution of the times between events that happen continuously and independently at a constant average rate.

The most commonly used queueing models assume that the customer arrival *rate* (i.e., the number of arrivals per time unit) can be described by a Poisson distribution and that the service *duration* can be described by an Exponential distribution. **Poisson distribution** is a one-parameter discrete probability distribution of a number of events occurring in an interval of time, provided that these events occur with a known average rate and independently of the time since the last event. **Exponential distribution** is the continuous probability distribution of the times between events that happen continuously and independently at a constant average rate. Figure 18-4 illustrates these distributions.

Figure 18-5A illustrates how Poisson-distributed customer arrivals might occur during a three-day period. In some hours, there are three or four arrivals, in some other hours one or two arrivals, and in some other hours no arrivals.

Figure 18-5B illustrates how Exponential service durations might appear for the same customers. Note that most service durations are very short but a few are relatively long.

Waiting lines are likely to occur when arrivals are bunched up and/or when service durations are particularly lengthy. For instance, note the long service duration of customer 7 on day 1 in Figure 18-5B. In Figure 18-5A, the seventh customer arrived just after 10 o'clock and the next two customers arrived shortly after that, making it very likely that a waiting line would form. A similar situation occurred on day 3 with the last three

Figure 18-4

Poisson and Exponential distributions

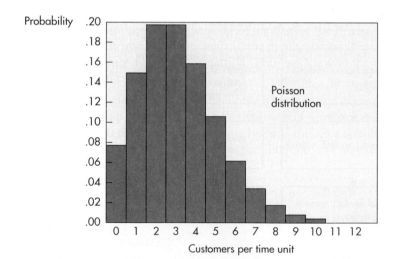

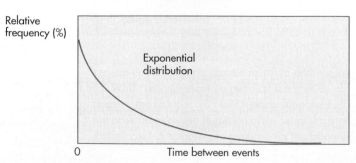

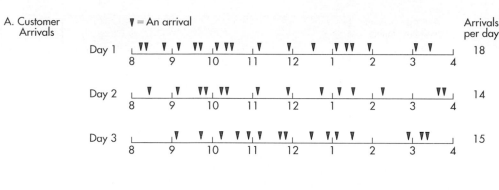

A. Customer Arrivals

▼ = An arrival

Arrivals per day

Day 1 — 18

Day 2 — 14

Day 3 — 15

Figure 18-5

Examples of Poisson customer arrivals (A) and Exponential service durations (B)

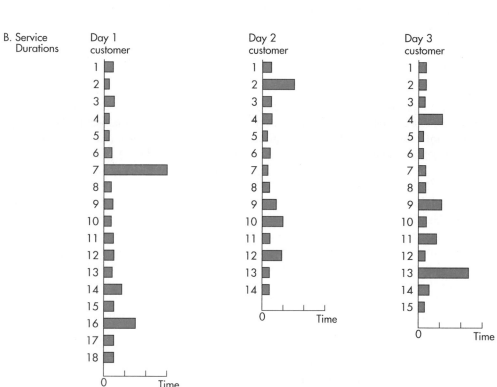

B. Service Durations

Day 1 customer

Day 2 customer

Day 3 customer

customers: the relatively long service duration for customer 13 (Figure 18-5B) and the short time before the next two arrivals (Figure 18-5A, day 3) would create (or increase the length of) a waiting line.

It is interesting to note that the Poisson and Exponential distributions are alternate ways of presenting the same basic information. That is, if service durations are Exponential, then the service rates (i.e., the number of services per time unit) are Poisson. Similarly, if the customer arrival rates are Poisson, then the inter arrival durations (i.e., the time between two consecutive arrivals) are Exponential. There is an inverse relationship between the means of these two distributions. For example, if a service facility can process 12 customers per hour, then average service duration is $1/12^{th}$ of an hour or five minutes. And if the arrival rate is 10 per hour, then the average duration between two consecutive arrivals is six minutes.

Most models described in this chapter require that arrival and service rates be approximately Poisson or, equivalently, that inter-arrival and service durations be approximately Exponential. In practice, it is necessary to verify that these assumptions are met. Sometimes this is done by collecting data and plotting them, although the preferred approach is to use a chi-square goodness-of-fit test for that purpose. A discussion of the chi-square test is beyond the scope of this text, but it is covered in most statistics textbooks.

Figure 18-6

The average time customers wait in line increases non-linearly as the server utilization increases.

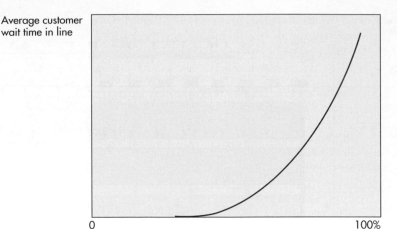

Average customer wait time in line

0   100%

Server utilization

Research has shown that these assumptions are often appropriate for customer arrival rates but less likely to be appropriate for service durations. In situations where the assumptions are not reasonably satisfied, the alternatives would be to use (1) an approximate model, or (2) computer simulation.

Queue Discipline (i.e., Order of Service)

queue discipline The order in which customers are served.

Queue discipline refers to the order in which customers are served. All but one of the models to be described assumes that service is provided on a *first-come, first-served* (FCFS) basis. This is the most commonly encountered rule at banks, stores, theatres, restaurants, four-way stop signs, registration lines, and so on. Examples of systems that do not serve on a FCFS basis include hospital emergency rooms, rush orders in a factory, and mainframe computer processing of jobs. In these and similar situations, customers do not all represent the same waiting costs; those with the highest cost (e.g., the most seriously ill) are processed first, even though other customers may have arrived earlier.

Performance Measures

Operations managers typically look at four measures when evaluating existing or proposed queuing systems. Those measures are:

1. The average number of customers waiting, either in line (not counting those being served) or in the system (including those being served)

2. The average length of time customers wait, either in line or in the system

3. **Server utilization**, i.e., the proportion of time a server will be busy

server utilization The proportion of time a server will be busy.

4. The probability that an arriving customer will have to wait for service or will have to wait more than a specified length of time before being served

Of these measures, server utilization bears some elaboration. It reflects the extent to which the servers are busy rather than idle. On the surface, it might seem that the operations manager would want to seek 100 percent utilization. However, as Figure 18-6 illustrates, increases in server utilization are achieved at the expense of greater increases in the average customer wait time. In fact, average customer wait time becomes exceedingly large as server utilization approaches 100 percent. Also, 100 percent utilization of servers leads to burnout. Instead, a utilization of 80 to 90 percent is appropriate for most queueing systems.

LO3 QUEUING MODELS: "INFINITE" SOURCE

Many "infinite"-source queuing models are available for a manager or analyst to choose from. The discussion here includes eight of the most basic and widely used models. All models discussed (except Model 7) assume Poisson arrival rates. Moreover, they assume that the average arrival and service rates are constant. If they are not, then the operating hours should be divided into sub-periods within which the rates are fairly constant. For example, each hour or half-hour may have a different average arrival rate. In addition, the results are for the steady state condition, i.e., the transient behaviour of the queuing system at the opening hour are ignored. The eight "infinite"-source models described are:

1. Single server, Exponential service durations
2. Single server, Exponential service durations, finite number in system
3. Single server, constant service durations
4. Single server, general service durations
5. Multiple servers, Exponential service durations
6. Multiple servers, Exponential service durations, finite number in system
7. Multiple servers, general inter-arrival and service durations
8. Multiple servers with priority, Exponential service durations

To facilitate your use of queuing models, Table 18-1 provides a list of the symbols used for the "infinite"-source models.

Symbol	Represents
λ	Average arrival rate
μ	Average service rate
L_q	Average number of customers waiting in line for service
L_s	Average number of customers in the system (waiting and being served)
ρ	Server utilization
W_q	Average length of time customers wait in line
W_s	Average length of time customers spend in the system (waiting in line and being served)
$1/\mu$	Average service duration
P_o	Probability of zero customers in the system
P_n	Probability of n customers in the system
M	Number of servers
r	Average number of customers being served at any time

Table 18-1

Symbols for "infinite"-source queueing models

Basic Relationships

There are certain basic relationships that hold for all "infinite"-source queuing models. Knowledge of these relationships can be very helpful in deriving the desired performance measures, given a few key values. Here are the basic relationships. Some are intuitive, others complex. For the latter, proof is omitted here.

Note: The average arrival and service rates, represented by λ and μ, respectively, must be in the same time units (e.g., per hour or per minute).

Server utilization, ρ (rho), is equal to the ratio of demand (as measured by the average arrival rate) to capacity (as measured by the product of the number of servers, M, and the average service rate, μ):

$$\rho = \frac{\lambda}{M\mu} \tag{18-1}$$

The average number of customers being served (at any point in time), r, is equal to each server's utilization times the number of servers = ρM, or:

$$r = \frac{\lambda}{\mu} \tag{18-2}$$

Six Flags

S ix Flags uses a waiting system similar to Disney's Fastpass. It is called Flash Pass and uses a virtual queuing system by Lo-Q Company (http://www.lo-q.com). Each customer can rent a pager at the park entrance, called Q-Bot. Then, at some popular rides, the pager can be used to reserve the person's spot in the line. The person can go away and enjoy other rides. Ten minutes before her actual turn, she will be notified via the pager.

Sources: T. O'Brien, "Six Flags Debuts Queue Management," *Amusement Business* 113(9), March 5, 2001, pp. 1, 26; http://themeparks.about.com/cs/sixflagsparks/a/blfastlanea.htm.

Figure 18-7

Basic relationships

	Line	+	**Service**	=	**System**
Customers $\longrightarrow$	000	$\rightarrow$	$\boxed{0}$	$\rightarrow$	
Average number waiting:	L_q	+	$\dfrac{\lambda}{\mu}$	=	L_s
Average time waiting:	$W_q = \dfrac{L_q}{\lambda}$	+	$\dfrac{1}{\mu}$	=	W_s

The average *number* of customers

waiting in line for service, L_q: L_q [Model dependent. Obtain using a table or formula.]

in the system (line plus being served), L_s: $\qquad L_s = L_q + r$ $\qquad\qquad$ (18-3)

The average length of time customers

wait in line, W_q: $W_q = \dfrac{L_q}{\lambda}$ $\qquad$ [Little's Formula] $\qquad\qquad$ (18-4)

spend in the system, W_s: $W_s = W_q + \dfrac{1}{\mu} = \dfrac{L_s}{\lambda}$ $\qquad$ [Little's Formula] $\qquad\qquad$ (18-5)

All "infinite"-source models require that server utilization be less than 1.0; the models apply only to underloaded systems.

The average number of customers waiting in line, L_q, is a key value because it determines the other measures of system performance. Hence, L_q will usually be one of the first values you will want to determine in problem solving. Figure 18-7 can help you relate the symbols to the basic relationships in a queuing system.

Example 1

Customers arrive at a bakery at an average rate of 18 per hour on weekday mornings. The arrival rate can be described by a Poisson distribution. Each server can serve a customer in an average of four minutes; service durations can be described by an Exponential distribution.

a. What are the average arrival and service rates?

b. Calculate the average number of customers being served at any time (assume that at least two servers will be working, resulting in server utilization < 1.0).

c. Suppose that the average number of customers waiting in line is 3.6. Calculate the average number of customers in the system (i.e., waiting in line or being served), the average length of time customers wait in line, and the average length of time customers spend in the system.

d. Determine the server utilization if there are $M = 2$, 3, or 4 servers.

Solution

a. The average arrival rate is given in the problem: $\lambda = 18$ customers per hour. Change the average service duration to a comparable *hourly* service rate by first restating the duration in hours and then taking its reciprocal. Thus, (4 minutes per customer)/(60 minutes per hour) = 1/15 hour per customer. Its reciprocal is $\mu = 15$ customers per hour, the average service rate.

b. $r = \dfrac{\lambda}{\mu} = \dfrac{18}{15} = 1.2$ customers

c. Given: $L_q = 3.6$ customers,

$L_s = L_q + r = 3.6 + 1.2 = 4.8$ customers

$W_q - \dfrac{L_q}{\lambda} - \dfrac{3.6}{18} = .20$ hour, or $\times 60$ minutes/hours

$= 12$ minutes

$W_s = W_q + \dfrac{1}{\mu} = .20 + \dfrac{1}{15} = .267$ hour, or 16 minutes

d. Server utilization is $\rho = \dfrac{\lambda}{M\mu}$.

For $M = 2$, $\rho = \dfrac{18}{2(15)} = .60$

For $M = 3$, $\rho = \dfrac{18}{2(15)} = .40$

For $M = 4$, $\rho = \dfrac{18}{2(15)} = .30$

Hence, as the system capacity, measured by $M\mu$, increases, the server utilization (for a given arrival rate) decreases.

 ## SINGLE-SERVER MODELS

Model 1: Single Server, Exponential Service Durations

The simplest model involves a system that has one server (or a single crew), the queue discipline is FCFS, and customer arrival rates can be approximated by a Poisson distribution and service durations by an Exponential distribution. The length of queue is not a constraint.

Table 18-2 lists some formulas for Model 1, which should be used in conjunction with formulas 18-1 through 18-5.

Performance Measure	Equation	
Average number in line	$L_q = \dfrac{\lambda^2}{\mu(\mu - \lambda)}$	(18-6)
Probability of zero customers in the system	$P_o = 1 - \left(\dfrac{\lambda}{\mu}\right)$	(18-7)
Probability of n customers in the system	$P_n = P_o \left(\dfrac{\lambda}{\mu}\right)^n$	(18-8)
Probability of fewer than n customers in the system	$P_{<n} = 1 - \left(\dfrac{\lambda}{\mu}\right)^n$	(18-9)
Probability that a customer waits at least t time units in queue	$P_{w \text{ in } Q > t} = \dfrac{\lambda}{\mu} e^{-(\mu - \lambda)t}$	(18-10)

Table 18-2

Formulas for Model 1: single-server, Exponential service durations

Example 2

A phone company is planning to open a kiosk in a new shopping mall, staffed by one sales agent. It is estimated that requests for phones, accessories, and information will average 15 per hour during peak period, and number of requests will have a Poisson distribution. Service durations are assumed to be Exponentially distributed. Previous experience with similar kiosks suggests that service duration should average about three minutes per request. Determine each of the following measures during the peak period:

a. Server utilization.

b. Percentage of time the sales agent will be idle.

c. The expected number of customers waiting in line to be served.

d. The average length of time customers will spend in the system.

e. The probability of zero customers in the system and the probability of four customers in the system.

f. The probability that a customer will have to wait.

g. The probability that a customer will have to wait more than 5 minutes.

Solution

$\lambda = 15$ per hour

$$\mu = \frac{1}{\text{Average service duration}} = \frac{1 \text{ customer}}{3 \text{ minutes}} \times 60 \text{ minutes per hour}$$

$$= 20 \text{ customers per hour}$$

a. $\rho = \dfrac{\lambda}{M\mu} = \dfrac{15}{1(20)} = .75$

b. Percentage idle time $= 1 - \rho = 1 - .75 = .25$, or 25 percent

c. $L_q = \dfrac{\lambda^2}{\mu(\mu-\lambda)} = \dfrac{15^2}{20(20-15)} = 2.25$ customers

d. $W_s = \dfrac{L_q}{\lambda} + \dfrac{1}{\mu} = \dfrac{2.25}{15} + \dfrac{1}{20} = .20$ hour, or 12 minutes

e. $P_0 = 1 - \dfrac{\lambda}{\mu} = 1 - \dfrac{15}{20} = .25$ and $P_4 = P_0\left(\dfrac{\lambda}{\mu}\right)^4 = .25\left(\dfrac{15}{20}\right)^4 = .079$

f. Probability that a customer will have to wait $= \rho = .75$

g. $P_{W \text{ in } Q > t} = \dfrac{\lambda}{\mu} e^{-(\mu-\lambda)t}$

$$= \dfrac{15}{20} e^{-(20-15)(5/60)}$$

$$= .494$$

Note that t should be in the same time unit as λ and μ.

Model 2: Single Server, Exponential Service Durations, Finite Number in System

In many cases, the number of customers or calls that can fit in the queuing system is limited. Let $K =$ maximum number of customers (or calls) that can fit in the queuing system (in line and being served). If there are K customers already in the queuing system, the next customer will not be allowed to enter the system and has to balk (leave). In this case, P_0 and L_q can be calculated using the following two formulas. The probability of a customer balking is the same as probability of K customers in the system, P_k. The effective average arrival rate in this case is $\lambda(1 - P_k)$, and should be used to relate W_q to L_q.

$$P_o = \left[1 + \frac{\left(\frac{\lambda}{\mu}\right)\left(1 - \left(\frac{\lambda}{\mu}\right)^K\right)}{\left(1 - \frac{\lambda}{\mu}\right)}\right]^{-1} \tag{18-11}$$

$$L_q = \frac{\left(\frac{\lambda}{\mu}\right)^2 P_o}{\left(1 - \frac{\lambda}{\mu}\right)^2}\left(1 - \left(\frac{\lambda}{\mu}\right)^K - K\left(1 - \frac{\lambda}{\mu}\right)\left(\frac{\lambda}{\mu}\right)^{K-1}\right) \tag{18-12}$$

OM in ACTION   http://www.q-matic.com/ca/

Qmatic

Qmatic, based in Sweden, is an international company that produces hardware and software for queue and customer flow management. When a customer comes in, she receives a ticket that puts her on a queue. Then, she can sit down (or go away and return later) until the ticket number is displayed on an LED display. The ticket number could also be called out. From management's point of view, Qmatic's major advantage is that it automatically collects data such as the number of customers arriving per period, waiting and transaction (service) durations, and the number of customers waiting. It also recommends the right number of servers to use. This allows the manager to add or remove servers as needed. Also, statistical data can be generated to devise better staffing plans and to measure employee productivity.

Qmatic is being used in thousands of companies where queues develop: banks; hospital receptions and pharmacies; government departments/agencies/institutions such as motor vehicle offices, post offices, embassies and consulates, colleges and universities, courts, and city hall; and retail stores and hotels.

A Qmatic ticket printer and waiting-line data collector

Source: http://www.q-matic.com/ca/

$$P_K = \left(\frac{\lambda}{\mu}\right)^K P_o \tag{18-13}$$

$$W_q = \frac{L_q}{\lambda(1 - P_K)} \tag{18-14}$$

Example 3

Reconsider Example 2, but assume that if there are already four customers in the system (three in line and 1 being served), then no new customer will join the line. Calculate

a. The average number in the line and compare it with Example 2.
b. The probability of balking.
c. The average time in the system and compare it with Example 2.

a. Recall $\lambda = 15$ per hour and $\mu = 20$ per hour. K = 4.

Solution

$$P_0 = \left[1 + \frac{\left(\frac{15}{20}\right)\left(1 - \left(\frac{15}{20}\right)^4\right)}{\left(1 - \frac{15}{20}\right)}\right]^{-1} = .327785$$

$$L_q = \frac{\left(\frac{15}{20}\right)^2 (.327785)}{\left(1 - \frac{15}{20}\right)^2} \left(1 - \left(\frac{15}{20}\right)^4 - 4\left(1 - \frac{15}{20}\right)\left(\frac{15}{20}\right)^3\right) = .7721 \text{ customers} < 2.25$$

customers in Example 2.

b. $P_K = \left(\dfrac{15}{20}\right)^4 (.327785) = 0.1037$ or 10%.

c. $W_s = \dfrac{L_q}{\lambda(1-P_k)} + \dfrac{1}{\mu} = \dfrac{.7721}{15(1-.1037)} + \dfrac{1}{20} = .10743$ hour or 6.4 minutes $<$ 12 minutes in Example 2.

Model 3: Single Server, Constant Service Durations

As noted previously, waiting lines are a consequence of random arrival and service rates. If we can reduce or eliminate the variability of either or both arrivals and services, then we can shorten the waiting line. A case in point is a queueing system with constant service durations (and Poisson arrival rates). The effect of constant service durations is to cut the average number of customers waiting in line in half (relative to Model 1):

$$L_q = \frac{\lambda^2}{2\mu(\mu - \lambda)} \tag{18-15}$$

The average length of time customers wait in line, W_q, is also cut in half.

Example 4

Consider a single bay automatic car wash that takes five minutes to wash a car. On a typical Saturday morning, cars arrive at a mean rate of eight per hour, according to Poisson distribution. Find:

a. The average number of cars in line.

b. The average length of time cars spend in line and service (i.e., system).

Solution

$\lambda = 8$ cars per hour

$\mu = 1$ per 5 minutes, or 12 cars per hour

a. $L_q = \dfrac{\lambda^2}{2\mu(\mu - \lambda)} = \dfrac{8^2}{2(12)(12 - 8)} = .667$ car

b. $W_s = \dfrac{L_q}{\lambda} + \dfrac{1}{\mu} = \dfrac{.667}{8} + \dfrac{1}{12} = .167$ hour, or 10 minutes

Model 4: Single Server, General Service Durations

For a general service durations with standard deviation $= \sigma_s$, it can be shown that

$$L_q = \frac{\lambda^2(\mu^2\sigma^2_s + 1)}{2\mu(\mu - \lambda)} \tag{18-16}$$

Note that when $\sigma_s = 0$, the above formula reduces to the L_q for Constant service durations (Model 3), and when $\sigma_s = \dfrac{1}{\mu}$, it reduces to the L_q for Exponential service durations (Model 1). Also, make sure that σ_s, λ and μ have the same time unit.

Example 5

At a small post office with one server, during the peak lunch period customers arrive according to Poisson distribution with an average rate of 30 customers per hour. Customers have a service time that is the sum of a constant 30 seconds and an Exponential service duration with average of 1 minute. Find:

a. The average number of customers in line during lunch time.

b. The average customer waiting time in line.

$\lambda = 30$ customers per hour

$1/\mu = .5 + 1 = 1.5$ minutes per customer or $\mu = 60/1.5 = 40$ customers per hour

$\sigma_s = 1$ minute or $1/60 = .0166667$ hour (because the constant 30 seconds time has zero variance and the standard deviation of an Exponential distribution equals its mean). Note that service duration is *not* Exponentially distributed.

a. $L_q = \dfrac{\lambda^2(\mu^2\sigma_s^2 + 1)}{2\mu(\mu - \lambda)} = \dfrac{30^2(40^2(.0166667)^2 + 1)}{2(40)(40 - 30)} = 1.625$ customers

b. $W_q = \dfrac{L_q}{\lambda} = \dfrac{1.625}{30} = 0.5417$ hour or 3.25 minutes.

LO5 MULTIPLE-SERVER MODELS

Model 5: Multiple Servers, Exponential Service Durations

A multiple server system exists whenever there are two or more servers working individually to provide service to customers. Use of the model involves the following assumptions:

1. Poisson arrival rates with average λ and Exponential service durations with average $\dfrac{1}{\mu}$.

2. All M servers work at the same average rate.

3. Customers form a single waiting line.

Formulas for the multiple-server, Exponential service durations model are listed in Table 18-3. Obviously, the multiple-server formulas are more complex than the single-server formulas for L_q and P_0. Fortunately, you can also determine their values using Table 18-4, given values of λ/μ and M.

Performance Measure	Equation	
Average number of customers in line	$L_q = \dfrac{\lambda\mu\left(\dfrac{\lambda}{\mu}\right)^M}{(M-1)!(M\mu - \lambda)^2}P_o$	(18-17)
Probability of zero customers in the system	$P_o = \left[\displaystyle\sum_{n=0}^{M-1}\dfrac{\left(\dfrac{\lambda}{\mu}\right)^n}{n!} + \dfrac{\left(\dfrac{\lambda}{\mu}\right)^M}{M!\left(1 - \dfrac{\lambda}{M\mu}\right)}\right]^{-1}$	(18-18)
Probability of n customers in the system	$P_n = \begin{cases} \dfrac{1}{n!}\left(\dfrac{\lambda}{\mu}\right)^n P_o & \text{if } n \leq M \\[2mm] \dfrac{1}{M!M^{n-M}}\left(\dfrac{\lambda}{\mu}\right)^n P_o & \text{if } n > M \end{cases}$	(18-19)
Average waiting time (before being served) for an arrival who is not immediately served	$W_a = \dfrac{1}{M\mu - \lambda}$	(18-20)
Probability that an arrival will have to wait for service	$P_W = \dfrac{W_q}{W_a}$	(18-21)
Probability that a customer waits at least t time units in queue	$P_{W\,in\,Q > t} = \dfrac{\left(\dfrac{\lambda}{\mu}\right)^M P_o}{M!\left(1 - \dfrac{\lambda}{M\mu}\right)}e^{-M\mu\left(1 - \frac{\lambda}{M\mu}\right)t}$	(18-22)

Table 18-3

Formulas for the multiple-server, Exponential service durations model (M = number of servers)

To use Table 18-4, calculate the value of λ/μ and round it to two decimal places if $\lambda/\mu < 1$ and one decimal place if $\lambda/\mu \geq 1$. Then, simply read the values of L_q and P_0 for the appropriate number of servers, M. For instance, if $\lambda/\mu = 0.50$ and $M = 2$, the table provides a value of 0.033 for L_q and a value of .600 for P_0. These values can then be used to calculate other measures of system performance. Note that Table 18-4 can also be used for the single server, Exponential service durations model (Model 1) (use $M = 1$ values).

Table 18-4

Multiple-server, Exponential service durations model values for L_q and P_0, given values for λ/μ and M (number of servers).

λ/μ	M	Lq	P_o	λ/μ	M	Lq	P_o	λ/μ	M	Lq	P_o
0.15	1	0.026	.850		4	0.003	.427	1.8	2	7.674	.053
	2	0.001	.860	0.90	1	8.100	.100		3	0.532	.146
0.20	1	0.050	.800		2	0.229	.379		4	0.105	.162
	2	0.002	.818		3	0.030	.403		5	0.023	.165
0.25	1	0.083	.750		4	0.004	.406	1.9	2	17.587	.026
	2	0.004	.778	0.95	1	18.050	.050		3	0.688	.128
0.30	1	0.129	.700		2	0.277	.356		4	0.136	.145
	2	0.007	.739		3	0.037	.383		5	0.030	.149
0.35	1	0.188	.650		4	0.005	.386		6	0.007	.149
	2	0.011	.702	1.0	2	0.333	.333	2.0	3	0.889	.111
0.40	1	0.267	.600		3	0.045	.364		4	0.174	.130
	2	0.017	.667		4	0.007	.367		5	0.040	.134
0.45	1	0.368	.550	1.1	2	0.477	.290		6	0.009	.135
	2	0.024	.633		3	0.066	.327	2.1	3	1.149	.096
	3	0.002	.637		4	0.011	.367		4	0.220	.117
0.50	1	0.500	.500	1.2	2	0.675	.250		5	0.052	.121
	2	0.033	.600		3	0.094	.294		6	0.012	.122
	3	0.003	.606		4	0.016	.300	2.2	3	1.491	.081
0.55	1	0.672	.450		5	0.003	.301		4	0.277	.105
	2	0.045	.569	1.3	2	0.951	.212		5	0.066	.109
	3	0.004	.576		3	0.130	.264		6	0.016	.111
0.60	1	0.900	.400		4	0.023	.271	2.3	3	1.951	.068
	2	0.059	.538		5	0.004	.272		4	0.346	.093
	3	0.006	.548	1.4	2	1.345	.176		5	0.084	.099
0.65	1	1.207	.350		3	0.177	.236		6	0.021	.100
	2	0.077	.509		4	0.032	.245	2.4	3	2.589	.056
	3	0.008	.521		5	0.006	.246		4	0.431	.083
0.70	1	1.633	.300	1.5	2	1.929	.143		5	0.105	.089
	2	0.098	.481		3	0.237	.211		6	0.027	.090
	3	0.011	.495		4	0.045	.221		7	0.007	.091
0.75	1	2.250	.250		5	0.009	.223	2.5	3	3.511	.045
	2	0.123	.455	1.6	2	2.844	.111		4	0.533	.074
	3	0.015	.471		3	0.313	.187		5	0.130	.080
0.80	1	3.200	.200		4	0.060	.199		6	0.034	.082
	2	0.152	.429		5	0.012	.201		7	0.009	.082
	3	0.019	.447	1.7	2	4.426	.081	2.6	3	4.933	.035
0.85	1	4.817	.150		3	0.409	.166		4	0.658	.065
	2	0.187	.404		4	0.080	.180		5	0.161	.072
	3	0.024	.425		5	0.017	.182		6	0.043	.074

Table 18-4

(continued)

λ/μ	M	Lq	P₀	λ/μ	M	Lq	P₀	λ/μ	M	Lq	P₀
	7	0.011	.074	3.6	4	7.090	.011		10	0.011	.014
2.7	3	7.354	.025		5	1.055	.023	4.4	5	5.268	.006
	4	0.811	.057		6	0.295	.026		6	1.078	.010
	5	0.198	.065		7	0.019	.027		7	0.337	.012
	6	0.053	.067		8	0.028	.027		8	0.114	.012
	7	0.014	.067		9	0.008	.027		9	0.039	.012
2.8	3	12.273	.016	3.7	4	10.347	.008		10	0.013	.012
	4	1.000	.050		5	1.265	.020	4.5	5	6.862	.005
	5	0.241	.058		6	0.349	.023		6	1.265	.009
	6	0.066	.060		7	0.109	.024		7	0.391	.010
	7	0.018	.061		8	0.034	.025		8	0.133	.011
2.9	3	27.193	.008		9	0.010	.025		9	0.046	.011
	4	1.234	.044	3.8	4	16.937	.005		10	0.015	.011
	5	0.293	.052		5	1.519	.017	4.6	5	9.289	.004
3.0	4	1.528	.038		6	0.412	.021		6	1.487	.008
	5	0.354	.047		7	0.129	.022		7	0.453	.009
	6	0.099	.049		8	0.041	.022		8	0.156	.010
	7	0.028	.050		9	0.013	.022		9	0.054	.010
	8	0.008	.050	3.9	4	36.859	.002		10	0.018	.010
3.1	4	1.902	.032		5	1.830	.015	4.7	5	13.382	.003
	5	0.427	.042		6	0.485	.019		6	1.752	.007
	6	0.120	.044		7	0.153	.020		7	0.525	.008
	7	0.035	.045		8	0.050	.020		8	0.181	.008
	8	0.010	.045		9	0.016	.020		9	0.064	.009
3.2	4	2.386	.027	4.0	5	2.216	.013		10	0.022	.009
	5	0.513	.037		6	0.570	.017	4.8	5	21.641	.002
	6	0.145	.040		7	0.180	.018		6	2.071	.006
	7	0.043	.040		8	0.059	.018		7	0.607	.008
	8	0.012	.041		9	0.019	.018		8	0.209	.008
3.3	4	3.027	.023	4.1	5	2.703	.011		9	0.074	.008
	5	0.615	.033		6	0.668	.015		10	0.026	.008
	6	0.174	.036		7	0.212	.016	4.9	5	46.566	.001
	7	0.052	.037		8	0.070	.016		6	2.459	.005
	8	0.015	.037		9	0.023	.017		7	0.702	.007
3.4	4	3.906	.019	4.2	5	3.327	.009		8	0.242	.007
	5	0.737	.029		6	0.784	.013		9	0.087	.007
	6	0.209	.032		7	0.248	.014		10	0.031	.007
	7	0.063	.033		8	0.083	.015		11	0.011	.077
	8	0.019	.033		9	0.027	.015	5.0	6	2.938	.005
3.5	4	5.165	.015		10	0.009	.015		7	0.810	.006
	5	0.882	.026	4.3	5	4.149	.008		8	0.279	.006
	6	0.248	.029		6	0.919	.012		9	0.101	.007
	7	0.076	.030		7	0.289	.130		10	0.036	.007
	8	0.023	.030		8	0.097	.013		11	0.013	.007
	9	0.007	.030		9	0.033	.014	5.1	6	3.536	.004

Table 18-4

(concluded)

λ/μ	M	Lq	P_o	λ/μ	M	Lq	P_o	λ/μ	M	Lq	P_o
	7	0.936	.005		8	0.483	.004	5.7	6	16.446	.001
	8	0.321	.006		9	0.178	.004		7	2.264	.002
	9	0.117	.006		10	0.066	.004		8	0.721	.003
	10	0.042	.006		11	0.024	.005		9	0.266	.003
	11	0.015	.006		12	0.009	.005		10	0.102	.003
5.2	6	4.301	.003	5.5	6	8.590	.002		11	0.038	.003
	7	1.081	.005		7	1.674	.003		12	0.014	.003
	8	0.368	.005		8	0.553	.004	5.8	6	26.373	.001
	9	0.135	.005		9	0.204	.004		7	2.648	.002
	10	0.049	.005		10	0.077	.004		8	0.823	.003
	11	0.017	.006		11	0.028	.004		9	0.303	.003
5.3	6	5.303	.003		12	0.010	.004		10	0.116	.003
	7	1.249	.004	5.6	6	11.519	.001		11	0.044	.003
5.3	8	0.422	.005		7	1.944	.003		12	0.017	.003
	9	0.155	.005		8	0.631	.003	5.9	6	56.300	.000
	10	0.057	.005		9	0.233	.004		7	3.113	.002
	11	0.021	.005		10	0.088	.004		8	0.939	.002
	12	0.007	.005		11	0.033	.004		9	0.345	.003
5.4	6	6.661	.002		12	0.012	.004		10	0.133	.003
	7	1.444	.004								

Two new measures are given in Table 18-3: W_a and P_W. W_a is the average wait time for only those customers who have to wait. Note that $W_a > W_q$ because W_q also contains those customers who do not have to wait. P_W is the probability that a customer has to wait. These three terms are related through the following relationship:

W_q = average wait time if customer does not have to wait × probability of not waiting
 + average wait time if customer has to wait × probability of waiting

$$= 0(1 - P_W) + W_a P_W \text{ or, } P_W = \frac{W_q}{W_a}.$$

Example 6

A taxi company has seven cars stationed at an airport during late evening hours on week-nights. The company has determined that customers request taxis during these times at rates that follow Poisson distribution with a mean of 6.6 per hour. Service durations are Exponential with a mean of 50 minutes (including the return time to the airport). Find each of the performance measures listed in Table 18-3, and each taxi's utilization. Use $t = 5$ minutes in formula 18-22.

Solution

$\lambda = 6.6$ per hour $M = 7$ taxis (servers)

$$\mu = \frac{1}{50 \text{ minutes} \div 60 \text{ minutes per hour}}$$

$$= 1.2 \text{ per hour}$$

$\lambda/\mu = \dfrac{6.6}{1.2} = 5.5$. From Table 18-4, for $\dfrac{\lambda}{M} = 5.5$ and $M = 7$ we get $L_q = 1.674$

and $P_0 = .003$

$$P_1 = \frac{1}{1!}(5.5)^1(.003) = .0176$$

$$P_2 = \frac{1}{2!}(5.5)^2(.003) = .0484$$

$$\ldots$$

$$W_a = \frac{1}{M\mu - \lambda} = \frac{1}{7(1.2) - 6.6} = .556 \text{ hour, or } 33.36 \text{ minutes}$$

$$W_q = \frac{L_q}{\lambda} = \frac{1.674}{6.6} = .2536 \text{ hour, or } 15.22 \text{ minutes}$$

$$P_W = \frac{W_q}{W_a} = \frac{.2536}{.556} = .456$$

$$\rho = \frac{\lambda}{M\mu} = \frac{6.6}{7(1.2)} = .786$$

$$P_{w\,in\,Q > \frac{5}{60}} = \frac{\left(\frac{6.6}{1.2}\right)^7 (.003)}{7!\left(1 - \frac{6.6}{7(1.2)}\right)} e^{-7(1.2)\left(1 - \frac{6.6}{7(1.2)}\right)\left(\frac{5}{60}\right)} = \left(\frac{456.73}{1080}\right) e^{-.15} = 0.364$$

$$\text{or } 36.4\%$$

The Excel template provided on *Connect* can also be used to solve Example 6. After entering $\lambda = 6.6$ and $\mu = 1.2$ at the top of the template, the queuing statistics for 7 servers are shown in the $M = 7$ column of the table in the template. Note that Excel is a little more accurate because it carries several decimal digits. The template also provides queuing statistics for 6 and 8 through 11 servers, although these are not required for this example. In addition, the template can be used to increment λ and μ by a small amount, to perform sensitivity analysis.

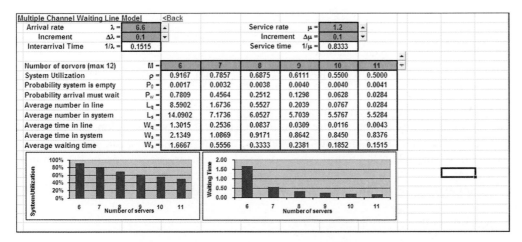

Multiple Channel Waiting Line Model	<Back						
Arrival rate	$\lambda =$	6.6		Service rate	$\mu =$	1.2	
Increment	$\Delta\lambda =$	0.1		Increment	$\Delta\mu =$	0.1	
Interarrival Time	$1/\lambda =$	0.1515		Service time	$1/\mu =$	0.8333	

		6	7	8	9	10	11
Number of servers (max 12)	$M =$	6	7	8	9	10	11
System Utilization	$\rho =$	0.9167	0.7857	0.6875	0.6111	0.5500	0.5000
Probability system is empty	$P_0 =$	0.0017	0.0032	0.0038	0.0040	0.0040	0.0041
Probability arrival must wait	$P_w =$	0.7809	0.4564	0.2512	0.1298	0.0628	0.0284
Average number in line	$L_q =$	8.5902	1.6736	0.5527	0.2039	0.0767	0.0284
Average number in system	$L_s =$	14.0902	7.1736	6.0527	5.7039	5.5767	5.5284
Average time in line	$W_q =$	1.3015	0.2536	0.0837	0.0309	0.0116	0.0043
Average time in system	$W_s =$	2.1349	1.0869	0.9171	0.8642	0.8450	0.8376
Average waiting time	$W_a =$	1.6667	0.5556	0.3333	0.2381	0.1852	0.1515

Determining the Number of Servers Using Wait Time Standards

So far we have determined the performance measures of Model 5 using λ, μ and M. However, we can also do the reverse; that is, we can determine the number of servers M needed to achieve specified levels of various performance measures. This approach is illustrated in the following example.

OM in ACTION   http://www.llbean.com

L.L. Bean

L.L. Bean is a catalogue phone-order outdoors-clothing company. It has two large call centres in Maine that receive orders and answer questions. Like other call centres, capacity issues for these call centres range from "long" term (i.e., number of phone lines, called trunks, to install) to "medium" term (i.e., number of agents to employ) to short term (i.e., staff scheduling). L.L. Bean determines the number of trunks to install (on a bi-weekly basis), the number of stations and agents to employ (on a weekly basis), and the maximum size of queue and the number of staff on duty (on a half-hour basis). These are determined hierarchically using a search procedure. L.L. Bean uses the finite line-length version of the multi server model (Model 6) for two of these (see the following diagram): (a) for determining the number of trunks s_t, (the line length is assumed to be zero, i.e., the number of calls in the trunks system = the number of trunks s_t); and (b) for determining the number of agents on duty s_a and maximum queue size $K - s_a$ (after getting in but before talking to an agent). For each two-week period, a search procedure uses both the trunks model and agents queue model (for every half-hour within the two-week period) with various values of s_t, s_a, and K, $s_a \leq K \leq s_t$. For each set of values for s_t, s_a, and K, the probability of being blocked (getting a busy signal) and average customer connect time are determined. The set of value (s_t, s_a, and K) over all half-hour periods of the two-week period that minimizes the total cost of lost orders (due to being blocked), connect time, and staff pay is the optimal solution. A small number of calls, about 1–2 percent, abandon the queue system because of excessive wait. These are ignored in the optimization. Before the above method, L.L. Beans used the following target service goal to determine the values for s_t, s_a, and K: the percent of calls that wait more than 20 seconds is at most 15 percent.

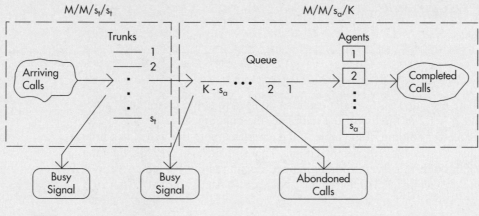

KEY:
s_t : number of trunks installed
s_a : number of agents on-duty
K : system capacity for calls waiting and in service

Source: P. Quinn, et al, "Allocating Telecommunications Resources at L. L. Bean, Inc.," *Interfaces*, 21(1), January–February 1991, pp. 75–91.

Example 7

The taxi company of Example 6 also plans to have taxis at a new rail station. The expected customer requests for taxis there during weekday mornings is 4.8 per hour, and the average service time (including the return time to the rail station) is expected to be 40 minutes. How many taxis will be needed to achieve an average customer wait time in line of close to but not exceeding 10 minutes during weekday mornings?

Solution

$\lambda = 4.8$ per hour

$\mu = \dfrac{1}{\left(\dfrac{40}{60}\right)} = 1.5$ per hour

$M = ?$

$W_q(\text{desired}) = 10$ minutes, or .167 hour

Using $L_q = \lambda W_q$, $L_q = (4.8/\text{hour})\ (.167\ \text{hour}) = .8$. Thus, the average number waiting should be close to but not exceed .8. Referring to Table 18-4, with $\lambda/\mu = 4.8/1.5 = 3.2$, we obtain $L_q = 2.386$ for $M = 4$ and 0.513 for $M = 5$. Hence, five taxis will be needed during weekday mornings.

Determining the Number of Servers by Minimizing Total Cost

Instead of achieving a performance measure standard (e.g., the average wait time should be close to but not exceed 10 minutes), we can determine the number of servers by minimizing the sum of total average customer wait cost and total servers pay cost. Thus, the goal is:

Minimize total cost = Total average customer wait cost + Total servers pay cost

An iterative process is used to identify the number of servers that will minimize the total cost. The number of servers is incremented one unit at a time and the total cost is calculated at each increment. Because the total cost curve is U-shaped, the total cost will initially decrease as number of servers is increased and then it will eventually begin to increase. The optimal number of servers is the value just before the total cost increases.

Total average customer wait time in the system during an hour is equal to the average number of customers arriving during the hour multiplied by the average wait time per customer in the system; that is, λW_s. But this equals L_s by Little's formula. To save on calculations, we will use the formula $L_s = L_q + \dfrac{\lambda}{\mu}$ to obtain the total average customer wait time in the system.

Example 8

Trucks arrive at a warehouse at an average rate of 15 per hour during business hours. A crew of four work together to unload the trucks at an average rate of five per hour. (Both distributions are Poisson.) Both the trucks and the warehouse belong to the same company. Recent changes in wage rates and truck and driver costs have caused the warehouse manager to re-examine the question of how many crews to use. The new rates are the following: a crew (of four) costs $100 per hour; truck and driver cost $120 per hour. Assuming there are enough unloading docks, how many crews should the manager use?

Solution

L_q values are from Table 18-4 using $\dfrac{\lambda}{\mu} = \dfrac{15}{5} = 3.0$.

Crew Size	Crew Cost	$\left[L_s = L_q + \dfrac{\lambda}{\mu} \right]$ Total Average Wait Time in System per Hour	$[L_s \times \$120]$ Total Average Driver/Truck Wait Cost per Hour	Total Cost
4	$400	$1.528 + 3.0 = 4.528$	$543.36	$943.36
5	500	$.354 + 3.0 = 3.354$	402.48	902.48 (minimum)
6	600	$.099 + 3.0 = 3.099$	371.88	971.88
7	700	$.028 + 3.0 = 3.028$	363.36	1,063.36

Five crews will minimize the total cost. Because the total cost will continue to increase once the minimum is reached, it is not necessary to calculate the total cost for crew sizes larger than six.

One additional point should be made concerning the total cost approach. Because customer wait cost is often estimated, the apparent optimal solution may not represent the true optimum. If wait cost estimates can be obtained as *ranges* (e.g., between $40 and $50 per hour), total cost should be calculated using both ends of the range to see whether the optimal solution is different. If it is, management must decide whether to expend additional effort to obtain more precise cost estimates or to choose one of the two indicated optimal solutions.

Model 6: Multiple Servers, Exponential Service Durations, Finite Number in System

In many cases, the number of customers or calls that can fit in the queuing system is limited. Let K = maximum number of customers (or calls) in the queuing system (in line and being served). Obviously, $K \geq M$, the number of servers. If there are K customers already in the queuing system, the next customer will not be allowed to enter the system and has to balk (leave). The probability of this is P_K. Because P_K proportion of customers are lost, the effective average arrival rate is $\lambda(1 - p_K)$. The formulas in this case are as follows:

$$P_o = \left[\sum_{n=0}^{M-1} \frac{\left(\frac{\lambda}{\mu}\right)^n}{n!} + \frac{\left(\frac{\lambda}{\mu}\right)^M \left(1 - \left(\frac{\lambda}{M\mu}\right)^{K-M+1}\right)}{M! \left(1 - \frac{\lambda}{M\mu}\right)} \right]^{-1} \tag{18-23}$$

$$L_q = \frac{\left(\frac{\lambda}{\mu}\right)^{M+1} P_o}{(M-1)! \left(M - \frac{\lambda}{\mu}\right)^2} \left(1 - \left(\frac{\lambda}{M\mu}\right)^{K-M+1} - (K-M+1)\left(1 - \frac{\lambda}{M\mu}\right)\left(\frac{\lambda}{M\mu}\right)^{K-M}\right) \tag{18-24}$$

$$P_K = \frac{\left(\frac{\lambda}{\mu}\right)^K P_o}{M^{K-M} M!} \tag{18-25}$$

$$W_q = \frac{L_q}{\lambda(1 - P_K)} \tag{18-26}$$

Example 9

Reconsider Example 6, but assume that no more than 15 customers will wait for a taxi (the 16th customer will use the more expensive limousine service). Calculate:

a. The average number of customers waiting and compare it with Example 6.

b. The probability of balking.

c. The average time a customer is in the system, and compare it with Example 6.

Solution

Recall that $\lambda = 6.6$ per hour, $\mu = 1.2$ per hour, and $M = 7$. Now, we also have $K = 15$.

a. $P_o = \left[1 + \left(\frac{6.6}{1.2}\right) + \frac{\left(\frac{6.6}{1.2}\right)^2}{2} + \frac{\left(\frac{6.6}{1.2}\right)^3}{6} + \frac{\left(\frac{6.6}{1.2}\right)^4}{24} + \frac{\left(\frac{6.6}{1.2}\right)^5}{120} + \frac{\left(\frac{6.6}{1.2}\right)^6}{720} + \frac{\left(\frac{6.6}{1.2}\right)^7 \left(1 - \left(\frac{6.6}{8.4}\right)^9\right)}{7!\left(1 - \frac{6.6}{8.4}\right)}\right]^{-1}$

$= [1 + 5.5 + 15.125 + 27.7292 + 38.1276 + 41.9404 + 38.4453 + 124.8784]^{-1} = .003416$

$L_q = \frac{\left(\frac{6.6}{1.2}\right)^8 .003416}{6!\left(7 - \frac{6.6}{1.2}\right)^2} \left(1 - \left(\frac{6.6}{8.4}\right)^9 - 9\left(1 - \frac{6.6}{8.4}\right)\left(\frac{6.6}{8.4}\right)^8\right) = 1.070$ customers < 1.674

customers in Example 6.

b. $P_{15} = \frac{\left(\frac{6.6}{1.2}\right)^{15} .003416}{7^8 7!} = .015$ or 1.5%. probability of balking.

c. $W_q = \frac{L_q}{\lambda(1 - P_K)} = \frac{1.070}{6.6(1 - .015)} = .1646$ hour or 9.88 minutes < 15.22 minutes

in Example 6.

For an application of Model 6, see the "L.L. Bean" OM in Action.

Model 7: Multiple Servers, General Inter-arrival and Service Durations[3]

The solution to this model is difficult to obtain. Thus, we will provide an approximate solution.

Let $\sigma_A =$ standard deviation of inter-arrival durations (i.e., the difference between arrival times of consecutive arrivals), and $\sigma_S =$ standard deviation of service durations.

Then,

$$L_q \approx \frac{\rho^{\sqrt{2(M+1)}}}{1-\rho} \times \frac{\mu^2 \sigma_S^2 + \lambda^2 \sigma_A^2}{2} \tag{18-27)[4]}$$

Example 10

An airport hotel receives groups of guests by airport shuttle vans. Each van may contain various numbers of guests arriving together. The average number of guests arriving per hour during workday afternoons is forecast to be 30 and the standard deviation of inter-arrival time is estimated to be three minutes. The check-in process takes a constant time of one minute plus an Exponential time with a mean of two minutes. According to hotel policy, the average waiting time in line should not exceed three minutes. Are two employees at the check-in counter adequate during workday afternoons?

Solution

$\lambda = 30$ guests per hour, $\sigma_A = 3$ minutes $= .05$ hour
$\mu = 60 / 3 = 20$ guests per hour, $\sigma_S = 2$ minutes $= .0333$ hour (Note: the constant part of service duration does not contribute to the standard deviation. The standard deviation of an Exponential distribution is equal to its mean).
$M = 2$.

$$\rho = \frac{\lambda}{M\mu} = \frac{30}{2(20)} = .75$$

$$L_q \approx \frac{.75^{\sqrt{2(2+1)}}}{1-.75} \times \frac{20^2(.0333)^2 + 30^2(.05)^2}{2} = 2.6627$$

$$W_q = \frac{L_q}{\lambda} = \frac{2.6627}{30} = .08876 \text{ hour or } 5.3 \text{ minutes} > 3 \text{ minutes} \rightarrow \text{No, 2 check-in counter}$$

employees are not adequate.

Model 8: Multiple Servers with Priority, Exponential Service Durations

In many queuing systems, processing occurs on a first-come, first-served (FCFS) basis. However, there are situations in which FCFS is inappropriate. The reason is that the waiting cost or penalty incurred may not be the same for all the customers. For example, in a hospital emergency waiting room, a wide variety of injuries and illnesses need treatment.

---

[3]R.B. Chase et al., *Operations Management for Competitive Advantage*, 10th ed. (Boston: Irwin, 2004).

[4]We will evaluate the performance of this approximation by comparing it with the results of Examples 6 and 7. In Example 6, $\lambda = 6.6$, $\mu = 1.2$, $M = 7$, and $\rho = .786$. It is well known that the standard deviation of an Exponential distribution equals its mean. Therefore, $\sigma_A = \frac{1}{\lambda}$ and $\sigma_S = \frac{1}{\mu}$. Substituting these in the L_q formula 18-27 results in:

$$L_q = \frac{0.786^{\sqrt{2(7+1)}}}{1-0.786} \times \frac{1+1}{2} = 1.784, \text{ which is very close to } L_q = 1.674 \text{ value obtained in Example 6.}$$

In Example 7, $\lambda = 4.8$, $\mu = 1.5$, $\rho = \frac{4.8}{5(1.5)} = .64$. Substituting these in the L_q formula 18-27 results in:

$$L_q = \frac{.64^{\sqrt{2(5+1)}}}{1-.64} \times \frac{1+1}{2} = .592, \text{ which is very close to } L_q = .513 \text{ value obtained in Example 7 for } M = 5.$$

multiple-server-with-priority model Customers (jobs) are processed not FCFS, but according to some measure of importance.

Some may be minor (e.g., sliver in finger) and others may be much more serious, even life threatening. It is more reasonable to treat the most serious cases first, letting the non-serious cases wait until all serious cases have been treated. Similarly, computer processing of jobs on large mainframe computers often follows rules other than FCFS (e.g., shortest job first). In such cases, a **multiple-server-with-priority model** is useful for describing the queueing system.

This model incorporates all of the assumptions of the multiple-server, Exponential service durations model (Model 5) except that it uses priority service rule instead of FCFS. Arrivals to the system are assigned a priority as they arrive (e.g., highest priority = 1, next priority class = 2, next priority class = 3, and so on). Let λ_k be the average arrival rate of priority class K. We have $\lambda = \Sigma \lambda_k$. An existing queue might look something like this:

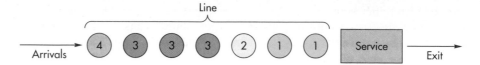

Within each class, waiting units are processed in the order they arrived (i.e., FCFS). Thus, in this sequence, the first 1 would be processed as soon as a server becomes available. The second 1 would be processed when that server or another one becomes available. We assume that each server can process any customer with any priority class and that the average service time is $\frac{1}{\mu}$ for any arrival. If, in the interim, another 1 arrived, it would be next in line *ahead of the first 2*. If there were no new arrivals, the only 2 would be processed by the next available server. At that point, if a new 1 or 2 arrived, it would be processed ahead of the 3s and the 4. We assume that any service already in progress would not be *preempted* or interrupted for another customer.

Obviously, a unit with a low priority could conceivably wait a rather long time for processing. In some cases, units that have waited more than a specified time are reassigned a higher priority.

Table 18-5 gives the appropriate formulas for the multiple-server-with-priority model.

Table 18-5	Performance Measure	Formula	Formula Number
Multiple-server-with-priority model	Server utilization	$\rho = \dfrac{\lambda}{M\mu}$	(18-28)
	Intermediate values (L_q from Table 18-4)	$A = \dfrac{\lambda}{(1-\rho)L_q}$	(18-29)
		$B_k = 1 - \displaystyle\sum_{c=1}^{k} \dfrac{\lambda_c}{M\mu}$ $(B_o = 1)$	(18-30)
	Average wait time in line for units in kth priority class	$W_k = \dfrac{1}{A \cdot B_{k-1} \cdot B_k}$	(18-31)
	Average time in the system for units in the kth priority class	$W = W_k + \dfrac{1}{\mu}$	(18-32)
	Average number of the kth priority class waiting in line	$L_k = \lambda_k \times W_k$	(18-33)

Example 11

A machine shop handles tool repairs in a large company. As each job arrives in the shop, it is assigned a priority based on urgency of the need for that tool: priority 1 is the highest and priority 3 is the lowest. Number of requests for repair per hour can be described by a Poisson distribution. Average arrival rates are: $\lambda_1 = 2$ per hour, $\lambda_2 = 2$ per hour, and

$\lambda_3 = 1$ per hour. The average service rate is one tool per hour for each mechanic, and the service rate has Poisson distribution. There are six mechanics in the shop. Determine the value of the following measures:

a. The server utilization.

b. The average time a tool in each of the priority classes will wait for repair.

c. The average time a tool spends in the system for each priority class.

d. The average number of tools waiting for repair in each class.

Solution

$$\lambda = \Sigma\lambda_k = 2 + 2 + 1 = 5 \text{ per hour}$$

$$M = 6 \text{ servers}$$

$$\mu = 1 \text{ tool per hour}$$

a. $\rho = \dfrac{\lambda}{M\mu} = \dfrac{5}{6(1)} = .833$

b. Intermediate values. For $\lambda/\mu = 5/1 = 5$ and $M = 6$, from Table 18-4, $L_q = 2.938$

$$A = \dfrac{5}{(1 - .833)2.938} = 10.19$$

$$B_0 = 1$$

$$B_1 = 1 - \dfrac{2}{6(1)} = \dfrac{2}{3} = .667$$

$$B_2 = 1 - \dfrac{2 + 2}{6(1)} = \dfrac{1}{3} = .333$$

$$B_3 = 1 - \dfrac{2 + 2 + 1}{6(1)} = \dfrac{1}{6} = .167$$

$$W_1 = \dfrac{1}{A \cdot B_0 \cdot B_1} = \dfrac{1}{10.19(1)(.667)} = .147 \text{ hour}$$

$$W_2 = \dfrac{1}{A \cdot B_1 \cdot B_2} = \dfrac{1}{10.19(.667)(.333)} = .442 \text{ hour}$$

$$W_3 = \dfrac{1}{A \cdot B_2 \cdot B_3} = \dfrac{1}{10.19(.333)(.167)} = 1.765 \text{ hours}$$

c. $W = W_k + 1/\mu$. In this case, $1/\mu = 1/1 = 1$. Thus:

Class	$W_k + 1 = W$ Hours
1	$.147 + 1 = 1.147$
2	$.442 + 1 = 1.442$
3	$1.765 + 1 = 2.765$

d. The average number of units waiting for repair in each class is $L_k = \lambda_k W_k$. Thus:

Class	$\lambda_k W_k = L_k$ Units
1	$2(.147) = .294$
2	$2(.442) = .884$
3	$1(1.765) = 1.765$

Using the Excel template on *Connect*, the solution to Example 11 would appear as follows:

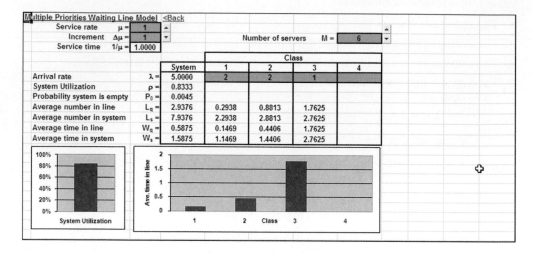

Note that the small differences between Excel and manual results are due to rounding.

Revising Priorities. If any of the wait times calculated in Example 11 are deemed too long by management (e.g., a wait time of .147 hour for tools in the first class might be too long), there are several options. One is to increase the number of servers. Another is to attempt to increase the service rate, say, by introducing new methods. If such options are not feasible, another approach is to re-examine the membership of each of the priority classes and relegate some jobs to lower priority classes. For example, if some repair requests in the first priority class can be reassigned to the second priority class, this will tend to decrease the average wait times for repair jobs in the highest priority class simply because the arrival rate of those items will be lower.

Example 12

The manager of the repair shop in Example 11, after consulting with the managers of the departments that use the shop's services, has revised the list of tools that are given the highest priorities. The revised average arrival rates are now: $\lambda_1 = 1.5$, $\lambda_2 = 2.5$, and λ_3 remains unchanged at 1.0. Determine the value of the following measures:

a. The server utilization.

b. The average waiting time for units in each priority class.

Solution

$$\lambda = \Sigma \lambda_k = 1.5 + 2.5 + 1.0 = 5.0$$
$$M = 6$$
$$\mu = 1$$

Note that these values are the same as in the previous example.

a. $\rho = \dfrac{\lambda}{M\mu} = 5.0/6(1) = .833$, the same as in the previous example.

b. The value of A, since it is a function of M, μ, and λ, is the same as in the preceding example because these values are the same. Therefore, $A = 10.19$ and

$$B_0 = 1 \text{ (always)}$$

$$B_1 = 1 - \frac{1.5}{6(1)} = .75$$

$$B_2 = 1 - \frac{1.5 + 2.5}{6(1)} = .333, \text{ same}$$

$$B_3 = 1 - \frac{1.5 + 2.5 + 1.0}{6(1)} = .167, \text{ same}$$

Then

$$W_1 = \frac{1}{10.19(1)(.75)} = .131 \text{ hour}$$

$$W_2 = \frac{1}{10.19(.75)(.333)} = .393 \text{ hour}$$

$$W_3 = \frac{1}{10.19(.333)(.167)} = 1.765 \text{ hour}$$

Example 12 offers several interesting results. One is that through reduction of the average arrival rate of the highest priority class, the average wait time for units in that class has decreased. In other words, removing some members of the highest class and placing them into the next lower class reduced the average wait time for units that remained in the highest class. It is interesting that the average wait time for the second priority class also was reduced, even though units were added to that class. Although this may appear counterintuitive, the *total* average wait time (or total average number waiting) will remain unchanged. We can see this by noticing that the average *number* waiting (see Example 11, part *d*) is .294 + .884 + 1.765 = 2.943. In Example 12, using the average wait times just calculated, the average number waiting in all three classes in total is

$$\sum_{k=1}^{3} \lambda_k W_k = 1.5(.131) + 2.5(.393) + 1.0(1.765) = 2.944.$$

Aside from a slight difference due to rounding, the totals are the same.

Another interesting observation is that the average wait time for customers in the third priority class did not change from the preceding example. The reason for this is that the *total* average arrival rates for the two higher-priority classes did not change and the average arrival rate for this class did not change.

LO6 QUEUING MODEL: FINITE SOURCE

The finite-source model is appropriate for cases in which the calling population is limited. For instance, in a queuing system for breakdowns of five machines, the size of the calling population is five.

As in the "infinite"-source models, arrival rates are assumed to be Poisson and service durations Exponential. A major difference between the finite- and "infinite"-source models is that the arrival rate of customers (machines) in a finite situation is *affected by* the length of the waiting line; the arrival rate decreases as the length of the line increases simply because there is a decreasing proportion of the population that is out and can generate calls for service. When *all* of the population is waiting in line, the arrival rate is zero because no additional units can arrive.

Because the mathematics of the finite-source model can be complex, analysts often use a table (Table 18-7) in conjunction with simple formulas to analyze these systems. Table 18-6 contains a list of the key formulas and definitions. The inputs to the model are the average service duration T, the average run duration U, the number of servers M, and total number of machines N. The desired quantities of interest are the average wait

	Formulas		Notation
Service factor	$X = \dfrac{T}{T+U}$	(18-34)	D = Probability that a machine will have to wait in line before service
Average number waiting	$L = N(1-F)$	(18-35)	F = Efficiency factor: proportion of machines being serviced or running
Average waiting time	$W = \dfrac{L(T+U)}{N-L} = \dfrac{T(1-F)}{XF}$	(18-36)	H = Average number of machines being serviced
Average number running	$J = NF(1-X)$	(18-37)	J = Average number of machines running
Average number being serviced	$H = FNX$	(18-38)	L = Average number of machines waiting for service
			M = Number of servers
Number in population	$N = J + L + H$	(18-39)	N = Number of machines
			T = Average service duration
			U = Average run duration
			W = Average wait duration
			X = Service factor; proportion of average service duration to sum of average service and average run durations

Cycle

	Running	Waiting	Being serviced
Average number:	J	L	H
Average time:	U	W	T

time (before service) W, average number running J, the average number in line L, and the average number in service H. You will find it helpful to study the diagram of a run-wait-service cycle that is presented in Table 18-6.

Table 18-7 is an abbreviated finite-source model table used to obtain values of D and F, given X and M. (Most of the formulas require a value for F.) In order to use this table, follow this procedure:

1. Identify the values for
   a. N, population size.
   b. M, number of servers.
   c. T, average service duration.
   d. U, average run duration.

2. Calculate the service factor, $X = T/(T+U)$.

3. Locate the section of the finite-source model table for population size N. (Only values for $N = 5$ and 10 are shown here because of space limitation.)

4. Using the value of X as the point of entry, find the values of F and D that correspond to M.

5. Use the value of F to determine the values of the desired measures of system performance using the formulas in Table 18-6.

Table 18-7

Finite-source model table; values for D and F, given values for X and M.

X	M	D	F	X	M	D	F	X	M	D	F	X	M	D	F
		Population 5		.110	2	.065	.996	.220	3	.036	.997		1	.911	.569
.012	1	.048	.999		1	.421	.939		2	.229	.969	.360	4	.017	.998
.019	1	.076	.998	.115	2	.017	.995		1	.735	.765		3	.141	.981
.025	1	.100	.997		1	.439	.933	.230	3	.041	.997		2	.501	.880
.030	1	.120	.996	.120	2	.076	.995		2	.247	.965		1	.927	.542
.034	1	.135	.995		1	.456	.927		1	.756	.747	.380	4	.021	.998
.036	1	.143	.994	.125	2	.082	.994	.240	3	.046	.996		3	.163	.976
.040	1	.159	.993		1	.473	.920		2	.265	.960		2	.540	.863
.042	1	.167	.992	.130	2	.089	.933		1	.775	.730		1	.941	.516
.044	1	.175	.991		1	.489	.914	.250	3	.052	.995	.400	4	.026	.997
.046	1	.183	.990	.135	2	.095	.933		2	.284	.955		3	.186	.972
.050	1	.198	.989		1	.505	.907		1	.794	.712		2	.579	.845
.052	1	.206	.988	.140	2	.102	.992	.260	3	.058	.994		1	.952	.493
.054	1	.214	.987		1	.521	.900		2	.303	.950	.420	4	.031	.997
.056	2	.018	.999	.145	3	.011	.999		1	.811	.695		3	.211	.966
	1	.222	.985		2	.109	.991	.270	3	.064	.994		2	.616	.826
.058	2	.019	.999		1	.537	.892		2	.323	.944		1	.961	.471
	1	.229	.984	.150	3	.012	.999		1	.827	.677	.440	4	.037	.996
.060	2	.020	.999		2	.115	.990	.280	3	.071	.993		3	.238	.960
	1	.237	.983		1	.553	.885		2	.342	.938		2	.652	.807
.062	2	.022	.999	.155	3	.013	.999		1	.842	.661		1	.969	.451
	1	.245	.982		2	.123	.989	.290	4	.007	.999	.460	4	.045	.995
.064	2	.023	.999		1	.568	.877		3	.079	.992		3	.266	.953
	1	.253	.981	.160	3	.015	.999		2	.362	.932		2	.686	.787
.066	2	.024	.999		2	.130	.988		1	.856	.644		1	.975	.432
	1	.260	.979		1	.582	.869	.300	4	.008	.999	.480	4	.053	.994
.068	2	.026	.999	.165	3	.016	.999		3	.086	.990		3	.296	.945
	1	.268	.978		2	.137	.987		2	.382	.926		2	.719	.767
.070	2	.027	.999		1	.597	.861		1	.869	.628		1	.980	.415
	1	.275	.977	.170	3	.017	.999	.310	4	.009	.999	.500	4	.063	.992
.075	2	.031	.999		2	.145	.985		3	.094	.989		3	.327	.936
	1	.294	.973		1	.611	.853		2	.402	.919		2	.750	.748
.080	2	.035	.998	.180	3	.021	.999		1	.881	.613		1	.985	.399
	1	.313	.969		2	.161	.983	.320	4	.010	.999	.520	4	.073	.991
.085	2	.040	.998		1	.683	.836		3	.103	.988		3	.359	.927
	1	.332	.965	.190	3	.024	.998		2	.422	.912		2	.779	.728
.090	2	.044	.998		2	.117	.980		1	.892	.597		1	.988	.384
	1	.350	.960		1	.665	.819	.330	4	.012	.999	.540	4	.085	.989
.095	2	.049	.997	.200	3	.028	.998		3	.112	.986		3	.392	.917
	1	.368	.955		2	.194	.976		2	.442	.904		2	.806	.708
.100	2	.054	.997		1	.689	.801		1	.902	.583		1	.991	.370
	1	.386	.950	.210	3	.032	.998	.340	4	.013	.999	.560	4	.098	.986
.105	2	.059	.997		2	.211	.973		3	.121	.985		3	.426	.906
	1	.404	.945		1	.713	.783		2	.462	.896	.560	2	.831	.689

Table 18-7
(continued)

X	M	D	F	X	M	D	F	X	M	D	F	X	M	D	F
	1	.993	.357	.038	2	.046	.999		2	.216	.986		3	.169	.987
.580	4	.113	.984		1	.337	.982		1	.722	.867		2	.505	.928
	3	.461	.895	.040	2	.050	.999	.095	3	.049	.998		1	.947	.627
	2	.854	.670		1	.354	.980		2	.237	.984	.160	4	.044	.998
	1	.994	.345	.042	2	.055	.999		1	.750	.850		3	.182	.986
.600	4	.130	.981		1	.371	.978	.100	3	.056	.998		2	.528	.921
	3	.497	.883	.044	2	.060	.998		2	.258	.981		1	.954	.610
	2	.875	.652		1	.388	.975		1	.776	.832	.165	4	.049	.997
	1	.996	.333	.046	2	.065	.998	.105	3	.064	.997		3	.195	.984
.650	4	.179	.972		1	.404	.973		2	.279	.978		2	.550	.914
	3	.588	.850	.048	2	.071	.998		1	.800	.814		1	.961	.594
	2	.918	.608		1	.421	.970	.110	3	.072	.997	.170	4	.054	.997
	1	.998	.308	.050	2	.076	.998		2	.301	.974		3	.209	.982
.700	4	.240	.960		1	.437	.967		1	.822	.795		2	.571	.906
	3	.678	.815	.052	2	.082	.997	.115	3	.081	.996		1	.966	.579
	2	.950	.568		1	.454	.963		2	.324	.971	.180	5	.013	.999
	1	.999	.286	.054	2	.088	.997		1	.843	.776		4	.066	.996
.750	4	.316	.944		1	.470	.960	.120	4	.016	.999		3	.238	.978
	3	.763	.777	.056	2	.094	.997		3	.090	.995		2	.614	.890
	2	.972	.532		1	.486	.956		2	.346	.967		1	.975	.890
.800	4	.410	.924	.058	2	.100	.996		1	.861	.756	.190	5	.016	.999
	3	.841	.739		1	.501	.953	.125	4	.019	.999		4	.078	.995
	2	.987	.500	.060	2	.106	.996		3	.100	.994		3	.269	.973
.850	4	.522	.900		1	.517	.949		2	.369	.962		2	.654	.873
	3	.907	.702	.062	2	.113	.996		1	.878	.737		1	.982	.522
	2	.995	.470		1	.532	.945	.130	4	.022	.999	.200	5	.020	.999
.900	4	.656	.871	.064	2	.119	.995		3	.110	.994		4	.092	.994
	3	.957	.666		1	.547	.940		2	.392	.958		3	.300	.968
	2	.998	.444	.066	2	.126	.995		1	.893	.718		2	.692	.854
.950	4	.815	.838		1	.562	.936	.135	4	.025	.999		1	.987	.497
	3	.989	.631	.068	3	.020	.999		3	.121	.993	.210	5	.025	.999
Population 10					2	.133	.994		2	.415	.952		4	.108	.992
.016	1	.144	.997		1	.577	.931		1	.907	.699		3	.333	.961
.019	1	.170	.996	.070	3	.022	.999	.140	4	.028	.999		2	.728	.835
.021	1	.188	.995		2	.140	.994		3	.132	.991		1	.990	.474
.023	1	.206	.994		1	.591	.926		2	.437	.947	.220	5	.030	.998
.025	1	.224	.993	.075	3	.026	.999		1	.919	.680		4	.124	.990
.026	1	.232	.992		2	.158	.992	.145	4	.032	.999		3	.366	.954
.028	1	.250	.991		1	.627	.913		3	.144	.990	.220	2	.761	.815
.030	1	.268	.990	.080	3	.031	.999		2	.460	.941		1	.993	.453
.032	2	.033	.999		2	.177	.990		1	.929	.662	.230	5	.037	.998
	1	.285	.988		1	.660	.899	.150	4	.036	.998		4	.142	.988
.034	2	.037	.999	.085	3	.037	.999		3	.156	.989		3	.400	.947
	1	.301	.986		2	.196	.988		2	.483	.935		2	.791	.794
.036	2	.041	.999		1	.692	.883		1	.939	.644		1	.995	.434
	1	.320	.984	.090	3	.043	.998	.155	4	.040	.998	.240	5	.044	.997

Table 18-7

(concluded)

X	M	D	F	X	M	D	F	X	M	D	F	X	M	D	F
	4	.162	.986		5	.135	.988		7	.058	.995		8	.072	.994
	3	.434	.938		4	.359	.952		6	.193	.979		7	.242	.972
	2	.819	.774		3	.695	.845		5	.445	.930		6	.518	.915
	1	.996	.416		2	.952	.617		4	.747	.822		5	.795	.809
.250	6	.010	.999	.330	6	.042	.997		3	.947	.646		4	.953	.663
	5	.052	.997		5	.151	.986		2	.998	.435		3	.996	.500
	4	.183	.983		4	.387	.945	.480	8	.015	.999	.650	9	.021	.999
	3	.469	.929		3	.723	.831		7	.074	.994		8	.123	.988
	2	.844	.753		2	.961	.600		6	.230	.973		7	.353	.954
	1	.997	.400	.340	7	.010	.999		5	.499	.916	.650	6	.651	.878
.260	6	.013	.999		6	.049	.997		4	.791	.799		5	.882	.759
	5	.060	.996		5	.168	.983		3	.961	.621		4	.980	.614
	4	.205	.980		4	.416	.938		2	.998	.417		3	.999	.461
	3	.503	.919		3	.750	.816	.500	8	.020	.999	.700	9	.040	.997
	2	.866	.732		2	.968	.584		7	.093	.992		8	.200	.979
	1	.998	.384	.360	7	.014	.999		6	.271	.966		7	.484	.929
.270	6	.015	.999		6	.064	.995		5	.553	.901		6	.772	.836
	5	.070	.995		5	.205	.978	.500	4	.830	.775		5	.940	.711
	4	.228	.976		4	.474	.923		3	.972	.598		4	.992	.571
	3	.537	.908		3	.798	.787		2	.999	.400	.750	9	.075	.994
	2	.886	.712		2	.978	.553	.520	8	.026	.998		8	.307	.965
	1	.999	.370	.380	7	.019	.999		7	.115	.989		7	.626	.897
.280	6	.018	.999		6	.083	.993		6	.316	.958		6	.870	.792
	5	.081	.994		5	.247	.971		5	.606	.884		5	.975	.666
	4	.252	.972		4	.533	.906		4	.864	.752		4	.998	.533
	3	.571	.896		3	.840	.758		3	.980	.575	.800	9	.134	.988
	2	.903	.692		2	.986	.525		2	.999	.385		8	.446	.944
	1	.999	.357	.400	7	.026	.998	.540	8	.034	.997		7	.763	.859
.290	6	.022	.999		6	.105	.991		7	.141	.986	.800	6	.939	.747
	5	.093	.993		5	.292	.963		6	.363	.949		5	.991	.625
	4	.278	.968		4	.591	.887		5	.658	.867		4	.999	.500
	3	.603	.884		3	.875	.728		4	.893	.729	.850	9	.232	.979
	2	.918	.672		2	.991	.499		3	.986	.555		8	.611	.916
	1	.999	.345	.420	7	.034	.993	.560	8	.044	.996		7	.879	.818
.300	6	.026	.998		6	.130	.987		7	.171	.982		6	.978	.705
	5	.106	.991		5	.341	.954		6	.413	.939		5	.998	.588
	4	.304	.963		4	.646	.866	.560	5	.707	.848	.900	9	.387	.963
	3	.635	.872		3	.905	.700		4	.917	.706		8	.785	.881
	2	.932	.653		2	.994	.476		3	.991	.535		7	.957	.777
	1	.999	.333	.440	7	.045	.997	.580	8	.057	.995		6	.995	.667
.310	6	.031	.998		6	.160	.984		7	.204	.977	.950	9	.630	.938
	5	.120	.990		5	.392	.943		6	.465	.927		8	.934	.841
	4	.331	.957		4	.698	.845		5	.753	.829		7	.994	.737
	3	.666	.858		3	.928	.672		4	.937	.684				
	2	.943	.635		2	.996	.454		3	.994	.517				
.320	6	.036	.998	.460	8	.011	.999	.600	9	.010	.999				

Source: L.G. Peck and R.N. Hazelwood, *Finite Queuing Tables* (New York: John Wiley & Sons, 1958). Reprinted by permission.

Example 13

One operator loads and unloads a group of five machines. Service durations (i.e., one unloading and loading) are Exponentially distributed with a mean of 10 minutes per machine. Machines run for an average of 70 minutes between loading and unloading, and this duration is also Exponential. Find:

a. The average number of machines waiting for the operator.

b. The expected number of machines running.

c. Average duration of downtime.

d. The probability that a machine will not have to wait for service.

Solution

$N = 5$

$T = 10$ minutes

$M = 1$

$U = 70$ minutes

$$X = \frac{T}{T+U} = \frac{10}{10+70} = .125$$

From Table 18-7, with $N = 5$, $M = 1$, and $X = .125$, we obtain $D = .473$ and $F = .920$.

a. Average number waiting, $L = N(1 - F) = 5(1 - .920) = .40$ machine.

b. Expected number running, $J = NF(1 - X) = 5(.92)(1 - .125) = 4.025$ machines.

c. Downtime = Waiting time + Service time:

$$\text{Average waiting time } W = \frac{L(T+U)}{N-L} = \frac{.40(10+70)}{5-.40} = 6.957 \text{ minutes}$$

Downtime = 6.957 minutes + 10 minutes = 16.957 minutes

d. Probability of not having to wait = 1 − Probability of having to wait

$$= 1 - D$$
$$= 1 - .473 = .527$$

Using the Excel template, the solution to Example 13 would appear as follows:

Finite Source Waiting Line Model					
<Back					
Population Size	N =	5	5		
Number of servers	M =	1	2		
Average service time	T =	10	10		
Average time between service calls	U =	70	70		
P(wait) - from table	D =	0.4730	0.0820		
Efficiency factor - from table	F =	0.9200	0.9940		
Service factor	χ =	0.125	0.125		
Average number waiting	L =	0.4000	0.0300		
Average waiting time	W =	6.9565	0.4829		
Average number running	J =	4.0250	4.3488		
Average number being serviced	H =	0.5750	0.6213		
	Per Time Unit				
Service cost =	10	10	20		
Downtime cost =	16	15.6	10.42		
Total Cost =		25.6	30.42		

Note: You must enter D and F (based on N, X, and M) from the table in the text.

Example 14

Suppose that in Example 13, the operator is paid $10 per hour and machine downtime costs $16 per hour. Should the department add another operator if the goal is total cost minimization?

Compare the total cost of the present system with the total cost of the proposed system: *Solution*

M	Average Number Down, $N-J$	Average Down Cost (per hour), $(N-J)$ X $16	Operator Cost (per hour)	Total Cost (per hour)
1	$5 - 4.025 = .975$	$15.60	$10	$25.60
2	.651	10.42	20	30.42

where $N-J$ for $M=2$ is obtained as follows: For $X=.125$ and $M=2$, from Table 18-7 $F=.994$; therefore $J=NF(1-X)=5(.994)(1-.125)=4.349$, and $N-J=5-4.349=.651$. Hence, the present system is superior because its total cost is less than the total cost of using two operators.

Summary

Analysis of waiting lines can be an important aspect of the design of service systems. Waiting lines have a tendency to form in such systems even though, in a macro sense, the system is underloaded. The arrival of customers together and variability of service durations combine to create temporary overloads. By the same token, at other times the servers are idle. The goal is to minimize total customer wait and server costs, but a standard on a performance measure such as "average wait time <3 minutes" is also used to determine the number of servers.

A major consideration in the analysis of queuing systems is whether the number of potential customers is limited (finite source) or unrestricted ("infinite" source). Nine queuing models are described, eight dealing with "infinite" source (four for single servers and four for multiple servers) and one dealing with finite source. Most models assume that customer arrival rates can be described by a Poisson distribution, that service durations can be described by an Exponential distribution, and customers are served FCFS. Basic relationships are given so that starting from the average queue length, other measures such as average wait time in the line or in the system and probability of having to wait can be determined.

Key Terms

Exponential distribution, 672
finite source, 670
"infinite" source, 670
multiple-server-with-priority model, 690

Poisson distribution, 672
queue discipline, 674
queuing theory, 667
server utilization, 674

Solved Problems

Problem 1

"Infinite"-source, Multiple servers, Exponential service durations (Model 5). One of the features of a new machine shop will be a well-stocked tool crib. The manager of the shop must decide on the number of attendants needed to staff the crib. Attendants will receive $9 per hour in wages and fringe benefits. Mechanics' time will be worth $30 per hour, which includes wages and fringe benefits. Based on previous experience, the manager estimates requests for tools will average 18 per hour with a service capacity of 20 requests per hour per attendant. How many attendants should be on duty in order to minimize total mechanics wait cost and attendants' wages? Assume that arrival and service rates will be Poisson. (Also assume that the number of mechanics is very large, in order for the infinite-source model to be appropriate.)

Solution

$\lambda = 18$ per hour

$\mu = 20$ per hour

Number of Attendants, M	L_q^*	$L_q + \dfrac{\lambda}{\mu} = L_s$	$9M:$ Attendant Cost (per hour)	$30L_s:$ Mechanic Cost (per hour)	Total Cost (per hour)
1	8.1	$8.1 + .9 = 9.0$	$9	$270	$279
2	.229	$.229 + .9 = 1.129$	$18	$33.87	$52^\dagger$
3	.03	$.03 + .9 = .93$	$27	$27.9	$55^\dagger$

*L_q from Table 18-4, with $\lambda/\mu = 18/20 = .9$.
†Rounded.

Hence, two attendants will produce the lowest total cost.

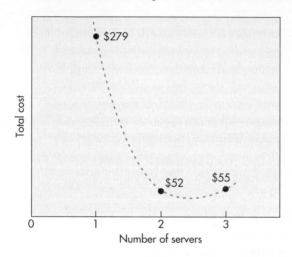

Problem 2

Infinite source. The following is a list of average service duration for three different operations:

Operation	Average Service Duration
A	8 minutes
B	1.2 hours
C	2 days

a. Determine the average service rate for each operation.

b. Would the calculated rates be different if these were inter-arrival durations rather than service durations?

Solution

a. The average service rate is the reciprocal of average service duration. Thus, the rates are:

A: 1/8 per minute = .125 per minute, or $\times 60 = 7.5$ per hour

B: 1/1.2 per hour = .833 per hour

C: 1/2 per day = .50 per day

b. No. In either case, the rate is simply the reciprocal of the duration.

Problem 3

Finite source. A group of 10 machines is loaded and unloaded by one of three servers. The machines run for an average of six minutes per cycle, and average time to unload and reload is nine minutes. Run and service durations can be described by Exponential distributions. While running, the machines produce a total of 16 units per hour if they did not have to pause to wait for a server and be loaded and unloaded. What is the average hourly output of each machine when waiting and serving are taken into account?

Solution

$T = 9$ minutes

$U = 6$ minutes; $X = \dfrac{T}{T+U} = \dfrac{9}{9+6} = .60$

$N = 10$ machines

$M = 3$ servers; from Table 18-7 (Population 10), we obtain $F = .500$, $D = .996$

Calculate the average number of machines running:

$$J = NF(1 - X) = 10(.500)(1-.6) = 2$$

Determine the percentage of machines running, and multiply by output while running:

$$\frac{J}{N} \times (16 \text{ per hour}) = \frac{2}{10} \times (16 \text{ units per hour}) = 3.2 \text{ units per hour}$$

Discussion and Review Questions

1. Give some examples of services where waiting lines are used. (LO1)
2. Why do waiting lines form even though the system is underloaded? (LO1)
3. What are the most common measures of system performance in queuing analysis? (LO2)
4. What information is necessary to analyze a queuing system? (LO2)
5. What effect would decreasing arrival and service variability have on the waiting line? (LO2 & 4)
6. What approach do supermarkets use to reduce waiting times? (LO2)
7. Contrast finite and "infinite" sources. (LO2)
8. In a multiple-server system, what is the rationale for having customers wait in a single joint line as is now done in many banks, rather than in multiple lines? (LO2)
9. What happens to the average wait time if a manager attempts to achieve a high capacity utilization? What happens if $\lambda \geq \mu$? (LO2)
10. Explain Little's formula: $L = \lambda W$. (LO3)
11. What is the difference between Wq and Ws? (LO3)
12. Will doubling the service rate of a single server system reduce the average waiting time in line by a factor of one-half? Explain briefly. (LO4)
13. Can a service duration be more variable than an Exponential distribution? Explain. (LO4)
14. Is Model 1 a special case of Model 5? Explain. (LO5)
15. Name two ways the number of servers can be determined. (LO5)
16. How can Model 6 be used to determine the maximum length of the line (size of waiting room)? (LO5)
17. Give an example where the distribution of inter-arrival times is not Poisson. (LO5)
18. A traffic light and the cars waiting at the traffic light on one side of the street form a queuing system. If there are two lines on this side of the street, what queuing model best describes this situation? (LO5)
19. Give an example of a situation where the finite-source model can be used. (LO6)

Taking Stock

1. What general trade-off is involved in waiting-line decisions? (LO1)
2. Who needs to be involved in assessing the waiting cost if the customers are (a) the general public and (b) employees of the organization? (LO1)
3. How has technology (a) had an impact on analyzing waiting-line systems? (b) improved waiting-line performance? (LO1)
4. During early November 2009, the threat of H1N1 and the fact that the vaccines were initially in short supply resulted in Public Health Agency of Canada prioritizing the people who would receive the vaccines first based on need: health professionals, children under five, people with chronic health conditions, and pregnant and breast-feeding women. However, there were numerous reports of other people jumping the queues, e.g., hockey players, executives, and patients of private

clinics. (See e.g., http://network.nationalpost.com/np/blogs/fullcomment/archive/2009/11/06/scott-stinson-h1n1-queue-jumping-and-the-fallacy-of-universal-health-care.aspx.)

a. Can a queuing model be used to describe this situation? If so, which one?

b. What is the implication of some people jumping queues on waiting times of various people?

c. Was the queue jumping ethical? Discuss. (LO5)

Critical Thinking Exercise

The owner of a restaurant implemented an expanded menu early last year. The menu was a success, drawing many more customers than the previous menu. But good news soon became bad news as long waiting lines began to deter customers, and business dropped off. Describe how waiting-line analysis can help the restaurant. (LO1 & 2)

Experiential Learning Exercise

Determine the average arrival rate and average service rate at one of these operations: a fast-food restaurant, supermarket, post office, or bank branch. (LO1 & 2)

a. For the arrival rate, observe for 15 one-minute intervals. Count the number of arrivals in each minute.
Construct a frequency distribution for arrivals. Does it resemble a Poisson distribution? Calculate its mean.

b. Now determine the service durations. To do this, observe the service time of 15 customers (e.g., how many minutes a teller at a bank spent with each customer). Make a frequency distribution. Does it look like Exponential distribution? Calculate its mean.

Internet Exercises

1. Visit http://www.q-matic.com/ca, find a case study, and briefly describe how the Qmatic system helped the operation. (LO2)

2. Visit http://www.waittimes.net/surgerydi/En/What.aspx?View=0&Type=0&Modality=&ModalityType=, choose a procedure and find the wait time in various hospitals in Toronto. Why do they have different wait times? How does this information help to decrease the average wait time of Ontario patients for the procedure you chose? (LO1, 2 & 5)

Problems

1. Repair calls for Xerox copiers in a small city are handled by one repair person. Repair duration, including travel time, is Exponentially distributed with a mean of two hours per call. Requests for copier repairs come in at a mean rate of three per eight-hour day (assume Poisson). Assume infinite source. Determine: (LO4)

    a. The average number of copiers waiting for repair.
    b. Server utilization.
    c. The amount of time during an eight-hour day that the repair person is not out on a call.
    d. The probability of two or more copiers in the system (waiting for or being repaired).
    e. The probability that a copier waits more than four hours for repair to begin.

2. A vending machine dispenses hot chocolate or coffee. Service duration is 30 seconds per cup and is constant. Customers arrive at a mean rate of 80 per hour (assume Poisson). Also assume that each customer buys only one cup. Determine: (LO4)

    a. The average number of customers waiting in line.
    b. The average time customers spend in the system.
    c. The average number of customers in the system.

3. Many of a bank's customers use its automated teller machine (ATM). During the early evening hours in the summer months, customers arrive at the ATM at the rate of one every other minute (assume Poisson). Each customer spends an average of 90 seconds completing his or her transaction. Transaction times are Exponentially distributed. Assume that the length of queue is not a constraint. Determine: (LO4)

   a. The average time customers spend at the machine, including waiting in line and completing transactions.

   b. The probability that a customer will not have to wait upon arrival at the ATM.

   c. Utilization of the ATM.

   d. The probability that a customer waits four minutes or more in the line.

4. A small town with one hospital has two ambulances. Requests for an ambulance during weekday mornings average .8 per hour and tend to be Poisson. Travel and loading/unloading time averages one hour per call and follows an Exponential distribution. Find: (LO5)

   a. Server utilization.

   b. The average number of patients waiting.

   c. The average time patients wait for an ambulance.

   d. The probability that both ambulances will be busy when a call comes in.

5. The following information pertains to telephone calls to a call centre on a typical workday. Assume Poisson arrivals and Exponential service durations. (LO5)

Period	Average Incoming Rate (calls per minute)	Average Service Rate (calls per minute per operator)	Number of Operators
Morning	1.8	1.5	2
Afternoon.	2.2	1.0	3
Evening	1.4	0.7	3

   a. Determine the average time callers wait to have their calls answered for each period and the probability that a caller will have to wait during each period.

   b. The call centre has seven leased phone lines (trunks). What is probability that a phone call will receive a busy signal during each of the three periods?

6. Trucks are required to check in a weigh station (scale) so that they can be inspected for weight violations. Trucks arrive at the station at the rate of 40 an hour in the mornings according to Poisson distribution. Currently two inspectors are on duty during those hours, each of whom can inspect 25 trucks an hour, according to Poisson distribution. (LO5)

   a. How many trucks would you expect to see at the weigh station, including those being inspected?

   b. If a truck were just arriving at the station, how many minutes could the driver expect to wait before being inspected?

   c. How many minutes, on average, would a truck that is not immediately inspected have to wait before being inspected?

   d. What is the probability that both inspectors would be busy at the same time (i.e., the probability that an arrival will have to wait for service)?

   e. What condition would exist if there were only one inspector?

   f. If only 13 trucks fit in the system, what is the probability that a truck cannot enter the system?

7. The manager of a new regional warehouse of a company must decide on the number of loading docks to request in order to minimize the sum of dock–crew and driver–truck costs. The manager has learned that each driver–truck combination represents a cost of $300 per day and that each dock plus crew represents a cost of $1,100 per day. (LO4 & 5)

   a. How many docks should she request if trucks will arrive at average rate of four per day, each dock can handle an average of five trucks per day, and both rates are Poisson?

   b. An employee has proposed adding new equipment that would speed up the service rate to 5.71 trucks per day. The equipment would cost $100 per day for each dock. Would this change the answer to part *a*? Should the manager invest in the new equipment?

8. The parts department of a large automobile dealership has a counter used exclusively for their own service mechanics requesting parts. The length of time between requests can be modelled by an Exponential distribution that has a mean of five minutes. A parts clerk can handle

requests at an average rate of 15 per hour, and this can be modelled by a Poisson distribution. Suppose there are two parts clerks at the counter. (LO5)

a. On average, how many mechanics would be at the counter, including those being served?

b. If a mechanic has to wait, how long would the average wait be?

c. What is the probability that a mechanic would have to wait for service?

d. What percentage of time is a clerk idle?

e. If clerks represent a cost of $20 per hour and mechanics represent a cost of $30 per hour, how many clerks would be optimal in terms of minimizing total cost?

9. One field representative services five customers for a computer manufacturer. Customers request assistance at an average (Poisson-distributed) rate of once every four workdays. The field representative can handle an average (Poisson-distributed) of one call per day. Determine: (LO6)

a. The expected number of customers waiting.

b. The average length of time customers must wait from the initial request for service until the service has been completed.

c. The percentage of time the service rep will be idle, i.e., the probability that a customer will not have to wait.

d. By how much would your answer to part *a* be reduced if a second field rep were added?

10. Two operators handle adjustments for a group of 10 machines. Adjustment time is Exponentially distributed and has a mean of 14 minutes per machine. The machines operate for an average of 86 minutes after an adjustment (Exponentially distributed). While running, each machine can turn out 50 pieces per hour. Find: (LO6)

a. The probability that a machine will have to wait for an adjustment.

b. The average number of machines waiting for adjustment.

c. The average number of machines being serviced.

d. The expected hourly output of each machine, taking adjustments into account.

e. Machine downtime represents a cost of $70 per hour; operator cost (including fringe benefits) is $15 per hour. What is the optimum number of operators?

11. One operator services a group of five machines. Machine run time and service durations are both Exponential. Machines run for an average of 90 minutes after a service, and service duration averages 35 minutes. The operator receives $20 per hour in wage and fringe benefits, and machine downtime costs $70 per hour per machine. (LO6)

a. If each machine produces 60 pieces per hour while running, find the average hourly output of each machine when waiting and service times are taken into account.

b. Determine the optimum number of operators.

12. A milling department has 10 machines. Each machine operates an average of eight hours before requiring adjustment, which takes an average of two hours. Both distributions are Exponential. While running, each machine can produce 40 pieces an hour. (LO6)

a. With one adjuster, what is the net average hourly output per machine?

b. If machine downtime cost is $80 per hour and adjuster cost is $20 per hour, how many adjusters would be optimal?

13. Trucks arrive at the loading dock of a wholesale grocer at an average rate of 1.2 per hour in the mornings. A single crew consisting of two workers can load a truck in about 30 minutes. Crew members receive $10 per hour in wage and fringe benefits, and trucks and drivers reflect an hourly cost of $60. The manager is thinking of adding another member to the crew. The average service rate would then be 2.4 trucks per hour. Assume both arrival and service rates are Poisson. (LO4)

a. Would the third crew member be economical?

b. Would a fourth member be justifiable if the resulting average service capacity were 2.6 trucks per hour?

14. Customers arriving at a service centre are assigned one of three categories (1, 2, and 3); category 1 is the highest priority. Records indicate that an average of nine customers arrive

per hour and that one-third are assigned to each category. There are two servers, and each can process customers at an average rate of five per hour. Arrival and service rates can be described by Poisson distributions. (LO5)

a. What is the utilization of a server?

b. Determine the average wait time for customers in each class.

c. Find the average number of customers in each class that are waiting for service.

15. A priority system is used to process customers, who are assigned one of two classes when they enter the processing centre. The highest-priority class has an average arrival rate of four per hour; the other class has an average arrival rate of two per hour. Both are Poisson. There are two servers, and each can process customers in an average of six minutes (Exponentially distributed). (LO5)

a. What is the server utilization?

b. Determine the average wait time for each class.

c. Determine the average number of customers of each class that would be waiting for service.

d. If the manager could alter the assignment rules so that arrival rates of the two classes were equal, what would be the revised average wait time for each priority class?

16. A priority waiting system assigns arriving customers one of four classes (class 1 has the highest priority). Arrival rates of the classes have Poisson distribution and their average are: (LO5)

Class	Average Arrivals per Hour
1	2
2	4
3	3
4	2

Five servers process the customers, and each can handle an average of three customers per hour. The service rate is Poisson.

a. What is the server utilization?

b. What is the average wait time for service by customers in the various classes? How many are waiting in each class on average?

c. If the average arrival rate of the second priority class could be reduced to three customers per hour by shifting some arrivals into the third priority class (which makes its average arrival rate 4 per hour), how would your answers to part *b* change?

d. What observations can you make based on your answers to part *c*?

17. Referring to Problem 16, suppose that each server could handle an average of four customers per hour. Answer the questions posed in Problem 16. Explain why the impact of reassigning customers in part *c* is much less in this case than in Problem 16. (LO5)

18. During the morning hours at a catalogue sales department, phone calls come in at an average rate of 40 per hour. Calls that cannot be answered immediately are put on hold. The system can handle eight callers on hold. If additional calls come in, they receive a busy signal. The three customer service representatives who answer the calls spend an average of three minutes with a customer. Both arrival and service rates are Poisson. What is the probability that a caller will get a busy signal? (LO5)

19. Since the terrorist attack of September 11, 2001, getting into the U.S. became more difficult, and hence slower for Canadian cars and trucks at border crossings. This resulted in long line-ups. One such case occurred on the Ambassador Bridge connecting Windsor to Detroit.[5] There were nine U.S. customs booths at the Detroit side of the bridge. Each truck took approximately two minutes to get cleared. During the busy hours, about 300 trucks (i.e., one every 12 seconds) arrived at the booths. Assuming that the standard deviation of getting cleared is 1 minute per truck and the standard deviation of inter-arrival durations is 6 seconds, how many more U.S. Customs Booths were needed at the Ambassador Bridge to provide a reasonable average wait time (e.g., less than 10 minutes)? (LO5)

---

[5]D. Battagello, *Windsor Star Border Reporter*, November 9, 2004, http://web2.uwindsor.ca/math/hlynka/qreal.html.

20. The number of customers coming to a bank between 1:00 and 1:30 p.m. of a "normal" day has a Poisson distribution with an average of 39 customers during the half hour. The length of time each customer spends with a teller is Exponential with an average of 45.5 seconds. The average time a customer spends in the line waiting is desired to be three minutes. The manager is wondering how many tellers are required during this time period. (LO5)

*21. Model 8300 Telemetry system used at Wesley Long Community Hospital, Greensboro, North Carolina, is a completely self-contained, wireless, one-patient cardiac monitor.[6] The system provides wireless transmission of a patient's heartbeat to a receiver either at a central station or at the bedside. A study was undertaken to analyze the service provided by the 18 currently held telemetry units and to investigate the cost/benefit of any additional units. During a 38-day reviewing period, there were 156 requests for service (telemetry units are requested and used 24 hours a day). The average service duration was 93.6 hours per patient. Both inter-arrival and service durations had Exponential distributions. (LO5)

   a. What is the average arrival rate per day of patients needing telemetry?
   b. What is the average service rate per day of patients needing telemetry?
   c. If the average wait time before service is desired to be less than 5 hours, are 18 telemetry units enough? (Hint: For $\lambda/\mu = 16$ and M = 18, it can be shown that $L_q = 4.29$.)

*22. The number of calls coming into a child abuse hotline during the 5 p.m. to 9 a.m. period on weekdays had a Poisson distribution with an average of 1.67 calls per hour. Call lengths had Exponential distribution with average of 5.4 minutes. It is considered important that a very high percentage of calls get through to the operator right away (as opposed to having to wait). If only one person is assigned to answer the phones, what is the probability that a call will have to wait because the operator is busy? (LO4)

*23. Becton-Dickinson manufactures medical supplies such as syringes.[7] In one plant it had 10 parallel syringe manufacturing lines. The problem was that syringes kept getting stuck in the lines, shutting the lines down. On average, a line got stuck again one minute after a blockage was removed (this time was distributed Exponentially). One operator was assigned to five lines (i.e., a total of two operators). The average time it took the operator to walk to the blocked line and fix the problem was 10 seconds (this time was distributed Exponentially). How long was a line expected to be down per hour? Assume that the two operators do not help each other. (LO6)

*24. Bendigo Health is a 672-bed hospital near Melbourne, Australia.[8] When the hospital administrators wanted to decide on the number of beds to set aside for a new program, transition care, some research staff suggested the use of queuing theory. Some hospital patients would qualify for the option of transition care before a group/nursing home is found for them. It is estimated that an average of $\lambda = 1.2$ patients per week would be eligible and interested for transition care (Poisson distribution). The average stay in transition care is estimated to be $(1/\mu) = 9.5$ weeks. If a bed is not available in transition care, the patient leaves for another facility (i.e., there is no wait). The research staff suggested the following method: first assume that the number of beds in transition care is infinite. Then, determine the average occupancy (i.e., the average number of patients in the system) = 1.2(9.5) = 11.4. Finally, use the fact that the distribution of number of patients in the system is Poisson with a mean of 11.4 to determine the probability that a bed will not be used, given various maximum number of beds. For example, "if the hospital allocates 9 beds to transition care, then in the long run there would be some empty beds on 19.84% of days, or about 1 day in 5." (LO5)

   a. Use Excel to verify the 19.84% result. Note that the Poisson table at the end of the textbook goes up to only a mean of 9.5. Hint : use = poisson(8,11.4,TRUE) in Excel, which gives

---

[6]T. Scott and W.A. Hailey, "Queuing Model Aids Economic Analysis of Health Centre," *Industrial Engineering*, February 1981, pp. 56–61.

[7]M.A. Vogel, "Queueing Theory Applied to Machine Manning," *Interfaces*, 9(4), August 1979, pp. 1–7.

[8]A. Crombie, et al, "Planning the Transition Care," *Australian Health Review*, August 2008, 32(3), pp. 505–508.

the cumulative Poisson probability of observing up to $x = 8$, given the average of 11.4. Note that a nine-bed transition care will have some empty beds if $x \leq 8$.

b. An alternative method is to use the following (Erlang B) formula,[9] where p_n = probability of n patients in the system and K = maximum number of beds (Note: this system is a special case of Model 6 where the finite size K equals the number of servers M, i.e., beds in this case):

$$p_n = \frac{\dfrac{\left(\frac{\lambda}{\mu}\right)^n}{n!}}{\displaystyle\sum_{j=0}^{K}\left(\dfrac{\left(\frac{\lambda}{\mu}\right)^j}{j!}\right)}$$

Which method is more appropriate for this problem?

*25. Bay of Plenty Electricity (BOPE) is an electrical utility company in the Bay of Plenty, New Zealand.[10] BOPE has 21 company cars that the head-office employees share for company business. However, BOPE has to reduce its costs. Assuming that the average number of employees needing a car per work-hour is 4, the average time they need the car is 2.5 hours, and the average utilization of cars is desired to be 83%, how many cars does BOPE need? (LO5)

*26. A Greek electrical appliance manufacturer has three trucks that its various departments, such as production, receiving, mould shop, and maintenance shop, use as needed.[11] The users have expressed that they wait an average of about nine minutes before a truck arrives (travel time is negligible). A study over 17 days (a day has 15 work hours) recorded 1,172 requests for truck service (randomly distributed over time, implying that the number of requests per hour was Poisson). The average service time was 20.3 minutes with a standard deviation of 10.6 minutes. (LO5)

a. Calculate the approximate average wait time in the queue for the truck users by using Model 7. Note: Variance of a Poisson distribution is equal to its mean.

b. Give some possible reasons for the actual wait time in the queue being so much larger than your answer to part *a*.

*27. The Department of Psychiatry in Cambridge Hospital (CH), Massachusetts, wanted to know the effect of the number of its beds on demand for beds in the local public mental hospital (PH).[12] A study was undertaken for one year that found that average number of in-state mental patients arriving at CH was 1.44 per day, and average number of out-of-state mental patients arriving at CH was .54 per day (both Poisson). CH had 46 beds for mental patients. If there was no free bed in CH, the patient was directed to PH. The average stay in CH was 37.1 days (the length of stay had close-to-Exponential distribution). Using the Erlang formula given in problem 24b above, calculate the probability that a patient finds CH full, i.e., P_{46}. (LO5)

28. A major New York bank commissioned a study to measure the service levels of its over 500 ATMs in N.Y.[13]. The ATMs were located in pairs inside vestibules attached to bank branches. The team used the finite queue version of multi server queuing model (i.e., Model 6) and suggested that the proportion of customers who balk (i.e., refuse to join the queue) should be used as the measure of service as opposed to the average wait time or average queue length. It was suggested that if the probability of balking during busiest times is greater than 5%, then a vestibule should be expanded and an additional ATM installed in it. Consider a specific

[9]S.C. Graves, et al, "A Simple Stochastic Model for Facility Planning in a Mental Health Care System," *Interfaces*, 13(5), October 1983, pp. 101–110.

[10]J. Buchanan and J. Scott, "Vehicle Utilization at Bay of Plenty Electricity," *Interfaces*, 22(2), Mar–Apr 1992, pp. 28–35.

[11]G.P. Cosmetatos, "The Value of Queueing Theory—A Case Study," *Interfaces*, 9(3), May 1979, pp. 47–51.

[12]S.C. Graves, et al, "A Simple Stochastic Model for Facility Planning in a Mental Health Care System," *Interfaces*, 13(5), Oct 1983, pp. 101–110.

[13]P. Kolesar, "Stalking the Endangered CAT: A Queuing Analysis of Congestion at Automatic Teller Machines," *Interfaces*, 14(6), November–December 1984, pp. 16–26.

vestibule with 2 ATMs in it. There is space for 10 people in the vestibule (2 being served, 8 in line); average service time is 1.28 minutes per customer (approximately Exponential), and average arrival rate is 86 customers per hour (approximately Poisson) during the busiest times of the week (noon–1pm or 1–2 pm weekdays). Determine the probability of balking at this vestibule. Should the vestibule be enlarged? (LO5)

29. The Columbia University Hospital wanted to know if it needed to have more than one operating room (OR) crew present during the night shift (11 p.m. to 7 a.m.)[14]. If the probability that one crew is busy is greater than 1 percent, then a second OR crew would be required. During one year, 62 patients required emergency operation during the night shift. The average operation took 80.79 minutes. Does the hospital need a second OR crew during the night shift? (LO4)

MINI-CASE

Big Bank

The operations manager of a soon-to-open branch of a large bank is in the process of configuring teller operations. Currently some branches have a separate teller line for customers who have a single transaction, while other branches do not have separate lines. The manager wants to avoid complaints about long waits that have been received at some branches. Because the demographics differ from location to location, a system that works at one branch will not necessarily work at another. The manager has obtained data on processing times from the bank's home office, and is ready to explore different options for configuring operations.

One time that will get special attention is the noon hour on Friday. The plan is to have five tellers available then. Under consideration are the following options:

a. Have one waiting line and have the first person in line go to the next available teller.

b. Have two waiting lines: one teller for customers who have a single transaction and four tellers who would handle customers who have multiple transactions.

An average of 80 customers are served during the noon hour. The average service duration for customers with a single transaction is 90 seconds, while the average service duration for customers with multiple transactions is 4 minutes. Sixty percent of the customers are expected to have multiple transactions.

Question

If you were the manager, which option would you select? Why? Explain the disparity between the results for the two options. What assumptions did you make in your analysis?

MINI-CASE   http://www.lourdes.com

Lourdes Hospital

When doctors referred their patients to the Lourdes Hospital in Binghamton, New York, for various services such as X-rays, their office had a tough time getting through to the centralized appointment office of Lourdes. Most of the time, the line was busy. The installation of a call waiting system did not improve the situation, because callers were put on hold for indefinite lengths of time. The poor service had resulted in numerous complaints. One of the managers was put in charge of finding a solution, and a goal of answering at least 90 percent of

calls without delay was set. The hospital was willing to employ more staff to receive calls. The manager studied this queuing problem by collecting data for 21 workdays during which additional staff was used to answer calls and no call received a busy signal or was put on hold. The number of calls per day ranged between 220 and 350, with no day-of-the-week seasonality. Most days, the number of calls was between 250 and 300. The average number of calls arriving during each 15-minute interval peaked at about 10 calls during 9:00–11:30 a.m. and 2:00–3:45 p.m. periods. The 944 service durations during the data collection period had a distribution similar to Exponential

---

[14]J.B. Tucker, et al, "Using Queuing Theory to Determine Operating Room Staffing Needs," Journal of Trauma, 46(1), 1999, pp. 71–79.

with a mean of 3.11 minutes. The manager also found out that previously the 6.5 full-time-equivalent employees usually spent half their time doing other tasks and turned off their phones while busy with other tasks. Using the multiple servers queuing model and a service goal of at least 90-percent probability of not having to wait, the manager determined the number of staff required during each 15-minute interval. When the original staffing levels were compared with the model-determined ones, it was discovered that more staff were required earlier in the day and later in the afternoon, and fewer were needed around noon. The problem was solved by rearranging work shifts.

Question

During busy periods (9:00 a.m.–11:30 a.m. and 2:00 p.m.–3:45 p.m.), the central appointment office receives 40 calls per hour, on average. Each call takes an average of 3.11 minutes to serve. It is desired that at least 90 percent of calls is received without waiting. What is the minimum number of staff needed during these busy times?

Source: S.R. Agnihothri and P.F. Taylor, "Staffing a Centralized Appointment Scheduling Department in Lourdes Hospital," *Interfaces* 21(5), September–October 1991, pp. 1–11.

MINI-CASE

Phoenix Mutual

Call volumes to Phoenix Mutual (now Phoenix Companies Inc.), a life insurance company based in Hartford, Connecticut, had doubled and the service representatives could not answer the calls as quickly as their goal indicated they should. This occurred even though the company had installed an automatic call sequencer the year before. Customers were on hold for too long and there were too many abandoned calls. Phoenix Mutual installed an automatic call distributor and started to analyze the work of service representatives and the queuing system. The goal was to answer 85 percent of the calls in 30 seconds. There also were other tasks required of a sales rep, such as making 150 to 200 outgoing calls per day. A 1.5-month study showed that only 38 percent of an employee's time was spent on answering calls, and another 31 percent of his or her time was classified as "available" for receiving calls. A graph of the number of incoming calls per half hour showed the peaks to be about 70 calls per half hour between 10:00 a.m.—noon and 1:00–4:00 p.m. Within each half-hour, the number of calls each day followed a Poisson distribution. Using the service goal of answering 85 percent of incoming calls within 30 seconds and the multiple-server queuing model, Phoenix Mutual was able

to determine the number of service representatives required to receive the forecasted incoming calls per half-hour of each day. These staff requirements were then increased to allow the service reps to also do the other required tasks. The result of the study was that the average service duration for incoming calls went down from approximately 4 minutes to 3.3 minutes, and the percentage of time a service representative was "available" to receive calls went down to approximately 20 percent because the number of service representatives was reduced from 33 to 29 even though service was improved.

Question

Assuming that 38 percent of the sales reps are available at any time to take a call, determine P_0 during a busy period using the Excel template on *Connect*, and then calculate the probability that a call during a busy period has to wait more than 30 seconds. (Note that Table 18-4 does not have the values for this λ/μ. Hint: use formula 18-22.) Does it appear that the service goal is satisfied?

Source: M.A. Yanke and J.D. Wehr, "The Queueing Method to Better Use of Your Phone System," *The Office* 96(5), November 1982, pp. 200, 204–5.

To access "Simulation," the supplement to Chapter 18, please visit *Connect*.

APPENDIX A

Answers to Selected Problems

CHAPTER 2 **Competitiveness, Strategic Planning, and Productivity**

2. A crew size of two has the highest productivity (250 m² per person per week installed).

3. Week 1: 5.62.
   Week 2: 5.45.
   Week 3: 5.20.
   Week 4: 5.01.
   Multifactor productivity is decreasing.

6. 4.3% increase.

CHAPTER 3 **Forecasting**

1. **a.** blueberry has no trend or seasonality; cinnamon has an increasing trend; cupcakes has 5-workday seasonality.
   b. blueberry = 33, cinnamon = 35, cupcakes = 47.
   c. For blueberry, could use an averaging technique such as moving average or exponential smoothing; for cinnamons, could use simple regression for linear trend; for cupcakes, could use the seasonality technique.

4. **a.** 22.   **b.** 20.75.   **c.** 20.72.

7. **a.** $Y_t = 195.47 + 7.00t$.
   $Y_{16} = 307.47$ $Y_{18} = 321.47$
   $Y_{17} = 314.47$ $Y_{19} = 328.47$
   b. 314.44

11. **a.** Fri. = 0.79, Sat. = 1.34, Sun. = 0.87.

14. **a.**

Day	Relative
1...	0.900
2...	0.833
3...	0.916
4...	1.031
5...	1.412
6...	1.482
7...	0.426

19. **b.**

Jan.	800
Feb.	810
Mar.	900
Apr.	809.6

24. **b.** -0.985. A strong negative relationship between sales and price.

29. **a.**

	MSE	MAD	MAPE
Forecast 1	9.4	2.8	.36%
Forecast 2	38.2	3.6	.46%

Forecast 1 is superior.

CHAPTER 5 **Strategic Capacity Planning**

4. **a.** A: 8,000 units.   **b.** 10,000 units.
   B: 7,500 units.
   c. A: $20,000.
   B: $18,000.
   A's profit would be higher.

6. **a.** A: $82.
   B: $92.
   C: $60.
   c. A: 0 to less than 88.
   B: Never.
   C: 89+

7. Vendor best for $Q \leq 63,333$. For larger quantities, produce in-house with process B

9. 3 machines.

11. **a.** one machine: BEP = 80.   two machines: BEP = 152.
    b. one machine.

CHAPTER 6 **Process Design and Facility Layout**

1. **a.** Eight.
   b. 3.6 minutes.
   c. (1) 50 units.
      (2) 30 units.

2. **a.**

Station	Tasks	Time
1	a	1.4
2	b, e	1.3
3	d, c, f	1.8
4	g, h	1.5

   b. 82%.

10.

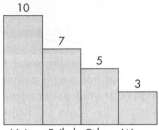

11.

4	3	1
5	8	6
7	2	

16. 3→A, 5→B, 1→C, 4→D, 6→E, 2→F.

CHAPTER 7   Design of Work Systems

2. **a.** 1.2 minutes.
   b. 1.14 minutes.
   c. 1.27 minutes.

4.

Task	OT
1	4.10
2	1.50
3	3.25
4	2.77

7. 5.85 minutes.

8. 7.125 minutes.

10. 57 observations.

11. 37 work cycles.

12. **a.** 12%.   **b.** 254 observations.

CHAPTER 8   Location Planning and Analysis

2. **a.** A: 16,854; B: 17,416; C: 17,753.   **b.** C, profit = $14,670.

4. **a.** B: 0 to 33; C: 34 to 400; A: 400+.   **b.** C
   c. Expansion leads to more control, whereas subcontracting leads to more flexibility.

9. A (Score = 87.02).

11. (5, 4).

CHAPTER 9   Management of Quality

2.

	Res.	Com.
Noisy	10	3
Failed	7	2
Odour	5	7
Warm	3	4

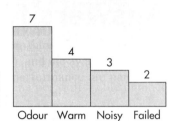

CHAPTER 10   Quality Control

1. **a.** 1.24%. **b.** 24.4 kg and 24.6 kg.

2. **a.** LCL: 1.991 litres.   **b.** Yes, process is in control.
      UCL: 2.009 litres.

3. **a.** Mean: LCL is 2.96, UCL is 3.24.
      Range: LCL is .099, UCL is 0.801.
   b. Yes.

6. **a.**
1	2	3	4
.020	.010	.025	.045
   b. .025.
   c. Mean = .025, standard deviation = .011.
   d. LCL = .001, UCL = .049.
   e. .0456.
   f. Yes.
   g. Mean = .02, standard deviation = .0099.
   h. LCL = .0002, UCL = .0399. No.

8. **a.** UCL = 16.266, LCL = 0, Yes.   **b.** No change

11. **35 pieces.**

16. **b.** 4.5, .192.
   c. 4.5, .086.
   d. 4.242 to 4.758.
   f. None.

17. **a.** 1.11.   **b.** Capable.

20. H: C_{pk} = .9375, incapable, K: C_{pk} = 1.0, capable, T: C_{pk} = 1.06, capable.

CHAPTER 11   Supply Chain Management

1. Use 2-day freight ($29.38 saving).

CHAPTER 12 **Inventory Management**

2. a.

Item	Class
Z45	A
F95	A
K35	A
P05	B
F14	B
D45	B
K36	B
D57	B
K34	C
D52	C
M20	C
F99	C
N08	C
D48	C
M10	C

4. a. 228 packages.
   b. $228
   c. Yes.
   d. Yes; TC = $310; save $82.

10. a. 1,633 bags.
   b. 490 bags.
   c. 3.27 days.
   d. 24.5 runs per year.
   e. $5,739.71

14. a. 600 stones (total cost = $41,120).
   b. 150 stones.

18. 6,600 metres.

20. a. 91 kg.
   b. ROP = 691 kg.

29. a. EOQ = 126 cases.   **b.** ROP = 81.6 cases.

31. K033:581; K144:458; L700:-16 (do not order).

34. 25 dozens, service level = 73%.

36. 78.85 kg.

CHAPTER 13 **Aggregate Planning**

7. Produce 25 units per month during overtime in months 2–4, and 20 units per month using part time workers in months 2–4 and 5 units in month 5, at total cost of $13,170.

13. Total cost = $124,960.

16. Projected on-hand, wk1 = 31, wk2 = 71, wk3 = 41, wk4 = 11, wk5 = 41, wk6 = 71, wk7 = 31, wk8 = 61.

CHAPTER 14 **MRP and ERP**

1. a. F = 12, G = 1, H = 1, J = 6, D = 10, L = 2, A = 4

2. a. E = 138.
   b. Week 5.

10. Order 160 units in Week 2; projected on-hand wk4 = 15, wk5 = 35, wk6 = 5, …

13. b. Production schedule for golf carts.

Week number			1	2	3	4	5	6	7	8	9
Quantity								100		100	100

Item: Golf cart LT = 1 week											
Gross requirements								100		100	100
Scheduled receipts											
Projected on-hand											
Net requirements								100		100	100
Planned-order receipts								100		100	100
Planned-order releases							100		100	100	

Item: Bases LT = 1 week											
Gross requirements							100		100	100	
Scheduled receipts											
Projected on-hand	20	20	20	20	50	100	50	100	50	0	
Net requirements											
Planned-order receipts				30	50	50	50	50	50		
Planned-order releases			30	50	50	50	50	50			

14. EPP = 79. Order 120 units in Month 2 and 60 units in Month 6.

CHAPTER 15 **Just-in-Time and Lean Production**

1. 4 or 5; fewer containers.
4. D, C, B, D, (C, D, A), D, B, C, D.

CHAPTER 16 **Job and Staff Scheduling**

1. **a.** SPT = D-C-B-A,
   EDD = C-B-D-A.

   b.

	SPT	EDD
Avg. flow time	19.75	21
Avg. days late	6	6

   c. SPT.

4. B-A-G-E-F-D-C. Makespan = 11.7 hours.
16. A-B-C, total setup time = 7 hrs.

CHAPTER 17 **Project Management**

1. **a.** S-9-10-11-12-13-End: 31 days.
   b. 1-2-5-7-8-9: 55 days.
   c. 1-2-3-4-End: 44 days.

3. critical path activities F, H, J, K.

8. **a.** .6881   **b.** .3978.   **c.** .0203.

14. **a.** wk1: act. 4, wk2: act. 1, wk3: act. 4 and 13, wk4: act. 9 and 12,
    wk5: act. 9 and 11, wk6: act. 1, 5, and 13.

CHAPTER 18 **Waiting-Line Analysis**

5. **a.** Morning: .375 minute; .45.
   Afternoon: .678 minute; .54.
   Evening: .635 minute; .44.
   b. Morning: .01; Afternoon: .05; Evening: .03.

9. **a.** .995 customer.
   b. 2.24 days.
   c. 31.1 percent.
   d. .875 customer less.

15. **a.** 0.30.
    b. W1 = .52 min.
    W2 = .74 min.
    c. L1 = .034.
    L2 = .025.
    d. W1 = .49 min.
    W2 = .69 min.

APPENDIX B

Tables

A. Areas under the Standardized Normal Curve, 0 to z,   715
B. Areas under the Standardized Normal Curve
   1. From $-\infty$ to $-z$, $z < 0$ 716
   2. From $-\infty$ to $+z$,   717
C. Cumulative Poisson Probabilities,   718

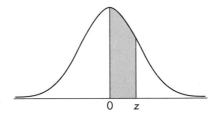

Table A										

Areas under the Standardized Normal Curve, 0 to z

z	.00	.01	.02	.03	.04	.05	.06	.07	.08	.09
0.0.	.0000	.0040	.0080	.0120	.0160	.0199	.0239	.0279	.0319	.0359
0.1.	.0398	.0438	.0478	.0517	.0557	.0596	.0636	.0675	.0714	.0753
0.2.	.0793	.0832	.0871	.0910	.0948	.0987	.1026	.1064	.1103	.1141
0.3.	.1179	.1217	.1255	.1293	.1331	.1368	.1406	.1443	.1480	.1517
0.4.	.1554	.1591	.1628	.1664	.1700	.1736	.1772	.1808	.1844	.1879
0.5.	.1915	.1950	.1985	.2019	.2054	.2088	.2123	.2157	.2190	.2224
0.6.	.2257	.2291	.2324	.2357	.2389	.2422	.2454	.2486	.2517	.2549
0.7.	.2580	.2611	.2642	.2673	.2703	.2734	.2764	.2794	.2823	.2852
0.8.	.2881	.2910	.2939	.2967	.2995	.3023	.3051	.3078	.3106	.3133
0.9.	.3159	.3186	.3212	.3238	.3264	.3289	.3315	.3340	.3365	.3389
1.0.	.3413	.3438	.3461	.3485	.3508	.3531	.3554	.3577	.3599	.3621
1.1.	.3643	.3665	.3686	.3708	.3729	.3749	.3770	.3790	.3810	.3830
1.2.	.3849	.3869	.3888	.3907	.3925	.3944	.3962	.3980	.3997	.4015
1.3.	.4032	.4049	.4066	.4082	.4099	.4115	.4131	.4147	.4162	.4177
1.4.	.4192	.4207	.4222	.4236	.4251	.4265	.4279	.4292	.4306	.4319
1.5.	.4332	.4345	.4357	.4370	.4382	.4394	.4406	.4418	.4429	.4441
1.6.	.4452	.4463	.4474	.4484	.4495	.4505	.4515	.4525	.4535	.4545
1.7.	.4554	.4564	.4573	.4582	.4591	.4599	.4608	.4616	.4625	.4633
1.8.	.4641	.4649	.4656	.4664	.4671	.4678	.4686	.4693	.4699	.4706
1.9.	.4713	.4719	.4726	.4732	.4738	.4744	.4750	.4756	.4761	.4767
2.0.	.4772	.4778	.4783	.4788	.4793	.4798	.4803	.4808	.4812	.4817
2.1.	.4821	.4826	.4830	.4834	.4838	.4842	.4846	.4850	.4854	.4857
2.2.	.4861	.4864	.4868	.4871	.4875	.4878	.4881	.4884	.4887	.4890
2.3.	.4893	.4896	.4898	.4901	.4904	.4906	.4909	.4911	.4913	.4916
2.4.	.4918	.4920	.4922	.4925	.4927	.4929	.4931	.4932	.4934	.4936
2.5.	.4938	.4940	.4941	.4943	.4945	.4946	.4948	.4949	.4951	.4952
2.6.	.4953	.4955	.4956	.4957	.4959	.4960	.4961	.4962	.4963	.4964
2.7.	.4965	.4966	.4967	.4968	.4969	.4970	.4971	.4972	.4973	.4974
2.8.	.4974	.4975	.4976	.4977	.4977	.4978	.4979	.4979	.4980	.4981
2.9.	.4981	.4982	.4982	.4983	.4984	.4984	.4985	.4985	.4986	.4986
3.0.	.4987	.4987	.4987	.4988	.4988	.4989	.4989	.4989	.4990	.4990

1. Areas under the Standardized Normal Curve, from $-\infty$ to z

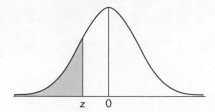

.09	.08	.07	.06	.05	.04	.03	.02	.01	.00	z
.0002	.0003	.0003	.0003	.0003	.0003	.0003	.0003	.0003	.0003	−3.4
.0003	.0004	.0004	.0004	.0004	.0004	.0004	.0005	.0005	.0005	−3.3
.0005	.0005	.0005	.0006	.0006	.0006	.0006	.0006	.0007	.0007	−3.2
.0007	.0007	.0008	.0008	.0008	.0008	.0009	.0009	.0009	.0010	−3.1
.0010	.0010	.0011	.0011	.0011	.0012	.0012	.0013	.0013	.0013	−3.0
.0014	.0014	.0015	.0015	.0016	.0016	.0017	.0018	.0018	.0019	−2.9
.0019	.0020	.0021	.0021	.0022	.0023	.0023	.0024	.0025	.0026	−2.8
.0026	.0027	.0028	.0029	.0030	.0031	.0032	.0033	.0034	.0035	−2.7
.0036	.0037	.0038	.0039	.0040	.0041	.0043	.0044	.0045	.0047	−2.6
.0048	.0049	.0051	.0052	.0054	.0055	.0057	.0059	.0060	.0062	−2.5
.0064	.0066	.0068	.0069	.0071	.0073	.0075	.0078	.0080	.0082	−2.4
.0084	.0087	.0089	.0091	.0094	.0096	.0099	.0102	.0104	.0107	−2.3
.0110	.0113	.0116	.0119	.0122	.0125	.0129	.0132	.0136	.0139	−2.2
.0143	.0146	.0150	.0154	.0158	.0162	.0166	.0170	.0174	.0179	−2.1
.0183	.0188	.0192	.0197	.0202	.0207	.0212	.0217	.0222	.0228	−2.0
.0233	.0239	.0244	.0250	.0256	.0262	.0268	.0274	.0281	.0287	−1.9
.0294	.0301	.0307	.0314	.0322	.0329	.0336	.0344	.0351	.0359	−1.8
.0367	.0375	.0384	.0392	.0401	.0409	.0418	.0427	.0436	.0446	−1.7
.0455	.0465	.0475	.0485	.0495	.0505	.0516	.0526	.0537	.0548	−1.6
.0559	.0571	.0582	.0594	.0606	.0618	.0630	.0643	.0655	.0668	−1.5
.0681	.0694	.0708	.0721	.0735	.0749	.0764	.0778	.0793	.0808	−1.4
.0823	.0838	.0853	.0869	.0885	.0901	.0918	.0934	.0951	.0968	−1.3
.0985	.1003	.1020	.1038	.1056	.1075	.1093	.1112	.1131	.1151	−1.2
.1170	.1190	.1210	.1230	.1251	.1271	.1292	.1314	.1335	.1357	−1.1
.1379	.1401	.1423	.1446	.1469	.1492	.1515	.1539	.1562	.1587	−1.0
.1611	.1635	.1660	.1685	.1711	.1736	.1762	.1788	.1814	.1841	−0.9
.1867	.1894	.1922	.1949	.1977	.2005	.2033	.2061	.2090	.2119	−0.8
.2148	.2177	.2206	.2236	.2266	.2296	.2327	.2358	.2389	.2420	−0.7
.2451	.2483	.2514	.2546	.2578	.2611	.2643	.2676	.2709	.2743	−0.6
.2776	.2810	.2843	.2877	.2912	.2946	.2981	.3015	.3050	.3085	−0.5
.3121	.3156	.3192	.3228	.3264	.3300	.3336	.3372	.3409	.3446	−0.4
.3483	.3520	.3557	.3594	.3632	.3669	.3707	.3745	.3783	.3821	−0.3
.3859	.3897	.3936	.3974	.4013	.4052	.4090	.4129	.4168	.4207	−0.2
.4247	.4286	.4325	.4364	.4404	.4443	.4483	.4522	.4562	.4602	−0.1
.4641	.4681	.4721	.4761	.4801	.4840	.4880	.4920	.4960	.5000	−0.0

(continued)

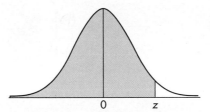

z	.00	.01	.02	.03	.04	.05	.06	.07	.08	.09
.0 ...	.5000	.5040	.5080	.5120	.5160	.5199	.5239	.5279	.5319	.5359
.1 ...	.5398	.5438	.5478	.5517	.5557	.5596	.5636	.5675	.5714	.5753
.2 ...	.5793	.5832	.5871	.5910	.5948	.5987	.6026	.6064	.6103	.6141
.3 ...	.6179	.6217	.6255	.6293	.6331	.6368	.6406	.6443	.6480	.6517
.4 ...	.6554	.6591	.6628	.6664	.6700	.6736	.6772	.6808	.6844	.6879
.5 ...	.6915	.6950	.6985	.7019	.7054	.7088	.7123	.7157	.7190	.7224
.6 ...	.7257	.7291	.7324	.7357	.7389	.7422	.7454	.7486	.7517	.7549
.7 ...	.7580	.7611	.7642	.7673	.7703	.7734	.7764	.7794	.7823	.7852
.8 ...	.7881	.7910	.7939	.7967	.7995	.8023	.8051	.8078	.8106	.8133
.9 ...	.8159	.8186	.8212	.8238	.8264	.8289	.8315	.8340	.8365	.8389
1.0 ...	.8413	.8438	.8461	.8485	.8508	.8531	.8554	.8577	.8599	.8621
1.1 ...	.8643	.8665	.8686	.8708	.8729	.8749	.8770	.8790	.8810	.8830
1.2 ...	.8849	.8869	.8888	.8907	.8925	.8944	.8962	.8980	.8997	.9015
1.3 ...	.9032	.9049	.9066	.9082	.9099	.9115	.9131	.9147	.9162	.9177
1.4 ...	.9192	.9207	.9222	.9236	.9251	.9265	.9279	.9292	.9306	.9319
1.5 ...	.9332	.9345	.9357	.9370	.9382	.9394	.9406	.9418	.9429	.9441
1.6 ...	.9452	.9463	.9474	.9484	.9495	.9505	.9515	.9525	.9535	.9545
1.7 ...	.9554	.9564	.9573	.9582	.9591	.9599	.9608	.9616	.9625	.9633
1.8 ...	.9641	.9649	.9656	.9664	.9671	.9678	.9686	.9693	.9699	.9706
1.9 ...	.9713	.9719	.9726	.9732	.9738	.9744	.9750	.9756	.9761	.9767
2.0 ...	.9772	.9778	.9783	.9788	.9793	.9798	.9803	.9808	.9812	.9817
2.1 ...	.9821	.9826	.9830	.9834	.9838	.9842	.9846	.9850	.9854	.9857
2.2 ...	.9861	.9864	.9868	.9871	.9875	.9878	.9881	.9884	.9887	.9890
2.3 ...	.9893	.9896	.9898	.9901	.9904	.9906	.9909	.9911	.9913	.9916
2.4 ...	.9918	.9920	.9922	.9925	.9927	.9929	.9931	.9932	.9934	.9936
2.5 ...	.9938	.9940	.9941	.9943	.9945	.9946	.9948	.9949	.9951	.9952
2.6 ...	.9953	.9955	.9956	.9957	.9959	.9960	.9961	.9962	.9963	.9964
2.7 ...	.9965	.9966	.9967	.9968	.9969	.9970	.9971	.9972	.9973	.9974
2.8 ...	.9974	.9975	.9976	.9977	.9977	.9978	.9979	.9979	.9980	.9981
2.9 ...	.9981	.9982	.9982	.9983	.9984	.9984	.9985	.9985	.9986	.9986
3.0 ...	.9987	.9987	.9987	.9988	.9988	.9989	.9989	.9989	.9990	.9990
3.1 ...	.9990	.9991	.9991	.9991	.9991	.9992	.9992	.9992	.9993	.9993
3.2 ...	.9993	.9993	.9994	.9994	.9994	.9994	.9994	.9995	.9995	.9995
3.3 ...	.9995	.9995	.9995	.9996	.9996	.9996	.9996	.9996	.9996	.9997
3.4 ...	.9997	.9997	.9997	.9997	.9997	.9997	.9997	.9997	.9997	.9998

Table C

Cumulative Poisson Probabilities

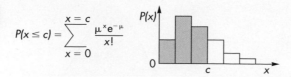

$$P(x \le c) = \sum_{x=0}^{x=c} \frac{\mu^x e^{-\mu}}{x!}$$

μ \ x	0	1	2	3	4	5	6	7	8	9
0.05....	.951	.999	1.000							
0.10....	.905	.995	1.000							
0.15....	.861	.990	.999	1.000						
0.20....	.819	.982	.999	1.000						
0.25....	.779	.974	.998	1.000						
0.30....	.741	.963	.996	1.000						
0.35....	.705	.951	.994	1.000						
0.40....	.670	.938	.992	.999	1.000					
0.45....	.638	.925	.989	.999	1.000					
0.50....	.607	.910	.986	.998	1.000					
0.55....	.577	.894	.982	.998	1.000					
0.60....	.549	.878	.977	.997	1.000					
0.65....	.522	.861	.972	.996	.999	1.000				
0.70....	.497	.844	.966	.994	.999	1.000				
0.75....	.472	.827	.960	.993	.999	1.000				
0.80....	.449	.809	.953	.991	.999	1.000				
0.85....	.427	.791	.945	.989	.998	1.000				
0.90....	.407	.772	.937	.987	.998	1.000				
0.95....	.387	.754	.929	.984	.997	1.000				
1.0....	.368	.736	.920	.981	.996	.999	1.000			
1.1....	.333	.699	.900	.974	.995	.999	1.000			
1.2....	.301	.663	.880	.966	.992	.998	1.000			
1.3....	.273	.627	.857	.957	.989	.998	1.000			
1.4....	.247	.592	.833	.946	.986	.997	.999	1.000		
1.5....	.223	.558	.809	.934	.981	.996	.999	1.000		
1.6....	.202	.525	.783	.921	.976	.994	.999	1.000		
1.7....	.183	.493	.757	.907	.970	.992	.998	1.000		
1.8....	.165	.463	.731	.891	.964	.990	.997	.999	1.000	
1.9....	.150	.434	.704	.875	.956	.987	.997	.999	1.000	
2.0....	.135	.406	.677	.857	.947	.983	.995	.999	1.000	
2.2....	.111	.355	.623	.819	.928	.975	.993	.998	1.000	
2.4....	.091	.308	.570	.779	.904	.964	.988	.997	.999	1.000
2.6....	.074	.267	.518	.736	.877	.951	.983	.995	.999	1.000
2.8....	.061	.231	.470	.692	.848	.935	.976	.992	.998	.999

(continued)

Table C (concluded)

μ \ x	0	1	2	3	4	5	6	7	8	9	10	11	12	13	14	15	16	17	18	19	20
3.0	.050	.199	.423	.647	.815	.916	.966	.988	.996	.999	1.000										
3.2	.041	.171	.380	.603	.781	.895	.955	.983	.994	.998	.999	1.000									
3.4	.033	.147	.340	.558	.744	.871	.942	.977	.992	.997	.999	1.000									
3.6	.027	.126	.303	.515	.706	.844	.927	.969	.988	.996	.999	1.000									
3.8	.022	.107	.269	.474	.668	.816	.909	.960	.984	.994	.998	.999	1.000								
4.0	.018	.092	.238	.433	.629	.785	.889	.949	.979	.992	.997	.999	1.000								
4.2	.015	.078	.210	.395	.590	.753	.868	.936	.972	.989	.996	.999	1.000								
4.4	.012	.066	.185	.359	.551	.720	.844	.921	.964	.985	.994	.998	.999	1.000							
4.6	.010	.056	.163	.326	.513	.685	.818	.905	.955	.980	.992	.997	.999	1.000							
4.8	.008	.048	.143	.294	.476	.651	.791	.887	.944	.975	.990	.996	.999	1.000							
5.0	.007	.040	.125	.265	.441	.615	.762	.867	.932	.968	.986	.995	.998	.999	1.000						
5.2	.006	.034	.109	.238	.406	.581	.732	.845	.918	.960	.982	.993	.997	.999	1.000						
5.4	.005	.029	.095	.213	.373	.546	.702	.822	.903	.951	.978	.990	.996	.999	1.000						
5.6	.004	.024	.082	.191	.342	.512	.670	.797	.886	.941	.972	.988	.995	.998	.999	1.000					
5.8	.003	.021	.072	.170	.313	.478	.638	.771	.867	.929	.965	.984	.993	.997	.999	1.000					
6.0	.002	.017	.062	.151	.285	.446	.606	.744	.847	.916	.957	.980	.991	.996	.999	.999	1.000				
6.2	.002	.015	.054	.134	.259	.414	.574	.716	.826	.902	.949	.975	.989	.995	.998	.999	1.000				
6.4	.002	.012	.046	.119	.235	.384	.542	.687	.803	.886	.939	.969	.986	.994	.997	.999	1.000				
6.6	.001	.010	.040	.105	.213	.355	.511	.658	.780	.869	.927	.963	.982	.992	.997	.999	.999	1.000			
6.8	.001	.009	.034	.093	.192	.327	.480	.628	.755	.850	.915	.955	.978	.990	.995	.998	.999	1.000			
7.0	.001	.007	.030	.082	.173	.301	.450	.599	.729	.830	.901	.947	.973	.987	.994	.998	.999	1.000			
7.2	.001	.006	.025	.072	.156	.276	.420	.569	.703	.810	.887	.937	.967	.984	.993	.997	.999	.999	1.000		
7.4	.001	.005	.022	.063	.140	.253	.392	.539	.676	.788	.871	.926	.961	.980	.991	.996	.998	.999	1.000		
7.6	.001	.004	.019	.055	.125	.231	.365	.510	.648	.765	.854	.915	.954	.976	.989	.995	.998	.999	1.000		
7.8	.001	.004	.016	.048	.112	.210	.338	.481	.620	.741	.835	.902	.945	.971	.986	.993	.997	.999	1.000		
8.0	.000	.003	.014	.042	.100	.191	.313	.453	.593	.717	.816	.888	.936	.966	.983	.992	.996	.998	.999	1.000	
8.2	.000	.003	.012	.037	.089	.174	.290	.425	.566	.692	.796	.873	.926	.960	.979	.990	.995	.998	.999	1.000	
8.4	.000	.002	.010	.032	.079	.157	.267	.400	.537	.666	.774	.857	.915	.952	.975	.987	.994	.997	.999	1.000	
8.6	.000	.002	.009	.030	.074	.150	.256	.386	.523	.653	.763	.849	.909	.949	.973	.986	.993	.997	.999	.999	1.000
8.8	.000	.002	.007	.024	.062	.128	.226	.348	.482	.614	.729	.822	.889	.935	.954	.981	.990	.995	.998	.999	1.000
9.0	.000	.001	.006	.021	.055	.116	.207	.324	.456	.587	.706	.803	.876	.926	.959	.978	.989	.995	.998	.999	1.000
9.5	.000	.001	.004	.015	.040	.089	.165	.269	.392	.522	.645	.752	.836	.898	.940	.967	.982	.991	.996	.998	.999

Acknowledgements

Chapter 1

Page 13, Figure 1-6: B. D'Netto, A.S. Sohal, and J. Trevillyan, "An Empirical Assessment of the Production/ Operations Manager's Job," *Production and Inventory Management Journal,* 1st Quarter 1998, 39(1), pp. 57–61. Reprinted with permission of APICS, The Association for Operations Management.

Chapter 3

Page 57, Figure 3 1: Steven Nahmias, *Production and Operations Analysis* (McGraw-Hil/Irwin, 1997) p. 61. Reprinted with permission of The McGraw-Hill Companies, Inc.

Chapter 4

Page 116, Figure 4-1: J. Ong, "Rapid Telecommunication Service Development," *Telecommunications* 31(11), November 1997, pp. 40–44; **Page 127, Figure 4-4:** J.G. Bralla, *Design for Manufacturability Handbook,* 2nd ed., New York: McGraw-Hill, 1999. Reprinted with permission from The McGraw-Hill Companies, Inc.; **Page 136 (unnumbered figure):** Design Concepts, Inc., http://www.design-concepts.com/portfolio/industry/sports-recreation/wilson-youth-batting-helmet.

Chapter 6

Page 169 (unnumbered figure): Plant floor plan image courtesy of Shane Korol; **Page 170 (unnumbered figure):** T. Feare, "Truck Plant Shifts into Overdrive," *Modern Materials Handling,* 55(2), Feb. 2000, pp. 73–76; **Page 172: (top)** Courtesy of Red Path Sugar Ltd.; **Page 176, Figure 6-2:** Roger G. Schroeder, *Operations Management,* 1st ed., (Boston: McGraw-Hill/Irwin, 2000), p. 96. Reproduced with permission of The McGraw-Hill Companies, Inc.; **Page 184, Figure 6-7:** Adapted from D. Fogarty and T. Hoffmann, *Production and Inventory Management* (Cincinnati-South-Western Publishing, 1983), p. 472; **Page 185, Figure 6-9:** Mikell P. Groover, *Automation, Production Systems, and Computer-Aided Manufacturing,* © 1980, p. 540. Reprinted by permission of Prentice-Hall, Inc., Englewood Cliffs, New Jersey; **Page 187, Figure 6-10:** "Computer Integrated Manufacturing," Vol. 1 in Revolution in Progress series, Chapman and Hall, London, 1990. Adapted from R.U. Ayres, Morris A. Cohen, and Uday M. Apte, *Manufacturing*

Automation (Burr Ridge, IL: McGraw-Hill, 1997), p. 175, **Page 193 (unnumbered figure): (top)** Adapted from Joseph S. Martinich, *Production and Operations Management: An Applied Modern Approach* (New York: John Wiley and Sons, Inc., 1997), p. 385. Reprinted with permission of John Wiley and Sons, Inc.; **Page 213 (unnumbered figure):** L. Ohm, "Automation Boosts Production 65 Percent," *FDM—The Magazine of Woodworking Production Management,* August 2003, 75(12), pp. 48–54; **Page 215 (unnumbered figure):** Processed Plastic Co., http://www.processedplastic.com; **Page 216 (unnumbered figure): (bottom)** Processed Plastic Co., http://www.processedplastic.com.

Chapter 7

Page 237 (unnumbered figure): Adapted from R.B. Chase et al., *Operations Management for Competitive Advantage,* 10th ed. (Boston: McGraw-Hill, 2004). Reprinted with permission of The McGraw-Hill Companies, Inc.

Chapter 9

Page 298 (unnumbered figure): http://www.inspection.gc.ca/english/anima/fispoi/qmp/files/tuna.pdf, accessed in 2005; http://www.cloverleaf.ca/en/company/seafood-school/tuna.html; **Page 299 (unnumbered figures):** http://www.nqi.ca/Certification/PEP/Overview.aspx.

Chapter 10

Page 344 (unnumbered figure): Figure reprinted with permission from *Six Sigma Forum Magazine.* © 2004 American Society for Quality; **Page 345 (unnumbered figure):** http://www.statease.com/e71ug/DE71-03A-TwoLevel-P1.pdf; **Page 359 (unnumbered figures): (top)** H.E. Ganley and J. Moxey, "Making Informed Decisions in the Face of Uncertainty," *Quality Progress,* Oct 2000, 33(10), pp. 76–78; **(bottom left and right)** D.E. Lighter and C.M. Tylkowski, "Case Study: Using Control Charts to Track Physician Productivity," *Physician Executive,* September/October 2004, 30(5), pp. 53–57.

Chapter 11

Page 368, Figure 11-2: G. Callioni and C. Billington, "Effective Collaboration—Hewlett-Packard Takes Supply Chain Management to

Another Level," *OR/MS Today,* October 2001 (Fig. 4), http://www.lionhrtpub.com/orms/orms-10-01/callioni-bilingtonfr.html; **Page 371, Figure 11-3:** http://www.ic.gc.ca/eic/site/dsib-logi.nsf/vwapj/pg00026_eng.pdf/$file/pg00026_eng.pdf; **Page 382, Table 11-1:** Reprinted by permission from David Simchi-Levi, Philip Kaminsky, and Edith Simchi-Levi, *Designing and Managing the Supply Chain: Concepts, Strategies, and Case Studies,* New York: Irwin/McGraw-Hill, 2000, p. 235; **Page 386, Table 11-3:** Based on information made available at http://www.supply-chain.org by the Supply Chain Council; **(unnumbered figure)** Figure reprinted with the permission of the Institute of Business Forecasting.

Chapter 12

Page 465 (unnumbered figure): Floor plan courtesy of McGraw-Hill Ryerson, Ltd.

Chapter 13

Page 470, Figure 13-2: T.F. Wallace, *Sales & Operations Planning* (Cincinnati: T.F. Wallace & Co., 2001). Figures reprinted courtesy of T.F. Wallace & Co.; **Page 471, Figure 13-3:** T.F. Wallace, *Sales & Operations Planning* (Cincinnati: T.F. Wallace & Co., 2001). Figures reprinted courtesy of T.F. Wallace & Co.; **Page 477, Figures 13 5A and 13 5B:** J.R. Edwards, et al., "Blue Bell Trims its Inventory," *Interfaces* 15(1), Jan/Feb 1985, pp. 34–52.

Chapter 14

Page 523, Figure 14-13: Stephen Love, *Inventory Control* (New York: McGraw-Hill, 1979), p.164. Reprinted by permission.

Chapter 15

Page 548, Figure 15-1: Adapted from Thomas E. Vollmann, William L. Berry, and D. Glay Whybark. *Manufacturing Planning and Control Systems,* 3rd ed. (McGraw-Hill/Irwin, 1992). Reprinted with permission of The McGraw-Hill Companies, Inc.; **Page 550 (unnumbered figure):** Courtesy of The Shingo Prize, www.shingoprize.org; **Page 552, Table 15-1:** Adapted from Edward M. Knod, Jr. and Richard J. Schonberger, *Operations Management: Meeting Customers' Demands,* 7th ed. (New York: McGraw-Hill, 2001); **Page 566 (unnumbered figures):** J.P. Womack, "Value Stream Mapping,"

Manufacturing Engineering, May 2006, 136(5), pp. 145–156; **Page 572 (unnumbered figure):** Figure reprinted with permission of APICS, The Association for Operations Management. *Production and Inventory Management Journal* 39(1), First Quarter, 1998, pp. 17–22.

Chapter 16

Page 576, Figure 16-1: R. Eade, "Cutting Lead Time through Smart Scheduling," *Manufacturing Systems* 11(11), November, 1993. Figure reprinted with permission. Rhythm (Demand Consolidation, Capacity Optimized Planner, and Dynamic Scheduler) is at the core of Black & Decker's computer-integrated manufacturing system.

Chapter 17

Page 618, Figure 17-1: Project Management Institute, *A Guide to the Project Management Body of Knowledge* (PMBOK® Guide), 3rd edition, 2004. Copyright and all rights reserved. Material from this publication has been reproduced with the permission of PMI; **Page 638, Figure 17-9:** Project Management Institute, *A Guide to the Project Management Body of Knowledge* (PMBOK® Guide), 3rd edition, 2004. Copyright and all rights reserved. Material from this publication has been reproduced with the permission of PMI.

Chapter 18

Page 694, Table 18-6: Adapted from L.G. Peck and R.N. Hazelwood, *Finite Queuing Tables* (New York: John Wiley & Sons, 1958). Reprinted by permission; **Page 695, Table 18-7:** L.G. Peck and R.N. Hazelwood, *Finite Queuing Tables* (New York: John Wiley & Sons, 1958). Reprinted by permission.

Photo Credits

Company Index

Subject Index

Areas under the Standardized Normal Curve, from $-\infty$ to $+z$

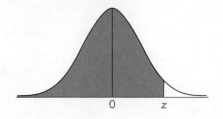

z	.00	.01	.02	.03	.04	.05	.06	.07	.08	.09
.0	.5000	.5040	.5080	.5120	.5160	.5199	.5239	.5279	.5319	.5359
.1	.5398	.5438	.5478	.5517	.5557	.5596	.5636	.5675	.5714	.5753
.2	.5793	.5832	.5871	.5910	.5948	.5987	.6026	.6064	.6103	.6141
.3	.6179	.6217	.6255	.6293	.6331	.6368	.6406	.6443	.6480	.6517
.4	.6554	.6591	.6628	.6664	.6700	.6736	.6772	.6808	.6844	.6879
.5	.6915	.6950	.6985	.7019	.7054	.7088	.7123	.7157	.7190	.7224
.6	.7257	.7291	.7324	.7357	.7389	.7422	.7454	.7486	.7517	.7549
.7	.7580	.7611	.7642	.7673	.7703	.7734	.7764	.7794	.7823	.7852
.8	.7881	.7910	.7939	.7967	.7995	.8023	.8051	.8078	.8106	.8133
.9	.8159	.8186	.8212	.8238	.8264	.8289	.8315	.8340	.8365	.8389
1.0	.8413	.8438	.8461	.8485	.8508	.8531	.8554	.8577	.8599	.8621
1.1	.8643	.8665	.8686	.8708	.8729	.8749	.8770	.8790	.8810	.8830
1.2	.8849	.8869	.8888	.8907	.8925	.8944	.8962	.8980	.8997	.9015
1.3	.9032	.9049	.9066	.9082	.9099	.9115	.9131	.9147	.9162	.9177
1.4	.9192	.9207	.9222	.9236	.9251	.9265	.9279	.9292	.9306	.9319
1.5	.9332	.9345	.9357	.9370	.9382	.9394	.9406	.9418	.9429	.9441
1.6	.9452	.9463	.9474	.9484	.9495	.9505	.9515	.9525	.9535	.9545
1.7	.9554	.9564	.9573	.9582	.9591	.9599	.9608	.9616	.9625	.9633
1.8	.9641	.9649	.9656	.9664	.9671	.9678	.9686	.9693	.9699	.9706
1.9	.9713	.9719	.9726	.9732	.9738	.9744	.9750	.9756	.9761	.9767
2.0	.9772	.9778	.9783	.9788	.9793	.9798	.9803	.9808	.9812	.9817
2.1	.9821	.9826	.9830	.9834	.9838	.9842	.9846	.9850	.9854	.9857
2.2	.9861	.9864	.9868	.9871	.9875	.9878	.9881	.9884	.9887	.9890
2.3	.9893	.9896	.9898	.9901	.9904	.9906	.9909	.9911	.9913	.9916
2.4	.9918	.9920	.9922	.9925	.9927	.9929	.9931	.9932	.9934	.9936
2.5	.9938	.9940	.9941	.9943	.9945	.9946	.9948	.9949	.9951	.9952
2.6	.9953	.9955	.9956	.9957	.9959	.9960	.9961	.9962	.9963	.9964
2.7	.9965	.9966	.9967	.9968	.9969	.9970	.9971	.9972	.9973	.9974
2.8	.9974	.9975	.9976	.9977	.9977	.9978	.9979	.9979	.9980	.9981
2.9	.9981	.9982	.9982	.9983	.9984	.9984	.9985	.9985	.9986	.9986
3.0	.9987	.9987	.9987	.9988	.9988	.9989	.9989	.9989	.9990	.9990
3.1	.9990	.9991	.9991	.9991	.9991	.9992	.9992	.9992	.9993	.9993
3.2	.9993	.9993	.9994	.9994	.9994	.9994	.9994	.9995	.9995	.9995
3.3	.9995	.9995	.9995	.9996	.9996	.9996	.9996	.9996	.9996	.9997
3.4	.9997	.9997	.9997	.9997	.9997	.9997	.9997	.9997	.9997	.9998

Areas under the Standardized Normal Curve, 0 to z

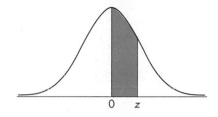

z	.00	.01	.02	.03	.04	.05	.06	.07	.08	.09
0.0	.0000	.0040	.0080	.0120	.0160	.0199	.0239	.0279	.0319	.0359
0.1	.0398	.0438	.0478	.0517	.0557	.0596	.0636	.0675	.0714	.0753
0.2	.0793	.0832	.0871	.0910	.0948	.0987	.1026	.1064	.1103	.1141
0.3	.1179	.1217	.1255	.1293	.1331	.1368	.1406	.1443	.1480	.1517
0.4	.1554	.1591	.1628	.1664	.1700	.1736	.1772	.1808	.1844	.1879
0.5	.1915	.1950	.1985	.2019	.2054	.2088	.2123	.2157	.2190	.2224
0.6	.2257	.2291	.2324	.2357	.2389	.2422	.2454	.2486	.2517	.2549
0.7	.2580	.2611	.2642	.2673	.2703	.2734	.2764	.2794	.2823	.2852
0.8	.2881	.2910	.2939	.2967	.2995	.3023	.3051	.3078	.3106	.3133
0.9	.3159	.3186	.3212	.3238	.3264	.3289	.3315	.3340	.3365	.3389
1.0	.3413	.3438	.3461	.3485	.3508	.3531	.3554	.3577	.3599	.3621
1.1	.3643	.3665	.3686	.3708	.3729	.3749	.3770	.3790	.3810	.3830
1.2	.3849	.3869	.3888	.3907	.3925	.3944	.3962	.3980	.3997	.4015
1.3	.4032	.4049	.4066	.4082	.4099	.4115	.4131	.4147	.4162	.4177
1.4	.4192	.4207	.4222	.4236	.4251	.4265	.4279	.4292	.4306	.4319
1.5	.4332	.4345	.4357	.4370	.4382	.4394	.4406	.4418	.4429	.4441
1.6	.4452	.4463	.4474	.4484	.4495	.4505	.4515	.4525	.4535	.4545
1.7	.4554	.4564	.4573	.4582	.4591	.4599	.4608	.4616	.4625	.4633
1.8	.4641	.4649	.4656	.4664	.4671	.4678	.4686	.4693	.4699	.4706
1.9	.4713	.4719	.4726	.4732	.4738	.4744	.4750	.4756	.4761	.4767
2.0	.4772	.4778	.4783	.4788	.4793	.4798	.4803	.4808	.4812	.4817
2.1	.4821	.4826	.4830	.4834	.4838	.4842	.4846	.4850	.4854	.4857
2.2	.4861	.4864	.4868	.4871	.4875	.4878	.4881	.4884	.4887	.4890
2.3	.4893	.4896	.4898	.4901	.4904	.4906	.4909	.4911	.4913	.4916
2.4	.4918	.4920	.4922	.4925	.4927	.4929	.4931	.4932	.4934	.4936
2.5	.4938	.4940	.4941	.4943	.4945	.4946	.4948	.4949	.4951	.4952
2.6	.4953	.4955	.4956	.4957	.4959	.4960	.4961	.4962	.4963	.4964
2.7	.4965	.4966	.4967	.4968	.4969	.4970	.4971	.4972	.4973	.4974
2.8	.4974	.4975	.4976	.4977	.4977	.4978	.4979	.4979	.4980	.4981
2.9	.4981	.4982	.4982	.4983	.4984	.4984	.4985	.4985	.4986	.4986
3.0	.4987	.4987	.4987	.4988	.4988	.4989	.4989	.4989	.4990	.4990